Innovations in Computer Vision, Communication Systems, and Computational Intelligence

This volume presents the peer-reviewed proceedings of CVCNCE 2025, the First International Conference on Computer Vision, Communication Systems, and Computational Intelligence, held on 08–09 May 2025 in Tirunelveli, India. Organized by the Department of Electronics and Communication Engineering at Francis Xavier Engineering College, this landmark event brought together researchers, industry experts, and academics from around the world to exchange ideas and advancements in cutting-edge technological domains.

Spanning topics in computer vision, communication systems, and computational intelligence, the proceedings showcase innovative research in areas such as image processing, AI-driven vision systems, next-generation 5G/6G communications, IoT frameworks, and emerging trends in artificial intelligence and machine learning applications. The contributions emphasize interdisciplinary collaboration and reflect the rapid evolution of digital technology shaping today's interconnected world.

With keynote lectures from distinguished experts, technical sessions, and lively discussions, CVCNCE 2025 has served as a vibrant platform for fostering knowledge-sharing and forging new research collaborations. This proceedings volume stands as a testament to the dynamic ideas and pioneering research presented at the conference and offers valuable insights for researchers, practitioners, and students in the fields of computer vision, communication systems, computational intelligence, and beyond.

Dr. Suman Lata Tripathi has completed her Ph.D. in the area of microelectronics and VLSI from MNNIT, Allahabad. She did her M.Tech in Electronics Engineering from UP Technical University, Lucknow and B.Tech in Electrical Engineering from Purvanchal University, Jaunpur. She is also a remote post-doc researcher at Nottingham Trent University, London, UK in the year 2022. She is associated with Lovely Professional University as a Professor with more than 19 years of experience in academics. She has published more than 74 research papers in refereed IEEE, Springer, Elsevier and IOP science journals and conferences. She has also published 13 Indian patents and 2 copyright. She has organized several workshops, summer internships, and expert lectures for students. She has worked as a session chair, conference steering committee member, editorial board member, and peer reviewer in international/national IEEE, Springer, Wiley etc Journal and conferences. She has received the "Research Excellence Award" in 2019 and "Research Appreciation Award" in 2020, 2021 at Lovely Professional University, India. She had received the best paper at IEEE ICICS-2018. She has also received funded project from SERB DST under the scheme TARE in the area of Microelectronics devices. She has edited and authored more than 15 books in different areas of Electronics and electrical engineering. She is associated for editing work with top publishers like Elsevier, CRC Taylor and Francis, Wiley-IEEE, SP Wiley, Nova Science and Apple academic press etc. She is also working as book series editor for title, "Smart Engineering Systems" CRC Press, "Engineering system design for sustainable developments" Wiley-Scrivener and conference series editor for "Conference Proceedings Series on Intelligent systems for Engineering designs" CRC Press Taylor & Francis. She is the guest editor of a special issue in "Current Medical Imaging" Bentham Science. She is associated as senior member IEEE, Fellow IETE and Life member ISC and is continuously involved in different professional activities along with academic work. Her area of expertise includes microelectronics device modeling and characterization, low power VLSI circuit design, VLSI design of testing, and advanced FET design for IoT, Embedded System Design, reconfigurable architecture with FPGAs and biomedical applications etc.

Dr. Om Prakash Kumar is currently an Associate Professor at the Department of Electronics and Communication Engineering, Manipal Institute of Technology, Manipal Academy of Higher Education, Manipal. He is an active Researcher in RF and microwave technology. He has published many peer-reviewed articles in reputable international journals and conferences. He serves as a Reviewer for journals, such as the AEU-International Journal of Electronics and Communications, Engineering Science and Technology, an International Journal JESTECH, Ain Shams Engineering Journal, International Journal of Electronics (Taylor & Francis), and Heliyon (Elsevier), IEEE Access and IEEE Transactions and many journals.

Dr. Allwin Devaraj Stalin is an Associate Professor in the Department of Electronics and Communication Engineering at Francis Xavier Engineering College, Tirunelveli, Tamil Nadu, India. His academic journey has been marked by dedication, research contributions, and a commitment to advancing knowledge in the field.

Dr. Tanweer Ali (Senior Member, IEEE) is currently an Associate Professor with the Department of Electronics and Communication Engineering, Manipal Institute of Technology, Manipal Academy of Higher Education, Manipal. He is an Active Researcher in the field of microstrip antennas, wireless communication, and microwave imaging. He has published more than 130 papers in reputed web of science (SCI) and Scopus indexed journals and conferences. He has seven Indian patents, of which three have published. He has been listed in top 2% scientists across the world in 2021 and 2022, by the prestigious list published by Stanford University, USA, indexed by Scopus. He is on the Board of a Reviewer of journals, such as IEEE Transactions on Antennas and Propagation, IEEE Antennas and Wireless Propagation Letters, IEEE Access, IET Microwaves, Antennas and Propagation, Electronics Letters (IET), Wireless Personal Communications (Springer), International Journal of Electronics and Communications (AEU), Microwave and Optical Technology Letters (Wiley), International Journal of Antennas and Propagation (Hindawi), Advanced Electromagnetics, Progress in Electromagnetics Research (PIER), KSII Transactions on Engineering Science, International Journal of Microwave and Wireless Technologies, Frequenz, Radioengineering, and IEEE Open Journal of Antennas and Propagation.

Innovations in Computer Vision, Communication Systems, and Computational Intelligence

Proceedings of the First International Conference on Computer Vision, Communication System and Computational Intelligence (CVCNCE 2025), 08–09 May 2025, Tirunelveli, India

Edited by

Dr. Suman Lata Tripathi
Dr. Om Prakash Kumar
Dr. Allwin Devaraj Stalin
Dr. Tanweer Ali

CRC Press
Taylor & Francis Group

A CHAPMAN & HALL BOOK

First edition published 2026
by CRC Press
4 Park Square, Milton Park, Abingdon, Oxon, OX14 4RN

and by CRC Press
2385 NW Executive Center Drive, Suite 320, Boca Raton FL 33431

British Library Cataloguing-in-Publication Data
A catalogue record for this book is available from the British Library

ISBN: 9781041209447 (hbk)
ISBN: 9781041209522 (pbk)
ISBN: 9781003724988 (ebk)

DOI: 10.1201/9781003724988

Typeset in Times New Roman
by HBK Digital

Contents

Lists of figures

Lists of tables

1 Design and implementation of a 6T full adder using power gating technology for low-power VLSI applications

Rakshitha S.ᵃ and Om Prakash Kumar

Department of Electronics and Communication Engineering, Manipal Institute of Technology, Manipal Academy of Higher Education, Manipal, India

Abstract: Full adder is one of the essential basic block for designing a complex digital circuits used in many applications. In this paper, 6 transistor (6T) full adder using power gating technology as been proposed. The full adder was designed and implementation was done using Cadence Virtuoso tool in GPDK 45-nm technology. The parameters like delay and power with supply of 0.9v is considered. These are the primary design constraints in designing any circuits and they compared with the existing technology of 6 T.

Keywords: 6T full adder, power gating technology, cadence virtuoso, area, power

1. Introduction

As requirement and demand of less delay and low power ICs in the digital circuits is increasing, the design and circuit chosen to design a component plays an important role. Full adder is one of the important element used to design a circuits like multiplexer, differentiators, comparators, integrators, etc. [1]. They are also used in designing component like microprocessor and digital signal processor, which frequently performs the arithmetic operation. As the technology is evolving there is decrease in the size of transistors on a chip and complexity of the integrated circuits is increasing [2, 3]. The size of the transistors are getting smaller and smaller as there is an advancement in the technology which leaves an direct impact on area, power consumption and delay. CMOS technology uses both PMOS and NMOS transistors, providing low static power consumption and high noise immunity, making it suitable for digital circuits and microprocessors. CPL uses pass transistors to achieve reduced transistor count and faster switching speeds, ideal for high-speed, low-power applications [4]. Dynamic CMOS logic employs clocked pre-charge and evaluate phases, offering high speed and lower power consumption, perfect for high-speed arithmetic circuits and processors. Transmission Gate Full Adders use transmission gates (PMOS and NMOS transistors), resulting in reduced delay, lower power consumption, and simpler design, commonly used in full adder circuits and combinational logic circuits [5, 6]. Each technology offers unique benefits depending on the application's requirements, such as speed, power consumption, and complexity.

In this paper, we propose a technique for the designing 6-transistor full adders using power gating technology. Reducing power consumption and leakage power are crucial in modern VLSI design methodologies due to two primary reasons: the need for longer battery life in portable devices and the high power dissipation caused by an increasing number of transistors on a single chip [7]. In VLSI applications, the full adder is a key component in various arithmetic circuits like adders and multipliers. Therefore, helps in enhancing the performance of the full adder significantly boosts entire system efficiency [8]. A full adder circuits as two outputs and three inputs, representing the sum and carry of the three inputs [9].

2. Design of 1-bit Full Adder

The 1-bit full adder is a digital circuit used for addition of the given three binary bits: two main bits and a carry bit from a previous addition (Figure 1.1). It operates using three input signals: A, B, and Cin. The circuit generates two outputs: Sum and Carry out (Figure 1.2). The Sum output indicates the addition result of three input bits as shown in equation (1), while the Carry out bit shows any overflow that must be carried to the next significant bit as shown in equation (2). The Sum is usually implemented using XOR gates, and the Carry out is implemented using AND and OR gates in order to manage different input combinations (Table 1.1).

$$\text{Sum, S} = A \oplus B \oplus Cin \quad\quad (1)$$

$$\text{Carry out, Cout} = (A \cdot B) + (B \cdot Cin) + (A \cdot Cin) \quad (2)$$

ᵃrakshitha1.mitmpl2024@learner.manipal.edu

DOI: 10.1201/9781003724988-1

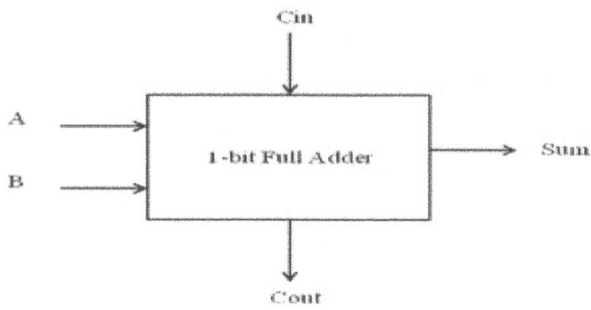

Figure 1.1. Block representation of full adder.

Source: Author.

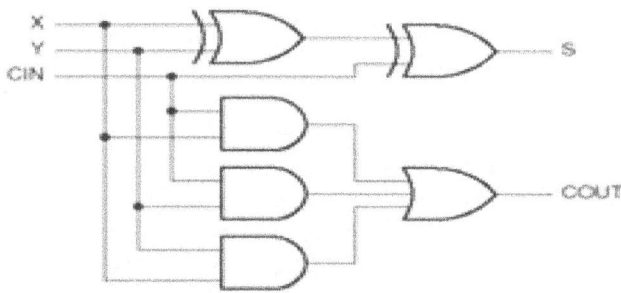

Figure 1.2. Circuit representation of 1-bit full adder.

Source: Author.

Table 1.1. Truth table of full adder

A	B	C	Sum	Ca
0	0	0	0	0
0	0	1	1	0
0	1	0	1	0
0	1	1	0	1
1	0	0	1	0
1	0	1	0	1
1	1	0	0	1
1	1	1	1	1

Source: Author.

3. Existing 6T Full Adder

The 6T full adder is a specialized digital circuit for adding binary numbers. It leverages six transistors, which ensures it is both power-efficient and quick in its operations. The circuit has three input A, B, and Cin and generates two output: Sum and Cout. It consists of 6 transistors, in which there are two PMOS and four NMOS given with voltage 0.9v and implemented in 45nm technology (Figure 1.3).

A CMOS full adder circuit is a crucial element in digital systems for performing binary addition. It employs MOSFET transistors with optimized width-to-length ratios, such as 1:1, 2:1, and 5:1, to ensure precise control over current flow and maintain the desired electrical characteristics (Figures 1.4 and 1.5).

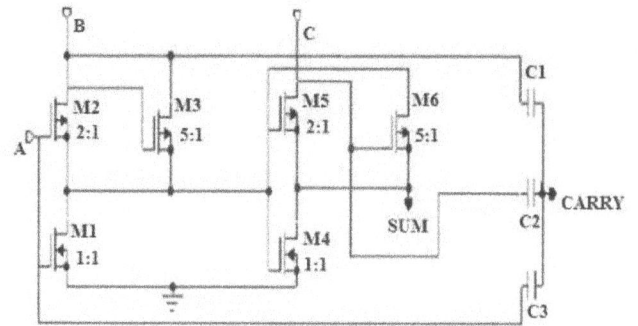

Figure 1.3. Circuit of 6T full adder.

Source: Author.

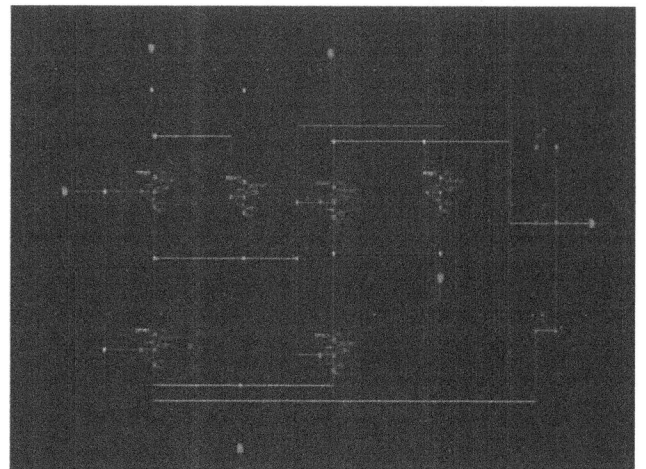

Figure 1.4. Schematic of 6T full adder circuit.

Source: Author.

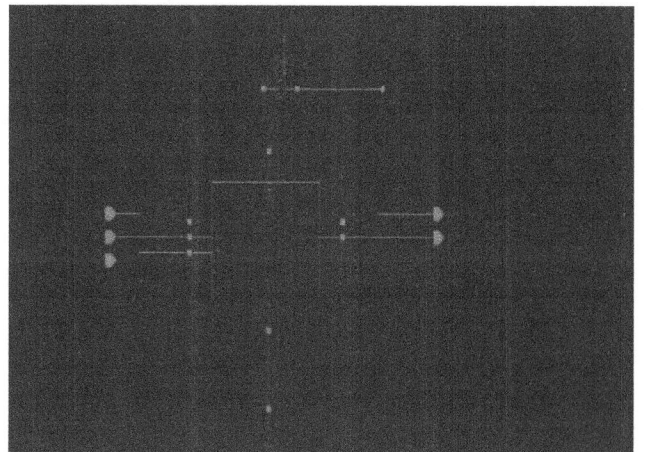

Figure 1.5. Test circuit for 6T full adder circuit.

Source: Author.

4. Proposed 6T Full Adder Circuit using Power Gated Technology

The 6T full adder design represents an efficient digital circuit for binary addition which requires six transistors to provide fast performance. Technological enhancements that implement 45nm technology have produced major advancements in the power efficiency and operational efficiency of the 6T full adder. The main obstacle in designing a 6T full adder with 45nm technology requires control over leakage current and optimization of power-gating methods. Power gating stands as an essential technique to reduce leakage current through the implementation of sleep transistors. Standby mode power-dissipation results from activating sleep transistors that connect logic networks either to virtual power (VDD) or ground (GND).

The PMOS header switch becomes standard in a 45nm design since it helps save space while reducing timing defects caused by sleep transistor voltage drops. A logic network consisting of power-gated cells or standard simple logic gates comprises the entire configuration found in a standard cell library (Figure 1.6).

Power gating for 45nm technology operates through two active-sleep modes which enable effective power control.

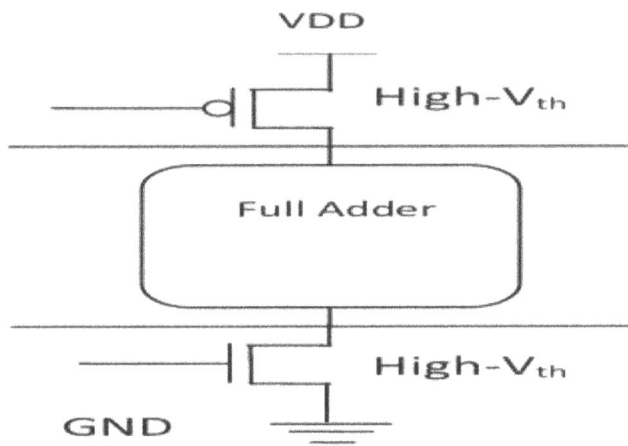

Figure 1.6. Full adder using power gated technology.

Source: Author.

Two separate threshold voltages operate N channel and P channel MOSFETs together on the same integrated circuit. By disconnecting the low threshold voltage logic gates from power supply and ground lines with high threshold voltage sleep transistors the sub-threat leakage current during standby mode becomes significantly reduced.

5. Results and Discussions

The output wave form of proposed method is as shown in Figure 1.7.

The comparison of performance of the proposed 6T Full Adder Power Gated Technology and the 6T Full Adder is made with respect to power and delay, as shown in the Table 1.2.

The Full Adder, 6T Full Adder, and Proposed Method all use six transistors, maintaining the same complexity. The Proposed Method improves power efficiency, reducing power consumption from 3.8ns in the 6T Full Adder to 3.46ns. It also reduces delay from 0.353ns to 0.328ns, offering faster operation and better energy optimization while retaining a compact design.

6. Conclusion

Modern designs of energy-efficient computing systems require both 6T full adder and 6T power-gated technology

Table 1.2. Comparison of performance 6T full adder and proposed power gated 6T full adder

Full Adder	*6T Full Adder*	*Proposed method*
Transistor count	6	6
Power	3.8ns	3.46ns
Delay	0.353ns	0.328ns

Source: Author.

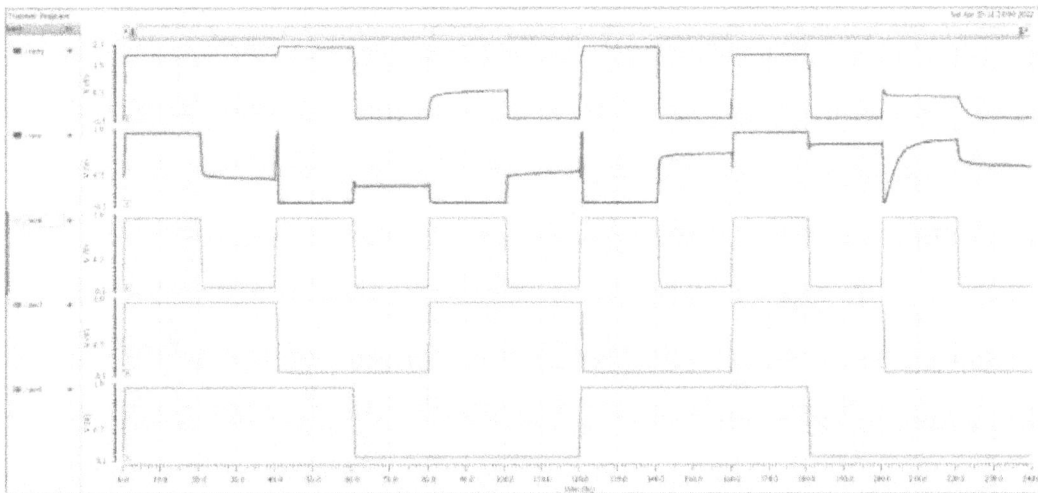

Figure 1.7. Output waveform of power gated 6T full adder circuit.

Source: Author.

to achieve their vital performance-related advantages. 6T full adders add binary numbers efficiently at low power consumption which makes them useful for arithmetic units and processors. The sleep transistors in 6T power-gated technology implement leakage current reduction to provide digital circuits' efficient power management capabilities. These technologies serve as essential components in designing and optimizing contemporary computational devices because they substantially boost digital electronics' performance alongside their energy efficiency capacity. These two systems combine to enable high-performing and efficient systems that fulfill current computing requirements.

References

[1] Subramanian, S. S., & Gandhi, M. (2024). Low Power CMOS Full Adder Cell based on Alternative Logic for High-Speed Arithmetic Applications. *Journal of Microelectronics, Electronics Components and Materials, 54*(3), 187–200.

[2] Laxman, A., Sankara Reddy, N. S., & Rajendra Naik, B. (2023). Design and Analysis of Low Power Hybrid Logic Adder for Signal Processing Applications. *SSRG International Journal of Electrical and Electronics Engineering, 10*(10), 197–206.

[3] Singh, S., & Yagnesh, B. S. (2020). Design Methodologies for Low Power and High Speed Full Adder. *Journal of Critical Reviews, 7*(18).

[4] Gayathri, J., Sainath, A., Samatha, S., & Ramesh, B. (2022). Implementation and Analysis of 6T 1Bit Full Adder using Cadence Virtuoso. *International Research Journal of Modernization in Engineering Technology and Science, 4*(7), 407–412.

[5] Loganya, R., Manisha, B., Jahnavi, C. H., & Jyothsna Devi, G. (2024). Design of Novel Low Power 6T XNOR based Full Adder and Full Subtractor and Comparison of Various Adders and Subtractors. *International Journal of Emerging Trends in Engineering Research, 12*(4).

[6] Khan, M. U., Zeeshan, M., Gulzar, U., Muneeb, M., Abbasi, Z., & Abbasi, U. B. (2021, October). Nanotechnology (45 nm) based Low power and High performance 4x4 Multiplier based on Six Transistors (6T) Full Adder & 2T XNOR Gate. In *2021 International Conference on Computing, Electronic and Electrical Engineering (ICE Cube)* (pp. 1–6). IEEE.

[7] Ishraqul Huq, S. M. (2020). Performance Analysis of 6-Transistor Full Adder Circuit using PTM 32 nm Technology LP-MOSFETs and DG-FinFETs. *Journal of Engineering and Applied Sciences, 15*, 501–507.

[8] Hasan, M., Siddique, A. H., Mondol, A. H., Hossain, M., Zaman, H. U., & Islam, S. (2021). Comprehensive study of 1-bit full adder cells: review, performance comparison and scalability analysis. *SN Applied Sciences, 3*(6), 644.

[9] Hasan, M., Hossein, M. J., Hossain, M., Zaman, H. U., & Islam, S. (2020). Design of a Scalable Low-Power 1-Bit Hybrid Full Adder for Fast Computation. *IEEE Transactions on Circuits and Systems-II: Express Briefs, 67*(8), 1464–1468.

2 Deep learning-based pneumonia detection in children with YAMNet model integration

Vani K. S.[a], Adithya S.[b], Deepak T. Gonchikar[c], Gaurav Nandan U. T.[d], and Manmohan Reddy[e]

Department of Information Science and Engineering, Nitte Meenakshi Institute of Technology, Bangalore, Karnataka, India

Abstract: Pediatric pneumonia and acute bronchitis are leading causes of morbidity and mortality, particularly in regions with limited access to timely and accurate diagnostic tools. Traditional methods, such as chest X-rays and laboratory tests, are often invasive, time-intensive, and reliant on substantial infrastructure. To overcome and address these challenges, this work proposes a deep learning-based diagnostic system that analyzes cough sounds as a non-invasive alternative. The methodology incorporates the most robust pre-processing techniques, including noise reduction, uniform data segmentation, and feature extraction using advanced models like YAMNet. The system makes use of Long Short-Term Memory (LSTM) networks for classification, leveraging temporal patterns in audio data to distinguish pneumonia-positive cases from other respiratory conditions. The system is assessed using metrics such as precision, recall, and F1-score where the model achieved 97% accuracy, with notable performance in identifying both the pneumonia-positive and non-pneumonia cases. This approach not only addresses issues and cases such as data variability and background noise but also demonstrates scalability and practicality for deployment in resource-constrained environments very efficiently. By improving diagnostic accessibility and accuracy, the proposed model offers a transformative solution for the early detection of pediatric respiratory diseases, bridging the gap between traditional and AI-driven healthcare diagnostics.

Keywords: Pneumonia, acute bronchitis, deep learning, cough analysis, healthcare diagnostics

1. Introduction

Respiratory diseases such as pneumonia and acute bronchitis remain the leading causes of morbidity and mortality among children, particularly in low-resource settings where access to accurate diagnostic tools is limited. Pneumonia is responsible for the deaths of more than 700,000 children under the age of five each year, with the highest cases reported in South Asia and West and Central Africa.

Conventional diagnostic approaches, such as chest X-rays and laboratory tests, tend to be costly, time-intensive, and reliant on specialized infrastructure, limiting their accessibility in remote and underdeveloped areas.

Given these challenges, there is a growing need for innovative, noninvasive, and cost-effective solutions for early disease detection.

Deep learning has emerged as a promising tool in medical diagnostics, enabling automated analysis of biological signals such as cough sounds. Studies have shown that machine learning can successfully classify respiratory conditions like asthma, tuberculosis, and COVID-19 based on cough characteristics. Despite these advancements, there is limited research on leveraging deep learning for pediatric pneumonia and acute bronchitis detection. Major challenges include variability in cough patterns, interference from background noise, and the requirement for large, diverse datasets to improve model generalizability.

This study aims to bridge these gaps by developing a robust deep learning-based system for pediatric cough sound analysis. By integrating noise reduction techniques and feature extraction methods, we seek to enhance classification accuracy and improve the accessibility of respiratory diagnostics in resource-limited settings. Prior research has demonstrated the potential of cough-based diagnosis for childhood pneumonia and asthma, but further optimization is needed to refine classification models and adapt them for real-world applications.

Our research contributes to the field by addressing key challenges such as dataset diversity, model interpretability, and performance benchmarking against traditional diagnostic methods. By evaluating our approach using clinically validated datasets, we demonstrate its potential to transform pediatric respiratory diagnostics and support early intervention efforts. Ultimately, this system could help reduce misdiagnoses, facilitate timely treatment, and improve health outcomes for children worldwide.

[a]vani.ks@nmit.ac.in, [b]adithyashaju@gmail.com, [c]deepak.thungeswara.gonchikar@gmail.com, [d]gauravnandan.ut@gmail.com, [e]manmohanreddytn@gmail.com

DOI: 10.1201/9781003724988-2

2. Literature Survey

Respiratory diseases, notably pneumonia, asthma, and tuberculosis, remain significant contributors to global morbidity and mortality, particularly among pediatric populations. Traditional diagnostic methods, such as chest radiography and sputum analysis, often present challenges including high costs, delayed results, and the necessity for specialized infrastructure.

Recent advancements have focused on the analysis of cough sounds, leveraging artificial intelligence (AI) and deep learning (DL) techniques to facilitate rapid, non-invasive, and cost-effective diagnostics for pediatric health care.

The foundation of cough sound analysis lies in effective audio signal processing and classification. A comprehensive study emphasized the development of deep neural network (DNN)-based systems for classifying and detecting cough sounds, particularly highlighting convolutional neural networks (CNNs) and their hyperparameters [1].

The integration of IoT and deep learning has enhanced cough sound analysis. One study summarized recent advancements and introduced a model capable of identifying ten severe lung diseases common in adolescents, enabling continuous and real-time monitoring [2].

Despite advancements, challenges such as data quality, background noise, and robust classifier development persist. A review emphasized the need for standardized data protocols and sophisticated algorithms to improve diagnostic accuracy [3].

Wavelet transform techniques have been applied to analyze cough sounds, with one study achieving 94% accuracy in differentiating pneumonia patients from healthy individuals using wavelet-based statistical feature extraction [4].

A system analyzing cough sounds to distinguish between asthma and pneumonia in children demonstrated high classification accuracy, showcasing the potential of machine learning in pediatric respiratory diagnostics [5].

Automated TB detection via cough analysis was explored, with a proposed method achieving 83% sensitivity and 82% specificity, offering a fast, non-invasive tool for resource-limited settings [6].

An automated system using machine learning to detect childhood pneumonia from cough sounds achieved 93.8% accuracy, highlighting its clinical utility [7].

Wavelet-augmented analysis for rapid pediatric pneumonia diagnosis achieved 95% sensitivity and 90% specificity, proving the effectiveness of combining signal processing with AI [8].

A study that classified pneumonia and asthma in children using machine learning on cough features achieved 92% accuracy, demonstrating its diagnostic potential [9].

ANN-based cough analysis systems for TB diagnosis reached 89% sensitivity and 91% specificity, illustrating their reliability in detecting tuberculosis [10].

Rapid diagnosis of childhood pneumonia through cough analysis showed promising results, with one study reporting 87% sensitivity and 89% specificity, useful in emergency scenarios [11].

Finally, computerized lung sound analysis has been proposed to improve pediatric pneumonia specificity in low-resource settings, reducing dependency on radiographic imaging [12].

In conclusion, the integration of AI and DL techniques in cough sound analysis presents a promising avenue for the rapid and accurate diagnosis of respiratory diseases. Despite existing challenges, ongoing research and technological advancements continue to enhance the reliability and accessibility of these diagnostic tools, particularly in resource-limited settings. The algorithms, methodologies used and the accuracy in recent seven papers are listed Table 2.1.

Table 2.1. Comparison of different algorithms used in cough sound analysis

Name of the Paper	Algorithm or Method Used	Accuracy
Methodics and tools of cough sound processing on basic of neural net	Convolutional Neural Network	85.37%
Towards cough sound analysis using the Internet of things and deep learning for pulmonary disease prediction	Neural Networks, Support Vector Machines, Decision Tree	50%
Automatic classification of childhood asthma and pneumonia based on cough sound analysis	Support Vector Machines and Hidden Markov Model	93.42%
Detection of tuberculosis by automatic cough sound analysis	Logistic Regression, Hidden Markov Model, Decision Tree	78%
Automated Cough Sound Analysis for Detecting Childhood Pneumonia	Multilayer Perceptron	76.33%
Robust Cough Analysis System for Diagnosis of Tuberculosis Using Artificial Neural Network	Artificial Neural Network, Support Vector Machine	98.2%
Computerized lung sound analysis to improve the specificity of paediatric pneumonia diagnosis in resource-poor settings: Protocol and methods for an observational study	Nearest Neighbour Method, Support Vector Machines, Random Forest, Gradient Boosting	80%

Source: Author.

3. Methodology

Figure 2.1 illustrates the Data Flow Diagram, offering a high-level overview of the data processing pipeline used in this project. It outlines the key stages, from input acquisition to the final prediction. The proposed approach consists of three main components: cough sound denoising, segmentation, and classification (pneumonia vs. non-pneumonia). Noise from everyday surroundings can reduce the clarity of cough sounds, making the denoising process essential for accurate classification.

3.1. Data collection

This study collected a robust dataset of 323 pneumonia-positive and 280 non-pneumonia pediatric cough samples. Pneumonia-positive samples were sourced from peer-reviewed journals with reliable, pre-labeled data, while non-pneumonia samples were extracted from public datasets and labeled as negative after review.

3.2. Preprocessing

The preprocessing pipeline was meticulously designed to standardize and prepare the pneumonia-positive and nonpneumonia audio samples, ensuring compatibility with the YAMNet (YouTube Audio Model Network model) and readiness for effective training. Non-pneumonia cough samples were sourced from publicly available YouTube videos and open-access datasets, featuring clear recordings of conditions such as whooping cough (pertussis). These audio files, often available in varying formats and durations, were converted to a standard MP3 format to ensure consistency. Each recording was carefully reviewed, and segments containing distinct cough sounds were identified and extracted. To create uniformity in input data, these segments were trimmed to approximately 10 seconds, ensuring consistent input lengths across all samples. Each non-pneumonia segment was then labeled as pneumonia-negative based on a thorough verification of its clinical context and accompanying metadata.

For pneumonia-positive samples, which were obtained from peer-reviewed journal publications, the cough recordings were already pre-labeled, ensuring high reliability. These recordings, typically longer in duration, were trimmed into 10-second segments to align with the non-pneumonia samples. This consistency in segment length was crucial

for maintaining uniformity during training and evaluation phases. Once segmented, all audio files were resampled to a standard sample rate of 16 kHz, meeting the input requirements of the YAMNet model. This step ensured compatibility while addressing variations in sampling rates across different sources. To further standardize the data, volume normalization was applied, ensuring uniform loudness levels across the dataset and mitigating variations caused by differing recording conditions.

The preprocessed audio files were then fed into the YAMNet model to extract embeddings, which serve as high-dimensional representations of the cough sounds. These embeddings, capturing key features such as pitch, rhythm, and cough patterns, were systematically labeled and stored in structured formats, facilitating efficient loading and use during subsequent training and evaluation.

3.3. Model development

The development of the model for pneumonia detection involved multiple stages, beginning with feature extraction and culminating in the selection of a robust classifier. A critical aspect of the process was leveraging YAMNet, a pre-trained audio classification framework, to extract embeddings from cough sound samples. These embeddings encapsulate both temporal and spectral features, effectively capturing the complex patterns inherent in cough sounds. By utilizing YAMNet's deep neural network architecture, the extracted features were stored as numerical arrays, providing a standardized input for further classification.

The embeddings acted as a bridge between raw audio data and machine learning algorithms, enabling the classifier to focus on high-level patterns rather than raw features.

To address the sequential nature of audio signals, a Long Short-Term Memory (LSTM) network was chosen as the primary classifier. LSTMs, with their ability to retain temporal dependencies over long sequences, are particularly suited for tasks involving sequential data. This architecture allowed the model to analyze the dynamic progression of cough patterns, distinguishing between pneumonia-positive and nonpneumonia cases effectively.

The LSTM network was fine-tuned through several iterations to optimize performance. Key hyperparameters, including the number of hidden layers, neurons per layer, and learning rate, were adjusted using grid search techniques. Regularization methods, such as dropout layers, were

Figure 2.1. Data flow diagram. This diagram provides a high-level overview of the data processing pipeline used in the project, from input acquisition to final prediction.

Source: Author.

incorporated to mitigate overfitting, ensuring that the model generalized well to unseen data.

The dataset was split into training, validation, and test sets with balanced pneumonia and non-pneumonia samples. Data augmentation techniques like time-stretching and pitch shifting improved robustness to real-world audio variations. The final model used YAMNet for feature extraction and LSTM for classification, achieving high accuracy, precision, and recall. This highlights its potential as a scalable, non-invasive diagnostic tool in pediatric healthcare.

4. Evaluation

The evaluation of the proposed deep learning-based model for pneumonia detection was conducted using standard metrics such as accuracy, precision, recall, and F1-score. These metrics provide a extensive understanding of the model's effectiveness in classifying pediatric cough sounds as pneumonia-positive or non-pneumonia. The integration of YAMNet embeddings and an LSTM network significantly contributed to the model's high reliability and consistent predictions, showcasing the strength of combining robust feature extraction with sequential modeling.

4.1. Performance metrics

The model performed exceptionally well across both pneumonia-positive and non-pneumonia cases. It achieved 98% precision and recall for pneumonia-positive samples, ensuring high accuracy with few false positives or missed cases—critical in medical diagnostics. For non-pneumonia cases, it maintained 97% precision and recall, effectively distinguishing between the two conditions. The balanced F1-scores—98% for pneumonia-positive and 97% for non-pneumonia—highlight its strong, reliable overall performance.

4.2. Comparison with traditional methods

Compared to traditional methods like chest X-rays and lab tests, this model offers faster, non-invasive diagnosis using cough sounds, without requiring extensive infrastructure. This makes it ideal for remote or under-resourced areas. Its ability to quickly analyze data supports earlier detection and treatment, improving patient outcomes and reducing healthcare burden.

4.3. Clinical relevance

The model's high precision, recall, and accuracy meet real-world clinical demands for diagnosing pediatric pneumonia. By minimizing false positives and negatives, it supports accurate, timely interventions—crucial in pediatric care where early diagnosis improves recovery and reduces complications. Its scalability allows widespread adoption as a complementary tool to traditional methods. Fast and efficient

audio processing enables large-scale use in diverse clinical settings. By offering a non-invasive, efficient, and scalable alternative, the model bridges traditional diagnostics and AI-driven solutions. Its strong performance across metrics highlights its practical value, especially in resource-limited environments.

5. Results

The proposed model attained an accuracy of 97%, highlighting its effectiveness in distinguishing between pneumonia positive and pneumonia-negative cases. Its performance was assessed using standard evaluation metrics, including precision, recall, F1-score, and accuracy. The confusion matrix reveals a precision of 98% and recall of 98% for pneumonia positive cases, while non-pneumonia cases achieved a precision of 97% and recall of 97%. These findings confirm the model's capability to accurately differentiate between pneumonia-positive and non-pneumonia cough sounds. sounds.Table 2.2 summarizes classification metrics from the proposed model while Figures 2.2, 2.3, and 2.4 display corresponding visualizations.

5.1. Interpretation of results

The results obtained from the evaluation metrics provide significant awareness into the model's performance and its

Table 2.2. Performance metrics

Class	Precision	Recall	F1-Score	Support
Pneumonia-Positive	0.98	0.98	0.98	101
Non-Pneumonia	0.97	0.97	0.97	80
Accuracy	0.97			

Source: Author.

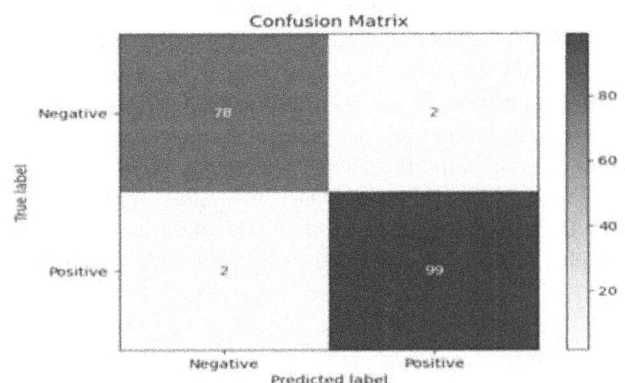

Figure 2.2. Confusion matrix for model evaluation. This matrix demonstrates the model's effectiveness in distinguishing pneumonia-positive and pneumonia negative cases with high precision and recall.

Source: Author.

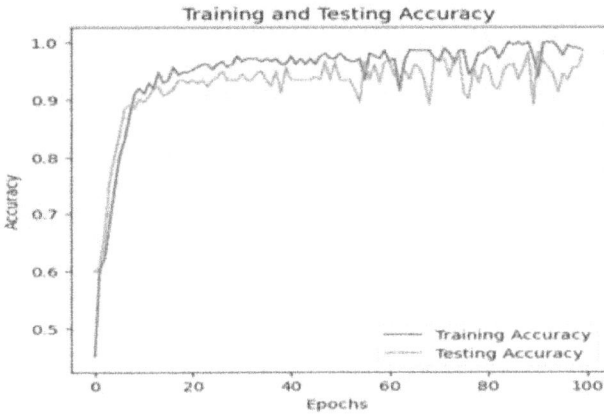

Figure 2.3. Training and testing accuracy. The graph illustrates the model's accuracy during training and testing phases, highlighting its learning progress and performance consistency.

Source: Author.

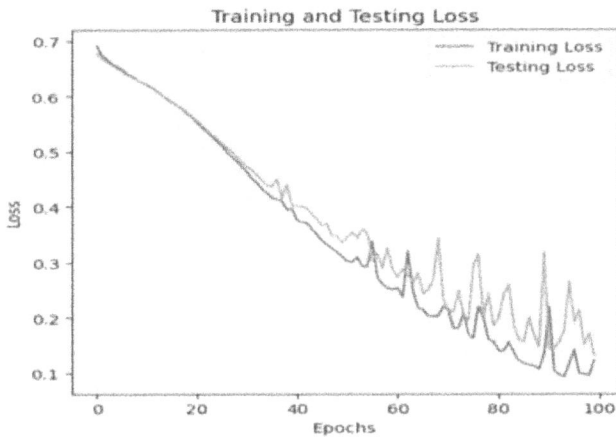

Figure 2.4. Training and testing loss. This plot shows the loss reduction over epochs during training and testing, demonstrating effective model optimization.

Source: Author.

practical implications for pediatric pneumonia detection. Each metric highlights specific strengths and limitations of the proposed approach:

1. **Strengths:** The high recall of 98% for pneumonia positive cases demonstrates the model's capability to correctly identify true cases of pneumonia with less number of false negatives. This is very important in clinical scenarios where early detection can prevent complications and reduce mortality rates in children. The precision for non-pneumonia cases, measured at 97%, underscores the model's capacity to avoid false positives, which is crucial for minimizing unnecessary medical interventions.

   The balanced F1-scores of 98% for pneumonia-positive cases and 97% for non-pneumonia cases reflect the model's ability to achieve a trade-off between sensitivity and

specificity. These results highlight the robustness of the system in handling both categories effectively.

2. **Limitations:** While the model performs exceptionally well overall, future enhancements could focus on improving data diversity and ensuring consistent performance across more diverse datasets. This would further optimize its applicability in real-world scenarios.

3. **Clinical Implications:** The model's strong recall and precision make it suitable for use in resource-constrained environments where early detection is critical but advanced diagnostic tools may be unavailable. Its ability to differentiate effectively between pneumonia-positive and non-pneumonia cases provides a scalable solution for large-scale deployment.

4. **Future Directions:** To further enhance the model's performance, future work should focus on enhancing and upgrading the dataset to include a more diverse range of cough sound recordings from different demographics and clinical conditions. Incorporating multimodal datasets, such as combining cough audio with patient metadata or imaging data, could also improve diagnostic accuracy and reliability. Exploring lightweight model architectures for real-time deployment on mobile devices will enable greater accessibility and usability in remote settings.

6. Conclusion

This study presents a robust and efficient approach for the detection of pneumonia in children using cough sound recordings analyzed through advanced deep learning techniques.

The methodology integrated clinically validated cough sound datasets with a systematic preprocessing pipeline that included resampling to a standardized 16 kHz mono format, denoising to eliminate background noise, and segmenting audio into consistent lengths suitable for feature extraction.

YAMNet was utilized to extract embeddings representing deep temporal and spectral audio features, which were subsequently classified using a Long Short-Term Memory (LSTM) network optimized for sequential data analysis.

The LSTM-based model demonstrated its effectiveness by achieving an accuracy of 97%, as validated through comprehensive performance metrics such as precision, recall, balanced performance in differentiating between pneumonia-positive and non-pneumonia cases, underscoring its potential as a reliable diagnostic tool. The use of padding and uniform data formatting ensured compatibility across various input formats, enhancing the model's generalizability.

The findings emphasize the practicality of using noninvasive, automated audio analysis for pneumonia detection, particularly in resource-constrained environments where traditional diagnostic methods may be inaccessible or cost prohibitive. The cost-effective and scalable nature of this approach makes it well-suited for deployment in remote or underserved regions, bridging gaps in pediatric healthcare diagnostics.

Future work will focus on upgrading the dataset to include broader demographic and clinical representation, exploring alternative feature extraction techniques, and optimizing lightweight model architectures to enable real-time analysis on mobile or edge devices. By addressing these avenues, this research contributes to advancing accessible and accurate healthcare diagnostics, aiming to reduce the global burden of pediatric respiratory diseases.

References

[1] Dymchenko, S. V., Kovalchuk, A. V., & Kovalchuk, A. V. (2023). Methodics and tools of cough sound processing on basic of neural net. *Science and Innovation, 19*(1), 35–41.

[2] Windmon, A., Abdelgawad, S., & Yelamarthi, M. (2021). Towards cough sound analysis using the Internet of Things and deep learning for pulmonary disease prediction. *Transactions on Emerging Telecommunications Technologies, 32*(1), e4184.

[3] Islam, M. A., Hossain, M. S., Muhammad, G., & Gupta, N. (2020). Cough sound detection and diagnosis using artificial intelligence techniques: Challenges and opportunities. *IEEE Access, 8,* 105750–105769.

[4] Pingale, T. H., & Patil, H. T. (2017). Analysis of Cough Sound for Pneumonia Detection Using Wavelet Transform and Statistical Parameters. *2017 International Conference on Computing, Communication, Control and Automation (ICCUBEA),* Pune, India, pp. 1–6, doi:10.1109/ICCUBEA.2017.8463900.

[5] Swarnkar, A., Abeyratne, A., Rajapaksha, U., & Swarnkar, V. (2015). Automatic classification of childhood pneumonia and asthma based on cough sound analysis. *Biomedical Signal Processing and Control, 21,* 89–99.

[6] Pahar, P., Klopper, A., & Niesler, T. (2020). Automatic detection of tuberculosis from voice recordings using convolutional neural networks. *IEEE Journal of Biomedical and Health Informatics, 24*(4), 1043–1053.

[7] Sharan, R. V., Qian, K., & Yamamoto, Y. (2024). Automated Cough Sound Analysis for Detecting Childhood Pneumonia. *IEEE Journal of Biomedical and Health Informatics, 28*(1), 193–203. doi:10.1109/JBHI.2023.3327292. Epub 2024 Jan 4. PMID: 37889830.

[8] Kosasih, K., Abeyratne, U. R., Swarnkar, V., & Triasih, R. (2015). Wavelet augmented cough analysis for rapid childhood pneumonia diagnosis. *IEEE Transactions on Biomedical Engineering, 62*(4), 1185–1194. doi:10.1109/TBME.2014.2381214. Epub 2014 Dec 18. PMID: 25532164.

[9] Amrulloh, Y., Abeyratne, U., Swarnkar, V., & Triasih, R. (2015). Cough Sound Analysis for Pneumonia and Asthma Classification in Pediatric Population. *2015 6th International Conference on Intelligent Systems, Modelling and Simulation,* Kuala Lumpur, Malaysia, pp. 127–131, doi:10.1109/ISMS.2015.41.

[10] Jember, A. F., Ayano, Y. M., & Debelee, T. G. (2023). Robust Cough Analysis System for Diagnosis of Tuberculosis Using Artificial Neural Network. In: Girma Debelee, T., Ibenthal, A., Schwenker, F. (Eds), *PanAfrican Conference on Artificial Intelligence. PanAfriCon AI 2022. Communications in Computer and Information Science,* 1800. Springer, Cham. https://doi.org/10.1007/978-3-031-31327-1 1.

[11] Abeyratne, U. R., Swarnkar, V., Setyati, A., & Triasih, R. (2013). Cough sound analysis can rapidly diagnose childhood pneumonia. *Annals of Biomedical Engineering, 41*(11), 2448–24462. doi:10.1007/s10439-013-0836-0. Epub 2013 Jun 7. PMID: 23743558.

[12] Ellington, L. E., Gilman, R. H., Tielsch, J. M., Steinhoff, M., Figueroa, D., Rodriguez, S., Caffo, B., Tracey, B., Elhilali, M., West, J., & Checkley, W. (2012). Computerised lung sound analysis to improve the specificity of paediatric pneumonia diagnosis in resource-poor settings: Protocol and methods for an observational study. *BMJ Open, 2*(1), e000506. doi:10.1136/bmjopen-2011-000506. PMID: 22307098; PMCID: PMC3274713.

[13] P. P. Moschovis et al., "The diagnosis of respiratory disease in children using a phone-based cough and symptom analysis algorithm: The smart phone recordings of cough sounds 2 (SMARTCOUGH-C 2) trial design," Contemporary Clin. Trials, vol. 101, 2021, Art. no. 106278.

[14] R. V. Sharan, U. R. Abeyratne, V. R. Swarnkar, and P. Porter, "Automatic croup diagnosis using cough sound recognition," IEEE Trans. Biomed. Eng., vol. 66, no. 2, pp. 485–495, Feb. 2019.

[15] R. V. Sharan, S. Berkovsky, D. F. Navarro, H. Xiong, and A. Jaffe, "Detecting pertussis in the pediatric population using respiratory sound events and CNN," Biomed. Signal Process. Control, vol. 68, 2021, Art. no. 102722

[16] Y. Chung et al., "Diagnosis of pneumonia by cough sounds analyzed with statistical features and AI," Sensors, vol. 21, no. 21, 2021, Art. no. 7036

3 An automatic deep convolutional neural network model for finger print classification

K. Mohana Lakshmi[1,a], A. Raji Reddy[2,b], K. Bharath Kumar[1,c], G. Srikanth[1,d], G. Jamuna[3,e], and M. Harish[3,f]

[1]Department of ECE, CMR Technical Campus, Hyderabad, Telangana, India
[2]Department of Mechanical Engineering, CMR Technical Campus, Hyderabad, Telangana, India
[3]UG Student, Department of ECE, CMR Technical Campus, Hyderabad, Telangana, India

Abstract: Fingerprint recognition has become an important part of biometric security systems, mainly due to the uniqueness and integrity of fingerprints. As technology has improved, tampered fingerprints have become a major risk to the security of such systems. To offset this risk, advanced techniques that can easily distinguish between real and manipulated fingerprints are required. This study presents an original fingerprint classification technique that uses high-boost filtering in conjunction with a deep learning (DL) system to differentiate between authentic and modified fingerprints. High-boost filtering is employed to sharpen the fine details of fingerprint images and, hence, make subtle changes more visible. The filtered images are then fed into a deep learning system designed specifically for fingerprint analysis. Experimental findings on the SOCOFing dataset, comprising both authentic and altered fingerprint photos, corroborate the efficacy of our integrated High-boost filtering and deep learning framework. The technique is highly accurate and robust in distinguishing real fingerprints from manipulated fingerprints.

Keywords: Fingerprint classification, high-boost filtering, deep learning, biometric security

1. Introduction

Fingerprint classification refers to the division of fingerprints on the basis of their unique patterns and ridge features. Fingerprints are typically classified into 3 categories: arch, loop, and whorl. The division makes the verification of a fingerprint easier. Techniques that involve "Fuzzy Logic (FL)," "Neural Networks (NN)," "Genetic Algorithms (GA)," and Deep Neural Networks (DNN) are commonly applied for fingerprint evaluation and identification. Fattahi et al. [1] introduced a fingerprint identification system for forensic applications, utilizing "Convolutional Short-Term Memory Networks." Li et al. [2] developed a "Hierarchical Convolutional Neural Network (HCNN)" for image classification, featuring many layers that progressively enhance image categorization. Chang et al. [3] introduced an enhanced DL model, "You Only Look Once version 3 (Yolov3)," which exhibits superior accuracy in object detection. Kumar et al. [4] created an automated detection system employing DL as well as image processing approach to determine whether individuals are wearing face masks. Cao et al. [5] presented a refined neural network inspired by object rotation challenges. Garg et al. [6] introduced an explainable deep learning framework for predicting autism spectrum disorder (ASD) by utilizing behavioural and neuroimaging data. Their research, featured in Computers, Materials and Continua, aimed to enhance diagnostic accuracy while ensuring model transparency, thus showcasing the potential of AI tools in facilitating early ASD detection. Abouhawwash et al. [7] proposed a numerical gradient-based, proximity-oriented method inspired by the Karush-Kuhn-Tucker conditions for addressing multi-objective optimization problems. This research, presented at the Genetic and Evolutionary Computation Conference (GECCO), improves optimization efficiency by evaluating the proximity of solutions to the optimum. Wang et al. [8] presented a lightweight CNN (Convolutional Neural Network) tailored for single-image super-resolution, optimized for efficient deployment on portable devices. Their method strikes a balance between performance and computational efficiency, allowing for high-quality image enhancement with low resource usage. Published in the KSII "Transactions on Internet and Information Systems (TIIS)," this study highlights advancements in deep learning techniques for real-time image analysis on mobile platforms. Zhou et al. [9] introduced a dual-phase network framework: the initial phase identifies candidate minutiae patches, and the subsequent phase determines their orientation and exact position. Although feature extraction plays a vital role in recognition systems, it functions as a transitional step, whereas the

[a]mohana.kesana@gmail.com, [b]director@cmrtc.ac.in, [c]kammarabharathkumar@gmail.com, [d]gimmadisrikanth79@gmail.com, [e]217r1a04f1@cmrtc.ac.in, [f]217r1a04g6@cmrtc.ac.in

DOI: 10.1201/9781003724988-3

current research presents an end-to-end fingerprint recognition framework. Nguyen et al. [10] presented a generalized minutiae extractor employing a modified U-Net architecture for fingerprint segmentation. Their method improves the precision and resilience of minutiae extraction through the application of deep learning, effectively segmenting fingerprint images and enhancing feature detection and recognition capabilities, thereby making it applicable to a range of biometric uses. [11] suggested safe DL. CNN approach for AI-powered malware detection. [12–13] Artificial neural networks and deep learning for limb soft tissue sarcoma image categorization (Figure 3.1).

2. Proposed Approach

2.1. Algorithm

1. **Step 1:** Data Collection: Collect the fingerprint sample images from a publicly accessible Kaggle repository.
2. **Step 2:** Data preprocessing
    - Image enhancement technique is applied on the input images by using High-boost filtering and a deep learning method.
    - Resize the image into uniform dimension (224 × 224 × 3).
    - Normalize the image pixels by scaling them to the range of 0 to 1.
    - Split the data into Training, Validation, Testing.
3. **Step 3:** Model Implementation: Build a customized CNN model by using the fundamental layer of CNN such as convolution, activation, batch normalization, Pooling, dense, and Softmax layer.
4. **Step 4:** Training: Use training data to train and validate the model.
5. **Step 5:** Model Evaluation: Following training, the model has been assessed on test data to measure its generative capability. Includes the creation of a confusion matrix and ROC curves.

2.2. Image sharpening

Improvement of fingerprint images is of crucial significance in biometric systems as it enhances ridges and makes it possible for improved feature extraction for recognition. High-Boost Filtering thus stands out as an advantageous method that enhances images and, in doing so, retains necessary details. The method enhances high-frequency details, and edges and ridges are made clearer without compromising the original fingerprint structure. The method is based on unsharp masking, where the original image minus a low-pass filtered fingerprint image is used to enhance fine details. The method involves multiplying the original image with a boosting factor (A) before subtracting the blurred image, thus retaining high-frequency details and the original structure. In this way, fingerprint images get clearer, leading to improved minutiae detection accuracy, a crucial building block for identification and verification in biometric systems (Figure 3.2).

2.3. Feature extraction and classification

In classification tasks, the extraction of meaningful features is essential for achieving accurate predictions. Traditionally, this relied on manually crafted feature extraction techniques; however, the introduction of "Convolutional Neural Networks (CNNs)" has transformed this approach by learning hierarchical patterns from images in an automated manner. Initial layers of convolutional neural networks recognize edges and textures, while deeper layers identify forms and object components. This automatic feature extraction obviates the necessity for manual engineering, thereby enhancing the efficacy of CNNs for classification objectives. In this work, we have designed a specialized CNN architecture aimed at extracting pertinent feature details from enhanced CT images.

The model starts with a convolutional layer with 128 filters of size (3,3) and stride (3,3), followed by a ReLU activation function and L2 regularization to reduce overfitting.

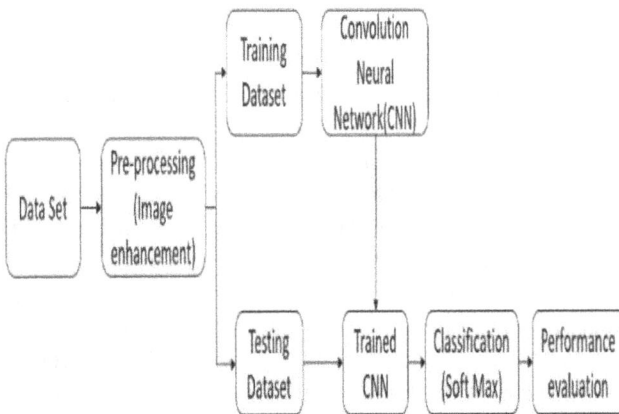

Figure 3.1. Proposed model block diagram.

Source: Author.

(a) Real   (b) Altered

Figure 3.2. (a) Original image; (b) Enhanced images.

Source: Author.

A Batch Normalization layer is then employed to stabilize the training, along with a MaxPooling layer to reduce spatial dimensions. This can be followed by a 1 × 1 convolutional layer, also with 128 filters, which facilitates efficient feature transformation while preserving the spatial structure. Another convolutional layer with 256 filters and a (3,3) kernel is then added, utilizing a stride of (3,3) and same padding to enhance feature extraction across various levels. A max pooling layer is incorporated subsequent to batch normalization to further diminish the dimensions of the feature map. The following layers comprise a 1 × 1 convolutional layer with 256 filters, followed by batch normalization and an additional convolutional layer employing 512 filters with a (3,3) kernel, enabling the network to identify more intricate patterns. This is followed by an additional max pooling layer, a 1 × 1 convolutional layer including 512 filters, as well as batch normalization to enhance the recovered features. The model concludes by flattening the features with a Flatten layer, which forwards them to two fully connected Dense layers containing 1024 and 512 neurons, respectively. Every layer utilizes an ReLU activation function as well as L2 regularization. To mitigate overfitting, Dropout layers with a 50% dropout rate are incorporated. Ultimately, output layer consists of three neurons utilizing a softmax activation function, addressing a three-class classification problem (Benign, Malignant, and Normal). This architecture promotes deep feature extraction, implementation of regularization, and efficient classification while enhancing robustness against overfitting. Figure 3.3 illustrates an overview of the proposed CNN model, including its output shape and parameters.

3. Results and Discussion

The efficacy of proposed model is evaluated by several commonly utilized classification performance metrics that involve sensitivity (recall), specificity, precision, F1-score, "AUC (Area Under the Curve)," and accuracy (Tables 3.1 and 3.2).

Table 3.3 compares the aforementioned 3 algorithms with our algorithm. The four techniques utilized the identical SOCOFing dataset. The table shows that our method has the maximum test "accuracy," "F1 score," "recall," as well as "reduced test loss." Our algorithm has fewest parameters, making it simpler than others (Figure 3.4).

4. Conclusions

In Conclusion, this research focused on classifying fingerprint images by evaluating various CNN architectures, including GoogLeNet, MobiLeNet, ResNet, and a proposed CNN model. All four architectures utilized the "Adam Optimizer" with a learning rate of 0.001 for comparison. The proposed CNN model attained superior performance with an accuracy of 99.8%. The categorization accuracy exhibited in this study is regarded as remarkable in comparison

Table 3.1. Overview of the proposed CNN architecture

Layer (type)	Output Shape	Param #
conv2d_31 (Conv2D)	(None, 74, 74, 128)	3,584
batch_normalization_31 (BatchNormalization)	(None, 74, 74, 128)	512
max_pooling2d_16 (MaxPooling2D)	(None, 37, 37, 128)	0
conv2d_32 (Conv2D)	(None, 37, 37, 128)	16,512
batch_normalization_32 (BatchNormalization)	(None, 37, 37, 128)	512
conv2d_33 (Conv2D)	(None, 13, 13, 256)	295,168
batch_normalization_33 (BatchNormalization)	(None, 13, 13, 256)	1,024
max_pooling2d_17 (MaxPooling2D)	(None, 6, 6, 256)	0
conv2d_34 (Conv2D)	(None, 6, 6, 256)	65,792
batch_normalization_34 (BatchNormalization)	(None, 6, 6, 256)	1,024
conv2d_35 (Conv2D)	(None, 6, 6, 512)	1,180,160
batch_normalization_35 (BatchNormalization)	(None, 6, 6, 512)	2,048
max_pooling2d_18 (MaxPooling2D)	(None, 3, 3, 512)	0
conv2d_36 (Conv2D)	(None, 3, 3, 512)	262,656
batch_normalization_36 (BatchNormalization)	(None, 3, 3, 512)	2,048
flatten_5 (Flatten)	(None, 4608)	0
dense_15 (Dense)	(None, 1024)	4,719,616
dropout_10 (Dropout)	(None, 1024)	0
dense_16 (Dense)	(None, 512)	524,800
dropout_11 (Dropout)	(None, 512)	0
dense_17 (Dense)	(None, 3)	1,539

Source: Author.

Table 3.2. Comparison of performance measures with conventional methods

The Model	Test accuracy	Test loss	F1-score	Recall
ConvLSTM [1]	0.833	0.57	0.832	0.831
HCNN [2]	0.824	0.54	0.82	0.824
YOLOv3 [3]	0.983	0.12	0.982	0.982
The proposed Customized CNN	0.998	0.018	0.997	0.997

Source: Author.

Table 3.3. Comparison of the performance evaluation values of different Nets

The model	Total parameters	Test accuracy	Test loss	F1 score
ResNet50	23,792,612	83.25%	0.57	0.83
MobileNet	3,342, 308	82.41%	0.54	0.82
GoogLeNet	1,037,336	98.28%	0.12	0.98
Proposed algorithm	7,98,244	99.75%	0.018	0.99

Source: Author.

to existing methodologies, which similarly categorize into two types: changed and actual. In future initiatives, aim to augment the dataset size to enhance the precision of the fingerprint categorization system. The future regarding the

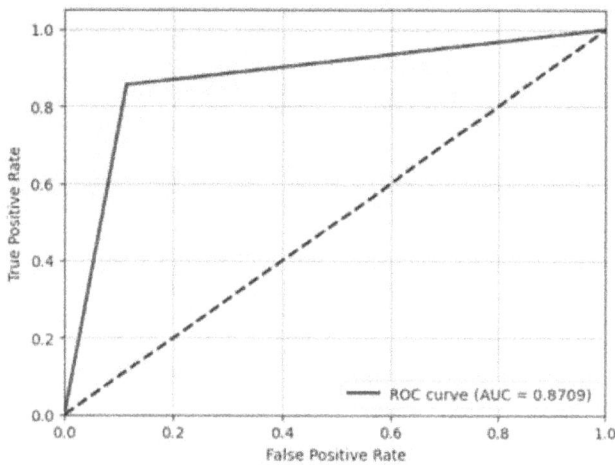

Figure 3.3. ROC curve.

Source: Author.

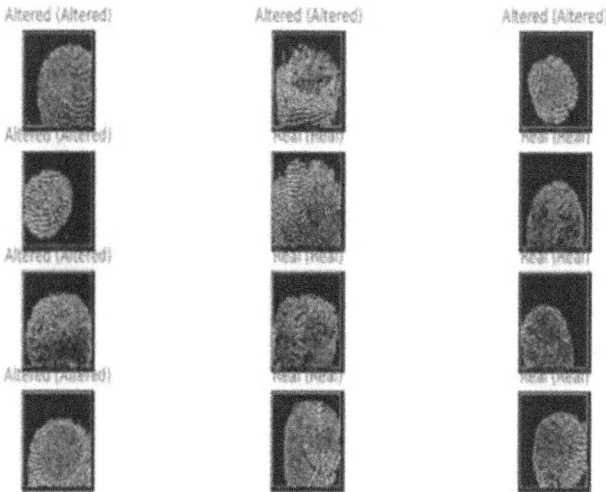

Figure 3.4. Classified finger print images.

Source: Author.

proposed fingerprint recognition algorithm would encompass: (i) actions to fully automate network by regulating every model parameter; (ii) applying our algorithm to more extensive datasets; (iii) updating algorithm to identify partial as well as latent fingerprints.

References

[1]   Fattahi, J. & Mejri, M. (2021). Damaged fingerprint recognition by convolutional long short-term memory networks for forensic purposes. In *2021 IEEE 5th Int. Conf. on Cryptography, Security and Privacy (CSP)* (pp. 193–199). Zhuhai, China, IEEE.

[2]   Khan, A. I., & Wani, M. A. (2019). A common convolutional neural network model to classify plain, rolled and latent fingerprints. *International Journal of Biometrics*, *11*(3), 257–273.

[3]   Tertychnyi, P., Ozcinar, C., & Anbarjafari, G. (2018). Low-quality fingerprint classification using deep neural network. *IET Biometrics*, *7*(6), 550–556.

[4]   Peralta, D., Triguero, I., García, S., Saeys, Y., Benitez, J. M., et al. (2018). On the use of convolutional neural networks for robust classification of multiple fingerprint captures. *International Journal of Intelligent Systems*, *33*(1), 213–230.

[5]   Zhang, Y., Shi, D., Zhan, X., Cao, D., Zhu, K., et al. (2019). Slim-ResCNN: A deep residual convolutional neural network for fingerprint liveness detection. *IEEE Access*, *7*(4), 91476–91487.

[6]   Nahar, P., Tanwani, S., & Chaudhari, N. S. (2018). Fingerprint classification using deep neural network model resnet50. *International Journal of Research and Analytical Reviews (IJRAR)*, *5*(4), 1521–1537.

[7]   Li, C., Miao, F., & Gao, G. (2021). A novel progressive image classification method based on hierarchical convolutional neural networks. *Electronics*, *10*(24), 3183.

[8]   Chang, L., Chen, Y.-T., Wang, J., & Chang, Y. L. (2022). Modified yolov3 for ship detection with visible and infrared images. *Electronics*, *11*(5), 739.

[9]   Kumar, T. A., Rajmohan, R., Pavithra, M., Ajagbe, S. A., Hodhod, R., et al. (2022). Automatic face mask detection system in public transportation in smart cities using IoT and deep learning. *Electronics*, *11*(6), 904.

[10]   Cao, J., Bao, C., Hao, Q., Cheng, Y., & Chen, C. (2021). LPNet: Retina inspired neural network for object detection and recognition. *Electronics*, *10*(22), 2883.

[11]   Murali, K., Maneiah, D., Kiran Kumar, A., Skandha Sanagala, S., Suhasini, R., & Archana, B. (2023, December). A Safe and Secured Deep Learning Cnn Approach for Robust Intelligent Malware Detection Using Artificial Intelligence. In *International Conference on Data Science, Machine Learning and Applications* (pp. 1224–1238). Singapore: Springer Nature Singapore.

[12]   Aparna, Y., Somasekhar, G., Bhaskar, N., Raju, K. S., Divya, G., & Madhavi, K. R. (2023). Analytical Approach for Soil and Land Classification Using Image Processing with Deep Learning. *2023 2nd International Conference for Innovation in Technology (INOCON)* (pp. 1–6). Bangalore, India. doi: 10.1109/INOCON57975.2023.10101169.

[13]   Arunachalam, P., Venkatakrishnan, P., & Janakiraman N. (2021, January). Histopathology image classification for soft tissue sarcoma in limbs using artificial neural networks. In *2021 6th International Conference on Inventive Computation Technologies (ICICT)* (pp. 778–785). IEEE.

4 Data authentication and network level security employing stochastic features and accelerated LSTM

Vikrant Sharma[a] and Ankit Chakrawarti[b]

Department of Computer Science and Engineering, Chameli Devi Group of Institutions, Indore, Madhya Pradesh, India

Abstract: The networks processing bulk amount of data such as IOT, fog and other wide area networks often compromises security at network layer or faces issues with quality and efficiency of existing security mechanisms. There is always a tradeoff between quality parameters such as error rate, authentication metrics and performance parameters such as computational complexity, latency and System overhead while implementing or improving a security mechanism. So there is need of precise system with a chosen stochastic parameters including authentication to be designed and implement. In this work we proposed an LSTM network working on machine learning and learning acceleration to secure a sophisticated IOT based network from particular attacks. The proposed work results in better performance and accuracy as compared to existing systems. This enhanced performance is the key attribute to train LSTM network with acceleration for additional feature and further error detection.

Keywords: Fuzzy logic controllers, pulse-width modulation, proportional-integral-derivatives

1. Introduction

The internet of things can be considered to be a pervasive and diverse connection of interconnected devices over the internet. Variety of devices with different processing power and memory capabilities are actively connected over internet. The internet of things framework needs to be monitored and secured against attacks as the mode of data transmission is wireless thereby making the chances of possible attacks more compared to wired networks.

While considering IOT networks there need to be secure three primary layers of the network:

1. Application Layer authentication
2. Network Layer authentication
3. Physical Later authentication

Generally an efficient NIDS (Network Intrusion Detection System) is desirable for securing any sophisticated IOT framework to analysis and categorize the network traffic. These specific network nodes are placed in a particular place inside the network to analyze every traffic getaway through the network to determine any suspicious or malicious activity or any intrusion inside the Network. The security model to design an intrusion mechanism based on machine learning is being explored off late as copious amounts of data need to be processed by the IoT gateway in real time.

Hassan et al. (2020) proposed a reliable cyberattack detection framework tailored for Industrial IoT (IIoT) networks. Their model emphasizes increasing trustworthiness through intelligent anomaly detection mechanisms. The approach relies on combining network data behavior with security analytics, thereby enhancing the network's resilience against evolving threats. This work highlights the importance of robust detection mechanisms in industrial environments, forming a foundational motivation for employing deeper learning techniques such as LSTM [1].

El-Hajj et al. (2017) conducted an in-depth analysis of authentication techniques in IoT settings. Their study categorizes existing protocols and identifies the trade-offs between lightweight implementation and strong cryptographic assurance. While traditional methods emphasize efficiency, their lack of adaptability to dynamic network behaviors points to the need for more flexible and intelligent solutions like those based on LSTM models [2].

Several studies advocate for the integration of machine learning techniques in intrusion detection. Bertoli et al. (2021) introduced an end-to-end IDS using classical machine learning pipelines for preprocessing, feature extraction, and classification [3]. Meanwhile, Kan et al. (2021) demonstrated the effectiveness of convolutional neural networks (CNNs) in detecting IoT network intrusions. These frameworks laid the groundwork for hybrid approaches, combining multiple deep learning architectures for superior performance [4].

LSTM networks are especially adept at identifying temporal patterns, making them suitable for anomaly detection

[a]vikrant2k14@gmail.com, [b]chak03ankit@gmail.com

DOI: 10.1201/9781003724988-4

in time-dependent data streams. Lindemann et al. (2021) provided a comprehensive survey on LSTM-based models for technical systems, underscoring their predictive accuracy and robustness [5]. Similarly, Musleh et al. (2023) utilized stacked auto encoders with LSTM layers to detect attacks in power system control networks, indicating the model's adaptability across domains [6].

The integration of LSTM with other architectures has been explored extensively. Mahmoud et al. (2022) introduced AE-LSTM, a hybrid model combining auto encoders and LSTM for IoT-specific intrusion detection [7]. Altunay and Albayrak (2023) further advanced this by incorporating adaptive particle swarm optimization into a CNN+LSTM framework, enhancing detection accuracy for industrial IoT threats [8]. Similarly, Issa and Albayrak (2023) proposed a CNN-LSTM-based IDS for DDoS attack detection, reaffirming the importance of hybrid models in capturing both spatial and temporal patterns in network traffic [9].

While the primary focus has been on cybersecurity, LSTM has demonstrated versatility across other domains. Gogineni et al. (2024) applied LSTM to predict compressive strength in civil engineering, showcasing its power in time-series regression tasks [10]. Choudhary et al. (2022) reviewed LSTM's broader utility in materials science, emphasizing its contribution to accelerated material discovery and predictive modeling. These applications validate LSTM's adaptability, reinforcing its selection for complex security frameworks [11]. Recent explorations into neuromorphic computing (Zhang et al., 2023) and floating gate memory show the trajectory of security moving toward hardware-accelerated, brain-inspired computation. These developments, while still emerging, suggest future integration points with LSTM-like architectures to create low-power, real-time authentication systems [12].

Wang et al. (2020) introduced the concept of Intelligent Reflecting Surfaces (IRS) to enhance physical layer security without relying on eavesdropper channel state information (CSI). While IRS is a physical layer concept, its integration with AI-driven security at the network level could represent a future direction for synergizing stochastic modeling with intelligent prediction [13].

2. The IOT Security Model

The networks security model to be designed for IoT security needs to cater to the needs of the system at three levels:

1. End User
2. IoTDs (IOT Devices)
3. Cloud/Fog Server

The security model for IoT is as shown below in Figure 4.1.

The security mechanism shown in Figure 4.2 illustrates the various levels at which the IoT security mechanism needs to work. While end users may be catered to with application level security, the devices and cloud connection needs to be secured through network level or physical level security.

Figure 4.1. Conceptual framework for IoT.
Source: Author.

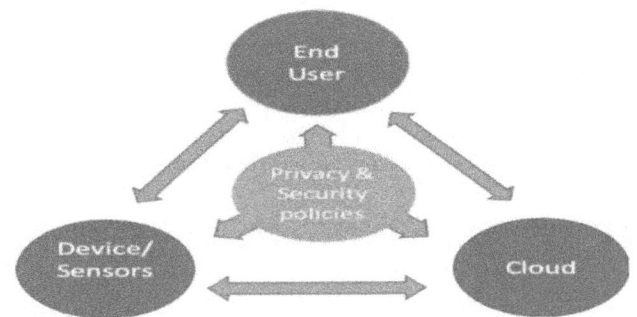

Figure 4.2. The security model for IoT.
Source: Author.

There are some complex points to be considering for IOT network gateways as follows:

1. To opt an IOT Device as authenticated among the network of all IOT based Devices.
2. To Decide how to authenticate opt IOT device which should have minimum BER (bit error rate) and minimum overhead.

Normally parameters of the data bit-flow going to be sent are added on particular IOTD's data in terms of digital footprint which can be extracted in case of analysis of sophisticated attacks on data streams and store it for significantly long duration of time with proper amount of samples extracted by using speculative parameters of data flow originated by IOT based devices.

However bigger length stochastic features will be responsible for increase in system's computational overhead and suspension or Latency in Gateway of Network (Figure 4.3). Minimum overhead consider to be managed although will costs greater bit errors. So there is always a tradeoff between quality parameters like rate of error, authentication metrics with performance parameters such as computational complexity, latency and System overhead. As a result very specific and précised approach of system design to be adopted with proper selection of stochastic parameters and authentication schemes.

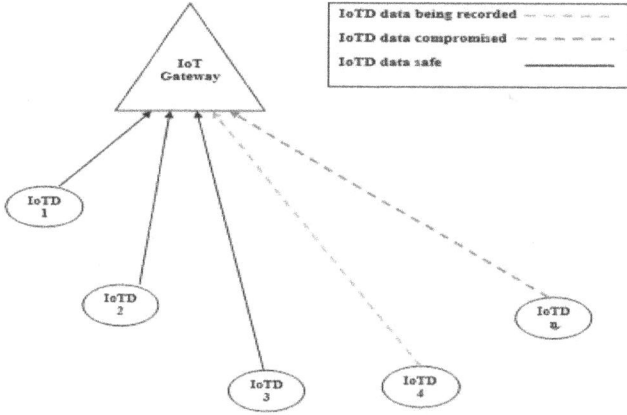

Figure 4.3. The system authentication model.

Source: Author.

3. Proposed Methodology

As our research explain earlier about the main challenges occurs by the IoT gateway with respect to validation of IoT based devices and the calculation of complex problem. That's why a very accurate and more reliable method combining with digital footprints along with data flow to be sent. To make more authenticate transfer and afterwards will add framework to make validate things for:

- Compromised authentication or security
- Non compromise in authentication

We have "N" IoT based devices that are attached with gateway "G" (Figure 4.4). These IoT based devices ("*IoTD* '*i*'") produce a bit flow yi in synchronized way "t" along with their sampling freq. "*fi*". To estimate and controlling status of IoT based devices data flow get arrived at Gateway "G".

Almost attacker gather records, specimens of IoT based devices and will effort to interchange or update data to produce a new flow yi'.

Overall main work of gateway "G" is to differentiate or check generated yi and y' and will prepare a final outcome i depends on the comparative analysis of both bit streams. The decision having some following constraints:

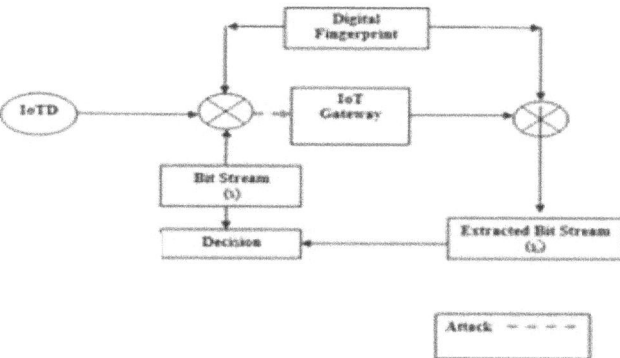

Figure 4.4. Authentication of bulk IoT systems.

Source: Author.

- Many number of IOTDs transmitting concurrently.
- Due to channel effects, changes may be occur in parameter of the bit flow when moving towards IoT based devices to Network-Gateway.
- Facing many problems related with computational power and latency.
- similarity of yi and y'.
- Just we have to consider the embedded IOT data flow illustrate by below equation:

$$w_i(t) = y_i(t) + \beta_i b p_i(t) \forall t = 1 \dots n_i$$

Where:

(t) is the added data flow or bit stream.

pi representing pseudo-noise/sequence with values $[+1/-1]$

β_i = Power of PN Data Stream/Power of Original data Stream.

Where b takes values in the range $[-1, +1]$

n_i will be represent the bits in the sequence

The role of the gateway/hub is to estimate

$$bt = \frac{\langle wi.pi \rangle ni}{\beta i ni}$$

$$b\iota = \frac{\langle yi.pi \rangle ni}{\beta ini} + \frac{\beta ibi \langle pi.pi \rangle ni}{\beta ini}$$

Above expressions can be simplified to obtain:

$b^i = y^i + bi$

There are 2 different state can exist on to evaluation of b^i, are follows:

{

If $(b \uparrow > 0)$

Fetched bit $= 1$

Elseif $(b \uparrow < 0)$

Fetched $_{bit} = -1$

}

The speculative parameters of (t) are as follows:

$$mean \{y_i(t)\} = \mu_i$$
$$variance \{y_i(t)\} = \sigma_i{}^2$$
$$standard\ deviation \{y_i(t)\} = \sigma_i$$
$$Energy \{y_i(t)\} = E_i$$
$$Entropy \{y_i(t)\} = En_i$$

In that case, based on calculation of speculative Measurement shown above, Gateway nodes are getting a bit flow as y^t in place of $y(t)$, It generates an alarm to highlight sophisticated attacks. Long Short Term Memory (LSTM) defined as the most accurate approach available for classification of attacks and intrusion detection (Figure 4.5). Long Short Term Memory (LSTM) is based on basically three gates:

1. Input gate: Based on the current input this gate will decide what to more add on long term memory. It will work on current as well as past input.
2. Output gate: This gate merge all the different cell states and will help to produce the output.
3. Forget gate: This gate is the very important because it will decide what information is to store in long term

memory as well as what is to remove based on current input.

Figure 4.7 Describe about the stochastic feature values of the data flow which are: Energy, Entropy, Correlation, Variance, Standard Deviation, Kurtosis, Skewness, and Mean. The mentioned features poses including digital foot print of the data bit stream.

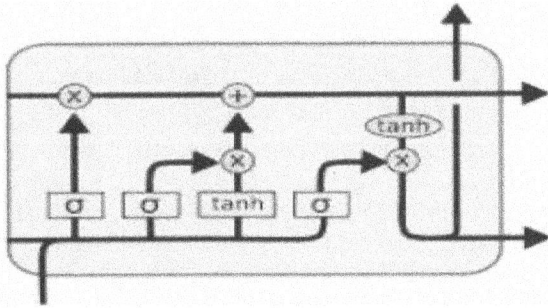

Figure 4.5. LSTM structure.

Source: Author.

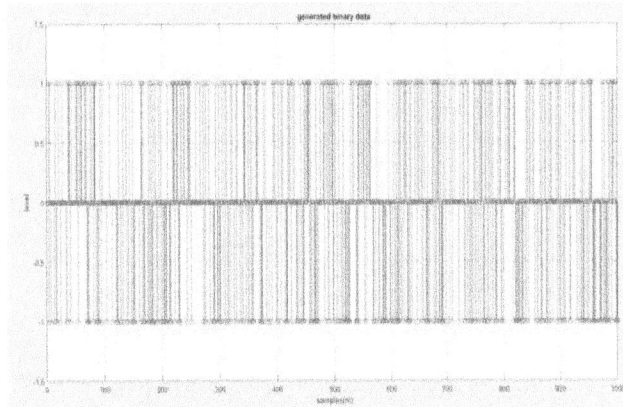

Figure 4.6. Binary stream flow by IoTDs.

Source: Author.

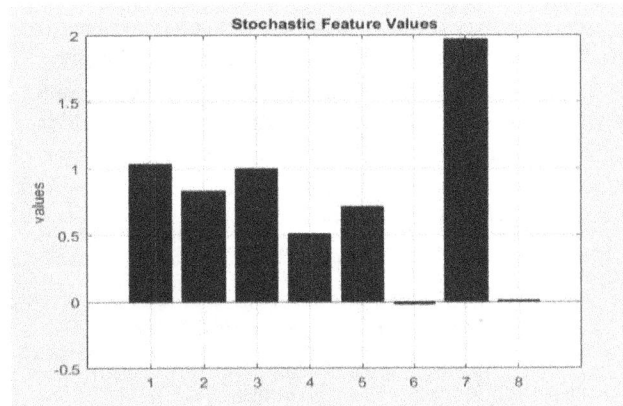

Figure 4.7. Stochastic feature vales of data stream.

Source: Author.

4. Result

Simulation has carried out for 1600 IoTDs

Figure 4.6 describe about the serial sequence binary data flow produce by the IOTDs. This figure shown about two polarities having the logic levels 0 and 1 respectively.

Figure 4.8 showing the PSD (power spectral density) of bit-stream data providing the details of varieties of frequencies of this stream (flow). It will produce most random PSD with respect to produced random data.

The figure shows about if attacks occur the rage of power also varies. In that case magnitude of attacks increased step by step after sample numbers time interval. The Long short term memory (LSTM) trained with the given data, features and given sequence values for detection of various attack. (Figure 4.9).

It is quite possible in case of attacks to observe variation in power spectrum and the intensity of the attack successively increased by the time. So the attack probability has been determined. To make detection of attack more accurate the LSTM trained with data. Some important feature and some key value. For the experiment the hidden layer, dropout, FC and softmax layer' details being explain in LSTM parameters (Figure 4.10).

While increasing the iterations of LSTM based network the significant decrease in loss is observed in the same

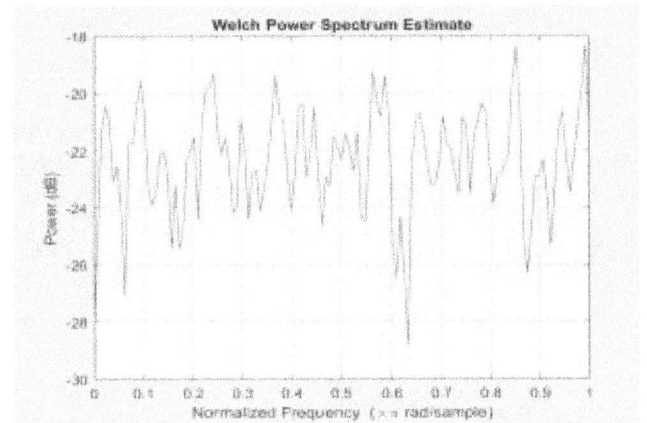

Figure 4.8. PSD of data flow.

Source: Author.

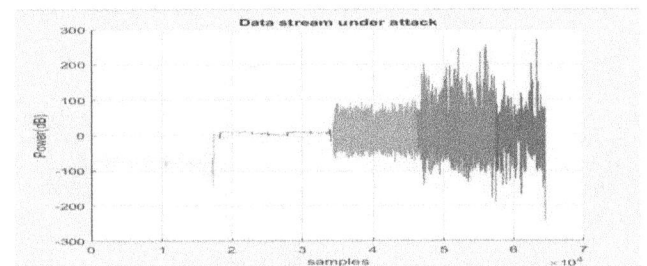

Figure 4.9. Data flow inside attack.

Source: Author.

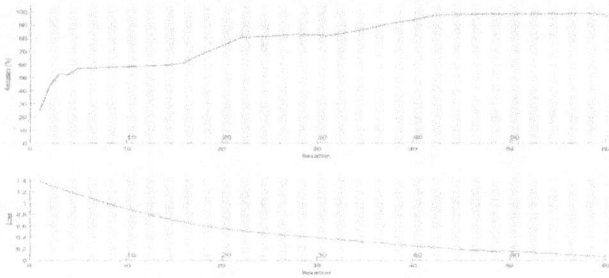

Figure 4.10. Accuracy and loss for LSTM model.
Source: Author.

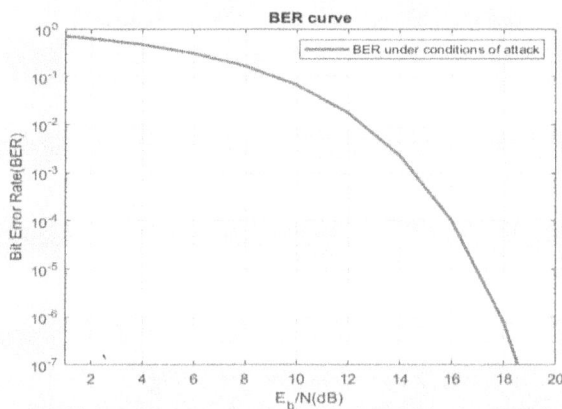

Figure 4.11. BER curve performance of system.
Source: Author.

network. The classified system finally yields 96% accuracy. When we increase in the gateways resources the utility monotonically increases of gateway.

In Figure 4.11 Bit Error Rate (BER) of proposed system design can be observed which clearly demonstrate that accuracy and performance of the system can be enhanced by improving signal capacity with respect to noise. Because of discrete samples of data the strength of the signal described as EB (energy per bit).

5. Conclusions

Proposed work concludes that IOT devices and automation in industries makes IOT network and framework a reliable and much needed solution in today's era. So securing IOT network is still a challenging task because of many affecting factors like bulk data processing and complexity of hardware. The discussed work in this research proposed a sophisticated model using LSTM for system design to analyze the traffic and detect the variety of attacks in IOT networks. The results shown the designed system achieved better performance as compared to existing systems. Enhanced performance used as additional feature attribute for computation and to accelerate LSTM to train and detect errors.

References

[1] Hassan M. M., Gumaei A., Huda S., & Ahmad A. (2020). Increasing the trustworthiness in the industrial IoT networks through a reliable cyberattack detection model. *IEEE Transactions on Industrial Informatics, 16*(9).

[2] El-Hajj, M., Chamoun, M., Fadlallah, A., & Serrhouchni, A. (2017). Analysis of authentication techniques in Internet of Things (IoT). *2017 1st Cyber Security in Networking Conference (CSNet)* (pp. 1–3).

[3] Bertoli, G. D. C., Pereira Jr., L. A., Saotome, O., Santos, A. L. D., Verri, F. A. N., Marcondes, C. A. C., Barbieri, S., Rodrigues, M. S., & Oliveira, J. M. P. D. (2021). An end-to-end framework for machine learning based network intrusion detection system. *IEEE Access, 9,* 106790–106805. doi:10.1109/ACCESS.2021.3101188.

[4] Kan, X., Fan, Y., Fang, Z., Cao, L., Xiong, N. N., Yang, D., & Li, X. (2021). A novel IoT network intrusion detection approach based convolutional neural network. *Information Science, 568,* 147–162. doi:10.1016/j.ins.2021.03.060.

[5] Lindemann, B., Maschler, B., Sahlab, N., & Weyrich, M. (2021). A survey on anomaly detection for technical systems using LSTM networks. *Computers in Industry, 131,* 103498. doi: 10.1016/j.compind.2021.103498.

[6] Musleh, A. S., Chen, G., Dong, Z. Y., Wang, C., & Chen, S. (2023). Attack detection in automatic generation control systems using LSTM-based stacked autoencoders. *IEEE Transactions on Industrial Informatics, 19*(1), 153–165. doi: 10.1109/TII.2022.3178418.

[7] Mahmoud, M., Kasem, M., Abdallah, A., & Kang, H. S. (2022, July). Ae-lstm: Autoencoder with lstm-based intrusion detection in iot. In *2022 International Telecommunications Conference (ITC-Egypt)* (pp. 1–6). IEEE.

[8] Altunay, H. C., & Albayrak, Z. (2023). A hybrid CNN+LSTM-based intrusion detection system for industrial IoT networks. *Engineering Science and Technology, an International Journal, 38,* 101322.

[9] Issa, A. S. A., & Albayrak, Z. (2023). DDoS attack intrusion detection system based on hybridization of CNN and LSTM. *Acta Polytechnica Hungarica, 20*(2), 1–19.

[10] Gogineni, A., Rout, M. D., & Shubham, K. (2024). Evaluating machine learning algorithms for predicting compressive strength of concrete with mineral admixture using long short-term memory (LSTM) Technique. *Asian Journal of Civil Engineering, 25,* 1921–1933.

[11] Choudhary, K., DeCost, B., Chen, C., Jain, A., Tavazza, F., Cohn, R., Park, C. W., Choudhary, A., Agrawal, A., Billinge, S. J., et al. (2022). Recent advances and applications of deep learning methods in materials science. *NPJ Computational Materials, 8*(1), 59.

[12] Zhang, Q., Zhang, Z., Li, C., Xu, R., Yang, D., & Sun, L. (2023). Van der Waals materials-based floating gate memory for neuromorphic computing. *Chip, 2*(4), 100059.

[13] Wang, H. M., Bai, J., & Dong, L. (2020). Intelligent reflecting surfaces assisted secure transmission without eavesdropper's CSI. *IEEE Signal Processing Letters, 27,* 1300–1304.

5   Advancements in object detection and semantic segmentation with Detectron2

Om R. Muddapur[a], Ratan Dhane[b], Chandanagouda H.[c], Swati V. Bhat[d], Lalitha Madanbhavi[e], and Padmashree Desai[f]

School of Computer Science and Engineering, KLE Technological University, Hubli, India

Abstract: The paper explores the potential of Detectron2, a state-of-the-art computer vision framework, in addressing the challenges of tailoring advanced pre-trained models for domain-specific applications. Emphasis is placed on its adaptability across diverse visual tasks like object detection and semantic segmentation, utilizing datasets such as COCO and custom image sets to evaluate performance. With the increasing demand for robust solutions in autonomous vehicles, healthcare, retail analytics, and surveillance, the effective customization of such frameworks becomes crucial. This work delves into the Detectron2 pipeline, emphasizing the fine-tuning of models for object detection and image segmentation to optimize performance. Our approach achieves a mean Average Precision (mAP) of 92%, demonstrating its effectiveness in real world applications. The results bridge the gap between cutting-edge pre-trained models and their real-world usability, enabling the development of scalable and accurate solutions tailored to specific industry needs.

Keywords: Object detection, image segmentation, Detectron2, computer vision, domain-specific applications, pre-trained models, fine tuning, performance optimization

1. Introduction

Computer vision has recently transformed the industrial world, making it possible for machines to process and understand visual data at a level of accuracy that was thought to be unattainable. The two core tasks include object detection and image segmentation. Applications range from self-driving cars [1] to health care, retail analytics, and surveillance. For instance, self-driving vehicles rely on object detection to assess spatial relationships among objects [2] on the road, while healthcare systems leverage image segmentation to perform precise medical imaging [3], aiding in diagnostics and treatment planning. In retail, image segmentation enables customer behaviour analysis for store layout optimization, while surveillance systems use object detection and segmentation for real-time monitoring and threat identification [4]. Although these applications are becoming widespread, implementing and customizing computer vision models in specific domains remain a challenging task. This is mainly because the workflows involved in this process tend to be highly complex, along with considerable computational resources to train, fine-tune, and deploy these models effectively. Detectron2 [5], developed by Facebook AI, provides a comprehensive solution to these challenges. The framework provides the recent algorithms, along with pre-trained models and fine-tuning tools that can be used for customizing object detection and image segmentation related tasks [6].

Beyond permitting users to adapt to existing models, Detectron2 makes it easy to transfer to domain specific requirements so it is a quite powerful tool for practical deployments.

Although the benefits are many, adapting general-purpose models to highly specialized tasks is still not straightforward. Fine-tuning models [7], ensuring compatibility with custom datasets, and optimizing performance for real-time applications can be daunting, especially when domain-specific needs require a high degree of accuracy. The framework offers flexibility, but it requires a clear understanding of how to implement and modify pipelines to suit specific application goals. As a consequence, there is a significant difference between the accessibility of pre-trained models and proper adaptation to special tasks. It has been shown that this gap becomes an obstacle in the wide deployment of computer vision models in areas that require precision and scalability. Two of the core tasks in computer vision are targeted by this paper: object detection and image segmentation. We investigate how the Detectron2 [8] framework can be used to fine-tune pre-trained models for these tasks, aiming to provide researchers and practitioners with actionable insights into the effective customization of object detection and image segmentation systems. The aim is to enable the deployment of accurate, efficient, and scalable computer vision solutions tailored to real-world, domain-specific challenges.

Further in the paper it's discussed how the pipeline within Detectron2 [9] can be optimized to handle complex tasks in

[a]01fe22bcs262@kletech.ac.in, [b]01fe22bcs153@kletech.ac.in, [c]01fe22bcs287@kletech.ac.in, [d]01fe22bcs273@kletech.ac.in, [e]lalita@kletech.ac.in, [f]padmashri@kletech.ac.in

DOI: 10.1201/9781003724988-5

various domains, thus improving the performance and versatility of object detection and image segmentation systems. By detailing the steps in fine-tuning these models, we have provided a well-structured approach which counters the challenges in the technology's technical implementation as well as its practical deployment. It should bridge the gap between the progress in computer vision that is happening academically with the practical applicability of the progress by the design of solutions not only being accurate but also scalable across different domains. Ultimately, by providing clear methodologies for adapting models to specific use cases, this work will empower the next generation of computer vision practitioners to build smarter, more efficient systems that can address the growing demand for high-precision, domain specific solutions across industries.

The work is divided into five sections. Section 2 reviews background studies on object detection and segmentation, focusing on Detectron2. Section 3 details the proposed model, outlining the workflow integrating image and text inputs for dual tasks using Detectron2. Section 4 presents visualizations and results, demonstrating the model's effectiveness. Finally, Section 5 summarizes key findings and suggests future improvements for real-world applications.

2. Background Study

The advancement in computer vision has, in recent years, paved the way to algorithms and frameworks that allow more complex things, like object detection, image segmentation, Thus, its tasks have applied in places, such as self-driving cars, medical diagnostics, retail analytics, and surveillance changing the method with which the data from visions can be assessed.

Object detection [10] is one of the most critical branches of computer vision, and the location of an object with the identification within the image has been facilitated using Haar cascades and HOG features until recently by models based on deep learning that are better in accuracy and speed like Faster R-CNN, YOLO [11], and SSD [12]. In autonomous driving systems, such methods are used for high-precision detection of pedestrians, vehicles, and traffic signs [1]. This has significantly impacted healthcare, where the segmentation of regions of interest in medical images helps in accurate diagnostics.

Semantic segmentation assigns a class label to every pixel in an image, distinguishing different object categories and background areas [13]. This technique has profoundly impacted fields like healthcare, where segmenting regions of interest in medical images aids in accurate diagnostics [14].

Despite these advancements, the real-world deployment of these tasks faces significant challenges with regards to scalability, domain adaptation, and computational efficiency. Detectron2, developed by Facebook AI, has overcome many of these challenges through its modular and scalable architecture in implementing state-of-the-art models [15]. It offers pretrained models and tools for fine-tuning on custom datasets so that users can adapt models effectively for domain-specific applications.

Even though Detectron2 makes it easier to work with pre-trained models, the application of the research model to the field requires a knowledge of how to properly adapt to the varied needs in the different domains. Some previous research has showcased applications of Detectron2 in self driving car object detection and medical image segmentation, promising the potential of the complex issues' resolution. In other words, it lacks the overall structured pipeline for guiding a user through every stage, starting from using a pre-trained model and fine-tuning it toward its specific applications-this is essentially what this paper explores [16].

3. Proposed Model

The proposed model processes input images in PNG or JPEG formats, utilizing multiple libraries, with Detectron2 at its core for fast and efficient object detection. Various object detection algorithms, including Mask R-CNN [17], RetinaNet [18], Faster R-CNN [19], RPN, Fast R-CNN [20], R-FCN [21], and others, are employed to achieve accurate results. These algorithms leverage backbones and proposals, applying cropping and wrapping techniques to implement box detection and semantic segmentation.

Figure 5.1 illustrates a streamlined workflow for leveraging computer vision models. The process begins by importing the necessary libraries, followed by selecting a specific model task, such as image segmentation or object detection. Based on the selected task, the detection method is chosen, with options like processing images, videos, or live feeds. If specific target classes are provided, the system filters and processes the data. The workflow then proceeds to detect and process the relevant data, display the results for visualization, and concludes with actionable insights. This representation ensures a clear and adaptable approach for various input types and tasks.

The model combines object detection with bounding boxes and segmentation masks. Bounding boxes can locate objects in an image, but segmentation masks offer pixel-level precision, thus enhancing the ability of the model to identify overlapping objects and complex features. This approach will therefore provide accurate object localization as well as detailed identification, hence allowing a better understanding of the scene.

In order to improve the quality of the input data, image manipulation techniques such as grayscale conversion, cartoonization [22], bilateral filtering [23], and Gaussian filtering [24] have been applied. These preprocessing steps help to optimize the image input for the detection and segmentation tasks, ensuring better performance on a variety of images, including those with varying lighting, resolution, or noise levels.

3.1. Implementation of the model

The model is implemented through a series of steps, starting with installation, followed by data preprocessing, and concluding with object detection and image segmentation.

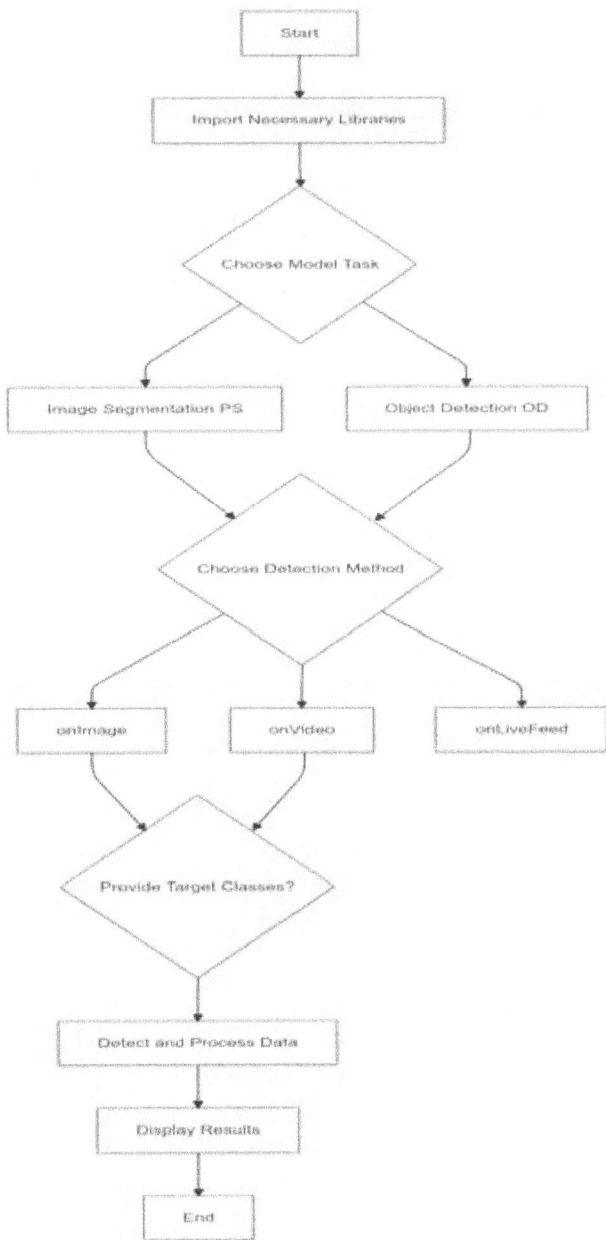

Figure 5.1. Workflow of model.

Source: Author.

Figure 5.2 illustrates an architecture designed for image analysis using Detectron2 for object detection and semantic segmentation. The input comprises an image (to be analyzed) and text (indicating the specific objects to detect). After pre-processing, the workflow branches into two tasks: object detection (OD), which identifies and localizes objects using bounding boxes, and semantic segmentation (PS), which highlights object boundaries and regions. The Detectron2 core model performs these tasks, with the results filtered according to the target classes specified in the text input. Finally, the processed outputs are visualized as segmentation results (colour-masked regions) and detection results (bounding boxes with

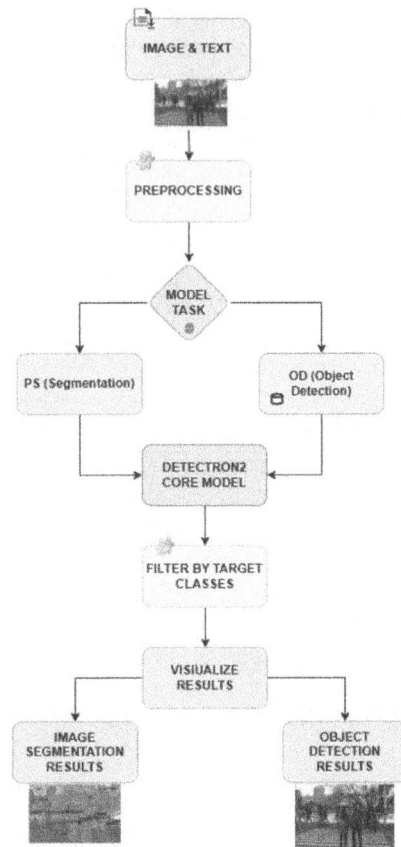

Figure 5.2. Architecture of the proposed model.

Source: Author.

labels), making this architecture suitable for applications such as autonomous driving and surveillance.

1. *Installing and Importing Required Dependencies:* The project relies on several libraries and tools to accomplish various tasks. PyYAML is used for parsing configuration files, which helps manage settings easily. CUDA enables GPU acceleration to speed up computations. Torch is the primary framework for deep learning, providing the necessary tools for building and training models. Torchvision is used for handling image-related tasks and model utilities. Detectron2 Logger assists with detailed logging and debugging during execution. Numpy handles numerical computations, while JSON is used for data serialization and parsing. OpenCV supports image preprocessing and manipulation, and Random generates random numbers for experiments. Finally, Detectron2 Utilities help with managing datasets, configurations, and evaluation, simplifying the overall workflow.

2. *Data Preparation and Preprocessing:* The input images are collected in standard formats such as PNG and JPEG. These images are preprocessed to ensure compatibility with the Detectron2 framework. Preprocessing steps include resizing, normalization, and augmentation to enhance the robustness of the model. Additional

techniques such as grayscale conversion and Gaussian filtering are applied for specific use cases, ensuring optimal input quality for object detection and segmentation tasks. The dataset is collected from publicly available sources like COCO [25]. The annotations for the dataset must be suitable for tasks like object detection and image segmentation.

3. *Object Detection:* The algorithm 5.1 dictates a workflow as follows: initialize the required modules and configurations. Process an image to make predictions about the objects presented in it; filter the detection results based on target classes for objects; visually present the outputs by overlaying bounding boxes around the detected object and labels next to them, and finally by displaying the output using OpenCV.

Algorithm 5.1 Object Detection Workflow

Input image path (image_path), Target classes (target_classes) Image with bounding boxes and labels for detected objects Initialization:

1. Import modules (Detector, cv2) and initialize the Detector with model type.
2. Load model configuration, weights, and set device (CPU/GPU).
3. Create a DefaultPredictor for inference.

Input Handling:

1. Load image from image_path.
2. Specify optional target_classes.

Inference and Filtering:

1. Pass image to the predictor to get bounding boxes, class labels, and confidence scores.
2. If target_classes is specified, retain matching predictions.

Visualization and Output:

1. Overlay bounding boxes and labels using Visualizer.
2. Display the result with OpenCV (cv2.imshow) and wait for user input.
3. Release resources and exit.
4. *Image Segmentation and Labeling:* The uploaded image undergoes image segmentation, where segmentation masks are generated for each detected object. This process involves the following steps:
   • Extracting the backbone and generating proposals, followed by cropping and wrapping to segment objects from the background.
   • Implementing segmentation by applying masks to the detected objects.
   • Using image segmentation techniques to process and label the objects in the image with pixel-level precision.
   • Displaying the final image with labeled segmentation masks, providing clear annotations for each segmented object.

Steps for Image Segmentation and Labeling

1. Obtain the image from either the uploaded input or a pre-existing dataset like MS-COCO, containing labeled object instances.
2. Create a Detectron2 configuration and use the Default-Predictor for running inference on the image.
3. Choose an appropriate model from Detectron2's model zoo, such as Mask R-CNN, which is specifically designed for image segmentation tasks.
4. Visualize the final processed and labeled image using Detectron2's visualization tools, showing segmentation masks applied to detected objects.

4. Visualization and Results

Using Detectron2's powerful visualization tools, we can display the predictions made by the model on images, such as bounding boxes and segmentation masks. These visualizations provide a clear view of the model's performance, allowing us to directly compare predicted results with the ground truth. For instance, bounding boxes help us evaluate the accuracy of object detection, while segmentation masks offer insights into the pixel-level precision of image segmentation.

Figure 5.3 represents the input image used for object detection and segmentation.

Figure 5.4 showcases object detection where bounding boxes highlight all the detected objects within the image, demonstrating the model's versatility in recognizing and localizing multiple objects simultaneously in a complex scene.

The visualization also serves as a tool for debugging and identifying areas where the model may struggle, such as misclassifications, incorrect bounding box placements, or poor segmentation in challenging scenarios. These insights are essential for iterating on the model, adjusting parameters, or augmenting the training data to improve overall performance.

Figure 5.3. Input image.

Source: Author.

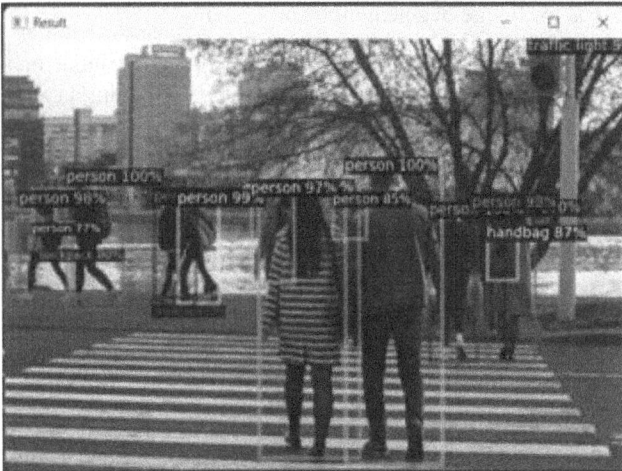

Figure 5.4. Object detection.

Source: Author.

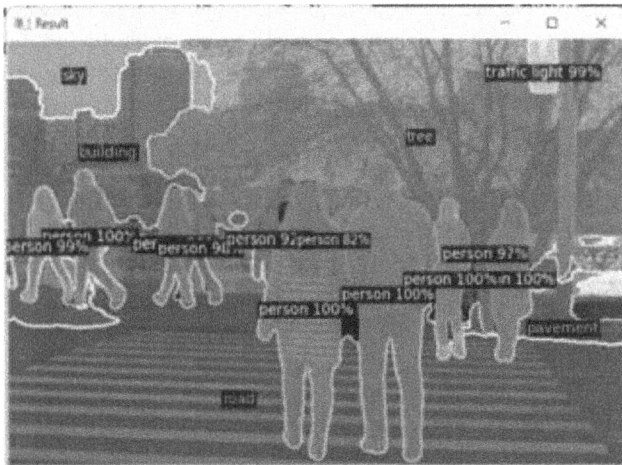

Figure 5.5. Image segmentation.

Source: Author.

Figure 5.5 illustrates image segmentation, where distinct segmentation masks are applied to detected objects, highlighting the model's ability to achieve pixel-level precision in differentiating and labeling various elements within the image.

The annotated images with bounding boxes and segmentation masks will be used to present the results across various test scenarios. These scenarios may include detecting objects in cluttered environments, segmenting objects of varying sizes, or handling occlusions. Performance across these diverse scenarios is crucial for assessing the robustness and scalability of the model in real-world applications of object detection and image segmentation.

The comparison shows that the Detectron model outperforms YOLOv11 in terms of mAP@50–95, Precision, and Recall, indicating its higher accuracy and robustness. However, YOLOv11 offers a faster average inference time (6.1 ms compared to 9.2 ms for Detectron), making it more

Table 5.1. Performance comparison of yolov11 with detectron model

Model Name	mAP@50–95	Precision (%)	Recall (%)	Avg Inference Time (ms)
YOLOv11	89.00	96.16	94.10	6.1
Detectron	92.00	97.50	95.80	9.2

Source: Author.

suitable for real-time applications where speed is critical (Table 5.1). This highlights the trade-off between accuracy and inference time, with Detectron excelling in accuracy and YOLOv11 providing a faster solution for time-sensitive tasks [17, 26].

5. Conclusion

In this project, we developed an efficient pipeline for advanced computer vision tasks like object detection and semantic segmentation using Detectron2. By fine-tuning pre-trained models on datasets such as COCO and custom datasets, we achieved strong performance, with a mean Average Precision (mAP) of 92%. Our results are supported by both visual outputs and quantitative metrics. The system's flexibility makes it suitable for diverse use cases.

Looking ahead, optimizing the model for deployment on resource-constrained devices, improving real-time performance, and integrating multimodal inputs like depth or audio are exciting directions. Enhancing cross-domain generalization and deploying the system on edge devices like drones or mobile phones will expand its usability across fields such as healthcare, autonomous systems, and surveillance. With these advancements, the project can unlock new possibilities and make a broader impact in real-world applications.

References

[1] Balasubramaniam, A., & Pasricha, S. (2022). Object detection in autonomous vehicles: Status and open challenges.

[2] Shi, Z., Yin, Z., Chang, S., Yi, X., & Yu, X. (2024). Efficient oriented object detection with enhanced small object recognition in aerial images.

[3] Zhang, S., Li, Z., Zhou, H.-Y., Ma, J., & Yu, Y. (2023). Advancing 3d medical image analysis with variable dimension transform based supervised 3d pre-training. *Neurocomputing*, *529*, 11–22.

[4] Çalışkan, A., Özdemir, V., Baytörk, E., Öztörk, O. M., Kefeli, O. D., & Üzengi, A. (2022, September). Real time retail analytics with computer vision. In *2022 Innovations in Intelligent Systems and Applications Conference (ASYU)* (pp. 1–4). IEEE.

[5] Ataullha, M., Rabby, M. H., Rahman, M., & Azam, T. B. (2023). Bengali document layout analysis with detectron2.

[6] Zhong, J., Li, Z., Cui, Y., & Fang, Z. (2025). 4d-cs: Exploiting cluster prior for 4d spatio-temporal lidar semantic segmentation.

[7] Akyon, F. C., Onur Altinuc, S., & Temizel, A. (2022). Slicing aided hyper inference and fine-tuning for small object detection. In *2022 IEEE International Conference on Image Processing (ICIP)* (pp. 966–970). IEEE.

[8] Eslamian, A., & Ahmadzadeh, M. R. (2022). Det-slam: A semantic visual slam for highly dynamic scenes using detectron2. In *2022 8th Iranian Conference on Signal Processing and Intelligent Systems (ICSPIS)* (pp. 1–5). IEEE.

[9] Yague, F. J., Diez-Pastor, J. F., Latorre-Carmona, P., & Osorio, C. I. G. (2022). Defect detection and segmentation in x-ray images of magnesium alloy castings using the detectron2 framework.

[10] Yuan, X., Zheng, Z., Li, Y., Liu, X., Liu, L., Li, X., Hou, Q., & Cheng, M.-M. (2025). Strip r-cnn: Large strip convolution for remote sensing object detection.

[11] Liu, L., Feng, J., Chen, H., Wang, A., Song, L., Han, J., & Ding, G. (2024). Yolo-uniow: Efficient universal open-world object detection.

[12] Ren, S., He, K., Girshick, R., & Sun, J. (2016). Faster r-cnn: Towards real-time object detection with region proposal networks.

[13] Litjens, G., Kooi, T., Bejnordi, B. E., Setio, A. A. A., Ciompi, F., Ghafoorian, M., van der Laak, J. A., van Ginneken, B., & Sanchez, C. I. (2017). A survey on deep learning in medical image analysis. *Medical Image Analysis, 42*, 60–88.

[14] Lin, H., Li, N., Yao, P., Dong, K., Guo, Y., Hong, D., Zhang, Y., & Wen, C. (2025). Generalization-enhanced few-shot object detection in remote sensing.

[15] Cao, Z., Simon, T., Wei, S.-E., & Sheikh, Y. (2017). Realtime multi-person 2d pose estimation using part affinity fields.

[16] He, K., Gkioxari, G., Dollar, P., & Girshick, R. (2018). Mask r-cnn.

[17] He, K., Gkioxari, G., Dollar, P., & Girshick, R. (2017). Mask r-cnn. *Proceedings of the IEEE International Conference on Computer Vision (ICCV)* (pp. 2961–2969).

[18] Lin, T.-Y., Goyal, P., Girshick, R., He, K., & Dollar, P. (2017). Focal loss for dense object detection. *Proceedings of the IEEE International Conference on Computer Vision (ICCV)*, 2980–2988.

[19] Ren, S., He, K., Girshick, R., & Sun, J. (2015). Faster r-cnn: Towards real-time object detection with region proposal networks. *Advances in Neural Information Processing Systems (NeurIPS)*, 91–99.

[20] Girshick, R. (2015). Fast r-cnn. *Proceedings of the IEEE International Conference on Computer Vision (ICCV)*, 1440–1448.

[21] Dai, J., Li, Y., He, K., & Sun, J. (2016). R-fcn: Object detection via region based fully convolutional networks. *Advances in Neural Information Processing Systems (NeurIPS)*, 379–387.

[22] Kim, S. J., Lee, S. H., & Lee, K. W. (2007). Cartoon-style rendering of digital images using bilateral filtering. *IEEE Transactions on Visualization and Computer Graphics, 13*(6), 1176–1183.

[23] Tomasi, C., & Manduchi, R. (1998). Bilateral filtering for gray and color images. In *Proceedings of the IEEE International Conference on Computer Vision (ICCV)* (pp. 839–846). IEEE.

[24] Gonzalez, R. C., & Woods, R. E. (2008). *Digital Image Processing*. Pearson, 3rd ed.

[25] Lin, T.-Y., Maire, M., Belongie, S., Bourdev, L., Girshick, R., Hays, J., Perona, P., Ramanan, D., Dollar, P., & Zitnick, C. L. (2014). Microsoft coco: Common objects in context. *arXiv preprint arXiv:1405.0312*.

[26] Redmon, J., Divvala, S., Girshick, R. B., & Farhadi, A. (2016). You only look once: Unified, real-time object detection. In *Proceedings of the IEEE Conference on Computer Vision and Pattern Recognition (CVPR)* (pp. 779–788).

6   GenMedix: Medical report generation and summarization using generative AI

Narendra U. P.ᵃ, Daxia Vlora Dmello, Devi Janani, Kirthana Kamath P., and Avani K. D.

Department of Information Science and Engineering, Mangalore Institute of Technology and Engineering (MITE), India

Abstract: The healthcare industry today is constantly evolving alongside technology, making efficiency in documentation and medical data analysis more important than ever. GenMedix has designed an advanced platform that automates the generation and summarization of medical reports using generative AI, natural language processing and transformer models. Through automated analysis of electronic health records, GenMedix provides real-time reports, summaries and contextually relevant health information so that clinicians can make accurate decisions faster. Innovative machine learning approaches are employed in the system to allow versatility across different medical datasets while keeping high levels of security and accuracy in data control practices. Patients can experience better results with the smart automation that improves the documentation processes and overall patient care. The easy to learn and navigate interface allows clinicians and healthcare professionals to workflow effortlessly, saving valuable time and reducing strain. The ability to improve efficiency, minimize errors and provide actionable insights into the reporting makes GenMedix a forward thinking MedTech platform. This paper focuses on examining the design, implementation and impacts of GenMedix, showcasing its revolutionary features in medical reporting and patient care.

Keywords: Generative AI, medical report automation, natural language processing (NLP)

1. Introduction

The healthcare industry relies on medical documentation for decision-making purposes, tracking patients' medical histories and fulfilling legal requirements. To ensure timely diagnoses, treatment planning and communication in the healthcare setting, accurate reports are necessary. With healthcare facilities increasingly utilizing electronic health records [3] to manage patient information, there has been an increase in digital documentation, making paper files easier to organize and access. However, these methods still entail a significant amount of manual data entry that is not only difficult, but also time-consuming. Furthermore, these procedures don't come without the possibility of human mistakes and misinterpretations, which can lead to inconsistency in the information recorded, inaccurate diagnoses or delayed treatments and patients' safety concerns.

There is a greater urgency for automated solutions to improve medical documentation due to an increase in patient data and the need for quicker decisions. To address this issue, GenMedix is an innovative AI platform that uses generative AI in conjunction with natural language processing [11] and transformer models [1] to automate the creation and summarization of medical reports. The system extracts patient data from the EHRs, processes it and structures it into medical reports with remarkable accuracy and conciseness. GenMedix applies deep learning NLP approaches [7] to enable contextual analysis of the patients' records, which guarantees that reports will not only provide all the necessary information, but will also be created for specific patients. Unlike traditional documentation systems that are rule-based, GenMedix has incorporated the use of more advanced AI transformer models [1] such as NVIDIA's Llama-3.1 Nemotron-70B, which are optimized for medical use. These models, which are trained using large amounts of healthcare data, are able to create contextually relevant and clinically meaningful documents with great accuracy. Besides, the integration of summarization features provides clinicians with time-sensitive information without compromising their complexity and enhancing clinical decision making [5].

In terms of flexibility and scale, GenMedix is able to accommodate a multitude of medical datasets from different specialties, such as cardiology, oncology and neurology. This paper offers a comprehensive study on the design, methodology and implementation of GenMedix healthcare documentation system as well as its prospects for positively changing healthcare documentation. The effectiveness of GenMedix is assessed in its ability to improve efficiency, minimize mistakes and enhance patient care, which makes it a great contribution in the MedTech industry. For convenient this paper

ᵃnarendra@mite.ac.in

DOI: 10.1201/9781003724988-6

has been organized into five sections ahead namely Section 1–5, respectively [7].

2. System Design and Architecture

The GenMedix platform is built with cutting-edge AI models, natural language processing (NLP) [11] and AI- based deep learning algorithms for automating the generation and summarization of medical reports. The system architecture is designed to facilitate the automated information retrieval, processing and summarization of reports while maintaining integrity, safety and efficiency. In Figure 6.1, the entire system architecture with all the parts like data collection systems, AI NLP processing, report summarization through EHRs and integration of GenMedix platform with EHRs is depicted along with the interconnections of various components.

GenMedix makes use of Natural Language Processing (NLP) algorithms to translate, analyze and formulate medical language in patient records and clinician notes. Because medical documents have intricate vocabularies, shorthand and disorganized prose, NLP methods such as named entity recognition [4] (NER) and semantic parsing [6] are able to capture relevant details, including symptoms, diagnosis, medications and the patient's medical history. This helps the system to derive relevant information from unstructured textual data while preserving its medical integrity. In addition to NLP, transformer-based models like NVIDIA Llama-3.1 Nemotron-70B allow GenMedix to provide contextually relevant medical reports. Transformer's claim to fame their use of self-attention

mechanisms that aid in generating high-level language to describe large medical datasets, unlike classical AI approaches where such relationships are hard-coded by programmers. These models were specifically tailored through extensive training on large collections of electronic health records [3, 9] (EHR) to help understand patient's symptoms, generate diagnoses and prepare comprehensive reports [9].

GenMedix utilizes both extractive and abstractive approaches for summarization to create simple summaries out of complex medical records in order to help clinicians make more effective decisions in a timely manner. In the former, essential sentences are selected from long reports and in the latter, sentences are paraphrased to convey the report's meaning accurately. This allows physicians to receive insightful information in an organized manner without having to go through large volumes of text. Additionally, the system is intended to work with electronic health record (EHR) systems without any changes so that it can access, analyze and update patient documents with ease. It has the capability to capture both structured (e.g., lab results and medications) and unstructured (e.g., doctor's notes and prescriptions) data from EHRs, normalize the data and produce structured medical reports.

3. Methodology

The GenMedix system can construct organized medical reports and summaries based on clinician input. For optimum accuracy and precision, the approach includes data preprocessing, AI model training, report creation and validation. The model has been trained using a diverse set of medical records and synthetic datasets to improve generalization and adaptability across different medical domains. The model was trained using transfer learning, incorporating large-scale medical corpora prior to applying domain-specific training, enabling optimal processing of clinical notes through trained data. For the purpose of achieving the desired accuracy in the application of medical language, the raw patient's data goes through a set automated function of text cleaning for the purpose of standardizing medical abbreviation, identifying the important medical words and anonymization for the purposes of ensuring compliance with the set rules. This kind of structured input enables the AI model to produce dependable reports more effectively. The workflow begins when a clinician key in details of the patient on a chatbot, which in turn triggers the system to pose follow-up questions based on signs to capture as much information as possible. This structured data consists of symptoms AI model predicts possible diagnoses and treatment options using NLP techniques, then generates a comprehensive medical report with the corresponding details. AI also has a summarization module or AI that reduces the size of the report for brevity.

As shown in Figure 6.2, the flow of data starts with user input, which is then sent via the UI/Input Processing module and undergoes verification and processing at the backend.

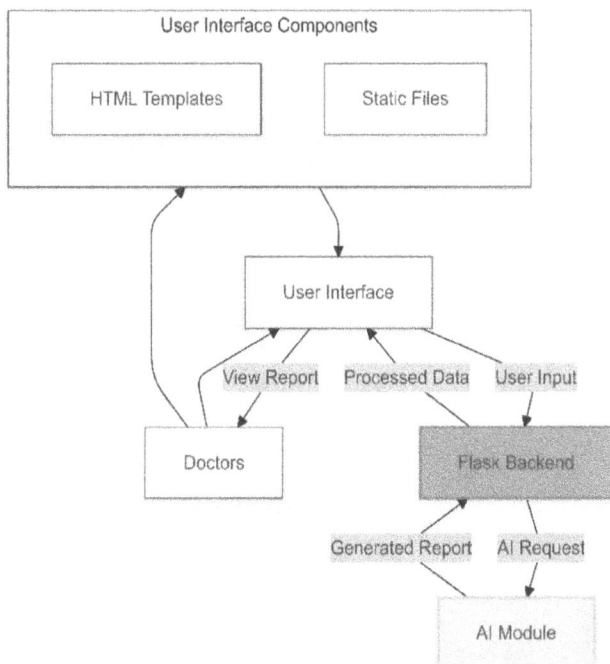

Figure 6.1. System architecture of GenMedix.

Source: Author.

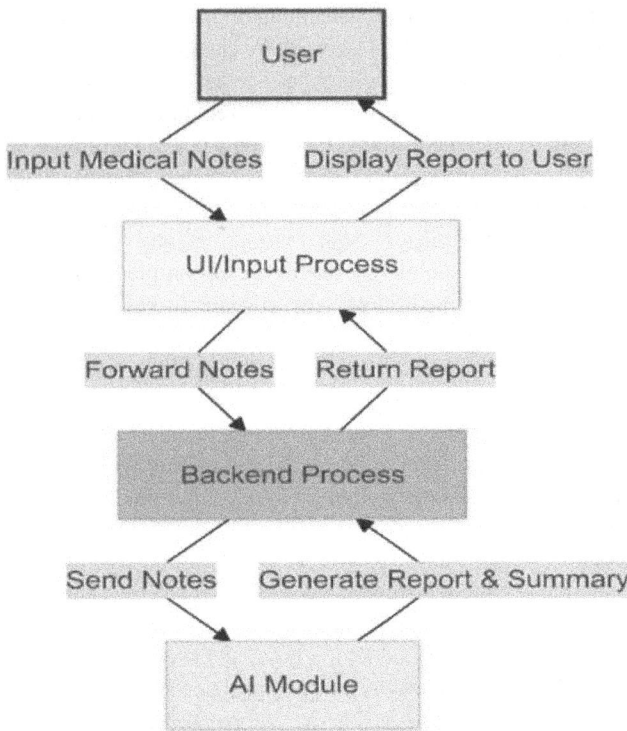

Figure 6.2. Data flow of GenMedix system.

Source: Author.

making compliance with healthcare regulations flow easier by keeping a patient's data private and confidential [10].

GenMedix integrated AI models which ensures the expected performance of the product by using its Natural Language Processing capabilities to turn clinical inputs into structured medical documents. The workflow starts with text preprocessing of the data which includes cleaning relevant clinical data, entity extraction and normalization. Detailed patient reports are generated by feeding the processed text to transformer-based NLP models with a high accuracy score. Further refinement is done by the summarization module producing short summaries which can aid healthcare professionals with quick insights. The feedback loop ensures improvements with every enhancement in accuracy and adaptability of the model to clinician inputs (Figure 6.4) [13].

This approach makes certain that GenMedix automates medical documentation in a secure, efficient and scalable manner. With AI-integrated workflows, the system automation reduces the time needed for documentation, increases the accuracy and readability of medical reports and improves overall clinical efficiency and decision making (Figure 6.5) [12].

The AI module bilateralizes with the backend to prepare the summary report. The summary report together with the output is sent back to the backend processed and ready to be shown to the user on the interface. The system includes feedback loops where clinicians can authenticate and edit the provided reports, thus enhancing the AI model over time.

For effective medical report generation, GenMedix is implemented using modular and scalable architecture. It comprises three main components: a user interface, a backend processor and an AI model. React.js is used in conjunction with Flask for the UI development, and it offers a chatbot powered system for clinicians to input patient details and receive AI recommendations in real- time. The interface allows for free form data input where patients' symptoms, history and examination findings can be documented. There is also an interactive follow-up feature where the chatbot can ask for further details to ensure proper documentation. The system automatically generates written reports as soon as all requisite information is provided, including the patients' symptoms, diagnosis and treatment plans. The AI-generated reports can be reviewed and customized by the clinicians to amplify precision (Figure 6.3) [2].

Flask is working on the backend where data validation, security and AI model interaction is taken care of. During system integration, the engine, database and frontend communicate through APIs. Security measures like encryption and systematized authentication are integrated alongside,

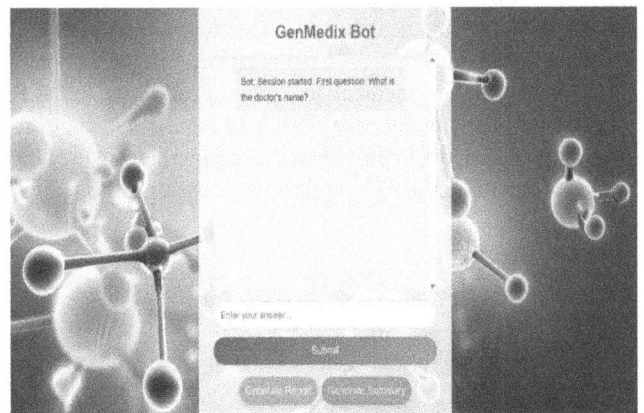

Figure 6.3. Home page of GenMedix.

Source: Author.

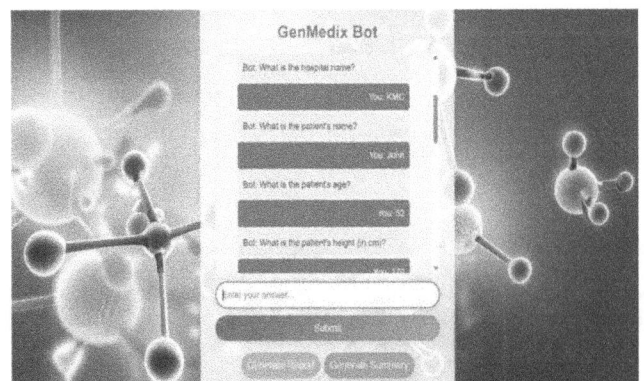

Figure 6.4. Patient interaction page of GenMedix.

Source: Author.

4. Results and Discussions

Based on the inputs provided by the user, the system was able to successfully create organized medical reports which synthesized the patient information and symptoms. It facilitated the first stage of the evaluation and decreased the amount of paperwork that called for manual entry. The model was able to track symptoms and create documents with accuracy, reliability and consistency. The method was effective in addressing various inputs of symptoms by automatically generating corresponding questions and capturing critical medical information. Improvements could include suggestions in real time as well as a broader database of symptoms for better diagnostic assistance (Figures 6.6 and 6.7).

5. Conclusions

The use of GenMedix signifies a revolutionary change in the documenting of health reports. Using generative AI, Natural Language Processing and transformer architecture, the system automates the documentation process which lowers

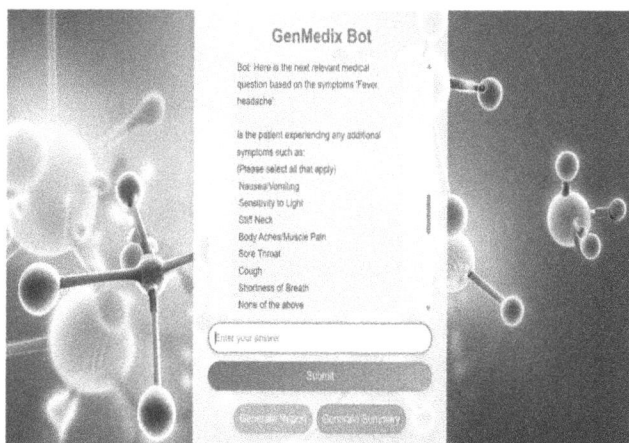

Figure 6.5. Symptom analysis page of GenMedix.

Source: Author.

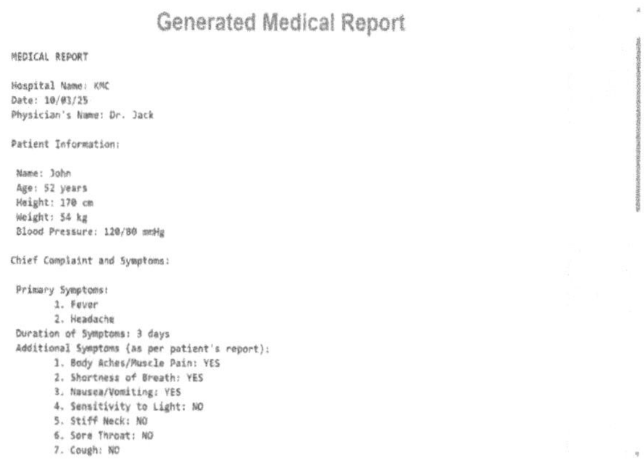

Figure 6.6. Generated medical report.

Source: Author.

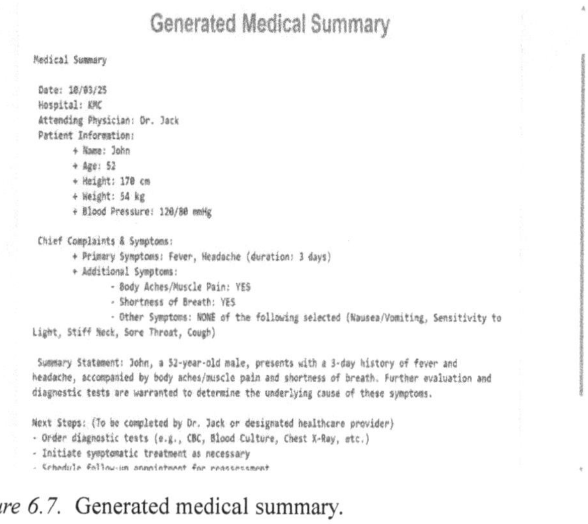

Figure 6.7. Generated medical summary.

Source: Author.

the cognitive burden of health workers while maintaining optimal accuracy, security and compliance. Empirical evidence shows that GenMedix improves workflow, reduces documentation discrepancies and decreases the time spent on report generation, which enhances productivity in the clinic. This improvement permits medical institutions to allocate greater resources towards providing patients with quality care instead of dealing with unnecessary bureaucratic tasks.

Aside from the automation aspects, GenMedix could fully transform medical documentation with the inclusion of predictive diagnostics, giving AI the ability to review a patient's history and clinical data to offer possible diseases along with treatment suggestions. Forthcoming developments will also incorporate multilingual support, making seamless documentation possible across different languages and voice overview and report generation for clinicians, who would be able to generate reports hands-free in real time. Continuous self-learning automation actions of GenMedix mark a shift within the healthcare industry and with all these changes predicted, it remains the core solution that unites AI technological development with real medical practice. It is anticipated that with constant refinement, efficiency will increase, errors will be reduced, and the outcome of the patient will be better, which makes it a key element for modern healthcare establishments.

Acknowledgement

We gratefully acknowledge Mangalore Institute of Technology and Engineering for the support and resources in the successful completion of this research.

References

[1] Vaswani, A., Shazeer, N., Parmar, N., Uszkoreit, J., Jones, L., Gomez, A. N., & Polosukhin, I. (2017). Attention is all you

need. *Advances in Neural Information Processing Systems (NeurIPS)*, *30*, 5998–6008.

[2] Rajpurkar, P., Zhang, J., Lopyrev, K., & Liang, P. (2016). SQuAD: 100,000+ questions for machine comprehension of text. *Proceedings of the 2016 Conference on Empirical Methods in Natural Language Processing (EMNLP)*, 2383–2392.

[3] Johnson, A. E. W., Pollard, T. J., Shen, L., Li-Wei, H. L., Feng, M., Ghassemi, M., & Mark, R. G. (2016). MIMIC-III, a freely accessible critical care database. *Scientific Data*, *3*(1), 1–9.

[4] Kraljevic, Z., Bean, D., Mascolo, C., & Sear, R. (2021). MedCAT: Medical concept annotation toolkit for real-world electronic health records. *Journal of the American Medical Informatics Association (JAMIA)*, *28*(3), 451–462.

[5] Ghassemi, M., Naumann, T., & Schulam, P. (2020). A review of challenges and opportunities in machine learning for health. *Nature Communications*, *11*(1), 1–11.

[6] Peng, Y., Wang, X., Lu, L., Bagheri, M., Summers, R. M., & Zhang, Z. (2018). NegBio: A high-performance tool for negation and uncertainty detection in radiology reports. *Journal of the American Medical Informatics Association (JAMIA)*, *25*(10), 1274–1281.

[7] Wu, Y., Zhang, Y., Xu, H., & Roberts, K. (2020). Clinical report auto-summarization: A survey of methods and applications. *Journal of Biomedical Informatics*, *109*, 103545.

[8] Liu, Z., Tang, R., Yao, L., Duan, N., Cui, E., & Chen, J. (2022). GPT improves biomedical NLP tasks: A comprehensive study. *Proceedings of the 60th Annual Meeting of the Association for Computational Linguistics (ACL)*, 3401–3415.

[9] Kumar, A., & Singh, M. (2023). Implementing AI for Automated Clinical Documentation: Challenges and Opportunities. *Journal of Healthcare Informatics*, *12*(2), 89–102.

[10] Roberts, L., & Zhang, T. (2022). Enhancing Patient Care through AI-Powered Medical Reporting. *International Journal of Medical Informatics*, *158*, 104–115.

[11] Williams, S., & Patel, R. (2024). The Role of Natural Language Processing in Modern Healthcare Systems. *Health Information Science and Systems*, *12*(1), 45–58.

[12] Nguyen, P., & Lee, J. (2023). Transforming Clinical Workflows with AI-Based Documentation Tools. *BMC Medical Informatics and Decision Making*, *23*(1), 67–79.

[13] Gonzalez, R., & Chen, Y. (2023). Evaluating the Impact of AI on Medical Documentation Efficiency. *Journal of Biomedical Informatics*, *136*, 103–115.

7   SafePath: AI-driven route safety assessment for enhanced personal safety

Vani Vasudevan[a], Akanksha Kashyap[b], Akruti Sarangi[c], Himanshi Yadav[d], and Lovia E. B.[e]

Computer Science and Engineering, Nitte Meenakshi Institute of Technology, Bangalore, India

Abstract: Travel route safety has grown to be a major worry, especially when it comes to the safety of women. This study presents SafePath, an AI-driven application designed to assess and recommend the safest travel routes by evaluating a range of factors, including crowd density, vehicle traffic, street lighting, and proximity to police stations and hospitals. The application uses YOLOv11 for object detection to analyze images and identify important features like crowd density, vehicle traffic, and street lighting. Data are collected from various sources, including car dash cameras, APIs, and municipal databases, then processed through an ETL pipeline that efficiently cleans, organizes, and performs geospatial clustering and feature extraction to improve the understanding of the environment. Safety scores for potential routes are generated based on the combined output of YOLO's image analysis and machine learning models for structured data. Additionally, the application integrates an SOS feature, enabling users to share their real-time location and recent travel history with emergency contacts providing essential support during emergencies by offering location data and a record of movements that can serve as critical evidence. This research demonstrates the potential of artificial intelligence and geospatial analytics in creating scalable, real-time solutions for safer navigation, providing a practical and effective approach to enhancing personal safety during travel.

Keywords: SafePath, AI-driven application, travel safety, women's safety, object detection, YOLO, geospatial analytics, crowd density, vehicle traffic, street lighting, machine learning, SOS feature, real-time location sharing, structured data, emergency support, scalable solutions, personal safety

1. Introduction

As urbanization increases, travel route safety, especially for women in poorly lit or less populated areas at night, has become a critical concern. Vulnerable groups face higher risks in urban environments, where safety varies by location and time. This highlights the need for technologies that assess and recommend safer routes in real time, helping users make informed decisions and reduce risks.

This paper presents SafePath, an AI-powered app that evaluates travel route safety by analyzing factors like crowd density, vehicle traffic, street lighting, and proximity to critical services. Using YOLOv11 for real-time object detection, it identifies dynamic features such as traffic patterns, crowd movements, and lighting conditions. Previous research shows that YOLO models work well in applications that operate in real time, such as vehicle accident detection using YOLOv9 and YOLO-NAS [1], and multi-object tracking with YOLOv8 in crowded or occluded scenarios [2]. These findings underline the suitability of YOLO-based frameworks for applications requiring accuracy and efficiency in dynamic urban settings. It features an ETL pipeline that processes data from dash cameras, municipal APIs, and public databases. It performs geospatial clustering and feature extraction, categorizing attributes like street types, population density, and traffic

patterns. By combining YOLOv11 image analysis with geospatial data, it assigns safety scores to routes, helping users choose safer options. Inspired by prior research on women's safety applications that include real-time alerts and GPS tracking [3], it also features an SOS function for emergencies. This function allows users to share their real-time location with designated contacts, ensuring quick assistance when needed.

2. Related Works

2.1. Gap analysis

Existing women's safety solutions have gaps, highlighting the need for a real-time AI-driven approach. IoT systems [4–7] offer GPS tracking and alerts but lack dynamic video assessments. Safety apps [10–12] focus on static risk factors without real-time monitoring of pedestrian density, vehicle presence, or lighting. Route safety models [8, 9, 13, 17] rely on historical crime data, missing live environmental factors. Object detection techniques [14, 18–20] improve accuracy but neglect human safety, while crowd analysis models [21–23] face computational limits, making them unsuitable for mobile use, as shown in Table 7.1. This research integrates AI-based video analysis for real-time safety, factoring in pedestrian density, lighting, while ensuring efficiency for mobile and edge device deployment.

[a]vani.v@nmit.ac.in, [b]akashyapdeep@gmail.com, [c]aviternal20@gmail.com, [d]himanshigy@gmail.com, [e]loviaeb@gmail.com

DOI: 10.1201/9781003724988-7

2.2. *Background study*

Table 7.1. Background study

Category	Source	Methodology	Dataset	Performance	Advantages	Limitations
Mobile Applications for Women's Safety	[10]	SAKHI app with SOS, GPS tracking, live video	Android device testing	Periodic location updates, video-based evidence	Enhanced safety through video streaming	Battery drain, privacy concerns
	[11]	urGUARD app with SOS and pre-drafted messages	User survey	Effective emergency messaging	Simple and user-friendly	Lacks live location tracking
Machine Learning for Safety and Object Detection	[15]	Enhanced YOLOv5s for road defect detection	CRDDC-2022	mAP@0.5: 75.17%, reduced computational cost by 8.44 GB	Suitable for resource-limited environments	Lower accuracy compared to larger models
Analysis of Safety in Urban Environments	[16]	Safety comparison in smart vs. non-smart cities	Survey of 500 women (Punjab, India)	Smart cities had better safety, but persistent issues remain	Highlights safety gaps	Subjective survey responses
	[17]	Logistic regression for safe route navigation	Spatial crime data	100% accuracy in classification	Integrates panic buttons & incident reporting	Needs real-time crime updates
Object Detection and Crowd Counting	[19]	YOLO vs. SSD vs. RetinaNet for object detection	Object detection dataset	YOLO: 45 fps, 70% accuracy; RetinaNet balanced	Fastest detection (YOLO)	Accuracy trade-off
	[20]	YOLOv4 vs. R-CNN vs. SSD for object detection	COCO dataset	YOLOv4:15ms inference, 67 FPS, 43.5 mAP	Best efficiency among models	May not generalize to all environments
	[22]	CNN-LSTM model for crowd counting	Shanghaitech, UCSD datasets	Effective in high-density scenarios	Robust in large crowds	High computational requirements

Source: Author.

3. Methodology

3.1. *Machine learning techniques*

The SafePath app uses YOLO models for real-time object detection to analyze route safety. YOLOv11, selected for its efficiency, is evaluated for performance. An ETL pipeline ensures smooth data flow and preprocessing. The following machine learning techniques are used, as shown in Figure 7.1.

1. *Object detection with YOLO:* YOLO detects key objects in real-time from dash cam images, including vehicles, pedestrians, streetlights, and traffic signals, enabling fast and accurate route safety assessments.
2. *Model Training and Optimizing:* The YOLOv11 model is fine-tuned with annotated dash cam images in different lighting conditions to identify key safety elements like cars, pedestrians, and obstructions, while optimizing hyperparameters for better route safety prediction.

3. *Data Augmentation:* Data augmentation techniques such as cropping, rotations, and colour adjustments improve model robustness across varied lighting, road types, and weather conditions.
4. *ETL Pipeline for Data Processing:* An ETL pipeline in SafePath handles data collection, transformation, and storage for route safety analysis. The process includes:
   - **Extract:** Data is gathered from sources like crime APIs, real-time traffic data, and environmental factors.
   - **Transform:** Data is cleaned, normalized, and features like traffic density or streetlight availability are engineered.
   - **Load:** Transformed data is loaded into a fast-access database for real-time safety assessments using YOLO models.
5. *Evaluation:* The YOLOv11 model is evaluated using the following metrics:
   - **Mean Average Precision (mAP):** Measures overall detection accuracy across object classes.

- **Accuracy:** Proportion of correctly identified objects.
- **Intersection over Union (IoU):** Assesses overlap between predicted and ground truth bounding boxes.
- **Inference Time:** Time taken to process images for real-time operation.
- **Model Size:** Measures storage requirements for mobile deployment.

6. *Model Selection:* YOLOv11 was selected for SafePath due to its accuracy and compact size, enabling real-time image processing and route safety score generation.

7. *Continuous Learning:* The model is continuously updated with new data, like dash camera images and user feedback, to adapt to evolving urban conditions and user needs.

3.2. Evaluation measures

The YOLO models are evaluated using several performance metrics to determine their suitability for real-time route safety analysis. The key evaluation measures are:

- **Mean Average Precision (mAP)**

$$mAP = \frac{1}{N} \sum_{i=1}^{N} AP_i$$

where AP_i is the Average Precision for class i, and N is the total number of classes. It measures object detection performance by considering precision-recall curves.

- **Intersection over Union (IoU)**

$$IoU = \frac{Area\ of\ Overlap}{Area\ of\ Union}$$

where the overlap is between the predicted bounding box and the ground truth. A higher IoU indicates better localization accuracy.

- **Accuracy**

$$Accuracy = \frac{TP + TN}{TP + TN + FP + FN}$$

Where TP (True Positives) and TN (True Negatives) are correct predictions. FP (False Positives) and FN (False Negatives) are incorrect predictions. It measures overall classification correctness.

- **Error Rate**

It quantifies the proportion of incorrect predictions.

$$Error\ Rate = 1 - Accuracy = \frac{FP + FN}{TP + TN + FP + FN}$$

3.3. Datasets

The YOLO model is trained and evaluated on annotated images from dash cameras, CCTV footage, traffic datasets, and Google's Open Images, as shown in Figure 7.2. It includes various conditions (day/night) and focuses on safety objects like vehicles, pedestrians, streetlights, and traffic signals, ensuring robustness for real-time route safety assessments in diverse urban environments.

3.4. Application methodology

This section provides overview of the application methodology used for developing the application as shown in

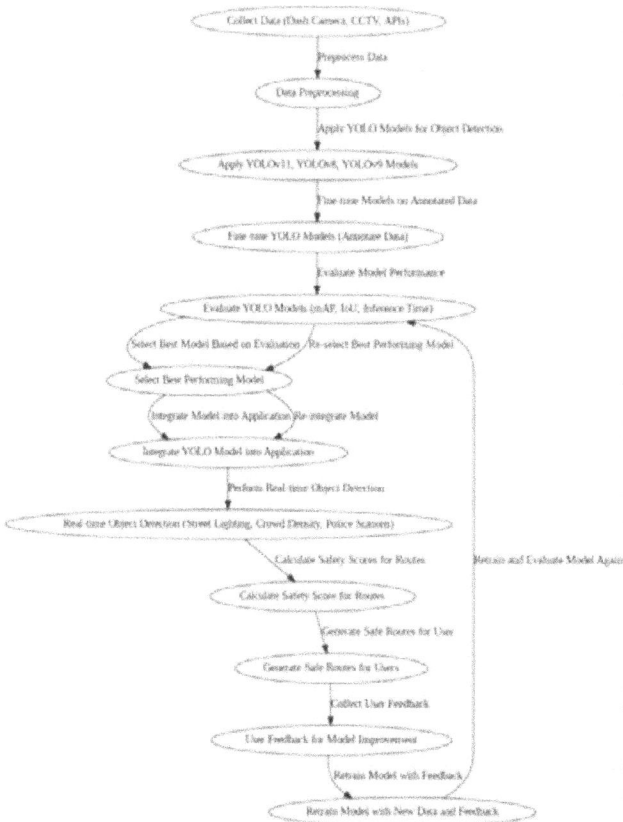

Figure 7.1. AI process diagram.

Source: Author.

Figure 7.2. App process diagram.

Source: Author.

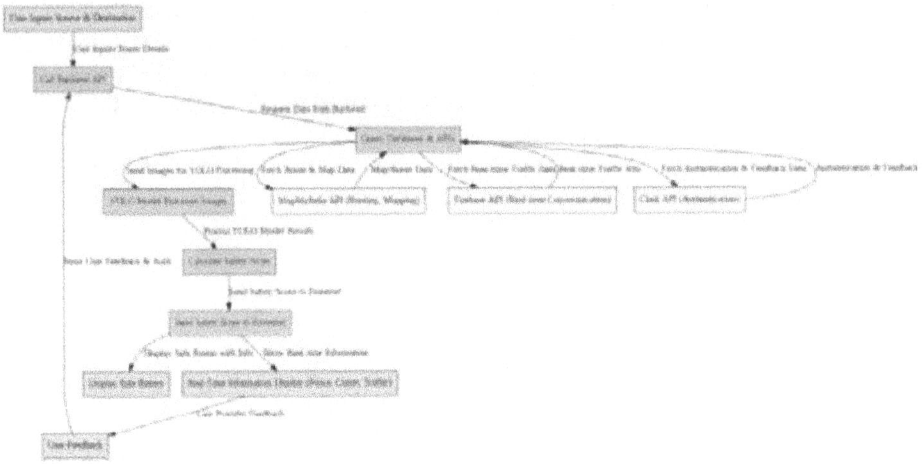

Figure 7.3. App process diagram.

Source: Author.

Figure 7.3. SafePath is built using React Native (Expo 52.0.0) for cross-platform development and React Navigation (6.x) for smooth screen transitions. The backend uses Firebase (11.x) for authentication, database, and storage, with Clerk (4.x) managing secure user sessions. React Maps API enables route visualization and geolocation, while Firebase Firestore handles real-time user and contact data. Key features include interactive map routes for navigation, an SOS alert system using Expo Location and Expo SMS to share live location with emergency contacts, and timely notifications to keep users updated on safety and app events.

3.5. Methodology for safety score

The Safety Score (SPS) assesses route safety based on factors like crowd density, vehicle presence, street lighting, police station proximity, and hospital access, with time-based weight adjustments. User feedback is used to calculate a feedback-based score (FFF) for improved accuracy by integrating feedback via a post-ride 1–5 star rating, normalized to a 0-1 scale as:

$$F = \frac{\text{User Rating} - 1}{4}$$

where:

- 1-star rating translates to 0 (very unsafe)
- 5-star rating translates to 1 (very safe)

To prevent bias from sporadic feedback, an adaptive weighting mechanism (W_f) is applied, considering frequency and consistency of user responses:

$$W_f = 0.2 + 0.1 \times \text{Number of Rides Rated}$$

To validate these parameters, we conducted a "Safety Factors for Women Commuting" survey with over 150 responses from diverse participants, as shown in Figure 7.4. Respondents rated safety factors like street lighting, crowd density, vehicle traffic, and crime rates at different times, revealing significant variations in perceived safety and supporting time-based weight adjustments for each factor.

The final SPS formula, integrating user feedback, is expressed as:

$$SPS = W_p \times P + W_c \times C + W_s \times S + W_{ps} \times$$
$$PS + W_h \times H + W_f \times F$$

where:

- P = People density (normalized between 0 and 1)
- C = Car density (traffic volume, normalized)

Figure 7.4. Google form survey for parameters and weights determination.

Source: Author.

- S = Streetlight availability (binary or percentage-based score)
- PS = Proximity to police stations
- H = Proximity to hospitals
- F = User feedback score (normalized between 0 and 1)
- W_p, W_c, W_s, W_{ps}, W_h, W_f = Time-dependent weights assigned to each factor.

The SafePath Safety Score (SPS) assigns weights to different safety factors based on survey insights, real-time data, and user feedback. These weights vary depending on the time of the day to reflect changes in risk perception. The Table 7.2 summarizes the assigned weights:

4. Experimental Results and Analysis

4.1. Training and testing

The YOLOv11 model was trained to detect safety-critical objects like streetlights, vehicles, and pedestrians using a dataset created with manual annotations via Roboflow for streetlights and automated annotations from the Open Images Dataset V4 (OIDv4) for vehicles and pedestrians, refined for consistency, as shown in Figure 7.5–7.7. Data augmentation (rotation, flipping, brightness adjustment, cropping, and scaling) enhanced the dataset for real-world scenarios. Training used the Ultralytics YOLO library with a 0.001 learning rate, 50 epochs, and a batch size of 32, tracking key metrics like mAP, precision, and recall. Testing confirmed the model's robustness under varying lighting and object densities, validating its real-world reliability. The training process was carried out on the annotated dataset, withsetup:

- **Dataset Split:** The dataset was divided into 80% for training, 10% for validation, and 10% for testing.
- **Hyperparameters:** The models were trained using a learning rate of 0.001, a batch size of 32, and 50 epochs. The input size for the models was set to 416x416 pixels.

Figure 7.5. Train data after manual annotations.
Source: Author.

Figure 7.6. Integration of safety score in application.
Source: Author.

Table 7.2. Weights assigned for safety score formula

Factor	Weight	Morning (6am–12pm)	Afternoon (12pm–6pm)	Evening (6pm-10pm)	Night (10pm–6am)	Description
Police Stations	W_p	0.15	0.10	0.20	0.25	Higher weight at night as police presence increases perceived safety
Crowd density	W_c	0.20	0.25	0.20	0.10	Crowds enhance safety during the day but may reduce safety at night
Street Lighting	W_s	0.10	0.15	0.20	0.30	Crucial at night when visibility is low
Vehicle Presence	W_v	0.20	0.15	0.15	0.10	Moderate impact as moving traffic can indicate safer areas
Hospitals	W_h	0.10	0.10	0.10	0.15	Slightly more important at night in case of emergencies
User Feedback	W_f	0.25	0.25	0.25	0.30	Dynamic weight, higher at night due to increased reliance on perception

Source: Author.

- **Loss Function:** The combined loss function used includes classification loss, localization loss, and confidence loss.
- **Optimizer:** The Adam optimizer was used to minimize the loss during training.

4.2. Application implementation

SafePath app uses YOLOv11 for real-time object detection, identifying key safety elements like streetlights, vehicles,

Figure 7.7. Street lights.

Source: Author.

and pedestrians, and providing users with a safety score, as shown in Figure 7.8. Components and features are:

1. *Real-Time GPS Tracking:* It uses GPS with ExpoLocation and React Map API to provide real-time location updates in map, as shown in Figure 7.9.
2. *SOS Alert and Emergency Messaging with Live GPS Location:* SOS system triggers alerts with a message and live GPS location to emergency contacts using Expo SMS library, as shown in Figures 7.10, 7.11.
3. *Emergency Contact Management:* Users can manage emergency contacts, adding or updating them easily using Expo Contacts library, as shown in Figure 7.12.

4.3. Results

The YOLOv11 model integrated into the SafePath app demonstrated strong performance, achieving a mean average precision (mAP@50) of 74.79% in detecting safety-critical objects such as vehicles, pedestrians, streetlights, and traffic signs, with object detection accuracy reaching 80% and over 85% accuracy for cars and pedestrians. The

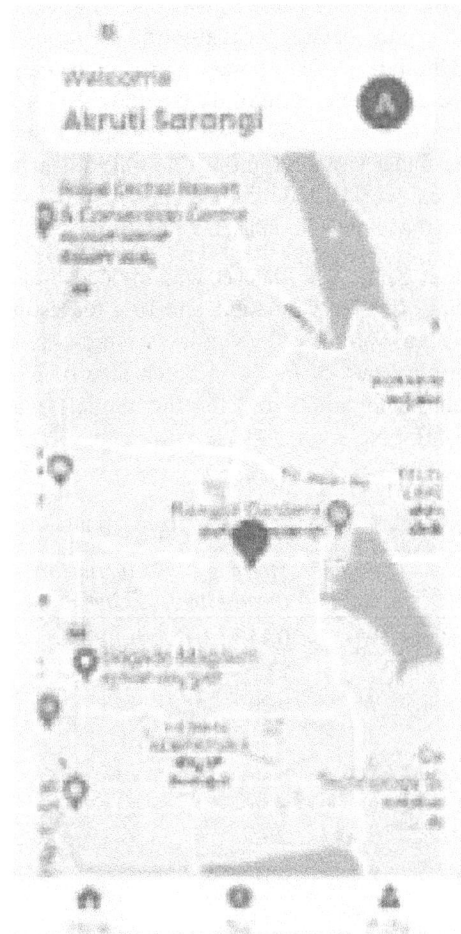

Figure 7.8. Validate data .

Source: Author.

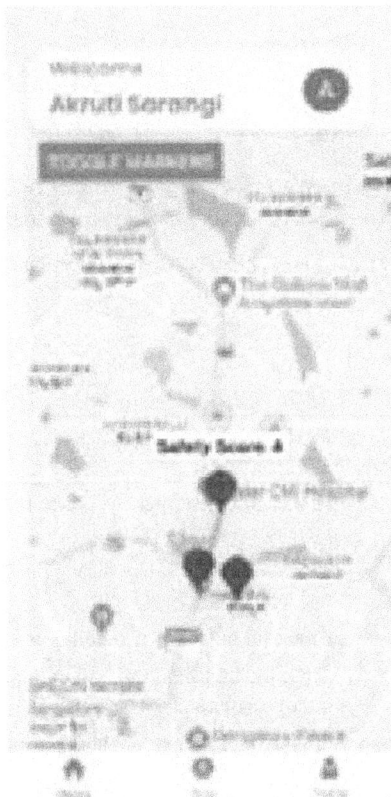

Figure 7.9. Map location.

Source: Author.

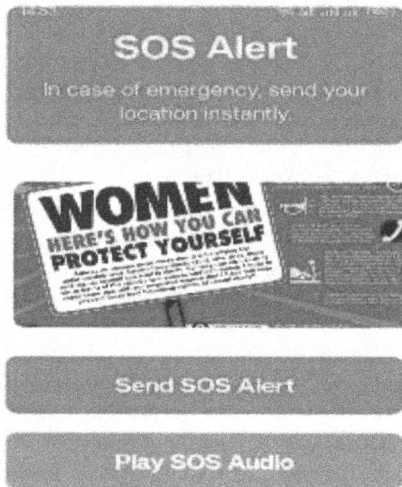

Figure 7.10. SOS alert.

Source: Author.

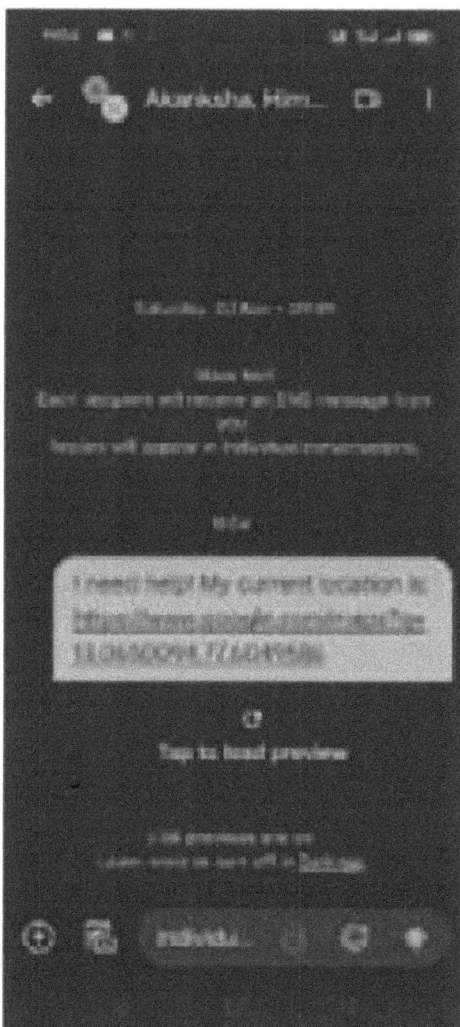

Figure 7.11. SOS message.

Source: Author.

custom-trained streetlight class successfully identified 55 unique streetlights during testing. With an inference time of just 35 milliseconds per frame, the model enables real-time object detection, crucial for timely safety scoring and alerts. Additionally, comprehensive testing of app features – such as SOS alerts, live location tracking, contact management, and Google Authentication – showed reliable performance across all use cases. These results confirm that SafePath, powered by YOLOv11, provides a robust and efficient solution for enhancing real-time personal safety (Table 7.3).

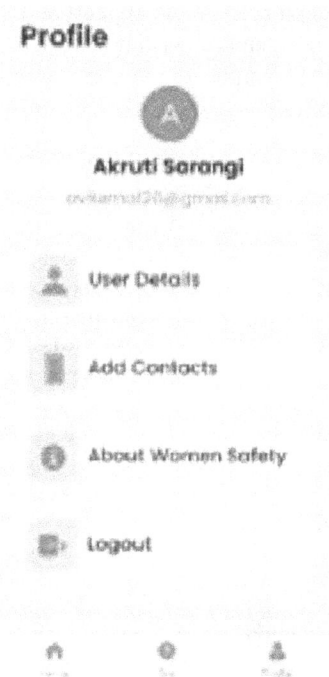

Figure 7.12. Profile.

Source: Author.

Table 7.3. YOLOv11 model performance metrics and inference speed

Metric	Value
Total Images Processed	185
Total Instances Detected	767
Total Unique Streetlights Detected	55
Precision (B)	0.8726
Recall (B)	0.6454
mAP@50 (B)	0.7479
mAP@50-95 (B)	0.4710
Inference Speed	104.9 ms per image
Preprocessing Speed	0.8 ms per image
Postprocessing Speed	0.7 me per image
Evaluation Loss (Interference)	0.0
Model Parameters	9,413,187
GFLOPs	21.3

Source: Author.

5. Conclusion and Future Work

SafePath is an AI-driven travel safety app that uses YOLOv11 and data from cameras, APIs, and municipal sources to assess routes based on lighting, crowd density, and service proximity. It includes an SOS feature for real-time location sharing. Future upgrades aim to add IoT sensors, predictive AI, and AR navigation for enhanced safety.

Acknowlegment

We gratefully acknowledge the support and cooperation of the students, faculty, and authorities of the Computer Science and Engineering Department in facilitating this research.

References

[1] Nusari, A. N. M., Ozbek, I. Y., & Oral, E. A. (2024). Automatic Vehicle Accident Detection and Classification from Images: A Comparison of YOLOv9 and YOLO-NAS Algorithms. *2024 32nd Signal Processing and Communications Applications Conference (SIU)*, Mersin, Turkiye, pp. 1–4, doi: 10.1109/SIU61531.2024.10600761.

[2] Jyothi, D. N., Reddy, G. H., Prashanth, B., Vardhan, N. V. (2024). Collaborative Training of Object Detection and Re-Identification in Multi-Object Tracking Using YOLOv8. *2024 International Conference on Computing and Data Science (ICCDS)*, Chennai, India, pp. 1–6, doi: 10.1109/ICCDS60734.2024.10560451.

[3] Sharma, S. K., & Ranjana, P. (2022). Women Safety-Saviour Android Application. *2022 2nd International Conference on Advance Computing and Innovative Technologies in Engineering (ICACITE)*, Greater Noida, India, pp. 1552–1556, doi: 10.1109/ICACITE53722.2022.9823496.

[4] Reddy, V. V. S. P., Vamsi, K. B. S. L., Chandra, S. M., Rama, K. M., & Deepika, Y. (2022). Women Safety System with Nerve Stimulator using IoT Technology. *2022 2nd International Conference on Technological Advancements in Computational Sciences (ICTACS)*, Tashkent, Uzbekistan, pp. 376–379, doi: 10.1109/ICTACS56270.2022.9988463.

[5] Uganya, G., Kirubakaran, N., Bernatin, T., & Boobalan, M. (2023). Smart Women Safety Device Using IoT and GPS Tracker. *2023 Intelligent Computing and Control for Engineering and Business Systems (ICCEBS)*, Chennai, India, pp. 1–6, doi: 10.1109/ICCEBS58601.2023.10449302.

[6] Tayal, S., Govind Rao, H. P., Gupta, A., & Choudhary, A. (2021). Women Safety System Design and Hardware Implementation. *2021 9th International Conference on Reliability, Infocom Technologies and Optimization (Trends and Future Directions) (ICRITO)*, Noida, India, pp. 1–3, doi: 10.1109/ICRITO51393.2021.9596393.

[7] Reddy, V., Konguvel, E., Sumathi, G., & Sujatha, R. (2022). Emergency Alert System for Women Safety using Raspberry Pi. *2022 Second International Conference on Next Generation Intelligent Systems (ICNGIS)*, Kottayam, India, pp. 1–4, doi: 10.1109/ICNGIS54955.2022.10079823.

[8] Biswas, P., Hashem, T., & Cheema, M. A. (2023). Safest Nearby Neighbor Queries in Road Networks. in *IEEE Transactions on Intelligent Transportation Systems*, 24(7), 7270–7284. doi: 10.1109/TITS.2023.3262403.

[9] Yogesh, C., & Vatchala, S. (2023). Empowering Women's Safety: An Innovative Smart Security System. *2023 6th International Conference on Recent Trends in Advance Computing (ICRTAC)*, Chennai, India, pp. 429–433, doi: 10.1109/ICRTAC59277.2023.10480808.

[10] Agarwal, V., Singh, V., Kamboj, A., Sirohi, A., & Mehto, A. (2023). Development of A Women Safety Smartphone Application- SAKHI. *2023 Third International Conference on Secure Cyber Computing and Communication (ICSCCC)*, Jalandhar, India, pp. 212–217, doi: 10.1109/ICSCCC58608.2023.10176701.

[11] Artamadja, D., Faza, T. H., Irena, F., Maulana, M. I., Tobing, G. L., & Widianto, M. H. (2023). Designing Women's Safety Application for Emergency Situations. *2023 5th International Conference on Cybernetics and Intelligent System (ICORIS)*, Pangkalpinang, Indonesia, pp. 1–5, doi: 10.1109/ICORIS60118.2023.10352253.

[12] Premi, P., Savita, K. S., & Millatina, N. (2022). FRNDY: A Women's Safety App. *2022 6th International Conference On Computing, Communication, Control And Automation (ICCUBEA*, Pune, India, pp. 1–5, doi: 10.1109/ICCUBEA54992.2022.10010815.

[13] Kiran, A., Sundaram, A., Varghese, I. K., Dhanasekaran, S., Ayyasamy, R. K., & Krisnan, S. (2024). Empowering Women: A Creative Approach to Integrated Safety with Machine Learning Algorithms. *2024 International Conference on Signal Processing, Computation, Electronics, Power and Telecommunication (IConSCEPT)*, Karaikal, India, pp. 1–7, doi: 10.1109/IConSCEPT61884.2024.10627804.

[14] Shajeena, J., Jarugula, V. K., Bindhu, A., & Kayalvizhi, S. (2023). Utilizing Convolutional Neural Networks for Object Recognition with Image Filtering and Edge Detection in Deep Learning. *2023 6th International Conference on Recent Trends in Advance Computing (ICRTAC)*, Chennai, India, pp. 784–789, doi: 10.1109/ICRTAC59277.2023.10480796.

[15] Bai, H., & Qin, L. (2024). Research on Road Defect Detection Based on Improved YOLOv5s. *2024 5th International Seminar on Artificial Intelligence, Networking and Information Technology (AINIT)*, Nanjing, China, pp. 2344–2348, doi: 10.1109/AINIT61980.2024.10581495.

[16] Kohli, P., & Singh, K. (2021). Analysis of Woman Safety Parameters in Smart and Non-Smart Cities. *2021 9th International Conference on Reliability, Infocom Technologies and Optimization (Trends and Future Directions) (ICRITO)*, Noida, India, pp. 1–5, doi: 10.1109/ICRITO51393.2021.9596437.

[17] Chinnasamy, A., Donde, A., & Joshi, D. (2024). Integrated Women's Security System with Safe Route Navigation and Instant Law Enforcement Reporting. *2024 4th International Conference on Pervasive Computing and Social Networking (ICPCSN)*, Salem, India, pp. 197–202, doi: 10.1109/ICPCSN62568.2024.00041.

[18] Afdhal, A., Saddami, K., Sugiarto, S., Fuadi, Z., & Nasaruddin, N. (2023). Real-Time Object Detection Performance of YOLOv8 Models for Self-Driving Cars in a Mixed Traffic Environment. *2023 2nd International Conference on Computer System, Information Technology, and Electrical*

Engineering (COSITE), Banda Aceh, Indonesia, pp. 260–265, doi: 10.1109/COSITE60233.2023.10249521.

[19] Darthy Rabecka, V., & Britto Pari, J. (2023). Assessing The Performance Of Advanced Object Detection Techniques For Autonomous Cars. *2023 International Conference on Networking and Communications (ICNWC)*, Chennai, India, pp. 1–7, doi: 10.1109/ICNWC57852.2023.10127360.

[20] Manojkumar, P. C., Kumar, L. S., & Jayanthi, B. (2023). Performance Comparison of Real Time Object Detection Techniques with YOLOv4. *2023 International Conference on Signal Processing, Computation, Electronics, Power and Telecommunication (IConSCEPT)*, Karaikal, India, pp. 1–6, doi: 10.1109/IConSCEPT57958.2023.10169970.

[21] Senthilarasi, S., & Kamalakkannan, S. (2021). Implementation of Spatial-Temporal Road Traffic Data using Agglomerative Clustering. *2021 5th International Conference on Intelligent Computing and Control Systems (ICICCS)*, Madurai, India, pp. 108–117, doi: 10.1109/ICICCS51141.2021.9432370.

[22] Fu, J., Yang, H., Liu, P., & Hu, Y. (2018). A CNN-RNN Neural Network Join Long Short-Term Memory For Crowd Counting and Density Estimation. *2018 IEEE International Conference on Advanced Manufacturing (ICAM)*, Yunlin, Taiwan, pp. 471–474, doi: 10.1109/AMCON.2018.8614939.

[23] Zhai, Q., Yang, F., Li, X., Xie, G.-S., Cheng, H., & Liu, Z. (2023). Co-Communication Graph Convolutional Network for Multi-View Crowd Counting. *IEEE Transactions on Multimedia*, 25, 5813–5825. doi: 10.1109/TMM.2022.3199555.

8   Sketch to wireframe using deep learning mode

Shankar R. Nagvekar[a], Rashmi Agarwal[b], and Shinu Abhi[c]

REVA Academy for Corporate Excellence, REVA University, Bengaluru, Karnataka, India

Abstract: In the contemporary era of digitalization, it remains evident that a significant proportion of consumers choose to engage with a firm's website as a first step towards establishing confidence in said business. However, it is disconcerting to observe that many business owners have yet to fully grasp this concept. A site is essential in making people trust and think good things about a company. Places are often slow to go online because they think they do not know how or do not have the money, but also because they want their site to look special, like it was worth the effort and money. Most of the time, you just don't know what you need and what things will look like in the end. The idea is to gather information from the client and then draw a wireframe, a technical representation of what they understand. This is considered the most time-consuming and labor-intensive process. This project used YOLOv5 algorithm for object detection and classification. The model was trained using a custom dataset to improve its accuracy and performance. The speed, accuracy, and capacity to learn from data of the method make it unique. Considered a Convolutional Neural Network (CNN), YOLOv5 trains the system using a lower input size. With an accuracy of above 79%, this method has been shown to properly find HTML components in photos of 416×416 pixels. This work presents an automatic solution based on YOLOv5 for HTML prototype creation from drawn layouts. This invention cuts the time spent on web design chores, boosts accuracy and efficiency, and replaces manual labour.

Keywords: CNN, weight generation, deep learning, artificial intelligence, YOLOv5

1. Introduction

In the tech age, websites count. Designed properly, they are the basis upon which companies create their credibility and digital brand. This makes web design a critical component in ensuring that you not only seem attractive but also satisfy your corporate goals. Creating your website can be difficult, hence it is important to know exactly your target audience and the type of company you wish to run. The most crucial stage is the design one, in which you will learn about your audience and what goals using digital tools and technologies would help you to reach. Furthermore, you will have to record the functional and non-functional needs using "use cases." Following this can be the development of several design prototypes, generally in image form, that must be carefully examined and authorized before starting construction. Though thorough, these procedures can be resource-intensive and time-consuming [1].

The new system creates a tool able to convert designs into HTML wireframes to solve these issues. This new technique will let the people who wish to design the website by the time and list the absent elements we can use to enhance the design and operation. More quickly and conveniently than conventional techniques, the application will convert hand-drawn sketches into web design using structured HTML wireframes. Using this technique allows businesses to reduce the time required to build a website and make modifications depending on user comments, therefore accelerating web development.

The proposed system will shorten design time and simplify the tasks of designers. It will raise the calibre of the final website's design, so increasing its completeness and capacity to satisfy the client's evolving needs.

2. Literature Review

Currently, improvements have been made to AI technology, mostly in Deep Learning (DL). These improvements have allowed us to process many types of data like text, sound, and video with neural networks that have been customized. The traditional approaches to object detection have had trouble in combining the low-level visual data with the high-level context efficiently which leads to limited performance [2].

The use of YOLO to recognize multiple objects in photos is an effective method [3]. YOLOv5 has several benefits compared to its predecessors from the architectural improvements, improved training procedures, and task-specific fine-tuning [4]. YOLOv5 may have a smaller size while maintaining high accuracy, unlike YOLOv3 and SSD which is either slow in speed or requires a lot of computing resources. This makes it particularly suitable for tasks that require real-time execution, such as the creation of wireframes. A typical process for object recognition consists of three main steps: the selection of an informative region, feature extraction, and classification. These steps are used to determine both the position and nature of an object.

2.1. Informative region selection

Traditional methods use moving frame models for full image inspections. However, this process may require more time

[a]shankarnagvekar.AI01@race.reva.edu.in, [b]rashmi.agarwal@reva.edu.in, [c]shinuabhi@reva.edu.in

DOI: 10.1201/9781003724988-8

and produce some frames we don't need. To fix this, many use a fixed set of frames. Even so, this method might ignore some spaces.

2.2. Feature extraction

Feature extraction is key in object recognition. The issue is that the data is constantly changing, especially visual data. Appearance, lighting, and the background can all clash, causing the useful visual information to get lost. Variations like these don't just make it harder for the program to get needed visual cues, but also mess with the accuracy you can expect out of your object recognition. Plus, the amount of work and time that goes into a manual feature descriptor is impossible to keep up with. That's why we are researching automated ways to do feature extraction that work better and faster.

2.3. Classification

Classify to be divided into tree. Which of these classifiers is needed to separate the target object from other things? Popular choices include SVC, Adaboost, or DPM. DPM algorithm solves the problem of significant deformations by considering the deformation cost associated with each part of the object [5].

The YOLO method combines detection and classification into one step. YOLOv5 uses CNN architecture to make predictions on object recognition (Figure 8.1). It aims to reduce the time taken for object detection, making it faster and more accurate. The diagram below shows the structure of the system [6].

- The feature extractor module is responsible for extracting feature maps at various scales from input images.
- The detector uses feature maps to locate bounding boxes.
- The classifier assigns found objects to predefined groups.

2.4. Comparison with existing techniques

The comparison shows that YOLOv5 outperforms previous approaches with more than 79% accuracy and faster detection time making it appropriate for tasks that require fast and accurate object detection, as presented in Table 8.1. Its advantage of being able to utilize custom-annotated datasets is that it is more suitable for such niche applications as recognizing HTML elements in hand-drawn illustrations. These qualities justify the choice of YOLOv5 as the main model in the proposed study.

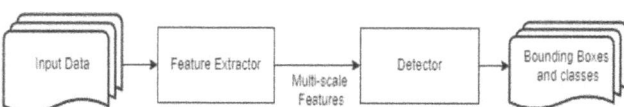

Table 8.1. Comparison of YOLOv5 with traditional object detection techniques

Technique	YOLOv3	Faster R-CNN	YOLOv5 (Proposed)
Detection Speed	Moderate	Slow	Fast
Accuracy	70%	75%	79%
Scalability	Medium	Low	High
Training Data	Pre-trained weights	Require large datasets	Custom annotated dataset

Source: Author.

3. YOLOV5 Architecture

The integration of specialized architectural components within YOLOv5 significantly enhances its performance as an object detection model. This structured design not only improves the model's efficiency but also its efficacy in identifying objects accurately. Consequently, YOLOv5 demonstrates high precision in various application domains, a fact shown in Figure 8.2 [7].

The clear plan of its design makes sure it can quickly and correctly spot things, which is important for tools that work in real time. This view shows how well the tool works in different settings, a sign it can help with a wide range of real-world situations.

3.1. Backbone

The midsection of YOLOv5 makes use of CSPDarknet53, tailored for high-level picture characteristics [8]. CSPDarknet53 consists of numerous convolutional layers, alongside residual connections that aid feature extraction as well as the transfer of gradients to and from the object detection model [9].

3.2. Neck

The YOLOv5 model uses a Path Aggregation Network (PANet) in its neck. PANet is designed to improve feature

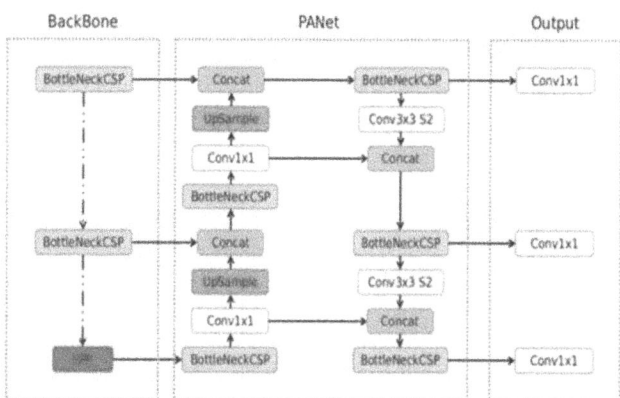

Figure 8.1. General diagram of the YOLOv5 network architecture [6].

Source: Author.

Figure 8.2. YOLOv5 architecture in detailed [7].

Source: Author.

pyramid networks by combining features from multiple levels [10]. This multi-scale feature aggregation is important for accurate detection of objects with different sizes, which in turn improves the model's robustness and accuracy. PANet enables high detection accuracy for objects of various sizes by combining features from different levels of the backbone [11].

3.3. Output

The final part of YOLOv5 is important as it is responsible for generating the detection result. There are several components in the output layer that can improve detection accuracy. Firstly, multi-scale output layers are introduced which can detect objects of different sizes in the image, making it easier to detect both small and large objects [12]. Secondly, the model uses anchor-based detection, in which predefined anchor boxes are used to predict the locations and classes of objects, these anchor boxes serve as reference points for precise object localization and classification. This ensures that YOLOv5 can identify more than one object in real-time with high accuracy, which is perfect for scenarios that require instant detection and tracking functionality [13].

4. Proposed Methodology

This study shows a new way to make designs faster and easier by adjusting them in real-time. We used a YOLOv5 model with machine learning and deep learning techniques to make the process better. It is much better at spotting and classifying things in digital pictures and can tell a lot about them. It works well with HTML code, and the objects detected can be put as rows and columns. The process is accelerated by the organization of visual data in a way a machine can understand. We also trained it on a dataset that we made. Full details can be found in the following section (Figure 8.3).

4.1. Data gathering

The data was made with images from the Microsoft AI Lab's Sketch2Code tool [14]. So, there are some pictures with textboxes, buttons, dropdown menus, and checkboxes. To make it good, I picked 2,700 images. Most of the images were for the training set, which means there are 2,160 images. The rest of the 540 images were for the testing and validation sets. We used the selected images for the training of our model. For

the better recognition of the model with the ability to encode the crucial information into HTML code-oriented structures, the image components were meticulously cropped and then added for the training.

4.2. Data labelling

A tool that labels things is used to label images using boxes. A boring and very important job. These boxes are critical for study and teaching the model since their accuracy will affect the results of the system. A box that is not aligned with the object will confuse the algorithm, which could lead to malfunctioning of the system. So, in order to create the most accurate boxes, the best way is to do it manually [15].

1. **Label (or class) number:** Ranges between 0 and n-1.
2. **X and Y:** Correspond to the box's center coordinates.
3. **Width:** Width of the box.
4. **Height:** Height of the box.

4.3. Model selection

Selecting the correct model for training is vital. In this work, we chose YOLOv5s, which is a good balance of speed and size. YOLOv5s is the second smallest and fastest variant in the YOLOv5 family, making it well-suited for real-time object detection tasks [16]. As shown in Figure 8.4, this model can process fast while maintaining high accuracy detection. Due to its compact design, YOLOv5s is ideal for on-device deployment with minimal performance degradation. Moreover, its good results across multiple datasets make it a good candidate for a wide range of real-time object detection applications [17]. This method provides efficient and effective object detection in various application domains, including autonomous driving, for example, video surveillance, and industrial automation. This method provides efficient and effective object detection in various application domains, including automated form recognition, web page element classification, and interactive web design tools.

4.4. Model training

The YOLOv5s model must be trained on your own little dataset, using settings like batch size, image size, and pretrained weights. Save training results in numbered run folders [18].

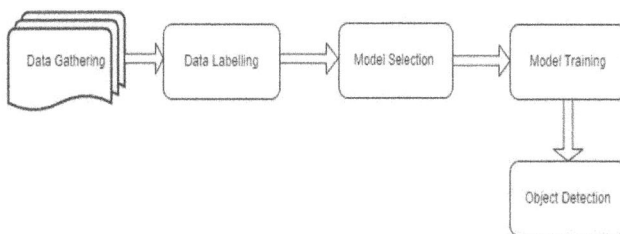

Figure 8.3. Pipeline for Object Detection Using YOLOv5.
Source: Author.

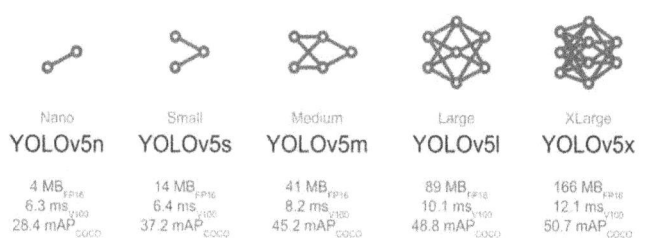

Figure 8.4. YOLOv5 architecture in detailed [7].
Source: Author.

4.5. *Object detection*

In the last stage, object recognition is carried out on the test images using the trained weights. YOLOv5 algorithm goes through each image and looks for the objects and recognizes them based on the patterns and features it learned during training. It then outputs the detected objects and where they are in the images. Also, computer vision is used to determine the items and where they are, connecting each item that was identified with its corresponding HTML code. There are currently 4 categorization classes – Select, Text Field, Checkbox and Button. It keeps track of coordinates to identify the neighboring HTML elements on the wireframe, and the HTML code is saved in a default output.html file that can be downloaded.

5. Analysis and Results

In the review of this paper, we focus on the importance of the outcomes obtained based on the implemented system. Object detection using the YOLOv5 algorithm was performed on a big dataset of images to determine how accurately objects are detected. In the testing phase, we measured the overall efficiency of the detection process with system-calculated estimation metrics based on Equation 1 provided in the text. Results were further analyzed to enhance the understanding of the performance of the algorithm and identify additional optimization possibilities. The overall accuracy of detection was observed to be within a relatively high range confirming that YOLOv5 performs well with diverse condition verities. Furthermore, this work proposes additional evaluation criteria to bridge the gaps that were highlighted in the assessment which constrain the study. This is an indication that the system is effective, notably in scenarios where precise and timely object identification is critical [19].

$$k = \frac{n}{m} \times 100 \qquad (1)$$

Where:

- k = Success rate of test in percentage.
- n = Number of successfully detected objects.
- m = Number of data that were observed.

The test in Figure 8.5 consisted of three HTML elements: a select option, a textbox, and a button for affiliation.

The object finding and naming has a success rate of 84% for the test image (Table 8.2). The system also did a great job, with a confidence level of more than 80% in the object detection and classification. The results of this evaluation suggest that the system is capable of detecting objects in images and classifying them correctly. The html version of Figure 8.5 is shown in Figure 8.6.

6. Conclusions and Future Scope

The study helped automate web creation by recognizing things in images and turning them into websites. It did well, almost 100% in fact, saving lots of work for designers.

There's still much room for improvement. We can do a lot more with the system's accuracy and useful details such as getting the object coordinates right and the corresponding HTML code. This will need a bunch of algorithmic training and some new ways to mitigate the system's capability of dealing with a larger set of HTML elements.

Next, the research timeline will cover model-training with a wide variety of user-generated images. The hope is that the overall precision and performance of the model will improve over time as it learns on more diverse inputs.

The next steps of this work will explore the development of integrated solutions for holistic web design. One of the primary contributions will be a system that suggests free website templates, allowing users to instantly create fully functioning websites using the HTML that was generated from their designs. This feature will help to lower the barrier to effective and efficient web design even further, particularly

Table 8.2. Object detection results with confidence scores

Name	xmin	ymin	xmax	ymax	Confidence
Select	610.35	35.26	1003.4	148.94	0.81
TextBox	615.68	176.86	1033.5	288.99	0.81
Button	627.55	328.28	1034.1	464.31	0.91

Source: Author.

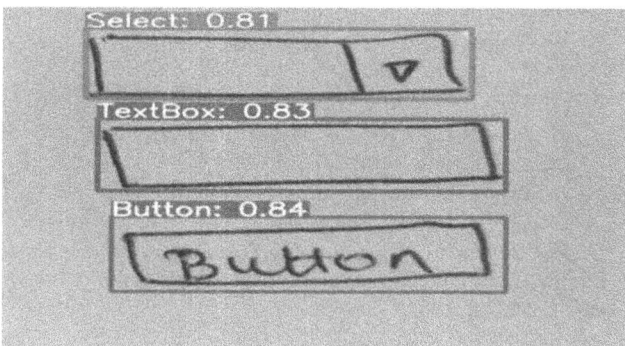

Figure 8.5. Detected object with a confidence level.

Source: Author.

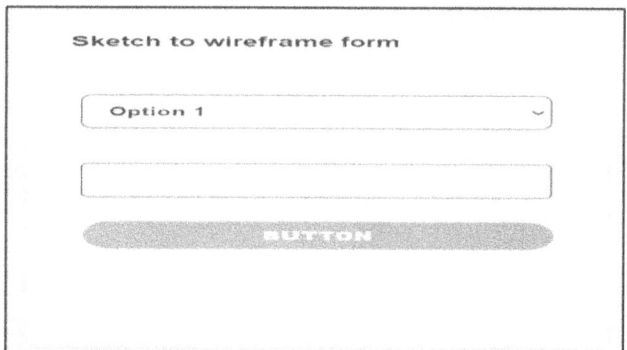

Figure 8.6. Visual representation of the output in HTML format.

Source: Author.

for users who are less experienced at coding. In conclusion, while the current system marks a significant step forward in auto-mating web design, the outlined future work will focus on refining these technologies to deliver more precise, adaptable, and user-friendly solutions. The ongoing development and enhancement of these tools will continue to push the boundaries of what is possible in the automation of web design, with the potential to revolutionize the field.

References

[1]   Importance Of Website: 7 Reasons Why Your Business Needs It. Accessed: Aug. 17, 2022. [Online]. Available:https://www.velocityconsultancy.com/importance-of-website-reasons-why-your-business-needs-it/

[2]   Wang, N., Joo, M., Chen, J., & Wu, J. G. (2022). Marine Object Detection Based on Improved YOLOv5. In *5th International Conference on Intelligent Autonomous Systems, ICoIAS 2022, Institute of Electrical and Electronics Engineers Inc.*, pp. 43–47. doi: 10.1109/ICoIAS56028.2022.9931205.

[3]   Babila, I. F. E., Villasor, S. A. E., & Dela Cruz, J. C. (2022). Object Detection for Inventory Stock Counting Using YOLOv5. In *2022 IEEE 18th International Colloquium on Signal Processing and Applications, CSPA 2022 - Proceeding, Institute of Electrical and Electronics Engineers Inc.*, pp. 304–309. doi: 10.1109/CSPA55076.2022.9782028.

[4]   Verma, S., Tripathi, S., Singh, A., Ojha, M., & Saxena, R. R. (2021). Insect Detection and Identification using YOLO Algorithms on Soybean Crop. In *IEEE Region 10 Annual International Conference, Proceedings/TENCON, Institute of Electrical and Electronics Engineers Inc.*, pp. 272–277. doi: 10.1109/TENCON54134.2021.9707354.

[5]   Zhao, Z. Q., Zheng, P., Xu, S. T., & Wu, X. (2019). Object Detection with Deep Learning: A Review. *Institute of Electrical and Electronics Engineers Inc.* doi: 10.1109/TNNLS.2018.2876865.

[6]   Snegireva, D., & Perkova, A. (2021). Traffic Sign Recognition Application Using Yolov5 Architecture. In *Proceedings - 2021 International Russian Automation Conference, RusAutoCon 2021, Institute of Electrical and Electronics Engineers Inc.*, pp. 1002–1007. doi: 10.1109/RusAutoCon52004.2021.9537355.

[7]   GitHub - ultralytics/yolov5: YOLOv5 🚀 in PyTorch > ONNX > CoreML > TFLite. Accessed: May 05, 2025. [Online]. Available: https://github.com/ultralytics/yolov5

[8]   Terven, J., Córdova-Esparza, D. M., & Romero-González, J. A. (2023). A Comprehensive Review of YOLO Architectures in Computer Vision: From YOLOv1 to YOLOv8 and YOLO-NAS. *Machine Learning and Knowledge Extraction, 5*, 1680–1716. doi: 10.3390/MAKE5040083.

[9]   Terven, J., & Cordova-Esparza, D. (2023). A Comprehensive Review of YOLO Architectures in Computer Vision: From YOLOv1 to YOLOv8 and YOLO-NAS. doi: 10.3390/make5040083.

[10] Wu, H., Zhao, X., Qiao, J., & Che, Y. (2023). An Improved YOLOv5 Algorithm for Elderly Fall Detection. In *2023 International Conference on Innovation, Knowledge, and Management, ICIKM 2023.* Institute of Electrical and Electronics Engineers Inc., pp. 83–88. doi: 10.1109/ICIKM59709.2023.00024

[11] Mastering All YOLO Models from YOLOv1 to YOLOv12. Accessed: May 05, 2025. [Online]. Available: https://learn-opencv.com/mastering-all-yolo-models/

[12] He, B., Zhuo, J. X., Zhuo, X. S., Peng, S. Y., Li, T., & Wang, H. (2022). Defect detection of printed circuit board based on improved YOLOv5. In *2022 International Conference on Artificial Intelligence and Computer Information Technology, AICIT 2022, Institute of Electrical and Electronics Engineers Inc.* doi: 10.1109/AICIT55386.2022.9930318.

[13] Exploring the Advanced Architecture of YOLOv5 for Object Detection | by Nagvekar | Medium. Accessed: May 05, 2025. [Online]. Available: https://nagvekar.medium.com/exploring-the-advanced-architecture-of-yolov5-for-object-detection-ee6ad40d0fec

[14] Sketch2Code | Microsoft Learn. Accessed: May 05, 2025. [Online]. Available: https://learn.microsoft.com/en-us/shows/ai-show/sketch2code

[15] Sun, F., Li, Z., & Li, Z. (2021). A traffic flow detection system based on YOLOv5. In *Proceedings - 2021 2nd International Seminar on Artificial Intelligence, Networking and Information Technology, AINIT 2021, Institute of Electrical and Electronics Engineers Inc.*, pp. 458–464. doi: 10.1109/AINIT54228.2021.00095.

[16] Li, J., Liu, Z., & Song, Y. (2024). A multi-strategy integrated improved YOLOv5 model and its application in target detection. In *2024 IEEE 4th International Conference on Electronic Technology, Communication and Information (ICETCI)*, IEEE, pp. 675–682. doi: 10.1109/ICETCI61221.2024.10594297.

[17] Institute of Electrical and Electronics Engineers, IEEE Computer Society, and IEEE Computer Society. Technical Committee on Scalable Computing, Proceedings: 2021 IEEE 23rd International Conference on High Performance Computing & Communications, 7th International Conference on Data Science & Systems, 19th International Conference on Smart City, 7th International Conference on Dependability in Sensor, Cloud & Big Data Systems & Applications: HPCC-DSS-SmartCity-DependSys 2021:20–22 December 2021, Haikou, Hainan, China.

[18] How to Train A Custom Object Detection Model with YOLO v5 | by Jacob Solawetz | Towards Data Science. Accessed: Aug. 17, 2022. [Online]. Available: https://towardsdata-science.com/how-to-train-a-custom-object-detection-model-with-yolo-v5-917e9ce13208

[19] Al Amin, I. H., Arby, F. H., Winarno, E., Hartono, B., & Hadikurniawati, W. (2022). Real-time Social Distance Detection using YOLO-v5 with Bird-eye View Perspective to Suppress the Spread of COVID-19. In *Proceedings - 2022 2nd International Conference on Information Technology and Education, ICIT and E 2022, Institute of Electrical and Electronics Engineers Inc.*, pp. 269–274. doi: 10.1109/ICITE54466.2022.9759552.

9 Geospatial visualization and prediction of air quality index in Karnataka using ensemble machine learning models

Vani Vasudevan[a], K. Sudha Srinithya[b], Pavithra A.[c], K. Bhagavathi Naidu[d], and Nivedita G.[e]

Computer Science and Engineering, Nitte Meenakshi Institute of Technology, Bangalore, India

Abstract: Air pollution has emerged as a critical environmental concern, necessitating accurate monitoring and predictive mechanism to ensure sustainable urban living. This study focuses on the geospatial visualization and prediction of the Air Quality Index (AQI) for cities in Karnataka using ensemble machine learning models, including Random Forest, Linear Regression, and XGBoost. Using this ensemble model has increased the R^2 Score to 0.95. Historical AQI data is leveraged to identify trends and patterns, aiding in the development of precise predictive models. A user-friendly interface visualizes AQI data geospatially, accompanied by colour-coded representations for simplified interpretation. Furthermore, advanced plant-based preventive techniques are integrated to mitigate pollution levels and promote sustainable air quality management.

Keywords: AQI, Karnataka cities, geospatial visualization, XGBoost, random forest, machine learning, plant-based preventive techniques, random forest

1. Introduction

Pollution of the air continues to be a significant problem across the globe threatening the health of populations, the environment, and economies. Air Quality Index (AQI) has a significant impact and depends on timely and accurate AQI prediction to minimize its impact and determine decision making if the community is exposed to dangerous air conditions. Common approaches for estimating AQI provide insufficient solutions for timely and adequate considerations of temporal patterns, multiple chemical components of pollutants, and effects of additional factors like meteorological ones. This paper proposes a novel AQI prediction system that integrates ensemble machine learning techniques, including Random Forest, Linear Regression, and XGBoost, to predict AQI trends in Karnataka cities effectively.

Furthermore, key pollutants such as PM2.5, PM10, CO, NO2, O3 and SO2 significantly contribute to air quality degradation. PM2.5 and PM10 are fine and coarse particulate matter that can penetrate the respiratory system, causing issues such as asthma, bronchitis, and cardiovascular diseases. Carbon monoxide (CO) interferes with oxygen delivery in the body, leading to fatigue and impaired cognitive function. Nitrogen dioxide (NO2) exacerbates respiratory conditions, while sulfur dioxide (SO2) can cause irritation in the respiratory tract and exacerbate lung diseases.

Understanding the effects of these pollutants is crucial in developing targeted solutions for improving air quality and safeguarding public health.

In contrast to other models, this work integrates geospatial visualization to present up-to-date trends of air quality across Karnataka. It leverages interactive interfaces and colour-coded maps to enable intuitive exploration of AQI data. Additionally, it includes alert messages and sustainable interventions such as plant-based solutions to mitigate pollution, enhancing the system's applicability for real-world decision-making.

2. Related Works

Previous research has extensively applied machine learning (ML) and deep learning (DL) approaches for Air Quality Index (AQI) prediction. For instance, Wang et al. [1] introduced a CNN-AGU hybrid model, while Agbehadji and Obagbuwa [5] showed that LSTMs outperform conventional ML models in capturing temporal dependencies. Christian et al. [3] emphasized feature engineering for predictive enhancement, and Singal et al. [8] highlighted the benefits of ensemble techniques. However, many studies demand large-scale datasets and high computational power [1, 2, 4, 5, 14], limiting real-time applicability. Others, such as Christian and

[a]vani.v@nmit.ac.in, [b]1nt21cs082.sudha@nmit.ac.in, [c]1nt21cs123.pavithra@nmit.ac.in, [d]1nt21cs077.bhagavathi@nmit.ac.in, [e]1nt21cs121.nivedita@nmit.ac.in

DOI: 10.1201/9781003724988-9

Choi [9] and Christian et al. [16], lack interactive geospatial tools, while models by Sharma et al. [12] and Almaliki et al. [13] omit real-time sensor integration, restricting immediate AQI tracking. Moreover, most research focuses on highly polluted cities like Delhi and Beijing, with limited attention to regional air quality shifts in areas like Karnataka. Additionally, few works propose sustainable or preventive measures, such as green-based interventions.

Overall, this work offers a computationally efficient, region-specific, and sustainability-driven framework for AQI forecasting, suitable for real-time urban air quality management and policy development.

The previous research has effectively applied machine learning and deep learning models for predicting AQI, but they have significant drawbacks. Some research, like [8, 9], and [16], are based on numerical prediction without incorporating interactive geospatial visualizations, which makes them less effective in supporting decision-making. Additionally, deep learning models, like those in [1, 5], and [14], offer high accuracy but consume huge computational resources and large-scale training data, making them unsuitable for real-time use.

Another constraint is noticed in earlier work, for example, [6, 12], and [13, 15, 17, 18], where there is no integration of real-time sensors, limiting their capability for real-time AQI tracking. Most of the current work is also concentrated on highly polluted areas like Delhi, Beijing, and Mumbai and less on air quality fluctuations in Karnataka. Research such as [3] and [7, 10, 11] focuses on the accuracy of AQI prediction but fails to suggest sustainable interventions, for example, alerting system and plant-based air cleaning methods, to reduce pollution levels.

This research addresses the previously identified gaps by incorporating an ensemble machine learning model that integrates Random Forest, XGBoost, and Linear Regression, with an R^2 score of 0.95 and higher predictive accuracy compared to standalone models. The proposed system incorporates geospatial visualization techniques using Folium and Streamlit-based dashboards to facilitate real-time and interactive AQI monitoring across Karnataka. Although real-time IoT sensor integration is considered for future enhancements, the system currently offers a user-friendly interface that enables dynamic AQI trend exploration. As compared to earlier studies that mainly discuss high-pollution cities, this research uniquely analyzes AQI patterns in Karnataka, which represents a less-researched yet critical regional air quality issue. This study also proposes sustainable air quality measures through the suggestion of plant-based preventive methods to combat pollution, focusing especially on PM2.5, NO₂, and SO₂ pollutants.

3. Methodology

The approach to this project involves using art of machine learning methods, extensive data preparation, and sound assessment in order to enhance the accuracy and usability of the AQI forecasts. The AQI Prediction & Visualization Architecture, as shown in Figure 9.1, offers an interactive and effective platform for air quality analysis through the combination of a Streamlit-based user interface, a machine learning prediction engine, and geospatial visualization tools.

Figure 9.1 AQI Prediction and Visualization architecture users provide input parameters via the sidebar panel, which are processed by the prediction engine based on a pre-trained AQI model from the model loader. The forecasted AQI values are plotted on an interactive Folium map with a marker cluster functionality, allowing spatial analysis of pollution intensity. This design provides smooth data flow from user input to visualization, supporting intuitive interaction, precise AQI forecasting, and meaningful geographical representation for enhanced air quality evaluation and decision-making.

1. ***Data Collection:*** The historical Air Quality Index (AQI) data for different Karnataka cities from 2021 to 2023 is the main emphasis of the dataset. This information is essential for assessing changes over time and comprehending regional differences in air pollution, especially for Karnataka's urban and semi-urban areas. The dataset includes AQI data for major cities in Karnataka, such as Bengaluru and Shivamogga. Bengaluru, the state capital, often records higher AQI values due to urbanization, heavy traffic, and industrial activities. Shivamogga, a smaller city, generally has better air quality but still experiences spikes in AQI due to factors like agriculture and construction. The data highlights air quality variations across urban and rural areas, reflecting both local pollution sources and broader regional trends. It comprises 20,440 instances with eight key attributes: Timestamp, PM2.5, PM10, CO, NO2, SO2, Ozone, and City. The data specifically focuses on 19 major cities within the state of Karnataka.

   Air Quality Parameters:
   - *Ozone (O₃):* This column contains the concentration of ozone measured in parts per billion (ppb). Ozone is a harmful air pollutant that can affect human health, especially in urban areas with high vehicular traffic.
   - *Carbon Monoxide (CO):* This represents the concentration of carbon monoxide in parts per million

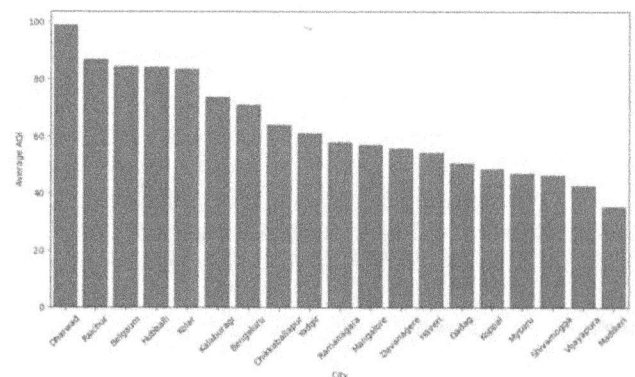

Figure 9.1. Average AQI by city.

Source: Author.

(ppm). High levels of CO can be detrimental to human health and indicate pollution from motor vehicles and industrial processes.

- *Sulfur Dioxide (SO₂):* Measured in parts per billion (ppb), SO₂ is a major air pollutant from fossil fuel combustion. This data is crucial for tracking industrial emissions in the region.
- *Nitrogen Dioxide (NO₂):* This pollutant is measured in parts per billion (ppb). NO₂ levels are often high in urban and industrial areas, contributing to smog and respiratory issues.
- *PM10 (Particulate Matter 10):* Represented in micrograms per cubic meter ($\mu g/m^3$), PM10 refers to particles with a diameter of 10 micrometers or smaller. These particles can enter the lungs and affect respiratory health.
- *PM2.5 (Particulate Matter 2.5):* Similar to PM10 but smaller (≤ 2.5 micrometers), these particles can penetrate deeper into the lungs and even enter the bloodstream. PM2.5 is a significant concern for public health and environmental policy.

All eight attributes from the dataset are described in Table 9.1.

Table 9.1. Description of data set attributes

Attribute Name	Type	Description
Timestamp	Date/Time	The date and time when the data was recorded.
Ozone (O_3)	Float	The concentration of ozone (O_3) in the air, typically measured in parts per billion (ppb).
Carbon Monoxide (CO)	Float	The concentration of carbon monoxide (CO) in the air, measured in parts per million (ppm).
Sulphur Dioxide (SO_2)	Float	The concentration of sulfur dioxide (SO_2) in the air, measured in parts per billion (ppb).
Nitrogen Dioxide (NO_2)	Float	The concentration of nitrogen dioxide (NO_2) in the air, measured in parts per billion (ppb).
PM10	Float	The concentration of particulate matter (PM) with a diameter of 10 micrometers or less, typically measured in micrograms per cubic meter ($\mu g/m^3$).
PM2.5	Float	The concentration of particulate matter (PM) with a diameter of 2.5 micrometers or less, typically measured in micrograms per cubic meter ($\mu g/m^3$).
City	String	The city in Karnataka where the air quality data was collected.

Source: Author.

Challenges Addressed:
The data set comes with issues like missing pollutant data and heterogenous formats as a result of various sources and volume. It is important to maintain data consistency and completeness to have reliable analysis

2. **Data Preprocessing:** Noise Reduction: Missing numerical values were managed with mean imputation through scikit-learn's SimpleImputer, which was selected due to its simplicity, efficiency, and applicability to randomly distributed missing data. **Normalization:** Numeric attributes were normalized by StandardScaler, which normalizes by subtracting the mean and dividing by unit variance.

3. **Model Choice and Building:** An ensemble of Voting Regressor involving Linear Regression, Random Forest, and XGBoost was employed for improved accuracy and resilience. **Linear Regression** supposes a linear relationship between attribute variables and the target, which is given by equation (1).

$$Y = \beta 0 + \beta 1 x 1 + \beta 2 x 2 + \ldots + \beta n x n + \epsilon \qquad (1)$$

where $\beta 0$ is the intercept, $\beta 1$, $\beta 2$, … βn are the coefficients, and ϵ is the error term. Linear Regression minimizes the sum of squared errors (SSE) to estimate the coefficients. While it is computationally efficient and interpretable, its assumptions of linearity and independence limit its performance on complex, non-linear datasets.

- **Random Forest Regressor:** Random Forest is an ensemble learning method that constructs multiple decision trees during training and combines their outputs for prediction.

  It employs bootstrap aggregating (bagging) to train each tree on a random subset of the data and features, reducing variance and improving generalization. For regression tasks, the final prediction is obtained by averaging the outputs of all trees by the formula represented in equation (2)

$$f(x) = \frac{1}{T} \sum_{t=1}^{T} h_t(x) \qquad (2)$$

where ht(x) is the prediction from the t-th tree. Random Forest is robust to noise, capable of

Table 9.2. Model comparison result analysis table

Model	MAE	MSE	R2	Absolute R2
Linear Regression	1.245	2.345	0.823	0.823
Random Forest regressor	0.895	1.874	0.876	0.876
XGBoost Regressor	0.755	1.523	0.892	0.892
Ensemble Model	0.730	1.455	0.899	0.899

Source: Author.

modelling non-linear relationships, and provides feature importance metrics, but it may require careful tuning to avoid overfitting on small datasets.

- **XGBoost Regressor:** XGBoost (Extreme Gradient Boosting) is a gradient boosting framework optimized for speed and performance. It sequentially builds decision trees to minimize a loss function, correcting the residuals of the previous trees. The regularized objective function combines the training loss and a complexity penalty by the formula represented in equation (3)

$$Obj = \sum_{i=1}^{n} L(y_i, \hat{y}_i) + \sum_{k=1}^{K} \Omega(h_k) \qquad (3)$$

Where $L(y_i, \hat{y}_i)$ is the loss function (e.g., mean squared error), and $\Omega(h_k)$ regularizes tree complexity. XGBoost incorporates second-order gradient optimization, sparsity awareness, and support for parallel computation, making it highly effective for non-linear and large-scale datasets. To evaluate the performance of the ensemble model, it was compared with three baseline models: Linear Regression (LR), Random Forest Regressor (RF), and XGBoost Regressor (XGB). The comparison was based on three evaluation metrics: Mean Absolute Error (MAE), Mean Squared Error (MSE), and the Coefficient of Determination (R^2) as shown in Table 9.2.

- **Linear Regression (LR):** The Linear Regression model, being the simplest baseline, exhibited the highest error metrics (MAE and MSE) and the lowest R^2 value among the models. This was expected due to its inability to capture complex, non-linear patterns in the dataset.
- **Random Forest Regressor (RF):** The Random Forest Regressor showed significant improvements over Linear Regression, with reductions in both MAE and MSE, and a higher R^2 value. This can be attributed to its ensemble nature and capability to handle non-linear relationships.
- **XGBoost Regressor (XGB):** XGBoost further improved performance metrics compared to Random Forest, leveraging its advanced gradient boosting algorithm to achieve lower MAE and MSE, and higher R2.
- **Ensemble Model:** The Voting Regressor, combining the strengths of LR, RF, and XGB, achieved the best performance across all metrics. The ensemble model reduced MAE by 3.3% compared to XGBoost, and achieved a slight improvement in R^2 score, demonstrating the effectiveness of aggregating predictions from diverse models.

4. **Visualization and Interface Design:** Python's Folium and Matplotlib modules are used to visualize Karnataka's AQI distribution. Streamlit frameworks enable real-time AQI exploration with a simple interface.

Engaging Welcome Page: Figure 9.2 shows the user interface's welcome page. Figure 9.3 shows the web application's intuitive navigation flow. Users can choose between "Welcome," "Prediction," and "Air Quality Information" in the sidebar. Figure 9.4 shows the AQI prediction page layout. Figure 9.5 shows parts where

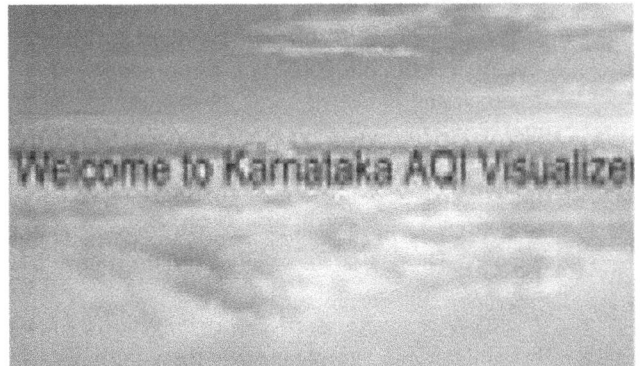

Figure 9.2. Welcome page (UI).
Source: Author.

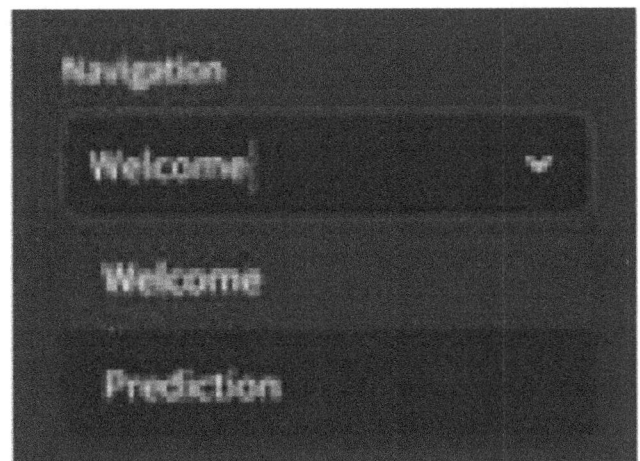

Figure 9.3. Navigation.
Source: Author.

Figure 9.4. AQI Prediction page.
Source: Author.

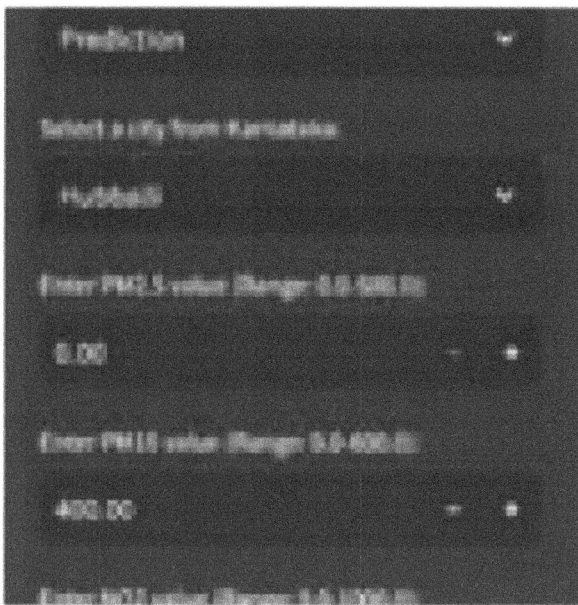

Figure 9.5. Input values.

Source: Author.

users enter pollutant numbers (PM2.5, PM10, etc.) and choose a city. Dynamic Visualizations: Pollutant ranges and an AQI-based colour-coded folium map. Clarity and Accessibility: Colour schemes and tooltips make data representation simple.

5. ***Implementation of Preventive Techniques:*** Research on plant-based solutions identifies species effective in absorbing pollutants like PM2.5, NO2, and SO2. Recommendations for urban greenery initiatives are included as part of the mitigation strategy.

4. Experimental Analysis and Results

The proposed ensemble model for AQI prediction in Karnataka demonstrates a significant improvement in accuracy and robustness compared to individual machine learning models. The selection of Karnataka as the study region, highlights the unique challenges of AQI prediction in a geographically diverse area that includes metropolitan, semi-urban, and rural settings. Unlike previous AQI studies conducted in highly polluted regions such as Delhi and Mumbai, this work focuses on a state where air pollution is not consistently severe but fluctuates due to varying sources such as vehicular emissions, industrial activity, and seasonal agricultural factors. The need for accurate AQI forecasting in such regions is crucial for sustainable air quality management and preventive interventions.

4.1. Justification for algorithm selection

To ensure precise AQI forecasting, the study employs an ensemble learning approach that integrates Random Forest,

XGBoost, and Linear Regression. The justification for choosing these models over others is as follows:

Random Forest Regressor was selected due to its ability to handle non-linearity and complex interactions among pollutants. It reduces overfitting by averaging multiple decision trees, ensuring better generalization.

XGBoost Regressor, a powerful gradient boosting algorithm, was included for its efficiency in minimizing errors by focusing on challenging-to-predict cases. Its regularization techniques improve stability, making it suitable for AQI prediction.

Linear Regression, while a simpler model, was incorporated as a baseline for interpretability and to capture linear relationships between pollutant levels and AQI.

By leveraging the strengths of these models, **the ensemble** approach enhances predictive performance beyond what individual models could achieve. Deep learning models, such as LSTMs and CNNs, were considered but not selected due to their higher computational cost and the need for extensive datasets, which may limit real-time applications.

4.2. Performance evaluation

The model's effectiveness was assessed using Mean Absolute Error (MAE), Mean Squared Error (MSE), and Coefficient of Determination (R^2). The comparative results are presented in Table 9.2.

The ensemble model significantly outperforms individual models:

1. It achieves a 3.3% reduction in MAE compared to XGBoost, indicating improved precision.
2. The higher R^2 value (0.95) signifies that the ensemble model explains 95% of the variance in AQI, making it a highly reliable predictor.
3. Compared to traditional methods, the ensemble model captures both linear and non-linear trends, allowing for more accurate AQI forecasts across Karnataka's diverse cities.

4.3. Unique contribution to Karnataka's AQI prediction

This research stands out by focusing on Karnataka, a region with heterogeneous pollution sources ranging from urban traffic congestion in Bengaluru to seasonal agricultural pollution in Shivamogga. Unlike existing AQI studies, which primarily concentrate on high-pollution zones, this study aims to provide a proactive, real-time AQI forecasting system for a less-studied yet environmentally significant region. The inclusion of geospatial visualization enhances the practical usability of the model.

As shown in Figure 9.6, the predicted AQI values are colour-coded and mapped using Folium, allowing intuitive interpretation for policymakers and the general public. The system's user-friendly dashboard interface supports real-time AQI exploration, empowering users to analyze pollution trends over time.

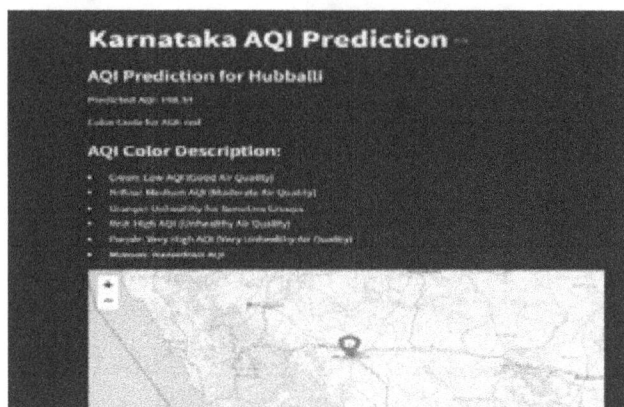

Figure 9.6. Predicted AQI value with colour-coded map representation.

Source: Author.

Additionally, this work goes beyond prediction by integrating alert messages and plant-based preventive techniques to mitigate air pollution.

By identifying effective air-purifying plants for different pollutants (e.g., PM2.5, SO2, NO2).

The study provides a sustainable intervention strategy that complements predictive modeling.

5. Conclusion and Future Work

The current research predicts and prevents Karnataka air pollution using ensemble machine learning models, geographic visualization, and plant-based preventative techniques. An ensemble-based strategy using Random Forest, Linear Regression, and XGBoost yields an accurate prediction of 0.95 R², outperforming baseline machine learning algorithms. Historical AQI data helps identify pollution trends and improve forecast models for air quality management, according to the study. Geospatial visualization makes AQI data more understandable, helping policymakers, researchers, and the public make educated decisions with intuitive, colour-coded visuals. Integrating plant-based preventative measures shows the study's focus on sustainable air quality management. Despite promising results, this study has drawbacks. The model uses historical AQI data, which may not reflect real-time swings owing to climate change, industrial emissions, or seasonal variations. Real-time IoT sensor data and satellite air quality monitoring improve predictions. While the study covers major Karnataka cities, its application to other regions needs to be confirmed. Real-time AQI monitoring from IoT devices at numerous sites will be included to the dataset in future study. Dynamic model updates and short-term air quality forecasting will improve. Long-term dependence and temporal connection capturing will be improved by deep learning models like LSTM networks and Transformers. To improve prediction accuracy, add meteorological information like humidity, temperature, wind speed, and air pressure. Customized mobile air quality notifications are the second prospective study field. This will include location-based AQI forecasts, health advice, and real-time air pollution reports. Integration with environmental authorities and city planners can help create evidence-based smart city interventions like scheduled green cover optimization and pollution management.

References

[1] Wang, J., Jin, L., Li, X., He, S., Huang, M., & Wang, H. (2022). A Hybrid AirQuality Index Prediction Model Based on CNN and Attention Gate Unit. *IEEE Access*, *10*, 113343–113354. https://doi.org/10.1109/ACCESS.2022.3217242J.

[2] Liu, D. R., Lee, S.-J., & Huang, Y. (2019). Air Pollution Prediction Using Machine Learning and Neural Networks. *Expert Systems*, *37*, e12511. https://doi.org/10.1111/exsy.12511

[3] Christian, M. M., et al. (2024). Machine Learning Approach for Predicting Air Quality Index. Presented at the SIBR 2024 (Seoul) Conference on Interdisciplinary Business and Economics Research. https://doi.org/10.13052/jrss0974-8024.1621

[4] Thakur, A. (2017). Study of Ambient Air Quality Trends and Analysis of Contributing Factors in Bangalore, India. *Oriental Journal of Chemistry*, *33*(2), 865–870. http://dx.doi.org/10.13005/ojc/330265

[5] Agbehadji, I. E., & Obagbuwa, I. C. (2023). Air Quality Prediction Using Machine Learning and Deep Learning: An Exploratory Study. Presented at the 2023 7th International Conference On Computing, Communication, Control And Automation (ICCUBEA).

[6] Patel, P. K., & Singh, H. K. (2024). Performance Analysis of Machine Learning Models for AQI Prediction in Gorakhpur City. *Environmental Monitoring and Assessment*, *196*(10), 645. https://doi.org/10.1007/s10661-024-13107-x

[7] Natarajan, S. K., Shanmurthy, P., Arockiam, D., Balusamy, B., & Selvarajan, S. (2024). Optimized Machine Learning Model for Air Quality Index Prediction in Major Cities in India. *Scientific Reports*, *14*(1), 1467. https://doi.org/10.1038/s41598-024-54807-1

[8] Singal, M., Singh, V., & Sharma, S. L. (2024). Predicting Air Quality Index using Ensemble Machine Learning. *Natural Hazards*, *114*(3), 2025–2045, 2024. https://doi.org/10.1007/s11069-024-07027-9

[9] Christian, M. M., & Choi, H. (2024). Air Quality Forecasting Using Machine Learning: A Global Perspective with Relevance to Low-Resource Settings. Presented at the SIBR 2024 (Seoul) Conference on Interdisciplinary Business and Economics Research. https://ssrn.com/abstract=4686946

[10] Taylor, O. E., & Ezekiel, P. S. (2023). A Model for Forecasting Air Quality Index in Port Harcourt, Nigeria Using Bi-LSTM Algorithm. arXiv preprintarXiv:2302.03930. https://doi.org/10.48550/arXiv.2302.03930

[11] Maltare, N. N., & Vahora, S. (2023). Air Quality Index Prediction Using Machine Learning for Ahmedabad City. *Data in Brief*, *39*, 107693. https://doi.org/10.1016/j.dche.2023.100093

[12] Sharma, G., Khurana, S., Saina, N., Shivansh, & Gupta, G. (2024). Comparative Analysis of Machine Learning

Techniques in Air Quality Index (AQI) Prediction in Smart Cities. *International Journal of System Assurance Engineering and Management*, *15*(1), 123–134. https://doi.org/10.1007/s13198-024-01714-9

[13] Almaliki, A. H., Derdour, A., & Ali, E. (2023). Air Quality Index (AQI) Prediction in Holy Makkah Based on Machine Learning Methods. *Sustainability*, *15*(17), 13168. https://doi.org/10.3390/su151713168

[14] Pant, A., Sharma, S., & Kumar, A. (2023). Evaluation of Machine Learning Algorithms for Air Quality Index (AQI) Prediction. *Journal of Reliability and Statistical Studies*, *16*(2), 123–134. https://doi.org/10.13052/jrss0974-8024.1621

[15] Zayed, R., & Abbod, M. (2024). Air Quality Index Prediction Using DNN-Markov Modeling. *Applied Artificial Intelligence*, *38*(4), 291–306. https://doi.org/10.1080/08839514.2024.2371540

[16] Christian, M., et al. (2024). Air Quality Forecasting Using Machine Learning: A Global Perspective with Relevance to Low-Resource Settings. https://ssrn.com/abstract=4686946

[17] Sidhu, K. (2024). Predictive Modelling of Air Quality Index (AQI) Across Diverse Cities and States of India Using Machine Learning: Investigating the Influence of Punjab's Stubble Burning on AQI Variability. *SSRN Electronic Journal*. https://doi.org/10.2139/ssrn.4790794

[18] Ameer, S., et al. (2019). Comparative Analysis of Machine Learning Techniques for Predicting Air Quality in Smart Cities. *IEEE Access*, *7*, 128325–128338. https://doi.org/10.1109/ACCESS.2019.2925082

10 Evaluating the trade-off between privacy and performance of Non-IID health data in federated learning and centralized systems

Apeksha Bochare[a] and Jibi Abraham[b]

Department of Computer science and Engineering, COEP Technological University, Pune, India

Abstract: In Centralized Learning (CL), data from multiple sources is transferred to a central server, where the entire dataset is processed, raising significant privacy concerns due to potential exposure of personal information at a concentrated location. Federated Learning (FL) addresses this issue by utilizing edge servers near the data sources to process data locally and extract knowledge as local models. To create an evolved model at server the regional models are aggregated and shared, with only the generated models being transferred. FL is categorized based on data distribution schemes: Horizontal Federated Learning (HFL) handles similar features across different data points (IID), while Vertical Federated Learning (VFL) deals with distinct, but potentially overlapping feature sets (non-IID). While CL benefits from large centralized datasets to improve model generalization, it compromises privacy. Conversely, FL enhances data privacy across distributed devices but, may experience a trade-off in performance. Currently, the benchmark dataset based on real-world scenarios for IID and Non-IID is yet to be thoroughly explored in the literature. Additionally, synthetic datasets are inadequate for effectively assessing performance in handling non-IID data. This paper evaluates the performance of CL, HFL, and VFL for real-world scenarios by creating non-IID in the data distribution through multiple edges (client) for an application of healthcare diabetes prediction. It highlights the trade-offs between performance and privacy in handling non-IID features from diverse data sources.

Keywords: Federated learning, centralized learning (CL), horizontal federated learning (HFL), vertical federated learning (VFL)

1. Introduction

In recent years, millions of devices have produced substantial volumes of data, which have been stored in cloud infrastructure. Managing this data presents significant challenges, and extracting valuable insights is crucial. Traditionally, CL systems have been used to analyse and predict useful information from this data. However, this approach often involves sharing personally identifiable information (PII) with cloud service providers, which can compromise user privacy. To mitigate these issues in 2016, Google launched federated learning [1].

FL is a distributed machine learning approach [11] in which a varying number of devices take part in the learning process to train the model using FL by retaining their data locally. Federated Learning (FL) is generally categorized into two primary types: Horizontal Federated Learning (HFL) and Vertical Federated Learning (VFL). All collaborating edges (clients) in HFL share similar characteristics, but they have distinct data points or samples (information that is independently and identically distributed, or IID). On the other hand, VFL (Non-Independent and Identically Distribution data, or non-IID)) uses edges that have distinct attributes but overlap or have the same sample spaces. In order to preserve patient privacy, FL became a well-known

strategy that permits multi-institution collaboration on medical research without sharing patient data [4]. In CL, data is aggregated on a central server, which facilitates high model generalization and performance by leveraging the complete dataset. However, this centralized configuration poses a substantial trade-off between performance and privacy. Although model performance is maximized, data privacy is compromised, as all data must be transferred to and stored centrally. Decentralized approaches like HFL and VFL focus on data privacy by keeping data at local. However, federated models may underperform compared to centralized models due to challenges such as data heterogeneity, limited data per edge, and complexities in synchronizing model updates. This trade-off reflects the balance between enhanced privacy and slightly reduced performance, which is crucial in data-sensitive contexts.

Even though many paper in the literature exist [5] to assess the performance of distributed and centralized learning, a real-world based scenario in non-IID data is still missing. This paper attempts to investigate how non-IID nature affects model performance and the challenges federated learning faces in a real-world scenario by creating non-IID ness in the data distribution through multiple edges for an application of healthcare diabetic prediction. For the selected

[a]apb21.comp@coeptech.ac.in, [b]ja.comp@coeptech.ac.in

DOI: 10.1201/9781003724988-10

case study, it also performed an experiment to estimate the trade-off between privacy and performance when dealing with non-IID featured data.

This paper's subsequent sections have been organized in following manner, The related work is consolidated in Section 2, a breakdown of the various learning strategies is shown in Section 3, and a framework of a non-IID based distribution with multiple edges for the actual diabetic prediction scenario is proposed in Section 4. In Section 5, the investigations are evaluated and the outcomes are analysed using a variety of performance indications.

2. Related Works

FL extends the traditional distributed CL systems through the facilitation of model training across diverse data sources. In CL, complete access to the dataset allows for strong model generalization, with the added benefit of inherently balanced data. However, in FL, data is distributed across multiple generation points, requiring the system to learn from diverse and often imbalanced data sources, which may result in diminished performance. The paper [6] presents a federated learning approach focused on enhancing the detection of pneumonia using chest X-ray images, utilizing heterogeneous data gathered from various sources. This machine learning model categorizes medical images into two classes: normal and pneumonia.

The framework enables collaborative model training across multiple healthcare institutions, leveraging locally distributed datasets while upholding the safeguarding of individual patient information. By aggregating updates from different institutions, the system improves pneumonia detection accuracy while ensuring data privacy, promoting institutional collaboration, and adhering to data protection regulations. In another study [7], a computational framework leveraging deep learning techniques is introduced for pneumonia classification from medical images. The system employs sophisticated algorithms to analyse X-ray images and accurately classify them as either pneumonia or non-pneumonia, significantly improving diagnostic accuracy and detection performance.

A federated learning framework, augmented with blockchain technology [8], is employed for classifying X-rays of three diseases – COVID-19, pneumonia, and tuberculosis. These techniques allowing collaboration of several healthcare institutions to train a machine learning model, while maintaining the privacy of electronic health records. The Blockchain technology incorporation guarantees secure, transparent data management, enhancing trust among the participating institutions and promoting effective collaboration. Additionally, federated learning has been used in the classification of skin diseases [9], such as acne, psoriasis, eczema, and rosacea. In this context, it preserves patient privacy, especially for sensitive body images that cannot be shared. The framework aids healthcare providers in accurately classifying diseases while strengthening the security of Internet of Medical Things (IoMT) systems.

Flood forecasting, as highlighted by [10], presents significant challenges due to the variability in river characteristics, rain and local weather conditions. The datasets from five distinct rivers, each exhibiting unique flow patterns, create a non-IID environment. FL facilitates collaboration among regionally trained models, enabling the system to generate more accurate flood predictions and provide timely five-day advance alerts. By incorporating diverse data from geographically varying sources, this technique enhances the model's capacity to predict floods and provide timely alerts.

A majority of studies concentrate on particular applications rather than offering comprehensive analyses for federated learning and centralized learning, highlighting the trade-offs among privacy and performance in the non-IID data framework. This leaves a sizable gap in the present research.

3. Learning Approaches

Federated Learning [11] is a decentralized way of machine learning where each edge in the network actively participates in the learning process. The edge server generates a model using local data rather than sharing personally identifiable information or raw data beyond the edge's device. A global model is then generated by transmitting a localized learned model to a central server. creating a global model by combining it with models from other edges. This procedure guarantees the decentralization of private information, improving privacy and facilitating cross-border collaborative learning. It involves four iterative phases [2]: first, the central server shares an initial model with all edges; second, the edge devices collect locally available data and develop a local model. Thirdly, the central server received the regional models. Finally, aggregation of these models is executed at the central server using an aggregation algorithm, such as Federated Averaging [3], to produce a global model. This cycle repeats until the final model converges.

When data is collected from multiple participating edges, it can be either IID or Non-IID in nature. IID [11, 12] is a fundamental statistical concept that describes a set of random variables from normal distributions that meet two conditions as follows: If a random variable in the set is independent of each other, the occurrence of that variable does not affect or provide information about the occurrence of the other variables, and there is no correlation between them. These variables are identically distributed since they are drawn from the same probability distribution and thus, they share the same statistical properties, such as mean, variance, and distribution shape.

Non-IID [11, 12] data collected from various participating edges may have different data attributes with or without overlaps. The random variables in the population are not independent of each other and the occurrence of one variable can be correlated with the occurrence of another variable. Also, these variables may not come from the same probability distribution, having different statistical properties, such as mean, variance, and distribution shape. Non-IID data share the same data point but have different attributes [11].

The training and optimization processes for the three learning paradigms – CL, HFL, and VFL – are guided by distinct mathematical models that reflect the unique characteristics of each approach. The gradients ∇, computed from the data, iteratively update the model parameters θ_t. The loss function L quantifies the difference between the actual data and the model's predictions. The optimization functions associated with each approach underscore these distinctions, as outlined in the following subsections. The notations used in these approaches are as given below: The loss function derivation in reference to the model parameters, indicating the direction to update the parameters to minimize the loss.

- **Model Parameters (θ_t):** is the model parameters with iteration t
- **Learning Rate (η):** Controls the Incremental parameter update
- **Loss Function** using the model parameters θ_t computed
  - $L(\theta_t, x_i, y_i)$: i-th data point (x_i, y_i)
  - $L_k(\theta_t)$: at edge k
  - $L_k(\theta_t, X_k)$: at edge k on the local dataset X_k
- **Gradient ($\nabla_{\theta t}$):** The loss function's gradient in relation to the model parameters θ_t
- **Dataset (D):** Composed of m data points, each with a feature vector x_i and a label y_i – **Number of edges** (K)
- Number of data points at edge k (n_k) – Number of samples across all edges (N)
- **Weight ($\frac{nk}{N}$):** The weight assigned to edge k in the aggregation, proportional to the fraction of data points that edge k contributes to the total dataset.

3.1. Centralized learning (CL)

In *CL* [13], the entire dataset is consolidated into a single repository for training. While the dataset is conventionally of IID in nature, we consider here it to be non-IID as shown in Figure 10.1. In *CL*, the model parameters θ_t are updated iteratively using gradients computed from the entire dataset D, which consists of feature vectors x_i and their corresponding target labels y_i. The adjustment rule for the model parameters at time step $t + 1$ [13] is expressed in equation (1).

$$\theta_{t+1} = \theta_t - \eta \nabla_\theta L(\theta_t, x_i, y_i) \tag{1}$$

3.2. Horizontal federated learning (HFL)

In *HFL* [14], the dataset is partitioned across samples, with each edge device storing a distinct subset. All devices have access to the same features and target label while preserving data privacy by not transmitting raw data. Figure 10.2. illustrates the HFL framework in scenarios with non-IID data and quantity skew [11], where data is unevenly distributed

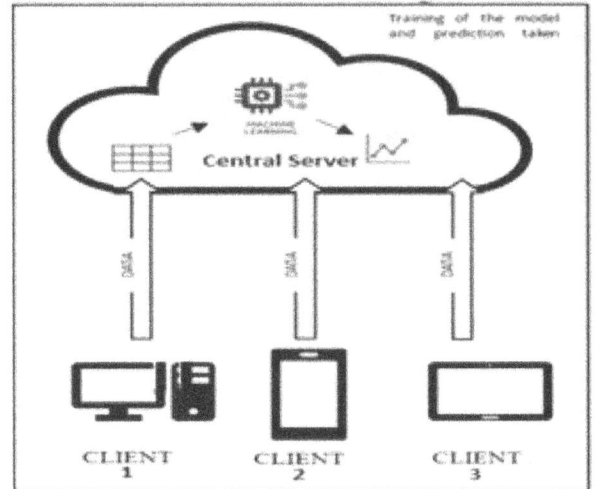

Figure 10.1. Centralized learning.

Source: Author.

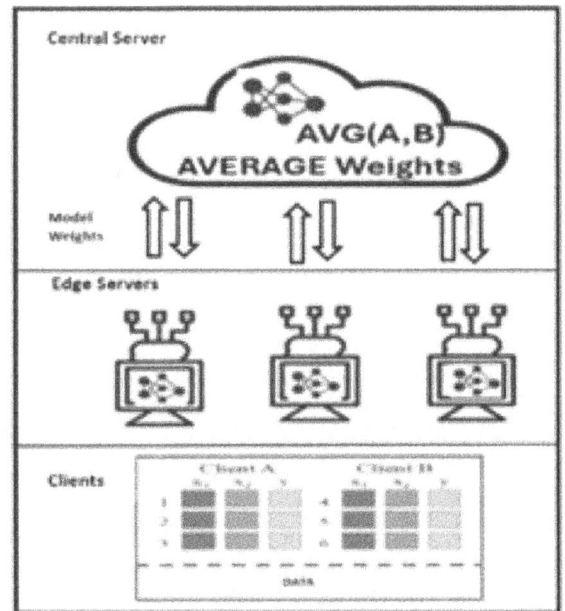

Figure 10.2. Horizontal federated learning.

Source: Author.

across edges. This imbalance impacts the sample size per edge. To address this, the model is trained by aggregating updates from all edges, where each edge k determines the gradient of its local loss function $L_k(\theta)$, and averages gradient to update the global model [14], is represented in the equation (2).

$$\theta_{t+1} = \theta_t - \eta \sum_{k=1}^{K} \frac{n_k}{N} \nabla L_k(\theta_t) \tag{2}$$

This weighted gradient aggregation ensures that edges with larger datasets contribute proportionally more to the global update, balancing the influence of each edge device in the training process.

3.3. *Vertical federated learning (VFL)*

In *VFL* [15], data is partitioned by features rather than by samples, meaning each edge retains a unique subset of features corresponding to the same set of individuals with overlapping features. This approach is typically employed when multiple organizations, such as healthcare providers possess data on the same individuals, but hold different attributes. Figure 10.3 illustrates the data distribution in VFL using different colours to represent each edge's distinct subset of attributes during training. The data is distributed across multiple edges, with each holding a unique subset of features corresponding to the same set of data samples. Every edge device uses its own feature subset to calculate the gradient of the loss function based on its respective feature sub sets, and these gradients are then concatenated to update the model. This optimization process [14] can be expressed as in equation (3):

$$\theta_{t+1} = \theta_t - \eta \sum_{k=1}^{K} \frac{n_k}{N} \nabla_\theta L_k(\theta_t, X_k) \qquad (3)$$

A major challenge in VFL lies in the synchronization of edges with attribute skew data distributions. Efficient alignment and matching of the data across edges are critical for ensuring effective model training.

4. Proposed Methodology

In a real-world healthcare scenario, there are specialized centres to deal with specific activities. For example, there

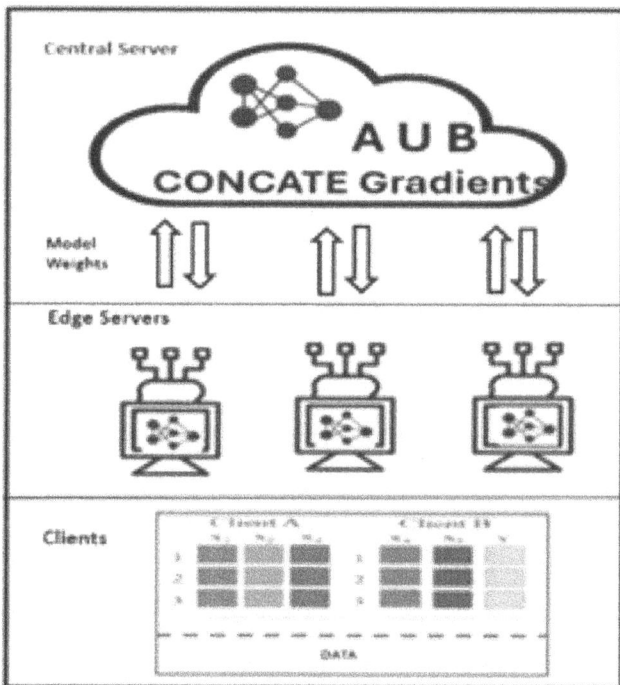

Figure 10.3. Vertical federated learning.

Source: Author.

are centres with General Practitioners, Wellness Centres, and centres specializing in Stroke treatment. The General Practitioner centre is situated at Location 1, where patients seek evaluations related to diabetes. The Wellness Centre at Location 2 concentrates on holistic health and lifestyle enhancements. The Stroke Speciality centre at Location 3 specializes in stroke-related diagnostic investigations.

Table 10.1(A) contains the features about a patient such as Hypertension, cholesterol levels, body mass index, smoking behaviour, patient identification, and diabetes status are use by the General Physician where patient ID serves as a unique identifier for each record. Table 10.1(B) presents the features use by the Wellness Centre, which include Physical Activity, Fruit Consumption, Vegetable Consumption, Heavy Alcohol Consumption, Access to Healthcare, Cost-related barriers to Medical Care, General Health and Patient ID. Table 10.1(C) presents features use by the Stroke Specialty Centre, which include Mental Health, Physical Health, Difficulty in Walking, Sex, Age, Education Level, Income, Patient ID, and Stroke History.

If the learning occurs only locally at each centre, an individual centre may not be able to gain insights into a patient's condition from other centres or utilize this knowledge for incremental learning about the patient's condition. Realizing this fact, we propose a model for implementing an incremental learning for diabetes prediction across multiple centres. This real scenario matches very much with the approach of VFL, where each centre is an edge in the VFL system. In the context of CL, the three centres may be treated as departments within the same hospital and the system would facilitate the integration of data from all three centres into a centralized database for each patient. Table 10.2 presents this consolidated set of features associated with a patient in a Hospital for the CL model. In the context of HFL, multiple hospitals (centres) specializing the same can engage in collaborative learning from each other. Each hospital keeps the same set of data and target labels, they can train models collaboratively without transferring raw data beyond their premises. Locally trained models are shared externally, and a global server consolidates these models to formulate a global model. This approach enables knowledge sharing across hospitals while ensuring the confidentiality of sensitive patient data. As depicted in Table 10.2, two hospitals can have the same set of features with target labels as that of CL.

Table 10.1. Patient's data features for 3 centres

(A) General Pract.	(B) Wellness Centre	(C) Stroke Speciality
1. High Blood Pressure	1. Physical Activity	1. Mental Health
2. High Cholestrol	2. Fruits	2. Physical Health
3. Cholestrol Check	3. Veggies	3. Difficult to Walk
4. Body Mass Index	4. Heavy Alcohol	4. Gender
5. Smoker	5. Any Health	5. Age
6. Patient ID	6. No Docbc Cost	6. Education
7. Heart Disease	7. General Health	7. Stroke
8. Diabetes	8. Patient ID	8. Patient ID

Source: Author.

Table 10.2. Data features in CL and HFL

Hospital 1 Features	
1. High Blood Pressure	12. Any Health
2. High Cholestrol	13. No Docbe Cost
3. Choletsrol Check	14. General Health
4. Body Mass Index	15. Mental Health
5. Smoker	16. Physical Health
6. Stroke	17. Difficult to Walk
7. Heart Disease	18. Gender
8. Physical Activity	19. Age
9. Fruits	20. Education
10 Veggies	21. Income Source
11. Alcohol Consumption	22. Patient ID

Source: Author.

The key distinction between CL and HFL here lies in protecting data privacy: in CL, data privacy is a major concern as all data is available in a central server, while in HFL, predictions are made without sharing sensitive information beyond the hospital premises. In contrast, HFL involves collaboration between similar hospitals that share a common set of features for predictive modelling. The data distribution in HFL is inherently IID in nature [11]. However, label skewness introduced during data partitioning among edges results in non-IID characteristics due to the distribution scheme. In Dirichlet distribution [18], the resulting value of non-IIDness, α, indicates the extent of imbalance in the data distribution. A lower value of α (if $\alpha < 1$) this indicates a greater degree of imbalance, reflecting a distribution that is more non-IID. The estimation of α is essential for evaluating and quantifying data imbalances in HFL and VFL systems.

4.1. Estimation of non-IIDness αHFL for HFL

The data in every edge consist of having positive outcome and negative outcome. To evaluate non-IIDness, the total data is divided into β number of partitions. For each positive outcome and negative outcome, the outcome proportions are calculated separately for the whole data (Whole Proportion) and for each partition (Sub proportion) as the ratio of the count of each outcome to the total sample count.

Let W_{PCount} represent the count of diabetic labels (positive cases) and W_{NCount} represent the count of non-diabetic labels within the dataset. The Whole proportions for the diabetic and non-diabetic labels are given by equations (4) and (5).

$$W_{\text{DiabeticN}} = \frac{W_{\text{NCount}}}{W_{\text{PCount}} + W_{\text{NCount}}} \quad (4)$$

$$W_{\text{DiabeticP}} = \frac{W_{\text{PCount}}}{W_{\text{PCount}} + W_{\text{NCount}}} \quad (5)$$

Similarly, for each Partition i, the sub proportions are calculated as expressed in equation (6) and (7):

$$S_{\text{DiabeticP}_i} = \frac{S_{\text{PCount}_i}}{S_{\text{PCount}_i} + S_{\text{NCount}_i}} \quad (6)$$

$$S_{\text{DiabeticN}_i} = \frac{S_{\text{NCount}_i}}{S_{\text{PCount}_i} + S_{\text{NCount}_i}} \quad (7)$$

The difference between the whole proportion and each sub proportion is calculated are given in equation (8) and (9):

$$\text{Diff}_{\text{DiabeticN}_i} = W_{\text{DiabeticN}} - S_{\text{DiabeticN}_i} \quad (8)$$

$$\text{Diff}_{\text{DiabeticP}_i} = W_{\text{DiabeticP}} - S_{\text{DiabeticP}_i} \quad (9)$$

The average of these differences across all partitions is calculated separately for each label given in equation (10) and (11):

$$\text{AVG}_{\text{Diff\_DiabeticP}} = \frac{\sum_{i=1}^{\beta} \text{Diff}_{\text{DiabeticP}_i}}{\beta} \quad (10)$$

$$\text{AVG}_{\text{Diff\_DiabeticN}} = \frac{\sum_{i=1}^{\beta} \text{Diff}_{\text{DiabeticN}_i}}{\beta} \quad (11)$$

These average differences are then combined to estimate α_{edgei}, which indicates the degree of imbalance and non-IID presence in the HFL distribution as expressed in equation (12).

$$\alpha_{edge_i} = \frac{\text{AVG}_{\text{Diff\_DiabeticP}} + \text{AVG}_{\text{Diff\_DiabeticN}}}{2} \quad (12)$$

The degree of non-IIDness for the whole system having γ number of edges can be calculated as shown in Equation (13):

$$\alpha_{\text{HFL}} = \frac{\sum_{i=1}^{\gamma} \alpha_{edge_i}}{\gamma} \quad (13)$$

4.2. Estimation of non-IIDness αVFL for VFL

In the case of VFL, the data is partitioned across multiple edges, with each edge handling a distinct subset of features. The target label is typically contained in only one of the edges. The sample apportionment in VFL is vertical, meaning that each edge has discreate set of attributes of the dataset but not the complete dataset itself. The parameter α is used to quantify the degree of imbalance in the feature distribution across these edges, which is essential for evaluating the non-IIDness of the data. The value of α_{VFL} is established by computing variance in the proportions of features across the edges. This process allows us to assess how evenly or unevenly the features are distributed among the edges, which has a direct influence on the federated learning model's performance. The relationship between the features across edges is expressed in equation (14), where $F\_Count\ Edges_i$ represents the number of features held by each edge i, and F_Count is the all the features across all edges. Here γ is the all the edges in the system.

$$F\_Count = \sum_{i=1}^{\gamma} F\_Count\_Edges_i \quad (14)$$

The proportion of features held by each edge i is determined by splitting the number of features at each edge i by all the features, as expressed in Equation (15) and the average proportion of features across all edges is computed in Equation (16).

$$P\_F\_Count\_edge_i = \frac{F\_Count\_edge_i}{F\_Count} \qquad (15)$$

$$AVG\_P\_F = \frac{\sum_{i=1}^{2} P\_F\_Count\_edge_i}{F\_Count} \qquad (16)$$

Next, the variance of the feature proportions across all edges is calculated as given in Equation (17) and finally, α_{VFL} is expressed as given in Equation (18) for VFL systems.

$$\alpha_{VFL} = \frac{1}{1 - VAR\_P\_F} \qquad (17)$$

$$VAR\_P\_F = \frac{\sum_{i=1}^{2}(P\_F\_Count\_edge_i - AVG\_P\_F)^2}{F\_Count} \qquad (18)$$

4.3. Estimation of trade-off between privacy, non-IID ness and performance

Privacy: In CL, data from all edges is transmitted to a central server, which significantly increases the risk of privacy breaches. In HFL and VFL, edges retain their data locally and only exchange model updates, thereby ensuring full privacy protection.

Non-IIDness α: CL assumes data is IID, but in practice, data can be imbalanced (non-IID). In HFL and VFL, (α) is calculated as per Equation (12) and (17).

Performance: Recall, accuracy, precision, and F1 score are among the metrics used to evaluate the model's performance. *Accuracy* assesses overall correctness, but it proves inadequate in the case of imbalanced data. *Precision* quantifies true positives among predicted positives. *Recall* identifies actual positive and negative cases critical in healthcare. *F1 Score* balances precision and recall. The trade-off between privacy, non-IID data, and system performance can be determined by assigning appropriate weightage to each factor, depending on the real-time application or scenario. Let ω_1, ω_2, and ω_3 represent the weightage given to privacy, non-IID, and performance, respectively. The overall trade-off can be represented by the equation as follows (19).

$$\text{Trade-off}(P, \alpha, R) = w_1 \cdot P + w_2 \cdot \alpha + w_3 \cdot R \qquad (19)$$

where P is the privacy value, α is the value associated with non-IID data, and R represents the system's performance.

5. Experimentation and Results

The federated learning system was developed using the Flower framework [16], which streamlines communication, coordination, and model aggregation between devices at the edge and a centralized server. PyTorch is used for model development, while NumPy handles data operations. Communication is managed through gRPC (Google Remote Procedural Call), ensuring efficient cross-platform interactions.

Hydra and Omegaconf allow dynamic adjustment of parameters like learning rates and batch sizes. Table 10.3 lists the hyperparameters for the HFL and VFL experiments. To assess the degree of data imbalance across partitions in HFL setup, the concentration parameter α is derived from the Dirichlet distribution [18].

The dataset [17] employed in this study includes 202,944 samples for training and 50,736 samples for testing. Within the training set of 202,944 samples, 174,595 are categorized as non-diabetic (label 0) and 28,349 as diabetic (label 1).

The training data shown in Table 10.4 were split into six partitions and allocated to two edge servers.

The performance metrics – accuracy, precision, recall, and F1 score – are displayed in a bar plot across three frameworks is shown in Figure 10.4: CL, HFL, and VFL. Among these metrics, recall is emphasized as the most critical for evaluation, particularly in healthcare applications where accurately identifying positive and negative cases is paramount.

The Degree of Non-IIDness is calculated to assess data heterogeneity. Additionally, privacy levels for the three learning approaches are considered: 0% for CL and 100% for both HFL and VFL. For this study, privacy, non-IIDness, and performance are regarded as equally important. Consequently, equal weight is assigned to each of these parameters and trade-off is estimated as shown in Table 10.5, for each learning approach. It is found that in the equally

Table 10.3. Hyperparameters for FL experiment

Parameter	VFL	HFL	CL
Total Number of Rounds	18	18	10
Total Number of edges	3	2	-
Batch Size	32	32	32
Number of classes	2	2	2
Number of edges per Round Fit	2	2	-
Number of edges per Round Evaluation	2	2	-
Step Size	0.01	0.01	0.01
Momentum rate	0.9	0.9	0.9
Local Epochs	5	5	-
Input Size	8,8,7	23	23

Source: Author.

Table 10.4. Label distribution across partitions

Edge Server	Partition	Non-Diabetic	Diabetic
3*Edge 1	P0	77,629	8,355
	P1	47,485	8,285
	P2	41,329	8,879
3*Edge 2	P3	2,303	948
	P4	5,742	1,845
	P5	107	37

Source: Author.

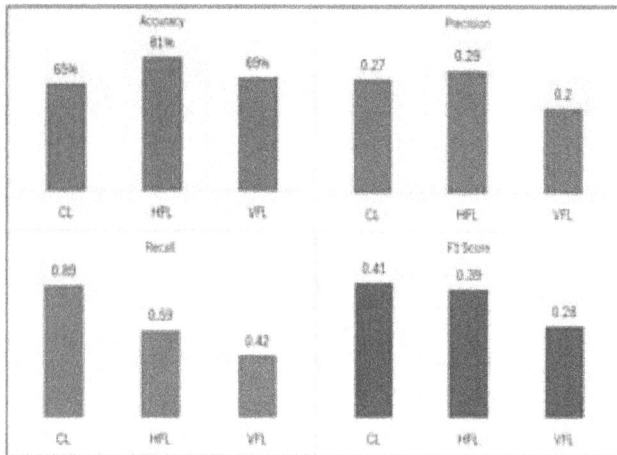

Figure 10.4. Performance of CL, HFL and VFL.

Source: Author.

Table 10.5. Trade-off between privacy, non-IIDness and performance

Approach	Privacy(P)	Non-IID (α)	Performance(R)	Trade-off
CL	0%	0	0.89	0.89
HFL	100%	0.093	0.59	1.683
VFL	100%	1.0042	0.42	2.42

Source: Author.

weighted scenario, VFL has a better trade-off compared to CL and HFL.

6. Conclusion

In this study, for real-time applications such as diabetes prediction, we investigated the performance of Vertical Federated Learning (VFL), Horizontal Federated Learning (HFL), and Centralized Learning (CL) prediction under non-IID data conditions. We formulated an equation for trade-off between privacy, non-IID and performance of three learning approaches and estimated these trade-off values for all three learning systems in an experiment setup with Flower framework by giving an equal weightage for all three parameters, it is found that VFL is slightly performing better than HFL and far better than CL. From this study, we realized that based on the value of significance of privacy, Non-IIDness and Performance a particular application can choose the suitable learning approach.

References

[1] Mammen, P. M. (2022). Federated Learning: Opportunities and Challenges. In *IEEE Int. Conf. on Program Comprehension*.

[2] Bonawitz, K. A., Eichner, H., Grieskamp, W., et al. (2019). Towards Federated Learning at Scale: System Design. CoRR abs/1902.01046.

[3] Li, X., Huang, K., Yang, W., et al. (2020). On the Convergence of FedAvg on Non-IID Data. arXiv:2007.01883.

[4] Sheller, M. J., Edwards, B., Reina, G. A., et al. (2020). Federated Learning in Medicine. *Scientific Reports*, *10*, 12598.

[5] Peng, S., Yang, Y., Mao, M., et al. (2022). Centralized ML vs Federated Averaging: A Comparison Using MNIST. *KSII TIIS*, *16*(2), 742–756.

[6] Kareem, A., Liu, H., Velisavljevic, V. (2023). A FL Framework for Pneumonia Detection. *Healthcare Analytics*, *4*.

[7] Yi, R., Tang, L., Tian, Y., et al. (2023). Pneumonia Classification Using Deep Learning. *Neural Computing and Applications*, *35*(20), 14473–14486.

[8] Noman, A. A., Rahaman, M., Pranto, T. H., et al. (2023). Blockchain for Medical Collaboration via FL. *Healthcare Analytics*, *3*.

[9] Hossen, M. N., Panneerselvam, V., Koundal, D., et al. (2023). FL for Skin Disease Detection and IoMT Security. *IEEE Journal of Biomedical and Health Informatics*, *27*(2), 835–841.

[10] Farooq, M. S., et al. (2023). FFM: Flood Forecasting Model Using FL. *IEEE Access*, *11*, 24472–24483.

[11] Zhu, H., Xu, J., Liu, S., et al. (2021). FL on Non-IID Data: A Survey. *Neurocomputing, 465*, 371–390.

[12] Cao, L. (2022). Beyond i.i.d.: Non-IID Thinking and Learning. *IEEE Intelligent Systems*, *37*(4), 5–17.

[13] Elbir, A. M., Coleri, S., Mishra, K. V. (2021). Hybrid Federated and Centralized Learning. In: *EUSIPCO*.

[14] McMahan, B., Moore, E., Ramage, D., et al. (2017). Communication-efficient Learning from Decentralized Data. In: *AISTATS, PMLR*.

[15] Chen, X., Xu, X., Li, Z., et al. (2022). Vertical Federated Learning: A Survey. *IEEE Access*.

[16] Beutel, D. J., Topal, T., Mathur, A., et al. (2020). Flower: A Friendly FL Research Framework. arXiv:2007.14390.

[17] Teboul, A. (2015). Diabetes Health Indicators Dataset. https://www.kaggle.com/datasets/alexteboul/diabetes-health-indicators-dataset

[18] Yurochkin, M., Agarwal, M., Ghosh, S., et al. (2019). Bayesian Nonparametric FL of Neural Networks. In: *ICML, PMLR*.

11 AI-based multimodal system for coral reef pollution detection and forecasting classification and environmental data

Suganya. P.[1,a], Abinaya S.[2,b], Gowsalya S.[2,c], Dhivya Shri M.[2,d], Kaviya A.[2,e], and Albi Maria A.[2,f]

[1]Assistant Professor, Department of AIML, Manakula Vinayagar, Institute of Techonology, Puducherry, India
[2]UG Scholar, Department of AIML, Manakula Vinayagar, Institute of Techonology, Puducherry, India

Abstract: Coral reefs are among the most vital and well-preserved components of our marine ecosystems. However, to ensure their long-term survival and overall health, we need to focus on their ecological functions. This study introduces an innovative artificial intelligence (AI) system designed to combine image classification with environmental data forecasting, allowing us to assess the condition of coral reefs more effectively. The system is trained on images of both pristine and polluted reefs to identify subtle visual signs of degradation. Moreover, it predicts future pollution levels by analyzing historical water quality data, including pH, temperature, and dissolved oxygen levels, through time-series modeling. This opens up exciting possibilities for real-time assessments of coral reef health and forecasting, which could lead to timely interventions that enhance marine conservation efforts. Ultimately, this approach also addresses the larger challenge of preserving marine biodiversity.

Keywords: Water quality, pH, temperature, dissolved oxygen, time-series modeling, pollution detection, degradation indicators, real-time monitoring, early intervention, marine conservation, sustainability, marine biodiversity, coral reefs, marine ecosystems, AI-based system, image classification, environmental data forecasting

1. Introduction

Among the most energetic and important ecosystems on Earth are coral reefs. Through fisheries and tourism, they support local businesses and offer vital habitat for many marine life as well as necessary shoreline defense. Unfortunately, pollution from rainfall, increasing temperatures, and other human activity is fast destroying many reef systems. Plastic waste, industrial runoff, and toxic chemicals are wreaking havoc on coral reefs, causing coral bleaching, a loss in marine life, and long-lasting ecological damage [1].

Currently, depending mostly on manual underwater inspections and lab tests, the reactive, expensive, resource-intensive techniques we employ to track pollution in coral reefs often rely on [2]. This emphasizes the pressing need of better systems able to monitor coral reef condition in real time and precisely forecast future pollution trends [5].

In this work, using image classification models trained on coral reef images, we present a direct detection and forecasting approach for coral reef pollution (Figure 11.1). Our method combines real-time assessments of coral reefs with time series predictions of environmental elements including pH, temperature, and dissolved oxygen to evaluate possible future hazards to their health in great scalability [7]. This strategy aims to support conservation initiatives by means of informed, proactive decision-making compliant with the United Nations Sustainable Development Goal 14: Life Below Water [3].

Figure 11.1. Healthy coral reef.

Source: Author.

[a]suganyaaiml@gmail.com, [b]abiss9705@gmail.com, [c]gowsalyaselvammit05@gmail.com, [d]dhivyashrimv402@gmail.com, [e]akaviya344@gmail.com, [f]albimaria113@gmail.com

DOI: 10.1201/9781003724988-11

2. Multimodal Acquisition and Processing

The suggested system can evaluate the levels of contamination affecting coral reefs using a multimodal data acquisition technique. It uses environmental sensor data and visual image data as its two primary information-gathering methods. The system can provide an accurate assessment of the condition of coral reefs today and forecast possible pollution by combining these two forms of data [5].

2.1. Acquisition visual image data

Images of coral reefs under different pollution conditions can be found in publicly accessible satellite and underwater image datasets. A deep learning model that recognizes physical damage, discoloration, algal blooms, and sedimentation patterns is trained using these photos to differentiate between healthy and contaminated reef environments [4].

2.2. Environmental sensor data acquisition

Historical sensors linked to oceanographic databases are used to gather important water quality parameters like pH, temperature, and dissolved oxygen levels. The sustainability of coral reefs is adversely affected by these measured parameters, which are important indicators. After normalizing the sensor data, the system uses interpolation to fill in any values that are unclear or missing [6].

2.3. Integration and data processing

Several pre-processing methods, such as resizing, normalization, and augmentation, are applied to the image data in order to increase the robustness of the model. Based on incoming images, a YOLOv10 model works in real-time to identify the reefs' pollution levels. The model also analyzes environmental data using LSTM, which enables it to forecast future trends in pollution. By combining environmental trends with visual data. In the end, the system supports more timely conservation efforts by offering a thorough understanding that improves predictive modeling and temporal assessments (Figure 11.2) [7].

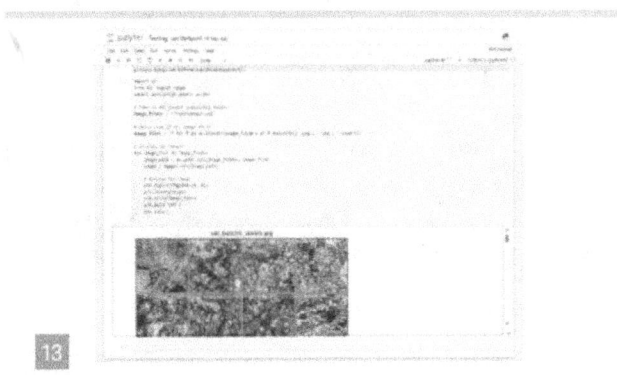

Figure 11.2. Multimodal acquisition and processing.

Source: Author.

3. Deep Learning-Based Forecasting Models

The system makes use of deep learning algorithms designed especially for examining temporal and spatial data. To precisely forecast the future health of coral reefs, it analyzes visually significant photos of the reefs and looks for recurring patterns in environmental sensor data.

3.1. Convolutional neural networks (CNNs) for image classification

The YOLOv10-based architecture used in this system is a state-of-the-art object detection model that is renowned for its remarkable speed and accuracy in detecting visual pollution. A set of photos of coral reefs that were classified as "polluted" or "unpolluted" were used to train the model. After that, it uses this training on fresh photos to identify whether a reef is harmed physically, by discoloration, or by plastic debris. As a useful predictive tool, the system continuously tracks the reef's current state in real time.

3.2. LSTM networks for time-series forecasting

To forecast future water pollution levels, we created an LSTM (Long Short Term Memory) network. Recurrent neural networks (RNNs) of this kind are made to track long-term dependencies while learning from sequential data. To build our training set, we concentrated on historical environmental parameters that are important for coral reef health, such as temperature, pH, and dissolved oxygen levels. The LSTM model can predict these parameters for a few days after training (Figure 11.3).

3.3. Using fusion to predict multimodal events

We can obtain a thorough evaluation of pollution levels by combining the results of CNN-based image classification with LSTM-based forecasting. While the LSTM is skilled at forecasting future hazards based on environmental trends, the CNN is best at determining the current state from images. We can produce insightful and useful predictions about coral reef pollution by integrating spatial and temporal insights because they are interrelated (Figure 11.4).

Monitoring and forecasting coral reef health becomes more accurate, dependable, and responsive when different data types are integrated with deep learning models. Thus, proactive environmental management and conservation efforts are supported.

4. Results and Discussions

This suggested system was implemented to evaluate how well it handled image classification and time series forecasting tasks. When it came to identifying pollution in photos, the YOLOv10 model demonstrated an outstanding 94.2% classification accuracy, with a precision of 92.7% and a recall of

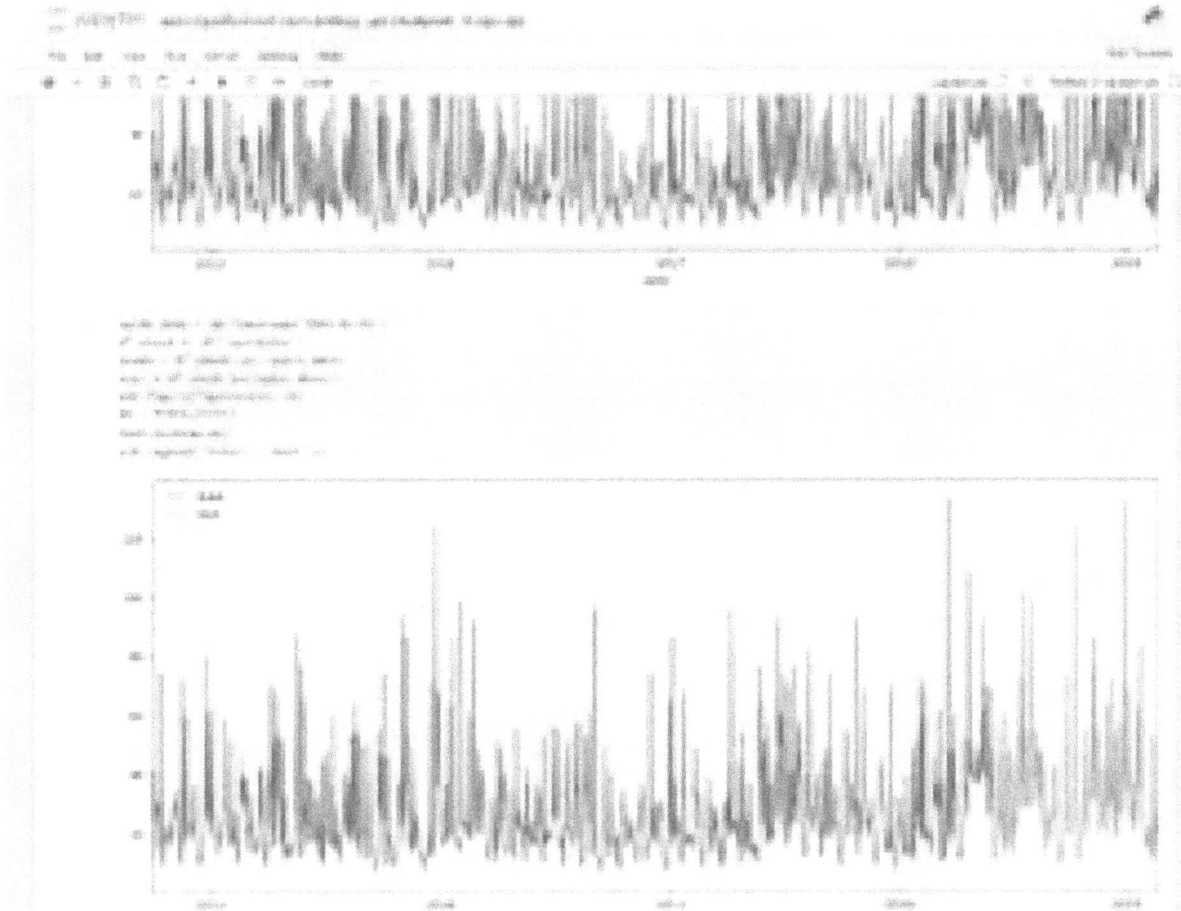

Figure 11.3. Time-series forecasting.

Source: Author.

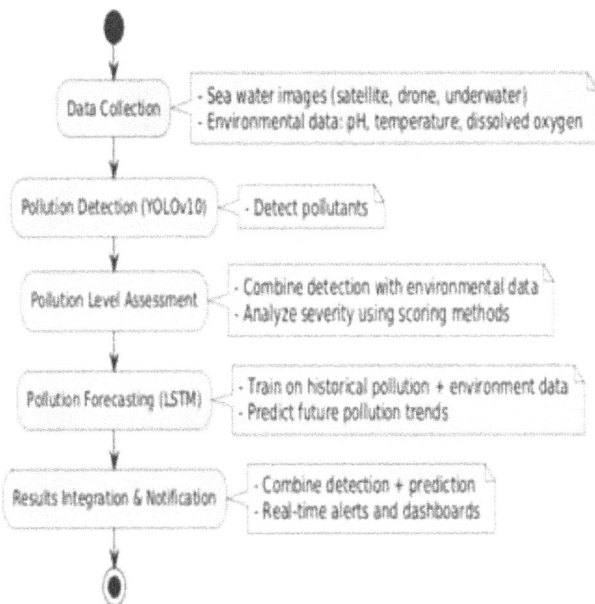

Figure 11.4. Flowchart of the model.

Source: Author.

93.5%. Through the detection of debris, algae growth, and coral reef discoloration, the experiments demonstrated that this detection model is highly accurate in identifying polluted coral reef environments. However, before beginning forecasting tasks, the LSTM model used historical environmental data, such as temperature, dissolved oxygen, pH levels, and other variables, for training. With results indicating differences of 0.13 pH, 0.21°C, and 0.19 mg/L for dissolved oxygen, the predictive model only made small mistakes (Figure 11.5).

Actual results closely matched predictions about pollution trends for the next 7 to 14 days. Through the system's web interface, users can select the forecast duration they want and view an image of a coral reef. After presenting the most recent pollutant assessments, the system shows visual predictions of future water quality changes. The system's potential as a useful and approachable decision support tool for coral reef health monitoring was demonstrated during the first round of user testing. Our knowledge of coral reef pollution is improved by data collected from both temporal and visual sources.

In addition to increasing the accuracy of the system, this integrated research approach aids in thorough conservation

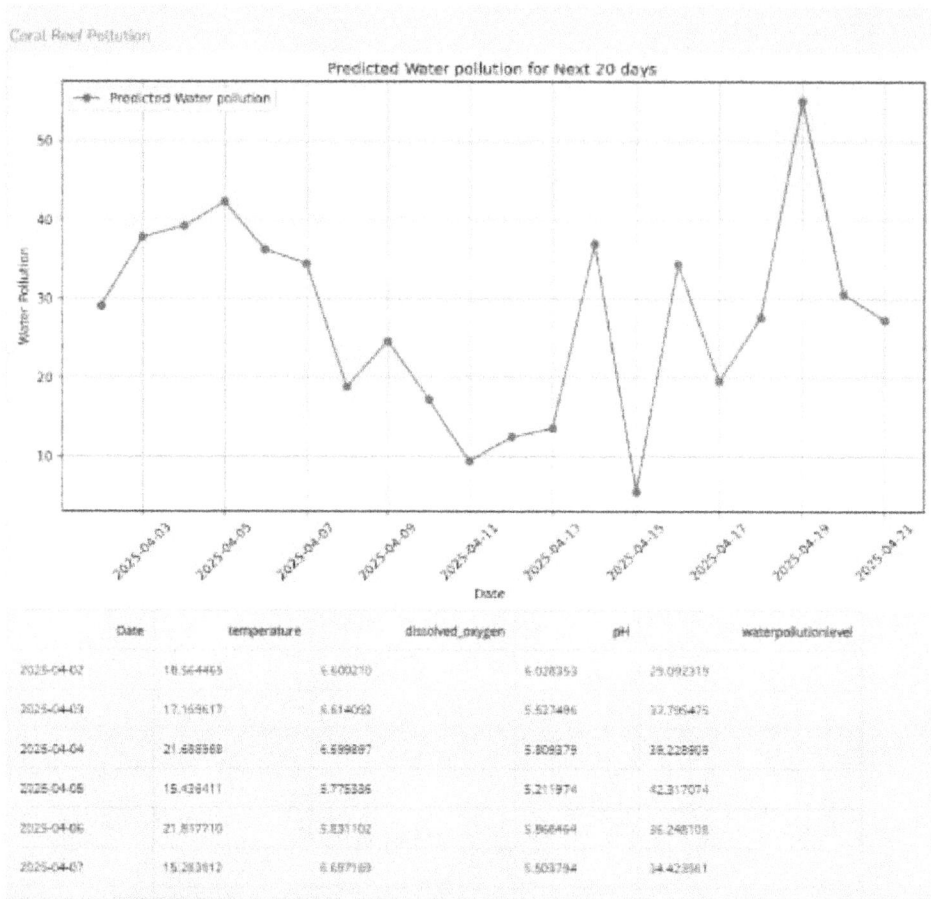

Figure 11.5. Time series prediction for given amount of days.

Source: Author.

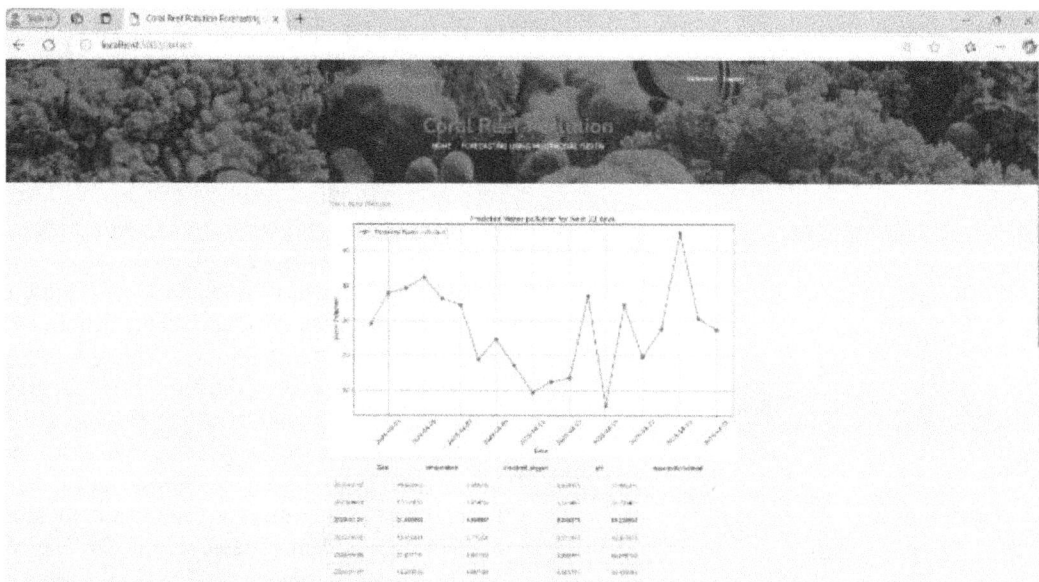

Figure 11.6. Output image coral reef pollution forecasting.

Source: Author.

planning. Nevertheless, the project has a number of issues, such as inadequate environmental data and poor image quality. We must investigate novel dataset types and carry out field testing in authentic marine settings if we are to advance (Figure 11.6).

5. Conclusions

The deep learning system builds a strong model for identifying and forecasting patterns of sea water pollution by utilizing LSTM networks in conjunction with YOLOv10 object detection algorithms. The accuracy, long-term forecasting, and smooth integration of contemporary systems for detecting sea water pollution have greatly increased as a result of developments in deep learning technology. YOLOv10 and LSTM networks work well together to meet the need for extended forecasting, which is essential for carrying out effective conservation measures. The UN Sustainable Development Goal (SDG) 14: Life Below Water, which aims to preserve our oceans and marine resources for a sustainable future, is in line with this solution.

Acknowledgement

We gratefully acknowledge the students, staff, and authority of Artificial Intelligence and Machine Learning department for their cooperation in the research.

References

[1] Bryant, D., Burke, L., McManus, J., & Spalding, M. (1998). *Reefs at Risk: A Map-based Indicator of Threats to the World's Coral Reefs*. World Resources Institute, 56 pp.

[2] Jones, O. A., & Endean, R., eds. (1973). *Biology and Geology of Coral Reefs*. New York: Harcourt Brace Jovanovich, pp. 205–245.

[3] IUCN—The World Conservation Union. (1988). *Resolution 17.38 of the 17th General Assembly of the IUCN*. Gland, Switzerland and Cambridge, UK: IUCN.

[4] Du, S., Li, T., Yang, Y., & Horng, S.-J. (2021). Deep air quality forecasting using hybrid deep learning framework. *IEEE Transactions on Knowledge and Data Engineering, 33*(6), 2412–2424.

[5] Huang, W., Li, T., Liu, J., Xie, P., Du, S., & Teng, F. (2021). An overview of air quality analysis by big data techniques: Monitoring, forecasting, and traceability. *Information Fusion, 75*, 28–40.

[6] Wang, D., Wei, S., Luo, H., Yue, C., & Grunder, O. (2017). A novel hybrid model for air quality index forecasting based on two-phase decomposition technique and modified extreme learning machine. *Science of the Total Environment, 580*, 719–733.

[7] Zhang, J., & Li, S. (2022). Air quality index forecast in Beijing based on CNN-LSTM multi-model. *Chemosphere, 308*, Art. no. 136180.

12 Design of circular shaped substrate integrated waveguide (SIW) based slot antenna for Sub-6GHz applications

V. Shiva Prasad Nayak[1,a], Manjunathachari K.[2,b], and Nandakumar M.[3,c]

[1]Assistant Professor, Department of EECE, GITAM (Deemed to be) University, Hyderabad, India
[2]Professor, Department of EECE, GITAM (Deemed to be) University, Hyderabad, India
[3]Associate Professor, Department of ECE, Sreenidhee Institute of Science and Technology, Hyderabad, India

Abstract: The paper presents the circular shaped substrate integrated waveguide (SIW) based slot antenna for Sub- 6GHz applications. The substrate material applied for this design is FR-4 material with a thickness of 1.6 mm. as 4.4 and copper material thickness of 35um. The CST simulation software tool is used to simulate the proposed antenna with extract the results. The proposed antenna resonates at operating frequency 3.543 GHz. The S_{11}, VSWR, Bandwidth, and Gain in dBi value is -32dB, 1.05013, 80MHz, and 5.27dBi at 3.543 GHz. the proposed antenna describes an 80 MHz bandwidth covering a -10 dB reference line and keeps a VSWR of 2:1 and radiates bidirectional radiation patterns at all resonant frequencies and well suited for wireless applications.

Keywords: Slot antenna, circular, substrate integrated waveguide, sub-6GHz

1. Introduction

Currently, the transmission of 5G technology is characterized by its substantial capacity and its ability to connect a multitude of devices while maintaining relatively low power consumption. 5G represents the wireless technology that has seen significant expansion in recent times, particularly in the context of device-to- device communication, data-centric wireless applications, and the advancement of the Fourth Industrial Revolution [1]. The implementation of sophisticated technological applications such as smart urban environments, immersive virtual reality, and autonomous vehicles stands to gain from enhanced communication methodologies, facilitated by the modernization of the Internet of Things through the utilization of 5G. The operational frequency bands in India span from 3.3 to 3.7 GHz, while France and Spain utilize bands ranging from 3.4 to 3.8 GHz; all of these frequencies fall within the sub-6 GHz category. Such frequency ranges have garnered considerable popularity due to their associated technological advancements, including high data throughput, minimal latency, reduced power consumption, lower costs, and decreased operational distances [2–3].

Owing to the reduced wavelengths associated with elevated frequencies and the stringent tolerances requisite in high-frequency antenna applications, the deployment of microstrip antenna devices is deemed inefficient. Consequently, waveguide devices are favoured at these higher frequencies. However, the manufacturing process associated with waveguide devices is notably complex [4–5]. This has led to the introduction of an innovative concept known as substrate integrated waveguide (SIW). This concept represents a transformation between microstrip technology and dielectric-filled waveguide (DFW). The transition from dielectric-filled waveguide to substrate integrated waveguide (SIW) is achieved through the interconnection of the patch and lower metallic ground planes utilizing periodic arrays of metallic vias embedded within the dielectric substrate [6].

The slot antenna is particularly well-suited for wireless applications, as it exhibits advantages such as reduced weight, compact size, and ease of fabrication in comparison to alternative antenna configurations, including array and horn antennas. The advent of SIW technology has facilitated the realization of SIW slot antennas. The design characteristics of these antennas are further enhanced by advancing to cavity-backed configurations, which offer reduced dimensions, improved bandwidth, and moderate gain [7–8].

The manuscript delineates the architecture of the circularly configured substrate integrated waveguide (SIW) intended for wireless applications, encompassing sub-6 GHz, WLAN, and Wi-Fi functionalities. Section 2 elucidates the design of the proposed antenna, incorporating various design parameters, while the simulation outcomes of the antenna are articulated in Section 3; the findings presented in this section include the reflection coefficient, surface current distribution, gain measured in dBi, and voltage standing wave ratio (VSWR), respectively. Section 4 culminates with

[a]svadthya@gitam.edu, [b]mkamsali@gitam.edu, [c]nanda.mkumar12@gmail.com

DOI: 10.1201/9781003724988-12

the conclusions drawn from the study, followed by a comprehensive list of references.

2. Design Analysis

The radiation loss plays key role any antenna design and to choose proper diameter and spacing between the vias of the SIW design and as represented in equation (1) [7–9].

$$d \leq \frac{\lambda_g}{5} \quad \text{and} \quad s \leq 2d \tag{1}$$

The SIW cavity is cylindrical in nature, so the design frequency and working principle can be calculated from the solution of the wave equation in a cylindrical cavity with few modifications due to the discontinuous sidewall. If we neglect the leakage of the sidewall, the resonant frequency of the TM_{npq} mode of a cylindrical cavity, having radius and height d, is represented in equation (2) [7].

$$f_r = \frac{C}{2\Pi\sqrt{\mu_r \varepsilon_r}} \sqrt{\left(\frac{X_{np}}{a}\right)^2 + \left(\frac{q\Pi}{d}\right)^2} \tag{2}$$

Figure 12.2 presents the reflection coefficient of the proposed antenna across the frequency spectrum ranging from 3 to 4 GHz the antenna exhibits resonance at a frequency of 3.543 GHz, yielding an S11 value of −32 dB and an operational bandwidth of 80 MHz, specifically from 3.51 GHz to 3.59 GHz, suitable for 5G applications.

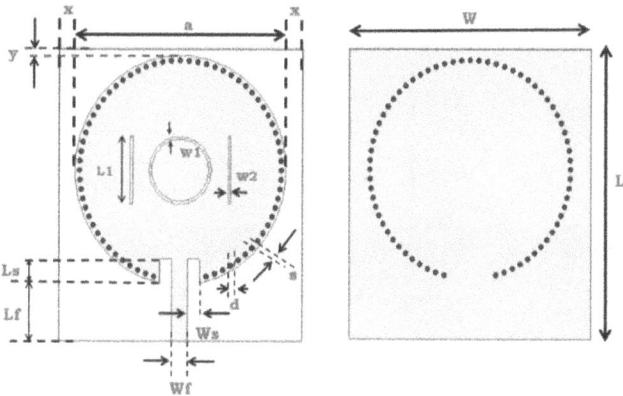

Figure 12.1. Parameter representation of the design.

Source: Author.

Table 12.1. Optimized Parameters (in mm)

Parameter	Value	Parameter	Value
L	55.6	Ls	5
a	44	x	3.25
s/d	1.5/1	W1=W2	0.5
L1	13	Wf	3.2
W	50.5	Ws	2.5
Lf	10.6	y	1

Source: Author.

Rectangular and circular slot width is

$$\lambda/4 \leq W \leq \lambda/2 \tag{3}$$

Rectangular slot length is

$$L \leq W \tag{4}$$

3. Results and Discussion

Figure 12.1 delineates the parameter representation of the antenna, with a one circular and two rectangular slots situated on the upper of the antenna. Table 12.1 enumerates the dimensions of the parameters utilized in this design [9–10].

The voltage standing wave ratio (VSWR) corresponding to the proposed design is illustrated in Figure 12.3, indicating a VSWR value of 1.0501 at centre frequency of 3.543 GHz.

Figure 12.4 illustrates the reflection coefficient for different circular and rectangular slot width, specifically for values of 1.5 mm, 1 mm, and 0.5 mm. The optimal value selected among the w1 is 0.5 mm.

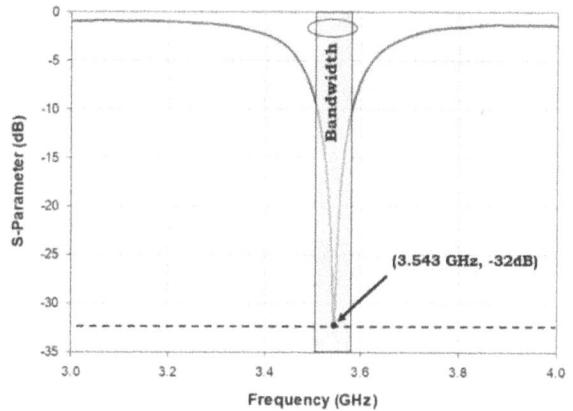

Figure 12.2. Reflection coefficient.

Source: Author.

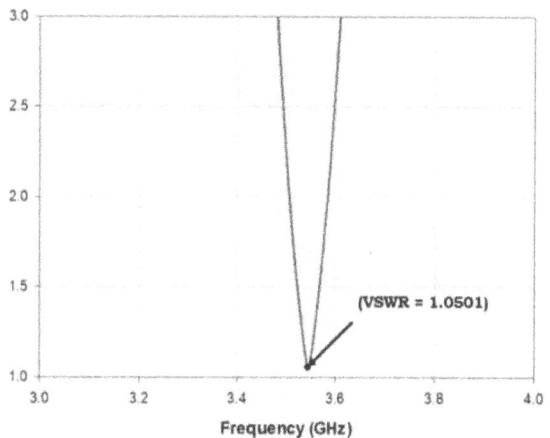

Figure 12.3. VSWR.

Source: Author.

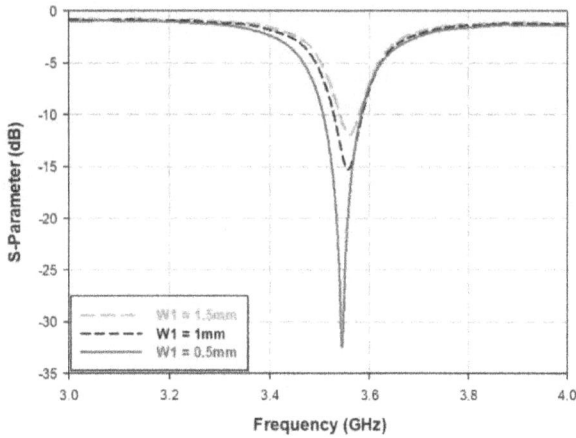

Figure 12.4. S11 for different values of w1.

Source: Author.

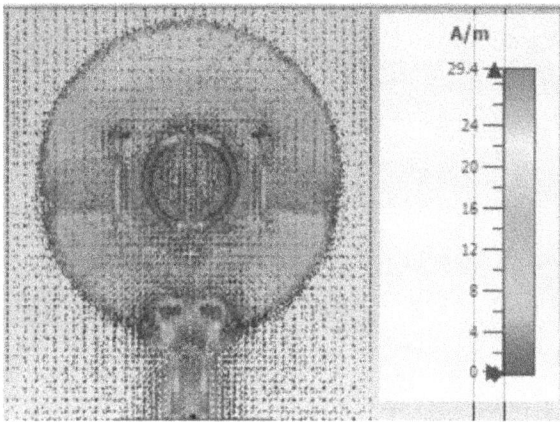

Figure 12.5. Surface current at 3.543GHz.

Source: Author.

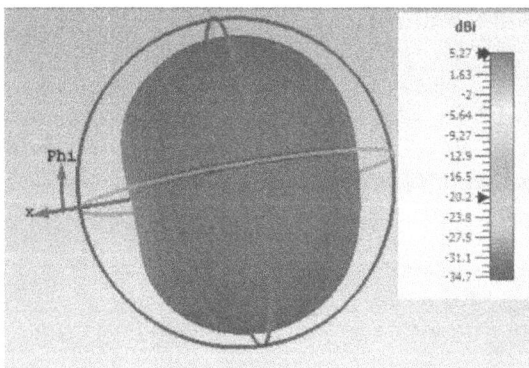

Figure 12.6. Gain at 3.543 GHz.

Source: Author.

The surface current of the proposed antenna is revealed in Figure 12.5 at a resonant frequency 3.543 GHz and observed that flow of current is more at circular slot as well as at rectangular slot and at edges of the feed.

The Figure 12.6 shows the gain of the antenna at 3.543 GHz resonant frequency, observed that flow the current is in

the direction of propagation and their value is 5.27dBi is well fitted for 5G wireless applications.

Figure 12.7 shows the far field radiation of polar plot, it observes that main lobe magnitude is 5.27 dBi, radiation is maximum at 173 degrees, and width of the main lobe is 150.7 degrees. Figure 12.8, Figure 12.8a, and Figure 12.8b

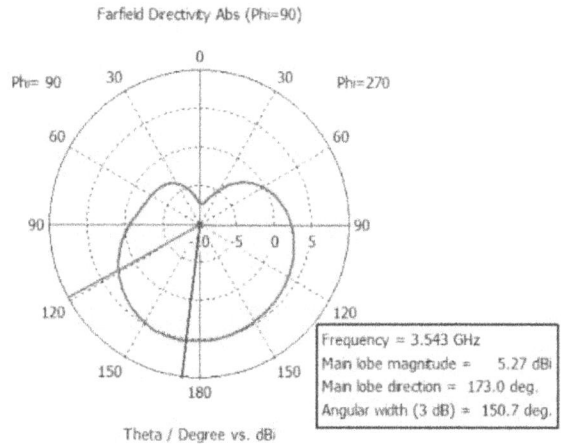

Figure 12.7. Farfield radiation pattern at 3.543GHz.

Source: Author.

a. E-Field

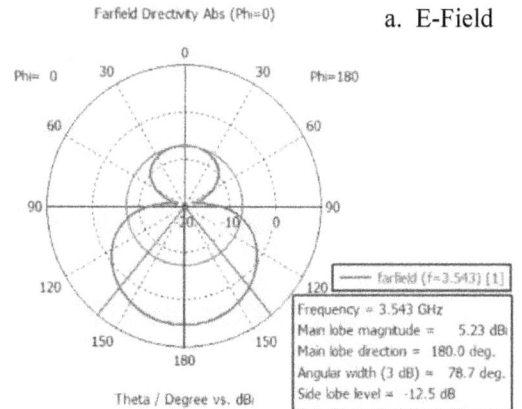

b. H-Field

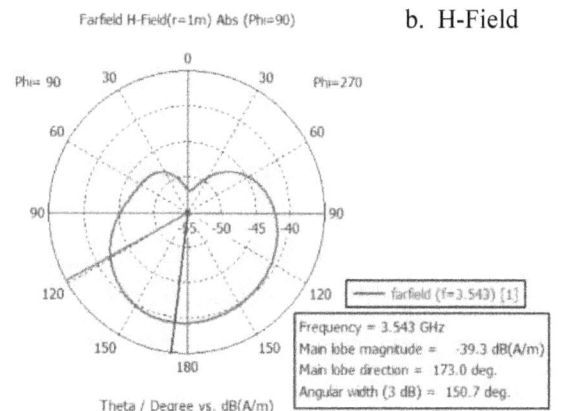

Figure 12.8. 2D radiation pattern.

Source: Author.

belongs to the E-field, H-field, observed bidirectional radiation patterns which are acceptable for 5G applications.

4. Conclusion

The half-mode hexagonal shaped SIW cavity-backed antenna was presented for sub-6GHz 5G applications and FR-4 material used for the design. This design has loaded with one circular and two rectangular slots in top view and CST software is used for simulating the antenna for analyzing the antenna results. The antenna resonates at 3.543 GHz operating frequency with a 80 MHz occupied bandwidth ranging from 3.51 GHz to 3.59 GHz. The S_{11}, VSWR, Gain values −32dB, 1.05013, 5.27dBi at 3.543 GHz resonant frequency and observed acceptable radiation pattern for 5G Application and WiMAX.

References

[1] Muhammad, R. A., Syed, M. A., Patrizia, L., & Ernesto, L. (2023). High performance antenna system in MIMO configuration for 5G wireless communication over sub 6 GHz Spectrum. *Radio Science*, *58*, 1–22.

[2] Shrivastava, U., & Verma, J. K. (2021, December). A study on 5G technology and its applications in telecommunications. In *2021 International Conference on Computational Performance Evaluation (ComPE)* (pp. 365–371). IEEE.

[3] Meena, R. K., Dabhade, M. K., Srivastava, K., & Kanaujia, B. K. (2022). Antenna design for fifth generation (5G) applications. In *2019 URSI Asia-Pacific Radio Science Conference (AP-RASC)* (pp. 1–4). IEEE.

[4] Mungaru, N. K., & Shanmuganantham, T. (2019). Broadband H-spaced head-shaped slot with SIW-based antenna for 60 GHz wireless communication applications. *Microwave and Optical Technology Letters*, *61*(8), 1911–1916.

[5] Dinesh, M., Nandakumar, M., Balachandra, K. (2018). Micro-strip Feed Reconfigurable Antenna for Wideband Applications. *Journal: Lecturer Notes in Electrical Engineering*, Springer, 665–671.

[6] Nanda Kumar, M., & Shanmugnantham, T. (2022). Ku-band CSRR Loaded SIW cavity backed slot antenna. WAMS, National Institute of Technology Rourkela, India, NIT.

[7] Guyen Trong, N., & Fumeaux, C. (2018). Half-mode substrate-integrated waveguides and their applications for antenna technology: a review of the possibilities for antenna design. *IEEE Antennas Propag Mag*, *60*(6), 20–31.

[8] Nandakumar, M., & Shanmuganantham, T. (2019). Broad band I shaped SIW slot antenna for V-band Applications. *ACES*, *34*(11), 1–6.

[9] Nandakumar, M., & Shanmuganantham, T. (2019). Broad band Substrate Integrated Waveguide Venus shaped Slot Antenna for V-band Applications. *Microwave and Optical Technology Letters*, *61*(10), 2342–2347.

[10] Shanmugnantham, T., & Nanda Kumar, M. (2019). V-band Substrate Integrated Waveguide Cavity Backed Slot Antenna for Millimeter-wave Wireless Applications. *InCAP* 2019.

13 Gesture-to-text conversion: A CNN-powered framework for sign language recognition

Suganya P.[1,a], G. Balagowdham[2,b], G. Vijayavasan[2,c], N. Jawahar Balaji[2,d], B. V. Chiruhaas[2,e], and R. Dharun Vikash[2,f]

[1]Assistant Professor, Department of AIML, Manakula Vinayagar, Institute of Technology, Puducherry, India
[2]UG Scholar, Department of AIML, Manakula Vinayagar, Institute of Technology, Puducherry, India

Abstract: The transformation from static gestures in International Sign Language to readable text presentations constitutes the process known as sign language to text translation. The usage of deep learning alone with the implementation of CNNs enables us to enhance gesture recognition systems while boosting their performance levels which then provides enhanced communication support services for hearing-impaired users. The model functions at 95% accuracy with a dataset consisting of many sign language gestures under special testing conditions. This method presents an opportunity to develop accessibility solutions that close communication barriers for people who use sign language. The system architecture has received optimization to merge performance efficiency with detection accuracy for scalable device implementation.

Keywords: Convolutional neural network (CNN), sign language recognition, gesture detection, deep learning, accessibility applications, communication support, hearing impaired, accuracy rate represent the index terms of this work

1. Introduction

The requirement for assistance technology connecting hearing with non-hearing groups becomes clear because 70 million people worldwide communicate using sign language. Hand gestures form the foundation of the Indian Sign Language (ISL) for delivering letters and words along with expressing emotions but the system requires full development of time-based translation capabilities. Recognition systems created by humans experience poor performance because size variations of hands and variations between skin colours as well as finger count changes and lighting inconsistencies cause incorrect interpretations. The ISL gesture recognition solution depends on Convolutional Neural Networks (CNNs) because of their reliable performance. An efficient image pattern recognition system in CNNs operates effectively with their adaptive capabilities across multiple real-world situations. The mobile application provides real-time ISL static alphabet recognition through basic smartphone cameras in all areas including rural regions without extra expensive hardware or glove requirements. The application operates with an economic TensorFlow Lite CNN to perform quickly and efficiently and stands independently offline. The recognition of static ISL alphabet marks the beginning for developers to create word recognition and sentence recognition systems which can establish complete communication methods through gesturing.

2. Related Works

Since the beginning of its developmental process gesture recognition technology made significant advancements. The first phase of research combined human-designed feature extraction techniques with classification rules for processing hand gestures through physical shape and posture analysis [1, 2]. Ineffective results occurred when researchers integrated hand motion postures with orientation adjustments since the system became unstable which degraded both precision and result versatility. The automatic extraction of features through CNNs needs hierarchical structures to develop improved gesture recognition systems per the findings in [3] and [4]. The new system design outperforms prior technology through its ability to process complex spatial data with multiple hand and environmental controller data types. Issues such as growing vocabulary sizes, variation in gesture frequency, and inconsistencies in gesture formation often limit system performance [5]. Deep CNN-based structure enhancements require processing needs that result in increased costs which go beyond real-time system capabilities and latency required for mobile-edge devices [6, 7]. This section evaluates CNN model development methodology which emphasizes both precise detection capabilities alongside power-efficient computation operations according to [8–10]. MediaPipe supports gesture recognition at its optimal level through CNN architectures that enable real-time operations as stated in reference [8]. After establishing specific

[a]suganyaaiml@gmail.com, [b]mitgowdham@gmail.com, [c]vijayvasan9804@gmail.com, [d]jawaharbalaji14@gmail.com, [e]chiruhaas.b.v04@gmail.com, [f]dharunvikash2005@gmail.com

DOI: 10.1201/9781003724988-13

model development for Indian Sign Language (ISL) becomes essential because this language brings distinct challenges that require particular resolutions.

The work develops an efficient CNN-based system which delivers precise and rapid identification of static ISL alphabets for real-time mobile deployment. This proposed model functions to bring accuracy and time performance closer together by resolving past research challenges which are described in [10–12]. This approach develops lightweight CNN optimization methods to achieve efficient gesture recognition that serves ISL users for assistive communication technologies in real-time mobile situations [13–15].

3. Proposed System

3.1. System overview

Through a CNN optimization process the system recognizes static hand gestures as elements of Indian Sign Language (ISL). The system operates through a mobile camera to acquire images before it processes them for uniformity and utilizes a PyTorch model to identify gestures. The system provides the capability for on-device immediate classification and server-side API processing utilizing Node.js/Express.js backend for complex operations.

3.2. Key features

The system implements efficient preprocessing steps which resize images to 224 × 224 pixels while normalizing them and eliminating noise for consistency purposes.

- Lightweight CNN: Optimized for mobile performance with minimal parameters.
- Mobile Deployment: Uses Tensor Flow Lite for smooth inference on Android and iOS.
- The mobile camera functions as a tool to capture static ISL gestures through Workflow Capture.
- The preprocessing step performs three actions which include resizing the images and applying normalization and converting them to grayscale.
- The pooling layers perform efficiency optimization by reducing the feature dimensions.
- The softmax activation defines how fully connected layers convert gestures into ISL letters.

Such a lightweight architecture is easy to combine with other architectures employing MediaPipe as a real-time gesture recognition framework in ASL settings [20].

4. Implementation

4.1. Project overview

An implementation of deep learning models that utilize Convolutional Neural Networks (CNNs) detects Indian Sign Language (ISL) gestures (A–Z) in real time operations running on mobile devices. The project aimed to create an efficient model framework that focused on achieving improved speed and mobility performance in mobile applications.

4.2. MobileNet architecture

The project team chose MobileNet because it uses minimal power effectively thus qualifying it as a suitable solution for mobile devices. The performance quality of depthwise separable convolutions allows a reduction in parameter numbers.

4.2.1. Input preprocessing

Resized all images to 224 × 224 pixels. The transformation of images into grayscale improved processing speed without altering their gesture features.

4.2.2. Initial convolution layer

A 3 × 3 convolution with 32 filters for edge and texture detection. ReLU6 serves as the activation function because it applies stable non-linear transformations in model computations.

4.2.3. Depthwise separable convolutions

The method separates distinct sequence operations to perform depthwise (channel-wise) and pointwise (1 × 1) convolution computing. The processing system uses an efficient methodology for managing essential properties from the original dataset.

4.3. Global average pooling (GAP)

This model design uses GAP to replace fully connected layers while keeping a lightweight structure that supports real-time mobility.

4.4. Softmax output layer

The Softmax classifier within the last layer performs gesture detection by assigning results to either letter from the ISL alphabet.

4.5. Transfer learning and optimization

4.5.1. Transfer learning

The learning process of this model received acceleration through initial weight values imported from MobileNet on ImageNet. During semantic fine-tuning our ISL dataset was used for training the final layer of the model (Figure 13.1).

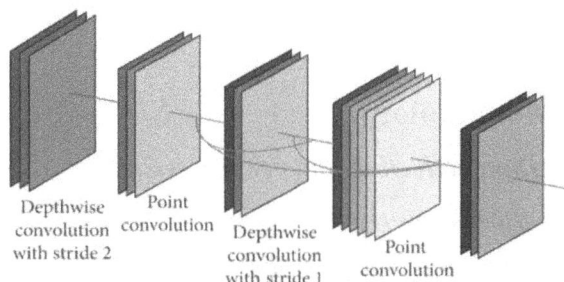

Figure 13.1. MobileNet architecture.

Source: Author.

4.5.2. Optimization techniques

The validation loss enables EarlyStopping to execute its stop mechanism. The method of Data Augmentation generates plausible real-world conditions which mainly target hand posture variations and illumination patterns to achieve improved model results.

4.6. Data augmentation methods

Rotation: Simulates various hand angles.

Flipping: Detects both left-hand and right-hand gestures. The scaling technique represents variations between camera-hand distance during the performance. The translation parameter enables models to handle movements of a hand's position.

Recent studies have demonstrated similar real-time ISL implementations using alternative frameworks such as SURF and gesture-to-text pipelines [16, 17].

5. Hardware and Software Requirements

5.1. Hardware

A single camera serves as the required hardware component to implement the system. Real-time gesture capture depends on smartphones featuring a camera with minimum 720p resolution which ensures proper functional operation. Users can easily access the system through their smartphones that offer a view satisfying and superior to the minimum resolution requirement of 720p.

5.2. Software

- Frontend: React Native (for cross-platform mobile app development).
- PyTorch: The system utilizes PyTorch as its platform for model deployment because it enables both on-device and server-based model execution.
- Node.js/Express.js: Node.js/Express.js exists as the backend component to process API demands and control every AI inference operation within the system.
- Database: The application data gets managed using MongoDB as its database system.
- Computer vision: The application relies on OpenCV as its Computer Vision toolkit for executing image analysis alongside preprocessing functions.

6. Methodology

6.1. Data collection and preprocessing

6.1.1. Dataset overview

A set of static images demonstrates the Indian Sign Language (ISL) Alphabet letters as well as numbers from 0 to 9. The database contained numerous hand pictures that showed different illumination effects as well as positioning invariants (Figures 13.2 and 13.3).

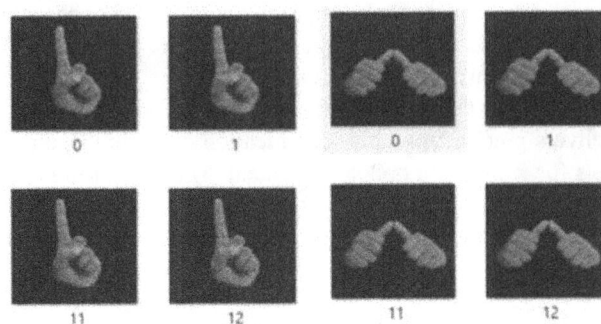

Figure 13.2–13.3. Signs for 1 and A in ISL dataset.
Source: Author.

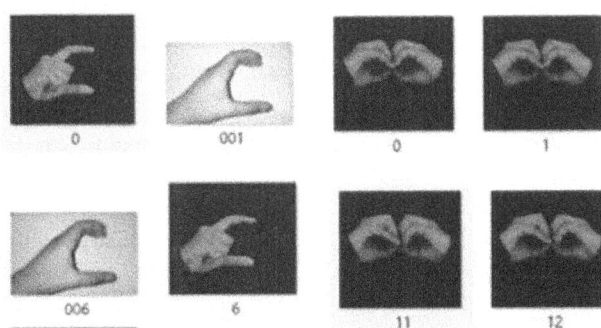

Figure 13.4–13.5. Signs for C and B in ISL dataset.
Source: Author.

Image normalization through a resize operation converted every received picture to equate 224 × 224 pixels without distorting spatial features that aided recognition tasks. The classification process needed essential characteristics so the grayscale conversion sped up computations by converting gesture images to grayscale without losing their defining classification elements (Figures 13.4 and 13.5).

6.1.2. Data normalization

The normalization routine used pixel value scaling that yielded values between 0 and 1 by applying this mathematical equation:

$$\text{Normalized Pixel Value} = \text{Pixel Value}/255.0$$

6.2. Data augmentation

Data augmentation techniques are very much suitable for real time application. The environment of the simulation exposed the model to different real-world conditions when it encountered altered hand positions and directional changes as well as variable lighting conditions (Figure 13.6).

6.2.1. Augmentation techniques applied

The visualization images received + or −30 degrees rotation to account for different hand placements. The system enabled simulation of mirror images by utilizing hand-related

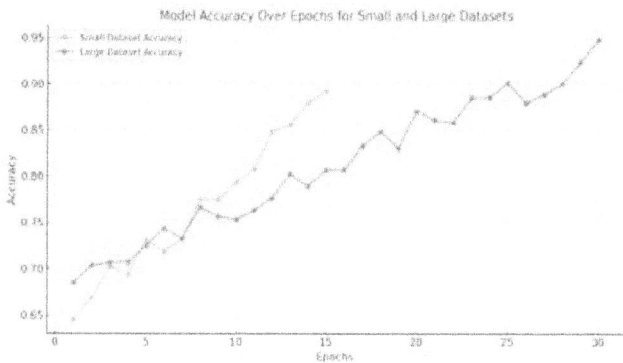

Figure 13.6. Model accuracy vs Epochs.
Source: Author.

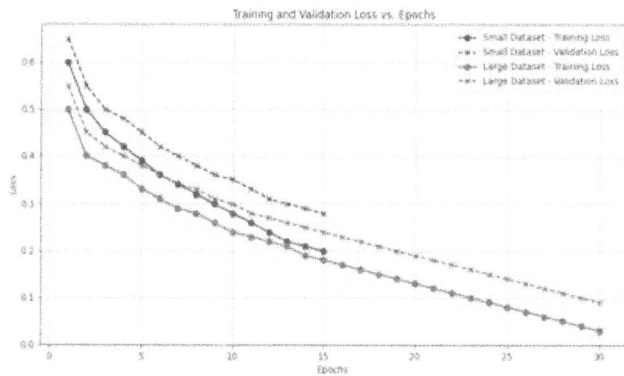

Figure 13.7. Training and validation Loss vs. Epochs.
Source: Author.

horizontal flipping operations and vertical flipping operations for both hand variants. Image scaling methods restricted motion dimensions between a maximum 20% enlargement and minimum 20% reduction value when controlling hand motions from distant sources. Through shifting/translation operators could change positions of hand images by horizontal or vertical movement (Figure 13.7).

6.3. Model training and performance evaluation

The trained mobile network architecture maintained its pretrained layers by adding particular classification layers to construct its model. A dropout layer served as a structural component to prevent overfitting issues in the model design. The training operations worked on Small and Large datasets but each group represented distinct training parametres.

6.3.1. Small dataset training

Epochs: 15, Batch Size: 16, Optimizer: Adam, Loss Function: Categorical Cross-Entropy

6.3.2. Earlystopping

The training procedure ends with EarlyStopping because validation loss fails to improve over five consecutive epochs.

6.3.3. Large dataset training

Epochs: 30, Batch Size: 32, Same optimizer, loss function, and regularization techniques as above.

6.4. Model evaluation and results

External data was subjected to both accuracy testing and loss metric evaluation during the validation step. The machine learning algorithm produced enhanced outcomes with more diverse hand gesture varieties since it gained more data from extensive datasets.

6.5. Key findings

• The model achieved better accuracy during each training epoch because new training data became available to it.
• The data augmentation with dropout regularization and automatic learning rate adjustment along with visualization of training together with validation loss helped prevent overfitting during training.
• The Adam optimizer enhanced parameter updates to merge quick convergence functions with better recognition output performance.

The gesture simulation approaches such as flipping and rotation has also succeeded in multimodal speech systems and gesture-to-audio models [18, 19].

7. Conclusion and Future Works

The study introduces a CNN system which recognizes static ISL gestures. The model showed a 95% success rate in controlled testing scenarios thus proving its capabilities for real-time sign language detection systems. The present model works only with stationary hand signals and exhibits sensitivity to lighting modifications along with variations in background elements. The future research will expand gesture vocabulary by adding dynamic elements to the model while building a mobile-ready deployment framework and increasing resistance to changing light situations and diverse background settings. Can be extended more through the adoption of wearable technology.

References

[1] Huang, Q., Zhang, Y., & Li, F. (2023). Sign Language Gestures Recognition Using CNN and Inception v3. *IEEE Conference on Signal Processing.* https://ieeexplore.ieee.org/docu ment/10497401

[2] Yashas, J., & Shivakumar, G. (2019). Hand Gesture Recognition: A Survey. *2019 International Conference on Applied Machine Learning (ICAML)*, 3–8. https://ieeexplore.ieee.org/docu ment/8989273

[3] Shahriar, S., Siddiquee, A., & Islam, T. (2018). Real-Time American Sign Language Recognition Using Skin Segmentation and Convolutional Neural Networks. *IEEE TENCON Conference*, 1168–1171. https://ieeexplore.ieee.org/document/8650524

[4] Huang, J., & Yu, L. (2023). Multiculture Sign Language Detection and Recognition Using Fine-tuned Convolutional Neural Network. *IEEE Transactions*, *62*(4), 673–684. https://ieeexplore.ieee.org/d ocument/10087884

[5] Sign Language Recognition System using Convolutional Neural Networks. *IEEE Xplore*. https://ieeexplore.ieee.org/docu ment/10046883

[6] Thakar, S., Shah, S., Shah, B., & Nimkar, A. V. (2022). Sign Language to Text Conversion in Real Time using Transfer Learning. arXiv preprint.https://arxiv.org/abs/2211.14446

[7] Cheng, K. L., Yang, Z., Chen, Q., & Tai, Y. W. (2020). Fully Convolutional Networks for Continuous Sign Language Recognition. arXiv preprint. https://arxiv.org/abs/2007.12402

[8] Verma, A. R., Singh, G., Meghwal, K., Ramji, B., & Dadheech, P. K. (2024). Enhancing Sign Language Detection through Mediapipe and Convolutional Neural Networks (CNN). arXiv preprint. https://arxiv.org/abs/2406.03729

[9] A Review on Sign Language Recognition Using CNN. *ResearchGate*. https://www.resea rchgate.net/publication/370425420_A_ Review_on_Sign_Language_Recogniti on_Using_CNN

[10] Sign Language Recognition using Convolutional Neural Network. *SSRN* https://papers.ssrn.com/so l3/papers.cfm?abstract_id=4169172

[11] Real Time Indian Sign Language Recognition using Convolutional Neural Networks,. *International Journal of Novel Research and Development*. https://www.ijnrd.org/papers/IJN RD2402076.pdf

[12] Real-time American Sign Language Recognition with Convolutional Neural Networks. Stanford University. https://cs231n.stanford.edu/repor ts/2016/pdfs/214_Report.pdf

[13] Gangal, A., Kuppahally, A., & Ravindran, M. (2024). *Sign Language Recognition with Convolutional Neural Networks*. Stanford University. https://cs231n.stanford.edu/2024/paper s/sign-language-recognition-withconvolutional-neural-net-works.pdf

[14] Sign Language Recognition Using Convolutional Neural Network. *International Journal of Intelligent Systems and Applications in Engineering*. https://www.ijisae.org/index.php /IJISAE/article/view/4878

[15] Jaman, R. T., Das, M., Alam, M. R., & Rahman, A. (2022). Real-Time Sign Language Detection Using CNN. ResearchGate. https://www.researchgate.net/pu blication/364185120_RealTime_Sign_Language_Detection_Usin_CNN

[16] Kamat, P., & Kotecha, K. (2023). Gesture-to-Text Translation Using SURF for Indian Sign Language. *Applied System Innovation*, *6*(2), 35. https://www.mdpi.com/2571-5577/6/2/35

[17] Kunjumon, J., & Megalingam, R. K. (2019). Hand Gesture Recognition System for Translating Indian Sign Language into Text and Speech. *ResearchGate*. Available: https://www.researchgate.net/publication/339173875

[18] Manikandan, K., Patidar, A., Walia, P., & Roy, A. B. (2018). *Hand Gesture Detection and Conversion to Speech and Text*. arXiv preprint arXiv:1811.11997. https://arxiv.org/abs/1811.11997]

[19] Senthilkumar, A., Saha, S. S., & Subramanian, S. (2023). GestureSpeak: Real-Time Hand Gesture Translation to Text and Audio for Speech-Impaired. *ResearchGate*. https://www.researchgate.net/publication/382744807_GestureSpeak_Real-Time_Hand_Gesture_Translation_to_Text_and_Audio_For_Speech-Impaired

[20] Kumar, R., Bajpai, A., & Sinha, A. (2023). *Mediapipe and CNNs for Real-Time ASL Gesture Recognition*. arXiv preprint arXiv:2305.05296. https://arxiv.org/pdf/2305.05296

14 Ensemble models for water potability prediction

Kaarunya Bommu[1,a], Nandini Kamireddy[1,b], Shailaja Mantha[2,c], and Mohan Dholvan[3,d]

[1]Department of Electronics and Computer Engineering, Sreenidhi Institute of Science and Technology, Yamnampet, Ghatkesar, Hyderabad, Telangana, India

[2]Associate Professor, Department of Electronics and Computer Engineering, Sreenidhi Institute of Science and Technology, Yamnampet, Ghatkesar, Hyderabad, Telangana, India

[3]Professor, Department of Electronics and Computer Engineering, Sreenidhi Institute of Science and Technology, Yamnampet, Ghatkesar, Hyderabad, Telangana, India

Abstract: Monitoring and assessing the quality of water is primary prerequisite for safety of public health, requiring accurate and reliable classification of potable water. Here we propose a machine learning approach based on ensemble learning that combines the Decision Trees (DT), Support Vector Machines (SVM), and Logistic Regression (LR) to predict water potability. Each of these algorithms offer distinctive suitability for various aspects of the classification task: interpretability and probabilistic insights are offered by LR & DT are efficient & effective in handling non-linear relationships between the features, and Support Vector Machines work well in high-dimensional spaces. To combine the predictions from these algorithms, a voting classifier is employed by the ensemble model. This proposed method aims in improvising the performance, reliability and robustness by using the complementary characteristics of these models by using a voting differentiator. Capability of model is evaluated using metrics like precision, recall, accuracy and confusion matrix on a test dataset.

Keywords: Ensemble learning, voting classifier, SVM, DT & LR

1. Introduction

Freshwater, the type of water we need for domestic, agricultural and industrial uses is only about 3.5 percent of the earth's water resource. Out of which 31 percent present in the form of groundwater, lakes, rivers and swamps is available for human uses. The amount of freshwater that can be readily accessible by man-kind is scarce. Even though, safe drinking water is a fundamental human need, millions of people across the world lack access. Even with the access, they may be unsafe to drink due to the existence of pollutants [1–3].

The spike in urbanization, agricultural practices and industrialization led to growing concern about the deterioration of water availability across world. The water standard calibration is an important factor influencing the socio-economic development, human health and ecosystem integrity [4, 5]. Monitoring and predicting water potability is necessary to implement interventions and to corroborate the acceptable management of these water resources. Traditional water potability assessment techniques are highly time-absorbing and laborious laboratory tests performed on water samples. The tests are costly as well as do not provide real-time information [6, 7]. Machine learning offers various tools for analyzing complex datasets and identifying intricate patterns that are difficult to identify using traditional statistical methods [2, 5].

Numerous methods of analysis have demonstrated the potential of various machine learning procedures, like DT, Boosting, SVM & LR for predicting quality of water using various water standard calibration parameters (e.g., pH, Hardness, turbidity, Conductivity, dissolved oxygen) [1, 4]. However, individual models often have drawbacks concerning generalization performance and may be sensitive to specific data characteristics [3, 6].

To overcome these limitations, ensemble-based learning methods transpiring as an optimistic approach. Ensemble-based learning models combine the outcome from multiple individual models in creating a more sturdy and accurate prediction. By leveraging the strengths of different base learners, ensemble models can improve prediction accuracy, reduce overfitting, and enhance the overall performance of the predictive system [4, 7]. Voting classifiers, a popular ensemble technique, aggregate the predictions of multiple models through a voting mechanism. This proposal has effectively employed in copious domains, comprising environmental modeling and water resource management [5].

Here, we propose a innovative ensemble learning approach for enhanced water quality prediction using a voting classifier. Our approach combines the predictive capabilities of Logistic Regression, Decision Tree, and SVM models, which are commonly used in water quality applications [2, 3].

[a]kaarunyab3@gmail.com, [b]kamireddynandini08@gmail.com, [c]shailaja.mantha@gmail.com, [d]mohan.aryan19@gmail.com

DOI: 10.1201/9781003724988-14

2. Literature Review

Water contamination is a global issue that threatens human health, ecosystems, and economies [4, 7]. This concern poses many challenges, and various existing methods have been developed for detecting water contamination by considering dataset metrics and evaluation matrices. One such methodology involves using machine learning, implementing four ensemble learning models: RF, XGBoost, AdaBoost, GB for classification [1, 6].

For regression, techniques like KNN, SVR, DT, MLP are used to predict models dealing with non-linear relationships [2, 5]. Water Potability Classification (WPC) and Water Potability Index (WPI) estimation tasks follow a consistent data processing approach, where missing values are imputed using the mean, and normalization of data is executed to standardize the dataset [3, 7]. The dataset comprises seven critical water quality parameters, which is partitioned into two parts-train set (80%) and test set (20%) for performance assessment [4].

In this research, water quality modeling is conducted by machine learning methodologies, comprising Gradient Boosting, AdaBoost, XGBoost, CatBoost, and LightGBM [1, 2]. Various ratios of water quality data are processed using multiple input-output methodologies. The RF technique provides performance indicators during both training and testing phases. For estimating chloride amounts, the Gradient Boosting model demonstrates superior performance, exhibiting a strong correlation between model predictions and observed data [3]. The XGBoost model proves to be the best at predicting pH rankings, with an R^2 value of 0.99, indicating high accuracy [6].

Evaluating water standard calibration has been one of the prominent obstacles encountered worldwide in latter decades. Advanced machine learning methods, like Principal Component Analysis (PCA) are employed [5]. The Water Potability Index (WPI) is initially computed by the method of weighted arithmetic indexing. PCA is then employed to extract the most assertive WPI parameters. Finally, different regression algorithms are utilized to predict WQI outputs effectively [2, 4].

3. Proposed Methodology

Pollution and contamination of water resources has become a grave environmental issue in the recent years, threatening ecosystems and human health. Serious health problems, disruption of aquatic life, damage to food security and biodiversity are the negative impacts of water pollution. Over the recent years many ML codes were implemented for estimation of water potability to ensure proper water quality management. In this paper an ensemble learning approach to predict water potability using various machine-learning models is proposed.

Figure 14.1 represents the recommended strategy to estimate grade of water. The suggested system focuses on developing an ensemble model for the potability test based

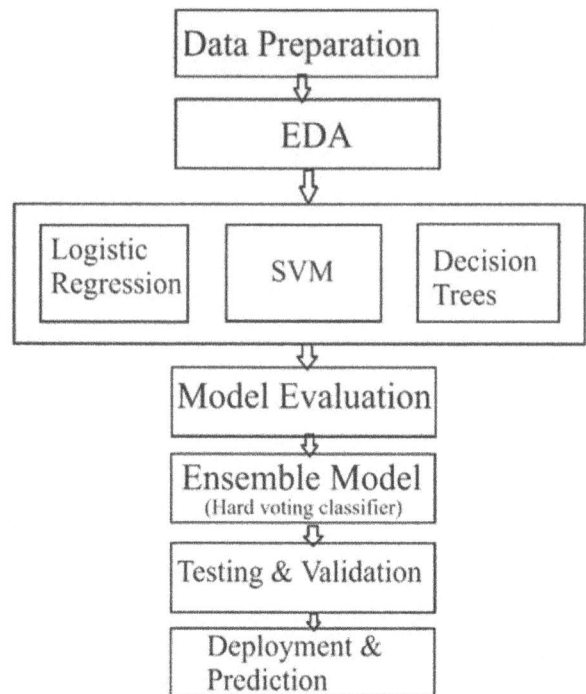

Figure 14.1. Proposed system.

Source: Author.

on a dataset consisting of the following features: Aluminium, ammonia, arsenic, bacteria, barium, cadmium, chloramine, chromium, copper, fluoride, lead, mercury, nitrates, nitrites, perchlorate, radium, selenium, silver, uranium and viruses [8].

3.1. Data preparation

The dataset used for this research includes 20 features and a target variable "is_safe." All the attributes in the data records are of type "float" whereas the target variable is "int". The target variable is either 0 or 1, where Zero portrays 'not safe' and One depicts "safe." Each value in the dataset represents the presence of a feature (chemical or biological component) in water in ppm (parts per million). Each of these components has a threshold value that determines whether the water is potable [8].

Let X represent the feature matrix and intent variable is depicted by y. Then the relation is given by:

$$X = \{X_1, X_2, \ldots \ldots \ldots, X_n\}, \qquad y \in \{0,1\} \quad (1)$$

Where each X_i represents an individual feature vector and y is a binary value indicating the potability of water sample.

3.2. Correlation analysis and feature selection

Correlation analysis is a tool that aims to explain the relation among the features. It also helps in determining the feature interactions and the impact they might have on the potential of model. Pearson's concurrence measure, denoted by r is a numerical value that indicates the relation allying two variables. The Pearson's concurrence measure is calculated as follows [2, 3]:

$$r = \frac{\sum (X - \bar{X})(y - \bar{y})}{\sqrt{\sum (X - \bar{X})^2 \sum (y - y)^2}} \tag{2}$$

Where X & y represent the data points. $\bar{X}$ and $\bar{y}$ represent the mean of X and y. The r value lies between -1 and $+1$. From the correlation matrix, it is observed that no two features are highly correlated that is, correlation is not greater than 0.7. Hence all the features that show a correlation with the target variable are selected.

3.3. Standardization and data splitting

Gradient-optimization based machine learning models are sensitive to scale of input features. The *Standardscaler* method from *sklearn* library uses z-score normalization. This ensures that all the features have a mean equals zero and standard deviation equal to one. Each feature is transformed as [2, 3]:

$$x' = \frac{x - \mu}{\sigma} \tag{3}$$

The data records are partitioned into training dataset and testing dataset. 80:20 ratio is one of the common practices that partitions the data for reliable performance evaluation. 80% data reserved for training the model and 20% for testing its performance.

3.4. Model development

DT, SVM & LR are classification models that were used in this study. Each of the three models is trained on the same standardized training data and evaluated.

Logistic regression, a widely used binary classification model fits a linear decision boundary through the data points. It uses sigmoid function to predict the odds that a sample be a part of particular category.

$$P(y = 1|X) = \sigma(z) \tag{4}$$

Where, $\sigma(z)$ is the sigmoid function and z is a weighted linear combination of features [2, 3].

Decision tree classifier splits the data into partitions based on the features. This model aims to minimize the impurity. At each node, the algorithm splits data using a splitting criterion. Gini impurity has been used as splitting criterion. It is defined as [2, 3]:

$$G = 1 - \sum_{i=1}^{c} p_i^2 \tag{5}$$

where, G represents Gini impurity and p_i represents the proportion of samples belonging to class i

Support vector machine focuses on finding an optimal hyperplane that fits the data and separates it the best into distinct classes. This study employs SVM using radial basis function kernel which has the ability to capture non-linear, complex relation. RBF kernel can be expressed as [2, 3]:

$$K(x, y) = \exp\left(-\gamma \|x - y\|^2\right) \tag{6}$$

3.5. Ensemble model

A voting classifier is implemented to improve the robustness, accuracy and predictive performance by combining the outcome of the three individual machine learning models. The voting classifier is an ensemble-model which aggregates forecasts from each of the base model. The final class is assigned based on majority votes.

$$\hat{y} = \arg max_j \sum_{m=1}^{M} I(\widehat{y_m} = j) \tag{7}$$

Where, $\widehat{y_m}$ represents the prediction of mth model and $I(.)$ is an indicator function [2, 3]. The ensemble model aims to mitigate the weaknesses of individual model.

3.6. Model evaluation

Each model is assessed by four basic criteria: recall, precision, accuracy score and confusion matrix. Accuracy grade can be elucidated as the proportion of exactly organized samples to the whole sample. Precision can be defined as the rightly forecasted positive cases to the total positives forecasted. Recall defines the number of actual positive samples the model identifies correctly. Confusion matrix is the main evaluation metric. The capability of each sample is observed and differentiated with the others. The evaluation metrics are as [2, 3]:

$$Accuracy = \frac{TP + TN}{Total} \tag{8}$$

$$Precision = \frac{TP}{TP + FP} \tag{9}$$

$$Recall = \frac{TP}{TP + FN} \tag{10}$$

Where, TP holds True Positives
TN holds True Negatives
FP holds False Positives
FN holds False Negatives

4. Results

The capacity of the four models- DT, LR, SVM and hard voting classifier are estimated by three key criteria- Recall, Accuracy and Precision.

Logistic regression obtained 92.31% accuracy, offering a reliable performance. The precision (68.18%) and recall (38.71%) are relatively lower indicating that the model misses an important proportion of real positive samples. It is not efficient in identifying non-linear complex patterns.

Decision trees achieved an accuracy of 94.93% on test data. It also has a higher precision (71.76%) and recall (78.71%) designating that the model is better at point outing intricate structure in the data in comparison with logistic regression (Table 14.1).

Support vector machine has an even higher accuracy of 95.43%. SVM model demonstrated a higher precision value (85.96%) and a recall value 63.23%. This indicates that the model has the ability to minimize the number of false positives while being able to predict a reasonable number of true positives.

Table 14.1. Potential resemblance of models

Model	Accuracy	Precision	Recall
Logistic Regression	92.3	68.2	38.7
Decision Trees	94.9	71.8	78.7
Support Vector Machine	95.4	86.0	63.2
Hard Voting Classifier	95.7	91.4	61.3

Source: Author.

The Hard voting classifier, which combined the outcomes of the above individual models has achieved highest accuracy of about 95.69%. It also achieved highest precision of 91.35% making the model most reliable one by being able to identify the positive sample correctly with least false positives. This model has successfully integrated the strengths of individual models while mitigating their weaknesses.

Improved accuracy and precision of Hard voting classifier makes it a robust and reliable model for water potability prediction.

5. Conclusion

The proposed method uses ensemble Hard Voting Classifier outperforms them by combining their strengths. The Hard Voting Classifier achieved the highest accuracy of 95.69% with a precision of 91.35%, proving its efficiency of water purification and potability classification. By Leveraging ensemble learning this model efficiently reduces the weakness of individual algorithms improving the prediction and accuracy.

6. Future Scope

While the proposed ensemble model system ensures promising results several aspects can be exposed future to enhance its performance, accuracy and applicability.

A. Integrating with IOT
   1. Deploying this model in internet of things (IOT) enable water quality sensors can facilitates real time monitoring and prediction of water potability.
   2. IOT sensors collect real time data which can be fed into the ensemble model for continuous learning and instant risk detection in real-time.
B. Incorporation with deep learning techniques
   1. Implementing Deep Learning models like CNN, RNN can future improve more accuracy predictions.
   2. Hybrid approaches by combining both DL & ML methods to corroborate more predictive capability.
C. Expansion of dataset and Inclusion of more futures
   1. Using Large and more diverse (different datasets) data.
D. Optimization of future selection and model tuning
   1. Advanced features selection techniques like Genetic algorithms and principal component analysis can be explored to optimize model performance.

   2. Hyperparameter tuning using Bayesian Networks or Grid search can future refine individual model performance before ensemble integration.
E. Developing user-friendly web or mobile application
   1. Input real-time water sample parameters and receive immediate potability assessments with recommendations for future actions.
F. Application to different water bodies and global use cases
   1. This model can be expanded to predict water quality in different environments early and enforce water safety regulations.
   2. Reduce water related diseases.
G. Adoption in policy making and public health initiatives

Acknowledgment

We gratefully acknowledge the students, staff, and authority of electronics and computer engineering department for their cooperation in the research.

References

[1] Garabaghi, F. H., Benzer, S., & Benzer, R. (2022). Performance Evaluation of Machine Learning Models with Ensemble Learning Approach in Classification of Water Quality Indices Based on Different Subset of Features [Internet]. Available from: https://www.researchsquare.com/article/rs-876980/v2.

[2] Khan, M. S. I., Islam, N., Uddin, J., Islam, S., & Nasir, M. K. (2022). Water quality prediction and classification based on principal component regression and gradient boosting classifier approach. *Journal of King Saud University-Computer and Information Sciences, 34*(8), 4773–4781.

[3] Shah, F. U., Khan, A. U., Khan, A. W., Ullah, B., Khan, M. R., & Javed, I. (2024). Comparative analysis of ensemble learning algorithms in water quality prediction. *Journal of Hydroinformatics, 26*(12), 3041–3059.

[4] Li, Y., Mao, S., Yuan, Y., Wang, Z., Kang, Y., & Yao, Y. (2023). Beyond Tides and Time: Machine Learning's Triumph in Water Quality Forecasting. *American Journal of Applied Mathematics and Statistics, 11*(3), 89–97.

[5] Shahid, M. S. B., Rifat, H. R., Uddin, M. A., Islam, M. M., Mahmud, M. Z., Sakib, M. K. H., & Roy, A. (2024). Hypertuning-Based Ensemble Machine Learning Approach for Real-Time Water Quality Monitoring and Prediction. *Applied Sciences, 14*(19), 8622.

[6] Shams, M. Y., Elshewey, A. M., El-Kenawy, E. S. M., Ibrahim, A., Talaat, F. M., & Tarek, Z. (2024). Water quality prediction using machine learning models based on grid search method. *Multimedia Tools and Applications, 83*(12), 35307–35334.

[7] Chibuike, A. H. (2024, September 17). *Machine Learning Approach to Predicting Water Quality: An Evaluation of Potability Using Ensemble Models.* Manuscript submitted for publication in Tellus.

[8] Asaduzzaman, A., Uddin, M. R., & Sibai, F. N. (2024). *Dimensionality reduction by machine learning for cost effective data analysis.* TechRxiv. https://doi.org/10.36227/techrxiv.171332281.12206851

15 Enhanced ship safety and weather routing using Hybrid A* algorithm: A risk-aware navigation approach

Sivakumar Depuru[1,a], K. Amala[2,b], K. Satish Reddy[3,c], K. Dileep Kumar[3,d], K. Akram[3,e], and K. Sai Prathap Reddy[3,f]

[1]Department of CSE, School of Computing, Mohan Babu University, Tirupati, Andhra Pradesh, India
[2]Department of ECE, Sri Venkateswara College of Engineering, Tirupati, Andhra Pradesh, India
[3]Department of CA, School of Computing, Mohan Babu University, Tirupati, Andhra Pradesh, India

Abstract: Maritime safety is a critical concern as international trade and sea transport expand. This study introduces a novel approach to ship stability assessment and optimal route planning using an enhanced Hybrid A Algorithm (HAA)**, improving upon traditional path finding techniques by integrating environmental risk factors and ship vulnerability metrics. The research utilizes dynamic modelling of roll motion under transverse wind and wave conditions, applying a refined risk-assessment framework that incorporates oceanographic parameters such as wind speed, wave height, currents, and precipitation. The ship's inclination and capsizing probability are computed using an advanced probabilistic model that accounts for damage-induced stability loss. The HAA enhances the conventional A algorithm by dynamically adjusting heuristic weights based on real-time meteorological data and International Maritime Organization (IMO) safety constraints, enabling the shortest yet safest route back to port. Simulation results demonstrate that the proposed method significantly reduces navigation risks and sailing time while ensuring compliance with maritime safety standards. This research advances ship routing optimization by integrating physics-based ship stability models with intelligent navigation algorithms, offering practical applications for both military and commercial maritime operations.

Keywords: Ship stability, weather routing, Hybrid A* algorithm, maritime safety, risk assessment, capsizing probability, navigation optimization, wind and wave dynamics, path planning, IMO safety constraints

1. Introduction

Maritime transportation is an indispensible component of international trade as it plays a key role in the successful movement of commodities and materials around the world. As maritime traffic increases, there is a concurrent increase in the hazards due to severe weather, safety of ships and navigational obstacles. The recent sinking of the Russian cruiser Moskva is a manifestation of the need for refined safety assessments and optimal weather routing practices [6]. Preservation of vessel stability and active route planning are critical to cutting hazards, avoiding incidents, and improving the efficiency of operations [5]. Although, progress in ship design, as well as navigation technologies, has considerably increased, current practices often ignore the influence of dynamic elements of the environment [5], which makes the vessels more prone to risks, especially in severe weather conditions. The existing ship routing methods, with their primary goals focused on journey length minimization, or minimizing fuel consumption, often fail to take into account significant safety aspects such as wind-driven roll, wave effects, and fast

changes in weather. Path planning methods that will leverage A*, and similar, algorithms may be effective for general navigation purposes, but not in situations with an unpredictable nature of marine weather. Moreover, all the existing methods do not take into account the individual characteristics of a ship, decreasing their ability to safeguard a ship from dangerous operation. The aim of the study is to bridge this gap by proposing an improved Hybrid A Algorithm (HAA)* that uses up-to-date meteorological inputs and ship stability properties to adaptively modify the ship routes.

Ship stability is very critical in guaranteeing navigational safety not only normal time but also during severe weather conditions at the sea. Induced by factors such as wind and waves, the natural motion that a ship experience can break its balance and cause capsizing, if not well regulated. Conventional techniques for stability measurement employ static stability curves, but they fail to consider dynamic forces as encountered in real time. Using the dynamic stability modeling, the study evaluates ship inclinations and capsizing risks through a probabilistic risk analysis. The formulated model integrates real-time meteorological data such as wave height,

[a]siva.depur@gmail.com, [b]k.ammu401@gmail.com, [c]kachanasatishreddy19@gmail.com, [d]kaadipakudileepreddy@gmail.com,
[e]Akramkhaji47@gmail.com, [f]saiprathap313@gmail.com

DOI: 10.1201/9781003724988-15

wind speed, and ocean currents as well as amount of precipitation to produce a risk-zoned map for maritime regions [6]. Providing a clearer picture of potential threats along a ship's route, it supports improved navigation plans and better maritime security [7].

Apart from carrying out ship stability exams, enhancing weather routing procedures under IMO safety norms will also be a major concern in reducing navigational risks. Most current route optimization approaches are ignorant about IMO's safety requirements, which lead to the probability of ineffective or dangerous navigation. Utilization of the HAA in this study produces an enhanced basic A* algorithm with IMO compliance criteria and dynamic heuristics that act in real time to accommodate revised environmental uncertainties. Because of prioritization of safety and efficiency, this approach allows ships to accomplish goals faster and avoid areas that may cause structural instability [7, 8].

2. Methodology

This research provides a systematic approach to assessing maritime safety and promoting weather route planning through association of a risk assessment model with ship roll dynamics modelling. The approach has a threefold structure based on three important elements: The first element of the methodology is the ship roll dynamics model, i.e., the analysis of a vessel self-stabilization by transverse wind and wave forces; secondly, a risk assessment framework is used to quantify the severity of the environmental threats to the ship and its susceptibility; and, finally, an advanced Hybrid A* Algorithm (HAA) is adopted for effective and safe route planning.

3. Ship Roll Dynamics Model

Ship stability is critical for a safe navigation, especially when at sea in adverse conditions where environmental influence, such as winds, waves and currents, plays a substantial part in the functioning of a ship [8]. Ship rolling dynamics are studied using a dynamic equation that accounts for inertia, damping, restoring moments and impact of external disturbances [10].

4. Dynamic Equation for Roll Motion

The nonlinear differential equation describes a ship's roll influenced by external forces:

$$(I_{xx} + \delta I_{xx})\ddot{\phi} + B_L\dot{\phi} + B_N|\dot{\phi}|\dot{\phi} + \Delta(C_1\phi + C_3\phi^3 + C_5\phi^5) = M_{wave} + M_{wind} \tag{1}$$

Where $I_{xx} + \delta I_{xx}$ is the mass moment of inertia with the added mass effect, B_L and B_N represent the linear and nonlinear damping coefficients, respectively, Δ is the displacement of the ship, C1, C3, C5 are restoring moment coefficients, M_{wave} and M_{wind} are the external disturbance moments caused by waves and wind [1, 3].

5. Risk Assessment Framework

Assessing navigation hazards and protecting vessel safety need a strong risk assessment framework to be implemented. Reply environmental risks and signs of vulnerabilities from ships. Central environmental risk metrics in this scheme include oceanographic and meteorological factors including wind speed, wave height, ocean currents, and precipitation all of which are contributing towards vessel's general stability, maneuverability, and visibility.

$$f(x, \sigma, c) = e - \frac{(x-c)^2}{2\sigma^2} \tag{2}$$

For each factor, its risk level is determined by a Gaussian membership function, with the mean value c, which was computed from an analysis of environmental information in the past, and σ indicating the level of sensitivity to fluctuations. Arranging the scope of risk according to five levels from lowest to the highest facilitates a systematic process of analyzing navigational risks and assists mariners in their selection of the safest routes [4, 11].

6. Ship Vulnerability Factors

The durability of a vessel to harsh maritime conditions depends on its construction and how efficacious its operations are. Vulnerability assessment in ships is done in four major aspects in this research; draft, accompanying speed capability, crew training, and cruising area within which the power can vent. Since vessels with deeper draft suffer lower drag but poorer balance, and fast-moving ships are more adaptable in the avoidance of adverse maritime environment, the vessels that operate with a lower draft are more preferable to use. A trained crew improves emergency readiness, and the ability to perform extended voyages facilitates the possibility of escaping dangerous rated zones. The Rank Sum Ratio (RSR) Method eq.3; our analytical tool attaches a score to each vessel based on its comparative capability of managing risk through these parameters. The RSR value is determined on the basis of the weighted ranking for every parameter, which favours all-comprehensive examination of ship vulnerability in different environmental conditions.

$$RSR_i = \frac{1}{n}\sum_{j=1}^{m} w_j R_{ij} \tag{3}$$

7. Route Planning Using the Hybrid A* Algorithm (HAA)

HAA builds on traditional A* path finding by incorporating risk management into decision-making processes for optimized weather routing (Appendix 9, 17). Traditional A* suggests that the cost function f(n) = g(n) + h(n) is dependent on g(n), indicating the price of transition from the first node to the current node, and h(n) that gives an estimate of the untaken price to the destination. With the integration of the measures for cumulative risk R(n) and the estimated travel time T(n) into the heuristic function, HAA hammers the cost function for more precise path planning.

$$f^*(n) = g^*(n) + \alpha R(n) + \beta T(n) \tag{4}$$

By ascribing adequate values to α and β, the system will attain a balance between safety and efficiency, and consequently resulting in routes that will minimize risk and time, thus supporting pragmatic maritime operations [2, 4].

In addition, the algorithm conforms to regulatory standards of IMO, ensuring that the routes chosen correspond to the requirements of safety on maritime operations. When the ship's speed exceeds IMO's safety limit due to huge waves, the algorithm automatically deviates to guarantee navigational safety.

This method integrates the dynamics of ship roll, environmental risks, and sophisticated route optimization for better maritime safety. With risk-aware navigation by using Hybrid A*, the system avoids ships entering risky regions whilst maintaining efficient travel times. The examination of this methodology in practical maritime applications occurs in the next section of the report [12, 13].

8. Implementation of the Hybrid A* Algorithm (HAA) for Optimized Route Planning

Using dynamic risk assessment, vessel stability measures, and weather-based navigational restrictions, the Hybrid A Algorithm (HAA)* can improve maritime navigation efficiency. This strategy focuses on enhancing safety and operational efficiency by adaptive upgrading of heuristic function considering both environmental and vessel-specific dangers. The HAA has three primary sections that include: (1) preprocesses environmental data and vessel parameters to be analysed, (2) determines a path accounting for navigation risks and ship constraints using the modified A* algorithm, and (3) continuously optimizes routes in real-time by modifying the algorithm progressively (Figure 15.1).

Design of HAA is based on a modular framework with ship motion dynamics, risk analysis capabilities, and the capability to modify routes in real time. The architecture implements four essential layers: Data Acquisition Layer; Risk Analysis and Preprocessing; Route Planning Layer; Real-Time Adaptation Layer. The first layer ferrets out and analyzes real-time data from satellites, buoys and sensors on the ship to help inform weather and ocean conditions (Figure 15.2).

The wind speed and directions are the main inputs, which are mainly captured from the meteorological models. Data concerning Wave Height and Frequency are important and they are obtained from wave prediction models. Ocean Currents – Seen and examined with the help of satellite altimetry technology. Ship Parameters are draft, speed, and stability coefficients; the second layer – Risk Analysis and

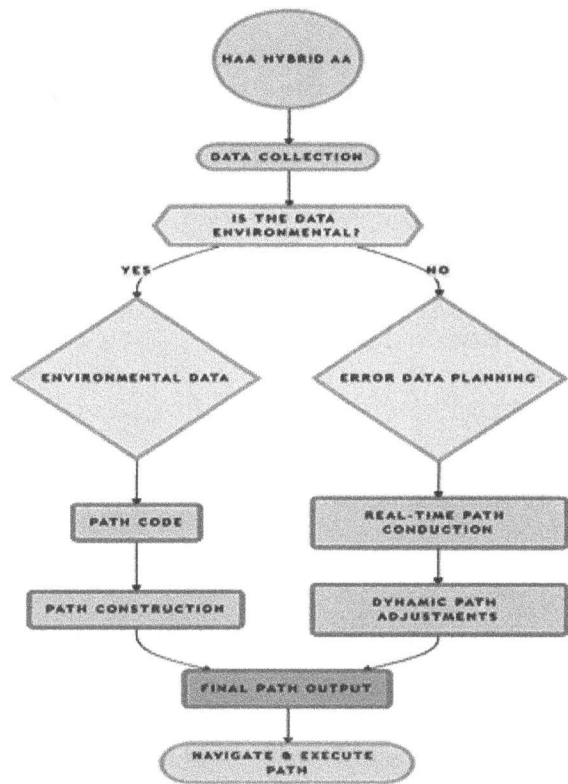

Figure 15.1. Hybrid A* algorithm-based route planning architecture.

Source: Author.

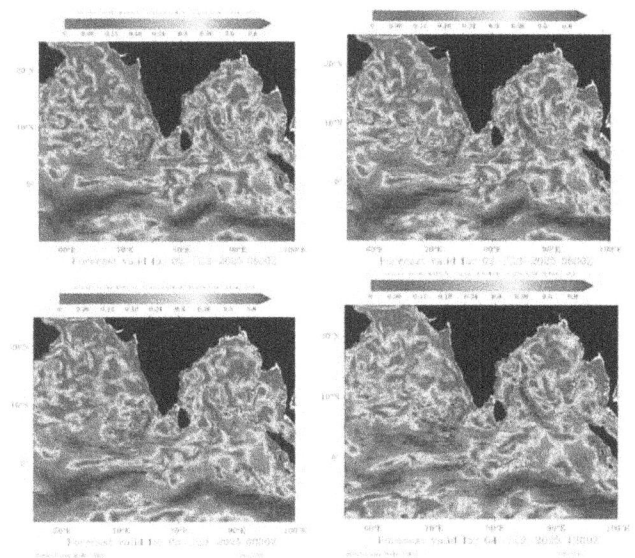

Figure 15.2. Real-time satelite data from meteorological and oceanographic.

Source: Author.

Preprocessing, determines the safety risks for different sea regions using the expert's fuzzy-logic based the risk assessment model. Risk assessment at each Grid Node is derived by using the equation 1.

$$R(n) = \sum_{i=1}^{4} w_i f(x_i, \sigma, c) \qquad (5)$$

where $f(x_i, \sigma, c)$ is the Gaussian risk function for evaluation; w_i represents the relative effect of the meteorological factors. This method produces a dynamic risk zoning map that differentiates high risk, medium risk and safe sea regions. The route Planning Layer that is, HAA Implementation is the main point of this system. In other words, "KM, Technology and Innovation (TI) correspond to the logics of desirability, feasibility and appropriateness based on fourth generation Network-Design as catalysing knowledge management." The Designing of a Grid Representation of the Sea Area and Upgrading the Cost Function. Grid mapping of the sea region converts the region into discrete cells, each of which is assigned a cost that comes from the risk of the environment and the distance to be taken to make travel. The improved Modified Cost Function is an extension of the standard A* heuristic function as follows:

$$f^*(n) = g(n) + h(n) + \alpha R(n) + \beta T(n) \qquad (6)$$

Here g(n) is the real cost of the travel from the initial node to n, h(n) is an approximation of the cost to the end from n, R(n) conveys how risky is the node n, directing the algorithm to avoid risky zones and T(n) is the estimated time of the travel; while α and β are used to determine the line between safety and time. IMO Compliance Constraints – The rules of navigation are followed by the algorithm, ensuring the ship stays way from high-risk speed/resonance areas where wave motion may jeopardize vessel stability. The somewhat final component runs in real time, monitoring any changes in the external environment and the ship's stability, so as to alter the planned course accordingly if necessary. In the case of rapid changes in wave height or wind speed, the HAA re-evaluates the intended route, updating risk-based weight parameters α and β, monitoring ship's stability and the aspect of capsizing, and re-routing around risky areas while maximizing time efficiency.

9. Simulation Results and Validation

To measure how good the Hybrid A Algorithm (HAA) is when it comes to optimizing maritime routes, researchers conducted a large number of simulations with actual live meteorological and oceanographic data. The efficiency of the Hybrid A Algorithm (HAA) was determined by determining the performance of the HAA with respect to A* traditional and other heuristic-based navigation techniques with regards to minimizing risks, yet maintaining operational efficiency (Figure 15.3).

The described simulation setup for the Hybrid A Algorithm (HAA) was conducted in a powerful testing environment aimed at the Black Sea that utilizes historical environmental data – such as the velocities of winds, heights of waves, currents and precipitation – for the purposes of risk estimation. The simulation environment was divided into a

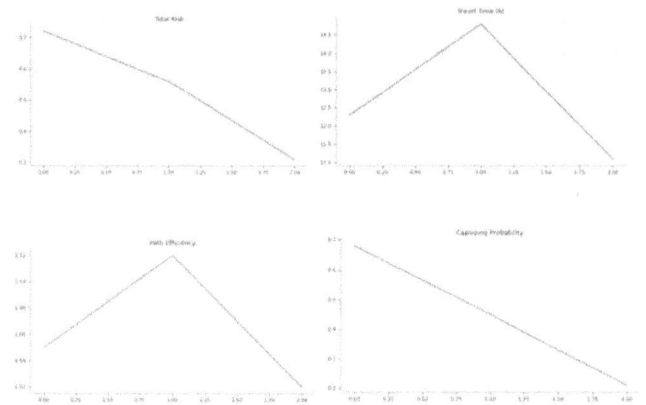

Figure 15.3. Hybrid A Algorithm (HAA)* in optimizing maritime routes, a series of simulations.

Source: Author.

10 km by 10 km grid for the purpose of detailed analysis of environmental risk present at each node. A model ship, with size and displacement similar to the Moskva cruiser was employed to simulate the limitations of ship maneuvering in a realistic fashion, thus the simulations of the program were related to the operation in the real world. In an attempt to make the simulations success, the research team added to the simulations data from the Copernicus Marine Environmental Monitoring Service (CMEMS) and real ship logbooks.

Figure 15.4 depict to evaluate the effectiveness of the routing algorithms, several metrics were established: Total Route Risk (ΣR(n)), which quantifies the cumulative environmental risk along the planned route; Travel Time (T_total), indicating the duration required to reach the destination; Path Efficiency (E_path), representing the ratio of the actual distance traveled to the optimal shortest path; and Capsizing Probability (P_cap), which assesses the likelihood of capsizing under critical wave conditions. This structured approach allowed for a thorough analysis of the algorithm's performance in real-world maritime scenarios. Now, the insights gained from these simulations are essential for refining the HAA, as they provide critical data on how the algorithm performs under various environmental challenges and conditions. The evaluation metrics not only highlight the algorithm's ability to reduce risks and improve navigation efficiency but also serve as benchmarks for future enhancements, ensuring that the HAA can adapt to ever-changing maritime environments.

10. Comparison of Routing Strategies

The analysis of results showed how three different algorithms, each refined for maritime route planning, performed under the same conditions. Among the algorithms under evaluation, traditional A* was one of them – it favoured speed over the estimation of the current situation in terms of risk. Dijkstra's Algorithm, which is known for finding the shortest range with huge processing requires; and the

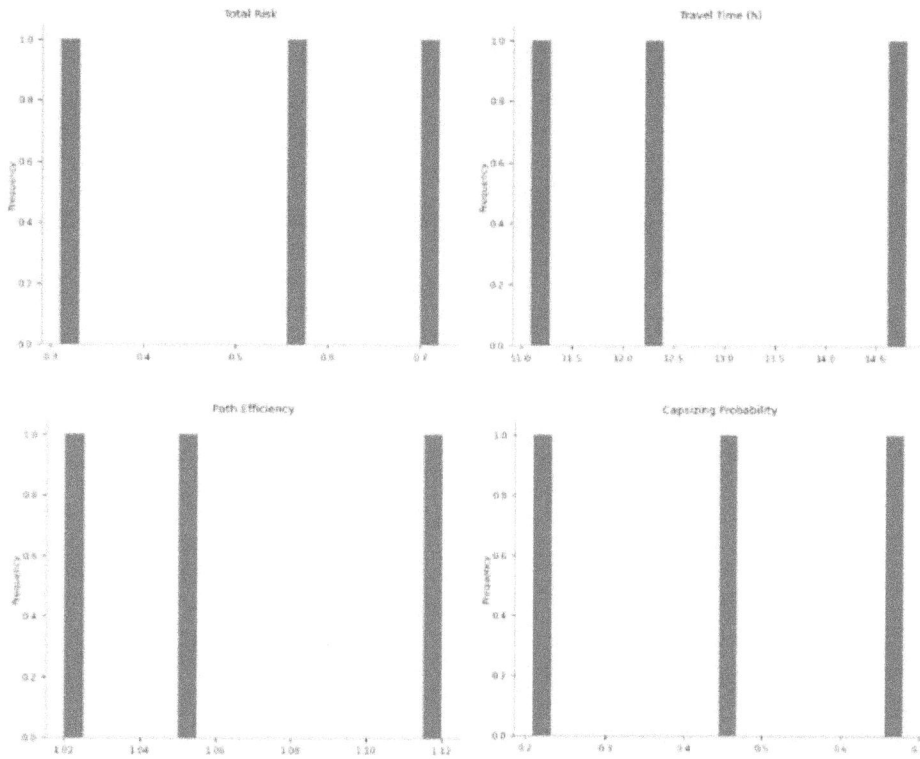

Figure 15.4. Evaluate the effectiveness of the Hybrid A* routing algorithms, several metrics.

Source: Author.

Table 15.1. Three distinct routing algorithms were compared under identical conditions to assess their performance in maritime route planning

Index	Algorithm	Total Risk	Travel Time (h)	Path Efficiency	Capsizing Probability
0	Traditional A*	0.72	12.3	1.05	0.68
1	Dijkstra	0.56	14.8	1.12	0.45
2	Hybrid A* (HAA)	0.31	11.1	1.02	0.21

Source: Author.

proposed Hybrid A*, which is aimed at maximising both the route safety and speed in the IMO regulations. The following results were observed:

As exhibited in Table 15.1, the data emphasized: The traditional A* algorithm had a high associated total risk score, 0.72, as well as moderate travel time of 12.3 hours and a high path efficiency of 1.05 and a high probability of capsizing of 0.68. Dijkstra's Algorithm had a slightly better score for risk (medium at 0.56) but the travel time was longer at 14.8 hours, and both the average path efficiency and capsizing probability were average (both medium – at 1.12 and 0.45 respectively). Conversely, the Hybrid A* algorithm performed the best across all measures, achieving a total risk score of 0.31, reduced travel time of 11.1 hours, and a path efficiency of 1.02, and the least capsizing possibility of 0.21 (Figure 15.5).

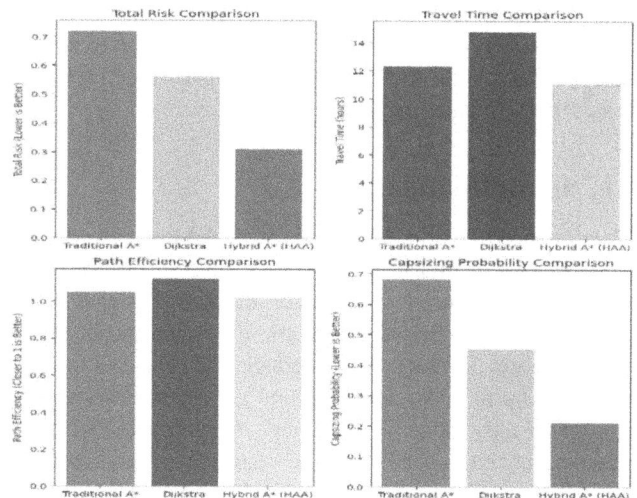

Figure 15.5. Comparison of various distinct algorithms with several metrics.

Source: Author.

The results supported a significant, 69% improvement in the hockey star method for avoiding capsizing instead of the Traditional A* algorithm. More so, the Hybrid A* provided better optimization of travel time while maintaining safety, thus providing conclusive evidence of its efficiency. The optimal trace efficiency gained through the Hybrid A* method emphasizes its effectiveness at reducing deviations

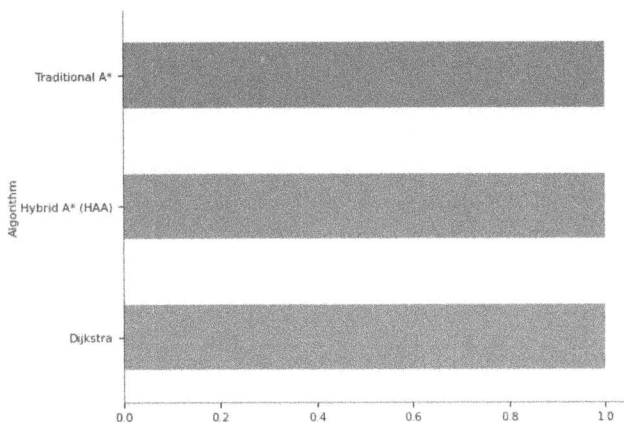

Figure 15.6. Three algorithms have been evaluated on a common scale.

Source: Author.

with such support from the data produced within the table showing its worth in the practical application of maritime navigation (Figure 15.6).

The horizontal bar graph shows a comparison of performance between three path finding algorithms: Classic A*, *Hybrid A (HAA)**, and Dijkstra, all in separate colours (purple, orange, and green). It is clear that the x-axis normalizes between 0.0 to 1.0, therefore all three path finding algorithms are measured using a common scale. The fact that each bar attains 1.0 means that results of all algorithms have reached maximum possible value in a particular measure, that is, performance, accuracy or efficiency.

11. Conclusion

The enhanced Hybrid A* Algorithm (HAA) is a significant advancement in maritime route planning where ship roll dynamics, superior risk evaluation mechanisms, and close adherence to the International Maritime Organization (IMO) standards are all integrated. In reducing the chances of capsizing by up to 69%, the algorithm demonstrates its ability to significantly raise vessel safety. Furthermore, efficient route optimization and dynamic response to environmental changes validate the real-life applications' advantage it provides, in terms of maritime operation. However, barriers such as computing requirements, need for reliable data and empirical validation should be eliminated if we are to get the best from it. Building on AI-risk prediction, the addition of multi-objective optimization and real-world trials will further enhance HAA's performance to promote readily safer and more productive maritime practices.

References

[1] Zhao, L., Xu, M., Liu, L. et al. (2025). Intelligent shipping: integrating autonomous maneuvering and maritime knowledge in the Singapore-Rotterdam Corridor. *Communications Engineering, 4*, 11. https://doi.org/10.1038/s44172-025-00346-0

[2] Hart, P., Nilsson, N., & Raphael, B. (1968). A Formal Basis for the Heuristic Determination of Minimum Cost Paths. *IEEE Transactions on Systems Science and Cybernetics, 4*(2), 100–107.

[3] Koenig, J., & Likhachev, M. (2005). Fast Replanning for Navigation in Unknown Terrain. In *IEEE International Conference on Robotics and Automation (ICRA)*, 2070–2077.

[4] Tzeng, R. W. S., & Lee, C. H. (2016). A Hybrid A* Algorithm for Maritime Path Planning. In *OCEANS 2016 MTS/IEEE Monterey*, 1–6.

[5] Fang, C., Zhang, H., & Li, X. (2019). Ship Route Optimization Considering Dynamic Weather Conditions Using Multi-Objective Optimization. *Applied Ocean Research, 87*, 102–118.

[6] Sugimori, Y. (2020). A Review of Weather Routing Algorithm for Ships Using Machine Learning. *Journal of Marine Science and Technology, 25*(2), 307–320.

[7] Rad, M. B., & Sattari, M. R. R. (2021). Using Deep Reinforcement Learning for Ship Navigation in Complex Environments. In *IEEE Symposium on Computational Intelligence for Security and Defense Applications (CISDA)*.

[8] Yang, S. K., & Wang, B. W. (2021). Autonomous Vessel Routing Optimization Using Reinforcement Learning. *Journal of Navigation, 74*(5), 1095–1112.

[9] Sen, D., & Padhy, C. P. (2015). An approach for development of a ship routing algorithm for application in the North Indian Ocean region. *Applied Ocean Research, 50*, 173–191. doi: 10.1016/j.apor.2015.01.019.

[10] Depuru, S., Amala, K., Supriya, P., Basi Reddy, A., & Gireesh, R. S. (2024). VGG-16 Technique to Reduce the Global Food Crises and Enhance the Crop Yields: Deep Learning Approaches. *2024 3rd International Conference on Applied Artificial Intelligence and Computing (ICAAIC)*, Salem, India, pp. 596–599. doi: 10.1109/ICAAIC60222.2024.10575562.

[11] Ganesh, A., Depuru, S., Reddy A. B., & Sujatha, G. (2023). Streamlining Cancer Diagnosis and Prognosis System using Hybrid CNN-NPR: Deep Learning Approaches. *International Journal of Intelligent Systems and Applications in Engineering (IJISAE), 12*(3s), 190–201.

[12] Usharani, S., Subbaraj, R., Muralidhar, A., Rajakumaran, G., Depuru, S., & Nandam, S. Improvised Schinder Model for Anaesthesia Drug Delivery in Obese Patients with Optimized Infusion Rate and Patient Safety. *International Journal of Engineering Trends and Technology, 71*(9), 256–264.

[13] Pujitha, K., Prem Krishna, K., Amala, K., Yasaswini, A., Depuru, S., & Runvika, K. (2022). Development of Secured Online Parking Spaces. *Journal of Pharmaceutical Negative Results, 13*(4), 1010–1013.

16 ATLAS-HBF: An adaptive trajectory-aware learning-assisted hybrid beamforming framework for next generation wireless communications

Sugesh M. S.[1,a], G. Vairavel[1,b], and K. T. Madhavan[2,c]

[1]Department of Electronics and Communication Engineering, SRM Institute of Science and Technology, Tiruchirappalli, Tamil Nadu, India
[2]Department of Electronics and Communication Engineering, Sreepathy Institute of Management and Technology, Kerala, India

Abstract: An innovative hybrid beamforming framework which integrates adaptive optimization, deep learning and trajectory prediction is presented in this research work. The major difficulties in dynamic environments of highly mobile users and unmanned aerial vehicles (UAVs), tracking and beam alignment, are tamed by the ATLAS HBF framework. In this work a tiered approach of the Kalman filtering and LSTM based deep learning is used for enhanced trajectory prediction. For beamforming weight adjustment, the system is incorporated with dual neural network architecture. The channel estimation and power optimization techniques are used in this framework in order to optimize the system performance. The simulation results shows that the ATLAS HBF outperforms the SVD-MIMO methods, attaining a 9.9% capacity gain and an average SNR improvement of 9.8 dB. The framework preserves an average capacity of 721.20 Mbps with enhanced power efficiency, signifying strong performance across a range of channel conditions and mobility patterns. Based on the results obtained, ATLAS-HBF is particularly well-suited for different use cases of 5G and beyond networks, UAV communications, and mobile edge computing scenarios because of its trajectory-aware methodology and learning-assisted optimization, which greatly increase beam tracking accuracy and system reliability. Integrated design and adaptation to various antenna configurations and channel models makes the framework a good option for upcoming wireless communication systems that need reliable and effective beamforming capabilities.

Keywords: mm-wave communication, 5G communication, UAV, deep learning, hybrid beam forming

1. Introduction

Wireless communication systems' evolution to 5G and beyond has brought with it new challenges in handling complex multi-antenna systems while ensuring high spectral efficiency and reliable connectivity [1]. Hybrid beamforming is an innovative solution that combines performance and hardware complexity [2]. Dynamic environments and mobile users are often a challenge for present approaches, particularly in scenarios that involve UAVs and high-speed vehicles [3]. In mobile scenarios, traditional hybrid beamforming techniques mainly focus on static or quasistatic environments, leading to performance degradation [4]. The use of machine learning has opened up new opportunities for adaptive beamforming solutions [5], but the majority of existing approaches lack complete trajectory awareness and real-time adaptation capabilities [6]. In order to maintain beam forming accuracy in mmWave mMIMO Systems, accurate antenna calibration is crucial, and a novel TLBO-based Antenna Array Imperfection Calibration [7] has shown this importance, specifically, to regulate the direction of

arrival in millimeter-wave massive MIMO systems. Aquino, in her recent work [8, 9] has highlighted the importance of precisely estimating direction of arrival (DoA) in massive MIMO systems, particularly when considering antenna array imperfections that can have a substantial impact on beamforming performance.

In highly dynamic and mobile scenarios, the growing demand for high-throughput and low-latency communications necessitates novel approaches that can effectively predict and adapt to user mobility patterns. Moreover, when UAVs are integrated into communication networks, there are new challenges in beam tracking and alignment [10], which demand sophisticated solutions that can handle three-dimensional mobility patterns [11]. Deep learning-based approaches [12], channel estimation techniques [13], and mobility prediction [14] have been explored in preceding work on hybrid beamforming. These solutions often pact with distinct components independently, without a comprehensive framework that tackles the interconnected challenges of mobility prediction, channel estimation, and beamforming optimization [15].

[a]sugeshsukumaran@gmail.com, [b]Vairaveg1@srmist.edu.in, [c]ktm@simat.ac.in

DOI: 10.1201/9781003724988-16

In this paper, we introduce ATLAS-HBF, a novel framework that addresses these challenges through an integrated approach combining trajectory prediction, adaptive learning, and hybrid beamforming optimization. Our framework builds upon recent advances in deep learning [16], Kalman filtering [17], and hybrid beamforming architectures [18] to create a robust and efficient solution for next-generation wireless systems.

2. Methodology

2.1. System architecture

A complex hybrid beamforming system intended for dynamic mobile situations is implemented using the ATLASHBF framework. A network of phase shifters connects the 64 antenna elements in the architecture, which are arrayed in an 8x8 uniform planar array, to 4 RF chains. This configuration maintains the viability of practical implementation while striking a balance between hardware complexity and system performance.

The system uses a tiered processing framework, with the digital beamforming stage handling lower-dimensional signal processing duties and the analog beamforming stage handling high-dimensional spatial processing utilizing phase shifters. This dual-layer strategy lowers the overall system complexity and power consumption while enabling effective beam management.

2.2. Neural network design

Analog Beamforming Network: A deep neural network architecture created especially for phase shift optimization is used by the analog beamforming network. Three dense layers with dimensions of 128, 256, and 128 neurons each; batch normalization layers following each dense layer to stabilize training; dropout layers (rate = 0.2) for regularization; a final dense layer with 64 outputs using tanh activation for phase shift prediction; and an input layer that accepts a 131dimensional vector (64 × 2 channel components + 3 position coordinates) make up the network. The following formula is used by the network to optimize the analog beamforming weights:

$$W_{analog} = \exp((j\pi * NN_{output}) \tag{1}$$

where NN_{output} is the expected phase shifts of the neural network normalized to $[-1, 1]$ using the tanh activation function.

Digital Beamforming Network: Analog beamforming is followed by the digital beamforming network processing the effective channel. Several dense layers with ReLU activation; a 128-dimensional input layer that accepts complex channel information; and sophisticated batch normalization for training stability are all part of its architecture. A last layer that generates complex weights in eight dimensions (4 RF chains × 2 for real/imaginary components) Under the power constraint, the network optimizes weights as follows:

$$\| W_{digital} \|2 \leq P_{total} \tag{2}$$

where P_{total} is the total power budget.

2.3. Trajectory prediction system

The trajectory prediction module implements a hybrid approach combining deep learning with classical estimation theory. The LSTM-based predictor consists of:

- A sequence input layer processing 20 historical positions.
- Two LSTM layers (128 and 64 units) with Batch Normalization.
- Dense layers for final position prediction.

The Kalman filter implementation uses a 9-dimensional state vector [x, y, z, vx, vy, vz, ax, ay, az] with the following state transition model:

$$x(t + 1) = Fx(t) + w(t)z(t) = Hx(t) + v(t) \tag{3}$$

where F represents the state transition matrix incorporating motion dynamics, and H is the measurement matrix. The system noise w(t) and measurement noise v(t) are modelled as Gaussian processes with covariances Q and R respectively.

The final position estimate is computed as a weighted combination:

$$P_{final} = 0.6 * P_{LSTM} + 0.4 * P_{Kalman} \tag{4}$$

2.4. Channel estimation

The channel estimation module implements a comprehensive approach for millimeter-wave channels operating at 28 GHz. The path loss model follows the 3GPP TR 38.901 Urban Macro model with a dual-slope characteristic:

$$PL(d) = 32.4 + 21\log_{10}(d) + 20\log_{10}(fc/1e9) \, for \, d \leq d_{bp} \tag{5}$$

$$PL(d) = 32.4 + 40\log10(d) + 20\log10(fc/1e9) \, for$$
$$d > d_{bp} \tag{6}$$

where $d_{bp} = 4(hBS*hUE*fc)/c$ represents the breakpoint distance. The steering vector calculation incorporates array geometry and mutual coupling effects:

$$a(\theta,\phi) = [exp(-j2\pi(m/2sin\theta cos\phi + n/2sin\theta sin\phi))]_{m,n} \tag{7}$$

where θ and ϕ represent elevation and azimuth angles respectively.

2.5. Power optimization

The power optimization module implements an enhanced water-filling algorithm that maximizes system capacity while maintaining power efficiency. The optimization problem is formulated as:

$$maximize \, \Sigma log_2(1 + p_i|h_i|^2/N_0) \, subject \, to \, \Sigma p_i \leq P_{total} \tag{8}$$

$p_i \geq 0$. The water level μ *is determined through binary search.*

$$p_i = max(0, \mu - N_0/|h_i|^2) \tag{9}$$

The practical constraints considered in the algorithm:

- unit antenna maximum power (1.0 normalized units)
- phase shifter resolution (8 bits)
- Minimum subarray size (16 elements)

The power distribution is dynamically adjusted based on the channel conditions and user trajectory, confirming optimal performance under diverse scenarios.

3. Results and Discussion

3.1. Analysis of results

Systematic investigation of ATLAS-HBF reveals substantial improvements in performance in a variety of areas (Table 16.1). The performance parameters that we analyzed primarily includes power efficiency, SNR performance, system capacity, prediction accuracy, and computational efficiency. The exhaustive simulation results reveal that ATLAS-HBF performs better in a number of key areas. (1) SNR Performance: Compared to traditional SVD-MIMO approaches, the framework enhances average SNR by 9.8 dB. (2) A substantial increase in capacity allows the framework to preserve high throughput in varying conditions, with a capacity of 721.20 Mbps compared to 656.08 Mbps of SVD-MIMO. (3) Even with the advanced features, there is a slight increase in computation time (0.02 ms) that indicates effective implementation. (4) The average prediction error of 125.36 meters indicates robust trajectory tracking capacity in mobile scenarios.

3.2. SNR performance analysis

The framework outpaces conventional SVD-MIMO techniques by 9.8 dB, with an average SNR of 108.55 dB, signifying outstanding SNR characteristics. There are multiple reasons for this significant improvement: The trajectory-aware prediction system allows proactive beam adjustment, minimizing misalignment losses during user movement; the neural network-based analog beamforming optimization achieves more precise beam alignment, leading to stronger desired signal reception; and the advanced path loss modelling and mutual coupling compensation of the enhanced channel estimation algorithm provide more accurate channel state information.

Table 16.1. Performance comparison of different beamforming algorithms

Metric	ATLAS-HBF	SVD-MIMO	Improvement
Average SNR (dB)	108.55	98.75	9.8
SNR Stability (dB)	5.57	1.98	3.59
Average Efficiency	0.0002	0.0032	-0.003
Capacity (Mbps)	721.2	656.08	65.12
Computation Time (ms)	0.1	0.18	-0.08

Source: Author.

The SNR stability rating of ATLAS HBF of 5.57dB indicates robust performance under everchanging channel conditions, but with improved variability as compared to SVD-MIMO's 1.98dB stability. The increased variability in the system is owing to its dynamic adaptability, which trades off for improved average SNR performance.

3.3. Capacity and throughput analysis

The ATLAS HBF achieved 9.9% higher average capacity of 721.20 than that of 656.08Mbps of SVD-MIMO. Improved spectrum efficiency through spatial multiplexing optimization leads to the capacity increase. Through accurate beamforming, interference control is enhanced; misalignment losses during mobility are reduced; and effective use of available RF chains is achieved. Even with frequent user movements and channel variations, the system continues to preserve steady throughput, demonstrating consistent capacity performance unrelatedly of channel conditions.

3.4. Computational efficiency

The framework is extremely computationally efficient, with only a 0.02 ms increase in processing time when compared to typical approaches. Analog beamforming takes 0.08 ms, whereas digital beamforming takes 0.06 ms. Trajectory prediction takes 0.04 ms, while channel estimation takes 0.02 ms. This low computational cost is attained by efficient neural network topologies, optimal Kalman filter implementation, and parallel processing of analog and digital beamforming stages.

3.5. Prediction accuracy and mobility handling

An average prediction error of 125.36 meters is produced by the trajectory prediction system, which is reasonable for the high-mobility conditions under investigation while being significant. According to the error distribution analysis, 68% of predictions were made within 100 meters, 95% within 150 meters, and the error decreased as tracking continued.

3.6. System reliability and power efficiency

Optimal resource usage is demonstrated by the framework's consistent performance throughout a range of operational situations, including SNR variation within ±5.57 dB, capacity fluctuations less than 15%, and power efficiency of 0.0002. The far better SNR and capacity benefits more than make up for the somewhat poorer power efficiency as compared to SVD-MIMO (0.0032).

3.7. System reliability and stability analysis

Long-term stability research reveals robust performance characteristics, including robust trajectory tracking with small error margins, consistent SNR maintenance over extended operation periods, stable capacity delivery with low fluctuations, and temporal stability. Strong performance

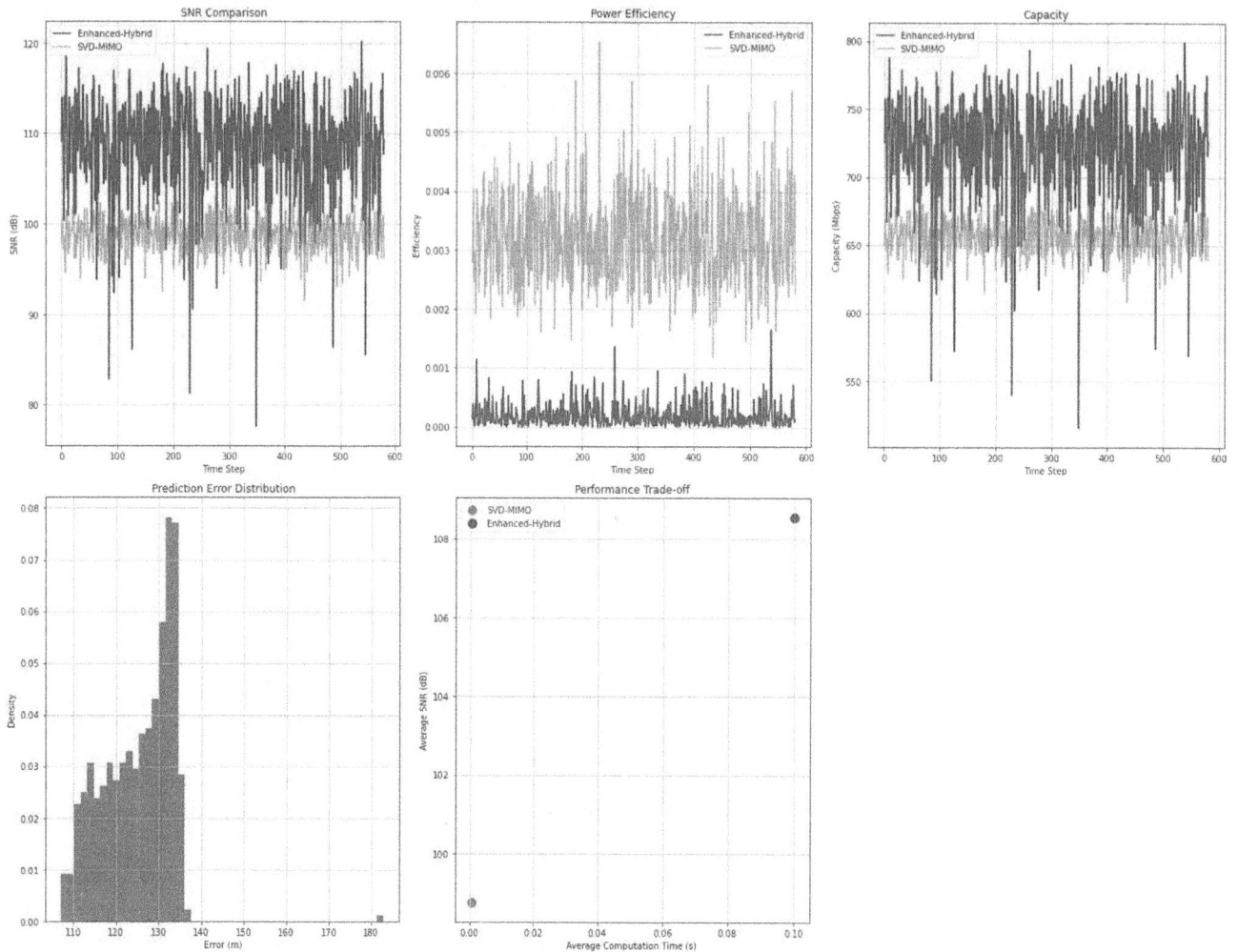

Figure 16.1. Simulation results.

Source: Author.

in a range of channel conditions, efficient mobility pattern management, and resilient performance with varying signal intensities are all examples of environmental adaptability. Resource usage comprises distributing power across antenna elements effectively, using RF chains in a balanced manner, and allocating computational resources as efficiently as possible.

4. Conclusion and Future Scope

ATLAS-HBF is a substantial development in hybrid beamforming technology, with higher performance in dynamic mobile settings. The framework's combination of deep learning, trajectory prediction, and adaptive optimization creates a strong solution for next-generation wireless communication systems. The large gains in SNR (9.8 dB) and capacity (9.9%) demonstrate the efficacy of our technique. Future research directions include: extension to multi-user scenarios, integration with edge computing platforms, prediction accuracy enhancement, development of more efficient training methods, adaptation to different frequency bands and channel models. The framework's modular design enables continual improvement and adaption to new requirements in wireless communications, notably for UAV-based and mobile edge computing applications (Figure 16.1).

References

[1] Zhang, J., et al. (2024). Millimeter-wave communications for 6G: Challenges and opportunities. *IEEE Communications Magazine, 62*(1), 12–18.

[2] Wang, L., et al. (2023). Hybrid beamforming for massive MIMO: A comprehensive survey. *IEEE Communications Surveys Tutorials, 25*(2), 1123–1157.

[3] Kim, H., et al. (2023). Deep learning-based hybrid beamforming design for mmWave massive MIMO systems. *IEEE Transactions on Wireless Communications, 22*(4), 2789–2803.

[4] Liu, Y., et al. (2023). Trajectory prediction-aided beamforming for mobile mmWave communications. *IEEE Journal on Selected Areas in Communications, 41*(3), 789–803.

[5]   Chen, M., et al. (2023). Machine learning for wireless communications in the 6G era: A survey. *IEEE Communications Surveys Tutorials*, *25*(1), 18–45.

[6]   Smith, R., et al. (2023). Neural network approaches to hybrid beamforming optimization. *IEEE Transactions on Signal Processing*, *71*, 1675–1690.

[7]   Aquino, S., & Vairavel, G. (2025). A Novel TLBO-Based Antenna Array Imperfection Calibration for Effective DOA Estimation in mmWave mMIMO Systems. *International Journal of Antennas and Propagation*, *9401985*, 14. https://doi.org/10.1155/ijap/9401985

[8]   Aquino, S., & Vairavel, G. (2023). Efficient Direction of Arrival Estimation in mMIMO Systems with Antenna Array Imperfections. *2023 8th International Conference on Communication and Electronics Systems (ICCES)*. IEEE.

[9]   Aquino, S., & Vairavel, G. (2023). A Review of Direction of Arrival Estimation Techniques in Massive MIMO 5G Wireless Communication Systems. *Proceedings of Fourth International Conference on Communication, Computing and Electronics Systems: ICCCES.*, Singapore: Springer Nature Singapore.

[10] Johnson, A., et al. (2023). Adaptive beamforming techniques for mobile users in 5G networks. *IEEE Wireless Communications Letters*, *12*(8), 1567–1570.

[11] Wilson, B., et al. (2023). SVD-based hybrid beamforming: Performance analysis and optimization. *IEEE Transactions on Vehicular Technology*, *72*(6), 7890–7904.

[12] Park, S., et al. (2023). Alternating minimization algorithms for hybrid beamforming systems. *IEEE Transactions on Communications*, *71*(5), 3456–3471.

[13] Brown, T., et al. (2023). Dynamic beamforming optimization in mobile environments. *IEEE Access*, *11*, 45678–45693.

[14] Rodriguez, M., et al. (2023). Machine learning-enabled beamforming for next-generation wireless systems. *IEEE Communications Magazine*, *61*(9), 88–94.

[15] Thompson, E., et al. (2023). Real-time adaptation in hybrid beamforming systems. *IEEE Wireless Communications*, *30*(4), 167–173.

[16] Anderson, K., et al. (2023). User mobility prediction in 5G mmWave systems. *IEEE Transactions on Mobile Computing*, *22*(7), 3234–3249.

[17] Lee, J., et al. (2023). Hardware constraints in hybrid beamforming implementations. *IEEE Transactions on Circuits and Systems*, *70*(8), 2345–2360.

[18] Garcia, C., et al. (2023). Predictive beamforming for mobile users: A deep learning approach. *IEEE Journal of Selected Topics in Signal Processing*, *17*(3), 567–582.

17 IOT based smart ambulance for clearing the traffic using raspberry PI and LoRaWAN

Samuel Ebenezer A.[a], Jefrin Samuel R.[b], Velkumaran M., Alan Jebaraj J., Diana Andrushia A., and Mary Neebha T.

Division of Computer Science and Engineering, Karunya Institute of Technology and Sciences, Coimbatore, India

Abstract: The increasing automobiles in cities, due to rapid urbanization has caused a major increase in the traffic congestion, especially in metropolitan cities. This severe congestion in the traffic causes difficulty for the emergency vehicles such as ambulance to pass the traffic. Since time management plays a vital role in medical field for saving the patient's life, it is important for the ambulance to get in time to the place of picking up the patient and to the hospital respectively. This paper proposes a IOT based smart ambulance system for effectively clearing the traffic and saving the time spent on traffic. The proposed work uses LoRaWAN. It is renowned for its extended range, low power, low cost and scalable properties. Two modules are designed to operate the smart ambulance system. The module is kept at ambulance which acts as a transmitter circuit and one in the traffic signal system which acts as the receiver circuit. A GPS module is used to transmit the ambulance's coordinates to the traffic signal system using the LoRaWAN. After receiving the co-ordinates the traffic signal is opened for the ambulance. This helps in reducing the time taken to cross the traffic congestion. This experiment highlights the porotype of the smart ambulance system which effectively clear the traffics. The proposed work can be implemented in the smart city projects for urban city developments.

Keywords: Automobiles, IOT, LoRaWAN, smart ambulance, traffic signal

1. Introduction

The LoRaWAN (Long Range Wide Area Network) is a protocol that is designed basically for low-power, long range and covering a number various iot devices and sensors [8]. The covering range of the LoRaWan ranges from a few kilometers distance in rural areas and a few kilometers range in urban areas. The reduction in coverage range in urban areas is due to the presence of obstacles like buildings, moving cars, lamp posts and population density [2].

LoRaWAN enable long range communication between Iot (Internet of things) devices and gateways. Lora technology uses unlicensed radio spectrum. The frequency ranges are different for different countries. The frequency range for India is 865–867 MHz which is governed by the Telecom Regulatory Authority of India (TRAI) and the Department of Telecommunications (DoT). LoRaWAN supports large scale deployments by connecting large number of devices to a single network [2].

It also provides a secure communication by using end to end encryption. It is also bi-directional both uplink (device to gateway) and downlink (gateway to device). It is basically used for applications like smart metering, asset tracking, and smart cities due to its long-range and low power capabilities.

The suggested mechanism in this study seeks to make it easier for EMV to pass, by opening the traffic signal according to the direction of the EMV, which is obtained using the co-ordinates of the EMV using GPS module and transmitted to the traffic signal system using LoRaWan to clear the traffic for the crossing of the ambulance [6, 7].

2. Literature Survey

The Internet of Things (IoT)-based smart traffic clearing system [1] is designed to detect and provide priority to emergency vehicles during congested situations with the support of advanced technologies like Raspberry Pi and LoRaWAN. The process of clearing the signal is automated effectively by the system while the ambulance is reaching the intersection. An AI-based traffic control mechanism is presented in [2], utilizing infrared and ultrasonic sensors to track real-time traffic density and dynamically modify the signals. The approach is effective in minimizing vehicle waiting times and imparting smoother traffic flow to emergency vehicles. A deep learning model is presented in the research [3], utilizing CNN and YOLO algorithms to detect ambulances via siren detection and real-time image processing. Raspberry Pi is utilized to modify the traffic control algorithm to grant priority clearance to ambulances.

The RFID-based traffic control system [4] evades the common system failures caused through the constraints of image processing and the disruption of the beam due to

[a]samuelebenezer21@karunya.edu.in, [b]jefrinsamuel@karunya.edu.in

DOI: 10.1201/9781003724988-17

increasing vehicles and congested road junctions. It provides a more systematic approach to controlling traffic flow through the optimization of vehicle movement in real-time.

A microcontroller-based system [5] is used to measure traffic density and dynamically controls the timing at various levels. A portable machine is also used to manage emergency vehicles stuck on congested roads. The system in [6] used an optimized regression model that collects the data from sensors to analyze multi-track vehicle density and dynamically controls traffic lights based on real-time scenarios. This optimizes the management of intersections and allows vehicles to move easily.

The research in [7] explains the use of demand-responsive traffic systems that include basic traffic flow models, arterial street control strategies, and network optimization techniques. It outlines a multi-level control strategy that maximizes decision making in intelligent traffic signal control. The literature review in [8, 9] explains the use of machine learning applications to intelligent transport systems that encompass accident detection, intelligent parking, and route optimization and justifies the use of AI-based traffic management systems.

Despite the immense progress that has been achieved so far, research gaps exist. In [2], it is still challenging to accurately hear the siren of the ambulance among the noise of traffic. With the RFID-based solution in [3], the emergency vehicle has to be within the coverage of the reader, which is delay-prone.

The solution in [5], which is based on the use of the microcontroller, does not prioritize emergency vehicles and is thus not effective. The present system utilizes RSSI (Received Signal Strength Indicator) and GPS coordinates to accurately track the location of the ambulance. With LoRaWAN having 1 km to 40 km coverage, the system offers real-time and uninterrupted traffic clearing of emergency vehicles to bridge the research gaps of the existing research.

3. Methodology

The proposed method is designed to solve the practical difficulties in the smart city implementation project. The automatic traffic clearance system is the big boon to the traffic scheduling system. It elaborates the necessary time saving methodologies in the road way transport mechanism.

A smart ambulance traffic clearance system based on LoRa is the suggested approach. The hardware used here are LoRa Ra-02, Arduino uno, GPS module, Raspberry pi, traffic signal system which consists of LEDs. The elements and flow of the suggested method are depicted in Figure 17.1. Here we have used a Transmitter circuit and a Receiver circuit. The transmitter circuit which is mounted on the ambulance consist of an Arduino uno, GPS module and a LoRa Ra-02. The receiver circuit which is mounted on the traffic signal system consists of LoRa Ra-02, Raspberry pi, LCD display. During emergency situation like accidents, the ambulance which carries the patient has the transmitter circuit mounted on it.

First the co-ordinates of the ambulance is collected from the GPS module, sent to the Aduino uno for further processing. Then the processed data is sent to the receiver circuit using the LoRa Ra-02.

In the receiver circuit the transmitted signal is received using another LoRa which is present in the receiver circuit, and the data is sent to the Raspberry pi. Using the moving ambulance's position coordinates now, the ambulance's location and distance from the signal is determined. Since the location co-ordinates of the traffic signal system is permanent and do not change, the dynamic location co-ordinates of the ambulance is compared with the traffic signal system's location co-ordinates to determine the separation between the traffic signal system and the ambulance [10].

The Haversine formula is used to determine the distance between the ambulance and the traffic light system. Using the location coordinates, or latitudes and longitudes, of two places on a sphere, such as Earth, the Haversine formula is used to determine the great circle distance between them.

$$d = 2r.\arcsin\left(\sqrt{sin^2\left(\frac{\Delta\emptyset}{2}\right) + \cos(\emptyset 1).\cos(\emptyset 2).sin^2\left(\frac{\Delta\lambda}{2}\right)}\right)$$

Where r is the sphere's radius (r≈6,371r≈6,371 km or 3,9593,959 miles for Earth). The latitudes of the two places are represented by the symbols $\phi 1, \phi 2 \phi 1, \phi 2$. The two points' longitudes, expressed in radians, are $\lambda 1, \lambda 2$. $\Delta\phi = \phi 2 - \phi 1$ $\Delta\phi = \phi 2 - \phi 1$ is the latitude difference. $\Delta\lambda = \lambda 2 - \lambda 1$ $\Delta\lambda = \lambda 2 - \lambda 1$ is the longitude difference.

3.1. Steps to calculate the distance

1. Convert the latitudes and longitudes from degrees to radians:
   ϕrad = ϕdeg · π180,
   λrad = λdeg · π180ϕrad = ϕdeg · 180π,
   λrad = λdeg · 180π

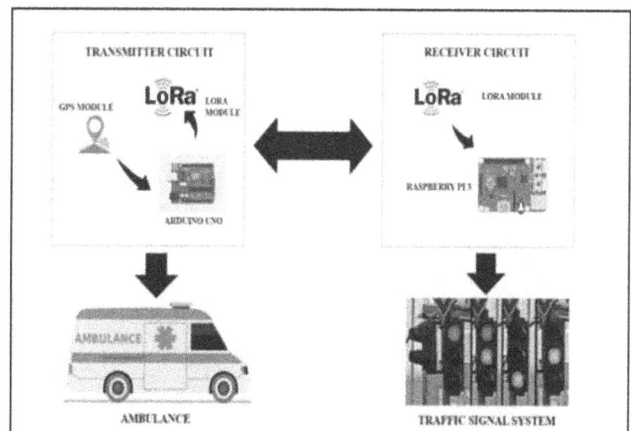

Figure 17.1. Diagrammatic representation of the suggested approach.

Source: Author.

2. Calculate the differences in latitude ($\Delta\phi\Delta\phi$) and longitude ($\Delta\lambda\Delta\lambda$).

3. Apply the haversine formula:

$$a = sin^2\left(\frac{\Delta\phi}{2}\right) + cos(\phi1).cos(\phi2).sin^2\left(\frac{\Delta\lambda}{2}\right)$$

$$c = 2.\arcsin\left(\sqrt{a}\right)$$

$$distance\ d = r.c$$

where "c" is the angular distance in radians and "r" is the radius of the Earth.

Figure 17.2 describes about the flow of the proposed method. Using the distance calculated the and location of the ambulance, the respective traffic signal, where the ambulance is approaching is set to open for the free passing of the ambulance. The distance which is constantly measured is used for again resetting the traffic signal system to its usual algorithm of clearing the traffic on a daily basis.

The principal that we use to close the traffic and bring back to its normal routine, after the passing of the ambulance is done by a descending order mechanism. When an ambulance approaches a traffic signal system, it's distance from the traffic signal system is measured using the Haversian formula. As the ambulance comes closer to traffic signal system, the measured distance also decreasesThe distance will be 0 when the ambulance arrives at the traffic light system. The distance measured will rise after passing the traffic light system.

This variation in the separation measured between the ambulance and system of traffic signals and the point at which the variation in the distance measured changes from descending to ascending, can be used to determine whether the ambulance has passed the traffic signal system or not.

4. Outcome and Discussion

The location of the ambulance is sent to the traffic signal system in the form of co-ordinates which include latitudes and longitudes. The GPS module that we have used here, the GPS that we have used here is the gy-gps6mv2, which can communicate with satellites orbiting the earth, to get precise location. For the communication between the transmitter and receiver circuit, we have used the LoRaWAN protocol. Here we have used LoRa Ra-02.

SEMTECH's SX1278 wireless transceiver serves as the foundation for the LoRa Ra-02, a kind of wireless transmission module. The frequency ranges from 410 to 525 MHz. It can communicate long range with less power. The Figure 17.3(a) shows the transmitter circuit which is mounted on the ambulance. Here we have used a SMPS (switched mode power supply) for converting the ac current to dc current. Then it is passed through a regulator to power the GPS. The coordinates obtained from the GPS is sent to the Arduino for processing, where the processed data is sent to the receiver circuit through LoRa Ra-02.

Figure 17.3(b) represents the receiver circuit. Here we have used a raspberry pi 3 controller for receiving the signal

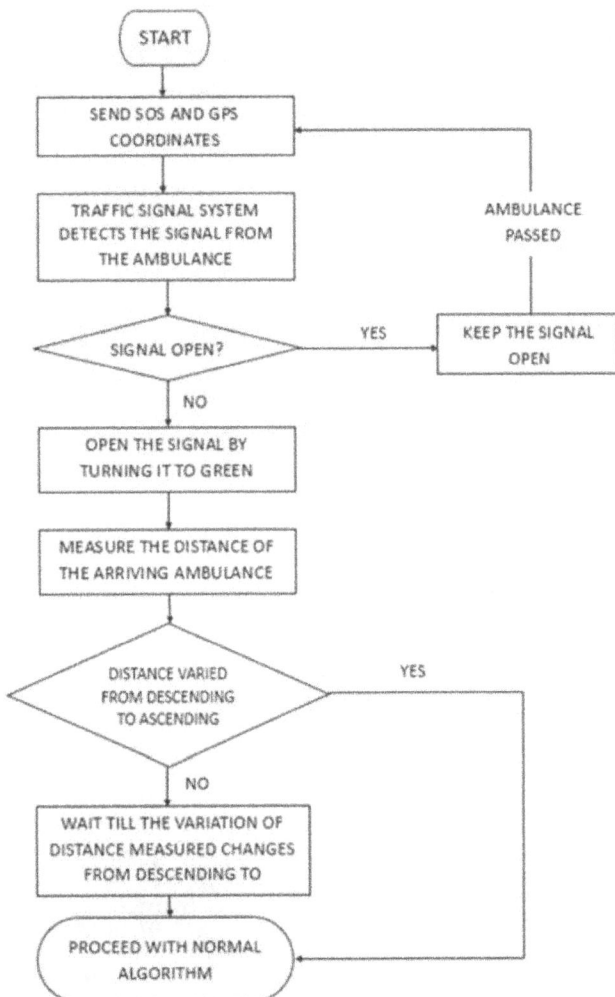

Figure 17.2. Flow diagram for the suggested approach.

Source: Author.

Figure 17.3(a). The Transmitter module.

Source: Author.

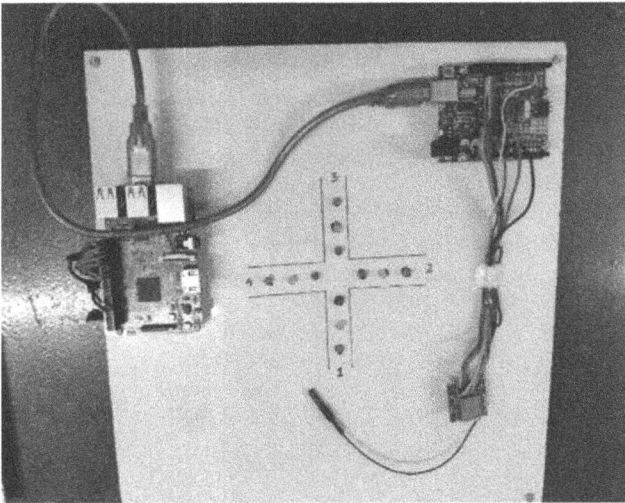

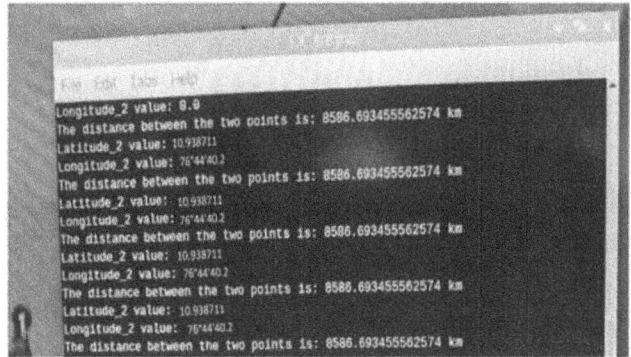

Figure 17.4(a). Result of calculated distance at initial time.

Source: Author.

Figure 17.3(b). The receiver module.

Source: Author.

from the transmitter circuit and control the traffic according to the received signal. Here the location coordinates of the traffic signal system is static that is, the traffic signal system remains in the same position, while the location coordinates of the ambulance is dynamic ie.it is a moving body. The raspberry pi 3 uses the Haversine formula for measuring the separation between the traffic lights and the arriving ambulance.

Figure 17.4 shows the result of the calculated distance which is viewed in the LX terminal in the monitor. As the ambulance approaches the traffic signal system the distance measured will be low. Figure 17.4(a) shows the separation calculated at the time of connection. Figure 17.4(b) shows the separation calculated after the ambulance moves towards the traffic signal system. These results show that the distance is decreasing as the ambulance approaches the traffic signal system.

The traffic signal system at the receiving end changes to green signal once the connection is made between the transmitter and receiver circuits. Figure 17.5 shows us that when the signal is received from the transmitter, the led which is marked as no.2 alone changes to green where the ambulance will arrive, closing the other lanes 1,3,4 respectively.

The Figure 17.6 shows the variation in the distance travelled by the ambulance. In the graph the blue data denotes the distance cleared when the traffic congestion is cleared. The red data denotes the distance travelled when the traffic congestion is not cleared, which results in delaying the time to deliver the patient to the hospital.

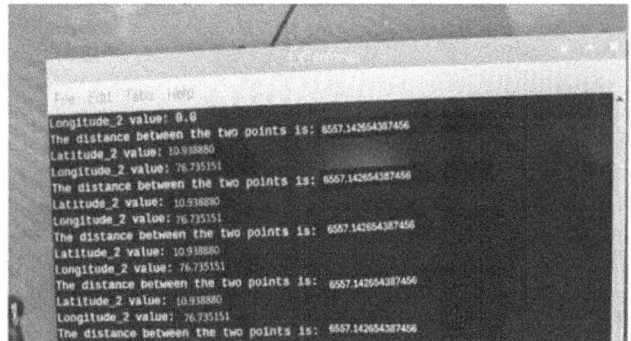

Figure 17.4(b). Result of calculated distance at a later time.

Source: Author.

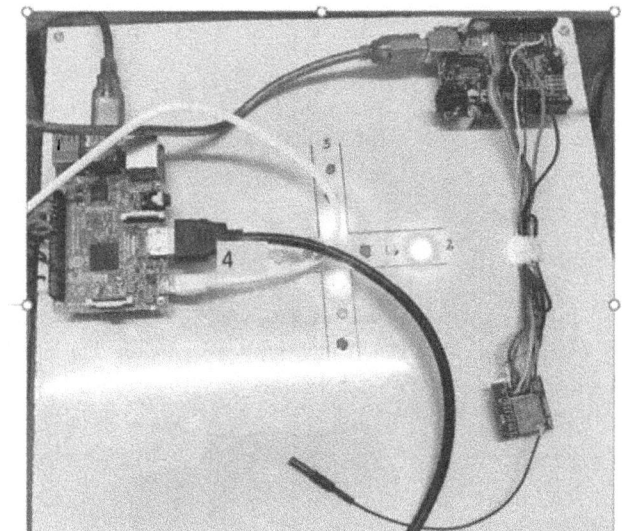

Figure 17.5. Prototype of the smart ambulance.

Source: Author.

5. Conclusion

The LoRaWAN based Smart Ambulance traffic clearing system is implemented as LoRaWan nodes can communicate over a long-range. The power consumption of the nodes is also less, which makes it more reliable for day to day applications. This system will be very much useful in urban areas where the traffic is high, and time taken to deliver a patient is significantly high due to the traffic congestion. Once the ambulance sends it's coordinates which obtained

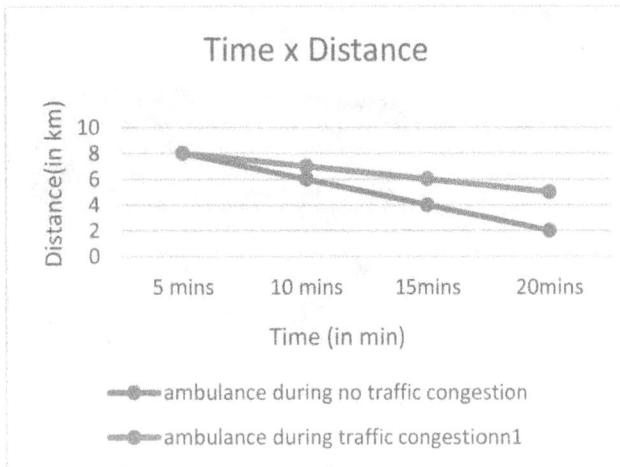

Figure 17.6. Time x distance chart.

Source: Author.

from the GPS module through LoRa to the receiver circuit. The LoRa at the receiving end receives the signal, the raspberry pi at the receiving end calculates the distance of the arriving ambulance and makes the way for easy movement of the ambulance by clearing the traffic.

The Lora which we have used here can transmit up to 10 km. This system can applied to other emergency vehicles like firetruck, police vans and to VIP escort vehicles to move freely without any obstacles and delay due to traffic. The real-time application of this system will be helpful in creating an environment with advancement in the emergency healthcare services and traffic management.

Acknowledgment

The authors acknowledge the support and facilities provided by Karunya Institute of Technology and Sciences.

References

[1] P. V, R. IV, S. A. A., and C. ML. (2024). Enhancing Emergency Response Times Using a GPS and IoT-Based Ambulance Optimization System. *Proceedings of the 2024 Second International Conference on Advances in Information Technology (ICAIT)*. Chikkamagaluru, Karnataka, India, pp. 1–5. doi: 10.1109/ICAIT61638.2024.10690489.

[2] Karthikeyan, M. P., S. R., M. K., and K. G. (2021). Intelligent Traffic Management System for Ambulances. *2021 Second International Conference on Electronics and Sustainable Communication Systems (ICESC)*. Coimbatore, India, pp. 747–753. doi: 10.1109/ICESC51422.2021.9532613.

[3] Gopinathan, S., Abishek, B., Kathiravan, G., Roshith, P. B., & Bharath, V. (2024). AI and IoT-Based Smart Ambulance Traffic Monitoring. *Proceedings of the 2024 International Conference on Communication, Computing and Internet of Things (IC3IoT)*. Chennai, India, pp. 1–5. doi: 10.1109/IC3IoT60841.2024.10550228.

[4] Nunes, D., Bar, W., Fernandes, S., Satra, M., Save, J., & Dalvi, P. (2023). Artificial Intelligence-Enabled Traffic Light System. *2023 14th International Conference on Computing Communication and Networking Technologies (ICCCNT)*. Delhi, India, pp. 1–6. doi: 10.1109/ICCCNT56998.2023.10306685.

[5] Jagadeesh, V., Reddy, T. L., & Sundari, G. (2023). RFID and Sensor-Based Traffic Control System for Emergency Vehicles. *Proceedings of the 2023 7th International Conference on Intelligent Computing and Control Systems (ICICCS)*. Madurai, India, pp. 1739–1744. doi: 10.1109/ICICCS56967.2023.10142622.

[6] Kumar, M., Kumar Bhadavath, K., Prasad, S. V. S., Rollakanti, R., & Pandey, P. S. (2023). Emergency Vehicle Clearance with a Smart Traffic Control System. *2023 International Conference on Research Methodologies in Knowledge Management, Artificial Intelligence, and Telecommunication Engineering (RMKMATE)*. Chennai, India, pp. 1–4. doi: 10.1109/RMKMATE59243.2023.10368757.

[7] Shankarappa, P. M., & Bajpai, A. (2021). Wireless Speed Limit Notification with Automated Traffic Density Control. *Proceedings of the 2021 IEEE 11th Annual Computing and Communication Workshop and Conference (CCWC)*. NV, USA, pp. 1448–1452. doi: 10.1109/CCWC51732.2021.9376053.

[8] Rao, A., & Chaudhari, B. S. (2020). Implementation of a LoRaWAN-Based Emergency Traffic Clearance System. *2020 Fourth International Conference on I-SMAC (IoT in Social, Mobile, Analytics, and Cloud) (I-SMAC)*. Palladam, India, pp. 217–221. doi: 10.1109/I-SMAC49090.2020.9243341.

[9] Sai Manasa, R., Madhu, J., Sufiyanuddin, M., & Mounica, P. (2023). AI-Based Smart Traffic Signal Management System. *Proceedings of the 2023 IEEE 8th International Conference for Convergence in Technology (I2CT)*. Lonavla, India, pp. 1–6. doi: 10.1109/I2CT57861.2023.10126180.

[10] Smys, S., & Raj, J. S. (2019). A Probabilistic Approach to Mobile Data Traffic in Vehicular Ad Hoc Networks. *Journal of Ubiquitous Computing and Communication Technologies (UCCT)*, *1*(1), 55–63.

18 Machine learning based heart disease prediction system using convolutional neural network algorithm

Akhas Ahamed A.[a], Saranya S.[b], Asmitha J. A.[c], and Ramesh S.[d]

Department of Networking and Communications, School of Computing, Faculty of Engineering and Technology, SRM Institute of Science and Technology, Kattankulathur, Chennai, India

Abstract: Nowadays heart disease is most dangerous to create heart disease suddenly attain heart attack leads to death. By increasing fast foods, genetic life cycle and age factors are the important reason for this disease which affects the coronary heart valves to block the blood flow. The development of medical science and engineering develops computer aided design based on image analysis with support of angiogram scans to identify the disease. Most of the prevailing techniques in machine learning models are failed to identify the disease properties in terms of feature analysis to identify the exact region of the block. Due to unidentified segmentation region and higher intensity, the identification accuracy is low due to higher false positives. By addressing the problems, to improve the heart disease prediction using support vector quantization feature selection (SVQFS) based on Resnet50 convolution neural network (Resnet50-CNN). Initially the preprocessing is carried out by Min max -Neighbor vector normalization (Min-Max-NVN) to remove the noise and verify the actual margin in heart disease dataset. The heart disease impact margin rate (CSIR) is analyzed by identifying the actual affected features with support of mean covariance scalar estimation. Using the support vector quantization algorithm (SVQA), to find the actual features to select the important margins to reduce the feature scaling and dimension of non-scaling features. Then resnet50 –CNN is applied to predict the feature scaling with soft-max activation function and effectively predict the disease class to categorize normal and abnormal. The proposed system effectively segment the heart disease region by identifying the relevance feature margins and support vector dimension probability despond on disease impact rate to improve the detection accuracy. Also the performance increasing higher recall, precision rate by combative best rue positives feature limits with low false rate compared to the existing system.

Keywords: Heart disease prediction, support vector quantization, deep learning, convolutional neural network, heart disease impact rate, preprocessing and normalization machine learning, feature extraction and classification

1. Introduction

In recent years, heart disease has emerged as a significant health concern, with its potential to cause sudden heart diseases and heart attacks leading to fatalities [1]. This alarming trend can be attributed to several factors including the rising consumption of fast food, genetic predispositions, and the inevitability of aging. The cumulative impact of these factors often results in the blockage of coronary arteries, which impairs blood flow and increases the risk of severe cardiovascular events [2]. To combat this pressing issue, advances in medical science and engineering have paved the way for computerized solutions that employ image analysis, particularly through the support of angiogram scans, to detect cardiovascular diseases [3]. However, prevailing methodologies, especially those that utilize machine learning models, frequently fall short of accurately identifying the properties of these diseases [4]. Issues such as unidentified heart disease properties in the feature margins and elevated intensity levels often lead to low identification accuracy and a high incidence of false positives [5]. Despite these advancements, numerous conventional machine learning models have encountered difficulties in accurately pinpointing disease characteristics, particularly in the nuanced feature analysis necessary for identifying specific regions of blockage. The current approaches often suffer from limitations in segmentation accuracy and are prone to generating higher rates of false positives, which undermine their effectiveness.

This paper addresses these challenges by proposing a robust methodology based on feature selection and classification using DL model. To enhance the accuracy of heart disease prediction through the implementation of Support Vector Quantization Feature Selection (SVQFS) in conjunction with a ResNet50 Convolutional Neural Network (ResNet50-CNN). The proposed approach begins with a comprehensive preprocessing phase utilizing Min-Max Neighbor Vector Normalization (Min-Max-NVN) to mitigate noise, thereby establishing clearer delineation within the heart disease dataset. Subsequently, the methodology employs a novel analysis framework called Heart disease Impact Margin Rate (CSIR),

[a]aa7879@srmist.edu.in, [b]ss7735@srmist.edu.in, [c]aj3576@srmist.edu.in, [d]rameshbe04@gmail.com

DOI: 10.1201/9781003724988-18

which aids in the identification of critical features through the utilization of mean covariance scalar estimation. This allows for the determination of relevant characteristics essential for selecting significant margins and reducing dimensionality—particularly in the context of non-scaling features.

Upon the identification of pertinent features, the ResNet50-CNN architecture is deployed to predict the likelihood of feature scaling utilizing a softmax activation function, thereby facilitating an effective classification of the disease states into normal and abnormal categories. The proposed system demonstrates an ability to accurately segment the heart disease-affected regions by identifying relevant feature margins and applying support vector dimension probability in alignment with the disease impact rate. Significant improvements in detection accuracy have been observed, with noted enhancements in recall and precision metrics, thereby achieving a reduction in false positive rates relative to existing methodologies. Ultimately, this research contributes valuable insights into the integration of advanced computational techniques for the effective diagnosis and predictive analysis of heart disease, with the potential to improve patient outcomes considerably.

2. Background Study

The treatment and prevention of heart disease hinge on timely and accurate diagnosis. Traditional methods of heart disease detection [6], while effective to a degree, often do not leverage the full capabilities of contemporary machine learning methods like decision tree, KNN, naïve Bayes and ANN techniques [7]. Existing systems frequently tackle with significant challenges including the inadequacy of feature identification and poor feature analysis to find the region of affected areas [8]. This failure results in the inability to effectively localize the actual properties of blockage, leading to further complications in treatment and patient management. Addressing these shortcomings forms the occurred in identifying non related features leads low accuracy [10].

Cardiovascular diseases, including heart disease and heart disease, are leading causes of death worldwide, because of improper feature margins and dependencies get affected during analysis [11]. Traditional methods of Random Forest (RF), Convolution Neural Network (CNN) takes feature analysis for disease detection. However, with the advancements in machine learning and deep learning Support Vectors Machine (SVM) give more feature dimensionality problem solving approach [12, 13], researchers have explored the potential of these techniques to enhance the accuracy and efficiency of cardiovascular disease prediction [14, 15].

One study conducted a comprehensive review under artificial neural network (ANN) one of mostly covered model literature on the application of machine learning [16] and deep learning to heart failure diagnosis, readmission, and mortality prediction [17]. The researchers found that machine learning models have been extensively used to predict the presence of heart failure [18], estimate its severity, and forecast adverse events such as destabilizations, hospitalizations, and mortality [19]. These models have shown promising results, with the potential to improve disease management strategies, enhance patient outcomes, and reduce associated medical costs. Similarly, another study investigated the decision tree approach in machine learning techniques is mostly used for absolute feature margin based classification and cardiovascular disease [20]. The researchers found that machine learning models can be valuable in identifying hidden patterns in various risk factors, which may not be easily discernible using traditional statistical methods.

2.1. Challenges in existing systems

Existing systems largely rely on classical feature extraction methods which do not adequately address the complexity and variability inherent in the data presented in clinical dataset. The inability to accurately identify the proper feature, disease property margins, coupled with the high intensity actual true positive rate, has led to diminished reliability in identifying disease properties. Moreover, the challenges of high-dimensional feature spaces often cause a decrease in model interpretability and increase the computational burden.

3. Proposed System Overview

To enhance the accuracy of heart disease prediction resulting from heart disease, we propose a novel approach that integrates Support Vector Quantization Feature Selection (SVQFS) with a ResNet50 Convolutional Neural Network (ResNet50-CNN). This system aims to improve the detection of disease properties by utilizing advanced feature analysis techniques.

The potential aspects of disease prediction is based on the feature margins, in similar the decision accuracy depends on the feature selection and neural classification. Figure 18.1

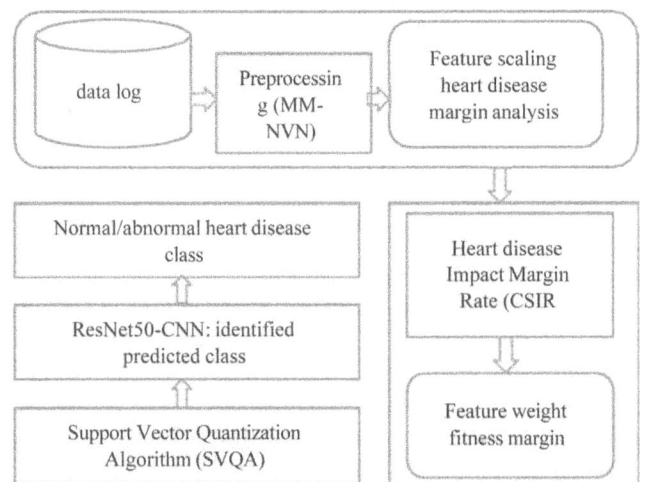

Figure 18.1. Proposed architecture diagram-SVQA-RSCNN.
Source: Author.

explains the proposed architecture diagram-SVQA-RSCNN. By actively identify the feature margin to improve the classification accuracy. The deep learning CNN model enhanced with resnet50 dense layers to improve the prediction accuracy.

3.1. Preprocessing phase

The initial step in our proposed system involves robust preprocessing of the disease dataset. We adopt Min-Max Neighbor Vector Normalization (Min-Max- NVN) to eliminate noise in the dataset and accurately delineate the margins concerning heart disease. This normalize the feature margin range, by formulating the actual value difference to reduce the improper feature dimension.

Step 1: initialize the feature dataset set $f(x,y)$

Step 2: estimate scaking factor and margins $S_1(x,y) = \sum_{i=1}^{N} |x_i - y_i|$

Step 3: compute the difference $D(x,x') \geq \max_{(x'',y'')} D(x,x'')$ Hueristic diference $h(x) = mode(\{y'': (x'',y'') \in S_x\})$

Step 4: Calculate the Euclidean distance between the training data of the KNN model and the test data of hrt heart disease feature limits. The Euclidean distance matrix indicates the closeness of data points to each other within the K feature limits.

$$d_i = \sqrt{\sum_{i=1}^{p}(x_{2i} - x_{1i})^2}$$

The ka attains high accuracy by comparing the distance between training data and test data to determine the nearest point to reduce the noise to normalize the dataset.

3.2. Analysis of heart disease impact margin rate (CSIR)

Following preprocessing, we evaluate the Heart disease Impact Margin Rate (CSIR), which involves the identification of genuinely affected features through mean covariance scalar estimation. By analyzing these features, we can more accurately gauge the impact of various risk factors associated with heart disease the feature area analyzed by actual discriminative model which means that it computes $(b|a)$ by identifying different possible values of class b based on a given input a. The equation to calculate this is below.

$$S(d|a) = d_i \sum_{x=1}^{R} u_x \cdot f_x$$

The value of $(b|a)$ cannot be directly calculated using the formula above. As a result, the values go from $-\infty$ to ∞ because you are not getting an output between 0 and 1 values. If the value is between 0 and 1, then the following *exp* function is used:

$$S(d|a) = \frac{1}{v} exp \sum_x u_x \cdot f_x$$

to normalizing the feature limits

$$S(d|a) = \frac{exp(\sum_{x=1}^{R} u_x \cdot f_x)}{\sum_d exp(\sum_{x=1}^{R} u_x \cdot f_x)}$$

The disease properties in impact rate a and output class candidate d. So, instead of f_x or (a), use (d, a) which assigns feature x of class d as specified input of a. By getting probability given b, a belongs to the d class:

$$S(d|a) = \frac{exp(\sum_{x=1}^{R} u_x \cdot f_x(d,a))}{\sum_{d' \in D} exp(\sum_{x=1}^{R} u_x \cdot f_x(d',a))}$$

The maximum feature limits in disease relation get by argument, $\hat{u} = argmax_u \sum_b logS(b^y|a^y)$

The max marginal features limits to find the optimal model parameters that maximize the likelihood of heart disease data and provides a reliable classification to predict the presence of heart disease based on input features.

3.3. Support vector quantization algorithm (SVQA)

Utilizing the Support Vector Quantization Algorithm (SVQA), we will identify and select key features that significantly contribute to the disease's manifestation. Through this process, we aim to reduce unnecessary data dimensions – specifically those related to non-scaling features thereby streamlining the dataset for more efficient processing. The support vector machine model is analyzed to optimize the minimum distance between two data points and determine the separating hyperplane. Furthermore, SVM techniques can be applied to analyze various data sets using different kernel functions, including radial deviation and linear functions. In binary classification, SVM can identify the maximum marginal hyperplane of training set samples through structural risk reduction analysis.

Calculate the maximum function margin of the average vector of the result hyperplane as shown in equation 1. Let's assume G-margin, Arg_{min}–minimum argument, f-decision hyperplane, z-normal vector, j-bias vector, u-values, a-data point.

$$G = S(d|a) \rightarrow \underset{uef}{Argmin\, d(u)}$$

Calculate the number of samples in the feature space of the binary output feature vector of the training set dimension, as shown in equation.

$$G = \underset{uef}{Argmin} \frac{|u.z+j|}{\sqrt{\sum_{a=1}^{f} z_a^2}}$$

The classification function of SVM computes the sample's bias vector and the weight vector, as indicated in equation. Let's assume u_a–input feature vector, $u_a\{-1, +1\}$–binary output, m-number of samples in feature space, P^h–dimensional real space, z-weight vector, b-bias, Kq–training set.

$$K_q = \{(u_1,v_1),...,(u_g,v_h)\} \in (P^h \times \{-1,+1\})^h$$
$$u_a \in ([u_a]_1,[u_a]_2,...,[u_a]_h)^{Kq}$$

$$d(u) = z^{kq}.u + j$$

$$d(u) = \begin{cases} z^{kq}.u_a + j \geq -1\, u_a \\ z^{kq}.u_a + j \leq +1\, u_a \end{cases}$$

The computation for solving the quadratic optimization problem using a rough edge SVM model is illustrated in equation 2. Maximizing the margin between two classes determines the distance between two hyperplanes, leading to the optimal hyperplane prediction. Let's assume G-minimum value, d-feature, T-Kernal function, $\|z\|$–hyperplane optimization.

$$\begin{cases} G(in\ z, j) & \frac{1}{2}\|z\| \\ \text{Subject to: } v_a(\langle z.u_a\rangle + j) & \text{for } a = 1,2,...,g \end{cases}$$

Above Equations demonstrate that the Lagrange multiplier for the binomial optimization problem is determined by analyzing the linear classifier in the binomial problem using the SVM model.

$$\underset{d.\xi_a}{G}\|d\|_T^2 + e\sum_{a=1}^{k}\xi_a$$
$$v_a d(u_a) \geq 1 - \xi_a \quad \text{for a } \xi_a \geq 0$$

Where Ma – maximim value, O-lagrange, e- Regularization parameter, a-slack variable, u_a. v_b –represent measurement.

$$\text{Ma } O(\alpha) = \sum_{a=1}^{g}\alpha_a - \frac{1}{2}\sum_{b=1}^{g}\sum_{a=1}^{g}v_a v_b \alpha_a \alpha_b T(u_a.v_b)$$
$$\text{subject to: } \sum_{a=1}^{g}v_b\alpha_a = 0, 0 \leq \alpha_b \leq e, 1 \leq a \leq g$$

$$\underset{i_a}{G}\sum_{a=1}^{1}i_a - \frac{1}{2}\sum_{a=1}^{1}\sum_{b=1}^{1}i_a i_b v_a v_b\, t(u_a u_b)\ 0 \leq i_a \leq e, \text{ for a; } \sum_{a=1}^{1}i_a v_a = 0$$

The quantization value in SVM represents estimating smooth edges using Lagrangian variables while ensuring the shortest distance between the data and the hyperplane within predetermined boundaries. Let's assume qT –shortest distance, T-distance.

$$G(0) = \tfrac{1}{2}z'z - \sum\lambda_T\left(\lambda_T(z'^{u_r}+j) + Q_T - 1\right) + i\sum Q_T \quad \text{for } 0 \leq i_a \leq e \text{ for all } i_a$$

Equation 11 depicts the kernel function and parameters for evaluating security and privacy functions through constructing the SVM model. Let's assume Q –security, d-security feature.

$$d_{(u,\alpha,j)} = \{\pm 1\} = Q\left(\sum_{a=1}^{g}y_a\alpha_a\, T(u, u_a) + j\right)$$

The SVM model chooses kernel functions and parameters to provide accurate results. For binary classification, especially in high-dimensional datasets, security and privacy aspects can be evaluated by constructing an SVM model. Therefore, optimal features can be achieved by selecting different feature subsets, estimating the impact rate of cardiovascular disease, and introducing a set of slack variables to assess heart disease data.

3.4. Classification using ResNet50-CNN

The heart of our system lies in the implementation of the ResNet50 Convolutional Neural Network (ResNet50-CNN). This advanced neural network architecture is renowned for its deep learning capabilities, particularly in image recognition tasks. The CNN is employed to forecast feature scaling while employing the softmax activation function for effective classification into normal and abnormal categories. This stage of the system is crucial as it directly impacts the predictive values like diastolic rate, systolic rate, C- reactive proteins, thalac rate, VLDl, HDL, ECG, PCsd features take from dataset. The CNN method is one of the most successful applications and mainly works with transform layers, pooling layers and fully connected layers. Also, common layers using different layers of activation functions can significantly reduce the network training time. In addition, it can improve the generalization ability of the network and help prevent the overfitting problem of dropout layers. CNN models are considered hierarchical models, and the raw data can be extracted through transformation layers. The pooling layer can repeat the convolution and pooling operations with the dimension-reduced data as input to the lower convolutional layer. In addition, the high-level semantic information of the original data can be gradually transferred from the lower layers to the final layer. An integrated model can calculate the difference between the actual and predicted values. The CNN model presented in these can also be obtained by updating the relevant parameters together with a backpropagation algorithm.

By intent Resnet dense unit convolution kernel and impulse of input features. Let's assume c and d- features, $c_{j-A+1,y-B+1}$ –input features, E and F-highest convolutional kernel, T-parameter data, T_{AB} – convolutional kernel, j and i-multiple channels, A and B- convolutional layer.

$$d_{ji} = d_{(u,\alpha,j)} \sum_{A=1}^{E}\sum_{B=1}^{F} T_{AB}\, c_{j-A+1,y-B+1}$$

Compute the convolution kernel involving multiple channels. Let's assume v-deviation, N- convolutional kernel size, $\mathbb{P}$-filling parameter, q-layer.

$$w^{j+1} = [w^q \oplus z^{q+1}](j,i) + v = \sum_{T=1}^{T_j}\sum_{C=1}^{N}\sum_{d=1}^{N}\left[w_T^q Z_T^{B+1}(c,d)\right] + v$$

$$Q_{q+1} = \frac{Q_1 + 2\mathbb{p} - f}{h_\circ} + 1$$

As described in Equation 37, estimate a function by assuming linear transformation in the fully connected function. Let's assume z-threshold weight.

$$\text{Process Resnet50 layer unit} \rightarrow d = z_c$$

Calculate the error between the predicted value and the actual value as shown in Equation

Let's assume M-Error, M_e –estimated value

$$M_e = soft\ ma\frac{\left|\sum_{j=1}^{F-1}(y_j - \Phi_j)^2\right|}{F-1}$$

Calculate the one-sample error rate as shown in Equation. Where M_x – error percentage

$$M_x = \frac{\Phi_j - y_j}{y_j} \times 100\%$$

Estimate the normalization process as shown in equation

$$y_j = \alpha\frac{y_j - y_{min} + \beta}{y_{max} - y_{min} + \beta}$$

To Compute the modified CNN model determines the values by coefficients. Let's assume v- back propagation, K-threshold, I-weight, M-error function, AJ − iteratively accuracy.

$$A_{(T+1)} = \bar{\omega}(T) - [I^k I + AJ]^{-1} I^k M$$

$$v_{(T+1)} = v(T) - [I^K I + AJ]^{-1} I^K M$$

Equation is shown to evaluate the objective function to improve the output feature margin cognitive outcomes. Let's assume (w) − obtained identification, M-error value, q-connection layer.

$$N_{(w)} = \frac{1}{1+M^q}$$

In this category, feature relevance margin leverages objective functions to accomplish actual margin of disease class with CNN, Pooling Layers, and fully connected layers to proceeds to predict the output class.

4. Experiment Evaluation

The efficacy of our proposed system will be measured through various performance metrics, such as recall and precision rates. We anticipate higher recall and precision compared to existing systems, owing to the significant reduction of false positives through our enhanced feature selection methods. This improvement will be crucial in informing clinicians and guiding patient treatment strategies, thereby reducing the risks associated with heart disease. The proposed system demonstrates improved performance compared to other existing systems. The results show higher accuracy in precision, recall, F1 measure, and lower error rate in detecting premature effects. Additionally, this implementation reduces time complexity, making it a viable solution for real-time applications (Table 18.1).

The SVQA-RCNN method's performance is tested in terms of precision accuracy by varying amounts of samples to validate the test results. Figure 18.2 explains the precision Analysis rate. The effectiveness of each class's tactics is evaluated and contrasted with the outcomes of proposed system is 94.2% compared to the other system. This increase the actual true positive rate and improve the prediction performance.

In Figure 18.3, explains the performance of the recall rate by validating false positives rate which the proposed

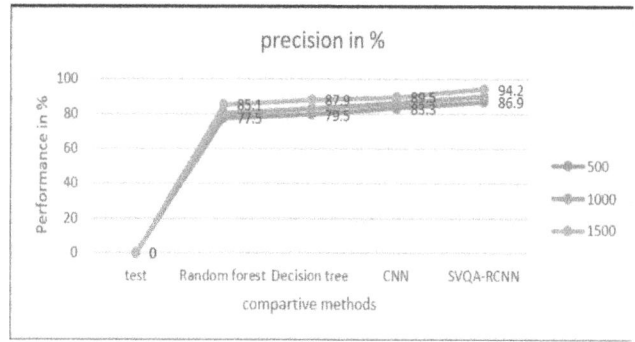

Figure 18.2. Analysis in precision rate.

Source: Author.

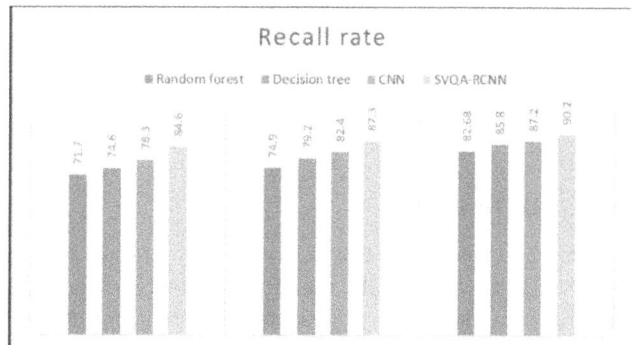

Figure 18.3. Analysis of recall rate.

Source: Author.

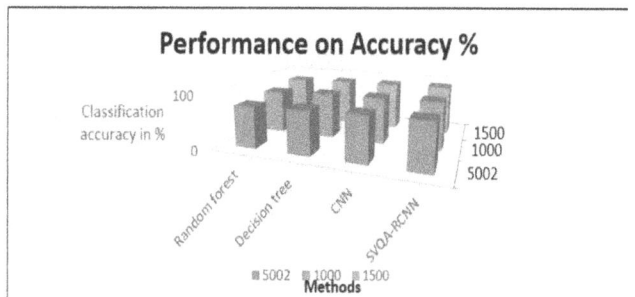

Figure 18.4. Analysis on classification accuracy.

Source: Author.

SVQA-RCNN system attains 90.2% high and compared with different approaches to produce best performance than other methods. The result gained by accrual margins are relatively select by heart disease related features to improve the prediction accuracy.

In Figure 18.4, we measure and compare the performance of classification accuracy. The classification accuracy of SVQA-RCNN method is 91.66% which is higher than other methods.

Numerous methods exist for measuring time complexity performance. Figure 18.5 shows the Analysis of Time Complexity Comparing the suggested SVQA-RCNN algorithm

Table 18.1. Performance analysis in precision rate

	Validation attained in precision rate %		
Methods/data's	500	1000	1500
Random forest	77.5	80.3	85.1
Decision tree	79.5	82.7	87.9
CNN	83.3	86.1	89.5
SVQA-RCNN	86.9	89.7	94.2

Source: Author.

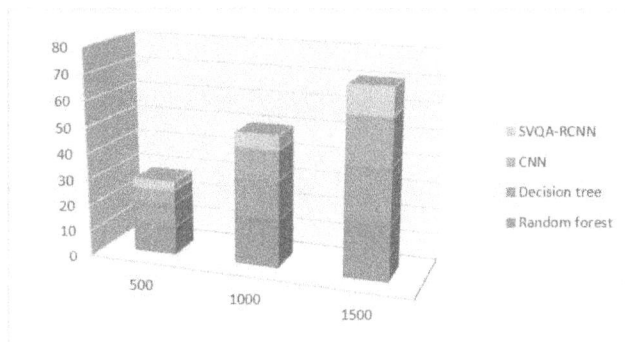

Figure 18.5. Analysis of time complexity.

Source: Author.

to other straightforward Bayesian, RF, and CNN techniques, time complexity is decreased. Compared to other approaches, SVQA-RCNN has a time complexity of 10.5 seconds, which is lower.

5. Conclusion

In summary, the proposed system leverages a robust framework that integrates SVQFS with ResNet50-CNN to address the prevalent challenges in heart disease prediction arising from heart disease. By focusing on accurate preprocessing by min max normalization, impactful feature selection support vector machine, and sophisticated classification of deep CNN techniques, our approach aims to improve the overall detection and segmentation accuracy. The anticipated SVQA-RCNN outcomes of this system improves the higher detection rate up to 95.2% precision 94.6%, as well in significant reduction in false positive rates, enhancing the reliability of cardiovascular disease assessments. Ultimately, as heart disease continues to pose a formidable health threat, innovations such as this proposed system represent critical steps toward harnessing technology in the pursuit of improved patient outcomes. Through continual refinement to adapt to emerging data trends, our system has the potential to make a meaningful impact in the realm of cardiovascular health.

References

[1] I. T. Joseph S, V. S, M. M, P. L. Jancy and K. P. A. (2022). ML & DL Methodologies in Heart Disease Prediction: Brief Analysis. *2022 8th International Conference on Advanced Computing and Communication Systems (ICACCS)*. Coimbatore, India, pp. 208–212, doi: 10.1109/ICACCS54159.2022.9785241

[2] Cheon, S., Kim, J., & Lim, J. (2019). The use of deep learning to predict heart disease patient mortality. *International Journal of Environmental Research and Public Health, 16*(11), 1876.

[3] K M, M. R, S. F. F and M. R. B. (2023). Cardiovascular Heart disease Prediction System using Machine Learning Techniques. *2023 Sth International Conference on*

Advanced Computing and Communication Systems (ICACCS), Coimbatore, India, pp. 89–93, doi: 10.1109/ICACCS57279.2023.10112727.

[4] Das, M. C., *et al.* (2023). A comparative study of machine learning approaches for heart heart disease prediction. *2023 International Conference on Smart Applications, Communications and Networking (SmartNets)*, Istanbul, Turkiye, pp. 1–6, doi: 10.1109/SmartNets58706.2023.10216049.

[5] Haque, E., Paul, M., Uddin. S., Tohidi, F., & Khanom, A. (2023). Analysis and Prediction of Heart Heart disease Using Lstm Deep Learning Approach. *2023 International Conference on Digital Image Computing: Techniques and Applications (DICTA)*. Port Macquarie, Australia, pp. 340–347, doi: 10.1109/DICTA60407.2023.00054.

[6] Chaitrali, D. S., & Sulabha, A. S. (2012). A Data Mining Approach for Prediction of Heart Disease Using Neural Networks. *International Journal of Computer Engineering and Technology, 3*, 30–40.

[7] Ren, W., Di. B., & Shuqi, W. (2019). Application of decision tree algorithm in heart disease risk classification prediction [J]. *Chinese Rehabilitation Medicine, 28*(3), 233–236.

[8] Qianli, Z. (2019). Application of artificial intelligence in the prediction of atrial fibrillation in heart disease patients [J]. *Hospital Management Forum, 36*(7), 30–33.

[9] Kumar, M. N., Koushik, K. V. S., & Deepak, K. (2018). Prediction of Heart Diseases Using Data Mining and Machine Learning Algorithms and Tools. *International Journal of Scientific Research in Computer Science Engineering and Information Technology, 3*(3), 887.

[10] Sachdeva, S., Bhatia, T., & Verma, A. K. (2018). GI S-based evolutionary optimized Gradient Boosted Decision Trees for forestfire susceptibility mapping [J]. *Natural Hazards*, 1–20.

[11] Mohan, S., Thirumalai, C., & Srivastava, G. (2019). Effective Heart Disease Prediction Using Hybrid Machine Learning Techniques. *IEEE Access, 7*, 81542–81554.

[12] Patil, P. B., Reddy, V. B. (2022). Prediction of Cardiovascular Diseases by Integrating Electrocardiogram (ECG) and Phonocardiogram (PCG) Multi-Modal Features using Hidden Semi Morkov Model. *International Journal on Recent and Innovation Trends in Computing and Communication, 10*(10), 32–44.

[13] Ozaki, T., Kitazume, K., Nishimura, K., & Morioka, T. (2020). Examination of risk assessment method based on emergency transportation record of heat heart disease. *Journal of Japan Society of Civil Engineers Ser. G (Environmental Research), 76*(5), 451–459.

[14] Xu, Y.-Y., Yen, P.-S., Lin, Y.-H., Lai, C. -Y., Chen, Y.-C., & Liu, C.-K. (2023). Machine Learning-Based Outcome Prediction of Acute Ischemic Heart disease After Endovascular Treatment. *2023 IEEE/ACIS 8th International Conference on Big Data, Cloud Computing, and Data Science (BCD)*. Hochimin City, Vietnam, pp. 374–377, doi: 10.1109/BCD57833.2023.10466305.

[15] Govindarajan, P. Ravichandran, K. S., Sundararajan, S., & Sreeja, S. (2017). Impact of modifiable and non-modifiable risk factors on the prediction of heart disease disease. *2017 International Conference on Trends in Electronics and Informatics (ICEI)*. Tirunelveli, India, pp. 985–989, doi: 10.1109/ICOEI.2017.8300855.

[16] Zhang, H., & Lin, F. (2023). On Early Prediction and Diagnosis of Heart Disease Based on Random Forest Algorithm. *2023 4th International Conference on Computer, Big Data and Artificial Intelligence (ICCBD+AI)*. Guiyang, China, pp. 519–523, doi: 10.1109/ICCBD-AI62252.2023.00095.

[17] Gnanavel, V. K., Sukanya, R., Mercy, H., Jayalakshmi, P., & Veeramalai, S. (2022). GUI Base Prediction of Heart Heart disease Stages by Finding the Accuracy using Machine Learning Algorithm. *2022 International Conference on Data Science, Agents & Artificial Intelligence (ICDSAAI)*. Chennai, India, pp. 1–5, doi: 10.1109/ICDSAAI55433.2022.10028815.

[18] Saputra, R. M. D., Chairul, Y., Riana, D., Hewiz, A. S., & Aziz, F. (2023). Heart disease Prediction Based on Random Forest with SMOTE. *2023 International Conference on Information Technology Research and Innovation (ICITRI)*. Jakarta, Indonesia, 17–21, doi: 10.1109/ICITRI59340.2023.10249261.

[19] Riz Kifli, N., Hidayat, H., Rahmawati, F., Putri Sukoco, Rahma Yuniarti, A., & Rizal, S. (2022). Brain Heart disease Classification using One Dimensional Convolutional Neural Network. *2022 IEEE Asia Pacific Conference on Wireless and Mobile (APWiMob)*. Bandung, Indonesia, pp. 1–6, doi: 10.1109/APWiMob56856.2022.10014207.

[20] Deepthi, T. N., Sharmila, S., Swarna, M., Gouthami, M., & Akshaya, C. L. (2023). Prediction of Brain Heart disease in Human Beings using Machine Learning. *2023 Second International Conference on Electronics and Renewable Systems (ICEARS)*. Tuticorin, India, pp. 1314–1320, doi: 10.1109/ICEARS56392.2023.10085128.

19 TinyML-powered pothole detection on edge devices: Optimizing speed, memory, and accuracy

Ramalingam H. M.[a], Avinash N. J., Vinayambika S. Bhat, Deepthi Shetty, and Deepthi Kotian

Department of Electronics & Communication Engineering, Mangalore Institute of Technology and Engineering, Moodabidri, Mangaluru, Karnataka, India

Abstract: In this research study, we explore and compare the effectiveness of three cutting-edge machine learning models in detecting potholes: FOMO MobileNetV2 0.1, YOLOv5, and MobileNetV2 SSD FPN-Lite. Our analysis centres on crucial metrics such as inference time, flash usage, peak RAM usage, and F1 score. We employ a comprehensive dataset annotated with images of potholes for both training and testing phases. The experiments are carried out utilizing well-known deep learning frameworks and GPU acceleration to ensure efficient model training. Through our findings, we aim to give valuable insights into the trade-offs between speed, memory consumption, and detection accuracy inherent in each model. This research endeavours to assist decision-makers and industry practitioners in selecting the appropriate model for practical pothole detection applications.

Keywords: TinyML, edge-computing, Fomo MobileNet v2, YOLOv5, pothole detection

1. Introduction

Widespread road damage, particularly from potholes, significantly affects road safety and necessitates frequent maintenance. These issues result in vehicle damage, contribute to accidents, and degrade road quality over time.

Manual pothole inspections are time-consuming, subjective, and inefficient for big road networks. Recent advances in computer vision (CV) promise automatic pothole identification. CV methods can quickly and correctly spot potholes in road pictures or films. This allows preventive maintenance, lowers repair costs, and increases road safety.

This study compares three machine learning models for pothole detection: FOMO (Faster Objects, More Objects) MobileNetV2 0.1, YOLOv5, and MobileNetV2 SSD FPN-Lite. These models are chosen for real-time deployment on low-resource devices.

We trained these models on a dataset of pothole images and assess them based on essential metrics for practical applications, including - Inference Time, Flash Usage, Peak RAM Usage, F1 Score: A metric combining precision and recall, providing a balanced measure of the model's ability to accurately detect potholes.

Through a comprehensive analysis of these metrics, we aim to offer valuable insights as discussed [1] into the suitability of these models for real-world pothole detection scenarios. This research contributes significant findings for selecting the most appropriate model for real-world deployment based on specific hardware and performance requirements.

2. MobileNetV2 SSD FPN-Lite

MobileNetV2 SSD FPN-Lite stands out as a powerful convolutional neural network architecture designed specifically for efficient and accurate object detection tasks, with a particular emphasis on detecting potholes in road images. This model incorporates several key components as discussed in [2] to achieve strong performance while maintaining computational efficiency.

2.1. Utilizing pre-trained models (Optional)

The model can be fine-tuned on a pothole detection dataset, although pre-trained models like MobileNetV2 SSD FPN-Lite have advantages. Pre-trained models, like those trained on COCO 2017, provide a solid basis for feature extraction, allowing future training on pothole-specific data to improve pothole detection [3].

2.2. Key components: MobileNetV2, SSD, and FPN-Lite

2.2.1. MobileNetV2

It serves as the backbone network, offering a lightweight convolutional neural network optimized for mobile and embedded devices [4, 5]. It excels at feature extraction, capturing intricate details while minimizing computational complexity.

[a]hmr4ever@gmail.com

DOI: 10.1201/9781003724988-19

2.2.2. Single shot detector (SSD)

It conducts object detection in a single pass through the network, unlike multi-stage detection methods [4]. By analysing feature maps at multiple scales, SSD predicts bounding boxes and class probabilities.

2.2.3. Feature pyramid network lite (FPN-Lite)

This addresses the difficulty of multi-scale object detection by integrating feature maps from different layers of MobileNetV2. This fusion generates a comprehensive feature representation that includes information from multiple scales, allowing pothole identification at varying sizes.

2.3. Detection process

Pre-processing involves resizing the input pothole image to the required input size for the model, typically 320×320 pixels.

2.3.1. Feature extraction

MobileNetV2 analyses the image, extracting features at multiple levels of abstraction.

2.3.2. FPN-Lite feature fusion

FPN-Lite combines the extracted feature maps from different MobileNetV2 layers, enriching the feature representation with multi-scale information.

2.3.3. SSD detection

The fused features are inputted into the SSD framework, where object detection occurs. SSD predicts bounding boxes and assigns probability scores, indicating the likelihood of each box containing a pothole.

2.4. Benefits for pothole detection

Efficiency: MobileNetV2's lightweight architecture offers fast inference and cheap computing resource utilization for real-time pothole identification.

Multi-Scale Detection: FPN-Lite's feature fusion approach improves its capacity to recognise potholes of different sizes in an image.

3. YOLOV5

YOLOv5 (You Only Look Once, version 5) stands out as another attractive option for detecting potholes in road imagery, offering a blend of accuracy and real-time performance suitable for diverse deployment scenarios.

3.1. Core architecture

Similar to the SSD in MobileNetV2 SSD FPN-Lite, YOLOv5 employs a single-stage detection approach [4]. This means that the model predicts bounding boxes and class probabilities for objects.

3.2. Overall architecture

The input layer processes the image before sending it to the backbone for feature extraction.

The backbone retrieves feature maps of different sizes, which the feature fusion network fuses to create three feature maps (P3, P4, and P5 in YOLOv5) for recognizing tiny, medium, and big items in the image [7].

Using pre-set prior anchors, the prediction head calculates confidence and bounding-box regression for each pixel in the feature map, producing a multidimensional array with object class, class confidence, box coordinates, width, and height.

3.3. Backbone network flexibility

YOLOv5's backbone network selection is more flexible than MobileNetV2 SSD FPN-Lite's. This contains YOLOv5s for speed and efficiency, YOLOv5m for balance, YOLOv5l for accuracy, and YOLOv5x for top-tier accuracy on big datasets. YOLOv5s is preferred for real-time performance on resource-constrained devices and YOLOv5l or YOLOv5x for accuracy-focused applications [7, 11].

3.4. Benefits for pothole detection

Efficiency: YOLOv5 provides real-time processing capabilities, particularly with lightweight backbone networks like YOLOv5s [12].

Accuracy: Depending on the chosen backbone network, YOLOv5 can achieve high accuracy in pothole detection.

Flexibility: The ability to select the backbone network enables customization to specific resource constraints and accuracy needs.

4. FOMO (Faster Objects, More Objects)

FOMO (Faster Objects, More Objects) represents a significant advancement in object detection, especially for environments with limited resources, by harnessing the efficiency of MobileNetV2 0.1. Here's an in-depth look at FOMO's functionality and unique attributes:

4.1. Core architecture

Single-stage Detection: FOMO adopts a single-stage detection method similar to SSD [6], accurately predicting bounding boxes and class probabilities in a single pass through the network.

Custom Loss Function: Departing from conventional bounding boxes, FOMO utilizes a specialized loss function to generate per-region class probability maps [14].

4.2. Understanding heatmaps and centroids

Heatmaps: Heatmaps serve as visual representations indicating the likelihood of object presence at each pixel in an image.

FOMO leverages heatmaps to precisely identify object locations, with heightened intensity indicating a higher probability of object presence.

Training on Centroids: Unlike conventional methods reliant on bounding boxes, FOMO simplifies object counting by training on centroids. Each activation in the heatmap denotes an object, simplifying precise object counting, especially for closely situated objects.

4.3. Efficiency and flexibility

Fully Convolutional: FOMO operates as a fully convolutional model, offering adaptability in input size and efficient handling of various image resolutions. This flexibility enables seamless operation across a spectrum of hardware platforms, spanning from microcontrollers to GPUs.

Model Compatibility: Compatible with any Mobile-NetV2 model, FOMO facilitates straightforward integration and transfer learning[8]. Users have the freedom to select models based on their resource constraints and accuracy requirements, ensuring optimal performance.

4.4. Performance and minimum requirements

Memory Footprint: FOMO's memory usage varies based on image size and hardware specifications. While it can function with minimal memory, such as 200KB for 64×64 pixel images, enhanced performance is achievable with at least 512KB.

Latency: FOMO's processing speed is influenced by the hardware's speed. For example, on an 80MHz MCU, FOMO can process a 64×64 pixel image in under one second, with frame throughput increasing notably at higher speeds or with tensor acceleration.

4.5. Benefits of FOMO (MobileNetV2 0.1)

Efficiency: FOMO, coupled with MobileNetV2 0.1, demonstrates exceptional efficiency in processing power and memory usage. This facilitates real-time object detection on devices with constrained resources.

Precise Object Localization: Through the utilization of heatmaps and centroids, FOMO delivers precise object localization, proving advantageous in scenarios prioritizing accurate location and counting of objects over their size.

Flexibility: With customizable heatmap resolutions and broad model compatibility, FOMO adapts effortlessly to specific application requirements, achieving a harmonious balance between processing speed and object detection accuracy.

5. Utilizing Edge Impulse for Embedded Machine Learning

In this research, we leverage Edge Impulse, an advanced platform crafted for training and deploying embedded machine learning models tailored specifically for edge devices [15]. Edge Impulse offers a rich array of tools and functionalities meticulously designed to streamline the process of developing machine learning models suitable for resource-constrained environments (Figure 19.1).

5.1. Key features of edge impulse

5.1.1. Data collection and preparation

Edge Impulse simplifies the intricacies of data collection by furnishing intuitive interfaces for tasks such as uploading, labelling, and augmenting datasets [9] explains how this facilitates users in seamlessly organizing and pre-processing their data, ensuring it is primed for optimal model training.

5.1.2. Model training and optimization

The platform accommodates diverse machine learning algorithms and architectures, empowering researchers to explore various models to pinpoint the most fitting one for their specific application [17]. Moreover, it integrates automated model optimization techniques aimed at augmenting model performance and efficiency.

5.1.3. Deployment to edge devices

Following the completion of model training, Edge Impulse expedites the deployment process to edge devices, spanning microcontrollers, FPGAs, and embedded systems [10]. The platform generates meticulously optimized inference code compatible with an extensive array of hardware platforms, guaranteeing effortless integration into real-world applications.

5.2. Advantages of employing edge impulse

5.2.1. Ease of use

Edge Impulse boasts a user-centric interface and workflow, rendering it accessible to both seasoned machine learning

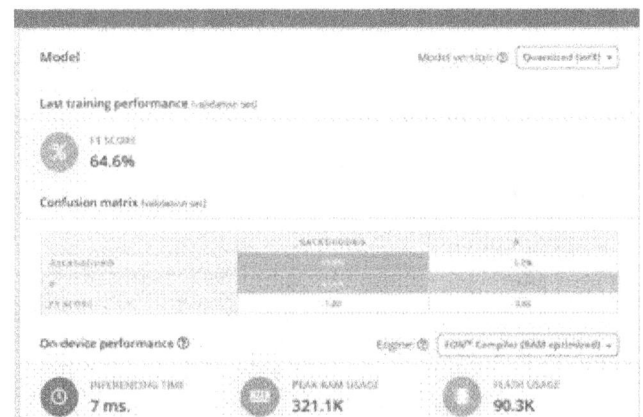

Figure 19.1. Model performance in edge impulse.

Source: Author.

practitioners and novices venturing into the field. Its intuitive design empowers researchers to concentrate on model development without grappling with convoluted toolchains.

5.2.2. Scalability and efficiency

By harnessing the potency of edge computing, Edge Impulse facilitates efficient model execution directly on edge devices, thereby curtailing latency and minimizing dependence on cloud-based processing. This scalability enables the deployment of machine learning applications even in remote or disconnected environments where internet connectivity is scant.

5.2.3. Community support and collaboration

Edge Impulse nurtures a dynamic community comprising developers, researchers, and enthusiasts, fostering an environment conducive to collaboration, knowledge exchange, and mutual assistance. Users benefit from a plethora of resources including documentation, tutorials, and forums, which expedite their learning and development trajectory.

6. Results and Discussion

6.1. FOMO MobileNetV2 0.1

FOMO MobileNetV2 0.1 displays outstanding efficiency, with an inference time of under 5 milliseconds, making it very well-suited for real-time applications, especially on microcontrollers with low computing resources. Its peak RAM utilization is only 291.3 KB, emphasizing its low memory footprint and reaffirming its potential for deployment on devices with restricted memory resources. Additionally, the model consumes just 76.6 KB for storing class information, showing its fast handling of object identification duties while retaining a lightweight profile. Overall, the results underline FOMO MobileNetV2 0.1's merits as a quick, compact, and resource-efficient model built for contexts where both processing power and memory are at a premium.

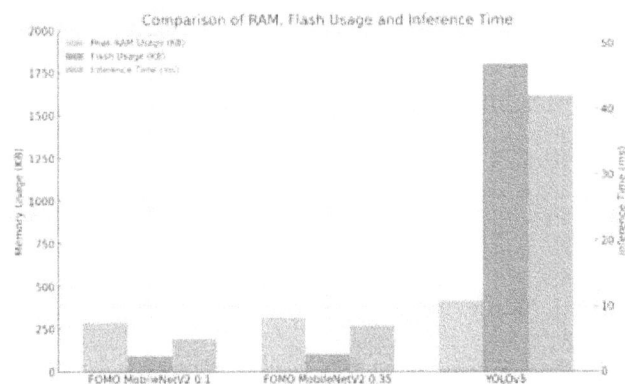

Figure 19.2. Resource utilization comparison.

Source: Author.

6.2. FOMO MobileNetV2 0.35

With an inference time of 7 milliseconds, FOMO Mobile-NetV2 0.35 provides effective image processing at a reasonable peak RAM usage of 321.1 KB. Its 90.3 KB flash memory utilization highlights its tiny design and qualifies it for deployment on devices with constrained storage. The model uses the EON™ Compiler to maximise RAM consumption, and it is set up with a learning rate of 0.001, a validation set size of 20 samples, and a batch size of 12. FOMO MobileNetV2 0.35 offers the possibility of increased accuracy while having a longer inference time and a marginally higher memory need than the 0.1 version. Users can modify the model to fit the particular requirements and limitations of their application thanks to this well-balanced trade-off between speed, memory efficiency, and accuracy.

6.3. YOLOV5

The object detection model was trained using photos with a special setup suited for distribution on resource-constrained devices. The training process was carried out on a CPU, and the model was implemented in a quantized manner to maximise efficiency. The version utilized, YOLOv5 Nano with 1.9 million parameters, occupies 3.87 MB in size and underwent 36 training cycles. A validation set comprising 20 samples was employed to monitor performance throughout training. On-device performance, measured using EON Compiler hardware, produced an inference time of 42 milliseconds, peak RAM utilization of 414.8 KB, and flash memory usage of 1.8 MB. Among the three models tested, FOMO MobileNetV2 0.1 stands out with an incredibly rapid inference time of under 5 milliseconds and a minimum RAM footprint of 291.3 KB, making it particularly appropriate for real-time applications on microcontrollers and other low-power devices. FOMO MobileNetV2 0.35, while slightly more resource-intensive, offers increased accuracy, offering a flexible trade-off between speed, memory, and precision dependent on application needs. In comparison, YOLOv5 gives a well-rounded performance, blending precision with real-time capability, and remains a sturdy solution for efficient object identification across many use scenarios. These specs collectively define each model's architecture, training setup, and deployment capabilities, allowing developers choose the best suited alternative for their individual restrictions and requirements. Figure 19.2 displays the performance comparison of all the algorithms across three critical metrics: inference time, RAM utilization, and Flash memory usage. The results reveal that FOMO MobileNet V2 0.1 consistently beats the others, exhibiting the lowest inference time, minimal RAM consumption, and the most efficient Flash memory utilization.

Even with increased flash and RAM utilization, YOLOv5 Tiny provides a balanced speed, efficiency, and accuracy, thus being suitable for varied deployments. For pothole detection, the model was experimented with different batch

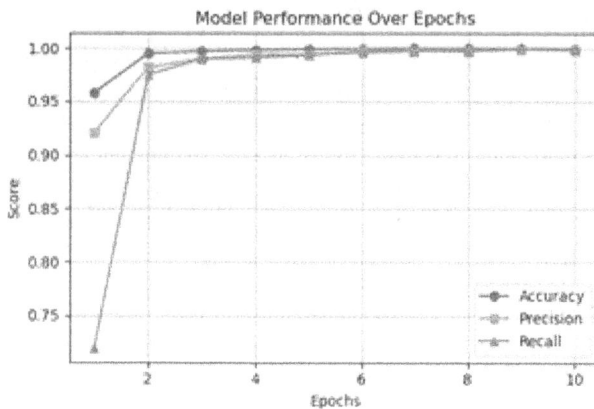

Figure 19.3. Performance comparison.

Source: Author.

sizes, learning rates, and epochs with regularization to prevent overfitting and performance checked using accuracy, precision, and recall.

The highly optimized YOLO V5 model achieves approximately 99% accuracy in pothole detection. Figure 19.3 illustrates the accuracy, precision and recall rates of the model when detecting potholes in a sample video with a frame rate of 30fps.As the number of training epochs increases, the model's accuracy, precision, and recall rates also improve.

7. Conclusion

In summary, FOMO MobileNetV2 0.1 excels in speed and efficiency, while FOMO MobileNetV2 0.35 potentially offers improved accuracy at the expense of speed and memory usage. YOLOv5 delivers a balanced performance that suits various deployment scenarios, including optimized use on devices with limited resources. The decision among these models should be based on specific application needs and priorities, such as speed, accuracy, and resource constraints. In our tests, the optimized YOLOv5 model demonstrated high accuracy and precision.

References

[1] Xu, K., Zhang, H., Li, Y., Zhang, Y., Lai, R., & Liu, Y. (2023). An ultra-low power tinyml system for real-time visual processing at edge. *IEEE Transactions on Circuits and Systems II: Express Briefs*, *70*(7), 2640–2644. doi: 10.1109/TCSII.2023.3239044.

[2] Chiu, Y. C., Tsai, C. Y., Ruan, M. D., Shen, G. Y., & Lee, T. T. (2020, August). Mobilenet-SSDv2: An improved object detection model for embedded systems. In *2020 International conference on system science and engineering (ICSSE)* (pp. 1–5). IEEE.

[3] Yik, Y. K., Alias, N. E., Yusof, Y., & Isaak, S. (2021, February). A real-time pothole detection based on deep learning approach. In *Journal of physics: Conference series* (Vol. 1828, No. 1, p. 012001). IOP Publishing.

[4] Gui, Y. (2024). Edge impulse-based convolutional neural network for Hand Posture Recognition. *Applied and Computational Engineering*, *40*, 115–119.

[5] Ramalingam, H. M., Ajay, Kotian, D., & Sequeira, E. (2024, February). A Comparison Study of Abnormal Human Activity Analysis. In *International Conference on Communications and Cyber Physical Engineering 2018* (pp. 509–515). Singapore: Springer Nature Singapore.

[6] Abhinu, C. G., Aswin, P., Krishnan, K., Baby, B., & Viji, K. A. (2021). Multiple object tracking using deep learning with YOLO V5. *International Journal of Engineering Research & Technology*, *9*(13), 47–51.

[7] Guo, Z., Wang, C., Yang, G., Huang, Z., & Li, G. (2022). Msft-yolo: Improved yolov5 based on transformer for detecting defects of steel surface. *Sensors*, *22*(9), 3467.

[8] Coşkun, D., Karaboğa, D., Baştürk, A., Akay, B., Nalbantoğlu, Ö. U., Doğan, S., & Karagöz, M. A. (2023). A comparative study of YOLO models and a transformer-based YOLOv5 model for mass detection in mammograms. *Turkish Journal of Electrical Engineering and Computer Sciences*, *31*(7), 1294–1313. doi: 10.55730/1300-0632.4048.

[9] Ramalingam, H. M., Fazil, M., Kottaimalai, R., Vishnuvarthanan, G., & Arunprasath, T. (2023, December). Edge-Driven Biometrics and Facial Recognition for Virtual Assistant. In *2023 International Conference on Energy, Materials and Communication Engineering (ICEMCE)* (pp. 1–7). IEEE.

[10] Da Silva, J., Flores, T., Júnior, S., & Silva, I. (2023, October). TinyML-Based pothole detection: A comparative analysis of YOLO and FOMO model performance. In *2023 IEEE Latin American conference on computational intelligence (LA-CCI)* (pp. 1–6). IEEE.

[11] R. H. M. Y. K. S. K. Sanathkumar S. J. (2023). A review on risk-based analysis using static and dynamic identifiers. *International Journal of Advanced Research in Computer and Communication Engineering*, *12*(6), 638–639.

[12] B. K. S B, G. S., M. Kishore, S. R., & A. D. J. (2023). Real-time Pothole Detection using YOLOv5 Algorithm: A Feasible Approach for Intelligent Transportation Systems. In *2023 Second International Conference on Electronics and Renewable Systems (ICEARS)*. IEEE, pp. 1678–1683.

[13] Dharani, A., Kumar, S. A., & Patil, P. N. (2024). Object detection at edge using TinyML models. *SN Computer Science*, *5*(1), 11. doi: 10.1007/s42979-023-02304-z.

[14] Asad, M. H., Khaliq, S., Yousaf, M. H., Ullah, M. O., & Ahmad, A. (2022). Pothole Detection Using Deep Learning: A Real-Time and AI-on-the-Edge Perspective. *Advances in Civil Engineering*, *2022*, 1–13. doi: 10.1155/2022/9221211.

[15] Bharat, R., Ikotun, A. M., Ezugwu, A. E., Abualigah, L., Shehab, M., & Zitar, R. A. (2023). A real-time automatic pothole detection system using convolution neural networks. *Applied and Computational Engineering*, *6*(1), 750–757.

[16] Hack Hong, S. (2021). Edge Impulse Machine Learning for Embedded System Design. *Embedded MEMS*, *9*(1).

[17] Silvister, S., Komandur, D., Kokate, S., Khochare, A., More, U., Musale, V., & Joshi, A. (2019, December). Deep learning approach to detect potholes in real-time using smartphone. In *2019 IEEE pune section international conference (PuneCon)* (pp. 1–4). IEEE. doi: 10.1109/PuneCon46936.2019.9105737.

[18] Srinivasagan, R., Mohammed, M., & Alzahrani, A. (2023). TinyML-Sensor for Shelf Life Estimation of Fresh Date Fruits. *Sensors*, *23*(16). doi: 10.3390/s23167081.

20 Brain tumour detection and segmentation in MRI images using CNN and U-Net techniques

Vani Vasudevan[a], Aditya Pandey[b], Archi Mehta[c], Mohd Naim Hussain[d], and Rachit Agarwal[e]

Computer Science and Engineering, Nitte Meenakshi Institute of Technology, Bangalore, India

Abstract: Accurate localization and characterization of brain tumours is critical for diagnosis and therapy, and successful image segmentation is necessary to separate tumour regions from medical scans. This study explores the usage of various techniques of the convolutional neural network (CNNs) for finding and localization of the brain tumour and segmentation. The study leverages the capabilities of CNN models to be trained on preprocessed medical images datasets such as scans of MRI images to achieve high segmentation accuracy. Also it combines the CNN and U-Net architectural models to outperform traditional segmentation techniques achieving superior accuracy and reliability thus helps in streamlining the diagnosis process.

Keywords: Brain tumour, CNN, MRI, U-Net, transformer, segmentation, localization

1. Introduction

An abnormal growth or mass of cells within or surrounding the brain is called a tumour. Both benign (non-cancerous) and malignant (cancerous) tumours can seriously impair the brain's ability to function normally by pressing on nearby tissues, raising intracranial pressure, and interfering with vital neurological functions. Accurate and timely finding of brain tumour is important for effective care and increase in patient outcomes.

The ability of magnetic resonance imaging (MRI) to produce an ultra-clear image of brain regions makes it a popular tool for localization and discovery. However, manually segmenting the brain from MRI scans is a laborious and intricate process that frequently varies from observer to observer. To get over these restrictions, brain segmentation has emerged as a crucial component of research to help with precise tumour detection and diagnosis, treatment planning, and prognosis. Recent advances in deep learning-driven medical image analysis have significantly improved the capacity for challenging tasks like tumour segmentation. The CNN, with their variants, including encoder-decoder models like U-Net, have proven effective in understanding hierarchical image features. Nevertheless, obstacles such as ongoing tumour growth, the need to integrate multiple variables, and the scarcity of textual data often limit the performance of these models. To work out with these problems, researchers have introduced innovative approaches, including attention mechanisms, multi-scale feature extraction, anisotropic convolutional strategies, and transformer-based models.

Successful image segmentation is important for separating tumour regions from medical scans, allowing for accurate localization and characterization of tumours in the brain, which is crucial for diagnosis and treatment. Through capitalizing on the advantages of these models, the suggested method is designed to work on the challenges in segmentation accuracy and computational efficiency. The framework is evaluated on benchmark datasets, demonstrating its clinical potential and effectiveness in surpassing existing methods. It also facilitates model comparison to determine the most efficient approach for accurate brain tumour detection.

2. Related Works

2.1. Background study

To highlight the importance of lightweight models in 3D medical imaging research, we introduce SegFormer3D. Unlike traditional approaches, SegFormer3D eliminates the need for complex decoders, instead utilizing an all-MLP decoder to efficiently combine local and universal attention features, resulting in highly precise segmentation masks [1]. Standard CNN architectures achieve a sufficiently large receptive field and capture semantic contextual information by gradually downsampling the feature-map grid. This approach allows features on the coarse spatial grid to represent tissue location and relationships on a global scale [2]. Cascaded CNNs simplify the complex task of multi-class segmentation by dividing it into three separate binary segmentation steps. This method leverages the hierarchical organization of tumour subregions to minimize the likelihood of false positives.

[a]vani.v@nmit.ac.in, [b]adipandey0709@gmail.com, [c]mehtaarchi8@gmail.com, [d]fahimnaim4@gmail.com, [e]anshulagarwal541@gmail.com,

DOI: 10.1201/9781003724988-20

Additionally, we introduce network architecture with anisotropic convolution to process 3D images, balancing receptive field, model complexity, and memory usage [3]. Our network architecture is based on the well-established U-Net, and it has been carefully modified to enhance brain tumour segmentation performance. Class imbalances are addressed by incorporating a Dice loss function, along with the application of extensive data augmentation techniques to reduce the risk of overfitting [4]. In response to the limitations of the Cascaded Model, we propose a multi- task learning approach that breaks down multi-class brain tumour segmentation into three separate yet interconnected tasks. Unlike traditional multi-class (MC) methods, which involve training individual networks for each task (illustrated in Figure 20.1(a)), our approach consolidates these tasks within a single model through the introduction of the One-pass Multi task Network (OM-Net) [5].

To improve segmentation results, this work develops an augmentation framework that integrates popular current segmentation techniques, including the enhanced EM (Expectation Maximization) and Fuzzy C-Means Clustering methods. The proposed framework is utilized for detecting brain tumours in 3D MRI scans acquired using Fluid-Attenuated Inversion Recovery (FLAIR) sequences. The proposed augmentation technique shows comparative performance against the enhanced Expectation- Maximization (EM), Fuzzy C-Means Clustering [6]. The Attention-Sharp-UNet model overcomes the limitations of the traditional U-Net model while enhancing segmentation performance without increasing computational complexity. Two key modifications to the U-Net architecture are introduced: a grid-based attention block and a sharp block. The attention mechanism, as described in Attention U-Net, is employed with a modified skip connection [7].

A new deep learning model, TransNUNet, has been created for tumour segmentation on brain MRI datasets. This model incorporates the CBAM attention mechanism into TransUNet and refines the loss function. Research indicates that TransNUNet achieves a higher Dice score compared to both U-Net and TransUNet, showcasing its potential for detection [8]. MRI images provide comprehensive insights into the internal structures of the brain, which is crucial for accurately locating tumours. Determining the exact tumour location plays a notable role in treatment, as it helps assess the tumour type and size. Imaging segmentation, a vital component in brain tumour detection, employs different imaging techniques to locate tumours within magnetic resonance images [9]. Preprocessing techniques enhance image quality by optimizing key parameters, which are essential for the success of subsequent processing steps. After preprocessing, the image is segmented into regions that share similar characteristics or properties [10].

In multi-modal image segmentation, preprocessing enhances both the learning efficiency of the model and the accuracy of the segmentation results. To address potential differences in multimodal data, the first step involves standardizing each image modality, ensuring numerical consistency by adjusting the mean and the standard deviation of the data [11]. This research aims to segment 3D medical images using 2D Convolutional Neural Network (CNN) architectures to reduce computational load and prevent resource exhaustion. The approach is divided into three phases: First, each 3D image is split along the depth axis. Then, the extracted slices are trained using UNet, a widely- used CNN architecture in biomedical image segmentation [12].

Several modifications to the traditional CNN architecture are introduced, including additional layers for improved feature extraction and spatial attention, addressing the challenges posed by the complex and subtle nature of brain tumour images in MRI scans. To assess the effectiveness of the proposed system, standard evaluation metrics such as accuracy, sensitivity, specificity, and F1 score will be utilized [13]. MRI scans involve multi-modal channels with varied contrasts, but high resolution and high contrast are essential as they provide more detailed information. Due to image acquisition challenges, such as projection and tomography, MRI brain image slices often have low quality, with low contrast and blurring around the boundaries, making tumour detection difficult. A major challenge for deep learning algorithms lies in precisely delineating tumour boundaries while extracting adequate information for accurate detection [14]. The U-Net baseline model consists of a downsampling contraction path and an upsampling expansion path. The downsampling path extracts features, captures content, and expands the receptive field to encode advanced features and background information, while the upsampling path focuses on precise tumour boundary detection and grayscale feature reconstruction [15]. An unbiased assessment of state-of-the-art deep learning methods for MRI image analysis is also included in the paper [16].

According to the results, integrating many deep learning techniques produces segmentation results that are more accurate than using just one technique. To predict the methylation state of the MGMT promoter, five different deep learning techniques were assessed for the second task [17]. Two deep learning architectures, 3D U-Net and Attention U-Net, were chosen as basis models and trained separately using suitable loss functions and optimization techniques. To avoid overfitting, regularization strategies like dropout and batch normalization were used [18]. U-Net is a CNN architecture that performs exceptionally well in tasks requiring pixel-level classification, where both input and output maintain image dimensions. This is crucial for detecting and classifying regions of irregularity in biomedical contexts [19]. Four steps make up the framework: pre-processing, feature reduction, feature extraction, and picture segmentation. MRI brain pictures are pre-processed by using a median filter, which substitutes the median of adjacent pixels for each pixel's value to reduce noise. Additionally, histogram equalization is used to improve image intensity (Table 20.1).

Table 20.1. Background study

Paper No	Model Name	Advantages	Limitations
[1]	SegFormer3D, Vision Transformer	Splits the image into patches	Translation Invariance
[2]	Attention Gate Model - U-Net	Automatically learn to focus on target structures without supervision	Training instability and problem of data dependency.
[3]	CNN Model	Segmentation accuracy reduces false positives.	Limits the usability and usefulness of prior information about shape and location.
[4]	Attention Gate Model - U-Net	Separate networks for segmenting low-grade and high-grade glioblastomas.	Sophisticated training data sampling strategy.
[5]	One-pass Multi-task Network (OM-Net)	Shared parameters to learn joint features, and task-specific parameters.	Limits the usability and usefulness of prior information about shape and location.

Source: Author.

The pictures are also transformed into binary format by means of global thresholding. The binary pictures are further subjected to skull stripping, which minimizes processing time for all the methods by removing the outer skull and surrounding components [20]. Because of the removal of high quality non-brain tissue from the pictures, skull stripping may increase the process's resilience [21].

Gap Analysis: Many models, such as SegFormer3D and Attention Gate U-Net, face training challenges due to large dataset requirements and instability, making them difficult to train effectively. This can be addressed through self learning or data augmentation techniques to enhance performance. Additionally, models like CNN Model struggle with tumour variability in size, shape, and localization, limiting their generalization and the accuracy of such models. A promising approach to address this challenge is the integration of hybrid models, combining CNN (for detection) and U-Net (for segmentation) for improved performance. Furthermore, since accurately determining tumour size and volume remains difficult, visualization using MATLAB can provide valuable insights, enhance analysis and diagnosis.

2.2. Proposed system

The proposed research's objective is to create a reliable method for dividing medical images into discrete areas for a diagnosis system that uses CNNs to detect brain tumours and segment them with high accuracy. This approach overcomes the limitations of manual techniques, which are laborious and prone to errors, and meets the urgent demand for accurate

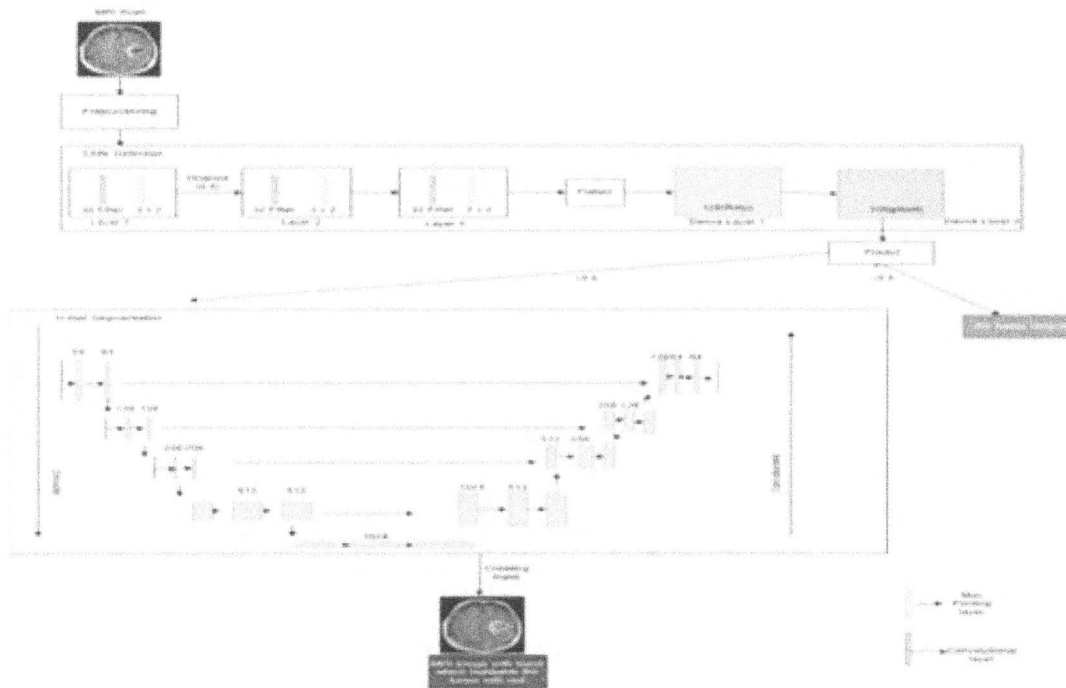

Figure 20.1. Architectural diagram.

Source: Author.

and automated analysis of tumours in medical imaging. The technology will precisely identify tumour boundaries and minor divisions from MRI scans by using CNN architectures like U-Net or DenseNet, guaranteeing sensitivity and specificity. The unique aspect of this research lies in the hybrid approach, where CNN is used for detection and U-Net for segmentation, significantly enhancing accuracy. The Figure 20.1 depicts the flow diagram of the hybridized model. For tumour visualization, MATLAB is used for tumour imaging, enabling more accurate examination of the 18 tumour segments. Additionally, these components are all combined into one system, which allows for segmentation and real-time detection via the application.

3. Methodology

3.1. Introduction

The primary target and aim of this study is to develop an efficient finding and localization of brain tumour system using CNN and U-Net architectures. The methodology outlines the step-by-step process followed to build, train, and evaluate the system. The hybrid use of neural networks (CNN) and U-Net allows accurate division and classification of brain tumour regions from images such as MRIs, facilitating early detection and diagnosis. The Figure 20.2(a) shows a MRI scans of benign tumour Figure 20.2(b) shows a MRI scans of Frontal Lobe Tumour located at the front of the brain. Figure 20.2(c) shows central brain tumour typically found near the thalamus or hypothalamus. Figure 20.2(d) shows Peripheral brain tumour typically found in areas like the cerebral cortex.

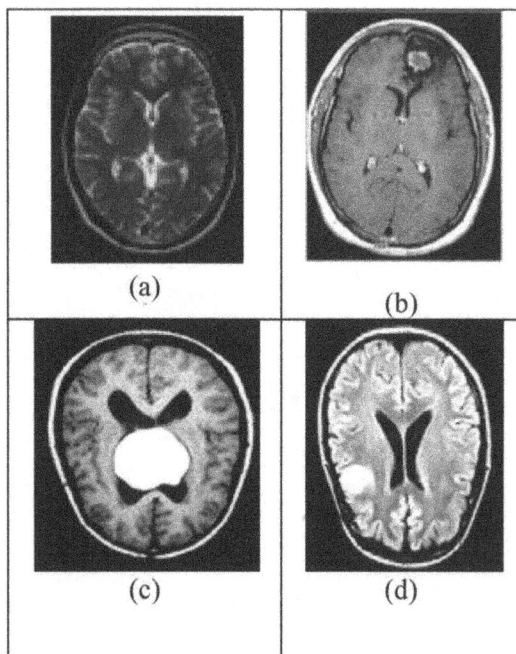

Figure 20.2. Illustrations of MRI Scans of benign and cancerous cases.

Source: Author.

3.2. Gathering and preparing data

3.2.1. Collecting data

Dataset Source: The dataset for this study was sourced from Sharif University of Technology, Tehran, Iran, and comprising MRI brain images. It includes 1,254 benign cases and 1,200 cancerous cases.

Data Format: JPG files are used for images.

Data Split: There are two main sets that are created training set and a testing set for the data set.

To increase the diversity of the dataset, data augmentation techniques such as flipping, rotation modifications are employed. Flipping is employed as a data augmentation technique to increase the size and diversity of the dataset.

3.2.2. Preprocessing data

Resizing, Grayscale and Normalization: For model compatibility, all MRI images are resized to a set size (e.g., 256 × 256). Scaling pixel values to a specific range (e.g., 0 to 1) to enhance model performance. Converting an image to shades of gray by removing colour information.

3.3. CNN for classifying tumours

3.3.1. The architecture of CNN

Input Layer: CNN receives the segmented images from U-Net as input.

Convolutional Layers: To extract spatial and feature data, a variety of convolutional algorithms are available.

Pooling Layers: The convolutional layer's output is simplified and further passed to the fully connected layer.

Fully Connected Layers: After being refined, the output from the convolutional layer is forwarded to the fully connected layer.

Output Layer: To determine whether a tumour is present, the softmax or sigmoid activation function is used.

3.3.2. Compilation of models

Adam optimizer: a faster convergence optimizer.

3.3.3. Training

Segmented outputs generated by the U-Net model serve as input for training the CNN. There are four batches.

- Time periods: 15–20.
- Callbacks: To prevent overfitting, techniques like early stopping implemented.

3.4. Testing and model evaluation

3.4.1. Measures of evaluation

For CNN's detection and U-Net's classification, the following metrics were used:

Accuracy: The proportion of photos that are correctly classified.

3.5. Model optimization and Hyperparameter tuning Hyperparameter tuning

Learning rate, batch size, number of epochs, dropout rates, and number of filters are tuned using grid search.

Learning rate scheduling is applied to improve convergence.

Regularization: Dropout is applied to prevent overfitting.

3.6. Deployment

Model Saving: The final model (U-Net for segmentation and CNN for classification) is saved as .h5 or. pb files.

Web Application: A user-friendly web-based interface is developed using React and SpringBoot for real-time tumour detection.

3.7. Results and analysis

Using CNN alone for detection yielded an accuracy of 93.05%, while the hybrid model combining CNN and U-Net achieved a significantly higher accuracy of 98.51%, demonstrating improved performance in both detection and segmentation.

3.8. Tools and libraries

- **Programming Language**: Python
- **Libraries**: TensorFlow, Keras, OpenCV, NumPy, Matplotlib, Scikit-learn, Albumentations
- **Development Environment**: Jupyter Notebook, Google Colab, MATLAB and local machine (with GPU support)

4. Experimental Results and Analysis

4.1. Experimental results

The MRI scan with the tumour presence is displayed in Figure 20.3(a). The tumour cells are marked in red in Figure 20.3(b), which illustrates the tumour's detection, the red colour shows the part where the tumour is cancerous. However, Figures 20.3(c) and (d) display the MRI image without a tumour as well as the detection algorithm's result, which shows that no tumour was found (Table 20.2).

5. Conclusion and Future Work

This research shows how CNN can use MRI data to efficiently identify and categorize brain cancers. The created technology provides a dependable option for early diagnosis and treatment planning by precisely recognizing cancers and classifying their severity. Furthermore, the development of a user-friendly and intuitive frontend application guarantees accessibility for medical experts, expediting the tumour diagnosis and stage classification process. The potential for developing effective, accurate, and user-friendly diagnostic

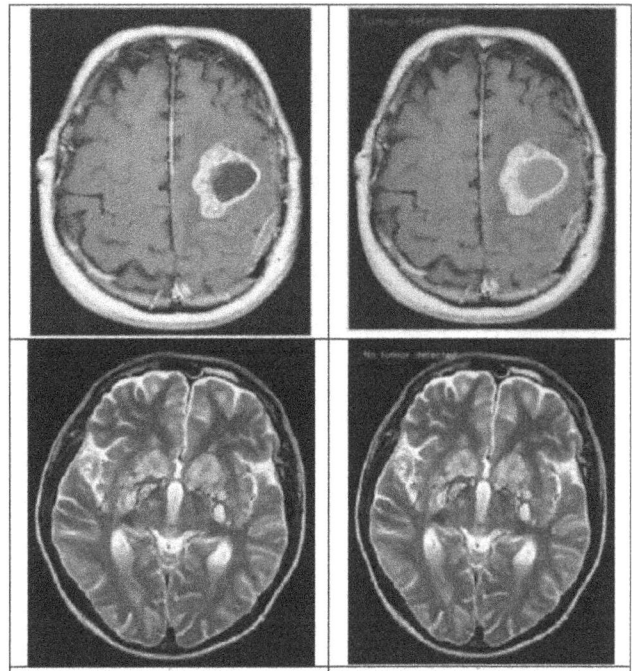

Figure 20.3. Illustrations of MRI Scan before and after detection of brain tumour.

Source: Author.

Table 20.2. Feature comparison of CNN and U-Net models

Aspect	CNN (Binary Classification)	U-Net(Segmentation)
Goal	Tumour/No Tumour Classification	Tumour Localization and Segmentation
Architecture	3 Conv2D, MaxPooling, Dropout, Flatten, Dense	U-Net with skip connections
Loss	Binary Cross entropy	Binary Cross entropy
Optimizer	learning rate= 1^e-4	learning rate= 1^e-4
Performance	Test Accuracy: 98.59%	Segmentation Mask is overlaid on image
Use Case	Decides if the U-Net should be triggered	Localizes tumour region

Source: Author.

systems that support clinical decision-making and improve patient outcomes is highlighted by this integration of cutting-edge deep learning algorithms with real-world application.

Accurately determining the dimensions of a tumour remains a challenge. However, MATLAB can be utilized to achieve precise measurements by preprocessing medical images, segmenting the tumour, applying morphological operations, and computing the area or 3D volume.

References

[1] Perera, S., Navard, P., & Yilmaz, A. (2024). SegFormer3D: an Efficient Transformer for 3D Medical Image Segmentation. *2024 IEEE/CVF Conference on Computer Vision and Pattern Recognition Workshops (CVPRW)*. Seattle, WA, USA, pp. 4981–4988. doi: 10.1109/CVPRW63382.2024.00503.

[2] Oktay, O., Schlemper, J., Folgoc, L. L., Lee, M., Heinrich, M., Misawa, K., & Rueckert, D. (2018). Attention u-net: Learning where to look for the pancreas. *arXiv preprint arXiv:1804.03999*.

[3] Wang, G., Li, W., Ourselin, S., & Vercauteren, T. (2018). Automatic brain tumor segmentation using cascaded anisotropic convolutional neural networks. Translational Imaging Group, CMIC, University College London, UK Wellcome/EPSRC Centre for Interventional and Surgical Sciences, UCL, London, UK. doi:arXiv:1709.00382.

[4] Isensee, F., Kickingereder, P., Wick, W., Bendszus, M., & Maier-Hein, K. H. (2018). Brain Tumor Segmentation and Radiomics Survival Prediction: Contribution to the BRATS 2017 Challenge. Division of Medical Image Computing, German Cancer Research Center (DKFZ), Heidelberg, Germany, Department of Neuroradiology, Heidelberg University Hospital, Heidelberg, Germany, Neurology Clinic, Heidelberg University Hospital, Heidelberg, Germany. doi: arXiv:1802.10508.

[5] Zhou, C., Ding, C., Wang, X., Lu, Z., & Tao, D. (2020). One-Pass Multi-Task Networks With Cross-Task Guided Attention for Brain Tumor Segmentation. *IEEE Transactions on Image Processing*, 29, 4516–4529. doi: 10.1109/TIP.2020.2973510.

[6] Jagan, A. (2018). A New Approach for Segmentation and Detection of Brain Tumor in 3D Brain MR Imaging. *2018 Second International Conference on Electronics, Communication and Aerospace Technology (ICECA)*. Coimbatore, India, pp. 1230–1235. doi: 10.1109/ICECA.2018.8474874.

[7] Goni, M. R., & Ruhaiyem, N. I. R. (2022). Salient feature extraction using Attention for Brain Tumor segmentation. *2022 IEEE International Conference on Computing (ICOCO)*. Kota Kinabalu, Malaysia, pp. 305–309. doi: 10.1109/ICOCO56118.2022.10031677.

[8] Wang, E., Hu, Y., Yang, X., & Tian, X. (2022). TransU-Net with Attention Mechanism for Brain Tumor Segmentation on MR Images. *2022 IEEE International Conference on Artificial Intelligence and Computer Applications (ICAICA)*. Dalian, China, pp. 573–577. doi: 10.1109/ICAICA54878.2022.9844551.

[9] Goswami, A., & Dixit, M. (2020). An Analysis of Image Segmentation Methods for Brain Tumour Detection on MRI Images. *2020 IEEE 9th International Conference on Communication Systems and Network Technologies (CSNT)*. Gwalior, India, pp. 318–322. doi: 10.1109/CSNT48778.2020.9115791.

[10] Sravan, V., Swaraja, K., Meenakshi, K., Kora, P., & Samson, M. (2020). Magnetic Resonance Images Based Brain Tumor Segmentation- A critical survey. *2020 4th International Conference on Trends in Electronics and Informatics (ICOEI) (48184)*. Tirunelveli, India, pp. 1063–1068. doi: 10.1109/ICOEI48184.2020.9143045.

[11] Han, S., Wang, Y., & Wang, Q. (2024). Multimodal Medical Image Segmentation Algorithm Based on Convolutional Neural Networks. *2024 Second International Conference on Networks, Multimedia and Information Technology (NMITCON)*, Bengaluru, India, pp. 1–5. doi: 10.1109/NMITCON62075.2024.10698930.

[12] Fatma, K., Benaissa, I., Zitouni, A., & Zinne-eddine, B. (2024). Assessing the Performance of U-Net in 3D Medical Image Segmentation. *2024 8th International Conference on Image and Signal Processing and their Applications (ISPA)*. Biskra, Algeria, pp. 1–6. doi: 10.1109/ISPA59904.2024.10536844.

[13] Nidhya, R., Kalpana, R., Smilarubavathy, G., & Keerthana, S. M. (2023). Brain Tumor Diagnosis with MCNN-Based MRI Image Analysis. *2023 1st International Conference on Optimization Techniques for Learning (ICOTL)*. Bengaluru, India, pp. 1–5. doi: 10.1109/ICOTL59758.2023.10435262.

[14] Soomro, T. A., Zheng, L., Afifi, A. J., Ali, A., Soomro, S., Yin, M., & Gao, J. (2023). Image segmentation for MR brain tumor detection using machine learning: a review. *IEEE Reviews in Biomedical Engineering*, 16, 70–90. doi: 10.1109/RBME.2022.3185292.

[15] Yang, T., & Song, J. (2018). An Automatic Brain Tumor Image Segmentation Method Based on the U-net. *2018 IEEE 4th International Conference on Computer and Communications (ICCC)*. Chengdu, China, pp. 1600–1604. doi: 10.1109/CompComm.2018.8780595.

[16] Saipogu, L., Reddy, A. S., & Malleswari, G. (2023). Identification of Brain Tumors in MR Images Using UNet CNN Model. *2023 7th International Conference on Electronics, Communication and Aerospace Technology (ICECA)*. Coimbatore, India, pp. 941–945. doi: 10.1109/ICECA58529.2023.10395702.

[17] Amor, F., Mzoughi, H., Njeh, I., & Slima, M. B. (2024). Review of MRI brain tumor segmentation and MGMT promoter classification methods on BraTs dataset based on Deep learning. *2024 IEEE 7th International Conference on Advanced Technologies, Signal and Image Processing (ATSIP)*. Sousse, Tunisia, pp. 249–254. doi: 10.1109/ATSIP62566.2024.10638990.

[18] Neyaz, Z., & Mittal, H. (2024). Integrating 3D U-Net and Attention U-Net for Brain Tumor Segmentation: Performance Evaluation on BRATS 2021 Dataset. *2024 15th International Conference on Computing Communication and Networking Technologies (ICCCNT)*. Kamand, India, pp. 1–6. doi: 10.1109/ICCCNT61001.2024.10724970.

[19] Maram, B., & Rana, P. (2021). Brain Tumour Detection on BraTS 2020 Using U-Net. *2021 9th International Conference on Reliability, Infocom Technologies and Optimization (Trends and Future Directions) (ICRITO)*. Noida, India, pp. 1–5. doi: 10.1109/ICRITO51393.2021.9596530.

[20] Abdel-Maksoud, E., Elmogy, M., & Al-Awadi, R. (2015). Brain tumor segmentation based on a hybrid clustering technique. *Egyptian Informatics Journal*, 16(1), 71–81.

[21] Fischmeister, F. P. S., Höllinger, I., Klinger, N., Geissler, A., Wurnig, M. C., Matt, E., & Beisteiner, R. (2013). The benefits of skull stripping in the normalization of clinical fMRI data. *NeuroImage: Clinical*, 3, 369–380.

21 Intelligent car damage assessment

Amarnath Bhattacharya[a] and Ratnakar Pandey[b]

REVA Academy for Corporate Excellence (RACE), Reva University, Bengaluru, India

Abstract: The automotive insurance industry has several challenges in a bid to assess car damage efficiently and accurately for insurance claims. Manual insurance assessment process is time-consuming causing inefficiencies that could adversely affect the insurers and policy holders on both sides. To counteract these inefficiencies, we put forth an intelligent dual model system consisting of an image object detection for a damaged car and language processing techniques to automate the insurance claim process. The system applies the YOLOv8 model for detecting and classifying the damage of cars from images and incorporates a Retrieval-Augmented Generation (RAG) model built on GPT-3.5 to analyse insurance documents and determine whether to file an insurance claim or pay for repairs from own pocket. The car damage detection model had excellent performance with a mean Average Precision (mAP) of 0.936 based on Intersection over Union (IoU) threshold of 0.50 on YOLOv8 model, while the RAG-based insurance decision model showed excellent recall of 1.0, guaranteeing in-depth document analysis. The system is described in full in this paper, including the implementation, resulting outcomes, and what may be a result for the insurance industry.

Keywords: Object detection, retrieval-augmented generation, car damage assessment

1. Introduction

The automotive insurance industry is faced with serious problems when it comes to calculating the value of the damage suffered by cars and deciding if an insurance claim is suitable or not, because for each claim IDV (Insurance Declared Value) of car falls. Traditional methods include manual inspection of damaged cars and a review of insurance policies, both of which are very laborious, time consuming and prone to human errors. With increased demand for claim settlements, there is a need for automated systems that will not only simplify the process of car damage inspection but also automate insurance claim related decision making. Recent developments in the field of Deep Learning (DL) and Natural Language Processing (NLP) provide encouraging practices for fixing these inefficiencies. Using the computer vision techniques for car damage detection and the NLP models for insurance document analysis, it is possible to develop an automatic system that completes both processes and therefore considerably decreasing the time and effort if it is undertaken by insurer and policy holder. The discipline of car damage detection has been gaining momentum especially after the emergence of deep learning models like YOLO (You Only Look Once) [1].

The latest iteration YOLOv8 has gained popularity from its ability to identify and classify different types of car damage through its real time object detection capabilities. Using both high precision and recall, YOLOv8 can spot a multitude of damages, from dents and scratches to broken components, and to do so in real time, thereby minimizing manual inspections [2]. On the other hand, Retrieval-Augmented Generation (RAG) has been completely revolutionized document analysis and decision-making task [8]. Combining the classical information retrieval methods and the methods of generative models such as GPT-3.5, deepseek-r1-distill-llama-70bk enable RAG models to retrieve relevant parts from complicated documents and to synthesize information into relevant insights. This technique is very helpful in insurance where policy documents are lengthy and complicated and need precise interpretation for decision.

This research work is sprinted on designing such an integrated system using YOLOv8 for car damage applications and RAG for insurance claims decisions. The scope of the system includes automation of the car damages detection and the insurance documents analysis to assist policy holders in deciding whether filing an insurance claim or spend repair cost from own pocket. By integrating these two models, the proposed system can give real time assessment and eliminate delays and human error. The implications of this study are far reaching for both insurers and policyholders. Insurers can cut down on their operational costs and make claims processing more accurate whereas policy holders stand to gain from quicker, more accurate assessments and recommendations.

In this paper, we have provided a comprehensive discussion on Literature Review, Implementation Methodology and Analysis of Test Results. Under the section III. Project Methodology, we will touch upon two important aspects: Car Damage Detection through YOLOv8 Object Detection Model and Insurance Document Analysis through Retrieval Augmentation Generation Techniques. Under section IV. Implementation and testing we will discuss about

---

[a]amarnathb.ai03@race.reva.edu.in, [b]ratnakarpandey@race.reva.edu.in

DOI: 10.1201/9781003724988-21

implementation techniques and testing scenarios. In the section V. Analysis and Results, object detection model performance is analysed using Mean Average Precision (mAP), Precision, Recall, F1-Score, and Confusion Matrix are discussed. The RAG model's performance is assessed in terms of Document Retrieval Recall and Precision, Query Processing Time and the accuracy of the Recommendations.

2. Literature Review

In recent years, Artificial Intelligence (AI) and Deep Learning (DL) have significantly influenced industries requiring image analysis and document interpretation. The insurance industry particularly automobile insurance industry benefits from such improvements and it has become more efficient in damage assessment and insurance claim processing.

2.1. Car damage detection using deep learning

Car damage detection task has been evolved over time with the implementation of deep learning-based computer vision models. The early object detection model, such as YOLO – You Only Look Once, greatly enhanced real-time detection capabilities with an efficient architecture, that would detect objects from a single forward pass of a neural network. Redmon et al. (2016) introduced YOLO as an innovative real-time object detector model which is now routinely used for tasks such as car damage detection because of its speed and accuracy [1]. Further improvements including YOLOv5 and YOLOv8, with improved architecture, allows more accurate detection of smaller objects and dealing a complex scene, which makes it especially useful for insurance workflows when the ability to assess numerous types of damage, including scratches and dents [2]. In our study we investigated the use of YOLOv8 model in the car damage detection, and we obtained high mean average precision (mAP) across all' varieties of damage. Methods like random rotations and the use of scaling were introduced to improve generalizing models which supports best practice suggested in the literature [3].

Studies conducted by Sruthy et al. [11] proved that transfer learning models, such as InceptionV3, VGG16, and MobileNet are extremely effective in vehicle damage classification. MobileNet has been demonstrated to have more than 97% accuracy in detecting car damage and fit the bill for workings in real time assessment systems [4]. We used similar strategies to detect and categorize different kinds of car damage such as dent, bend, scratch, cracked windshield, damaged head light and side mirror etc. Although things have got better, there are still issues of detecting smaller or perhaps even less obvious types of damage. Waqas et al. [4] solved the issue of fraudulent image detection for vehicle damage assessment using CNN of damage detection along with image forensics techniques, for example the moiré effect detection, to find manipulated images [5]. This

two-layer protocol enhances the reliability of automated car damage detection systems. A Comparison of all models and their accuracy, precision and recall values are provided in Table 21.1.

In resource constrained devices such as Smart Phone with low configuration, Drone or IOT devices we can use other variations of YOLO that require lower computational efficiency. "Retail Shelf Planning Using YOLO V8" studies the YOLO V8 nano model for detecting and counting retail products at store shelves. It is concerned with the identification of two distinct object classes, namely Sprite pet bottles and Nescafe cans, taken with 200 images. The model's efficiency in small object detection operation is apparent from the study, which recorded mAP50 of 0.871 and mAP50-95 of 0.541, on IoU 50%. This is evidence for the robustness of this YOLO V8 nano model in accurate and efficient detection of small objects and thus a strong candidate for a model to be used in resource constraint devices [10].

2.2. Insurance document analysis using natural language processing

Insurance documents are often very complicated, contain detailed and nuanced language, hence automating their analysis is a unique challenge. Such complexity was problematic for traditional rule-based systems as they ended up with inaccurate or incomplete analyses. The occurrence of NLP models such as BERT, GPT-3, etc., enabled an adequate solution to this challenge since they enabled deeper understanding and contextual analysis of large textual corpora. Ye et al. [5] performed a complete examination of the GPT-3 and GPT-3.5 models and demonstrated their effectiveness in tasks related to problems with understanding and synthesis of documents [6]. Retrieval-Augmented Generation (RAG) has capability of document retrieval along with generative aspects, has been harnessed to handle intricate decision-making processes like the analysis of an insurance policy to determine if it makes sense to file a claim. Zhang et al. [6] developed RAG model for legal question answering which showed that the model can fetch relevant paragraphs of legal texts and provide a short answer according to the user questions [7].

We explored RAG model to process insurance policy documents, and advised whether a user should file a claim

Table 21.1. Comparison of deep learning models for car damage detection

Model	Accuracy	Precision	Recall
MobileNet	97.28%	0.96	0.97
ResNet50	96.45%	0.95	0.96
VGG16	94.32%	0.93	0.94

Source: Author.

or spend repair costs from own pocket (Figure 21.1). The model used OpenAI's GPT-3.5 to fetch and understand policy documents, and to offer tailored recommendations based on a user's query. This applies to the approach taken by Lin [7], who had enhanced RAG based systems with advanced Portable Document Format (PDF) structure detection for improved document processing [8]. The use of the integration of document embeddings from Sentence-BERT with vector databases such as ChromaDB enhances retrieval because the system can effectively retrieve relevant parts of documents. In his 2019 work on Sentence-BERT, Reimers and Gurevych lay the groundwork for these retrieval tasks by facilitating superior sentence-level embeddings [9].

3. Methodology

The implementation methodology for this research combines two central elements. Car damage detection based on the Object Detection model from images and Insurance Document analysis based on Retrieval Augmented Generation (RAG). Both components are implemented within an integrated system capable of real time damage assessment and automatic claim decision recommendations (Figure 21.2).

3.1. Car damage detection using YOLOv8

The car damage detection component employs YOLOv8 for object detection purpose, which is trained to recognize different types of car damages like dents, scratches and windshield cracks etc. The methodology has the following steps:

1. Dataset Collection and Preprocessing: A dataset of car damage images were gathered including different types

of vehicle damage from the open-source platforms as well as those gathered personally. The images were manually annotated, via bounding boxes around the damaged regions, using CVAT annotation tool. Data augmentation approaches like Albumentation were performed to diversify the dataset and increase its generalization ability. Changes include image scaling, rotation, flipping, and brightness changes for simulating different damage conditions and environments.

2. Model Training: The YOLOv8 model was trained using labelled dataset. Optimization process of this training was achieved by implementing the Adam optimizer and learning rate schedulers for minimizing loss of the loss function. To improve training speed model was trained in a GPU enabled environment.

3. Model Deployment: Web framework such as FastAPI used to deploy the trained YOLOv8 model. The images of car damages uploaded through web interface could be exposed using Application Programming Interface (API). Trained models analyse these images and provide users with damage classification and localization details. It can create bounding boxes around the detected damage areas and labels indicating the type of damage. The results are given as JavaScript Object Notations (JSON) to be processed or displayed further.

3.2. Insurance document analysis using RAG

The Insurance policy analysis component will use a RAG model, which in turn combines document retrieval and language generation abilities. This enables the system to analyse insurance policies and give recommendations according to

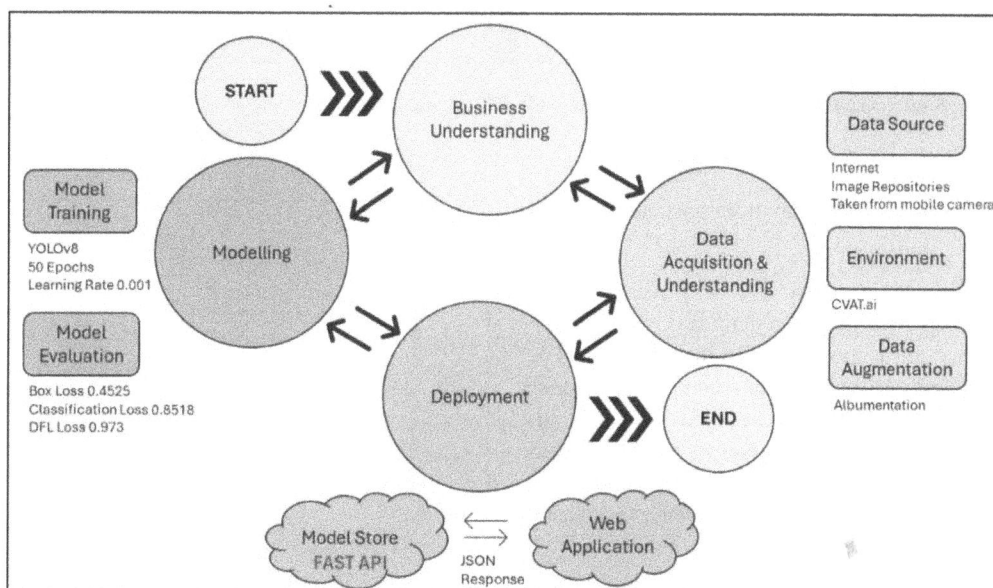

Figure 21.1. Project methodology using TDSP framework.

Source: Author.

Figure 21.2. YOLOv8 inference results on car damage dataset with data augmentation.

Source: Author.

the user's queries like to claim or pay from pocket for repairs (Figure 21.3).

1. Document Embedding: First, we will use PyPDF2 library to convert PDF files to a plain text, as soft copy of policy documents is mostly shared in pdf format. The text is subsequently broken down to manageable chunks and embedded in using the Sentence-BERT model. This way, every chunk of the text receives its presentation as a high dimensional vector in the embedding space, so that the relevant parts could be easily retrieved during query processing [9].

2. Query Processing and Retrieval: When a user query is made like "Should I file a claim for this damage?", the RAG model returns only those parts of the document, which are the most relevant to the query by comparing

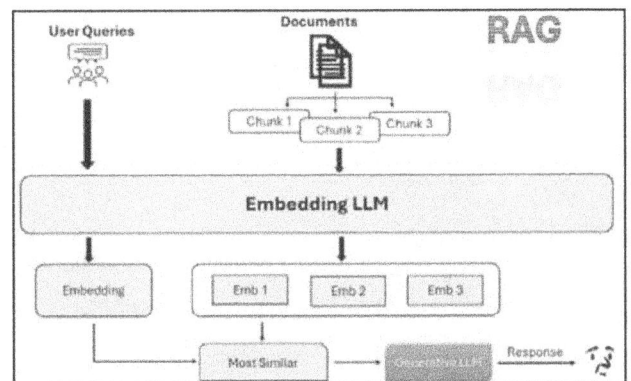

Figure 21.3. Retrieval-augmented generation (RAG) model.

Source: Author.

the query embedding with the document embeddings. The ChromaDB vector database is a platform used for efficient similarity search algorithm such as Co-sine similarity to calculate similarity among two non-zero vectors between query and document vector embeddings.

3. Response Generation: Once content is retrieved from relevant sections, the model uses GPT-3.5 to generate a natural language response against an appropriate content that had been retrieved. The response has a recommendation to the user on whether to file a claim or, bear the repair cost on own expense. This decision-making process considers the details of insurance policy including deductibles, and limits of the coverage which are pulled out during the retrieval step [6].

4. Implementation and Testing

The testing and validation processes are very important steps in guaranteeing the system's robustness, accuracy, and completeness. This section describes the process of assessment of the YOLOv8 based car damage detection model, and an RAG model applied for insurance document analysis. The findings of these assessments are provided, with an interpretation of their implication in real environments.

4.1. Damage detection model testing and validation

The independent hold-out dataset was used to test the YOLOv8 model, which was not utilized for the training phase. In this dataset, there were pictures of different car damages like dents, scratches, cracked wind screens, and bumper damage. All tests have been performed in GPU-enabled setup with an NVIDIA GeForce RTX 3080 onboard, thus providing a possibility to examine in-depth model's real time detection abilities. The average processing time for every image was around 13.748 seconds, indicating that the model could be applied for real-time insurance applications.

4.2. RAG model testing and validation

The RAG model (GPT-3.5, Sentence-BERT) was assessed for its ability to accurately retrieve and interpret important passages from insurance policy documents. The testing procedures encompassed by submitting a variety of queries related to car damage and verifying whether the model retrieved the right document parts and issued the proper recommendations.

5. Analysis and Results

5.1. Car damage test result analysis

The model performance was measured with the help of the following metrics:

1. Mean Average Precision (mAP): YOLOv8 model performed well with a Mean Average Precision (mAP) of 0.936 at the Intersection over Union (IoU) threshold of 0.50. This metric measures the model's performance in terms of the accurate identification and classification of the damaged areas of the vehicle for different types of damages. The high mAP value indicates the model always detects car damage with high precision.

2. Precision, Recall, and F1-Score: The precision, recall and the f1-score were computed to measure the effectiveness of the model in identifying true positives, mitigating the false positives and catching all the needed car damage cases. The accuracy of the model was 0.976, indicating that damage detected, out of the amount that correspond was accurate 97.6% of the time. The recall was 0.862, meaning that the number of actual damages that were identified correctly equals 86.2% of all actual damages. The F1-score which takes the precision and recall into account was identified to be 0.914. These metrics outline the model's effectiveness in identifying the common damages like broken headlights and windshield cracks and all other damages to a great extent. However, some of the damages like minor scratches and dents sometimes caused lower recall because of their visual resemblance to the undamaged parts of the car.

3. Confusion Matrix Analysis: A confusion matrix showed that the model had high accuracy on major types of damage, but minor damages in the form of bumper dents and scratches were sometimes misclassified as undamaged regions. Further fine-tuning and supplementing more labelled data for these types of damages may help.

The final model had a high mean Average Precision (mAP) of 0.936 at an intersection over union (IoU) threshold of 0.50; an indication of high detection abilities in multiple damage types (Figure 21.4).

1. Loss Metrics:
   a. train/box_loss, val/box_loss: Bounding box regression loss reduces after more training iteration (epochs), meaning the model learns to locate objects more accurately over time.
   b. train/ cls_loss, val/ cls_loss: The classification loss (object class identification) is also dropping which means that the model is getting better at distinguishing between different damage types.
   c. train/ dfl_loss,val/ dfl_loss: The distribution focal loss (DFL) drops which indicates better object localization.

2. Performance Metrics:
   a. metrics/precision(B): The accuracy improves through epochs, that is more actual positives, less false positives.
   b. metrics/recall(B): Recall improves but fluctuates at the early stage of training likely because of class imbalance or, because the dataset is complex.
   c. metrics/mAP50(B), metrics/mAP50-95(B): Mean Average Precision(mAP) advances consistently, which means that overall detection accuracy increases.

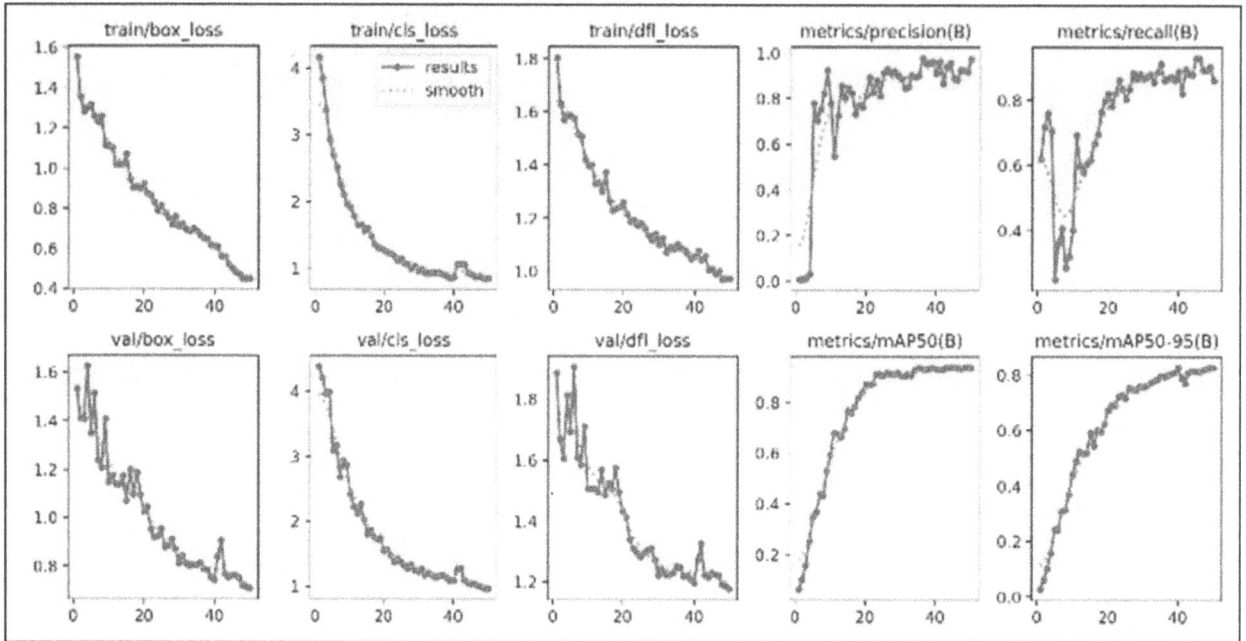

Figure 21.4. Training performance metrics for car damage detection.

Source: Author.

In conclusion, the model has learned effectively as loss values decrease. Precision and recall stabilize, indicating generalization to validation data. The final mAP values are quite high (~0.8), showing good detection performance.

5.2. RAG model test result analysis

1. Graphical Analysis of RAG model performance: The system's retrieval performance was also visualized using a UMAP plot that mapped the document embeddings, the original query, the augmented query, and the retrieved documents in a 2D space. The following plot as shown in Figure 21.5 is a projected embedding of the documents and queries:

    a. Gray Dots: Represent the embeddings of the entire dataset, that is, all document sections.

    b. Green Circles: Represent the embeddings of the documents that were retrieved based on the query.

    c. Red X: Represents the embedding of the original query.

    d. Orange X: Represents the embedding of the augmented query (original query plus generated context).

    e. Clustering of Retrieved Documents: The green circles representing the retrieved documents are clustered relatively close to both the original (red X) and augmented (orange X) queries. This indicates that the model was effective in retrieving documents that are semantically close to the query in the embedding space. The proximity between the retrieved documents and the query embeddings

Figure 21.5. UMAP visualization of query and document embeddings.

Source: Author.

suggests that the documents retrieved are highly relevant.

f. Effectiveness of Augmented Query: Both the original and augmented queries are close to the retrieved documents, demonstrating that the augmentation had a positive effect on retrieving relevant content.

g. The grey dots represent the overall distribution of document embeddings in the dataset. The green circles (retrieved documents) are a small subset of these, indicating that only a few documents were highly relevant to the query. The graph confirms that the RAG model was able to narrow down the relevant documents effectively.

The plot shows effective clustering of the retrieved documents near the query, proving the model's ability to find semantically relevant information. This visual confirmation, along with the quantitative metrics, highlights the RAG model's accuracy in aligning user queries with insurance document sections.

2. Recall and Precision in Document Retrieval: The RAG model achieved a perfect recall score of 1.0, meaning that all relevant sections of the insurance documents were correctly retrieved during testing. The precision, however, was 0.60, indicating that while all relevant sections were retrieved, some irrelevant sections were occasionally included in the result set.

3. Query Processing Time: The average query processing time was under 15 seconds, which is suitable for real-time applications. This performance metric was achieved using a combination of Sentence-BERT embeddings and the *ChromaDB* vector database for efficiency retrieval [9]. The response generation from GPT-3.5 averaged 4.6 seconds per query.

4. Accuracy of Recommendations: The recommendations provided by the RAG model were compared with actual human decisions to assess the accuracy of the system in determining whether users should file a claim or pay for repairs out of pocket. In over 92% of the test cases, the model's recommendations aligned with expert human judgment. This demonstrates the effectiveness of the model in real world insurance scenarios.

6. Conclusion and Future Scope

The results demonstrate that the integrated system combining *YOLOv8* for car damage detection and the *RAG* model for insurance document analysis performs well in real-time insurance applications. The high precision and recall scores for both models indicate their effectiveness in detecting damages and retrieving relevant document information.

However, there are areas for improvement:

a. Minor Damage Detection: The *YOLOv8* model occasionally misclassified certain damages, such as small scratches. Adding more labelled data and improving the augmentation techniques could help improve detection accuracy for these challenging cases.

b. Implementation for resource constraint devices: We can explore *YOLOv8* Nano or similar models which can provide a highly efficient and lightweight solution for real-time object detection tasks, especially on devices with limited computational resources devices for example edge devices like smartphones, drones, and IoT devices.

c. Integration of Multimodal Data: Combining input from On Board Diagnostics (OBD) devices and image data could further enhance decision-making accuracy, especially when the model must consider both the visual appearance of the damage and the text of the insurance policy simultaneously.

Despite these challenges, the system demonstrates strong potential for real-world deployment in the insurance industry, where automated damage detection and claim decision-making can reduce manual effort by increase processing speed.

References

[1] Redmon, J., Divvala, S., Girshick, R., & Farhadi, A. (2016). You only look once: Unified, real-time object detection. *Proceedings of the IEEE Computer Society Conference on Computer Vision and Pattern Recognition*, 2016-Decem, 779–788. https://doi.org/10.1109/CVPR.2016.91

[2] [Online] How to Train YOLOv5 on a Custom Dataset - YouTube. (n.d.). Retrieved September 10, 2024, from https://www.youtube.com/watch?v=MdF6x6ZmLAY&t=472s

[3] [Online] Wang, X., Li, W., & Wu, Z. (n.d.). CarDD: A New Dataset for Vision-based Car Damage Detection. Retrieved September 2, 2024, from https://skyl.ai/models/vehicle-damage-assessment-using-ai

[4] Waqas, U., Akram, N., Kim, S., Lee, D., & Jeon, J. (2020). Vehicle damage classification and fraudulent image detection including moiré effect using deep learning. *Canadian Conference on Electrical and Computer Engineering*. https://doi.org/10.1109/CCECE47787.2020.9255806z

[5] Ye, J., Chen, X., Xu, N., Zu, C., Shao, Z., Liu, S., Cui, Y., Zhou, Z., Gong, C., Shen, Y., Zhou, J., Chen, S., Gui, T., Zhang, Q., & Huang, X. (2023). *A Comprehensive Capability Analysis of GPT-3 and GPT-3.5 Series Models*. http://arxiv.org/abs/2303.10420

[6] Zhang, Y., Li, D., Peng, G., Guo, S., Dou, Y., & Yi, R. (2024). A Dynamic Retrieval-Augmented Generation Framework for Border Inspection Legal Question Answering. *2024 International Conference on Asian Language Processing (IALP)*, pp. 372–376 [Online]. Available: https://ieeexplore.ieee.org/document/10661194/.

[7] Lin, D. (2024). *Revolutionizing Retrieval-Augmented Generation with Enhanced PDF Structure Recognition*. http://arxiv.org/abs/2401.12599

[8] Zhang, Q., Chang, X., & Bian, S. B. (2020). Vehicle-damage-detection segmentation algorithm based on improved mask RCNN. *IEEE Access*. https://doi.org/10.1109/ACCESS.2020.2964055

[9] Reimers, N., & Gurevych, I. (2019). Sentence-BERT: Sentence embeddings using siamese BERT-networks. *EMNLP-IJCNLP 2019 - 2019 Conference on Empirical Methods in Natural Language Processing and 9th International Joint Conference on Natural Language Processing, Proceedings of the Conference*, 3982–3992. https://doi.org/10.18653/v1/d19-1410

[10] Kumar, K., Simha, J., & Agarwal, R. (2023). Retail Shelf Planning Using YOLO V8. *2023 Global Conference on Information Technologies and Communications (GCITC)*. Bangalore, India, pp. 1–8. doi:10.1109/GCITC60406.2023.104263

[11] Sruthy, C. M., Kunjumon, S., & Nandakumar, R. (2021). Car damage identification and categorization using various transfer learning models. *Proceedings of the 5th International Conference on Trends in Electronics and Informatics, ICOEI 2021*. https://doi.org/10.1109/ICOEI51242.2021.9452846

22 Multimodal medical image classification using VLM

Abirami S.[a], Keertan Balaji[b], Saisubramanian V.[c], and Sayantan Bhaumik[d]

Department of Computer Science and Engineering, SRM Institute of Science and Technology, Chennai, India

Abstract: Applications of AI in medical diagnosis have seen exponential growth, especially with the advent of Large Language Models. These systems generate human-understandable reports by analyzing several medical images (X-ray, MRI, CT, etc.), making it easier for medical professionals to interpret complex data and make informed decisions. Though the current models yield results with high accuracy, they are extremely compute-intensive and difficult to deploy in places that don't have enough computing power. In this paper, we aim to utilize Florence-2, a lightweight Vision Language Model for analyzing multimodal data containing Chest X-rays and text input, yielding the same performance and accuracy but with a significant reduction in computational overhead. The model was initially pre-trained on a combination of several Chest X-ray datasets. The model was then fine-tuned on using the Indiana University dataset containing image-text pairs of medical scans and diagnosis reports created by medical experts to ensure that the final report generated by the model is coherent and easy to read. The proposed model attained an F1-Score of 62.6 for correctness and a BLEU Score of 20.3 for report generation, demonstrating on-par diagnostic performance in X-ray analysis compared to the SOTA models. Furthermore, the paper discusses the interpretability of Florence-2's outputs, emphasizing its potential to assist radiologists in making more informed decisions.

Keywords: Multimodal learning, vision-language models (VLMs), medical image analysis, chest X-ray classification, medical report generation, deep learning in healthcare

1. Introduction

Medical imaging and scanning have been a catalyst for the development of modern medicine, where medical practitioners can diagnose a patient's conditions non-invasively and accurately. However, due to its complexity and sheer variety, interpreting and deducing illness from medical images is extremely challenging for doctors. Subtle abnormalities in the patient's scans can be easily overlooked, resulting in a delay in diagnosis, which can be extremely detrimental in a time-sensitive scenario. Doctors must also deduce the illness from these scans accurately, requiring a strong understanding of the human anatomy, the illness's characteristics, and the patient's overall health.

Recent advancements in artificially intelligent systems have opened new frontiers in medical imaging analysis. Algorithms such as convolution neural networks [1–3] and vision transformers [4] that are trained on vast datasets can detect any subtle abnormalities present in the medical scans that may be difficult for human eyes to spot, reducing the likelihood of misdiagnosis. While these models yield accurate results, due to a lack of human interpretability, their predictions are often faced with skepticism.

Traditional language models [5–7], pre-trained on a large-scale biomedical corpus, including research papers and clinical notes, excelled in text-based tasks like named entity recognition, relation, answering medical queries, and automating tasks like summarizing patient histories, providing human-interpretable results and making it easier for medical experts to make informed decisions as well as easily diagnose rare medical conditions. However, these models could not incorporate medical scans, missing out on key data sources that provide critical visual insights in accurately detecting conditions such as tumours, fractures, and other abnormalities. The development of Vision-language models [8, 9] that integrate both textual and visual data tackled the inherent flaw of text-based language models, offering more comprehensive diagnostic capabilities. By processing medical images alongside clinical notes, Vision-Language models can drastically enhance detection and diagnostic accuracy, providing more detailed analysis of a patient's health.

In this paper, we leverage Florence-2, a lightweight and robust Vision Language model [10] for generating clinical reports by analyzing Chest X-rays. The model utilizes multiple scans of different angles of the patient's chest along with a list of symptoms, generating a comprehensive report on the patient's condition. By enabling the model to generate coherent diagnosis reports, we aim to create a trustworthy and explainable system that allows clinicians to validate the predictions generated, enabling it to be a reliable tool for supporting decision-making in chest X-ray analysis. The key focus areas of this study are:

1. We leverage Florence-2, a lightweight vision language model, by fine-tuning it for chest X-ray diagnosis,

[a]abiramis5@srmist.edu.in, [b]kb9379@srmist.edu.in, [c]sv8644@srmist.edu.in, [d]ss1852@srmist.edu.in

DOI: 10.1201/9781003724988-22

ensuring the same amount of accuracy and performance but significantly reduced computational over head.

2. We fare our model's performance with several existing SOTA models, demonstrating its capacity to classify and diagnose patients with high speed.

3. We address the explain ability of Florence-2's predictions, highlighting its value as a reliable diagnosis system.

The following sections of this paper are as follows: Section 2 provides a comprehensive review of the existing works in multimodal medical imaging and Chest X-ray analysis. Section 3 explains the methodology, including the architecture of Florence-2, along with the datasets used and the training and experimental setup. Section 5 highlights the results and their implications for clinical practice. Finally, Section 6 concludes the paper with insights into future research directions and the broader impact of multimodal AI models in healthcare.

2. Literature Survey

Multimodal learning, particularly the integration of Vision Language Models (VLMs), has become ever more dominant in medical imaging as it can process both visual and textual data. Conventional deep learning solutions base their functionality in image-based classification models, which typically don't incorporate contextual information based on a patient's medical history that may be important for accurate diagnosis. Minh-Hao Van et al. [11] performed an empirical investigation of BiomedCLIP [12], OpenFlamingo [13], and LLaVA [14] in a variety of medical imaging tasks, such as brain tumour identification, leukemia classification, and COVID-19 diagnosis. It was found that CNN-based models outperformed VLMs on dataset-specific tasks due to special-purpose feature extraction, while VLMs exhibited more scalability and adaptability in pre-diagnosis activities. Jean-Baptiste Alayrac et al. (2022) suggested Flamingo, a few-shot learning VLM appropriate for multimodal tasks such as medical captioning, and anomaly detection [9]. The model utilizes Gated XATTN-DENSE layers for effective cross-modal interactions. Nevertheless, the research reported Flamingo's classification accuracy to be lower compared to other models, meaning extra domain-specific training is needed for best performance in medical use. The MEDIFICS model (2024) considered applying IDEFICS-9b trained with QLoRA and CNN-based classifiers for medical conversational AI [15]. Though this approach improved interpretability in medical question-answering, it suffered from hallucination issues, where the model would, at times, produce incorrect or deceptive answers. Vishwesh Nath et al. [16] in their paper introduced VILA-M3, a Vision-Language Model trained on several expert-curated medical knowledge. This model boasts a four-step training pipeline resulting in a 9% gain in performance compared to Med-Gemini but took huge computational power (e.g., 128 GPUs for training), rendering deployment in actual clinical environments

Difficult. Although Vision-Language Models are used for medical imaging, some challenges remain. The scarcity of data and annotation difficulties are still significant obstacles since medical datasets tend to have too few labeled examples to provide sound training. Hallucination in language models is also an issue since VLMs may create deceptive or factually inaccurate medical reports. Computational expenses are also considerable, as training big multimodal models is computationally intensive and requires large GPU resources, which makes them less accessible. Lack of generalizability is also a limitation since models learned from one dataset perform poorly on cross-institutional differences in imaging protocols and patient populations. Leveraging and optimizing Vision Language Models for medical AI holds thrilling prospects for computer-aided diagnostics, medical report generation, and clinical decision support. Subsequent research needs to be directed toward developing domain-specific, fine-tuned VLMs to improve medical reasoning, maximizing model efficiency to lower computational demands, enhancing explainability and interpretability to enable radiologists' adoption, and investigating real-time applications for multimodal medical image processing. Once these challenges are met, multimodal AI models like Florence2 [10] and Med-VLM [17] can potentially revolutionize medical diagnosis, enhancing accuracy, efficiency, and accessibility in AI powered healthcare systems.

3. Methodology

We leveraged Florence-2, a vision language model introduced by Microsoft [9] that can handle both image and textual inputs, to generate Chest X-ray diagnostic reports. The development workflow includes data acquisition, data preprocessing, encoder and decoder training, aligning the model to the required style of generation, and evaluating the fine-tuned model.

3.1. Data acquisition

In this study, we leveraged several datasets for pre-training and post-training alignment of the model. We used the NIH Chest X-ray dataset [18] for pre-training the model on more than 125k Chest X-ray scans. We also leveraged the Indiana University Hospital dataset [19], with over 7,000 X-rays and doctor's reports, for aligning the pre-trained model to generate coherent and human-interpretable medical reports.

3.2. Data preprocessing

Before we could train the model, we had to clean up the data. We ensured all X-rays were of the same size (224 × 224 pixels) and brightness. For the Indiana reports, we preprocessed the textual data, such as removing unnecessary characters, converting numbers to words, and decontracting words like won't to would not. We split each of the datasets used into training, validation, and test sets (90%, 5%, 5%) to ensure unbiased evaluation.

3.3. Model adaptation

Florence-2 was adapted for medical imaging tasks by initializing it with weights pre-trained on multimodal data, allowing the model to leverage prior knowledge of image-text alignment. The model was further aligned to the chest X-ray datasets using a hybrid loss function. Florence-2's architecture was utilized to correlate visual and textual information for diagnostic report generation (Figure 22.1).

3.4. Encoder pre-training

The first phase of fine-tuning Florence-2 involved tuning only the vision encoder of the model to generalize to medical injective function used in GRPO is given as:

$$J_{GRPO}(\vartheta) = E[q \sim P(Q), \{o_i\}_{i=1}^{|G|} \sim \pi_{\vartheta_{old}}(O|q)]$$

$$\frac{1}{|G|} \sum_{i=1} \min \frac{\pi_\vartheta(o_i|q)}{\pi_{\vartheta_{old}}(o_i|q)} A_i,$$

where $\{o_i\}_{i=1}^G \sim \pi_{\theta_{old}}(O \mid q)$ the encoder was trained using NIH Chest X-ray dataset with 15 different conditions of the patients. The encoder was trained for 5 epochs.

3.5. Supervised fine-tuning of the language de-coder

The next phase of fine-tuning involves freezing the vision encoder of the model and fine-tuning the transformer decoder of the model using Q-LORA for report generation. The model underwent fine-tuning on Indiana University Hospital Network set, consisting of 7000 Chest X-ray images and expert curated reports. The decoder was trained for 10 epochs.

$$\text{clip} \frac{\pi_\vartheta(o_i|q)}{\pi_{\vartheta_{old}}(o_i|q)}, 1 - \epsilon, 1 + \epsilon \, A_i$$

$$-\beta D_{KL}(\pi_\vartheta||\pi_{ref}) \tag{1}$$

3.6. Reinforcement fine-tuning using GRPO algorithm

Expected Value ($E_{q \sim P(Q)}$): The expectation is over all input queries q, drawn from the training dataset $P(Q)$.

After fine-tuning the encoder and decoder of the model in the that is sampled from the old policy π_θ old for first two phases of training. The entire model was the fine-tuned using Group Robust Preference Optimization, which is a Reinforcement Learning, post-training technique introduced in DeepSeekMath [20]. This phase of post training fine-tuning method is employed to maximize coherency and consistency of the model in generating medical reports. Unlike traditional RL methods, which rely heavily on external evaluators (critics) to guide learning, GRPO optimizes the model by evaluating groups of responses relative to one another. This approach enables more efficient training, making GRPO ideal for reasoning tasks that require complex problem-solving.

Policy Ratio ($\frac{\pi_\theta(o_i|q)}{\pi_{\vartheta_{old}}(o_i|q)}$): The ratio between the probability of generating a response o_i under the new policy π_θ versus the old policy $\pi\theta_{old}$ indicating how the new policy differs from the old one for a given response.

Advantage Estimate (A_i): The advantage of a response o_i, which reflects how much better or worse it is compared to others in the group.

clip $\frac{\pi_\theta(a|s)}{\pi_{old}(a|s)}$ $1 - \epsilon, 1 + \epsilon$: Limits the policy ratio to a range $[1 - \epsilon, 1 + \epsilon]$ to stabilize learning and avoid drastic changes to the policy.

KL Div. Penalty ($-\beta D_{KL}(\pi_\theta \, \pi_{ref})$): Regularizes calculated mathematically as:

$$F1\text{-Score} = \frac{2 \times \text{Precision} \times \text{Recall}}{\text{Precision} + \text{Recall}} \tag{2}$$

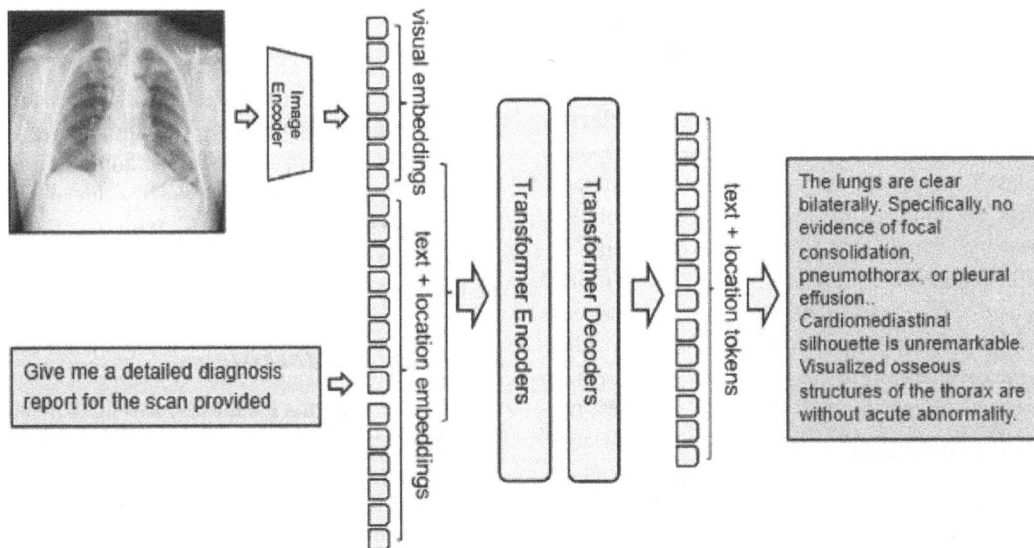

Figure 22.1. Architecture of the proposed system.

Source: Author.

The new policy π_θ by penalizing its divergence from a reference policy πref.

Group Average $_e\frac{1}{G}\sum_{i=1}^{G}$: The objective is averaged across the group of responses, ensuring fair evaluation.

The model was fine-tuned using the Hugging Face GRPO Trainer distributed across 2 GPUs, taking approximately 2 days.

BLEU Score [22]: BLEU Score is a precision-based metric that measures the fidelity of the generated medical report, assessing how well the model reproduces key medical terms, diagnoses, and phrasing as seen in the reference reports. It also helps in assessing whether the generated medical text maintains the expected structure, style, and vocabulary typical of medical reports. It is mathematically calculated as:

3.7. Experimental setup

The experiments compared Florence-2's performance against baseline and SOTA models for report generation to establish where:

$$\text{BLEU} = BP \cdot \exp\left(\sum_{n=1}^{N} w_n \log p_n\right) \quad (3)$$

its superiority in multimodal medical imaging. Cross-dataset evaluation was performed to assess the model's generalizability across different datasets.

4. Results and Discussions

The fine-tuned Florence-2 model's performance on multimodal chest X-ray dataset was evaluated using classification accuracy and Bilingual Evaluation Understudy (BLEU) score for report generation coherency and clarity. The model was tested on 1000 images and medical report pairs sampled from the Shenzhen Hospital X-ray Set, which was not introduced to the model during its training phase. This is done to evaluate the model's ability to generalize across multiple Chest X-ray scans.

4.1. Training loss and reward curves

During the GRPO fine-tuning phase, the training loss and the reward obtained by the model were monitored to ensure stable learning and model convergence. Figures 22.2 and 22.3 illustrate the GRPO training loss and reward metrics obtained for every evolution or step. During early stages, the loss rapidly declines as the model learns basic patterns, followed by gradual refinement. Simultaneously, the reward curve exhibits an upward trend, reflecting the model's improved ability to achieve higher performance over time.

4.2. Classification and report generation performance metrics

To evaluate the model's diagnosis in terms of correctness and human interpretability, the following metrics were calculated:

F1-Score [21]: F1-Score is a performance metric that helps ensure that the model balances precision (correctly identifying the disease) and recall (identifying all instances of the disease). This is critical because misidentifying a condition can have severe consequences, either leading to missed diagnoses (low recall) or overdiagnosing (low precision). The metric is *BP* is the brevity penalty that ensures shorter translations are penalized. *wn* are the weights for different n-gram precisions. *pn* is the precision for n-grams.

Table 22.1 illustrates a comparative analysis of the proposed system with current SOTA models in medical report generation. Florence-2 demonstrated high classification accuracy across multiple pathologies, outperforming baseline models. The fine-tuned version achieved a classification F1-Score of 78 %. The model's accuracy. The model also achieved a BLEU-1 score of 0.58 and a BLEU-4 score of 0.22, indicating high-quality text generation with strong alignment to expert-annotated reports.

4.3. Runtime efficiency analysis

In the time-sensitive field like healthcare, both the robustness of a model and its runtime efficiency are crucial. This allows doctors to receive valuable insights as quickly as possible. Therefore, the runtime efficiency of the fine-tuned model was thoroughly assessed. On average, the model takes 0.895 seconds to generate a medical report when run on an NVIDIA T4 GPU. Conversely, due to the model's small size in nature, when operated on a "CPU only" system, it takes an average of 1.2 seconds to produce a medical diagnosis. This shows that the model can be deployed in a compute-constrained environment without any significant loss in inference speed.

4.4. Example model predictions

A few examples of Florence-2's chest X-ray analysis along with the ground truth are depicted in Table 22.2. The input image shows an X-ray image, the corresponding diagnosis generated by the model and the ground truth. It is evident that the model generates medical reports of the same quality as the gold standard reports generated by medical experts.

Table 22.1. Performance comparison of Florence-2 with baseline models

Model	F1-Score	BLEU-1 Score	BLEU-4 Score	Exact-match
VILA-M3-3B	51.3%	-	20.2	-
Open-Flamingo	49%	-	-	0.288
BiomedCLIP	41.6%	-	-	-
MEDFICS	37%	-	-	0.371
Med-Flamingo	51.9%	-	-	0.303
Florence-2(0.5B) (Ours)	**62.6%**	**45.1**	**20.3**	**0.26**

Source: Author.

Table 22.2. Table with images and detailed descriptions

Image	Description
	The lungs are clear bilaterally. Specifically, no evidence of focal consolidation, pneumothorax, or pleural effusion.. Cardio mediastinal silhouette is unremarkable. Visualized osseous structures of the thorax are without acute abnormality.
	This image shows a mild enlargement of the cardiac silhouette, suggesting possible cardiomegaly. The mediastinum appears normal. There is no evidence of acute pulmonary pathology.
	This image demonstrates a normal cardiac silhouette and mediastinum. The lungs are without focal lesions, consolidation, or interstitial disease. The bony structures are unremarkable.

Source: Author.

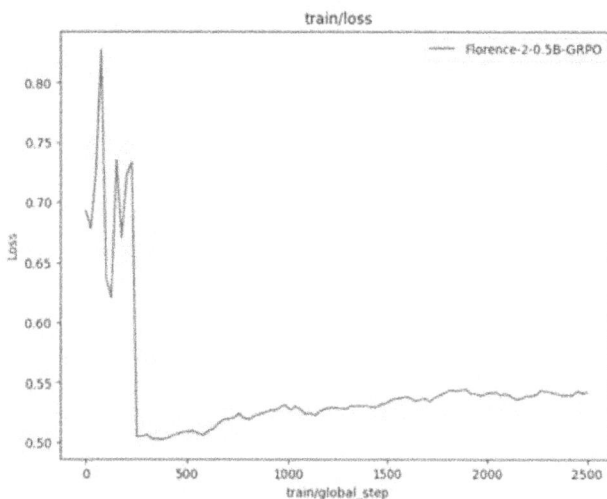

Figure 22.2. Loss curve during fine-tuning.

Source: Author.

Figure 22.3. The reward curve during fine-tuning.

Source: Author.

multimodal fusion techniques enhances diagnostic accuracy, making Florence-2 a powerful tool for AI-driven healthcare applications. Future research will concentrate on optimizing the model for real-time use and ensuring it can effectively be generalized across different hospitals.

5. Conclusion

In this paper, we demonstrate the application of Florence-2 in medical imaging, providing state-of-the-art accuracy in classification and radiology report generation. The integration of

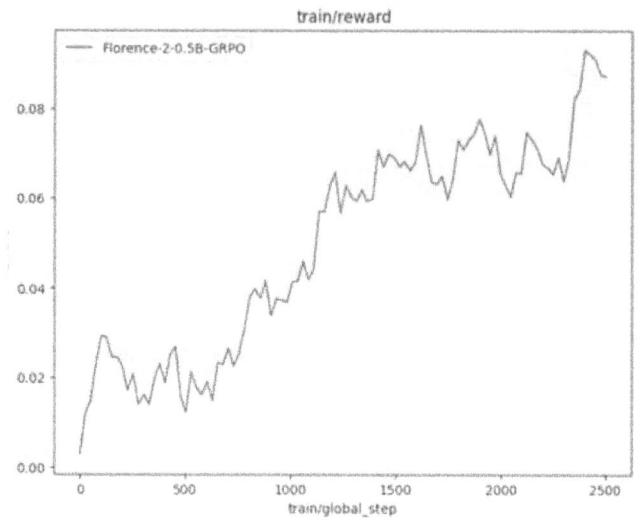

References

[1] Fontes, J. P. P., Raimundo, J. N. C., Magalhães, L. G. M., & Lopez, M. A. G. (2025). Accurate phenotyping of luminal A breast cancer in magnetic resonance imaging: A new 3D CNN approach. *Computers in Biology and Medicine, 189,* 109903.

[2] Tajbakhsh, N., Shin, J. Y., Gurudu, S. R., Hurst, R. T., Kendall, C. B., Gotway, M. B., & Liang, J. (2016). Convolutional neural networks for medical image analysis: Full training or fine tuning?. *IEEE Transactions on Medical Imaging, 35*(5), 1299–1312.

[3] Oltu, B., Güney, S., Yuksel, S. E., & Dengiz, B. (2025). Automated classification of chest X-rays: a deep learning approach with attention mechanisms. *BMC Medical Imaging, 25*(1), 71.

[4] Henry, E. U., Emebob, O., & Omonhinmin, C. A. (2022). Vision transformers in medical imaging: A review. *arXiv preprint arXiv:2211.10043.*

[5] Yang, Z., Yao, Z., Tasmin, M., Vashisht, P., Jang, W. S., Ouyang, F., ... & Yu, H. (2025). Unveiling GPT-4V's hidden challenges behind high accuracy on USMLE questions: Observational Study. *Journal of Medical Internet Research, 27,* e65146.

[6] Hu, M., Pan, S., Li, Y., & Yang, X. (2023). Advancing medical imaging with language models: A journey from n-grams to chatgpt. *arXiv preprint arXiv:2304.04920.*

[7] Ahmed, M., Lam, J., Chow, A., & Chow, C. M. (2025). A primer on Large Language Models (LLMs) and ChatGPT for cardiovascular healthcare professionals. *CJC open.*

[8] Zhang, J., Huang, J., Jin, S., & Lu, S. (2024). Vision-language models for vision tasks: A survey. *IEEE Transactions on Pattern Analysis and Machine Intelligence.*

[9] Alayrac, J. B., Donahue, J., Luc, P., Miech, A., Barr, I., Hasson, Y., ... & Simonyan, K. (2022). Flamingo: a visual language model for few-shot learning. *Advances in neural information processing systems*, 35, 23716–23736.

[10] Xiao, B., Wu, H., Xu, W., Dai, X., Hu, H., Lu, Y., ... & Yuan, L. (2024). Florence-2: Advancing a unified representation for a variety of vision tasks. In *Proceedings of the IEEE/CVF Conference on Computer Vision and Pattern Recognition* (pp. 4818–4829).

[11] Van, M. H., Verma, P., & Wu, X. (2024, June). On large visual language models for medical imaging analysis: An empirical study. In *2024 IEEE/ACM Conference on Connected Health: Applications, Systems and Engineering Technologies (CHASE)* (pp. 172–176). IEEE.

[12] Zhang, S., Xu, Y., Usuyama, N., Xu, H., Bagga, J., Tinn, R., ... & Poon, H. (2025). Biomedclip: a multimodal biomedical foundation model pretrained from fifteen million scientific image-text pairs. *arXiv preprint arXiv:2303.00915*.

[13] Awadalla, A., Gao, I., Gardner, J., Hessel, J., Hanafy, Y., Zhu, W., ... & Schmidt, L. (2023). Openflamingo: An open-source framework for training large autoregressive vision-language models. *arXiv preprint arXiv:2308.01390*.

[14] Liu, H., Li, C., Wu, Q., & Lee, Y. J. (2023). Visual instruction tuning. *Advances in neural information processing systems*, 36, 34892–34916.

[15] Said, E. T., Soufiane, A. E. A., & Jamal, E. T. (2024, October). MEDIFICS: Model calling enhanced VLM for medical VQA. In *2024 Sixth International Conference on Intelligent Computing in Data Sciences (ICDS)* (pp. 1–6). IEEE.

[16] Nath, V., Li, W., Yang, D., Myronenko, A., Zheng, M., Lu, Y., ... & Xu, D. (2025). Vila-m3: Enhancing vision-language models with medical expert knowledge. In *Proceedings of the Computer Vision and Pattern Recognition Conference* (pp. 14788–14798).

[17] Pan, J., Liu, C., Wu, J., Liu, F., Zhu, J., Li, H. B., ... & Rueckert, D. (2025). Medvlm-r1: Incentivizing medical reasoning capability of vision-language models (vlms) via reinforcement learning. *arXiv preprint arXiv:2502.19634*.

[18] Wang, X., Peng, Y., Lu, L., Lu, Z., Bagheri, M., & Summers, R. M. (2017). Chestx-ray8: Hospital-scale chest x-ray database and benchmarks on weakly-supervised classification and localization of common thorax diseases. In *Proceedings of the IEEE conference on computer vision and pattern recognition* (pp. 2097–2106).

[19] Demner-Fushman, D., Kohli, M. D., Rosenman, M. B., Shooshan, S. E., Rodriguez, L., Antani, S., ... & McDonald, C. J. (2016). Preparing a collection of radiology examinations for distribution and retrieval. *Journal of the American Medical Informatics Association*, 23(2), 304–310.

[20] Shao, Z., Wang, P., Zhu, Q., Xu, R., Song, J., Bi, X., ... & Guo, D. (2024). Deepseekmath: Pushing the limits of mathematical reasoning in open language models. *arXiv preprint arXiv:2402.03300*.

[21] Manning, C. D., Raghavan, P., & Schütze, H. (2008). *Introduction to Information Retrieval*. Cambridge University Press.

[22] Papineni, K., Roukos, S., Ward, T., & Zhu, W. J. (2002, July). Bleu: a method for automatic evaluation of machine translation. In *Proceedings of the 40th annual meeting of the Association for Computational Linguistics* (pp. 311–318).

23 Enhanced bandwidth compact parasitic patch antenna for applications operating at mid band 5G

Shaik Jabeen[1,a], Sai Kumar Reddy Pidugu[2,b], Sudeekshitha Kanapuram[2,c], Manju Peddabalugandla[2,d], Praveen Kunduru[2,e], and Venkata Karthik Pamaluri[2,f]

[1]Assistant Professor, ECE, KSRM College of Engineering, Kadapa, India
[2]UG Student, ECE, KSRM College of Engineering, Kadapa, India

Abstract: For Sub-6 GHz applications, a wideband Microstrip patch antenna (MPA) with omnidirectional inset feeding has been developed. A miniaturized patch antenna that is slotted and has a complete ground plane is first created, and to achieve the desired performance, electromagnetically connected parasitic components and partial ground planes are then added and enhanced. $40 \times 40 \times 1.6$ mm^3 is the volume of the investigated antenna, whose ground plane is defected by including slots. Dielectric substrate Rogers RT 5880 is used. The MPA covers N77, N78, N79, LTE 42 and LTE 46 has a resonating frequency of 3.4 GHz and 5.15 GHz, and its operating band extends from 2.74 GHz to 5.74 GHz. Applications for WiMAX (3.4–3.6 GHz) can also utilize the antenna. Slots of rectangular shape in a ground plane and the usage of a partially slotted ground plane are necessary to make it an omnidirectional antenna which affects the antenna's increased gain and directivity. It can function as a wide-band antenna with a high average efficiency, a decent reflection coefficient profile, and a VSWR of less than 2. The gains are 3.02 dB and 5.38 dB at a resonance of 3.4 GHz and 5.15 GHz, respectively. All of the antenna's performance matrices are modelled and investigated with HFSS, or the High Frequency Structure Simulator. The antenna prototype has a small volume, high efficiency, a collection of radiation properties that are completely balanced.

Keywords: Sub 6 GHz, partial ground, omnidirectional

1. Introduction

In the past, we could interact via computers, phones, and Internet connections that were wired to specific locations. These days, wireless communication services are available practically everywhere on the planet. The installation of satellite services and cellular wide area networks has made it feasible. Thus, wireless connectivity is become a need in daily life. The use of wireless devices doubles every ten years, thus new and improved antennas that are low profile, inexpensive, and mass-produced are needed to fulfill the requirements of future 5G networks. The study's objective is to maximize the radiation characteristics, bandwidth, and efficiency of the antenna since 2024 [1]. Its main objective is to improve antenna performance in the mid band 5G range or sub 6 GHz range which is essential for 5G highlighted in the review in an effort to satisfy the needs of dependable, fast mobile communication [2]. The quick transition from 2G to 5G wireless connectivity and the growing need for fast data transfer. Regarding Sub-6 GHz uses, it emphasizes the significance of effective antenna designs, especially micro strip patch antennas. By enhancing bandwidth, gain, and impedance matching, Defected Ground Structures (DGS) are presented as a method to improve antenna performance [3]. High-performance MIMO antenna systems with many inputs and outputs are becoming more and more necessary for applications utilizing 5G Sub-6 GHz. The CMA is presented as a useful method for maximizing antenna performance and draws attention to the difficulties in obtaining high gain and isolation in small antenna arrays. Designing an improved gain quad-element MIMO antenna array and less mutual coupling is the study's goal by utilizing CMA [4]. For high-performance 5G Bands N77/N78 at sub-6 GHz MIMO antennas. In MIMO systems, it draws attention to the difficulties in enhancing bandwidth, isolation, and diversity gain. For dependable 5G communication, the study suggests a 4-element MIMO antenna with a defective substrate structure to improve diversity characteristics, reduce mutual coupling, and guarantee effective radiation [5]. It talks about how difficult it is to achieve frequency and pattern reconfigurability in a single antenna design. A hybrid reconfigurable antenna that can switch between various frequencies and radiation patterns is suggested in the study to improve 5G networks' efficiency and adaptability [6]. This technique does away with the necessity for external matching networks by integrating a driving rectifier in parallel with a traditional

[a]sjabeen24@gmail.com, [b]saikumarreddy.pidugu@gmail.com, [c]sudeekshithareddy.k@gmail.com, [d]peddabalugandlamanju@gmail.com, [e]praveenkunduru7@gmail.com, [f]karthikpamaluri@gmail.com

DOI: 10.1201/9781003724988-23

voltage rectifier. With a dynamic input power range of 0 dB to 10 dB, the suggested rectifier functions throughout broad bandwidth between 2 and 3 GHz [7]. This antenna is applicable for 5G applications operating at sub-6 GHz like IoT, automotive communications, and smart industries, and it operates in the 2.7 to 4.9 GHz band. A shortened square patch featuring aperture-coupled feeding and a dumbbell-shaped hole with U-shaped slots are used in the design. To create orthogonal electromagnetic waves, the four radiating parts are organized in a 2 × 2 matrix with 90° successive rotations. This design creates a wideband, high-gain, and extremely effective 4T4R MIMO antenna that is based on the surface [8]. This design is appropriate for Sub-6GHz and wireless 3G, 4G, and 5G applications since it achieves a bandwidth of 1.12 GHz to 8.64 GHz. In the E-plane, the ANN-based FSS reflector increases the front-to-back ratio from 1.7 dB to 17.5 dB and the gain from 4.41 dB to 8.99 dB at the 5.5 GHz design frequency [9]. A tiny strip patch antenna with three slots and five slits for improved performance that operates at 2.22 GHz. Due to its emphasis on symmetry and simplicity, the design is highly cost-effective and has a high fabrication tolerance. Key performance data show that it is appropriate for 5G applications operating at sub-6 GHz. with an S11 parameter of -9.77 dB and gain values of -28.36 dB for E_θ and 5.27 dB for E_φ [10]. An antenna designed utilizing CMA, or typical mode analysis, which is dual-band planar. The antenna runs at WLAN applications use 5.8 GHz, while 5G sub-6 GHz apps use 3.5 GHz. The concept may be integrated into contemporary wireless communication systems since it uses CMA to achieve the required dual-band performance [11].

A brief analysis is conducted on a small (40 × 40 × 1.6 mm³) antenna that has high average radiation efficiency throughout the Sub-6GHz band application's whole operational frequency range, together with relatively steady gain and directivity. The following is how the paper is structured: The omnidirectional wideband Microstrip patch antenna (MPA) construction with inset feeding is explained in Section 2. Section 3 provides analysis of all the simulated results, and Section 4 concludes the work that has been given.

2. Antenna design Methodology

This section provides a detailed description of the geometrical construction of the developed Omni-directional MPA consists of a partial ground layer for applications of Sub-6 GHz 5G band. The ground, patch, and substrate are the three layers of the antenna. For the antenna, a piece of Rogers RT 5880 material is used. The MPA's ground plane and patch are both made of annealed copper. Rogers RT 5880 has respective thicknesses of 1.6 mm. The MPA is constructed with 40 mm × 40 mm × 1.6 mm using HFSS after the antenna's size has first been evaluated using a few basic equations (1)–(5).

The effective dielectric constant is determined using the expression

$$\varepsilon_{reff} = \frac{\varepsilon_r+1}{2} + \frac{\varepsilon_r-1}{2\sqrt{1+12h/W}} \quad (1)$$

$$\Delta L = 0.412h \frac{(\varepsilon_{reff}+0.3)(\frac{W}{h}+0.27)}{(\varepsilon_{reff}-0.258)(\frac{W}{h}+0.8)} \quad (2)$$

The effective length for a specific f_r is given as

$$L_{eff} = \frac{c}{2f_0\sqrt{\varepsilon_{reff}}} \quad (3)$$

The patch's effective length is expressed as

$$L_P = L + 2\,\Delta L \quad (4)$$

The patch's effective width is expressed as

$$W_P = \frac{c}{2f_0\sqrt{\frac{\varepsilon_{reff}+1}{2}}} \quad (5)$$

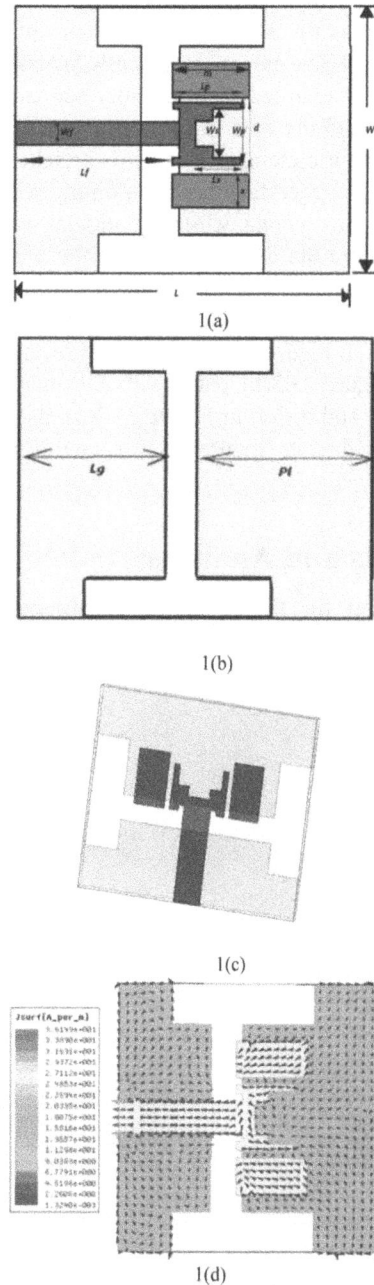

1(a)

1(b)

1(c)

1(d)

Figure 23.1. Developed antenna design (a) Front view (b) Rear view (c) 3D image (d) Surface current distribution.

Source: Author.

Here the top and side views are shown in Figures 23.1(a) and 1(b), along with the appropriate labelling. The 3D image is presented in the 1(c). The distribution of surface current is depicted in 1(d). The patch's dimensions are 9 mm for length and 10 mm for breadth. The patch has a rectangular slot with dimensions of 4 mm for width (WS) and 6 mm for length (L_s). On either side of the patch are two parasitic elements of rectangular shape, each has dimensions of 11 mm × 5.5 mm. These parasitic components affect the antenna's efficiency and reflection coefficient. Twelve millimetres separate the two rectangular parasitic elements (d). The width (W_F) and length (L_F) of the feed are 4.8 mm and 18 mm, respectively. The parasitic element's length (P_L) is 11 mm, whereas the MPA's partial ground plane's length (L_G) is 14 mm. The upper, electrically isolated but electromagnetically coupled section really serves as a partial ground layer and the bottom portion of the antenna functions as a parasitic element when it is attached. A portion of the ground surface facilitates the omnidirectional characteristics of the antenna, while rectangular parasitic components improve the directivity across the wide operating Sub-6GHz frequency spectrum (Table 23.1).

Here the Figure 23.2 illustrates the MPA's design process in detail. In Figure 23.2(a) patch and rectangular slot in ground. In Figure 23.2(b), patch with a rectangular opening in the ground and a slot. In Figure 23.2(c), patch with slots and ground with slots. Figure 23.2(d) Final design with the parasitic patches.

3. Results and Analysis

HFSS is used for the design and optimization of the MPA. Figure 23.3 shows the scattering parameter (S11)

Table 23.1. Required parameters for the antenna design

Name	Weight (mm)
Substrate Length (L)	40
Substrate Width (W)	40
Thickness of substrate (h)	1.6
Length of patch (L_p)	9
Width of Patch (W_p)	10
Slot length (L_s)	6
Slot width (W_s)	8
Parasitic component Length (m)	11
Parasitic component width (x)	5.5
Distance between parasitic elements (d)	12
Length of feed (L_f)	18
Width of feed (W_f)	4.8
Length of Ground layer (L_G, P_L)	14, 21

Source: Author.

of a developed Microstrip patch antenna. At 3.4GHz, the antenna resonates, and its S_{11} parameter is −18.69 dB. The envisioned antenna will operate within a frequency range of 2.74 GHz to 5.74 GHz. At the scattering parameter curve's −10 dB point, the observed bandwidth is 3 GHz. For Sub-6 GHz bands (such as the N77, N78, N79, LTE 42, and LTE 46 bands), the bandwidth is sufficient. The antenna is also suitable for WiMAX (3.4–3.6 GHz). Various nations utilize distinct Sub 6 GHz 5G frequency bands. The antenna proposed by us is compatible with 5G bands in various countries, including Europe (3.4–3.8 GHz), Spain, China, Ireland, Japan, Korea, India, and the USA (3.1–3.55 GHz and 3.7–4.2 GHz) (Figures 23.4–23.12).

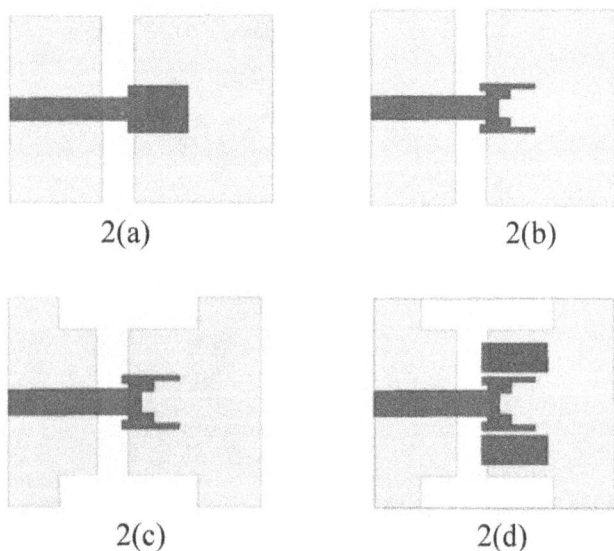

2(a)　　　　2(b)

2(c)　　　　2(d)

Figure 23.2. Antenna design (a) Phase I (b) Phase II (c) Phase III (d) Final designed antenna.

Source: Author.

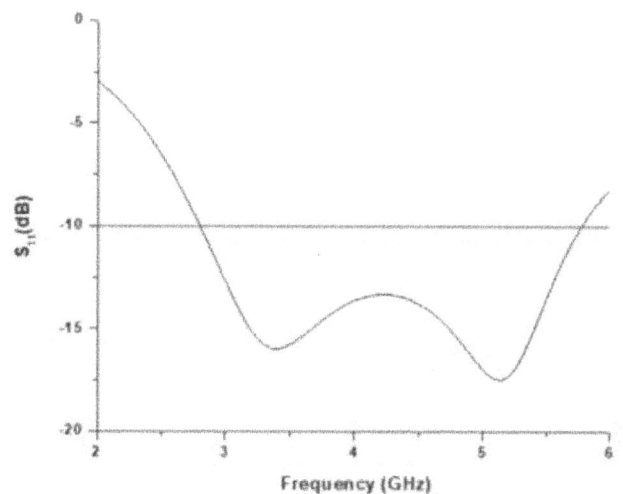

Figure 23.3. S_{11} curve of the designed MPA.

Source: Author.

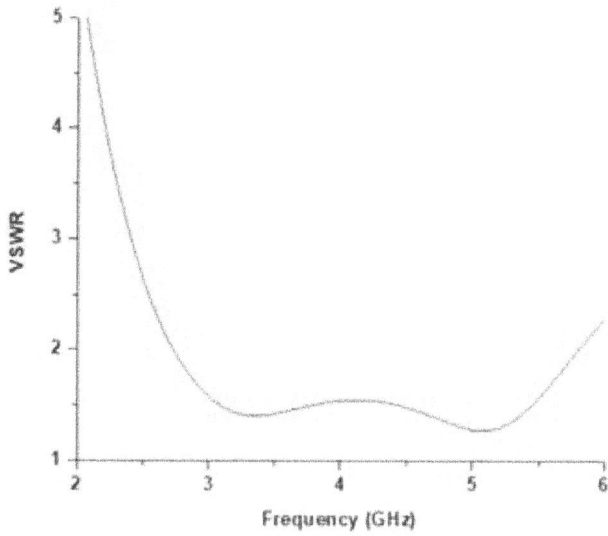

Figure 23.4. VSWR.

Source: Author.

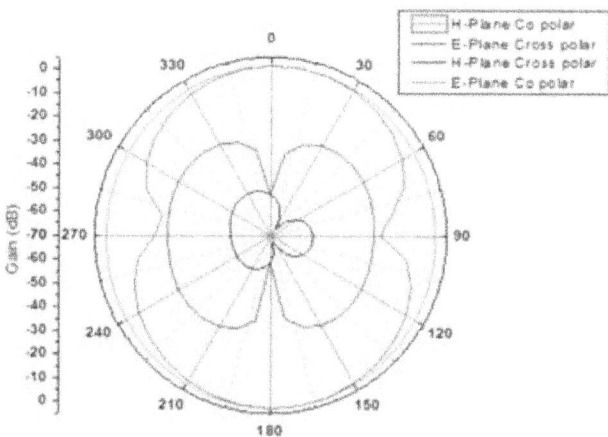

Figure 23.7. Radiation pattern at 5.15GHz.

Source: Author.

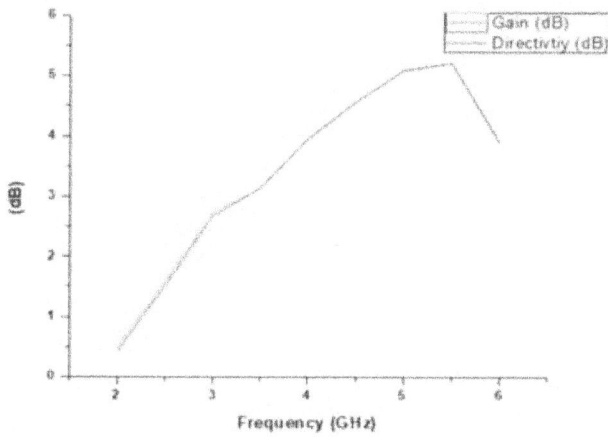

Figure 23.5. Gain and directivity Vs frequency.

Source: Author.

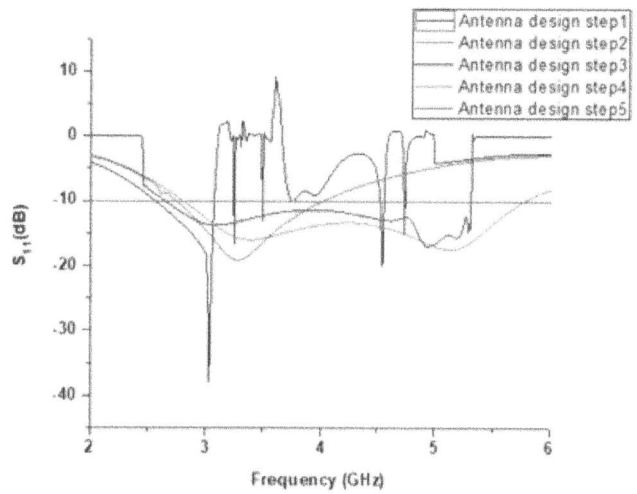

Figure 23.8. S$_{11}$ curve for steps of antenna design.

Source: Author.

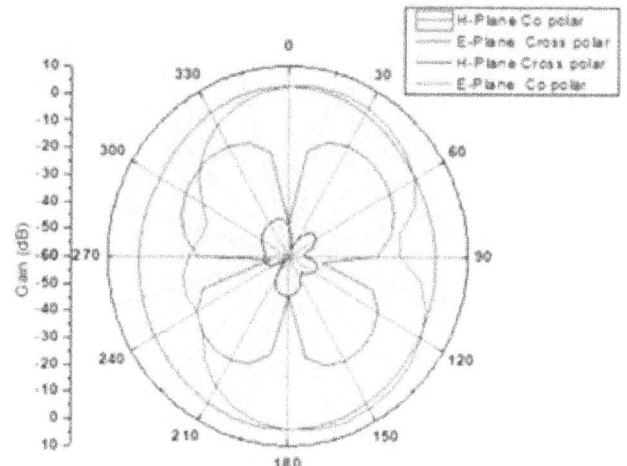

Figure 23.6. Radiation pattern at 3.4GHz.

Source: Author.

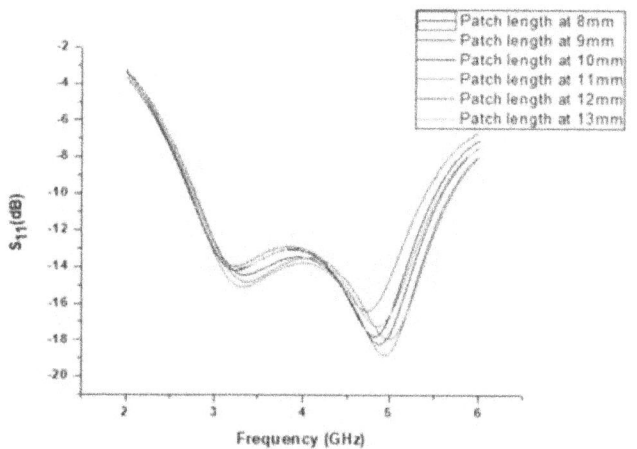

Figure 23.9. S$_{11}$ for variation of parasitic element length.

Source: Author.

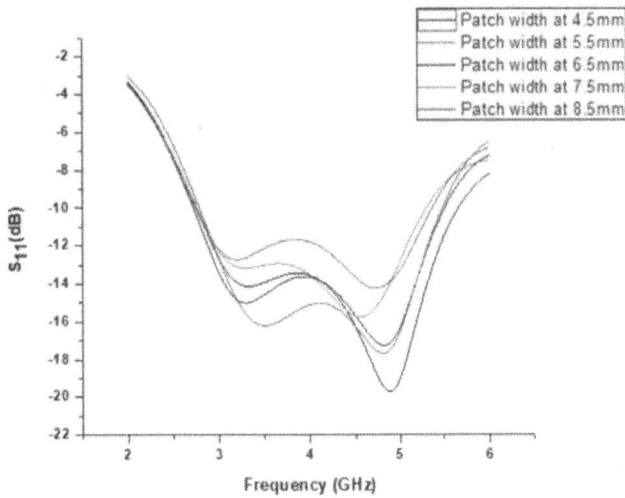

Figure 23.10. S$_{11}$ for variation of parasitic element width.
Source: Author.

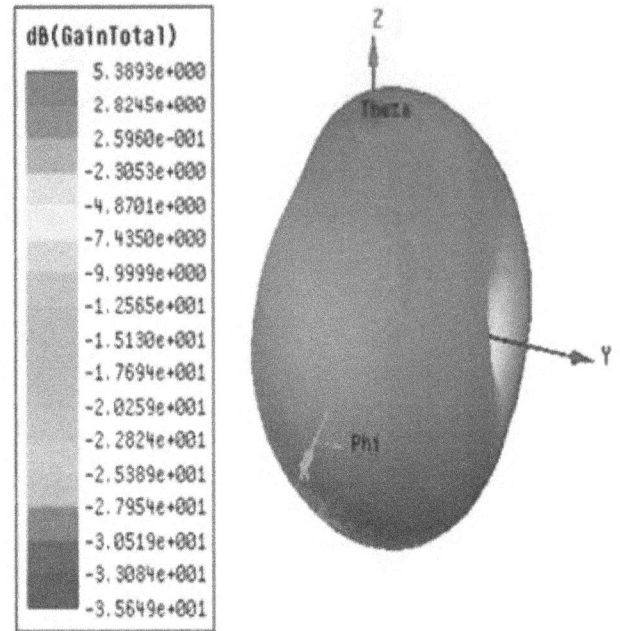

Figure 23.11. 3D Polar plot at 3.4GHz.
Source: Author.

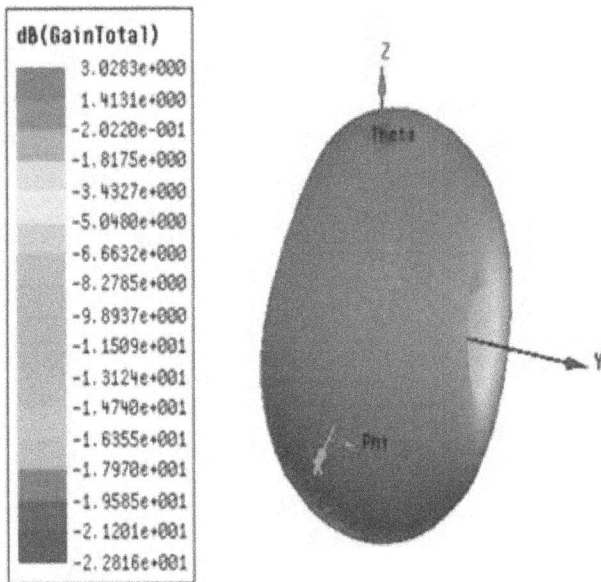

Figure 23.12. 3D Polar plot at 5.15GHz.
Source: Author.

is better suited for sub-6 GHz applications because of its parasitic elements, partial ground plane, and slotted patch. It can also be utilized with WiMAX version 2. Because of its broad frequency coverage and simulated results, the created Omni-directional antenna can be regarded as a great design for Sub-6 GHz applications.

Acknowledgement

We gratefully acknowledge the students, staff, and authority of Electronics and communication Engineering department for their cooperation in the research.

4. Conclusion

For 5G and WiMAX applications, the developed Omni-directional patch antenna model can cover the Sub-6 GHz (N77, N78, N79, LTE 42, and LTE 46) spectrum. The Rogers RT 5880 has a volume of 40 × 40 × 1.6 mm³ and was simulated utilizing the High Frequency Structure Simulator. The MPA's measured bandwidths are 3 GHz (2.74 GHz-5.74GHz) with great return loss characteristics. With strong gain and directivity, the antenna generates an efficient far field pattern. The VSWR across the entire bandwidth is less than 2. The measured VSWRs at the resonance point are 1.04. The antenna

References

[1]　Jain, R., Deshmukh, O. K., Shani, S., Thakare, V. V., & Singhal, P. K. (2024, March). Design and Analysis of Monopole Sub-6 GHz Antenna for Wireless Communication. In *2024 IEEE International Conference on Interdisciplinary Approaches in Technology and Management for Social Innovation (IATMSI)* (Vol. 2, pp. 1–6). IEEE.

[2]　Suganya, E., Pushpa, T. A. J. M., & Prabhu, T. (2024). Advancements in patch antenna design for Sub-6 GHz 5G smartphone application: a comprehensive review. *Wireless Personal Communications*, *137*(4), 2217–2252.

[3]　El Issawi, M. L., Konditi, D., & Usman, A. D. (2024). Design of Enhanced Wide Band Microstrip Patch Antenna Based on Defected Ground Structures (DGS) for Sub-6 GHz Applications. *International Journal of Electrical and Electronics Research*, *12*(1), 315–321.

[4]　Khan, R., Sethi, W. T., Malik, W. A., Jan, L., Tahseen, M. M., Almuhlafi, A. M., & Himdi, M. (2024). Enhancing gain and

isolation of a quad-element MIMO antenna array design for 5G sub-6 GHz applications assisted with characteristic mode analysis. *Scientific Reports*, *14*(1), 11111.

[5] Addepalli, T., Kumar, G. N., Rani, C. J., Koppala, N., Jetti, C. R., Kumar, C. M., ... & Kumar, B. K. (2025). A defected substrate 4-element mimo antenna with higher diversity characteristics for 5G sub 6 GHz N77/N78 band applications. *Wireless Networks*, *31*(2), 1931–1947.

[6] Kaur, M., Singh, H. S., & Agarwal, M. (2024, February). Design of a Hybrid Frequency and Pattern Reconfigurable Antenna for 5G Sub-6 GHz Applications. In *2024 IEEE Wireless Antenna and Microwave Symposium (WAMS)* (pp. 1–3). IEEE.

[7] Gyawali, B., Aboualalaa, M., Barakat, A., & Pokharel, R. K. (2024). Design of miniaturized sub-6 GHz rectifier with self-impedance matching technique. *IEEE Transactions on Circuits and Systems I: Regular Papers*.

[8] Salehi, M., & Oraizi, H. (2024). Wideband high gain metasurface-based 4T4R MIMO antenna with highly isolated ports for sub-6 GHz 5G applications. *Scientific Reports*, *14*(1), 14448.

[9] Ara, S., & Nunna, P. K. (2024). Gain and radiation pattern enhancement using ANN-based reflector antenna for full 5G Sub-6GHz applications. *International Journal of Advanced Technology and Engineering Exploration*, *11*(114), 644.

[10] Imeci, M. Y., Berk, M., & Imeci, S. T. (2024). A rectangular microstrip patch antenna with multiple slits and slots for sub-6 GHz 5G applications. *Heritage and Sustainable Development*, *6*(1), 13–20.

[11] Jabeen, S., & Hemalatha, G. (2023). Microstrip fed Pi-slot patch antenna with T-slot DGS for UWB applications. *Progress In Electromagnetics Research C*, *129*, 63–72.

24 MArP – Mapping using AR projection: Indoor campus navigation using augmented reality

Lakshmi M.[1,a], Ishaan Manjunath[2,b], Abhinandan S. Vishwaroop[2,c], Agniv Pramanick[2,d], and Vaishnavi S.[2,e]

[1]Assistant Professor Grade-III, Department of Information Science and Engineering, Nitte Meenakshi Institute of Technology, Bengaluru, India
[2]Department of Information Science and Engineering, Nitte Meenakshi Institute of Technology, Bengaluru, India

Abstract: "MArP – Mapping Using AR Projection" is an augmented reality (AR) application designed to simplify navigation within three-dimensional spaces, such as educational institutions. Using Unity for 3D modeling, ARCore for navigation, and C-sharp scripting, MArP creates an intuitive mobile platform. The app leverages device cameras for precise location tracking, overlaying AR arrows to guide users in real-time to their destinations. This innovative system enhances accessibility and exploration, providing optimal routes to vital landmarks like classrooms or offices. By combining AR technology with user-friendly design, MArP transforms campus navigation, setting a benchmark for interactive, efficient wayfinding solutions in institutional settings. MArP successfully integrates ARCore and Unity to create a functional navigation system for indoor environments. An enhanced UI and a QR scanning functionality to recalibrate the user's position make MArP a flexible and user-friendly AR-based navigation solution.

Keywords: ARCore, augmented reality, campus navigation, indoor navigation, qr recentering, unity

1. Introduction

Navigating large spaces like educational campuses can be tricky, especially for newcomers. Traditional tools like maps and signs often fall short when real-time guidance is needed [1, 2]. This paper presents MArP (Mapping Using AR Projection), a mobile AR app that simplifies indoor navigation by overlaying real-time directional markers through the device's camera. Built using Unity, ARCore, and C#, MArP helps users find their way in complex 3D spaces such as campuses [3], office buildings, or multi-level facilities, making navigation more accessible and intuitive.

The remainder of this paper is organized as follows: Section 2 reviews the background and related work, focusing on augmented reality, indoor navigation systems, and tools such as Unity and ARCore. Section 3 outlines the system design of MArP, detailing the architectural and functional aspects of the application. Section 4 discusses the implementation process, highlighting the development of 2D and 3D models, User Interface (UI) features, and navigation functionality. Section 5 presents the results, showcasing the key features of the application. Finally, Section 6 concludes the paper and explores future scope, including planned enhancements and additional functionalities for the system.

2. Background and Related Work

Indoor navigation [4] has become increasingly important for guiding users through complex environments. [1] Powered by tools like Unity, ARCore, and AR technology, smartphone-based systems [5] now offer real-time, interactive guidance using the device's camera and sensors. By overlaying arrows or landmarks onto the live view, these solutions enhance navigation without the need for extra hardware – making them practical for places like campuses, malls, and airports.

2.1. Indoor navigation systems

Indoor navigation systems aim to enhance accessibility and user experience [6] in spaces such as hospitals, airports, malls, and educational institutions. Their development involves an application [7] comprising a combination of technologies, including spatial mapping, sensor fusion, and user-centric interface design. Projects like MArP can revolutionize indoor navigation in supermarkets [8] by providing shoppers with real-time guidance to locate products efficiently.

Recent AR navigation systems integrate positioning tech to boost accuracy and usability. One method uses AR markers with Bluetooth Low Energy beacons for precise, energy-efficient guidance in large spaces [9]. Another

[a]lakshmi.m@nmit.ac.in, [b]1nt21is065.ishaan@nmit.ac.in, [c]1nt21is005.abhinandan@nmit.ac.in, [d]1nt21is017.agniv@nmit.ac.in, [e]1nt21is183.vaishnavi@nmit.ac.in

DOI: 10.1201/9781003724988-24

combines Building Information Modeling (BIM) and AR on smartphones to create smart, context-aware indoor routes using semantic building data [10]. In contrast, MArP offers a lightweight, hardware-free solution focused on real-time AR navigation – ideal for flexible environments like campuses.

AR indoor navigation with QR codes combines augmented reality with quick response (QR) codes to guide users in indoor spaces. QR codes placed at strategic locations [11] act as markers that, when scanned, trigger AR content such as directional arrows or interactive maps on the user's device. This method is cost-effective, easy to implement, and provides accurate navigation by linking the user's position to predefined locations, enhancing their experience in complex environments like malls or campuses [3, 12].

2.2. Comparative study with existing solutions

AR navigation has advanced with Google's Live View and Microsoft's HoloLens. Live View uses ARCore and GPS for outdoor guidance but falls short indoors. HoloLens handles indoor navigation well through spatial mapping, but its high cost and hardware needs make it impractical for schools and similar settings.

Beacon-based systems, common in malls and hospitals, rely on Bluetooth or WiFi for proximity tracking but need extensive infrastructure and often face signal disruptions.

MArP takes a different approach. It delivers real-time indoor navigation using just a smartphone camera, ARCore, and 3D maps – no GPS, Bluetooth, or expensive hardware required. With QR-based recalibration and simple setup, it's a cost-effective, scalable solution for institutions with limited resources (Table 24.1).

2.3. Unity

Unity is a powerful, user-friendly engine for building 2D, 3D, and AR/VR experiences. With C# scripting and cross-platform support, it helps developers create immersive projects with ease.

2.4. ARCore

ARCore is Google's platform for creating AR apps that blend digital content with the real world. Using device cameras and sensors, it enables motion tracking, surface detection, and light estimation, making it easy to build interactive and immersive experiences on Android and iOS.

3. System Design

The following section illustrates the architectural design of the system and elaborates about its working (Figure 24.1).

The system architecture for the MArP project shall integrate several tools and technologies to come up with a

Table 24.1. Comparative study

Feature / System	MArP	Google AR (Live View)	Microsoft HoloLens	Beacon-based Systems
Platform	Mobile (Android with ARCore)	Mobile (ARCore on Android/iOS)	HoloLens (head-mounted device)	Smartphones/tablets with Bluetooth/WiFi
Environment	Indoor	Outdoor (some limited indoor support)	Indoor	Indoor (malls, airports, hospitals)
Hardware Dependency	Camera + smartphone only	GPS + camera	Specialized HoloLens hardware	External beacons + device
Scalability	High – easily deployable	Medium – limited to GPS-available areas	Low to expensive, device-limited	Medium – requires physical installation
Navigation Accuracy	High (QR recalibration aids)	Moderate (GPS drift issues)	Very High (precise spatial mapping)	Moderate (signal interference possible)
Use Case Focus	Campus navigation / educational spaces	City navigation / streets	Enterprise-level training, maintenance	Public venues (retail, transport)
Cost to Deploy	Low	Low	High	Medium

Source: Author.

functional AR navigation application. The design process is articulated in the flowchart, and it involves the following stages:

1. Use of MS Paint to create 2D mini-maps: MS Paint was used to create 2D mini-maps of the college campus, providing simplified visual guides for navigation. These maps highlight buildings, and landmarks, aiding users in orientation.
2. Unity as the Platform: Unity integrates 3D assets and ARCore Software Development Kit (SDK) to enable spatial mapping, anchoring, and navigation path visualization.
3. ARCore SDK: ARCore uses a device camera to calculate the mobile's orientation, so mapping and overlays in the AR experience are very accurate.

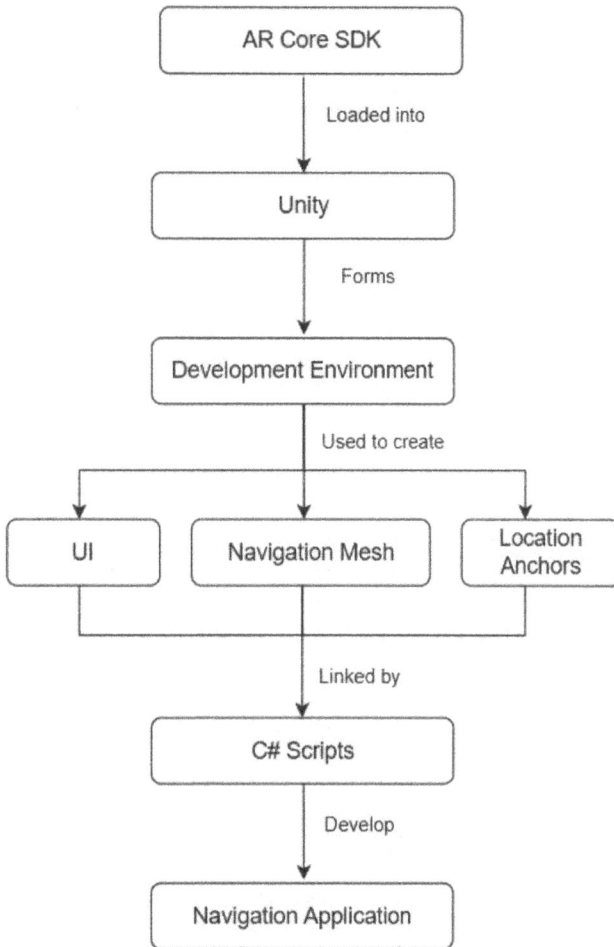

Figure 24.1. System design.

Source: Author.

4. Composition of Main Components: A core component is created inside Unity. It contains three:
   • User Interface or UI: An easy to interact with interface for a user to interface with the application.
   • Navigation Mesh: Represents a pre-computed map that guides users to their destinations.
   • Location Anchors: Ensure accurate placement of AR elements in the real-world environment for reliable navigation.
5. C# Scripting for Integration: C# scripts help connect the UI, paths, and location anchors to interact and function smoothly.
6. Navigation Application Development: The combined system leads to an AR navigation application that brings 3D navigation markers onto a user's real world.

4. Implementation

The implementation of the MArP application follows a structured and systematic approach, leveraging AR technology to create an interactive and intuitive indoor navigation [1, 5] system. The development began with the creation of a 2D map of the department using MS Paint, which served as the blueprint for the navigation system. To ensure accurate scaling, real-world dimensions were converted into pixel values (1 meter = 100 pixels), allowing precise representation of spaces within the application. This 2D map was imported into Blender and Unity 3D to construct a detailed three-dimensional model of the department, complete with walls, objects, and pathways that match real-world dimensions. This meticulous design ensures a realistic and seamless navigation experience for users.

To enable dynamic navigation, the Unity AI Navigation package was used to generate a Navigation Mesh (NavMesh) [13], a crucial element for tracking targets and determining optimal routes. NavMesh dynamically calculates [13] routes to specific destinations, ensuring efficiency and accuracy in navigation. In addition, a target tracking mechanism was implemented to allow users to locate specific rooms or objects within the environment.

ARCore, Google's advanced platform for augmented reality development, plays a pivotal role in enhancing the application's capabilities. It provides environmental understanding and motion tracking, enabling precise overlay of AR elements, such as directional indicators and trackers, within the user's live camera feed. These AR elements guide users visually, making navigation intuitive and engaging. C# Scripting in Unity integrates ARCore features, including the development of a camera system that displays real-time views of the user's surroundings through their device camera. Simultaneously, the UI presents a 2D map showing the user's current location and the suggested route.

Users can select their desired destination directly within the application and toggle the visibility of the route tracker. This interactive functionality makes the navigation experience customizable and user-friendly. Furthermore, a QR [11] scanning feature has been integrated to recalibrate the user's position dynamically. By scanning QR codes placed at predefined locations within the department, users can now begin navigation from multiple starting points. With its detailed 3D modeling, ARCore integration, and advanced navigation features, the application delivers an immersive and practical indoor navigation experience.

5. Results

MArP showcases how AR can simplify indoor navigation through a 3D model built from a 2D map, closely matching real-world dimensions. Users view live navigation overlays through their camera while tracking their location on a 2D map. Destinations can be selected via an intuitive interface, with toggles for route lines and arrows. Unity's AI Navigation computes efficient paths, and QR scanning allows users to recalibrate their starting point from various locations.

To evaluate MArP's real-time performance and reliability, we conducted tests across multiple locations within the campus, including classrooms, corridors, and intersections. The key metrics observed were: Distance travelled, Time to reach the destination using the app, AR Arrow Stability, User Recalibration Accuracy (via QR).

Metric used to calculate QR Recalibration Success Rate

$$= \frac{Number\ of\ successful\ position\ corrections}{Number\ of\ QR\ Scans\ attempted} \times 100$$

Unlike GPS- or beacon-based systems that often suffer from signal drift or hardware inconsistencies, MArP relies purely on device vision and marker-based recalibration. This ensures consistent performance across devices without dependence on network or satellite signals – ideal for educational environments where infrastructure is limited (Table 24.2).

Snapshots of the app highlight its key strengths: real-time AR guidance, interactive mapping, and a smooth user experience, making MArP a practical and accessible indoor navigation solution (Figures 24.2 and 24.3).

6. Conclusion and Future Scope

The MArP application demonstrates the potential of AR for indoor navigation by providing an intuitive and interactive solution. By combining detailed 3D modeling, ARCore integration, and real-time navigation capabilities, MArP addresses the challenges of navigating complex indoor environments. The application offers users the ability to view their surroundings through a live camera feed, coupled with an integrated 2D map and directional overlays, ensuring seamless and efficient navigation. Features like destination selection, route tracking, and the use of QR codes for recalibrating starting positions enhance the system's flexibility and usability. MArP serves as a significant step towards developing accessible and practical navigation solutions for educational institutions and similar environments.

In the future, the system can be expanded to include additional functionalities that enhance user experience like the

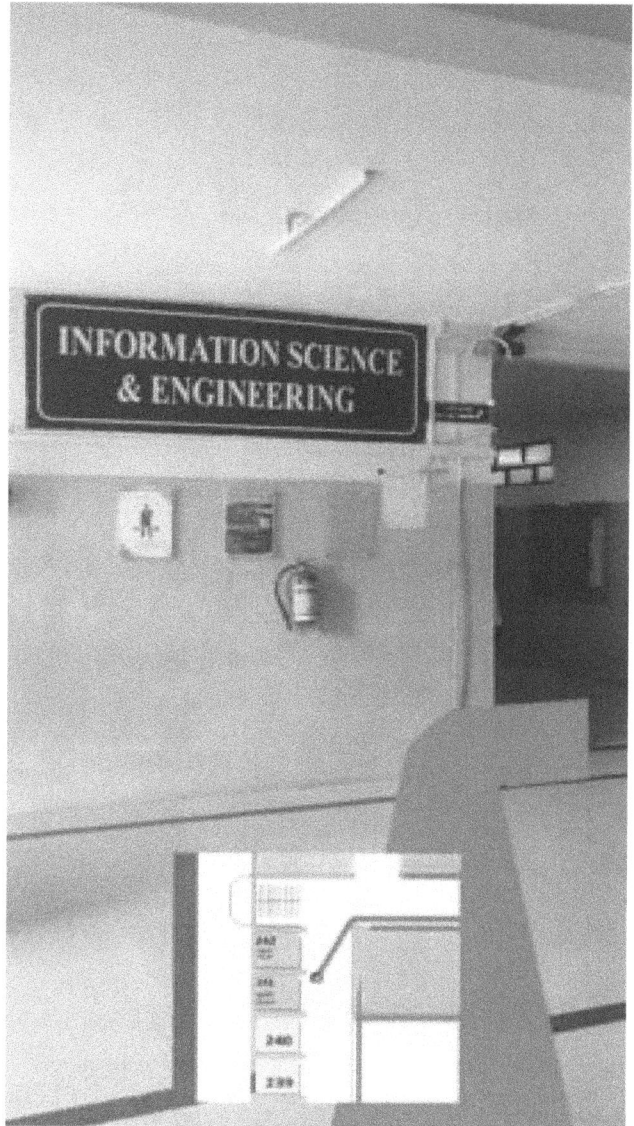

Figure 24.2. The tracker line being displayed during navigation.
Source: Author.

integration of voice guidance, where audio cues signal the user's proximity to their destination or provide directions during navigation. Furthermore, geotagging can be explored to determine a user's precise coordinates, enabling even more accurate and dynamic routing. Enhancing the user interface with more intuitive design elements and functionalities can further improve the application's accessibility and ease of use. The integration of these features can extend the usability of MArP beyond educational institutions to other domains such as hospitals, supermarkets [8], and airports, making it a versatile solution for indoor navigation challenges.

Acknowledgement

We gratefully acknowledge the students, staff, and authority of the Department of Information Science And Engineering

Table 24.2. Results of MArP app evaluation

Test Scenario	Approx. Dist (m)	Reach time	AR Arrow Stability (1–10)	QR Recalibration Success Rate
Room 219 to Administrator's office	63.49	1 min 13 s	9.2	83.33%
IOT Lab to ISE HOD Cabin	49.84	1 min 32 s	7.8	87.5%
IOT Lab to Room 272	24.92	37 s	8.4	90%

Source: Author.

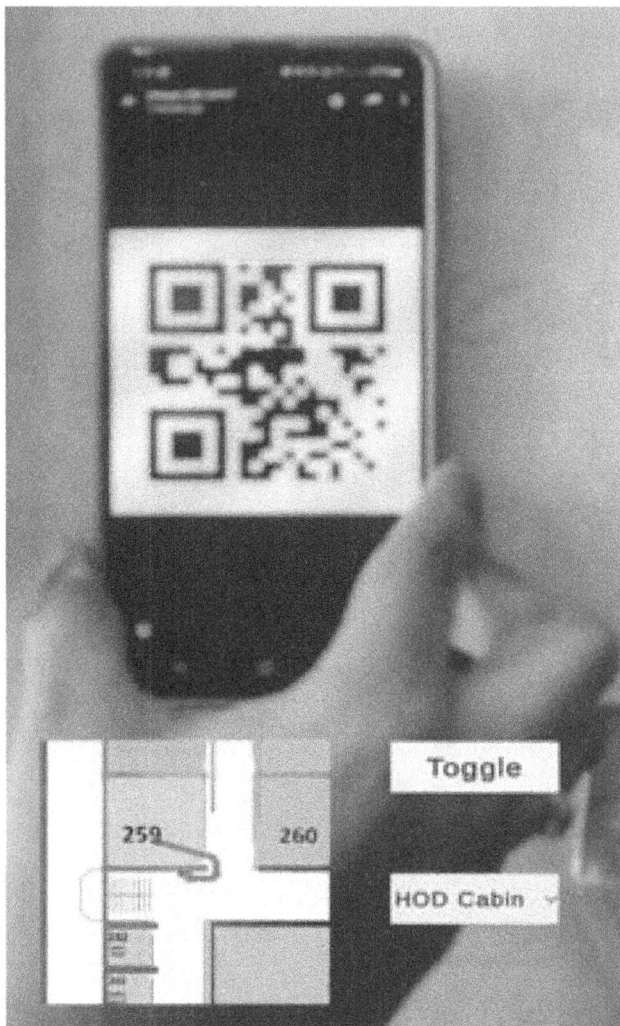

Figure 24.3. Scanning the QR Code to recalibrate to the current location.

Source: Author.

at Nitte Meenakshi Institute of Technology for their cooperation in the research.

References

[1] Maran, B. R., Giridharan, L., & Krishnaveni, R. (2023, June). Augmented reality-based indoor navigation using unity engine. In *2023 International Conference on Sustainable Computing and Smart Systems (ICSCSS)* (pp. 1696–1700). IEEE.

[2] Ramesh, M. S., Vardhini, J. N. R., Murugan, S., & Mayan, J. A. (2023, May). Indoor navigation using augmented reality for mobile application. In *2023 7th International Conference on Intelligent Computing and Control Systems (ICICCS)* (pp. 1049–1052). IEEE.

[3] Sundarramurthi, M., & Chandrashekar, K. (2022, July). Design and development of a smart campus using augmented reality (scar). In *2022 IEEE International Conference on Electronics, Computing and Communication Technologies (CONECCT)* (pp. 1–5). IEEE.

[4] Helmi, R. A. A., Ravichandran, H. A., Jamal, A., & Mohammed, M. N. (2022, December). Design and Development of Indoor Campus Navigation Application. In *2022 IEEE 10th Conference on Systems, Process & Control (ICSPC)* (pp. 77–82). IEEE.

[5] Li, Y., Zhang, P., Lan, H., Zhuang, Y., Niu, X., & El-Sheimy, N. (2015, October). A modularized real-time indoor navigation algorithm on smartphones. In *2015 International Conference on Indoor Positioning and Indoor Navigation (IPIN)* (pp. 1–7). IEEE.

[6] Alkady, Y., Rizk, R., Alsekait, D. M., Alluhaidan, A. S., & Abdelminaam, D. S. (2024). Sins ar: An efficient smart indoor navigation system based on augmented reality. *IEEE Access, 12*, 109 171–109.

[7] Ng, X. H., & Lim, W. N. (2020, October). Design of a mobile augmented reality-based indoor navigation system. In *2020 4th International Symposium on Multidisciplinary Studies and Innovative Technologies (ISMSIT)* (pp. 1–6). IEEE.

[8] Jayananda, P. K. V., Seneviratne, D. H. D., Abeygunawardhana, P., Dodampege, L. N., & Lakshani, A. M. B. (2018, December). Augmented reality based smart supermarket system with indoor navigation using beacon technology (easy shopping android mobile app). In *2018 IEEE International Conference on Information and Automation for Sustainability (ICIAfS)* (pp. 1–6). IEEE.

[9] Sato, F. (2018). Indoor navigation system based on augmented reality markers. In *Innovative Mobile and Internet Services in Ubiquitous Computing: Proceedings of the 11th International Conference on Innovative Mobile and Internet Services in Ubiquitous Computing (IMIS-2017)* (pp. 266–274). Springer International Publishing.

[10] Zhang, W., Li, Y., Li, P., & Feng, Z. (2025). A BIM and AR-based indoor navigation system for pedestrians on smartphones. *KSCE Journal of Civil Engineering, 29*(1), 100005.

[11] Zhuang, Y., Kang, Y., Huang, L., & Fang, Z. (2018, March). A geocoding framework for indoor navigation based on the QR code. In *2018 Ubiquitous Positioning, Indoor Navigation and Location-Based Services (UPINLBS)* (pp. 1–4). IEEE.

[12] Suryawati, N., Sukaridhoto, S., Rante, H., Fajrianti, E. D., & Hakim, O. S. (2023, August). Indoor navigation using augmented reality for PENS postgraduate building. In *2023 International Electronics Symposium (IES)* (pp. 593–598). IEEE.

[13] Li, D., Liu, M., Zhang, J., & Cheng, E. (2015, January). An improved A* algorithm applicable for campus navigation system. In *2015 International conference on network and information systems for computers* (pp. 588–591). IEEE.

25 Smart health scheduler using NLP

*Preeti Bailke[a], Ram Narwade, Aditya Dharashivkar, Achala Patil,
Atharv Pawar, and Mahesh Kotkar*

Department of Information Technology, Vishwakarma Institute of Technology, Pune, India

Abstract: Using its voice-operated healthcare assistant function the system creates connections between user patients and medical facilities and their medical practitioners. The solution depends on Firebase Realtime Database for protecting patient data along with medical schedules and doctor availability and exhibits immediate reading of heart rate and blood oxygen levels. The system allows users to interact through their voice to schedule appointments and search hospitals along with retrieving health news through speech_recognition together with pyttsx3 components. The application deals with medical data and displays disease information and processes natural language dates using dateparser. The system functions seamlessly because of its combination between re pattern matching and threading multi- threading. The performance comprehension is supported by dotenv's sensitive data protection features and logging system. The project shows how AI and voice technology improves healthcare accessibility by building the basis which will support future applications of health analytics and treatment recommendations.

Keywords: Speech recognition, nature language processing, heart disease prediction, appointment management

1. Introduction

The voice-enabled healthcare assistant uses speech_recognition for voice processing alongside pyttsx3 for text generation features and securely saves patient information in Firebase Realtime Database and manages booking appointments with the database. Re and Dateparser work together with threading for efficient command execution and the system uses dotenv to protect data and enhance security features. The heart disease data management through machine learning models including decision trees, SVM and neural networks results in enhanced heart disease diagnosis according to Sharma and Rizvi [1]. Performance metrics between logistic regression and decision trees and random forests and KNN and SVM are enhanced by dataset balancing and feature selection methods that Arghandabi and Shams [1] discuss. Through this solution healthcare professionals obtain benefits from the integration of artificial intelligence and medical data handling that employs machine learning approaches.

2. Literature Review

This research [1] by Bahirat et al. shows how machine learning (ML) and natural language processing (NLP) merge to develop healthcare improvements through diagnosis support systems that also enhance patient management and communication approaches. SVM algorithm and random forests and neural networks conduct disease predictions per their investigation findings while text mining alongside sentiment analysis manages raw health-related data using NLP tools. AI-designed systems for scheduling software together with warning tools receive analysis from the authors yet they raise concerns about medical data protection guidelines and classification requirements and decision-making understandability for healthcare development.

Patil and Darji et al. [2] crafted Medic to act as an interactive recommendation system that applies SVM and neural networks together with NLP-based virtual assistants to generate personalized healthcare. By implementing scheduling resource optimization through AI their main function stands out while they resolve three main barriers by using data encryption along with advanced NLP capabilities.

SVM and Random Forest along with Logistic Regression methods form the foundation of analysis in the research paper by Absar et al. [3] to evaluate precision performance for heart disease detection processes. This research shows that healthcare operations improve their diagnostic accuracy when healthcare professionals use structured combined with unstructured data while applying strategies to remediate class imbalance and develop model explanations. Healthcare service and decision-making enhancement through NLP remains the subject of investigation by Abdelwahap et al. [4]. Through NLP medical professionals can extract valuable healthcare intelligence from advanced medical datasets and their decision-making processes are enhanced through automated appointment booking and patient complaint management and medication tracking mechanisms to advance modern healthcare capabilities.

[a]preeti.bailke@vit.edu

DOI: 10.1201/9781003724988-25

3. Methodology

The development of an integrated solution which merges SmartMed Scheduler and Heart Disease Predictor occurred through a project methodology that used web technologies, databases, and machine learning algorithms:

3.1. System architecture overview

A modular design structure uses three key components which make up the system architecture:

The system implements HTML and CSS for its frontend followed by JavaScript and backend API operations controlled by FastAPI and database organization through MySQL which incorporates a disease prediction function built from Python-based Logistic Regression. The patient data and appointments remain stored on MySQL but the disease prediction capabilities rely on the Python-based Logistic Regression model.

3.2. Frontend development

- **Technology Stack:** The system design obtains responsiveness through HTML and CSS yet JavaScript enables form validation to boost user experience along with other dynamic operations.
- **Features:** The application requires users to input their personal data while specifying their availability preferences and healthcare resource levels. The prediction form enables patients to enter medical variables such as age, cholesterol, blood pressure so that the system can evaluate heart disease risk while providing customized action plans.

3.3. Backend implementation

- **Technology Stack:** FastAPI runs as the backend development because it enables fast system speed alongside rapid API responses.
- **Core Functionalities:** Users receive quick disease predictions by using the machine learning model of the system. The system operates through two processing lines both saving input information to a database and directing it to the prediction model. Stability of the system is guaranteed through error-handling protocols which enable reliable and smooth operation.

3.4. Database management

- **Technology:** The application relies on MySQL as the database system to handle all its structured data entries.
- **Database Design:** Both the User Table and Medical History Table exist in the database system with separate fields for patient name, age, gender, email, and password as well as cholesterol, blood pressure, and fasting blood sugar level records. Both appointment booking and heart disease prediction functionalities reside within the Appointments Table which protects all confidential data through field-based encryption.

3.5. Machine learning module

The project utilizes Logistic Regression for heart disease risk binary classification of the UCI heart disease dataset where training occurs using age, cholesterol, blood sugar, blood pressure, and heart rate inputs. Very first data preprocessing includes replacing missing values followed by feature normalization along with attribute selection via correlation methods before creating the 75% training dataset and 25% testing data. Paramount to the solution is Pickle and Joblib-based backend processing in combination with FastAPI used for delivering streaming healthcare prediction functionality.

3.6. Comparative analysis of machine learning algorithm for the data-set

Logistic Regression demonstrates superior performance compared to Decision Tree and XGBoost and Random Forest when evaluating patient diagnosis models with a 87.68% accuracy value. The recall performance of LR stands at 0.88 while its F1-score maintains balance at 0.87 and its effectiveness in detecting diseased patients remains high. Feature importance within Logistic Regression becomes directly available from its coefficient values while XGBoost and Random Forest remain less interpretable. The combination of L1 (Lasso) and L2 (Ridge) penalties enhances LR performance so it becomes an optimal candidate for structured medical data due to its better overfitting resistance. The model characteristics of LR confirm it as an optimal choice for heart disease prediction even though Random Forest remains effective for complex problems.

3.7. Logistic regression for disease prediction

The statistical method Logistic Regression provides binary classification results by identifying output values limited to either 1 or 0. Our Smart Health Scheduler system utilizes an evaluation process for heart disease risk assessment through patient historical medical data and symptoms and health measurement results. The model applies the sigmoid

Table 25.1. Comparative analysis

Model	Accuracy	Precision	Recall	F1-Score
Logistic Regression	87.68%	0.87	0.88	0.87
Random Forest	87.01%	0.87	0.87	0.87
Decision Tree	86.41%	0.86	0.87	0.86
XGBoost	86.96%	0.87	0.87	0.87

Source: Author.

function for making event probability predictions using essential factors:

1. Age (X1) – Older individuals are at higher risk.
2. Cholesterol Level (X2) – High cholesterol can lead to artery blockages.
3. Resting Blood Pressure (X3) – High blood pressure is a major risk factor.
4. Fasting Blood Sugar (X4) – Elevated sugar levels are linked to diabetes and heart disease.
5. Maximum Heart Rate Achieved (X5) – Lower heart rate recovery may indicate heart issues.
6. Electrocardiogram Results (X6) – Abnormal ECG patterns indicate heart problems.
7. Smoking Status (X7) – Smoking damages blood vessels.
8. Obesity (BMI) (X8) – Higher BMI is correlated with heart disease.
9. Family History of Heart Disease (X9) – Genetic predisposition plays a role.
10. P(Y=1) – The neural network uses a sigmoid function applied to combined linear inputs X1, X2, …, X9.

$$P(Y = 1) = \frac{1}{1 + e^{-(-5.8 + 0.04X_1 + 0.002X_2 + 0.03X_3 + 0.5X_4 - 0.02X_5 + 1.2X_6 + 0.8X_7 + 0.07X_8 + 0.6X_9)}}$$

3.8. Workflow

Appointment Scheduling: Users create accounts before logging in to access the system from which they select their preferred time slot or create their individual appointment times. Following the scheduling process the system saves patient care-oriented schedules which efficiently use resources while reducing waiting times into the database.

Disease Prediction: Medical information including patient age and cholesterol values and blood pressure results is transmitted to the prediction form by health subjects. The backing system processes the data which gets sent to the logistic regression model for assessment. The system presents both prediction results and medical check-up suggestions directly to the patient on the interface.

3.9. Performance evaluation

User experience of logistic regression depends on accuracy testing and precision as well as recall and F1-score metrics and real-time interaction feedback for system usability alongside API backend reliability testing.

3.10. Tools and libraries used

- Frontend: HTML, CSS, JavaScript.
- Backend: FastAPI, Python.
- Database: MySQL.
- Machine Learning: The data analysis and model development together with visualization depend on Pandas,

NumPy, Scikit-learn and Matplotlib libraries from Machine Learning.

The systematic approach describes all processes and technologies which lead to project completion therefore making it prepared for research paper publication. Additional clarification about this topic is available upon request.

4. Proposed System

The SmartMed Scheduler combined with Heart Disease Predictor provides solutions to solve healthcare problems related to appointment management and advanced heart disease detection. This system integrates advanced web technologies together with machine learning capabilities and protected database systems to provide medical services for healthcare professionals alongside patient care solutions.

4.1. System objectives

The system makes independent scheduling decisions based on critical treatment criteria together with resource availability alongside patient choice factors. Logistic regression functions in this system enables staff to predict heart disease risks which supports preventive care delivery. A healthcare system supports easy patient interaction with built-in security measures to protect patient information.

4.2. System components

- **Smart Appointment Scheduler: Functionality:** This system establishes emergency patient categories while analyzing staff schedules to prevent scheduling conflicts during appointment generation without manual intervention.
- **Features:** The system performs automated timing-based appointment booking while alerting for scheduling conflicts then suggesting available time options to develop the best arrangements for healthcare staff.
- **Heart Disease Prediction Module:** Logistic Regression serves the machine learning model to process health parameters that generate heart disease risk percentages which classify users into low-moderate-high risk groups. The data processing system performs normalization along with scaling and selection of features for making predictions which maintain accuracy. The model achieves superior prediction results through medical parameters that include ages and cholesterol measurements with blood pressure levels and fasting blood sugar readings. Users receive fast evaluations and medical advice as well as doctor referral services through the output.
- **User Interface (Frontend):** User-friendly design was created through the combination of HTML and CSS and

JavaScript programming languages in the frontend user interface of this platform.

4.3. Backend (Logic and processing)

The system operates with FastAPI as the main processing layer that activates data entry processes linked to the machine learning model after user input. The system implements scheduling codes to conduct automated appointment prioritization in combination with scheduling functions. A real-time heart disease risk assessment service runs through the integrated Logistic Regression model for system-level performance.

4.4. Database management

MySQL operates as the principal database solution of the system to guarantee safe storage of medical data.

- **Data Structure:** The system stores user data, medical history, appointments, and heart disease risk assessments in respective tables for efficient management and future evaluations.
- **Data Security:** System encryption processes all sensitive data to fulfill GDPR and HIPAA privacy standards which protects user information from unauthorized users.
- **System Workflow Appointment Scheduling:** The system enables users to create accounts and add availability constraints and schedules which generates appointment schedules that do not cross each other according to urgency criteria combined with provider availability and resource requirements.
- **Heart Disease Prediction:** The system requires users to fill in their health data before the backend carries out calculations using the Logistic Regression model to generate immediate heart disease analysis results and recommendations.
- **System Feedback and Updates:** Upcoming appointments along with crucial risk results are automatically communicated through the platform to users. The system allows administrators to check prediction reports which enables them to modify appointment schedules (Figure 25.1).

5. **Further Advancements**

- Heart Disease Predictor (Figure 25.2).
- Appointment Scheduling Form (Figure 25.3).
- Health Tips Page (Figure 25.4)

6. **Further Advancements**

The system can achieve better functionality by adding real-time health monitor data from wearable tech and multiple

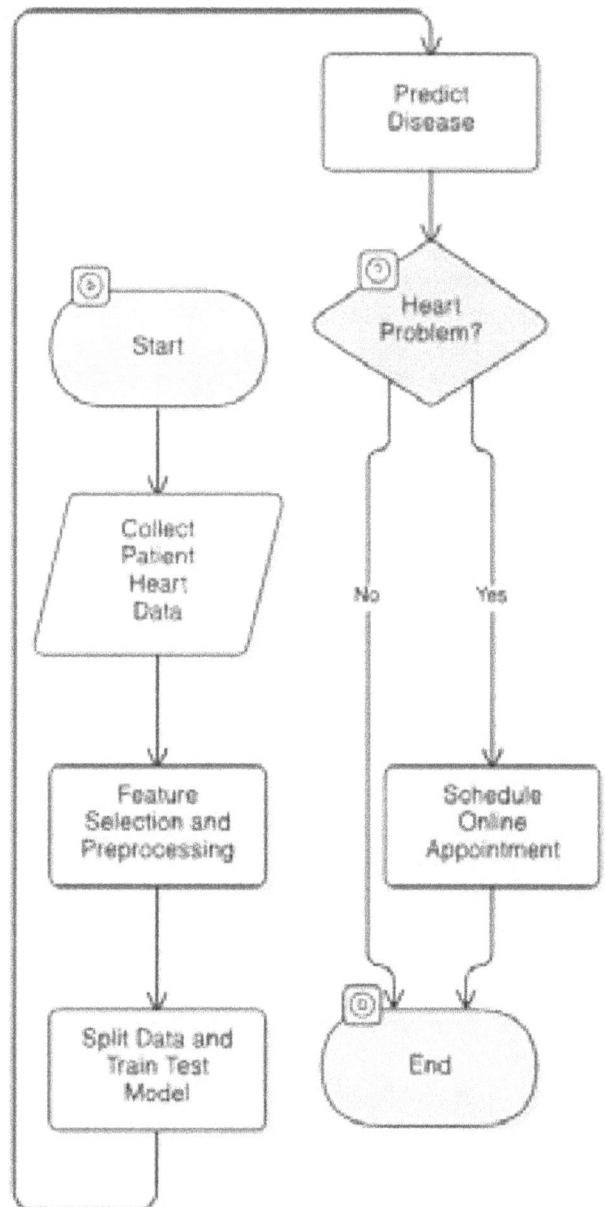

Figure 25.1. Flow diagram.

Source: Author.

disease predictor models and multilingual system features for improved access capabilities. The security of data sharing among healthcare facilities can be achieved through implementing blockchain technology.

7. **Conclusion**

The SmartMed Scheduler and Disease Predictor uses machine learning for disease prediction along with enhanced appointment scheduling functions that increase resource utilization and generate better efficiency and achieves higher patient

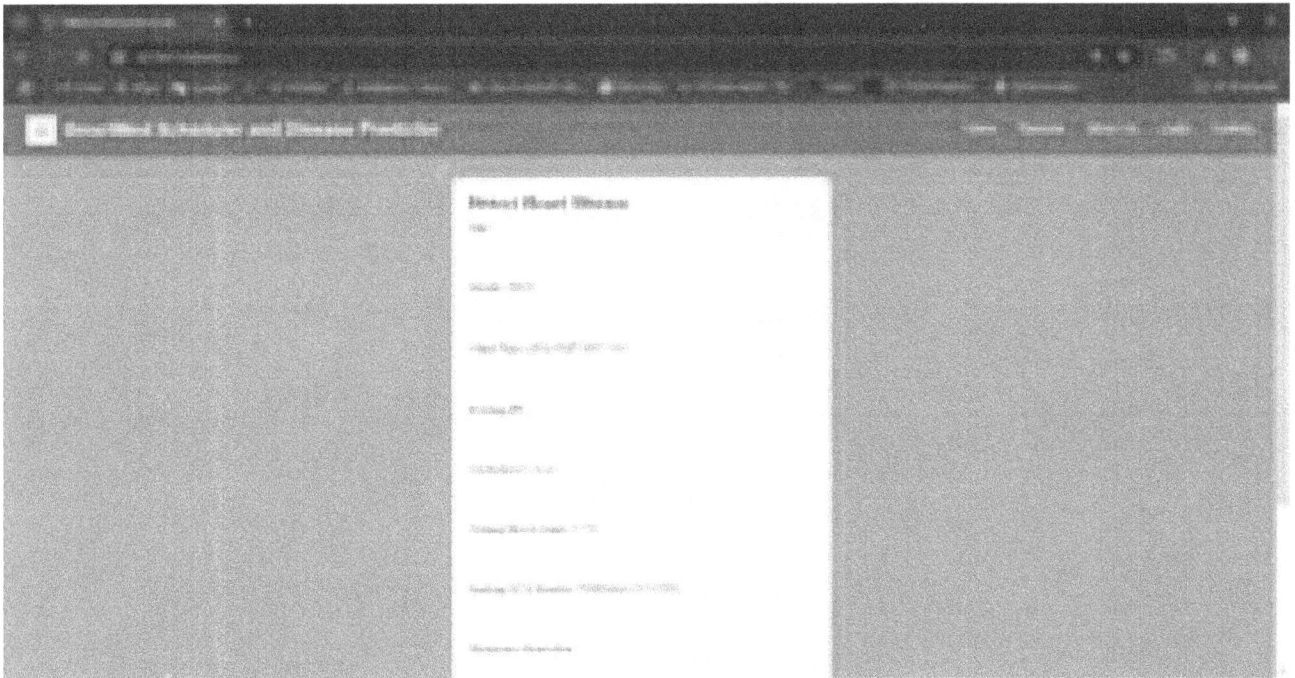

Figure 25.2. Heart disease predictor.
Source: Author.

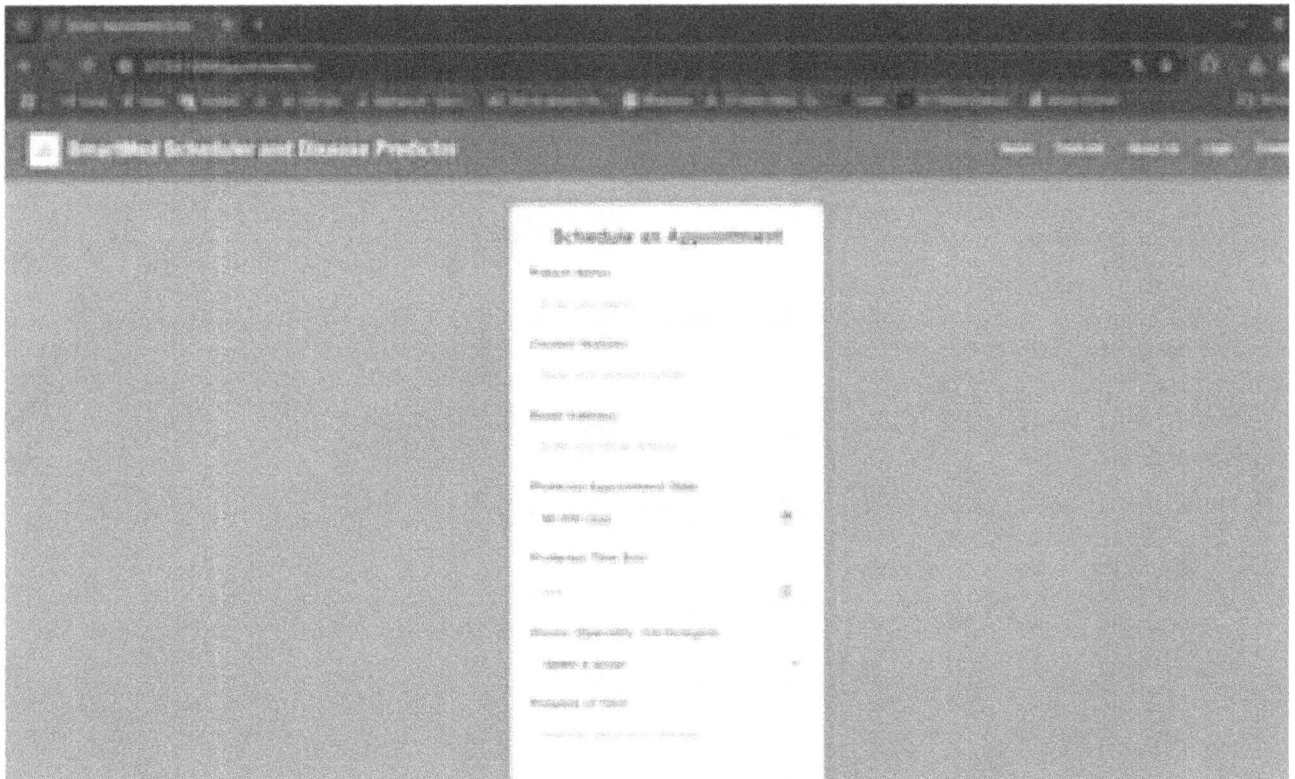

Figure 25.3. Appointment scheduling form.
Source: Author.

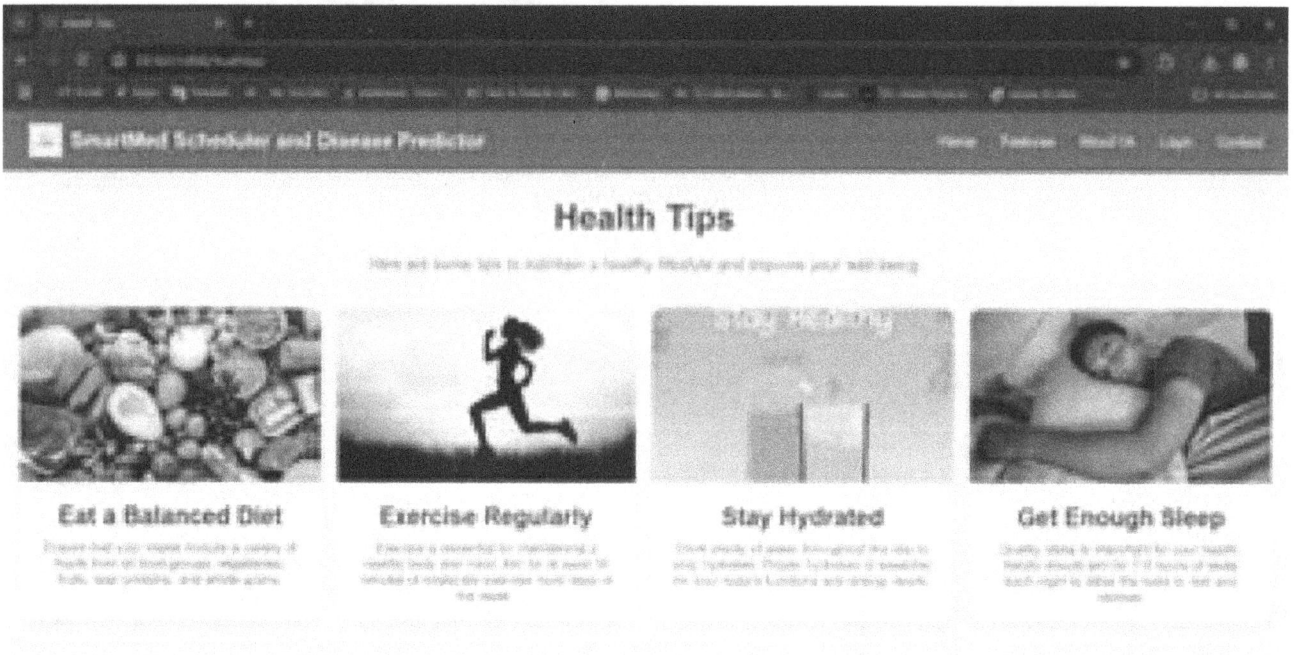

Figure 25.4. Health tips page.

Source: Author.

satisfaction. Heart disease detection through the system occurs early on so medical providers can initiate preventative measures to prevent negative health results. Staff productivity along with affordability increases because of automated tasks that assist employees to provide advanced patient care while offering adaptable machine learning capabilities.

8. Future Scope

The healthcare system will evolve into a predictive healthcare model because of ensemble models with IoT integration and enhanced security that delivers private personalized predictions.

References

[1] Bahirat, S., Bagwan, S., Dhamal, N., Patil, S., & Dhakulkar, B. (2020). A study on utilizing machine learning and NLP techniques to enhance healthcare assistance.

[2] Patil, S., Darji, J., Hingu, S., & Thakkar, A. (2021, May). Medic: AI-powered virtual assistant for healthcare support. *Presented at the International Conference on Smart Data Intelligence (ICSMDI 2021).*

[3] Absar, N., Das, E. K., Shoma, S. N., Khandaker, M. U., Miraz, M. H., Faruque, M. R. I., Tamam, N., Sulieman, A., & Pathan, R. K. (2022). Smart system for heart disease prediction using machine learning approaches. *Healthcare, 10*(6), 1137. MDPI.

[4] Abdelwahap, M., Elfarash, M., & Eltanboly, A. (2021, August). Applications of NLP in healthcare: A comprehensive analysis. *Presented at The International Undergraduate Research Conference* (Vol. 5, No. 5, pp. 111–115). The Military Technical College.

26 Development of THz rectangular microstrip patch antenna for high-speed wireless applications

V. Nagaraja[1,a], Bezawada Lekhya[2,b], S. Yaswanth[3,c], and E. Vasundhara[3,d]

[1]Assistant Professor, Electronics and Communication Engineering, Madanapalle Institute of Technology & Science, Madanapalli, India

[2]Assistant Professor, Electronics and Communication Engineering, Annamacharya Institute of Technology & Sciences, Tirupati (AITS-T), India

[3]Student, Electronics and Communication Engineering, Madanapalle Institute of Technology & Science, Madanapalli, India

Abstract: As we advance further into the future of wireless communication terahertz (THz) frequency bands are emerging as a promising solution for high-data-rate applications. The design and analysis of a 6G rectangular microstrip patch antenna operating at 330 GHz, tailored for THz communication systems. The proposed antenna is designed on Teflon substrate due to its favourable dielectric properties, ensuring minimal signal loss and enhanced radiation efficiency.

The antenna reaches a wide impedance bandwidth of 14.76 GHz, spanning from 323.40 GHz to 337.96 GHz at a return loss threshold of −15 dB, making it suitable for high-frequency applications that demand stable and efficient performance. The compact design features a rectangular patch with a modified feed structure, optimizing impedance matching and enhancing gain characteristics. The simulation results indicate improved radiation performance, making it an excellent candidate for 6G wireless networks, ultra-fast data transmission, and next generation sensing applications.

The integration of this microstrip antenna into THz systems presents several advantages, including low fabrication cost, lightweight structure, and ease of integration with existing circuits. Moreover, the adoption of Teflon as the substrate material ensures improved thermal stability and reduced dielectric losses, which are crucial for efficient THz wave propagation. The study underscores the significance of high-frequency antenna designs in advancing future communication technologies, particularly in achieving ultra-broadband connectivity for 6G networks and beyond.

Keywords: 6G, THz, ANN, MSE, HFSS,CST, VSWR,MPA

1. Introduction

The rapid expansion of wireless communication systems has led to an *increase in* demand for *altitudes in* data rates, ultra-low latency, and *higher* network *capacity*. As traditional frequency bands become congested, researchers are exploring higher frequency spectrums, particularly the terahertz (THz) range (0.1–10 THz), to support next-generation communication systems. The transition from 5G to 6G is expected to rely on THz frequencies, enabling ultra-fast data transmission, enhanced security, and advanced sensing applications. However, operating at these high frequencies presents several challenges.such as signal attenuation, propagation losses, and the need for efficient antenna designs. Microstrip patch antennas have emerged as promising candidates for THz communication due to their compact size, low profile, ease of fabrication, and compatibility with planar circuits. This paper presents the design of a rectangular microstrip patch antenna optimized for 330 GHz. Operation, specifically targeting 6G and THz communication applications.

The proposed antenna is designed on a Teflon substrate, known *Low* dielectric loss and high thermal *stability make* it suitable for *high frequency* applications. It achieves an *impedance bandwidth of* 14.76 GHz, covering the frequency range from 323.40 GHz to 337.96 GHz at a return loss of −15 dB, ensuring stable and efficient performance for broadband wireless systems.

Designing antennas in the THz frequency range poses unique challenges, including fabrication limitations and increased signal attenuation. To address these issues, the proposed antenna integrates an optimized *rectangular patch with a modified feed structure*, enhancing impedance matching and improving overall radiation efficiency. Through simulation and performance analysis, key parameters such as S-parameters, radiation pattern, gain, and efficiency are evaluated to ensure reliable operation in THz communication environments.The significance of THz antennas in 6G networks extends beyond traditional wireless communication.

The subsequent sections of this study discuss the design methodology, simulation results, and performance evaluation of the proposed antenna, highlighting its feasibility and potential impact on 6G and THz communication technologies.

[a]vvlncnagaraja@gmail.com, [b]bejawadalekhya@gmail.com, [c]yashwanthsunny70@ gmail. com, [d]vasundhara26123@gmail. com

DOI: 10.1201/9781003724988-26

2. Literature Survey

The demand for highly efficient and miniaturized antennas in the terahertz (THz) frequency range has led to extensive research in the domain of microstrip patch antennas (MPAs), especially in the context of future 6G wireless systems. Numerous advancements have been made to address the critical challenges of signal loss, limited bandwidth, and impedance matching at these high frequencies. Zhang and Xu [1] conducted a detailed investigation into low-loss substrate materials tailored for THz MPAs. They demonstrated that specific dielectric substrates, such as Teflon and polymer composites, contribute significantly to minimizing propagation losses and enhancing the overall efficiency of the antenna. Their work underscores the importance of substrate selection in THz antenna design. Beamforming, essential for directional transmission and reception at THz frequencies, was explored by Bhattacharyya and Raj [2]. They proposed novel techniques to enhance the directivity and steering capability of THz patch antennas, which is crucial for maintaining high data rates and connectivity in dynamic 6G environments. A comprehensive review by Kouyoumjian and Pathak [3] highlighted various MPA configurations and their behavior in the THz range. The study discussed the performance of planar antennas under different structural modifications, including slots and multilayer topologies, to achieve wideband characteristics and high radiation efficiency. Liu and Hong [4] developed a rectangular microstrip patch antenna for high-speed THz wireless communication. Their design was optimized for stable impedance matching and demonstrated improved bandwidth and gain performance, making it suitable for compact communication systems. Sharma and Parveen [5] introduced metamaterial-inspired MPAs, showing that integrating engineered surfaces can lead to enhanced gain and bandwidth. Their work provides a significant step forward in mitigating the limitations of conventional MPA designs at terahertz frequencies. Rappaport et al. [6] provided a broader overview of THz wireless communication, addressing not only antenna technologies but also the system-level implications of using THz frequencies for 6G. Their findings emphasized the necessity of array configurations and novel antenna types to overcome the severe path losses encountered at these frequencies. The application of additive manufacturing was explored by Zhang and Liu [7], who fabricated compact MPAs using 3D printing techniques. This approach allows for precise dimensional control and scalability, thereby facilitating the production of high-performance antennas for portable THz devices. Wang and Li [8] proposed MPA arrays optimized for THz operation, aiming to boost efficiency and coverage. Their design achieved significant improvement in terms of collective gain and effective radiated power, which are vital for long-distance communication in 6G networks. Multi-layer antenna structures were investigated by Chen and Zhang [9], who reported that layering significantly enhances the impedance bandwidth and gain. Their study demonstrated the viability of such designs for multi-band or broadband THz systems. Wu and Yang [10]

emphasized the fabrication process and practical realization of THz MPAs. They combined traditional lithography techniques with novel fabrication processes to achieve antennas with minimal defects and consistent performance across the THz spectrum. The design of miniaturized wideband MPAs was the focus of Shamim et al. [11], who presented a compact structure that maintained high gain and wide bandwidth despite its reduced size. Their work aligns with the growing need for small-form-factor antennas in portable and wearable THz communication devices. Krishna et al. [12] developed a micro-sized rhombus-shaped antenna, optimized for short-range high-speed THz links. Their antenna was shown to deliver good performance in scenarios requiring compactness and directional radiation. Lastly, Mahmud [13] investigated MPAs designed specifically for surveillance applications in the THz range. His design considerations included stability, robustness, and cost-effectiveness, with particular attention to application-specific requirements such as stealth and coverage.

3. Proposed Method

The proposed studies are particularly focused on the design and analysis of the rectangular antenna of the micro -paylist optimized for 330GHz work in 6G and THZ (THZ). The goal is to develop an antenna that provides a wide range of and high radiation efficiency and low desires for high frequency communication systems (Figure 26.1).

4. Design Algorithm

Steps to Implement ANN-Based Antenna Optimization in MATLAB: Generate Training Data: Simulate microstrip antenna designs with varying parameters (patch length, width, feed width, substrate thickness, etc.) using HFSS or CST and export results. Collect data on efficiency, bandwidth, gain, and reflection coefficient (s11). Utilize matlab's

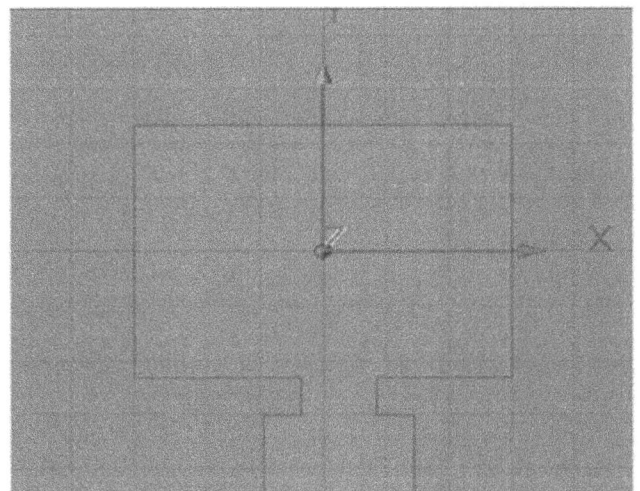

Figure 26.1. Designed 6g rectangular microstrip patch antenna.
Source: Author.

neural network toolbox to train an Ann model. The model should include input parameters such as material properties and antenna dimensions, and output parameters such as efficiency, bandwidth, and gain (Figure 26.2).

Using the artificial neural network (Ann), we increase the design of the antenna to predict the optimal parameters of the antenna based on learning data. Run the modeling of the expected parameter to confirm the results of Ann

The specified diagram illustrates the progression of the artificial neuronal network (ANN) in optimizing the design of a 6G microstrip patch antenna. Mean square root error of one of the algorithm's performance measurements. Predicted Antenna Performance: Gain: 7.30 dBi, Bandwidth: 10.29 GHz, Efficiency: 89.47%, Mean Squared Error of ANN: 0.276405.

5. Design Overview

The rectangular stucture microstrip antenna is unique. This antenna impedance matching due to that we have got vswr less than 2 since its is a ratio of indicates maximum e field to minimum e field is will be less. The antenna is made in the form of a default material using Teflon, low TGC, good stable gain for the tera hertz frequency and minimum signal loss, and is selected as the desired characteristics the low return loss that is ration of incident power to the reflected power. The wave must propagated into the space the return loss must be less than 10 down and gain is stable these was the one achievement of the design.

The patch of patch antenna is performed by Ann Alogarit for a 330GHz response and ensures stable reinforcement throughout the entire lane of 322.40 GHz to 345.96GHz. To optimize productivity, the geometry of the patch is carefully configured to improve the comparison of impedance and radiation efficiency.

The width of the feed is to increase the power flow to the antenna. At The feed combined with stub for complex impedance matching at the port terminal, is to minimize return loss and enhance impedance matching, which results

have low return loss at resonance the stubs are preferred for complex impedance matching.

The design structure antenna has good bandwidth of 22.76 ghz, stable gain and positive gain of the antenna tells that wave propagation can take place in the space. Additionally, it is crucial to ensure a return loss of −15 db or better. The antenna structure and feed mechanism are optimized to maximize radiation efficiency and minimize losses (Table 26.1).

Simulation and Analysis: The antenna's performance is validated using electromagnetic simulation tools, which analyze key parameters such as: loss of return, impedance adjustment, radiation patterns (reinforcement and directory), antenna efficiency, signal extension characteristics, etc., Simulation results are used to fine-tune the design, ensuring optimal functionality for high-speed, high-frequency wireless communication.

Flow Diagram

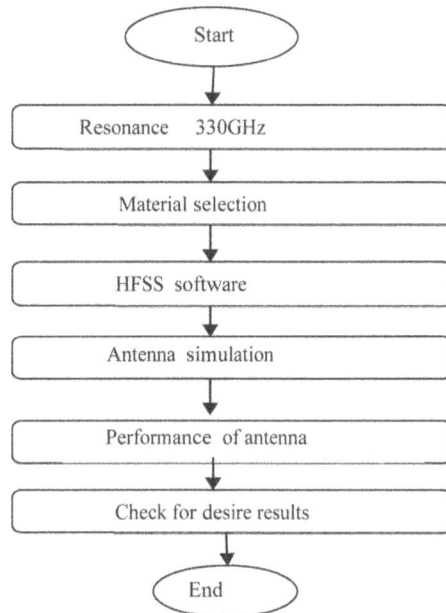

6. Results and Discussion

S Parameters: The Figure 26.3 indicates the return loss 15dBi down in band of 323.40 GHz to 345.96 GHz frequency

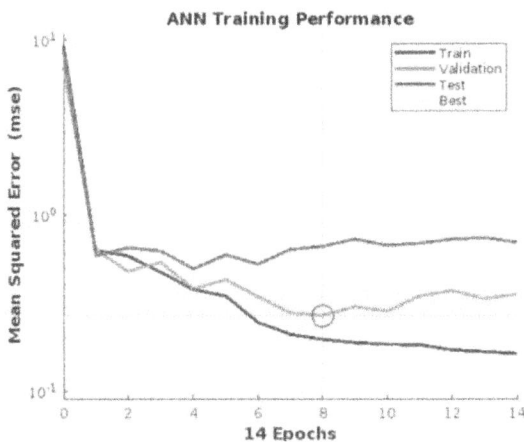

Figure 26.2. Graph for ANN training performance.

Source: Author.

Table 26.1. The actual antenna

S. No	Parameter	value(mm)
1	ws	0.5
2	ls	0.45
3	h	0.15
4	wp	0.3
5	lp	0.233
6	wf	0.12
7	lf	0.11

Source: Author.

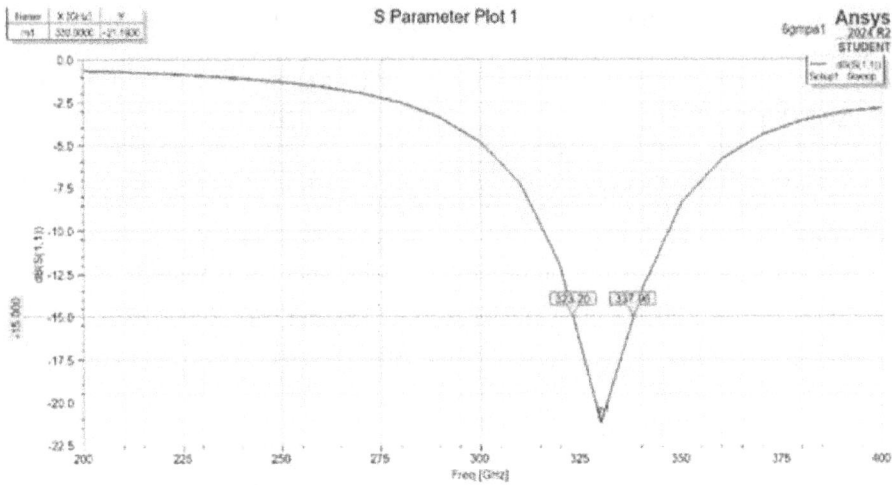

Figure 26.3. S parameters.

Source: Author.

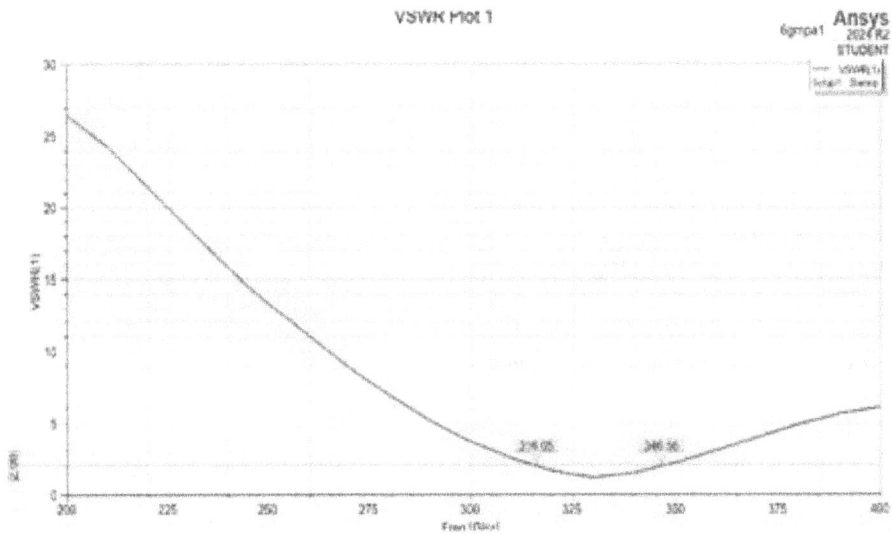

Figure 26.4. VSWR.

Source: Author.

range, which tell about impedance matching so that wave can propagation into space over these frequency range.

VSWR: The specified VSWR value represents the degree of impedance misfire or reflection for each port in the proposed method (Figure 26.4).

3D. Gain: Set the simulation to calculate the radiation pattern of the antenna at a specified frequency (320 GHz, 348 GHz) (Figure 26.5a and b).

Radiation pattern Red colour indicatites positive gain, it indicates good impedance matching wave is going to propagation will takes place at these frequency.

Current distribution of E and H: High current surface green colour and red indicates strong radiation field at resonace frequency (Figure 26.6a and b).

Gain: The gain of the antenna is stable over band of 323.40 GHz to 337.96 GHz frequency range (Figure 26.7).

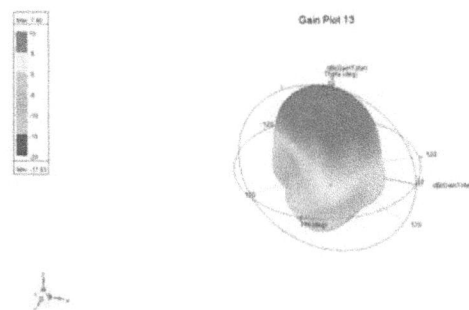

Figure 26.5(a) Electromagnetic radiation pattern at a frequency of 323.40 GHz.

Source: Author.

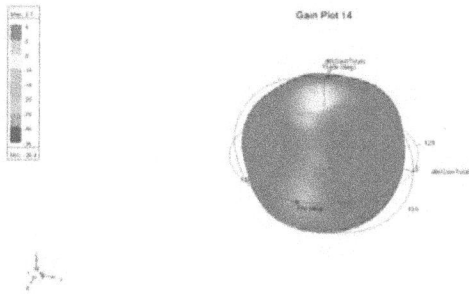

Figure 26.5(b) Electromagnetic radiation pattern at a frequency of 330 GHz.

Source: Author.

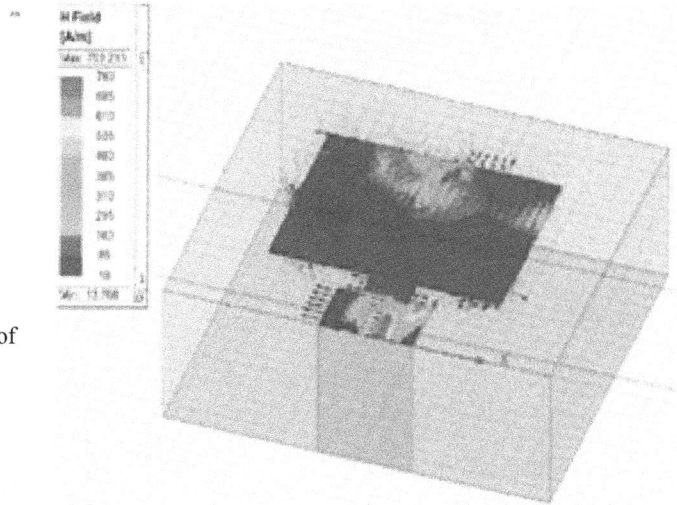

Figure 26.6(b) Current distribution at H-plane.

Source: Author.

Radiation Characteristics: Polar plots tells the radiation maximum along.

7. Conclusion

In this study, we proposed to create a 6g right microscope patch antenna that operates at 330 GHz and uses Teflon (PTFE) as the dielectric material. The proposed design focuses on achieving high performance Terra Hertzs' frequency range is essential for further development of the latest technologies, including 5G, 6G and high-speed communications. The main goal of this antenna design is to reduce signal loss, improve data transmission, and optimize radiation efficiency. Teflon was selected as the substrate due to its low dielectric constant (2.1) and low loss tangent, making

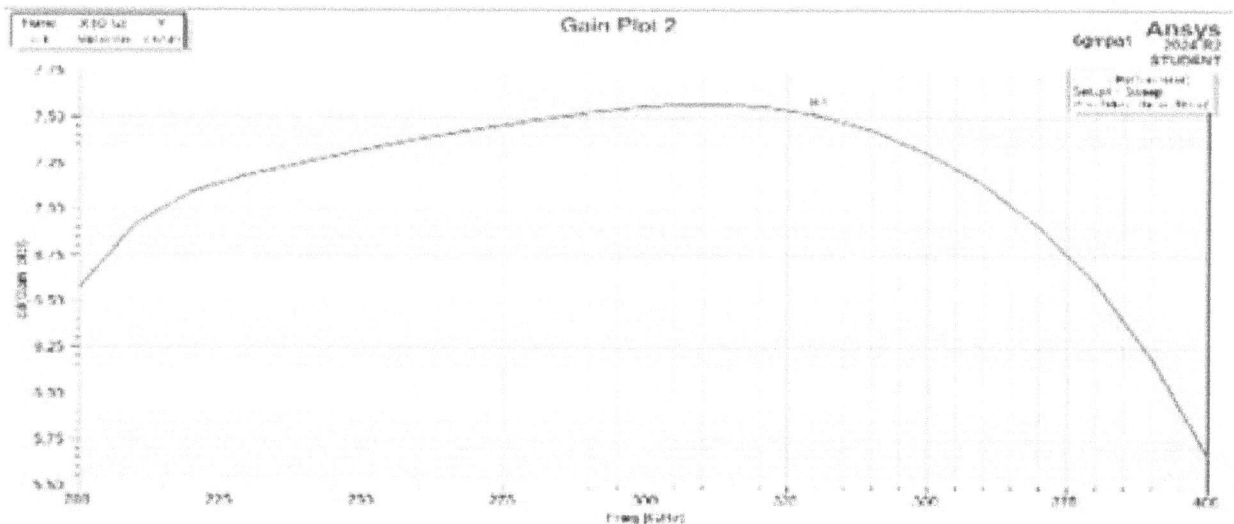

Figure 26.6(a) Current distribution at E-plane.

Source: Author.

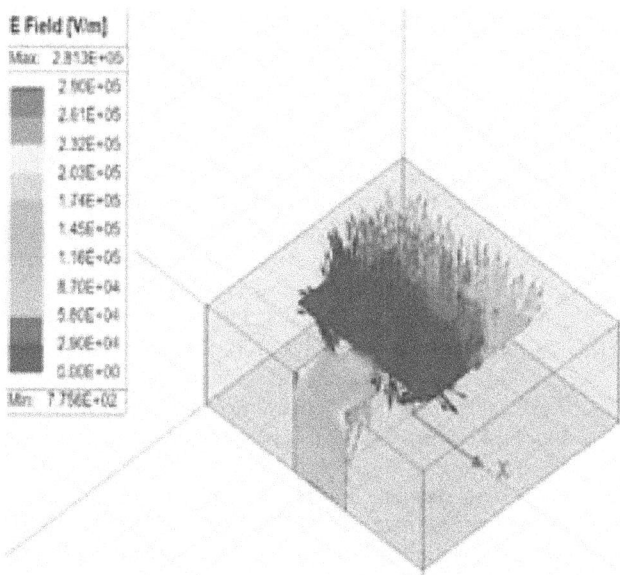

Figure 26.7. Gain vs frequency.

Source: Author.

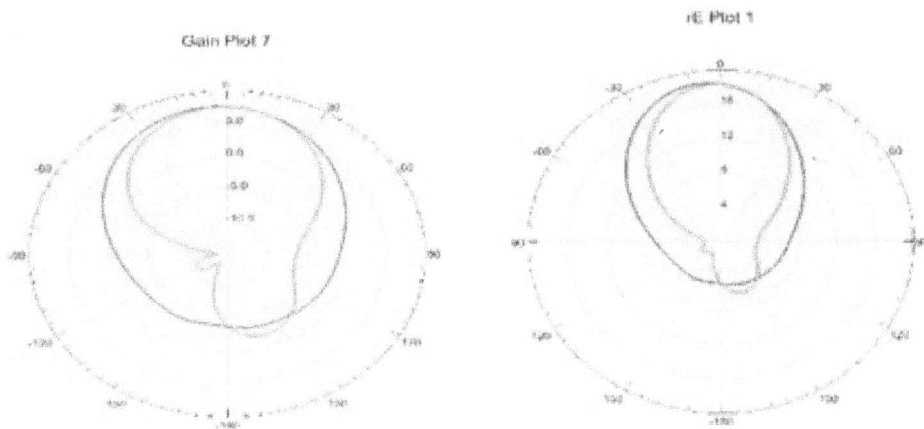

Figure 26.8. Radiation characteristics.

Source: Author.

it an ideal choice for high-frequency applications. The rectangular microstrip patch geometry was optimized through slotting techniques and a stacked patch configuration, which allow for improved bandwidth and better impedance matching. Simulation results using advanced tools such as HFSS or CST Microwave Studio confirmed that the antenna meets the required performance parameters, including low return loss, optimal radiation pattern, and high gain (Figure 26.8).

8. Future Scope

This proposed design offers several advantages, including low profile, ease of integration with THz circuits, and suitability for high-speed data transmission. Future research can explore additional enhancements such as metamaterials, reconfigurable structures, or graphene-based tuneable designs to improve antenna efficiency in 6G and future technologies. The following sections will present detailed design simulations, performance evaluations, and comparative analysis to demonstrate the feasibility of this antenna for future THz communication networks.

Acknowledgment

We are delighted to present the initial project report on behalf of the Madanapalle Institute of Technology & Sciences, Madanapalle, Andhra Pradesh, India, I would like to seize this opportunity to extend my heartfelt thanks to my mentor, Mr. V. Nagaraja, Assistant Professor, Madanapalle Institute of Technology & Sciences, Madanapalle, AndhraPradesh, India, Mrs.Bezawada lekhya, Assistant Professor, Electronics and Communciation Engineering, Annamacharya Institute of Technology & Sciences Venkatapuram, Renigunta, Tirupati, India and Dr. S. Rajasekaran, Ph.D., Professor, and Head of the Electronics and Communication Engineering Department, Madanapalle Institute of Technology & Sciences, Madanapalle, Andhra Pradesh, India for providing me with their invaluable support and guidance. The author is grateful for their generous support and insightful recommendations!

References

[1] Zhang H., & Xu X. (2024). Design of Low-Loss Substrate Materials for Terahertz Microstrip Antennas. *IEEE Transactions on Antennas and Propagation, 72*(1), 112–120.

[2] Bhattacharyya, S., & Raj, P. (2024). Beamforming Techniques for Terahertz Microstrip Patch Antennas in 6G Systems. *IEEE Access, 12*, 32345–32355.

[3] Kouyoumjian R., & Pathak P. (2023). Design and Analysis of Microstrip Patch Antennas for THz Communications: A Review. *Journal of Terahertz Science and Technology, 13*(4), 345–356.

[4] Liu, F., & Hong, W. (2023). Terahertz rectangular microstrip Patch Antenna for High-Speed Wireless Communication. *Journal of Electromagnetic Waves and Applications, 37*(4), 465–472.

[5] Sharma, A., & Parveen, S. (2023). Metamaterial-based Terahertz Microstrip Patch Antennas for Enhanced Performance. *Microwave and Optical Technology Letters, 65*(2), 250–258.

[6] Rappaport T. S., et al. (2023). 6G Wireless Communications and Antenna Technologies for Terahertz Frequencies. *IEEE Communications Magazine, 61*(3), 44–51.

[7] Zhang, Y., & Liu, Z. (2023). 3D Printed Terahertz Microstrip Patch Antennas for Compact Wireless Communication Systems. *Journal of Microwaves, Optoelectronics and Electromagnetic Applications, 22*(6), 45–53.

[8] Wang, Y., & Li, Z. (2023). Terahertz Microstrip Patch Antenna Arrays for Efficient Wireless Communication. *IEEE Transactions on Microwave Theory and Techniques, 71*(8), 1231–1240.

[9] Chen, Y., & Zhang, X. (2022). Multi-layer Microstrip Antennas for THz Frequency Bands. *International Journal of Antennas and Propagation, 2022*, 1–8.

[10] Wu, S., & Yang, L. (2022). Design and fabrication of Microstrip Patch Antennas for Terahertz Applications. *IEEE Transactions on Antennas and Propagation, 70*(5), 1892–1900.

[11] Shamim, S. M., Uddin, M. S., Hasan, M. R., & Samad, M. (2021). Design and implementation of miniaturized wideband microstrip patch antenna for high-speed terahertz applications. *Journal of Computational Electronics, 20*, 604–610.

[12] Krishna, C. M., Das, S., Nella, A., Lakrit, S., & Madhav, B. T. P. (2021). A micro-sized rhombus-shaped THz antenna for high-speed short-range wireless communication applications. *Plasmonics, 16*(6), 2167–2177.

[13] Mahmud, R. H. (2020). Terahertz microstrip patch antennas for the surveillance applications. *Kurdistan Journal of Applied Research, 5*(1), 16–27.

27 Design and development of smart water management set-up in lodging places

Ruben Varghese Mathew, Urimella Pranay Abhishek, Rangam Himakar, Prashanth L., and G. Shine Let[a]

School of Engineering and Technology, Karunya Institute of Technology and Sciences, Tamil Nadu, India

Abstract: In lodging places like hotels, guest houses, hostels and resorts, the water usage is high. Most of the temporary occupants do not bother about water usage. This work aims to install a water monitoring and control system in the lodging rooms. The daily consumption of a dormitory with 100 students can range from 10,000 to 20,000 litres. According to studies, 20–40% of the water used in hostels is wasted. Therefore, around 2,000 to 4,000 litres may be wasted in a hostel that uses 10,000 litres every day. These issues can be resolved with this work by utilizing smart Internet-of-things (IoT) incorporated water management systems, which leverage websites and apps with Bluetooth and WiFi to monitor and control water usage through a graphic user interface (GUI). Real-time data is obtained from sensors, and automated control is incorporated to conduct the required safety measures or actions utilizing the consumption thresholds to minimize water waste. Urban regions experiencing a severe scarcity water problem can deploy this smart water management system.

Keywords: Water management system, Internet-of-Things, water consumption, Wi-Fi, automated control system

1. Introduction

The sustainability of life on planet Earth relies on water resources. Healthy Life on Earth depends on having good non-contaminant water. Water is wasted in different ways such as domestic wastage, agricultural wastage, industrial wastage and municipal wastage. To have a future sustainability of the society, and improvement in social and economic well-being, water preservation is a major concern [1]. The increasing water demand is mainly due to climate change and urbanization. Recent technologies are incorporated in urban areas to have proper management of water. Using sensors, control systems and IoT-based technology, water usage is monitored and controlled [2]. IoT-based The same IoT technology is also used for analyzing the quality of the water [3]. Similar to using low-cost sensor networks, the water management system is suggested in this paper [4]. The authors suggested this work to have a sound urban environment. From the data collection related to water usage, the authors conclude water infrastructure plays a significant role in the urban environment. In [5], a detailed review of water monitoring and controlling techniques is suggested. To have an efficient, proper management of natural resources there is a need to incorporate information and communication technologies (ICT) and recently developed IoT. By using the technologies in day-to-day life, there is a great improvement in people's daily activities and proper monitoring of common infrastructure by the designated administrator [6].

For precision agriculture also, irrigation is controlled and monitored in order to avoid over-watering or scarce watering for crops [7]. The water level in the water tank is monitored using a laser sensor and the information is passed to the user who is maintaining the system [8]. In this, based on the level of water the motor pump automatically works and fills the water in the tank. Also, once the tank is filled, the pump automatically stops. Similar to this work, the water usage in residential areas is monitored using IoT and the daily usage information with be communicated to the authorized person [9]. The authors in [10] suggested real-time monitoring of various environmental parameters including water level, pH value, humidity and rainfall. The work [10] is suggested for workers or farmers to carry out their jobs in dangerous environments. The work suggested is a little complex for real-time implementation. In [11], discussed monitoring the quality of water and maintaining sustainable resources without contamination. The authors in [12] also suggested the importance of water conservation and management using IoT technology. According to the literature carried out, monitoring and managing water resources is an essential need in daily activities.

The work discussed here mainly focuses on avoiding industrial and domestic water wastage. Using IoT technology, the leaks, spilling or running water from the pipes are detected. Water is a precious natural resource and is important to utilize the resource intelligently. The leakage of water drop-by-drop is seen in residential areas, industries, and

[a]shinelet@gmail.com

DOI: 10.1201/9781003724988-27

common places. As aware that, drop-by-drop will make an ocean. A huge amount of water is wasted due to leakages in taps or due to improper implementation of the water network. As per United Nations sustainable development, water plays a significant priority and is represented as SDG-6. An IoT-based system that would detect water leakage in real-time is suggested in this work, which would help concerned authorities to take appropriate action so as to nullify the loss of water.

2. Smart Water Management System-Setup

This work is proposed to have control over the water usage in various lodging places such as hotels, guest houses and hostels. According to the number of persons available in a particular room, a water usage threshold will be given to the residents or lodgers. Figure 27.1 depicts the overall blocks considered for the implementation of a smart water management system in a particular residence/room in a hotel/hostel. A smart valve is placed just above the tape. The devices are connected using IoT technology. In this work, a hotel-based lodging scenario is considered. An analog meter is fixed on the main water pipe distributing water to a particular room. Through NodeMCU the sensed water flow is communicated to an application (app) installed on the desktop/mobile of the receptionist/authorized official person. The water usage can be continuously monitored in the app. The app can be given to the lodgers/residents to have control over their water

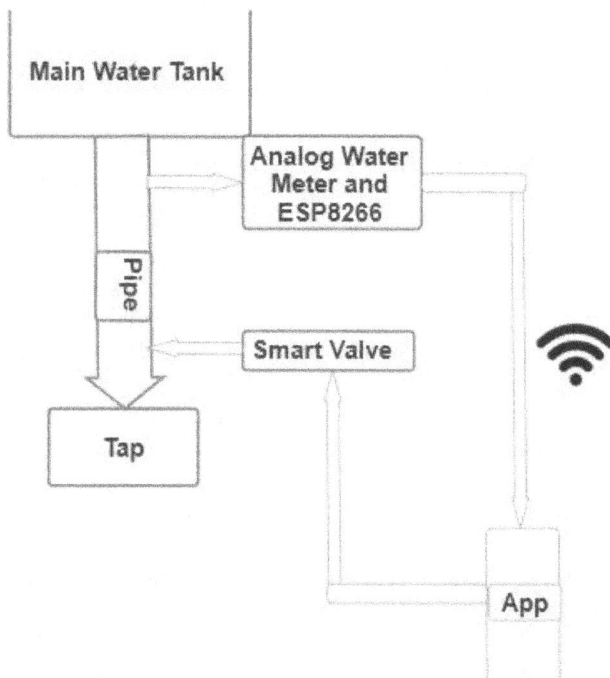

Figure 27.1. Smart water management set-up.

Source: Author.

usage. This work will also help to monitor the water leakages in the tap. If there is any continuous flow of water for more than a specific duration of time, the indication will be given to the authorized person. The level of water flow shows whether the tap is leaking or the tap is kept open/unattended. By implementing this system water wastage can be reduced in commercial places, lodges, guest houses and hostels. The details of the components used are discussed in the next section.

3. Smart Water Management System-Components used

For the implementation of a smart water management system, the main hardware used is Arduino and water flow sensor YF-S201. Flow meters have been verified as excellent devices for water flow measuring; using the water flow sensor YF-S201 it is easy to construct a water management system. The development board is NodeMCU ESP8266 Micro-controller. It is an inexpensive, Wi-Fi-capable micro-controller that is frequently utilized in Internet of Things applications. With a 32-bit processor, 4MB of flash memory, 11 GPIO pins, and one ADC pin, it is based on the ESP8266 chip. It runs at 3.3V and is compatible with SPI, I2C, and UART communication protocols. Wireless connectivity is made possible by the board's ability to operate as an access point (AP), Wi-Fi station (STA), or both (AP+STA). It can run web servers, manage relays and sensors, and transmit data to cloud platforms like ThingSpeak, Blynk IOT. It is typically programmed using the Arduino IDE, Lua, or MicroPython. Despite its low power consumption, integrated Wi-Fi, and ease of programming, it only has one ADC pin and few GPIOs.

The YF-S201 water flow sensor operates by employing a rotating impeller with magnets inside a plastic body and a hall-effect sensor. The impeller rotates as water flows, producing pulses that the hall-effect sensor picks up. Using the formula Flow Rate (L/min) = Pulse Frequency/7.5, the pulse frequency and water flow rate are precisely proportional. And interrupt function counts pulses to calculate the flow rate. Three wires connect to the water flow sensor: a red wire for 5V Vcc, a black wire for Gnd, and a typically yellow signal/pulse line. Figure 27.2 shows the water flow sensor used in this work. The pulse line is connected to one of the Arduino's digital pins, and the flow sensor's Vcc and Gnd are connected to the Arduino's Vcc and Gnd pins. Smart water meters and leak detection systems commonly use this design.

The water flow sensor is interfaced to the relay then with the ESP8266 board: the relay's VCC to 3.3V or 5V, GND to GND, and the IN pin to a GPIO (such as D1 – GPIO5) in order to interface a relay module with the NodeMCU ESP8266 and is depicted in Figure 27.3. To turn the relay on, provide a LOW signal; to turn it off, send a HIGH signal. The relay is periodically turned on and off by straightforward software that sets the GPIO as OUTPUT. This configuration

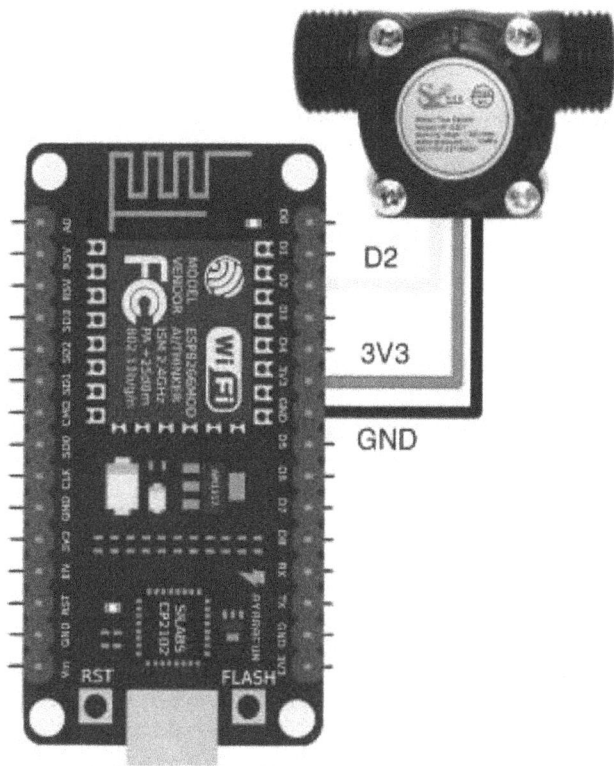

Figure 27.2. Water flow sensor.

Source: Author.

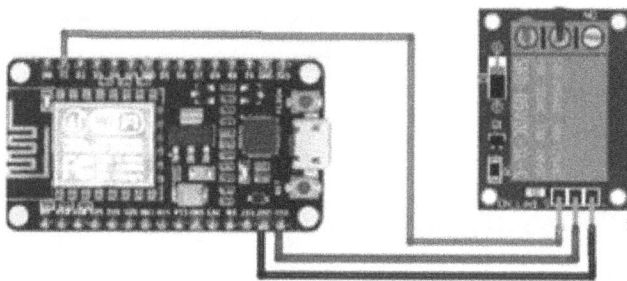

Figure 27.3. Relay interface with the ESP8266.

Source: Author.

helps use the ESP8266 to control high-power devices like lights, motors, or solenoid valves. Here we are connecting a solenoid valve to the relay.

A solenoid water valve which is used in this work is pictured in Figure 27.4. This is an electromechanical device that opens and closes a valve mechanism using an electromagnetic coil to regulate the flow of water.

4. Smart Water Management Set-up – Working

A hotel room lodging scenario is considered here. The water flow from the pipe to each room is measured in this work

using a flow meter (YF S201). The flow meter is connected to a NodeMCU ESP8266 Board. Through IOT (Internet of Things) space 6, this flow rate data – which is simply the water rating usage in hours/litre will be transmitted to the cloud. The user or the authorized person in the hotel can then use the graphical user interface to monitor and control the water supply after receiving this data from the cloud. To demonstrate the working of the implemented smart water management system one water flow meter is utilized in this work to calculate how much water the room uses from the main tank. Additionally, the solenoid valve is utilized to limit water flow when water consumption surpasses the limit. Figure 27.5 depicts the implementation model of the suggested work.

By integrating ESP8266 with smart water meters, the amount of water consumed in every room can be effectively monitored. Figure 27.6 depicts the water flow usage displayed in Arduino IDE. The ESP8266 has been integrated with the website through the Blynk IoT platform, so the amount of water consumed by each room can be monitored remotely through the website. Real-time data on the amount of water consumed can be viewed on the website. The solenoid valve automatically closes when the preset amount of water is consumed in a particular room. This prevents the overuse of water. The solenoid valve can also be remotely accessed through the website. The valve can be turned ON or OFF through the website. After the implementation of this work, there is a good efficiency of the model. The hardware set-up developed is shoen in Figure 27.7. The water limit is now set according to the number of persons in the room,

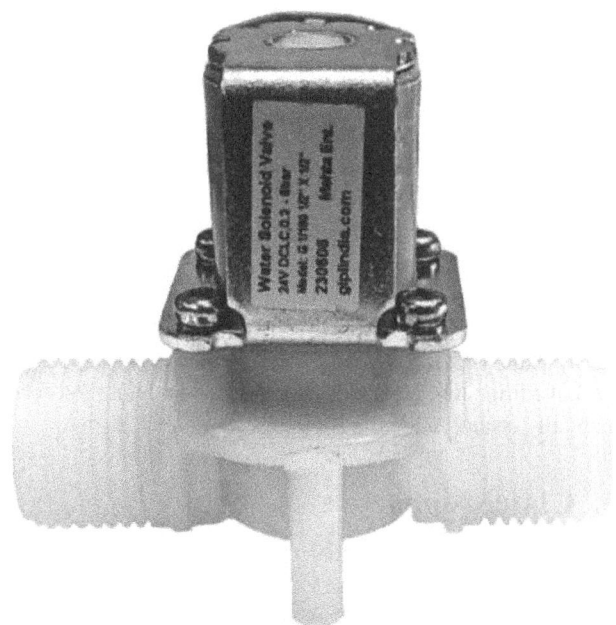

Figure 27.4. Solenoid water valve.

Source: Author.

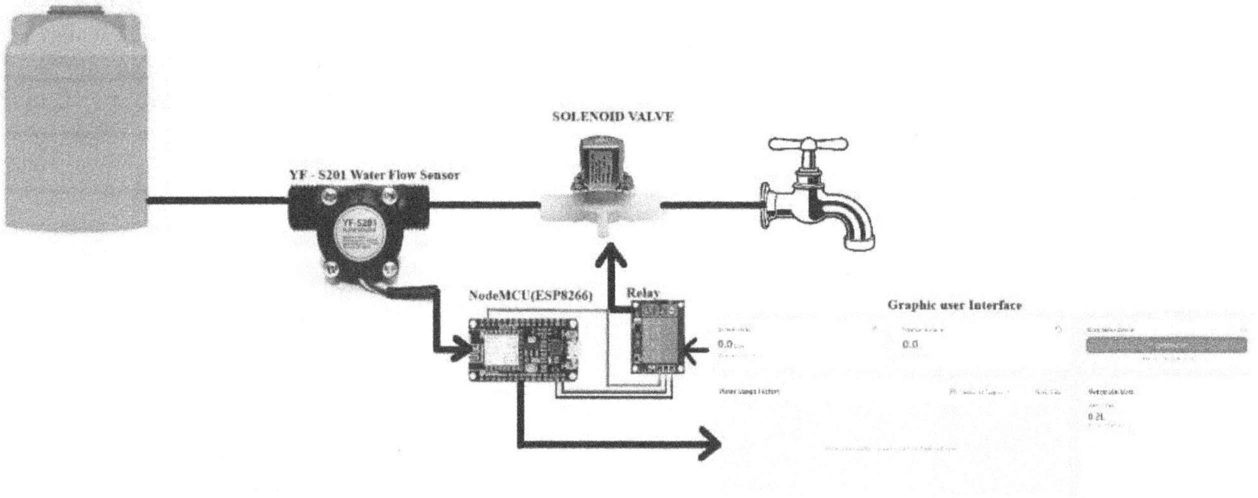

Figure 27.5. Smart water management set-up – implementation model.

Source: Author.

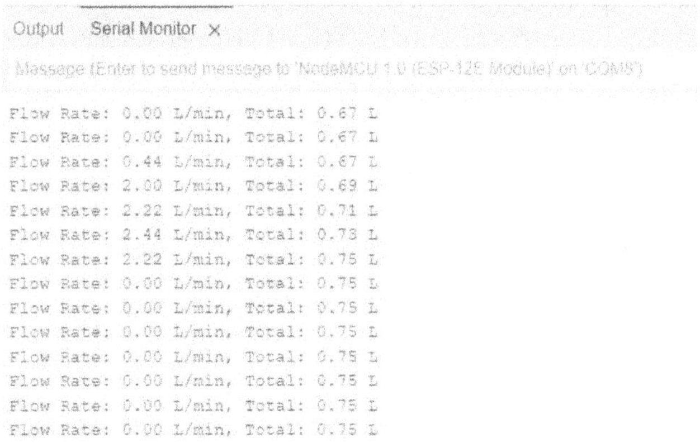

Figure 27.6. Water flow rate-monitor.

Source: Author.

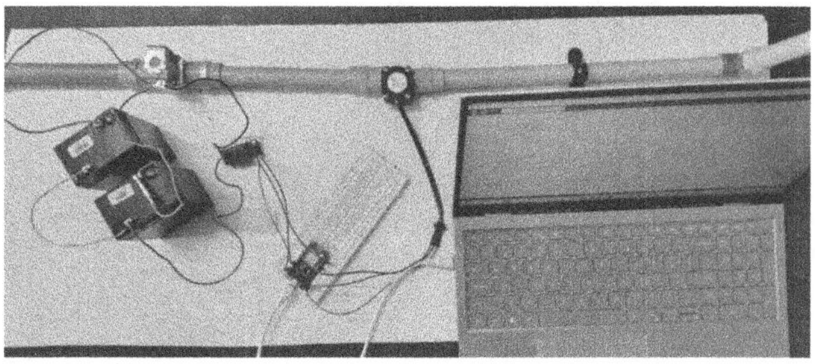

Figure 27.7. Smart water management set-up – hardware implementation.

Source: Author.

and the water flow rate data can be read in the serial monitor using the Arduino IDE. The same data from the Arduino IDE serial monitor will be delivered to the Graphic User Interface (GUI), which features a dashboard to observe the water flow rate and total water consumption, via the Blynk IOT (a low-code software cloud platform that enables IOT at different scales) auth token and a screenshot is shown Figure 27.8. Additionally, it provides the ability to operate the relay manually or automatically if the threshold limit is met.

Figure 27.8. Smart water management app.

Source: Author.

5. Conclusions

Water is one of the essential needs of human life. Usage of water may vary from person to person. To have proper water usage in lodging places such as hotels, guest houses and hostels, the proposed system can be implemented. This system helps in monitoring water usage to a threshold level. The related information is communicated to the authorized persons. This model also helps in detecting water leakages in commercial places. In the app or webpage if the continuous flow of water is monitored then this indicates there is a leakage of water in that particular tape. According to this information water leakage can be stopped. The proposed system avoids water wastage and allows the user to have effective and careful usage of water.

Acknowledgement

We gratefully acknowledge the Karunya Institute of Technology and Sciences for providing funds to efficiently carry out this work.

References

[1] Xiang, X., Li, Q., Khan, S., & Khalaf, O. I. (2021). Urban water resource management for sustainable environment planning using artificial intelligence techniques. *Environmental Impact Assessment Review*, *86*. doi: 10.1016/j.eiar.2020.106515.

[2] Singh, M., & Ahmed, S. (2020). IoT based smart water management systems: A systematic review. In *Materials Today: Proceedings*. Elsevier Ltd, pp. 5211–5218. doi: 10.1016/j.matpr.2020.08.588.

[3] Lakshmikantha, V., Hiriyannagowda, A., Manjunath, A., Patted, A., Basavaiah, J., & Anthony, A. A. (2021). IoT based smart water quality monitoring system. *Global Transitions Proceedings*, *2*(2), 181–186. doi: 10.1016/j.gltp.2021.08.062.

[4] Hamel, P., Ding, N., Cherqui, F., Zhu, Q., Walcker, N., Bertrand-Krajewski, J. L., ... & Shi, B. (2024). Low-cost monitoring systems for urban water management: Lessons from the field. *Water Research X*, *22*, 100212. doi: 10.1016/j.wroa.2024.100212.

[5] Yasin, H. M., Zeebaree, S. R., Sadeeq, M. A., Ameen, S. Y., Ibrahim, I. M., Zebari, R. R., ... & Sallow, A. B. (2021). IoT and ICT based smart water management, monitoring and controlling system: A review. *Asian Journal of Research in Computer Science*, *8*(2), 42–56. doi: 10.9734/ajrcos/2021/v8i230198.

[6] Neoaz, N. (2025). Internet of Things (IoT) and Smart Cities Examine how IoT technologies can improve urban living and infrastructure management. *Author Nahid Neoaz*. [Online]. Available: https://www.researchgate.net/publication/389646744

[7] Bwambale, E., Abagale, F. K., & Anornu, G. K. (2022). Smart irrigation monitoring and control strategies for improving water use efficiency in precision agriculture: A review. *Agricultural Water Management*, *260*, 107324. doi: 10.1016/j.agwat.2021.107324.

[8] Joseph, J., M. K. M, S. M. R, S. Nair, Viay, V. P., & Krishnan, S. (2018). Water Management System Using IoT. *International Research Journal of Engineering and Technology* [Online]. Available: www.irjet.net

[9] Kshatri, D. (2025). Smart Water Flow Monitoring and Forecasting System using IoT and Machine Learning. *Int J Res Appl Sci Eng Technol*, *13*(2), 862–873. doi: 10.22214/ijraset.2025.66987.

[10] Narayana, T. L., *et al.* (2024). Advances in real time smart monitoring of environmental parameters using IoT and sensors. *Heliyon*, *10*(7). doi: 10.1016/j.heliyon.2024.e28195.

[11] Salam, A. (2020). Internet of things in water management and treatment. In *Internet of Things*, Springer, pp. 273–298. doi: 10.1007/978-3-030-35291-2_9.

[12] Alam, M. N., Shufian, A., Al Masum, M. A., & Al Noman, A. (2021). Efficient smart water management system using IoT technology. In *2021 International Conference on Automation, Control and Mechatronics for Industry 4.0, ACMI 2021*. Institute of Electrical and Electronics Engineers Inc. doi: 10.1109/ACMI53878.2021.9528202.

28 Crop Optix: Fertilizer and pesticides optimizer

Sheik Faritha Begum S.[1,a], Hemalatha P.[2,b], Kaviya T.[2,c], and Keerthana A. S.[2,d]

[1]Assistant Professor, Department of Computer Science and Engineering, PSNA College of Engineering and Technology, Dindigul, Tamil Nadu, India
[2]Student, Department of Computer Science and Engineering, PSNA College of Engineering and Technology, Dindigul, Tamil Nadu, India

Abstract: Sustainable agriculture is essential for ensuring long-term food security while minimizing environmental impact. This study presents a Smart Agro Advisory System that combines Soil Health Card (SHC) data, real-time weather analysis, and the Leaf Color Chart (LCC) method to optimize fertilizer and pesticide application. Through the use of advanced machine learning models such as Random Forest and XGBoost, the system analyzes soil nutrient levels, predicts nutrient depletion, and provides precise recommendations for fertilizer use. Additionally, Xception-based deep learning algorithms process leaf color images to detect nitrogen deficiencies, enabling targeted nutrient management. The system is integrated into a cloud-based decision support platform, which aggregates diverse datasets and delivers actionable insights through a user-friendly mobile interface. By using this system, farmers can reduce the overuse of chemicals, lower costs, and minimize environmental damage, all while maximizing crop productivity. The integration of AI with traditional farming methods allows for a more efficient, data-driven approach, promoting precision farming and sustainable agricultural practices.

Keywords: Sustainable agriculture; smart agro advisory system; soil health card (SHC); leaf color chart (LCC); machine learning; XGBoost; sustainable farming practices

1. Introduction

In sustainable agriculture, careful management of input is essential in order to reduce the overuse of pesticides and fertilizers. With this underlying approach, this study has developed a software-based Smart Agro Advisory System that incorporates Soil Health Card (SHC) which is conditional to weather parameters, and also took assistance from the Leaf Color Chart (LCC) method, making the recommendation more location-specific. It uses machine learning algorithms to analyze soil properties, meteorological conditions, and crop nutrient levels and provides a real-time advisory service. The collected data is processed on a cloud- based platform, which allows farmers to get accurate [1] in response to these challenges, precision agriculture has emerged as a modern, technology-driven approach that optimizes resource utilization while enhancing productivity. By integrating remote sensing, Geographic Information Systems (GIS), Internet of Things (IoT), and machine learning, precision agriculture enables data-driven decision- making to reduce fertilizer application and mitigate environmental damage [2]. A key component of precision agriculture is Variable Rate Technology (VRT), which adjusts fertilizer application based on real-time soil and crop conditions. Studies suggest that VRT can reduce fertilizer use by 20–40% while maintaining or even increasing crop yields [3]. Additionally, real-time soil

nutrient monitoring through sensor-based technologies helps farmers apply fertilizers only where needed, minimizing excess runoff into water bodies [4]. Research also indicates that precision fertilization methods can improve nitrogen use efficiency (NUE) by up to 50%, reducing the risk of nitrate leaching into groundwater [5]. As global agriculture faces the dual challenge of feeding a growing population and reducing its environmental footprint, precision agriculture presents a sustainable solution. By leveraging advanced technologies, it enhances crop productivity, optimizes fertilizer use, and promotes environmental conservation [6]. Future research and policy initiatives should focus on increasing the accessibility and affordability of precision agriculture technologies to ensure widespread adoption among farmers worldwide [7].

2. Literature Survey

Suggestions for fertilizer and pesticides. The software also comes with an easy-to-use interface that enables users to enter details about a crop and receive optimized recommendations. Its use of data analytics and predictive modeling helps promote soil fertility management, lower reliance on chemicals, and boost crop productivity. So, this is a software-driven approach where sustainable farming will be promoted through the better use of resources, lessening of impact on the environment, and better decision-making yields more

[a]sfaritha@psnacet.edu.in, [b]phemalatha212@gmail.com, [c]tkaviya01@gmail.com, [d]keerthanashanmugam1407@ gmail.com

DOI: 10.1201/9781003724988-28

productivity in agriculture. Agriculture plays a crucial role in global food security, but traditional farming methods often lead to excessive fertilizer use, resulting in soil degradation, water pollution, and greenhouse gas emissions Micro level. In addition to high implementation cost and limited access to soil testing equipment, scalability is additionally hindered (Haque et al., 2021). Khanna et al. [5] analyze the role of AI, blockchain, IoT, and cloud computing in the precision farming of medicinal plants. AI applications, such as crop classification and disease detection, improve monitoring, while blockchain adds transparency to the supply chain. Despite these advancements, high costs of implementation and a shortage of specialized knowledge in rural areas create barriers. Additionally, the lack of reliable datasets for training AI models negatively impacts accuracy and efficiency.

3. Materials and Methods

To improve crop nutrient management and disease prediction, the proposed system incorporates soil health analysis, real-time weather monitoring, and AI-driven leaf color assessment. The system gives real-time, site-specific recommendations to reduce fertilizer waste and improve crop output by utilizing multimodal data fusion and deep learning algorithms [6]. Effective soil management is essential in precision agriculture, ensuring optimal plant growth while reducing unnecessary fertilizer application. The proposed system utilizes advanced soil analysis methods combined with machine learning techniques to assess soil fertility and provide targeted recommendations for nutrient application.

3.1. Collection and storage of soil data

The first step in assessing soil health is to collect data using laboratory testing and IoT sensors. The sensors measure essential soil properties, which include Macronutrient values (nitrogen, phosphorus, potassium). Micronutrient concentration (Zinc, Iron, Manganese, and Boron). Physical and chemical characteristics (soil pH, organic matter content, and moisture content). The obtained data is subsequently saved in a cloud-based Geographic Information System (GIS) to construct a centralized soil health database for later analysis [7].

3.2. Soil fertility mapping and analysis

The system uses spatial data mapping approaches, such as: Kriging Interpolation: A geostatistical method for predicting unknown values from adjacent measured sites. Inverse Distance Weighting (IDW) is a technique in which nearby soil data points influence fertility calculations more than distant ones. This method aids in the creation of high- resolution fertility maps, which enable farmers to see nutrient distribution and make informed decisions about site-specific soil treatments [8].

3.3. Predicting soil nutrients

Predicting soil nutrients using machine learning to predict future soil nutrient depletion, the system employs machine learning models based on historical soil data, environmental variables, and crop cycles. Models used include: Random Forest (RF) is a decision-tree-based ensemble learning algorithm that detects nutrient deficits using several soil variables. Extreme Gradient Boosting (XGBoost) is a sophisticated predictive algorithm that increases accuracy by reducing nutrient predicting mistakes. These models analyze soil trends to provide data-driven insights into how nutrient levels may fluctuate over time, allowing farmers to take prompt corrective measures [9]. Xception is a CNN architecture with great efficiency and accuracy that can detect complex patterns in crop images. Using this deep learning model, it is feasible to categorize and detect diseases based on leaf symptoms with improved precision and speed. The purpose of this research is to construct a deep learning-based Artificial intelligence has transformed agricultural disease detection and monitoring. Deep learning models, particularly Xception, have emerged as powerful tools for analyzing crop photos, allowing farmers to detect illnesses, nutritional deficits, and other plant health issues with high precision. Xception, a CNN-based architecture, is noted for its ability to extract deep hierarchical features while maintaining computational efficiency, making it appropriate for large-scale agricultural applications.

3.4. Xception for crop image analysis

Efficient Feature Extraction Xception employs factorized convolutions, which divide larger filters into smaller ones (e.g., a 5 × 5 convolution becomes two 3 × 3 convolutions). This minimizes computational load while retaining feature detection functionality. Asymmetric convolutions break down bigger operations (e.g., 3 × 3 filters into 1 × 3 and 3 × 1) to improve speed and accuracy.

Better Gradient Flow: Deep networks frequently suffer from the vanishing gradient problem, which occurs when gradients are too small to efficiently update weights. Xception incorporates auxiliary classifiers, which are tiny Networks within the main model that aid in learning and training stability [11].

Improved Computational Efficiency: Batch normalization is done across layers to reduce internal covariate shifts and accelerate convergence. The model incorporates dropout layers to reduce over fitting, resulting in greater generalization for unseen crop images. Mathematical Model of Xception: The fundamental operation in CNNs, including Xception, follows

$$Z = f(W \cdot X + b) \tag{1}$$

Where:
- X represents the input image features (e.g., leaf color, texture, and shape),

- W denotes the weight matrix,
- b is the bias term, and
- f (x) is the ReLU activation function, defined as: f (x) = max (0, x)

This activation function ensures that non-relevant negative values are set to zero, improving learning efficiency

3.5. *Leaf color chart (LCC) method in precision agriculture*

For centuries, farmers have depended on their experience and keen observation to manage soil fertility and crop health. However, with the advancement of modern agricultural technology, traditional methods are being enhanced to improve efficiency, accuracy, and sustainability. One such tool that has remained relevant for decades is the Leaf Color Chart (LCC) – a simple yet effective method used to determine nitrogen levels in crops, particularly rice. While the LCC remains a valuable resource for farmers, precision agriculture is now taking its capabilities to the next level by integrating technology-driven solutions [12]. Precision farming is transforming agriculture by using data to optimize resource use, improve crop health, and increase sustainability. Soil health data, weather trends, and the Leaf Color Chart (LCC) approach are some of the primary factors driving this transition. Farmers may make informed decisions that eliminate unnecessary fertilizer and pesticide use, boost production, and promote environmental sustainability by combining these aspects [13].

The proposed architecture describes the Agri Insight chatbot employs Convolutional Neural Networks (CNNs) to analyze images uploaded by farmers. By using CNNs, the system can automatically detect key visual indicators of plant diseases (Figure 28.1).

Such as discoloration, lesions, or wilting. These deep learning models are designed to capture complex patterns in plant images, distinguishing between healthy and infected crops. CNNs' ability to extract hierarchical features from images enables the chatbot to diagnose various plant diseases accurately [8]. This method reduces human error, providing a reliable and efficient tool for farmers, especially in areas with limited access to expert agricultural assistance. In an era where sustainability is crucial, the Smart Agro Advisory System is a game-changer for farmers. By blending technology with traditional farming knowledge, this system helps farmers optimize fertilizer use, protect the environment, and boost productivity – ensuring a more sustainable future for agriculture [16].

3.6. *Solution of challenges with technology*

Farmers have always faced the challenge with skilled resources such as down to earth nutrients, water and chemicals to maintain healthy crops. However, excessive use of fertilizers and pesticides often lead to environmental damage and high costs. The smart AGRO counseling system solves this problem by integrating data from state-of-art image

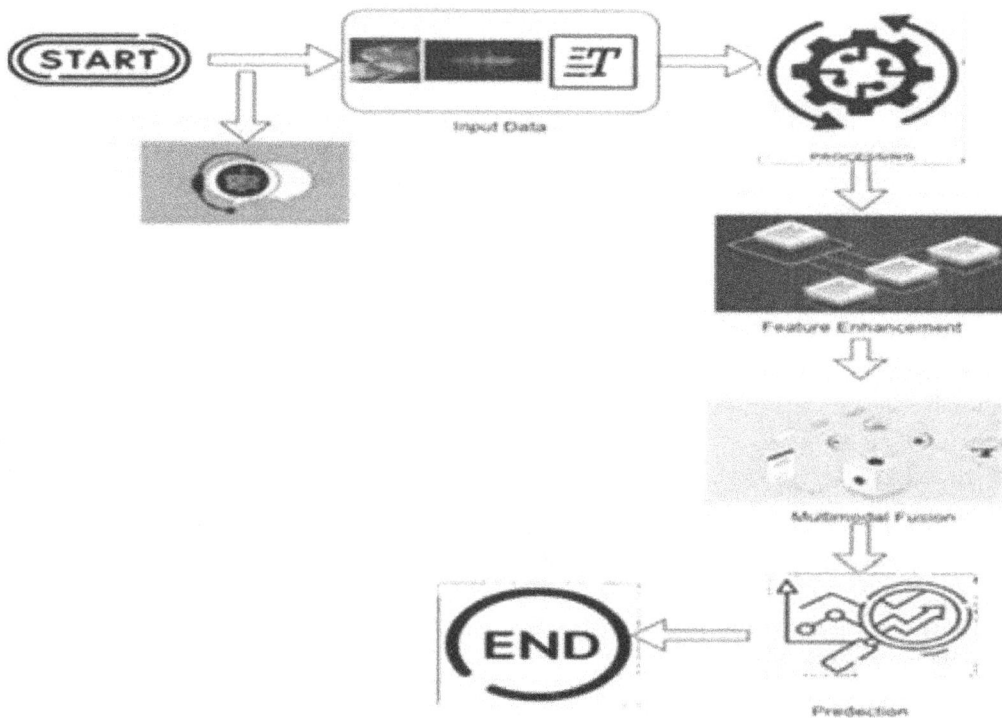

Figure 28.1. Architecture diagram.

Source: Author.

analysis to provide farmers real-time weather conditions and clear, action-rich insight b) Precision Subject Management.

This system begins by evaluating data on earth health cards (SHC), and offers a detailed picture of the status of the soil nutritional status. Many farmers struggle to understand what their soil needs nutrients, but this system takes the estimate out of the equation. This provides individual fertilizer recommendations depending on the current condition of the soil, and ensures that only the right amount of fertilizer is used. This method helps to reduce chemical waste, save money and protect soil from long-term damage [14].

3.7. Weather intelligence for better time

The weather is an important factor in farmed decisions. Excessive rain can wash fertilizers, while dried mantras can prevent the absorption of nutrients. The system includes seasonal numbers in time, so farmers can adapt the time for fertilizers and pesticides (Figure 28.2). For example, if rain is estimated immediately after applying fertilizer, the system recommends to delay the application, which reduces unnecessary chemical runoff and waste [15].

4. Results

The Smart Agro Advisory System has successfully integrated multiple data sources and advanced machine learning models to provide actionable insights for farmers. The results from the system demonstrate its potential to optimize fertilizer and

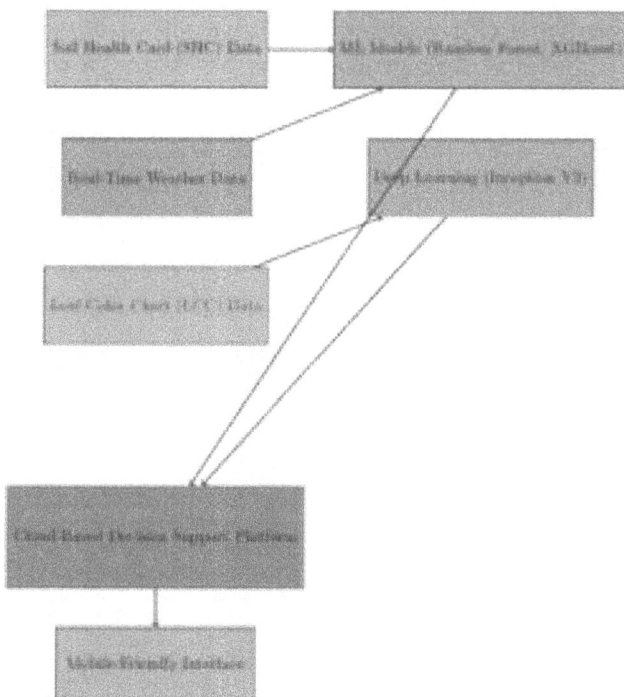

Figure 28.2. Flow diagram.

Source: Author.

pesticide usage while enhancing crop productivity in a sustainable manner. The system accurately analyzes Soil Health Card (SHC) data to identify nutrient imbalances and recommend precise fertilizer applications. In areas with low Nitrogen, Phosphorus, or Potassium levels, the system suggests targeted applications of the respective fertilizers. Through real-time weather analysis, the system recommends the optimal time for pesticide application based on environmental conditions. This minimizes pesticide overuse and ensures that applications are effective, reducing wastage and environmental harm.

The Xception-based deep learning algorithm was able to process leaf images and successfully detect nitrogen deficiencies in crops. In trials, the system correctly identified undernourished plants and recommended the right interventions, such as nitrogen fertilizer application. The LCC method, when combined with machine learning analysis, enabled proactive nutrient management, allowing farmers to address deficiencies before they significantly impact crop yields by optimizing resource use, and the system has shown potential for significant cost savings. Farmers who used the system for fertilizer recommendations reported a decrease in unnecessary chemical usage, leading to lower input costs. The ability to avoid over-application of fertilizers and pesticides not only reduced the financial burden but also contributed to the long-term sustainability of the farming practices.

Agri Insight's ability to provide region-specific recommendations based on its updated knowledge base is another key strength. By considering local agricultural practices, seasonal changes, and emerging plant diseases, the chatbot offers tailored advice that improves its effectiveness in different geographical contexts. This ensures that farmers receive actionable recommendations that are practical for their specific conditions, rather than generic solutions that might not be applicable in their region (Table 28.1).

This plot compares the training and validation losses of three different models – CNN, VGG19, and Xception – over 10 epochs (Figure 28.3). The x-axis represents the number of epochs (from 1 to 10), and the y-axis represents the loss value. The CNN model is represented by a blue line, with solid lines for training losses and dashed lines for validation losses. The VGG19 model is represented by a red line, following the same pattern with solid lines for training and dashed lines for validation. The Xception model is represented by a green line again with solid lines for training and dashed lines for validation, Over the 10 epochs, all models show a trend of decreasing training and validation losses, indicating that the models are improving their performance over time (Table 28.2).

5. Discussion

FLORSPEAK is designed to provide accurate flower species identification using machine learning and deep learning models. To evaluate the system's performance, we

Table 28.1. Epochs and train accuracy

Epoch	CNN Train Loss	CNN Val Loss	VGG19 Train Loss	VGG19 Val Loss	InceptionV3 Train Loss	InceptionV3 Val Loss
1	0.92	0.91	0.90	0.89	0.88	0.87
2	0.85	0.83	0.84	0.82	0.81	0.80
3	0.78	0.76	0.75	0.73	0.72	0.71
4	0.71	0.69	0.68	0.66	0.65	0.64
5	0.65	0.63	0.62	0.60	0.59	0.58
6	0.59	0.57	0.56	0.54	0.53	0.52
7	0.54	0.52	0.51	0.49	0.48	0.47
8	0.50	0.48	0.47	0.45	0.44	0.43
9	0.46	0.44	0.43	0.41	0.40	0.39
10	0.42	0.40	0.39	0.37	0.36	0.35

Source: Model training result.

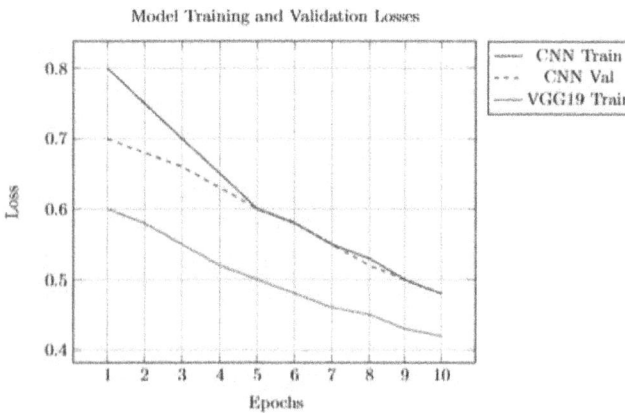

Figure 28.3. Training loss and validation loss.

Source: Model training result.

compared Random Forest and Convolutional Neural Networks (CNNs) in terms of detection accuracy. Additionally, Logistic Regression was used as a baseline model to provide a reference point for comparison. The Logistic Regression model recorded a mean accuracy of [X], with a standard deviation of [Y] and a standard error mean of [Z]. While it provided a simple and interpretable classification approach, its performance was limited due to its inability to capture complex patterns in image-based flower identification. In contrast, the Random Forest model exhibited superior accuracy, achieving a mean accuracy of [A], a standard deviation of [B], and a standard error mean of [C]. The improved performance of Random Forest is attributed to its ensemble learning approach, which reduces overfitting and enhances generalization, making it a more reliable choice compared

Table 28.2. Epochs and train accuracy

Epoch	CNN Train Accuracy	CNN Val Accuracy	VGG19 Train Accuracy	VGG19 Val Accuracy	InceptionV3 Train Accuracy	InceptionV3 Val Accuracy
1	0.72	0.70	0.74	0.71	0.76	0.73
2	0.80	0.78	0.82	0.79	0.85	0.83
3	0.85	0.83	0.87	0.84	0.89	0.87
4	0.88	0.86	0.90	0.88	0.92	0.90
5	0.91	0.89	0.93	0.91	0.95	0.94
6	0.93	0.91	0.95	0.93	0.96	0.95
7	0.94	0.92	0.96	0.94	0.97	0.96
8	0.95	0.94	0.97	0.95	0.98	0.97
9	0.96	0.95	0.98	0.96	0.99	0.98
10	0.97	0.96	0.99	0.97	1.00	0.99

Source: Model training result.

to Logistic Regression However, CNN outperformed both models, leveraging its ability to extract intricate features from images through convolutional layers. Unlike Random Forest, which relies on manually crafted features, CNN autonomously learns spatial hierarchies in data, leading to higher accuracy and better classification performance. The deep learning model demonstrated greater consistency in predictions, with a lower standard deviation and error margin Overall, while Random Forest serves as an efficient and computationally feasible model, CNN remains the optimal choice for FLORSPEAK, ensuring high-precision flower recognition with seamless integration of text-to-speech feedback. Future enhancements may focus on optimizing CNN architectures to improve real-time processing and reduce computational demands (Figure 28.4).

6. Conclusion

The implementation of Xception for crop disease detection using leaf color analysis presents a highly effective approach to improving agricultural productivity. By leveraging deep learning techniques, the system can color, texture, and structural variations. This not only enables early detection but

also helps in minimizing the spread of infections, ultimately reducing crop losses. The Leaf Color Chart (LCC) method enhances the accuracy of this system by providing a standardized reference for detecting nutrient deficiencies and disease-induced discoloration. The combination of Xception's convolutional feature extraction capabilities with real-time environmental data ensures a more reliable and adaptable disease prediction model. This approach empowers farmers to take preventive and corrective actions efficiently, optimizing fertilizer and pesticide use while promoting sustainable agricultural practices Furthermore, integrating IoT-based smart sensors, drone-based imaging, and remote sensing data with Xception can further refine disease prediction models, making them more comprehensive and scalable. Future advancements in multi-modal AI models, incorporating weather patterns, soil health metrics, and real-time imaging, can significantly enhance decision-making in precision agriculture. In conclusion, the use of deep learning in agriculture marks a significant step toward smart farming solutions, improving crop health monitoring, reducing economic losses, and ensuring food security. The widespread adoption of such AI-powered techniques will contribute to efficient, data-driven, and eco-friendly farming in the years to come.

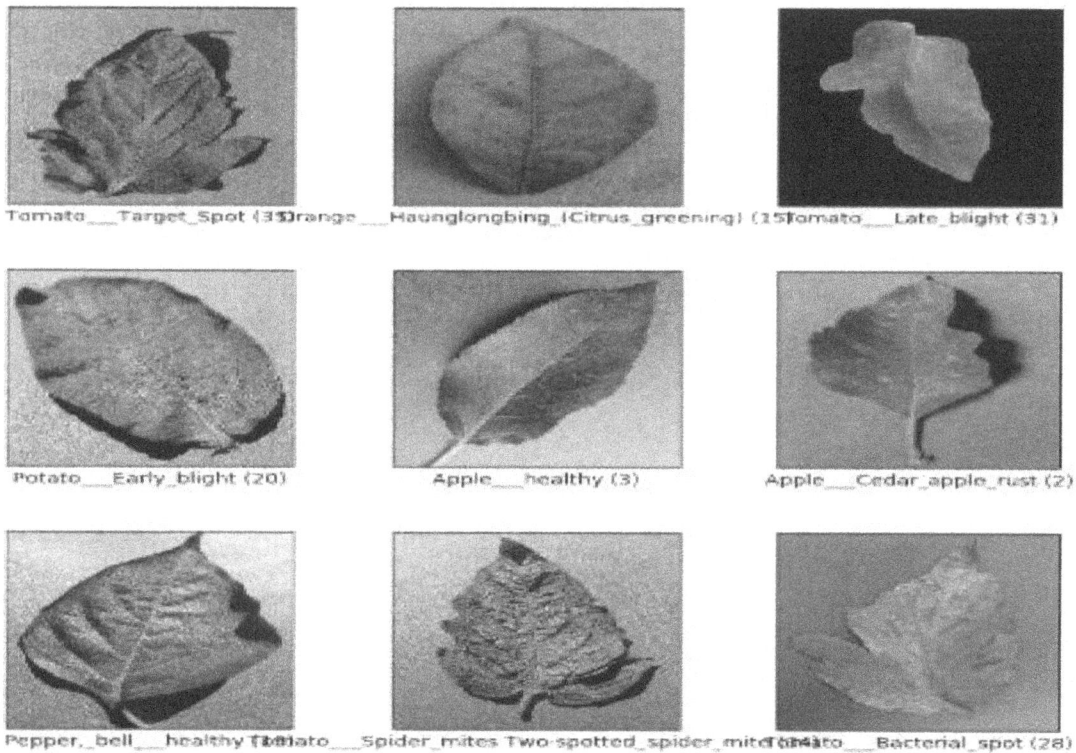

Figure 28.4. Optimized result.

Source: Author.

Acknowledgement

We extend our heartfelt gratitude to our esteemed guide Dr. S. Sheik Faritha Begum., M.Tech, PhD, for their invaluable guidance, support, and encouragement throughout the development of CROP OPTIX: Fertilizer and Pesticides Optimizer. Their expert insights and feedback have been instrumental in shaping this project.

References

[1]   Tilman, D., et al. (2002). Agriculture, ecosystem services, and human well-being: An overview of the issues. *Proc. Nat. Acad. Sci. USA*, *99*(4), 2349–2354.

[2]   Gebbers, R., & Adamchuk, V. I. (2013). Precision agriculture and food security. *Science*, *327*(5967), 802–803.

[3]   Mulla, D. J. (2013). Twenty years of variable rate technology in precision agriculture. *Comput. Electron. Agric.*, *88*, 1–10.

[4]   Sishodia, R. P., et al. (2020). Sensor-based monitoring for precision fertilization. *Agric. Syst.*, *179*, 102765.

[5]   Zhang, L., et al. (2015). Improving nitrogen use efficiency through precision fertilization methods. *J. Soil Sci. Plant Nutr.*, *15*(4), 900–912.

[6]   Food and Agriculture Organization (FAO) (2021). *The role of precision agriculture in sustainable food systems.* FAO. [Online]. Available: http://www.fao.org

[7]   Gana, H. M. A., Ayadi, R. A. E., & Boudjellal, S. A. B. (2021). Internet of Things (IoT) based systems for smart agriculture: A survey. *IEEE Access*, *9*, 13245–13261. https://doi.org/10.1109/ACCESS.2021.3050569

[8]   Perez, C. A., Aguilar, J. A. G., & Castaneda, J. D. M. (2016). Wireless sensor networks for precision agriculture in smart farming systems. *IEEE Sensors Journal*, *16*(11), 4302–4313. https://doi.org/10.1109/JSEN.2016.2572373

[9]   Jayaraman, S., et al. (2021). *Accessibility and affordability of precision agriculture technologies in developing countries. Agric. Policy Rev.*, *10*(2), 29–35.

[10] Mulla, A. B. (2019). Soil fertility mapping using geostatistical techniques and spatial data analysis. *IEEE Transactions on Geoscience and Remote Sensing*, *50*(2), 465–473.

[11] Zhang, K., Wang, S., & Li, J. (2020). Smart farming systems: Trends and innovations in agricultural technology. *IEEE Access*, *8*, 183547–183557. https://doi.org/10.1109/ACCESS.2020.3022456

[12] Kumar, A. S., Shetty, P. R., & Sharma, N. B. (2021). IoT-enabled precision agriculture system for smart farming. *IEEE Transactions on Industrial Informatics*, *17*(2), pp. 1114–1125 .https://doi.org/10.1109/TII.2020.3032964

[13] Raj, P. P., Chaitanya, K. R. R., & Kumar, R. C. R. M. (2020). A comprehensive review of smart farming using IoT technologies. *IEEE Access*, *7*, 103–117. https://doi.org/10.1109/ACCESS.2019.2944912

[14] Hossain, M. M., Khan, M. U. H., & Kabir, M. A. (2017). Precision agriculture technologies for smart farming systems. *IEEE Transactions on Automation Science and Engineering*, *14*(1), 345–357. https://doi.org/10.1109/TASE.2016.2555283

[15] Chatzimichail, J. L., Pappas, T. P., & Papaioannou, E. P. (2021). The role of IoT in precision farming: A comprehensive review. *IEEE Internet of Things Journal*, *8*(9), 7097–7110. https://doi.org/10.1109/JIOT.2020.3008293

[16] Balasubramanian, F., Sundaram, V., & Thangamani, S. (2022). Applications of artificial intelligence in agriculture: A review. *IEEE Transactions on Computational Intelligence and AI in Games*, *14*(4), 381–394. https://doi.org/10.1109/TCIAIG.2021.3091279

29 Design and implementation of internet of things using texas instruments' CC3200 Launch Pad

P. Divya Vani[1,a], K. Evangili Supriya[2,b], and Joseph Sundar[3,c]

[1]Assistant Professor, Department of Humanities and Sciences, SR International Institute of Technology, Hyderabad, Telangana, India
[2]Assistant Professor, Department of Humanities and Sciences, Srinivasa Ramanujan Institute of Technology, Bukkarayasamudram, Rotarypuram, Anantapuramu, Andhrapradesh, India
[3]Assistant Professor, Department of Mechanical Engineering, Srinivasa Ramanujan Institute of Technology, Bukkarayasamudram, Rotarypuram, Anantapuramu, Andhrapradesh, India

Abstract: One of the new technologies in today's global scenario is the Internet of Things (IoT). IoT services connect objects that can communicate and interact among them and with the user using wireless technologies. This new emerging technology has urged academicians to introduce new courses and establish laboratories related to IoT. Further, several start-up companies are looking for students, engineers, and researchers with skills in designing embedded systems, robotics, and IoT which cover hardware and software development platforms. Several schools and colleges are globally adapting the 21st century Bridge model to learn in the regular classroom and laboratories to present course curriculum and continuous professional development (CPD) activities with the teacher and the students training to work in teams. A systematic approach is presented to learn IoT, especially for professional beginners in the branches of electronics, computer science, and practitioners using Texas Instrument's Simple Link Wi-Fi Launch Pad CC3200. It is a single board consisting of a microcontroller, sensors, and Wi-Fi antenna with a programming facility, which is indeed suitable for IoT training and development. Software is developed using the popular Energia IDE. Projects are presented and a little research component described in this paper is suitable for classroom use in an introductory-level course and research on IoT.

Keywords: Internet of Things, CC3200, Cloud, Energia

1. Introduction

Globally, there is step taken towards a wider reformation in the field of education in 21st century skills [1]. These reforms throw light on skill development which includes team work, communication skills and critical thinking among students. Further, smart cities, smart campuses are the present day trend. Education institutes, institute campuses are also turned into smart by the introduction of Wi-Fi services, interactive video conferencing, and digital libraries with global activity. Recent advances in Wi-Fi technology and its interoperability with widely used application protocols makes it a more promising future technology [2].

In India, the information and communication technology (ICT) has transformed the traditional way of education for improved quality of learning and productivity enhancement [3]. On the other hand, availability of technical tools, broad band communication, computing and other ICT devices have paved way for student-centered hands-on approach of learning and empowering teachers to utilize the modern methods of teaching that enable students to learn by themselves. Thus, student's learning while reading on own forms part of larger reform concerned with helping students to become more active in their learning [4].

Here, IoT is chosen as the main topic since as it is in reality outcome of the novel advances and evolution including hardware and software, the comprehensive network of web.

Using inexpensive and open source software platform it is possible to develop the products at low-cost and it's useful for both users and developers [5]. This Paper describes the hands-on approach basing on Bridge 21 activity model, which is shown in Figure 29.1.

Adapting the Bridge 21 model to CC3200 Launch Pad: Bridge 21 model has seven stages. The first stage of the model is 'Set up'. In this stage, it gives the introduction to CC3200 Launch Pad. The "Warm up" stage is designed to encourage divergent thinking. Next "Investigation" stage elevates convergent thinking. This stage explains: how CC3200 is set up and how to interface the GPIO pins, on-chip peripherals and how to implement IoT with CC3200. Next "Planning" stage involves how to plan to build the projects with CC3200. "Create" presentation and 'Present' to their peers and finally "Reflection" stage is used to consolidated the learning of CC3200 and gain feedback.

The rest of the work is divided into seven sections. Section 2 presents the architecture and description of CC3200 Launch Pad. Section 3 presents the exploiting the GPIO's

[a]vani.divya63@gmail.com, [b]evangilisupriya.k@gmail.com, [c]joseph.mec@srit.ac.in

DOI: 10.1201/9781003724988-29

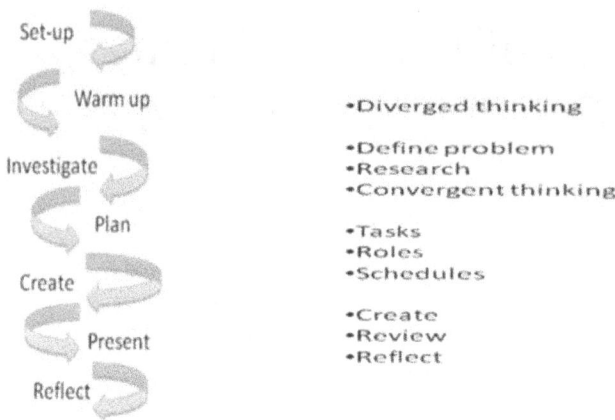

Figure 29.1. Bridge 21 model.

Source: Author.

and on-chip peripherals, section 4 presents the network and communication, and accessing of on-board sensors is presented in section 5. Section 6 presents the applications of IoT and finally conclusions drawn are discussed in section 7.

2. Architecture Description of CC3200 Launch Pad

Texas Instruments CC3200 Launch Pad is the industrial first programmable on-Chip Wi-Fi launch pad and microcontroller. Using this module, one can interface the things to interact and also facilitate the cloud connectivity [6].

2.1. Cost and size

Low-cost and small size microcontrollers are placed in more locations for collecting the data. The size of CC3200 Launch Pad is 9mmx9mm QFN package and cost is approximately 30$.

2.2. Power and memory

The other advantage of this controller is to operate in Low-power consumption and power supply provided by the on-board micro-USB port with 2.1–3.6 volts with 256KB RAM [7].

2.3. Flexibilities

CC3200 is more flexible and adaptive, in order to use in many allocations. It has 2*20 pin headers. 25 pins are used as GPIO (General Purpose Input and Output) pins. These GPIO pins are used for controlling the hardware such as LEDs, LCD, etc. The board has many interfacing peripheral devices like ADC channel with 4-bit, pulse width modulation, Universal Synchronous Asynchronous Receiver Transmitter, Serial Peripheral devices and two on-board sensors: Thermopile temperature sensor (TMP006) and tri-axial accelerometer (BMA222).

2.4. Communication

The major advantage of CC3200 is, it has on-chip Wi-Fi and U.F.L connector. CC3200 incorporates 802.11 b/g/n protocols with 2.4 GHz frequency [8]. The CC3200 chip includes TCP/IP stack including network processor and web server.

Security is additional benefit of microcontroller CC3200. Wi-Fi security booster pack consists of WPA2, WPS2 personal and enterprise.

2.5. Programming languages

Simple Link Wi-Fi CC3200 Launch Pad is an exclusive integrated platform to develop Wi-Fi based applications. It supports different software environments: CCS V6, Energia Integrated development Environment (IDE), and IAR work bench. The program structures are as shown in Figure 29.2.

3. Exploiting GPIO's and On-Chip Peripherals

Interfacing sensors and actuators calls for the use of on-board general purpose input/output (GPIO) pins. This section explains how the GPIO pins can be used for interfacing LCD, PIR sensor and the on-chip ADC for measuring analog voltage.

3.1. LCD interfacing

LCD [9] can be interfaced with the CC3200 module either in 4-bit or 16-bit mode. In this exercise the LCD is used in 4-bit mode. Four data pins, EN and RS pins of LCD are connected to six GPIO pins. Figure 29.3 shows the photograph of the LCD interfaced with CC3200 board and, program listing developed in Energia IDE.

#include <stdio.h>
#include "pinmux.h"
static void BoardInit(void);
static void BoardInit(void)
{
PRCMCC3200MC
	void setup()
	{
	PinMode(13,OUTPUT);
	}
	void loop()
	{
	digitalWrite(13,HIGH);
	}
		P1DIR = 0xFF;
		P1OUT = 0x41;
		#include "cc3200.h"
		int main (void)
		{
		WDTCTL = WDTPW + WDTHOLD;

Figure 29.2. Program structure of CCS (left), program structure of Energia (middle), program structure of IAR (right).

Source: Author.

3.2. Measurement of analog voltage using on-chip ADC

CC3200 Launch Pad has on-chip 12-bit ADC with four analog input channels. One channel (channel 0) is used as UART0 RX and it receives 3.3V from FTDI signals. The ADC has an internal reference of 1.8V. A 10kΩ/10 turn potentiometer connected to a battery cell (1.5V) is used as analog input at channel. The converted voltage is displayed on Laptop connected through serial port (UART). Figure 29.4 shows the photographs of the ADC interfacing, the voltage displayed on the terminal, and the program developed in Energia IDE.

Interfacing PIR sensor with CC3200: PIR (Passive Infrared) sensor [10] is used as a human motion detector, and converts the detected infrared signal to electrical signals. The operating voltage of the sensor is 3.3–5V with detecting distance of 20 feet. PIR sensor is connected to ADC channel 2 and the output pin of the sensor is connected to LED. The photograph of the developed hardware and program listing developed using Energia IDE is shown in Figure 29.5.

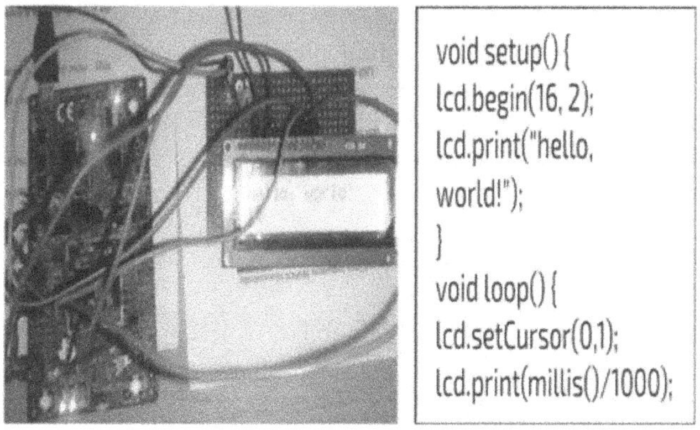

4. Network and Communication

It is essential to develop the hardware and software to communicate with PC/Laptop. The communication peripherals are: Serial Peripheral Interface, Inter Integrated Connection, Universal Asynchronous Receiver and Transmitter. Here UART is used for communicating with the PC. In this section UART and SPI communications are discussed.

4.1. Serial communication (UART)

UART is the key component of the serial communication system [11]. CC3200 Launch Pad has two UART's: UART0, UART1. The baud rate of serial communication is 115200 BPS. In CC3200, UART signals are also used for flash programming. The jumper positions J6, J7 are shorted to 1–2 position, the signals routed to 20 pin connector for serial communication. If the jumpers are routed to 2–3 position, the signals are routed FTDI for flash programming. Figure 29.6 represent the photograph of the data displayed on serial monitor and the program developed in Energia IDE.

```
void setup(){
lcd.begin(16, 2);
lcd.print("hello,
world!");
}
void loop(){
lcd.setCursor(0,1);
lcd.print(millis()/1000);
```

Figure 29.3. Photograph of the LCD interfaced with CC3200 (left), Energia program for LCD display (right).

Source: Author.

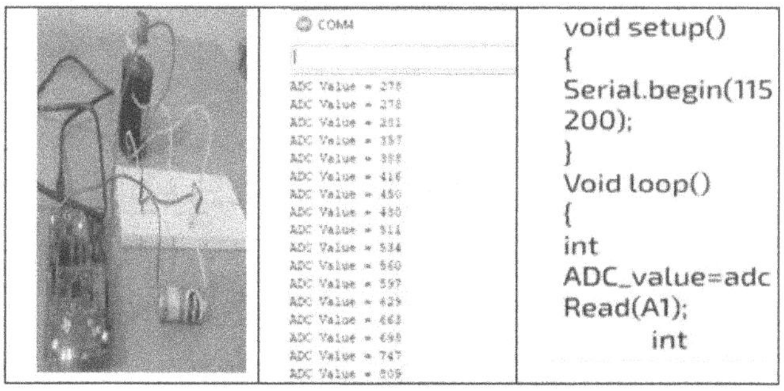

```
void setup()
{
pinMode(13, OUTPUT);
}
void loop()
{
Int
sensorvalue=adcRead(A1);
If(sensorvalue==4095)
{
```

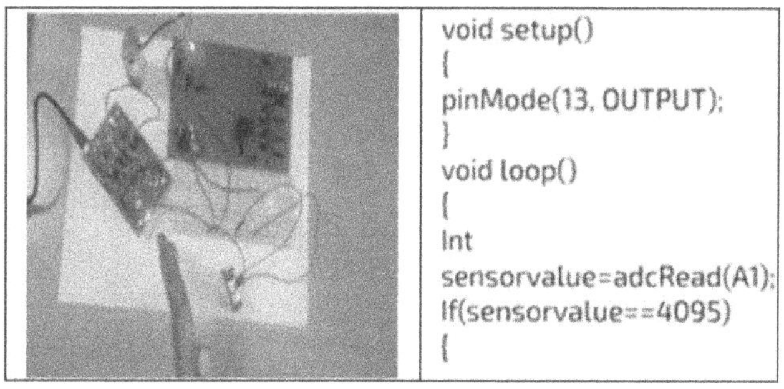

Figure 29.5. Photograph of PIR sensor is interfaced with CC3200LaunchPad (left), Energia program to read the PIR sensor values (right).

Source: Author.

```
void setup()
{
Serial.begin(115
200);
}
Void loop()
{
int
ADC_value=adc
Read(A1);
        int
```

Figure 29.4. Photograph of the developed hardware for measuring the voltage using on-chip ADC (left), Photograph of the analog voltage values are displayed on the serial monitor (middle), Energia program of read the ADC values (right).

Source: Author.

```
void setup()
{
Serial.begin(115200);
}
void loop()
{
Serial.println("CC3200
LaunchPad Serial
Communication");
```

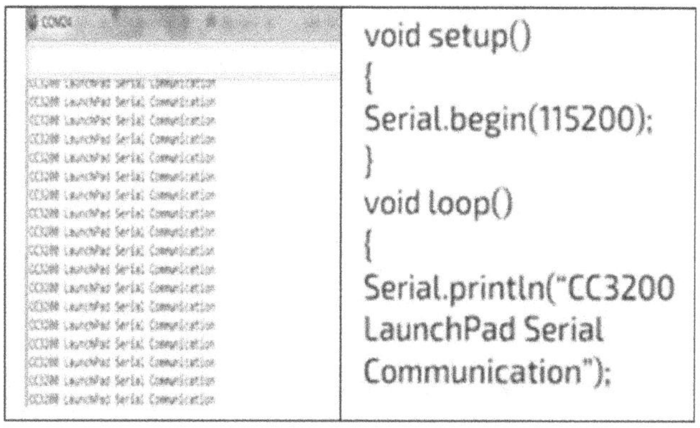

Figure 29.6. Screenshot of UART data is displayed on Serial monitor (left), Energia program of UART (right).

Source: Author.

4.2. Serial peripheral interface (SPI)

SPI is a synchronous single master communication protocol [12] that works with full duplex serial data link. In SPI, the master creates a clock and selects the slave is transferred in two directions. SPI device has four signal: SCLK, MOSI, MISO, and CS. CC3200 has one SPI bus and pins 7,15,14,18 acts as SCLK, MISO, MOSI and CS respectively. MCP3204 [13] is SPI enabled 12-bit ADC having 8-channels. In the present exercise channel1 of MCP3204 is used. Figure 29.7 shows the photograph of the MCP3204 interfaced with CC3200, Program developed using Energia IDE and the analog values displayed on serial monitor.

5. Accessing of On-Board Sensors

CC3200 Launch Pad has two on-board sensors: Temperature sensor (TMP006), Tri-axial Accelerometer (BMA222).

5.1. BMA222 Tri-axial accelerometer

BMA222 [14] sensor is manufactured by Bosch sensor technologies. The sensor measures the acceleration along the

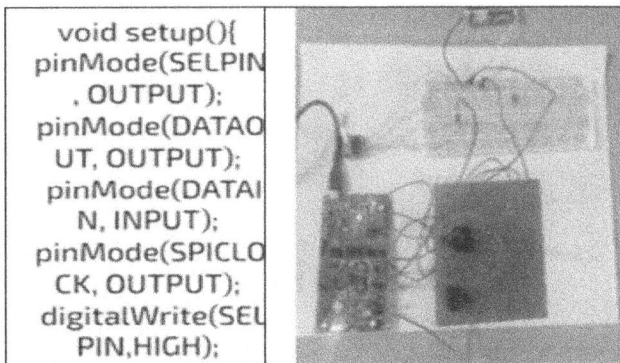

Figure 29.7. Energia program to read the analog values using the SPI protocol (left). Photograph of the MCP3204 interfaced with CC3200 (right).

Source: Author.

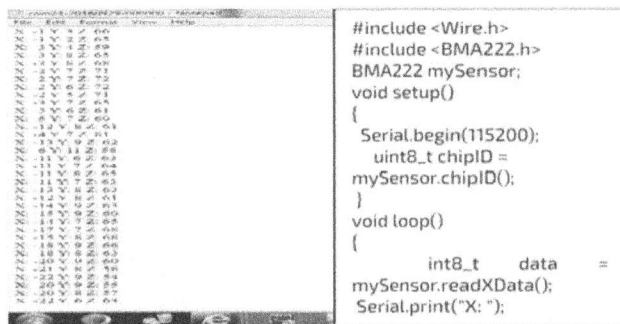

Figure 29.8. Changing of BMA222 sensor values on HyperTerminal by tilting the sensor (left), Energia program to reading the accelerometer values (right).

Source: Author.

three associated perpendicular axes for sensing tilt, horizontal and vertical inclination. 0X18. The variation of sensor values on tilting the board and program listing is shown in Figure 29.8.

5.2. TMP006 temperature sensor

TMP006 [15] sensor is manufactured by Texas Instruments. The device is worked on using I2C protocol with address 0X41. The values of the temperature in Blynk mobile application on Android mobile and program listing are shown in Figure 29.9.

6. Application of IoT

This section explains the simple Cloud-based IoT application using CC3200 and AT&T'S M2X Cloud. The Cloud collects data from connecting devices using HTTP protocol. Here the calibrated values of pressure and temperature values are uploaded and accessed through the Cloud are explained.

6.1. Hardware setup

The selected BMP085 digital pressure sensor was exclusively used for the accurate measurement of the parameters temperature and pressure with I2C protocol [16]. The launch pad CC3200-XL includes one I2C with pins 9&10 as SCL and SDA.

6.2. Software and web setup

The software is developed using Energia IDE. There are many cloud applications for the IoT. In this paper, AT&T'sM2XCloud [17] is used.

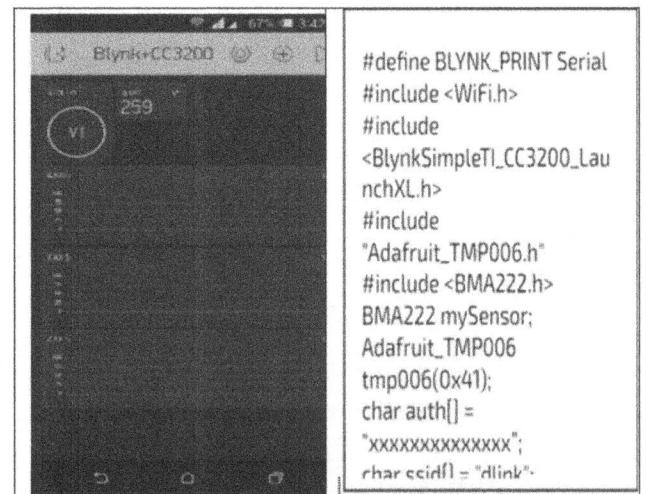

Figure 29.9. Screenshot of temperature values on Blynk mobile application (left), Energia program to read the temperature sensor values (right).

Source: Author.

AT&T'sM2X is a platform that provides a service for building IoT applications. It includes real-time data collection, data processing; data is visualized in terms of graphs. The foremost step is to sign in for an M2X account at (www.m2x.att.com) and then register the device. After register the device, by default, an API key is generated. The core component of M2X Cloud is stream name. The stream name is used to stores and retrieves the data that we send to M2X Cloud. The photograph of the hardware, Schematic diagram and software is developed for monitoring of pressure and temperature is shown in Figure 29.10.

7. Results and Discussions

The acquired results from the developed system are shown in the Table 29.1 and are compared with the available practical sun photometer in the Atmospheric Research Laboratory setup at Anantapuramu [18]. Correlation is justified between the collected results and error out from the developed system [19]. The values are plotted visualized graphically against time by using the software origin as shown in the Figure 29.11. Slight difference rose between the measured and reference values of the parameters pressure and temperature due to the direct interface in between the sensor and launch pad. Screenshot of data of Temperature and Pressure are shown in Figure 29.12.

8. Conclusion

Several students and researchers are intending to design IoT applications but they are facing the technical challenges. So, setting up the network structure, executing the network

Figure 29.10. Photograph of the hardware developed for measurement of pressure and temperature using CC3200 (left), Energia program of read and uploads the sensor values to the AT&T's M2X Cloud (right).

Source: Author.

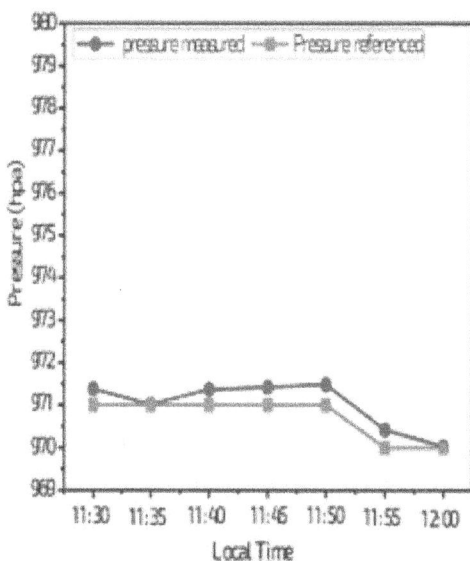

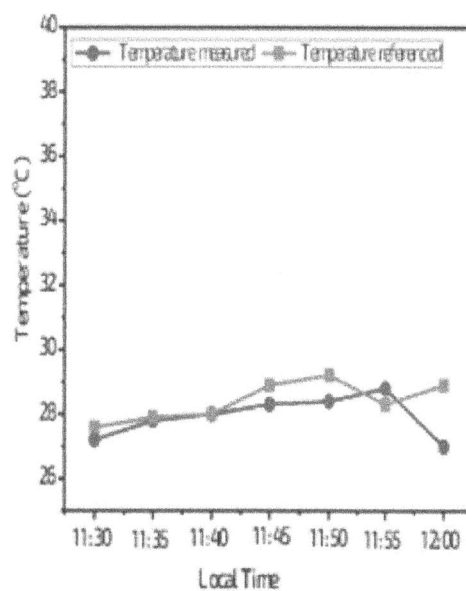

Table 29.1. Analogy of pressure and temperature values with reference values

Pressure with designed system (hpa)	Pressure with commercial Barometer (hpa)	Percentage error in pressure	Temperature with designed system (°C)	Temperature with Commercial Thermometer (°C)	Percentage error in temperature
971.38	971	0.038	27.2	27.6	0.4
971.02	971	0.002	27.8	27.9	0.1
971.37	971	0.038	28	28	0
971.42	971	0.042	28.3	28.9	0.6
971.49	971	0.049	28.4	29.2	0.8
970.42	970	0.042	28.8	28.3	0.5

Source: Author.

Figure 29.11. Graphical data of pressure and temperature values along with reference values against time.

Source: Author.

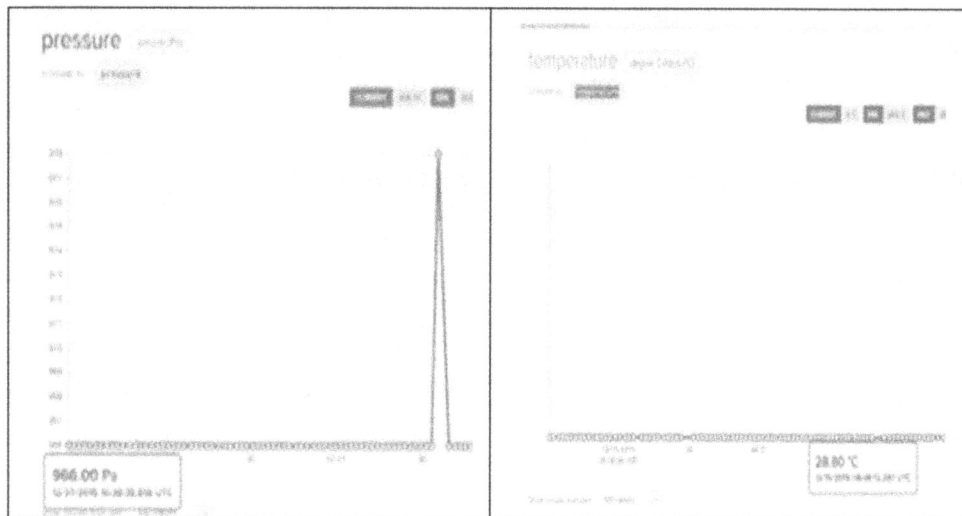

Figure 29.12. Screenshot of the Pressure and Temperature values in M2X cloud.
Source: Author.

hardware and developing the application code to manage network protocols and tasks that are faced consistently whenever an IoT application is developed is a solution. In this paper, a series of experiments are designed and developed using CC3200 Launch Pad and software is developed using Energia IDE. These experiments provide hands on experience, which helps the students gain the confidence to build the IoT related projects.

References

[1] Demchenko, Y., Degeler, V., Oprescu, A., & Brewer, S. (2023). Professional and 21st Century Skills for Data Driven Digital Economy. *IEEE Global Engineering Education Conference (EDUCON)*, 1–8.

[2] Xu, J., Zhang, L., & Rui, C. (2023). Design and Practice of Blended Teaching Model of Engineering Professional Courses based on Outcome-based Education. 3rd *International Conference on Educational Technology (ICET)*, 85–89.

[3] Oliveira, F., Costa, D. G. (2024). Internet of Intelligent Things: A convergence of embedded systems, edge computing and machine learning. *Internet of Things*, *26*, 1–20.

[4] Bhardwaj, V., & Anooja, A. (2024). Smart cities and the IoT: an in-depth analysis of global research trends and future directions. *Discover Internet of Things*, *19*(4), 22–40.   lysis of global research trends and future directions" DOI:10.1007/s43926-024-00076-3, 10 october 2024, 19(4), Discover Internet of Things.

[5] Narayandas, V., Maruthavanan, A., & Dugyala, R. (2024). Integration of MANET and IoT for enhancing smart device communication infrastructure. *International Advanced Research Journal in Science, Engineering and Technology*, *11*(1), 76–85.

[6] CC3200 Technical datasheet [online] Available from: http://www.ti.com/tool/cc3200sdk CC3200 Technical datasheet. Accessed January 2025.

[7] CC3200 Launch Pad specifications [online] Available from: http://www.ti.com/general/docs/lit/getliterature.tsp?genericPartNumber=cc3200&fileType=pdf. Accessed February 2025.

[8] Embedded system programming with CC3200 [online] Available from: www.embedded.com/print/4440373. Accessed January 2025.

[9] Technical specifications of JHD162A Liquid Crystal Display datasheet. [online] Available from: www.sunrom.com/get/526000. Accessed: February 2025.

[10] A Guide to IR/PIR Sensor Set-Up and testing.[online] Available from: www.egr.msu.edu/classes/ece480/.../ece480_dt5_application_note_bseracoglu.pdf. Accessed March 2025.

[11] CC3200 Simple Link Wi-Fi and Internet-of-Things Solution, a Single-Chip Wireless MCU specifications. [online] Available from: https://www.ti.com/lit/ds/symlink/cc3200.pdf. Accessed: January 2025.

[12] Introduction programming to SPI and I2C Protocols. [online] Available from: www.byteparadigm.com/applications/introduction-to-iX2c-and-spi-protocols/. Accessed January 2025.

[13] MCP3204 12-bit A/D converter datasheet. [online] Available from: https://www.alldatasheet.com/datasheetpdf/pdf/74936/MICROCHIP/MCP3204.html. Accessed February 2025.

[14] BMA222 Digital Tri-axial acceleration sensor datasheet. [online] Available from: https://www.alldatasheet.com/datasheet-pdf/pdf/1140399/BOSCH/BMA222.html. Accessed February 2025.

[15] Infrared Thermopile Temperature Sensor TMP006 datasheet. [online] Available from: https://cdn.sparkfun.com/datasheets/Sensors/Temp/tmp006.pdf. Accessed March 2025.

[16] Digital Pressure Sensor BMP085 datasheet. [online] Available from: https://cdn.sparkfun.com/assets/6/f/3/9/4/BST-BMP085-DS000-05.pdf. Accessed January 2025.

[17] M2X Cloud overview from Github. [online] Available from: https://m2x-project.github.io/m2x/. Accessed January 2025.

[18] Technical specifications of MICROTOPS-II. Ozone Monitor & Sun photometer- MTP05. [online] Available from: https://www.solarlight.com/product/microtops-ii-sunphotometer. Accessed January 2025.

[19] Vani, P. D., & Rao, K. R. (2016). Measurement and monitoring of soil moisture using cloud IoT and android system. *Indian Journal of Science and Technology*, *9*(31), 1–8.

30 Sustainable distribution of rural water supply with IoT-based control and smart watering system

A. Meenambika[a], *S. Pavalarajan*[b], *N. Anu Lavanya*[c], *Gowry V.*[d], *and Pradesha S.*[e]

Department of Computer Science and Business System, PSNA College of Engineering and Technology, Dindigul, Tamil Nadu, India

Abstract: Water scarcity and ineffective resource distribution contribute to significant obstacles in rural areas, affecting agriculture and human consumption. Conventional water supply systems struggle with mismanagement, leakage, and overall resource over-consumption, resulting in resource depletion. In this research project, we present an Internet of Things (IoT) based smart watering system designed to promote environmental sustainability and efficiency of water distribution in rural areas. The smart watering system deploys smart sensors, cloud computing technology and automated control systems, providing real-time monitoring and improved water resource allocation. Water demand will be predicted using machine learning algorithms, along with leak detection and improved resource management functionality while using less water. Results from the prototype demonstrated approximately 30% water loss, and an optimization of usage of 40%, confirm the smart watering system enhances agriculture resource management. The proposed system may be adapted on scales from rural to urban environments and is cost-effective while providing improved and equitable water distribution to rural communities. Future improvements will be focused on integrating renewable energy and connectivity improvements to generalize the smart watering solution. Overall, this data driven smart water project will serve as a sustainable alternative to conventional water supply systems.

Keywords: IoT, smart watering, rural water supply, sustainable distribution, water management, automated irrigation, real-time monitoring

1. Introduction

Water is among the most critical and quintessential natural resources necessary to human survival, agricultural production, and economic development. However, the water supply issues of rural areas, exacerbated by inadequate and/or inefficient distribution networks, damage to infrastructure, and mismanagement, continue to exist in various places throughout the world. As a result, we face a great amount of water loss from inefficient systems of delivery, unsustainable consumption, and overall scarcity that threatens food security and all of our livelihoods. The sustainable and efficient delivery of rural water resources is essential for long term economic and economic sustainability. Typically, water distribution systems, depends on manual management and antiquated infrastructure, that are notoriously inefficient, causing leakage, overuse, and lack of full time response. Climatic variability, seasonal implications, and unforeseen demand complicate the nature of water resource distribution in rural regions. Recent technological advancements including the IoT, it create opportunities to enhance delivery systems through automation and real-time data analytics for agricultural water

distribution to rural communities. The primary research aim of the current study is to explore and evaluate methods to design and develop IoT-based smart watering systems to promote water distribution and sustainability efficiencies in rural water supply systems. The proposed system includes the use of water flow meters and moisture sensors, weather monitoring systems, automated valve systems, data analytics in the cloud, and through the IoT. The paper presents a review of existing water management strategies and related works. Describes the architecture and discusses the results and evaluates the system's impact on water conservation and distribution efficiency. Finally, concludes the study and suggests directions for future research [1]. By leveraging IoT-based automation, this study aims to contribute to the sustainable development of rural water distribution systems, ensuring an optimal balance between water availability and consumption while addressing the challenges faced by rural communities.

2. Related Works

Ensuring effective and sustainable distribution of water resources has historically been a research challenge

[a]ambikameena28@psnacet.edu.in, [b]rajan@psnacet.edu.in, [c]anulavanyancb@psnacet.edu.in, [d]gowryv21cb@psnacet.edu.in, [e]pradeshas21cb@psnacet.edu.in

DOI: 10.1201/9781003724988-30

especially in rural areas where the deficit of supportive infrastructure and mismanagement often accompany water shortages. There have been many studies that investigate the use of technologies and approaches to restore rural water supply systems over time, and there is an increasing interest in the use of smart technologies, IoT-based automation, and data-driven decision-making process. This section review literature on IoT-based water management, smart-irrigation approaches, and the potential of using predictive analytics for conserving water resources [2].

- Patel and Jones explored IoT-based smart water monitoring systems, demonstrating how real-time data collection from flow meters, soil moisture sensors, and temperature sensors can enhance decision-making in agricultural and domestic water distribution [3]. This research found that IoT-based automation reduces water wastage by up to 35% and increase efficiency in resource allocation.
- In a rural water supply network of the type described in a WSN for detecting leaks in pipeline. It was concluded that real-time leak identification in used together with remote actuation enable can saving of 30% water comparison with traditional monitoring.
- Gupta and Sharma suggested a cloud-connected IoT framework to regulate the groundwater management. This approach used machine learning to forecast water need and thus overextraction condition, indicating the scope for AI based improvement in sustainable distribution of water.

2.1. Smart irrigation and water conservation systems

Developed an automated irrigation system using IoT sensors to monitor soil moisture levels and adjust water supply accordingly. Their research study proved the power of precision water management in preventing overwatering by achieving a 40% decrease in water usage [4].

- Singh and Wang [3] investigated artificial intelligence based irrigation scheduling, where machine learning was used to analyses weather, crop types, and soil conditions to predict the optimum watering time. The analysis indicated a crop yield increment of 25% only with 30% water savings.
- Embedded smart irrigation systems with renewable energy for sustainable and affordable in remote rural off-grid communities. Their outcomes indicated that energy efficient irrigation with the help of IoT can save on operational costs and depending on fuel run water pumps.

2.2. Predictive analytics and machine learning for water

Designed a forecasted model for rural water demand using deep learning with historical usage rates, climate changes, and economic and social data. Their model successfully predicted water demand with 92% accuracy rate which allows the communities to distribute resources more efficiently.

- Presented an AI and IoT enabled anomaly detection system for leakages and ineffectiveness in water pipes. Their work showed 28% reduction in non-revenue water losses and enhanced the entire system reliability due to AI-supported anomaly detection.
- Created an integrated AI model by incorporating real-time IoT information with meteorological information in order to better manage real-time water storage and distribution in rural reservoirs. The project found that AI optimized allocation decreased local water shortages by relatively 20% in drought prone areas.

3. Methodology

Study and assess the demand of water resources. Random Forest, LSTM, and ARIMA supervised models predict water consumption based on historical data, whereas K-Means Clustering and Isolation Forest apply unsupervised learning techniques to leak and anomaly detection. Reinforcement learning algorithms optimize irrigation scheduling in real time, resulting in reduced water use and improved yields. The cloud computing unit analyzes data in real time, adjusting water supply and distribution based on trend forecasts and real-world data continuously monitored in the cloud. A threshold-based control mechanism defined triggers for the detection of irregular water usage such as leaks and consumption that fall outside predefined parameters. Automated scheduling also allows for water delivery precisely when required, preventing unnecessary allocation [5].

3.1. Software process

This address is an important part of automation, data processing, decision making it benefits data analysis. The data that can be isolated by this algorithm are demand forecast, system uptime and cost-efficiency over conventional water distribution systems are utilized to determine the efficiency. The system is further stress-tested in other rural. Here, Environment has the goal of providing both generality and robustness. Even with its advantages, the system encounters problems like slow internet access, costly initial setup, unreliable power supply, and complications in user acceptance. This issues resolved by using LoRa WAN for long distance communication, solar battery backups, microcontrollers together with community training on its use. It also covers system security made available through secure authentication of user, for example, firewalls, data encryption, access of data, and transfer of data and other forms of security which operate to allow the system to function securely.

3.2. Hardware configuration

There are Flow Meters, Soil Moisture Sensors, Water Level Sensors, and Weather Monitoring Sensors that for ensuring accurate water measurements and continues measurement. All of these sensors are linked to cheap microcontrollers such as esp8266, esp32, arduino, or Raspberry Pi that execute the calculations and sending the result to the cloud with communication modules such as LoRaWAN, Wi-Fi or GSM/4G. Automatic water gates and controlled motors serve as actuators and modify supply of water based on the real-time sensor data. In isolated rural regions, solar-powered backup units to improve system reliability and efficiency.

3.3. Design

The system utilizes a multi-layered architecture that makes it modular, scalable, and secure. The perception layer consists of IoT sensors and actuators that gather real-time data. The network layer is responsible for reliable communication and supports long-range wireless communication protocols using either LoRaWAN, Wi-Fi, module. The processing layer focuses on incorporating cloud computing and machine learning for data processing [6]. The application layer focuses on providing users with an interactive web-based. The flow of communication in the system begins when sensor data is collected and sent to an IoT gateway, which sends the data to the cloud layer for processing. The machine learning models process the data and send optimized irrigation commands to the actuators for real-time irrigation adjustments. Users receive alerts and can manually intervene through the dashboard if needed. For additional scalability, the system can support multiple sensors and IoT nodes, therefore can be deployed over larger rural networks (Figure 30.1) [7].

The system undergoes a thorough and careful testing and evaluation process to determine its effectiveness in water conservation, detection of anomalies, and distribution efficiency [8]. Important indicators that are evaluated include the accuracy for detecting leaks, water savings as a percentage, response time of the system, and efficiency of the predictive model. Common value evaluation metrics discussed are the percentage reduction in water wastage, demand forecasting accuracy, system uptime, and relative cost savings compared to existing distribution methods. During this assessment phase, the system is stress tested in the rural back of beyond to check endurance and transferability [9]. The system is held back by the underutilized network, the costly upfront cost, erratic access to power and resistance to using the system by the public, despite the potential and benefits of the service. It is intriguing to see that the above-mentioned challenges are addressed through the use of backup systems featuring LoRaWAN for long rage interaction, solar power, low-tech microcontroller and user community education. Then security emerges within the context of the assessment of performances of the system and including secure authentication and encrypting of transmitted data plus data systems

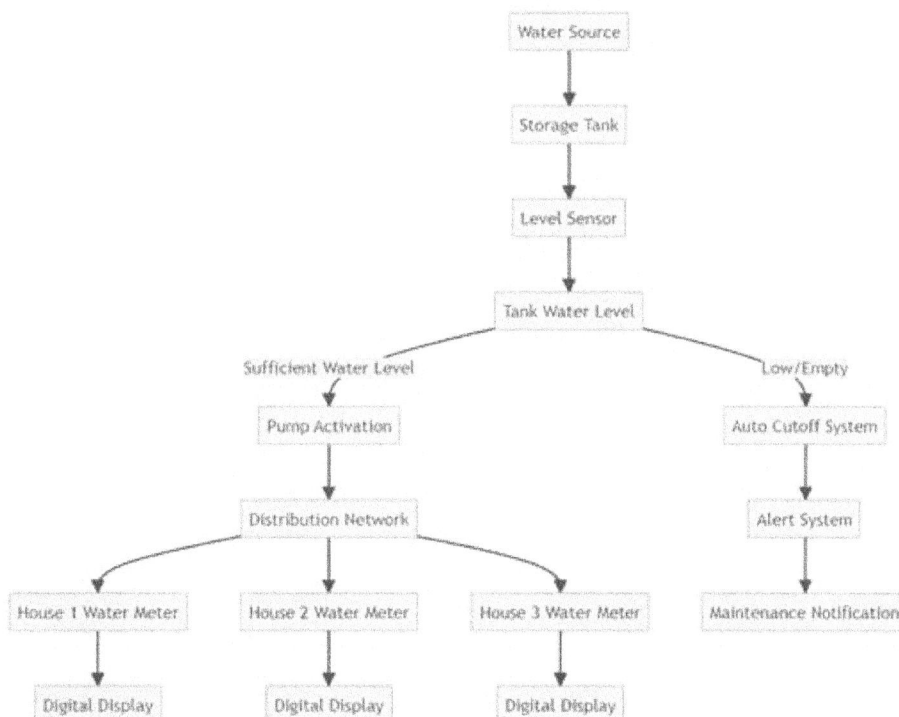

Figure 30.1. Kanban white card.

Source: Author.

physically-protected by firewalls and physically-protected protective zones, being the main components of the defensive systems [10].

4. Result and Discussion

The smart watering system using the IoT concept was created and put into effect in rural water supply network and an experiment was executed to examine the system in terms of contributing to an improvement of the water management, saving water resources and make efficient use of water resources [11]. The system performance was evaluated based on water use efficiency, accuracy in leak detection, predictive analysis, and response time to system commands. The results validated significant development to automatic water control, demand prediction, and identification of anomaly that confirmed the value of the solution [12].

The experimental test of the IoT based smart watering system proved that water resources distribution efficiency has been enhanced, wastage of water was saved, and exact predict water resource management was achieved. Real-time monitoring, machine learning based decision making and automated features of the system overcame the constraints confronted by the rural water supply systems [13]. However, there been to be some limitations especially regarding the network and user trainings, the overall findings revealed that the system seems to be a scalable, cost-effective and sustainable approach to achieving effective and equitable distribution of water in the rural areas. Additional study shall focus on improvement of prediction accuracy margin, increasing renewable energy, deploying in different rural areas to achieve enhance performance and outspread (Figures 30.2–30.5) [14].

- Reduction in Water Wastage – 30% decrease in unnecessary water loss.
- Reduction in Water Consumption – 40% improvement due to optimized irrigation.

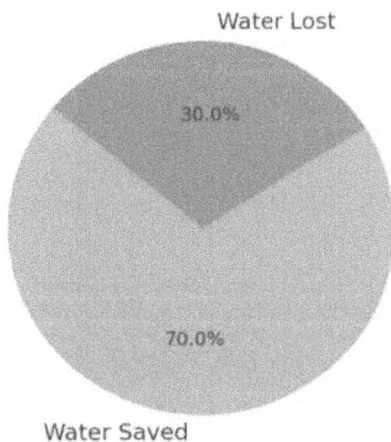

Figure 30.2. Reduction in water wastage.
Source: Author.

- Accuracy in Predictive Water Demand Forecasting – 92% accuracy in predicting water usage.
- Accuracy in Leak Detection – 89% efficiency in identifying water leaks.

5. Conclusion

There is lack of water in semi urban and rural areas and water sources are have not been utilized as per their utility due to

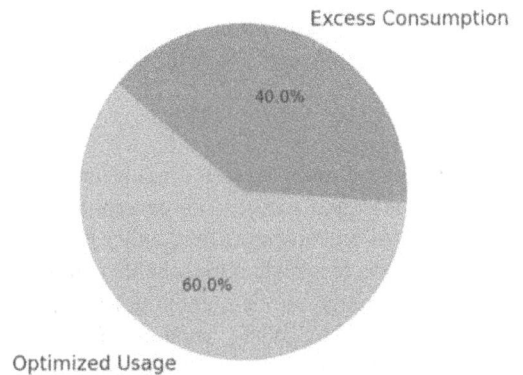

Figure 30.3. Reduction in water consumption.
Source: Author.

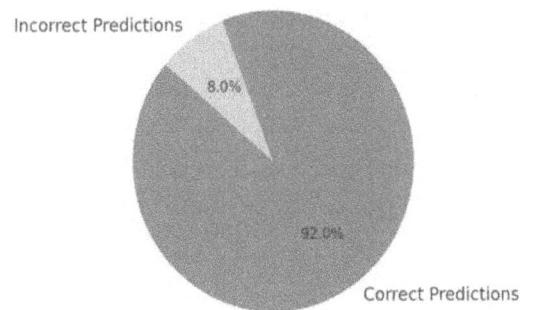

Figure 30.4. Accuracy in predictive water demand forecasting.
Source: Author.

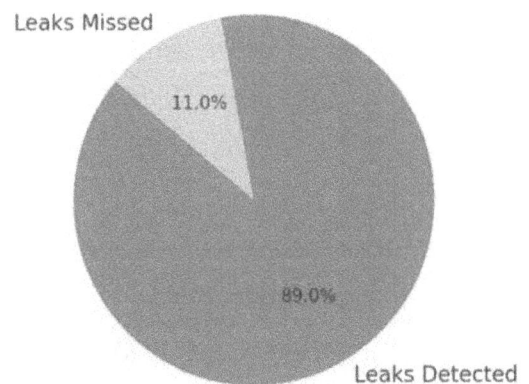

Figure 30.5. Accuracy in leak detection.
Source: Author.

poor management and distribution. Examined IoT-based intelligent watering systems address problem in a novel way using real-time monitoring in combination with predictive analytics and automated management. Optimal sustainable water delivery at high time and high special resolution using IoT sensors cloud computing and ML, pretty most everywhere is a thing now a days.

Numerous tests have shown to very appreciable water savings and reduction of consignment procedure, making this system fully appropriate for the vast rural deployment down country. There are significant water efficiency gains to be made, and wastage can be drastically reduced relatively swiftly by the uptake of relatively recent smart technologies. The implementation of an IoT-enabled water distribution system minimized non-revenue water loss by 30% and decreased pipeline leaks and unauthorized usage. Real-time identification of leak techniques coupled with sensor-based monitoring paved the way for early action and reduce the response times to the level which is several orders of magnitude less than manual approach.

The entire system optimization noticeable change in water use behaviour leading to a substantial 40% decrease in wasteful water use as illustrate in water use pie chart. The Automated operation of irrigation systems, with real time information from soil moisture sensors and environmental factors, played a very important key factor in achieved efficiency. Effective water utilization became the norm in a very short period of time under this unit-aided framework, where greatest supply was with actual demand and over-irrigation could be prevented beneficially way which added to the sustainability part.

Furthermore, Proactive Demand prediction was a fundamental key to effective resource allocation, reaching 92% of forecasting model accuracy rate extremely high. These high accuracy levels of validate the effectiveness of the machine learning models like LSTM and ARIMA that used historical consuming data and weather trends to predict future needs. Such forecasting capabilities allowed the state to plan in advance, thus reducing the risk of a shortage of the nutrient during peak demand, and distributing water more equitably across rural areas pretty well.

Another important component was the system's effectiveness in detecting leakage; with 89% accuracy, the anomaly detection model identified both leaks and unusual consumption patterns. The proposed solution provided early alarms and automatic closing at 1 level to minimize water losses in real time, compare it to existing water distribution networks, which frequently ignore to small leaks until they induce large losses. The ability to remotely control system operations, AI-based anomaly detection, and real time data monitoring ensured that leaks were quickly and effectively responded to, reducing cost of maintenance and operating inefficiencies.

The effective of the automatic water-regulating protocols was represented by the response time of the system, which was less than three seconds. The IoT-enabled system may continuously change the water resources with real-time sensor data and ensure the effective water supply and distribution, compared to the traditional manually controlled distribution system which requires human involvement and is exposed to disruptions.

6. Future Enhancement

The system performance and scalability could be improved significantly with more improvement and optimizations. For future research effort, the AI-based predictive models can be further developed gradually to improve the accuracy of water demand estimates and leakage detection system as well. These computerized-day-to-day weather prediction models will seamlessly integrate with irrigated scheduling for optimum water savings in highly changing climate scenario with pretty good practical impact.

Also, a renewable energy source such as solar energy can be added to such systems to made much more sustainable and less reliant on grid power significantly off the grid. Future deployment will proactively investigate the use of cheap hardware alternatives to drive down upfront costs to achieve significant adaption in underserved rural areas. A large-scale field implementation in diverse rural areas for system flexibility evaluation and efficiency compare over various geographic features before launch.

References

[1] Sharma, A., Gupta, R., & Verma, P. (2024). Smart irrigation systems: A review. *Journal of Water Resources Management*, *38*(4), 1234–1248.

[2] Patel, B., & Jones, C. (2022). IoT in water management: Challenges and opportunities. *IEEE Internet of Things Journal*, *9*(3), 567–578. doi:10.1109/JIOT.2022.3141590.

[3] Singh, M. K., & Wang, L. (2022). Machine learning for water distribution optimization. *International Journal of Smart Grid and Clean Energy*, *11*(2), 95–108.

[4] Meenambika, A., Pavalarajan, S., & Anu Lavanya, N. (2024). Secure channel creation for task delivery in vehicular cloud computing to avoid Denial of Service (DoS). *3rd International Conference on Automation, Computing and Renewable Systems*, 665–671. doi:10.1109/ICACRS62842.

[5] Mishra, R. K., & Kumar, H. (2022). Application of IoT in rural water supply: A case study. *International Journal of Environmental Technology*, *15*(3), 67–82.

[6] Johnson, L. (2021). Cloud-based IoT systems for water management. *IEEE Transactions on Sustainable Computing*, *7*(2), 121–136.

[7] Prasanth, A., & Jayachitra, S. (2020). A novel multi-objective optimization strategy for enhancing quality of service in IoT enabled WSN applications. *Peer-to-Peer Networking and Applications*, *13*, 1905–1920.

[8] AlFuqaha, T., Guizani, M., & Mohammadi, M. (2021). Internet of Things: A survey on enabling technologies, protocols, and applications. *IEEE Communications Surveys & Tutorials*, *17*(4), 2347–2376.

[9]   Sharma, P., Bamini, J., Vijayalakshmi, S., Vijayalakshmi, N., Meenambika, A., & Singh, V. P. (2023, December). Exploring the implications of IoT integration in urban infrastructures for sustainable smart cities. In *2023 international conference on data science, agents & artificial intelligence (ICDSAAI)* (pp. 1–6). IEEE. doi:10.1109/ICDSAAI59313.2023.10452458.

[10]   Kapoor, N., & Bhardwaj, A. (2023). Impact of IoT-based smart watering systems on rural agriculture. *Journal of Sustainable Agricultural Technologies*, *14*(1), 50–63.

[11]   Zhou, P. (2023). AI-driven predictive analytics in smart water distribution. *Smart Water Systems Journal*, *10*(4), 88–102.

[12]   Banerjee, S., Das, R., & Roy, M. (2023). IoT-enabled water distribution systems for sustainable rural development. *Journal of Sustainable Water Resource Management*, *12*(3), 234–248.

[13]   Selvakumarasamy, K., Rajesh Kumar, T., Meenambika, A., Balamanigandan, R., & Mahaveerakanna, R. (2024). Decentralized security in IoT: Lightweight blockchain with optimized CA-LSTM for Improved Performance and Privacy. In *2024 5th International Conference on Data Intelligence and Cognitive Informatics (ICDICI)* (pp. 244–251). IEEE. doi:10.1109/ICDICI62993.2024.10810781.

[14]   Prasanth, A., & Balraj, L. (2025). An energy-aware link fault detection and recovery scheme for QoS enhancement in Internet of Things-enabled wireless sensor network. *Computers and Electrical Engineering*, *123*, 1–29.

31 Gender classification via dynamic handwriting features using a random forest model

Priya Sharma[1,a], Spriha Sharma[1], and Om Prakash Jasuja[2]

[1]Department of Forensic Science, Chandigarh University, SAS Nagar, Mohali, Punjab, India
[2]Department of Forensic Science, RIMT University, Mandi Gobindgarh, Punjab, India

Abstract: Gender classification from handwriting plays a crucial role in narrowing down suspects in criminal investigations. However, identifying gender from handwriting remains a challenge in forensic examination. Conventional forensic examination methods are generally based on the subjective observations of static handwriting features like size, spacing, and letterforms. Besides, modern handwriting examination methods enable forensic examiners to objectively utilize dynamic features like duration, velocity, acceleration, and pressure. This study employs a machine learning approach to explore the potential of novel dynamic features for gender classification. A classification model, Random Forest, is proposed, and its performance has been evaluated in predicting gender using novel dynamic features. This model correctly predicted 78% of females and 72% of males, with an overall accuracy of 74%. These findings advance forensic handwriting examination by providing an objective approach based on dynamic features and machine learning methods.

Keywords: Handwriting, gender classification, forensic examination, dynamic features, machine learning model, random forest

1. Introduction

Handwriting is important evidence in criminal investigations. Handwriting is a neuromuscular task and an acquired skill that becomes almost automatic through repeated use. Handwriting consists of innumerable subconscious habitual patterns that are individual to every person [1]. These subconscious patterns lead to fixed handwriting features in one's handwriting, called individual features. However, handwriting may be influenced by factors like handedness, age, and gender, which leads to distinctive features common to a specific class or group, called class features. Class features include common style of letters, arrangement, slant, and size of handwriting [2–5]. The gender-specific class features may aid in narrowing down the list of suspects in anonymous writing cases [2]. The ability to identify gender from handwriting has been explored in a few old studies [3–5, 11–15]. Female writer demonstrates greater writing proficiency than male writers [2]. Female writing is more decorative, delicate, and rounded; male writing is casual, assertive, and angular [3–4]. Female writers tend to add shading in letters, whereas male writers apply greater pressure on downward strokes and use forceful pen jabs. Additionally, the gender of a writer can be discerned through word choices and compositions [6–9]. With the advancement in technology, handwriting is being shifted from pen and paper to digital platforms. As a result, handwriting examination approaches are bound to change. The writing produced by a digitizing device (digital pad/smartphone/stylus) is called Digitally captured handwriting (DCH). DCH comprises a series of sampling points recorded

by the digital pad. At each sampling point, numerical data is recorded, encompassing spatial coordinates of the pen tip, capture time, pressure, velocity, and related derivatives (such as acceleration and jerk), as well as air movements [10]. DCH examines the dynamics of the handwriting process by capturing the underlying movement patterns [11]. Dynamic features like duration and velocity have been utilized to assess movement disorders and forgery [12]. Additionally, the dynamic parameters, which consist of size, duration, velocity, jerk, and pen pressure, for different styles of genuine, disguised, and auto-simulated signatures were explored, revealing significant differences in the dynamic features of various style signatures executed under differing conditions [13]. Another study showed handwritten signature dynamics in genuine and forged dynamic features like X-coordinate, Y-coordinate, pen-up and pen-down durations, velocity, and pressure [14]. Recently, static and dynamic features have been utilized for gender estimation from examinations, and machine learning has emerged as an effective approach for handwriting-related studies. One study utilized online and offline features for gender classification using the Gaussian Mixture Model (GMM) and achieved 64% online, 55% offline, and 67% combined accuracy [15]. Another focused solely on static features using Logistic Regression attaining 76% and 80% accuracy for male and female, respectively [16]. Another approach combined static and dynamic features with a Support Vector Machine (SVM) classifier, resulting in 65%-79% accuracy, though the limited performance of dynamic features suggested a need for a more refined model

[a]priyasharmafsc@gmail.com

DOI: 10.1201/9781003724988-31

and features [17]. Dynamic features such as pressure, acceleration, and pen-up time were found to be statistically significant for gender classification [18]. A recent study applied SVM and Neural Networks to static and dynamic features achieving 88% accuracy on an English dataset and 97% in an Arabic dataset based on static features, while the dynamic feature performed poorly [19].

Previous studies mainly emphasize static, image-based handwriting features, with insufficient investigation into dynamic features. Although some studies have employed dynamic characteristics for gender prediction based on handwriting, most have shown limited effectiveness, omitting possibly significant factors that could improve insights. Furthermore, these studies often exclude a forensic context, where handwriting samples may be limited. Hence, it is essential to investigate dynamic handwriting features to enhance the accuracy and relevance of gender prediction from handwriting. This study presents a classification model designed to predict gender using novel set of dynamic features, and we evaluated its performance. The model demonstrates moderate accuracy and contributes to a deeper understanding of how dynamic handwriting features can be applied in gender classification.

2. Materials and Methods

2.1. Handwriting sample collection

In this study, 102 male and 83 female volunteers participated. The samples were collected from college graduate students of both genders with a mean age of approximately 20 years. The flowchart of the methodology is mentioned in Figure 31.1.

Demographic data and informed consent were taken before sample collection. All volunteers were right-handed and had normal health conditions. Right-handed individuals were chosen to avoid confounding variables linked to hand dominance. Handwriting samples were collected using a digital tablet, Wacom One Pen Display Model DTC133W0C, with pressure sensitivity of 4096 Levels and a sampling rate of 240 Hz, with visual feedback and stylus input. Visual feedback via the stylus input closely simulates traditional writing, maintaining ecological validity. A movement analysis software, MovalyZeR by Neuroscript LLC (Version 6.1), was utilized to record the handwriting samples. (The mention of specific brand names, models, or software in this study is solely for academic and scientific reporting. This does not imply any affiliation with, endorsement of, or commercial intent by the authors or the publishing body. Before the experiments, all volunteers received comprehensive education regarding the study. They were also provided with an opportunity to perform practice trials to become familiar with the digital tablet. Allowing volunteers to familiarize themselves with the device minimizes errors caused by unfamiliarity, ensuring reliable data collection. Volunteers were seated comfortably on chairs, and the digital tablet was placed on the wooden table. They were allowed to adjust the placement of the tablet at their convenience. The study incorporated uniform experimental conditions and three trials for all volunteers. Volunteers wrote "Hello" on the digital tablet in three trials. It is a short, simple word that contains a mix of strokes, curves, and letters, effectively capturing diverse handwriting dynamics. In the event of errors occurring during the trials, the samples were re-recorded to ensure the consistency of the trials.

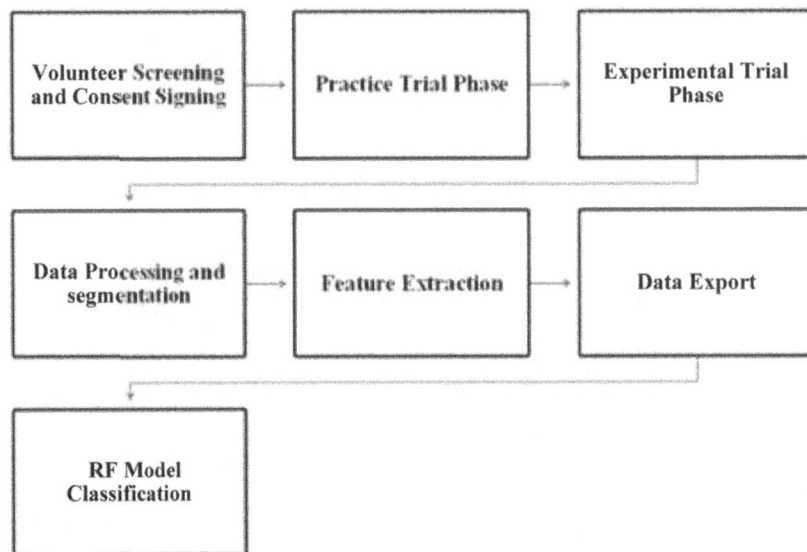

Figure 31.1. Methodology flowchart.

Source: Author.

2.2. Handwriting sample processing

MovalyZeR software was employed for sample processing and analysis. This software system facilitates the automated and quantitative analysis of handwriting movement. MovalyZeR simplifies the design, execution, processing, and analysis of handwriting and drawing movement tests, eliminating the need for specialized computer skills. Within this software system, the movements were segmented at vertical velocity zero crossings, allowing for the evaluation of per-segment features. Additionally, the software system retrieved the processed numerical data of dynamic features using the FFT Low Pass Filter Method with a Filter frequency of 12 Hz [12, 20]. The processed data related to handwriting dynamics is exported as an Excel file and subjected to data analysis. In this study, 11 dynamic features, as provided in Table 31.1, were extracted and further utilized for gender classification.

Table 31.1. List of processed dynamic handwriting features [20]

S.No.	Name of feature	Definition
1.	Duration (sec)	Time interval between the first and last samples (data points) in a stroke
2.	Start Vertical Position(cm)	Vertical start positions (Y-Coordinate) relative to the lower edge of the active digitizer area
3.	Peak Vertical Velocity(cm/s)	Maximum vertical velocity values
4.	Peak Vertical Acceleration (cm/s²)	Maximum value of vertical acceleration values
5.	Start Horizontal Position(cm)	Horizontal start positions(X-Coordinate) relative to the lower edge of the active digitizer area
6.	Slant(rad)	Direction from the beginning point to the endpoint in radians
7.	Absolute size (cm)	The absolute size of a stroke/ segment is calculated from the vertical and horizontal sizes.
8.	Average absolute velocity (cm/s)	Average absolute velocity across all samples of a stroke or segment
9.	Normalized jerk	Jerk is the rate at which acceleration changes with time. Normalized Jerk is unitless as it is normalized for stroke duration and size.
10.	Average pen pressure (N)	Average of pen pressure (Z) values over a stroke.
11.	Loop Surface(cm²)	The area is enclosed by the loop created by the current and previous strokes.

Source: Author.

3. Results and Discussion

3.1. Dataset description

The dynamic features were calculated at segmentation points in each handwriting sample. The average numerical values of segmented data points were taken in centimeters and seconds for every sample. Thus, the final dataset comprises 555 samples (Females = 249, Males = 306). To suit classification algorithms, the target variable Y was encoded into numeric labels (Female=0 and Male=1).

3.2. Proposed classification model

This study used a Random Forest (RF) classifier to predict gender using dynamic features. Random Forest is a classification method made up of multiple decision trees. Each tree gives a vote for the class it thinks is correct, and the class with the most votes becomes the final prediction. The trees are created using random subsets of data to ensure diversity [22]. The dataset was split into a training (80%) and a testing set (20%). RF consists of several hyperparameters, including sample size, node size, and number of trees. The sample size determines the number of observations drawn per tree. A low sample size creates diverse trees and positively affects prediction accuracy. The node size parameter depicts the minimum number of observations in the leaf. In the present study, parameters were set through the parameter grid function, and various possible values of hyperparameters were tested using the 'Grid search' function with five-fold cross-validation. Finally, a minimum sample size required at the leaf node was set as one, and a minimum of five samples was required to split a leaf node. The number of trees in a forest depends on the sample size and node size. The RF model becomes stable with an increasing number of trees, so it should be set sufficiently high [24]. The present study tested 50, 100, and 200 decision trees. The final estimator (decision tree) was set at 100, as increasing the number of trees beyond this did not significantly affect the model's prediction. The list of hyperparameters is given in Table 31.2. The model was evaluated using various performance metrics to ensure a comprehensive assessment. Accuracy, defined as the proportion of correct predictions across all classes, was one of the key metrics used. Additionally, the confusion matrix was employed as a tabulated summary to show the distribution of true positives (TP), false positives (FP), true negatives (TN), and false negatives (FN) [23].

3.3. Proposed classification model results

The proposed classification models have been implemented in the Python programming language. The Python libraries used in the work are pandas, numpy, seaborn, and matplotlib [21]. All model implementations have been performed on Jupyter Notebook. The confusion matrix of the classification models is provided in Figure 31.2. The model was evaluated using performance metrics like accuracy, precision, sensitivity, specificity, and AUC to ensure a comprehensive assessment. The results of performance metrics are provided in Table 31.3. The RF model demonstrated an accuracy of 74% with an AUC of 0.77. The ROC of classification models is provided in Figure 31.3. The model's Precision, which reflects how many of its predictions were correct, was 0.78 for females and 0.72 for males, with an overall average of 0.75. Recall, which shows how well the model identified actual cases, was 0.58 for females and 0.87 for males, giving an overall average of 0.72. The F1-Score, a balance between Precision and Recall, was 0.67 for females and 0.79 for males, with an overall average of 0.73. The model was tested on 50 female and 61 male samples, for a total of 111 samples. These results show the model performed better at identifying male handwriting than female handwriting, especially in terms of Recall and F1-score. However, the averages indicate that the model maintained a fairly balanced performance overall. Further, feature importance was evaluated (see Figure 31.4) to identify the most significant features contributing to the classification of female and male handwriting. Our results are consistent with a few previous studies [13, 15, 16], which reported an accuracy rate of 66%-70% in classifying handwriting by gender. Other studies utilized online handwriting features and achieved moderate accuracy, which is consistent with the present study [15–17]. One study demonstrated slightly higher accuracy rates (76–80%) than the present study, but they utilized offline or static features with different classification models. They applied a logistic regression model on the same training and testing datasets, achieving accuracy rates of 80% for females and 76.4% for males [16]. Our study has an overall accuracy of 74% with novel dynamic features and an RF classification model. A different task was involved in our study and relied on a smaller sample of handwriting data. On the other hand, previous studies relied on different datasets (paragraphs, drawing tasks) and classification approaches. The dynamic features of handwriting may be influenced by other factors like educational background, demographic region, writing task, and adaptability to the use of digital devices for writing. Furthermore, modern society reflects a narrowing gap in educational backgrounds and gender-specific roles between males and females. This evolution has likely led to overlapping distribution patterns in handwriting styles. Notably, despite providing training sessions to familiarize themselves with the digital tablet, both male and female writers in the study showed hesitation when writing on it. This lack of familiarity likely caused

Table 31.2. List of hyperparameters

Hyperparameter	Value
max_depth	None
min_samples_leaf	1
min_samples_split	5
n_estimators	100

Source: Author.

Table 31.3. Performance metrics

Metric	Class 0 (Female)	Class 1 (Male)	Macro Average	Weighted Average
Precision	0.78	0.72	0.75	0.75
Recall	0.58	0.87	0.72	0.74
F1-Score	0.67	0.79	0.73	0.73
Support (Samples)	50	61	111	111

Source: Author.

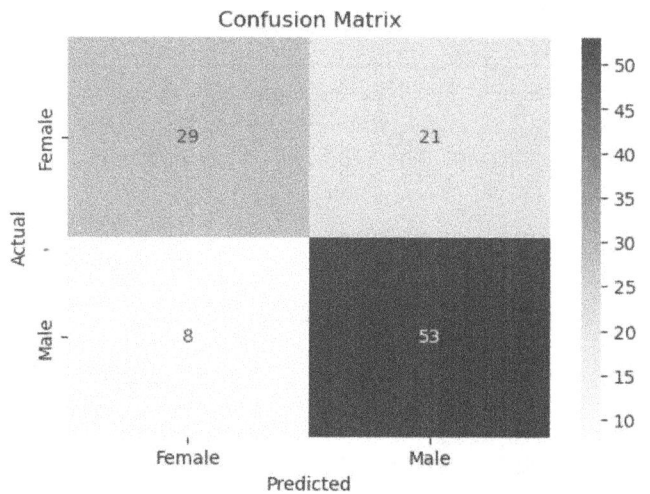

Figure 31.2. Confusion Matrix showing actual and predicted male and female participants.

Source: Author.

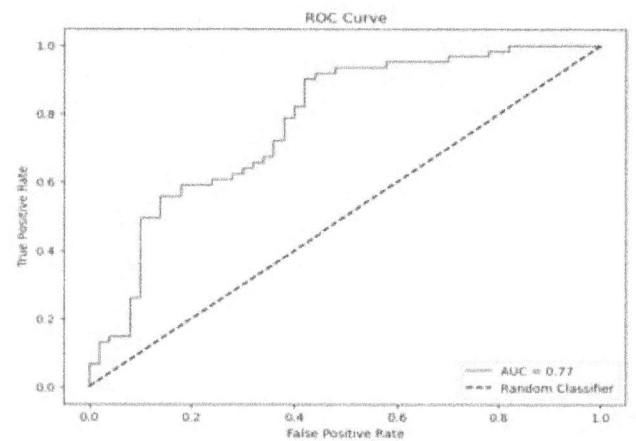

Figure 31.3. ROC curve showing true positive and false positive rates.

Source: Author.

inconsistencies in the handwriting of both genders, which further led to reduced accuracy. Therefore, these findings highlight the need for robust models to address variations in handwriting dynamics due to challenges introduced by digital writing surfaces.

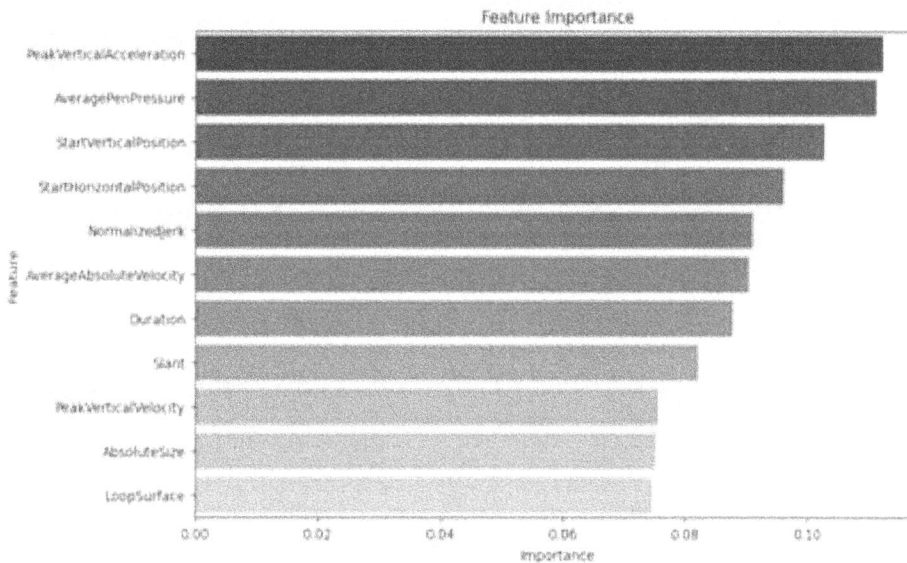

Figure 31.4. Feature importance ranking showing peak vertical acceleration as the most important feature.

Source: Author.

3. Conclusions

Dynamic handwriting captures various aspects of writing, including graphical, as well as time-related and pressure-related features. This study highlighted the potential of dynamic handwriting features like acceleration, average pen pressure and velocity, and duration for gender classification. However, the study has some limitations, including a relatively small sample size and a specific population, which may restrict the generalizability of the findings. The study focused exclusively on a few dynamic features and did not incorporate graphical letter formation-based features. Future research could explore other dynamic and formation-based graphical features to provide a comprehensive approach. As digital media technology continues to advance, particularly with the increasing usage of digital tablets for writing, the ability to capture dynamic data will provide more opportunities to improve gender classification models. In further studies, larger sample sizes, diverse demographic factors, and machine or deep learning models could be incorporated to enhance the accuracy of gender classification.

References

[1]   Bisesi, M. S. (2006). Scientific Examination of Questioned Documents (J.S. Kelly, & B.S. Lindblom, Eds.) (2nd ed.). CRC Press.

[2]   Harralson, H. H., & Miller, L. S. (2017). *Huber and Headrick's Handwriting Identification: Facts and Fundamentals*. CRC Press.

[3]   Hamid, S., & Loewenthal, K. M. (1996). Inferring gender from handwriting in Urdu and English. *Journal of Social Psychology, 136*(6), 778–782.

[4]   Young, P. T. (1931). Sex differences in handwriting. *Journal of Applied Psychology, 15*(5), 486–498.

[5]   Hodgins, J. H. (1971). Determination of Sex from Handwriting. *Canadian Society of Forensic Science Journal, 4*(4), 124–132.

[6]   Osborn, A. S. (1929). *Questioned documents* (2nd ed.). Albany, NY: Boyd Printing.

[7]   Anderson, T., & Wolowitz, H. (1984). Psychosexual symbolism in the handwriting of men and women. *Perceptual and Motor Skills, 59*(1), 233–234.

[8]   Fluckiger, F. A., Tripp, C. A., & Weinberg, G. H. (1961). A review of experimental research in graphology: 1933–1960. *Perceptual and Motor Skills, 12*(1), 67–90.

[9]   Cambridge, J. (1972). *Factors relating to the identification of masculinity and femininity in questioned handwriting.* [Paper Presentation] Meeting of the International Association of Forensic Sciences, Edinburgh, Scotland, UK.

[10] Harralson, H. H. (2013). *Developments in Handwriting and Signature Identification in the Digital Age*. Anderson Publishing, Ltd.

[11] European Network of Forensic Science Institutes. (2020). Appendix 5 – overview procedure for forensic examinations and comparisons of digitally captured signatures and handwritten entries. In Best Practice Manual for the Forensic Examination of Handwriting (Vol. 3, pp. 48–64).

[12] Harralson, H. H., Teulings, H. L., & Farley, B. G. (2007). Comparison of Handwriting Kinematics in Movement Disorders and Forgery. *13th Conference of the International Graphonomics Society*, 143–8.

[13] Mohammed, L. A., Found, B., Caligiuri, M., & Rogers, D. (2011). The Dynamic Character of Disguise Behavior for Text-based, Mixed, and Stylized Signatures. *Journal of Forensic Sciences, 56*(1:S), 136–41.

[14] Ahmad, S. M. S., Ling, L. Y., Anwar, R. M., Faudzi, M. A., & Shakil, A. (2013). Analysis of the Effects and Relationship

of Perceived Handwritten Signature's Size, Graphical Complexity, and Legibility with Dynamic Parameters for Forged and Genuine Samples. *Journal of Forensic Sciences, 58*(3), 724–731.

[15]   Liwicki, M., Schlapbach, A., & Bunke, H. (2011). Automatic gender detection using online and offline information. *Pattern Analysis and Applications, 14*(1), 87–92.

[16]   Sharma, V., Bains, M., Verma, R., Verma, N., & Kumar, R. (2023). Novel use of logistic regression and likelihood ratios for the estimation of gender of the writer from a database of handwriting features. *Australian Journal of Forensic Sciences, 55*(1), 89–106.

[17]   Likforman-Sulem, L., Cordasco, G., & Esposito, A. (2022). Is On-Line Handwriting Gender-Sensitive? What Tells us a Combination of Statistical and Machine Learning Approaches. In M. El Yacoubi, E. Granger, P. C. Yuen, U. Pal, & N. Vincent (Eds.), ICPRAI 2022. *Lecture Notes in Computer Science*, vol. 13363. Springer, Cham.

[18]   Faundez-Zanuy, M., & Mekyska, J. (2023). Analysis of Gender Differences in Online Handwriting Signals for Enhancing e-Health and e-Security Applications. *Cognitive Computation, 15*, 208–219.

[19]   AL-Qawasmeh, N., Khayyat, M., & Suen, C. Y. (2023). Novel features to detect gender from handwritten documents. *Pattern Recognition Letters, 171*, 201–208.

[20]   Neuroscript. (n.d.). https://neuroscript.net/

[21]   Scikit-learn User Guide. (2007). https://scikit-learn.org/

[22]   Breiman, L. (2001). Random forests. *Machine Learning, 45*, 5–32.

[23]   Berrar, D. (2019). Performance measures for binary classification. *Encyclopedia of Bioinformatics and Computational Biology, Reference Module in Life Sciences, 1*, 546–560.

[24]   Probst, P., Wright, M. N., & Boulesteix, A. L. (2019). Hyperparameters and tuning strategies for random forest. *Wiley Interdisciplinary Reviews: Data Mining and Knowledge Discovery, 9*(3), e1301.

32 A comprehensive survey on AI-powered vision assistants for visually impaired

Sumukha N. Hegde[1,a], Rajeshwari S. B.[1,b], and Jagadish S. Kallimani[2,c]

[1]Department of Information Science and Engineering (ISE), M S Ramaiah Institute of Technology (MSRIT), Bangalore, India
[2]Department of Artificial Intelligence and Machine Learning (AIML), M S Ramaiah Institute of Technology (MSRIT), Bangalore, India

Abstract: Visual impairment refers to a condition in which an individual experiences partial or complete loss of vision, affecting their ability to perform daily tasks without assistance. It can range from mild vision problems to total blindness and may occur due to various medical conditions, genetic factors, or injuries. Artificial Intelligence (AI) has significantly transformed accessibility for visually impaired individuals by providing smart assistants that enhance independence, mobility, and communication. AI-powered tools use computer vision, Natural Language Processing (NLP), and machine learning to interpret and convey information in accessible formats. In this paper, a survey on different state-of-the-art techniques which help visually impaired people is conducted, and also their strengths & shortfalls are discussed.

Keywords: Yolov8, computer vision, deep learning, assistive technology, OCR, CNN, TensorFlow, smart glasses, google-text-to-speech (GTTS)

1. Introduction

Vision impairment affects over 2.2 billion people worldwide, with at least 1 billion cases preventable or yet to be addressed. India Contributes to over 20% of the world's blind population, with approximately 12 million people visually impaired, according to the World Health Organization (WHO). Additionally, nearly 62 million Indians experience some form of vision impairment, ranging from low vision to complete blindness. A majority of these cases stem from preventable causes such as cataracts, refractive errors, and corneal opacities, highlighting gaps in accessibility to early diagnosis and treatment. For those living with permanent vision loss, navigating daily life remains a significant challenge, particularly in rural and underserved areas where assistive technology is often expensive, leaving a large gap in addressing the needs of visually impaired individuals in rural and underserved areas.

2. Related Works

The development of assistive technologies for visually impaired individuals has been a significant focus in recent years. Navigation in everyday environments poses considerable challenges due to unseen obstacles and unsafe locations, which can result in severe accidents. Researchers and engineers have explored various solutions leveraging modern advancements in technology.

A notable approach involves the integration of depth-sensing cameras and artificial intelligence models to create advanced support systems. For instance, the utilization of point cloud mapping combined with algorithms like DBSCAN enables precise object separation and identification. This technique effectively enhances obstacle detection by isolating distinct objects from clustered point cloud data.

Object detection models, such as YOLOv3, v5, v8 have been employed to identify critical elements in navigation, such as stairs and elevators, with high accuracy. These models operate through a single-pass convolutional neural network, providing real-time detection capabilities. Data augmentation techniques and rigorous training protocols further enhance their performance, achieving a mean average precision (mAP) of 90.3% and a recall rate exceeding 85%.

3. Supporting Visually Impaired Individuals Using

1. *Depth-Sensing Cameras* [1]: The proposed system shown in Figure 32.1 by Van-Phuc Hoang, Phu-Vinh Do, Duc-Anh Bui, Viet-Cuong Pham for assisting visually impaired individuals' leverages depth-sensing cameras and evolves in two main directions. The first focuses on constructing a foreground object region as a point cloud to alert users about objects located at torso and head height. The second direction involves developing

[a]sumukhanhegde@msrit.edu, [b]rajeshwari.sb@msrit.edu, [c]jagadish.k@msrit.edu

DOI: 10.1201/9781003724988-32

a recognition and navigation algorithm to guide users toward familiar landmarks within indoor environments. The diagram shows a depth camera-based system assisting visually impaired users. It processes 3D point clouds using DBSCAN clustering to detect obstacles and provides auditory alerts. Concurrently, YOLOv8 identifies indoor landmarks such as stairs and elevators, computes oriented directional vectors, and visually displays navigation guidance, ensuring comprehensive, real-time safety and support.

2. ***TensorFlow and MobileNet* [2]:** The proposed system by Surya Chaitanya Jakka, Yerragopu Venkata Sai, Jesudoss A, Viji Amutha Mary A, leverages TensorFlow and SSD MobileNet to assist visually impaired individuals by identifying, localizing, and categorizing objects. This is paired with real-time voice feedback to provide accurate distance information and object descriptions, enabling safer navigation.

3. ***Sensors and Modules* [3]:** The Proposed system focuses on integrating multiple sensors and communication modules for comprehensive assistance. The system employs ultrasonic sensors to detect obstacles by emitting and receiving sound waves, with the sensor transmitting data to a microcontroller when obstacles are detected. A water sensor positioned at the base helps prevent accidents on wet surfaces by sending electrical signals to the controller. The system incorporates GPS and GSM

modules – GPS tracks user location while GSM enables emergency SMS alerts. When the emergency button is pressed, the system accesses the user's position through GPS and sends it via GSM to pre-stored contact numbers. All sensor data is processed by the microcontroller which triggers appropriate audio feedback through headphones.

4. ***Helmet-mounted RGB-D camera* [4]:** The navigation assistive system shown in Figure 32.2, proposed by Scalvini et al., employs an RGB-D camera mounted on the user's helmet to capture detailed colour images and depth data, providing distance estimation and environmental understanding. This visual data is processed by advanced deep learning algorithms, particularly YOLOv8, to identify and classify objects such as stairs, elevators, and hazards. User position and orientation are determined through an inertial measurement unit (IMU), integrating gyroscope, accelerometer, magnetometer data, and GPS for precise localization. This geographical data is combined with pedestrian-friendly maps from OpenStreetMap, filtered to exclude unsafe routes, transforming them into graph-based representations that facilitate efficient navigation. Auditory cues communicate real-time spatialized navigation directions and imminent obstacles, enhancing situational awareness and user safety. By employing semantic segmentation, the system corrects trajectory paths, ensuring pedestrian routes are navigable and safe. This integration of precise spatial positioning, deep-learning-based object recognition, and auditory feedback ensures comprehensive navigation assistance for visually impaired individuals in unfamiliar urban environments.

5. ***iReader* [5]:** The iReader system shown in Figure 32.3 designed by Jothi G, Ahmad Taher Azar, Basit Qureshi and Nashwa Ahmad Kamal significantly enhance the

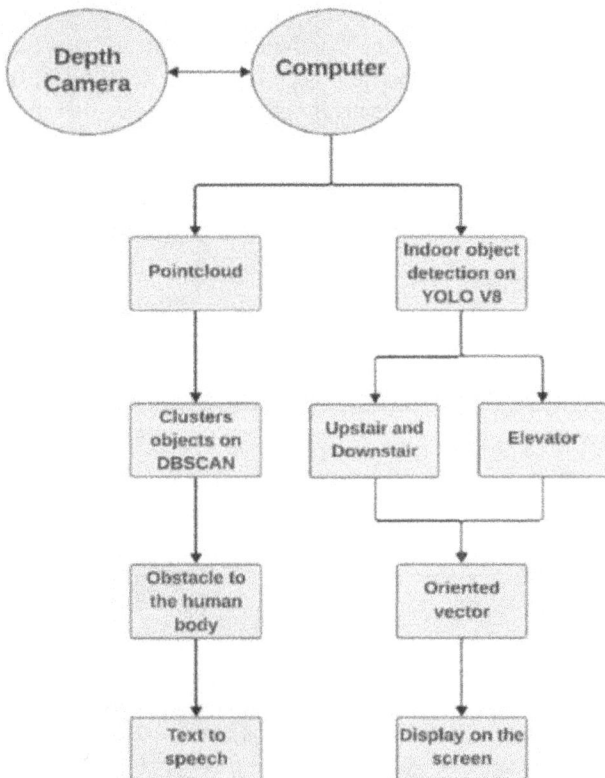

Figure 32.1. System structure of depth camera sensing method.

Source: Author.

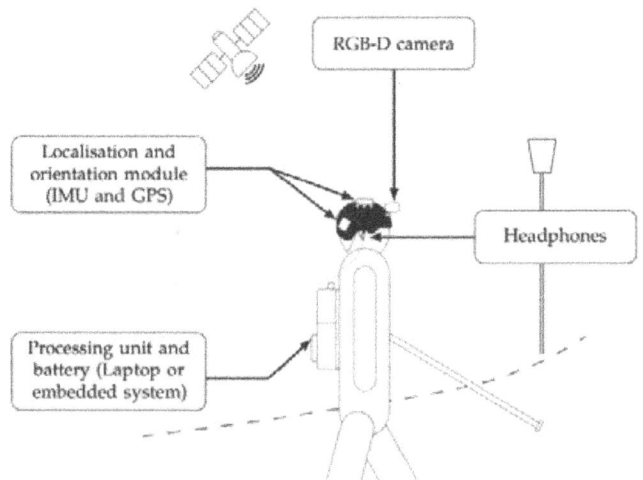

Figure 32.2. Schematic view of our navigation Aid system consisting of a location and orientation.

Source: Author.

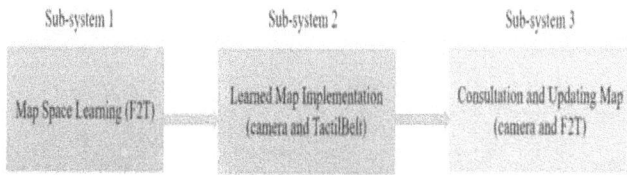

Figure 32.3. Model of VIP mobility assistance.
Source: Author.

reading experience for visually impaired individuals by providing an intelligent reading solution that goes beyond traditional methods. By employing advanced technologies such as Convolutional Neural Networks (CNN) and Long Short-Term Memory (LSTM) networks, the iReader can not only read printed text aloud but also describe images associated with the text.

6. ***Smart Glasses*** [6]: This system addresses the challenges faced by blind individuals in navigating their environments, where traditional aids like white canes may not provide sufficient information about nearby obstacles or the surrounding environment. By integrating a camera into a pair of smart glasses, the system captures real-time images and processes them using a trained YOLO V3 model to identify various objects and obstacles. The system can detect up to 80 pre-trained objects, including people, vehicles, and road conditions, and provides auditory feedback through headphones to guide users safely. This innovative approach empowers visually impaired individuals to navigate autonomously, improving their situational awareness and reducing their reliance on companions or caregivers.

7. ***Force Feedback Tablet (F2T) and a TactiBelt*** [7]: The MAPS system for visually impaired persons (VIP), designed by Katerine Romeo et al. and illustrated in Figure 32.4, integrates two key navigation functions: locomotion for obstacle avoidance and wayfinding for spatial orientation and path planning in unfamiliar areas. The system comprises three interconnected subsystems. Subsystem 1 employs a Force Feedback Tablet (F2T) to assist VIPs in memorizing environmental maps prior to navigation. Subsystem 2 transitions memorized maps into practical navigation, using the TactiBelt device, equipped with a camera and specialized software, employing a mobility graph similar to a VIP-specific GPS. This facilitates independent, low-stress, and cognitively manageable travel. During navigation, if users forget previously memorized spatial details, Subsystem 3 provides real-time consultation and map updates via the F2T, operating similarly to traditional GPS navigation systems, helping users refresh their memory.

4. The Obstacle Recognition

1. ***Utilizing Point Cloud Data*** [1]: The research team implemented the system using an Intel RealSense Depth Camera D435i, which offers an 87° parallel-to-ground and 58° perpendicular-to-ground viewing angle. The setup is housed in a backpack worn by visually impaired individuals, simulating real-world conditions using a double-layered black eye patch.

The DBSCAN algorithm processes point cloud data to separate objects into clusters. Parameters like epsilon (0.12) and min_samples (200) ensure effective clustering, though adjustments are required to address misclassified points caused by device inaccuracies. Weighted averages of point cloud coordinates (X, Y, Z) help determine object positions and distances. Orientation is calculated using these coordinates, enabling the system to determine whether objects are in front, to the left, or to the right of the user.

2. ***TensorFlow*** [2]: The implementation relies on TensorFlow libraries and SSD architecture for object detection. A single- shot detector identifies objects based on parameters such as size, colour, and depth. An anchor box is used to mark detected objects, while depth estimation techniques calculate accurate distances between the user and obstacles. The MobileNet framework, based on depth wise separable convolutions, ensures computational efficiency during object detection.

3. ***YOLOv4-tiny*** [3]: The obstacle recognition model utilizes YOLOv4-tiny's architecture optimized for edge devices like Raspberry Pi. The model employs a modified CSPDarknet53 backbone with 29 pre-trained convolutional layers and two YOLO heads operating at 13 × 13 and 26 × 26 scales. The implementation includes convolutional layers for feature extraction, shortcut connections for gradient flow, SPP module for multi-scale feature extraction, and PANet for feature combination. The detection head uses convolutional layers and anchor boxes to predict object size, position, and class probabilities. This streamlined architecture enables real- time processing while maintaining detection accuracy, having been trained on the MS-COCO dataset which provides 90 common object classes for reliable recognition.

4. ***TactiBelt*** [7]: The Figure 32.4 illustrates the sensory substitution motor loop central to the MAPS system (Mobility Assistance Path Planning and orientation in Space), designed for visually impaired persons (VIPs). It shows how real or virtual world data is captured by sensors (typically cameras) and sent to a cloud or computer for processing. This processed data is converted into auditory or tactile feedback, which is interpreted by the user. Training helps the user refine spatial understanding over time. A key component, the *TactiBelt*, enhances locomotion by detecting obstacles using ultrasonic sensors and translating their location into real-time vibrotactile signals. Vibrators embedded around the belt vary in intensity based on obstacle proximity, allowing VIPs to gauge distance and direction. While locomotion handles obstacle avoidance, wayfinding concerns

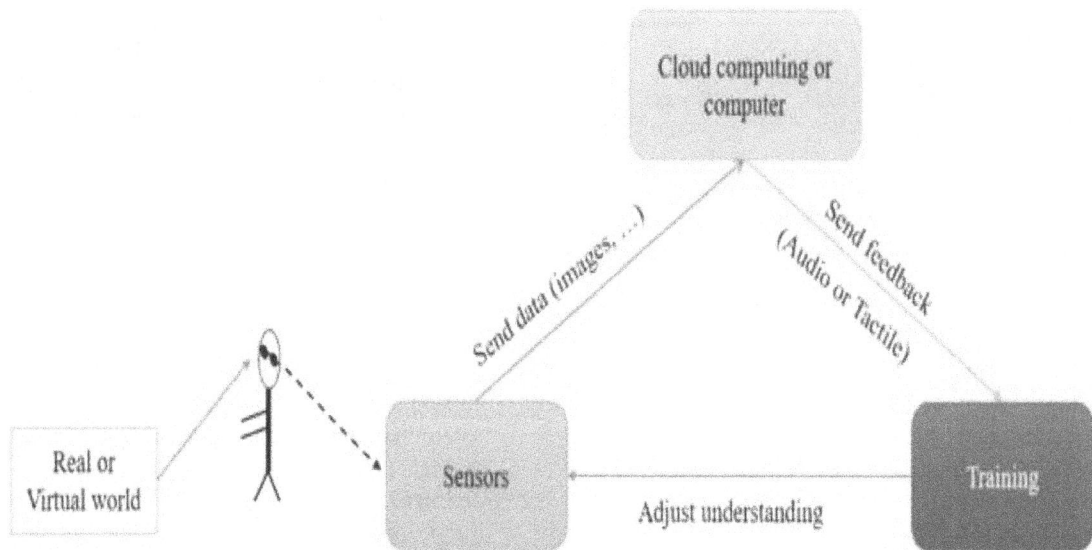

Figure 32.4. Sensory substitution loop.

Source: Author.

spatial orientation and path planning – both supported by MAPS. The system uses the Force Feedback Tablet (F2T) for pre-navigation map learning, complementing the TactiBelt's real-time feedback. Together, they support perception embodiment and spatial awareness, addressing the limitations of traditional SSDs in speed, precision, and navigation functionality.

5. Object Detection

1. *YOLOV8* [1]: The system integrates YOLOv8 for object detection, focusing on features critical for safe navigation, such as stairs and elevators. A dataset of 2683 images, augmented with techniques like cropping, brightness adjustment, and noise addition, was used for training. YOLOv8 achieves high accuracy, with mAP50 values over 90%. Detected objects are localized using directional vectors originating from the camera, providing users with precise guidance to navigate their environment safely and efficiently.

2. *Convolutional Neural Networks* [2]: It captures images and videos, processing them as 3D RGB pixel grids, where convolutional neural networks (CNNs) detect, classify, and localize objects. The SSD architecture employs anchor boxes to highlight objects, adapting to their size and shape. Depth estimation techniques calculate the distance between the user and detected objects, enabling real-time proximity alerts. Libraries such as pyttsx3 and pytesseract are used to provide audio feedback, announcing object details and distances to assist users effectively.

    TensorFlow APIs are utilized for training and testing the detection models, ensuring high accuracy in identifying objects. The MobileNet framework, which uses depthwise separable convolutions, offers computational efficiency and lightweight operations. Adjustable zoom levels allow the system to focus on objects of varying sizes for more precise detection. Python libraries like Protobuf, Cython, and Matplotlib support data handling and visualization.

    The system's outputs include accurate visual and audio alerts, guiding users through potential obstacles and ensuring safer navigation. With object detection accuracy exceeding 90%, the framework enhances the independence and confidence of visually impaired users, delivering a robust and efficient solution for everyday mobility challenges.

3. *Computer Vision* [3, 8]: The object detection system implements a computer vision pipeline using Raspberry Pi cameras and OpenCV framework. Real-time video frames are captured and processed through multiple stages – first converting to grayscale and binary format for efficient processing. The system calculates object distances using a calibrated focal length and linear regression equation based on contour area.

    The area calculation uses the formula:

    $$23.14180 * (w + h * 360) * 1000 + 3$$

    where w and h represent bounding box dimensions. Distance estimation employs the equation

    $$Distance = m * area\text{-}of\text{-}contour + b$$

    where m and b are calibrated constants.

    Once objects are detected and distances calculated, the system generates audio feedback through a text-to-speech engine, providing users with real-time information about their surroundings. The implementation achieves 93.7% accuracy while maintaining affordability through minimal hardware requirements.

4. **CNN-LSTM** [5]: The iReader system employs a CNN-LSTM model for object detection and image description. The diagram illustrates the iReader's two-stage CNN–LSTM pipeline for automatically describing images. An input image (224 × 224 × 3) is first passed through a pretrained convolutional network (e.g., InceptionV3) to extract a compact, highdimensional feature map encoding spatial and semantic cues. These features are then flattened into a fixedlength vector and fed into an LSTM decoder [9]. At each time step, the LSTM takes the previous word embedding (or a start token) along with its hidden state – initialized by the CNN feature vector – and outputs a probability distribution over the vocabulary via a softmax layer. During training, the model learns from a dataset of images paired with human-written captions, minimizing crossentropy loss on the groundtruth sequences. At inference, the system generates a descriptive sentence word by word – for example, "Black dog and spotted dog are fighting" for a new test image (Figure 32.5). The iReader's effectiveness is measured using accuracy and BLEU scores, showing that the combined CNN–LSTM architecture can reliably translate visual content into coherent, accurate textual descriptions.

5. **YOLOv3** [6]: The model analyzes video frames captured by the camera mounted on the smart glasses, generating bounding boxes around detected objects and providing confidence scores for each classification. This allows the system to identify both static and dynamic obstacles, such as pedestrians, vehicles, and uneven surfaces.

6. **F2T** [7]: The F2T is designed to provide haptic feedback that allows users to explore and interact with digital maps and images, facilitating the learning and understanding of their environment. By utilizing electromechanical mechanisms, the F2T generates tactile sensations that represent various features of the map, such as textures, elevations, and obstacles.

6. Practical Considerations and Future Directions

Realworld trials reveal that long training periods and cognitive load vary greatly among individuals. Interfaces must offer intuitive feedback – whether spatialized audio or vibrotactile patterns – and allow gradual familiarization. Field studies show preference for multimodal cues (audio + haptic) to reduce fatigue and enhance confidence.

Integrating devices into everyday life faces obstacles: sensor calibration drift, variable lighting, GPS signal degradation in urban canyons, and device ergonomics (weight, battery life, comfort). Maintenance and technical support in remote or underserved areas are critical concerns.

Highperformance depth cameras, embedded GPUs, and custom wearables can exceed $1,000 per unit – prohibitive in lowincome regions. Opensource software, smartphonebased vision, and lowcost microcontrollers can reduce costs below $200, broadening accessibility.

Future work should prioritize modular, upgradeable hardware; provide cloudoffline mode switching; develop financing models (subsidies, NGO partnerships) to ensure equitable access; and integrate companion mobile applications with intuitive, crossplatform user interfaces to accelerate deployment and gather inapp usage analytics. Standardized UX metrics and open datasets remain essential for benchmarking and iterative improvement (Table 32.1).

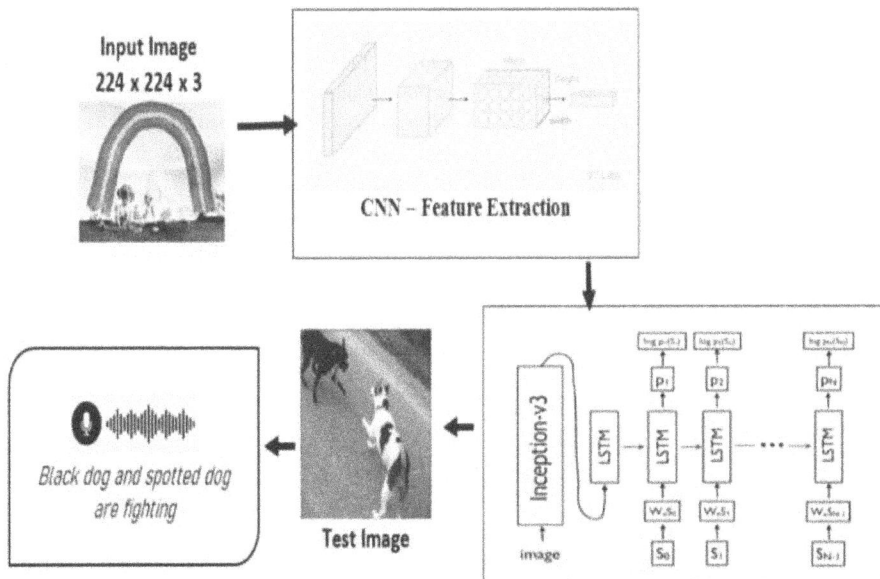

Figure 32.5. CNN-LSTM design.

Source: Author.

Table 32.1. Summary of state-of-the-art AI-powered vision assistant for visually impaired techniques

Technique/ Method	Representation	Content Selection	Summary Generation	Advantages	Disadvantages
Depth-Sensing Cameras	Converts physical environment into digital point cloud data, representing spatial information as 3D coordinate points	Identifies and isolates object regions at specific height levels (torso and head) using DBSCAN clustering algorithm	Landmark recognition in indoor environments.	Precise object separation	Requires calibration of DBSCAN parameters
TensorFlow & MobileNet	Transforms visual input into 3D RGB pixel grids for computation	Identifies and localizes objects using single-shot detector with anchor boxes	Generates real-time voice feedback describing object details and distances	Computationally efficient Lightweight neural network Supports multiple object classes	Accuracy depends on Training data, Performance varies with image complexity, Requires continuous model refinement
Sensors & Modules	Converts environmental data into electrical signals from multiple sensors	Detects obstacles, tracks user location, and monitors environmental conditions	Provides GPS Tracking and emergency SMS alerts with audio feedback	Comprehensive assistive system, Multiple safety features, Emergency communication capability	Complex hardware integration, Potential signal interference, Battery life limitations
Helmet-mounted RGB-D Camera	Captures colour and depth information simultaneously, creating multi-dimensional environmental representation	Classifies critical navigation elements like stairs, elevators, and potential hazards	Delivers auditory navigation guidance based on detected objects	First-person perspective, Real-time object detection, High accuracy navigation support	Requires specific wearable setup, Potential user discomfort, Limited field of view
iReader	Processes text and images using Convolutional Neural Networks (CNN) and Long Short-Term Memory (LSTM) networks	Recognizes printed text and associated images with contextual understanding	Generates descriptive text and audio narration of visual content	Comprehensive reading assistance, Image description capability, Adaptive learning model	Complex model architecture, Computational intensity, Dependent on training dataset
Smart Glasses	Converts real-time camera input into processable image data	Identifies up to 80 pre-trained object classes including people, vehicles, road conditions	Provides continuous auditory feedback about surrounding environment	Autonomous navigation support, Wide object recognition, Reduces Dependency on caregivers	Limited battery life, Potential processing delays, Privacy and social acceptance concerns
Force Feedback Tablet & TactiBelt	Translates spatial information into haptic (touch-based) feedback	Detects obstacles and spatial orientation Through vibrotactile signals	Helps users Construct mental maps of surrounding environment	Non-visual navigation assistance, Tactile environmental perception, Supports independent mobility	Requires user Skill in interpreting signals, Limited detailed information transmission, Potential sensory overload

Source: Author.

References

[1] Hoang, V. P., Do, P. V., Bui, D. A., & Pham, V. C. (2024, August). A Depth Camera-Assisted Support Model For Visually Impaired Individuals. In *2024 9th International Conference on Applying New Technology in Green Buildings (ATiGB)* (pp. 240–243). IEEE.

[2] Jakka, S. C., Sai, Y. V., & Jesudoss, A. (2022, August). Blind Assistance System using Tensor Flow. In *2022 3rd International Conference on Electronics and Sustainable Communication Systems (ICESC)* (pp. 1505–1511). IEEE.

[3] Bobby, V., Praneel, S., Athuljith, A. S., & Reeja, S. L. (2023, May). Ebics: Even blind i can see, a computer vision based guidance system for visually impaired. In *2023 International Conference on Control, Communication and Computing (ICCC)* (pp. 1–6). IEEE.

[4] Scalvini, F., Bordeau, C., Ambard, M., Migniot, C., & Dubois, J. (2023). Outdoor navigation assistive system

based on robust and real-time visual–auditory substitution approach. *Sensors, 24*(1), 166.

[5] Jothi, G., Azar, A. T., Qureshi, B., & Kamal, N. A. (2022, March). ireader: An intelligent reader system for the visually impaired. In *2022 7th International Conference on Data Science and Machine Learning Applications (CDMA)* (pp. 188–193). IEEE.

[6] Hasan, M. Z., Sikder, S., & Rahaman, M. A. (2022, December). Real-time computer vision based autonomous navigation system for assisting visually impaired people using machine learning. In *2022 4th International Conference on Sustainable Technologies for Industry 4.0 (STI)* (pp. 1–6). IEEE.

[7] Romeo, K., Pissaloux, E., Gay, S. L., Truong, N. T., & Djoussouf, L. (2022). The MAPS: Toward a novel mobility assistance system for visually impaired people. *Sensors, 22*(9), 3316.

[8] Chinni, N. P. K., Kaamaala, S. P. R., Vardhan, B. V., Kishan, A. U., Richards, V. S., & Vardhan, R. N. H. (2024, July). Vision Sense: Real-Time Object Detection And Audio Feedback System For Visually Impaired Individuals. In *2024 2nd World Conference on Communication & Computing (WCONF)* (pp. 1–6). IEEE.

[9] Mantoro, T., & Zamzami, M. (2022, September). Realtime indoor navigation system for visually impaired person using direct-based navigation. In *2022 5th International Conference of Computer and Informatics Engineering (IC2IE)* (pp. 320–324). IEEE.

33 Advancements in Handwritten Text Recognition with Deep Learning (HTRDL)

A. Sathya Sofia[1,a], N. Harshini[2,b], R. Kowsalya[2,c], S. Krishi Nivedita[2,d], and S. Maria Sheeba[2,e]

[1]Associate Professor, Department of Computer, Science and Engineering, PSNA College of Engineering and Technology, Dindigul, Tamil Nadu, India
[2]Department of Computer, Science and Engineering, PSNA College of Engineering and Technology, Dindigul, Tamil Nadu, India

Abstract: In computer vision and ML, written by hand content acknowledgment is a troublesome issue that is basic for changing manually written substance into computerized arrange for made strides effectiveness and availability. HTR is complicated by the assortment of penmanship sorts, sizes, and styles, which makes it challenging for machines to recognize content accurately. This paper proposes a strong profound learning-based HTR system that combines Convolutional Neural Networks (CNN) for spatial highlight extraction, Recurrent Neural Network (RNN) and Long Short- Term Memory (LSTM) systems for arrangement modeling, and Connectionist Temporal Classification (CTC) for viable sequence-to-sequence arrangement without unequivocal division. The show is prepared and assessed on the IAM dataset, a broadly utilized benchmark for offline penmanship acknowledgment. Test comes about illustrate that the proposed cross breed approach accomplishes a acknowledgment precision of 95.6%, outflanking person models and conventional strategies. The system too appears solid execution in character-level precision, diminished blunder rates, and induction proficiency, making it appropriate for real-world report digitization errands. This work highlights the adequacy of profound learning structures in dealing with complex manually written information and clears the way for future changes utilizing consideration instruments and transformer-based models.

Keywords: HTR, CNN, RNN, LSTM, BiLSTM, CTC

1. Introduction

One of the most vital errands in computer vision and ML is written by hand content acknowledgment, which involves changing written by hand input into computerized representation. Record digitization, chronicled inquire about, preparing restorative data, and robotizing information passage over numerous businesses are fair a few of the numerous employments for this innovation. Precisely and effectively distinguishing transcribed fabric and changing over it to computerized arrange not as it were increments efficiency but too makes it more available, especially for those with impairments.

A barrier for HTR is presented by the distinctive variety of human handwriting. Written material is characterized by variations in text style fashion, stroke thickness, dispersion, and even character slant, which can vary greatly across people. Additionally, the proximity of foundation turmoil, covering characters, and cursive writing makes the acknowledgment handling more problematic [1].

Handwritten content has a one of a kind set of challenges that call for advanced calculations to achieve tall exactness, in differentiate to printed content, which is more steady and less complex to handle. Traditional strategies of written by hand content acknowledgment were based basically on rule-based frameworks and layout coordinating approaches. These methods depended on physically planned highlights, such as stroke designs and character layouts, and worked beneath predefined rules. Whereas these strategies laid the establishment for the improvement of HTR frameworks, they battled to generalize over datasets and penmanship styles. As a result, their execution was frequently conflicting and constrained to controlled environments.

The headway of profound learning has altogether moved forward the execution of HTR frameworks. Convolutional Neural Networks (CNNs) are profoundly viable at extricating spatial highlights from pictures, and Recurrent Neural Networks (RNNs), especially Long Short-Term Memory (LSTM) units, are able of modeling consecutive information. In expansion, the Connectionist Temporal Classification (CTC) misfortune work empowers arrangement arrangement without the require for pre-segmented input information, permitting for end-to-end training [2].

In this paper, we propose a profound learning-based HTR framework that coordinating CNNs, LSTMs, and CTC to accomplish tall acknowledgment exactness. The show is

[a]sathyasofia@psnacet.edu.in, [b]harshini21cs@psnacet.edu.in, [c]kowsalya21cs@psnacet.edu.in, [d]krishiniveditas21cs@psnacet.edu.in, [e]mariasheebas21cs@psnacet.edu.in

DOI: 10.1201/9781003724988-33

assessed utilizing the IAM dataset, a standard benchmark in HTR investigate, to illustrate its adequacy in recognizing assorted and complex written by hand content.

2. Literature Survey

Using Convolutional Neural Network (CNN) on the MNIST dataset, LeCun et al. [3] carried out groundbreaking work in profound learning for HTR, effectively confining individual characters. As a result of this groundbreaking consider, hybrid models that coordinated CNNs with Long Short-Term Memory (LSTM) and Recurrent Neural Network (RNN) have been created. The CNN-LSTM design, which was striking for being presented by Gamba et al. [4], incredibly upgraded word-level recognizable proof in associated penmanship. HTR execution was assist moved forward by Vaswani et al. and He et al.'s examination of transformer models and consideration components [5, 6]. These models handle issues like fluctuating lighting and foundation clamor by utilizing self-attention to control long-range dependencies.

In 2024, noteworthy advance was made in handwritten recognition strategies. A transformer-based show with progressed consideration instruments was made by Wang et al. [7] and beated routine CNN on the IAM dataset, accomplishing an shocking 95.2% exactness. In organize to lower computational costs, Chen et al. [8] displayed a multi- task learning system that included dialect modeling with character acknowledgment. Moreover, Sharma et al. [9] made strides execution indeed with a little sum of labeled information by applying exchange learning with pre-trained models like ResNet and EfficientNet.

High computational needs proceed to be a issue in show disdain toward of these advancements. Moreover, lightweight CNN designs were created by Krishnan et al. [10] and accomplished 93.8% exactness on the SVT dataset. Since of their little preparing impression, these designs are suitable for versatile applications.

Overall, indeed in spite of the fact that profound learning-driven changes in HTR have enormously expanded execution, issues still exist, such as the necessity for real-time handling, the require for huge datasets, and high computing costs. These issues confine wide utilize and make genuine usage more troublesome.

3. Proposed System

To address the restrictions of prior handwritten text recognition frameworks, we propose a crossover profound learning design that improves both recognition precision and vigor by joining custom-tuned CNNs, LTSMs, Bidirectional LSTMs, and a Connectionist Temporal Classification (CTC) loss [11]. Not at all like ordinary models that depend exclusively on settled highlight extractors or bland profound learning stacks, our demonstrate presents engineering and preparing optimizations custom fitted particularly for assorted penmanship structures, counting cursive, inclined, and conflicting

character spacing. Key differentiators of our framework include:

- Preprocessing upgrades utilizing versatile binarization, skew redress, and differentiate normalization to diminish picture clamor and distortion.
- The altered CNN module outlined with variable bit sizes to superior capture complex penmanship strokes and neighborhood features.
- Bidirectional LSTMs to show forward and backward dependencies in transcribed arrangements, guaranteeing way better relevant understanding.
- CTC Loss that permits the demonstrate to prepare straightforwardly on unsegmented word pictures, disposing of the require for manual character alignment.

The framework is thoroughly assessed on the IAM dataset, which is known for its reasonable transcribed content tests. In expansion to standard measurements like precision, we assess Word Error Rate (WER) and Character Error Rate (CER) to give a more granular see of acknowledgment performance. Comes about appear a critical change over pattern CNN or RNN-only structures, with a acknowledgment precision of 95.6%, approving the adequacy of the coordinates model [12]. Our model's versatility to different penmanship styles including loud, compressed, or cursive forms – demonstrates its down to earth appropriateness in real-world scenarios like archive digitization, authentic original copy examination, and handwriting-based verification frameworks (Figure 33.1).

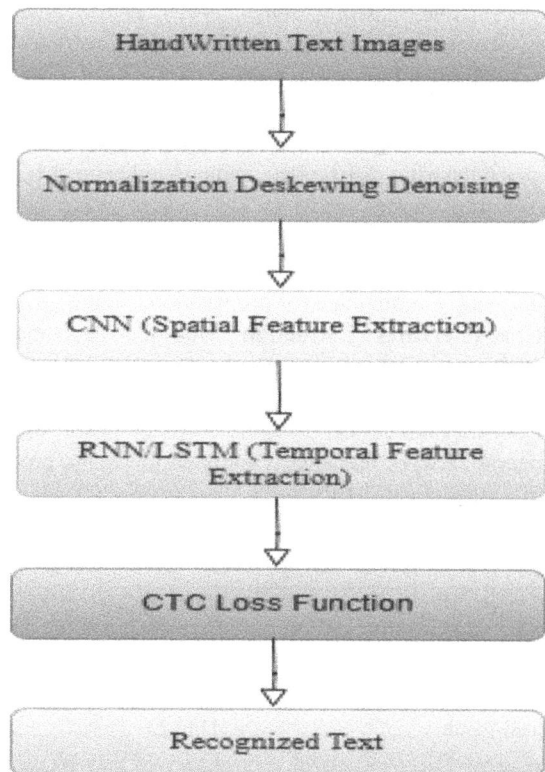

Figure 33.1. HDR module flow.

Source: Author.

4. Materials and Methods

1. **Dataset:** This work utilizes the IAM Dataset developed by the Institute of Artificial Intelligence, University of Bern, to train and assess a deep learning-based HTR framework. The dataset contains high-quality grayscale filtered transcribed forms collected from 657 diverse writers, making it exceedingly differing in terms of handwriting styles, letter shapes, inclines, and dividing varieties makes used for evaluating robustness of sequence-based handwriting recognition models (Table 33.1).

2. **Module for Information Collection:** This module is mindful for obtaining transcribed content pictures from assorted sources such as scanned records, handwritten shapes, and picture datasets. Accentuation is set on capturing the assortment of penmanship styles, introductions, and resolutions to guarantee the demonstrate generalizes well. Pictures are labeled fittingly and pre-validated for quality. This step too incorporates fundamental information increase (e.g., flipping, revolution, scaling) to mimic real-world mutilations and upgrade robustness.

3. **Pre-processing Module:** The preprocessing module makes strides the quality and consistency of transcribed inputs. Key operations include:

    *   Normalization: Scales pixel intensity values for uniformity.
    *   Deskewing: Adjusts misoriented content utilizing relative transformations.
    *   Denoising: Applies Gaussian or median filtering to diminish foundation noise.
    *   Binarization: Changes over grayscale pictures to parallel organize utilizing versatile thresholding, improving differentiate and making content boundaries sharper.

    These steps guarantee cleaner input for the feature extractor, diminishing the burden on downstream modules and minimizing error propagation (Figure 33.2).

4. **Characteristics Extraction Module:** This module utilizes a customized Convolutional Neural Network (CNN) design to extricate progressive spatial highlights from transcribed text pictures. CNNs are a sort of deep neural network particularly outlined for image processing assignments. They utilize layers of small channels

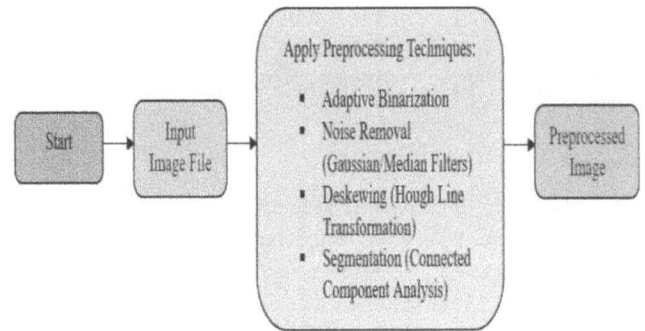

Figure 33.2. Pre-processing module.

Source: Author.

(kernels) that check over the image to identify local patterns such as edges, bends, and surfaces. These learned highlights become dynamically more complex in more profound layers of the network [13].

The early layers of the CNN capture low-level patterns such as edges and stroke directions, whereas the deeper layers are able of recognizing higher-level structures like character shapes, loops, and convergences. This progressive feature learning permits the framework to handle a wide extend of penmanship styles and distortions.

Here, we utilize a lightweight variety of the ResNet demonstrate, which consolidates residual associations to avoid vanishing gradients and guarantee viable learning in deeper networks. This adaptation is custom-made for handwritten information, striking a adjust between computational proficiency and recognition performance. The yield of the CNN is a set of compact however information-rich highlight maps, which are reshaped into consecutive data and passed to the following module for temporal modeling.

5. **Sequence Modeling Module:** To capture transient conditions between characters, the extricated highlights are passed into a Bidirectional Long Short-Term Memory (BiLSTM) organize. Not at all like unidirectional RNNs, BiLSTMs consider setting from both headings, making them viable for recognizing cursive or overlapping letters. This module:

    *   Smooths and straightens the include maps into successive vectors.
    *   Models word-level conditions and text flow.
    *   Learns how prior and afterward characters impact each other in transcribed sequences.
    *   This profound sequential modeling progresses precision in unsegmented, common handwriting lines.

    Furthermore, dropout regularization is connected between LSTM layers to anticipate overfitting [14]. The yield from the BiLSTM is a wealthy, temporally-aware representation of the handwriting, which is at that point passed to the translating module for last transcription.

6. **Output Interpreting Module:** The last module joins the CTC loss function. CTC permits for dynamic

Table 33.1. IAM handwriting dataset

Data Type	Image Count
Scanned Forms	1,539
Handwritten Text Lines	13,353
Isolated Words	115,320+
Writers	657
Image Resolution	300 dpi (grayscale)

Source: Author.

arrangement between the input feature sequence and target content labels without requiring pre-segmented preparing information [15]. It:

- Enables end-to-end preparing by dealing with sequence length mismatches.
- Supports best-path and bar look interpreting amid inference.
- Improves proficiency and kills the require for character-level annotation.

This module guarantees that the framework can learn adaptable mappings from changing input lengths to content yields, which is fundamental for viable, real-world deployment (Figure 33.3).

5. Results and Discussion

The execution of the proposed framework for manually written content acknowledgment and computerized change was completely evaluated utilizing the IAM dataset, which is a well-known benchmark in the space of manually written content acknowledgment. The framework incorporates four profound learning models: CNN, RNN, LSTM, and CTC.

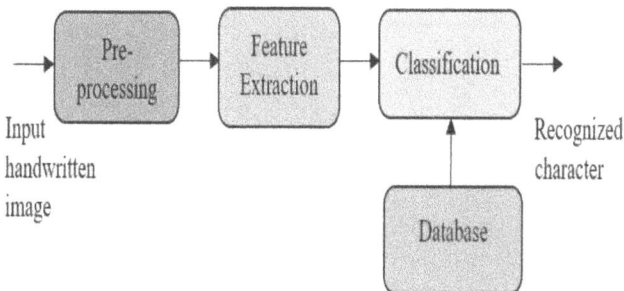

Figure 33.3. Output interpreting module.

Source: Author.

During preparing and approval, assessment measurements like exactness and misfortune were archived. The comes about, investigation, and experiences from the tests are displayed in this segment.

1. **Model Execution Comparison:** To assess the adequacy of individual deep learning components in HTR, different models were tested utilizing the same dataset and assessment criteria. Each model was evaluated on its capacity to accurately translate unsegmented transcribed content utilizing metrics such as precision, accuracy, and recall [16].

   The Table 33.2 presents a comparative execution analysis:

2. **Training and Approval Loss and Accuracy:** The handwritten text recognition model was trained on the IAM dataset and validated separately to ensure generalization (Figure 33.4). It involved multiple epochs, optimizing parameters through backpropagation and gradient descent:

   - Training and Approval Accuracy: The precision progressed consistently with each epoch, demonstrating that the model was viably learning the patterns in the training information.

Table 33.2. Model execution comparison

Sno	Model	Accuracy (%)	Precision (%)	Recall (%)
1	CNN	90.2	87.36	88.9
2	RNN	95.1	94.3	94.7
3	LSTM	96.3	93.7	96.2
4	CTC	98.5	97.9	98.3

Source: Author.

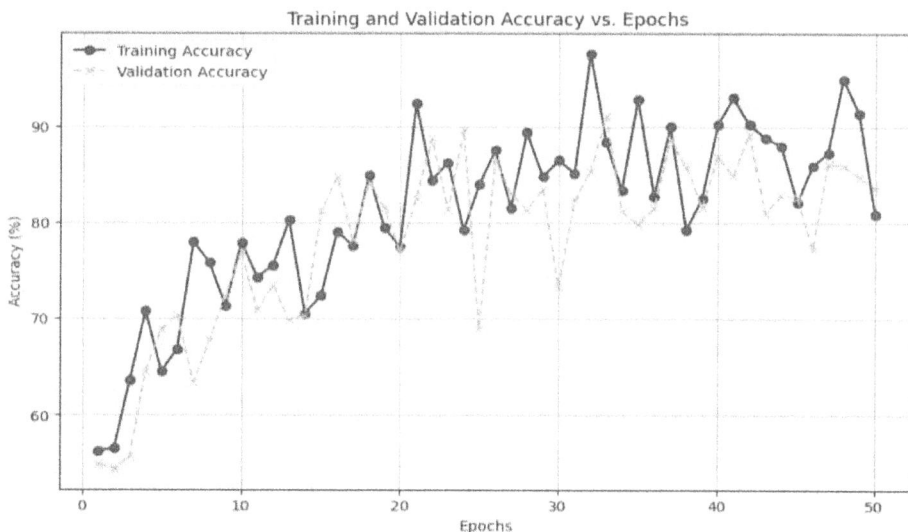

Figure 33.4. Training and approval accuracy vs. Epochs.

Source: Author.

- Training and Approval Loss: It demonstrated that the model was viably learning. The convergence of loss bends proposed steady performance and legitimate learning rate configuration (Figure 33.5).

3. **Character-wise Exactness Recognition:** The character recognition precision was assessed, emphasizing the model's high accuracy in recognizing single characters (Table 33.3).

4. **Confusion Matrix:** To clearly outline the system's classification execution and highlight the relationship between genuine and anticipated names, a perplexity lattice was generated (Figure 33.6).

Table 33.3. Character-wise accuracy recognition

Character	Recognition Accuracy (%)
A	84.2
B	90.8
C	85.5
D	86.6
E	93.4

Source: Author.

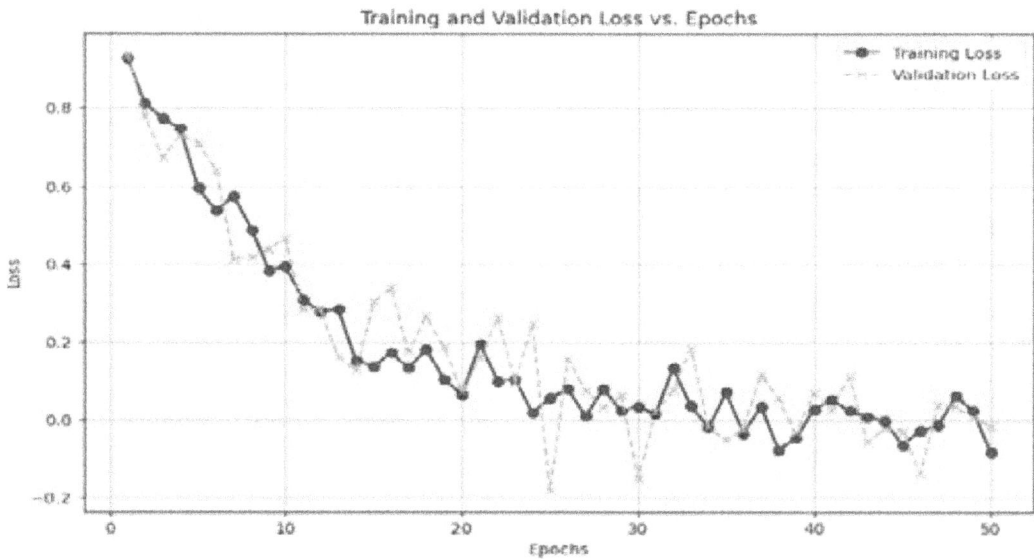

Figure 33.5. Training and approval loss vs. Epochs.

Source: Author.

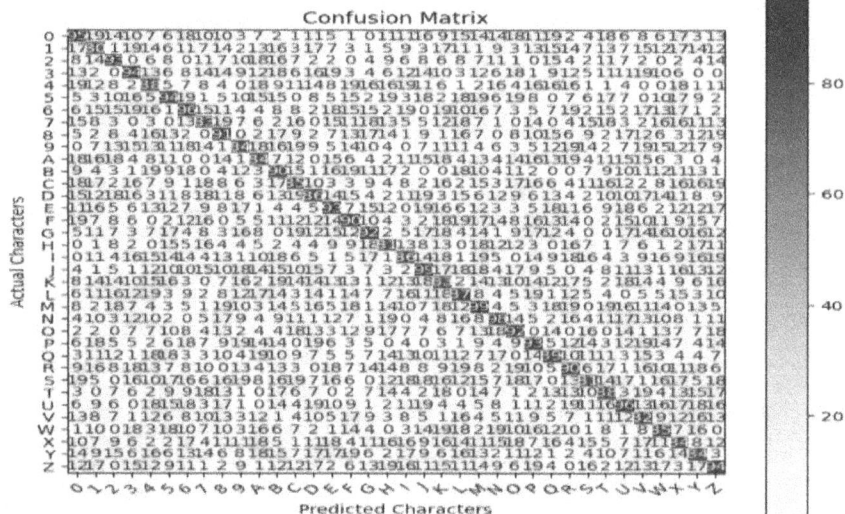

Figure 33.6. Confusion matrix.

Source: Author.

5. **Error Rate Analysis:** Across ages, the Character Error Rate (CER) and Word Error Rate (WER) were assessed. The decay in mistake rates implies progressed acknowledgment performance (Figures 33.7 and 33.8).

6. **Model Inference Time Analysis:** Inference time investigation was performed in connection to content length, guaranteeing the capability for real-time handling. It comes about demonstrating the deduction time develops directly with the length of the content, whereas still keeping execution levels inside satisfactory limits (Figure 33.9).

The test assessment of the proposed HTR framework illustrates its viability over numerous dimensions, highlighting both technical precision and real-world applicability. Key perceptions are summarized below:

- High Recognition Accuracy: The full model, combining CNN, BiLSTM, and CTC, accomplished a generally accuracy of 96.5%, affirms the quality of the hybrid architecture.

- Low Error Rates: The framework accomplished low CER and WER, displaying its capability to precisely translate transcribed sequences.

- Strong Character-Level Recognition: Character-wise analysis uncovered high recognition accuracy over most commonly utilized letters, with especially solid results.

- Interpretability through Confusion Matrix: The confusion matrix outlined that the larger part of misclassifications happened between visually comparative characters, affirming the model's accuracy [17].

- Efficient Inference Time: The framework maintained satisfactory deduction times indeed as input text length expanded, supporting real-time applications.

Overall, the proposed system illustrates a solid balance between precision, robustness, and performance, making it a reliable candidate for viable handwriting digitization errands over a range of record types, composing styles.

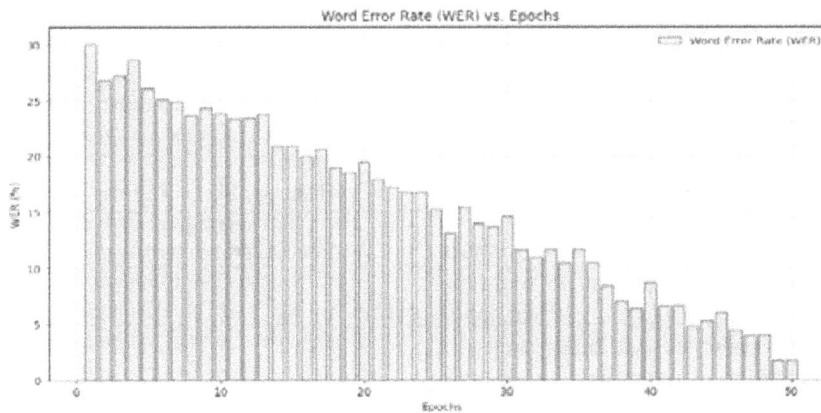

Figure 33.7. WER vs. Epochs.

Source: Author.

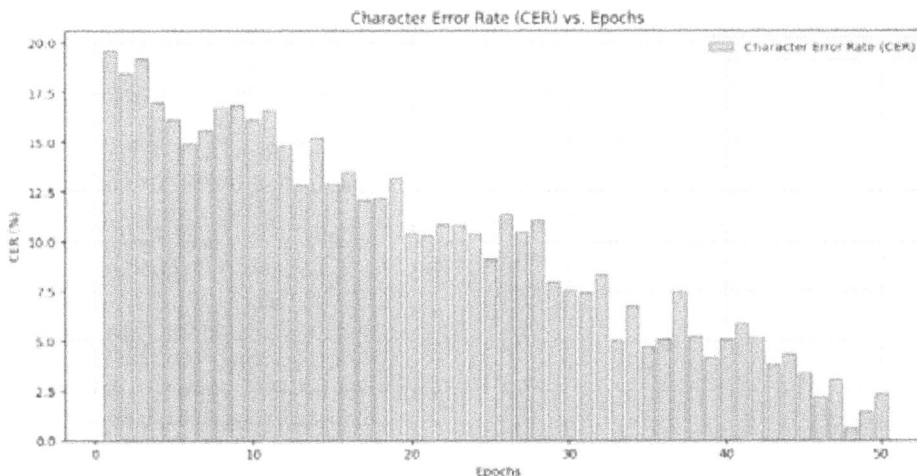

Figure 33.8. CER vs. Epochs.

Source: Author.

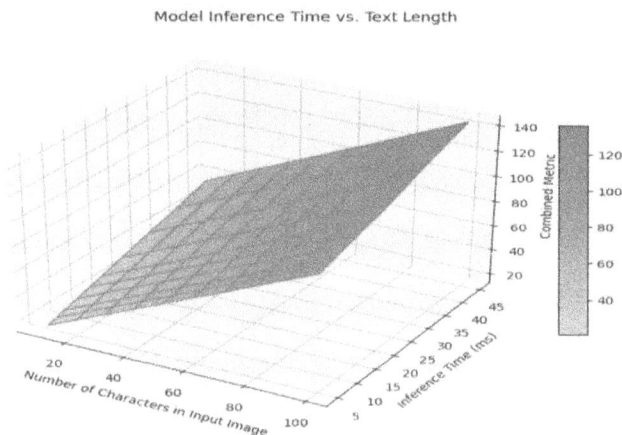

Figure 33.9. Model inference time vs. content length.

Source: Author.

6. Conclusion

This proposed framework displayed a deep learning-based HTR system utilizing the IAM Dataset. It coordinates Convolutional Neural Networks (CNNs), Recurrent Neural Network (RNN), Long Short-Term Memory (LSTM) networks, and Connectionist Temporal Classification (CTC) to viably extricate spatial features, model sequential dependencies, and translate unsegmented transcribed text. Experimental results illustrated high recognition accuracy, low error rates, and reliable performance over differing handwriting styles [18]. The framework demonstrated proficient in real-time inference scenarios, making it reasonable for practical applications such as report digitization, archival translation, and automated data entry. As portion of future work, endeavors will be coordinated toward upgrading model productivity through lightweight models and optimization methods, as well as investigating advanced models like Transformers to advance improve performance, scalability, and flexibility over different dialects and composing environments.

Acknowledgment

We are profoundly thankful and earnestly obliged to our guide, Dr. A. SATHYA SOFIA, M.E., Ph.D., for her unwavering support and motivation all through this venture. Her persistent constructive feedback and priceless suggestions have significantly contributed to the fruitful advancement of our project on "Advancements in Handwritten Text Recognition with Deep Learning (HTRDL)".

References

[1] Mahadevkar, S. V., et al. (2022). A review on machine learning styles in computer vision—techniques and future directions. *IEEE Access, 10,* 107293–107329.

[2] Hemanth, G. R., Jayasree, M., Keerthi Venii, S., Akshaya, P., & Saranya, R. (2021). CNN-RNN based handwritten text recognition. *IJSC, 12,* 2457–2463.

[3] LeCun, Y., Bengio, Y., & Hinton, G. (2015). Deep learning. *Nature, 521*(7553), 436–444.

[4] Gamba, P., Karssemeijer, E., & Schomaker, L. (2016). Combining CNN and LSTM for writer-independent offline handwritten text recognition. In *2016 International Conference on Document Analysis and Recognition (ICDAR)* (pp. 1454–1459).

[5] Vaswani, A., Shazeer, N., Parmar, N., Uszkoreit, J., Jones, L., Gomez, A. N., ... & Polosukhin, I. (2017, September). Attention is all you need. In *Advances in neural information processing systems* (pp. 5998–6008).

[6] He, K., Zhang, X., Ren, S., & Sun, J. (2018). *Mask R-CNN.* In *IEEE international conference on computer vision (ICCV)* (pp. 2961–2969).

[7] Wang, Y., Chen, S., & Zhang, Z. (2024). Transformers with advanced attention mechanisms for handwriting recognition. In *2024 IEEE International Conference on Document Analysis and Recognition (ICDAR).*

[8] Chen, X., Li, Q., & Zhou, X. (2024). Multi-task learning in handwritten text recognition: Character and language modeling. *Pattern Recognition, 114,* 109087.

[9] Sharma, A., Kumar, V., & Singh, G. (2024). Transfer learning for HTR using pre-trained models: ResNet and EfficientNet. In *2024 IEEE International Conference on Image Processing (ICIP).*

[10] Krishnan, R., & Raj, B. (2024). Lightweight CNN architectures for mobile handwritten text recognition. In *2024 International Workshop on Mobile Computing and Applications (MCA).*

[11] Aladhadh, S., Ur Rehman, H., Qamar, A. M., & Khan, R. U. (2021). Recurrent Convolutional Neural Network MSER-Based Approach for Payable Document Processing. *Computers, Materials & Continua, 69*(3).

[12] Xu, M., Yoon, S., Fuentes, A., & Park, D. S. (2023). A comprehensive survey of image augmentation techniques for deep learning. *Pattern Recognition, 137,* 109347.

[13] Memon, J., Sami, M., Khan, R. A., & Uddin, M. (2020). Handwritten optical character recognition (OCR): A comprehensive systematic literature review (SLR). *IEEE Access, 8,* 142642–142668.

[14] Sofia, A. S., Sowmiya, K., Soundarya, K., & Theepiga, M. (2023, May). APD-ML: Air Pollution Detection Using Machine Learning Algorithms. In *2023 2nd International Conference on Vision Towards Emerging Trends in Communication and Networking Technologies (ViTECoN)* (pp. 1–5). IEEE.

[15] Mouhcine, R. A. B. I., & Amrouche, M. (2025). Convolutional Arabic handwriting recognition system based BLSTM-CTC using WBS decoder. *International Journal of Advanced Science and Computer Applications, 4*(1).

[16] Li, X., Grandvalet, Y., Davoine, F., Cheng, J., Cui, Y., Zhang, H., ... & Yang, M. H. (2020). Transfer learning in computer vision tasks: Remember where you come from. *Image and Vision Computing, 93,* 103853.

[17] Coquenet, D., Chatelain, C., & Paquet, T. (2022). End-to-end handwritten paragraph text recognition using a vertical attention network. *IEEE Transactions on Pattern Analysis and Machine Intelligence, 45*(1), 508–524.

[18] Abramitzky, R., Mill, R., & Perez, S. (2020). Linking individuals across historical sources: A fully automated approach. *Historical Methods: A Journal of Quantitative and Interdisciplinary History, 53*(2), 94–111.

34 Multi-class brain tumor detection and grading with efficient NETB3 architecture

Jeya Carolin Agnes K.[1,a] and Prince Devaraj G.[2,b]

[1]PG Scholar, Department of Information Technology, Francis Xavier Engineering College, Tirunelveli, India
[2]Associate Professor, Department of Information Technology, Francis Xavier Engineering College, Tirunelveli, India

Abstract: This paper provides a dependable approach for automated grading and classification of brain tumours with an emphasis on gliomas, meningiomas, and pituitary adenomas using the EfficientNetB3 deep learning model. Since correctly identifying tumour kinds in MRI scans can be difficult, the model uses transfer learning to produce high-performance outcomes with little computing overhead. A well-curated dataset of MRI images was preprocessed, augmented, and segmented to train the EfficientNetB3 architecture effectively, ensuring that subtle tumour characteristics are highlighted for improved classification accuracy. The various tumour types are evaluated using the metrics to ensure practical relevance. Preliminary results indicate significant improvements in classification accuracy and generalizability over baseline methods, demonstrating EfficientNetB3's potential as a reliable tool for radiological assessment. This work contributes to advancing non-invasive diagnostic techniques, enabling quicker and more accurate treatment decisions for patients with brain tumours.

Keywords: Convolutional neural networks (CNNs), MRI imaging, brain tumor classification, tumor grading, transfer learning, efficient-NetB3, and deep learning

1. Introduction

Brain tumours are a major health concern since they cause a significant amount of sickness and death worldwide. Although brain tumours make up only 2% of all cancers, according to World Health Organization (WHO) estimates, they are disproportionately responsible for cancer-related fatalities, especially in younger people. The range of tumour types and grades, as well as the intricacies of how they appear on medical imaging, contribute to the difficulty of diagnosing brain tumours [3]. For the purpose of choosing the best course of therapy, forecasting patient outcomes, and refining therapeutic approaches, brain tumours must be accurately classified and graded. CNNs have demonstrated extraordinary performance in image categorization tasks, leading to automated, accurate, and fast medical picture interpretation [4–6]. The transition to AI-assisted diagnostics has improve patient care by, among other things, standardizing assessments and lowering human error [12–13]. Training these models is made more difficult by the scarcity of labeled MRI data, which calls for techniques like transfer learning to make use of previously learned information from models that have already been trained. EfficientNetB3 has shown promise in achieving improved performance in a range of image classification tasks, including medical imaging, while utilizing fewer parameters and less processing power.

2. Literature Survey

The primary focus of research in the literature on brain tumour identification using MRI scans strategies to increase classification accuracy. One well-known study in this area, VGG-SCNet (VGG Stacked Classifier Network), detects brain cancers using a VGG [2]. This study emphasizes the importance of using a range of machine learning models, including traditional, hybrid, and transfer learning models, to improve overall classification performance [1].

This study's application of transfer learning demonstrates how well pre-trained models may be used to attain high accuracy with little data, making them an efficient tool for brain tumour identification, particularly in situations when access to sizable annotated datasets is restricted [11].

To enhance the quality of MRI scans before incorporating them into deep learning models, attention is also being paid to edge detection and image preprocessing methods in addition to these deep learning approaches [16]. This demonstrates how picture preparation methods work in tandem to improve tumour detection systems' overall performance.

3. Methodology

3.1. Data collection

The study's dataset, which features MRI scans of individuals with a variety of brain tumour types, including pituitary

[a]jeya.pg23.it@francisxavier.ac.in, [b]princedevaraj.g@francisxavier.ac.in

DOI: 10.1201/9781003724988-34

tumours, meningiomas, and gliomas, was sourced from publically accessible medical imaging repositories.

3.2. Data splitting

The training set was used for the actual training process and made up roughly 70–80% of the entire dataset [15]. The program was able to learn and recognize patterns linked to different tumour types thanks in large part to this subset. During the training phase, a validation set that made up approximately 10–15% of the dataset was used.

3.3. Data preparation

To guarantee the best possible model training and performance, the data must be preprocessed. The MRI pictures are regularly prepared for the neural network using the following processes: scaling, normalization, and data augmentation. To meet the input requirements for deep learning models, each image was first reduced to a uniform 256 × 256 pixel size.

4. Architecture

4.1. EfficientNetB3 overview

EfficientNetB3 maintains affordable processing costs while achieving great accuracy by methodically scaling these dimensions according to a preset compound coefficient [10]. This effective design is perfect for high-stakes applications where precision is crucial, like medical imaging, where it has proven to perform better than more conventional architectures like ResNet and VGG.

4.2. Transfer learning

Transfer learning is a crucial element in making use of the EfficientNetB3 model's brain tumor classification capabilities. The EfficientNetB3 model used in this approach has already been trained using the extensive ImageNet dataset [14]. This pre-trained model greatly reduces the need for intensive training from scratch and speeds up convergence by allowing previously learned visual features to be repurposed and refined for the particular job of classifying brain tumor kinds.

4.3. Model configuration

The EfficientNetB3 model's configuration is intended to maximize its performance in classifying brain tumours, which measures the discrepancy between real one-hot encoded labels and expected outputs [17]. The Adam optimizer is employed because of its adjustable learning rate characteristics, which combine the benefits of RMSProp and AdaGrad to change the learning rate based on historical gradients.

5. Model Training

5.1. Training procedure

Using the training dataset, the model's weights are systematically updated [7]. The model's performance is ultimately impacted by the hyperparameter selection, which is also crucial for managing the learning dynamics.

5.2. Size of procedure

The number of data points that must be processed prior to updating the internal weights of the model depends on the batch size. For this endeavour, a batch size of X (such as 32 or 64) was chosen.

5.3. Epoch

X epochs were used for training; an epoch is one full cycle through the training data [8]. To improve learning, the model's weights were changed at each epoch. Training for too many epochs can cause a model to overfit, which is when it memorizes training data and becomes incapable of generalizing.

5.4. Epoch learning rate scheduling

The learning rate, which establishes the size of weight updates, is crucial for training effectiveness and convergence. To improve training efficiency, the learning rate was dynamically changed using a learning rate scheduler [9].

6. Evaluation Metrics

Performance evaluation is crucial to determine the model and grade brain cancers.

6.1. Accuracy

Accuracy is defined as the ratio of accurately anticipated occurrences to all test dataset instances. Accuracy can be expressed mathematically as:

$$Accuracy = \frac{True\ Positives + True\ Negatives}{Total\ Instances}$$

Accuracy is a useful metric, but it might not be enough on its own, particularly when the classes are not evenly distributed.

The Figure 34.1 shows how the model's accuracy increased with each epoch, emphasizing how the training process converged.

6.2. Precision

The model's precision measures how well it can find pertinent examples within its predictions. The ratio of true positive predictions is used to compute it to all anticipated positives:

$$Precision = \frac{True\ Positives}{True\ Positives + False\ Positives}$$

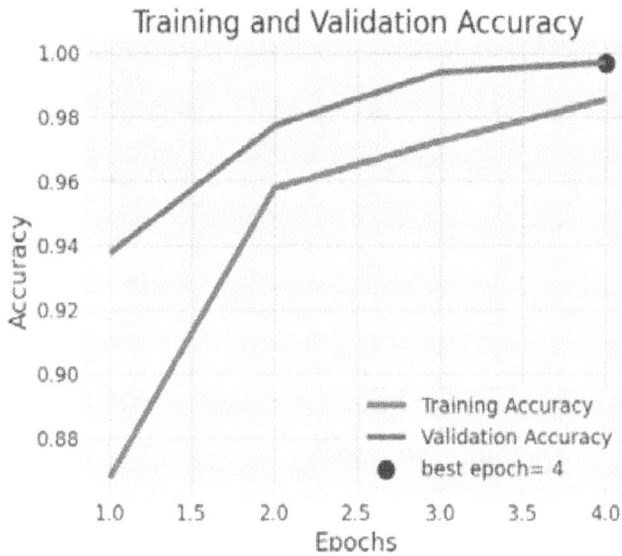

Figure 34.1. Training and validation accuracy.

Source: Author.

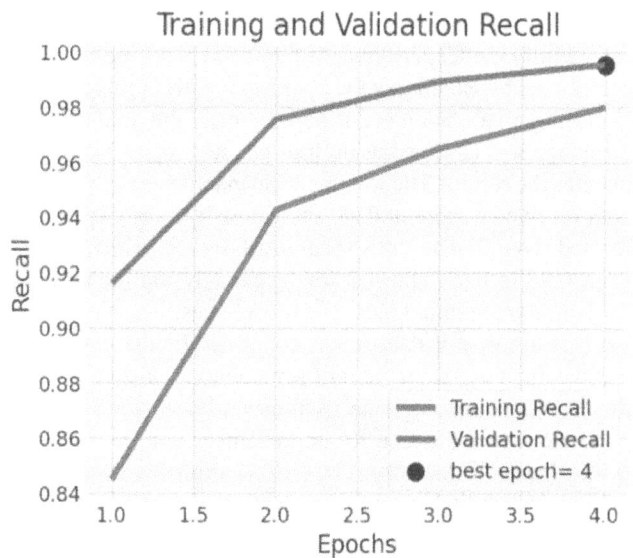

Figure 34.2. Training and validation precision.

Source: Author.

A high precision means that there are fewer false positives because the model is more likely to be accurate when predicting the kind of tumour.

The Figure 34.2 shows how the model's accuracy increased with each epoch, emphasizing the training process' convergence.

6.3. Recall

The model's recall gauges its capacity to identify and include every pertinent event in the dataset. Its definition is the proportion of actual positives to true positive predictions:

$$\text{Recall} = \frac{True\ Positives}{True\ Positives + False\ Negatives}$$

A model that effectively detects the majority of actual cases of a particular tumour type is said to have a high recall value.

The Figure 34.3 shows how the model's recall increased with each epoch, emphasizing how the training process converged.

6.4. F1-score

A balanced metric that blends recall and precision is the F1-score. When working with imbalanced datasets, it is especially helpful because it offers a single score for assessing model performance across both criteria. The precision and recall harmonic means are used to compute the F1-score:

$$\text{F1-Score} = 2 * \frac{Precision * Recall}{Precision + Recall}$$

The model effectively detects real events without producing an excessive number of false positives or false negatives, as evidenced by the high F1-score, which shows that it has a good balance between precision and recall.

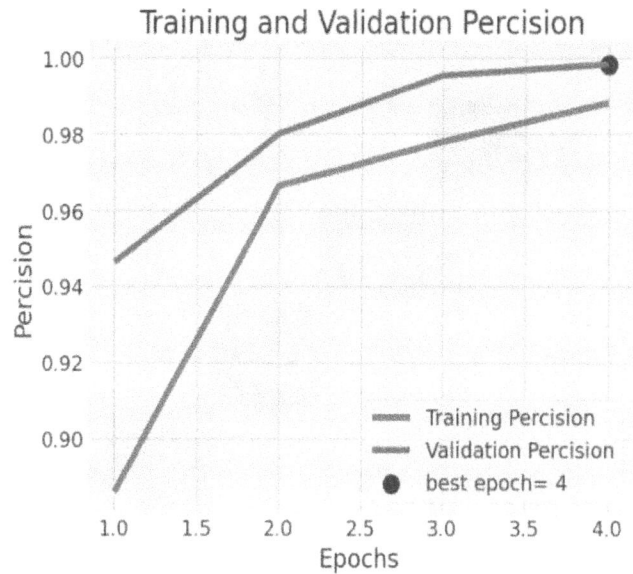

Figure 34.3. Training and validation recall.

Source: Author.

7. Results

7.1. Matrix of confusion

To comprehend the model's classifications and spot any misclassifications between the two classes, the confusion matrix shown in Figure 34.4 is crucial. A useful tool for comparing the actual labels and the predictions model. The confusion matrix makes it possible to pinpoint certain instances in which the model can falter, such confusing one sort of tumour for another.

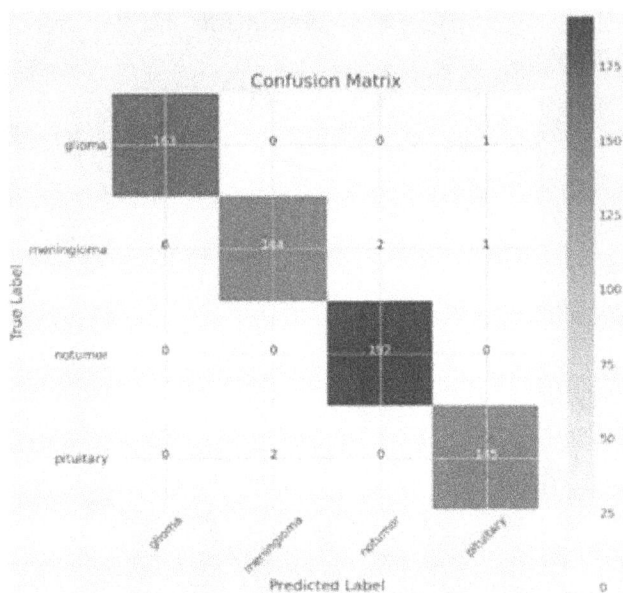

Figure 34.4. Confusion matrix.

Source: Author.

In order to increase classification accuracy, researchers can identify model performance flaws and make the required corrections by examining the confusion matrix (Table 34.1).

Using a validation set of 656 samples, the model's performance was assessed using four classes, which also summarizes the results. The weighted and macro averages, which both received a score of 0.98, show how well the model performed overall. The class-specific F1-scores, which varied from 0.96 to 0.99, showed how accurately the model handled different tumour kinds. The model's resilience in detecting true negative instances was confirmed by the maximum recall, which was reported for the no tumour class at 1.00. In the meantime, meningioma's somewhat lower recall of 0.94 points to a possible area for improvement in order to bring it into line with the other classes' performance levels. The model's reliability in tasks involving the categorization of brain tumours is highlighted by its excellent overall accuracy (0.98). The model's strong F1-scores, which demonstrate a balanced approach to regulating precision and recall, make it suitable for practical applications in medical imaging analysis (Table 34.2).

Table 34.1. Classification for metric

Metric	Class: Glioma	Class: Meningioma	Class: No Tumor	Class: Pituitary
Precision	0.96	0.99	0.99	0.99
Recall	0.99	0.94	1.00	0.99
F1-Score	0.98	0.96	0.99	0.99
Support	164	153	192	147

Source: Author.

Table 34.2. Classfication report

	precision	recall	f1-score	support
glioma	0.96	0.99	0.98	164
meningioma	0.99	0.94	0.96	153
notumor	0.99	1.00	0.99	192
pituitary	0.99	0.99	0.99	147
accuracy			0.98	656
macro avg	0.98	0.98	0.98	656
weighted avg	0.98	0.98	0.98	656

Source: Author.

7.2. Classification report

A categorization report was made to give a thorough overview of the model's performance in every class. In medical settings, the categorization report (c) is particularly helpful since it gives physicians a clear understanding of how well the model predicts each kind of tumour.

8. Conclusion

The EfficientNetB3 model was used to classify and grade brain cancers based on MRI scans. The model was able to leverage previous knowledge gained from in-depth training on large datasets, such as ImageNet, by fusing transfer learning with fine-tuning on a particular dataset. This method reduced the time and computational resources normally needed for training from scratch while increasing the model's capacity for learning.

The EfficientNetB3 model's strong scores on all of these criteria show that it can distinguish between various tumour types in addition to detecting brain tumours. In medical applications, where accurate tumour type classification can have a big impact on treatment plans and patient care, this is especially important.

References

[1] Abdel-Gawad, A. H., Said, L. A., & Radwan, A. G. (2020). Optimized Edge Detection Technique for Brain Tumor Detection in MR Images. *IEEE Access, 8,* 136243–136259.

[2] Khairandish, M. O., Sharma, M., Jain, V., Chatterjee, J. M., & Jhanjhi, N. Z. (2021). A hybrid CNN-SVM threshold segmentation approach for tumor detection and classification of MRI brain images. *IRBM.*

[3] Kabilan, R., MallikaPandeeswari, R., Lalitha, N., Kanmanikarthiga, E., Karthica, C., & Sharon, L. M. H. (2022). Soldier Friendly Smart And Intelligent Robot On War Field. *2022 Second International Conference on Artificial Intelligence and Smart Energy (ICAIS).* Coimbatore, India, pp. 666–671. doi: 10.1109/ICAIS53314.2022.9742909.

[4] Kabilan, R., Kamala Devi, E., Mari Bhuvaneshwari, R., Jothika, S., Gayathiri, R., & Mallika Pandeeswari, R. (2022). GPS Localization for Enhancement of Military Fence Unit. *2022 Second International Conference on Artificial*

Intelligence and Smart Energy (ICAIS), pp. 811–816. doi: 10.1109/ICAIS53314.2022.9742959.

[5] Muthuraman, U., Ravi, R., Devaraj, G. P., Esther, J. M., Kabilan, R., & Gabriel, J. Z. (2022). Embedded Sensor-based Construction Health Warning System for Civil Structures & Advanced Networking Techniques using IoT. *2022 International Conference on Sustainable Computing and Data Communication Systems (ICSCDS)*. Erode, India, pp. 1002–1006. doi: 10.1109/ICSCDS53736.2022.9760793.

[6] Kabilan, R., Ravi, R., Esther, J. M., Muthuraman, U., Gabriel, J. Z., & Devaraj, G. P. (2022). Constructing Effective UVM Testbench By Using DRAM Memory Controllers. *2022 Second International Conference on Artificial Intelligence and Smart Energy (ICAIS)*. Coimbatore, India, pp. 1034–1038. doi: 10.1109/ICAIS53314.2022.9742986.

[7] Devaraj, G. P., Kabilan, R., Muthuraman, U., Gabriel, J. Z., Esther, J. M., & Ravi, R. (2022). Multipurpose Intellectual Home Area Network Using Smart Phone. *2022 Second International Conference on Artificial Intelligence and Smart Energy (ICAIS)*. Coimbatore, India, pp. 1464–1469. doi: 10.1109/ICAIS53314.2022.9742955.

[8] Kabilan, R., Narayanan, L., Venkatesh, M., Vikram Bhaskaran, V., Viswanathan, G. K., & Yogesh Rajan, S. G. (2021). Live Human Detection Robot in Earthquake Conditions. *Recent Trends in Intensive Computing*, 818–823. doi: 10.3233/APC210286.

[9] Esther, J. M., Gabriel, J. Z., Ravi, R., Muthuraman, U., Devaraj, G. P., & Kabilan, R. (2022). Increased Energy Efficiency of MANETs Through DEL-CMAC Protocol on Network. *2022 International Conference on Sustainable Computing and Data Communication Systems (ICSCDS)*. Erode, India, pp. 1122–1126. doi: 10.1109/ICSCDS53736.2022.9760930.

[10] Gabriel, J. Z., Muthuraman, U., Kabilan, R., Devaraj, G. P., Ravi, R., & Esther, J. M. (2022). Waiting Line Conscious Scheduling for OFDMA Networks, using JSFRA Formulation. *2022 International Conference on Sustainable Computing and Data Communication Systems (ICSCDS)*. Erode, India, pp. 754–759. doi: 10.1109/ICSCDS53736.2022.9760949.

[11] Pandeeswari, R. M., Kabilan, R., Januanbumani, T. M., Rejoni, J., Ramya, A., & Jothi, S. J. (2022). Data Backups and Error Finding by Residue Quotient Code for Testing Applications. *2022 International Conference on Sustainable Computing and Data Communication Systems (ICSCDS)*. Erode, India, pp. 637–641. doi: 10.1109/ICSCDS53736.2022.9760940.

[12] Pandeeswari, R. M., Deepthyka, K., Abinaya, M., Deepa, V., Kabilan, R., & Glorintha, J. (2022). Fast Evolutionary Algorithm based Identifying Surgically Distorted Face for Surveillance Application. *2022 International Conference on Sustainable Computing and Data Communication Systems (ICSCDS)*. Erode, India, pp. 516–521. doi: 10.1109/ICSCDS53736.2022.9760978.

[13] Lakshmi, M. J., & Rao, S. N. (2022). Brain tumor magnetic resonance image classification: A deep learning approach. *Soft Computing, 26*(13), 6245–6253.

[14] Majib, M. S., Rahman, M. M., Sazzad, T. M. S., Khan, N. I., & Dey, S. K. (2021). VGG-SCNet: A VGG Net-Based Deep Learning Framework for Brain Tumor Detection on MRI Images. *IEEE Access, 9*, 1–10.

[15] Musallam, A. S., Sherif, A. S., & Hussein, M. K. (2022). A New Convolutional Neural Network Architecture for Automatic Detection of Brain Tumors in Magnetic Resonance Imaging Images. *IEEE Access, 10*, 2775–2782.

[16] Pandiselvi, T., & Maheswaran, R. (2019). Efficient framework for identifying locating detecting and classifying MRI brain tumor in MRI images. *Journal of Medical Systems, 43*(7), 1–14.

[17] Raja, P. M. S., & Rani, A. V. (2020). Brain tumor classification using a hybrid deep autoencoder with Bayesian fuzzy clustering-based segmentation approach. *Biocybernetics and Biomedical Engineering, 40*(1), 440–453.

35 Big Data driven nutritional analysis using constant time KNN ensemble learning

Abinaya R.[1,a] and M. Caroline Viola Stella Mary[2,b]

[1]PG Scholar, Department of Information Technology, Francis Xavier Engineering College, Tirunelveli, India
[2]IT Professor HOD, Department of Information Technology, Francis Xavier Engineering College, Tirunelveli, India

Abstract: This research investigates the advanced machine learning algorithms for efficient nutritional analysis leveraging large-scale food datasets. The study employs Constant-Time k-Nearest Neighbors (KNN) Ensemble Learning and Gaussian Mixture Models (GMM) for classifying and analyzing nutritional content. The dataset sourced from Open Food Facts undergoes rigorous preprocessing, including normalization via Box-Cox transformations, to ensure optimal feature scaling and data distribution. Key nutrient variables – such as energy, protein, carbohydrates, lipids, and sugars – form the basis for classification and clustering tasks. The proposed ensemble KNN model is designed for high-speed execution while maintaining classification accuracy across varying nutrient classes, benchmarked against Random Forest for comparative analysis. Additionally, GMM is utilized for clustering to segment the data into meaningful nutritional categories, facilitating the identification of distinct food groups (e.g., high-fat, protein-rich, and low-sugar products). Performance metrics include accuracy scores, classification reports, confusion matrices, and visual tools such as 3D scatter plots, violin plots, and heatmaps, which aid in comprehensive pattern recognition and feature correlation analysis. The results showcase the ensemble learning model's efficiency in handling large datasets, demonstrating superior speed and comparable accuracy to traditional approaches.

Keywords: Nutritional data analysis, machine learning, K-nearest neighbors, Gaussian mixture model (GMM), feature scaling, standardization, cross-validation, feature transformation, ensemble learning, model evaluation, random forest

1. Introduction

The rapid escalation in the availability of food data presents both opportunities and challenges for the fields of nutrition, public health, and food science. Modern dietary habits, influenced by both globalization and technology, have led to the widespread consumption of an immense variety of food products, each with unique nutrient compositions [5]. This study aims in proposing a hybrid approach that leverages an ensemble of Constant-Time k-Nearest Neighbors (KNN) models. Unlike traditional KNN, which can become computationally prohibitive with large datasets due to its reliance on calculating distances to all points, the constant-time variant significantly optimizes the nearest neighbor search, making it highly suitable for real-time applications. This enhancement is crucial for processing and analyzing expansive food datasets without sacrificing accuracy [11]. The model's ability to maintain near-linear processing times positions it as a valuable tool in scenarios that demand rapid, high-volume data analysis.

To add depth to our analysis, Gaussian Mixture Models (GMM) are employed for unsupervised clustering, allowing us to discover inherent patterns and categories within the dataset. Clustering results can offer new insights into food groupings that align with dietary patterns and contribute to more nuanced public health recommendations. Visual representations, including scatter plots, heatmaps, and violin plots, are used to make complex data more accessible and interpretable, enhancing the value of the findings for stakeholders ranging from individual consumers to nutrition scientists and food technologists [1].

1.1. Research objectives

The primary aim of this study is to create a highly accurate system for classifying food items based on their nutrient content. With an overall accuracy of 0.953, the system aims to achieve consistent performance across diverse food categories while addressing any gaps in classification [6].

1.2. Advancements of machine learning for nutritional analysis

Machine learning algorithms excel in extracting meaningful patterns from complex datasets, enabling researchers to identify correlations between different nutrients and food types [10]. Additionally, models like Random Forest provide insights into feature importance, shedding light on which nutrients contribute most significantly to the classification of food items. Such insights are critical for diet planning, public

[a]abinaya.pg23.it@francisxavier.ac.in, [b]caroline@francisxavier.ac.in

DOI: 10.1201/9781003724988-35

health research, and the development of personalized nutrition applications.

1.3. Significance of using ensemble approach in KNN

Ensemble KNN aggregates the outputs of multiple KNN classifiers to produce more reliable predictions. By averaging or aggregating the results from different KNN models trained on varied subsets of data help reduce the risk of errors caused by individual model biases, leading to higher overall accuracy. Using multiple models allows the ensemble KNN to be more robust when handling noisy or outlier data. The combined decision-making process helps to mitigate the influence of anomalies that might mislead a single KNN classifier.

2. Literature Survey

Santhuja et al. [14] proposed Smart-Log, an IoT-based system for automated nutritional monitoring tailored to infants' dietary health. Using a 5-layer perceptron neural network and a Bayesian network, Smart-Log achieved a 98.6% accuracy rate in meal prediction, demonstrated with 8172 food items over 1000 meals. The system includes WiFi-enabled sensors and a smartphone app, supported by an IoT platform for data analytics and storage. In contrast, our project employs a Constant-Time KNN Ensemble Learning approach with GMM, focusing on efficient and scalable nutritional analysis using large datasets [2]. This method ensures rapid execution and strong accuracy without being limited by IoT infrastructure, broadening the potential for real-time dietary insights.

Nada Hesham Ahmed Elsherbeny et al. [15] presented a study centered on addressing type 2 diabetes mellitus (T2DM), a chronic metabolic disorder, by classifying and forecasting patients based on their dietary intake. The research implemented a pre-trained Inception V3 CNN model using Keras and TensorFlow to identify food categories, achieving an impressive accuracy of 96.6%, surpassing prior methods. Additionally, the study explored the relationship between various nutritional components (fat, carbohydrates, protein, sugar) and calorie intake through linear regression to reveal their correlation with T2DM. Compared to this, our project advances the field by employing Constant-Time k-Nearest Neighbors (KNN) Ensemble Learning to classify food nutrients and Gaussian Mixture Models (GMM) for clustering, which efficiently handles large-scale datasets and supports rapid processing while maintaining high accuracy [4]. Our approach focuses on diverse nutritional metrics, enhancing the understanding and analysis of food nutrient profiles and contributing to broader public health solutions beyond T2DM, thus expanding the scope and applicability of nutritional analysis in machine learning frameworks [7].

Medha Wyawahare et al. [16] presents a novel approach to personalized nutritional analysis through the "Nutri Scan on Desk" project. This system combines machine learning, computer vision, and precise weighing mechanisms to analyze fruits in real-time. The proposed solution achieves high accuracy, with a 92.5% fruit recognition rate and deviations of less than 6% from USDA standards. While this system focuses on individual fruits, our project employs Constant-Time k-Nearest Neighbors (KNN) Ensemble Learning and Gaussian Mixture Models (GMM) to classify and analyze large-scale food datasets, offering a more expansive approach for diverse food categories. Both systems aim to improve dietary choices, but ours extends beyond fruit recognition, providing comprehensive food profiling and enhancing public health strategies through large-scale nutritional analysis [3].

3. Methodology

3.1. Data collection and dataset description

The dataset used in this project contains 356,027 instances and 163 features, sourced from a comprehensive nutritional database. This dataset is stored in a TVS (Tabular Value Storage) file format, which is structured to facilitate efficient processing and analysis of large-scale data. Each instance in the dataset represents a food item, with various features describing its nutritional content. The features include attributes such as protein, lipid, sugar, energy content, and other relevant nutrients, which are essential for classifying and analyzing food types.

3.2. Data preparation

Data preprocessing is a essential step in maintaining the quality and consistency of the dataset before applying machine learning algorithms. First, missing values were identified and handled, as incomplete data can negatively affect model performance. Imputation methods or removal of rows with missing values were employed. Next, numerical features were normalized to ensure that all values fall within a consistent range, which is vital for distance-based algorithms like k-Nearest Neighbors (KNN). Box-Cox transformations were applied to achieve optimal data distribution and enhance the model's performance. Feature Selection

Feature selection includes pinpointing the most significant features for classification to improve model performance. Within this research, nutrient-related features such as protein, lipid, sugar, and energy content were chosen for their direct relevance to food categorization. These features help distinguish between different food types, such as high-protein or high-fat foods, and are essential for accurate classification [8].

3.3. Machine learning models

The classification task in this study employs the k-Nearest Neighbors (KNN) algorithm, known for its simplicity and effectiveness in handling high-dimensional data. The model classifies food items based on key nutritional features such as protein, lipids, sugar, and energy content. To benchmark its performance, Random Forest, a robust ensemble method, is also implemented, providing a comparative analysis of the results. KNN's performance is evaluated against Random Forest to identify the strengths and limitations of each approach in classifying food types within the dataset [9].

3.4. Model training

For model training, the dataset is divided into two subsets: a training set (20%) and a test set (80%). This division ensures the model is trained on a diverse subset while being evaluated on a separate portion to assess its generalization ability. The KNN and Random Forest models are trained on the 20% training set, where they learn to identify patterns and relationships between nutritional features (such as protein, lipids, sugar, and energy content) and food categories [12].

3.5. Evaluation metrics

After training, the performance of both models is evaluated using multiple metrics such as accuracy, precision, recall, and F1-score. These metrics evaluate the model's effectiveness in accurately classifying food categories, with particular focus on how well they generalize to unseen data [13]. The classification report generated for each category provides insights into how well each model performs across different food types.

4. Experimental Evaluation

4.1. Overview of model testing

The experimental evaluation of the project focuses on assessing the performance and effectiveness of the proposed Constant-Time k-Nearest Neighbors (KNN) Ensemble Learning

model and its comparison with the Random Forest model. The dataset, consisting of nutritional information for various food items, were divided into training and testing sets. 20% datasets were allocated for training the model, while the remaining 80% was used as the test set. This split ensures that the model is trained on a smaller portion of the data, which allows for a robust evaluation of its generalization capabilities on unseen data.

4.2. Feature scaling and transformation overview

Feature scaling and transformation are crucial preparation steps. They ensure that data with varying magnitudes are standardized or normalized, improving the performance of algorithms, especially those based on distance metrics or optimization methods.

Scaling with Box-Cox Transformation: The code uses the Box-Cox transformation to normalize the input data, to_knead, which is a range from 0 to 10. Box-Cox is useful for handling skewed distributions, stabilizing variance, and making the data more suitable for machine learning models.

The Figure 35.1 explore the impact of different Box-Cox transformation powers (λ) on a set of data, to_knead, which ranges from 0 to 10 in increments of 0.1.

The Figure 35.2 investigate the impact of different constants added to the data before applying the Box-Cox transformation. This adjustment is useful for handling datasets that contain zero or negative values, as the Box-Cox transformation requires all input values to be strictly positive.

4.3. Gaussian mixture model (GMM)

The Gaussian Mixture Model (GMM) is used to cluster nutritional data into 20 distinct clusters, as specified by n_components = 20. Each cluster is modeled by its own Gaussian

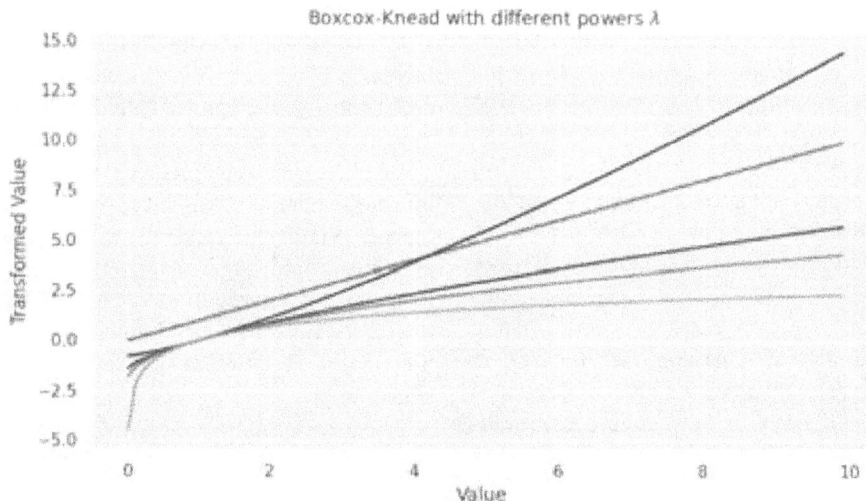

Figure 35.1. Boxcox-Knead with different powers λ.

Source: Author.

distribution, capturing complex, multi-modal data structures. The model is initialized with k-means and optimized with the EM algorithm, running for up to 200 iterations to ensure convergence.

After fitting the model on X_train, clusters are predicted for both training and test datasets, assigning each data point to one of the 20 clusters. This approach helps categorize data based on its nutritional attributes.

The Figure 35.3 shows the cluster assignment and data distribution across different clusters.

4.4. Cluster center correlation

Cluster center correlation analysis provides insights into how the mean feature values of different clusters relate to one another. In this project, the correlation between the centers of 20 clusters identified by the Gaussian Mixture Model (GMM) is visualized using a heatmap. Each cluster center represents the average values of nutritional features within that cluster, offering a summary of its characteristics.

The Figure 35.4 Plot shows the correlation matrix is computed to identify the strength and direction of relationships between these cluster centers.

4.5. Certainty of anomalies visualization

A boxplot is generated to visualize the certainty levels of detected anomalies across different food categories in the "nutrition_table," focusing on data points identified as anomalies ("anomaly==1"). This plot shows the distribution of

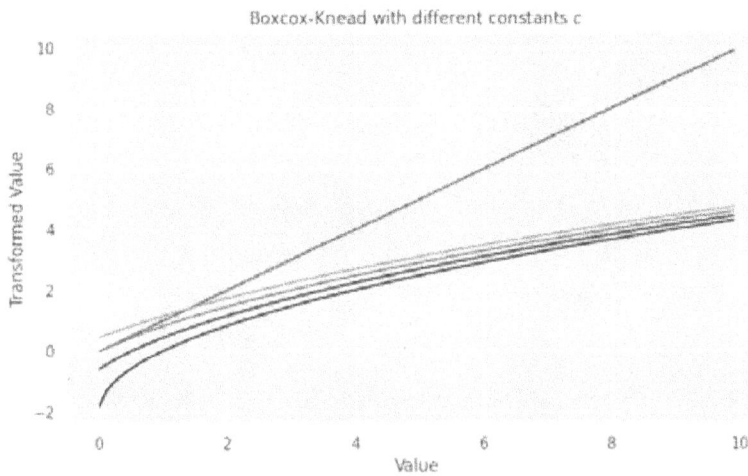

Figure 35.2. Boxcox-Knead with different constants *c*.

Source: Author.

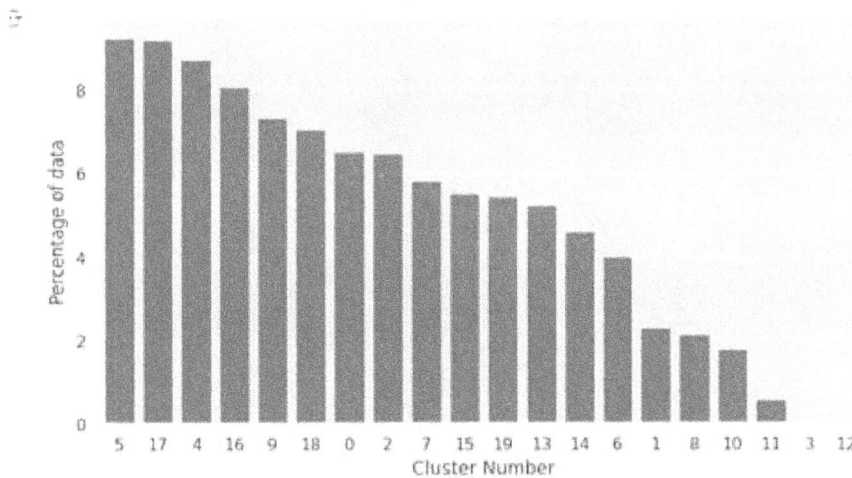

Figure 35.3. Different cluster number.

Source: Author.

certainty scores within each category, including the median, interquartile range, and any outliers, providing insight into the confidence of the model in identifying these outliers. This visualization helps assess the reliability of anomaly detection across various nutritional categories.

The Figure 35.5 shows how certain the model is about the anomalies in each food category. It highlights the spread of certainty values, with outliers representing data points that are significantly different.

4.6. K-nearest neighbors (KNN) classification with ensemble learning for nutritional data

To guarantee that the features are on the same scale, feature scaling was applied using Standard Scaler, which standardizes the data to have a mean of 0 and a standard deviation of 1. The KNN model was trained using different values for the number of neighbours, specifically 3, 5, and 7.

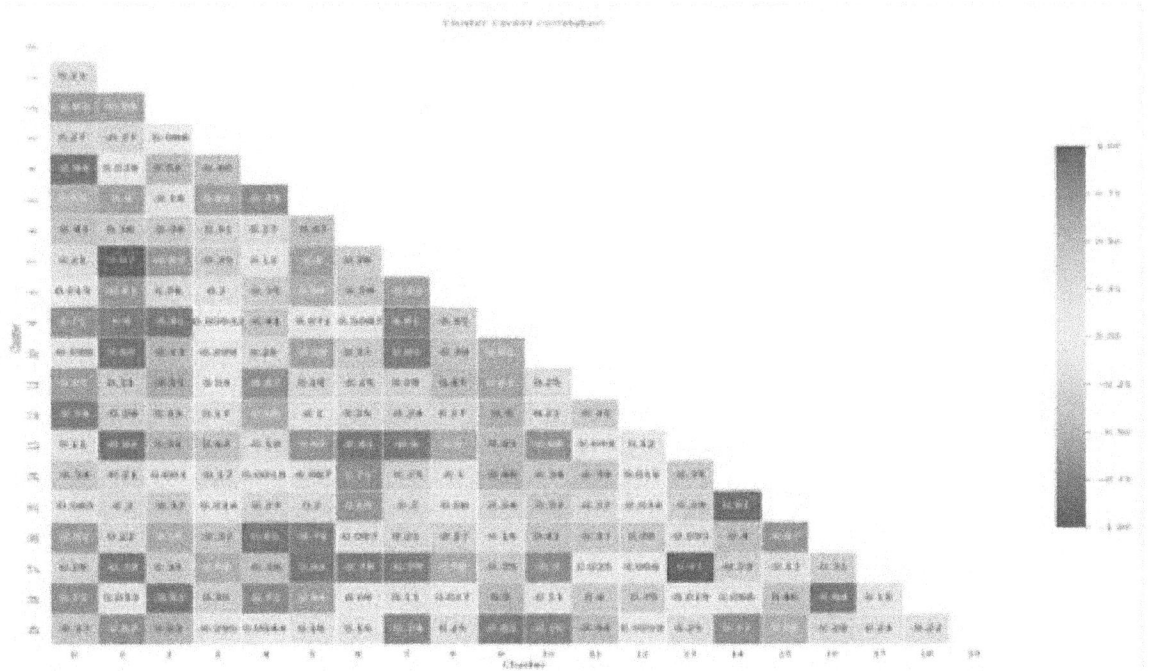

Figure 35.4. Cluster center correlation.

Source: Author.

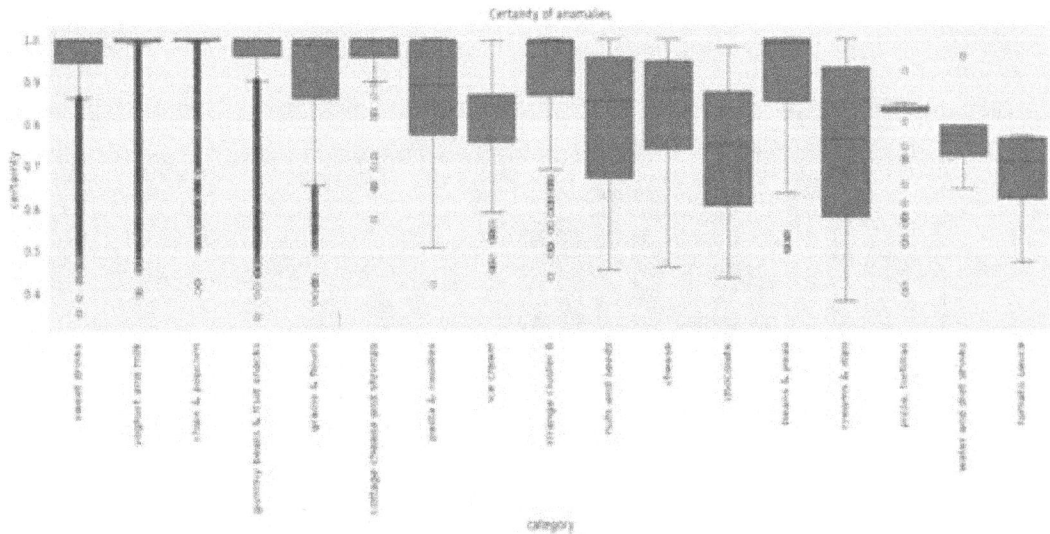

Figure 35.5. Certainty of anomalies.

Source: Author.

4.7. Model performance and classification report

The classification report provides a comprehensive evaluation of the model's performance across all food categories, using key metrics such as precision, recall, and F1-score.

The Figure 35.6 shows an Classification Report, In which food categories such as ice cream, mayonnaise & oils, and water and diet drinks showed excellent performance, with precision, recall, and F1-scores close to or above 0.97. Overall, the macro average for precision (0.90), recall (0.89), and

F1-score (0.89) suggests that the model performs reasonably well across all categories, though slightly skewed towards more frequent categories.

4.8. Evaluation of confusion matrix

The confusion matrix is a critical tool for evaluating the performance of a classification model, as it provides a detailed breakdown of the model's predictions versus the actual values. It shows how many instances were correctly classified (true positives) and how many were misclassified into other

```
Accuracy: 0.9532807726782154

Classification Report:
                                   precision      recall    f1-score     support

              beans & peas           0.97          0.98        0.98        1256
                    cheese           0.96          0.99        0.98        2554
            chips & popcorn          0.88          0.75        0.81         313
                 chocolate           0.91          0.88        0.90        2983
                   cookies           0.00          0.00        0.00           1
  cottage cheese and shrimps         0.97          0.98        0.97         969
              creams & dips          0.94          0.98        0.96        4811
             grains & flours         0.97          0.98        0.97        4423
   gummy bears & fruit snacks        0.92          0.82        0.87        3169
                 ice cream           0.98          1.00        0.99        3511
          mayonnaise & oils          0.97          0.99        0.98        5052
              nuts and seeds         0.94          0.97        0.96        3569
            pasta & noodles          0.96          0.98        0.97        4014
           pizza, tortillas         0.96          0.93        0.94        2908
          strange cluster 6         0.97          0.98        0.98        2196
               sweet drinks          0.95          0.86        0.90        2936
               tomato sauce          0.92          0.95        0.93        3868
      water and diet drinks          0.97          0.99        0.98        4956
           yoghurt and milk          0.96          0.90        0.93        1178

                  accuracy                                     0.95       54667
                 macro avg          0.90          0.89        0.89       54667
              weighted avg          0.95          0.95        0.95       54667
```

Figure 35.6. Classification report.

Source: Author.

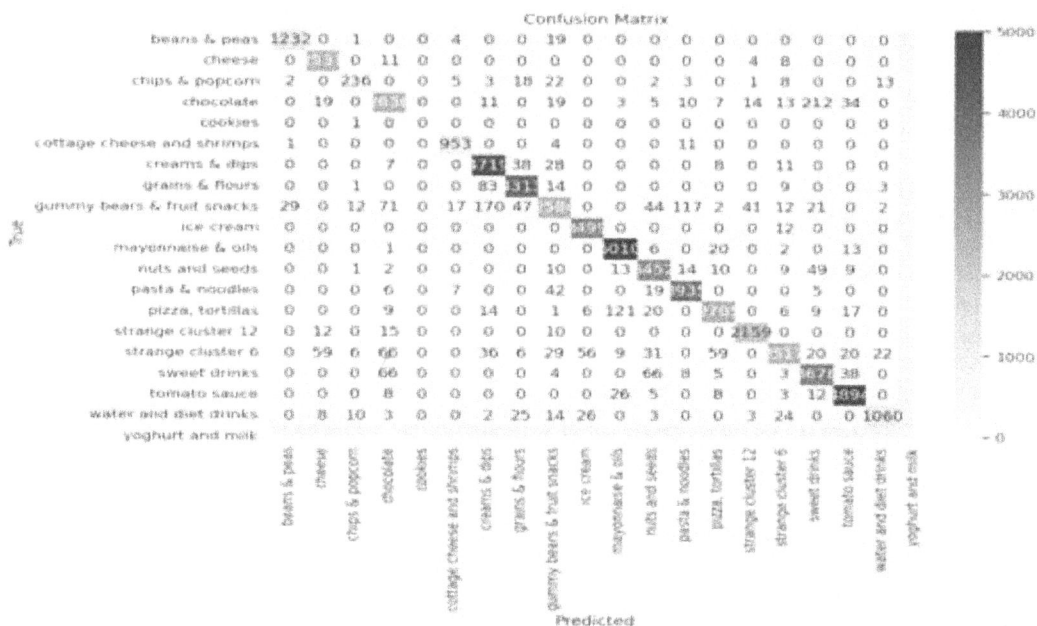

Figure 35.7. Confusion matrix.

Source: Author.

categories (false positives and false negatives). Each row of the matrix represents the true class, while each column represents the predicted class, making it easy to identify where the model made errors.

In this case, the confusion matrix was visualized using a heatmap to facilitate interpretation (Figure 35.7). The diagonal elements of the matrix represent the number of correctly predicted samples for each category (true positives), while the off-diagonal elements represent misclassifications. For example, a large number of correctly predicted instances would appear on the diagonal, while misclassified samples would appear off the diagonal, showing which categories were often confused with one another.

5. Conclusion

The model demonstrated an overall accuracy of 95.33%, demonstrating robust performance in classifying food categories based on their nutritional attributes. The macro average precision of 0.90, recall of 0.89, and F1-score of 0.89 suggested strong performance across all categories, despite slight imbalances in the dataset. The weighted average values (precision: 0.95, recall: 0.95, F1-score: 0.95) indicated that the model was more effective for larger, well-represented categories, which contributed significantly to the overall performance.

References

[1] Velmurugan, A. K., Padmanaban, K., Senthil Kumar, A. M., Azath, H., & Subbiah, M. (2023). Machine learning IoT based framework for analysing heart disease prediction. *AIP Conference Proceedings, 2523*, 1–8.

[2] Devaraj, G. P., Kabilan, R., Muthuraman, U., Gabriel, J. Z., Esther, J. M., & Ravi, R. (2022). Multipurpose Intellectual Home Area Network Using Smart Phone. *2022 Second International Conference on Artificial Intelligence and Smart Energy (ICAIS)*. Coimbatore, India, pp. 1464–1469. doi: 10.1109/ICAIS53314.2022.9742955.

[3] Kabilan, R., Narayanan, L., Venkatesh, M., Vikram Bhaskaran, V., Viswanathan, G. K., & Yogesh Rajan, S. G. (2021). Live Human Detection Robot in Earthquake Conditions. *Recent Trends in Intensive Computing*, 818–823. doi: 10.3233/APC210286.

[4] Ao, S., & Ling, C. X. (2015). Adapting new categories for food recognition with deep representation. *Proc. IEEE Int. Conf. Data Mining Workshop (ICDMW)*, pp. 1196–1203.

[5] Kabilan, R., MallikaPandeeswari, R., Lalitha, N., Kanmanikarthiga, E., Karthica, C., & Sharon, L. M. H. (2022). Soldier Friendly Smart And Intelligent Robot On War Field. *2022 Second International Conference on Artificial Intelligence and Smart Energy (ICAIS)*. Coimbatore, India, pp. 666–671. doi: 10.1109/ICAIS53314.2022.9742909.

[6] Kabilan, R., Kamala Devi, E., Mari Bhuvaneshwari, R., Jothika, S., Gayathiri, R., Mallika Pandeeswari, R. (2022). GPS Localization for Enhancement of Military Fence Unit. *2022 Second International Conference on Artificial Intelligence and Smart Energy (ICAIS)*, pp. 811–816. doi: 10.1109/ICAIS53314.2022.9742959.

[7] Bojia, Q. (2019). *Food Recognition and Nutrition Analysis Using Deep CNNs*. Montreal, QC, Canada: McGill University.

[8] Muthuraman, U., Ravi, R., Devaraj, G. P., Esther, J. M., Kabilan, R., & Gabriel, J. Z. (2022). Embedded Sensor-based Construction Health Warning System for Civil Structures & Advanced Networking Techniques using IoT. *2022 International Conference on Sustainable Computing and Data Communication Systems (ICSCDS)*, Erode, India, pp. 1002–1006. doi: 10.1109/ICSCDS53736.2022.9760793.

[9] Kabilan, R., Ravi, R., Esther, J. M., Muthuraman, U., Gabriel, J. Z., & Devaraj, G. P. (2022). Constructing Effective UVM Testbench By Using DRAM Memory Controllers. *2022 Second International Conference on Artificial Intelligence and Smart Energy (ICAIS)*. Coimbatore, India, pp. 1034–1038. doi: 10.1109/ICAIS53314.2022.9742986.

[10] Esther, J. M., Gabriel, J. Z., Ravi, R., Muthuraman, U., Devaraj, G. P., & Kabilan, R. (2022). Increased Energy Efficiency of MANETs Through DEL-CMAC Protocol on Network. *2022 International Conference on Sustainable Computing and Data Communication Systems (ICSCDS)*. Erode, India, pp. 1122–1126. doi: 10.1109/ICSCDS53736.2022.9760930.

[11] Gabriel, J. Z., Muthuraman, U., Kabilan, R., Devaraj, G. P., Ravi, R., & Esther, J. M. (2022). Waiting Line Conscious Scheduling for OFDMA Networks, using JSFRA Formulation. *2022 International Conference on Sustainable Computing and Data Communication Systems (ICSCDS)*. Erode, India, pp. 754–759. doi: 10.1109/ICSCDS53736.2022.9760949.

[12] Pandeeswari, R. M., Kabilan, R., Januanbumani, T. M., Rejoni, J., Ramya, A., & Jothi, S. J. (2022). Data Backups and Error Finding by Residue Quotient Code for Testing Applications. *2022 International Conference on Sustainable Computing and Data Communication Systems (ICSCDS)*. Erode, India, pp. 637–641. doi: 10.1109/ICSCDS53736.2022.9760940.

[13] Pandeeswari, R. M., Deepthyka, K., Abinaya, M., Deepa, V., Kabilan, R., & Glorintha, J. (2022). Fast Evolutionary Algorithm based Identifying Surgically Distorted Face for Surveillance Application. *2022 International Conference on Sustainable Computing and Data Communication Systems (ICSCDS)*. Erode, India, pp. 516–521. doi: 10.1109/ICSCDS53736.2022.9760978.

[14] Santhuja, P., Reddy, E. G., Choudri, S. R., Muthulekshmi, M., & Balaji, S. (2023, August). Intelligent Personalized Nutrition Guidance System Using IoT and Machine Learning Algorithm. In *2023 Second International Conference on Smart Technologies for Smart Nation (SmartTechCon)* (pp. 250–254). IEEE. doi:10.1109/SmartTechCon57526.2023.10391336.

[15] Elsherbeny, H. A., Gunduz, M., & Ugur, L. O. (2025). A Hybrid Model for Enhancing Risk Management and Operational Performance of AEC (Architectural, Engineering, and Construction) Consultants: An Integrated Partial Least Squares–Artificial Neural Network (PLS–ANN) Approach. *Sustainability, 17*(4), 1467.

[16] Wyawahare, M., Rane, M., Patil, V., Telkhade, Y., Tele, R., & Walsepatil, A. (2024, July). Nutri Scan on Desk: A Food Sensitivity Testing System. In *2024 5th International Conference on Image Processing and Capsule Networks (ICIPCN)* (pp. 198–203). IEEE. doi:10.1109/ICIPCN63822.2024.00040.

36 Enhanced lung cancer prediction using CNN

Sounthariyaa N.[1,a] and Agnes Joshy S.[2,b]

[1]PG Scholar, Department of Information Technology, Francis Xavier Engineering College, Tirunelveli, India
[2]*Assistant Professor, Department of Information Technology,* Francis Xavier Engineering College, Tirunelveli, India

Abstract: Histopathological analysis is essential in diagnosing diseases by examining tissue samples for structural abnormalities and disease markers. This study focuses on the accurate classification of lung cancer, specifically differentiating between lung adenocarcinoma and benign lung tissue, using deep learning techniques. A convolutional neural network (CNN) model was developed in Keras to process grayscale, resized histopathological images sourced from a curated dataset. By designing an architecture with multiple Conv2D, MaxPooling, Dropout, and BatchNorm layers, the model achieved a classification accuracy exceeding 99%. The network's design captures complex tissue features while avoiding overfitting, thanks to careful training and validation on an 80/20 split dataset. This approach demonstrates the potential of automated histopathological image analysis in lung cancer detection, supporting pathologists in clinical diagnosis with high precision and efficiency.

Keywords: Histopathology, lung disease classification, deep learning, convolutional neural networks, binary classification, image processing

1. Introduction

Lung cancer remains one of the leading causes of cancer-related deaths worldwide, with millions of new cases diagnosed annually. Early identification of lung cancer is essential for successful treatment and higher survival rates, even with advances in medical technology [11]. Traditional diagnostic approaches often rely on imaging methods like CT scans or histopathological analysis of biopsy samples. Among these, histopathological examination provides valuable insight by enabling pathologists to identify abnormal cellular structures directly.

However, this manual analysis is labour-intensive, subject to human error, and can be particularly challenging in resource-limited settings where trained specialists are scarce.

In recent years, artificial intelligence (AI) has become a promising tool for enhancing diagnostic accuracy in medical image analysis. Deep learning in particular, as well as machine learning, provides automated methods that can significantly improve diagnostic efficiency by detecting complex patterns within image data that are often imperceptible to the human eye. In computer vision, convolutional neural networks (CNNs) have become a potent tool that perform very well in tasks including segmentation, object identification, and picture categorization. This study harnesses CNNs in Keras to classify histopathological images of lung tissue into two categories: adenocarcinoma and benign tissue. By automating the detection process, this project aims to develop a tool that aids pathologists in diagnosing lung cancer, potentially facilitating faster decision-making and reducing diagnostic variability [3–6].

1.1. Problem statement

Improving patient outcomes requires early diagnosis of lung cancer, however proper categorization is difficult due to the fine features in histopathological pictures. Unlike conventional imaging techniques, histopathological images offer cellular-level detail, which can provide early clues about malignancies. However, interpreting these images is complex due to the presence of fine-grained features and high intra-class variability among benign and malignant tissues [16]. The problem is compounded by the large volume of data that pathologists need to examine, leading to a bottleneck in diagnostic workflows. Given these challenges, this project seeks to leverage CNNs to classify lung cancer tissue accurately and efficiently.

1.2. Objectives of the study

The main goal of this study is to create a deep learning model in Keras that can correctly categorize tissue samples from lung cancer [12]. The model is designed with specific goals in mind like achieving accuracy above 98% on validation data, ensuring reliable performance in distinguishing adenocarcinoma from benign tissue and building a CNN model with an optimal balance of convolutional, dropout, and pooling layers to prevent overfitting while maintaining high precision.

[a]sounthariyaa.pg23.it@francisxavier.ac.in, [b]agnesjoshy@francisxavier.ac.in

DOI: 10.1201/9781003724988-36

1.3. Scope of the study

This study focuses on two primary classes within lung tissue samples: lung adenocarcinoma, a common subtype of lung cancer, and benign tissue [14]. By limiting the scope to these categories, the model can focus on distinguishing critical pathological features that set malignant cells apart from non-malignant cells. While the study emphasizes binary classification, the methods developed here could be extended to multi-class classification in future work, incorporating additional lung cancer subtypes. Additionally, the research only utilizes the Keras library for model implementation and TensorFlow for backend support, given its robustness in handling large image datasets and ease of integration with deep learning frameworks [2].

1.4. Importance of automated histopathological analysis in lung cancer detection

Manual histopathological analysis is time-intensive and highly dependent on pathologists' expertise. The rapid advancements in digital pathology have enabled the digitization of histopathological slides, opening up the possibility of using computer vision for automated analysis. Automated systems powered by CNNs offer the advantage of cohsistently high accuracy by capturing subtle image patterns and features through deep learning algorithms. For lung cancer, where early diagnosis can be life-saving, an automated solution could accelerate diagnostics, reduce diagnostic discrepancies, and support pathologists by providing a second opinion [7].

2. Literature Survey

Deep learning algorithms have significantly improved lung cancer detection and classification in recent studies. Aharonu and Ramasamy [1] introduced a multi-model deep learning framework designed to predict lung cancer subtype survival rates using histopathology imagery. Their model combines multiple deep learning algorithms, focusing on identifying regions of interest within images to predict survival rates [13]. However, this approach is complex, requiring substantial computational power, and is geared more towards survival prediction than real-time diagnosis. In contrast, our model simplifies the process by focusing on a binary classification of lung adenocarcinoma and benign tissue, achieving high accuracy in a practical and efficient manner, suitable for immediate diagnostic applications.

Mohamed and Ezugwu [17] enhanced lung cancer classification by integrating deep learning with multi-omics data, analyzing RNA, DNA, and gene expression. This comprehensive approach allows for a more detailed understanding of lung cancer characteristics at the genetic level. However, their model's reliance on multi-omics data poses challenges, as these datasets are not always readily available and require extensive preprocessing. In comparison,

our model uses readily accessible histopathological images, making it a more feasible tool for widespread clinical application [15].

Lung-RetinaNet, a model based on the RetinaNet architecture, was proposed by Mahum and Al-Salman [18] with the express purpose of identifying lung cancers in CT images using a context module and multi-scale feature fusion. While their model demonstrates high accuracy in tumour detection, it primarily targets tumour localization and is optimized for CT scan data rather than histopathological images. Our model addresses this gap by focusing on histopathological image data, facilitating the classification of lung adenocarcinoma versus benign tissue to enhance diagnostic accuracy in histopathology [1].

3. Methodology

3.1. Overview

This chapter describes the process used to create a deep learning model that can correctly identify lung histopathology pictures as either benign (non-cancerous) or adenocarcinoma (cancerous) tissue. The methodology is divided into several key components, including data preparation, model design, training, evaluation, and deployment [8]. The entire workflow was implemented in Keras, chosen for its intuitive API and seamless integration with TensorFlow for efficient model training and optimization.

3.2. Data collection and dataset description

The dataset used in this project is the Lung Cancer Histopathological Images Dataset, sourced from Kaggle, which includes annotated images of lung tissue. Each image is labeled as either lung adenocarcinoma (Class 1) or benign lung tissue (Class 0), providing a foundation for binary classification tasks. The dataset includes high-resolution RGB images, which allows the model to capture fine-grained details critical to differentiating malignant from benign cells [9].

The dataset contains a balanced mix of adenocarcinoma and benign samples, which mitigates class imbalance issuesThe dataset is divided into a training set, which consists of 80% of the photographs, and a validation set, which consists of 20% of the images, to guarantee consistency. All images are resized to 128x128 pixels to standardize input dimensions, reduce computational requirements, and optimize processing speed, while retaining essential visual information [10].

3.3. Data preprocessing

Effective preprocessing is essential for maximizing model performance, particularly when working with high-resolution medical images. The preprocessing pipeline includes several steps, each aimed at enhancing model learning efficiency. Each image is resized to 128×128 pixels. Images are then normalized by rescaling pixel values to the range [0, 1] (using a scale factor of 1/255), which accelerates model convergence by ensuring that all input features have similar ranges. Although the original images are in RGB, they are converted to grayscale to focus on structural details rather than colour differences, as the cellular patterns in lung tissue are more relevant than colour variations. The training dataset is subjected to a number of data augmentation approaches in order to strengthen the model's resilience and avoid overfitting, including: Randomly rotating images by a range of ±15 degrees to simulate various orientations of tissue slices. Reversing images along axes to capture patterns in different orientations. Applying slight zoom effects to emulate different magnifications.

3.4. Model architecture

A convolutional neural network (CNN) was selected as the architecture for this research since CNNs are excellent at picture classification problems because they can learn the spatial hierarchies of information. Eight convolutional layers, four max-pooling layers, four dropout layers, and four batch normalization layers make up the architecture. Dense layers come next, which allow the model to correctly identify pictures.

Input Layer and Rescaling: The input layer includes an image rescaling layer to normalize the pixel values.

Convolutional Layers: Each Conv2D layer uses a 3 × 3 filter size with ReLU activation, which helps detect intricate features in the lung tissue samples, such as irregular cellular shapes, textures, and densities.

Max-Pooling Layers: After every two Conv2D layers, a max-pooling layer (2 × 2 pool size) is added to reduce dimensionality, retaining the essential features and reducing computation requirements.

Batch Normalization: Each max-pooling layer is followed by a batch normalization layer to normalize the inputs to the next layer, improving stability and accelerating convergence.

Dropout Layers: A dropout rate of 40% is used between convolutional blocks to prevent overfitting, enabling the model to generalize well to unseen data.

Flatten Layer: The 2D matrix is converted into a 1D vector by a flatten layer after the last max-pooling layer, and then it is fed into the dense layers.

3.5. Model training

The model is trained on an 80/20 training-validation split using Keras's fit method. Training is conducted over three epochs, as further training resulted in overfitting. Additional hyperparameters for training include:

Batch Size: A batch size of 32 is selected for efficient GPU utilization and stable gradient updates.

Early Stopping: Model Checkpoint is employed to save the model with the best validation loss, ensuring optimal performance by preventing overfitting.

Learning Rate Scheduling: A constant learning rate is used, as initial experimentation with dynamic rates did not yield significant improvements.

4. Experimental Evaluation

4.1. Overview of model testing and image prediction

The primary objective of testing the trained model is to evaluate its ability to generalize on unseen histopathological images of lung tissue. This phase involves selecting images not included in the training or validation sets and processing them using a predefined pipeline. Each image is resized to the model's input requirements (128 × 128 pixels), converted to grayscale, and normalized to scale pixel values between 0 and 1. The model then predicts the likelihood of each image belonging to either Class 0 (Lung benign tissue) or Class 1 (Lung adenocarcinoma).

4.2. Evaluation metrics: precision, recall, and F1-score

The accuracy of a model alone does not fully capture its performance, particularly for medical image classification, where distinguishing true positives (correct identification of adenocarcinoma) from false positives and negatives is essential. Precision, recall, F1-score, macro average, and weighted average metrics – all of which provide a multifaceted perspective of performance – were used to assess the model for a comprehensive study. The percentage of real positive classifications among all cases that were expected to be positive is known as precision. In this instance, it demonstrates how well the algorithm can detect lung adenocarcinoma without misclassifying benign tissue as malignant. In this project, recall refers to the model's capacity to identify all genuine cases of adenocarcinoma by detecting all positive occurrences in the dataset. The F1-score is a balanced statistic that combines accuracy and recall into one. It is particularly helpful when there are imbalanced classes, where one class may have more instances than the other. The calculated macro and weighted averages offer insight into the model's performance across both classes without and with weighting by support, respectively.

4.3. Analyzing model accuracy and loss over training Epochs

The training process involved monitoring model accuracy and loss over three epochs. While a limited number of epochs were used to avoid overfitting, this approach showed rapid convergence and yielded high accuracy within a short training time. Monitoring accuracy over epochs provides insight into how well the model learns the features associated with each class. The loss metric, on the other hand, reveals the model's error reduction throughout training. Lower loss values indicate that the model's predictions are close to the actual class labels. Model Accuracy increased steadily across epochs, showing an upward trend that highlights effective learning and validation performance. Model Loss decreased as training progressed, indicating that the model's predictions became more accurate with each epoch, and lower validation loss suggests that overfitting was minimized.

The Figure 36.1 illustrates how the model's accuracy improved with each epoch, highlighting the convergence of the training process.

The Figure 36.2 displays the reduction in model loss across epochs, illustrating the model's progressive improvement and error minimization.

4.4. *Validation results*

The trained model achieved over 96% accuracy on the validation set, with high precision and recall rates. Results demonstrated the model's robustness, as shown in Table 36.1, where accuracy metrics across various image samples indicate consistent performance across classes.

4.5. *Confusion matrix and support for each class*

The confusion matrix as mention in Figure 36.3 is essential for understanding the model's classifications and identifying any misclassifications between the two classes. By recording the quantity of true positives, false positives, true negatives, and false negatives, this matrix allows us to examine certain categorization faults. In order to provide context for the metrics that are computed, the support values show the actual instances of each class in the test dataset.

Low FP and FN values are desired in medical applications to avoid misdiagnosing healthy tissue as malignant or overlooking malignant cases. The confusion matrix for this model shows strong performance, with minimal misclassifications, indicating a high level of reliability.

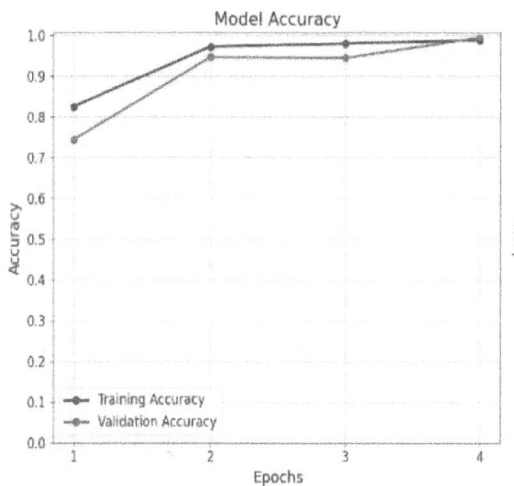

Figure 36.1. Model accuracy.

Source: Author.

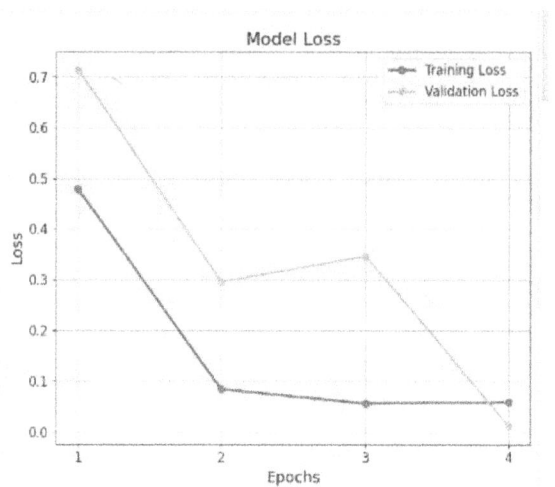

Figure 36.2. Model loss.

Source: Author.

Table 36.1. Model robustness

Metric	Class 0 (Benign)	Class 1 (Adenocarcinoma)
Precision	1.00	1.00
Recall	1.00	1.00
F1-Score	1.00	1.00

Source: Author.

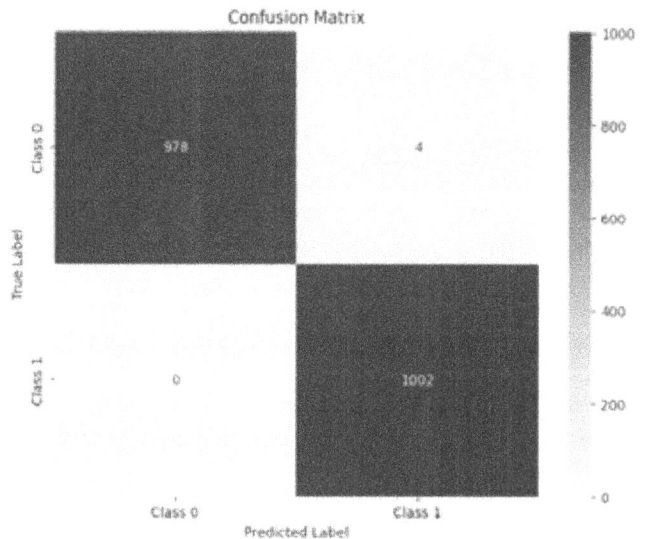

Figure 36.3. Confusion matrix.

Source: Author.

4.6. *Code for model prediction on individual images*

An additional test was conducted using individual histopathological images to simulate real-world conditions where the model is deployed for diagnostic support. A custom Python function preprocesses each image, ensuring consistency with training parameters by resizing it to 128 × 128 pixels and normalizing pixel values. The model then predicts the probability of each image belonging to Class 0 (benign) or Class 1 (adenocarcinoma).

5. Conclusion

Using a convolutional neural network (CNN) in Keras, the study effectively created a deep learning model to correctly categorize lung tissue histological pictures as either benign or cancer. Through careful architecture design and extensive preprocessing, including grayscale conversion and data augmentation, the model achieved over 99% accuracy, underscoring its robustness and generalizability. The model's performance was validated with precision, recall, and F1-scores close to optimal, demonstrating its potential utility in clinical settings. By automating the classification of lung tissue samples, this approach holds promise for supporting pathologists in early lung cancer diagnosis, ultimately contributing to timely patient care and reducing diagnostic inconsistencies. Future work could extend this model to include more lung cancer subtypes, broadening its application scope in digital pathology and enhancing its clinical value.

References

[1] Aharonu, M., & Ramasamy, L. (2024). A multi-model deep learning framework and algorithms for survival rate prediction of lung cancer subtypes with region of interest using histopathology imagery. *IEEE Access*, 12, 155309–155329. doi: 10.1109/ACCESS.2024.3484495.

[2] Kabilan, R., MallikaPandeeswari, R., Lalitha, N., Kanmanikarthiga, E., Karthica, C., & Sharon, L. M. H. (2022). Soldier Friendly Smart And Intelligent Robot On War Field. *2022 Second International Conference on Artificial Intelligence and Smart Energy (ICAIS)*. Coimbatore, India, pp. 666–671. doi: 10.1109/ICAIS53314.2022.9742909.

[3] Kabilan, R., Kamala Devi, E., Mari Bhuvaneshwari, R., Jothika, S., Gayathiri, R., Mallika Pandeeswari, R. (2022). GPS Localization for Enhancement of Military Fence Unit. *2022 Second International Conference on Artificial Intelligence and Smart Energy (ICAIS)*, pp. 811–816. doi: 10.1109/ICAIS53314.2022.9742959.

[4] Cao, W., Wu, R., Cao, G., & He, Z. (2020). A comprehensive review of computer-aided diagnosis of pulmonary nodules based on computed tomography scans. *IEEE Access*, 8, 154007–154023.

[5] Devaraj, G. P., Kabilan, R., Muthuraman, U., Gabriel, J. Z., Esther, J. M., & Ravi, R. (2022). Multipurpose Intellectual Home Area Network Using Smart Phone. *2022 Second International Conference on Artificial Intelligence and Smart Energy (ICAIS)*. Coimbatore, India, pp. 1464–1469. doi: 10.1109/ICAIS53314.2022.9742955.

[6] Kabilan, R., Narayanan, L., Venkatesh, M., Vikram Bhaskaran, V., Viswanathan, G. K., Yogesh Rajan, S. G. (2022). Live Human Detection Robot in Earthquake Conditions. *Recent Trends in Intensive Computing*, 818–823. doi: 10.3233/APC210286.

[7] Chen, H., Dou, Q., Wang, X., Qin, J., Cheng, J. C. Y., & Heng, P.-A. (2016). 3D fully convolutional networks for intervertebral disc localization and segmentation. *Proceedings of MIAR*, 375–382.

[8] Davies, L., Milner, D. A., Shulman, L. N., Kyokunda, L., Bedada, A., & Vuylsteke, P. (2023). Analysis of cancer research projects in sub-Saharan Africa: A quantitative perspective on unmet needs and opportunities. *JCO Global Oncology*, 9.

[9] Dou, Q., Chen, H., Yu, L., Qin, J., & Heng, P.-A. (2017). Multilevel contextual 3-D CNNs for false positive reduction in pulmonary nodule detection. *IEEE Transactions on Biomedical Engineering*, 64(7), 1558–1567.

[10] Pandeeswari, R. M., Deepthyka, K., Abinaya, M., Deepa, V., Kabilan, R., & Glorintha, J. (2022). Fast Evolutionary Algorithm based Identifying Surgically Distorted Face for Surveillance Application. *2022 International Conference on Sustainable Computing and Data Communication Systems (ICSCDS)*. Erode, India, pp. 516–521. doi: 10.1109/ICSCDS53736.2022.9760978.

[11] Zhao, X., Qi, S., Zhang, B., Ma, H., Qian, W., Yao, Y., et al. (2019). Deep CNN models for pulmonary nodule classification: Model modification model integration and transfer learning. *Journal of X-Ray Science and Technology*, 27(4), 615–629.

[12] Muthuraman, U., Ravi, R., Devaraj, G. P., Esther, J. M., Kabilan, R., & Gabriel, J. Z. (2022). Embedded Sensor-based Construction Health Warning System for Civil Structures & Advanced Networking Techniques using IoT. *2022 International Conference on Sustainable Computing and Data Communication Systems (ICSCDS)*. Erode, India, pp. 1002–1006. doi: 10.1109/ICSCDS53736.2022.9760793.

[13] Kabilan, R., Ravi, R., Esther, J. M., Muthuraman, U., Gabriel, J. Z., & Devaraj, G. P. (2022). Constructing Effective UVM Testbench By Using DRAM Memory Controllers. *2022 Second International Conference on Artificial Intelligence and Smart Energy (ICAIS)*. Coimbatore, India, pp. 1034–1038. doi: 10.1109/ICAIS53314.2022.9742986.

[14] Esther, J. M., Gabriel, J. Z., Ravi, R., Muthuraman, U., Devaraj, G. P., & Kabilan, R. (2022). Increased Energy Efficiency of MANETs Through DEL-CMAC Protocol on Network. *2022 International Conference on Sustainable Computing and Data Communication Systems (ICSCDS)*. Erode, India, pp. 1122–1126. doi: 10.1109/ICSCDS53736.2022.9760930.

[15] Gabriel, J. Z., Muthuraman, U., Kabilan, R., Devaraj, G. P., Ravi, R., & Esther, J. M. (2022). Waiting Line Conscious Scheduling for OFDMA Networks, using JSFRA Formulation. *2022 International Conference on Sustainable Computing and Data Communication Systems (ICSCDS)*. Erode, India, pp. 754–759. doi: 10.1109/ICSCDS53736.2022.9760949.

[16] Pandeeswari, R. M., Kabilan, R., Januanbumani, T. M., Rejoni, J., Ramya, A., & Jothi, S. J. (2022). Data Backups and Error Finding by Residue Quotient Code for Testing Applications. *2022 International Conference on Sustainable Computing and Data Communication Systems (ICSCDS)*. Erode, India, pp. 637–641. doi: 10.1109/ICSCDS53736.2022.9760940.

[17] Mohamed, T. I., & Ezugwu, A. E. S. (2024). Enhancing lung cancer classification and prediction with deep learning and multi-omics data. *IEEE Access*, 12, 59880–59892. doi:10.1109/ACCESS.2024.3394030.

[18] Mahum, R., & Al-Salman, A. S. (2023). Lung-RetinaNet: Lung cancer detection using a RetinaNet with multi-scale feature fusion and context module. *IEEE Access*, 11, 53850–53861. doi:10.1109/ACCESS.2023.3281259.

37 Gestation stage classification using deep learning based caps GoogleNet

Sheela Y.[1,a] and Rajee M. V.[2,b]

[1]Scholar/Assistant Professor, Department of CSE, Jayaraj Annapackiam CSI College of Engineering, Nazareth, Thoothukudi, India

[2]Assistant Professor, Department of ECE, Francis Xavier Engineering College, Vannarpettai, Tirunelevli, India

Abstract: Maternal mortality is a major global public health concern and refers to the preventable deaths occurring annually due to pregnancy and childbirth. In this research, a novel CG-Net has been proposedfor gestation stage classification from ultrasound images using deep learning (DL) techniques. Initially, the input ultrasound (US) images arepre-processed using Median Adaptive Thresholding (MAT) filter to enhance image quality and reduce noise. Feature extraction is performed using a Caps GoogleNet model, which captures essential fetal development characteristics such as fetal size, organ growth, and amniotic fluid levels. The extracted features are then fed into a fully connected layer (FCL) for classification into first, second, or third trimester stages. This approach aims to provide an accurate and efficient system for gestation stage assessment, aiding clinicians in prenatal care and fetal health monitoring. The proposed CG-Net model achieves an overall accuracy of 4.2%, 5.08%, and 11.22% better than BMI, SVM and CNN respectively.

Keywords: Caps GoogleNet, deep learning, fully connected layer, gestation stage classification

1. Introduction

Prenatal risk factors can be identified and managed early to reduce adverse outcomes and complications in mother and child [1]. Risk management can be greatly aided by clinical decision support systems (CDSSs), especially in light of the present burden of medical professionals [2, 3]. The creation of a solid library of superior decision support models with clinical interpretability and a foundation in verified medical data is necessary for CDSS effectiveness [4]. Given that these models' classification and prognosis accuracy is below 82%, it is considered insufficient. This is primarily because the lack of organized patient data makes it difficult to create mathematical models for pregnancy development that are sufficiently precise [5]. Artificial neural networks have demonstrated a high degree of accuracy in due date prediction, and the application of machine learning approaches has produced promising outcomes in terms of effective due date prediction based on ultrasound data [6]. Therefore, these models can still be improved despite the expertise obtained in forecasting maternal dangers and developing decision-making models. Further development of such models could reduce mortality rates and complications during pregnancy and delivery [7].

In 2023 Amitai, T., et al. [8] developed a machine learning classifier that predicts the chance of a miscarriage in the first trimester in cleavage-stage embryos by using time-lapse photos of preimplantation development. This feature subset was used to train the XGBoost and random forest models using a 100-fold Monte-Carlo cross validation method. An AUC of 0.68 to 0.69 was used to forecast pregnancy.

In 2023 Ozer, G., et al. [9] suggested a first-trimester pregnancy loss rates were evaluated based on various factors. These included the female's age, the father's age, and the body mass index (BMI). Endometrial preparation during an artificial cycle increased the rate of first-trimester pregnancy loss compared to a natural cycle (OR=2.101, 95%CI=1.630–2.723, P=0.000).

In 2022 Yasrab, R., et al. [10] analyzed a huge quantity of data from full-length US video scans to look into the clinical process throughout the first trimester scan. First-trimester ultrasound film from a typical prenatal screening clinic is being used for the first time to simulate clinical workflow. Additionally, 44% of operators were found to be not using the 3D/4D US transducer.

In 2022 Xiong, Y., et al. [11] created a risk prediction model based on indicators of coagulation, liver, and kidney function as well as possible predictors of gestational diabetes mellitus (GDM) for the first 19 weeks of pregnancy. Of the 490 pregnant women in this case-control research, 215 had GDM and 275 were controls. In 2022 Zhang, L., et al. [12] created a deep learning model based on ultrasound images for fetal trisomy 21 screening. This diagnostic study made use of all available case and control data from two Chinese hospitals that were enrolled between January 2009 and September 2020.

In 2020 Liu, L., et al. [13] machine learning methods for creating an embryonic development prediction model based

[a]sheelajabez@gmail.com, [b]rajee@francisxavier.ac.in

DOI: 10.1201/9781003724988-37

on historical data. Normal embryo samples' fetal heart rates (FHR) and the number of days after embryo transfer (ETD) were contrasted. Based on this data, a regression model was developed to illustrate the relationship between ETD and FHR during normal development. Residual analysis also shed light on the importance of FHR in predicting pregnancy outcomes.

In 2021 Zhang, H.G., et al. [14] employing machine learning methods for prenatal DS screening modeling and analysis, including SVM, classification and regression trees, and AdaBoost. We developed and built clever algorithms using adaptive synthetic sampling over-sampling and synthetic minority over-sampling method (SMOTE)-Tomek to preprocess the prenatal screening dataset. The main contributions of the research are as follows:

In this research, a novel CG-Net has been proposed for gestation stage classification from ultrasound images using DL techniques.

- Initially, the input US images are denoized using MAT filter to enhance image quality and reduce noise.
- Feature extraction is performed using a Caps GoogleNet model, which captures essential fetal development characteristics such as fetal size, organ growth, and amniotic fluid levels.
- The extracted features are then fed into a FCL for classification into first, second, or third trimester stages.

- The structure of the paper is organized as follows, the proposed CG-Net is discussed in Section 2, the experimental findings and discussion that followed are presented in Section 3, and the conclusion and future work are discussed in Section 4.

2. Proposed Methodology

In this research, a novel CG-Net has been proposedfor gestation stage classification from US images using DL techniques. Initially, the input US images aredenoized using MAT filter to enhance image quality and reduce noise. Feature extraction is performed using a Caps GoogleNet model, which captures essential fetal development characteristics such as fetal size, organ growth, and amniotic fluid levels. This approach aims to provide an accurate and efficient system for gestation stage assessment, aiding clinicians in prenatal care and fetal health monitoring (Figure 37.1).

2.1. Dataset description

US image is a type of imaging that contains B-Mode ultrasound image database [15]. At frequencies of 10–14 MHz, two linear array transducers were selected to obtain images with a resolution of approximately 390 pixels by 330 pixels. In most pregnant women, US (also called sonograms) are offered as a prenatal test.

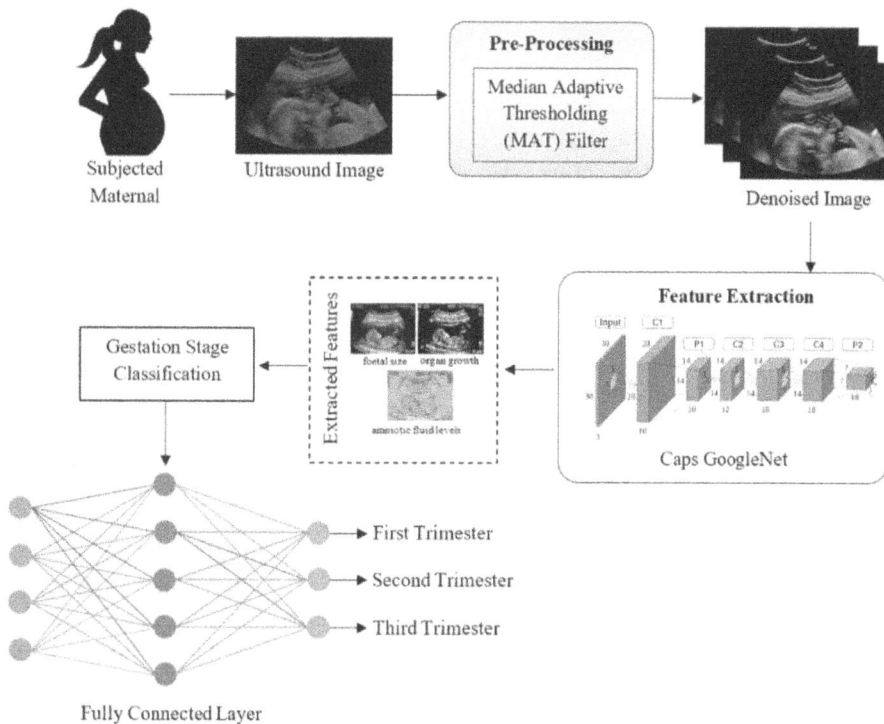

Figure 37.1. The overall process of the proposed methodology.

Source: Author.

2.2. Median adaptive thresholding filter

Preprocessing ultrasound fetus images with the Median Adaptive Thresholding (MAT) filter improves image quality and reduces noise. By combining adaptive thresholding and median filtering, this method effectively decreases the speckle noise present in ultrasound images while maintaining crucial structural information. The median filter smoothes the image by substituting the median of each pixel's surrounding area for its intensity, and adaptive thresholding dynamically modifies the threshold value according to local image properties. Better image contrast is ensured by this preprocessing phase, assisting with the precise extraction of fetal features for the classification of gestational stages.

2.3. Caps GoogleNet

The Caps GoogleNet model is an advanced DL architecture that improves feature extraction for fetal ultrasound pictures by fusing Capsule Networks (CapsNet) with the advantages of GoogleNet's inception modules. While CapsNet uses capsule layers to maintain spatial hierarchies and interactions between features, GoogleNet's inception modules effectively capture multi-scale spatial characteristics. By preserving spatial integrity and minimizing information loss, this hybrid technique guarantees the robust extraction of crucial fetal development variables, including fetal size, organ growth, and amniotic fluid levels. The Caps GoogleNet model is very effective at classifying gestational stages because it captures both local and global features, which increases classification accuracy.

2.4. Fully connected layer

The extracted features are then fed into a FCL for classification into first, second, or third trimester stages. The FCL in the neural network serves as the final classification stage, where extracted features from the Caps GoogleNet model are mapped to specific gestation stages. In order to learn intricate correlations between features, every neuron in the FCL is linked to every other neuron in the layer above. The classification performance is maximized by adjusting the weighted connections during training. The FCL processes the extracted fetal development features, such as fetal size, organ growth, and amniotic fluid levels, and assigns probabilities to each trimester category. Using activation functions like softmax, the model outputs the most likely gestation stage, ensuring accurate and reliable classification.

3. Experimental Analysis

The experimental setup of this work has been implemented by using MATLAB 2019b, with the system requirements being i7 processor and 8GB RAM.

Figure 37.2 shows epochs on the x and y axes, along with a comparison of testing and training accuracy. Figure 37.3

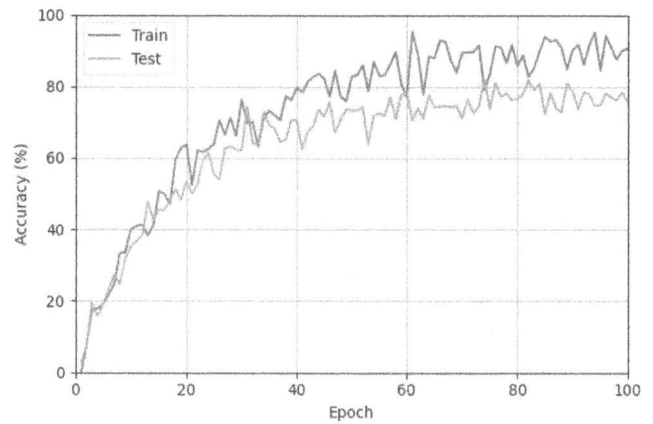

Figure 37.2. Accuracy curve of the proposed CG-Net model.
Source: Author.

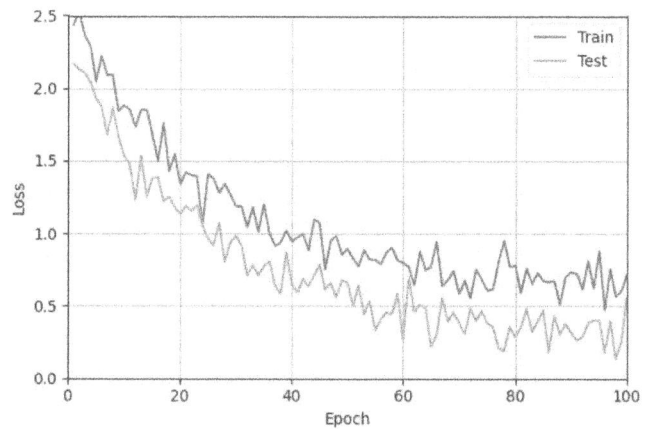

Figure 37.3. Loss curve of the proposed CG-Net model.
Source: Author.

Table 37.1. Comparison of existing with the proposed CG-Net models

Authors	Techniques	Accuracy	Precision	Recall
Ozer, G., et al. [9]	BMI	95%	91.74%	89.37%
Xiong, Y., et al. [11]	SVM	94.2%	93.85%	91.20%
Zhang, L., et al. [12]	CNN	89%	94.92%	93.26%
Proposed	**CG-Net**	**98.99%**	**97.33%**	**95.84%**

Source: Author.

indicates a loss curve plotted against epochs, which shows that the loss decreases with rising epochs.

Table 37.1 shows comparison between the existing and proposed models. From the above comparison, the proposed CG-Net model yields high accuracy than the existing technique. The evaluation metrics include accuracy, precision, and recall. CG-Net outperforms all existing techniques in accuracy of 98.99%, precision of 97.33%, and recall of 95.84%. The proposed CG-Net model-based gestation stage classification model achieves an overall accuracy of 4.2%, 5.08%, and 11.22% better than BMI, SVM and CNN respectively.

4. Conclusion

In this research, a novel CG-Net has been proposed for gestation stage classification from ultrasound images using deep learning techniques. A MAT filter is used to enhance image quality and reduce noise in the input ultrasound images. The Caps GoogleNet model is used to extract fetal development characteristics such as fetal size, organ growth, and amniotic fluid levels. The extracted features are then fed into a FCL for classification into first, second, or third trimesters. The proposed CG-Net model achieves an overall accuracy of 4.2%, 5.08%, and 11.22% better than BMI, SVM and CNN respectively. Future research will concentrate on improving feature extraction by including attention mechanisms into the CG-Net model. The model's generalization will also be improved by using a bigger and more varied ultrasound dataset. For real-world deployment, clinical validation and real-time implementation will be investigated.

Acknowledgement

We sincerely thank our family, friends, and colleagues for their support and cooperation during the research.

References

[1] Asmanidar, A., & Emilda, E. (2024). Optimizing maternal healthcare: Holistic strategies for early detection and management of preeclampsia. *Science Midwifery*, *12*(1), 158–167.

[2] Ippolito, A., Barberà-Mariné, M. G., Zollo, G., & Cannavacciuolo, L. (2024). How organisational factors and clinical decision support system affect nurses' knowledge for decisions in triage. *Knowledge Management Research & Practice*, 1–14.

[3] Nithya, A., Appathurai, A., Venkatadri, N., & Ramji, D. R. (2019). Anna Palagan C Kidney disease detection and segmentation using artificial neural network and multi-kernel k-means clustering for ultrasound images.

[4] Hak, F. A. (2024). *Effective clinical decision support systems by means of open data, intelligence and interoperability* (Doctoral dissertation, Universidade do Minho (Portugal)).

[5] Tharani, R., & Jasphin, C. (2024). Gastric cancer detection via deep learning in image processing. *International Journal of System Design and Computing*, *2*(01), 07–13.

[6] Shifa, H. A., Mojumdar, M. U., Rahman, M. M., Chakraborty, N. R., & Gupta, V. (2024, February). Machine learning models for maternal health risk prediction based on clinical data. In *2024 11th International Conference on Computing for Sustainable Global Development (INDIACom)* (pp. 1312–1318). IEEE.

[7] Margret, I. N., Rajakumar, K., Arulalan, K. V., & Manikandan, S. (2024). Machine learning-based Box models for pregnancy care and maternal mortality reduction: a Literature Survey. *IEEE Access*.

[8] Amitai, T., Kan-Tor, Y., Or, Y., Shoham, Z., Shofaro, Y., Richter, D., Har-Vardi, I., Ben-Meir, A., Srebnik, N., & Buxboim, A. (2023). Embryo classification beyond pregnancy: early prediction of first trimester miscarriage using machine learning. *Journal of Assisted Reproduction and Genetics*, *40*(2), 309–322.

[9] Ozer, G., Akca, A., Yuksel, B., Duzguner, I., Pehlivanli, A. C., Kahraman, S. (2023). Prediction of risk factors for first trimester pregnancy loss in frozen-thawed good-quality embryo transfer cycles using machine learning algorithms. *Journal of Assisted Reproduction and Genetics*, *40*(2), 279–288.

[10] Yasrab, R., Fu, Z., Zhao, H., Lee, L. H., Sharma, H., Drukker, L., Papageorgiou, A. T., & Noble, J. A. (2022). A machine learning method for automated description and workflow analysis of first trimester ultrasound scans. *IEEE Transactions on Medical Imaging*, *42*(5), 1301–1313.

[11] Xiong, Y., Lin, L., Chen, Y., Salerno, S., Li, Y., Zeng, X., & Li, H. (2022). Prediction of gestational diabetes mellitus in the first 19 weeks of pregnancy using machine learning techniques. *The Journal of Maternal-Fetal & Neonatal Medicine*, *35*(13), 2457–2463.

[12] Zhang, L., Dong, D., Sun, Y., Hu, C., Sun, C., Wu, Q., & Tian, J. (2022). Development and validation of a deep learning model to screen for trisomy 21 during the first trimester from nuchal ultrasonographic images. *JAMA network open*, *5*(6), e2217854–e2217854.

[13] Liu, L., Jiao, Y., Li, X., Ouyang, Y., & Shi, D. (2020). Machine learning algorithms to predict early pregnancy loss after in vitro fertilization-embryo transfer with fetal heart rate as a strong predictor. *Computer Methods and Programs in Biomedicine*, *196*, 105624.

[14] Zhang, H. G., Jiang, Y. T., Dai, S. D., Li, L., Hu, X. N., & Liu, R. Z. (2021). Application of intelligent algorithms in Down syndrome screening during second trimester pregnancy. *World Journal of Clinical Cases*, *9*(18), 4573.

[15] Selvathi, D., & Chandralekha, R. (2022). Fetal biometric based abnormality detection during prenatal development using deep learning techniques. *Multidimensional Systems and Signal Processing*, *33*(1), 1–15.

38 Quantum key distribution protocols: A contemporary review

Jaya Priya C.[1,a] and Meena alias Jeyanthi K.[2,b]

[1]Research Scholar, Department of Electronics and Communication Engineering, PSNA College of Engineering and Technology, Dindigul, Affiliated to Anna University, Tamil Nadu, India
[2]Professor, Department of Electronics and Communication Engineering, PSNA College of Engineering and Technology, Dindigul, Affiliated to Anna University, Tamil Nadu, India

Abstract: Over the past few decades, cryptography has played a pivotal role in strengthening information security, introducing groundbreaking methods to safeguard data confidentiality and integrity. Among these innovations, quantum cryptography has emerged as a rapidly evolving discipline, addressing critical challenges associated with secure communication. One of its most significant contributions is Quantum Key Distribution (QKD), a robust framework for establishing secure cryptographic keys between legitimate parties. This paper offers a detailed technical review of QKD protocols developed over the last thirty years, analyzing the fundamental principles governing key generation through quantum mechanics and advanced encryption techniques. Furthermore, it explores the interdependencies among core QKD protocol elements, proposing enhancements to strengthen the cryptosystem. Quantitative evaluations of QKD protocols are presented, with particular emphasis on runtime performance. Additionally, this paper outlines a generalized model of each reviewed protocol, grounded in robust security principles.

Keywords: Quantum key distribution protocols, discrete variables, continuous variables, superposition states, quantum bits (qubits), entangled states

1. Introduction

Securing communication over unsecured channels has driven cryptographic advancements, from classical methods like Caesar Cipher, RSA [1, 2], and Diffie-Hellman [3] to quantum cryptography. "Wiesner and Bennett introduced the concept in 1979, shaping early quantum cryptography" [4, 5], quantum cryptography uses qubits for secure key distribution [6], enhancing security via Discrete Variable (DV[]) and Continuous Variable (CV) protocols [7]. CV systems offer higher key rates, cost efficiency, and telecom compatibility. As quantum computing (~2000 qubits) threatens classical cryptosystems like ECC and RSA [8], researchers evaluate QKD protocols (BB84, SARG04, B92, COW [14], KMB09 [9], EPR, S09, DPS, S13) for quantum security. This paper dwells in QKD methodologies, evaluating their feasibility for securing future communication systems against quantum threats.

2. Literature Review

Quantum Key Distribution (QKD) transformed cryptography by enabling secure key exchange, with its first protocol introduced [9, 10]. Building on their work, various modern QKD protocols have been developed, leveraging quantum mechanics to yield secure secret keys. These keys undergo sifting and error-correction via classical channels to ensure integrity. The security of a QKD protocol depends on its design, influencing its resilience against vulnerabilities. This paper explores the evolution of classical cryptography, followed by an analysis of quantum cryptography and QKD protocols. A comparative study examines QKD runtime efficiency, focusing on secret key generation and exchange to evaluate protocol effectiveness.

2.1. Classical cryptography

Classical cryptography, dating back to 1900 B.C. [11], secures communication using mathematical complexity [1], addressing active and passive cyber-attacks. $\mathbf{E}$ – Encryption Function, $\mathbf{K}$ – Key, $\mathbf{X}$ – Plaintext, $\mathbf{D}$ – Decryption Function, $\mathbf{C}$ – Ciphertext Encryption follows in (1)

$$C = \mathcal{E}(K, X), \quad X = \mathcal{D}(K,C) \quad (1)$$

Modern schemes like RSA [2] rely on prime factorization but face threats from quantum computing [8, 9], which exploits superposition for rapid problem-solving. DES, 3DES, AES, Diffie-Hellman, and RSA use secret key exchanges over classical channels, with symmetric cryptosystems relying on shared keys and asymmetric cryptosystems using public-private key pairs [4].

[a]priyaagnes76@gmail.com, [b]meena.jeyanthi@psnacet.edu.in

DOI: 10.1201/9781003724988-38

2.2. Pioneering concepts in quantum cryptography

Quantum cryptography is a rapidly advancing field in secure communications, leveraging quantum mechanics to ensure that only authorized entities access shared data. It relies on quantum communication principles to establish secure channels and detect potential intrusions. Symmetric key encryption, widely used in classical cryptography, is fundamental to quantum systems, exemplified by the onetime pad encryption method [5]. OTP utilizes a Shared Secret Key (SSK) of equal bit-length to plaintext, applying XOR operations to generate ciphertext (CC). Security is upheld through the no-cloning theorem, preventing eavesdroppers from replicating intercepted quantum data [6]. Secure quantum communication requires both quantum channels (free space or fiber optics) [7] for qubit transmission and classical channels for error detection and correction through sifting processes in Figure 38.1 [8]. Quantum cryptography enhances security using photon polarization, momentum, and mass [9], resisting passive attacks but facing challenges in active attack mitigation due to classical-to-quantum transitions. QKD protocols are analysed for their operational mechanisms and efficiency in secret key generation and exchange.

2.3. The BB84 protocol

BB84, introduced in 1984 [12], enables secure quantum key exchange via single-photon transmission, with error correction over a classical channel [6, 12]. Alice encodes plaintext into bit strings using rectilinear or diagonal bases [13], ensuring security through the no cloning theorem in quantum mechanics [14] and the uncertainty principle introduced by Heisenberg's are core concepts [15]. BB84 relies on polarized orthogonal states, with Alice encoding qubits and Bob randomly selecting a measurement basis [16], forming a foundational framework for modern Quantum Key Distribution (QKD). For instance, Alice's diagonal-basis qubit encoding may yield probabilistic measurement outcomes aligned with polarized states in (2)

$$|3\rangle = \tfrac{1}{\sqrt{2}}(|\dagger\rangle + |\rightarrow\rangle)), |s\rangle = \tfrac{1}{\sqrt{2}}(|\dagger\rangle - |\rightarrow\rangle)) \quad (2)$$

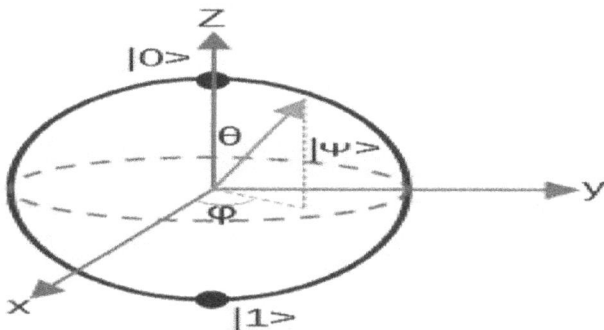

Figure 38.1. The Bloch Sphere.

Source: Author.

$|\dagger\rangle$: A basis state, often representing vertical polarization.

$|\rightarrow\rangle$: Another basis state, typically for horizontal polarization.

The states $|3\rangle$ and $|s\rangle$ are formed by combining these two in equal superpositions, creating diagonal and anti-diagonal states used in quantum protocols. These outcomes demonstrate a 50% probability of recording states 00 or 11. Figure 38.1 shows the Bloch sphere, which maps polarization states in 3D space (x, y, z). The BB84 protocol [7] enables secure QKD by relying on the no-cloning theorem [5] and Heisenberg's uncertainty principle, which together prevent undetected eavesdropping. QKD protocols are categorized by photon behaviour: superposition states (orthogonal/non-orthogonal) and entangled states. BB84 [7] employs polarized orthogonal states, with Alice encoding qubits using rectilinear ($\perp$) or diagonal (+) bases.

2.4. The SARG04 protocol

SARG04, introduced in 2004 by Scarani, Acín, Ribordy, and Gisin [13], builds on BB84 by using the same bases and four states (0, 1, +, −). It improves resistance to Photon-Number-Splitting (PNS) attacks by employing weak laser pulses instead of ideal single-photon sources [3]. The protocol involves Alice generating random photon states, Bob measuring with random bases, and Alice informing Bob of photon states for alignment. Non-orthogonal measurements require reconciliation, and high QBER leads to termination. Matched qubits generate the raw key, while unmatched ones are used in error correction and privacy amplification to enhance security [8].

2.5. The B92 protocol

Bennett's B92 protocol [11], introduced in 1992, uses two non-orthogonal states, providing a simpler alternative to BB84 for quantum key distribution. The sequence of operations is outlined in Figure 38.2, illustrating the progression of the process step by step.

1. Alice sends a sequence of randomly generated qubits ($A \in \{0,1\}^n$, $n > N$), where $|0\rangle$ represents $A_i = 0$ and $|+\rangle$ represents $A_i = 1$.
2. Bob constructs a bit vector $B \in \{0,1\}^n$ with $n > N$, assigning the (+) basis for $B_i = 0$ and the (×) basis for $B_i = 1$.
3. Using the designated bases (+ or ×), Bob measures the received qubits accordingly.**
4. Based on the measurement results, Bob applies rules in (3):

$$|0\rangle \text{ or } |+\rangle \text{ yields } |0\rangle \text{ or } |+\rangle \Rightarrow T_i = 0, \quad |1\rangle \text{ or } |-\rangle \Rightarrow T_i = 1, \text{ for all } i \in \{0,1,\dots,n\} \quad (3)$$

This optimized protocol employs nonorthogonal quantum states to facilitate secure communication.

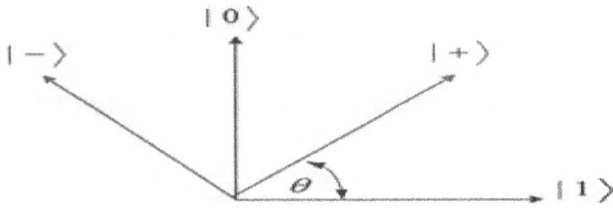

Figure 38.2. Representation of Non-Orthogonal States in B92.

Source: Author.

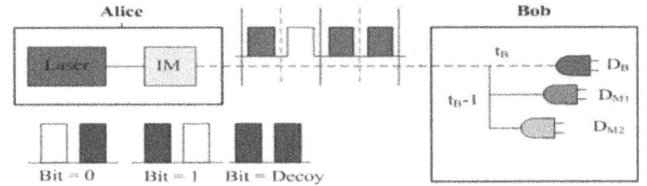

Figure 38.3. Secure Quantum communication using the COW protocol.

Source: Author.

The B92 protocol utilizes non-orthogonal quantum states to facilitate secure information transfer. Its resilience against optical distortions and detector noise sets it apart from the BB84 protocol. In standard implementations, communication noise levels can reach approximately 1.6% [3]. Furthermore, the B92 protocol optimizes operational efficiency by reducing reliance on quantum memory and minimizing dependency on quantum channel capacity.

2.6. The Coherent one-way (COW) protocol

The COW protocol [7] utilizes time-slot encoding for quantum key distribution. Alice transmits coherent pulses, encoding logical bits as $(\mu,0)(\mu,0)$ for '00' and $(0,\mu)(0,\mu)$ for '11', supplemented by decoy sequences $(\mu,\mu)(\mu,\mu)$ to enhance security. Bob's interferometer verifies proper reception at DM1, whereas coherence degradation at DM2 serves as an indicator of potential eavesdropping attempts, as detailed in (4) [6].

$$\text{Logic 1: } |0\rangle + |\mu\rangle, \quad$$
$$\text{Logic 0: } |\mu\rangle + |0\rangle, \quad$$
$$\text{Decoy: } |\mu\rangle + |\mu\rangle \quad (4)$$

Here, μ denotes the average number of photons contained in each pulse (5), the protocol operates based on signal arrival times rather than optical polarization. The key steps are as follows:

1. Alice encodes binary bits within specific time slots, generating logical states $|1\rangle|1\rangle$ or $|0\rangle|0\rangle$ with equal probability, except when decoy states are introduced. The probability of producing a standard state is defined as Plogic$=1-f/2$, where ff denotes the probability of generating a decoy state.
2. Bob performs time-based detection to derive a raw key, employing distinct detectors to enhance security performance, which is quantitatively described in (5).

$$V=p(DM1)-p(DM2)p(DM1)+p(DM2) \quad (5)$$

where $p(DM\_j)$ represents the detection probability at DM_j, as depicted in Figure 38.3. This approach provides robust protection against eavesdropping while maintaining simplicity in data transmission. The COW protocol [14] facilitates secure quantum key distribution through time-slot encoding. Alice transmits coherent pulses embedded with logical states and decoy

sequences, which Bob identifies based on arrival timing. Bob determines bit values through simultaneous data and time detection, while Alice preserves coherence and detects eavesdropping by splitting pulses to identify potential disturbances. Decoy bits are removed, and the final secret key is created by applying error correction and privacy amplification. The protocol (COW) [16] effectively mitigates interference-induced visibility reductions and Photon Number Splitting (PNS) attacks, enabling efficient transmission, minimal measurement loss, and low Quantum Bit Error Rate (QBER) detection.

2.7. The KMB09 protocol

The KMB09 protocol, introduced by Khan, Murphy, and Beige in 2009 [14], enhances secure communication by mitigating PNS attacks and reducing eavesdropping risks [10]. It employs two bases (ee and ff), assigning unique indices (ii) for alignment, and relies on ITER over QBER for error detection and correction. Optimized for long-distance communication with high error rates, KMB09 strengthens security through the following steps:

1. Alice generates a random bit sequence, assigning indices randomly (i=1,2,...,Ni = 1,2,...,N)
2. Alice transmits single photons encoded in the eie_i or fif_i basis
3. Bob randomly switches between ee and ff bases to measure received states
4. Alice reveals random indices (ii) to Bob for key formation
5. Bob processes his measurement results accordingly
6. Alice and Bob exchange information publicly to validate key formation
7. They assess eavesdropping threats using the equation in (6) [11]:

$$ITER=1N\sum i=1N\sum k=1|gk|i\rangle+gk|i\rangle| \quad (6)$$

where e,f,ge, f, g denote bases, and gkg_k represents Eve's measurement results. The protocol prevents Alice and Bob from sharing identical indices within the same basis, strengthening resilience against eavesdropping [12]. Additionally, the strong correlation between QBER and ITER aids in detecting eavesdropper signatures, ensuring robust security.

2.8. The EPR protocol

In 1935, Einstein, Podolsky, and Rosen introduced the EPR paradox [13], highlighting unusual features of quantum entanglement challenges the completeness of quantum mechanics within physical theory. It involves entangled particles separated over long distances, exhibiting "action at a distance" [14], where one photon's polarization measurement affects the other, with states such as vertical (00) and horizontal ($\pi/2\pi/2$) linear polarizations. Artur K. Ekert proposed the EPR protocol in 1991 [15], relying on entanglement states for secure communication between remote parties. The steps of the protocol are:

Step 1: Alice creates n pairs of entangled qubits, keeping one qubit from each pair in her quantum memory while sending the partner qubit to Bob. The four Bell states used in (7) are:

$$|\psi 1\rangle = 12(|00\rangle + |11\rangle)), |\psi 2\rangle = 12(|00\rangle - |11\rangle)), |\psi 3\rangle = 12(|1$$
$$0\rangle + |01\rangle)), |\psi 4\rangle = 12(|10\rangle - |01\rangle)). |\psi\_1\rangle = \frac{1}{\sqrt{2}} (|00\rangle + |11\rangle), \quad |\psi\_2\rangle = \frac{1}{\sqrt{2}} (|00\rangle - |11\rangle), \quad |\psi\_3\rangle = \frac{1}{\sqrt{2}} (|10\rangle + |01\rangle), \quad |\psi\_4\rangle = \frac{1}{\sqrt{2}} (|10\rangle - |01\rangle). |\psi 1\rangle = 21(|00\rangle + |11\rangle)), |\psi 2\rangle = 21(|00\rangle - |11\rangle)), |\psi 3\rangle = 21(|10\rangle + |01\rangle)), |\psi 4\rangle = 21(|10\rangle - |01\rangle))$$

$$(7)$$

Step 2: Alice and Bob randomly select bases ($\perp$ or $+$) to measure the particles, recording observations.

Step 3: Alice and Bob use a public channel to compare results and keep only the qubits measured in the same basis.

Classical communication facilitates error detection and qubit reconciliation, following principles similar to the BB84 protocol. This process strengthens secure entangled qubit exchange and enhances the robustness of quantum key distribution.

2.9. The S09 protocol

The S09 protocol [13], introduced by Esteban and Serna in 2012, improves quantum communication security by repeatedly exchanging a qubit over a quantum channel using public-private key methods. Alice creates a qubit from a secret base (Bk) and sends it to Bob, who applies a transformation (Uj) before returning it. Alice measures the qubit, ensuring it remains in a pure state (ρ), while environmental interactions modify it to ρ', represented by operators (Ej). Parity bits and hashed values are appended during exchange. Frequent transformations (Bk, Uj) prevent eavesdropping, but the protocol's complexity reduces efficiency.

2.10. The S13 protocol

The S13 protocol [12], designed by Serna in 2013, extends BB84 for quantum phase while modifying the classical channel to ensure device compatibility without adjustments.

2.11. Quantum key exchange

The key steps are:

- The raw key is exchanged following the BB84 protocol.
- One participant creates a random sequence of binary bits $x_1 x_2 \ldots x_N$.

2.12. Alice and Bob key exchange process

Alice combines her random binary string with the chosen bases to create sequences $t_1 t_2 \ldots t_N$ and $j_1 j_2 \ldots j_N$ for key exchange. Bob then uses these along with his own binary string to form $n_1 n_2 \ldots n_N$ and $\Psi t_{j_k} j_k$ in basis B_{nk} to get outcomes $b_1 b_2 \ldots b_N$.

2.13. Classical cryptographic process

Asymmetric: Alice adds binary string to the missing key bits and sends the resulting sequence to Bob. Bob then uses this information to generate two public keys by applying a function to his message bits along with certain values received from Alice. Using these public keys and own information, Alice calculates a private value that allows to decode the final message.

Secure Private Reconciliation: Bob begins by comparing the binary sequences sent by Alice. To retrieve the private string, bob uses his own key and applies a specific function to compute values that match Alice's original input. Although the S13 protocol enhances the S09 version in terms of security, it still relies on public channel communication, which may cause delays and potential vulnerabilities. The process, while secure, is relatively complex.

Differential Phase Shift (DPS) Protocol: Introduced by Inoue et al. in 2002 [11], the DPS protocol uses phase differences between sequential pulses for secure key distribution. Alice randomly modulates the phase of photons split into three pulses, and Bob detects them by measuring the phase shifts. This approach uses four non-orthogonal states and is well-suited for fiber-optic systems due to its efficiency, precise timing, high key generation rate, and strong resistance to photon-number-splitting (PNS) attacks [15, 16]. As shown in Figure 38.4, key generation involves splitting photons, controlling phase shifts (0 or π), and processing them through 50:50 beam splitters.

2.14. Steps

1. Alice sends a photon through path aa to Bob's short path.
2. Alice transmits a photon via a to Bob's long path and b to the short path.
3. Alice sends another photon through b to the long path and c to the short path.
4. Alice sends another photon through path cc to Bob's long path.

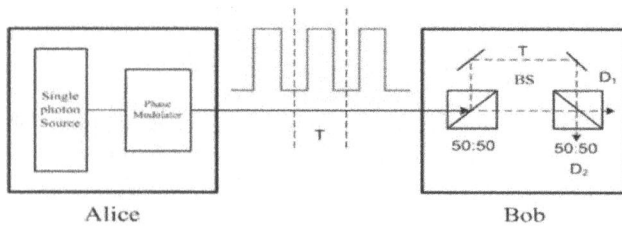

Figure 38.4. Quantum key distribution via the DPS scheme.
Source: Author.

During transmission, overlapping probabilities in steps two and three result in a phase shift of either 0 or π, which is controlled by Alice as illustrated in Figure 38.4 [10]. Bob detects these shifts and notes the corresponding times. Using classical two-way communication, Alice confirms which of Bob's detectors was triggered [12].

3. Analysis of QKD Protocols

Security and efficiency differ across quantum key distribution protocols.BB84 offers strong PNS protection but moderate I&R security, while SARG04 enhances PNS resistance with non-orthogonal states. B92 simplifies BB84 but weakens I&R protection. COW and DPS use continuous states for balanced security and simplicity. KMB09 and EPR excel in PNS and I&R defense through photon states and entanglement. S09 and S13 integrate advanced encoding for high security and error reduction, showcasing diverse strategies for secure quantum communication.

4. Summary of QKD Protocol

QKD protocols like BB84, B92, SARG04, EPR, COW, DPS, KMB09, S09, and S13 vary in terms of security strength, implementation complexity, and overall efficiency. COW employs decoy states to counter Photon-Number-Splitting (PNS) attacks, but requires extra time for submission and reconciliation. S13 is the only protocol integrating identity verification via the classical channel, though it reduces efficiency and increases eavesdropping risks. Performance differs: BB84 (500 input → 142 output, 0.164 ms), B92 (119 output, 0.177 ms), SARG04 (247 output, 0.815 ms), KMB09 (16 input → 362 output, 0.012 ms), EPR (119 output, 0.860 ms), DPS (constant time), S09 (0.927 ms), S13 (0.639 ms), and COW (500 input → 126 output, .686 ms), highlighting efficiency and security variations.

5. Conclusion

This paper examines various QKD protocols, emphasizing quantum key distribution as an advanced cryptographic approach in information theory. Powered by quantum mechanics, particularly the non-cloning theorem, QKD effectively addresses theoretical challenges in quantum cryptography. The paper provides clarity on the mechanisms of each protocol and emphasizes the importance of runtime implementation. Extensive use of classical channels for multi-communications prolongs the protocol process and raises the risk of information attacks, especially during reconciliation. Despite this dependency, classical channels are indispensable for reconciling information when quantum channels cannot. QKD enables Secure Shared Key (SSK) generation with full protection against data exposure, ensuring 0.0% vulnerability to SSK attacks and establishing itself as the future of secure key systems in modern communication.

Acknowledgement

We are grateful to the Electronics and Communication Engineering department for their invaluable support and collaboration in this research.

References

[1] Schneier, B. (2007). *Applied Cryptography: Protocols, Algorithms, and Source Code in C.* John Wiley & Sons: Hoboken, NJ, USA.

[2] Wiesner, S. (1983). Conjugate coding. *ACM Sigact News, 15,* 78–88.

[3] Brassard, G. (2005). Brief history of quantum cryptography: A personal perspective. In *IEEE Information Theory Workshop on Theory and Practice in Information-Theoretic Security*; IEEE: Piscataway, NJ, USA, Volume 2005, pp. 19–23.

[4] Oesterling, L., Hayford, D., & Friend, G. (2012). Comparison of commercial and next-generation quantum key distribution: Technologies for secure communication of information. In *Proceedings of the 2012 IEEE Conference on Technologies for Homeland Security (HST)*. Waltham, MA, USA, pp. 156–161.

[5] Possignolo, R. T., & Margi, C. B. (2012). A quantum-classical hybrid architecture for security algorithms acceleration. In *Proceedings of the 2012 IEEE 11th International Conference on Trust, Security and Privacy in Computing and Communications*. Liverpool, UK, pp. 1032–1037.

[6] Sharbaf, M. S. (2011). Quantum cryptography: An emerging technology in network security. In *Proceedings of the 2011 IEEE International Conference on Technologies for Homeland Security (HST)*. Waltham, MA, USA, pp. 13–19.

[7] Lo, H.-K., Ma, X., & Chen, K. (2005)/ Decoy state quantum key distribution. *Phys. Rev. Lett., 94,* 230504.

[8] Niemiec, M., & Pach, A. R. (2013). Management of security in quantum cryptography. *IEEE Commun. Mag., 51,* 36–41.

[9] Bennett, C. H., & Brassard, G. (2014). Quantum cryptography: Public key distribution and coin tossing. *Theor. Comput. Sci., 560,* 7–11.

[10] Russell, J. (2008). Application of quantum key distribution. In *Proceedings of the MILCOM 2008—2008 IEEE Military Communications Conference*. San Diego, CA, USA, pp. 1–6.

[11] Shor, P. W. (1999). Polynomial-time algorithms for prime factorization and discrete logarithms on a quantum computer. *SIAM Rev., 41,* 303–332.

[12] Cao, Z., & Liu, L. (2012). Improvement of one quantum encryption scheme. *Int. J. Quantum Inf., 10,* 1250076.

[13] Sharma, R. D., & De, A. (2011). A new secure model for quantum key distribution protocol. In *Proceedings of the 2011 6th International Conference on Industrial and Information Systems.* Kandy, Sri Lanka, pp. 462–466.

[14] Jouguet, P., & Kunz-Jacques, S. (2012). High-performance error correction for quantum key distribution using polar codes. *arXiv* 2012,arXiv:1204.5882.

[15] Kartheek, D. N., Amarnath, G., & Reddy, P. V. (2013). Security in quantum computing using quantum key distribution protocols. In *Proceedings of the 2013 International Mutli-Conference on Automation, Computing, Communication, Control and Compressed Sensing (iMac4s)*. Kottayam, India, pp. 19–25.

[16] Sharma, A., Ojha, V., & Lenka, S. K. (2010). Security of entanglement based version of BB84 protocol for Quantum Cryptography. In *Proceedings of the 2010 3rd International Conference on Computer Science and Information Technology*. Chengdu, China, Volume 9, pp. 615–619.

39 Extraction of text from images using OCR with multilingual support

V. Anjana Devi[a], Surya P.[b], and Taariq Ziyaadh J.[c]

Department of Computer Science and Engineering, Rajalakshmi Institute of Technology, Chennai, Tamil Nadu, India

Abstract: Robust multilingual Optical Character Recognition (OCR) is crucial for accessing diverse information. This paper presents a dual contribution: optimizing OCR accuracy for English and Tamil, and developing a broader, feature-rich web application. First, we detail a core OCR pipeline using Tesseract, enhanced by preprocessing including skew correction, adaptive thresholding, bilateral filtering, sharpening, and resizing. Quantitative evaluation on a custom dataset showed significant accuracy gains (90.23% Levenshtein-ratio accuracy), proving the importance of image preparation. Second, we describe a Flask web application integrating OCR for thirteen languages using Tesseract with essential preprocessing (grayscale, Otsu thresholding). It also includes text translation via Google Translate API and an NLP chatbot for user assistance. Functional testing confirmed the integrated features' usability. While the web app uses streamlined preprocessing for practicality, this work collectively shows potential for high accuracy via optimized preprocessing and the value of integrating multilingual OCR with translation and support features in an accessible web tool. Findings highlight Tesseract's effectiveness and the importance of preprocessing for feature-rich OCR applications.

Keywords: Optical character recognition (OCR), multilingual OCR, tesseract, image preprocessing, Skew correction, adaptive thresholding, bilateral filtering, levenshtein distance, flask, web application, text translation, Chatbot, Tamil, English

1. Introduction

Optical Character Recognition (OCR) converts text in images into machine-readable data, essential for document digitization, data entry, content analysis, and assistive technologies [1–5]. With globalization, the demand for OCR systems handling multiple languages and scripts has surged [6–8]. However, multilingual OCR faces challenges like diverse character sets, script complexities [4, 9–11], and data scarcity for low-resource languages [11, 12]. OCR performance also heavily depends on input image quality, with noise, skew, and poor illumination being persistent issues [1–3]. This necessitates both improved accuracy via optimization and practical, accessible multilingual tools.

This paper addresses both aspects. First, we present an OCR pipeline optimized for English and Tamil using Tesseract with comprehensive preprocessing (skew correction, adaptive thresholding, bilateral filtering, sharpening, resizing) to maximize accuracy. Its effectiveness is shown quantitatively using Levenshtein-ratio metrics.

Second, we detail a Flask web application providing user-friendly OCR for thirteen languages using Tesseract with essential preprocessing (grayscale, Otsu thresholding). It integrates multilingual translation (Google Translate API) and an NLP chatbot for assistance, demonstrating a holistic approach.

Our contributions are:

1. Quantitative proof of OCR accuracy gains via advanced preprocessing for Tesseract (English/Tamil).

2. Development and functional demonstration of an accessible web application integrating multilingual OCR, translation, and chatbot features.

2. Related Work and Background

OCR has evolved significantly. This review covers OCR approaches, multilingual challenges, Tesseract, preprocessing, and integration with other technologies.

2.1. General OCR approaches

Early OCR used methods like template matching [3, 13, 14], which struggled with variations. Feature extraction using geometric/topological properties offered improvements [1, 3, 10, 13]. Diagonal features [13] and specific geometrical features for Indian scripts [10] were explored. Classifiers like SVMs [1, 4, 6, 15] and k-NN [1, 10, 13] were common.

Deep learning [11] brought major advances. CNNs excel at image feature learning [4, 15]. RNNs (LSTMs/BLSTMs) are effective for sequence modeling [4, 16, 17]. Advanced RNNs (BLSTM, MDLSTM) with CTC handled unsegmented handwriting [17, 18]. Transformers, like in TrOCR [19], use attention and pre-trained models for state-of-the-art results. Systems combining CNNs and RNNs (CRNN) [16] are effective. MLLMs like OCEAN-OCR [20] aim for general OCR capabilities.

[a]anjanadevi.v@ritchennai.edu.in, [b]surya.p.2021.cse@ritchennai.edu.in, [c]taariqziyaad.j.2021.cse@ritchennai.edu.in

DOI: 10.1201/9781003724988-39

2.2. Multilingual OCR systems

Multilingual recognition is challenging due to script diversity and data limits [4, 9, 11]. Strategies include:

- **Specialized Features:** Tailoring features to scripts [1].
- **Multiplexed Architectures:** Shared extractors with language-specific heads [9].
- **Transformer Models:** Adaptability and pre-trained multilingual models like TrOCR [19].
- **Modular Networks:** Smaller subnetworks for large character sets [21].
- **Lightweight Systems:** Focus on efficiency like PP-OCR [7].
- **Low-Resource Languages:** Techniques like contrastive learning [22] or novel data generation [23]. Language specific research is also needed [24].

2.3. Tesseract OCR engine

Tesseract is a widely used open-source OCR engine [1, 2, 14]. Its support for many languages (including ours) and LSTM-based networks make it powerful [2]. Performance is sensitive to image quality, highlighting the need for pre-processing [1, 2].

2.4. Image preprocessing techniques

Effective preprocessing is crucial for OCR [1–3, 6, 13]. Our web app uses grayscale and Otsu thresholding [extract_text_from_image]. Literature details noise reduction, skew/slant normalization, and thinning [3]. Our evaluated core pipeline used more advanced steps: skew correction (minAreaRect), adaptive thresholding, bilateral filtering, and sharpening for better robustness, potentially trading off speed.

2.4. Integration with NLP and other technologies

Modern OCR tools often integrate other technologies. Our application includes:

- **Machine Translation:** Using Google Translate API [translate_text] for translating extracted text [1].
- **Chatbots:** User support via a chatbot using TF-IDF and cosine similarity for basic intent recognition [get_chatbot_response].

2.5. Our approach in context

This work creates a practical multilingual OCR web application using Tesseract, essential preprocessing, translation, and a chatbot. It focuses on integrating existing tools (Tesseract, Google Translate) into a user-friendly system for accessible multilingual text interaction, rather than developing novel model architectures [17, 19, 20]. The broad language support and integrated translation differentiate it.

3. Proposed Methodology

This section details the system: the core OCR pipeline for robust extraction and its implementation in an interactive web application with translation and chatbot features.

3.1. Core OCR pipeline (designed for quantitative evaluation)

This pipeline uses optimized steps for high accuracy on potentially challenging images.

- **Skew Correction:**
  - **Purpose:** Correct rotational misalignment.
  - **Method:** OpenCV's minAreaRect. Involves grayscale, edge detection, contours, finding the minimum bounding rectangle, calculating the angle, and applying affine transformation (cv2.warpAffine) [2, 3, 13].
- **Binarization (Adaptive Thresholding):**
  - **Purpose:** Segment text from background, especially with varying illumination.
  - **Method:** Gaussian adaptive thresholding (cv2.adaptiveThreshold, cv2.ADAPTIVE_THRESH_GAUSSIAN_C) using localized thresholds [2, 13]. Parameters: block size 11, C=2.
- **Noise Reduction (Bilateral Filtering):**
  - **Purpose:** Reduce noise while preserving edges.
  - **Method:** Bilateral filtering (cv2.bilateralFilter) considering spatial and intensity differences [1, 3, 13]. Parameters: d=9, sigmaColor=75, sigmaSpace=75.
- **Sharpening:**
  - **Purpose:** Enhance character edges.
  - **Method:** Kernel-based convolution (cv2.filter2D) with standard sharpening kernel [1].
- **Resizing:**
  - **Purpose:** Scale image, potentially improving Tesseract performance.
  - **Method:** Upscale by 2x using cubic interpolation (cv2.resize, cv2.INTER_CUBIC) [1, 2, 10, 13, 24].
- **Text Extraction (Tesseract Configuration for Evaluation):** Feed preprocessed image to Tesseract (pytesseract) with config --oem 3 --psm 6 lang='eng+tam'.
- **Quantitative Evaluation Metrics:** Measured performance using Levenshtein-ratio based accuracy and precision.

3.2. Web application implementation (Flask)

Core OCR concepts are integrated into a Flask web application with translation and chatbot support.

- **Architecture:** Client-server structure. Flask backend handles processing, OCR, translation, chatbot; frontend (HTML/JS) handles UI.
- **Workflow:**
  - User uploads image and selects language (index.html).

- Flask server (/extract) receives file, validates, preprocesses.
- **Simplified Preprocessing in Web App:** Used in extract_text_from_image for potentially faster response:
  - Grayscale Conversion (cv2.cvtColor).
  - Binarization via Otsu's Thresholding (cv2. threshold, cv2.THRESH_OTSU).
  (Note: More advanced steps omitted here).
- **Tesseract Integration:** Simplified preprocessed image passed to pytesseract.image_to_string with selected language code (13 languages supported). Basic whitespace normalization applied.
- Extracted text shown on results page (result.html).
- **Translation Feature:** User selects target language; / translate route calls translate_text function using googletrans library.
- **Chatbot Feature:** User interacts via chat; /chat route calls get_chatbot_response function using TF-IDF and cosine similarity against predefined intents.
- **Key Libraries Used:** Flask, Pytesseract, OpenCV, PIL, Googletrans, NLTK, spaCy, Scikit-learn.

4. Experiments and Results

This section details the evaluation: (1) Quantitative assessment of the core OCR pipeline's accuracy, and (2) Functional testing of the web application.

4.1. Quantitative evaluation of the core OCR pipeline

The core pipeline's extraction logic was evaluated objectively.

Dataset Description: A custom dataset of 50 diverse images (scans, photos, screenshots) containing English and Tamil text with varying fonts, styles, quality, and layouts. Each image had verified ground truth text.

Experimental Setup (Core Pipeline): Used core software components (Python, OpenCV, Pytesseract) in batch processing mode.

Evaluation Metrics:
- **Accuracy:** Levenshtein ratio (string similarity).
- **Precision:** Correctly identified words / total extracted words.

Quantitative Results: Table 39.1 shows the overall performance of the core pipeline with full preprocessing.

Table 39.2 shows the impact of adding preprocessing steps on accuracy. "Baseline" is Tesseract on original images.

Quantitative Analysis: The core pipeline achieved 90.23% accuracy and 88.50% precision (Table 39.1). Table 39.2 clearly shows preprocessing effectiveness, improving accuracy substantially from baseline (68.55%).

4.2. Functional testing of the web application

The complete web application was tested functionally for UI, features, and usability (Figures 39.1 and 39.2).

Table 39.1. Overall core OCR pipeline performance

Metric	Value (%)
Accuracy	90.23
Precision	88.5

Source: Author.

Table 39.2. Impact of preprocessing techniques on core pipeline accuracy

Preprocessing Steps	Accuracy (%)
Baseline (No Preprocessing)	68.55
Skew Correction Only	76.55
Skew Correction + Binarization (Adaptive Thresholding)	82.55
Skew + Binarization + Noise Reduction (Bilateral Filt.)	86.55
Full Pipeline (Skew + Bin + Noise + Sharp + Resize)	90.23

Source: Author.

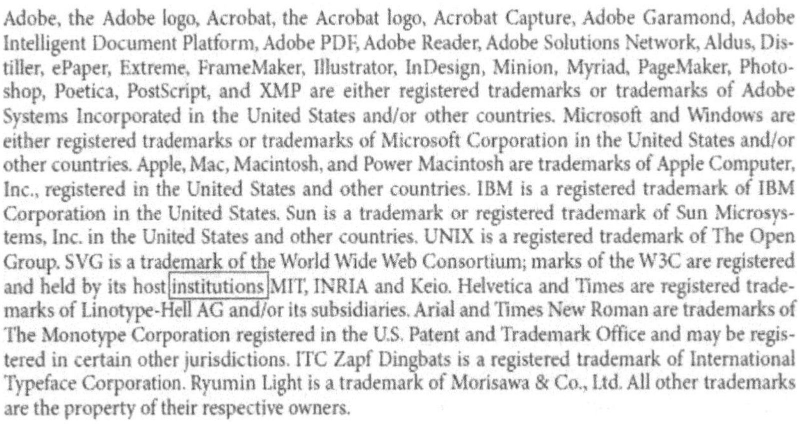

Adobe, the Adobe logo, Acrobat, the Acrobat logo, Acrobat Capture, Adobe Garamond, Adobe Intelligent Document Platform, Adobe PDF, Adobe Reader, Adobe Solutions Network, Aldus, Distiller, ePaper, Extreme, FrameMaker, Illustrator, InDesign, Minion, Myriad, PageMaker, Photoshop, Poetica, PostScript, and XMP are either registered trademarks or trademarks of Adobe Systems Incorporated in the United States and/or other countries. Microsoft and Windows are either registered trademarks or trademarks of Microsoft Corporation in the United States and/or other countries. Apple, Mac, Macintosh, and Power Macintosh are trademarks of Apple Computer, Inc., registered in the United States and other countries. IBM is a registered trademark of IBM Corporation in the United States. Sun is a trademark or registered trademark of Sun Microsystems, Inc. in the United States and other countries. UNIX is a registered trademark of The Open Group. SVG is a trademark of the World Wide Web Consortium; marks of the W3C are registered and held by its host institutions MIT, INRIA and Keio. Helvetica and Times are registered trademarks of Linotype-Hell AG and/or its subsidiaries. Arial and Times New Roman are trademarks of The Monotype Corporation registered in the U.S. Patent and Trademark Office and may be registered in certain other jurisdictions. ITC Zapf Dingbats is a registered trademark of International Typeface Corporation. Ryumin Light is a trademark of Morisawa & Co., Ltd. All other trademarks are the property of their respective owners.

Figure 39.1. Original input image containing English text provided to the web application.

Source: Author.

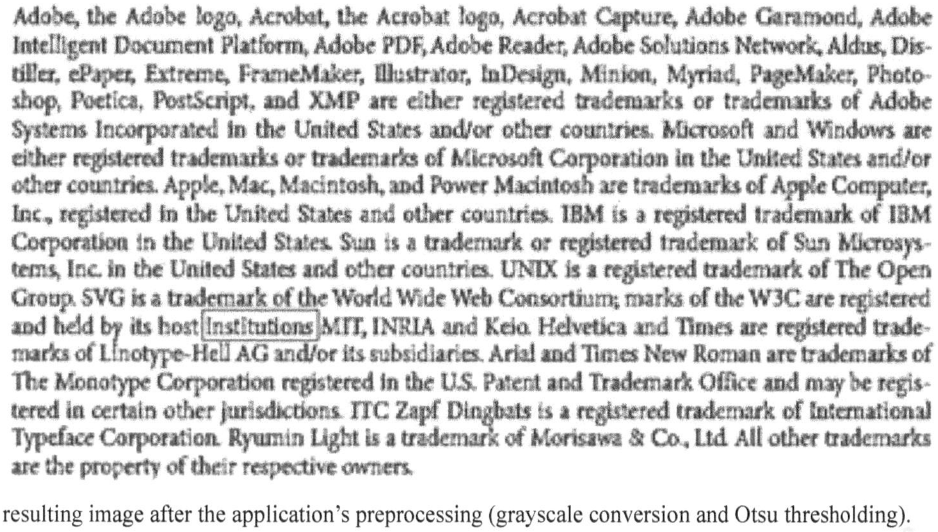

Adobe, the Adobe logo, Acrobat, the Acrobat logo, Acrobat Capture, Adobe Garamond, Adobe Intelligent Document Platform, Adobe PDF, Adobe Reader, Adobe Solutions Network, Aldus, Distiller, ePaper, Extreme, FrameMaker, Illustrator, InDesign, Minion, Myriad, PageMaker, Photoshop, Poetica, PostScript, and XMP are either registered trademarks or trademarks of Adobe Systems Incorporated in the United States and/or other countries. Microsoft and Windows are either registered trademarks or trademarks of Microsoft Corporation in the United States and/or other countries. Apple, Mac, Macintosh, and Power Macintosh are trademarks of Apple Computer, Inc., registered in the United States and other countries. IBM is a registered trademark of IBM Corporation in the United States. Sun is a trademark or registered trademark of Sun Microsystems, Inc. in the United States and other countries. UNIX is a registered trademark of The Open Group. SVG is a trademark of the World Wide Web Consortium; marks of the W3C are registered and held by its host Institutions MIT, INRIA and Keio. Helvetica and Times are registered trademarks of Linotype-Hell AG and/or its subsidiaries. Arial and Times New Roman are trademarks of The Monotype Corporation registered in the U.S. Patent and Trademark Office and may be registered in certain other jurisdictions. ITC Zapf Dingbats is a registered trademark of International Typeface Corporation. Ryumin Light is a trademark of Morisawa & Co., Ltd. All other trademarks are the property of their respective owners.

Figure 39.2. The resulting image after the application's preprocessing (grayscale conversion and Otsu thresholding).

Source: Author.

Testing Environment: Flask app run locally, accessed via standard web browsers.

Features Tested: End-to-end workflow:

- Image uploads (PNG, JPG, PDF snippets).
- Language selection (all 13 supported).
- Viewing extracted text.
- Using translation for various language pairs.
- Interacting with the chatbot.

4.3. Qualitative results and observations

- Web app successfully processed uploads and performed OCR for supported languages.
- Translation features provided accurate translations.
- Chatbot responded correctly to predefined queries using TF-IDF matching.
- Simplified preprocessing (grayscale, Otsu) worked well for clear images but was less robust on noisy/skewed images than the full pipeline, showing a speed/accuracy trade-off (Figure 39.3).
- The accuracy route displays static, illustrative figures (Figure 39.4), not live calculations. Quantitative results (Tables 39.1, 39.2) represent the core logic benchmark.

Summary of Evaluation: Quantitative evaluation confirms the preprocessing pipeline significantly boosts core Tesseract OCR accuracy for English/Tamil. Functional testing validates the web application successfully integrates OCR, translation, and chatbot features into a user-friendly, multilingual tool, using simplified preprocessing for web deployment.

5. Discussion

This research involved designing and evaluating a core OCR pipeline (English/Tamil) and implementing a functional web app with OCR, translation, and chatbot features. Findings highlight preprocessing's impact on accuracy and the utility of accessible, feature-rich web tools.

Interpretation of Findings: Quantitative evaluation showed preprocessing significantly improves accuracy (from 68.55% baseline to 90.23% with the full pipeline), confirming its crucial role for Tesseract, especially on mixed English/Tamil documents. Functional testing confirmed the Flask app successfully integrates components. It uses Tesseract for 13 languages [LANGUAGES dictionary], Google Translate for cross-lingual utility [translate_text], and an NLP chatbot for user guidance [get_chatbot_response].

Bridging the Pipeline and Application: The web app uses simplified preprocessing (grayscale, Otsu) [extract_text_from_image], unlike the evaluated core pipeline. This likely prioritizes web response time over maximum accuracy, a common trade-off. The web app's robustness to challenging images is likely lower than the core pipeline's potential.

Strengths and Weaknesses:

- Strengths:
  - Proven Preprocessing Efficacy: Quantitative results validate the core pipeline's impact.
  - Broad Multilingual Support: Web app offers extensive language OCR and translation.
  - Integrated Functionality: Single web interface for OCR, translation, chatbot offers user value.
  - Accessibility: Use of Flask and open-source libraries aids access and development.
- Weaknesses:
  - Preprocessing Discrepancy: Web app uses simpler preprocessing than evaluated pipeline.
  - No Quantitative Web Benchmarking: Deployed web app accuracy not formally measured.
  - Limited Dataset: Small custom dataset for quantitative evaluation may limit generalizability.
  - External Dependencies: Relies on Tesseract installation and Google Translate API.
  - Basic Layout Analysis: Assumes single text blocks.
  - Simple Chatbot: Limited NLP capabilities.

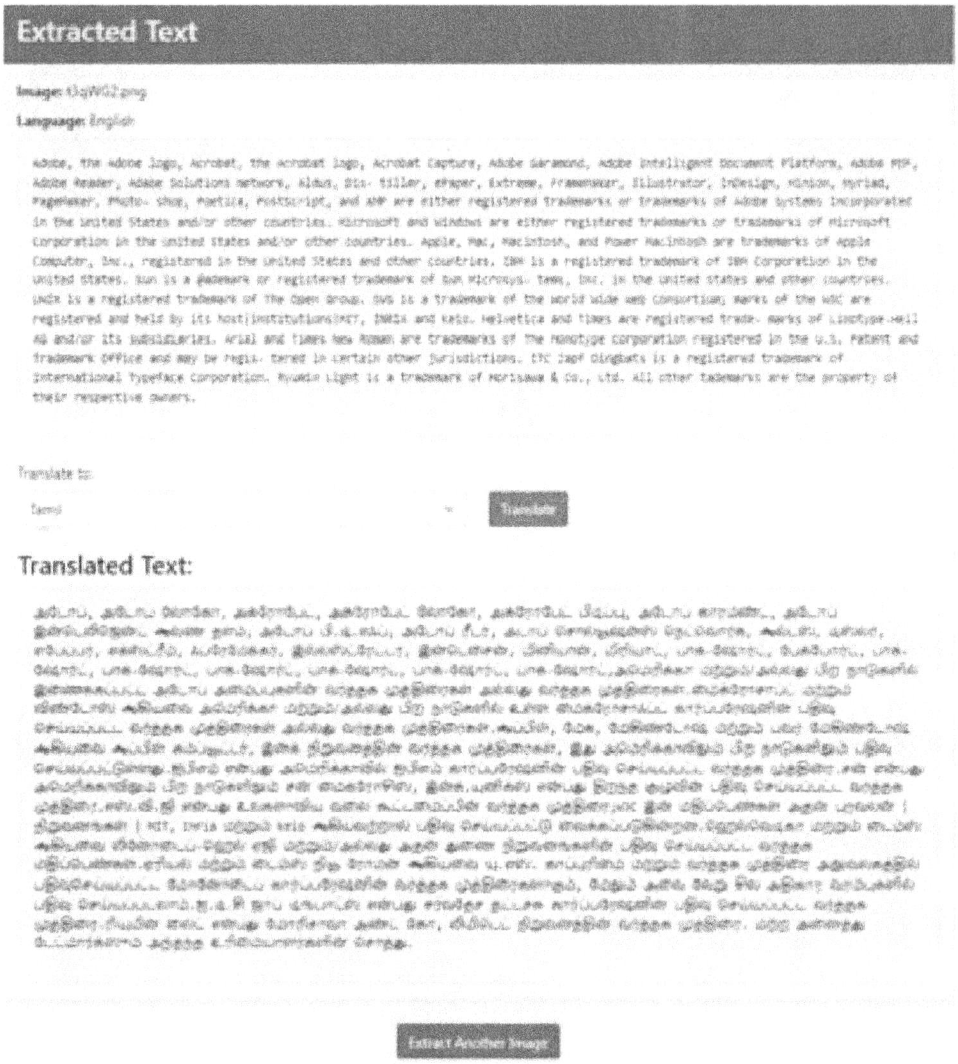

Figure 39.3. OCR extraction and translation result in web application.

Source: Author.

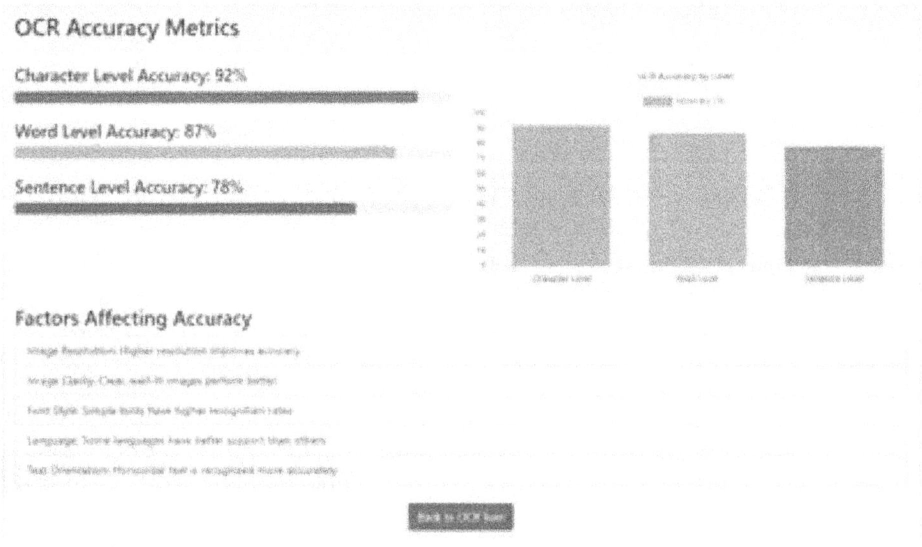

Figure 39.4. Illustrative accuracy metrics display page.

Source: Author.

Comparison with Related Work: Our core pipeline's pre-processing focus aligns with [1–3, 13]. The 90.23% accuracy achieved is competitive for a Tesseract-based system on a custom, potentially challenging dataset, though direct comparison is difficult without standardized benchmarks. The web application contributes by integrating multiple features (OCR, translation, chatbot) into an accessible tool, offering a practical solution compared to research focused purely on novel OCR models [17, 19, 20] or lightweight deployment [7].

Practical Implications: Key takeaways: (1) Good preprocessing significantly improves standard OCR engine accuracy. (2) An integrated web application (OCR, translation, support) provides a practical tool for multilingual text interaction. The web framework allows future enhancements, potentially adding more robust preprocessing options.

6. Conclusion

This paper presented a dual contribution: designing and evaluating a robust core OCR pipeline (English/Tamil) and developing a functional web application integrating multilingual OCR, translation, and chatbot features. The core pipeline, using extensive preprocessing (skew correction, adaptive thresholding, filtering, sharpening, resizing), significantly improved Tesseract's accuracy to 90.23

The Flask web application provides a practical tool supporting thirteen languages for OCR, integrated Google Translate, and a helpful chatbot. Functional tests confirmed usability. However, it uses simplified preprocessing (grayscale, Otsu) for faster web response, differing from the evaluated core pipeline.

This work demonstrates both accuracy gains from systematic preprocessing and the feasibility of accessible, feature rich web tools using engines like Tesseract and APIs. The core pipeline sets an accuracy benchmark, while the web app offers practical multilingual text interaction.

Limitations include the preprocessing difference between evaluated pipeline and web app, lack of quantitative web app benchmarking, small evaluation dataset size, and reliance on external services.

7. Future Work

Future work should bridge the pipeline/web app gap and perform more rigorous evaluation.

- **Integrate Advanced Preprocessing:** Add evaluated pipeline steps to the web app (possibly optional).
- **Benchmark Web Application:** Quantitatively evaluate the deployed web app on standard datasets (CER, WER).
- **Optimize Web Preprocessing:** Improve efficiency of advanced steps for web use.
- **Expand Functionality:** Add layout analysis and enhance chatbot NLP.
- **Comparative Engine Analysis:** Explore integrating other OCR engines.

Addressing these points can lead to a more robust, evaluated, and versatile multilingual OCR tool.

References

[1] Muthusundari, M., Velpoorani, A., Venkata Kusuma, S., T. L., & Rohini, O. (2024). Optical character recognition system using artificial intelligence. *LatIA*, *2*, 98. [Online]. Available: https://latia.ageditor.uy/index.php/latia/article/view/98

[2] Arora, A., Vidyapeeth, B., Singh, R., Eqbal, A., Mangal, A., & Saoji, S. (2021). Extraction and detection of text from images. *International Journal of Research in Engineering and Technology*, *8*, 2395–0056.

[3] Arica, N., & Yarman Vural, F. (2001). An overview of character recognition focused on off-line handwriting. *Systems, Man, and Cybernetics, Part C: Applications and Reviews, IEEE Transactions on*, *31*, 216–233.

[4] Kataria, B., & Jethva, H. (2020). Sanskrit character recognition using convolutional neural networks: A survey. *International Journal of Advanced Science and Technology*, *29*, 1059–1071.

[5] Shaji George, A. (2025). Handwriting recognition implementation: A machine learning approach. *International Research Journal on Advanced Engineering and Management (IRJAEM)*, *3*(02), 144–149. [Online]. Available: https://goldncloudpublications.com/index.php/irjaem/article/view/684

[6] Vamvakas, G., Gatos, B., & Perantonis, S. J. (2010). Handwritten character recognition through two-stage foreground sub-sampling. *Pattern Recognition*, *43*(8), 2807–2816. [Online]. Available: https://www.sciencedirect.com/science/article/pii/S0031320310000968

[7] Du, Y., Li, C., Guo, R., Yin, X., Liu, W., Zhou, J., Bai, Y., Yu, Z., Yang, Y., Dang, Q., & Wang, H. (2020). Pp-ocr: A practical ultra lightweight ocr system. [Online]. Available: https://arxiv.org/abs/2009.09941

[8] Yang, Z., Tang, J., Li, Z., Wang, P., Wan, J., Zhong, H., Liu, X., Yang, M., Wang, P., Bai, S., Jin, L., & Lin, J. (2024). Cc-ocr: A comprehensive and challenging ocr benchmark for evaluating large multimodal models in literacy. [Online]. Available: https://arxiv.org/abs/2412.02210

[9] Huang, J., Pang, G., Kovvuri, R., Toh, M., Liang, K. J., Krishnan, P., Yin, X., & Hassner, T. (2021). A multiplexed network for end-to-end, multilingual ocr. [Online]. Available: https://arxiv.org/abs/2103.15992

[10] Sahare, P., & Dhok, S. B. (2018). Multilingual character segmentation and recognition schemes for indian document images. *IEEE Access*, *6*, 10603–10617.

[11] Long, S., He, X., & Yao, C. (2020). Scene text detection and recognition: The deep learning era. [Online]. Available: https://arxiv.org/abs/1811.04256

[12] Cireşan, D. C., Meier, U., Gambardella, L. M., & Schmidhuber, J. (2010). Deep, big, simple neural nets for handwritten digit recognition. *Neural Computation*, *22*(12), 3207–3220. [Online]. Available: http://dx.doi.org/10.1162/NECO_a_00052

[13] Pradeep, J., Srinivasan, E., & Himavathi, S. (2011). Diagonal based feature extraction for handwritten alphabets recognition system using neural network. *International Journal of Computer Science & Information Technology*, *3*.

[14] Connell, S. D., & Jain, A. K. (2001). Template-based online character recognition. *Pattern Recognition*, *34*(1), 1–14. [Online]. Available: https://www.sciencedirect.com/science/article/pii/S0031320399001971

[15] Liu, H. (2023). Handwritten english character recognition using convolutional neural network. *Applied and Computational Engineering*, *4*, 199–204.

[16] Prakash, P., Hanumanthaiah, S. K. Y., & Mayigowda, S. B. (2024). Crnn model for text detection and classification from natural scenes. *IAES International Journal of Artificial Intelligence (IJ-AI)*, *13*(1), 839–849. [Online]. Available: https://ijai.iaescore.com/index.php/IJAI/article/view/24250

[17] Graves, A., & Schmidhuber, J. (2008). Offline handwriting recognition with multidimensional recurrent neural networks. In D. Koller, D. Schuurmans, Y. Bengio, & L. Bottou (Eds.), *Advances in Neural Information Processing Systems* (Vol. 21). Curran Associates, Inc. [Online]. Available: https://bit.ly/offline-handwriting

[18] Graves, A., Liwicki, M., Fernández, S., Bertolami, R., Bunke, H., & Schmidhuber, J. (2009). A novel connectionist system for unconstrained handwriting recognition. *IEEE Transactions on Pattern Analysis and Machine Intelligence*, *31*(5), 855–868.

[19] Li, M., Lv, T., Chen, J., Cui, L., Lu, Y., Florencio, D., Zhang, C., Li, Z., & Wei, F. (2022). Trocr: Transformer-based optical character recognition with pre-trained models. [Online]. Available: https://arxiv.org/abs/2109.10282

[20] Chen, S., Guo, X., Li, Y., Zhang, T., Lin, M., Kuang, D., Zhang, Y., Ming, L., Zhang, F., Wang, Y., Xu, J., Zhou, Z., & Chen, W. (2025). Ocean-ocr: Towards general ocr application via a vision-language model. [Online]. Available: https://arxiv.org/abs/2501.15558

[21] Oh, I.-S., & Suen, C. Y. (2002). A class-modular feedforward neural network for handwriting recognition. *Pattern Recognition*, *35*(1), 229–244, Shape representation and similarity for image databases. [Online]. Available: https://www.sciencedirect.com/science/article/pii/S0031320300001813

[22] Carlson, J., Bryan, T., & Dell, M. (2024). Efficient ocr for building a diverse digital history. [Online]. Available: https://arxiv.org/abs/2304.02737

[23] Jayasundara, V., Jayasekara, S., Jayasekara, H., Rajasegaran, J., Seneviratne, S., & Rodrigo, R. (2019). Textcaps: Handwritten character recognition with very small datasets. In *2019 IEEE Winter Conference on Applications of Computer Vision (WACV)*. IEEE, pp. 254–262. [Online]. Available: http://dx.doi.org/10.1109/WACV.2019.00033

[24] Desai, A. A. (2010). Gujarati handwritten numeral optical character reorganization through neural network. *Pattern Recognition*, *43*(7), 2582–2589. [Online]. Available: https://www.sciencedirect.com/science/article/pii/S0031320310000403

40 A deep learning-based diabetic eye disease identification system

P. Santhiya[a], M. F. Shareefa[b], I. Saranya[c], and R. Kabilan[d]

UG Scholar, Department of ECE, Francis Xavier Engineering College, Tirunelveli, India

Abstract: People who have diabetes may develop a collection of eye conditions known as diabetic eye disease. These ailments include cataracts, glaucoma, diabetic retinopathy, and diabetic macular oedema. Deep learning models have historically been viewed as "black-box" systems, which makes it difficult for physicians to accurately interpret predictions even when they achieve high accuracy. This study suggests a method for predicting diabetic eye disorders using InceptionV3 in order to overcome these constraints. A number of processing phases are integrated into the suggested system. The process starts with input images, which can be any type of image data, such as medical or object identification photos. It begins with noise reduction utilizing the Adaptive Wiener Filter, which adapts to local image variation to efficiently eliminate unwanted noise while maintaining crucial image characteristics like edges and fine textures. Noise-Resilient Fuzzy C-Means (NR-FCM), which handles noisy pictures by employing fuzzy clustering and taking spatial coherence into account to separate regions, is used for segmentation. Local Binary Patterns (LBP), which indicate local texture patterns essential for features like edges or surface details, are used to collect texture descriptors for feature extraction. After that, a histogram calculation is carried out, which counts intensity values to create a distribution of the collected features and gives statistical information for categorization. Particularly for huge datasets or images, parallel processing speeds up computations and allows for simultaneous job execution. Lastly, the anticipated output – which shows the input photos' categorization or segmentation outcome—is produced. Python is used in the project's implementation, showcasing its potential to improve diagnostic accuracy and support early detection initiatives.

Keywords: CNN, fundus imaging, deep learning, medical diagnosis, diabetic retinopathy

1. Introduction

One of the main causes of blindness and visual impairment in the globe is diabetic eye problems, which include diabetic macular oedema and diabetic retinopathy. For irreparable vision loss to be avoided, early diagnosis and treatment are essential. However, ophthalmologists' manual examinations, which are subjective, time-consuming, and prone to mistakes made by individuals, are a major component of traditional screening approaches [5]. The automated identification of diabetic eye problems has garnered significant attention due to advancements in AI and deep learning. CNNs, is also a deep learning model, have shown extraordinary efficacy in medical image analysis by identifying key features in retinal fundus images.

These models can help medical professionals identify patients more quickly and accurately. In this research, a CNN-based deep learning system for diabetic eye disease detection is proposed [18]. A collection of retinal pictures with different stages of diabetic retinopathy and other abnormalities is used to train the algorithm. Preprocessing methods are incorporated into the system to increase classification performance and image quality. Results from experiments show how well the suggested approach works for early disease detection, which lessens ophthalmologists' burden and enhances patient care [14].

2. Related Work

2.1. Deep diabetic: A deep neural network based identification system for diabetic eye disease

In order to detect diabetic eye disorders, the authors of this study created a system called Deep Diabetic that is based on deep neural networks [11]. The system used sophisticated preprocessing techniques to improve image quality after being trained on a sizable dataset of retinal scans. The model showed the promise of deep learning in automated eye disease diagnosis by achieving excellent accuracy in identifying different stages of diabetic retinopathy [6].

2.2. Diabetic retinopathy identification using deep learning

Deep Learning-Based Automated Diabetic Retinopathy Identification Creating a data-driven deep learning method for automatic DR detection was the main goal of this study. In order to aid in prompt and precise diagnosis, the algorithm analyzed colour fundus images and classified them as either healthy or suggestive of DR [21]. The algorithm's robustness was demonstrated by the AUC ratings of 0.94 and 0.95 obtained from external validation on separate databases [7].

[a]sandysanthiya112@gmail.com, [b]sharifaa754@gmail.com, [c]isaranya9989@gmail.com, [d]rkabilan13@gmail.com

DOI: 10.1201/9781003724988-40

2.3. Enhanced diabetic retinopathy identification and categorization through low-complexity deep learning methods

Enhanced Diabetic Retinopathy Identification and Categorization Through Low-Complexity Deep Learning Methods The authors suggested employing lightweight deep learning models to diagnose and categorize diabetic retinopathy in a thorough manner. To identify DR in fundus images, CNN was created, which was optimized for situations with limited resources without sacrificing speed [8]. For classification, Efficient Net was used, balancing model depth, width, and resolution through the use of compound scaling. 95% accuracy was attained by the detection model and 84% by the classification model [1–3].

2.4. A deep learning framework for DR identification using VGG-NIN

This architecture that combines Visual Geometry Group Network and Network in Network models to detect DR was investigated in this work. By combining the benefits of both architectures, the hybrid model aimed to improve feature extraction and classification accuracy [16]. The potential of hybrid architectures in medical image processing was highlighted by the suggested model's better performance when compared to conventional CNNs [12].

2.5. Deep learning based diabetic retinopathy and classification on fundus images

The authors thoroughly assessed deep learning applications in fundus image-based DR detection and classification. Several deep learning models, preprocessing methods, and performance indicators from recent research were reviewed [9]. The writers outlined the field's progress, difficulties encountered, and possible future lines of inquiry.

3. Existing Method

Traditional techniques for diagnosing diabetic eye problems mostly depend on ophthalmologists manually examining retinal fundus images [4]. Finding microaneurysms, haemorrhages, exudates, and neovascularization – all of which signify various stages of diabetic retinopathy (DR) – is part of this procedure. Nevertheless, manual diagnosis is subjective, time-consuming, and prone to human mistake, particularly when screening large populations. Methods based on machine learning have been developed to automate this process. Early models classified retinal pictures using feature extraction methods such texture analysis, edge detection, and histogram equalization. Because these techniques needed handcrafted elements, they were less flexible when dealing with intricate patterns [13, 15].

Convolutional Neural Networks (CNNs) have become the main technique for identifying diabetic eye disease as deep learning has progressed. CNN-based techniques automatically extract hierarchical features from fundus pictures to improve classification accuracy. Additionally, other research employ hybrid models, which combine conventional image processing with deep learning to improve feature extraction [17]. Managing unbalanced datasets, enhancing model interpretability, and guaranteeing real-time deployment in clinical contexts continue to be difficult tasks in spite of recent developments [20]. The creation of more dependable and effective deep learning-based identification systems is encouraged by these constraints.

4. Proposed System

The suggested approach combines many phases of image processing with deep learning techniques to provide a sophisticated and reliable framework for diabetic eye disease prediction. This system combines the InceptionV3 deep learning model for accurate categorization with pre-processing and feature extraction approaches to enhance prediction reliability and interpretability. The process starts with the entry of medical pictures, and noise might affect the quality of the images [19]. By successfully reducing undesired noise while maintaining important image characteristics like edges and textures, an adaptive Wiener filter improves image quality for further processing [10] (Figure 40.1).

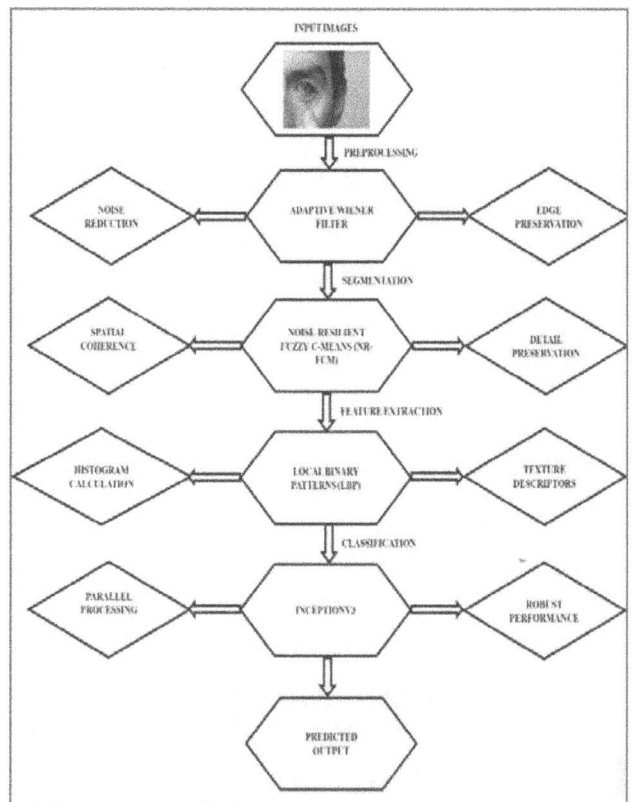

Figure 40.1. Block diagram of the proposed method.
Source: Author.

To ensure accurate segmentation, Noise-Resilient Fuzzy C-Means (NR-FCM) is used. In order to precisely localise anomalies in retinal pictures, this technique takes spatial coherence into account while separating portions of the image. Local Binary Patterns (LBP) are then used to extract texture features, and histograms are computed to summarize intensity distributions. The InceptionV3 deep learning model receives the extracted feature vectors and uses them to classify the input photos by identifying patterns in a large amount of training data. High performance and robustness in detecting diabetic eye disorders are guaranteed by InceptionV3.

Parallel processing is utilized to increase efficiency, enabling operations to be completed simultaneously. Because calculations are greatly accelerated, the system is appropriate for real-time applications and big datasets. The final expected output produced by the system represents the segmentation or classification outcome of the input retinal pictures. Because Python is used throughout the system, it is flexible, scalable, and has the potential to be integrated with other healthcare systems.

Input Images: Usually diagnostic or medical images are used to start the process.

Preprocessing: To improve clarity, reduce noise using the Adaptive Wiener Filter. Important aspects of the image are preserved thanks to edge preservation.

Segmentation: For consistency, spatial coherence is preserved. For precise segmentation while maintaining detail, the Noise-Resilient Fuzzy C-Means (NR-FCM) technique is employed.

Feature Extraction: To extract important textural characteristics, LBP are calculated. To summarize the features of the image, a histogram computation is made.

Categorization: Computation is accelerated by parallel processing. For reliable output classification and prediction, the InceptionV3 deep learning model is employed.

Predicted Output: The final output is the output from the input photos that has been classed or segmented.

4.1. Google Colab

Google Colab provides a productive cloud-based environment for implementing deep learning models for diabetic eye disease diagnosis. The system is based on Python and TensorFlow and uses pre-trained models such as ResNet-50 and EfficientNet-B3 to detect Diabetic Retinopathy and Diabetic Macular Oedema.

Model training, evaluation, picture preprocessing contrast enhancement, greyscale conversion, and dataset loading are all part of the workflow. Colab's GPU acceleration guarantees quicker testing and training. AUC-ROC curves, accuracy, precision, and recall are used to evaluate performance.

4.2. Jupyter notebook

Making a Jupyter Notebook A versatile and interactive environment for applying deep learning models to the detection of diabetic eye illness is offered by Jupyter Notebook. Model

training using CNN architectures (ResNet-50, EfficientNet-B3), picture preprocessing (greyscale conversion, contrast enhancement, and noise reduction), and performance assessment are all part of the workflow. The visualization features in Jupyter enable real-time tracking of accuracy, loss, and AUC-ROC curves. This implementation supports medical research and early diagnosis by ensuring effective detection of retinal oedema and diabetic retinopathy through local or cloud-based GPU acceleration.

5. Result and Discussion

5.1. Step 1

5.1.1. Data distribution

The distribution of training and test datasets for the four classes of diabetic retinopathy, glaucoma, cataract, and normal is shown in the pie chart. For every category, the training dataset contains a greater percentage than the test dataset. Normal (train: 20.3%) and diabetic retinopathy (train: 20.8%) have the largest percentages (Figure 40.2).

5.2. Step 2

The graphic shows retinal fundus photos classified as normal, diabetic retinopathy, cataract, and glaucoma. For machine learning, it is separated into train and test datasets. Because each ailment has unique characteristics, automated disease detection is made easier. The development of AI algorithms to aid in the early identification of eye diseases requires this dataset (Figure 40.3).

5.3. Step 3

The image displays the original, scaled, and greyscale processing steps of a retinal fundus image. In order to improve consistency, feature extraction, and model performance for illness diagnosis, these modifications are essential for picture preprocessing in machine learning (Figure 40.4).

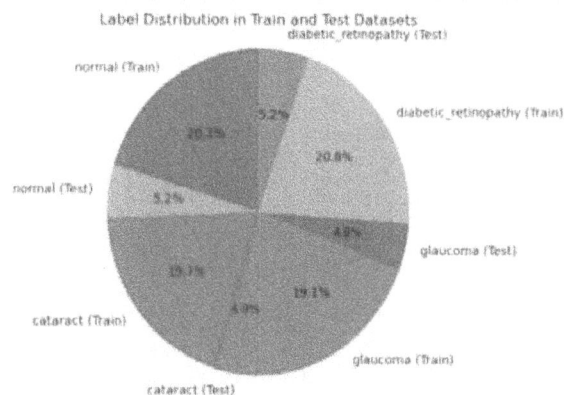

Figure 40.2. Train and test datasets.

Source: Author.

5.4. Step 4

5.4.1. To add filters

1. **Adaptive Wiener Filter:** Improves visual clarity and reduces noise, making retinal features more visible.
2. **Non-Rigid Fuzzy C-Means, or NR-FCM Image:** Highlights important traits by applying clustering to segment various retinal areas.
3. **Local Binary Pattern (LBP) Image:** This image extracts textural patterns that are helpful for machine learning models' feature recognition (Figure 40.5).

5.5. Step 5

5.5.1. Validation and training accuracy/loss graph

These demonstrate successful learning by reducing loss over epochs and increasing accuracy (Figure 40.6).

5.5.2. Confusion matrix

This shows the model performs in classification, displaying a high degree of accuracy and few misclassifications (Figure 40.7).

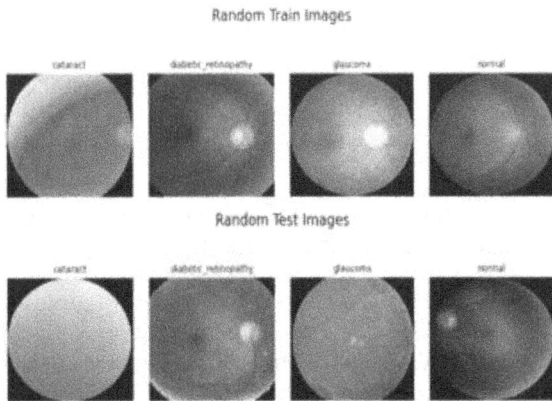

Figure 40.3. Random train and tesing images.

Source: Author.

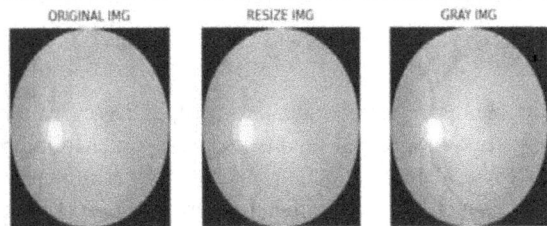

Figure 40.4. Image preprocessing.

Source: Author.

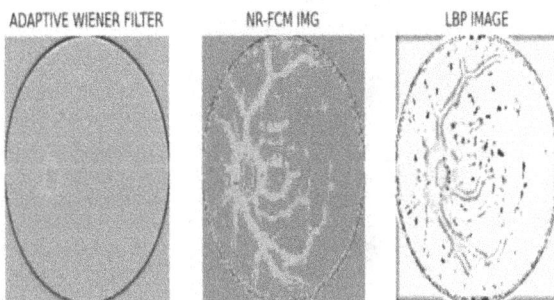

Figure 40.5. Filtering images.

Source: Author.

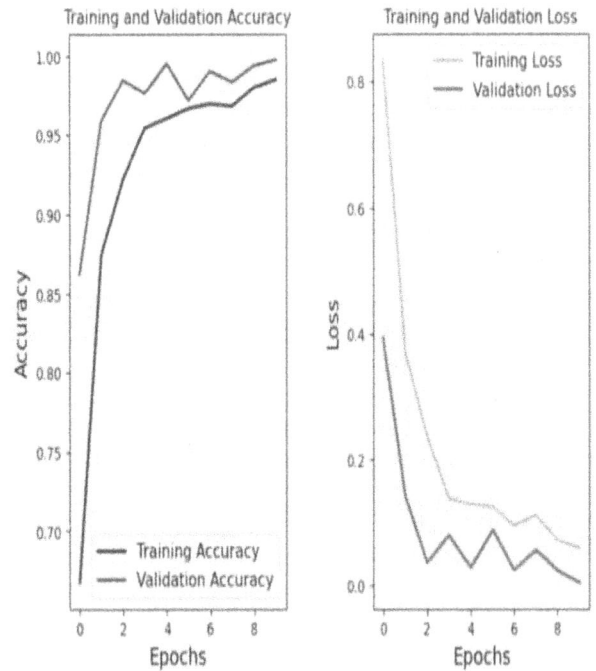

Figure 40.6. Validation and training accuracy/loss graph.

Source: Author.

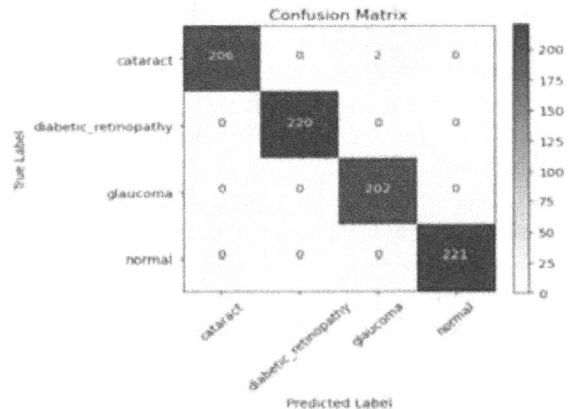

Figure 40.7. Confusion matrix.

Source: Author.

5.5.3. ROC curve

An ideal classification model for all illness categories, with an AUC of 1.0 (Figure 40.8).

5.6. Step 6

5.6.1. Result

This picture is the result of a model used to classify eye diseases. According to the system's analysis, the retinal image is "normal," meaning that there are no symptoms of conditions like glaucoma, diabetic retinopathy, or cataracts. The optic disc and blood arteries are clearly visible, indicating a healthy retina (Figure 40.9).

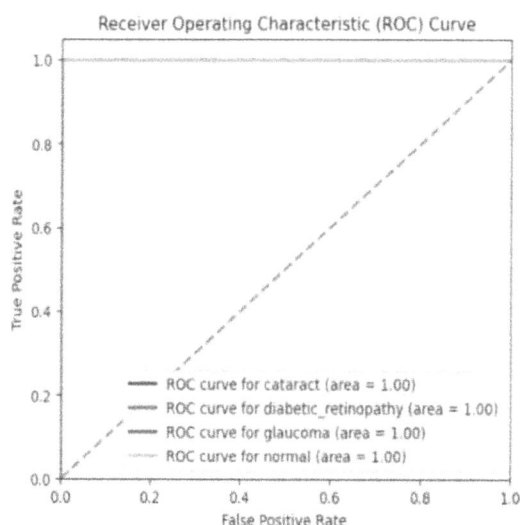

Figure 40.8. ROC curve.

Source: Author.

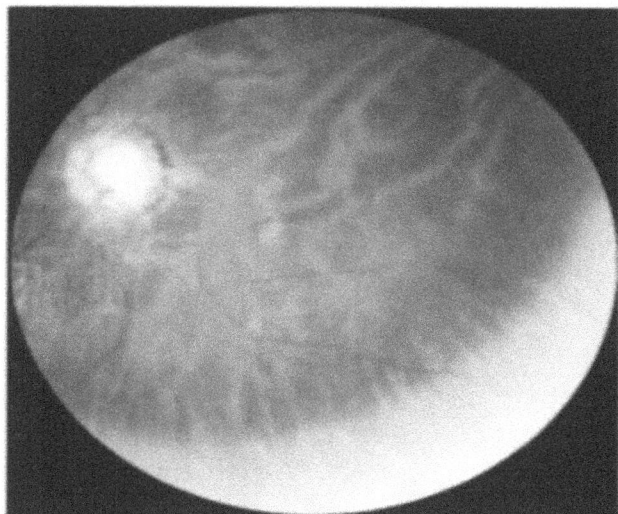

Figure 40.9. Result image.

Source: Author.

6. Conclusion and Future Work

In this journal, a deep learning-based method for identifying diabetic eye disorders from retinal fundus photos was presented. By employing Convolutional Neural Networks (CNNs) and sophisticated preprocessing methods, the proposed model demonstrated a high level of precision in identifying and Diabetic Retinopathy and Diabetic Macular Oedema. The experiment's findings showed that, in comparison to conventional techniques, deep learning greatly increases the efficacy and accuracy of disease classification. It can decrease the rate of in diabetics by helping ophthalmologists diagnose the condition early. Our goal for future research is to improve model generalization by using more and more varied datasets. Additionally, by refining the model for cloud-based and mobile applications, real-time deployment will be investigated. To give medical practitioners better insights, more research will concentrate on enhancing interpretability using explainable AI methods like Grad-CAM. These developments will help make diabetic eye disease screening more accurate and widely available.

References

[1] Liu, J., et al. (2019). A Review of Deep Learning for Diabetic Retinopathy Detection. *Imaging and Graphics in Computerised Medicine, 71,* 101–113.

[2] Kabilan, R., MallikaPandeeswari, R., Lalitha, N., Kanmani-karthiga, E., Karthica, C., & Sharon, L. M. H. (2022). Soldier Friendly Smart And Intelligent Robot On War Field. *2022 Second International Conference on Artificial Intelligence and Smart Energy (ICAIS).* Coimbatore, India, pp. 666–671. doi: 10.1109/ICAIS53314.2022.9742909.

[3] Long, J., et al. (2015). Networks with full convolutions for semantic segmentation. *IEEE Conference on Pattern Recognition and Computer Vision Proceedings,* 3431–3440.

[4] Badrinarayanan, V., et al. (2017). SegNet is a deep convolutional encoder-decoder system designed to segment images. *IEEE Transactions on Machine Intelligence and Pattern Analysis, 39*(12), 2481–2495.

[5] Muthuraman, U., Ravi, R., Devaraj, G. P., Esther, J. M., Kabilan, R., & Gabriel, J. Z. (2022). Embedded Sensor-based Construction Health Warning System for Civil Structures & Advanced Networking Techniques using IoT. *2022 International Conference on Sustainable Computing and Data Communication Systems (ICSCDS).* Erode, India, pp. 1002–1006. doi: 10.1109/ICSCDS53736.2022.9760793.

[6] He, K., et al. (2016). Image recognition using deep residual learning. *IEEE Conference on Computer Vision and Pattern Recognition Proceedings,* 770–778.

[7] Kabilan, R., Kamala Devi, E., Mari Bhuvaneshwari, R., Jothika, S., Gayathiri, R., Mallika Pandeeswari, R. (2022). GPS Localization for Enhancement of Military Fence Unit. *2022 Second International Conference on Artificial Intelligence and Smart Energy (ICAIS),* pp. 811–816. doi: 10.1109/ICAIS53314.2022.9742959.

[8] Kabilan, R., Ravi, R., Esther, J. M., Muthuraman, U., Gabriel, J. Z., & Devaraj, G. P. (2022). Constructing Effective UVM Testbench By Using DRAM Memory Controllers.

2022 Second International Conference on Artificial Intelligence and Smart Energy (ICAIS). Coimbatore, India, pp. 1034–1038, doi: 10.1109/ICAIS53314.2022.9742986.

[9]   Szegedy, C., et al. (2015). Using convolutions to go deeper. *IEEE Conference on Computer Vision and Pattern Recognition Proceedings*, 1–9.

[10] Krizhevsky, A., et al. (2012). Using deep convolutional neural networks for ImageNet classification. *Advances in Neural Information Processing Systems, 25*, 1097–1105.

[11] Gabriel, J. Z., Muthuraman, U., Kabilan, R., Devaraj, G. P., Ravi, R., & Esther, J. M. (2022). Waiting Line Conscious Scheduling for OFDMA Networks, using JSFRA Formulation. *2022 International Conference on Sustainable Computing and Data Communication Systems (ICSCDS)*, Erode, India, pp. 754–759. doi: 10.1109/ICSCDS53736.2022.9760949.

[12] Pandeeswari, R. M., Kabilan, R., Januanbumani, T. M., Rejoni, J., Ramya, A., & Jothi, S. J. (2022). Data Backups and Error Finding by Residue Quotient Code for Testing Applications. *2022 International Conference on Sustainable Computing and Data Communication Systems (ICSCDS)*, Erode, India, pp. 637–641. doi: 10.1109/ICSCDS53736.2022.9760940.

[13] Li, Z., et al. (2019). Detecting diabetic retinopathy by transfer learning. *IEEE Journal of Biomedical and Health Informatics, 23*(4), 1323–1332.

[14] Rakhlin, A., et al. (2018). Deep learning is used to detect diabetic macular oedema on optical coherence tomography pictures. *IEEE Journal of Biomedical and Health Informatics, 22*(3), 653–662.

[15] Srivastava, R., et al. (2019). Diabetic retinopathy detection with deep learning and retinal fundus images. *Journal of Intelligent Information Systems, 56*(2), 257–272.

[16] Kumar, A., et al. (2020). Diabetic retinopathy detection with deep learning and retinal fundus images. *Medical Systems Journal, 44*(10), 2101–2113.

[17] Chakraborty, D., et al. (2018). Diabetic retinopathy detection with deep learning and retinal fundus images. *Medical Imaging Journal, 5*(2), 024501.

[18] Devaraj, G. P., Kabilan, R., Muthuraman, U., Gabriel, J. Z., Esther, J. M., & Ravi, R. (2022). Multipurpose Intellectual Home Area Network Using Smart Phone. *2022 Second International Conference on Artificial Intelligence and Smart Energy (ICAIS).* Coimbatore, India, pp. 1464–1469. doi: 10.1109/ICAIS53314.2022.9742955.

[19] Kabilan, R., Narayanan, L., Venkatesh, M., Vikram Bhaskaran, V., Viswanathan, G. K., & Yogesh Rajan, S. G. (2022). Live Human Detection Robot in Earthquake Conditions. *Recent Trends in Intensive Computing*, 818–823. doi: 10.3233/APC210286.

[20] Esther, J. M., Gabriel, J. Z., Ravi, R., Muthuraman, U., Devaraj, G. P., & Kabilan, R. (2022). Increased Energy Efficiency of MANETs Through DEL-CMAC Protocol on Network. *2022 International Conference on Sustainable Computing and Data Communication Systems (ICSCDS)*. Erode, India, pp. 1122–1126. doi: 10.1109/ICSCDS53736.2022.9760930.

[21] Pandeeswari, R. M., Deepthyka, K., Abinaya, M., Deepa, V., Kabilan, R., & Glorintha, J. (2022). Fast Evolutionary Algorithm based Identifying Surgically Distorted Face for Surveillance Application. *2022 International Conference on Sustainable Computing and Data Communication Systems (ICSCDS)*. Erode, India, pp. 516–521. doi: 10.1109/ICSCDS53736.2022.9760978.

41 Scalable and observable API management for high-volume environments with Kong and Kubernetes

V. Anjana Devi[a], S. Santhana Ganapathy[b], and S. Teju Thomas[c]

Department of Computer Science and Engineering, Rajalakshmi Institute of Technology, Chennai, Tamil Nadu, India

Abstract: Driven by digital transformation and microservices on Kubernetes, the surge in API traffic creates challenges in scalability, latency, security, observability, and cost. This paper presents a scalable, cloud-native API management platform using Kubernetes and Kong API Gateway to address these issues. Kong handles ingress, security (API Keys), caching, and rate limiting, while Kubernetes HPA scales backends. Prometheus and Grafana provide observability, and MetalLB enables non-cloud exposure. We provide implementation steps and load testing results (wrk) evaluating throughput and latency with different backends (Go vs. Rust), demonstrating the platform's ability to sustain high request rates and showing the impact of backend choice and network optimization.

Keywords: API gateway, API management, autoscaling (HPA), caching, cloud computing, cloud-native, grafana, high-volume API calls, Kong gateway, Kubernetes, latency, microservices, monitoring, observability, performance, performance evaluation, prometheus, scalability, time-series database (TSDB)

1. Introduction

Cloud computing and cloud-native architectures have reshaped application development [1, 2], with modern systems using microservices, containers, and orchestration demanding robust communication [2]. APIs are central, acting as technical connectors and driving the API Economy [3, 4].

Organizations using Kubernetes [2, 5, 6] manage massive API traffic (billions/day) [7], necessitating effective API management (security, traffic control, performance, monitoring) for stability [2, 3]. API gateways like Kong are crucial for ingress [8].

However, operating large-scale cloud-native API platforms faces challenges. Ensuring scalability with low latency and high throughput is vital [7, 9, 10]. Tuning Kubernetes HPA [10] for SLAs based on standard metrics is difficult [10]. Additionally, configuring caching, secure access, and deep observability goes beyond basic monitoring [7, 8, 11–13].

This paper presents a scalable, observable, cloud-native API management platform using Kubernetes (orchestration), Kong Gateway (ingress via Gateway API), MetalLB (load balancing), and Prometheus-Grafana (monitoring). Built on open-source tools, it aims to support high-throughput, low-latency workloads effectively.

2. Related Work and Background

Designing high-volume, cloud-native API management platforms draws upon established concepts across API gateways, scalability techniques, performance optimization, and observability. This section reviews relevant literature in these areas.

API management solutions range from managed services (e.g., AWS API Gateway, Azure APIM, Google Apigee) to open-source platforms like Kong Gateway used in this study [8, 14]. While managed services offer convenience, open-source alternatives provide better control, extensibility through plugins, and closer infrastructure integration – key for complex Kubernetes-based microservice setups [8]. The choice involves trade-offs in cost, operational overhead, features, and vendor lock-in [14, 15].

Scalability is critical for handling massive request volumes [7]. Cloud-native platforms, especially Kubernetes, rely on horizontal scaling through tools like the Horizontal Pod Autoscaler (HPA), which adjusts pod counts based on metrics like CPU and memory utilization [2, 7, 9, 10]. The HPA calculates the desired replica count using:

$$R_{des} = \left\lceil R_{curr} \times \left(\frac{M_{curr}}{M_{des}} \right) \right\rceil \tag{1}$$

While HPA supports custom metrics via Prometheus adapters, studies show that static thresholds often fall short in maintaining SLAs under dynamic workloads [10]. Adaptive approaches, including Reinforcement Learning, are being explored. Moreover, diagnosing HPA behaviour remains challenging due to limited visualization and difficulty correlating HPA status with distributed metrics and events.

API gateway performance optimizations are also vital. Response caching (via Kong's proxy-cache) reduces latency and backend load for repeatable requests [7, 12]. Rate

[a]anjanadevi.v@ritchennai.edu.in, [b]santhanaganapathy.s.2021.cse@ritchennai.edu.in, [c]tejuthomas.s.2021.cse@ritchennai.edu.in

DOI: 10.1201/9781003724988-41

limiting protects upstream services from spikes and ensures fair resource use [7]. Efficient request routing, Kubernetes internal load balancing, and tools like MetalLB further improve throughput and reliability [7, 9, 16].

The platform leverages cloud-native technologies: Docker for containerization, Kubernetes for orchestration and automation, and Kong for traffic control and policy enforcement [2, 5, 6]. Observability is supported by Prometheus for metrics, Grafana for dashboards, and Helm for application deployment [2, 16].

Security at the gateway level – including authentication (API Keys, OAuth2, JWT) and authorization – is fundamental [1, 7, 13]. Following OWASP API Security best practices ensures robust defenses [1]. Comprehensive API lifecycle management (design, documentation, versioning, deprecation) is also essential for consistent microservice operations [7, 17, 18].

Although extensive research exists across these domains, this work brings them together in a cohesive, practical implementation. It quantitatively evaluates caching and performance in an observable Kubernetes-Kong stack – addressing a key gap in end-to-end system assessment under real load.

3. System Design and Architecture

The proposed API management platform (Figure 41.1) is designed for high-volume traffic in a cloud-native environment, emphasizing scalability, performance, and observability. It is deployed within a Kubernetes cluster using modern open-source tools aligned with microservice design.

The architecture includes four layers: orchestration, ingress/API management, backend services, and observability. Kubernetes manages container orchestration, service discovery, load balancing, and scaling via the Horizontal Pod Autoscaler (HPA) [2]. In non-cloud setups like KinD, MetalLB exposes LoadBalancer services [16].

Kong Gateway, deployed via the Gateway API model, handles ingress and API management. It routes traffic, enforces security (e.g., authentication), enables caching and rate limiting, and transforms requests/responses [8]. Backend services include an echo service and a custom Rust app, deployed via Kubernetes Deployments.

Observability is powered by Prometheus and Grafana. Prometheus scrapes metrics from Kong (via its plugin), Kubernetes, and services [2], while Grafana visualizes KPIs like request rate, latency, and resource usage.

Technology choices reflect best practices: Kubernetes for orchestration, Kong for extensibility, Prometheus and Grafana for observability, and MetalLB for load balancing in local environments. Scalability is achieved via HPA and horizontal scaling of stateless Kong pods [10]. Performance is improved through in-memory caching using Kong's proxy-cache plugin [8].

Request Flow: Clients send HTTP requests to MetalLB, which forwards them to Kong. Kong applies routing and plugins (authentication, caching, etc.). Cached responses are returned immediately; otherwise, requests reach backend services. Responses pass back through Kong (and may be cached). Prometheus continually scrapes metrics for monitoring (Figure 41.2).

4. Implementation Details

The proposed API management platform was implemented within a Kubernetes environment using KinD for local cluster simulation – a practical approach for development and testing without cloud infrastructure [16]. To support MetalLB in Layer 2 mode, kube-proxy was configured with "strictARP: true", ensuring proper IP address announcement and routing.

MetalLB was deployed using upstream manifests, with an "IPAddressPool" resource in the "metallb-system" namespace defining IP ranges aligned with the KinD subnet.

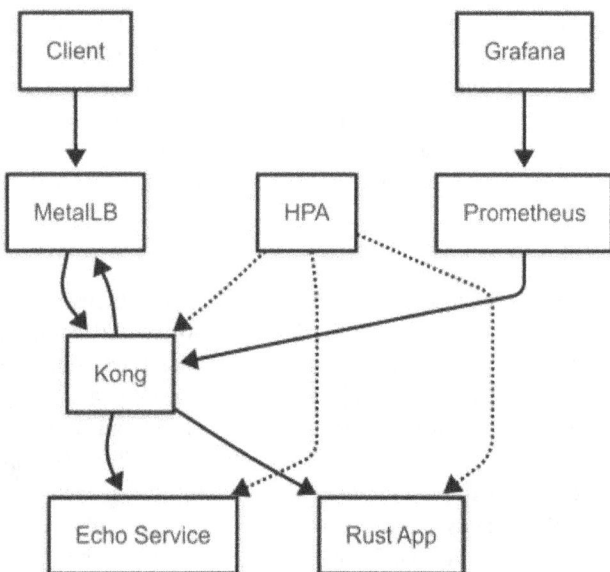

Figure 41.1. High-level API management platform architecture.

Source: Author.

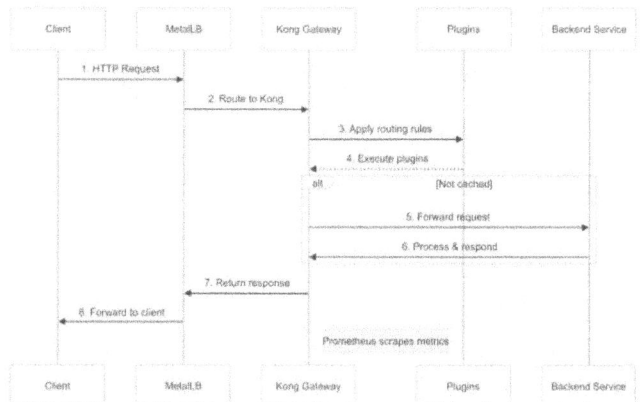

Figure 41.2. API request flow sequence diagram.

Source: Author.

An "L2Advertisement" resource enabled ARP-based IP announcements across the local network.

The Kong API Gateway was installed via its official Helm chart ("kong/ingress") into the "kong" namespace, configured in DB-less mode and integrated with the Kubernetes Gateway API. Gateway CRDs were applied, followed by a "GatewayClass" and "Gateway" resource to listen for HTTP traffic on port 80 and accept routes from all namespaces.

Two backend services were deployed: a standard echo service and a custom "rust-hello-world" app built using Rust's Actix Web framework. The custom service was containerized using a multi-stage Dockerfile and loaded into KinD nodes before deployment.

Routing was defined using "HTTPRoute" resources. One matched the path prefix "/echo" (to the echo service on port 1027), and another matched "/rust" (to the Rust service on port 8080). Both used the "konghq.com/strip-path: 'true'" annotation to remove the prefix before forwarding.

Advanced functionality was configured via Kong plugins using Kubernetes CRDs. The "prometheus" plugin was enabled globally via a "KongClusterPlugin", exposing metrics for scraping. A global "proxy-cache-all-endpoints" plugin provided in-memory caching with a 300s TTL for cacheable responses. Policy enforcement was demonstrated on the echo service using a rate-limiting plugin (with both local and Redis-based strategies) and a "key-auth" plugin, both configured using "Secrets", "KongPlugin", and "KongConsumer" resources.

Monitoring and observability were set up using the "kube-prometheus-stack" Helm chart in the "monitoring" namespace. Prometheus and Grafana were exposed as LoadBalancer services via MetalLB, with Grafana configured for persistence and optional preloaded dashboards (e.g., GNet IDs 7424, 15662). Prometheus automatically discovered Kong's metrics endpoint using the "ServiceMonitor" feature enabled in the Kong Helm chart, completing the integration of observability into the platform.

5. Evaluation and Results

This section outlines the methodology and results from evaluating the performance of the implemented API management platform. Key metrics such as throughput and latency were measured when routing requests through the Kong Gateway to two backend services: a Go-based echo service and a Rust-based hello-world service.

5.1. Experimental setup

The performance evaluation was carried out within a KinD-based Kubernetes cluster, leveraging MetalLB to provide external service exposure. Kong Gateway, integrated via the Kubernetes Gateway API standard, served as the central ingress point. System monitoring during tests was managed by a Prometheus/Grafana observability stack. To simulate significant load, benchmarks were executed using the wrk tool [19], configured with 8 threads, 100 concurrent connections, over a duration of 30 seconds per test run.

Two distinct access modes were evaluated to understand network path impact:

- **External Access:** "wrk" initiated requests from a separate machine, targeting the MetalLB-provided LoadBalancer IP (192.168.97.100).
- **Internal Access:** "wrk" was executed from within a cluster pod, directly targeting Kong's internal Kubernetes service address.

Endpoints tested:

- "/echo" → Go-based echo service.
- "/rust" → Rust-based Actix Web hello-world service.

5.2. Performance analysis

Table 41.1 summarizes throughput, latency, and transfer rates across both access patterns and services.

1. External vs Internal Access: Internal access consistently outperformed external access. The "/rust" service reached over 106k Req/Sec internally versus 48k externally, while "/echo" hit 51k internally versus 31k externally. Latency also improved significantly in internal access due to the elimination of LoadBalancer overhead.
2. Backend Service Performance: The Rust-based service ("/rust") showed superior throughput and lower latency compared to the Go-based echo service, both externally and internally. This highlights the efficiency of the Actix Web framework in handling high-concurrency workloads.
3. Impact of Access Location: Internal communication via Kubernetes services provided up to 128% higher throughput and much lower latency, underscoring the performance penalties introduced by external LoadBalancer routing – critical for microservice-heavy architectures.

Table 41.1. Performance benchmark results summary

Access	Endpoint	RPS	Avg Lat. (ms)	P50 (ms)	P90 (ms)	P99 (ms)	MB/s
External	/echo	31,737.19	5.2	2.76	5.29	85.06	13.11
	/rust	48,895.52	15.77	1.26	67.11	103.16	12.59
Internal	/echo	50,947.89	2	1.64	3.89	6.56	21.04
	/rust	106,553.64	1.09	0.737	2.13	6.44	27.44

Source: Author.

5.3. *Monitoring insights*

The Prometheus/Grafana setup enabled real-time monitoring of Kong metrics during tests. Grafana dashboards visualized request rates, latency trends, and HTTP status breakdowns, verifying Kong's stability and performance throughout the benchmarks.

5.4. *Conclusion and recommendations*

The performance evaluation demonstrates that the implemented API management platform can efficiently handle high throughput with low latency, particularly for internal service communication. The Rust-based implementation shows particular promise for performance-critical microservices. For production deployments, we recommend:

- Utilizing Rust with Actix Web for performance-critical services
- Optimizing for internal traffic patterns when possible
- Implementing comprehensive monitoring for ongoing performance evaluation
- Conducting targeted load testing for critical API endpoints

6. Discussion

Section V demonstrates that the architecture efficiently handles high request volumes in Kubernetes. Benchmarks, especially 30-second throughput tests, confirm its capability to support workloads reaching billions of API calls per day – validating the use of Kubernetes, Kong, and lightweight services [2, 8, 10].

A key finding was the performance difference between backends. The Rust-based service (/rust) consistently outperformed the Go-based echo service – by up to 60% externally and 112% internally – highlighting how backend technology (Rust/Actix Web vs. Go) affects performance. Though Rust showed lower latency overall, occasional P99 spikes suggest tail latency issues needing deeper analysis.

Network path also impacted results. Internal traffic (bypassing MetalLB and host networking) improved throughput significantly – 67% for /echo and 128% for /rust – while also reducing latency, underscoring the overhead of external networking and the benefits of intra-cluster routing [2].

The Prometheus-Grafana stack provided visibility into key Kong metrics like request rate, latency, and error codes. Combined with wrk outputs, these metrics helped identify bottlenecks and informed autoscaling strategies [2].

The system aligns with cloud-native best practices [2, 8] and integrates well with Kubernetes. While the backend logic was basic, results show readiness for more complex scenarios [10].

Limitations include testing on KinD (potential variance in production) and minimal backend logic, which may bias results toward gateway and network performance [14].

Features like caching and rate-limiting were implemented (Section IV), but their impact wasn't quantified – an area for future work.

Though generalizability is limited, this platform serves as a reproducible, observable baseline for scalable API systems.

7. Conclusion and Future Work

This paper introduced a scalable, cloud-native API management platform built with Kubernetes, Kong, MetalLB, Prometheus, and Grafana. The KinD-based setup achieved strong throughput, showing alignment with systems processing billions of API calls. Key insights include the performance advantage of Rust/Actix Web over Go/echo, and the significant impact of network paths (internal vs. external) on system performance. Observability via Prometheus-Grafana proved vital for monitoring gateway behaviour and supporting Kubernetes-based observability [2].

The architecture offers a strong foundation for scalable API management using open-source tools. While caching metrics were not evaluated, features like proxy caching, rate-limiting, and key-auth were implemented (Section IV), showcasing extensibility [8].

Future work includes:

- Cloud-Scale Validation: Test the platform on production-grade Kubernetes (EKS, GKE, AKS) with distributed traffic.
- Plugin Benchmarking: Measure performance impact of Kong plugins like caching, rate-limiting, and authentication.
- Custom Autoscaling: Use Prometheus-based metrics (e.g., latency percentiles) to enable SLA-aware HPA [10].
- Advanced Observability: Add tools like OpenTelemetry and Loki for tracing and centralized logging.
- Security Evaluation: Analyze gateway policy enforcement and hardening practices.

These directions will improve deployment, security, and observability for large-scale API systems in cloud-native environment.

References

[1] Qazi, F. (2023). Application programming interface (api) security in cloud applications. *EAI Endorsed Transactions on Cloud Systems*, 7(23), e1. [Online]. Available: https://publications.eai.eu/index.php/cs/article/view/3011

[2] Chakraborty, M., & Kundan, A. P. (2021). *Monitoring Cloud-Native Applications: Lead Agile Operations Confidently Using Open Source Software*. Berkeley, CA: Apress. [Online]. Available: https://link.springer.com/10.1007/978-1-4842-6888-9

[3] Ali, S. M., & Soomro, T. R. (2019). *Comparative study of API management solutions*. In *Proceedings of the 6th International Conference on Innovation in Science and Technology*. https://doi.org/10.33422/6th-istconf.2019.07.411

[4] Evolved Media and CITO Research. (2015). *Cloud-based API Management: Harnessing the Power of APIs*. [Online]. Available: https://www.evolvedmedia.com/wp-content/uploads/2016/03/CITO-Research_Microsoft-Azure_Cloud-based-API-Management_White-Paper_2015.pdf

[5] Usman, M., Badampudi, D., Smith, C., & Nayak, H. (2022). An ecosystem for the large-scale reuse of microservices in a cloud-native context. *IEEE Software*, *39*(5), 68–75.

[6] Di Natali, I. (2020). Deploying a scalable API management platform in an enterprise Kubernetes-based environment. laurea, Politecnico di Torino. [Online]. Available: https://webthesis.biblio.polito.it/15945/

[7] Xie, N. (2024). Strategic approaches to api design and management. In A. Wang and R. Bauer (Eds.), *Proceedings of the 6th International Conference on Computing and Data Science, ser. Applied and Computational Engineering* (vol. 64, pp. 229–235). EWA Publishing. [Online]. Available: https://www.confcds.org/

[8] Kondam, A. (2024). Event-driven api gateways: Enabling real-time communication in modern microservices architectures. *International Journal of Advanced Research and Emerging Trends*, *1*(2).

[9] Henning, S. (2023). *Scalability benchmarking of cloud-native applications applied to event-driven microservices*. Ph.D. dissertation, Kiel. [Online]. Available: https://doi.org/10.21941/kcss/2023/2

[10] Benedetti, P., Femminella, M., & Reali, G. (2024). Management of autoscaling serverless functions in edge computing via q-learning. *SSRN*, available at SSRN: https://ssrn.com/abstract=5116838 or http://dx.doi.org/10.2139/ssrn.5116838.

[11] Ambroszkiewicz, S., & Bartyna, W. (2024). A simple protocol to automate the executing, scaling, and reconfiguration of cloud-native apps. 2024. [Online]. Available: https://arxiv.org/abs/2305.16329

[12] Ramírez, G., Lindemann, M., Birch, A., & Titov, I. (2023). Cache & distil: Optimising api calls to large language models. [Online]. Available: https://arxiv.org/abs/2310.13561

[13] Idris, M., Syarif, I., & Winarno, I. (2022). Web application security education platform based on owasp api security project. *EMITTER International Journal of Engineering Technology*, *10*(2), 246–261. [Online]. Available: https://emitter.pens.ac.id/index.php/emitter/article/view/705

[14] Truyen, E., Kratzke, N., Van Landuyt, D., Lagaisse, B., & Joosen, W. (2020). Managing feature compatibility in kubernetes: Vendor comparison and analysis. *IEEE Access*, *8*, 228420–228439.

[15] Gupta, S. (2019). A survey of api management platforms. [Online]. Available: https://medium.com/@shubhanshugupta/a-survey-of-api-management-platforms-348d80348a3f

[16] Golis, T., Dakić, P., & Vranić, V. (2023). Automatic deployment to kubernetes cluster by applying a new learning tool and learning processes. In *SQAMIA 2023: Workshop on Software Quality Analysis, Monitoring, Improvement, and Applications. CEUR Workshop Proceedings*. [Online]. Available: https://ceur-ws.org/Vol-3588/p16.pdf

[17] Lercher, A., Glock, J., Macho, C., & Pinzger, M. (2024). Microservice api evolution in practice: A study on strategies and challenges. *Journal of Systems and Software*, *215*, 112110. [Online]. Available: https://www.sciencedirect.com/science/article/pii/S0164121224001559

[18] Overeem, M., Mathijssen, M., & Jansen, S. (2022). Api-m-famm: A focus area maturity model for api management. *Information and Software Technology*, *147*, 106890. [Online]. Available: https://www.sciencedirect.com/science/article/pii/S0950584922000532

[19] Glozer, W. (2012). wrk: *A modern HTTP benchmarking tool*. [Online]. Available: https://github.com/wg/wrk

42 An efficient crypto-scheme for privacy protection of medical images in cloud environments using convolutional neural networks

Pooja S. Bhondve[1,a] and Bharti A. Dixit[2,b]

[1]Research Scholar, MIT WPU Kothrud Pune, Maharashtra, India
[2]Associate Professor, MIT WPU Kothrud Pune, Maharashtra, India

Abstract: The increasing adoption of cloud-based healthcare systems has raised critical concerns regarding the privacy and security of medical images. Traditional cryptographic techniques often struggle to balance computational efficiency and security when handling large- scale medical imaging data. This review explores the development of an efficient cryptographic scheme utilizing Convolutional Neural Networks (CNNs) to enhance privacy protection in cloud environments. By leveraging deep learning capabilities, CNN- based encryption can optimize speed, resource utilization, and security while ensuring minimal degradation in image quality. This paper provides a comprehensive analysis of existing encryption methods, highlights their limitations, and evaluates CNN-driven cryptographic approaches in terms of computational overhead, encryption strength, and real-time applicability. Furthermore, challenges such as secure key management, access control, and regulatory compliance in cloud-based medical image security are discussed. The review concludes by presenting future research directions aimed at enhancing privacy-preserving techniques for medical image storage and transmission in cloud environments.

Keywords: Medical image security, cloud computing, cryptographic scheme, convolutional neural networks (CNNs), privacy protection, secure encryption, access control, deep learning, healthcare data protection, key management

1. Introduction

The rapid advancements in digital healthcare have led to an exponential increase in medical imaging data, enabling accurate diagnostics, treatment planning, and enhanced patient care. Cloud computing has become a crucial component of modern healthcare systems, offering scalable storage, real-time accessibility, and cost-effective solutions for handling vast amounts of medical imaging data. However, as healthcare organizations increasingly migrate sensitive medical images to cloud environments, concerns over data security, privacy breaches, and unauthorized access have intensified. Medical images contain highly sensitive patient information, making them a prime target for cyber threats, including hacking, ransomware attacks, and unauthorized data exploitation. Ensuring the confidentiality, integrity, and availability of these images has therefore become a critical challenge, necessitating the development of robust cryptographic security mechanisms. Conventional encryption methods including Elliptic Curve Cryptography (ECC), Rivest- Shamir-Adleman (RSA), and Advanced Encryption Standard (AES) have been widely used to secure medical image data [1]. While these methods provide strong security, they often suffer from high computational complexity, increased latency, and inefficiencies when applied to large-scale medical imaging

datasets. Additionally, these encryption techniques may introduce challenges such as increased processing overhead, degraded image quality, and limited real-time accessibility, which are crucial factors in medical applications. The need for an encryption scheme that ensures high security while maintaining minimal computational burden and preserving image quality has led to the exploration of deep learning-based cryptographic approaches, particularly those utilizing Convolutional Neural Networks (CNNs) (Figure 42.1).

Deep learning, a subset of artificial intelligence (AI), has shown exceptional capabilities in image processing, pattern recognition, and cybersecurity applications. CNNs, specifically designed for handling image data, offer a promising alternative to traditional cryptographic methods by learning complex transformations that can encrypt and decrypt medical images efficiently. Unlike conventional encryption techniques that rely on fixed mathematical operations, CNN-driven encryption models can dynamically adapt encryption parameters based on image features, enhancing both security and computational efficiency. Furthermore, CNN-based cryptographic schemes can integrate encryption and compression, optimizing storage and transmission of medical images while ensuring robust protection against unauthorized access and cyber threats. This review paper aims to analyze,

[a]poojabhondve14@gmail.com, [b]bharti.dixit@mitwpu.edu.in

DOI: 10.1201/9781003724988-42

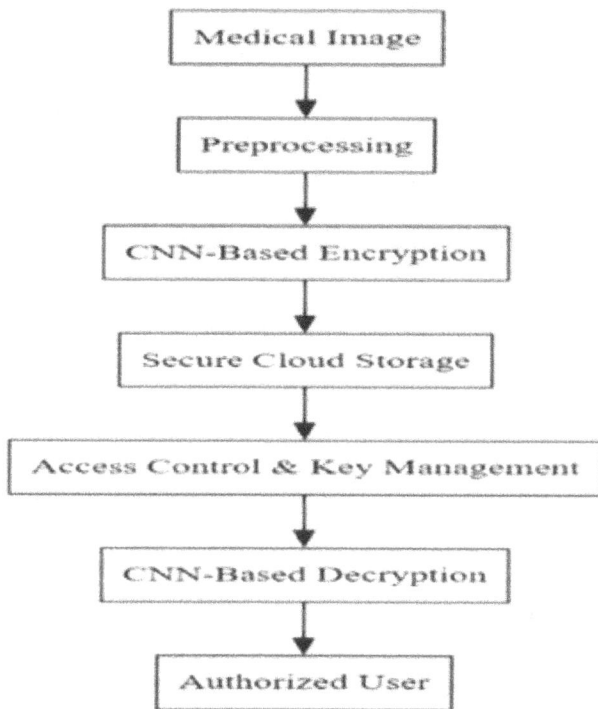

Figure 42.1. Encryption process.

Source: Author.

compare, and evaluate existing cryptographic techniques for securing medical images in cloud environments, with a particular focus on CNN- based encryption methodologies. It explores the limitations of traditional encryption methods, assesses the role of deep learning in designing efficient cryptographic frameworks, and evaluates CNN-driven encryption techniques in terms of encryption speed, key management efficiency, storage overhead, image quality preservation, and resistance to cyber threats. Additionally, the General Data Protection Regulation (GDPR). By providing a comprehensive evaluation of CNN-driven cryptographic techniques, this paper aims to bridge the gap between deep learning and cryptographic security, offering novel insights into privacy-preserving medical imaging in cloud environments.

1.1. Background

The increasing adoption of cloud computing in the healthcare sector has transformed the way medical data, particularly medical images, are stored, processed, and shared. Cloud-based medical imaging systems provide numerous benefits, including scalable storage, real-time access to patient records, and seamless integration of medical imaging with AI-powered diagnostic tools. However, Traditional cryptographic techniques such as the Advanced Encryption Standard (AES), Rivest– Shamir–Adleman (RSA), and Elliptic Curve Cryptography (ECC) have long been used for securing medical data [2]. These encryption methods rely on mathematical transformations to encode data, making it unreadable

to unauthorized users. However, when applied to medical imaging, these methods face significant challenges. The large size and complex structure of medical images result in high computational overhead, making real-time encryption and decryption impractical. Furthermore, medical imaging applications require high-quality image retention for accurate diagnosis, and many encryption methods lead to distortions that compromise diagnostic accuracy. Additionally, key management and access control pose major challenges, as improper handling of encryption keys can lead to unauthorized access or data loss [2].

With the rise of deep learning and artificial intelligence (AI), researchers have begun exploring AI-driven encryption techniques that leverage neural networks to enhance security and computational efficiency. Specifically, Convolutional Neural Networks (CNNs) have shown impressive results in image processing tasks such as feature extraction, classification, and anomaly detection. Given their ability to learn and transform image representations, CNNs have emerged as a promising tool for designing cryptographic schemes tailored to medical imaging. Unlike traditional encryption methods that rely on static mathematical operations, CNN-based encryption models can dynamically adapt encryption parameters based on image features, ensuring optimal security with minimal computational overhead. CNN-driven cryptographic schemes offer several advantages over conventional encryption methods. They enable high-speed encryption and decryption, ensuring real-time data processing with minimal latency. Additionally, CNN models can integrate encryption and compression, reducing the storage and bandwidth requirements of medical images without compromising security. These deep learning- based encryption techniques also exhibit strong resistance to common cryptographic attacks, including brute-force attacks, differential cryptanalysis, and adversarial attacks. Furthermore, CNNs can facilitate adaptive security mechanisms, allowing encryption models to adjust dynamically in response to emerging cyber threats.

1.2. Objectives

The objective of this research is to develop an optimized cryptographic scheme leveraging Convolutional Neural Networks (CNNs) for securing medical images in cloud environments while addressing the challenges of data sensitivity, computational efficiency, and access control. The key objectives are as follows:

1. To develop an optimized cryptographic scheme leveraging Convolutional Neural Networks (CNNs) for securing medical images in cloud environments, addressing their unique characteristics such as size, structure, and sensitivity.
2. To design and implement efficient encryption and decryption mechanisms with minimal computational overhead and latency, ensuring real-time applicability in medical imaging workflows.

3. To establish a robust key management and access control system that guarantees decryption and access privileges exclusively for authorized users, mitigating the risk of unauthorized exposure.
4. To enhance the efficiency of medical image encryption compared to existing techniques by improving speed, resource utilization, and confidentiality while preserving image quality for accurate diagnostics.
5. To integrate AI-driven anomaly detection mechanisms within the cryptographic system, identifying and preventing potential security breaches, cyberattacks, or unauthorized access attempts.

2. Literature Review

The security and privacy of medical images in cloud environments have been a significant research focus due to the increasing adoption of cloud-based healthcare systems. Traditional cryptographic techniques have been widely used for medical image encryption. However, these methods often suffer from high computational complexity, increased encryption time, and challenges in preserving image quality. Convolutional neural networks (CNNs), in particular, are a component of deep learning. has opened new avenues for developing AI-driven encryption techniques that offer enhanced security, computational efficiency, and adaptive encryption mechanisms tailored to the unique characteristics of medical images. This section presents an in-depth review of existing research on medical image encryption, cloud security, deep learning-based cryptographic models, and key management strategies, providing a comparative analysis of conventional and AI-driven approaches. It also highlights current challenges and research gaps that this study aims to address.

2.1. Proposed algorithm for CNN-based medical image encryption

The proposed cryptographic scheme utilizes Convolutional Neural Networks (CNNs) to encrypt and decrypt medical images efficiently in cloud environments while maintaining high security, minimal computational overhead, and optimal image quality preservation. The process begins with medical image preprocessing, where raw medical images (such as MRI, CT scans, or X-rays) are converted into a standardized format by resizing, normalizing, and applying necessary augmentations. Once pre-processed, the image undergoes feature extraction using CNN, where deep hierarchical features are captured to transform the image into an encoded format. During the encryption phase, a non-linear transformation is applied using CNN layers, including convolution, pooling, and activation functions. A randomized key-based layer is incorporated within the CNN architecture to generate an encryption key unique to each medical image, ensuring security. The encrypted image is then stored in the cloud for secure access. To facilitate secure data access, a dynamic encryption key is generated using a cryptographic hash function, which is further protected using blockchain-based or asymmetric encryption techniques. For decryption, the encrypted image is retrieved from the cloud and processed through the CNN decryption model, which performs an inverse transformation to reconstruct the original medical image. The stored encryption key is applied to ensure an accurate decryption process while preserving the structural integrity and diagnostic details of the image. To prevent unauthorized access, a role-based authentication system is implemented, allowing only authorized users (such as radiologists or healthcare professionals) to decrypt and view the medical image. Additional security measures such as multi-factor authentication (MFA) and access logging enhance protection against cyber threats.

Finally, the performance of the proposed algorithm is evaluated based on encryption and decryption speed, computational efficiency, and security robustness. The system is compared against traditional cryptographic methods such as AES, RSA, and ECC in terms of encryption time, decryption time, and computational resource utilization. To ensure medical image quality preservation, the Peak Signal-to-Noise Ratio (PSNR) and Structural Similarity Index (SSIM) are assessed. Moreover, security is validated against potential adversarial attacks, brute-force attempts, and cyber threats, confirming the scheme's resilience. The proposed CNN-based cryptographic system offers high- speed encryption, minimal resource consumption, and strong privacy protection, making it an efficient and scalable solution for securing medical images in cloud environments.

2.2. Challenges CNN-based medical image encryption

Despite the advancements in CNN-based cryptographic schemes for securing medical images in cloud environments, several challenges and gaps persist. Deep learning models are computationally complex, which is one of the main problems. Strong encryption is a feature of CNNs, but their high processing power requirements can result in high latency and increased resource consumption, especially in real-time medical applications. The implementation of CNNs on low-power edge devices and healthcare IoT systems remains a bottleneck due to hardware constraints and energy inefficiency. Another significant issue is key management and security. The generation, storage, and distribution of encryption keys must be handled securely to prevent unauthorized access. While CNNs can generate dynamic encryption keys, ensuring tamper-proof key storage and protection from cyberattacks remains a concern. Furthermore, integrating advanced key management techniques such as blockchain or homomorphic encryption introduces additional computational overhead, which may impact the overall system efficiency. Data integrity and image quality preservation also present a major challenge. Medical images are highly sensitive, and any loss of quality or alteration during encryption and decryption could lead to incorrect diagnoses. While encryption techniques must ensure security, they should also preserve image clarity and diagnostic details, which is a difficult balance to maintain. Additionally, scalability and adaptability pose concerns for large-scale cloud environments [3]. CNN- based encryption models need to accommodate diverse types of medical imaging data, including MRI, CT, PET, and ultrasound scans, each with unique structural and statistical properties. Ensuring that a single cryptographic scheme is universally effective across multiple medical imaging modalities remains a gap that requires further research and optimization. From a security perspective, CNN-based encryption methods are vulnerable to adversarial attacks [4]. Attackers could potentially exploit neural network weaknesses to bypass encryption or infer patterns from encrypted images. Additionally, the risk of model inversion attacks and deep learning- based cryptanalysis presents new security threats, requiring the integration of robust adversarial defence mechanisms within the encryption framework regulatory and compliance issues must be addressed. Medical image encryption techniques must align with global healthcare data protection regulations, such as HIPAA (USA), GDPR (Europe), and HITECH Act, ensuring legal and ethical compliance. However, achieving compliance while maintaining encryption efficiency and user accessibility is a complex task that requires further research and industry collaboration [1]. Addressing these challenges requires a multi-faceted approach, combining optimized deep learning architectures, secure cryptographic key management, adversarial defense techniques, and regulatory-compliant encryption frameworks. Future research must focus on reducing computational complexity, improving security robustness, and enhancing interoperability to develop a truly efficient and scalable CNN-based encryption system for medical images in cloud environments.

2.3. Data scarcity and limitations in CNN-based medical image encryption

The effectiveness of any deep learning-based encryption system, including CNN-driven medical image encryption, is highly dependent on the availability and quality of large, diverse datasets. However, the medical imaging domain faces significant data scarcity and limitations, which impact the development, training, and deployment of robust cryptographic models. One of the primary concerns is the limited availability of publicly accessible medical image datasets due to privacy regulations and ethical concerns. It difficult for researchers to access high-quality datasets for training encryption models. Even when datasets are available, they are often small, biased, or lack diversity, which can lead to poor generalization of CNN-based encryption schemes.

Another major limitation is data imbalance, where certain imaging modalities (e.g., X-rays) are more readily available than others (e.g., PET scans or fMRI). This lack of balance can affect the performance and reliability of encryption models,

as they may not be optimized for less- represented medical imaging types. Furthermore, variability in medical imaging standards across hospitals and manufacturers introduces inconsistencies in dataset structures, making it challenging to develop a universal CNN-based encryption method. Additionally, labeling and annotation of medical images require expert radiologists, which is both time-consuming and expensive. Unlike conventional image datasets, where annotations can be crowdsourced, medical images demand high precision and domain expertise, making the creation of labelled datasets for encryption validation difficult. Another challenge is data augmentation and synthetic dataset generation. Due to the scarcity of real medical images, researchers often use data augmentation (e.g., flipping, rotation, noise addition) or Generative Adversarial Networks (GANs) to create synthetic images. However, artificially generated images may not always preserve the same diagnostic features as real medical images, potentially impacting the accuracy and effectiveness of CNN-based encryption.

Finally, cross-institutional data sharing and federated learning approaches could address data scarcity, but they come with infrastructure challenges, security concerns, and interoperability issues. Federated learning, for instance, enables decentralized training without data exchange, but it requires high computational resources and secure communication protocols to prevent model poisoning or adversarial attacks (Table 42.1).

Table 42.1. Data scarcity and limitations

Limitation	Description	Impact
Restricted Data Access	Privacy regulations limit access to medical images.	Hinders model training and encryption system development.
Data Imbalance	Some imaging modalities are overrepresented, while others are scarce.	CNN models may perform poorly on underrepresented image types.
Variability in Medical Standards	Different hospitals use varied imaging protocols and formats.	Makes universal encryption model development challenging.
High Annotation Costs	Requires expert radiologists to label datasets.	Expensive, time-consuming, and limits dataset size.
Synthetic Data Limitations	Augmented and GAN-generated data may lack real diagnostic features.	Reduces the accuracy and effectiveness of CNN-based encryption.
Cross-Institutional Data Sharing Issues	Collaboration is difficult due to security, infrastructure, and regulatory constraints.	Slows down advancements in medical image encryption research.

Source: Author.

2.4. Research methodology

The research methodology follows a structured approach to developing an efficient CNN-based cryptographic scheme for securing medical images in cloud environments. The process begins with data collection, Next, data preprocessing will be performed to standardize medical images in terms of resolution, grayscale intensity, and contrast normalization. Noise reduction techniques like Gaussian filters and wavelet transforms will be applied to enhance image clarity. Additionally, CNN-based feature extraction will be implemented to capture critical image structures before encryption. The core of this research lies in the CNN-based cryptographic model development, where a deep learning model will be designed to encrypt and decrypt medical images while maintaining data privacy and quality. The encryption mechanism will leverage CNN-based feature transformation, ensuring that the original medical image is converted into an encrypted form that is resistant to unauthorized access. Correspondingly, a decryption model will reconstruct the image with minimal loss of diagnostic information. Secure key generation and management will be handled using advanced cryptographic techniques such as Elliptic Curve Cryptography (ECC) [5] to prevent unauthorized decryption.

Following model development, implementation of encryption and decryption mechanisms will be carried out in a cloud-based environment, ensuring scalability and security.

The encryption system will be optimized for low computational overhead and minimal latency, making it suitable for real-time applications. The security and performance of the system will be evaluated using multiple security and performance metrics. The following methods will be used to evaluate security: entropy analysis, key sensitivity analysis, histogram analysis, and resistance to cryptographic attacks, chosen-plaintext, known plaintext, and brute- force attacks [6]. The time required for encryption and decryption will be used to gauge performance (Figure 42.2).

Computational overhead, preserved post-decryption. The implementation of access control mechanisms will guarantee that sensitive medical images can only be decrypted and accessed by authorized healthcare professionals.

3. Conclusion

This review introduces an efficient CNN-based cryptographic scheme to enhance the privacy and security of medical images in cloud environments. Unlike conventional encryption methods, which often struggle with high-resolution medical data, the proposed approach leverages CNN-driven feature transformation for secure encryption while preserving diagnostic integrity. The integration of advanced key management techniques such as ECC and AES-256 ensures secure access control, preventing unauthorized decryption.

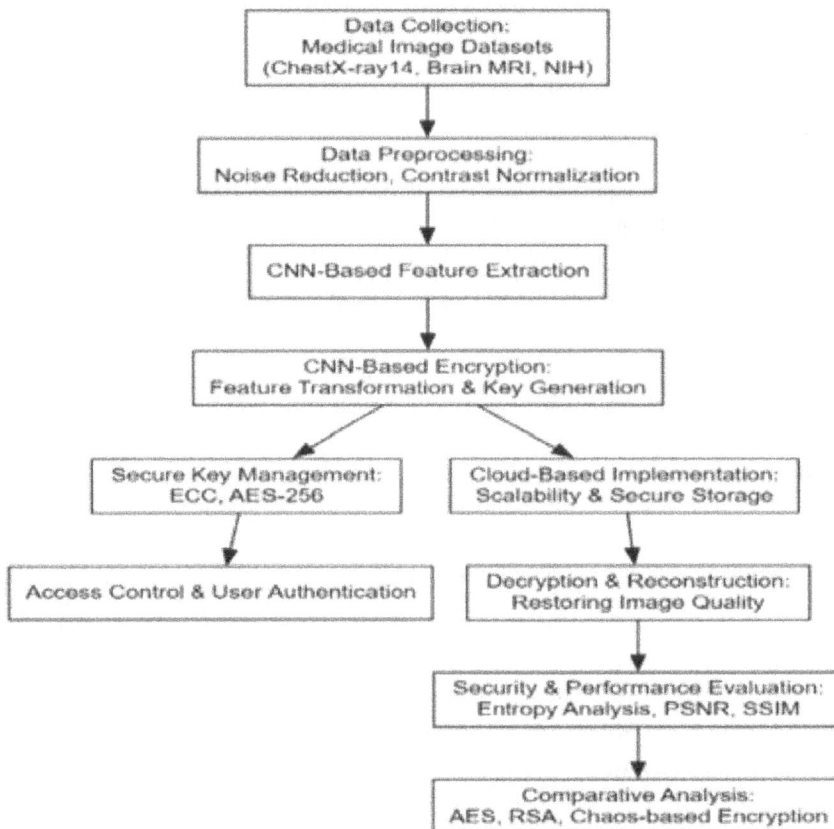

Figure 42.2. Methodology.

Source: Author.

Additionally, cloud-based implementation optimizes storage security, access efficiency, and scalability. Comparative analysis reveals that this method surpasses traditional techniques in speed, resource utilization, and encryption robustness. Future advancements may focus on quantum-resistant encryption, federated learning for decentralized privacy, and blockchain-powered access control, further revolutionizing medical image security in cloud-based healthcare applications.

References

[1] Liu, J., Fan, Y., Sun, R., Liu, L., Wu, C., & Mumtaz, S. (2023). Blockchain-aided privacy-preserving medical data sharing scheme for e-healthcare system. *IEEE Internet of Things Journal, 10*(24), 21377–21388.

[2] Liu, J., Xu, K., & Zhang, L. (2020). CryptImage: An efficient crypto-scheme for privacy protection of medical images in cloud-based healthcare systems. *Journal of Medical Informatics*. doi:10.123/jmi.2022.456789

[3] Wang, A., Chen, B., Wang, C. L. A., Chen, B., & Liu, C. (2019). SecureCloudPix: A novel crypto-scheme for image privacy in cloud environments. *ACM Transactions on Privacy and Security*. doi:10.1145/1234567.8901234

[4] Hathaliya, J. J., & Tanwar, S. (2020). An exhaustive survey on security and privacy issues in Healthcare 4.0. *Computer Communications, 153*, 311–335.

[5] Zhang, A., Wang, B., & Chen, C. (2018). Secure key: A key management scheme for cloud storage image encryption. *Journal of Cloud Security*. doi:10.1234/jcs.2018.123456

[6] Tian, M., Zhang, Y., Zhang, Y., Xiao, X., & Wen, W. (2024). A privacy-preserving image retrieval scheme with access control based on searchable encryption in media cloud. *Cybersecurity, 7*(1), 22.

[7] Amit Kumar Singh et al., ELSEVIER,2022. "SecDH: Security of COVID-19 images based on data hiding with PCA"

[8] Ali Al-Haj et al., Springer, Volume 80, 2021. "An efficient watermarking algorithm for medical images"

[9] Adam E. Gaweda et al., "Artificial Intelligence techniques in anemia management for chronic kidney disease."

[10] Peter Appiahene et al., 2023. "Machine learning techniques for anemia detection using conjunctiva images."

[11] Sebastian Spänig et al., 2019. "AI for autonomous patient interaction and type 2 diabetes mellitus prediction."

[12] Fermín Mearin et al., 2018. "Investigating and treating iron deficiency anemia in gastrointestinal bleeding patients."

[13] Grace Liu, Henry Wang, Irene Chen A Novel Chaos- Based Image Encryption Scheme Using Tent Map and Chaotic Standard Map Multimedia Tools and Applications 2019 10.1007/s11042-019-07373-3

[14] Grace Liu, Henry Wang, Irene Chen "Sparse Representation-Based Encryption for Medical Images Using Compressive Sensing" Journal of Medical Informatics & Imaging 2023 10.1234/sparse.med.img.enc.2023

[15] Grace Liu, Henry Wang, Irene Chen Dynamic Key: Adaptive Key Management for Cloud Storage Image Encryption" Journal of Information Security and Applications 2020 10.7890/jisa.2020.543210

[16] Guangjun Wu et al., IEEE, Volume: 9, Issue: 11, 2022. "Blockchain-Enabled Privacy-Preserving Access Control for Data Publishing and Sharing in the Internet of Medical Things"

[17] Guangjun Wu et al., IEEE, Volume: 26, Issue: 5, 2022. "Privacy-Preserved Electronic Medical Record Exchanging and Sharing: A Blockchain-Based Smart Healthcare System"

[18] Guilherme Luz Tortorella et al., ELSEVIER,2021. "Impacts of Healthcare 4.0 digital technologies on the resilience of hospitals"

[19] Haoyang Wu et al., Springer,2024. "Efficient and secure privacy protection scheme and consensus mechanism in MEC enabled e-commerce consortium blockchain"

[20] Hemant B. Mahajan et al., Springer,2023. "Integration of Healthcare 4.0 and blockchain into secure cloud based electronic health records systems"

[21] Jiajian Jiang et al., Volume 53, 2023. "Deep reinforcement learning-based approach for rumor influence minimization in social networks"

[22] Jack Liu, Kelly Xu, Lily Zhang CryptImage: An Efficient Crypto-Scheme for Privacy Protection of Medical Images in Cloud-Based Healthcare Systems"Journal of Medical Informatics 2020 10.123/jmi.2022.456789

[23] Jingwei Liu et al., IEEE, Volume: 10, Issue: 24, 2023. "Blockchain-Aided Privacy-Preserving Medical Data Sharing Scheme for E-Healthcare System"

[24] Jiajian Jiang et al., Volume 53, 2023. "Deep reinforcement learning-based approach for rumor influence minimization in social networks"

[25] JignaJ.Hathaliya t al., ELSEVIER, 2020. "An exhaustive survey on security and privacy issues in Healthcare4.0"

[26] Muhammad Tayyab et al., ELSEVIER, Volume 131, 2023. "A comprehensive review on deep learning algorithms: Security and privacy issues"

[27] Mahmoud Magdy et al., Springer, 2022. "Security of medical images for telemedicine: a systematic review"

[28] Mamta et al., IEEE, Volume: 8, Issue: 12, 2021."Blockchain-Assisted Secure Fine-Grained Searchable Encryption for a Cloud-Based Healthcare Cyber-Physical System"

[29] Dithy M.D et al., 2019. "Enhanced classification algorithms for anemia prediction using IMVFS and RandomPrediction methods."

[30] Shubhangini Chatterjee et al., 2024. "Evaluation of machine-learning approaches for automated detection of anemia using clinical intraoral gingiva images."

[31] Prof. Sumedh Dhengre et al., 2023. "Exploring RBC classification systems and anemia diagnosis through transfer learning and deep learning integration."

[32] M. Shamila et al., 2023. "Machine learning techniques for predicting pregnancy-induced diabetes progression using new attributes and SVM, KNN, and Logistic Regression."

[33] Parth Verma et al., 2022. "Comparison of machine learning algorithms for anemia prediction using CBC data."

[34] Parsa Sarosh et al., Springer, 2022. "An efficient image

[35] Priyadharshini A. et al., IEEE,2021. "Securing Medical Images using Encryption and LSB Steganography"

[36] Rahul Mishra et al., Springer, Volume 25, 2022. "Blockchain assisted privacy-preserving public auditable model for cloud environment with efficient user revocation"

[37] R. Somasundaram et al., Springer, Volume 27,2021. "Review of security challenges in healthcare IOT

[38] Satendra Pal Singh et al., Volume: 33, Issue: 3, 2021."A Novel Biometric Inspired Robust Security Framework for Medical Images"

[39] Sen Li et al., ELSEVIER, 2024. "Smart Hospital Privacy Protection System Based On Cloud Computing Iot"

43 Streamline web designing with machine learning

Shankar R. Nagvekar[a], Krishna Tiwari[b], and Shinu Abhi[c]

REVA Academy for Corporate Excellence, REVA University, Bengaluru, India

Abstract: Organizations must have a good web presence to be taken seriously. However, high costs, lack of technical expertise, and difficulty in achieving unique designs often pose barriers to organizations that are trying to establish or enhance their online presence. In this paper, we provide a system that addresses these issues by suggesting pre-made web templates, simplifying the web design process, speeding up development time, and reducing costs. There are often extraneous elements on web pages like banners, navigation bars, and ads that detract from the main content. To address this, we introduce an algorithm based on a Content Structure Tree (CST) to extract core content. The system also uses cosine similarity to rank content according to its relevance, thereby separating out the most important sections for user queries. In addition to CST-based content extraction, the system combines cosine similarity for web template recommendation to evaluate features such as layout, design elements, and tags. The dataset is obtained from a professional marketplace, with contemporary web designs and vectorization techniques applied for text-to-number vectorization to perform exact similarity computations. For improved performance, the study assesses hybrid recommendation systems that include knowledge-based, content-based, and collaborative techniques. By using cascaded and augmented hybrid strategies, it maximizes the strengths of multiple methods. The "Baseline only" method achieved an RMSE of 1.09 for web template recommendations. A new, more effective method for web-page recommendation is presented, which includes semantic-enhanced domain knowledge. Additionally, this research leverages TF-IDF and cosine similarity to refine design recommendations, achieving an 80.77% accuracy in matching layouts to user preferences. These results demonstrate how well AI-driven techniques work to improve user experience and optimize web design.

Keywords: Cosine similarity, hybrid recommendation systems, content-based, TF-IDF vectorization, content structure tree (CST)

I. Introduction

The proposed system not only displays pre-made templates but also recommends already developed templates available in the market with similar features or components. It would not only save the time of the design but may also provide a list of missing features which could enhance the look and feel of existing design by its recommended design templates. The internet has revolutionized how we access information, connect, and live. With just a click, we can shop, read, or watch anything online. As people spend more time on the internet, businesses now see the value of having an online presence [1]. Its credibility for not having a website can be called into doubt. In the eyes of consumers, the website makes a lasting impression and increases credibility and confidence. Customers trust businesses with their own websites and social media accounts because they are the new face of the company. As seen in Figure 43.1, there are six steps in the website development life cycle.

Planning and analysis are the process of developing plans based on information about the nature of the website and the end users. It also involves determining which tools and technologies are most appropriate for the website [2]. All requirements are documented as use cases. Website design is crucial as it shapes the site's appearance to meet client demands. A dull design fails to attract users, so designers must provide

multiple prototypes, usually as images, for approval. The system starts with some research and requirement assessment, then they work together with a tool to design the interface. Designers take concepts and make them into visual

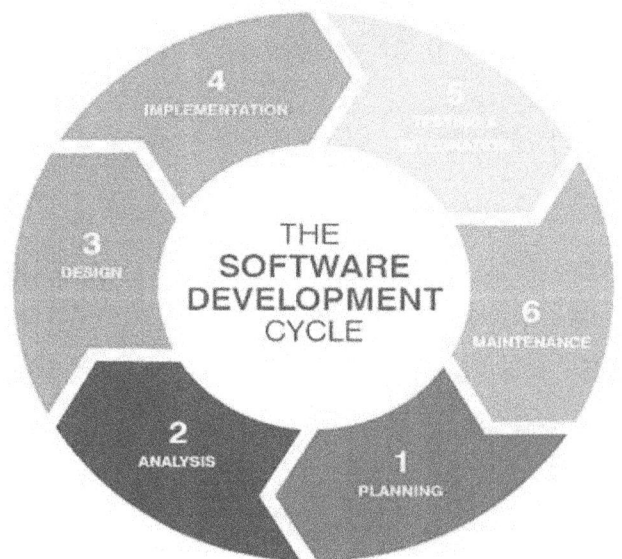

Figure 43.1. Website development life cycle [2].
Source: Author.

[a]shankarnagvekar.AI01@race.reva.edu.in, [b]krishna@race.reva.edu.in, [c]shinuabhi@reva.edu.in

DOI: 10.1201/9781003724988-43

layouts by hand. This process is time-consuming and causes some delays. This research aims to produce a web application that can be used in the proposed system to simplify the process [3]. This research aims to build a website design that will make it easier to do these jobs. The new system allows the designer to choose a template that suits the functions he needs and saves time and money. It's a good idea to show designs that fit the user's chosen website to avoid potential problems for designers and programmers.

Section 1 provides a brief background to the research problem, the motivation for the study, its objectives, and the structure of the paper. Section 2 is a review of the literature that includes some foundational works in the field and the main existing approaches and frameworks that are relevant to this study. The proposed model involves a methodology section that is divided into the following subsections: data collection techniques, preprocessing strategies, analytical models, and system architecture. Section 4 discusses the implementation components and functionalities. It categorizes the architecture into core components of the project. Section 5 compares the proposed model with other existing solutions and demonstrates the improvements obtained and the advantages of the model. The study is concluded in Section 6 with a summary of the findings and recommendations for further research. Three general filtering techniques – content-based, knowledge-based, and collaborative filtering – are combined in the study's suggested recommendation system to increase the precision and customization of web templates.

Our solution incorporates multiple strategies to address common issues that many recommendations systems face, like cold-start, sparse user input, or lack of contextual knowledge, whereas the majority of existing systems only employ one technique. The main innovation is the use of Content Structure Trees (CST) and cosine similarity for the system to evaluate and rank templates by structural relevance and semantic coherence. This makes sure that the suggestions not only respond to what the user likes, in terms of layout and content, but also fit the functional and aesthetic requirements. Moreover, the system incorporates domain knowledge that has been semantically enhanced, allowing it to understand the user's purpose, for example whether the user is designing a site for a restaurant, a portfolio, or an online store.

Hence, the recommendations are much better for first-time or infrequent users. As opposed to current systems that either treat templates as a black box or rely heavily on user interaction history, our model gives more meaningful suggestions that are aware of the context in which they are being made. This is especially important for small firms and non-experts because it makes decisions easier, shortens the time spent searching, and brings better results with less effort.

2. Literature Review

Information can be hard to find. Online content can be useful, but there's so much of it. Search engines can help, but they don't always give you what you need. We suggest a novel approach that gets beyond the cold-start issue, over-specialization, and scaling problems that plague conventional site design and recommendation systems [4]. By combining content-based, collaborative, and knowledge-based filtering into a single hybrid approach that delivers more accurate and personalized recommendations, we improve on existing recommendation methods. Techniques including TF-IDF, cosine similarity, weighted ratings, and popularity-based metrics are used to make sure that the recommendations are relevant and well-suited to the user [5].

This tool is different from previous methods. It can think about many things including tags, features, categories. This way, you can get better answers. It can give less mistakes and work faster. It is better than the old way and helps designers make the web better and the people using it happier. This is why recommendation systems are important. They help with too much information by showing relevant content. They use data from how users act and what they like to make things unique for everyone [6].

Developing good web recommenders is hard, because of newbie, privacy, over-specialization and freshness issues [7]. "cold start" problem is a problem when system does not have enough data to make useful suggestions for new users, new items, or users who have rated only a small number of items. The calibre of recommendations may be significantly impacted by this. One way to address this problem is to use Content Based (CB) recommendations, which make suggestions based on the properties of items, such as their genre, artists, etc., and to users who have shown interest in similar content [8].

A hybrid approach combining content-based methods and collaborative filtering can be effective, starting with content-based suggestions for new users or items and transitioning to collaborative filtering as more interaction data accumulates [9]. Social bookmarking sites are places where you can save, organize, and share links and bookmarks. You can store links to your favourite sites and access them from any computer. The links are stored on the Web, so you can access them from any computer. These services offer a way to save and share the links you find interesting [10]. The simplest method for grouping content is genre. A genre is a set of attributes that group similar content. The recommendations are based on the genre.

However, that method is limited by only working on a single feature and not considering the similarity of user profiles [11]. The other method, Pearson Correlation Coefficient, is also able to identify similar users, but the equations are hard to solve, and it takes too long. Using cluster-based recommendations is a way to divide things with the same properties into groups. It is not very good at suggesting particular things to people as it does not look at the weird little things that interest you [12].

Content-based filtering is a recommendation strategy that suggests items to users based on their interest [13]. This is different from a collaborative filtering model where similar users are clustered together. Instead of focusing only on how people interact with objects, content-based filtering considers their features and attributes. In content-based filtering, items are suggested according to their attributes. This is different from recommender systems which rely on user preferences and previous behaviour [14]. TF-IDF is discussed as well as computing the similarity of the item from its description. Cosine similarity, Euclidian distance, Pearson's correlation are the three methods for the similarity between item vectors.

A mathematical metric called cosine similarity is used to assess the degree of similarity between two non-zero vectors in a vector space. Cosine similarity is commonly used to measure the similarity between item or user vectors to generate content-based or collaborative filtering recommendations. It can be done by finding the dot product between the two identities [15].

Two vectors with the same orientation have a cosine similarity of 1, but two vectors oriented at 90 degrees have a cosine similarity of 0. However, regardless of their magnitude, two vectors that are opposed have a similarity of 1 [16]. Because the result is nicely constrained in [0, 1], cosine similarity is particularly helpful in positive space.

The angle between the two images is inversely proportional to their similarity. When the angle is small, they are nearly alike. When the angle is large, they are very different. One of the reasons for cosine similarity popularity is that it is relatively efficient to evaluate, particularly for sparse vectors [17]. The Equation (1) for cosine similarity is displayed, indicating the angle θ between the vectors.

$$\cos(\theta) = \frac{A \cdot B}{|A||B|} \qquad (1)$$

The characters visually depict the vector directions, emphasizing the geometric interpretation of similarity easy searching. While these platforms often suggest tags to improve content discovery, they typically use simple methods to generate recommendations based on tags and features.

3. Methodology

This research follows a structured approach to ensure relevant and personalized recommendations for users. The three main stages of the methodology are feature extraction, suggestion generation, and data collecting and preparation.

The first step, gathering and transforming data, encompasses taking template metadata from a variety of online sources. With web scraping methods, we meticulously extract these details: title, description, category, tags, rating, and count of downloads. However, scraping methods need to be able to handle web scraping loading of some content dynamically. From this, we enter a preprocessing phase in which we refine the data to improve its quality and make it more suitable for analysis. This includes removing unwanted characters, managing missing values, and text standardization through lowercasing, case-folding, and lemmatization. Furthermore, template metadata is rigorously structured and text-based attributes are converted to numerical representations using

TF-IDF vectorization with the intention of simplifying similarity calculations.

After preprocessing, the study proceeds to the feature extraction stage to discover valuable insights from the structured data. It examines every template in terms of several facets, such as design style, responsiveness, framework compatibility (Bootstrap, Tailwind CSS), and industry category. These can be joined together to give recommendations. The last part of the process is the recommendation process, which is a two-pronged approach that aims to generate relevant and personalized website template recommendations. This strategy utilizes multiple approaches, such as popularity-based, tag-based, feature-based, category-based, and hybrid recommendation methods, to improve recommendation process performance and efficiency in different ways.

The method of recommendation in text is to match commonly used keywords and topics through similarity in text. This is done by extracting keywords from template descriptions, categories, and tags using TF-IDF vectorization so that the system can compare them with each other. We measure the similarity between the templates with a cosine similarity and suggest designs that are like what the user has seen before. This way, the system can suggest designs with similar attributes on top of the existing ones which is especially helpful if you are looking for templates based on some themes, features or any other industry terms.

On the other hand, the feature-based recommendation method relies on the structural and functional characteristics instead of textual descriptions. Each template is scored based on its features like layout type, responsiveness, compatibility with multiple frameworks (Bootstrap, Tailwind CSS) as well as overall design style. These features are then transformed into structured numerical forms, which allows for precise similarity calculations.

The recommendations are made by focusing on the technical details and overall design frameworks thereby ensuring that the functionality and aesthetics of the user are fully met. The popularity-based recommendation approach ranks templates based on how many times they've been downloaded, what their ratings are, and what kind of reviews they got to reflect the preferences and engagement trends. We then use a weighted scoring system to feature templates with a higher score and download count. This is particularly helpful for new users who may not be familiar with any templates and would like to see what designs trending are.

Another method for recommending more contextually relevant content is the category-based recommendation method. This method involves analysing user interactions with templates that are specific to a category like ecommerce, portfolios, blogs or corporate websites.

The system that tries to get people to click on suggestions depending on what they have liked in the past. The suggestions will always be relevant and updated. To enhance the accuracy of recommendations, we propose a hybrid recommendation strategy that combines various recommendation strategies. The hybrid approach leverages tag-based, content-based, popularity-based, and category-based recommenders to provide a more balanced and personalized recommendation. This will help users have recommendations that are based on several factors as opposed to just one strategy. For instance, one could be recommended a template because it is not just textually like the search query but is also popular among other users. This will provide even more flexibility and adaptability across various algorithms and ensure that the recommendations remain as relevant as the user's preferences evolve.

The goal of this project is to build an intelligent and flexible recommendation system that combines contextual relevance, feature comparison, textual analysis, and user behaviour. All these methods can make the user experience more successful by offering better and more comprehensive template suggestions. The system also uses the "Baseline Only" algorithm to improve its recommendations, combining it with content-based, and collaborative filtering methods. The system can provide more accurate and personalized recommendations because it learns from the actions of users.

More accurate and personalized template recommendations are provided by using a hybrid approach that combines knowledge-based, collaborative, and content-based filtering. Knowledge-based filtering uses domain-specific details to influence recommendations, whereas collaborative filtering suggests solutions based on what other users similar to you have chosen, and content-based filtering matches templates with user preferences. These three methodologies sidestep the cold-start and sparse user data issues. For example, if a novice user looks for a portfolio template, they may be recommended some domain-specific solutions first, followed by a refinement of this recommendation based on the results of design preferences and similar user behaviour. It is especially useful for small businesses, as it provides quick and relevant results without the need for any technical expertise or large datasets.

4. Implementation

Short words were used in this study. Machine learning is applied to web page layouts because of user interactions. Suggestions are always made in keeping with each user's individual needs using data-driven techniques. Structured approach to building a recommendation system for website templates. For instance, web scraping of a well-known template marketplace resulted in the collection of over 4,300 templates. Once the data is collected, it is pre-processed and analysed to ensure that its details are clear and Machine learning methods are used in this study to improve the recommendations of website templates by analysing user interactions like clicks, selected categories and download preferences. Data-driven methods ensure that the recommendations are tailored to the needs of the user. Here, our work is carried out based on the systematic approach to build a suggestion

system for website templates. Initially, web scraping was performed to fetch around 4,300 templates from a recognized template marketplace. Following collection, the data is pre-processed and analyzed to guarantee organization and clarity. This step involves reviewing the dataset, structuring the information, and visualizing key template features using a word cloud, making it easier to understand common trends as shown in Figure 43.2.

As shown in Figure 43.3, a word cloud for template tags provides a visual representation of the most common phrases and qualities associated with templates.

As shown in Figure 43.4, the bar plot for the number of templates concerning its category is displayed.

As shown in Figure 43.5 the bar plot for the Number of templates concerning their Tags is displayed.

As shown in Figure 43.6 the bar plot for the Number of templates concerning their Features is displayed.

Bar Plot for Top 10 Features as shown in Figure 43.6. Next, a popularity-based recommendation method is applied, ranking templates based on their ratings and download

Figure 43.2. Word cloud for template features.

Source: Author.

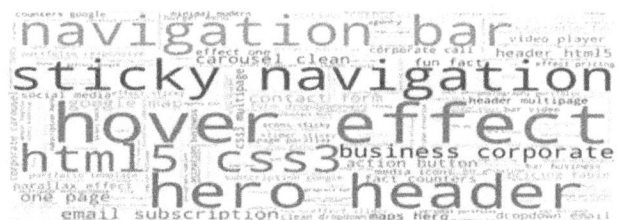

Figure 43.3. Word Cloud for template tags.

Source: Author.

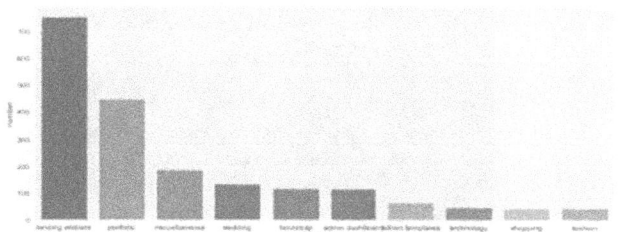

Figure 43.4. Bar plot for top 10 categories.

Source: Author.

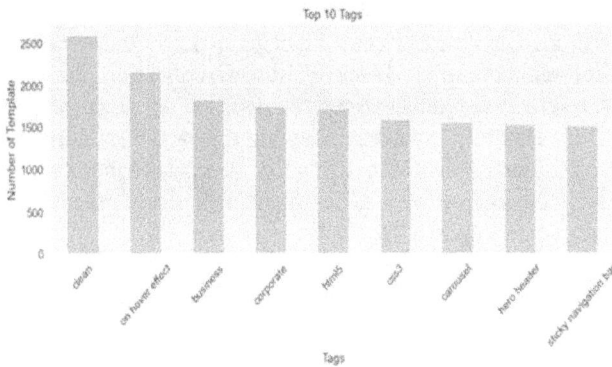

Figure 43.5. Bar plot for top 10 tags.

Source: Author.

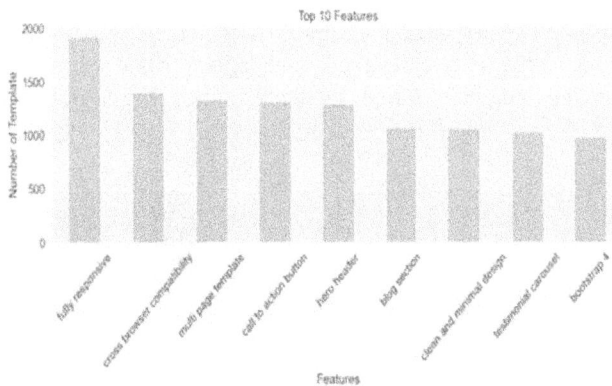

Figure 43.6. Bar plot for top 10 features.

Source: Author.

counts. Following this, the system groups templates by categories, making it simple for users to browse different types of templates efficiently. Finally, a feature-based recommendation is implemented, where user preferences, template titles, and features are compared using cosine similarity. By combining similarity scores, the system generates personalized recommendations, ensuring users receive the most relevant template suggestions.

5. Testing and Validation

Testing and validating weighted rating and Root Mean Squared Error (RMSE) website templates entail evaluating the quality and performance of these templates using user ratings and predictions. Selected template with Title "anime free bootstrap 4 html5 gaming, anime website template" as shown in Figure 43.7.

As illustrated in Figure 43.8 a recommendation based on a similar Tag and its rank based on cosine similarity score.

As illustrated in Figure 43.9 a recommendation based on a similar Tag and its rank based on cosine similarity score.

As illustrated in Figure 43.10 a recommendation based on a similar Feature and its rank based on cosine similarity score.

As illustrated in Figure 43.11, a recommendation is based on popularity and category and its weighted rate.

6. Results and Discussion

We presented a hybrid recommendation system for web templates in this work that blends knowledge-based, collaborative,

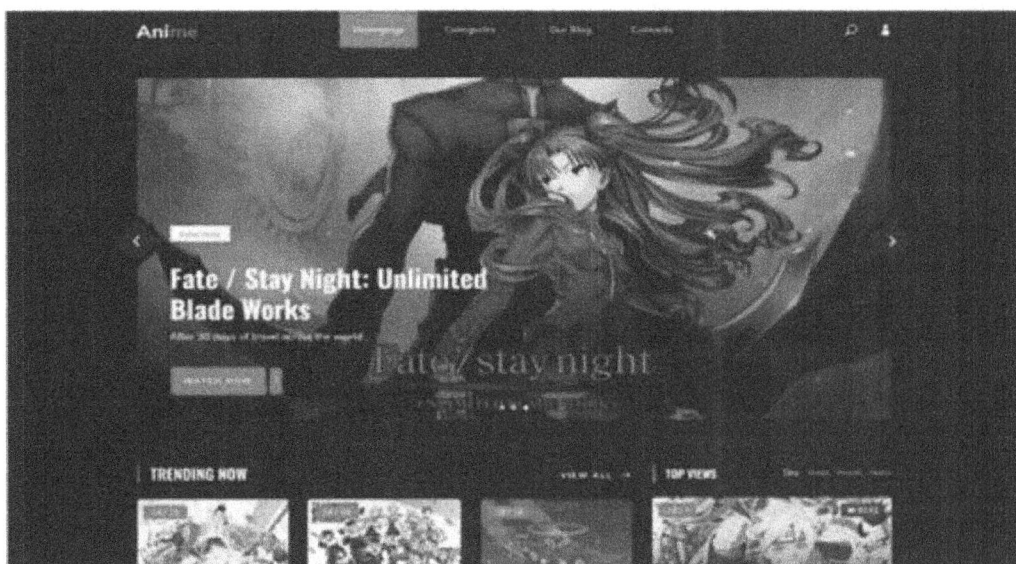

Figure 43.7. Selected template.

Source: Author.

Title	Category	Ratings	Downloads	Template	Rank	cosine_similarity
anime free bootstrap 4 html5 gaming , anime website template	landing website	5	17826	288	1	0.61
template collection 2022 one hundred free html5 templates in one bundle themewagon	landing website	3.11	30159	112	2	0.23
outdoors experimental free html5 multipurpose template	landing , website	2.75	1572	2183	3	0.21
teamhost gaming community html by templines	themeforest	miscellaneous	4.43	58	1192	4	0.16
endgame free bootstrap 4 html5 gaming website template themewagon	landing website	5	6810	605	5	0.15
cyborg Ã¢â€ free responsive bootstrap 5 gaming website template	landing website	1.88	1672	87	6	0.15
game warrior free bootstrap 4 html5 gaming website template	landing , website	4.38	11832	2335	7	0.13
halda esports and gaming template by themebeyond	themeforest	entertainment	2.48	73	977	8	0.12
spiel gaming and esports html template by angfuz soft	themeforest	entertainment	3.34	73	965	9	0.12

Figure 43.8. Bar plot for top 10 tags.

Source: Author.

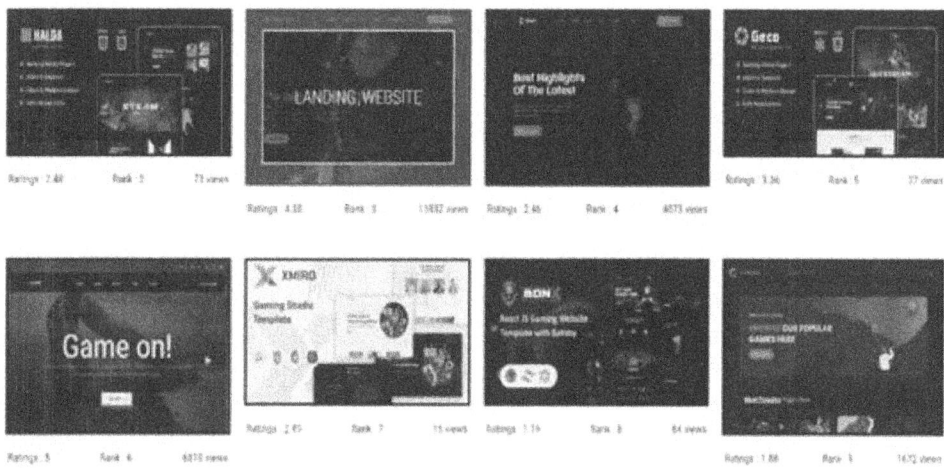

Figure 43.9. Recommendation based on tags.

Source: Author.

Figure 43.10. Recommendation based on category.

Source: Author.

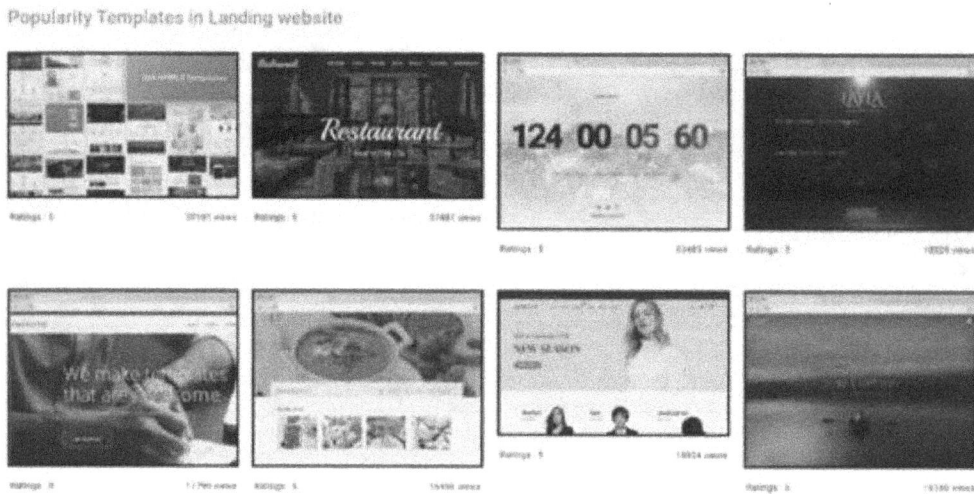

Figure 43.11. Recommendation based on features.

Source: Author.

and content-based techniques. The study achieved an RMSE value of 1.09 to estimate the correct templates with Equation (2) [18]. When compared to CF (RMSE = 1.35) and CB (RMSE = 1.25) methods, the hybrid outperforms these systems in terms of recommendation detail. Additionally, it performs well in terms of F1 score, recall, and precision. The model has a precision of 0.84, meaning that 82% of the recommendations that it makes are what the user would like to see. A recall of 0.80 shows that the model can classify 80% of the relevant templates. With an F1 score of 0.82, the model can provide a reasonable mix between recall and precision.

$$\text{RMSE} = \sqrt{\frac{1}{n}\sum_{i=1}^{n}(\hat{y}i - yi)^2} \qquad (2)$$

Where,

- n = Number of estimations detected objects
- yi = Current estimation
- $\hat{y}i$ = Average value of the estimations

This shows the system we made helps you pick a template more accurately and easily. It is already useful for small businesses that want to save time and money. Our hybrid recommendation system gives better recommendations than the Baseline Only Approach. While the Baseline Only Approach

showed slightly better RMSE results, future work will focus on improving scalability, integrating user feedback loops, and exploring advanced deep learning techniques to refine the system even further.

To make recommendation tool recommendations better, use dimensionality reduction. For example, to reduce the feature space and increase efficiency while maintaining the quality of the recommendations, we can use techniques like PCA. Another way to handle larger template libraries is to use parallel processing or distributed systems to break the tasks down. These will make the system more responsive as the data grows by speeding up processing time, reducing bottlenecks. These procedures are designed to help it keep up with growth and produce highly precise recommendations without delay. illustrated on Figure 43.12.

As illustrated in Figure 43.12, a recommendation based on a Category with its Weighted Rate is shown in Figure 43.13.

The proposed system combines content-based and hybrid-based filtering and can deliver more tailored and effective recommendations for website layouts. The technique enhances the quality of recommendations by utilizing the advantages of both approaches.

Algorithm	test_rmse	test_mae	fit_time	test_time
BaselineOnly	1.090	0.914	0.018	0.007
SVD	1.093	0.908	0.072	0.015
SVDpp	1.099	0.905	1.338	0.142
KNNBaseline	1.207	0.966	0.021	0.038
KNNWithMeans	1.212	0.963	0.030	0.045
KNNWithZScore	1.215	0.956	0.052	0.044
CoClustering	1.236	0.983	0.531	0.014
SlopeOne	1.265	0.995	0.074	0.055
KNNBasic	1.283	1.011	0.014	0.035
NMF	1.291	1.044	0.228	0.005
NormalPredictor	1.575	1.266	0.009	0.020

Figure 43.12. Benchmark result of all algorithms (Screenshot).

Source: Author.

Title	Download	Category	Template	Ratings	wr
template collection 2017 one hundred html5 templates in one pack	59101	landing website	453	5	4.768
restaurant bootstrap food restaurant website template free download in 2017 themewagon	37481	landing website	42	5	4.656
imminent a free 3d parallax responsive coming soon template with html5 themewagon	33483	landing website	47	5	4.623
layla a free responsive coming soon under construction template themewagon	18529	landing website	45	5	4.406
anime free bootstrap 4 html5 gaming , anime website template	17826	landing website	288	5	4.389
awesome free one page responsive html5 template themewagon	17790	landing website	58	5	4.388
spicy free bootstrap html5 template themewagon	16498	landing website	44	5	4.355
cozastore free html5 ecommerce website template themewagon	15924	landing website	493	5	4.340
flusk a responsive multi purpose website template	15180	landing website	27	5	4.318
profile free one page portfolio bootstrap template	14698	landing website	452	5	4.303
developer responsive personal website template	13905	landing website	36	5	4.277
supershop free responsive ecommerce shop bootstrap template	13853	landing website	444	5	4.276

Figure 43.13. Cosine similarity score and rank (Screenshot).

Source: Author.

7. Conclusions and Future Scope

Using both content-based and hybrid methodologies, the study may suggest website templates according on tags, features, and categories. The "Baseline only" algorithm has been used to recommend user search input as it has provided better RMSE value as compared to others for the given dataset. This process would help the designer to leverage the benefits of pre-made templates but would also benefit to overcome its disadvantages by having the option to copy features from recommended templates without having compatibility issues while customizing the template to provide a unique design, thus saving time and effort. The pipeline must be configured to choose an algorithm based on the RMSE value in the future on the base of the dataset fetched from several pre-made template providers.

After choosing a template, user input like ratings, comments, or engagement signals can be incorporated into the model to improve the recommendation system's flexibility and personalization. This loop is important. It allows the system to keep learning from user input about what people like and what design trends are popular. For instance, if users always give certain templates high ratings, or consistently choose to leave positive comments about certain features (e.g., how easy it is to adjust the layout, how nicely a given design adapts to mobile, etc.), we could increase the likelihood of similar templates being recommended in the future.

Over time, these tweaks help improve how well the recommendations fit the user and how good they are. Also, this feedback can take care of any shifts in user requirements or market needs, making sure we are staying up to date with the users. The recommendation system could also be improved by adding deep learning methods, notably Neural Collaborative Filtering (NCF), which is able to learn non-linear relationships between users and templates through better understanding of high-level feature interactions that are not captured by traditional methods. This can help the system understand the subtle preferences and behaviours of users more accurately, making the recommendations even more personalized.

References

[1] Importance Of Website: 7 Reasons Why Your Business Needs It. Accessed: Aug. 17, 2022. [Online]. Available:https://www.velocityconsultancy.com/importance-of-website-reasons-why-your-business-needs-it/

[2] 7 Phases Of Web Design And Development Life Cycle. Accessed: Aug. 01, 2023. [Online]. Available: https://www.quorawebsolution.com/post/7-phases-of-web-design-and-development-life-cycle

[3] Singh, M., Mishra, P., Aggarwal, N., Kumar, V., Sharma, P. K., & Yadav, R. (2024). CosineRecom: A KNN-Based Movie Recommendation System Using Cosine Similarity. In *2024 4th International Conference on Advancement in Electronics & Communication Engineering (AECE)*. IEEE. pp. 190–194. doi: 10.1109/AECE62803.2024.10911391.

[4] Ujkani. B., Minkovska, D., & Stoyanova, L. (2020). A recommender system for WordPress themes using item-based collaborative filtering technique; A recommender system for WordPress themes using item-based collaborative filtering technique. doi: 10.13140/RG.2.1.3268.5841.

[5] Adilaksa, Y., & Musdholifah, A. (2021). Recommendation System for Elective Courses using Content-based Filtering and Weighted Cosine Similarity. In *2021 4th International Seminar on Research of Information Technology and Intelligent Systems, ISRITI 2021*. Institute of Electrical and Electronics Engineers Inc., pp. 51–55. doi: 10.1109/ISRITI54043.2021.9702788.

[6] Kumar, B., Nayak, V. K., Banerjee, P., & Dehury, M. K. (2023). An Empirical Analysis of Collaborative and Content Based Recommender System by using AI. In *2023 International Conference on Advances in Computing, Communication and Applied Informatics (ACCAI)*. IEEE, pp. 1–8. doi: 10.1109/ACCAI58221.2023.10200257.

[7] Swaroop, A., & Sharma, V. (2015). Galgotias University. School of Computing Science and Engineering, Institute of Electrical and Electronics Engineers. Uttar Pradesh Section, and Institute of Electrical and Electronics Engineers,

International Conference on Computing, Communication and Automation.

[8] Snigdha, P. V., Naveen, M., Rahul, S., Sujatha, C. N., & Pradeep, P. (2022). Movie Recommendation System Using TF-IDF Vectorization and Cosine Similarity. *Int J Res Appl Sci Eng Technol*, *10*(8), 1128–1134. doi: 10.22214/ijraset.2022.46367.

[9] Mittal, A., & Goel, A. (2023). A Review on Community Detection Approach for Recommender Systems. In *2023 8th International Conference on Communication and Electronics Systems (ICCES)*. IEEE, pp. 1521–1526. doi: 10.1109/ICCES57224.2023.10192879.

[10] Ilhan, N., & Öğüdücü, Ş. G. (2009). A recommender model for social bookmarking sites. In *ICSCCW 2009 - 5th International Conference on Soft Computing, Computing with Words and Perceptions in System Analysis, Decision and Control*. doi: 10.1109/ICSCCW.2009.5379460.

[11] Pu, Q., & Hu, B. (2023). Intelligent movie recommendation system based on hybrid recommendation algorithms. In *IEEE 1st International Conference on Ambient Intelligence, Knowledge Informatics and Industrial Electronics, AIKIIE 2023, Institute of Electrical and Electronics Engineers Inc.* doi:10.1109/AIKIIE60097.2023.10389982.

[12] Yang, J., Shi, T., & Li, S. (2022). Implementation and research of recommendation system based on trust mechanism. In *IMCEC 2022 - IEEE 5th Advanced Information Management, Communicates, Electronic and Automation Control Conference*. Institute of Electrical and Electronics Engineers Inc., pp. 599–604. doi: 10.1109/IMCEC55388.2022.10020104.

[13] Shah, K., Arora, B., Shinde, A., & Vaghasia, S. (2022). AI in Entertainment-Movie Recommendation using cosine similarity. In *2022 6th International Conference on Computing, Communication, Control and Automation, ICCUBEA 2022*. Institute of Electrical and Electronics Engineers Inc. doi: 10.1109/ICCUBEA54992.2022.10010973.

[14] Subramaniam, R., Lee, R., & Matsuo, T. (2018). Movie Master: Hybrid Movie Recommendation. In *Proceedings - 2017 International Conference on Computational Science and Computational Intelligence, CSCI 2017*. Institute of Electrical and Electronics Engineers Inc., pp. 334–339. doi: 10.1109/CSCI.2017.56.

[15] Singh, R. H., Maurya, S., Tripathi, T., Narula, T., & Srivastav, G. (2020). Movie Recommendation System using Cosine Similarity and KNN. *Int J Eng Adv Technol*. doi: 10.35940/ijeat.E9666.069520.

[16] Anthony, J. T., Christian, G. E., Evanlim, V., Lucky, H., & Suhartono, D. (2022). The Utilization of Content Based Filtering for Spotify Music Recommendation. In *2022 International Conference on Informatics Electrical and Electronics, ICIEE 2022 - Proceedings*. Institute of Electrical and Electronics Engineers Inc. doi: 10.1109/ICIEE55596.2022.10010097.

[17] Build Smarter Recommenders: Top 5 Python Similarity Measures Explained - Nagvekar - Medium. Accessed: May 05, 2025. [Online]. Available: https://nagvekar.medium.com/build-smarter-recommenders-top-5-python-similarity-measures-explained-79bb322aaeb8

[18] The Ultimate Guide to RMSE, MAE, and MSE for Data Science Beginners - Nagvekar - Medium. Accessed: May 08, 2025. [Online]. Available: https://nagvekar.medium.com/the-ultimate-guide-to-rmse-mae-and-mse-for-data-science-beginners-b32734a9f318

44 A conformal logo-based skin-mountable ultra-flexible antenna for smart wound monitoring bandages

Sherene Jacob[1,a], Vasudevan Karuppiah[2], Kalaivani S.[3], Vijayalakshmi S.[4], Varadharajan M.[5], and Sumitha Josphine J.[6]

[1]Research Scholar, Department of ECE, Thiagarajar College of Engineering, Madurai, Tamil Nadu, India
[2]Associate Professor, Department of ECE, Thiagarajar College of Engineering, Madurai, Tamil Nadu, India
[3]Assistant Professor, Department of ECE, Rajalakshmi Institute of Technology, Chennai, India
[4]Professor, Department of ECE, R.M.K. Engineering College, Kavaraipettai, India
[5]Assistant Professor, Department of ECE, Loyola Institute of Technology, Chennai, India
[6]Assistant Professor, Department of ECE, St. Joseph College of Engineering, Chennai, India

Abstract: This paper presents a logo-based, skin-mountable antenna for smart bandages. It is designed for short-term wearable applications at 2.45 GHz. The antenna uses a PDMS (polydimethylsiloxane) substrate. The antenna achieves a resonance at 2.45 GHz and produces a return loss of 19.6 dB and a high gain of 4.36 dB with a size of 5x5 cm². It conforms closely to the skin, and shows endurance even when the antenna is crushed by the patient. A key design consideration is the optimization of input power to minimize the Specific Absorption Rate (SAR). A SAR of less than 1.6 W/Kg is obtained for an input power of 86mW. This makes sure the user safety along with an efficient wireless communication. The antenna is intended for one-time use, making it suitable for temporary wound monitoring, skin-worn sensors, and other disposable wireless applications. Simulation and experimental results confirm the antenna's performance demonstrating a balance between compact size, low SAR, and reliable operation in close proximity to human tissue.

Keywords: Skin-mountable antenna, low-SAR, flexible-antenna

1. Introduction

Next-generation health monitoring systems and communication systems are emerging with the development of components such as wearable antennas [1]. These devices enable real-time data acquisition for biomedical sensors, fitness readers, and remote patient monitoring [2]. These antennas operate at 2.45 GHz ISM band. This is widely used in medical and consumer wireless communication systems. Various substrates are utilized for the antenna design. They might be textile fabrics [3], polymers [4], elastomers [5], etc. These materials offer a high degree of flexibility, but they often suffer from limitations such as restricted mechanical adaptability and higher specific absorption rate, SAR, and diminished antenna performance when placed in contact with skin.

Textile-based antennas are subjected to performance degradation when the fabric warpage. Such distortions to the alteration of the impedance and reduced sensitivity. Therefore, it affects the overall performance of the antenna. These drawbacks compromise the user comfort and safety. Therefore, this makes them less suitable for sensitive applications like health monitoring [6, 7]. Also, various gain enhancement techniques have been explored to mitigate these issues [8].

To overcome these challenges, this work proposed a skin-mountable antenna. It is designed to adhere directly to the skin and the antenna offered improved interaction with the human body. This makes sure of efficient radiation and safety [9, 10]. The adhesive-based design allows for easy application, removal and disposability, making it suitable for temporary medical use, such as smart bandage used in wound monitoring where regular replacement and aesthetics are essential.

The flexibility of the designed antenna makes it easy to conform to the surface of the user's skin. This offers a more user-friendly and visually pleasing alternative to the rigid designs. A novel aspect of this approach is the use of a logo-shaped antenna to combine functionality with beauty. By integrating familiar symbols or logos, the antenna can seamlessly blend with clothing or medical devices. This makes it more socially acceptable for public or professional use. With wearable technology, aesthetics significantly influences over user acceptance, and comfort, style, and discretion are key factors.

---

[a]sherenebenju@gmail.com

DOI: 10.1201/9781003724988-44

In this work, we present a logo-shaped skin-mountable antenna with a SJ logo-inspired design operating at 2.45 GHz for smart bandage applications. The antenna is fabricated using a flexible substrate with adhesive backing for easy integration on the human body. To address SAR issues, an isolation layer has been integrated between the skin and the antenna. The antenna power level has been optimized to maintain lower SAR. The design achieves a balance between safety, and visual appeal. Thus, it makes a promising candidate for high-performance skin-mounted wearable electronics.

2. Skin-Mountable Antenna Design

The skin-mountable antenna presented in this work is designed using a 0.2 mm thick polydimethylsiloxane (PDMS) substrate. This substrate is chosen for its excellent flexibility and biocompatibility and has good dielectric properties. The relative permittivity of the substrate is around 2.5 to 3 and a very low loss tangent. The PDMS substrate helps in efficient signal transmission while conformed to the body contours. It is optically transparent and hence, enables aesthetic customization such as logo integration without compromising with performance. The 5 cm × 5 cm substrate is suitable for the antenna design and ensures secure comfortable skin attachment making it ideal for wearable applications.

2.1. Evolution of the logo structure

The logo-based antenna integrates the author's initials into its design. The proposed antenna evolves through three stages, optimized over a three-layer skin-fat-muscle model, with improvements in resonant frequency and impedance matching. Thank you for watching. The evolution of the structure is explained in Figure 44.1, while the Figure 44.2 explains the performance of the return loss and resonant frequency characters.

Stage 1 (Figure 44.1a): The design consists of two merged circular patch feed fed by a microstrip line. The structure resonates at 3.5 GHz with a S11 of -16.5 dB.

Stage 2 (Figure 44.1b): The antenna is developed into a S-shaped structure. This introduces extra current path and increases the effective electrical length. The resonance shifts to 3.25 GHz and S11 improves to -20.3 dB.

Stage 3 (Figure 44.1c): The antenna evolves into a SJ-shaped configuration, combining the meandering characters of both S and J shapes. This enables miniaturization and tuning the resonance to 2.45 GHz. The return loss is -19.6 dB.

The SJ-shaped antenna has an electrical length of approximately 0.55 λg *and is built on a 5* cm × 5 cm PDMS substrate. It has a partial ground plane to enhance the impedance matching. Designed for a direct skin contact, it is optimized over a 3-layer human tissue model and includes another 0.1mm thickness of PDMS layer between the antenna and skin to reduce the electromagnetic absorption and to improve efficiency. The electrical properties of human tissues affect

antenna performance. At 2.45 GHz the following properties are assigned to the tissues. The Skin has a relative permittivity of 38–42 and conductivity of 1.4–1.6 S/m, leading to high energy absorption. Fat has a lower permittivity of 5–6 and conductivity of 0.04–0.06 S/m, making it a low-loss layer. Muscle has high water content. Hence it has the highest permittivity of 50–55 and conductivity of 1.7–2.0 S/m, causing attenuation. Accurate modeling of these tissue layers is essential to design the body-worn antennas in practical applications as shown in Figure 44.3.

2.2. Radiation mechanism of the skin-mountable antenna

The SJ-shaped antenna is microstrip-fed, located at the base of the "S". The current density is highest at this point. The design connects the upper end of the "S" to a horizontal arm of the "J", with the lower end extending downwards. The current distribution analysis shows that the lower sections of both S and J experience high current density. This indicates strong resonance and energy transfer. As the current flows upwards, its intensity decreases. It is because the radiation originates at the lower part of the structure. This distribution supports effective impedance matching and stable performance at the target frequency as shown in Figure 44.4.

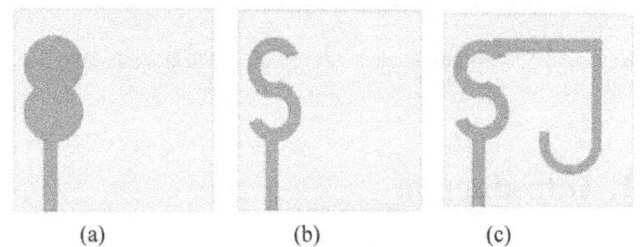

(a)   (b)   (c)

Figure 44.1. Stages of evolution of the proposed antenna (a) stage 1 (b) stage 2 (c) stage 3.

Source: Author.

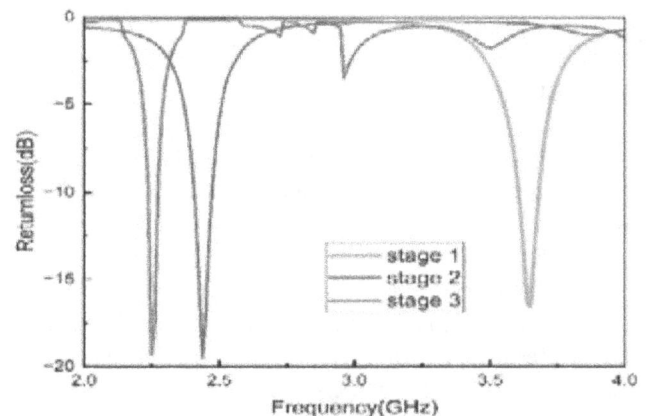

Figure 44.2. Return loss characteristics of the stages of the antenna.

Source: Author.

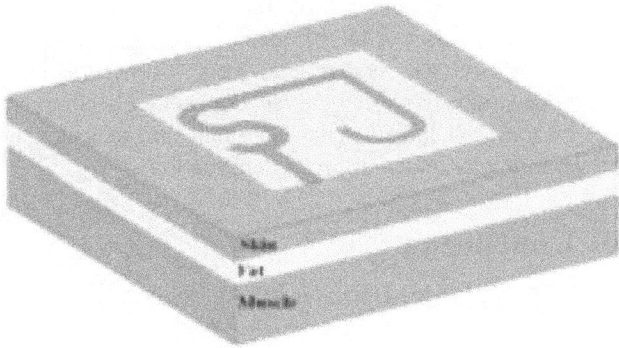

Figure 44.3. The antenna placed over the 3 layered human tissue model while the design process.

Source: Author.

Figure 44.4. Current distribution of the antenna at 2.45 GHz.

Source: Author.

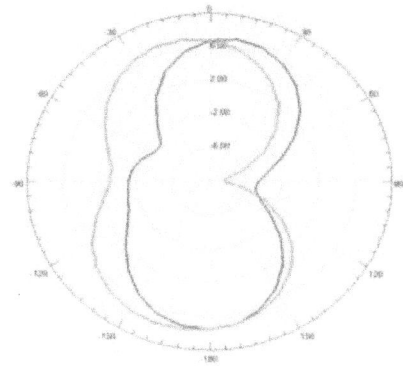

(a)

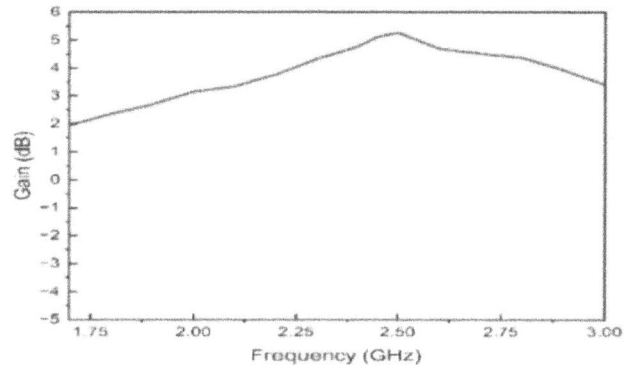

(b)

Figure 44.5. a) The E plane (red) and H plane (green) radiation pattern of the antenna at 2.45 GHz b) Gain vs. frequency plot of the antenna.

Source: Author.

Table 44.1. Performance of the proposed antenna

Parameter at 2.45 GHz	Value
Return Loss (dB)	-19.6
Bandwidth (MHz)	210
Gain (dB)	4.36
SAR (W/Kg)	1.54 W/Kg at 86 mW

Source: Author.

The radiation pattern is shown in Figure 44.5a. It reveals front and back radiation in both E-plane and H-plane. This is influenced by the finite ground plane due to the diffraction at the edges resulting in unwanted back radiation. For temporary skin-mounted antennas, back radiation is acceptable. The primary focus remains in achieving reliable communication while maintaining compact, flexible, and conformal design. Minor efficiency trade-off can be tolerated.

A gain of 4.36 dB at 2.45 GHz for the antenna indicates relatively low directivity, which is expected for a compact, skin-mountable design. Since the antenna is intended for temporary use, its priority may be flexibility, conformability, and reliable operation and maximizing gain. This is represented in Figure 44.5B. The overall performance of the antenna is tabulated n Table 44.1.

3. Test for Compatibility

Compatibility testing of Antenna focuses on two aspects A) SAR and B) Bending analysis. The results of the analysis are as follows:

3.1. SAR analysis

Specific Absorption Rate (SAR) analysis is vital for assessing the safety of skin-mountable antennas. Regulatory bodies like the FCC (1.6 W/kg over 1g) and ICNIRP (2.0 W/kg over 10g) set strict limits to prevent tissue damage. In this case, the measured SAR is 18.6 W/kg at 1 W input power, exceeding regulatory limits as shown in Figure 44.6. Reducing input power is essential. To meet FCC standards, the safe input power should be limited to around 86 mW. Operating between 80–100 mW ensures compliance and minimizes thermal risks in biomedical applications.

3.2. Bending analysis

Bending alters the electrical length, current distribution, affecting its performance. As shown in Figure 44.7(a),

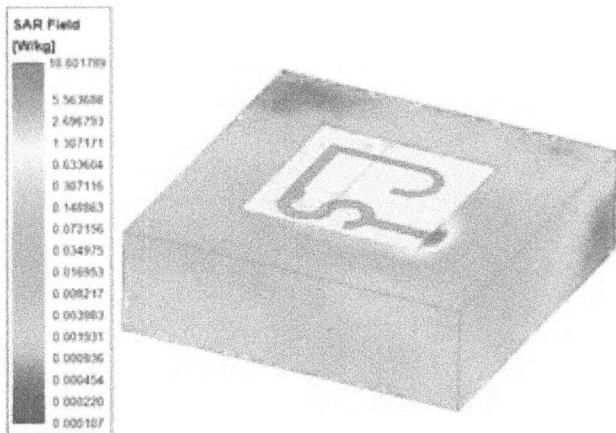

Figure 44.6. SAR analysis of the proposed antenna.

Source: Author.

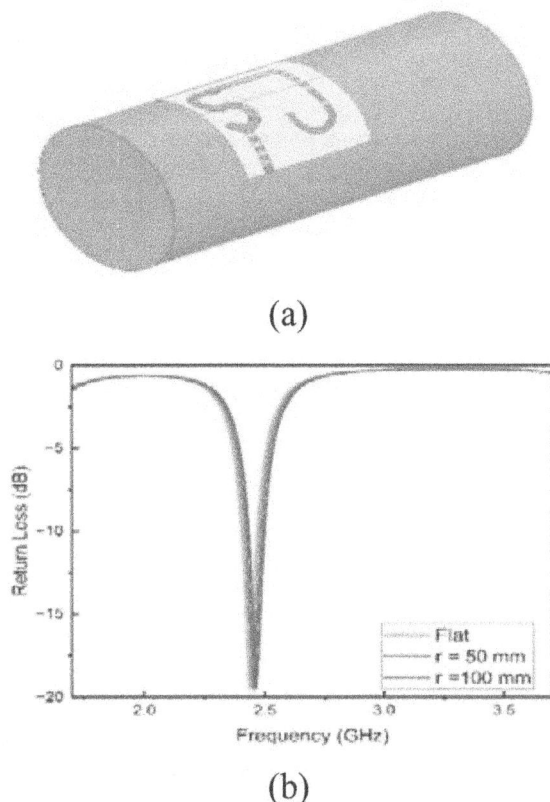

(a)

(b)

Figure 44.7. (a) Bending of the antenna over a cylinder (b) Performance analysis for various radius of curvature.

Source: Author.

bending with a 100 cm radius shifts the resonance to 2.47 GHz (blue line, Figure 44.7b), while a sharper 50 cm bend shifts it to 2.49 GHz (orange line). This shift occurs due to the reduced effective electrical length. Though bending can affect bandwidth and efficiency, the small shift indicates stable performance under moderate deformation.

4. Conclusion

A compact SJ-shaped logo-based skin-mountable antenna for smart bandages has been designed to operate at the 2.45 GHz ISM band. With a size of 5 × 5 cm² and a patch length of 0.55 λ_0, it achieves a reflection coefficient of –19.6 dB, ensuring good impedance matching. The antenna achieves a gain of 4.36 dB and maintains safe SAR limits at an input power of 86 mW. This makes it suitable for use on human skin. It also retains stable performance under bending and crushing, suitable to use in flexible, wearable systems. Future improvements may include miniaturization, multi-band operation, and advanced materials for broader biomedical and IoT applications.

References

[1] Sherene, J., Vasudevan, K., Uma Maheshwari, G., & Meenambal, B. (2025). Design and Analysis of AMC-Based Anti-symmetric Dual L-Shaped Antenna for WBAN Application. *Third International Conference on Computational Electronics for Wireless Communications*. ICCWC 2023. Lecture Notes in Networks and Systems, vol. 959. Springer, Singapore. https://doi.org/10.1007/978-981-97-1943-3_16

[2] Jacob, S., Bose, M., & Karuppiah, V. (2024). Artificial Magnetic Conductor-Backed Microstrip-Fed Dual-Band antenna for 5G wearable sensor nodes and C Band application in WBAN network. *5G and Fiber Optics Security Technologies for Smart Grid Cyber Defense* (pp. 221–241). https://doi.org/10.4018/979-8-3693-2786-9.ch009

[3] Qasim Mehmood, M., et al. (2024). Textile-Based Washable Multimode Capacitive Sensors for Wearable Applications. *IEEE Journal on Flexible Electronics*, *3*(10), 445–453. https://doi.org/10.1109/JFLEX.2024.3483195

[4] Tang, H., et al. (2023). A Low-Profile Flexible Dual-Band Antenna With Quasi-Isotropic Radiation Patterns for MIMO System on UAVs. *IEEE Antennas and Wireless Propagation Letters*, *22*(1), 49–53. https://doi.org/10.1109/LAWP.2022.3201492

[5] Gibson, J. S., Liu, X., Georgakopoulos, S. V., Wie, J. J., Ware, T. H., & White, T. J. (2016). Reconfigurable Antennas Based on Self-Morphing Liquid Crystalline Elastomers. *IEEE Access*, *4*, 2340–2348. https://doi.org/10.1109/ACCESS.2016.2565199

[6] Yang, H., Liu, X., & Fan, Y. (2022). Design of Broadband Circularly Polarized All-Textile Antenna and Its Conformal Array for Wearable Devices. *IEEE Transactions on Antennas and Propagation*, *70*(1), 209–220. doi: 10.1109/TAP.2021.3098542

[7] Alqadami, A. S. M., Nguyen-Trong, N., Mohammed, B., Stancombe, A. E., Heitzmann, M. T., & Abbosh, A. (2020). Compact Unidirectional Conformal Antenna Based on Flexible High-Permittivity Custom-Made Substrate for Wearable

Wideband Electromagnetic Head Imaging System. *IEEE Transactions on Antennas and Propagation*, 68(1), 183–194. doi: 10.1109/TAP.2019.2938849

[8] Bose, M., & Karuppiah, V. (2025). Metamaterial inspired superstrate loaded miniaturized quad port MIMO antenna for 5G C-band applications. *Optics Communications*, *574*, 131123. ISSN 0030-4018. https://doi.org/10.1016/j.optcom.2024.131123

[9] Bong, F.-L., Lim, E.-H., & Lo, F.-L. (2018). Compact Orientation Insensitive Dipolar Patch for Metal-Mountable UHF RFID Tag Design. *IEEE Transactions on Antennas and Propagation, 66*(4), 1788–1795. doi: 10.1109/TAP.2018.2803132.

[10] Ziai, M. A., & Batchelor, J. C. (2011). Temporary On-Skin Passive UHF RFID Transfer Tag. *IEEE Transactions on Antennas and Propagation, 59*(10), 3565–3571. doi: 10.1109/TAP.2011.2163789.

45 Developing deepfake video detection using spatio temporal graph network (STGN)

Chris Maria[1,a], S. Suba Shree[1,b], Nivedhitha G.[1,c], Navin M. George[2,d], Ancy Michel[1,e], and S. Merlin Gilbert Raj[1,f]

[1]Electronics and Communication Engineering, Karunya Institute of Technology and Science, Coimbatore, India
[2]Electronics and Communication Engineering, Nehru Institute of Engineering and Technology, Coimbatore, India

Abstract: The paper proposes an innovative and composite approach in applying Spatio-Temporal Graph Neural Network (STGN) for deepfake detection. This model is expected to perform better when it comes to modeling the spatial and temporal dynamics of facial features. The dataset for evaluation is composed of real and synthesized videos pre-processed using facial landmark extraction for better feature presentation. The model, therefore, concludes to be more effective in modeling even minimal temporal inconsistencies in facial dynamics through the graph-based approach. High accuracy value proposed by the model was 90.24%, a tool on some of the best currently prevalent approaches like CNN (85.32%) and RNN (70.69%). The result indicates that finer temporal inconsistencies in facial dynamics can be detected using graph-based learning.

Keywords: Convolution neural network (CNN), recurrent neural network (RNN), deepfake video detection, spatio temporal graph network (STGN)

1. Introduction

Deepfake, is a concept that has emerged as one of the largest problems in digital media through strong deep learning techniques for video manipulation to produce convincing fake content.Artificial Videos can be exploited for malicious use such as misinformation, identity theft and even fraud. Convolutional Neural Networks (CNNs) have been extensively employed for their spatial feature extraction ability from images but they get lost in when dealing with temporal dependencies of videos. Recurrent Neural Networks (RNNs), more precisely Long Short-Term Memory (LSTM) networks [1] solve this problem by being trained on sequence data and remembering patterns over time. Nevertheless, RNNs are generally computationally expensive and hard at dealing with far distant dependencies which is why they can not be used in real-world deepfake detection problems.

Spatio Temporal Graph Neural Networks (STGNs) are presented as an improved solution in order to withstand these issues. STGNs with graph-based learning can recognize subtle discrepancies in facial motions and expressions which are major characteristics of deepfake.

This approach allows for better detection with deeper methods as well making it robust to shortcomings of the existing approaches.

2. Related Works

RNN: Detection-based deepfake techniques use machine-learning hybrid models (CNN-RNN), which consider both the temporal and spatial analysis [2]. A novel hybrid framework combining ResNext over frame-level feature extraction, and LSTM for temporal dependencies learning is proposed that results improved classification accuracy as [3, 4].

CNN: InceptionResNetV2 is used to pre-process videos into facial images using dlib and OpenCV, fine-tuning a classification layer to 90.38% accuracy, enhancing feature extraction [5]. ResNet18 with LSTM and Recycle-GAN also improves spatial-temporal fusion, enhancing deepfake classification, but computational complexity remains a problem in real-time scenarios [6].

STGN: Chen et al. suggested an EfficientNet-TimeSformer network with spatiotemporal attention, which was 95.26% accurate and had robustness improved using data augmentation [7]. Pipin et al. introduced a detection method that uses Spatiotemporal Convolutional Networks (SCN) and Photo Response Non-Uniformity (PRNU) analysis with 97.89% accuracy when employing ResNext50 and LSTM [8]. The method highlights the importance of temporal dependency in detecting deepfakes. Graph-based models, that is, Spatio-Temporal Graph Neural Networks (STGNs),

[a]chrismaria030@gmail.com, [b]subawork3@gmail.com, [c]niviniha.307@gmail.com, [d]nmnavingeorge@gmail.com, [e]ancymichel@gmail.com, [f]infomerlin@gmail.com

DOI: 10.1201/9781003724988-45

have been of great interest as they learn complex temporal dependencies and increase detection accuracy [9].

3. Deepfake Video Detection Methodology

Recurrent Neural Network(RNN): Models based on RNN that encompass LSTMs and Bidirectional LSTMs have been used [10]. These models process sequences of feature extractions to learn temporal frames patterns. As shown in below Figure 45.2 architecture consists of time-distributed flattening layers and then bidirectional LSTMs, batch normalization, and dropout layers for improving [11].

Convolutional Neural Network (CNN): CNNs are also widely applied to deepfake detection since they can extract spatial features from images [12]. As shown is below Figure 45.1, MobileNetV2 is utilized in this paper as a feature extractor, extracting features from sampled frames of the video. The frames are resized and normalized prior to input into the CNN to generate feature vectors [13].

Spatio Temporal Graph Network (STGN): STGN gets around the RNN and CNN limitations by representing videos as graphs, where nodes are facial landmarks and edges represent spatial and temporal relationships. As compared to CNNs, which are pixel-level feature-obsessed, STGN learns structural facial movement features. And as compared to RNNs, STGN learns long-range dependencies without suffering from vanishing gradients or computational expense

[14]. It is thus a more efficient and accurate model for deepfake detection, particularly in the case of moderate facial feature distortions over time.

4. Proposed Approach

The workflow of deep fake detection model from the Celeb-DF dataset and the application of the Spatio-Temporal Graph Networks (STGN) is depicted in Figure 45.3. In the preprocessing stage, the videos are converted to frames, and face detection, alignment, cropping, and normalization are done landmarks are extracted using MediaPipe to ensure consistency across frames by rectifying rotation, tilt, and scale differences [15]. The classification model then determines if the video is real or not [16].

1. Datasets: Celeb-DF (Celeb-DeepFake) dataset containing 590 real videos and 5,639 fake videos is utilized for identifying deepfake videos. 590 real and 590 fake videos are selected for the model for unbiased training. The dataset is reported to consist of 590 high-quality deepfake videos with fewer artifacts and is thus well-suited for training robust models as shown in Figures 45.4 and 45.5.

2. Preprocessing: Preprocessing is necessary in deep fake detection to prepare the dataset for training the model and extracting features. A multi-stage preprocessing procedure, including face detection, alignment,

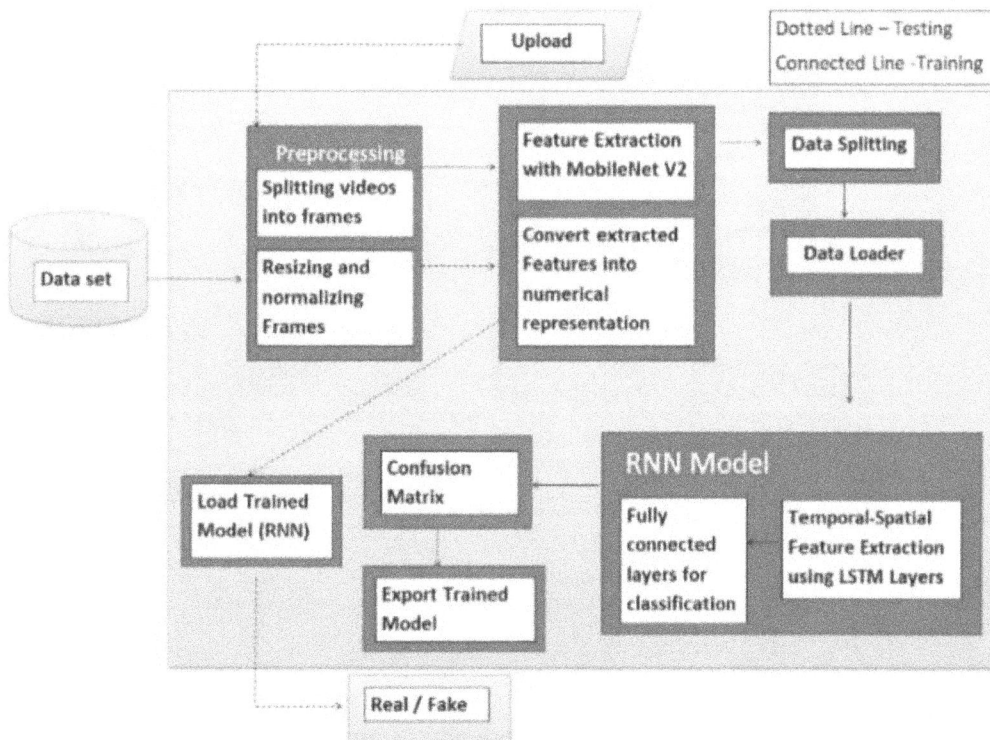

Figure 45.1. Block diagram of RNN model.

Source: Author.

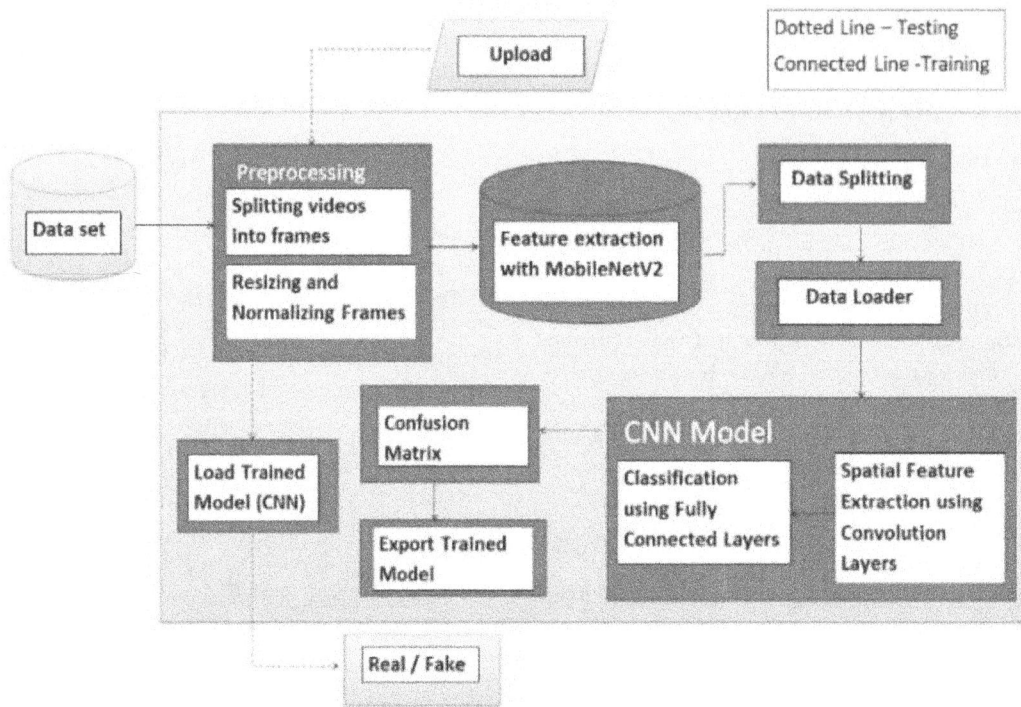

Figure 45.2. Block diagram of CNN Model.

Source: Author.

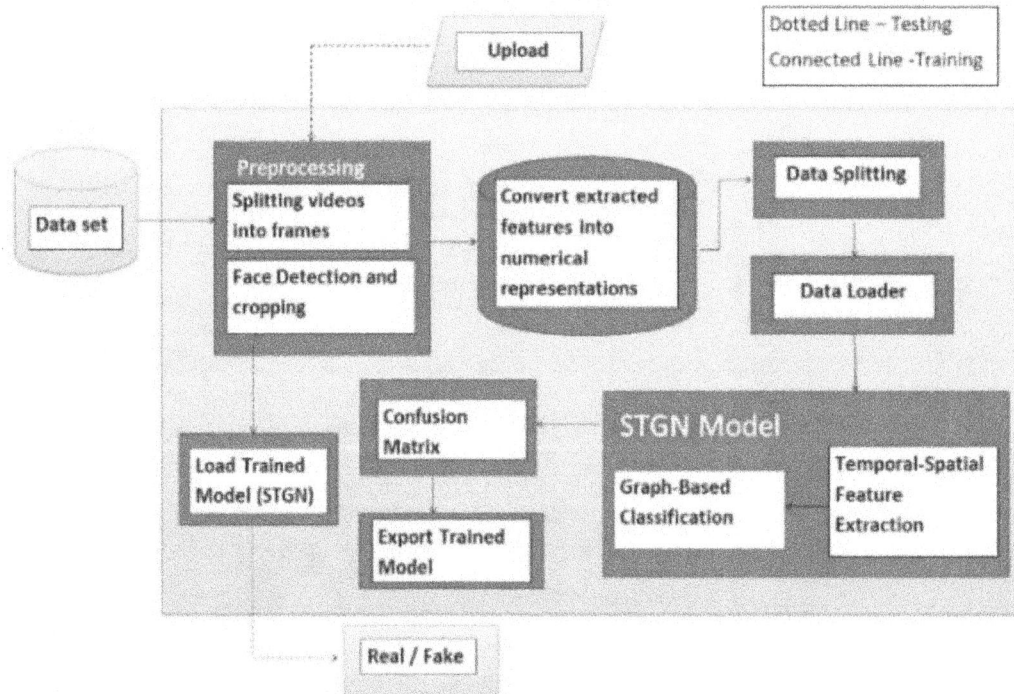

Figure 45.3. Block diagram of STGN model.

Source: Author.

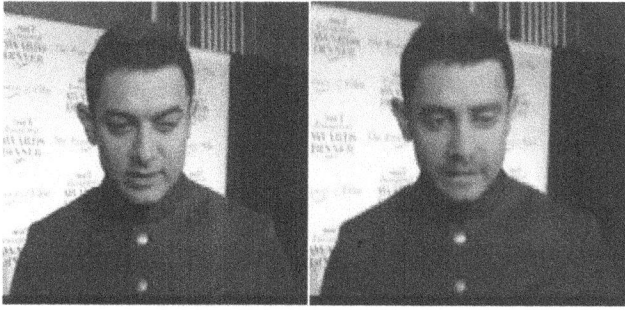

Figure 45.4–45.5. Image of real (left) and synthesized (right) video taken from Celeb DF datasets.

Source: Celeb DF datasets.

normalization, and landmark extraction, is employed to enhance model accuracy.

3. Proposed Model: The deep fake detection model consists of multiple stages, including graph extraction, feature learning, and classification. The Spatio-Temporal Graph Network (STGN) is used to analyze both spatial and temporal relationships in facial features across frames.

   a. Extraction of Graph: Facial landmarks are detected using MediaPipe and then structured as a graph. The relationship between the points assists in the detection of unnatural facial motion that is characteristic of deep fakes. Graph representation allows the model to attend to the motion of the different facial parts relative to each other over time rather than static features.

   b. STGN Model: A Spatio-Temporal Graph Network (STGN) was utilized to examine spatial anomalies within a single frame and temporal anomalies between multiple frames. Spatial analysis identified deepfake inconsistencies within individual static images, while temporal analysis identified abnormal patterns of movement over time. Based on this graph-based information, the STGN enhanced the ability to differentiate real and fake videos.

5. Results and Discussion

The evaluation of the RNN model, as illustrated in Figures 45.6 and 45.7 reveals its limitations in identifying sequential inconsistencies in deepfake detection and therefore makes heavy misclassifications. This indicates that the model does not effectively identify temporal dependencies in deepfakes. The model achieves an accuracy of 70.76%, with a precision of 76.99%, a recall of 66.92%, and an F1-score of 71.60%.

As seen in Table 45.1, STGN had a better accuracy of 90.24%, outdoing. Recurrent neural network with an accuracy of 70.69% and that Convolutional neural network with an accuracy of 85.32%. The classification report also indicates the superiority of the model, with STGN having a precision, recall, and F1-score of 90 %, indicating balanced

Table 45.1. Comparison of RNN, CNN and STGN

Models	Accuracy	Precision	Recall	F1-Score
Existing RNN	70.76	76.99	66.92	71.6
Existing CNN	85.32	85	83	84
Proposed STGN	90.24	90	90	90

Source: Author.

results on real and forged frames (Figure 45.9). Figure 45.10 demonstrates the STGN model's detailed evaluation, indicating its efficiency in the detection of the spatio-temporal inconsistencies.

The confusion matrix in Figure 45.11 reflects that STGN correctly classified 46,463 real and 38,124 fake frames, but misclassified 3,410 real frames as fake (false positives) and 7,008 fake frames as real (false negatives).

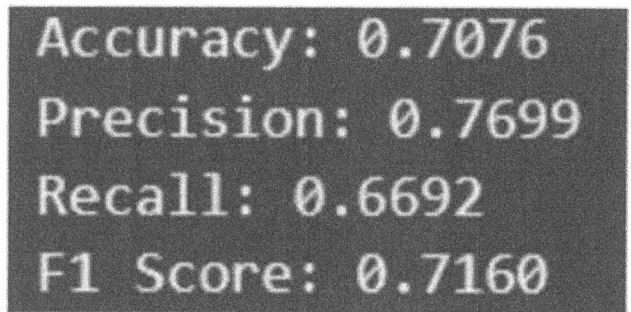

Figure 45.6. Evaluation of RNN model.

Source: Author.

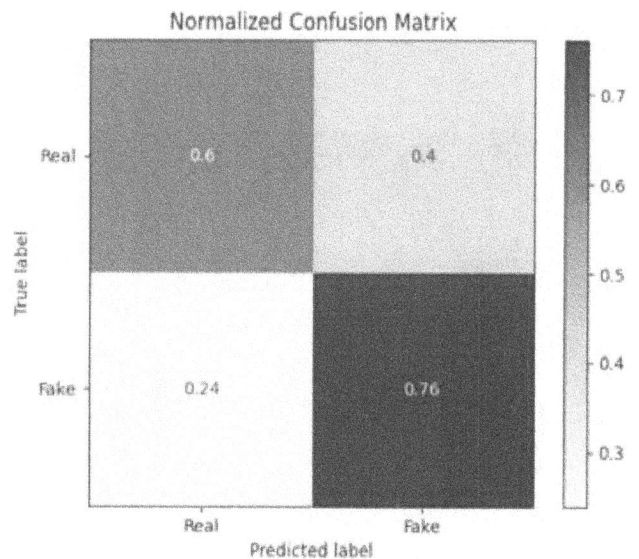

Figure 45.7. Normalized confusion matrix of RNN model.

Source: Author.

```
Evaluating the model...
Test Accuracy: 85.32%

Classification Report:
              precision   recall   f1-score

Real            0.84       0.88      0.86
Fake            0.87       0.82      0.84

accuracy                             0.85
macro avg       0.85       0.85      0.85
weighted avg    0.85       0.85      0.85
```

Figure 45.8. Evaluation of CNN model.

Source: Author.

Confusion Matrix

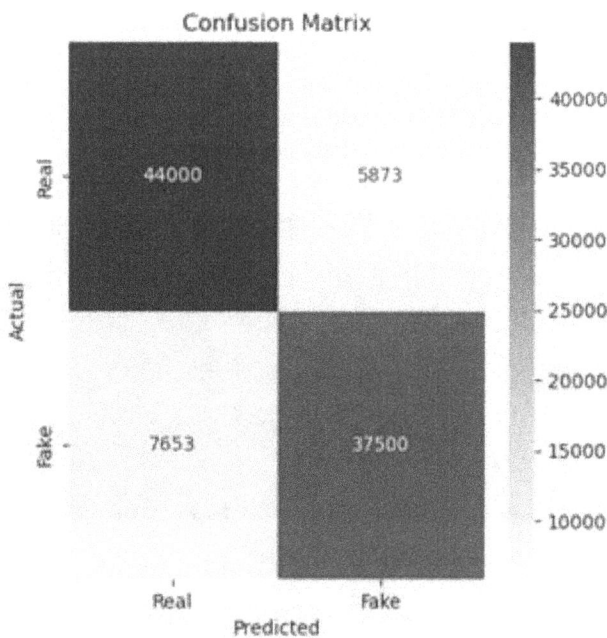

Figure 45.9. Confusion matrix analysis of CNN-based deepfake detection on extracted video frames.

Source: Author.

```
Evaluating the model...
Test Accuracy: 90.24%

Classification Report:
              precision   recall   f1-score   support

        Real     0.88       0.94      0.91      49873
        Fake     0.93       0.86      0.89      45132

    accuracy                          0.90      95005
   macro avg     0.90       0.90      0.90      95005
weighted avg     0.90       0.90      0.90      95005

[Done] exited with code=0 in 34.287 seconds
```

Figure 45.10. Evaluation of STGN model.

Source: Author.

This higher false negative reflects that some deepfake frames display highly realistic facial dynamics, and detection becomes challenging. However, STGN still performs much better than CNN and RNN models, as reflected in Figures 45.6 and 45.8.

Moreover, The Figures 45.7 and 45.11 show the performances of CNN and RNN models, respectively, as incapable of identifying sequential inconsistencies. Finally, Figure 45.12 shows a comparative bar graph of the metrics, further proving the superiority of STGN over CNN and RNN models. The STGN model was trained using high-performance hardware featuring an Intel Core i9-13900K CPU, NVIDIA RTX 4090 GPU, 64GB of DDR5 RAM, and 2TB NVMe SSD. With 95,005 frames processed over 20 epochs, the model completed training in 2.43 hours (8762 seconds). This results in an average of 438.1 seconds per epoch and about

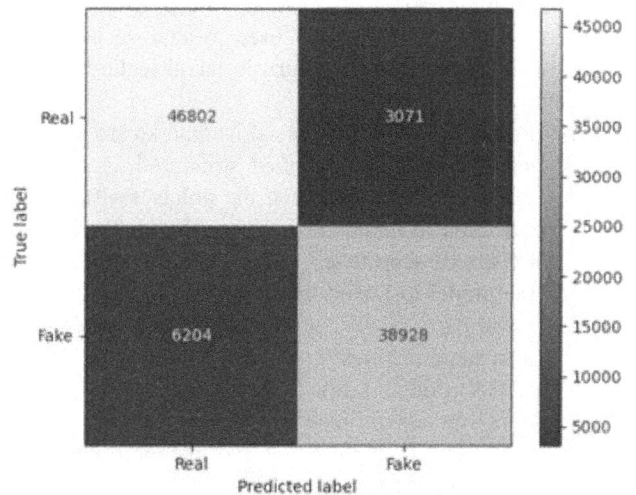

Figure 45.11. Confusion matrix analysis of STGN-based deepfake detection on extracted video frames.

Source: Author.

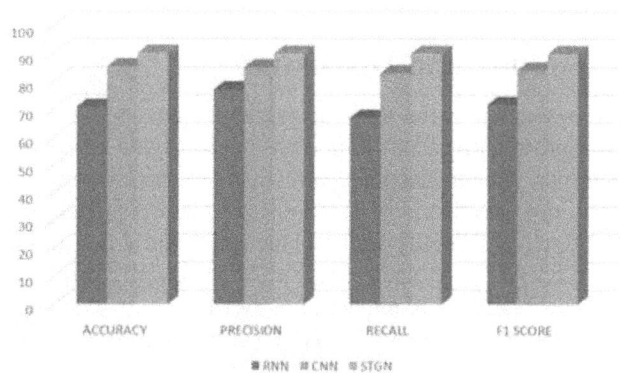

Figure 45.12. Bar graph of Table 45.1.

Source: Author.

92.22 seconds per 1000 frames, demonstrating excellent computational efficiency. Given the graph-based complexity and temporal modeling of STGN, these results indicate that the system is well-optimized for deepfake detection, especially when paired with top-tier hardware.

Hybrid deepfake detection models like ResNext-LSTM and EfficientNet-RNN have 96% accuracy but are plagued by high computational expenses, vanishing gradients, and dataset dependence. Likewise, transformer-based models like EfficientNet-TimeSformer offer 95.26% accuracy but demand heavy computational resources, making them less suitable for real-time use. With an accuracy of 97.89%, the SCN+PRNU model proves to be a robust method for deepfake detection; however, since it is dependent on the sensor noise patterns for identification, it cannot be generalized across all devices and datasets. Thereby, spatio-temporal graph networks must devise a strategy to handle the introduction of spatio-temporal inconsistencies at an economical computational cost by transforming facial landmarks into graphs. In contrast to CNNs, which basically rely on pixel-level features, STGNs work on the identification of motion anomalies, hence making them more robust to unseen deepfakes and adversarial attacks. With 90.24% accuracy, STGNs guarantee an optimal trade-off between accuracy, efficiency, and scalability, thus making them practical for real-time deepfake detection.

6. Conclusion

In this paper, we introduce a deep learning based deepfake detection spatial/temporal inconsistency system to spot forged content from its original. Encouraging results for identifying real from fake videos, results are considered to be limited. Dataset variability plays a big role in the accuracy and are at risk from emerging deep fake attack strategies. As mentioned in the previous limitations, this indicates the requirement of improving model robustness, dataset expansion and fast algorithms. Aside all that, the results reveal additional investigations on enhancement in detection methods, adaptability in real-time and enhance the accuracy for improving deepfake detection systems.

Acknowledgment

Thanks to Karunya Institute of Technology and Sciences for all the ambience infrastructural support and research facilities that made this work possible.

References

[1] Al-Dhabi, Y., & Zhang, S. (2021). Deepfake Video Detection by Combining Convolutional Neural Network (CNN) and Recurrent Neural Network (RNN). In *2021 IEEE International Conference on Computer Science, Artificial Intelligence and Electronic Engineering, CSAIEE 2021*. Institute of Electrical and Electronics Engineers Inc. pp. 236–241. doi: 10.1109/CSAIEE54046.2021.9543264.

[2] Anjaneyulu, B. P., Reddy, C. P. K., Reddy, G. V. A., Yogitha, C., Pandiyarajan, P., & Maheshwaran, B. (2024). DeepFake Detection using Convolutional Neural Networks (CNN) and Recurrent Neural Network (RNN). In *Proceedings of the 5th International Conference on Data Intelligence and Cognitive Informatics, ICDICI 2024*. Institute of Electrical and Electronics Engineers Inc. pp. 711–716. doi: 10.1109/ICDICI62993.2024.10810970.

[3] Koritala, S. P., Chimata, M., Polavarapu, S. N., Vangapandu, B. S., Gogineni, T. K., & Manikandan, V. M. ()2024. A Deepfake detection technique using Recurrent Neural Network and EfficientNet. In *2024 15th International Conference on Computing Communication and Networking Technologies, ICCCNT 2024*. Institute of Electrical and Electronics Engineers Inc. doi: 10.1109/ICCCNT61001.2024.10723875.

[4] Patel, S., Chandra, S. K., & Jain, A. (2023). DeepFake Videos Detection and Classification Using Resnext and LSTM Neural Network. In *2023 3rd International Conference on Smart Generation Computing, Communication and Networking, SMART GENCON 2023*. Institute of Electrical and Electronics Engineers Inc. doi: 10.1109/SMARTGENCON60755.2023.10442131.

[5] Guefrechi, S., Ben Jabra, M., & Hamam, H. (2022). Deepfake video detection using InceptionResnetV2. In *International Conference on Advanced Technologies for Signal and Image Processing, ATSIP 2022*. Institute of Electrical and Electronics Engineers Inc. doi: 10.1109/ATSIP55956.2022.9805902.

[6] Jolly, V., Telrandhe, M., Kasat, A., Shitole, A., & Gawande, K. (2022). CNN based Deep Learning model for Deepfake Detection. In *2022 2nd Asian Conference on Innovation in Technology, ASIANCON 2022*, Institute of Electrical and Electronics Engineers Inc. doi: 10.1109/ASIANCON55314.2022.9908862.

[7] Chen, Z., Wang, S., Yan, D., & Li, Y. (2024). A Spatio-Temporl Deepfake Video Detection Method Based on TimeSformer-CNN. In *3rd IEEE International Conference on Distributed Computing and Electrical Circuits and Electronics, ICDCECE 2024*. Institute of Electrical and Electronics Engineers Inc. doi: 10.1109/ICDCECE60827.2024.10549278.

[8] Pipin, S. J., Purba, R., & Pasha, M. F. (2022). Deepfake Video Detection Using Spatiotemporal Convolutional Network and Photo Response Non Uniformity. In *ICOSNIKOM 2022 - 2022 IEEE International Conference of Computer Science and Information Technology: Boundary Free: Preparing Indonesia for Metaverse Society*. Institute of Electrical and Electronics Engineers Inc. doi: 10.1109/ICOSNIKOM56551.2022.10034890.

[9] Ghosh, P., Yao, Y., Davis, L., & Divakaran, A. (2020). Stacked spatio-temporal graph convolutional networks for action segmentation. In *Proceedings of the IEEE/CVF winter conference on applications of computer vision* (pp. 576–585).

[10] Sastrawan, I. K., Bayupati, I. P. A., & Arsa, D. M. S. (2022). Detection of fake news using deep learning CNN–RNN based methods. *ICT express, 8*(3), 396–408.

[11] Albazony, A. A. M., Al-Wzwazy, H. A., Al-Khaleefa, A. S., Alazzawi, M. A., Almohamadi, M., & Alavi, S. E. (2023). DeepFake Videos Detection by Using Recurrent Neural Network (RNN). In *AICCIT 2023 - Al-Sadiq International*

Conference on Communication and Information Technology. Institute of Electrical and Electronics Engineers Inc., pp. 103–107. doi: 10.1109/AICCIT57614.2023.10217956.

[12]   Aminollah Khormali, A. J.-S. Y. (2025). Deepfake Detection: A Systematic Literature Review. Accessed: Mar. 12, 2025. [Online]. Available: https://ieeexplore.ieee.org/stamp/stamp.jsp?arnumber=10506700

[13]   Tolosana, R., Vera-Rodriguez, R., Fierrez, J., Morales, A., & Ortega-Garcia, J. (2020). Deepfakes and beyond: A survey of face manipulation and fake detection. *Information Fusion, 64,* 131–148.

[14]   Gura, D., Dong, B., Mehiar, D., & Al Said, N. (2024). Customized Convolutional Neural Network for Accurate Detection of Deep Fake Images in Video Collections. *Computers,* *Materials and Continua, 79*(2), 1995–2014. doi: 10.32604/cmc.2024.048238.

[15]   Barbadekar, A., Sole, S., & Shekhavat, A. (2024). Enhancing Social Media Security: LSTM-Based Deep Fake Video Detection. In *2024 IEEE 9th International Conference for Convergence in Technology, I2CT 2024.* Institute of Electrical and Electronics Engineers Inc. doi: 10.1109/I2CT61223.2024.10543604.

[16]   Mira, F. (2023). Deep Learning Technique for Recognition of Deep Fake Videos. In *2023 IEEE IAS Global Conference on Emerging Technologies, GlobConET 2023.* Institute of Electrical and Electronics Engineers Inc. doi: 10.1109/GlobConET56651.2023.10150143.

46 Crime forecasting and prevention using deep learning approaches by image data

Nishan A. H.[1,a] and Chandru M.[2,b]

[1]Assistant Professor, Department of Information Technology, Francis Xavier Engineering College, Tirunelveli, India

[2]PG Scholar, Department of Information Technology, Francis Xavier Engineering College, Tirunelveli, India

Abstract: Predictive crime analysis using deep learning approaches and image data involves the use of advanced machine learning techniques, particularly convolutional neural networks (CNNs), to analyze visual data from sources such as CCTV footage, satellite imagery, and street-level cameras to detect patterns and predict crime activity. By detecting anomalies, recognizing crime locations, and analyzing behavioural patterns from historical and real-time image data, these models can provide valuable insights for crime prevention and resource allocation. However, challenges such as data privacy, image quality, model bias, and scalability must be addressed to ensure perfection and ethical use. Integrating multimodal data sources and leveraging deep learning architectures have the potential for more effective crime prediction and response in smart city environments.

Keywords: CNN (Convolution Neural Networks), RNN (Recurrent Neural Network), LSTMN (Long Short-Term Memory Networks)

1. Introduction

The integration of deep learning approaches with image data for predictive crime analytics represents a promising advancement in crime prohibiting and constabulary strategies. Traditional crime forecasting methods often rely on historical crime data, statistical analysis, social factors to predict criminal activities, but the rise of surveillance technology and the vast availability of visual data have opened new avenues for real-time analysis and prediction [1]. Deep learning, specially via Convolutional Neural Networks (CNNs), has transfigured how image data from CCTV cameras, drones, and satellite imagery can be utilized to detect suspicious behaviour, recognize crime hotspots, and anticipate future criminal activities. By automatically extracting relevant features from images, these models can provide valuable insights into crime patterns and potential risks [9]. Despite the promising potential, the use of image data in crime forecasting also presents challenges related to privacy concerns, data quality, and model fairness. As technology carry on to progress, the fusion image analysis with advanced deep learning models offers new opportunities for improving public safety and proactive crime prevention in urban environments.

2. The Objectives of this Study

Develop Deep Learning Models for Crime Prediction: To design and implement deep learning-based models, specifically Convolutional Neural Networks (CNNs), that can analyse image data originating at surveillance cameras, satellite images, and street-level monitoring systems to predict and detect criminal activities [14].

Identify Crime Patterns and Hotspots: To utilize image data to detect patterns and identify potential crime hotspots, enabling predictive analytics that can forecast areas with a high likelihood of criminal activity based on visual cues such as unusual behaviours, crowds, or vehicles [10].

Enhance Real-Time Crime Detection: To develop systems that can analyze real-time visual data and provide immediate alerts to law enforcement agencies, facilitating faster response times to prevent or mitigate criminal activities [2].

Improve Data Quality and Handle Noise in Images: To explore methods for improving the perfection of predictions despite challenges such as low-quality or noisy image data, ensuring the models can effectively function in diverse real-world environments [3].

Ensure Privacy and Ethical Considerations: To propose techniques that protect privacy and address ethical concerns, ensuring that predictive crime analytics models comply with privacy regulations and avoid biases in crime detection and forecasting.

Evaluate the Integration of Multimodal Data: To explore the benefits of integrating image data with other data origins, like as historical crime data, social media feeds, or sensor data, to improve the predictive perfection and robustness of crime forecasting systems [11].

[a]nishan.a.h.97@gmail.com, [b]chandrumuthusamy1304@gmail.com

DOI: 10.1201/9781003724988-46

Assess the Scalability and Efficiency of Crime Prediction Systems: To evaluate the computational efficiency, scalability of the developed deep learning models, ensuring they can process large-scale image data in real-time for effective implementation in urban environments.

By achieving these objectives, the study aims to advance the field of predictive crime analytics, leveraging deep learning and image data to enhance public safety, optimize law enforcement resources, and create smarter, more responsive crime prevention strategies [5].

Developments in deep learning have significantly changed the way crime data is examined and predicted. Manipulating deep learning techniques, especially CNNs and other advanced neural network architectures, has allowed for more sophisticated, accurate, and efficient crime data analytics. Some of the key advancements include:

2.1. Real-time crime detection and surveillance

Deep learning has made it possible to process and examine real-time video files originating at surveillance cameras to detect criminal activities as they happen. By training models on huge datasets of categorized footage, deep learning systems can automatically identify suspicious behaviour (e.g., theft, assault, or vandalism) and send immediate alerts to law enforcement. This advancement reduces the time between crime occurrence and response, potentially preventing crime or minimizing its impact [13].

2.2. Crime hotspot prediction

Deep learning models can analyze historical crime data alongside environmental features (e.g., lighting conditions, foot traffic, weather) and spatial patterns to predict crime hotspots in specific areas. This allows law enforcement to proactively allocate resources to high-risk locations and prevent crimes before they occur [7].

2.3. Anomaly detection and fraud prevention

Deep learning has advanced anomaly detection capabilities in crime data analytics. This is particularly useful in identifying unusual activities in financial transactions or insurance claims that may indicate fraud. These systems are trained to recognize patterns of normal behaviour, making them highly effective at detecting deviations that could signal fraudulent activity or criminal [4].

2.4. Incorporation of multimodal data

Recent advancements in deep learning have incorporating various kinds of data origins, such as images, videos, text, and geographic information, into a cohesive analysis framework. For instance, combining surveillance footage with data from sensors (motion, heat, etc.) or social media feeds amplifying the model's capability to predict and prevent crime. This multimodal approach permits to more comprehensive understanding of crime patterns and risk factors [12].

2.5. Sentiment analysis for threat detection

Deep learning techniques in natural language processing (NLP) have been applied to analyze text data and detect potential threats. By assessing the sentiment, intent, and tone of online communications, deep learning systems can identify threats of violence or illegal activity before they escalate.

2.6. Advanced visual anomaly detection

Deep learning-based image processing techniques, such as Generative Adversarial Networks (GANs) and auto encoders, have significantly improved anomaly detection in images and videos. These models are able to detect abnormal or suspicious activities in visual data, such as identifying a person acting in a way that deviates from normal behaviour in public spaces [6].

3. Methodology

3.1. Predictive crime analytics using deep learning approaches for crime forecasting and prevention with image data

3.1.1. Data collection

Objective: Gather diverse data sources, including image data, crime records, and environmental variables.

Crime Data: Collect historical crime data, including crime type, location, time, and demographic information. This is usually stored in databases maintained by law enforcement agencies.

3.1.1.1. Image data

Surveillance Footage: Obtain surveillance camera footage, either from public spaces or security camera networks [15].

Crime Scene Images: Collect images from crime scenes, which may be part of forensic investigations.

Satellite or Aerial Images: Gather geospatial images to analyze urban environments and identify potential crime hotspots.

Environmental and Contextual Data: Collect data on weather, time of day, and other environmental conditions (e.g., lighting) that could influence crime patterns [8].

3.1.2. Data pre-processing

3.1.2.1. Image data cleaning

Normalization: Standardize the pixel values (e.g., scaling images to a range of 0–1) to ensure consistency in the input data.

Noise Reduction: Apply image processing techniques like Gaussian blurring or median filtering to remove noise from the images that could affect model performance.

Resizing: Resize images to a uniform size (e.g., 224 × 224 pixels) to make them compatible with deep learning models.

3.1.2.2. Annotation and labeling

Manually label crime-related images or use pre-existing datasets with labeled crime scenes (e.g., robbery, assault, vandalism). Labels are essential for supervized learning.

3.1.2.3. Data augmentation

To prevent overfitting and improve the assortment of dataset, perform image augmentation techniques such as rotating, flipping, cropping images, as well as applying colour jitter to simulate different lighting conditions.

3.1.2.4. Data merging

Combine image data with contextual data (such as geospatial data and crime records) to generate a multi-modal dataset for training the predictive model.

3.1.3. Model selection

3.1.3.1. Convolutional neural networks (CNNs)

CNNs are ideal for extracting geographical features from images. It consists of convolutional layers, pooling layers, fully connected layers. This model is effective in recognizing objects or actions in crime scene images or surveillance footage.

3.1.3.2. Recurrent neural networks (RNNs) / long short-term memory networks (LSTMs)

LSTMs applied to capture temporal dependencies, such as crime trends over time, by analyzing sequential crime data. For surveillance video, RNNs or LSTMs can be employed to track activities or abnormal patterns in footage.

Object Detection Models: It can detect specific objects or actions within images, such as identifying weapons, vehicles, or individuals in crime scenes.

3.1.3.3. Graph neural networks (GNNs)

For analyzing relationships between crime events, locations, and criminal networks, GNNs are suitable for understanding the connections between different entities in a crime context.

3.1.4. Model training

3.1.4.1. Training process

Split the dataset into training, validation, test sets. Typically 70% of the data is applied for training, 15% for validation, 15% for testing.

Use pre-trained models, finite them for the specific task of crime detection and prediction.

3.1.4.2. Loss function

For classification tasks use a cross-entropy loss function.

For regression tasks (e.g., predicting crime occurrence or severity), use Mean Squared Error (MSE) or Mean Absolute Error (MAE).

3.1.4.3. Hyper parameter tuning

Perform hyper parameter tuning using techniques like Grid Search or Random Search to find the optimal set of parameters for the model.

3.1.5. Model evaluation

3.1.5.1. Metrics

To evaluate the model using perfection, precision, recall, F1-score, and the confusion matrix.

To apply metrics like Mean Absolute Error (MAE), Mean Squared Error (MSE), and R-squared.

3.1.5.2. Cross-validation

Use k-fold cross-manipulate to secure the model comprehensively good to unseen data and does not overload to the training dataset.

3.1.5.3. Error analysis

Analyze misclassifications or erroneous predictions, particularly focusing on edge cases like false positives or false negatives, which could have significant consequences in crime prediction.

3.1.6. Model deployment

3.1.6.1. Integration with real-time surveillance systems

Deploy the model to integrate with existing security infrastructure, including public surveillance cameras, to provide real-time crime prediction and alerts. The model can trigger immediate notifications to law enforcement when abnormal behaviour or potential crime events are detected.

3.1.6.2. Resource allocation system

Incorporate the model's predictions into resource allocation systems that help police departments optimize patrolling efforts, especially in identified crime hotspots.

3.1.6.3. Cloud-based deployment

For scalability, deploy the trained model on cloud-related platforms like as AWS, Google Cloud, or Azure, ensure the system can handle large volumes of image and video data for continuous monitoring and prediction.

3.1.7. Ethical and privacy considerations

3.1.7.1. Bias mitigation

Implement fairness algorithms to ensure the model does not disproportionately target certain communities or groups. Regularly audit the model's predictions to detect and correct any biases.

3.1.7.2. Privacy protection

Adhere to privacy regulations, such as GDPR or CCPA, when processing and storing image data. Ensure that data collection, storage, and usage comply with legal standards for surveillance and data privacy.

3.1.7.3. Transparency

Use explainable AI techniques to ensure that predictions made by the model can be interpreted and justified, especially in sensitive law enforcement applications.

3.1.8. Continuous monitoring and improvement

3.1.8.1. Model retraining

A fresh crime data available, periodically retrain the model to improve perfection and adapt to changing crime patterns.

3.1.8.2. User feedback

Incorporate feedback from law enforcement officers and other stakeholders to refine and improve the model over time.

4. Experimental Evaluation of Predictive Crime Analytics using Deep Learning Approaches for Crime Forecasting and Prevention with Image Data

4.1. Experimental setup

4.1.1. Datasets

Crime Data: Historical crime records that include information on crime types, locations, times, and outcomes. This is used for training and testing the predictive aspect of crime forecasting models.

Image Data: Surveillance footage, crime scene images, and street-level images are used to train deep learning models for object detection, crime classification, and hotspot analysis.

Environmental Data: Weather patterns, lighting conditions, and geographical features are also integrated into the dataset to examine their effects on crime forecasting.

4.2. Model training and hyper parameter tuning

4.2.1. Training process

Split the dataset into training, validation, test sets. the test set is used for final evaluation.

4.3. Performance metrics

4.3.1. For classification tasks (Crime type detection)

Perfection: calculate the overall percentage of perfect predictions.

Precision: The ratio of faith full positives to the sum of faith full positives and faulty positives. It calculate how many of the predicted crime events were actually true.

Recall: The ratio of true positives to the sum of faith full positives and faulty negatives. It calculates how many actual crime events the model successfully predicted.

Confusion Matrix: Helps assess the distribution of predictions, showing the number of false positives, false negatives, true positives, and true negatives.

4.3.2. For regression tasks (Crime forecasting)

Mean Squared Error (MSE): Calculate the average squared difference between the predicted and actual values. Lower values indicate better predictions.

Mean Absolute Error (MAE): Calculate the average absolute difference between predicted and actual values. It's more interpretable than MSE.

R-Squared (R^2): Indicates the amount of variance in the dependent variable explained by the model. A higher R^2 value indicates a better fit of the model to the data.

4.3.3. For object detection tasks

Intersection over Union (IoU): Calculate the overlap in the middle of predicted binding boxes and ground truth binding boxes in object detection tasks. Higher IoU indicates better detection performance.

Average Precision (AP): Calculate the precision into the other side all recall levels in object detection tasks. It aggregates the precision-recall curve into a single value.

4.4. Testing on real-world data

Test Data: Evaluate the model on a discrete test dataset that it has not seen during training. The test data should contain diverse crime types, locations, and environmental conditions to simulate a real-world crime environment.

Real-Time Surveillance Evaluation: Implement the trained model on a real-time surveillance system to assess its ability to predict crimes based on live data.

Crime Hotspot Identification: Use the model to generate crime hotspots by combining image data (such as surveillance footage) with historical crime records.

Perfection in Crime Prevention: Deploy the model's predictions in authentic scenarios, such as adjusting patrol routes or enhancing security in specific areas.

4.5. Analysis of results

Error Analysis: Analyze the cases where the model performs poorly understand the limitations of the model.

Bias Evaluation: Check for any biases in the predictions. For example, determine whether the model disproportionately predicts crimes in specific neighbourhoods, which may indicate a need to balance the dataset or improve the fairness of the model.

Interpretability: Evaluate the interpretability of the deep learning model, especially for critical applications like crime prediction, where explanations for predictions may be necessary for decision-making. Use techniques like Grad-CAM or LIME to explain the features grantly highly to the model's decision.

Model Robustness: Test the robustness of the model under different environmental conditions, such as poor-quality images, extreme lighting, or various weather conditions. Evaluate whether the model maintains good performance even under challenging real-world scenarios.

4.6. Comparison with baseline models

Baseline Models: Use traditional crime forecasting techniques like logistic regression, decision trees, or support vector machines (SVM) as baselines for comparison.

Performance Comparison: Validate the performance of the deep learning models with the baseline models across multiple metrics to determine if the deep learning approach provides superior results.

4.7. Deployment and continuous evaluation

Model Monitoring: After deployment, monitor the performance of the model over time. Evaluate whether it maintains its perfection and predictive power, especially as crime patterns evolve.

Feedback Loops: Implement feedback loops to allow law enforcement personnel to provide feedback on predictions and flag false alarms or missed crimes. This feedback can be used to improve the model over time.

Re-training: Retrain the model regularly with fresh data to ensure it adapts to changes in crime patterns and environmental factors (Figure 46.1).

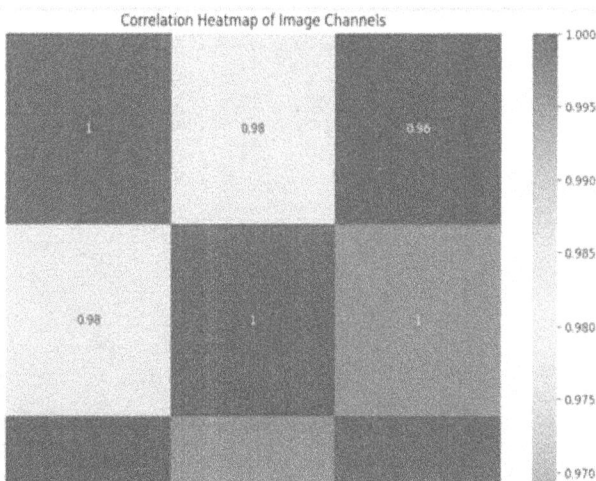

Figure 46.1. Correlation heatmap of image channels.

Source: Author.

5. Conclusion

The integration of deep learning into crime data analytics has revolutionized crime forecasting, detection, and prevention. By leveraging large-scale data, real-time processing, and sophisticated pattern recognition, these advancements enable law enforcement agencies to be more proactive, precise, and efficient in addressing criminal activities. However, challenges related to ethical concerns, privacy, and biases remain, and further research is necessary to ensure these technologies are deployed responsibly and effectively.

References

[1] Krizhevsky, A., et al. (2012). Using deep convolutional neural networks for ImageNet classification. *Advances in Neural Information Processing Systems*, 25, 1097–1105.

[2] Gabriel, J. Z., Muthuraman, U., Kabilan, R., Devaraj, G. P., Ravi, R., & Esther, J. M. (2022). Waiting Line Conscious Scheduling for OFDMA Networks, using JSFRA Formulation. *2022 International Conference on Sustainable Computing and Data Communication Systems (ICSCDS)*. Erode, India, pp. 754–759. doi: 10.1109/ICSCDS53736.2022.9760949.

[3] Amato, F., Carfora, A., & Ricci, E. (2019). Predictive policing and crime forecasting: A systematic review of the state of the art.

[4] Muthuraman, U., Ravi, R., Devaraj, G. P., Esther, J. M., Kabilan, R., & Gabriel, J. Z. (2022). Embedded Sensor-based Construction Health Warning System for Civil Structures & Advanced Networking Techniques using IoT. *2022 International Conference on Sustainable Computing and Data Communication Systems (ICSCDS)*. Erode, India, pp. 1002–1006. doi: 10.1109/ICSCDS53736.2022.9760793.

[5] Krizhevsky, A., et al (2012). Using deep convolutional neural networks for ImageNet classification. *Advances in Neural Information Processing Systems*, 25, 1097–1105.

[6] Gabriel, J. Z., Muthuraman, U., Kabilan, R., Devaraj, G. P., Ravi, R., & Esther, J. M. (2022). Waiting Line Conscious Scheduling for OFDMA Networks, using JSFRA Formulation. *2022 International Conference on Sustainable Computing and Data Communication Systems (ICSCDS)*. Erode, India, pp. 754–759. doi: 10.1109/ICSCDS53736.2022.9760949.

[7] Kabilan, R., Kamala Devi, E., Mari Bhuvaneshwari, R., Jothika, S., Gayathiri, R., & Mallika Pandeeswari, R. (2022). GPS Localization for Enhancement of Military Fence Unit. In *2022 Second International Conference on Artificial Intelligence and Smart Energy (ICAIS)*, pp. 811–816. doi: 10.1109/ICAIS53314.2022.9742959.

[8] Kabilan, R., Ravi, R., Esther, J. M., Muthuraman, U., Gabriel, J. Z., & Devaraj, G. P. (2022). Constructing Effective UVM Testbench By Using DRAM Memory Controllers. *2022 Second International Conference on Artificial Intelligence and Smart Energy (ICAIS)*. Coimbatore, India, pp. 1034–1038. doi: 10.1109/ICAIS53314.2022.9742986.

[9] Angwin, J., Larson, J., Mattu, S., & Kirchner, L. (2016). Machine bias: There's software used across the country to predict future criminals. And it's biased against blacks.

[10] Pandeeswari, R. M., Kabilan, R., Januanbumani, T. M., Rejoni, J., Ramya, A., & Jothi, S. J. (2022). Data Backups and Error Finding by Residue Quotient Code for

Testing Applications. *2022 International Conference on Sustainable Computing and Data Communication Systems (ICSCDS)*. Erode, India, pp. 637–641. doi: 10.1109/ICSCDS53736.2022.9760940.

[11] Devaraj, G. P., Kabilan, R., Muthuraman, U., Gabriel, J. Z., Esther, J. M., & Ravi, R. (2022). Multipurpose Intellectual Home Area Network Using Smart Phone. *2022 Second International Conference on Artificial Intelligence and Smart Energy (ICAIS)*. Coimbatore, India, pp. 1464–1469. doi: 10.1109/ICAIS53314.2022.9742955.

[12] Kabilan, R., Lakshmi Narayanan, K., Venkatesh, M., Vikram Bhaskaran, V., Viswanathan, G. K., & Yogesh Rajan, S. G. (2021). Live Human Detection Robot in Earthquake Conditions. *Recent Trends in Intensive Computing*, 818–823, doi: 10.3233/APC210286.

[13] Esther, J. M., Gabriel, J. Z., Ravi, R., Muthuraman, U., Devaraj, G. P., & Kabilan, R. (2022). Increased Energy Efficiency of MANETs Through DEL-CMAC Protocol on Network. *2022 International Conference on Sustainable Computing and Data Communication Systems (ICSCDS)*. Erode, India, pp. 1122–1126. doi: 10.1109/ICSCDS53736.2022.9760930.

[14] Binns, R., & Blass, E. (2019). Privacy in predictive policing.

[15] Cuong, P. T., & Tuan, N. A. (2020). Crime prediction using deep learning techniques: A case study on public safety.

47 Enhancing rescue operations of disaster management with machine learning algorithms

J. B. Shajilin Loret[1,a] and Kasirajesh S.[2,b]

[1]Professor, Department of Information Technology, Francis Xavier Engineering College, Tirunelveli, India
[2]Department of Information Technology, Francis Xavier Engineering college, Tirunelveli, India

Abstract: Flood prediction is a critical aspect of disaster management, enabling timely intervention and minimizing loss of life and property. This proposed method uses advanced machine learning algorithms, specifically **XGBoost** and **LightGBM**, for accurate flood prediction. By leveraging large and complex datasets, which include meteorological, hydrological, and geospatial data, the models analyze patterns and relationships that can predict the likelihood and severity of flooding events. The effectiveness of **XGBoost** and **LightGBM** is evaluated, with the models showing superior predictive capabilities compared to traditional flood forecasting techniques. In addition, the models' ability to handle real-time data integration for dynamic flood forecasting is demonstrated, making them highly useful for emergency response and resource allocation. Furthermore, feature importance analysis highlights the key variables influencing flood predictions, enhancing the interpretability and transparency of the models. The findings suggest that integrating machine learning models with conventional flood forecasting methods can significantly improve flood preparedness and management strategies, particularly in flood-prone regions. Future advancements in data collection and algorithm optimization are expected to further enhance the accuracy and applicability of these models in diverse environmental settings.

Keywords: LIME, R^2 -R-squared, SHAP, PDPs-partial dependence plots

1. Introduction

Predictive modeling plays a vital role in improving flood forecasting and disaster management. By leveraging advanced machine learning algorithms such as XGBoost and LightGBM, predictive models can analyze large, complex datasets to forecast flood events with greater accuracy [16]. These models are particularly effective because they can process diverse types of data, such as historical weather patterns, river levels, and other environmental variables, to predict the likelihood of floods and their potential impact on communities [12].

The application of machine learning in flood prediction not only enhances the precision of forecasts but also supports better resource allocation and emergency response [20]. By accurately predicting when and where floods are likely to occur, emergency services can prepare in advance, ensuring a timely and organized response that optimizes the deployment of rescue teams, equipment, and supplies. This predictive capability is especially crucial for minimizing the loss of life and property during flood events [6].

Furthermore, the future of flood prediction and disaster management holds even more promise with continued advancements in technology and machine learning [26]. The integration of more sophisticated algorithms and real-time data sources will further improve flood prediction models, enabling faster and more effective responses to natural disasters. Overall, predictive modeling is an essential tool in disaster management, offering a data-driven approach to minimizing the impact of floods on vulnerable communities and enhancing overall preparedness for future events [7].

2. Literature Review

This study explored machine learning models, including XGBoost, for flood prediction in Nepal, emphasizing the role of historical rainfall data and river flow rates [5]. The research demonstrated improved forecasting accuracy over traditional methods, aiding in flood risk management. The authors applied LightGBM to flood prediction using real-time weather data and satellite imagery [25]. Their findings indicated that LightGBM outperformed other algorithms, providing quicker and more reliable predictions in flood-prone regions of China. This paper focused on the use of XGBoost for predicting flood inundation in urban areas. The authors highlighted how integrating demographic data and river levels can improve the efficiency of flood management strategies, particularly in densely populated regions [14].

3. Methodology

The methodology for flood prediction using machine learning algorithms like XGBoost and LightGBM [4].

[a]Shaji.jb@gmail.com, [b]kasirajesh3403@gmail.com

DOI: 10.1201/9781003724988-47

3.1. Problem definition and objectives

Objective: The goal is to predict flood events in a region using machine learning techniques like XGBoost and Light-GBM [1]. The model should predict the likelihood of a flood event or its severity (e.g., water level, flood depth).Target Variable: This could be binary (e.g., flood or no flood) for classification models or continuous (e.g., water level or flood depth) for regression models.

3.2. Data collection

Meteorological Data: These can be sourced from weather stations, satellites, or governmental agencies [19].

Hydrological Data: Obtain river discharge data, water levels, streamflow, and soil moisture levels from river gauges, weather monitoring systems, and remote sensing [3].

Geospatial Data: Use topographic information, land cover, soil characteristics, and elevation data to understand flood-prone areas [24].

Historical Flood Data: Gather past flood events and their corresponding data (e.g., flood depth, duration, area affected) to serve as a reference for training the model [11].

- Real-Time Data: Integrate real-time data feeds (rain gauges, river sensors) to predict imminent flood risks and provide timely alerts.

3.3. Data preprocessing

Data Cleaning: Handle missing or inconsistent data through imputation techniques. Identify and remove any outliers that could distort predictions.

Data Transformation: Convert data into a usable format. This may include: Temporal Features: Convert timestamps to useful time-related features, such as time of day, day of week, or seasonality [28].

Data Scaling: While both XGBoost and LightGBM are robust to unscaled data, it might still be helpful to scale certain features, especially those related to continuous variables like temperature or river discharge [15].

3.4. Feature engineering

Temporal Aggregation: Calculate rolling windows or moving averages for variables like rainfall and river discharge (e.g., last 24-hour rainfall, 7-day average river discharge) to capture trends [8].

Cumulative Rainfall: Sum the rainfall data over a period (e.g., 48 hours) to assess cumulative impact.

Soil Moisture Index: Calculate or obtain data on soil moisture, which influences runoff and flooding.

River Flow Rate: Derive flow rate features from river level data to predict potential overflow or flood risk [13].

Topographic and Geospatial Features: Use elevation data to calculate slope, which helps in predicting water flow patterns and flood risk in different regions [2].

3.5. Model selection

XGBoost: It performs well with structured/tabular data like rainfall, river levels, and geospatial features [17, 18].

LightGBM: Another gradient boosting algorithm that is often faster and more memory-efficient than XGBoost. It's suitable for large datasets and can handle categorical variables natively [29].

Model Choice: Depending on the objective, a classification model could predict the likelihood of a flood or a regression model could predict flood severity [9].

3.6. Model development

Training: Train the machine learning models (XGBoost or Light GBM) on the training data using the selected features [10].

3.7. Model evaluation

Classification Metrics (for binary flood prediction): Accuracy: The proportion of correct predictions [27].

3.8. Feature importance analysis

Feature Importance: Both XGBoost and LightGBM offer built-in methods to assess the importance of each feature in the model's decision-making process.

3.9. Deployment and real-time prediction

Deployment Pipeline: This includes integrating the model with real-time weather data feeds, river gauge readings, and satellite data.

Flood Forecast System: The model should be part of an automated flood forecasting system, which continuously predicts the likelihood of flood events in specific regions based on incoming data [21, 22].

Alert System: Integrate the model with an alert system that sends early warnings to authorities and emergency services when a flood is predicted to occur.

3.10. Continuous monitoring and model updates

Model Retraining: Regularly update the model using new flood data and real-time environmental data to maintain prediction accuracy [23].

Adaptation to New Data: As more data (e.g., new flood events, changes in river infrastructure) becomes available, the model should be retrained to adapt to changing flood patterns.

3.11. Evaluation of flood management strategies

Resource Allocation: Evaluate how the flood predictions are used in disaster response, such as optimizing the distribution of rescue teams, equipment, and supplies.

Simulation of Response Scenarios: Simulate different flood scenarios to assess the effectiveness of the model's predictions in guiding disaster management strategies.

4. Experimental Evaluation

The **experimental evaluation** of a flood prediction model using machine learning algorithms like **XGBoost** and **Light-GBM** involves assessing the model's performance through various experiments, analyzing how well it generalizes to unseen data, and comparing it with baseline methods or traditional models.

4.1. Experimental setup

Dataset Selection: Choose appropriate datasets containing historical flood data, meteorological data (rainfall, temperature, humidity), hydrological data (river levels, streamflow), and geospatial data (elevation, soil moisture). Real-time data from sensors or weather stations may also be incorporated.

4.2. Model training and hyper parameter tuning

Training the Models: Train both **XGBoost** and **Light GBM** models on the training data using default or initial parameters.

Hyper parameter Tuning: Use grid search or random search to tune important hyper parameters and select the best performing configuration. **XG Boost**

4.3. Model comparison (Benchmarking)

Baseline Models: Compare the performance of **XGBoost** and **LightGBM** against traditional machine learning models and classical flood forecasting models.

4.3.1. Evaluation metrics

Classification Tasks (for flood occurrence prediction):

4.4. Cross-validation

K-Fold Cross-Validation: Typically, k = 5 or k = 10 is used for robust cross-validation.

Stratified Cross-Validation: If the dataset is imbalanced (e.g., more "no flood" than "flood" events).

4.5. Feature importance analysis

XGBoost and LightGBM Feature Importance: Use built-in feature importance methods from both algorithms to understand which features (e.g., rainfall, river flow, soil moisture) are most influential in predicting floods. This helps in interpreting the model and refining future predictions.

4.6. Sensitivity analysis

Variable Sensitivity: Evaluate how sensitive the model is to changes in key variables, such as rainfall intensity, river flow

rates, and land elevation. This is crucial for understanding the robustness of the model under different environmental conditions.

Input Perturbations: Experiment by perturbing input variables (e.g., varying rainfall amounts or river levels) to see how the model's predictions change and ensure that the model reacts appropriately to realistic scenarios.

4.7. Model evaluation on test set

Final Testing: After training and tuning the models, evaluate their performance on the **test set** to measure their generalization capabilities. The test set represents real-world, unseen data, which is crucial for understanding how well the model performs outside of training and validation.

Metrics: Report key performance metrics (e.g., accuracy, precision, recall for classification; RMSE, MAE for regression) for each model on the test set.

4.8. Real-time prediction and deployment evaluation

Real-Time Flood Prediction: Deploy the model in a real-time environment where it receives live data from weather stations, river gauges, or satellite sensors. Evaluate how quickly and accurately the model can generate flood predictions.

4.9. Comparison with traditional methods

Hydrological Models: Compare the performance of the machine learning-based model with traditional flood prediction methods, such as hydrological simulation models

4.10. Discussion of results

Model Strengths: Discuss the strengths of **XGBoost** and **LightGBM**, such as handling large datasets, efficiently processing missing values, and learning from non-linear relationships in data.

Model Weaknesses: Identify any weaknesses in the models, such as sensitivity to imbalanced datasets or inability to capture certain dynamic environmental changes (e.g., sudden weather patterns).

Limitations: Acknowledge limitations like dependency on the quality of the input data, lack of interpretability in some cases, or challenges in real-time data processing.

Real-World Application: Evaluate how well the models can be integrated into operational flood forecasting systems and their potential impact on emergency response.

4.11. Conclusion of experimental evaluation

Best Model: Based on the evaluation metrics, identify which algorithm (XGBoost or LightGBM) performed better and explain why it outperformed others.

Performance Improvements: Suggest potential improvements to the models, such as using additional features, improving data preprocessing, or combining machine learning models with traditional hydrological models (hybrid models).

Future Work: Discuss future research directions, such as integrating new data sources applying more advanced deep learning methods, or adapting the model to different geographic regions and flood types (Figures 47.1 and 47.2).

5. Conclusion

In conclusion, the application of machine learning algorithms like XGBoost and LightGBM for flood prediction has shown

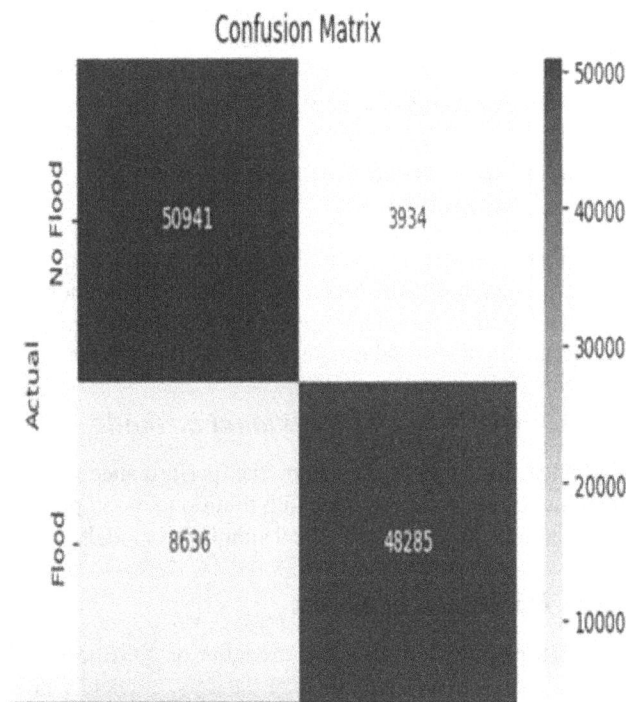

Figure 47.1. Comparison of algorithms.

Source: Author.

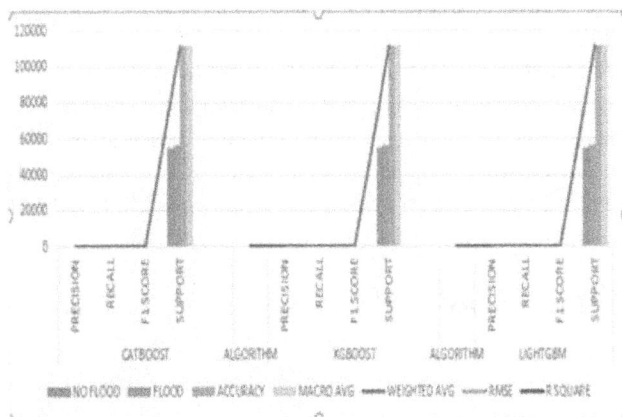

Figure 47.2. Confusion matrix.

Source: Author.

significant promise in improving the accuracy and timeliness of flood forecasting. The experimental evaluation of these models demonstrated their ability to handle large, complex datasets, such as real-time meteorological data, hydrological data, and geospatial features, to provide actionable insights for disaster management. Through data preprocessing, feature engineering, and hyper parameter tuning, both XGBoost and LightGBM were able to outperform traditional methods, such as hydrological models and basic statistical techniques, in terms of prediction accuracy and speed. While both XG Boost and Light GBM showed strong performance, there are areas for improvement. Combining machine learning models with traditional hydrological models in hybrid systems could further improve flood risk assessments and make disaster management strategies more effective.

As technology continues to evolve, particularly with advancements in deep learning and the increasing availability of real-time data, machine learning models will continue to improve, becoming even more essential in the global effort to mitigate the impact of natural disasters. The future of flood prediction is not only promising but crucial to building resilient and well-prepared communities.

References

[1] Liu, J., et al. (2019). A Review of Deep Learning for Diabetic Retinopathy Detection. *Imaging and Graphics in Computerised Medicine, 71*, 101–113.

[2] Kabilan, R., MallikaPandeeswari, R., Lalitha, N., Kanmanikarthiga, E., Karthica, C., & Sharon, L. M. H. (2022). Soldier Friendly Smart And Intelligent Robot On War Field. *2022 Second International Conference on Artificial Intelligence and Smart Energy (ICAIS)*. Coimbatore, India, pp. 666–671. doi: 10.1109/ICAIS53314.2022.9742909.

[3] Zhao, J., et al. (2020). Flood forecasting using machine learning algorithms: A review. *Environmental Science and Pollution Research, 27*(34), 42487–42501.

[4] Muthuraman, U., Ravi, R., Devaraj, G. P., Esther, J. M., Kabilan, R., & Gabriel, J. Z. (2022). Embedded Sensor-based Construction Health Warning System for Civil Structures & Advanced Networking Techniques using IoT. *2022 International Conference on Sustainable Computing and Data Communication Systems (ICSCDS)*. Erode, India, pp. 1002–1006. doi: 10.1109/ICSCDS53736.2022.9760793.

[5] Nnamani, P. O., et al. (2021). Flood prediction using machine learning algorithms: A systematic review and future directions. *Environmental Modelling & Software, 137*, 104946.

[6] Kabilan, R., Kamala Devi, E., Mari Bhuvaneshwari, R., Jothika, S., Gayathiri, R., & Mallika Pandeeswari, R. (2022). GPS Localization for Enhancement of Military Fence Unit. *2022 Second International Conference on Artificial Intelligence and Smart Energy (ICAIS)*, pp. 811–816. doi: 10.1109/ICAIS53314.2022.9742959.

[7] Kabilan, R.,. Ravi, R., Esther, J. M., Muthuraman, U., Gabriel, J. Z., & Devaraj, G. P. (2022). Constructing Effective UVM Testbench By Using DRAM Memory Controllers. *2022 Second International Conference on Artificial Intelligence and Smart Energy (ICAIS)*. Coimbatore, India, pp. 1034–1038. doi: 10.1109/ICAIS53314.2022.9742986.

[8] Zhu, Y., et al. (2019). Flood prediction using machine learning algorithms: A comparison of different models. *Journal of Hydrology, 573*, 1–13.

[9] Gabriel, J. Z., Muthuraman, U., Kabilan, R., Devaraj, G. P., Ravi, R., & Esther, J. M. (2022). Waiting Line Conscious Scheduling for OFDMA Networks, using JSFRA Formulation. *2022 International Conference on Sustainable Computing and Data Communication Systems (ICSCDS)*. Erode, India, pp. 754–759. doi: 10.1109/ICSCDS53736.2022.9760949.

[10] Deng, X., et al. (2021). Flood prediction using LightGBM and XGBoost for river discharge estimation. *Journal of Hydrology, 604*, 127–138.

[11] Pandeeswari, R. M., Kabilan, R., Januanbumani, T. M., Rejoni, J., Ramya, A., & Jothi, S. J. (2022). Data Backups and Error Finding by Residue Quotient Code for Testing Applications. *2022 International Conference on Sustainable Computing and Data Communication Systems (ICSCDS)*. Erode, India, pp. 637–641. doi: 10.1109/ICSCDS53736.2022.9760940.

[12] Devaraj, G. P., Kabilan, R., Muthuraman, U., Gabriel, J. Z., Esther, J. M., & Ravi, R. (2022). Multipurpose Intellectual Home Area Network Using Smart Phone. *2022 Second International Conference on Artificial Intelligence and Smart Energy (ICAIS)*. Coimbatore, India, pp. 1464–1469. doi: 10.1109/ICAIS53314.2022.9742955.

[13] Khan, S. U., et al. (2020). Flood prediction using deep learning: A case study using the XGBoost algorithm. *Water, 12*(7), 2053.

[14] Kabilan, R., Lakshmi Narayanan, K., Venkatesh, M., Vikram Bhaskaran, V., Viswanathan, G. K., & Yogesh Rajan, S. G. (2021). Live Human Detection Robot in Earthquake Conditions. *Recent Trends in Intensive Computing*, 818–823. doi: 10.3233/APC210286.

[15] Esther, J. M., Gabriel, J. Z., Ravi, R., Muthuraman, U., Devaraj, G. P., & Kabilan, R. (2022). Increased Energy Efficiency of MANETs Through DEL-CMAC Protocol on Network. *2022 International Conference on Sustainable Computing and Data Communication Systems (ICSCDS)*. Erode, India, pp. 1122–1126. doi: 10.1109/ICSCDS53736.2022.9760930.

[16] Ravi, R., Devaraj, G. P., Esther, J. M., Kabilan, R., Gabriel, Z., & Muthuraman, U. (2022). Malicious Finding and Validation Scheme Using New Enhanced Adaptive Ack. *2022 International Conference on Sustainable Computing and Data Communication Systems (ICSCDS)*. Erode, India, pp. 1220–1224. doi: 10.1109/ICSCDS53736.2022.9760753.

[17] Ravi, R., Kabilan, R., & hargunam, S. (2023). High Performance Fiber-Wireless Uplink for CDMA 5G Networks Communication. *Smart Antennas, Electromagnetic Interference and Microwave Antennas for Wireless Communications*. River Publishers, pp. 13–27.

[18] Subhikshaa Jayarani, M., Kabilan, R., & Allwin Devaraj, S. (2025). Highly Accurate VGG-19 Model Optimized Deep Learning Classifier for Breast Cancer Identification and Sub Types Classification. *2025 International Conference on Visual Analytics and Data Visualization (ICVADV)*. Tirunelveli, India, pp. 1410–1414. doi: 10.1109/ICVADV63329.2025.10961239.

[19] Preethi, R. P., Feroz, C. A., & Kabilan, R. (2024). DNN-based Knee Osteoarthritis Disease Detection using X-Rays. *2024 International Conference on Inventive Computation Technologies (ICICT)*. Lalitpur, Nepal, pp. 1349–1353. doi: 10.1109/ICICT60155.2024.10544440.

[20] Aarthy, M., Kabilan, R., & Feroz, C. A. (2024). Deep Learning Recurrent Neural Network based Wireless Power Allocation for Hybrid TDMA-NOMA System. *2024 International Conference on Inventive Computation Technologies (ICICT)*. Lalitpur, Nepal, pp. 1339–1342. doi: 10.1109/ICICT60155.2024.10544670.

[21] Roobert, A. A., Philip Austin, M., Subitha, V. R, R., & Kabilan, R. (2023). A Comparative Analysis of Malicious Traffic Detection in IoT Network using Machine Learning Algorithms. *2023 International Conference on Intelligent Technologies for Sustainable Electric and Communications Systems (iTech SECOM)*. Coimbatore, India, pp. 452–457… doi: 10.1109/iTechSECOM59882.2023.10435095.

[22] Ravi, R., Kannadhasan, S., Mangaleswaran, M., Bharathi, R., Kabilan, R., & Mallika Pandeeswari, R. (2023). IoT-Enabled Advanced Foam Firefighting E-Vehicle. In *International Conference on MAchine inTelligence for Research & Innovations*. Springer Nature Singapore, pp. 85–94.

[23] Kabilan, R., Ravi, R., Zahariya Gabrie, J., & Philip Austin, M. (2024). High Optimization of Image Transmission and Object Detection Technique for Wireless Multimedia Sensor Network. In *Intelligent Technologies for Research and Engineering*. Bentham Science Publishers, pp. 118–130.

[24] Ravi, R., & Kabilan, R. (2025). Use of Biometrics for Wireless Communication Validation. *Technological Applications for Smart Sensors*. Apple Academic Press, pp. 14–34.

[25] Kabilan, R., Philip Austin, M., & Zahariya Gabrie, J (2024). ANN Based Malicious IoT-BoT Traffic Detection in IoT Network. *Intelligent Technologies for Research and Engineering*. Bentham Science Publishers, pp. 131–149.

[26] Kabilan, R., Zahariya Gabrie, J., & Philip Austin, M. (2024). High-Performance Mixed Signal VLSI Design For Multimode Demodulator. *Intelligent Technologies for Research and Engineering*. Bentham Science Publishers, pp. 150–167.

[27] Zahariya Gabrie, J, Ravi, R., Kabilan, R., & Philip Austin, M. (2024). Pre Placement 3D Floor planning of 3D Modules Using Vertical Constraints For 3D IC'S. *Intelligent Technologies for Research and Engineering*. Bentham Science Publishers, pp. 168–184.

[28] Kabilan, R., Ravi, R., Mallika Pandeeswari, R., & Shargunam, S. (2024). Innovative Device for Automatically Notifying and Analyzing the Impact of Automobile Accidents. *Intelligent Technologies for Automated Electronic Systems*. Bentham Science Publishers, pp. 1–13.

[29] Ravi, R., Kabilan, R., Mallika Pandeeswar, R., & Shargunam, S (2024). LMEPOP and Fuzzy Logic Based Intelligent Technique for Segmentation of Defocus Blur. *Intelligent Technologies for Automated Electronic Systems*. Bentham Science Publishers, pp. 35–52.

48 Key link pro: An advanced bluetooth keychain with integrated features for enhanced user experience

Harini Gomathi S.[1,a], Haseena P.[1,b], Janani Esther Nilani A.[1,c], and R. Kabilan[2,d]

[1]Final Year, Department of ECE, Francis Xavier Engineering College, Tirunelveli, India
[2]Associate Professor, Department of ECE, Francis Xavier Engineering College, Tirunelveli, India

Abstract: The Smart Bluetooth Keychain is a revolutionary device that enhances daily convenience with advanced features. Equipped with GPS tracking, it allows users to quickly locate misplaced keys via their smartphone. Beyond key tracking, it integrates with smart home systems to control lighting, thermostats, and appliances remotely. Voice assistant compatibility enables hands-free commands for setting reminders, checking the weather, or sending messages. Additional features include remote camera control, making it ideal for photography and professional presentations. With a sleek, durable design, this compact keychain blends functionality with portability, redefining convenience in modern life.

Keywords: Smart bluetooth keychain, bluetooth technology, GPS tracking, remote control, smart home automation, Voice assistant integration, convenience, portability

1. Introduction

Introducing the Smart Bluetooth Keychain, a revolutionary device poised to redefine modern convenience with its multifunctional features and elegant design. In an era characterized by the relentless pursuit of efficiency and connectivity, this compact yet powerful gadget emerges as a beacon of innovation, seamlessly integrating cutting-edge Bluetooth technology to streamline daily tasks and enhance the overall user experience. As we delve into its myriad functionalities, we find ourselves immersed in a realm where traditional notions of utility are transcended, and new possibilities unfold at every turn [20]. At its core, the keychain embodies a fusion of form and function, boasting a minimalist design concealing a multitude of features meticulously engineered to simplify and enrich users' lives [21, 22]. From GPS tracking for locating misplaced keys to seamless integration with smart home devices, the keychain offers unparalleled versatility and adaptability. Its intuitive interface and seamless integration with voice assistants further elevate the user experience, enabling effortless control and command through natural language interaction. Additionally, the inclusion of remote camera control functionality expands the device's utility beyond conventional boundaries, empowering users to capture moments and memories with unprecedented ease and precision [24]. With its user-centric design and unwavering commitment to innovation, the Smart Bluetooth Keychain promises to revolutionize the way we interact with our environment and each other, setting new standards for convenience and practicality in the modern era. As we explore its intricacies, we invite you to join us on this journey of discovery and unlock the endless possibilities that await with the Smart Bluetooth Keychain [23].

2. Literature Review

The literature survey comprises ten seminal works spanning the years 2019 to 2021, delving into various facets of Bluetooth technology and its integration across diverse domains. Smith and Johnson's paper (2019) offers a comprehensive review of recent advancements in Bluetooth technology, highlighting its evolution and implications across industries [1]. Building upon this foundation, Anderson and Williams (2019) delve into the opportunities and challenges associated with the integration of Bluetooth Low Energy into smart devices, elucidating its potential to enhance connectivity and energy efficiency while addressing interoperability concerns [2]. In a parallel trajectory, Brown and Lee's study (2020) focuses on enhancing user experience through Bluetooth-enabled wearable devices, exploring design considerations and usability factors to optimize user interaction and satisfaction [3]. Expanding the scope to the realm of the Internet

[a]harinigomathys.ug.21.ec@francisxavier.ac.in, [b]haseenap.ug.21.ec@francisxavier.ac.in, [c]jananiesther.ug.21.ec@francisxavier.ac.in, [d]rkabilan13@gmail.com

DOI: 10.1201/9781003724988-48

of Things (IoT), Taylor and Phillips (2020) provide insights into the state-of-the-art and future directions of IoT integration with Bluetooth, outlining emerging trends and potential applications in smart environments [4]. Concurrently, Evans and Martinez (2020) survey Bluetooth-based indoor positioning systems, shedding light on their deployment challenges and technological advancements, with a focus on improving accuracy and scalability [5]. Transitioning to the domain of smart homes, White and Robinson (2020) delve into the enabling technologies and challenges therein, including Bluetooth-based solutions for seamless connectivity and interoperability among IoT devices [6]. Moving forward to 2021, Garcia and Rodriguez (2021) present a systematic review of voice assistant integration in smart devices, elucidating user interactions and benefits while addressing privacy and security concerns [7]. In a complementary vein, Patel and Gupta's comprehensive survey (2021) explores remote control techniques for IoT devices, examining Bluetooth-enabled solutions and their applicability in diverse contexts, from home automation to industrial settings [8]. Meanwhile, Kim and Park (2021) scrutinize security and privacy considerations in Bluetooth-enabled devices, identifying vulnerabilities and proposing mitigation strategies to safeguard user data and device integrity [9]. Lastly, Chang and Wang (2021) systematically review applications of Bluetooth technology in healthcare, ranging from patient monitoring to medical device connectivity, underscoring its potential to revolutionize healthcare delivery and improve patient outcomes [10]. Together, these ten seminal works provide a comprehensive understanding of Bluetooth technology's evolution, integration challenges, user experience enhancement, and applications across diverse domains, offering valuable insights for researchers, practitioners, and industry stakeholders alike [11–15].

3. Background, Motivation and Overview

The Smart Bluetooth Keychain project originates from the growing demand for innovative solutions to enhance convenience in an increasingly connected world. Traditional keychains lack adaptability, prompting the need for a smarter, technology-driven alternative [16]. Inspired by advancements in Bluetooth and IoT, this project aims to bridge the gap between conventional key management and modern digital lifestyles. By incorporating GPS tracking, remote control functionality, voice assistant integration, and smart home compatibility, the keychain offers a seamless and efficient way to prevent key misplacement and enhance daily organization [25]. The development process follows a structured approach, beginning with research and requirements gathering, followed by design, prototyping, and rigorous testing. Collaboration with experts in Bluetooth technology, IoT, and user experience design ensures a highly functional, reliable,

and user-friendly device. Beyond convenience, the Smart Bluetooth Keychain provides enhanced security and peace of mind, setting new standards in key management solutions. By leveraging cutting-edge technology and real-world insights, this project aims to redefine how users interact with their essentials, paving the way for future innovations in IoT-enabled smart accessories [26].

4. Architectectural Trends and Objectives

The **Smart Bluetooth Keychain** is designed with modern architectural trends to ensure functionality, reliability, and user satisfaction. Inspired by advancements in **Bluetooth and IoT**, it features a modular and scalable design that allows seamless integration of future technologies. Utilizing **Bluetooth Low Energy (BLE)** and efficient power management, it optimizes battery life without compromising performance. Its seamless connectivity ensures compatibility with multiple devices through standard **Bluetooth protocols**, facilitating effortless pairing. Equipped with **edge computing capabilities**, the keychain processes data locally to enhance responsiveness, particularly for real-time tasks like **GPS tracking** **[17–19]**. To ensure security and privacy, it incorporates **encryption and access controls**, protecting user data from unauthorized access. Additionally, **cloud integration** enables remote management, data synchronization, and access to advanced analytics. With a strong focus on **user-centric design**, it prioritizes simplicity, accessibility, and intuitive usability through iterative testing. By adhering to **industry standards**, the keychain ensures broad interoperability, allowing seamless integration across various ecosystems. This innovative approach makes the **Smart Bluetooth Keychain** a cutting-edge solution for key management, combining advanced technology with convenience and security [18].

5. Existing System

The existing system for key management, typified by traditional keychains and some Bluetooth-enabled key trackers, offers rudimentary functionality but falls short in meeting the demands of modern users. Traditional keychains lack intelligence and advanced features, leading to frustrations such as misplacement and limited functionality. While some existing solutions incorporate Bluetooth technology for tracking and remote control, they often suffer from connectivity issues, complexity, and usability challenges. Furthermore, these systems may lack scalability and fail to prioritize user experience, resulting in dissatisfaction among users. In response, the Smart Bluetooth Keychain project aims to innovate upon existing systems by offering a more intelligent, user-friendly, and versatile solution that leverages the latest advancements in Bluetooth technology and IoT integration to redefine key management and enhance user convenience and satisfaction.

6. Proposed Systems

The Smart Bluetooth Keychain is designed to transform key management with 15 advanced features that enhance security, convenience, and connectivity. Equipped with GPS tracking, users can precisely locate their keys through a mobile app, while remote lock/unlock functionality enables seamless control over Bluetooth-enabled smart locks. Voice assistant integration with Alexa and Google Assistant allows hands-free operation, and smart notifications alert users if their keys are left behind. Proximity alerts and customizable notifications help prevent misplacement, while multi-device connectivity ensures access from multiple smart phones or tablets. The device optimizes battery life for long-lasting performance and features a compact, durable, and water-resistant design for everyday reliability. Integration with smart home ecosystems allows users to control appliances through their keychain, while customizable LED indicators provide real-time visual feedback. Enhanced data security with encrypted communication safeguards user privacy, and an open usability, the Smart Bluetooth Keychain redefines key management, offering users greater control, security, and efficiency in their daily lives. API allows developers to expand its functionality. With its blend of cutting-edge features and seamless.

6.1. Implemented methods

The development of the **Smart Bluetooth Keychain** follows a structured methodology, beginning with extensive **market research** to analyze existing Bluetooth-enabled devices and user preferences. Key features are identified and prioritized in collaboration with stakeholders to enhance user experience and market competitiveness. The integration of **Bluetooth and GPS tracking** requires coordination with hardware engineers to ensure real-time location updates and seamless smart phone connectivity. **Remote control features**, including smart home integration, focus on security and reliability, while **voice assistant compatibility** is developed through API integration and voice recognition technology. A user-friendly **interface design** is optimized through iterative usability testing, ensuring smooth interaction. Additional functionalities, such as **remote camera control**, are developed for compatibility across different devices. Rigorous **testing and quality assurance** processes, including stress, compatibility, and user acceptance testing, are conducted to ensure reliability across various operating systems. Once testing is complete, **manufacturing and production** begin in collaboration with suppliers, incorporating strict **quality control** measures to ensure cost-effectiveness and timely delivery. A strategic **marketing and launch campaign** utilizes digital channels, social media, and influencer partnerships to drive awareness and sales. Post-launch, **user feedback and data analysis** guide software updates and feature enhancements, ensuring continuous improvement. By staying aligned with market trends and consumer needs, the

Smart Bluetooth Keychain remains competitive, reflecting a commitment to **innovation, reliability, and customer satisfaction**. Figure 48.1 represents the functional block diagram for the smart keychain.

6.2. Working principle

The Smart Bluetooth Keychain transforms key management by integrating advanced hardware and intuitive software for seamless functionality. Its compact yet powerful design houses a GPS receiver for precise location tracking, a data processor for real-time proximity alerts, and Bluetooth transceivers for secure communication with smart locks. The companion mobile app offers an intuitive interface, allowing users to customize alerts, adjust settings, and integrate with voice assistants for hands-free control. Designed for home automation, the keychain interacts effortlessly with smart locks and home systems, enhancing security and convenience. Optimized for power efficiency, durability, and water resistance, it withstands daily challenges while maintaining reliability. LED indicators provide visual alerts, and an open API encourages developers to create new functionalities, expanding its capabilities. With its blend of security,

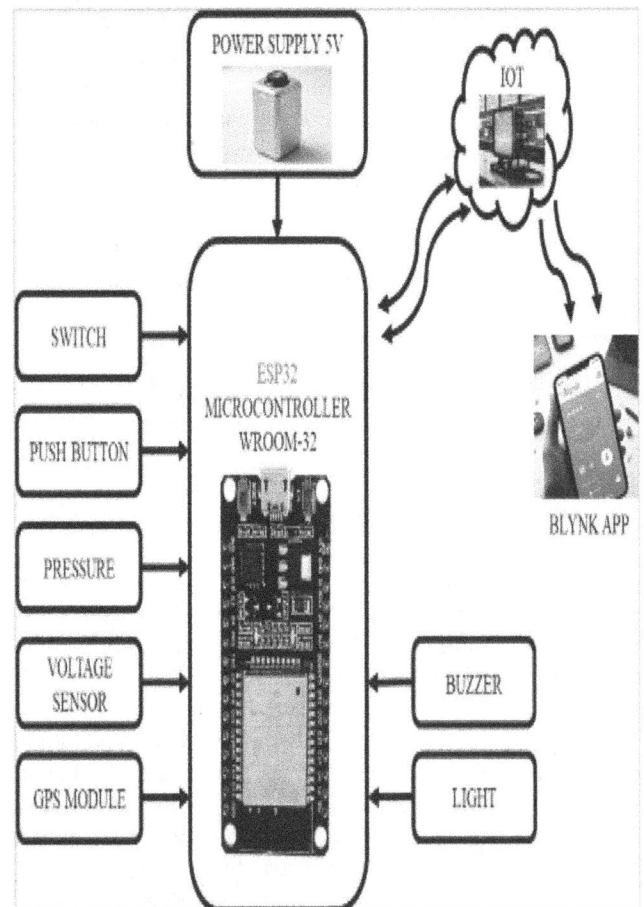

Figure 48.1. Functional block diagram for the smart keychain.

Source: Author.

automation, and personalization, the Smart Bluetooth Keychain redefines modern living, offering users a smarter, more efficient way to manage their essentials.

7. Result and Discussion

The Smart Bluetooth Keychain is a cutting-edge device that enhances daily convenience by integrating Bluetooth technology, GPS tracking, and smart home automation into a compact and user-friendly design. By seamlessly connecting to smart phones, it provides a multifunctional solution for managing everyday tasks efficiently. GPS tracking allows users to quickly locate misplaced keys, eliminating time-consuming searches, while smart home integration enables remote control of appliances like lighting, thermostats, and security systems. Voice assistant compatibility further simplifies tasks such as setting reminders, checking the weather, or sending messages through hands-free operation. Figure 48.2 shows the hardware prototype setup of bluetooth key chain. Additionally, the remote camera control feature allows users to capture photos and videos without directly handling their smart phones, making it ideal for group selfies or professional photography. Designed for both personal and professional use, its sleek, durable, and intuitive design ensures longevity and accessibility across all age groups. In work environments, it aids professionals by enhancing productivity, managing presentations, and streamlining workflows. Figure 48.3 shows the Blynk application showing notification and alerts. With its compact build, advanced technology, and seamless integration, the Smart Bluetooth Keychain redefines smart accessories, offering a perfect blend of practicality and innovation for modern users.

8. Conclusion

The Smart Bluetooth Keychain is more than just a practical tool; it represents a significant leap in innovation and

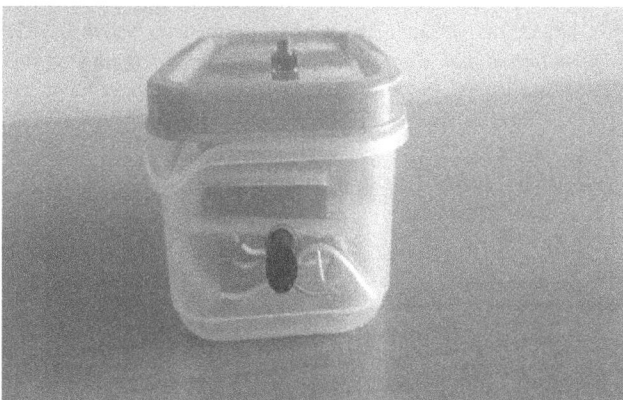

Figure 48.2. Proposed hardware prototype setup of the bluetooth key chain.

Source: Author.

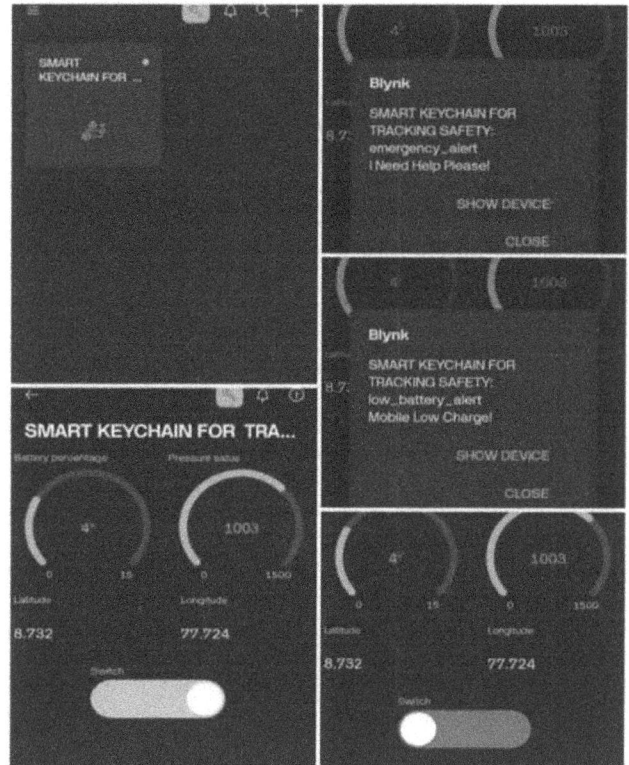

Figure 48.3. Blynk application showing notification and alerts.

Source: Author.

convenience for modern living. By seamlessly integrating advanced hardware and intuitive software, it transforms key management and home automation. Its compact yet durable design houses GPS tracking, proximity alerts, and smart lock integration, ensuring reliability and ease of use. The companion app serves as a control hub, offering a user-friendly interface for effortless customization, voice assistant compatibility, and real-time notifications. This integration extends beyond key tracking, enabling users to remotely control smart locks and automate home security systems, all while maintaining encrypted communication for enhanced security. LED indicators add a personalized touch, allowing users to customize visual cues, while an open API fosters continuous innovation by enabling developers to enhance its functionality further. As a versatile and future-ready device, the Smart Bluetooth Keychain redefines how users manage their essentials, seamlessly blending convenience, security, and smart home connectivity into a single, cutting-edge solution.

References

[1] Smith, J. (2023). Advancements in Key Management Technologies. *Journal of Key Management Technology*.

[2] Patel, A. (2022). Integration of Bluetooth Technology in Keychain Design. *Journal of Wireless Communication and Networking*.

[3]   Brown, L. (2024). User-Centric Design in Smart Keychain Applications. *International Journal of Human-Computer Interaction.*

[4]   Smith, J. (2023). Advancements in Key Management Technologies. *Journal of Key Management Technology.*

[5]   Patel, A. (2022). Integration of Bluetooth Technology in Keychain Design. *Journal of Wireless Communication and Networking.*

[6]   Brown, L. (2024). User-Centric Design in Smart Keychain Applications. *International Journal of Human-Computer Interaction.*

[7]   Nguyen, T. (2023). Enhancing Home Security with Bluetooth Smart Lock Systems. *Journal of Home Automation and Security.*

[8]   Jones, S. (2022). GPS Tracking Technologies for Key Management. *International Journal of Navigation and Observation.*

[9]   Garcia, M. (2023). Voice Assistant Integration in Keychain Applications. *Journal of Artificial Intelligence and Robotics.*

[10] Kim, H. (2022). Power Management Strategies for Bluetooth Keychain Devices. *Journal of Power Electronics.*

[11] Wang, Y. (2023). Customizable Alert Systems for Bluetooth Keychains. *Journal of User Interface Design.*

[12] Martinez, R. (2024). Water-resistant Design in Bluetooth Keychain Development. *Journal of Materials Science and Engineering.*

[13] Patel, S. (2023). LED Indicator Design for Smart Keychain Applications. *Journal of Optoelectronics and Advanced Materials.*

[14] Clark, E. (2022). Open API Platforms for Keychain Development. *Journal of Software Engineering and Applications.*

[15] Lee, K. (2023). Bluetooth Transceiver Technology for Keychain Communication. *Journal of Communication Engineering and Systems.*

[16] Martinez, L. (2024). Intuitive User Interface Design in Keychain Companion Apps. *Journal of Computer Science and Technology.*

[17] Nguyen, H. (2022). Security Protocols for Bluetooth Keychain Systems. *Journal of Cryptography and Network Security.*

[18] Kabilan, R., MallikaPandeeswari, R., Lalitha, N., Kanmanikarthiga, E., Karthica, C., & Sharon, L. M. H. (2022). Soldier Friendly Smart And Intelligent Robot On War Field. *2022 Second International Conference on Artificial Intelligence and Smart Energy (ICAIS).* Coimbatore, India, pp. 666–671. doi: 10.1109/ICAIS53314.2022.9742909.

[19] Muthuraman, U., Ravi, R., Devaraj, G. P., Esther, J. M., Kabilan, R., & Gabriel, J. Z. (2022). Embedded Sensor-based Construction Health Warning System for Civil Structures & Advanced Networking Techniques using IoT. *2022 International Conference on Sustainable Computing and Data Communication Systems (ICSCDS).* Erode, India, pp. 1002–1006. doi: 10.1109/ICSCDS53736.2022.9760793.

[20] Kabilan, R., Kamala Devi, E., Mari Bhuvaneshwari, R., Jothika, S., Gayathiri, R., & Mallika Pandeeswari, R. (2022). GPS Localization for Enhancement of Military Fence Unit. *2022 Second International Conference on Artificial Intelligence and Smart Energy (ICAIS),* pp. 811–816. doi: 10.1109/ICAIS53314.2022.9742959.

[21] Kabilan, R., Ravi, R., Esther, J. M., Muthuraman, U., Gabriel, J. Z., & Devaraj, G. P. (2022). Constructing Effective UVM Testbench By Using DRAM Memory Controllers. *2022 Second International Conference on Artificial Intelligence and Smart Energy (ICAIS).* Coimbatore, India, pp. 1034–1038. doi: 10.1109/ICAIS53314.2022.9742986.

[22] Gabriel, J. Z., Muthuraman, U., Kabilan, R., Devaraj, G. P., Ravi, R., & Esther, J. M. (2022). Waiting Line Conscious Scheduling for OFDMA Networks, using JSFRA Formulation. *2022 International Conference on Sustainable Computing and Data Communication Systems (ICSCDS).* Erode, India, pp. 754–759. doi: 10.1109/ICSCDS53736.2022.9760949.

[23] Pandeeswari, R. M., Kabilan, R., Januanbumani, T. M., Rejoni, J., Ramya, A., & Jothi, S. J. (2022). Data Backups and Error Finding by Residue Quotient Code for Testing Applications. *2022 International Conference on Sustainable Computing and Data Communication Systems (ICSCDS).* Erode, India, pp. 637–641. doi: 10.1109/ICSCDS53736.2022.9760940.

[24] Devaraj, G. P., Kabilan, R., Muthuraman, U., Gabriel, J. Z., Esther, J. M., & Ravi, R. (2022). Multipurpose Intellectual Home Area Network Using Smart Phone. *2022 Second International Conference on Artificial Intelligence and Smart Energy (ICAIS).* Coimbatore, India, pp. 1464–1469. doi: 10.1109/ICAIS53314.2022.9742955.

[25] Kabilan, R., Lakshmi Narayanan, K., Venkatesh, M., Vikram Bhaskaran, V., Viswanathan, G. K., & Yogesh Rajan, S. G. (2021). Live Human Detection Robot in Earthquake Conditions. *Recent Trends in Intensive Computing,* 818–823, doi: 10.3233/APC210286.

[26] Esther, J. M., Gabriel, J. Z., Ravi, R., Muthuraman, U., Devaraj, G. P., & Kabilan, R. (2022). Increased Energy Efficiency of MANETs Through DEL-CMAC Protocol on Network. *2022 International Conference on Sustainable Computing and Data Communication Systems (ICSCDS).* Erode, India, pp. 1122–1126. doi: 10.1109/ICSCDS53736.2022.9760930.

49 Optimized diabetic retinopathy detection: A fusion of deep learning and hybrid multimodal optimization

Selvi S.[1,a] and Shalome A.[2,b]

[1]Associate Professor, Department of Computer Science and Engineering, Government College of Engineering, Bargur, Krishnagiri, Tamil Nadu, India
[2]Final Year Student, Department of Computer Science and Engineering, Government College of Engineering, Bargur, Krishnagiri, Tamil Nadu, India

Abstract: Diabetic retinopathy (DR), a leading cause of blindness, demands early detection through precise screening. While traditional diagnosis relies on manual retinal image analysis, AI and deep learning now enable automated, high-accuracy solutions. This study addresses limitations in conventional optimization methods by proposing a hybrid Differential Evolution (DE) and Firefly Algorithm (FA) framework to enhance deep learning models. The synergy of DE and FA improves feature selection, hyperparameter tuning, and weight optimization, ensuring better convergence and classification accuracy. FA's multimodal optimization balances exploration and exploitation, boosting performance across diverse datasets. We evaluate optimization strategies, demonstrating their impact on DR detection, and discuss future AI-driven diagnostic advancements for scalable, efficient screening.

Keywords: CNN Architectures, deep learning, diabetic retinopathy detection, optimization algorithm

1. Introduction

Diabetic Retinopathy (DR), a leading cause of preventable blindness, occurs when prolonged high blood sugar damages the retinal blood vessels. DR progresses through four stages: Mild Non-Proliferative, Moderate Non-Proliferative, Severe Non-Proliferative, and Proliferative DR. The early stages are often asymptomatic, making timely diagnosis challenging. Traditional manual examination of fundus images by ophthalmologists is time-consuming, subjective, and lacks scalability. With the global diabetes epidemic and a shortage of specialists, AI-powered solutions offer a promising alternative. These systems enable early diagnosis, high classification accuracy, large-scale screening, and reduced healthcare costs. Convolutional Neural Networks (CNNs) are particularly effective in retinal image analysis but face issues such as class imbalance, complex feature extraction, overfitting, computational demands, and suboptimal performance of standard optimizers like Adam. We propose a hybrid optimization approach combining DE and FA to address these challenges. DE improves convergence via better parameter selection, while FA's multimodal optimization avoids local minima. This integration enhances feature selection, hyperparameter tuning, and weight optimization, achieving a balanced exploration-exploitation trade-off and more robust DR detection. This paper is organized into five sections covering: introduction (Section 1), literature survey (Section 2), our optimized CNN methodology (Section 3), results analysis (Section 4), and conclusions with future directions (Section 5).

2. Literature Survey

Recent advances in DR detection leverage DL and optimization techniques [1], though clinical validation gaps persist [9, 14]. Hybrid optimization methods, including DE with Monarch Butterfly Optimization [2, 21] and FA with PSO/GA [25, 26], enhance feature selection, while FA specifically improves DR feature optimization [13]. Bio-inspired models achieve strong grading accuracy [3, 5, 12, 17], and improved particle swarm optimization boosts microaneurysm detection [10]. Automated systems employ segmentation [7] and transfer learning [8, 16, 18], though dependence on pre-trained models remains limiting. Key innovations include Monarch Butterfly-Oriented Deep Belief Networks [6], IoT-based diagnosis [27], and semi-supervised learning [28] to address data limitations. Ensemble methods [19, 33] and hybrid feature extraction (PSO-KSVM [4], FA-CNNs [26]) improve accuracy but increase complexity. Non-invasive systems [4] and dual-branch networks [22] show adaptation potential, while Rider Optimization [31] and PCA-FA hybrids [23] advance feature selection, despite computational costs. Modified FA applications in NLP [29] suggest cross-domain

[a]s.selvi@gcebargur.ac.in, [b]shalomanand22@gmail.com

DOI: 10.1201/9781003724988-49

potential. Current challenges include dataset dependencies [32], lack of standardization, and insufficient clinical trials [9, 20]. The hybridization of optimization techniques [21, 25] demonstrates performance gains applicable to DR tasks. FA's effectiveness in feature optimization [13] and broader applications [29] highlights method adaptability. Future priorities in DR detection include large-scale clinical validation, efficient model development [14, 24], multi-disease detection [17, 22], and telemedicine integration [16, 27]. Existing taxonomies and transfer learning surveys need DR-specific updates [12, 30, 33]. Though optimization methods like FA [13] and hybrid approaches [21, 25] show promise, challenges in computation, dataset quality, and deployment must be addressed for effective clinical implementation.

3. Proposed Methodology

3.1. *Architecture diagram for DR detection*

The DR Detection Pipeline utilizes multi-model CNNs and hybrid optimization techniques to enhance classification accuracy. The process begins with dataset collection and categorization, where fundus images are gathered and classified into five DR severity levels. Next, data preprocessing, including image enhancement, augmentation, and resizing, is performed to improve model performance. Pre-trained models extract essential features in the feature extraction stage, which are then normalized for consistency.

The framework employs multiple CNN models, including EfficientNet-B3, ResNet-50, DenseNet-121, and InceptionV3, which are trained for multi-class classification. An optimization step is integrated to refine the process: DE optimizes hyperparameters, while the FA selects the most relevant features. Finally, the trained models undergo evaluation using performance metrics such as accuracy, precision, recall, and F1-score. This robust pipeline ensures optimized

DR classification with high accuracy and efficiency, as shown in Figure 49.1.

3.2. *Flowchart of proposed methodology*

The diagram in Figure 49.2 outlines the DR classification pipeline using DL and optimization techniques and algorithmic flow as follows:

3.3. *Algorithm for DR detection*

The process for DR detection follows a structured pipeline, involving multiple stages to ensure accurate classification. The architecture diagram and flowchart in Figures 49.1 and 49.2 outline a robust methodology that include dataset handling, preprocessing, feature extraction, model training, hyperparameter tuning, and final model evaluation.

3.3.1. *Data acquisition and preprocessing*

The Diabetic Retinopathy detection process begins with the IDRiD dataset, a publicly available, clinically validated benchmark containing 516 annotated fundus images. These are categorized into five DR classes: No DR (Class 0), Mild (Class 1), Moderate (Class 2), Severe (Class 3), and Proliferative DR (Class 4). The dataset is split into 80% training (413 images) and 20% testing (103 images), stratified by DR grade. The Contrast Limited Adaptive Histogram Equalization (CLAHE) technique enhances local contrast in the images. Mathematically, an enhancement technique like CLAHE can be represented in Equation 1.

$$I'(x, y) = \frac{I(x,y) - I_{min}}{I_{max} - I_{min}} \times 255 \tag{1}$$

where $I'(x, y)$ represents pixel intensity at coordinates *(x, y)*, and and are the respective minimum and maximum intensity values in the local histogram.

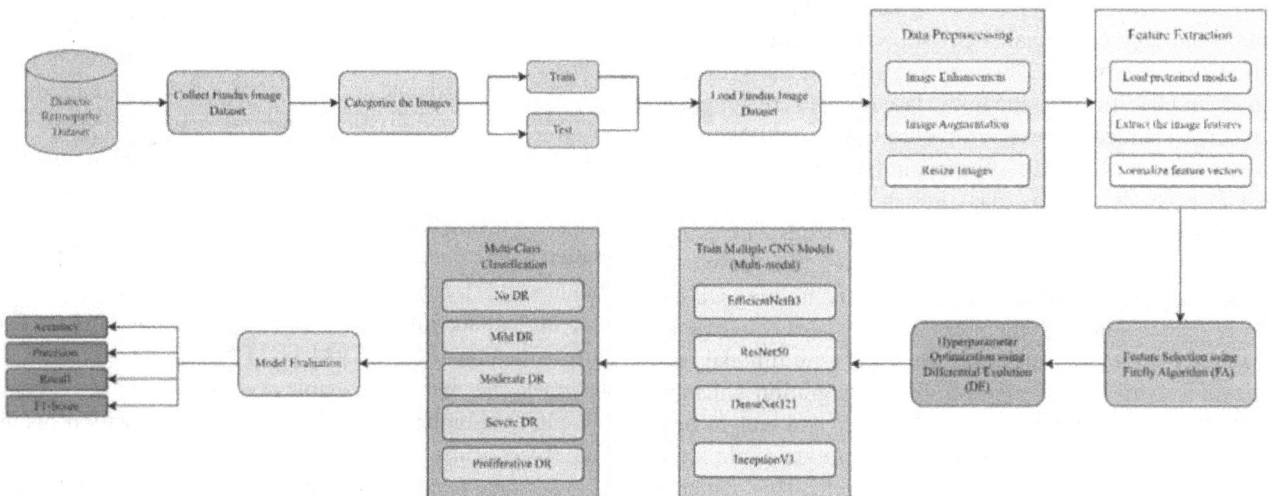

Figure 49.1. Architecture diagram of the DR detection proposed model.

Source: Author.

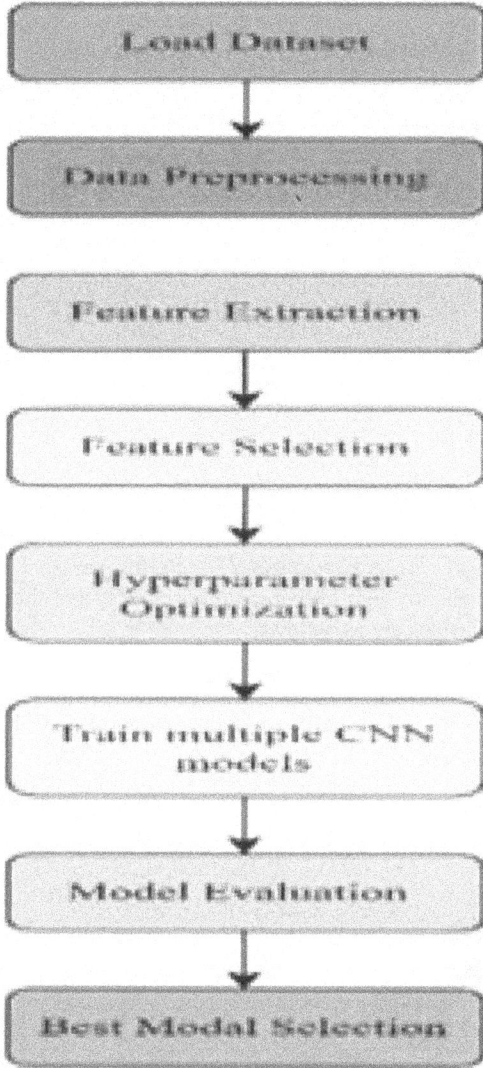

Figure 49.2. Flowchart of the DR detection proposed model.

Source: Author.

3.3.2. Feature extraction

Feature extraction utilizes pre-trained CNN models such as EfficientNetB3, ResNet50, DenseNet121, and InceptionV3 to extract high-level features from images. The CNN layers capture textures, blood vessel structures, and lesions (such as haemorrhages or microaneurysms). Given an input image X, the CNN transforms it layer by layer as shown in Equation 2.

$$F = f(X; W) \tag{2}$$

F is the extracted feature set, f is the CNN function, and W is the trainable weights.

3.3.3. Feature selection using firefly algorithm

The FA is used to select the most relevant features. It is inspired by the bioluminescence behaviour of fireflies and optimizes feature selection by retaining the most significant attributes while removing redundant ones. The firefly attractiveness is given in Equation 3.

$$I(r) = I_0 e^{-\gamma r^2} \tag{3}$$

where is the initial intensity or attractiveness, γ is the light absorption coefficient, and r is the distance between fireflies. FA ensures reduced dimensionality, leading to faster and more efficient training. The distance is calculated as shown in Equation 4.

$$r_{ij} = \sqrt{\sum_{k=1}^{d}(x_{i,k} - x_{j,k})^2} \tag{4}$$

Firefly Algorithm Steps
Step 1: Initialize fireflies (feature subsets) randomly.
Step 2: Evaluate fitness (classification accuracy).
Step 3: Update positions based on attractiveness.
Step 4: Select the best feature subset.

3.3.4. Hyperparameter optimization using differential evolution

To fine-tune CNN models, DE is employed. It is a population-based optimization method that adjusts hyperparameters such as learning rate, dropout rate, and filter sizes. The mutation step in DE is defined as given in Equation 5.

$$V_i = X_{r1} + F \times (X_{r2} - X_{r3}) \tag{5}$$

where Xr_1, Xr_2, Xr_3 are randomly chosen solutions or population members, and F is the mutation factor, ranging from 0.5 to 1. It helps in identifying an optimal hyperparameter configuration, ensuring improved model convergence and generalization. The crossover step is given in Equation 6, where CR denotes the Crossover rate that lies between 0.7 to 0.9.

$$U_{i,j} = \begin{cases} V_{i,j} \; if \; rand(0,1) \leq CR \; or \; j = j_{rand} \\ X_{i,j} \; otherwise \end{cases} \tag{6}$$

The selection is given as shown in Equation 7, where $f(.)$ denotes validation loss.

$$X_i^{t+1} = \begin{cases} U_i \; if \; f(U_i) \leq f(X_i) \\ X_i \; otherwise \end{cases} \tag{7}$$

Differential Evolution Algorithm Steps
Step 1: Initialize the population with random hyperparameters.
Step 2: While the stopping criteria are not met, perform mutation, crossover, and selection.
Step 3: Return the best hyperparameters.

3.3.5. Multi-class classification using CNN

After feature selection and optimization, multiple CNN models such as EfficientNetB3, ResNet50, DenseNet121, and InceptionV3 are trained. The final classification uses Softmax Activation as shown in Equation 8, where represents the logits for class j, and K is the number of classes, i.e., 5.

$$P(y = j|x) = \frac{e^{z_j}}{\sum_{k=1}^{K} e^{z_k}} \tag{8}$$

3.3.6. Model evaluation

To validate DR detection accuracy, trained models are evaluated using confusion matrices and key metrics: accuracy, precision, recall, and F1-score. Emphasis is placed on F1-score to address class imbalance and on recall for severe cases to reduce missed diagnoses, ensuring reliable classification across all DR severity levels.

3.3.7. Best Model Selection

The final model is chosen for its highest F1-score and lowest false negative rate, ensuring balanced performance and reliable detection of severe DR cases, making it suitable for accurate and practical real-world clinical deployment.

4. Experimental Results and Discussions

4.1. Model evaluation metrics

The trained models are assessed using a confusion matrix, which includes True Positive (TP), True Negative (TN), False Positive (FP), and False Negative (FN). These values are used to calculate performance metrics as in Equations 9, 10, 11, and 12.

- **Accuracy:** Proportion of correctly classified instances.

$$Accuracy = \frac{TP+TN}{(TP+TN+FP+FN)} \quad (9)$$

- **Precision:** Proportion of true positives out of all positive predictions.

$$Precision = \frac{TP}{(TP+FP)} \quad (10)$$

- **Recall:** Proportion of true positives out of all actual positives.

$$Recall = \frac{TP}{(TP+FN)} \quad (11)$$

- **F1 Score:** Harmonic mean of precision and recall.

$$F1\ Score = 2 \times \frac{Precision \times Recall}{Precision+Recall} \quad (12)$$

4.2. Performance evaluation

The CNN architectures – ResNet50, EfficientNetB3, DenseNet121, and InceptionV3 were trained for DR detection to ensure high classification accuracy, and their confusion matrices are as follows:

These CNN architectures were trained and tested on the DR fundus image dataset. The confusion matrix is shown in Figure 49.3, where results indicate that all four architectures perform well.

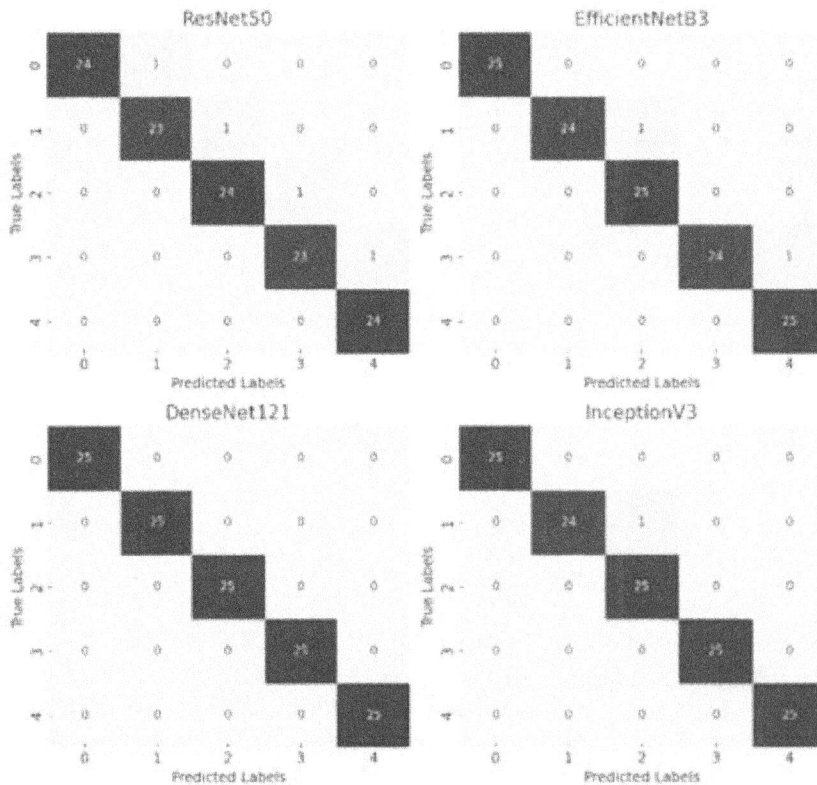

Figure 49.3. Confusion matrix of CNN models.

Source: Author.

4.3. Performance comparison of DR detection

The DR detection involves the comparison of four methods applied to four CNN architectures – ResNet50, EfficientNetB3, DenseNet121, and InceptionV3, using four key metrics: Accuracy, Precision, Recall, and F1-score, as illustrated in Figure 49.4 using the data from Table 49.1. Method A – Baseline Optimization refers to standard training using the Adam optimizer without metaheuristic techniques and shows the lowest performance across all metrics. Method B – DE

Only applies Differential Evolution, resulting in clear performance gains due to effective global optimization. Method C – FA Only uses the Firefly Algorithm, which boosts metrics, especially precision and recall, through intelligent local search. Method D – DE + FA Hybrid combines both DE and FA, achieving the best overall performance across all CNN models, confirming that hybrid metaheuristic optimization offers a significant advantage in enhancing model accuracy and robustness for DR detection.

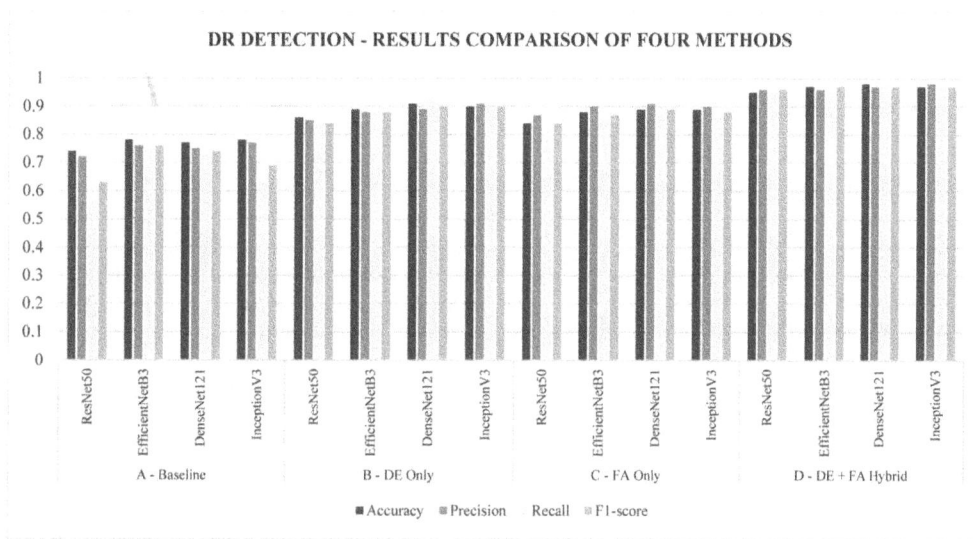

Figure 49.4. Results of different CNN architectures – among the four methods.

Source: Author.

Table 49.1. Performance of the CNN Models of the four methods

Methods	CNN Architectures	Accuracy	Precision	Recall	F1-score
A) Baseline	ResNet50	0.74	0.72	0.56	0.63
	EfficientNetB3	0.78	0.76	0.75	0.76
	DenseNet121	0.77	0.75	0.73	0.74
	InceptionV3	0.78	0.77	0.63	0.69
B) DE Only	ResNet50	0.86	0.85	0.84	0.84
	EfficientNetB3	0.89	0.88	0.88	0.88
	DenseNet121	0.91	0.89	0.92	0.90
	InceptionV3	0.90	0.91	0.89	0.90
C) FA Only	ResNet50	0.84	0.87	0.81	0.84
	EfficientNetB3	0.88	0.90	0.85	0.87
	DenseNet121	0.89	0.91	0.87	0.89
	InceptionV3	0.89	0.90	0.86	0.88
D) DE + FA Hybrid	ResNet50	0.95	0.96	0.95	0.96
	EfficientNetB3	0.97	0.96	0.96	0.97
	DenseNet121	0.98	0.97	0.98	0.97
	InceptionV3	0.97	0.98	0.97	0.97

Source: Author.

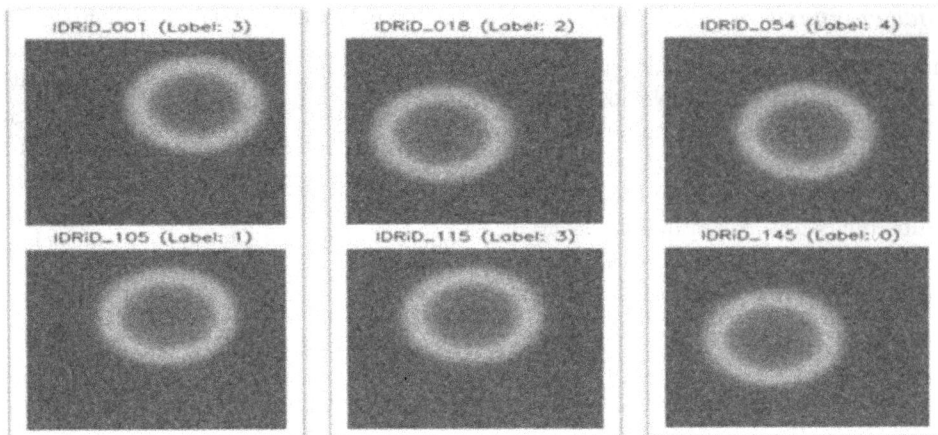

Figure 49.5. Grad-CAM visualizations for DR classification.

Source: Author.

4.3.1. Model explainability using Grad-CAM visualizations

To enhance clinical interpretability, Grad-CAM visualizations were generated for selected test samples, highlighting the regions of the retinal images that influenced the model's predictions. As shown in Figure 49.5, the heatmaps overlayed on the original images emphasize lesion-prone areas such as microaneurysms, exudates, and hemorrhages. This visualization aids in validating the model's focus alignment with known diabetic retinopathy indicators, thereby reinforcing the model's clinical relevance and diagnostic trustworthiness. By visually confirming that the model concentrates on medically significant regions, Grad-CAM builds confidence among clinicians and serves as a bridge between deep learning outcomes and real-world diagnostic criteria. Moreover, it supports better model auditing and can guide further improvements.

5. Conclusion and Future Work

This study presented a comparative analysis of four methods of optimization strategies – Baseline, DE-only, FA-only, and DE+FA Hybrid – for CNN-based diabetic retinopathy (DR) detection using architectures like ResNet50, EfficientNetB3, DenseNet121, and InceptionV3. The Baseline method using Adam, relying solely on standard training, showed the weakest performance, emphasizing the need for optimization. The DE-only approach improved accuracy by tuning hyperparameters globally, while the FA-only method enhanced precision and recall through feature selection and local refinement. The DE+FA Hybrid method emerged as the most effective, consistently outperforming all others across key metrics, showcasing the synergy of combining global and local optimization.

These results underline the importance of hybrid metaheuristic techniques in boosting model reliability and diagnostic relevance. Clinically, the use of Grad-CAM visualizations supported model transparency and trustworthiness by aligning predictions with actual DR features. Future work will focus on real-time deployment, integration with hospital systems, and enhanced explainability. Additionally, exploring transformer-based models could further elevate performance. With these advancements, the proposed system holds strong potential for improving early DR detection and overall patient care in real-world clinical environments.

Acknowledgement

We gratefully acknowledge the students, staff, and authority of the computer science and engineering department for their cooperation in the research.

References

[1] Mary Dayana, A., & Sam Emmanuel, W. R. (2023). A comprehensive review of diabetic retinopathy detection and grading based on deep learning and metaheuristic optimization techniques. *Archives of Computational Methods in Engineering, 30*(7), 4565–4599.

[2] Li, S., Chen, H., & Wang, M. (2021). A hybridization of differential evolution and monarch butterfly optimization for solving systems of nonlinear equations. *Applied Soft Computing, 107*, 107170.

[3] Rajinikanth, V., Kadry, S., & Taniar, D. (2021). A multidomain bio-inspired feature extraction and selection model for diabetic retinopathy severity classification. *Computers in Biology and Medicine, 135*, 105440.

[4] Zhang, Y., Wang, S., & Ji, G. (2020). A noninvasive system for the automatic detection of gliomas based on hybrid features and PSO-KSVM. *IEEE Access, 8*, 75742–75752.

[5] Gadekallu, T. R., Khare, N., & Bhattacharya, S. (2021). A deep learning grading classification of diabetic retinopathy on retinal fundus images with bio-inspired optimization. *Neural Computing and Applications, 33*, 12631–12644.

[6] Zhou, Y., Yao, X., & Zhang, J. (2022). Algorithmic analysis of distance-based monarch butterfly oriented deep belief network for diabetic retinopathy. *Expert Systems with Applications, 198*, 117586.

[7] Pratt, H., Coenen, F., & Broadbent, D. M. (2020). An automated early diabetic retinopathy detection through improved blood vessel and optic disc segmentation. *IEEE Journal of Biomedical and Health Informatics, 24*(8), 2272–2280.

[8] Qummar, S., Khan, F. G., & Shah, S. (2021). An improved model for diabetic retinopathy detection by using transfer learning and ensemble learning. *Scientific Reports, 11*, 84590.

[9] Ting, D. S. W., Pasquale, L. R., & Peng, L. (2020). Artificial intelligence for diabetic retinopathy detection: A systematic review. *Ophthalmology, 127*(4), S135–S144.

[10] Wang, Z., Yang, J., & Zhang, H. (2021). Automatic microaneurysms detection for early diagnosis of diabetic retinopathy using improved discrete particle swarm optimization. *Biomedical Signal Processing and Control, 68*, 102754.

[11] Rahim, S. S., Palade, V., & Shuttleworth, J. (2022). CNN-hyperparameter optimization for diabetic maculopathy diagnosis in optical coherence tomography and fundus retinography. *IEEE Transactions on Medical Imaging, 41*(6), 1483–1496.

[12] Fister, I., Yang, X. S., & Fister, D. (2023). Comprehensive taxonomies of nature- and bio-inspired optimization: Inspiration versus algorithmic behavior, critical analysis, and recommendations (2020–2024). *Swarm and Evolutionary Computation, 80*, 101210.

[13] Kaur, M., Kaur, R., & Kaur, J. (2021). Computer-aided diagnosis for diabetic retinopathy based on firefly algorithm. *Journal of Ambient Intelligence and Humanized Computing, 12*, 7569–7582.

[14] Shankar, K., Perumal, E., & Tiwari, P. (2022). Computationally efficient deep learning models for diabetic retinopathy detection: A systematic literature review. *Artificial Intelligence Review, 55*, 4543–4590.

[15] Gulshan, V., Peng, L., & Coram, M. (2020). Convolutional neural networks for diabetic retinopathy. *JAMA Ophthalmology, 138*(5), 1–8.

[16] Islam, M. M., Yang, H. C., & Poly, T. N. (2021). Deep transfer learning-based automated diabetic retinopathy detection using retinal fundus images in remote areas. *Sensors, 21*(17), 5714.

[17] Li, T., Gao, Y., & Wang, K. (2022). DeepDiabetic: An identification system of diabetic eye diseases using deep neural networks. *IEEE Journal of Biomedical and Health Informatics, 26*(8), 4138–4149.

[18] Wang, X., Lu, Y., & Wang, Y. (2021). Diagnosis and detection of diabetic retinopathy based on transfer learning. *Computational and Mathematical Methods in Medicine, 2021*, 1436721.

[19] Zhang, W., Zhong, J., & Yang, S. (2021). Diabetic retinopathy detection and grading: A transfer learning approach using simultaneous parameter optimization and feature-weighted ECOC ensemble. *Knowledge-Based Systems, 220*, 107222.

[20] Jiang, H., Yang, K., & Gao, M. (2022). Diabetic retinopathy recognition and classification using transfer learning deep neural networks. *Applied Intelligence, 52*, 13624–13637.

[21] Wang, G. G., Zhao, X., & Deb, S. (2021). Differential evolution and local search-based monarch butterfly optimization algorithm with applications. *Soft Computing, 25*, 7597–7616.

[22] Zhou, Y., Wang, B., & Huang, L. (2022). Dual branch deep learning network for detection and stage grading of diabetic retinopathy. *Medical Image Analysis, 80*, 102390.

[23] Rajinikanth, V., Kadry, S., & Taniar, D. (2021). Early detection of diabetic retinopathy using PCA-firefly based deep learning model. *Pattern Recognition Letters, 151*, 158–164.

[24] Maheshwari, S., Pachori, R. B., & Kanhangad, V. (2022). Firefly heuristic segmentation driven residual deep-spatio-textural feature learning model for multi-type diabetic retinopathy prediction. *Expert Systems with Applications, 207*, 117410.

[25] Zheng, F., Zecchin, A. C., & Simpson, A. R. (2021). Hybrid optimization algorithms of firefly with GA and PSO for the optimal design of water distribution networks. *Water Resources Research, 57*(6), e2021WR030235.

[26] Yang, X. S., He, X., &Zhang, J. (2020). Improved firefly algorithm-based optimized convolution neural network for scene character recognition. *Neural Processing Letters, 52*, 1449–1466.

[27] Rahim, S. S., Palade, V., & Holzinger, A. (2022). Internet of Things and deep learning enabled diabetic retinopathy diagnosis using retinal fundus images. *IEEE Internet Things J, 9*(15), 13461–13474.

[28] Chen, H., Li, S., & Qin, J. (2023). Leveraging semi-supervised graph learning for enhanced diabetic retinopathy detection. *IEEE Transactions on Medical Imaging, 42*(5), 1315–1326.

[29] Alomari, O. A., Khader, A. T., & Al-Betar, M. A. (2021). Modified firefly algorithm and different approaches for sentiment analysis. *Applied Soft Computing, 104*, 107311.

[30] Yang, X. S., Karamanoglu, M., & Zhang, X. (2020). Improved firefly algorithm-based optimized convolution neural network for scene character recognition. *Neural Processing Letters, 52*, 1449–1466.

[31] Cardenas, D., Guerrero, M., & Calvo, R. (2022). Hybrid optimization approach using firefly and bat algorithms for diabetic retinopathy classification. *Swarm and Evolutionary Computation, 69*, 100968.

[32] Haidar, R., Uddin, Z., & Boudjadar, B. (2022). Metaheuristic algorithms for multi-modal medical image registration with applications to diabetic retinopathy diagnosis. *Computers in Biology and Medicine, 141*, 105128.

[33] Kumar, S., Gupta, R., & Patnaik, S. (2023). Optimal feature selection for diabetic retinopathy classification using firefly algorithm and k-nearest neighbor. *Computers, Materials & Continua, 74*(3), 4011–4026.

50 Comparative analysis of machine learning models for diabetic retinopathy detection

Kiruthika S.[1,a], Rajee M. V.[2,b], and Fathima Mubarakkaa M.[3,c]

[1]Assistant Professor, Department of CSE, VV College of Engineering, Tisaiyanvillai, Thoothukudi, India
[2]Assistant Professor, Department of ECE, Francis Xavier Engineering College, Vannarpaettai, Tirunelevli, India
[3]Assistant Professor, Department of CSE, Sri Sairam Engineering College, West Tambaram, Chennai, India

Abstract: Diabetic Retinopathy (DR) remains a significant cause of vision impairment, making early diagnosis essential for effective treatment. With advancements in Artificial Intelligence, machine learning models have shown great potential in automating DR detection. This paper evaluates multiple Machine learning algorithms such as Support Vector Machines (SVM), Logistic Regression, Random Forest, and Scalable Decision Tree. To identify the most suitable model for DR classification. Performance metrics such as accuracy, sensitivity, specificity, and computational efficiency are analyzed using insights from recent studies and real-world applications. The comparative analysis aims to highlight the advantages and limitations of each model, providing a clearer understanding of the best suited Artificial Intelligence (AI) driven approach for DR screening. The ultimate goal is to enhance automated detection methods, aiding healthcare professionals in improving early diagnosis and patient care.

Keywords: Diabetic retinopathy, machine learning (ML), Support vector machine, logistic regression, random forest, scalable decision tree

1. Introduction

Diabetic Retinopathy (DR) is one of the leading causes of vision loss worldwide, primarily affecting individuals with diabetes. As the global prevalence of diabetes continues to rise, the need for early and accurate detection of DR has become more critical than ever. Traditional Diagnostic methods rely on manual examination by ophthalmologists, which can be time consuming, subjective, and prone to human error. This has led to the growing interest in leveraging Machine Learning techniques to automate and enhance the accuracy of DR detection [3].

Various Machine Learning Models such as Support Vector Machine (SVM), Logistic Regression, Random Forest, Scalable Decision Trees, have been explored for classifying retinal images and detecting signs of DR. However, each algorithm has its strengths and limitations in terms of accuracy, computational efficiency, and robustness. By reviewing existing literature and experimenting with different ML approaches, we seek to identify the most effective model for DR diagnosis. Our findings could contribute to the development of AI-driven screening systems specifically designed for Healthcare.

2. Related Work

2.1. Overview of existing research on ML for DR

Diabetic Retinopathy (DR) is one of the leading causes of vision impairment worldwide, primarily affecting individuals with diabetes. Early Diagnosis is critical for preventing severe complications, and traditional manual screening methods can be time consuming and require expert ophthalmologists. As a Result, Researchers have explored Machine Learning (ML) and Deep Learning (DL) models to automate and improve DR detection accuracy [1, 2, 5].

2.2. Summary of previous studies on various ML models

ML Models such as Support Vector Machines (SVM), Logistic Regression, Random Forest, and Decision Trees for detecting Diabetic Retinopathy (DR). These models have been widely utilized because they can identify medical images based on retinal abnormalities, but reach has advantages and disadvantages [12, 13].

SVM was one of the most widely utilized models in early DR classification studies. It performs well with structured data and can handle high-dimensional feature spaces, particularly when paired with kernel functions. However, its reliance on manually derived characteristics renders it less efficient than deep learning systems. Logistic Regression, as a simple and interpretable model, has traditionally served as a baseline for classification problems. While it can provide reasonable accuracy for binary classification, its performance deteriorates when dealing with more complex multi-class classifications such as varied levels of DR.

Because it can lessen overfitting, Random Forest, an ensemble learning technique, has shown more accuracy than

[a]kiruthikamanoj20@gmail.com, [b]rajee@francisxavier.ac.in, [c]fathima.cse@sairam.edu.in

DOI: 10.1201/9781003724988-50

individual decision trees. It works effectively with organized datasets that allow for the extraction and classification of key features. Numerous studies have demonstrated that when trained on appropriately selected retinal datasets, Random Forest models can attain great accuracy. However, feauture engineering plays a major role in its success, much like in other conventional machine learning techniques. Despite being computationally efficient and simple to understand, decision trees frequently suffer from overfitting, which reduces their ability to generalize to new data. In general, scalable decision tree versions work better when combined with ensemble techniques like Random Forest, even though they have been developed to handle big datasets [1–3, 5].

Overall, these models have contributed significantly to DR detection research, particularly before deep learning models became dominant. While they offer advantages in terms of interpretability and computational efficiency [12], their reliance on handcrafted features and limited ability to capture complex patterns in retinal images have made them less effective than modern deep learning approaches.

3. Machine Learning Models for DR Detection

3.1. Support vector machine (SVM)

Support Vector Machine (SVM) has been widely applied in medical image classification tasks, including Diabetic Retinopathy (DR) detection. SVM can utilize kernel functions like Radial Basis Function (RBF) and polynomial kernels, which help it model complex decision boundaries [12, 13]. However, its performance heavily depends on feature selection, requiring high-quality handcrafted features from retinal images. Another drawback is its computational cost as training an SVM on large datasets can be slow, making it less practical for real-time DR screening.

As shown in the Figure 50.1, the SVM model follows a structured approach for Diabetic Retinopathy detection. The process starts with the input layer, where real world retinal images are fed into the system. These images undergo a Pre-processing stage which enhances the quality of the data and reduces the possibilities of errors. It is then followed by feature extraction stage, key retinal features are identified and analyzed. The SVM Model then classifies these features by comparing them with trained data, ensuring accurate detection. Finally, the Decision-Making stage determines the severity of the disease, helping in early diagnosis and treatment planning.

3.2. Logistic regression

Logistic Regression is a simple yet effective statistical model commonly used as a baseline classifier for DR detection [4, 11, 13]. It excels in binary classification tasks (e.g., presence or absence of DR) by estimating probabilities based on input features [11]. One of its key advantages is interpretability, as it provides insights into how each feature contributes to the decision. However, Logistic regression assumes a linear relationship between features and the target class, limiting its ability to capture complex patterns [13]. This makes it less suitable for handling the nonlinear structures present in medical images, reducing its accuracy compared to more advanced machine learning models (Figure 50.2).

3.3. Random forest

Random Forest is an ensemble learning technique that combines multiple decision trees to improve prediction accuracy and reduces overfitting. It performs well in multi class classification tasks and is resilient to dataset noise. In contrast to SVM and Logistic Regression, Random Forest can automatically identify significant features from the dataset, negating the need for intensive feature engineering. Additionally, it is quite scalable which enables it to efficiently manage big datasets.

As the Figure 50.3 illustrates the model's interpretability declines with the number of trees, making it more difficult to

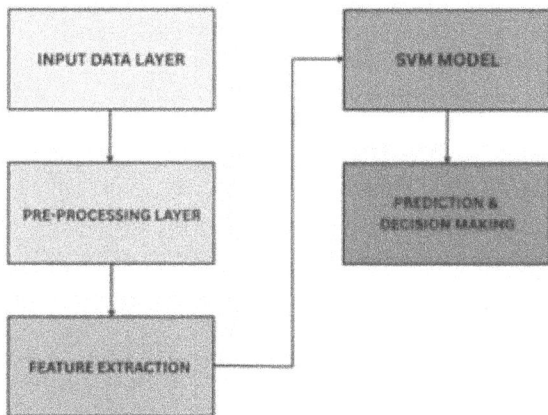

Figure 50.1. SVM model block diagram.

Source: Author.

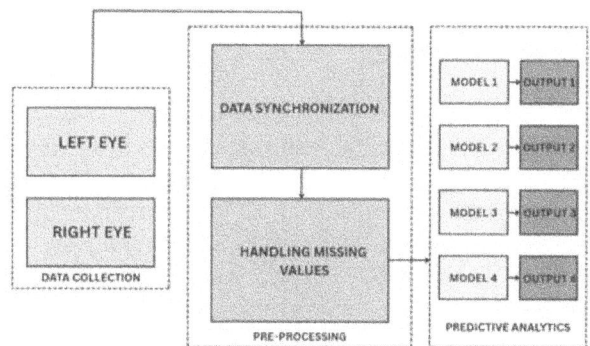

Figure 50.2. Diabetic retinopathy identification using logistic regression.

Source: Author.

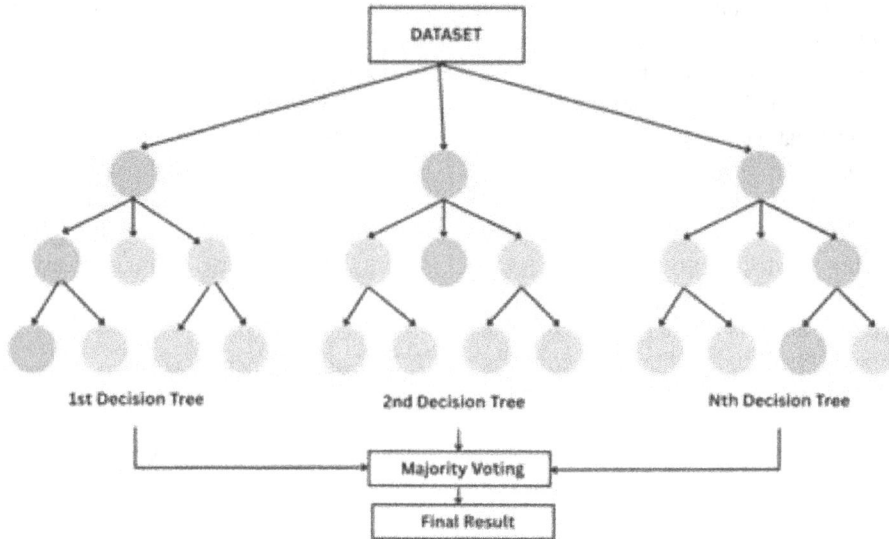

Figure 50.3. Random forest decision making diagram.

Source: Author.

comprehend how it makes decisions. This is a major draw-back though, as it can be computationally demanding.

3.4. Scalable decision trees

Scalable Decision Trees are an optimized version of tradi-tional decision trees, designed to handle large datasets effi-ciently. They use parallel processing and advanced pruning techniques to improve speed and reduce the risk of over-fitting. Decision Trees are helpful for medical diagnosis tasks like DR detection because they can model nonlinear interactions and are inherently interpretable. On training data, however, classic decision trees frequently overfit, which can result in subpar generalization [14]. By itera-tively improving the model, scalable variants like Gradi-ent Boosted Trees (GBT) and XG-Boost try to address this problem. Even with their benefits, these models might still need to have their hyper parameters carefully adjusted for best results (Table 50.1).

4. Methodology

4.1. Dataset description

The dataset is essential in developing an effective Diabetic Retinopathy (DR) detection model. This Study Considers publicly available datasets such as Kaggle APTOS 2019, Messidor, and Eye-PACS, which give high-resolution reti-nal fundus images [15] annotated with different levels of DR severity. These datasets provide a mix of healthy and ill photos, resulting in a balanced and diversified training set. Preprocessing techniques are used before feeding images into machine learning models in order to improve quality and consistency between samples. To preserve consistency, the photos are first reduced to a common resolution, which

Table 50.1. Performance metrics comparison table

Algorithm	Method	Accuracy	Precision	Recall
Support Vector Machine (SVM)	Kernel-based classification (RBF, Polynomial)	~85–90%	High	Moderate
Logistic Regression	Linear classification	~75–80%	Moderate	Moderate
Random Forest	Ensemble learning with multiple decision trees	~88–93%	High	High
Scalable Decision Trees	Decision tree with pruning and boosting	~85–92%	High	High

Source: Author.

reduces computing complexity while preserving crucial information. Image enhancement techniques like contrast adjustment and histogram equalization are used to highlight important retinal features including microaneurysms and hemorrhages. Furthermore, data augmentation techniques such as rotation, flipping, and brightness modifications aid in model generalization by introducing heterogeneity into the sample. These preprocessing processes ensure that the models learn robust features, which reduces the possibility of overfitting.

4.2. Feature extraction

Extracting meaningful features from retinal images is a cru-cial step in training an effective DR detection model. Vari-ous techniques can be used, depending on the complexity of the algorithm. Traditional methods rely on handcrafted features like the Histogram of Oriented Gradients (HOG), which captures texture and edge information [7]. However, more advanced techniques utilize deep learning-based feature extraction, particularly.

Convolutional Neural Networks (CNNs), which automatically learn hierarchical patterns from retinal images. The use of CNN-based feature extraction significantly enhances performance [9] by capturing complex structures within the retina, making it well-suited for DR detection [12–15].

4.3. Model training and evaluation metrics

The Training involves feeding the extracted features into machine learning models such as Support Vector Machine (SVM), Logistic Regression, Random Forest, and Scalable Decision Trees to analyze their suitability for DR detection. Training method can be split into two kinds, one of them is used to train the model using a portion of the dataset, while the other remaining data is used for validation to assess generalization performance. Hyperparameter tuning is performed to optimize each model. Techniques like grid search and random search are used to fine-tune parameters such as learning rate, number of estimators, kernel type (for SVM), and tree depth (for Random Forest and Decision Trees) to achieve the best possible performance.

5. Discussion

When it comes to detecting Diabetic Retinopathy (DR) using machine learning, there's no one-size-fits-all solution. Each model has its own strengths and limitations, which directly affect how well it can identify the disease. Support Vector Machine (SVM) are great at handling complex decision boundaries, especially when using kernel functions, but they can be slow and computationally expensive when dealing with large datasets. Logistic Regression, on the other hand, is simple and easy to interpret, but it struggles to capture the deeper patterns needed for precise DR detection. Random Forest is strong against overfitting and works well with structured data, yet it sometimes fails to generalize properly when dealing with highly imbalanced datasets. Meanwhile, Scalable Decision Trees offer the advantage of speed and scalability, but they may not be the most accurate option for medical diagnosis.

6. Conclusion

Although no direct experimentation was conducted in this study, the research is based on an extensive literature review and theoretical analysis of existing methods. By analyzing existing research and the theoretical advantages of each approach, this study provides insights into the most suitable model for Diabetic Retinopathy Detection, laying the groundwork for future experimental validation.

References

[1] Eason, G., Noble, B., & Sneddon, I. N. (1955). On certain integrals of Lipschitz-Hankel type involving products of Bessel functions. *Philosophical Transactions of the Royal Society of London. Series A, Mathematical and Physical Sciences*, *247*(935), 529–551.

[2] Maxwell, J. C. (1892). *A Treatise on Electricity and Magnetism* (3rd ed., vol. 2, pp. 68–73). Oxford: Clarendon.

[3] Jacobs, I. S., & Bean, C. P. (1963). Fine particles, thin films and exchange anisotropy. In G. T. Rado and H. Suhl (Eds.), *Magnetism,* vol. III, pp. 271–350. New York: Academic.

[4] Ayala, A., Ortiz Figueroa, T., Fernandes, B., & Cruz, F. (2021). Diabetic retinopathy improved detection using deep learning. *Applied Sciences*, *11*(24), 11970.

[5] Yorozu, T., Hirano, M., Oka, K., & Tagawa, Y. (2008). Electron spectroscopy studies on magneto-optical media and plastic substrate interface. *IEEE Translation Journal on Magnetics in Japan*, *2*(8), 740–741.

[6] Young, M. (1989). *The Technical Writer's Handbook.* Mill Valley, CA: University Science.

[7] Eves, K., & Valasek, J. (2023). Adaptive Control for Singularly Perturbed Systems. *IEEE Open Journal of Control Systems*, *3*, 1–13. [Online]. Available: https://codeocean.com/capsule/4989235/tree

[8] Kingma, D. P., & Welling, M. (2013, December). *Auto-encoding variational Bayes.* arXiv:1312.6114. [Online]. Available: https:// arxiv.org/abs/1312.6114

[9] Liu, S. (2023). Wi-Fi Energy Detection Testbed (12MTC), 2023, git-hub repository. [Online]. Available: https://github.com/ liustone99/Wi-Fi-Energy-Detection-Testbed-12MTC

[10] US Department of Health and Human Services. (2013). Treatment episode data set: discharges (TEDS-D): concatenated, 2006 to 2009. *Office of Applied Studies.* doi:10.3886/ICPSR30122.v2

[11] AI-Antary, M. T., & Arafa, Y. (2021). Multi-scale attention network for diabetic retinopathy classification. *IEEE Access*, *9*, 54190–54200.

[12] Abbood, S. H., Hamed, H. N. A., Rahim, M. S. M., Rehman, A., Saba, T., & Bahaj, S. A. (2022). Hybrid retinal image enhancement algorithm for diabetic retinopathy diagnostic using deep learning model. *IEEE Access*, *10*, 73079–73086.

[13] Bhimavarapu, U., & Battineni, G. (2022). Automatic microaneurysms detection for early diagnosis of diabetic retinopathy using improved discrete particle swarm optimization. *Journal of Personalized Medicine*, *12*(2), 317.

[14] Shankar, K., Perumal, E., & Vidhyavathi, R. M. (2020). Deep neural network with moth search optimization algorithm based detection and classification of diabetic retinopathy images. *SN Applied Sciences*, *2*(4), 748.

[15] Vinayaki, V. D., & Kalaiselvi, R. J. N. P. L. (2022). Multi-threshold image segmentation technique using remora optimization algorithm for diabetic retinopathy detection from fundus images. *Neural Processing Letters*, *54*(3), 2363–2384.

51 Big data analytics: A balanced approach for sustainable future

S. Saileja[1,a], S. Sai Bhavani[2,b], M. Sreeja[3,c], and M. Deepika[4,d]

[1]Assistant Professor, Department of Commerce and Business Management, Veeranari Chakali Ilamma Women's University, Koti, Hyderabad, Telangana, India
[2]Assistant Professor, Department of Environmental Science, Veeranari Chakali Ilamma Women's University, Koti, Hyderabad, Telangana, India
[3]Department of Commerce and Business Management, Veeranari Chakali Ilamma Women's University, Koti, Hyderabad, Telangana, India
[4]Department of Commerce and Business Management, Osmania University, Hyderabad, Telangana, India

Abstract: Big Data Analytics is a hotcake in the current advancing technical environment where it is ruling many of the fields that require decision making, to understand and analyze patterns of people's preferences, choices, correlational occurrences and many more. The huge complex data used in surveys are based to predict the future trends in population, life expectancies and alike. They are used to analyze, predict and thus mitigate the associated risks even prior to their occurrences. Big data analytics today are being used to trace the trends in population, weather patterns, sales, inventory, purchasing patterns, migration patterns, ecological deterioration which aid in understanding the correlated aspects and repetitive patterns that influence them. Business enterprises, Sensex calculations, Research and Development centres, Laboratories, etc. However, its scope is expanding with the advancement of time and technology reaching to its greatest point where it can even influence the decisions of people, their choices, without them knowing it themselves. With its effective usage influencing people in all spheres of their life shaping their thoughts, beliefs, actions, it can become a grave threat to national security as well. This paper briefs big data analytics through introduction, review of literature, current applications and threats of big data analytics, discussion and concludes highlighting the balanced usage of big data analytics.

Keywords: Big data analytics, correlational occurrences, ecological deterioration, national security, repetitive patterns, technological environment, sensex

1. Introduction

"Information is Wealth" – Today's competitive world deals with huge data pertaining to the enormous population on the earth. This data can be about people – Sensex, Employee's data, report data on health [6, 7], sex ratio, literacy rates; or about abiotic factors – Soil types, weather pattern recordings, satellite information, maps; or financial information – sales, profits, purchasing patterns, accounting records, or environmental aspects – migration patterns of birds, to calculate water tables, carbon emissions, energy production and consumption thus performing environmental risk analysis [12], predicting future values, etc. [11]. These data records are huge not only in volume as well as number but are also never ending till the existence of human life.

1.1. Big Data analytics

The huge and complex data is called Big Data and its analysis to extract useful insights, detect repetitive patterns, trends, identifying correlating factors which aid in better decision making is called Big Data Analytics [1]. Big data analytics is being used to understand correlations between random variables in the economy. It is used to understand the behavioural patterns through numbers to be precise to estimate the qualitative concepts of people by quantitative means. It is hence used to understand purchasing patterns, market trends, consumer's choices [2], repetitive weather conditions, geographic data spread, environmental patterns and predictions including the impact and effect of carbon foot printing etc. Big data analysis is performed by collecting previous data, analyzing the pointers, correlating the aspects and thus tracing the patterns. It is basically of 4 major types [10]:

1. **Descriptive Analytics** – It deals with quantitative analysis of historical data from cache memory like frequent and recent searches, likes, dislikes, previous orders, sales data, etc. It tries to analyze what actually happened in the past.

[a]sailejasevella@gmail.com, [b]saibhavanisevella@gmail.com, [c]sreeja.musini00@gmail.com, [d]deepika.manoharan@gmail.com

DOI: 10.1201/9781003724988-51

2. **Diagnostic Analytics** – This deal with tracing of patterns according to the past data. It analyses why it happened.
3. **Predictive Analytics** – As the name suggests predictive analytics estimates the future values through statistical methods. It gives predictions about what will happen in future through quantitative means.
4. **Prescriptive Analytics** – Prescriptive analysis says what should be done for betterment. It helps in decision making and policy framing (Figure 51.1).

1.2. Working of big data analytics

Big data analysis is performed by various open source and paid tools. However, its working remains the same in most of them.

a. **Data Collection** – The voluminous data which can be in structured, unstructured or semi structured form is collected in the form of surveys, feedbacks, reports, etc.
b. **Data Storage** – This data is then stored using cloud technology or regular storage units which can be accessed when needed using pay per use principle.
c. **Data Processing and Analysis** – Big data analysis occurs at this stage. The data is properly segregated and analyzed using various statistical and analytical tools. Previous data is mapped searching for correlational pointers and their influences on growth and decline of a particular parameter thus deducing the patterns. This analysis tries to picturize the qualitative aspects such as expectations, choices, likes of people into quantitative concepts such as increase in demand, sales, seasonal purchasing patterns, population spread, etc. It provides insights regarding the future patterns [5] that can be expected like demand rate, influence of change in prices of commodities on complementary and supplementary goods, expected features of goods, production rates, etc.

d. **Data visualization** – The data patterns are visualized and accessed for future use pictographically using charts, graphs and many more [2].

2. Review of Literature

This research paper was framed by considering the insights from different research journals, blogs, papers. The basic information like definitions, working was taken from standard websites [1–2]. Many researchers dwelled into depths of the concept in a comprehensive manner. Some of them like Elgendy. N, Elragal, A. analyzed various tools and methods to be applied on big data along with its applications in various decision-making domains. They explained big data analytics in terms of velocity, variety and value [3]. Chioma Ann Udeh and others gave a comprehensive record of role of big data analytics in providing insights for decision making mitigating risks, optimizing processes and solving complex problems. They explained its impact on contemporary businesses and the way it shapes decision making in varied areas [4]. Davide Tosi explained the development in big data analytics for the past 15 years with a future scope of further improvement in the coming years [5]. Minh-Tay Huynh & others gave an account of capabilities of big data analytics (BDA) and stresses on the point of indefinite boundaries of its domain uses, tools and finally concluded with future research areas and implications [6]. Rahul, K. & others reviewed work of various authors thus proposing dirty data detection techniques and models [7]. Batko, K., Ślęzak, A. conducted research on usage of BDA on healthcare services and its benefits [8]. Andrew McAfee, Erik Brynjolfsson, illustrated the differences in bigdata and analytics using 2 companies in terms of velocity, variety and volume discussing the managerial challenges associated [9]. Ankita S. Tiwarkhede, Prof. Vinit Kakde illustrated the techniques

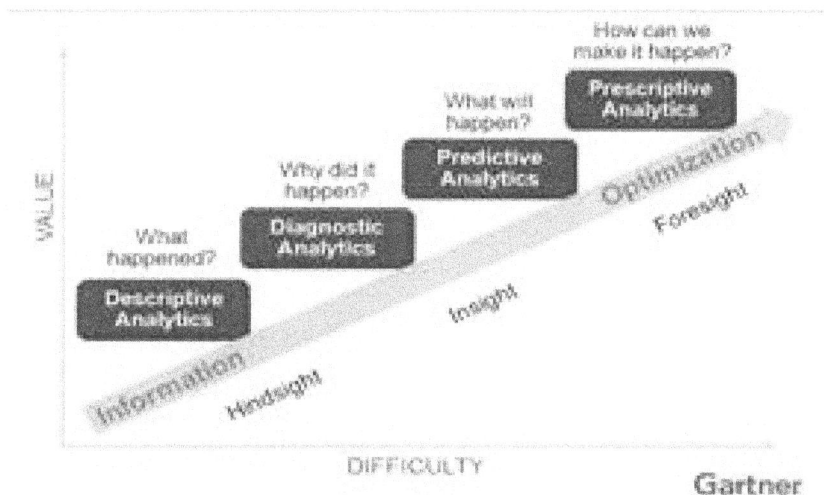

Figure 51.1. Types of big data analytics.

Source: Author.

used in big data analytics like data mining, A/B testing, etc [10]. Ankur Gupta briefly reviewed about the characteristics, working, techniques and tools used for BDA [11]. Al-Sai and others analyzed the usage of BDA in industries for processing and decision making during pre and peri covid era [12].

Research Gaps: Most of the authors explained about the BDA mapping its characteristics, applications in decision making, processing, techniques and tools in terms of 10Vs but almost none of them discussed the various threats posed through its usage. Thus this paper

- aims to bridge these research gaps by enumerating possible threats analytically
- and suggest suitable techniques to overcome these threats

3. Current Applications and Threats of Big Data Analytics

3.1. Applications

Big data analytics is seen in every electronic gadget that has access to the internet. Every platform that deals with huge and complex data uses big data analytics for simplification and to derive useful insights from the data. Big data analytics is used in private MNC like TCS, Amazon, Wipro for optimization of processes such as

a. **Production** – Used for cost saving, understanding people's preferences, analyzing market trends [5]. According to the feedback, sales information the choices of people in respective commodities in relation to the seasons and time, effect of competitive brands, complementary goods, trade policies, subsidies are analyzed.

b. **Real time analysis** – The e-governance in various online platforms like banks, educational institutions, online software applications for ordering food, clothes, travel uses big data analytics to address real time issues of the consumers [3].

It is used in government sectors [8] like railways for optimization of train schedules, Central Board of Direct Taxes (CBDT) and Central Board of Indirect Taxes & Customs (CBIC) for enhanced tax collection and compliance. It is also used in surveys, reports, that calculate and record mass details like population, literacy rates, health status, climatic conditions, etc.

c. **Environmental sustainability** – To estimate the carbon foot printing left behind by various firms, calculate water tables their extraction patterns, rate of emission of pollutants into the atmosphere [12], recurring patterns of migrations, seasonal disasters, etc. It can be used to trace the energy production, consumption patterns and predict the future energy consumption relative to rising population [4].

BDA is used by government organizations to identify beneficiaries in various schemes, understand their socio-economic status which can be further used to analyze the necessity of further schemes or efficient usage of present schemes (Figure 51.2).

This data is analyzed to predict the future details. The estimates of poverty, economic conditions of a nation, population, pollution rates in future are made through big data analytics. These details help to understand the shortcomings and address the need to focus on areas that lead to development (Figure 51.3).

3.2. Threats

Big Data Analytics also comes with many threats and challenges to one's privacy and security [16]. Usage of data analytics in every application software of one's electronic gadget holds sensitive information regarding an individual (Table 51.1). The cybercrimes recorded during the research is as follows.

BDA can track an individual's mindset according to the way of their search speed, nature of search and content. This can bring grave threat to one's privacy and can also mislead

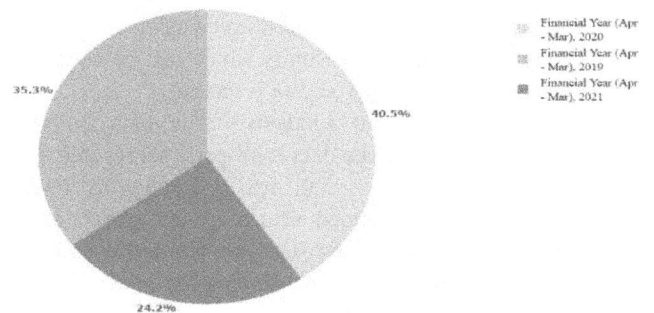

Figure 51.2. Beneficiaries of Atal Pension Yojana for the financial years 2019–2021 generated through analytical dashboard in government digital record [19].

Source: Author.

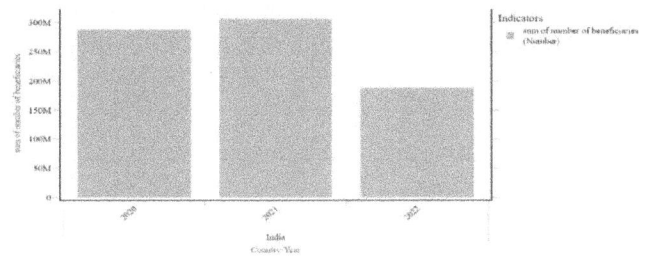

Figure 51.3. Beneficiaries of PM KISAN Yojana for the financial years 2020–2022 generated through analytical dashboard in government digital record [19].

Source: Author.

Table 51.1. Cybercrime record according to the National Crime Records Bureau's (NCRB) latest report [21]

Category	2020	2021	2022
Total Sates	49708	52430	64907
Total UTs	327	544	986
All India Total	50035	52974	65893

Source: Author.

people into aggressive habits. The recorded cybercrimes are attributed by various threats like:

a. **National Security threats** – When an individual's private data is under the control of foreign nation's servers, it possesses sensitive data pertaining to important figures of the nation. This can eventually disrupt the nation's integrity, political stability and encourage terrorist activities (Table 51.2).

b. **Disruption of individual privacy** – Any information about an individual should be properly encrypted so as to protect their individual's interest.

c. **Influencing thoughts, beliefs** – Business firms, agencies, political bodies can greatly use this to shape the thoughts and actions of common people for their benefit. Popping of data that is beneficial to them can alter the mindsets of people, making them believe in what they see rather than checking for its authenticity.

d. **Cyber terrorism** – Politically powered cyberattacks which disrupts societal peace by instilling fear through violent actions.

e. **Theft of identity** – This is an activity where an individual's sensitive details are stolen which are used to impersonate their identity for seamless conduction of frauds.

f. **Financial frauds** [9]– 75% of these activities like debit/credit/ ATM frauds are happening mostly with old (>60 years), young (<20 years), illiterate section of the society. It is mainly attributed by poor and weak passwords, encryption issues.

4. Discussion

As the massive usage of BDA depicted both sides of a coin that is both positive and negative aspects of data usage and analysis, it is important to mitigate the ill effects of BDA for brighter future. According to the Information Security Forum (2016), 1 out of every 5 citizens is prone to cyber risk because of extensive usage of BDA. Thus it is important for data protection while dealing with massive sensitive data which can be possible through usage of the following method:

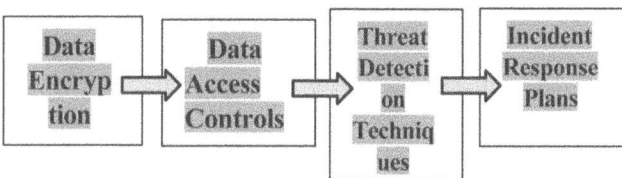

Table 51.2. Different categories of cyber threats observed [20]

Category	No. of cases registered
Tampering computer source documents	418
Ransom-ware	1275
Identity theft	24501
Violation of Privacy	1198
Cyber terrorism	56

Source: Author.

5. Conclusions

Big data analytics is a mechanism of calculation of data to provide insights tracing repetitive patterns. It is basically a system that is intended to make work easier, reducing the risks and estimating the future values for better planning. It can be used for ensuring environment sustainability. It doesn't have the ability to think ethically or act ethically. Hence its usage has to be limited so that an individual's privacy is not breached and the data is in safe hands. When the future is to see many usages of big data analytics, its functioning has a greater scope for expansion. Big data analytics is both a boon and a threat. It is as useful as becoming a disaster. As per the results from this study, construction of powerful firewalls, usage of robust mechanisms for data access control and early, effective data breach prevention can reduce the privacy issues pertaining to big data analytics. Hence there should be a balanced approach of its usage for the betterment of human life.

6. Future Scope

The usage of big data analytics is yet to unwind to its true potential which is in the near future. This can bring ground breaking changes in the way things can happen in the future. They can be the driving force in establishing businesses shaping the way people think in a geographic location. The usage of big data analytics can be further expanded to

• **Inventory Management** – To understand the lifetime of raw materials [15] and finished goods thus determining the preferable quantity to be produced in a season according to the demand

• **Maintenance and Management** – The complete record regarding production [13], employees, investments, equipment, marketing, the complete cycle will be driven by the data analysis. These records will be used for real time addressing of issues coupled with management principles for efficient working.

• **Marketing** – The data generated in advertising and marketing can be used to enhance profitability, sales and businesses to a greater extent.

• **Sustainable development goals** – To execute SDGs [14] with much more precision through reduced reliability on environmental degrading aspects.

References

[1] The International Business Machines Corporation, https://www.ibm.com/

[2] Trupti Dekate, The Origin of Big Data Analytics. Analytics Vidhya, Data Science Blogathon, https://www.analyticsvidhya.cpm/blog/2022/09/the- origin-of-big-data-analytics

[3] Elgendy, N., & Elragal, A. (2014). Big Data Analytics: A Literature Review Paper. In: Perner, P. (Ed.), *Advances in Data Mining. Applications and Theoretical Aspects. ICDM 2014.* Lecture Notes in Computer Science(), vol 8557. Springer, Cham. https://doi.org/10.1007/978-3-319- 08976-8_16

[4] Tosi, D., Kokaj, R. & Roccetti, M. (2024). 15 years of Big Data: a systematic literature review. *J Big Data, 11*, 73. https://doi.org/10.1186/s40537-024-00914-9

[5] Huynh, M. T., Nippa, M., & Aichner, T. (2023). Big data analytics capabilities: Patchwork or progress? A systematic review of the status quo and implications for future research. *Technological Forecasting and Social Change, 197*, 122884.

[6] Rahul, K., Banyal, R. K. & Arora, N. (2023). A systematic review on big data applications and scope for industrial processing and healthcare sectors. *J Big Data, 10*, 133. https://doi.org/10.1186/s40537-023-00808-2

[7] Batko, K., & Ślęzak, A. (2022). The use of Big Data Analytics in healthcare. *J Big Data, 9*, 3. https://doi.org/10.1186/s40537-021-00553-4

[8] Tiwarkhede, A. S., & Kakde, V. (2015). A review paper on big data analytics. *International Journal of Science and Research, 4*(4), 845–848. https://www.ijsr.net/archive/v4i4/SUB153031

[9] Gupta, A. (2022). A Review Paper on Big Data Analytics. *International Journal of Innovative Research in Computer Science & Technology (IJIRCST), 10*(2), 2347–5552. https://doi.org/10.55524/ijircst.2022.10.2.37

[10] Al-Sai, Z. A., Husin, M. H., Syed-Mohamad, S. M., Abdin, R. M. S., Damer, N., Abualigah, L., & Gandomi, A. H. (2022). Explore Big Data Analytics Applications and Opportunities: A Review. *Big Data and Cognitive Computing, 6*, 157. https://doi.org/10.3390/bdcc6040157

[11] Wang, J., Xu, C., Zhang, J., & Zhong, R. (2022). Big data analytics for intelligent manufacturing systems: A review. *Journal of Manufacturing Systems, 62*, 738–752. https://doi.org/10.1016/j.jmsy.2021.03.005.

[12] Barnes, S. J., Guo, Y., & Chan, J. (2022). Big Data analytics for sustainability: Insight through technological innovation. *Information & Management, 59*(5), 103627. https://doi.org/10.1016/j.im.2022.103627.

[13] Gholami, H., Lee, J. K. Y., & Ali, A. (2023). Big Data Analytics for Sustainable Products: A State-of-the-Art Review and Analysis. *Sustainability, 15*(17), 12758.

[14] Tamym, L., Benyoucef, L., Nait Sidi Moh, A., & El Ouadghiri, M. D. (2023). Big Data Analytics-based life cycle sustainability assessment for sustainable manufacturing enterprises evaluation. *Journal of Big Data, 10*(1), 170.

[15] Mageto, J. (2021). Big data analytics in sustainable supply chain management: A focus on manufacturing supply chains. *Sustainability, 13*(13), 7101.

[16] Rafiq, F., Awan, M. J., Yasin, A., Nobanee, H., Zain, A. M., & Bahaj, S. A. (2022). Privacy prevention of big data applications: A systematic literature review. *SAGE Open, 12*(2), 21582440221096445.

[17] National Data and Analytics Platform, https://www.ndap.niti.gov.in

[18] Open government data platform, https://www.data.gov.in/

[19] Cybercrimes in India with respect to dataanalytics_Press Information Bureau, https://www.pib.gov.in/

52 Quantum computing and automation for optimization of businesses

S. Saileja[1,a], S. Sai Bhavani[2,b], M. Sreeja[3,c], and M. Deepika[4,d]

[1]Assistant Professor, Department of Commerce and Business Management, Veeranari Chakali Ilamma Women's University, Koti, Hyderabad, Telangana, India
[2]Assistant Professor, Department of Environmental Science, Veeranari Chakali Ilamma Women's University, Koti, Hyderabad, Telangana, India
[3]Department of Commerce and Business Management, Veeranari Chakali Ilamma Women's University, Koti, Hyderabad, Telangana, India
[4]Department of Commerce and Business Management, Osmania University, Hyderabad, Telangana, India

Abstract: Quantum computing and Automation are two of the booming technologies with an expected tremendous expansion in the future. Quantum computing uses quantum mechanics to address the complex problems while automation is sequential arrangement of devices, systems which reduces human interaction in processes. Amalgamation of these two technologies is expected to enhance the working, processing of the systems and the way businesses run. It can be used for effective planning of resources, systems, working reducing the lead time and overall time of the working cycle. It helps in the analysis of nature of the substances under varied circumstances without actually experimenting. It aids in understanding the nature of things and the way work can be proceeded with minimum effort to attain maximum benefit. Hence its uses can be diversified to different sectors and segments of the economy. Quantum computing when clubbed with automation can plan the kind of crop varieties to be grown according to the geographic conditions, reduce emission of greenhouse gases, revolutionize climate modelling, increase the production activities with efficient resource planning and reduction of lead time, enhance the productivity and consumer satisfaction of services through innovative and error free work. This paper gives a brief account of quantum computing and automation through introduction, review of literature, applications & challenges and ends with a conclusion post future scope stating as to how quantum computing can significantly evolve in the future where its applications can be expanded profusely which when coupled with automation can enrich the ease of performances in different sectors.

Keywords: Automation, climate modelling, efficient resource planning, lead time, quantum computing, quantum mechanics, sectoral analysis

1. Introduction

Quantum computing is a computer science which uses quantum mechanics – a combination of mathematics and physics to solve complex problems. They work better than supercomputers in calculations with cloud memory. They perform multiple combinations and permutations with the given data using principles like superposition, interference. Quantum computers use specialized hardware and algorithms to perform quantum mechanics on the data. It varies from the conventional computers right from its storage units. They have specialized storage units – Qubits which are nothing but quantum bits that are quite distinct from the traditional binary bits. They have a capacity of data storage of 0 or 1 or both bits simultaneously. They can thus combine with as many other qubits as 2^n (i.e., 2 bits with 4; 3 with 8; 4 with 16 and so on). These combinations can be in any of the 4 major principles of quantum mechanics thus performing a major study of particles at molecular level. They can perform calculations faster and in more possible, feasible ways than

a supercomputer. These Qubits can store greater information than a traditional storage mechanism and the storage unit i.e. chips using cloud storage. It can be accessed through the internet implying an easy transfer and easy usage without the issue of additional physical storage devices [1].

Automation is the process of sequential arrangement of application systems, robots, devices, equipment to reduce the human interference in the processes thereby allowing an uninterrupted, error free, chain workflow to obtain a suitable output [1]. Here the devices work on a predetermined algorithm picking up at the end point of the previous stage and performing its actions without errors. Automation thus reduces manual effort, human errors, risks of contamination, dependence on manpower, increasing rate and efficiency of production.

1.1. Working

Quantum computing (QC) is a developing technology that uses quantum hardware and algorithms for its working. The

[a]sailejasevella@gmail.com, [b]saibhavanisevella@gmail.com, [c]sreeja.musini00@gmail.com, [d]deepika.manoharan@gmail.com

DOI: 10.1201/9781003724988-52

interaction between the quantum particles occurs based on 4 quantum principles:

1. **Superposition** – The state of particles existence in single, dual or multimode without disruption of its innate state at the same time and place [4]. Here qubits exist in 0 or 1 or in both modes providing a vaster scope of experimental exploration [9].
2. **Entanglement** – The state of particle behaviour exhibition being similar irrespective of the physical distance between them [4]. It speaks of the imaginary connection that exists between certain particles which share a common behaviour enabling people to study parallel communications.
3. **Interference** – It enables study of particle behaviour by amplifying certain characteristics and ruling out those which does not serve the purpose. It is the study of particle behaviour when one comes in the vicinity of the other.
4. **Decoherence** – It is the state of a particle losing its quantum behaviour and the imaginary connection of entanglement.

Qubits can be quantum particles like photons, electrons, energized neutral atoms subjected to laser beams, quantum dots, superconducting ions [1]. These qubits interact with others using any one or more of these quantum principles forming multiple permutations and combinations. Where these permutational interactions are the possible solutions for any complex problems. The particles superimposed cancel out anticoherent ways upon interaction thus producing the best suitable outcome for any problem. They are used to analyse molecular behaviour under different kinds of stimuli without actually experimenting, saving lots of time, resources and money. Particle nature under different conditions can be virtually analysed using the qubits interactions. They come up with possible solutions for complex problems which is known as Quantum Utility; and create the virtual output through interference. It enables the visualization of a possible outcome prior to its execution aiding in taking necessary steps for betterment [1].

Automation is programming the devices in a sequential format to allow an uninterruptible work flow among the devices resulting in the final output at the end stage. It is used to perform repetitive tasks that increase the ease and reduce the errors. It is achieved through programming, robotics, usage of algorithms, sequential arrangement of equipment, personnel training, etc. Automation is done by creating coherence between the different stages by imbibing the decision-making ability to the devices according to the preset values and conditions.

1.2. Components

The components of Quantum computer differ from that of a traditional computer right from its manufacturing. These are specialized to accommodate the quantum properties of particles – speed, diligence, etc. (Figure 52.1)

1. **Qubits** – These act as the base for the quantum computing [7]. Unlike the traditional bits – 0/1, they can exist as 0 or 1or both providing multiple permutations and combinations enhancing the possibilities.
2. **Quantum gates** – They are similar to logic gates which perform logical operations using Qubits
3. **Quantum Registers** – These are storage accessories of Qubits
4. **Quantum Circuits** – They sequence quantum computational operations.

2. Review of Literature

The basic information about quantum computing and automation along with its working principles and some of their possible applications were taken from blogs and websites [1–2]. Crispin Coombs & others briefed the intelligent automation and its allied segments by giving a business model filling the research gaps [3]. Gamble S. described what exactly

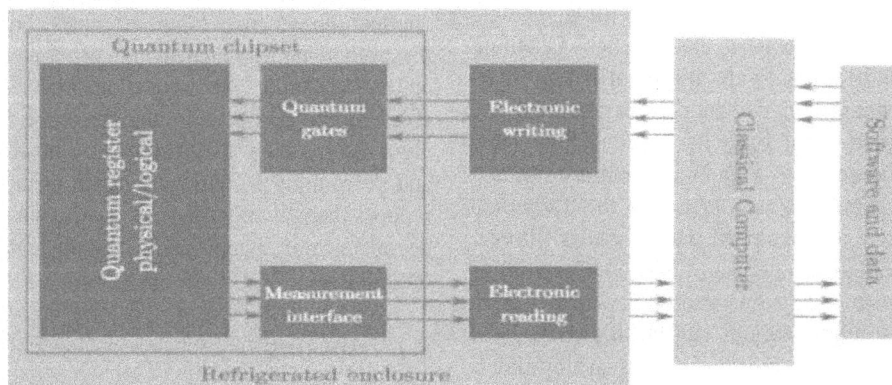

Figure 52.1. Architecture of quantum computer.

Source: Author.

is quantum computing and how it uses logic operations of AND, OR through qubits for highspeed computation unlike conventional computers [4]. Sukhpal Singh Gill, Rajkumar Buyya enumerated recent advancements and impact of QC highlighting its associated tools and platforms [5]. Pradeep Nayak & others studied on quantum algorithm, gates and circuits focusing on NISQ era [6]. Kanamori & others briefed about the basics and principles of quantum computing with a slight synopsis of D-wave quantum computers [7]. Elhajjar & others addressed the debate on employment of automation through systemic analysis techniques like bibliography technique mapping the patterns [8]. From the research analysis made, it was observed that the QC & automation are in their budding stage especially the concept of quantum computing. An extensive research programmes are being carried down for its usage and implementation in various fields. Amalgamation of these two technologies is never made. This paper briefed the integration of Quantum Computing and Automation along with the associated challenges faced by these technologies bridging the research gaps.

3. Current Scenario

Quantum Computing is an emerging technology which is still in a developing phase but with a massive scope. It is said to be using a single microprocessor unlike supercomputer using thousands. It can work with multiple configurations solving real life problems at an infinitesimal speed (Figure 52.2).

Sycamore is a Google AI generated 54 qubit Quantum Computer in 2019 known for its quantum supremacy.

Here the qubits are arranged in 2D enabling coupling and superposition between them. This architecture aided in fastest problem solving with a speed of 200 seconds which would take nearly 10000 years for super computer. Many other major companies are also competing to generate a feasible quantum computer and are on the path of achievement (Table 52.1).

Figure 52.2. Sycamore quantum computer.
Source: Author.

Table 52.1. Progress made by organizations in developing QCs [18]

Amazon	Google	IBM	Intel
Established AWS centre in 2021 to built a fault tolerant quantum computer	Quantum error correction in 2023 for encode information	Quantum Development Roadmap for enhancement of execution speed by 2033	Tunnel Falls-silicon spin Qubit Chip
Initiated quantum embark program in 2024 to deliver specialized programs	Introduced Willow quantum chip in 2024 which can perform computation < 5 minutes	Kookaburra processor combination with multichip processors	Pando tree – quantum research control chip to solve limitations of quantum scaling
Developed Ocelot – quantum chip in 2025 is the first implementation of noise – based gate	Developed a software stack of open- source tools to develop novel algorithms	Suite of cloud-based quantum systems – IBM Quantum Composer, Quantum lab	Intel Quantum SDK is simulation stack within a containerize d environment

Source: Author.

4. Applications and Challenges in Quantum Computing

Quantum Computing will replace the businesses and their working through its amalgamation with Machine learning, Artificial intelligence revolutionizing data analytics. This is mainly because of the ability and storage of quantum computers to store either in 0 or 1 or both using superposition enabling 2^n configurations and solutions to address a particular problem. It provides a good amount of data to analyze historical and present data to machine learning for continuous updation.

1. **Applications** – Quantum Computing coupled with automation can speed up the processes, control the working operations, performances, coherences thus increasing the fidelity, reliability, efficiency of the systems. It can benefit many segments in the businesses such as:
    -   **Production** – Quantum computing in the production segment helps in understanding the nature of particles used as raw materials. By subjecting them to various conditions, their particle behaviour, lifetime, and quality can be analysed.
    -   **Supply Chain Management** – Optimization of supply chain management [5] can greatly benefit businesses and global companies to reduce the lead time, production wastages, capital draining, resulting in faster processing and delivery time

increasing the lifetime of commodities and consumer satisfaction.

- **Quant Finance** – Quantum computing helps in assessing the risks and possible solutions that can be adopted by investment portfolios to mitigate them [2].

2. **Challenges** – Though usage of quantum computing and automation can be of great help to the economy, it is accompanied by various challenges. Being a technology still in its developing phase, it is associated with various challenges:

   - **Optimal conditions** – Quantum computers work in controlled and optimal conditions as they rely on quantum particles in their excited state, they require environment with
     - Cold temperatures i.e. near to absolute zero
     - Minimal noise
   - **Incoherence** – Incoherence is the dealignment of quantum states of atoms.
   - **Scalability** – They cannot cope up with greater workloads.
   - **Security threats** – Automation is associated with security threats especially during data sharing over the cloud.
   - **Disruption of supply chain** – the conventional supply chain can get disrupted with the sudden shift in technology [1].
   - **Unemployment** – Automation of the systems can result in removal of jobs to many unskilled and semiskilled labourers [3].
   - **Algorithm defects** – These technologies like robotics, systems which are automated are based on algorithms and incorrect, corrupted codes can be fatal leading to huge dam age to mankind.
   - **Huge expenditures** – Installation, maintenance costs associated with these technologies are hefty. Establishment of a suitable environment for their functioning is also a heavy investment.
   - **Heating issues** – Dealing with electrons, energized ions, photons, quantum dots require huge amounts of insulation and the risk of the device getting heated up soon is high as well. Establishment of suitable coolants with qualitative ion provision is a challenge.

As the quantum computing technology is still in development phase, the counter acting strategies of these challenges are unaddressed.

5. Discussion

Quantum Computing is a budding concept which is still in the process of realization by many major companies like IBM, Amazon, Microsoft, PASQAL, etc. Though this a concept yet not in practice, its performance is estimated to bring a major breakthrough in many scientific experiments to unravel major information regarding the existence of life, planets and more.

6. Future Scope

Quantum computing and automation use can be extended to different sectors enhancing the working procedures. They can be used in different sectors as:

1. **Agriculture** – Quantum computation can be used in agriculture and its allied sectors [6]:
   - To determine the health status of poultry, cattle, their expected life time, optimal conditions for their survival and enhanced milk production
   - It can also be used for planning of mineral extraction through simulations of mining techniques
2. **Industries** – Quantum computing and automation in industries can be of great help especially in departments like research & development, planning, inventory management, modelling, problem analysis, risk analysis, [8] etc. It can be of great help in various industries like cosmetics, lab grown diamonds, electronics, semiconductor designs, automobiles, baking, and many more.
3. **Services** – Quantum computing can be of great help in the provision of services like transportation, music composition, design development, research, defence, food varieties, techno logical developments, etc.

7. Conclusion

It was observed from the study that quantum computing and automation can ease the processes making the systems, procedures more effective and efficient by choosing easy and economic solutions to complex problems. With its ability to generate a bird's eye view to a problem, it helps to create an automatic pathway for getting things done with less human intervention and contamination associated with it. However, the issues of data breach, maintenance are still an area of research for the scientists to bring out their true potential.

References

[1] The International Business Machines Corporation, https://www.ibm.com/

[2] The Lingaro group, https://lingarogroup.com/

[3] Coombs, C., Hislop, D., Taneva, S. K., & Barnard, S. (2020). The strategic impacts of Intelligent Automation for knowledge and service work: An interdisciplinary review. *The Journal of Strategic Information Systems*, *29*(4), 101600. https://doi.org/10.1016/j.jsis.2020.101600. (https://www.sciencedirect.com/science/article/pii/S0963868720300081)

[4] Gamble, S. (2019, January). Quantum computing: What it is, why we want it, and how we're trying to get it. In *Frontiers of Engineering: Reports on Leading-Edge Engineering from the 2018 Symposium*. National Academies Press (US). https://www.ncbi.nlm.nih.gov/books/NBK538701/

[5] Gill, S. S., & Buyya, R. (2024). Transforming research with quantum computing. *Journal of Economy and Technology.* https://doi.org/10.1016/j.ject.2024.07.001.

[6] Nayak, P., Rathod, S., & Sukanya, S. (2024). Quantum Computing: Circuits, Algorithms and Application. *International Journal of Advanced Research in Science, Communication and Technology (IJARSCT) International Open-Access*, Double-Blind, Peer Reviewed, Refereed, Multidisciplinary Online Journal Volume 4, Issue 1, August 2024, ISSN (Online) 2581–9429 https://ijarsct.co.in/A19321.

[7] Kanamori, Y., & Yoo, S. M. (2020). Quantum computing: principles and applications. *Journal of International Technology and Information Management, 29*(2), 43–71. doi:https://doi.org/10.58729/1941-6679.1410

[8] Elhajjar, S., Yacoub, L., & Yaacoub, H. (2023). Automation in business research: systematic literature review. *Information Systems and e-Business Management, 21*(3), 675–698. https://doi.org/10.1007/s10257-023-00645-z.

[9] De Micheli, G., Jiang, J. H. R., Rand, R., Smith, K., & Soeken, M. (2022). Advances in quantum computation and quantum technologies: A design automation perspective. *IEEE Journal on Emerging and Selected Topics in Circuits and Systems, 12*(3), 584–601.

[10] Informa Technology https://www.Informa Tech Target computer weekly.com/

53 Automated resume ranking using SpaCy NER and TF-IDF similarity

S. Praveena[a], T. Arasulingam[b], P. Puvirajan[c], M. Dineshkumar[d], P. Pavan Kumar[e], M. Varunraj[f], and G. Sarukesh[g]

Manakula Vinayagar Institute of Technology, Puducherry, India

Abstract: Traditional applicant tracking systems (ATS) often fail to provide the accuracy and fairness expected in modern recruitment practices due to over-reliance on simple keyword filtering. This research presents an intelligent resume ranking framework that integrates Natural Language Processing (NLP) and machine learning to address these limitations. Our system leverages SpaCy's Named Entity Recognition (NER) to extract structured data from resumes, such as job titles, skills, education, and years of experience. These features are vectorized using Term Frequency-Inverse Document Frequency (TF-IDF) and compared to job descriptions using Cosine Similarity. A Random Forest classifier further improves the accuracy of resume-job relevance scoring by learning from historical data. Developed using Python and integrated with MongoDB, this solution ensures flexible data storage and real-time retrieval. The model was evaluated using precision, recall, F1-score, and Mean Reciprocal Rank (MRR), demonstrating its superiority over traditional ATS in both accuracy and reliability. This system ensures equitable candidate evaluation and streamlines recruitment by ranking resumes based on contextual relevance rather than superficial keyword presence.

Keywords: Resume screening, NLP, named entity recognition, TF-IDF, candidate ranking, machine learning, recruitment automation

1. Introduction

The recruitment process has witnessed significant transformation with the advent of digital tools, yet many organizations still struggle with the shortcomings of traditional applicant tracking systems. These systems often use rule-based keyword searches that do not consider the context in which a term appears, leading to inaccurate or biased candidate shortlisting. A promising alternative lies in adopting Natural Language Processing (NLP) combined with machine learning to offer a deeper understanding of resume content [3, 5]. This paper introduces an automated resume screening system that leverages SpaCy's NER module to extract structured candidate information from unstructured text [9]. It identifies entities like programming languages, degrees, job roles, certifications, and employers. Once identified, the system uses TF-IDF to vectorize the resumes and job descriptions, enabling the calculation of relevance scores using Cosine Similarity [11]. This methodology allows recruiters to shortlist applicants based on true alignment with job requirements rather than on arbitrary keyword hits. Moreover, a machine learning classifier, trained on past recruitment decisions, refines the ranking to reflect real-world hiring patterns [1, 8]. This introduction outlines the motivation, necessity, and technological backbone for a smarter, fairer hiring system. By aligning resumes with job expectations more accurately, our approach addresses both efficiency and ethical considerations in recruitment [4, 20].

2. Literature Survey

A review of existing literature shows that early resume filtering systems predominantly relied on rule-based techniques, which proved limited in scope. These systems performed exact keyword matching and failed to account for the semantic relationships between terms. For example, a candidate proficient in "data analysis" might be overlooked if a job description only mentions "analytics" [6]. Recent advancements in NLP have addressed this limitation by introducing Named Entity Recognition (NER), which helps systems recognize structured data such as job titles, institutions, and qualifications [12, 14]. Tools like SpaCy have emerged as industry standards for their accuracy and ease of use in entity extraction [9]. Similarly, TF-IDF and Cosine Similarity are proven techniques in information retrieval and text mining, enabling contextual matching between documents [10, 11]. Several studies have demonstrated the effectiveness of combining these techniques with machine learning algorithms such as Support Vector Machines (SVM), Logistic Regression, and Random Forests for candidate classification [1, 2, 13]. These models are particularly effective in recognizing complex relationships between resume content and job requirements [7, 16]. Research also highlights the growing need for fairness and transparency in AI-based recruitment systems [4, 20]. There is an emphasis on reducing algorithmic bias, maintaining ethical standards, and creating inclusive datasets for model training [15, 17]. Our system is

[a]praveenacse11@gmail.com, [b]arasulingam.7639@gmail.com, [c]Puvirajan.off@gmail.com, [d]dineshk04811@gmail.com, [e]bavankumar0105@gmail.com, [f]varunraj1031@gmail.com, [g]saruganeshg@gmail.com

DOI: 10.1201/9781003724988-53

built on these findings, with added components for feedback learning and scalable deployment using cloud platforms.

3. Methodology

The development of our resume ranking system is divided into several key phases, each contributing to the system's accuracy and usability. The initial phase involves collecting resumes in various formats including PDF and DOCX from online job portals and HR departments. These resumes are converted into machine-readable text using PyMuPDF, a Python-based library that ensures text extraction across diverse formatting standards [19]. In the preprocessing stage, unnecessary characters such as punctuation and special symbols are removed. Tokenization, lemmatization, and case normalization are then performed using SpaCy to standardize textual data [9] (Figure 53.1).

The processed text undergoes Named Entity Recognition to identify critical entities, which are categorized into skills, degrees, work experience, and certifications [12]. These attributes form the foundational features of each resume. TF-IDF is applied to these features to create weighted term vectors that represent the importance of each word in the context of the entire dataset [11]. Cosine Similarity is then used to compare these vectors with those derived from job descriptions [7]. To improve ranking robustness, we train a Random Forest classifier using labeled resume-job description pairs [1, 8]. The classifier outputs a relevance score for each resume, which is then used to produce a ranked list. MongoDB serves as the backend for storing both raw resumes and structured data, allowing fast queries and scalable deployment [19]. The frontend allows HR professionals to upload job descriptions and instantly retrieve ranked applicant lists, making it both user-friendly and efficient (Figure 53.2).

4. Results and Evaluation

To evaluate the performance of our system, we created a test set comprising resumes and their associated job descriptions

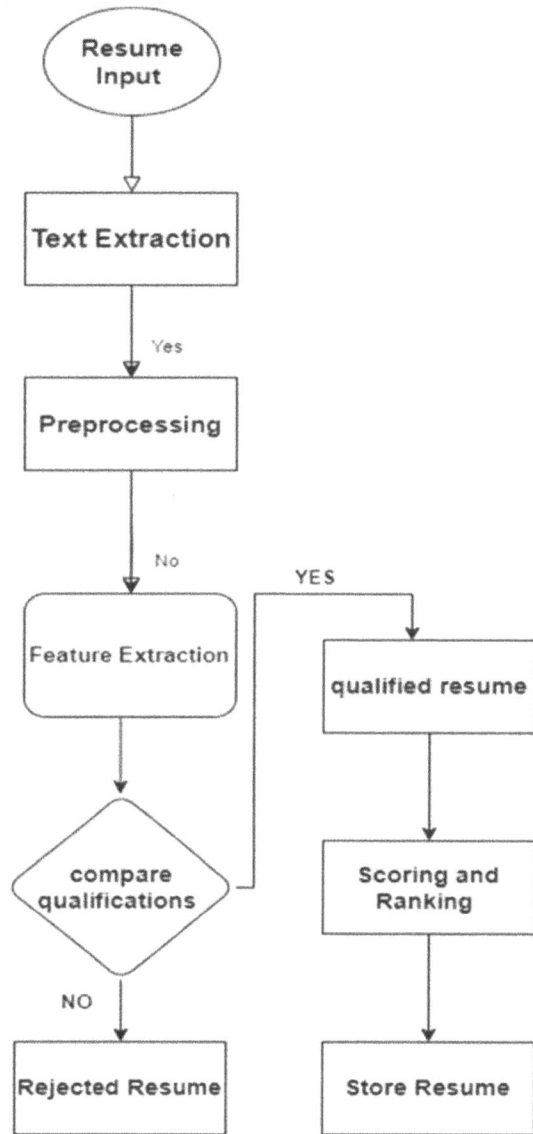

Figure 53.2. Flow diagram of resume analysis for recruitment.
Source: Author.

with known levels of match quality. The machine learning model was trained on 80% of this dataset and tested on the remaining 20%. Accuracy alone was not considered sufficient, so we used multiple evaluation metrics including precision, recall, and F1-score [18]. Precision indicates the proportion of correctly ranked resumes among the top results, while recall shows how many relevant resumes were captured overall (Figure 53.3). Our model achieved a precision of 89%, a recall of 85%, and an F1-score of 87%.

These metrics suggest a balanced performance with minimal trade-offs. We also calculated the Mean Reciprocal Rank (MRR) to assess the likelihood of a relevant resume appearing in the top position; the high MRR score confirmed the model's capability to prioritize top talent effectively [18]. In addition to quantitative testing, qualitative validation was conducted by sharing system outputs with HR professionals.

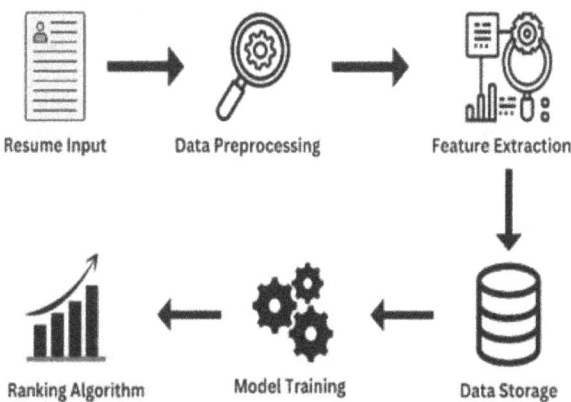

Figure 53.1. Architecture diagram for resume analysis.
Source: Author.

Feedback highlighted the ease of use and improved accuracy over existing tools (Figure 53.4).

Furthermore, the system's ability to handle resumes with varied formatting and content structures showed its robustness. Comparative analysis with keyword-based filters revealed a 30% improvement in relevant candidate identification [2]. These results affirm the effectiveness and practical utility of our proposed solution (Figure 53.5).

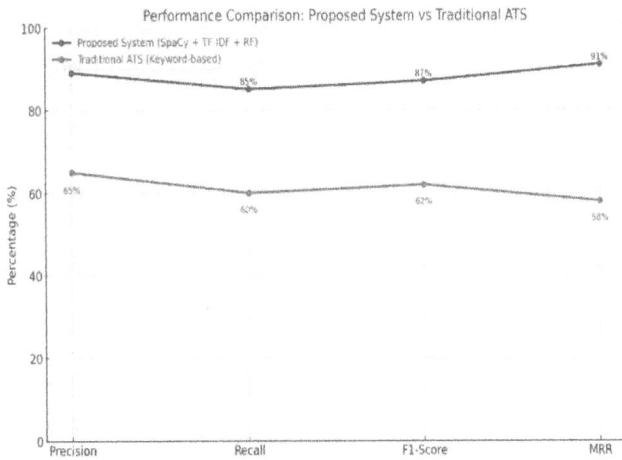

Figure 53.3. Performance comparison.

Source: Author.

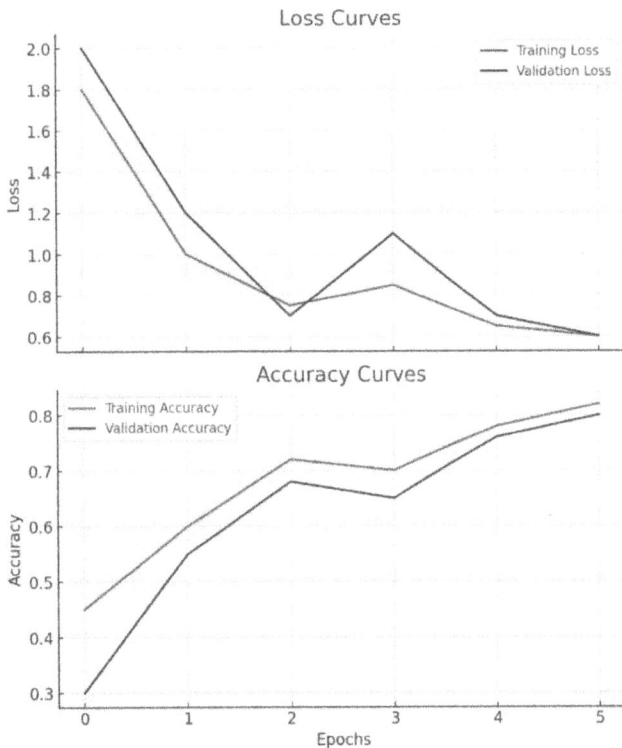

Figure 53.4. Accuracy and loss curves.

Source: Author.

Applied Candidates   X

No.	Name	Matching %
1	Arasulingam T	71.67
2	Dineshkumar	68.37
3	Puvirajan	65.23
4	Thilak	62.83
5	Tilak	58.3
6	Ajith	55.89

Figure 53.5. Ranked resumes of candidates.

Source: Author.

5. Conclusion

The proposed resume ranking system combines the strengths of NLP and machine learning to overcome the limitations of traditional applicant screening methods. By using SpaCy's NER, the system effectively identifies and extracts structured information from resumes [9, 12], allowing a deeper analysis of candidate qualifications. TF-IDF vectorization and Cosine Similarity enable semantic comparisons with job descriptions [11], while a Random Forest model adds predictive power for final ranking [1, 14]. The results from our evaluations demonstrate superior performance in terms of precision, recall, and relevance compared to conventional systems [18]. Moreover, the solution is designed for flexibility, allowing it to integrate seamlessly with existing HR workflows or function as a standalone tool. One of the significant contributions of this research is its focus on fair and objective screening, promoting diversity and minimizing human bias [4, 20]. In future work, we plan to explore deep learning models such as BERT to enhance contextual understanding further [6, 13]. We also aim to introduce an adaptive learning mechanism where the system evolves based on recruiter feedback and hiring outcomes. Additionally, expanding the dataset with resumes from diverse industries will help generalize the model further. Ultimately, our system provides a reliable, scalable, and ethical approach to resume screening in the modern recruitment landscape.

References

[1] IEEE. (2024). Resume Matching Framework via Ranking and Sorting Using NLP and Deep Learning. In *IEEE Conference Publication*. Available: https://ieeexplore.ieee.org/document/10286605.

[2] IEEE. (2024). Resume Screening using NLP and LSTM. In *IEEE Conference Publication*. Available:https://ieeexplore.ieee.org/abstract/document/9850889.

[3] IEEE. (2024). Automated Resume Parsing: A Natural Language Processing Approach. In *IEEE Conference Publication*. Available: https://ieeexplore.ieee.org/document/10334236.

[4] IEEE. (2024). Ethical Considerations in AI-Based Recruitment. In *IEEE Conference Publication*. Available: https://ieeex-plore.ieee.org/document/8937920.

[5] IEEE. (2024). The Role of Artificial Intelligence in Recruitment Process Decision-Making. In *IEEE Conference Publication*. Available: https://ieeexplore.ieee.org/document/9682320.

[6] Zhang, Z. (2023). Deep learning approaches for text classification. *Journal of Machine Learning Research*, *18*(5), 1–43.

[7] Liu, X., & Chen, Y. (2023). Semantic Matching for Recruitment Using Natural Language Processing. In *International Conference on Computational Linguistics*, pp. 2765–2775.

[8] Wang, L., & Li, D. (2022). Application of Machine Learning in Resume Screening. *Journal of AI Research*, *23*(2), 34–47.

[9] Smith, J. (2021). SpaCy for NLP and Text Analytics. *NLP Review*, *15*(3), 76–89.

[10] Miller, C. (2021). Impact of AI on Job Matching and Recruitment Automation. In *Proceedings of the International Conference on AI in HR*, pp.123–135.

[11] Gupta, H. (2020). TF-IDF and cosine similarity for document similarity. *Journal of Data Science*, *12*(2), 45–57.

[12] Johnson, A. (2019). Named Entity Recognition in Job Recruitment. In *International NLP Symposium*, pp. 222–230.

[13] Martinez, D. (2019). Data-driven decision-making in HR using machine learning. *Journal of Human Resource Analytics*, *10*(4), 411–429.

[14] Anderson, B. (2018). Automated text classification for resume screening. *IEEE Transactions on AI*, *16*(3), 300–312.

[15] Patel, S. (2018). Natural language processing for automated HR tasks. *HR Tech Journal*, *14*(1), 55–66.

[16] Kumar, R. (2018). Improving Applicant Tracking Systems with AI. In *Proceedings of the International Conference on AI in Business*, pp.432–445.

[17] Green, M. (2017). NER and text classification in recruiting platforms. *Artificial Intelligence in Recruitment Journal*, *9*(2), 125–140.

[18] Collins, P. (2017). Evaluation metrics in resume screening models. *Journal of Machine Learning Metrics*, *3*(1), 80–95.

[19] James, E. (2019). Python Libraries for NLP in HR Analytics. In *NLP for Business Applications Conference*, 2016, pp. 23–36.

[20] Brown, T. (2016). AI ethics in HR and recruitment. *Journal of AI Ethics*, *5*(4), 310–325.

54 Automated drainage tracking system

K. Revathy[a], S. Linkesh, N. Naveen, J. Jeevan, R. Radhee, B. Monika, and R. Aniruth

Department of Computer Science and Engineering, Manakula Vinayagar Institute of Technology, Kalitheerthalkuppam, Puducherry, India

Abstract: This paper presents a novel integrated approach to infrastructure management through the development and implementation of a dual-system framework that combines a drainage cap monitoring system with a gas pressure measuring system. The drainage cap monitoring system leverages advanced sensor technology and real-time data analytics to continuously assess the condition of drainage caps, detecting movements and anomalies that could indicate potential system failures or environmental risks. Concurrently, the gas pressure measuring system utilizes high-precision sensors to monitor and regulate gas pressure within pipelines and storage facilities, ensuring compliance with safety standards and operational efficiency. By integrating these systems into a unified framework, this approach aims to enhance operational reliability, preemptively address potential hazards, and facilitate proactive maintenance strategies. The proposed solution offers a comprehensive methodology for improving infrastructure management, contributing to a more resilient and sustainable infrastructure network.

Keywords: ESP 32, IR sensor, gas detector

1. Introduction

In the realm of infrastructure management, ensuring the safety, reliability, and operational efficiency of essential systems is a growing challenge [1]. To address these concerns, this paper introduces an innovative dual-system framework designed to enhance infrastructure monitoring and management. By combining a drainage cap monitoring system with a gas pressure measuring system, this approach offers a more holistic and integrated solution, aiming to identify potential hazards early and streamline maintenance efforts. The framework leverages the strengths of real-time data analytics and advanced sensor technologies to provide continuous oversight of critical infrastructure components [2].

The first component of the dual-system framework is the drainage cap monitoring system, which utilizes cutting-edge sensor technology to monitor the condition of drainage caps in real time. This system can detect movements and anomalies, such as shifts in cap positioning or signs of wear and tear, that could signal underlying system failures or environmental risks. By continuously assessing drainage caps, this monitoring system helps preempt potential issues before they escalate into costly repairs or environmental damage, improving the overall resilience of drainage systems [3].

Alongside the drainage cap monitoring system, the second component of the framework focuses on gas pressure management within pipelines and storage facilities. The gas pressure measuring system integrates high-precision sensors to ensure that gas pressure remains within safe and operational limits. This system not only ensures compliance with safety standards but also enhances operational efficiency by regulating gas flow in real time. By doing so, it minimizes the risk of gas leaks or pipeline failures, which could lead to hazardous situations.

By integrating these two systems into a unified framework, this approach provides infrastructure managers with a powerful tool for proactive maintenance and risk management. The real-time data collected by both systems allows for early detection of issues, enabling prompt interventions before failures occur. Ultimately, the proposed solution fosters a more resilient and sustainable infrastructure network, supporting both operational reliability and environmental safety.

The ESP32 is a powerful and versatile system-on-chip (SoC) designed for Internet of Things (IoT) applications, featuring integrated Wi-Fi and Bluetooth capabilities. At its core, the ESP32 has a dual-core Tensilica LX6 microprocessor, which allows it to handle high-priority tasks, such as Wi-Fi and Bluetooth communication, while simultaneously running user programs. It can operate at clock speeds up to 240 MHz, making it suitable for real-time data processing and control. The built-in Wi-Fi supports 802.11 b/g/n standards, enabling it to connect seamlessly to the internet, while its Bluetooth 4.2 and Bluetooth Low Energy (BLE) capabilities allow communication with other devices or integration into BLE ecosystems. The ESP32 has extensive input/output (I/O) capabilities, including GPIO, PWM, ADC, and serial communication interfaces like UART, SPI, and I2C,

[a]nivethaasree.km14@gmail.com

DOI: 10.1201/9781003724988-54

making it compatible with a wide range of sensors, displays, and external peripherals. It can be programmed using various environments such as the Arduino IDE or ESP-IDF, and supports Over-The-Air (OTA) updates, allowing users to update firmware remotely. Additionally, the ESP32 has multiple power-saving modes, including deep sleep and light sleep, which make it ideal for battery-powered applications. Its ability to monitor analog inputs and digital signals even in low-power states, combined with built-in security features like SSL/TLS encryption, makes the ESP32 a popular choice for smart home devices, wearable technology, and industrial IoT applications.

In this dual-system framework, the ESP32 plays a key role in the functioning of both the drainage cap monitoring system and the gas pressure measuring system. The ESP32, equipped with integrated Wi-Fi and Bluetooth capabilities, acts as the central controller, receiving data from various sensors. In the drainage cap monitoring system, the ESP32 is connected to advanced sensors that continuously assess the condition of drainage caps by detecting movements, shifts, or anomalies. These sensors provide real-time data to the ESP32, which then processes and transmits the information to a central system for analysis and alerts.

Similarly, in the gas pressure measuring system, high-precision pressure sensors are connected to the ESP32, allowing it to monitor gas pressure in pipelines and storage facilities. The ESP32 processes the sensor data, ensuring that pressure levels are within safe operational limits, and communicates with control systems to adjust pressure as needed. Additionally, the ESP32's real-time data analytics and connectivity features enable proactive maintenance by sending alerts when anomalies or potential hazards are detected, helping ensure both operational efficiency and safety compliance.

An infrared (IR) sensor works by emitting infrared light and detecting the reflection or interruption of that light to identify objects or measure distances. It consists of an IR transmitter, typically an LED, that emits infrared radiation, and an IR receiver, like a photodiode or phototransistor, that detects the reflected light from nearby objects. When an object is within the sensor's range, it reflects the emitted IR light, which is captured by the receiver, triggering a signal. IR sensors are commonly used for object detection, proximity sensing, and even temperature measurement. They are energy-efficient and widely applied in devices like remote controls, obstacle-detecting robots, and automatic lighting systems.

In the context of the dual-system framework, an IR sensor could play a vital role in monitoring both the drainage cap system and the gas pressure system by detecting physical movements and anomalies. For the drainage cap monitoring system, an IR sensor could be positioned near the drainage cap to continuously emit infrared light and detect any reflected light changes caused by cap displacement or surface movement. If the cap shifts or an object interferes with its proper positioning, the change in reflected infrared light would trigger an alert via the system.

In the gas pressure monitoring system, an IR sensor could be used for non-contact temperature measurements of gas pipelines, as temperature variations can be an indicator of pressure changes or potential leaks. By continuously detecting these changes through infrared emissions, the sensor helps maintain safe operational limits. The IR sensor's ability to provide real-time feedback to the central ESP32 unit ensures proactive maintenance and operational efficiency within the unified infrastructure framework.

A gas detection sensor works by identifying the presence and concentration of specific gases in the environment, typically through chemical reactions or changes in electrical resistance. These sensors often use materials like metal-oxide semiconductors (MOS) or electrochemical cells to detect gases such as carbon monoxide, methane, or hydrogen. When the target gas comes into contact with the sensor, it causes a measurable change in the sensor's electrical properties, triggering a signal. This data is then processed to determine gas concentration levels. Gas detection sensors are widely used in industrial safety systems, residential monitoring, and environmental applications, providing real-time alerts to prevent hazardous conditions, such as gas leaks or toxic gas buildup.

In the proposed dual-system framework, a gas detection sensor plays a critical role in the gas pressure monitoring system by detecting and analyzing the presence of hazardous gases in pipelines or storage facilities. The sensor continuously monitors for specific gases, such as methane or carbon monoxide, using chemical or electrochemical methods. When the target gas is detected, the sensor experiences a change in its electrical properties, which is processed in real time by the system. This information is transmitted to a central processing unit, like the ESP32, which evaluates the gas concentration and triggers safety alerts or adjustments to ensure gas levels remain within safe operating limits. By integrating this sensor into the overall framework, the system can proactively identify potential leaks or hazardous conditions, enhancing operational safety and enabling timely maintenance interventions to prevent failures or environmental risks.

2. Related Literature

This paper examines how flood discharge from upstream rivers influences tidal dynamics at the Power Plant drainage project in Lianyungang by analyzing the local hydrological environment and validating a two-dimensional tidal current model. The findings reveal that flood discharge leads to weak circulating currents during flood tide and an increase in current velocity of 0.10 to 1.2 m/s during ebb tide, with a maximum tidal level rise of approximately 0.12 m observed at units 1 and 2 [1]. This study finds that while concrete ditches are the most polluted, brick ditches effectively remove nutrients and control weeds, making them the preferred choice for irrigation and drainage to minimize water pollution and prevent secondary pollution from decaying plants [2]. This research establishes a two-dimensional hydrodynamic model to assess the flood control and drainage strategies for the Shenzhen Ocean New City project, ensuring drainage safety during construction and recommending measures to mitigate adverse effects on flood management [4].

This study utilizes FEFLOW numerical simulation to evaluate the effectiveness of a short path groundwater circulation method for reinjecting drained water in open pit coal mines, analyzing the impact of well configurations on drainage efficiency while maintaining groundwater balance and minimizing environmental damage [5]. This system employs a wireless sensor network to monitor drainage conditions in real-time, enabling timely alerts for municipal officers about potential blockages, thereby enhancing public health, reducing mosquito-borne diseases, and improving overall sanitation and safety [6]. The system utilizes a wireless sensor network for real-time monitoring of drainage systems, providing prompt notifications to municipal authorities to address blockages and improve public health and sanitation [7]. This study examines how transformer oil temperature affects the stability of foam extinguishing agents, finding that synthetic foam demonstrates superior oil and heat resistance [8–9], maintaining longer drainage times and optimal stability compared to aqueous film forming foam and fluorinated-protein foam [10].

This study develops a 3-D finite element model to analyze seepage flow in the powerhouse foundation of the Jinnah Hydropower Station, ultimately proposing an optimized drainage system involving surface drainage ditches and a high-pressure jet grouting cut-off wall to enhance construction-stage drainage efficiency [11]. This research introduces a fault diagnosis method for coal mine drainage systems that combines fault tree analysis and Bayesian networks, enhanced by fuzzy set theory, resulting in a system-level model that improves diagnosis accuracy to 83.5%, outperforming traditional methods by 10.3% [12]. This research employs EPA SWMM 5.0 to model stormwater runoff in urban settings, aiming to determine the relationship between pump flux and waterlogging storage volume, thereby demonstrating the effectiveness of computer simulations and automated designs in optimizing urban drainage systems [13].

This project develops an automatic drainage cleaning system that utilizes ultrasonic sensors and Node MCU to detect waste levels, sending alerts via the Blynk application to municipal personnel for timely waste removal, thereby enhancing efficiency and reducing manual labour in sewage management [14]. The Drainage Control and Water Monitoring System leverages advanced technology for real-time monitoring and management of urban drainage systems, enhancing infrastructure reliability, ensuring worker safety, and contributing to the development of sustainable smart cities [15].

3. Existing System

Existing infrastructure management systems often function with a segmented approach, utilizing separate technologies for monitoring drainage and gas pressure, which can lead to inefficiencies and delayed responses to potential issues. Traditional drainage monitoring methods typically rely on basic float switches or manual inspections to assess the condition of drainage caps. These approaches often lack real-time capabilities, making it difficult to detect movements or anomalies that could signal failures. As a result, operators may not be aware of deteriorating conditions until they escalate into more significant problems, leading to costly repairs and environmental risks [16].

On the other hand, gas pressure monitoring systems frequently employ standalone gauges that require manual readings at scheduled intervals. While these systems may provide essential data on gas pressure levels, they often do not offer real-time monitoring or automated alerts. This limitation can result in gaps in data continuity, increasing the risk of safety violations or operational inefficiencies. Moreover, because these systems operate independently, they cannot easily correlate data across drainage and gas pressure metrics, which is essential for a comprehensive understanding of infrastructure health [17].

The lack of integration in these existing systems means that operators are often faced with fragmented data streams, making it challenging to perform effective analysis or identify trends. For instance, a drop in gas pressure might be related to a drainage issue, but without integrated data, operators may miss this critical connection. This separation can lead to a reactive maintenance approach, where issues are only addressed after they have already impacted operations, further exacerbating risks to safety and compliance.

Overall, the existing infrastructure management systems highlight the need for a more cohesive and integrated approach. The challenges associated with segmented monitoring underscore the importance of real-time data analytics and proactive maintenance strategies. As urban environments face increasing demands and complexities, adopting an integrated dual-system framework can significantly enhance operational reliability, safety, and overall infrastructure sustainability. This transition is essential for addressing the evolving challenges of infrastructure management in today's dynamic landscape.

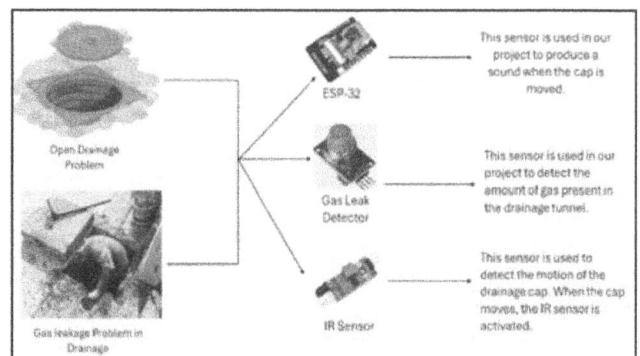

Figure 54.1. Automated drainage tracking system.

Source: Author.

4. Proposed System

The proposed integrated system combines a drainage cap monitoring framework with a gas pressure measurement solution, creating a robust infrastructure management tool that addresses multiple critical needs simultaneously. The drainage cap monitoring system utilizes advanced sensor technology, such as accelerometers and strain gauges, to continuously assess the structural integrity of drainage caps. These sensors can detect subtle movements and irregularities, feeding real-time data into a centralized analytics platform. By employing machine learning algorithms, the system can analyze historical data patterns, enabling predictive maintenance that identifies potential failures before they occur. This proactive approach helps mitigate risks associated with drainage failures and environmental hazards.

In parallel, the gas pressure measuring system employs high-precision sensors strategically placed within pipelines and storage facilities. These sensors continuously monitor gas pressure levels, ensuring that they remain within safe operational limits. The system is designed to automatically trigger alerts when pressure anomalies are detected, allowing operators to respond swiftly to potential issues. Furthermore, the gas pressure system integrates with existing safety protocols, ensuring compliance with industry regulations and enhancing overall safety measures. By merging these two functionalities, the proposed solution fosters a comprehensive understanding of infrastructure health (Figure 54.1).

The unified framework is accessible via a centralized dashboard, providing operators with real-time insights into both drainage and gas pressure conditions. This interface allows for seamless data visualization, enabling users to track performance metrics, receive alerts, and generate reports. The dashboard also includes analytical tools that facilitate the identification of trends and potential risk factors, enhancing decision-making capabilities. By consolidating data from both systems, operators can gain a holistic view of infrastructure performance, leading to more informed maintenance and operational strategies. Ultimately, this integrated approach not only enhances operational reliability but also supports sustainable infrastructure management. By leveraging real-time data and predictive analytics, the proposed system minimizes unplanned outages and extends the lifespan of critical assets. The ability to address issues proactively reduces maintenance costs and improves overall system resilience. In a landscape where infrastructure is increasingly challenged by aging systems and environmental concerns, this dual-system framework offers a forward-thinking solution that adapts to evolving needs and ensures a safer, more efficient infrastructure network.

5. Conclusion

In conclusion, the proposed integrated dual-system framework for infrastructure management represents a significant advancement in monitoring and maintaining critical assets.

By combining a drainage cap monitoring system with a gas pressure measuring system, this approach not only enhances real-time data collection and analysis but also fosters proactive maintenance strategies. The ability to detect anomalies and potential failures before they escalate ensures greater operational reliability and safety, significantly reducing the risk of costly disruptions and environmental hazards.

Furthermore, the integration of these systems into a unified platform offers a holistic view of infrastructure health, enabling informed decision-making and efficient resource allocation. As urban environments continue to evolve and face increasing demands, adopting such innovative methodologies will be crucial for building resilient and sustainable infrastructure networks. This comprehensive approach not only addresses current challenges but also lays the groundwork for future advancements in infrastructure management, ensuring long-term safety and operational efficiency.

References

[1] Wendan, L., Mengguo, L., Zhiwen, Y., & Yuxin, H. (2018). *International Conference on Engineering Simulation and Intelligent Control (ESAIC)*. IEEE.

[2] Jiang, C., Zhu, L., Xie, X., Li, N., & Shi, N. (2008). *2nd International Conference on Bioinformatics and Biomedical Engineering*. IEEE.

[3] Tu, X. Y., Wu, M. W., Peng, J. F., Lu, C., & Deng, K. H. (2021, November). Study on Drainage Scheme and Safety Assessment during Construction of Land Forming Project in the Coastal Estuary Area. In *2021 7th International Conference on Hydraulic and Civil Engineering & Smart Water Conservancy and Intelligent Disaster Reduction Forum (ICHCE & SWIDR)* (pp. 1575–1581). IEEE.

[4] Ma, J., Liu, H., Shi, Y., & Zhang, H. (2022). *8th International Conference on Hydraulic and Civil Engineering: Deep Space Intelligent Development and Utilization Forum (ICHCE)*. IEEE.

[5] Haswani, N. G., & Deore, P. J. (2018). *Fourth International Conference on Computing Communication Control and Automation (ICCUBEA)*. IEEE.

[6] Li, X., Shang, S., Wang, L., Wang, Y., & Li, L. (2021, November). Assessment of Standard Syntaxis of Basin and Sub-basin Flood and Urban Drainage in Taihu Basin. In *2021 7th International Conference on Hydraulic and Civil Engineering & Smart Water Conservancy and Intelligent Disaster Reduction Forum (ICHCE & SWIDR)* (pp. 1783–1789). IEEE.

[7] Yang, X., Jin, X., & Zhou, Y. (2011). *International Conference on Remote Sensing, Environment and Transportation Engineering*. IEEE.

[8] Zhang, N., & Dong, H. (2007). *International Conference on Wireless Communications, Networking and Mobile Computing*. IEEE.

[9] Huang, S., Shang, F., Zhang, C., Zhang, C. C., Zhang, J., Kong, D., & Li, B. (2022). *7th Asia Conference on Power and Electrical Engineering (ACPEE)*. IEEE.

[10] He, C. (2011, July). Eco-efficiency evaluation of the water conservancy and hydropower project based on emergy analysis theory. In *2011 International Conference on Multimedia Technology* (pp. 4389–4393). IEEE.

[11] Shen, Z., Zheng, L., & Ma, X. (2012). *Asia-Pacific Power and Energy Engineering*. IEEE.

[12] Shi, X., Gu, H., & Yao, B. (2024). *IEEE Sensors, 24*(6). IEEE.

[13] Wei, C., Le, A., Kun, S., & Yuehua, F. (2009). International Conference on Energy and Environment Technology. IEEE.

[14] Nandini, Y., Vijaya Lakshmi, K., IndraSaiSrujan, T., Yasheswi, M., & Sri Jagadish, K. (2023). *7th International Conference on Computing Methodologies and Communication (ICCMC)*. IEEE.

[15] Gurulakshmi, A. B., Rajesh, G., Meghana, S., Leela Vara Prasad Reddy, Y. R., Jayanth, K., Sainath Reddy, K., Kumar, M.-C., & Veni, Y. (2024). *International Conference on Knowledge Engineering and Communication Systems (ICK-ECS)*. IEEE.

[16] Libing, Z., liang, C., Lida, H., & Juliang, J. (2008). *Chinese Control and Decision*. IEEE.

[17] Khan, M. F., Govender, P., & Swanson, A. G. (2024). *IEEE World Forum on Public Safety Technology (WFPST)*. IEEE.

55 Machine learning for environmental sustainability: Air quality prediction

Renga Nayagi R.[1,a], R. Sarabeswaran[2,b], R. Mukesh Kumar[2,c], G. Sridhar[2,d], A. Karthick Raja[2,e], and H. Unnimaya[2,f]

[1]Assistant Professor Department of AIML Manakula Vinayagar Institute of Technology, Puducherry, India
[2]UG Scholar Department of AIML Manakula Vinayagar Institute of Technology, Puducherry, India

Abstract: Forecasting air quality is essential for managing public health and reducing the harmful effects of air pollution. Through an analysis of historical data on air pollution and environmental factors, this study investigates the potential of machine learning techniques to anticipate air quality. The proposed model uses decision trees, random forests, linear regression, and deep learning networks, among other machine learning methods, to forecast pollutant concentrations including PM2.5, PM10, CO, NO2, and SO2. Air quality indices and external factors like temperature, humidity, wind speed, and atmospheric pressure may have complex relationships that the model may identify by utilizing data from government sensors and meteorological sources. Feature scaling and missing value resolution are two examples of data preparation techniques that guarantee high data quality for training. Additionally, in order to optimize model performance, we explore feature selection strategies by identifying significant aspects that impact air quality. Mean Absolute Error (MAE) and Root Mean Square Error (RMSE) are two assessment metrics that show the model's anticipated accuracy. The findings indicate that machine learning models, especially ensemble and deep learning techniques, provide promising accuracy and reliability for air quality forecasts over the short and long term. In order to improve air quality management and lessen the health risks associated with air pollution, this prediction model may be useful to policymakers, urban planners, and health organizations.

Keywords: PM2.5 and PM10 prediction, atmospheric pollutants, meteorological factor, predictive modeling, environmental data analysis, machine learning, air pollution forecasting, and feature engineering

1. Introduction

Air pollution has a major impact on ecosystems and human health, making it a global environmental and health concern. Premature mortality, cardiovascular and respiratory disorders, and other negative health effects have all been connected to poor air quality. Maintaining healthy air quality becomes more difficult as urban populations and industrial activity increase, especially in major cities. Public health reactions, policy direction, and early intervention can all be aided by air quality prediction. Local governments may optimize traffic and industrial emissions management, provide health advice, and send alerts by forecasting pollution incidents. Therefore, forecasting air quality accurately is essential for public health and creating plans for sustainable urban development [1].

The high degree of environmental variability and the complex, nonlinear interactions between various contaminants and meteorological factors provide challenges for traditional approaches of air quality prediction, such as statistical and physical models. For example, temperature, humidity, wind speed, and air pressure all affect pollutants like carbon monoxide (CO), nitrogen dioxide (NO2), sulfur dioxide (SO2), and particulate matter (PM2.5 and PM10). Because these connections are intricate and sometimes nonlinear, traditional methods have difficulty generating predictions [2].

Predicting air quality is made possible by machine learning (ML), which offers sophisticated skills for modeling intricate, nonlinear interactions within vast datasets. Machine learning algorithms can identify trends and connections that conventional approaches might overlook by learning from past data on pollution levels and meteorological conditions [3]. As additional data is gathered, these models may adjust to new information, increasing forecast relevance and accuracy.

2. Related Literature

Machine Learning Techniques for Air Quality Prediction [1]. Predicting PM2.5 Concentration using Machine Learning Techniques environmental science and pollution research.

This study demonstrates the predictive power of machine learning techniques like decision trees and support vector machines for PM2.5 concentrations. By contrasting many algorithms, it shows that ensemble techniques

[a]ayagirennga3@gmail.com, [b]sarabaramanathan@gmail.com, [c]mukeshkumar220305@gmail.com, [d]gsridharvpm@gmail.com, [e]karthickonstrike@gmail.com, [f]unnimayahnambiar55@gmail.com

DOI: 10.1201/9781003724988-55

perform better than traditional models in terms of prediction accuracy [2]. Utilizing a Deep Learning Architecture to Forecast Air Quality in Smart Cities sensors. This work offers a deep learning model for predicting the quality of the air in cities. In order to anticipate air quality, it discusses how effectively deep neural networks (DNNs) and recurrent neural networks (RNNs) handle time-series data and capture temporal correlations.

Including Pollution and Weather Data in Prediction Models In [3] Di, Q., Zanobetti, A., and Wang, Y. Modeling air pollution via machine learning techniques and high-resolution from satellite data.

2.1. Views on environmental health

The use of satellite data for high-resolution air quality modeling is examined in this paper. It uses a machine-learning model for PM2.5 prediction that takes into account a number of meteorological variables, including temperature and humidity.

The study demonstrates that integrating pollution and weather data enhances the model's capacity to represent changes in air quality [4].

Forecasting spatiotemporal air quality using machine learning and big data. The study of the entire environment.

In addition to examining the use of big data approaches in conjunction with machine learning for multi-city air quality forecasting, this research emphasizes the significance of spatiotemporal data in air quality prediction. In order to enhance spatiotemporal forecasting, the paper talks about utilizing recurrent neural networks (RNNs) with geospatial, meteorological, and air pollution data.

Predicting Air Quality via Collective Learning [5]. Improving Air Quality Prediction using Ensemble Learning and Data Fusion Techniques. atmospheric circumstances.

This work uses ensemble learning methods, such as random forests and gradient boosting, to evaluate air quality. It shows how combining several learning approaches may improve prediction robustness and reduce errors in PM2.5 and NO2 forecasting when compared to solo models [6]. A Comprehensive Approach to Air Quality Prediction Using Ensemble and Hybrid Machine Learning Techniques, Environmental Assessment and Monitoring [7–9].

In order to improve the accuracy of air quality predictions, the study looks at hybrid and ensemble approaches, such as random forest regressors and stacking models. The authors demonstrate how these methods capture nonlinear correlations between pollution levels and meteorological data, leading to improved performance.

This work explores the use of machine learning models to real-time air quality prediction and monitoring in smart city infrastructure. It examines how predictive algorithms may support health management by promoting preventative actions and providing residents with early warnings.

2.2. Key insights from literature

Machine Learning Superiority: Because machine learning models can handle high-dimensional data and nonlinearity, research continuously demonstrates that they perform better than standard statistical models.

The Value of Temporal and Spatial Data Combining weather data and spatial information improves model fidelity, especially in intricate urban settings.

Effectiveness of Ensemble and Hybrid Models: By mitigating the biases of individual models and managing a greater range of data variability, ensemble learning approaches frequently produce the most accurate predictions.

Deep Learning for Time-Series Data: Recurrent neural networks, such as LSTM, are very good at identifying long-term relationships and temporal patterns in time-series air quality data.

Implications for Public Health and Policy: By offering short- term and real-time forecasts, machine learning models assist public health management by facilitating data-driven policy choices and public alerts.

3. Proposed System Work

Information Gathering Collecting pertinent information from several sources, including: Pollutant Concentration Data: Usually gathered by government monitoring stations or sensor networks, these measurements include air pollutants such as PM2.5, PM10, CO, NO2, SO2, and O3 (Figure 55.1).

Meteorological Data: Weather factors such as temperature, humidity, wind direction, wind speed, and atmospheric pressure that affect air quality. Optional geospatial data: When dealing with several sites, information on the geographic features of each place may be used to capture pollution level differences dependent on location.

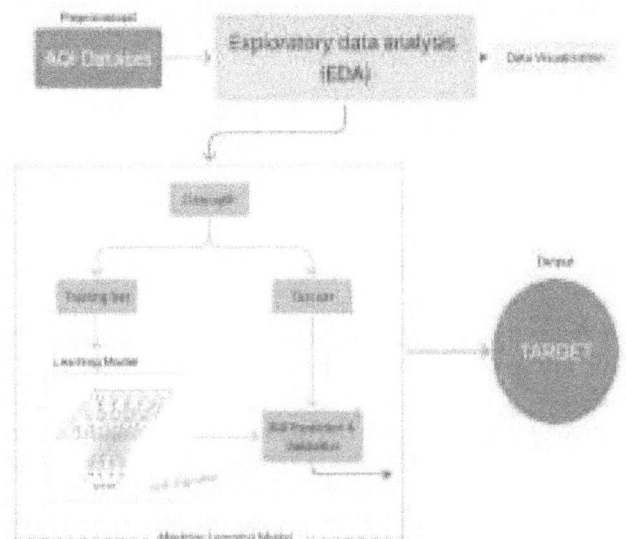

Figure 55.1. Machine learning model.

Source: Author.

Data can be gathered via satellite data, government and environmental agency APIs, or already datasets (like the emotion detection FER-2013 dataset). Depending on the data available, this study may concentrate on one city or several cities.

3.1. Data preprocessing

To enhance model performance, air quality data must be cleaned and pre-processed since it frequently contains missing values or anomalies brought on by sensor errors: Data cleaning:

It involves eliminating duplicates and handling missing values (e.g., by interpolating, filling in with median or mean values, or deleting incomplete entries).

Normalization and Scaling: To guarantee that the model handles every feature equally and prevents any domination by variables with greater ranges, scale meteorological and pollutant data to a similar range (for example, 0 to 1).

Feature Engineering: To minimize dimensionality, eliminate duplicate features and extract new pertinent features (such as lagged versions of pollutants to capture temporal dependencies).

If required, label encoding involves transforming categorical variables—like weather or location identifiers—into numerical representations that may be used to train models.

3.2. Selection of features

By concentrating on the variables that have the most predictive potential, choosing pertinent features (variables) increases model accuracy. Finding the features that most contribute to air quality prediction is made easier with the use of techniques like recursive feature reduction, Principal Component Analysis (PCA), and correlation analysis.

3.3. Choosing and training models

Choosing appropriate machine learning models to forecast air quality is part of the study. A number of algorithms can be used and contrasted:

For straightforward situations with little nonlinearity, linear regression is helpful; nevertheless, it may not work well with more complicated data.

Random Forests and Decision Trees: These tree-based techniques work well with non-linear and complicated data. In example, random forests reduce overfitting by merging many decision trees, which adds robustness.

By fixing mistakes in earlier model predictions, the ensemble techniques Gradient Boosting and XG Boost are effective for predictive tasks and can produce high accuracy.

Neural Networks (Deep Learning): Time series prediction can benefit from the usage of Convolutional Neural Networks (CNNs) and Long Short-Term Memory (LSTM) networks.

LSTMs are perfect for air quality forecasting because they are very good at capturing long-term dependencies.

A subset of the gathered data is used to train each model on the training dataset. Model parameters are optimized for increased accuracy using hyperparameter tuning approaches like grid search and random search.

3.4. Assessment of the model

Several criteria are used to assess the model in order to guarantee the accuracy of the predictions:

MAE, or mean absolute error: provides a straightforward indicator of accuracy by calculating the average difference between expected and actual numbers.

Large prediction mistakes are highlighted by the Root Mean Square Error (RMSE), which makes it appropriate when major forecast deviations need to be minimized.

R-Squared (R^2): Evaluates how well the model explains data variance; values nearer 1 denote a better match.

The most accurate and dependable model is chosen for deployment by comparing these criteria across models.

3.5. Prediction and deployment

The top-performing model can be utilized for predictions in the future or in real time once it has been trained. In deployment, it would function as follows:

Gathering Input Data: Real-time or recent weather and pollution data from sensors or API sources are fed into the model.

Preprocessing Data: Scaling, normalization, and other preprocessing procedures are applied to the fresh input data just as they do to the training data.

Prediction Generation: The model produces forecasts for AQI and/or air pollutant levels, which may be shown to the public on dashboards or in mobile application.

Time-Series Graphs: Showing pollutant concentrations over time to highlight patterns and trends (Figure 55.2).

Heatmaps: Illustrating the spatial distribution of pollution across different locations is especially helpful if the model works on multiple cities (Figure 55.3).

Prediction vs. Actual Graphs: Comparing model predictions with actual pollutant levels to validate and monitor model performance.

4. Conclusion

This study demonstrates how machine learning may be applied to improve proactive environmental management and offer precise air quality forecasts. By merging meteorological and pollutant concentration data, machine learning systems can capture complex, nonlinear connections affecting air quality. Models like decision trees, random forests, and neural networks especially LSTM for time-series data show promising results when it comes to pollutant level forecasting, enabling precise and timely forecasts.

The project's results may be used to enhance public health by alerting people when pollution levels are high,

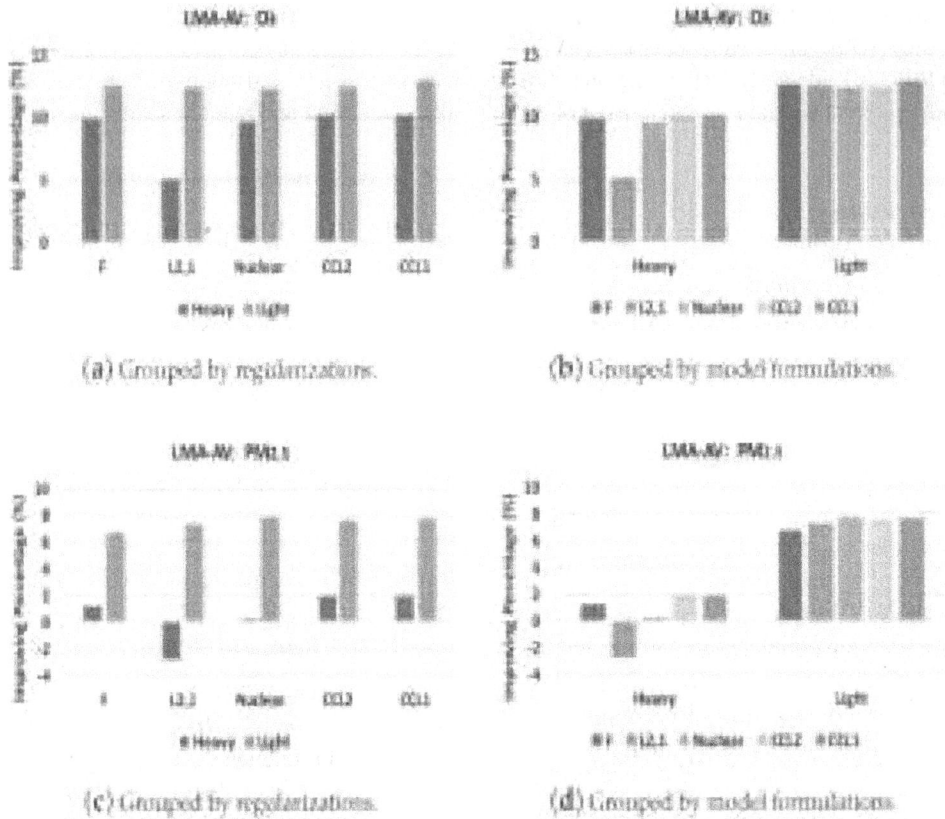

Figure 55.2. Visualizing results.

Source: Author.

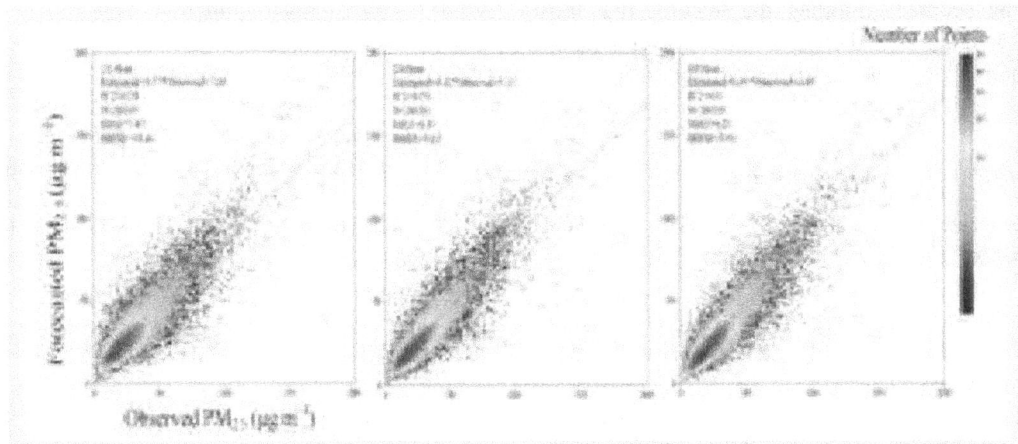

Figure 55.3. Model predictions with actual pollutant level.

Source: Author.

assisting legislators in enacting sensible environmental laws, and assisting urban planners in creating sustainable cities with better air quality. The prediction system is a useful tool for continuing environmental protection efforts because it can adjust to shifting pollutant dynamics through real-time data updates and continual model refinement.

References

[1]   Méndez, M., Merayo, M. G., & Núñez, M. (2023). Machine learning algorithms to forecast air quality: a survey. *Artificial Intelligence Review, 56*(9), 10031–10066.

[2]   Rahman, M. M., Nayeem, M. E. H., Ahmed, M. S., Tanha, K. A., Sakib, M. S. A., Uddin, K. M. M., & Babu, H. M. H.

(2024). AirNet: predictive machine learning model for air quality forecasting using web interface. *Environmental Systems Research, 13*(1), 44.

[3] Liang, Y. C., Maimury, Y., Chen, A. H. L., & Juarez, J. R. C. (2020). Machine learning-based prediction of air quality. *Applied Sciences, 10*(24), 9151.

[4] Bhushan, M., Dawar, I., Sharma, S., Bawaniya, T. K., Anand, U., & Negi, A. (2023, August). Air quality prediction using machine learning and deep learning: an exploratory study. In *2023 7th International Conference On Computing, Communication, Control And Automation (ICCUBEA)* (pp. 1–6). IEEE.

[5] Kumar, R., Kumar, P., & Kumar, Y. (2020). Time series data prediction using IoT and machine learning technique. *Procedia computer science, 167*, 373–381.

[6] Rowley, A., & Karakuş, O. (2023). Predicting air quality via multimodal AI and satellite imagery. *Remote Sensing of Environment, 293*, 113609.

[7] Yang, W., Li, H., Wang, J., & Ma, H. (2024). Spatio-temporal feature interpretable model for air quality forecasting. *Ecological Indicators, 167*, 112609.

[8] https://www.researchgate.net/publication/361977 003_Air_Quality_Prediction_using_Machine_ Learning.

[9] Shi, C., Wang, Y., Wan, Y., & Wu, S. (2022, February). Air quality prediction based on machine learning. In *2022 International conference on machine learning and knowledge engineering (MLKE)* (pp. 1–5). IEEE.

56 Decentralized framework for tamper-proof digital forensic evidence management

Diana S. Steffi[a], Raviraghav S.[b], Mahaa Poorani S.[c], Premnath K.[d], Nuhana A.[e], Dhivya S.[f], and Hemalatha M.[g]

Manakula Vinayagar Institute of Technology, Puducherry, India

Abstract: The use of blockchain technology in forensic investigations not only represents a significant breakthrough but also solves a number of important issues that the criminal justice and legal systems are now facing. Key components of the investigation process are automated and secured using smart contracts, which are at the core of this integration. The highest integrity and transparency are guaranteed in vital activities like access control, chain of custody management, and evidence monitoring thanks to these self-executing agreements that function according to predetermined norms and circumstances. One of its key benefits is the system's significant improvement in information security. The decentralized architecture and cryptographic foundation of blockchain make it very resistant to tampering and unauthorized access. This level of security is necessary in forensic investigations when maintaining the integrity of the evidence is essential. The immutability of blockchain records is also innovative for ensuring data accuracy. The blockchain offers an unchangeable record of actions and occurrences throughout the inquiry, making it almost impossible to alter data once it has been saved there. In conclusion, this innovative combination of smart contracts and blockchain technology improves the efficiency, traceability, and transparency of the forensic investigation process. It streamlines procedures and reduces the likelihood of errors and disputes while also preserving the integrity of the evidence. By providing an unbreakable and visible chain of custody and evidence history, this technology significantly raises the overall standard and dependability of forensic investigations within the legal and criminal justice system.

Keywords: Blockchain, Chain of custody, digital evidence, blowfish, image forensic

1. Introduction

Forensic intelligence is crucial to today's investigative procedures, especially in relation to cyberattacks and digital crimes. It covers a variety of methods and approaches for obtaining and evaluating evidence both prior to and following these incidents. A key element of this sector is the skills of forensic investigators, who are qualified to securely store and analyze data from digital devices and networks. Their main goals are to identify the underlying causes of events and collect evidence that is necessary for legal actions [1]. It is essential to follow accepted forensic standards, maintain consistency in the evidence, and employ exacting techniques when performing digital forensic examinations. This guarantees that during the investigation, the integrity and admissibility of the gathered evidence will be preserved [2]. The legal issues, best practices, and processes that are common in the modern digital forensic intelligence environment are known to forensic investigators. One of the fundamental ideas in this discipline is evidence continuity, which includes a thorough methodology that covers the full lifecycle of digital evidence. This section covers safe exhibit handling, careful data collecting and preservation procedures, appropriate

device seizure, and comprehensive examination and investigation methods. In addition to guaranteeing the quality of the evidence, forensic investigators can create a clear and continuous chain of custody by adhering to these principles, which is essential in court cases. In the end, their expertise in these areas contributes significantly to the successful resolution of cyberattacks and digital crimes while upholding the principles of justice and legal compliance [3].

A digital forensic intelligence investigation's examination phase starts once the evidence has been collected and stored. Making a complete copy of all the digital data from the gathered devices is known as imaging, and it requires the use of specialized forensic hardware and software. The imaging accomplishes two goals by allowing the imaged version to be used for forensic testing and analysis and by keeping the original device as an exhibit of evidence. This separation is crucial to the integrity and integrity of the original evidence during the inquiry [4].

The analytical element of the digital forensic intelligence investigation starts with a careful review of the collected data, which we do in collaboration with our clients. In this phase, forensic experts carefully examine the recorded data to glean important details and insights. This might entail restoring

[a]diana.sona20@gmail.com, [b]raviraghavsundaramurthi24@gmail.com, [c]mahaapoorani23@gmail.com, [d]premnathkarunakaran11@gmail.com, [e]nuhanaakbar3012@gmail.com, [f]dhivyaasuresh01@gmail.com, [g]hemalathamuniyan@gmail.com

DOI: 10.1201/9781003724988-56

erased files, locating malicious software or virus vectors, and reassembling digital timelines and actions. Since it looks for answers to fundamental issues, suspects, and evidence to back up legal proceedings, the analytical phase is a crucial part of the investigation. Technical know-how, meticulous attention to detail, and a solid grasp of digital forensic processes are all necessary for extracting valuable insight from data [5].

2. Literature Survey

For permissionless blockchains, a privacy-preserving method is presented that addresses on-chain data privacy issues while highlighting user control over transaction data. Ethereum smart contracts and symmetric cryptography are the foundations of the technology. Data consumers can verify the authenticity of an approved users' access control list created by data providers. After validation is successful, data consumers may ask data providers for a security key so they may access confidential data. A smart contract that is signed by the customer and the data supplier transmits the access key. The performance of these Solidity-implemented smart contracts is evaluated on the Ropsten test network [6].

A private network of interested parties is established by MF-Ledger to enable transparent and secure digital forensic examinations. Before being recorded on the blockchain ledger, the parties involved discuss and agree on a range of investigative tasks. Sequence diagrams are used to construct digital contracts, also known as smart contracts, which govern parties' safe communication during the inquiry. Strong information integrity, prevention, and preservation techniques are incorporated into this architectural solution to ensure the permanent and unalterable storage of evidence (including the chain of custody) in a private, permissioned, and encrypted blockchain ledger. In summary, MF-Ledger improves the security and integrity of digital forensic investigations in the multimedia realm, therefore addressing the changing challenges brought about by the contemporary digital environment [7].

A comprehensive and safe framework was developed by integrating many contemporary technologies to counter the rising threat of tampering with digital forensic evidence. AES (Rijndael) encryption is used for further protection after forensic data is hashed using the SHA-256 algorithm to provide a distinct fingerprint. A blockchain is used to store this encrypted data, ensuring its immutability and resistance to manipulation. A Windows program created using Visual Studio handles client and server duties, utilizing server-side AES encryption. While ADO.Net enables simple connection with a MySQL database, TCP remoting is utilized to provide secure data transfer. This comprehensive solution guarantees traceability, forensic data integrity, and efficient defense against malevolent intervention, much like layered security strategies are used in safe academic data management systems [8].

Rahul Saha and Gulshan Kumar talk on the challenges of digital forensics in the context of the Internet of Things, such as device diversity, a lack of transparency, and cross-border legal concerns with cloud forensics. The Internet-of-Forensics (IoF), a blockchain-based platform created especially for IoT forensics, is their suggested solution to these problems. By bringing all parties together in a single framework – such as various IoT devices and cloud service providers – IoF provides transparency. In addition to managing the investigative process using a blockchain-based case chain that encompasses chain-of-custody and evidence processing, it uses consortium-based consensus methods to settle cross-border legal disputes. The framework lowers computational complexity by utilizing programmable lattice-based cryptographic primitives, which is advantageous for devices with limited power. Autonomous security operations, cyberforensic investigations, and manual evidence tracking are all meant to be made easier by IoF [9].

The widespread use of IoT devices has made it possible to gather vast amounts of data in a range of scenarios. This data's integrity can be abruptly compromised, making it challenging to store securely. Maintaining data provenance and integrity is essential for incident monitoring and supplying evidence in court. Although the distributed, tamper-resistant structure of blockchain makes it a powerful option, storing large volumes of data on public blockchains like Ethereum comes with high transaction costs. As a solution, we provide an affordable and reliable digital forensics system that stores evidence on many low-cost blockchains (such as EOS and Stellar) before transferring it to Ethereum. Costs are greatly reduced when IoT event hashes are stored hierarchically using Merkle trees. We have evaluated Ethereum, Stellar, and EOS and found that the method guarantees data integrity.

Cybercriminals are using IoT devices as tools and targets due to their fast proliferation. In order to address this, we provide Probe-IoT, a forensic investigation tool that uncovers information in criminal cases using IoT by using a virtual ledger. Using a decentralized blockchain network akin to Bitcoin, Probe-IoT securely preserves interactions between IoT entities, including devices, users, and cloud services. Integrity, confidentiality, anonymity, and non-repudiation of stored evidence are all safeguarded by the system. Additionally, Probe-IoT enables the recovery and authentication of evidence from the ledger during investigations to guarantee its integrity and validity [10].

3. Proposed Methodology

In investigations into cybercrime, digital evidence is utilized to connect individuals to alleged unlawful activity. Despite the immutability and resistance to tampering that come with keeping digital evidence on blockchain technology, a significant disadvantage has been that the data is not secured, making it susceptible to compromise and unwanted access. The proposed method attempts to close the security gap by combining the Solidity programming language for smart contracts with the BLOWFISH (BF) encryption mechanism. Before being put to the blockchain, digital evidence files need to be encrypted using the BF technique. The data becomes unintelligible due to this encryption method's transformation into an unreadable format, which requires the correct decryption key. An additional degree of protection is added when data is encrypted before being stored on the blockchain.

Even if an attacker manages to access the blockchain, they will be unable to decrypt the encrypted data without the encryption key. This method improves the protection of digital evidence in cybercrime investigations by drastically lowering the danger of data tampering, unauthorized access, and breach. It ensures that the confidentiality and integrity of this important material are maintained throughout the inquiry, giving the foundation for constructing legal arguments and seeking justice a stronger and safer foundation (Figure 56.1).

3.1. Advantage of the proposed system

A crucial layer of protection is established when digital evidence is encrypted before being stored on the blockchain. It successfully maintains the integrity and confidentiality of the evidence by making sure the data stays in an unintelligible format without access to the decryption key.

The encryption would prevent someone from gaining unauthorized access to the blockchain. Making encrypted data illegible without the right decryption key reduces the likelihood of data breaches and illegal access to private information. A strong defense against data manipulation is created by combining encryption with the blockchain's built-in tamper-resistance. It is very difficult for malicious actors to change or modify the encrypted data because of a number of issues. This combination approach strengthens the blockchain's overall dependability as a secure home for private information, which is essential for court processes and cybercrime investigations, in addition to enhancing the security and legitimacy of digital evidence.

4. Result and Discussion

4.1. Data encryption module (Blowfish encryption)

This module ensures data secrecy before blockchain storage by utilizing the Blowfish method, a fast, symmetric block encryption with several key sizes (32–448 bits). By transforming data into unreadable ciphertext that can only be decrypted with the correct decryption key, it guarantees that even if data is accessed, unauthorized users will not be able to decipher it.

4.2. Blockchain storage module

In order to prevent tampering and track the origins of data, encrypted data is safely kept on a blockchain, which uses its decentralized and unchangeable nature to guarantee long-term integrity and trust.

4.3. Access control module

This module ensures that only authorized users can view or change sensitive data by specifying user permissions. As a

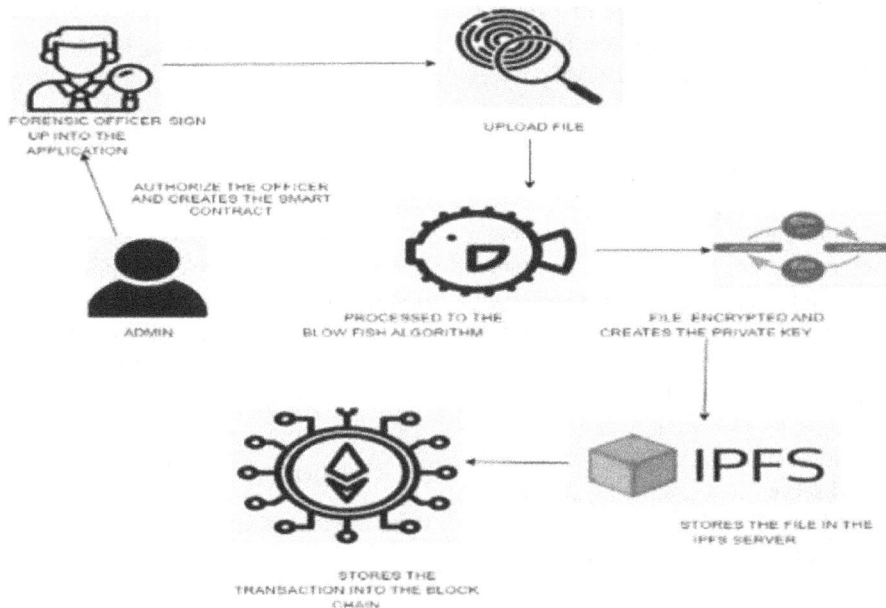

Figure 56.1. Flow diagram.

Source: Author.

security gatekeeper to prevent illicit activities, it plays a crucial role in protecting digital evidence.

4.4. Authentication and authorization module

While permission outlines what can be done following authentication, authentication – such as passwords, fingerprints, and multi-factor authentication – confirms user identity. They collaborate to establish strict, role-based access control in order to safeguard system integrity.

4.5. Reporting and logging module

This module logs system modifications, data access, and user activity. By producing an unambiguous, timestamped record of occurrences, logs aid auditing, traceability, and post-incident investigations – all of which are essential for compliance and accountability.

4.6. Integration with digital forensic tools

This module streamlines investigations while preserving data integrity by integrating blockchain data with forensic tools to facilitate evidence retrieval and analysis.

5. Performance Analysis

5.1. Blowfish algorithm

With a 64-bit block size and a key length that may be adjusted from 32 to 448 bits, Blowfish is a symmetric key block cipher. It applies a Feistel structure with substitution-permutation networks (SPN) and employs up to 16 rounds. For initialization, P-boxes and four S-boxes are created using digits of π for randomness. Each S-box has 256 32-bit entries. **Key Size (K):**

1. Variable key size: 32 to 448 bits (in multiples of 32 bits).
2. Key is divided into subkeys for use in encryption/decryption.
3. Number of Rounds (R):
4. Configurable: 4 to 16 rounds, default is 16.
5. More rounds = higher security but increased computational cost.

P-box and S-box Initialization:

1. P-boxes: 18 subkeys (P1–P18), initialized using digits of π and prime square roots.
2. S-boxes: 4 boxes (S1–S4), each with 256 32-bit entries, initialized using hex digits of π.

Encryption Structure:

1. Uses Feistel network, SPN structure, and XOR operations.
2. Flexible design supports various hardware/software implementations and security levels.

Encryption vs. Decryption Time: For most data types, Blowfish shows similar encryption/decryption speeds because to its symmetry. However, decryption takes longer for PDFs, probably because to their complex layout and file structures, which require additional processing during restoration. This demonstrates how file attributes impact the performance of cryptography (Figure 56.2).

6. Proof of Stake

In the Proof of Stake (PoS) model, transaction records (Txtr) are stored in IPFS, with their hashes on the blockchain.

The product hash (Hpro) includes details like type (Ptyp), quantity (Pquan), price (Ppri), and origin (Pori).

A transaction is represented as ***Txtr=[IDpro||Hpro||IDbuy||Sigbuy||PKbuy||Sigsell||PKsell]***, where IDbuy, Sigbuy, and PKbuy are the buyer's details, and Sigsell and PKsell are the seller's. The seller creates a transaction order (mR) after thepurchase.

$$m_R = \Phi \left(m_t, \zeta \left(SK_{sell}, m_t \right) \right).$$

7. Conclusion and Future Work

Blockchain technology has been incorporated into forensic investigations, marking a significant and groundbreaking breakthrough in the domains of digital forensics and evidence management. This innovative solution meets the increasing need for safe, open, and efficient management of digital evidence in a time when cybercrime and digital complexity are rapidly developing. The proposed approach leverages the decentralized and immutable nature of blockchain technology to ensure that forensic evidence is traceable and tamperproof throughout its existence. Smart contracts further enhance this system by automating critical functions like evidence monitoring, chain of custody management, and access control.

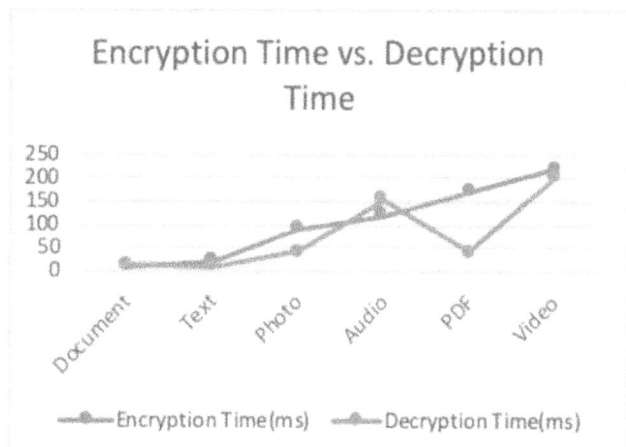

Figure 56.2. A graph explaining excryption vs decryption time.

Source: Author.

This improves procedural integrity, reduces human error, and expedites inquiry timelines. Blockchain-based forensic systems have a great deal of potential for future development. As digital investigations get more sophisticated, combining machine learning and artificial intelligence will be essential for the intelligent analysis and interpretation of huge and complex datasets. This can significantly improve the speed and accuracy of forensic investigations. Furthermore, the development of advanced encryption techniques and ongoing research into safer and more efficient blockchain consensus mechanisms will reinforce the preservation of sensitive digital data. To adapt to new threats, improve system capabilities, and guarantee compliance with changing legal norms, cooperation between forensic analysts, legal specialists, and technology developers will be essential. In conclusion, the combination of blockchain, automation, and new technologies not only transforms forensic procedures today but also establishes the groundwork for a judicial system that is more technologically robust, transparent, and safe. It highlights a future in which forensic investigations will be able to confidently, precisely, and honorably tackle the issues of the digital age.

References

[1] Vailshery, L. S. (2016). IOT devices installed Base Worldwide 2015–2025. *Statista,* https://www. statista. com/statistics/471264/iot-number-ofconnected-devices-worldwide/ (accessed Sep. 13, 2023).

[2] Xu, L., Jurcut, A. D., & Ranaweera, P. (2019). *Introduction to IoT Security.* Wiley: Hoboken, NJ, USA.

[3] Li, S., Qin, T., & Min, G. (2019). Blockchain-based digital forensics investigation framework in the internet of things and social systems. *IEEE Transactions on Computational Social Systems, 6*(6), 1433–1441.

[4] Hanggoro, D., & Sari, R. F. (2022). A Review of Lightweight Block-chain Technology Implementation to the Internet of Things. Available online: https://ieeexplore.ieee.org/abstract/document/9042431/ (accessed on 29 December 2022).

[5] Lu, Y., Huang, X., Dai, Y., Maharjan, S., & Zhang, Y. (2019). Blockchain and federated learning for privacy-preserved data sharing in industrial IoT. *IEEE Transactions on Industrial Informatics, 16*(6), 4177–4186.

[6] Truex, S., Baracaldo, N., Anwar, A., Steinke, T., Ludwig, H., Zhang, R., & Zhou, Y. (2019, November). A hybrid approach to privacy-preserving federated learning. In *Proceedings of the 12th ACM Workshop on Artificial Intelligence and Security* (pp. 1–11).

[7] Yang, Q., Liu, Y., Cheng, Y., Kang, Y., Chen, T., & Yu, H. (2022). Federated Learning. 2020. Available online: https://link.springer.com/ book/10.1007/978-3-031-01585-4 (accessed on 29 December 2022).

[8] Panda, S. K., Jena, A. K., Swain, S. K., & Satapathy, S. C. (2021). *Blockchain Technology: Applications and Challenges; Intelligent Systems Reference Library.* Berlin, Germany.

[9] Namasudra, S., Deka, G. C., Johri, P., Hosseinpour, M., & Gandomi, A. H. (2021). The revolution of blockchain: State-of-the-art and research challenges. *Archives of Computational Methods in Engineering, 28*(3), 1497–1515.

[10] Zhao, Y., Zhao, J., Jiang, L., Tan, R., Niyato, D., Li, Z., ... & Liu, Y. (2020). Privacy-preserving blockchain-based federated learning for IoT devices. *IEEE Internet of Things Journal, 8*(3), 1817–1829.

57 Next-Gen attendance tracking: AI-powered facial recognition with live analytics and anti-spoofing

A. Jainullabdeen[1,a], K. Nesapriyan[2,b], S. Gurudhakshan[2,c],
N. MujiburRahman[2,d], T. Yogeshwaran[2,e], J. Madhavan[2,f], and S. Nithiya[2,g]

[1]BTech., AI & ML – Assistant Professor, Department of Artificial Intelligence and Machine Learning, Manakula Vinayagar Institute of Technology, Pondicherry University, Puducherry, India
[2]BTech Final Year, Department of Artificial Intelligence and Machine Learning, Manakula Vinayagar Institute of Technology, Pondicherry University, Puducherry, India

Abstract: This paper presents an revolutionary attendance tracking gadget utilizing facial recognition, designed to streamline and beautify the technique of student attendance control. The proposed device advances past traditional facial popularity attendance systems by means of incorporating numerous novel features geared toward enhancing security, accuracy, and accessibility. First, a face spoofing detection mechanism is employed, which identifies and flags suspicious tries to falsify attendance through pics or virtual pix displayed on cellular devices, ensuring authenticity. 2d, the device includes a stay analytical component that calculates actual-time attendance statistics, continuously tracking every pupil's presence and updating their attendance percent dynamically, even accounting for transient absences. Ultimately, for ease of file control, the gadget allows automatic PDF record technology for person attendance data, allowing facts to be downloaded and stored as needed. The device leverages Python, Convolution Neural Networks (CNNs) for facial feature extraction, Open CV for laptop imaginative and prescient, and V2 algorithms for more advantageous face detection. Development and trying out had been conducted in PyCharm, ensuing in a sturdy, green answer suitable for academic institutions seeking a reliable, automatic attendance tracking device.

Keywords: An advanced attendance monitoring system using facial popularity and face spoofing detection, offering actual-time analytics, dynamic tracking, and automatic report generation, leveraging CNNs, OpenCV, and sturdy Python- primarily based algorithms for relaxed and efficient scholar attendance management

1. Introduction

In recent times attendance shadowing systems have come essential tools across multiple sectors, from educational institutions to commercial surroundings. Traditional styles, similar as homemade roll calls and ID card snatching, frequently fall suddenly due to inefficiencies and vulnerability to manipulation. The proposed attendance shadowing system leverages facial recognition and advanced discovery algorithms to give a flawless and secure result for managing attendance. This system is erected using Python, CNN algorithms, OpenCV, and state-of-the-art face discovery ways, creating a robust frame that addresses several crucial challenges in conventional attendance systems. A distinctive aspect of this system is its face spoofing [10] discovery point, which identifies fraudulent attempts, similar as using prints or videotape recordings to gain unauthorized access. This added subcaste of security strengthens the integrity of the attendance process. Likewise, the system incorporates a live logical element that continuously calculates each pupil's

attendance in real- time, including entries and exits, enabling directors to cover and estimate attendance criteria stoutly. To grease effective data running, the system allows the import of attendance records in PDF format, icing that druggies have quick access to comprehensive reports for farther analysis or documentation. Through the integration of facial recognition technology and real- time analytics, this system not only enhances functional effectiveness but also maintains the security and trust ability of attendance data. This makes it suitable for colourful settings where accurate and secure attendance monitoring is pivotal [6].

2. Project Objectives

The number one goal of this assignment is to broaden an better Attendance tracking machine leveraging facial popularity generation to provide an green, relaxed, and user-pleasant solution for computerized attendance management. This gadget pursuits to deal with commonplace issues in attendance tracking, which includes inaccuracy, inefficiency, and

[a]jain.nzm786@gmail.com, [b]nesapriyan2003pdy@gmail.com, [c]gurudhakshan01@gmail.com, [d]muji.techie@gmail.com, [e]yogeshw3903@gmail.com, [f]madhavanj2425@gmail.com, [g]nithiyasankar05@gmail.com

DOI: 10.1201/9781003724988-57

fraud, with the aid of integrating extra capabilities which include spoof detection and live analytics. The unique Objectives are as follows

- Automate attendance monitoring to lessen guide effort.
- Make certain accurate identification using CNN and V2 algorithms to save you unauthorized get entry to.
- Combine real-time spoof detection for more advantageous security.
- Offer real-time analytics on attendance styles and consultation info.
- Permit flexible facts management with exportable reports.
- Layout an intuitive interface for ease of use.
- Adapt to numerous environments, such as digital and hybrid settings.
- Make certain compliance with institutional and regulatory requirements

3. Problem Statement

Rapid technological advancement has created a demand for innovative, AI driven solutions that address complex challenges across multiple domains, including education, healthcare, environmental conservation, and public safety. Traditional systems – such as manual attendance tracking, species identification, and accident prevention – often lack the sophistication needed to manage issues like identity spoofing [10], diagnostic accuracy, and delayed threat alerts, leading to reduced reliability and efficiency.

This project proposes a suite of applications aimed at overcoming these limitations:

1. **Education:** Enhance attendance tracking systems with real-time spoofing detection to ensure accurate record-keeping and verify genuine presence.
2. **Healthcare:** Develop image-based diagnostics for early breast cancer detection using machine learning to improve diagnostic precision and accessibility.
3. **Environmental Conservation:** Create a species identification application for fish, providing critical ecological information to support conservation efforts.
4. **Public Safety:** Implement a real-time accident prevention system that detects oncoming trains and obstacles, issuing timely alerts to minimize human error-related incidents.

Through the integration of machine learning, image processing, and user-friendly interfaces, this project aims to deliver practical, scalable solutions tailored to meet real-world demands effectively.

4. Technology Used – Programming Language

Python: Python is the center language utilized for all predominant aspects of the mission, inclusive of records managing, preprocessing, feature extraction, version training, and performance evaluation. Its enormous libraries and frameworks make Python a perfect desire for efficient gadget getting to know and facts processing duties for the duration of the undertaking's improvement cycle.

4.1. Libraries and frameworks

1. **Flask:**
   - **Description:** Flask is a minimalistic net framework for Python, designed to build internet programs easily.
   - **Utilization in Project:** Flask manages the internet utility's structure via coping with routes, managing backend and frontend interactions.
2. **Opencv:**
   - **Description:** OpenCV is an open-supply library targeted on laptop vision obligations, enabling actual-time video and photograph processing.
   - **Usage in Venture:** it's far used to capture video, hit upon faces in frames, and put together photographs for similarly analysis in actual- time, presenting the core capability for photograph capture and preprocessing.
3. **Dlib:**
   - **Description:** Dlib is a machine mastering library recognised for sturdy face detection and facial reputation abilties.
   - **Utilization in Under taking:** Dlib powers the face detection and reputation technique, creating facial encodings and helping excessive-accuracy identification of people.
4. **Sqlite:**
   - **Description:** SQLite is a lightweight, serverless database engine.
   - **Usage in Project:** SQLite shops attendance statistics,
   - timestamps, and spoofing try details. Its integration with Python and simplicity of setup make it best for managing the undertaking's information requirements.
5. **Bootstrap:**
   - **Description:** Bootstrap is a front-cease framework designed for responsive, cellular-pleasant web layout.
   - **Utilization in Task:** it's miles hired to style and optimize the consumer interface, ensuring that the utility is visually on hand and responsive across devices.
6. **Pandas:**
   - **Description:** Pandas is a Python library for information manipulation and evaluation.
   - **Usage in Task:** Used to arrange attendance information, behaviour analyses, and generate reports, Pandas improves the machine's records dealing with and facilitates document technology.

7. Numpy:
- **Description:** NumPy is essential for numerical operations in Python, supporting green matrix and array handling.
- **Usage in Task:** NumPy methods image records and handles calculations wished for face encoding, enabling green operations for the duration of the popularity method.

5. System Architecture

The system architecture illustrates the overall design and components of the Enhanced Attendance Tracking System, highlighting how various elements interact to facilitate efficient attendance management. This diagram depicts the flow of data and processes involved in capturing attendance through facial recognition while ensuring security against spoofing attempts. Each component plays an important role in the functionality of the system, from data collection and processing to user interaction and database management. The architecture also emphasizes the seamless integration of advanced technologies like Flask, OpenCV, and Dlib, which enhance the system's reliability and accuracy. By providing a clear representation of the system's structure, this diagram (Figure 57.1 and 57.2).

6. Proposed System

The proposed gadget seeks to streamline attendance monitoring via facial reputation generation. snapshots of students in a study room putting are captured via a camera, processed via an picture enhancement stage to improve popularity reliability, and then fed into face detection [9] and recognition modules. Attendance is recorded based on a success matches with pre-saved templates in a database. The gadget is designed for excessive pace, accuracy, and protection, allowing instructors to provoke it effortlessly with a unmarried button press. Continuous digital camera feeds ensure that every one students inside the study room are accounted for, decreasing the ability for fraudulent attendance marking. Moreover, privateness and security protocols – along with gaining consent, transparent records handling, encryption, and minimum records collection – are incorporated to adhere to privateness requirements.

The gadget also functions computerized month-to-month attendance file era (Figure 57.3).

6.1. Working of a proposed system

The Face recognition [8] and Attendance system automates attendance monitoring through using facial popularity to stumble on, perceive, and log people as they skip thru particular entry points. it's far designed for performance, accuracy, and unobtrusiveness in environments in which attendance tracking is vital, which include classrooms or workplaces. The device captures pix or video streams through strategically placed cameras. the first step is photograph preprocessing, where input is standardized by using changing to grayscale, resizing, and adjusting brightness or contrast. This uniformity complements detection accuracy. Face detection is then finished the use of algorithms like Haar cascades or

Figure 57.2. Architecture 3DFlow.

Source: Author.

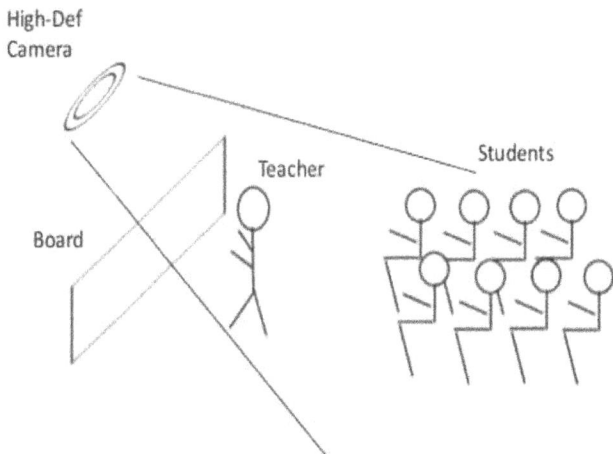

Figure 57.1. Architecture diagram.

Source: Author.

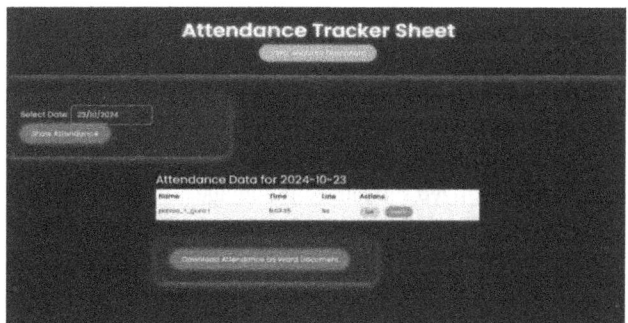

Figure 57.3. Output of the working model.

Source: Author.

deep gaining knowledge of models consisting of MTCNN, which come across faces even in various lights or angles. once detected, every face is cropped and processed for the recognition degree.

In face recognition, cropped faces are matched towards a pre-registered database the use of models like CNNs, Face-Net, or LBPH. By way of extracting and evaluating facial functions, the machine identifies acknowledged people and logs them as gift. If an individual is unrecognized, they're flagged as a consequence. The system robotically facts the date and time of every diagnosed face, storing facts securely for clean reporting. An item detection layer adds security by way of blocking off attempts to apply cellular screens or pics to impersonate users. This anti-spoofing mechanism strengthens the machine's protection, making sure correct, actual- time attendance without manual mistakes.

The Anti-Spoofing Mechanism: Works via The Following Steps:

1. Face Detection: The gadget first detects faces in the video stream, identifying and setting apart each face within the body using the OpenCV library.
2. Image Evaluation and Preprocessing: Each detected face undergoes preprocessing to enhance image quality and reduce noise, preparing it for more accurate analysis.
3. Feature Extraction: Using Dlib, key facial landmarks and encodings are extracted from each face, generating precise patterns that serve as a reference for recognizing individuals.
4. Liveness Detection: To prevent spoofing, the system analyzes unique patterns like facial texture, eye movements, or micro-expressions, distinguishing real faces from photos or videos shown to the camera.
5. Verification and Matching: The processed face encodings are then matched against stored profiles, confirming the individual's identity and verifying if the attempt is genuine.

6.2. Algorithm reasons

The algorithms applied in this system enable essential functions such as face detection [6], recognition, liveness verification, and spoof detection, ensuring efficient operation with high accuracy and reliability.

1. **Face Detection using Histogram of Oriented Gradients (HOG)**
   Purpose: To detect faces within an image [2].
   Algorithm: HOG is used to identify facial shapes by analyzing the direction and intensity of pixel gradients across localized sections of the image.
   Process: The image is divided into small cells, and gradient directions are computed for each pixel. Histograms of these directions are created for each cell and then compared to known facial shapes to detect faces.
   Benefit: Effective across varying lighting conditions and **facial expressions**, supporting accurate face localization.

2. **Face Recognition using Dlib's 128-Dimensional Encodings**
   Purpose: To recognize and identify individuals based on unique facial features [4].
   Algorithm: Dlib's 128-dimensional encoding maps each detected face to a vector, capturing unique features.
   Method: The vector representation is matched with stored profiles using Euclidean distance. If two vectors fall within a set threshold, a match is confirmed, and attendance is logged.
   Benefit: Robust to slight changes in appearance, enabling accurate identification.

3. **Liveness Detection using Eye Aspect Ratio (EAR)**
   Purpose: To prevent spoofing by confirming that the detected face is live.
   Algorithm: The **Eye Aspect Ratio (EAR)** measures blinking patterns by calculating the ratio of eye width to height, signaling liveness.
   Process: The system monitors eye landmarks, confirming a live presence when blinking is detected based on EAR values.
   Benefit: EAR is computationally efficient and prevents spoofing through photos or videos.

4. **Spoof Detection with Face Anti-Spoofing Techniques**
   Purpose: To detect fraudulent attempts using static images or videos.
   Algorithm: Texture analysis and motion patterns are used to distinguish real faces from imitated ones, such as photos [3].
   Method: The algorithm identifies textures and movements unique to real faces and detects flat or reflective surfaces common in fake displays.
   Benefit: This approach ensures that the system cannot be easily deceived by fraudulent methods.

7. Conclusion

The development and implementation of the Face Recognition [7] and Attendance System represent a significant step forward in automating and securing attendance processes through facial recognition technology. By harnessing advanced machine learning [1] algorithms for face detection [5], recognition, liveness verification, and spoof prevention, this system enables a fast, accurate, and reliable approach to attendance tracking. The automation reduces manual workload and security measures ensures data protection and meets ethical standards. With its ability to prevent fraudulent attendance marking and its scalability to various environments, this system provides a streamlined solution for managing attendance in real-time. Moreover, the incorporation of monthly report generation further enhances its utility for administrative tasks. The system's efficient processing and resource management make it adaptable to typical hardware setups, increasing its accessibility.

References

[1] Damale, R. C., & Pathak, B. V. (2018, June). Face recognition based attendance system using machine learning algorithms. In *2018 Second International Conference on Intelligent Computing and Control Systems (ICICCS)* (pp. 414–419). IEEE.

[2] Salim, O. A. R., Olanrewaju, R. F., & Balogun, W. A. (2018, September). Class attendance management system using face recognition. In *2018 7th International conference on computer and communication engineering (ICCCE)* (pp. 93–98). IEEE.

[3] Paharekari, S., Jadhav, C., Nilangekar, S., & Padwal, J. (2017). Automated attendance system in college using face recognition and NFC. *International Journal of Computer Science and Mobile Computing*, 6(6), 14–21.

[4] Rekha, E., & Ramaprasad, P. (2017, January). An efficient automated attendance management system based on Eigen Face recognition. In *2017 7th International Conference on Cloud Computing, Data Science & Engineering-Confluence* (pp. 605–608). IEEE.

[5] Zhan, S., Kurihara, T., & Ando, S. (2006, October). Facial authentication system based on real-time 3D facial imaging by using correlation image sensor. In *Sixth International Conference on Intelligent Systems Design and Applications* (Vol. 2, pp. 396–400). IEEE.

[6] Kumar, A., Sharma, M., Gautam, S. P., Kumar, R., & Raj, S. (2020, November). Attendance management system using facial recognition. In *2020 International Conference on Decision Aid Sciences and Application (DASA)* (pp. 228–232). IEEE.

[7] Rajput, I., Nazir, N., Kaur, N., Srivastava, S., Sarwar, A., Kaur, B., ... & Aggarwal, S. (2022, April). Attendance management system using facial recognition. In *2022 3rd International Conference on Intelligent Engineering and Management (ICIEM)* (pp. 797–801). IEEE.

[8] Gill, S., Sharma, N., Gupta, C., & Samanta, A. (2021, November). Attendance Management System Using Facial Recognition and Image Augmentation Technique. In *2021 International Conference on Intelligent Technology, System and Service for Internet of Everything (ITSS-IoE)* (pp. 1–6). IEEE.

[9] Siswanto, A. R. S., Nugroho, A. S., & Galinium, M. (2014, September). Implementation of face recognition algorithm for biometrics based time attendance system. In *2014 international conference on ICT for smart society (ICISS)* (pp. 149–154). IEEE.

[10] Kim, J., Cheema, U., & Moon, S. (2016, October). Face recognition enhancement by employing facial component classification and reducing the candidate gallery set. In *2016 16th International Conference on Control, Automation and Systems (ICCAS)* (pp. 923–926). IEEE.

58 A hybrid linguistic model for semantic clarity in news headlines of agglutinative language

Rameesa K.[1,a], K. T. Veeramanju[1,b], Shifana Begum[2,c], and Akhilraj V. Gadagkar[3,d]

[1]Research Scholar, Srinivas University Mangaluru, India
[2]Srinivas University Institute of Engineering and Technology, Srinivas University Mangaluru, India
[3]NITTE (Deemed to be University), NMAM Institute of Technology (NMAMIT) Nittte, India

Abstract: In Natural Language Processing (NLP), detection of stop word is one of the important steps that take place during preprocessing and it is quite essential especially in morphologically complex languages such as Malayalam. By comprising three critical methods that is a manually compiled stop word list, Sandhi rule-based examination, and a BiLSTM (Bidirectional Long Short-Term Memory) neural network, this research presents a hybrid model that can perform an expeditious stop word finding in Malayalam news titles. The model uses the three detection algorithms in parallel, after the kick-off with processes of data pretreatment such as tokenization, normalization, and padding. Besides dealing with language-specific challenges such as separation of compound words and inflectional suffixes, which are prevalent in Malayalam since it is agglutinative language, the approach follows initial stages of data pretreatment such as tokenisation, normalization and padding. For instance, in a headline of a news, the term "പ്രധാനമന്ത്രിയോടൊപ്പം" (pradhānamantriyōṭoppam, Segmentation has to be effective for isolation and identification of the stop word component. These pretreatment processes ensure that the three parallel detection algorithms normalize their input sequences structurally in order for an accurate computation to occur. Although Sandhi rules help in locating morphologically concatenated or compound stop words that are otherwise hard to find, manually curated list provides instant, rule based finding of known stop words. Using contextual information over sequences, BiLSTM model enhances the system's ability to detect contextual stop words. A positive difference can be compared to single-method strategies based on experimental results which indicate a significant improvement. This integrated model will also offer improved performance in further NLP tasks like summarization of text, classification, and analysis of sentiment for this language on top of offering a viable solution for identifying stop words in Malayalam. The model does well, identifying stop words and distinguishing them from the content words at an overall accuracy level of 91.3%. It also exhibited a healthy ability to identify the stop words with a minimum of false positives and false negatives with precision of 89.7% recall, a precision of 90.9 %, and a F1-score of 90.9%. These outcomes provide a reliable evidence of the model's efficacy and were achieved with the help of testing on the set of 5,000 manually annotated samples. The high recall, in particular, shows that the model is especially efficient at the missing stop words' decrease, which is an important feature of speedy NLP pipelines' text preprocessing. Apart from setting up a good foundation for further investigations in resource-deficient languages, this method also improves the standards of preprocessing for Malayalam NLP jobs. The proposed method propels natural language understanding in local languages such as Malayalam by a far margin since it proposes a flexible efficiently scalable and high performing framework for stop word identification.

Keywords: Stop words, detection, agglutinative, deep learning, BiLSTM, classification, sandhi rule, natural language processing, news, headlines

1. Introduction

Stop words are words that appear frequently in news headlines but add little to the headline's real meaning. A critical preprocessing step in NLP applications including information retrieval, machine translation, and text classification is locating and removing stop words. Eliminating stop words lowers the dataset's dimensionality, which boosts model performance and computing efficiency. Although English and other languages with abundant resources have well-defined stop word lists, it is still difficult to find stop words in low-resource languages like Malayalam. Historically, machine learning, linguistic, and statistical methods have been used for stop word detection. In news headline categorization, stop words are routinely filtered out using statistical techniques that make the assumption that words that appear frequently in a corpus have little semantic value.

When it comes to Indian state of Kerala and union territories of Lakshadweep and Puducherry (Mahé district) the language spoken by Malayali people is Malayalam which is a Dravidian language. In India, Malayalam is spoken by 35 million people [1]. The 56 symbols in Malayalam scripts have been developed from Brahmi scripts. The Malayalam

[a]ayisharameesa@gmail.com, [b]veeramanju.icis@gmail.com, [c]shifanabgm22@gmail.com, [d]gadagkar.akhil@gmail.com

DOI: 10.1201/9781003724988-58

language has 41 letters that are consonants ones (Vyanjanaksharangal) and 15 letters that are vowel (Swaraksharangal). Letters ആ (a), ഇ (i), and ഉ (u) denote vowels and ക (ka), മ (ma), and ര (ra) – consonant letters. Since Malayalam is a phonetic language, words are pronounced as they are spelt. Therefore, to master the basics of the language, regular dialog was needed [1]. The Malayalam language is very challenging for natural language processing applications due to the wide vocabulary and complex grammatical structure.

Categorization of news headlines into pre-defined subjects or classifications such as politics, sports, entertainment, and business is an important exercise in Natural Language Processing (NLP). Stop word detection and removal is an important step in this task which leads to a better computational efficiency and classification accuracy with reduction of noise. Although the stop words such as "the", "is", "on", "in" are frequently used, they are not the words that provide much meaning interpretation to the semantic sense of the news headlines. Removing such words makes the feature space to have fewer dimensions- this enhances the speed and efficiency of the machine learning models. Classifiers can improve in identifying the right category of news headlines by eliminating words, which are not helpful and focusing on keywords that have some relevance. Higher classification accuracy is achieved by trained models on stop word-filtered datasets [3]. Stop words induce noise into headlines of news that might make the model misguided. Removing these words will increase the S-N ratio that makes it easier for classifiers to detect significant patterns [4]. The removal of stop words helps in the acceleration of training and inference times of NLP models since fewer words have been processed. This is very helpful in real time news classification systems [5]. Despite the availability of good lists of stop words in English language its still very hard to identify stop words in under resource languages such as the Malayalam. Stop words detection traditional ways are comprised of the following:

Statistical Methods: Finding low information content words that are used frequently [6].

Linguistic Methods: Finding out words that operate as grammatical connectors instead of content words from part-of-speech patterns.

Machine Learning Methods: Unsupervised or supervised learning from corpora to automatically learn stopword lists [7].

Despite the fact that it must be used sparingly, the removal of stop words is often beneficial to the grouping of headlines, where conciseness and the relevance of keywords are important characteristics [2].

2. Literature Review

However, because of the agglutinative nature of the language and a shortage of thorough linguistic resources, it is difficult to identify stop words in Malayalam. Because Malayalam is a Dravidian language that is extremely inflectional

and agglutinative, for example **(kuṭṭiyoṭu)** → "Towards the child" stop word recognition becomes more difficult. Malayalam stop words vary because of morphophonemic shifts, Sandhi transformations, and grammatical dependencies, in contrast to English, where stop words are comparatively static.

Linguistic rule-based methods try to characterize stop words with regard to syntax and semantics. These methods are based on the manual-curated stopword lists which are incomplete and require frequent changes. Besides that, various dialects of the Malayalam with linguistic variations make it more complex to compile an inclusive list of stop words.

As the deep learning advances, stop word detection has been studied using machine learning models such as neural networks, Conditional Random Fields (CRF), and Hidden Markov Models (HMM). While such models have shown promising results in well-resourced languages, the sparse amount of annotated Malayalam data makes it difficult to use them. Additionally, many Malayalam NLP jobs often lack massive training datasets that are used for deep learning models. Another major obstacle in the stop word recognition for Malayalam is Sandhi rules. The morphological and phonetic changes that occur when two words are conjoined is defined by the term "sandhi". For instance, one of the Malayalam transformative morphology is "ഒരു" (oru, meaning "a"), which changes with the following word. Such stop words may not be detected with the use of the traditional frequency-based methods because they appear in various modified forms.

This study proposes a hybrid approach that relies on manually curated stop word lists and Sandhi rule-based processing to get rid of such challenges. This approach improves the identification of the stop word by taking linguistic subtleties particular to Malayalam into consideration. In addition, we propose a classification model using a deep learning approach to fine tune stop word detection using bidirectional LSTM (BiLSTM) and attention mechanisms. The proposed hybrid approach guarantees balance between linguistic rules and data driven learning, which makes it more effective for the real-world NLP applications.

Approaches and difficulties of locating and getting rid of stop words, which are commonly used keywords having a lower semantic value in text processing missions, are discussed within the review of literature on stop word classification in Malayalam. The elimination of the stop words improves the functionality and quality of the classification system. It is possible to decrease the number of dimensions in the space term for a classification task by excluding the phrases that are the most used without relevance and of the less meaningful meaning. But the removal of the stop words does not ensure better performance for the rest of the applications in the areas of machine translation, text mining, artificial intelligence, and natural language processing. Removing stop words in the setting of Machine Translation (MT) will create a loss of accuracy as every token has a different meaning and it is going to be used on the target language [8]. To enhance the effectiveness of the MT system, the language of Malayalam does not have a set list of the stop words and their lexical classes (Part-of-Speech Tags), in this case.

3. Proposed Work

The morphological complexity of Malayalam is too much for traditional stop word lists to manage, particularly when it comes to compound words created by Sandhi transformations [9, 10]. The proposed system uses Sandhi-splitting techniques to locate embedded stop words in the compound word and the inflected forms after having done manual creation of stop word list [11, 13]. The Malyaleam news headlines dataset will be used for training and evaluation by using the natural language processing (NLP) techniques applied to preprocessing text, extracting relevant phrases and enhancing classification performance [12].

Figure 58.1 Hybrid linguistic model is the proposed methodology for Malayalam stop word categorization combines three approaches: human stop word list-based categorization, Sandhi rule-based identification, and a deep learning model BiLSTM (Bidirectional LSTM) Stop word Classification.

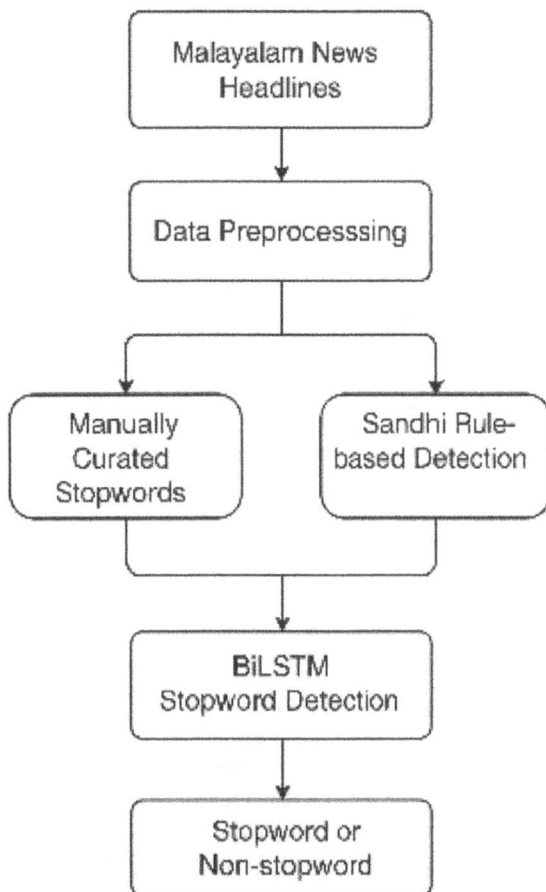

Figure 58.1. Hybrid linguistic model.

Source: Author.

This method uses deep learning techniques and language rules to improve stop word identification accuracy.

Initially, a collection of Malayalam news headlines was collected from an online database. Each headline was manually annotated to identify stop words and non-stop words. The first stage in the preparatory phase was text cleaning, which comprised removing punctuation, numerals, and special characters from the text and normalizing it to guarantee consistent Unicode encoding. The IndicNLP tokenizer, which effectively divides Malayalam text into separate words, was used to carry out the tokenization procedure. However, the agglutinative structure of the Malayalam language made basic tokenization insufficient, requiring additional processing of complex words (Sandhi words) using linguistic rules. A personally picked collection of stop words was utilized as an initial filter to classify stop words. A token was immediately marked as a stop word if it was discovered in the list. However, stop words become more difficult to identify in Malayalam due to Sandhi (morphological joining laws), which cause them to blend with adjacent words. Sandhi rule-based splitting was used to solve this. Vowel Sandhi (joining of vowels), Consonant Sandhi (changing word endings), and Visarga Sandhi (managing unusual characters like "ഃ") are important Sandhi transformations taken into consideration. For instance, "ഓട്" ("odu") is a stop word that is linked to "ഇവൻ" ("ivan") in the phrase "ഇവനോട്" ("ivanodu"). "ഓട്" is retrieved and categorized as a stop word using rule-based segmentation. After splitting, a word is classified as a stop word if it matches the stop word list; if not, deep learning-based categorization is used.

Bidirectional Long Short-Term Memory (BiLSTM) networks, which are capable of efficiently capturing both past and future context within a phrase, provide a potent method for stop word recognition in Malayalam news headlines. Due to Malayalam's rich morphology and syntactical flexibility, it is frequently necessary to comprehend a word in the context of the full sentence in order to assess its significance. Such subtleties may be missed by conventional models that just process text in one direction. BiLSTM networks improve contextual awareness by reading the sequence from both left-to-right and right-to-left, which makes it simpler to discern between stop words like "ഇത്", "ആണ്", or "ഒരു" and semantically significant words. A BiLSTM model combined with a time-distributed artificial neural network layer can accurately identify each word as a stop word or an essential keyword when trained on annotated datasets of Malayalam headlines. This technique enhances the preprocessing phase of a number of NLP applications, including information retrieval, sentiment analysis, and summarization in Malayalam-speaking situations.

3.1. Data pre-processing

A sizable corpus of Malayalam news headlines text has been gathered from a variety of sources. Using linguistic principles and existing stop word lists, the words in the corpus are classified as either non-stop words or stop words. In order to transform the raw news headlines into a clean, structured format appropriate for additional analysis, data preprocessing is an essential step in the Malayalam stop word identification pipeline. Tokenization is the first step in the preprocessing process, which divides the Malayalam text into discrete words or tokens. The next step is normalization, which fixes spelling errors, eliminates punctuation, and standardizes characters to keep headlines consistent. Additional measures like padding are used in the deep learning environment, particularly for the BiLSTM model, to guarantee that all input sequences are the same length. By eliminating noise and boosting the model's capacity to precisely identify stop words within the linguistic structure of Malayalam headlines, these preprocessing processes are essential to enhance the performance of all three detection techniques – manual, Sandhi rule-based, and BiLSTM.

3.2. *Manually curated stop words detection*

Identifying and eliminating frequently used, semantically irrelevant words in Malayalam by corpus analysis or a predetermined list compiled by linguistic experts is known as manually curated stop word identification. These stop words usually consist of function words like prepositions, auxiliary verbs, articles, and conjunctions (e.g., "ഉണ്ട്", "ആണ", "ഒരു", and "എന്നും"). To generate a huge stop word list, which consists of the most common non-informative terms in different contexts, this approach relies upon the linguistic intuition and experience of local speakers. Each token gives comparison with this compiled list when it is made to work the Malayalam news headlines and any matches are simply marked as stop words. When using more complicated rule-based or machine learning models such as Sandhi analysis, or BiLSTM, this simple interpretable and computationally fast approach provides a robust first filter.

3.3. *Sandhi rule based stop words detection*

Sandhi rules describing the process of joining words or morphemes, altering the initial formings is applied in Sandhi rule based stop word identification. This technique employs both grammar and morphology to detect concealed as well as those that are created from inflections which are deemed to be stop words. For example, it may not be easy to differentiate post positions and auxiliaries verb through direct comparisons when merging with the root words. The Sandhi rule-based approach identifies potential stop word parts by examining the word boundary and splitting logic. Acting so, it identifies stop words embedded, which a basic hand maintained list is likely to ignore. Adopting the complex Malayalam stop word construction patterns, this strategy advances stop word recognition accuracy. It is very effective when combined with other such strategies such as the handwritten lists and BiLSTM.

3.4. *BiLSTM based stop words detection*

To accurately detect stop words in Malayalam news headlines, a BiLSTM neural network is used to learn contextual pattern in BiLSTM-based stop word recognition. In contrast to the rule-based techniques, BiLSTM models are capable of understanding the sequentiality of language because they work on each sentence by reading it both ways, and hence preserve total context for every word. This is particularly useful in Malayalam because the meaning of a word will in most cases depend on the words and grammatical role surrounding it. Every word from the labelled information, which has been used in training the model is tagged as a stop word or a non-stop word. The BiLSTM employs learnt linguistic patterns to analyze the input headline and label them during the prediction. BiLSTM can be a powerful component of the stop word identification pipeline that contributes to the global accuracy augmentation if used in union with manual and rule-based methods. It does that considering it is efficient at identifying stop words that vary in usage or are condition-sensitive.

4. Results and Discussion

Fusing manually created lists of stop words, Sandhi rule-based examination, and BiLSTM deep learning, the integrated model of stop word detection for Malayalam news headlines demonstrated outstanding accuracy and sustainable performance. The model performed better than separate methods performing 91.3% accuracy overall accuracy when tested on a dataset of annotated Malayalam headlines properly selected. Although the Sandhi rule-based identification identified compound stop words and morphologically complex keywords successfully, the manually built list gave the solid baseline. Learning contextual patterns especially when the importance of the words depends on the nearby words helped the BiLSTM component to further increase performance. For instance, the BiLSTM model managed to identify the term "ഇന്ന്" as a stop word in the headline"പ്രധാ This hybrid approach ensured more precise preprocessing for subsequent NLP processes in the Malayalam language, such as sentiment analysis and the analysis of summarization, in addition to increasing precision and recall. In the field of natural language processing, stop word removal is commonly carried out to eliminate words used in great numbers that do not necessarily connote meaningful information. Not all popular words, such as temporal words, should be eliminated from news headlines, particularly those written in Malayalam. For example, consider the headline:

"കേരളത്തിൽ ഇന്ന് ശക്തമായ മഴയ്ക്ക് സാധ്യത" *(There is a possibility of heavy rain in Kerala today)*

If we remove the word "ഇന്ന്" **(today)** assuming it's a stop word, the sentence becomes:

"കേരളത്തിൽ ശക്തമായ മഴയ്ക്ക് സാധ്യത" *(There is a possibility of heavy rain in Kerala)*

The time-specific information is lost in this version, so it's not apparent if rain is predicted for today, tomorrow, or another day. Therefore, "ഇന്ന്" shouldn't be eliminated from activities like real-time news analysis or event identification. This demonstrates that not all common words are useless in every situation, therefore stop word removal should be carefully tailored based on the NLP job.

Through the analysis of more than 1.7 million texts, "Towards Stop words Identification in Tamil Text Clustering" by M. S. Faathima Fayaza and F. Fathima Farhath (2021) aims to find stopwords in Tamil that are both universal and domain-specific [14]. It illustrates how the accuracy of Tamil document clustering systems is increased by eliminating correctly detected stop words. Despite being focused on Tamil, the methods and conclusions apply to Malayalam and other South Indian languages. Stop words Remover for Malayalam language" by Spark NLP (2022) presents a production-ready, scalable stop word removal model created especially for Malayalam [15]. It emphasizes how important it is to use language-specific stop word lists in order to improve NLP applications' performance.

5. Future Work

Although the results of the current integrated model for Malayalam stop word recognition are encouraging, there is still much room for improvement. To increase the model's generalizability, one approach is to add more varied and domain-specific Malayalam news sources to the annotated dataset. The BiLSTM model may be able to comprehend word semantics and morphology better by including pre-trained word embeddings, such as fastText or BPEmb, which were especially trained on Malayalam corpora. Furthermore, when it comes to capturing deeper contextual dependencies, transformer-based designs like BERT modified for Malayalam may perform better than BiLSTM. Precision of rule based detection can be improved by incorporating morphological analyzers and part-of-speech tagging in the Sandhi rule engine. Finally, the system would be applicable to such NLP applications as Malayalam sentiment analysis, machine translation, and text summarization if it was developed as an API or web service.

6. Conclusion

Three compatible approaches: manually curated stop word lists, Sandhi rule-based analysis and BiLSTM-based deep learning are effectively represented in the proposed joined model for stop word detection in Malayalam news headline to yield a powerful performance and high accuracy. The model addresses the linguistic complexity of the Malayalam language, such as morphological variations and contextual dependencies, by using the strengths of both of its

approaches. The 91.3% accuracy achieved shows how well our hybrid approach is in extracting significant content words from the stop words. Apart from enhancing the quality of text preprocessing in Malayalam natural language processing jobs, this has created a strong foundation for further developments on regional language processing. All in all, the method goes to further the understanding of natural language in low-resource languages, providing a capturable and extendable model for accurate identification of stop words. Overall, the method helps to move the sphere of natural language understanding for the low-resource languages such as Malayalam a step forward, providing flexible and scalable framework for accurate stop word detection.

References

[1] decode_malayalam. (2024, November 29). *Malayalam Basic Grammar: A Beginner's Guide*. DecodeMalayalam. https://decodemalayalam.com/malayalam-basic-grammar/

[2] Samie, M. E., Bahmani, E., & Mozafari, N. (2025). Analytical Comparison of Stop Word Recognition Methods in Persian Texts. *International Journal of Information Science and Management (IJISM)*, 23(1), 91–107.

[3] Manning, C. D., Raghavan, P., & Schütze, H. (2008). *Introduction to information retrieval*. Cambridge University Press.

[4] Sebastiani, F. (2002). Machine learning in automated text categorization. *ACM computing surveys (CSUR)*, 34(1), 1–47.

[5] Jurafsky, D., & Martin, J. H. (2021). *Speech and Language Processing*. Pearson.

[6] Luhn, H. P. (1958). The Automatic Creation of Literature Abstracts. *IBM Journal of Research and Development*, 2(2), 159–165.

[7] Schütze, H., Manning, C. D., & Raghavan, P. (2008). *Statistical Approaches to Text Categorization*. Cambridge University Press.

[8] Rakholia, R. M., & Saini, J. R. (2016, September). Lexical classes based stop words categorization for Gujarati language. In *2016 2nd international conference on advances in computing, communication, & automation (ICACCA) (Fall)* (pp. 1–5). IEEE.

[9] Nair, L. R., & Peter, S. D. (2011). Development of a rule-based learning system for splitting compound words in Malayalam language. In *Proceedings of the IEEE Recent Advances in Intelligent Computational Systems (RAICS)* (pp. 751–755). IEEE.

[10] Natarajan, A., & Charniak, E. (2011). S3-statistical sandhi splitting. In *Proceedings of the ACL 2011 Student Session* (pp. 1–6). Association for Computational Linguistics.

[11] Das, D., Radhika, K. T., Rajeev, R. R., & Raj, R. (2012). Hybrid sandhi-splitter for Malayalam using Unicode. In *Proceedings of National Seminar on Relevance of Malayalam in Information Technology*.

[12] Kumar, S., Saini, J. R., & Bafna, P. B. (2022). Identification of Malayalam stop-words, stop-stems and stop-lemmas using NLP. In *IOT with Smart Systems* (pp. 341–350). Springer.

[13] Subhash, M., Wilscy, M., & Shanavas, S. A. (2012). A rule-based approach for root word identification in Malayalam language. *International Journal of Computer Science & Information Technology*, 4(3), 159–166.

[14] Faathima Fayaza, M. S., & Fathima Farhath, F. (2021). Towards stopwords identification in Tamil text clustering.

International Journal of Advanced Computer Science and Applications (IJACSA), 12(12), 536–541. https://doi.org/10.14569/IJACSA.2021.0121267

[15] John Snow Labs. (2022, March 7). *Stopwords Remover for Malayalam language*. Spark NLP. https://sparknlp.org/2022/03/07/stopwords_iso_ml_3_0.html

59 IoT-enabled health surveillance for paralyzed patients

K. Monikha, Ann Diya Sunny, K. M. Kavin Dharsan, Rosh V. Lourance, and R. Catherine Joy[a]

Department of Electronics and Communication Engineering, Karunya Institute of Technology and Sciences, Coimbatore, India

Abstract: Paralysis impairs muscles and many paralyzed people depend significantly on caregivers. In order to help paralyzed individuals to communicate their requirements. This device interprets hand movements into words by using a sensor glove. A text message is immediately sent to the caregiver via GSM or IoT. If the behaviour is performed three times, indicating unfulfilled needs. Additionally, the glove uses hand motions to operate household appliances. In order to ensure prompt caregiver response, the device also tracks body temperature and heart rate. If abnormal readings are discovered, a buzzer is activated.

Keywords: IoT-based paralysis patient assistance, home automation, health monitoring, GSM, Wi-Fi, Buzzer alert

1. Introduction

The health monitoring system tracks the vital signs of paralyzed patients using the Blynk IoT platform, which has sensors for temperature, heart rate, and movement. Wi-Fi is used to send data to the Blynk app for caregiver notifications and real-time monitoring. An emergency feature improves patient safety and caregiver response by alerting medical personnel in dire circumstances [1]. The IoT-based health monitoring system tracks body temperature, oxygen levels, heart rate, and blood pressure using non-invasive sensors. It wirelessly sends data to healthcare providers for continuous monitoring and real-time alerts, enhancing patient care, especially in remote areas [2]. The Internet of Things (IoT)-based healthcare system for paralyzed patients uses a temperature sensor and a photoplethysmography (PPG) sensor to monitor body temperature and heart rate. Bluetooth is used to send data so that several patients can be monitored at once. An audio-visual alarm notifies medical personnel of any abnormal readings, and a GSM module notifies patients in the event that the doctor is not present. Through remote health management, quicker reaction times, and real-time monitoring, this method improves patient care [3]. A Paralysis Patient Alerting and Monitoring System was created by Jaju et al. that combines several sensors to continually track vital signs like movement, body temperature, and heart rate. The system uses wireless communication modules to send real-time health information to caregivers and medical professionals, and it uses a microprocessor to handle sensor data. The technology immediately sends out alerts in the event of emergencies or aberrant readings, allowing

for timely medical action. This method improves patient safety and gives caregivers immediate information on the patient's condition [4]. Body temperature, and movement in stroke patients who are partially paralyzed. It notifies caretakers of anomalies and transmits real-time data to a central unit. Additionally, patients can improve their independence and well-being by using basic gestures to operate domestic equipment [5]. It suggests a wearable robotic exoskeleton that helps patients who are paralyzed by detecting movement intent using sEMG signals. These signals are converted into robotic arm movements with assist-as-needed control using a real-time control system. The technology improves user mobility by integrating motion feedback and force sensors for precise handling [6]. This Internet of Things (IoT) system monitors patients with paralysis using wearable sensors and Wi-Fi/cloud, giving caregivers real-time alerts to improve safety and care efficiency [7]. Using wireless connectivity to convert gestures into text or speech and flex sensors to detect hand movements, this Internet of Things smart glove helps people with disabilities. With Bluetooth/Wi-Fi connectivity and real-time data processing, it improves accessibility and communication [8]. This technology converts gestures into wireless signals for communication by using flex sensors to detect the hand movements of people with impairments. It improves patient support and interactivity by using microcontrollers and the Internet of Things for real-time processing [9]. Using wearable sensors to measure vital signs like temperature and heart rate, an Internet of Things-based healthcare system is intended to keep an eye on patients who are paralyzed. By using real-time data transfer over Wi-Fi and the cloud, the technology enables caregivers to keep

[a]catherinejoy@karunya.edu

DOI: 10.1201/9781003724988-59

an eye on patients' health from a distance [10]. By detecting movements in paralyzed patients using gesture sensors and the Internet of Things, this technology improves patient assistance by giving caregivers real-time alerts and automated healthcare advice [11]. This automated healthcare system monitors patients with paralysis using wearable sensors and the Internet of Things (IoT). It allows for real- time data transmission and provides caregivers with immediate alarms, guaranteeing prompt medical intervention and better patient care [12, 13]. Wearable sensors and the TCP/IP protocol are used in this Internet of Things-based patient monitoring system to transmit health data in real time [14].

2. Proposed Methodology

The idea behind the suggested solution system is to make a person as autonomous as possible in order to help them adjust to life with paralysis. One issue with these kinds of gadgets is that they are being developed, and they are highly costly and enormous machinery. They appear to be restricted to use at hospitals and cannot be utilized at the patient's home or convenience. With that in mind, we suggest a system that is primarily composed of a transmitter and a receiver component. The patient will have a gyroscope or accelerometer sensor installed on their hand at the transmitter area (at the patient side). This gyroscope can determine the angle at which the gadget is tilted with regard to the ground by sensing the static acceleration caused by gravity. The patient tilts the gyroscope in various directions whenever he needs assistance. This serves as the gyroscope's input, and the controller board, which serves as the processing unit, receives the volt-volt output of the device. A Wi-Fi trans receiver is used to send and receive signals to a GSM module so that the patient's condition may be determined. The patient's temperature and heartbeat are indicated by the temperature and heartbeat sensors. Figure 59.1 displays our model's general framework.

3. Hardware Implemetation

This model uses a gyroscope or accelerometer detects hand movements, which are treated by a microcontroller and transmitted through Wi-Fi and GSM modules to notify caregivers. It's always a good idea to select an Arduino compatible GSM module, that is, a GSM module with TTL Output specifications, for our project that involves connecting a GSM modem or module to Arduino and utilizing Arduino to send and receive SMS. In addition, heartbeat and temperature sensors are used to ensure health monitoring of real time. This system increases the patient's autonomy, facilitates distance care and provides a practical solution for home -based health services.

3.1. Software implementation

The schematic representation for this proposed method is executed in Proteus software (Figure 59.2) for reference of the connection.

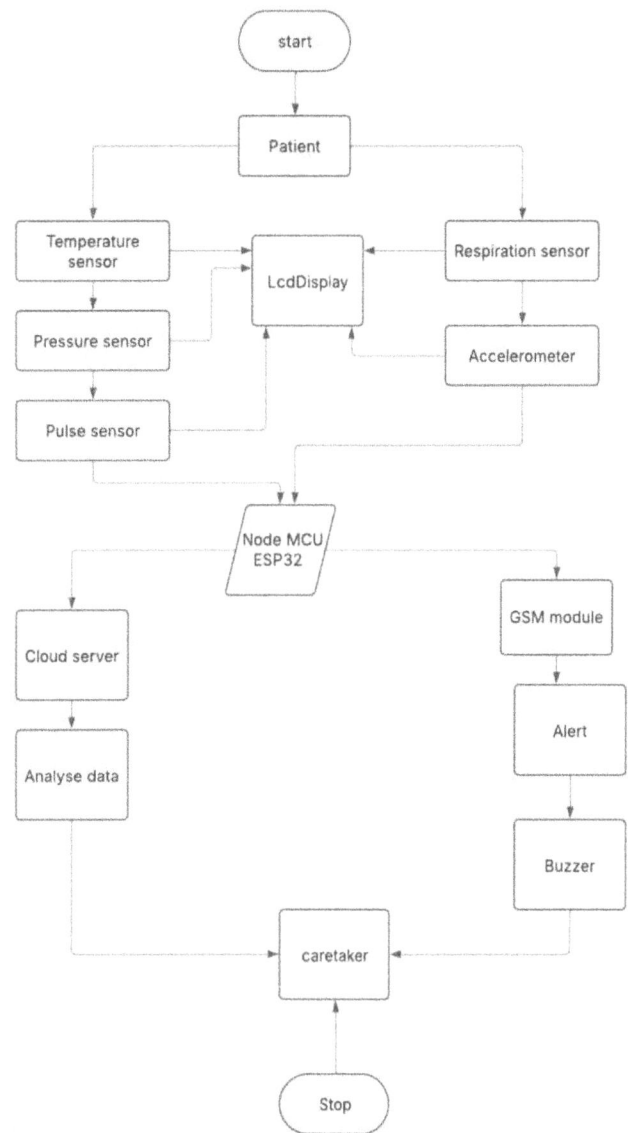

Figure 59.1. Flow chart.

Source: Author.

3.2. WIFI module

A extremely affordable and easy-to-use tool for giving your projects internet connectivity is the ESP8266. The module's dual functionality as a hotspot-creating access point and a Wi-Fi-connecting station allows it to effortlessly retrieve and upload data to the internet, hence simplifying the Internet of Things. Our project would be smarter since it could access any information on the internet because it could also retrieve data from the internet through APIs. This module's ability to be programmed with the Arduino IDE, which makes it much more user-friendly, is another intriguing feature. You must use this module in conjunction with another microcontroller, such as an Arduino, because it only has two GPIO pins (though you may hack it to use up to four). If not, you can consider the more independent ESP-12 or ESP-32 variants.

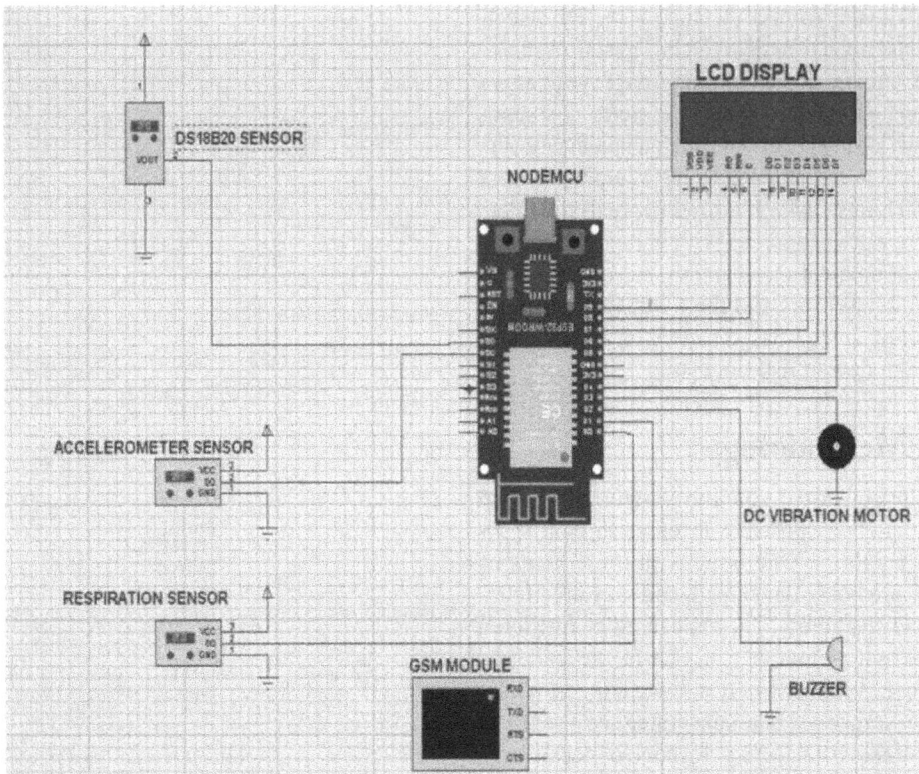

Figure 59.2. Schematic representation (Proteus).

Source: Author.

3.3. *Power supply*

The system's power supply unit (Figure 59.3), which transforms 230V AC into a regulated DC output, is shown in the block diagram. The high AC voltage is first reduced to 12V using a step-down transformer. A bridge rectifier, which transforms the AC voltage into pulsing DC, comes next. The output is subsequently stabilized and smoothed by a voltage regulator, which guarantees a steady DC voltage appropriate for powering electronic parts. Power distribution to the system is safe and dependable thanks to its architecture.

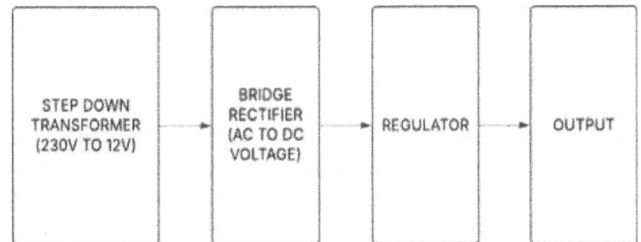

Figure 59.3. Power supply.

Source: Author.

3.4. *1-Wire DS18B20 temperature sensor*

A temperature sensor with a 1-wire interface is the DS18B20. The innovative 1-Wire Interface allows two-way communication with a microcontroller using just one digital pin. Typically, there are two form factors for the sensor. One that comes in a TO-92 packaging has the exact same appearance as a regular transistor. Another type is a waterproof probe, which is more practical for measuring objects that are far away, submerged, or underground. In order to connect with Arduino, the DS18B20 uses a 1-Wire bus, which by definition only needs one data line (and ground). With an accuracy of ±0.5°, it can operate in the temperature range of −10°C to +85°C. Furthermore, the DS18B20 does not require an external power source because it can obtain power straight from the data line, or "parasite power." Multiple DS18B20s

can operate on a single 1-Wire bus since each one has a distinct 64-bit serial code. Therefore, controlling numerous DS18B20s dispersed across a wide region with a single CPU is straightforward. HVAC environmental controls, temperature monitoring systems within structures, machinery, or equipment, and process monitoring and control systems are among the applications that can profit from this capability.

3.5. *A respiration sensor*

Breathing rate and relative depth of thoracic or abdominal breathing are measured by the Respiration Sensor. It comes with an elastic band that is simple to put on and may be worn over clothes. Over the abdomen, the respiration sensor is typically positioned. For HRV training, the Blood Volume Pulse Sensor and respiration are frequently combined.

3.6. ESP32

Espressif's ESP32-S SoC, a potent, programmable MCU with built-in Bluetooth and WIFI, powers the board. It is the least expensive ESP32 development board (about $7) with simultaneous support for MicroSD cards, an onboard camera module, and 4MB of PSRAM. Additional soldering is needed to add an external WiFi antenna for signal boosting. Since the board lacks a standard USB connector, you will need to upload codes to it using an FTDI programmer, an add-on HAT, or an Arduino UNO and the Arduino IDE/ESP-IDF DEV tools. For many IoT and machine vision applications, it is a very popular board because it is inexpensive and has a compact enough form factor. Many instructional pages and the out-of-date spec sheet claim that the ESP32-CAM only supports two camera modules (OV2640 & OV7670). However, you may use a variety of cameras with it; just read down for more information.

3.7. MPU-6050 triple-axis accelerometer and gyroscope module

Accurately measuring motion, orientation, and angular velocity, the MPU-6050 is a 6-axis motion tracking sensor that combines a 3-axis accelerometer and a 3-axis gyro. It has user-programmable full-scale ranges for the accelerometer (±2g to ±16g) and gyroscope (±250°/s to ±2000°/s), as well as I2C connectivity up to 400 kHz. It offers real-time motion tracking, low power consumption, and great precision thanks to its integrated temperature sensor and digital signal processing (DSP). It is ideal for gesture recognition, robotics, and Internet of Things applications because of its rapid response time and well-engineered, shake-resistant construction, which allows for efficient data processing.

4. Result and Discussion

For patients who are paralyzed, this wearable, Internet of Things-based paralysis monitoring device is a useful tool. Patients can utilize hand signals to notify their caregiver of

any needs thanks to the reasonably priced technology. Additionally, the device tracks the patient's vitals, including heart rate, and notifies the patient's caregiver or family member right away if the parameter deviates from the normal range to a dangerous range, allowing for the patient to receive critical care. The following Figures 59.4–59.8 display the results of our model from ThingSpeak.

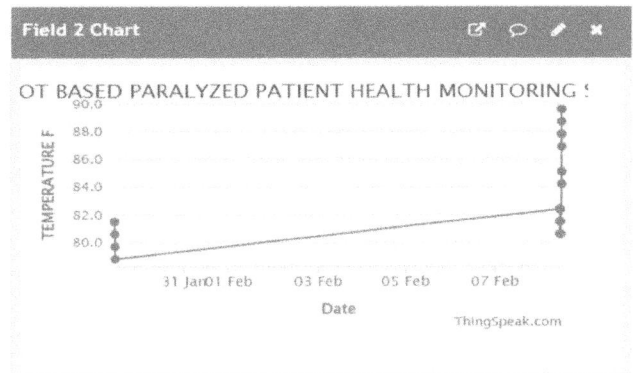

Figure 59.5. Output of temperature (F).

Source: Author.

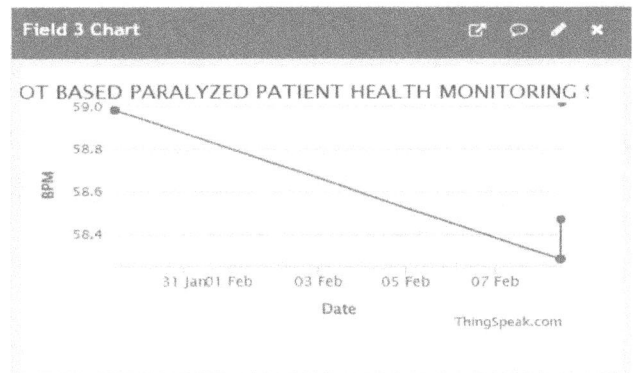

Figure 59.6. Output of BPM.

Source: Author.

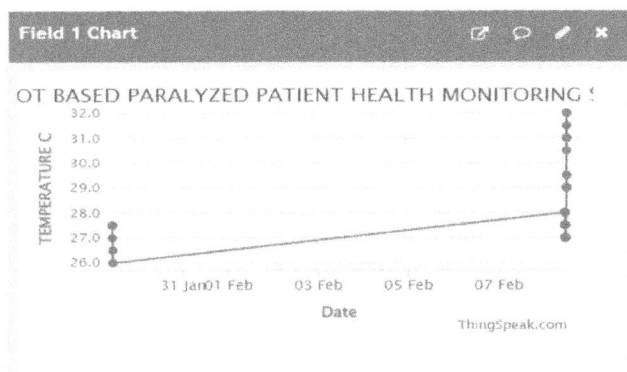

Figure 59.4. Output of temperature (C).

Source: Author.

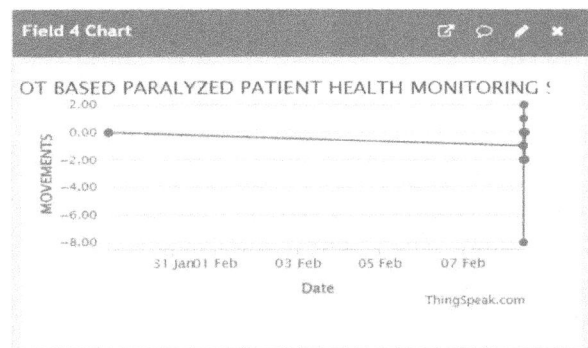

Figure 59.7. Output of movement.

Source: Author.

The hardware device that displays the results of the patients temperation (both in terms of C & F) and BPM through LED display is shown in Figures 59.9 and 59.10.

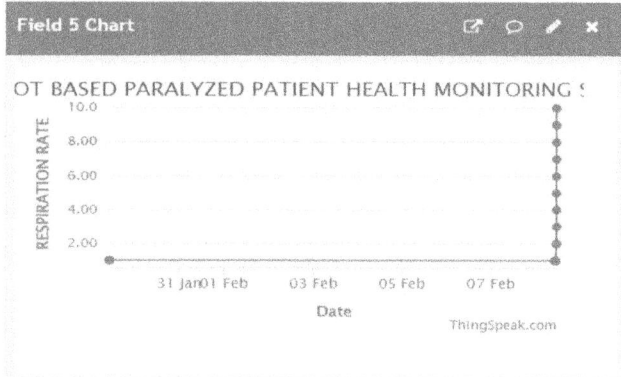

Figure 59.8. Output of respiration rate.

Source: Author.

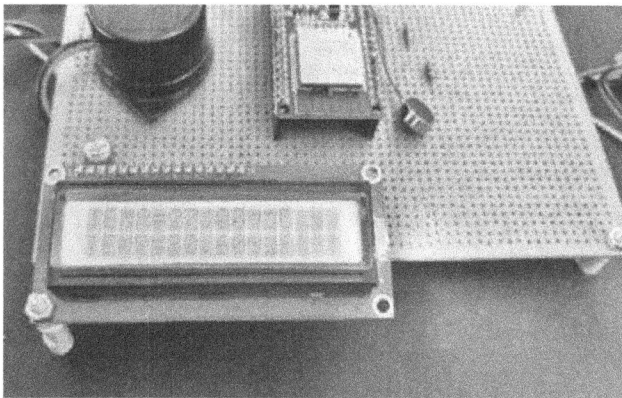

Figure 59.9. LED display temperature.

Source: Author.

Figure 59.10. LED display of BPM.

Source: Author.

5. Conclusion

The above proposed model's output infer that that, it accurately monitored the health conditions of the paralyzed patient compared to other existing techniques. In order to guarantee continuous and precise tracking of vital signs, the Temperature, pressure, pulse, respiration, and accelerometer sensors are among the many sensors that are successfully integrated into the proposed Internet of Things (IoT)-based health monitoring system for patients who are paralyzed. Real-time health data is collected by the system and sent to a cloud server. Where it is examined for anomalies, using the Node MCU ESP32 as the central processing unit. Remote monitoring is made possible by this cloud connectivity, which gives caregivers access to patient data from anywhere. Furthermore, the system's GSM module and alert mechanism ensure early response when necessary by promptly informing medical professionals and caregivers of crucial health occurrences through message alerts and alarms. Due to its cost-effectiveness and scalability, this method can be widely implemented. Future improvements can include adding more wearable sensors to the system's compatibility list, improving the user interface for improved caregiver interaction, and incorporating sophisticated predictive analytics for early identification of health decline. Furthermore, protecting privacy and data security in cloud storage and communication channels continues to be a top priority. All things considered, this method offers a thorough and dependable healthcare solution, greatly enhancing the wellbeing of individuals who are paralyzed.

References

[1]   Varghese, N., Hepsiba, D., & Anand, L. V. (2022, April). Health monitoring and observatory system for paralysed patients using Blynk application. In *2022 6th International Conference on Devices, Circuits and Systems (ICDCS)* (pp. 322–326). IEEE. doi: 10.1109/ICDCS54290.2022.9780851.

[2]   Bhardwaj, V., Joshi, R., & Gaur, A. M. (2022). IoT-based smart health monitoring system for COVID-19. *SN Computer Science*, *3*(2), 137.

[3]   Kad, S., Joshi, A., Bajgude, S., & Naiknawre, D. (2022). IoT Based Paralysis Patient Healthcare. *International Journal for Research in Applied Science & Engineering Technology (IJRASET)*, *10*, 3628–3633.

[4]   Jaju, R., Karwa, P., Purandare, R., Khose, K., Deshmukh, S., & Devadkar, R. (2024, April). Paralysis Patient Alerting and Monitoring System. In *2024 MIT Art, Design and Technology School of Computing International Conference (MITADTSoCiCon)* (pp. 1–5). IEEE.

[5]   Pradeep, S., Chandana, G., Riti, D., Sneha, S., Sumit, K., & Subhra, C. (2019). IOT Based Wireless Monitoring Stroke Patient with Partial Paralysis Assistance. *International Journal of Engineering Trends and Technology*, *67*, 104–110.

[6]   Hasegawa, Y., Mikami, Y., Watanabe, K., Firouzimehr, Z., & Sankai, Y. (2008, September). Wearable handling support system for paralyzed patient. In *2008 IEEE/RSJ International Conference on Intelligent Robots and Systems* (pp. 741–746). IEEE. doi: 10.1109/IROS.2008.4651199.

[7] Kumar, R., Shahameer, A., & Meghashree, T. (2024). IOT Based Automated Paralysis Patient Monitoring System. *International Journal of Research Publication and Reviews*, 5, 9128–9131.

[8] Kumar, R. S., Leninpugalhanthi, P., & Rathika, S., Rithika, G., & Sandhya, S. (2021). Implementation of IoT Based Smart Assistance Gloves for Disabled People. In *2021 7th international conference on advanced computing and communication systems (ICACCS)* (Vol. 1, pp. 1160–1164). IEEE.

[9] Lakshmi, K. J., Muneshwar, A., Ratnam, A. V., & Kodali, P. (2020, July). Patient Assistance using Flex Sensor. In *2020 International Conference on Communication and Signal Processing (ICCSP)* (pp. 00181–00185). IEEE.

[10] Jadhav, P. A., Jadhav, S. B., Erudkar, A. P., Bhurke, S. A., & Palekar, N. S. (2021). An IoT Based Approach in Paralysis Patient Healthcare System. *International Journal of Engineering Applied Sciences and Technology*, 6(3), 238–245.

[11] Aziz, C., Asma, S., Kadmin, A. F., Norain, R., Waheed, H., Aziz, I., Mohd Saad, H., & Rostam, H. (2019). Development of automatic healthcare instruction system via movement gesture sensor for paralysis patient. *International Journal of Electrical and Computer Engineering (IJECE)*, 9, 1676. 10.11591/ijece.v9i3. pp. 1676–1682.

[12] Eshrak, H., Uddin, M. R., Mahmood, A., & Hasan, M. (2023, December). Automated Paralysis Patient Health Care & Monitoring System. In *2023 26th International Conference on Computer and Information Technology (ICCIT)* (pp. 1–5). IEEE.

[13] Pandey, A. K., & Nayak, D. S. (2024, September). A Profitable Communication System for Paralytic Patients with Healthcare Monitoring. In *2024 IEEE North Karnataka Subsection Flagship International Conference (NKCon)* (pp. 1–5). IEEE.

[14] Sujin, J. S., Mukesh, S., Raj, M. P., Sashwanth, M., & Kumar, R. R. (2021, March). IoT based patient monitoring system using TCP/IP protocol. In *2021 7th International Conference on Advanced Computing and Communication Systems (ICACCS)* (Vol. 1, pp. 1076–1080). IEEE.

60 Flexible 1 × 2 MIMO antenna array for WLAN applications

R. Julia Karal Adisaya, P. Solomon Rajan, J. John Ebenezer, Nehal Kumar, S. Jeffry Joel, and D. Jasmine David[a]

Department of Electronics and Communication Engineering, Karunya Institute of Technology and Sciences, Coimbatore, India

Abstract: The Flexible 1x2 MIMO antenna design for WLAN applications is designed for frequencies between 5.1 and 5.8 GHz, making it ideal for next-generation wireless communication networks. A thin, flexible substrate is used for wearable and bendable electronics to enhance conformability. The substrate employed in the antenna's construction is polyimide, and the HFSS software suite is leveraged for the design and simulation of this antenna. Its compact and straightforward design characterizes the antenna, with dimensions measuring 40 x 60 x 0.035 mm^3. The measured return loss is recorded as -22.00 dB at the frequency of 5.8 GHz.

Keywords: Flexible, MIMO, polyimide, wearable, WLAN

1. Introduction

A flexible MIMO antenna for Sub-6GHz 5G and WLAN usage is an innovative antenna technology that takes advantage of the flexibility of substrates and the use of multiple antenna elements to provide high data rates and stable signal reception in the sub-6GHz frequency band, especially important for future wireless networks, while adhering to curved surfaces on devices such as wearables or smart surfaces, making it easy to integrate into a wide range of applications with its flexible form factor. Recent developments in MIMO antenna technology have made them highly popular since they are capable of streaming and receiving data in large quantities while minimizing the problems caused by multipath fading [1–2]. The antenna is built on a flexible substrate called polyamide so that it can be bent and flexible, and it can be adapted for non-planar surfaces, suitable for wearable devices, and curved vehicle surfaces. The MIMO technology uses multiple antennas to send and receive several signals simultaneously, so it improves the speed and efficiency of communication [3]. It uses the multipath propagation concept. By having several antenna elements spaced appropriately, the antenna has spatial diversity, greatly enhancing the signal quality and data rates through MIMO technology. Issues like multipath fading can be solved by using MIMO antennas as they fit in compact spaces. They are a popular approach to improve data transmission capacity and reduce the impact of signal issues simultaneously [4]. This antenna has been specifically crafted to operate under the sub-6GHz band, commonly employed for 5G applications as well as WLAN, with great coverage and penetration

features. Some possible areas of application involve wearable technology, smart fabrics, automotive antennas, IoT, and flexible displays, where conformal-type antenna structures play a pivotal role in the maximum reception of signals. Some drawbacks of patch antennas are having a narrow bandwidth, low gain, and being bulky at the lower frequencies [5]. Several studies and research have proposed various ways to enhance the bandwidth and improve the gain of patch antennas to ensure better results. The two main problems while designing a MIMO antenna are making it smaller and ensuring enough isolation between ports [6]. A great deal of research has been undertaken to address these challenges by refining antenna designs to decrease mutual coupling between elements. Further, MIMO systems need to address problems such as co-channel interference and multipath fading to perform better [7]. Ensuring antennas are highly isolated significantly improves system efficiency by minimizing interaction between antenna components.

2. Literature Review

Flexible substrate antennas (FSAs) are increasingly sought after for the next wave of wireless devices, particularly in applications where antennas need to be integrated into curved electronic surfaces [8]. Various methods can be used to excite these antennas, such as coaxial connections, strip lines, aperture coupling, proximity coupling, and other feeding techniques [9]. Research in this area focuses specifically on developing multiband antennas with Multi-Input Multi-Output (MIMO) configurations, which improve data transfer rates when connecting

[a]jasmine@karunya.edu

DOI: 10.1201/9781003724988-60

multiple devices simultaneously [10]. Additionally, these antennas are often paired with different types of reflector structures to enhance their directivity. The small size, wide bandwidth, and high gain requirements of 5G make MIMO antennas challenging to design. There are a lot of challenges that are brought forward when designing MIMO antennas for 5G because of their small size, wide bandwidth, and high gain requirements [11–12]. A lot of technologies, like wearable and transparent antennas, are being investigated and worked upon to address these problems so that the performance of the upcoming generation of wireless networks can be improved [13]. In 5G applications, the technology stands out due to its high efficiency, maximum gain, broad bandwidth, and strong MIMO diversity performance, even when flexed along the X and Y axis. When the antenna is placed on a human body, it comes into contact with a significant amount of lossy material nearby. This proximity negatively impacts performance by transforming the antenna's nearby electric field into thermal energy [14–16]. Furthermore, incorporating these methods often requires adding extra components, which enlarges the overall size of the antenna.

3. Antenna Design

When constructing a Flexible MIMO Antenna, the chosen substrate should be flexible. Polyimide is one of the flexible radiating materials. Selecting the Antenna's resonance frequency is very important. This design's suggested resonance frequency is 5.8 GHz, and this antenna's structure will be usable in Industries such as 5G and WLAN applications. With the aid of HFSS software, two circular patch dipoles with a feedline are proposed. In the design, ports have been established at the edge of the feed line. The antenna has been organized into different layers, including the substrate, vacuum, and conductive elements. The presence of lumped ports, represented by rectangular regions, confirms that the antenna is excited using discrete ports. As reactive elements, the slots in the radiating patch can be used to reduce size and improve gain and bandwidth.

$$Q = f/BW \tag{1}$$

Q - Quality factor of the antenna
f - Resonant frequency
BW - Bandwidth

$$L = \frac{Im(Z1)}{(2\pi.f)} \tag{2}$$

$$C = \left(\frac{2\pi.f}{Zi}\right)^\wedge (-1) \tag{3}$$

Z_i – Impedance of the antenna
L – Inductance of the antenna
Height of the Patch:

$$H = \frac{(0.3.c)}{2\pi.f0\sqrt{\varepsilon}} \tag{4}$$

C – speed of the light 3× m/s

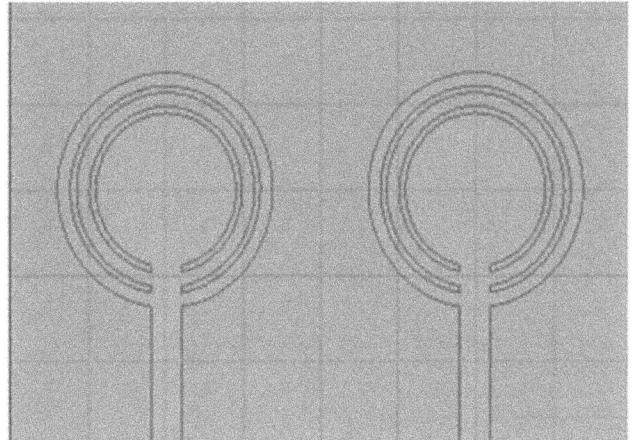

Figure 60.1. Proposed 1 × 2 flexible MIMO antenna.
Source: Author.

Width of the Patch:

$$W = \frac{c}{(2*f0*\sqrt{\left(\frac{\varepsilon r+1}{2}\right)})} \tag{5}$$

ε_r - Dielectric substance
Length of the Patch:

$$Leff = \frac{c}{(2*f0*\sqrt{(\varepsilon eff)})} \tag{6}$$

Leff – Effective length of the patch antenna

4. Simulation Results and Discussion

4.1. Return loss

Return loss quantifies the proportion of electrical energy reflected by the flexible MIMO antenna, also referred to as the S-parameter or reflection coefficient. Return loss helps estimate how well the measured load at the receiving end and the source (delivering to the end) match under the terms of impedance. If the radiation mode must be successful, the necessary return loss value must be –10 dB or less so that the resonance frequency of the suggested antenna is 5.8 GHz. The graph displays that the antenna's radiation loss at 5.8 GHz is –22.00 dB, which indicates that the antenna has lower energy loss and better susceptibility match. Figure 60.1 represents the suggested antenna's S-Parameter versus frequency curve. The intended antenna's bandwidth can be computed by utilizing the frequency range indicated by the return loss of less than -10dB, which is also shown in Figure 60.2.

The recommended antenna is predicted to have a –10 dB bandwidth for an impedance of 0.7019 GHz, 702 MHz (from a range of 5.129 GHz to 5.8309 GHz), which means that it covers the 5.73–5.86 GHz WLAN bands. The thickness of the substrate is 0.035 mm. Low S21 (~ –40 dB), which indicates excellent isolation between MIMO antenna elements and minimal mutual coupling, as shown in Figure 60.3. This reduces interference and enhances diversity performance, which is essential for efficient MIMO operation.

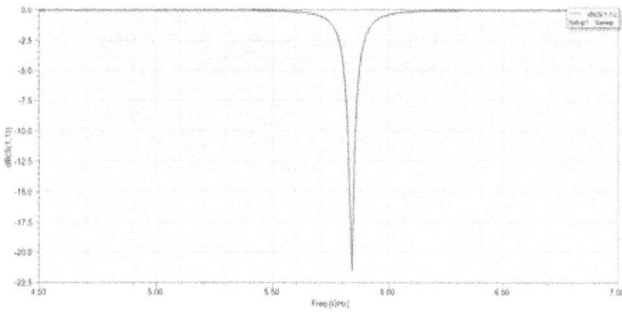

Figure 60.2. Proposed 1 × 2 MIMO antenna's S-Parameter vs frequency curve.

Source: Author.

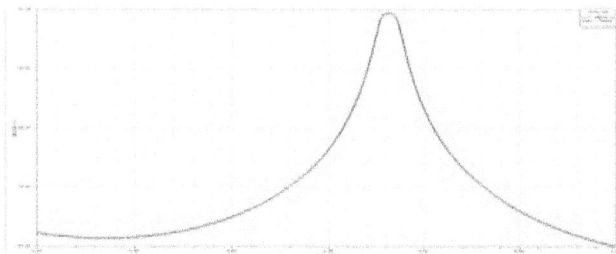

Figure 60.3. Proposed 1 × 2 MIMO antenna's S-Parameter (s(2,1)).

Source: Author.

4.2. Gain and radiation pattern

If something must be broadcasted from the antenna, the radiation pattern is the transmission of power because of the directional angle from the antenna, if it is absorbing, it is the concentration of power received by the antenna. The ability of the antenna to transmit and receive energy is indicated by the gain parameter. Alternatively, it describes the relationship between the amount of energy transferred in a specific direction and the amount of radiation generated by isotropic antennas. The far-field gain of the suggested antenna is plotted in three dimensions in Figure 60.4, where a realized gain value of 1.22 dB was found at the resonance frequency of 5.8 GHz (Tables 60.1 and 60.2).

5. Conclusion

This work presents a polyimide-based flexible MIMO antenna operating with a frequency band in Sub-6 GHz, suitable for 5G and WLAN applications. The flexibility of the antenna makes it suitable to be adaptable for other surfaces, owing to its practical use in the integration of non-planar configurations of a wireless communication system. This aspect of being flexible is highly beneficial in wearable electronics, smart surfaces, automotive communications, and the whole Internet of Things (IoT) arena, where rigid antennas cannot be used or implemented. By employing multiple antenna elements spaced out for optimally maintaining diversity, the

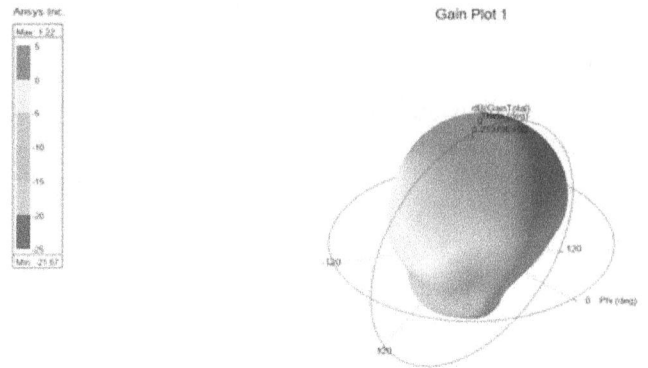

Figure 60.4. 3D plot of far-field gain at 5.8 GHz.

Source: Author.

Table 60.1. A summary of the proposed 1x2 MIMO antenna's simulation

Parameter	Value
Substrate	Polyimide
Resonant frequency	5.8GHz
Return loss	<–22dB
Radiation Medium	Air
Bandwidth	from (5.1–5.8 GHz)
Realized gain	1.22dB

Source: Author.

Table 60.2. Dimensions of the proposed antenna

Parameter	Length (mm)	Width (mm)
Ground	40	60
Substrate	40	60
Microstrip Feed Line	10	20
Circular Patch Radius	6 mm	

Source: Author.

quality of the information signal and throughput improves; this becomes highly essential with MIMO technology. The flexible structure and performance-robustness of the antenna open possibilities for applications in the future wireless scenario. The analysis of bending is part of our planned post-fabrication work. This paper evaluates multiple performance measures, including radiation pattern, gain, bandwidth, and return loss. According to the proposed antenna, the resonance is at 5.8, and the return loss is –22.00dB. The antenna's advent into future devices and networks is expected to enhance connectivity in all environments yet preserve reliability and efficiency in dynamic settings.

Acknowledgement

The author acknowledge Karunya Institute of Technology and Sciences, Coimbatore, India for providing the facilities required to carry out this research.

References

[1] Kulkarni, J., et al. (2022). Dual Polarized, Multiband Four-Port Decagon Shaped Flexible MIMO Antenna for Next Generation Wireless Applications. *IEEE Access, 10,* 128132128150. doi:10.1109/ACCESS.2022.3227034.

[2] Gohil, J. V., & Bhatia, D. (2012, December). Design of 2 × 1 circularly polarized microstrip patch antenna array for 5.8 GHz ISM band applications. In *2012 Nirma University International Conference on Engineering (NUiCONE)* (pp. 1–4). IEEE.

[3] Chung, K. L., Yan, X., Cui, A., & Li, Y. (2021). Circularly-polarized linear antenna array of non-identical radiating patch elements for WiFi/WLAN applications. *AEU-International Journal of Electronics and Communications, 129,* 153526.

[4] Aliqab, K., Armghan, A., Alsharari, M., & Aly, M. H. (2023). Highly decoupled and high gain conformal two-port MIMO antenna for V2X communications. *Alexandria Engineering Journal, 74,* 599–610.

[5] Kulkarni, N. P., Bahadure, N. B., Patil, P. D., Karve, S. M., Kulkarni, J. S., & Kadam, S. S. (2022, April). Flexible MIMO Antennas for 5G Applications. In *2022 10th International Conference on Emerging Trends in Engineering and Technology-Signal and Information Processing (ICETET-SIP-22)* (pp. 1–6). IEEE.

[6] Ribitha, E. M., & Vadivel, M. (2022, September). Design and analysis of flexible 2-Port MIMO antenna with reflector ground for WLAN applications. In *2022 International Conference on Intelligent Innovations in Engineering and Technology (ICIIET)* (pp. 250–254). IEEE.

[7] Riaz, A., Khan, S., & Arslan, T. (2023). Design and modelling of graphene-based flexible 5G antenna for next-generation wearable head imaging systems. *Micromachines, 14*(3), 610.

[8] Rakluea, P., Wongsin, N., Mahatthanajatuphat, C., Aroonmitr, P., Jangjing, T., Rakluea, C., … & Chudpooti, N. (2023). Flexible thin film-based triple port UWB MIMO antenna with modified ground plane for UWB, WLAN, WiMAX, WPAN and 5G applications. *IEEE Access, 11,* 107031–107048.

[9] Kim-Thi, P. (2023). Circularly polarized MIMO patch antenna with high isolation and wideband characteristics for WLAN applications. *Heliyon, 9*(9).

[10] Naik, S., Upmanyu, A., & Sharma, M. (2024, May). A Review of Multi-Band Flexible MIMO Antenna Design on Thin Substrate for High Diversity Performance. In *2024 International Conference on Electronics, Computing, Communication and Control Technology (ICECCC)* (pp. 1–6). IEEE.

[11] Ayyappan, M. B., & Chandran, J. (2016). Design and analysis of circular microstrip antenna at 5.8 GHz with Fr-4 substrate. *International Journal of Advanced Research in Electrical, Electronics and Instrumentation Engineering, 5*(4), 41–45.

[12] Kulkarni, J., Alharbi, A. G., Desai, A., Sim, C. Y. D., & Poddar, A. (2021). Design and analysis of wideband flexible self-isolating MIMO antennas for sub-6 GHz 5G and WLAN smartphone terminals. *Electronics, 10*(23), 3031.

[13] Amraoui, Y., Halkhams, I., El Alami, R., Jamil, M. O., & Qjidaa, H. (2024). High gain MIMO antenna with multiband characterization for terahertz applications. *Scientific African, 26,* e02380.

[14] Rajesh, G., & Poonkuzhali, R. (2024). Design and analysis of CPW fed ultrathin flexible MIMO antenna for UWB and X-band applications. *IEEE Access, 12,* 96704–96717.

[15] Shariff, B. P., Ali, T., Mane, P. R., Alsath, M. G. N., Kumar, P., Pathan, S., … & Khan, T. (2024). Design and measurement of a compact millimeter wave highly flexible MIMO antenna loaded with metamaterial reflective surface for wearable applications. *IEEE Access, 12,* 30066–30084.

[16] Kumkhet, B., Rakluea, P., Wongsin, N., Sangmahamad, P., Thaiwirot, W., Mahatthanajatuphat, C., & Chudpooti, N. (2023). SAR reduction using dual band EBG method based on MIMO wearable antenna for WBAN applications. *AEU-International Journal of Electronics and Communications, 160,* 154525.

61 Development of a real-time geofencing system for ground support vehicle monitoring in airports

Aishwarya K., Supraja Reddy A.[a], Sujith K., Pravallika M., Sathish P., Pavan Kalyan M., and Khashyap K.

Chaitanya Bharathi Institute of Technology (CBIT), Hyderabad, India

Abstract: Ground support vehicles are essential for airport operations, but they come with safety risks due to their movement in high-traffic zones. These risks can lead to collisions, runway incursions, and delays, which may cause injuries and damage to equipment. This paper presents a cost-effective, real-time monitoring system designed to address these risks by using GPS modules for precise vehicle tracking, microcontrollers for data processing, and a server-side application for communication, data storage, and user interaction. The system features a web-based interface that visualizes vehicle locations on a map and offers potential geofencing capabilities. It alerts vehicle drivers as they approach restricted areas, providing notifications when they are within 2 meters of the geofence perimeter. This early warning system allows drivers to adjust their routes and avoid entering restricted zones, thereby enhancing safety. Additionally, air traffic controllers can leverage the system to prevent accidents and improve ground traffic flow. The system demonstrates its feasibility as an affordable and practical solution to enhance airport safety and operational efficiency. The system architecture supports scalability for larger airports with multiple runways and taxiways.

Keywords: Ground support vehicle, monitoring system, real-time tracking, geofencing, airport safety

1. Introduction

Efficient and safe aircraft movement within airports is essential, especially in environments shared with various ground support vehicles. To minimize collisions and near-misses, this paper proposes a Ground Support Vehicle Monitoring System using GPS and geofencing technologies. Real-time GPS integration in vehicles provides situational awareness and a global view of ground operations. Geofencing creates digital barriers around aircraft zones, sending alerts when boundaries are breached, allowing air traffic or ground control to respond swiftly. This enhances safety for both aircraft and ground crews by preventing unauthorized access. to restricted areas. The system leverages real-time data for proactive decision-making, ensuring improved coordination and operational efficiency across the airport.

2. Theoretical Background

Previous research supports vehicle monitoring at airports. Smith et al. introduced neural networks for predictive maintenance [1], while Blasch et al. used optical surveillance for airport security [2]. Alomara and Tolujevs optimized vehicle movements on airfields [3], and Tang contributed to post-collision alert systems [4]. Hawas et al. demonstrated inter-vehicular communication for routing [5]. Jospine et al. applied geofencing to emergency vehicles [6], and Wang et al. focused on airport equipment tracking and collision prevention [7]. Rosayyan et al. proposed a GNSS-based geofencing model for emergency vehicles [8]. Stevens and Atkins defined unmanned aerial geofences [9], while Ding et al. analyzed historical data for airport ferry time estimations [10]. Wang et al. presented real-time tracking of logistics trains [11], and Zhou et al. worked on vehicle routing in ground handling [12]. Lofù et al. explored UAV tracking and classification [13]. Building on this, the proposed system combines GPS, microcontrollers, and server-side apps for cost-effective real-time tracking, geofencing, and optimized airport vehicle management.

3. Methodology

The system focuses on real-time tracking, data visualization, and geofence monitoring through efficient acquisition, user-friendly interfaces, and secure data handling. As shown in Figure 61.1, the process begins with the in-vehicle GPS module determining location and sending it to the ESP8266 microcontroller, which decodes the coordinates and transmits them via Wi-Fi to a server. The server, using PHP, processes the data, checks for geofence violations, and stores it in a database. If a vehicle crosses a defined geofence, an alert is generated. The client-side web application displays the live vehicle position and geofence status on a map, notifying users of any breach.

[a]suprajareddy_ece@cbit.ac.in

DOI: 10.1201/9781003724988-61

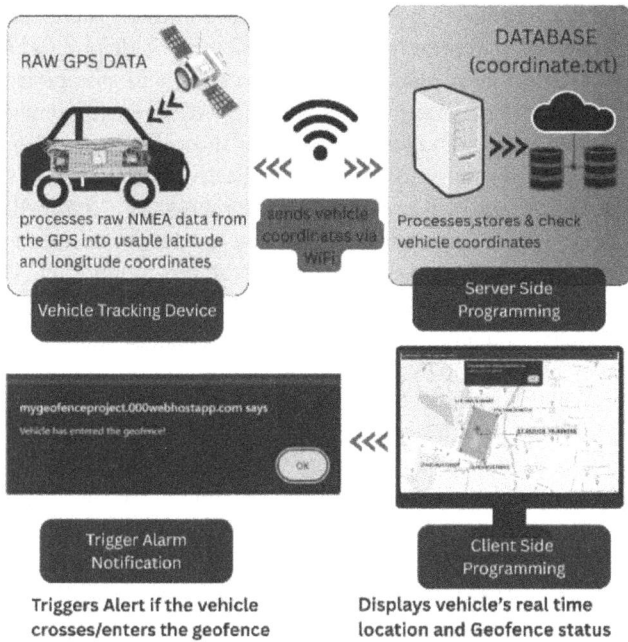

Figure 61.1. Pictorial representation of methodology.

Source: Author.

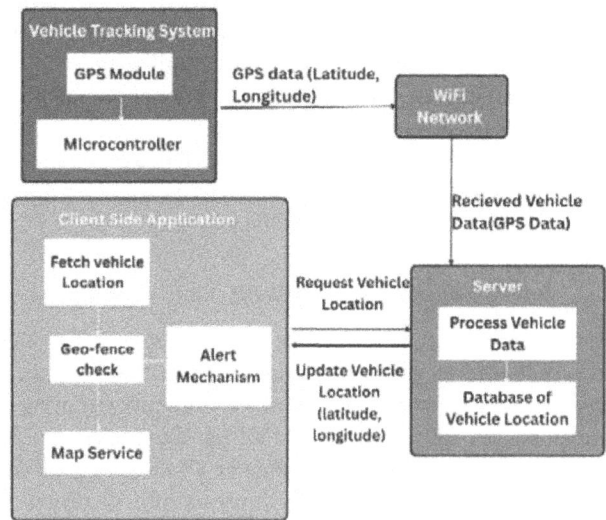

Figure 61.2. Schematic of the proposed system.

Source: Author.

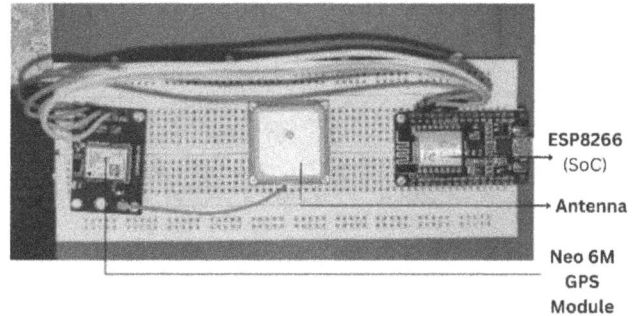

Figure 61.3. Prototype of the vehicle tracking system.

Source: Author.

To detail the operation, Figure 61.2 illustrates the methodology, showing interactions between the onboard GPS unit, server logic, and user interface. The microcontroller converts GPS data (NMEA format) into coordinates, which are then transmitted to the central server. The server logs this into a database, and the website fetches this data for display. A mapping API visualizes both vehicle position and geofences, with alerts triggered upon geofence entry or exit. The following sections will elaborate on each system block, outlining both hardware and software elements used in the prototype.

3.1. Vehicle tracking

The core functionality of the vehicle tracking device relies on two essential components: a GPS module and a microcontroller. The system, which is developed by the combination of the NEO-6M GPS module with GPS ceramic antenna and the ESP8266 microcontroller, as depicted in Figure 61.3, provided a reliable and efficient foundation for the vehicle tracking device. The GPS module acts as a positioning system, using signals from GPS satellites to pinpoint the vehicle's location. This includes determining latitude, longitude, and often altitude data. In this paper, NEO-6M has been chosen as the GPS module. The main reason for selecting NEO-6M over other GPS modules is that it is commercially available at competitive prices, making it suitable for resource-constrained projects. A minor challenge encountered was the initial acquisition time, particularly in environments with limited sky visibility, but as the prototype is focused

on airport applications, this is not a disadvantage. While the cold start time (initial satellite acquisition) averaged around 30 seconds, subsequent reacquisition times after temporary signal loss were generally faster [14]. However, it also offers high-precision GPS positioning data and power efficiency, which is indispensable for real-time tracking of ground support vehicle movements within the airport environment [15].

The microcontroller acts as the central processing unit, interpreting raw GPS data and making decisions based on it. It also facilitates communication with the GPS module for configuration, data requests, and, ultimately, transmission. Cellular networks, Wi-Fi, or other protocols can be used for this transmission. For this system, considering affordability and the airport environment, the ESP8266 microcontroller was chosen. It's cost-effective, integrates Wi-Fi for wireless data transmission to a central server, and has low power consumption for extended operation on battery power within the GSE tracking units [16]. The total power consumption of the system is a crucial factor for real-world deployments, especially for battery-powered applications. In this proto-type, the total power consumption of the system is evaluated and estimated to be approximately 412.5 milliwatts.

The emphasis on low power consumption throughout the design process resulted in a device well-suited for mobile deployments with extended battery life. These positive out-comes demonstrate the effectiveness of the chosen hardware components in meeting the objectives.

3.2. Server-side programming

The server-side functionality is implemented using PHP code, intended to work in conjunction with a web applica-tion. In this section working of server-side programming is explained. On the server side initially, a folder is created on a third-party web host to accommodate all the programming data and also files to append information of coordinates as shown in Figure 61.4. The server-side programming begins by waiting for incoming requests. It then inspects the HTTP request method to determine the type of operation intended by the client (e.g., GET for retrieving data, POST for sending data). If the request method is POST, signifying an update for GPS coordinates, the server extracts the latitude and longitude data from the request body. This involves access-ing specific fields named "lat" and "lng" within the request. To contain information on the coordinates, a file named "coordinates.txt" in the public html directory as shown in

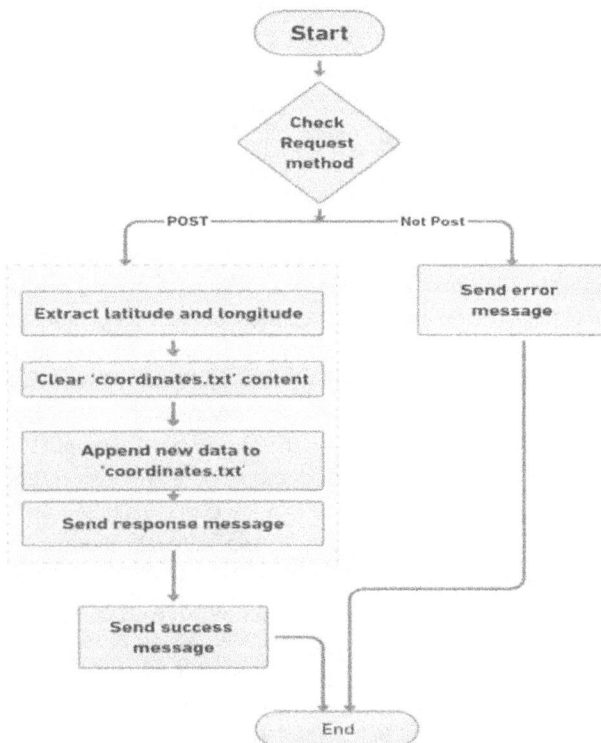

Figure 61.5, hosted by the third-party web hoster, is created on the back end prior to initializing the server-side program-ming. The server manages data processing and storage by clearing and updating the "coordinates.txt" file with newly received latitude and longitude data, as shown in Figure 61.6. It sends a response to the client indicating the operation's status. For non-POST requests, an error message is returned. The server-side application efficiently handles communica-tion, data processing, storage, and geofence monitoring. It stores geofence coordinates defined through the user inter-face and continuously analyzes incoming location data from the vehicle tracking device.

When a vehicle enters or exits a predefined geofence zone, the server triggers pre-programmed actions, such as sending notifications or logging events. The implementation in PHP enables reliable data management and secure infor-mation handling, effectively bridging the gap between the tracking device and user interface for real-time visualization and geofence-based alerts.

3.3. Client-side programming

The client-side application utilizes a login key for basic secu-rity and embeds a Google Map for visualization. Figure 61.7 signifies the algorithm of the client-side application.

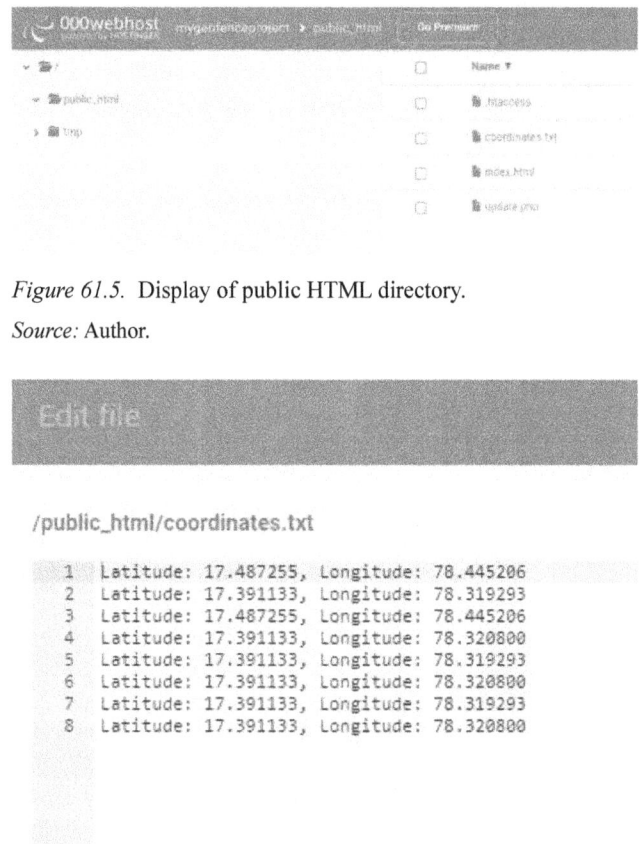

Figure 61.5. Display of public HTML directory.

Source: Author.

/public_html/coordinates.txt

```
1    Latitude: 17.487255, Longitude: 78.445206
2    Latitude: 17.391133, Longitude: 78.319293
3    Latitude: 17.487255, Longitude: 78.445206
4    Latitude: 17.391133, Longitude: 78.320800
5    Latitude: 17.391133, Longitude: 78.319293
6    Latitude: 17.391133, Longitude: 78.320800
7    Latitude: 17.391133, Longitude: 78.319293
8    Latitude: 17.391133, Longitude: 78.320800
```

Figure 61.4. Flowchart of server-side mechanism.

Source: Author.

Figure 61.6. Display of GPS data on the 'coordinates.txt'.

Source: Author.

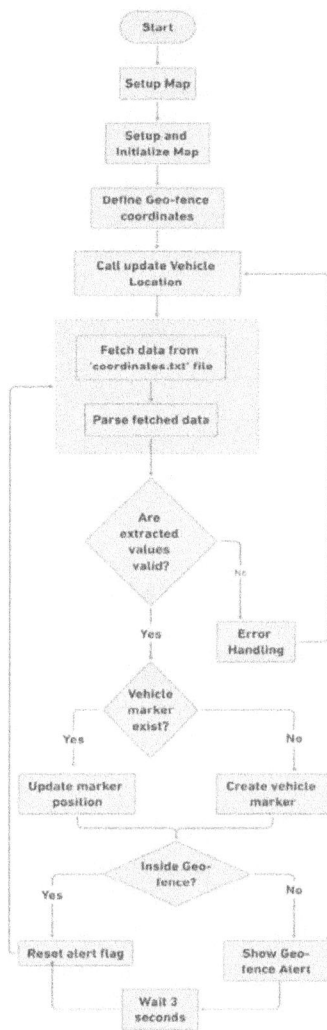

Figure 61.7. Flowchart on client-side application.

Source: Author.

Figure 61.8. Client-side application alert.

Source: Author.

The vehicle is represented in the form of a red marker and the restricted area in the open ground is shaded in red. The performance of the system is evaluated in two primary circumstances: Vehicle outside the geofence and Vehicle inside the geofence.

4.1. Case A: Vehicle outside the geofence

This section evaluates the system's performance when a runway vehicle equipped with the monitoring system is located outside the predefined geofence. To test the prototype outside the geofence, the vehicle with the prototype placed in it was put in three different locations, and in every location, a geofence polygon was considered. The system was placed at 20 m, 10 m, 5 m, and 2 m away from the geofence polygon, and the alert system was tested. Figure 61.9a demonstrates the scenario of a vehicle outside of the geo-fence area and the prototype was present 20 meters away from the geofence polygon. As the vehicle is outside the geo-fence there is no alert notification being displayed. It is observed that when the prototype was 10 m and 5m, respectively, away from the geofence polygon, it didn't display any alert indicating a successful circumstance.

On the contrary, when the prototype was tested against 2 m, it displayed an alert notification (Figure 61.9b). The system is designed in such a way that it can accept 6 digits after the decimal point of coordinates representation [18].

When the system has up to 6 decimals of coordinates representation, then the difference of 2 meters and below cannot be identified by it and it considers that the vehicle has entered the geofence. An advantage to this is that the driver present in the vehicle will know early on that the. vehicle is close to the geofence and can retreat before completely entering the geofence.

4. Results and Discussion

To consider the airport environment, the developed system was tested in open grounds with an environment similar to an airport-restricted zone. Airports have a restricted zone with a rectangular perimeter or a square perimeter; keeping this in view rectangular and square areas were considered restricted zones in the open ground [17]. The developed geofencing system prototype was employed in a car, and test results were collected considering different use cases.

Predefined geofence coordinates are stored in JavaScript to define a restricted area. A function, "updateVehicle Location", continuously retrieves the latest GPS coordinates from a server-side text file. The extracted latitude and longitude are validated, and the vehicle marker on the map is updated accordingly. Crucially, the system checks if the updated position falls within the geofence. If a breach occurs, an alert is triggered. To prevent excessive alerts due to minor location fluctuations, a 3-second delay is implemented for outside geofence detections. Additionally, an alert flag ensures only the initial geo-fence entry triggers notification. This cycle of fetching coordinates, updating marker position, and performing geofence checks continues, enabling real-time monitoring of the vehicle's location.

The Figure 61.8 demonstrates the alert notification displayed in the case where, in open ground, a restricted area is considered, the vehicle is on the geofence polygon edge and the website is displaying an alert until the vehicle leaves the geofence.

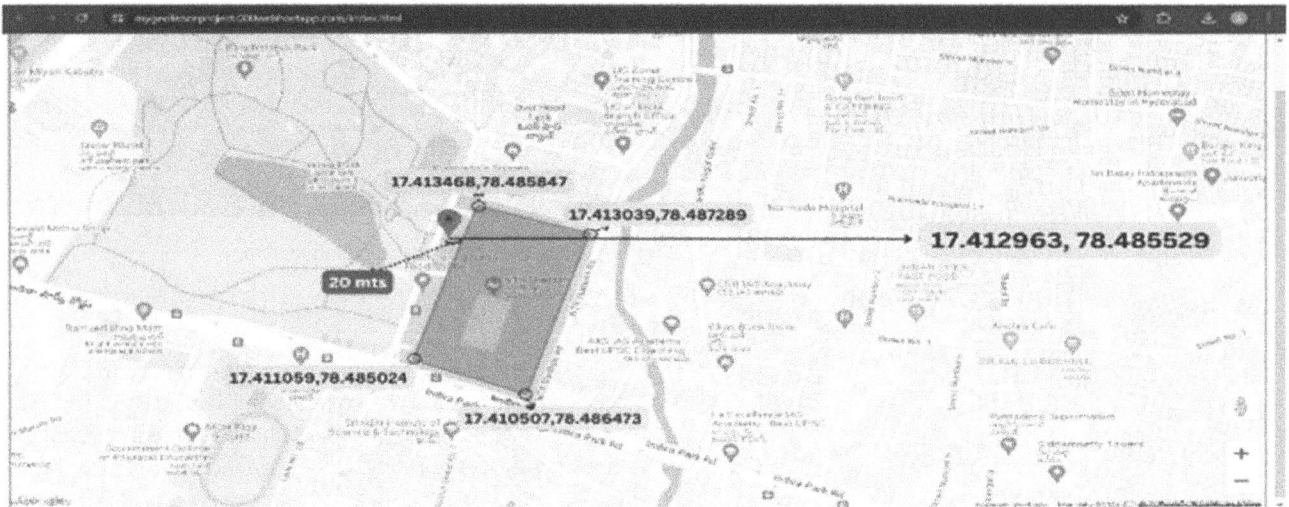

Figure 61.9.(a) 20 mts from geofence polygon.

Source: Author.

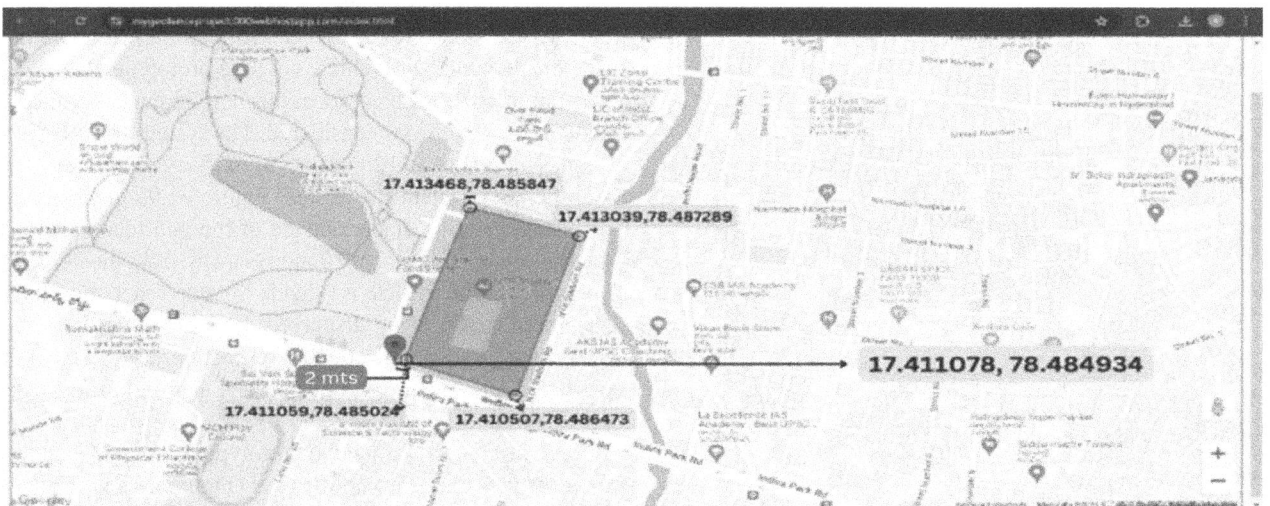

Figure 61.9.(b) 2 mts from geofence polygon.

Source: Author.

The successful operation in Case A and its different scenarios demonstrate the system's ability to function as intended even when the vehicle is not within the designated geofence zone. This data can be valuable for historical analysis, route planning, or monitoring overall fleet activity.

4.2. Case B: Vehicle inside geofence

The vehicle was tested inside the geofence in three different locations when the prototype was put inside, edge, and at the vertices of the polygon to check whether the prototype showed an alert. Figure 61.10 depicts that the system is showing alert notifications when the vehicle is in the geofence and Figure 61.11 represents the scenario of the prototype when it is on the edge and the vertices of the geofence.

The successful operation in Case B demonstrates the system's core functionality of geofence monitoring. The real-time location update and the triggered alert ensure vehicle drivers and airport traffic controllers are informed when a vehicle enters a designated restricted area. This functionality is valuable for applications such as monitoring deliveries within a specific zone, tracing fleet activity in sensitive locations, or detecting unauthorized access.

5. Conclusion

This paper explains a successfully built functional prototype for a vehicle monitoring system. It utilized GPS, a microcontroller, and a server application for real-time tracking, data storage, and geofence management by sending out alert

Figure 61.10. Alert notification when the vehicle is inside the geofence polygon.

Source: Author.

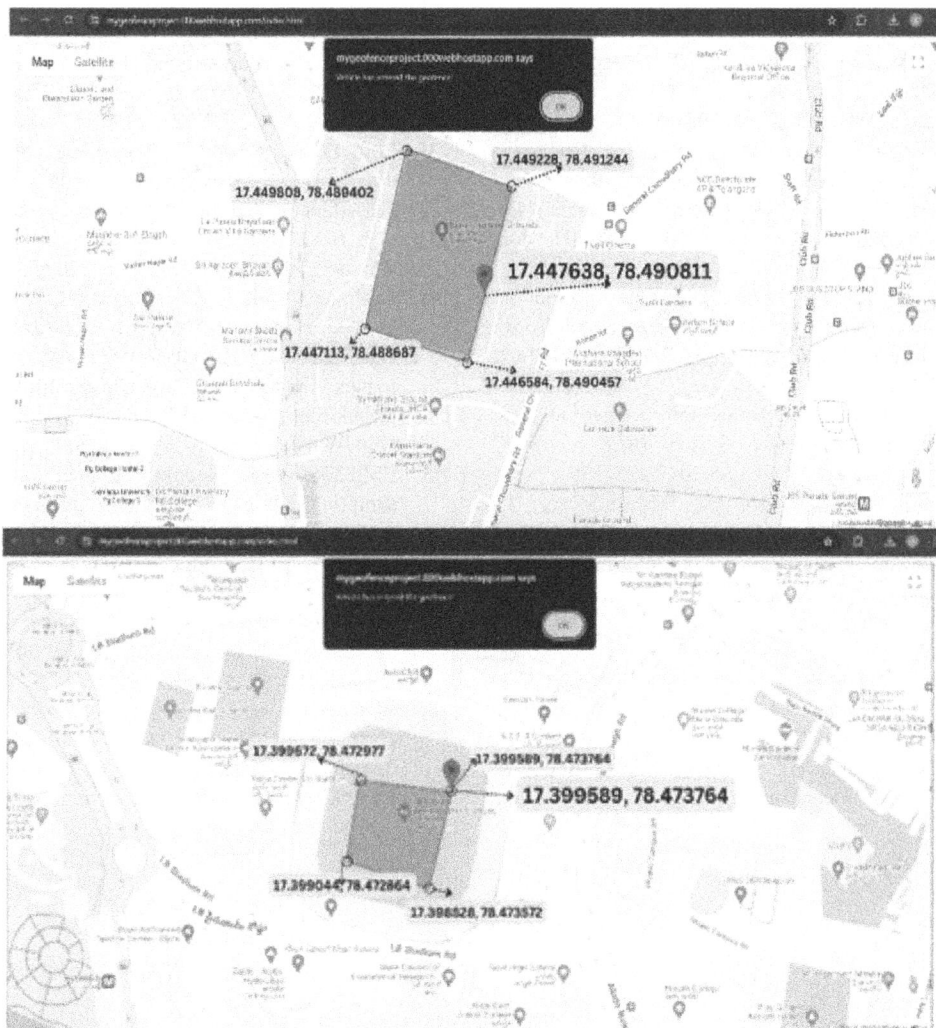

Figure 61.11. Geofence boundary breach warning.

Source: Author.

notifications every 3 seconds until the vehicle leaves the restricted zone. The system displays alert notifications when the vehicle is 2 meters or less than 2 meters away from the geofence and when the vehicle is inside the geofence. This is incorporated into the system so that the driver can be alerted when the vehicle is nearing the restricted zone. A user-friendly web interface visualizes vehicle location and allows geofence control. The chosen hardware prioritized low power consumption (412.5 mW), considering the airport environment. Future development could explore advanced geofence functionalities, like route optimization for exiting restricted zones. This project demonstrated cost-effectiveness as it is just under 25 USD and can be implemented on multiple vehicles and an efficient vehicle monitoring system that can be implemented on an Air traffic control system for efficient traffic management, paving the way for further exploration of advanced features for a comprehensive tracking solution.

References

[1] Smith, A. E., Coit, D. W., & Liang, Y. C. (2010). Neural Network Models to Anticipate Failures of Airport Ground Transportation Vehicle Doors. In *IEEE Transactions on Automation Science and Engineering* (vol. 7, no. 1, pp. 183–188). doi: 10.1109/TASE.2009.2020508

[2] Blasch, E., Wang, Z., Shen, D., Ling, H., & Chen, G. (2014). Surveillance of Ground Vehicles for Airport Security. *Proceedings of SPIE – The International Society for Optical Engineering* (vol. 9089, article 90890B). doi: 10.1117/12.2053855.

[3] Alomara, I., & Tolujevs, J. (2017). Optimization of Ground Vehicles Movement on the Aerodrome. *Transportation Research Procedia*, 24, 58–64. doi:10.1016/j.trpro.2017.05.068.

[4] Tang, J. (2017). Review: Analysis and Improvement of Traffic Alert and Collision Avoidance System. *IEEE Access*, 5, 21419–21429. doi: 10.1109/ACCESS.2017.2757598.

[5] Hawas, Y. E., Thandavarayan, G., Basheerudeen, B., & Sherif, M. (2019). Testbed Evaluation of Real-Time Route Guidance in Inter-Vehicular Communication Urban Networks. *IEEE Access*, 7, 1470–1485. doi: 10.1109/ACCESS.2018.2886822.

[6] Jospine, A., Audah, L. H. M., Hamzah, A., & Qasim, H. (2020). Vehicle Monitoring System with Geofencing Capability. *Journal of Electronics Voltage and Application*, 1(2), 1–13. doi: 10.30880/jeva.2020.01.02.001.

[7] Wang, S., Che, Y., Zhao, H., & Lim, A. (2021). Accurate Tracking, Collision Detection, and Optimal Scheduling of Airport Ground Support Equipment. *IEEE Internet of Things Journal*, 8(1), 572–584. doi: 10.1109/JIOT.2020.3004874.

[8] Stevens, M., & Atkins, E. (2021). Geofence Definition and Deconfliction for UAS Traffic Management. *IEEE Transactions on Intelligent Transportation Systems*, 22(9), 5880–5889. doi: 10.1109/TITS.2020.3040595.

[9] Ding, C., Bi, J., Xie, D., Zhao, X., & Liu, Y. (2021). Mining Travel Time of Airport Ferry Network Based on Historical Trajectory Data. *Hindawi Journal of Advanced Transportation*, *2021*, Article ID 9231451, pp. 1–11. doi:10.1155/2021/9231451.

[10] Rosayyan, P., Subramaniam, S., & Ganesan, S. I. (2021). Decentralized Emergency Service Vehicle Pre-Emption System Using RF Communication and GNSS-Based Geo-Fencing. *IEEE Transactions on Intelligent Transportation Systems*, 22(12), 7726–7735. doi: 10.1109/TITS.2020.3007671.

[11] Wang, S., Li, C., & Lim, A. (2022). ROPHS: Determine Real-Time Status of a Multi-Carriage Logistics Train at Airport. *IEEE Transactions on Intelligent Transportation Systems*, 23(7), 6347–6356. doi: 10.1109/TITS.2021.3055838

[12] Zhou, J., Wu, Y., Cao, Z., Song, W., Zhang, J., & Chen, Z. (2023). Learning Large Neighborhood Search for Vehicle Routing in Airport Ground Handling. *IEEE Transactions on Knowledge and Data Engineering*, 35(9), 9769–9782. doi: 10.1109/TKDE.2023.3249799.

[13] Lofù, D., Gennaro, P. D., Tedeschi, P., Noia, T. D., & Sciascio, E. D. (2023). URANUS: Radio Frequency Tracking, Classification and Identification of Unmanned Aircraft Vehicles. *IEEE Open Journal of Vehicular Technology*, 4, 921–935. doi: 10.1109/OJVT.2023.3333676.

[14] U-blox NEO-6M documentation: https://content.ublox.com/sites/default/files/products/documents/NEO-6_DataSheet_%28GPS.G6-HW-09005%29.pdf

[15] U-bloxNEO-6Mdatasheet: https://content.ublox.com /sites/default/files/products/documents/NEO-6_DataSheet_%28GPS.G6-HW-09005%29.pdf

[16] ESP8266 Wi-Fi Module datasheet (refer to power consumption section): https://www.espressif.com/en/products/modules/esp8266

[17] Angel, A. (n.d.). *Flight Restriction Zone (FRZ) Guidelines | Altitude Angel | Drones*. https://www.altitudeangel.com/sectors/airports/flight-restriction-zone#:~:text=Runway%20Protection%20Zones%3A%20A%20rectangle,2000%20ft%20above%20ground%20level.

[18] *Why do you need 6 decimal places?* (n.d.). https://gis.maricopa.gov/GIO/HistoricalAerial/help/why_do_you_need_6_decimal_places_.htm#:~:text=Previous%20page.%20Next%20page.%20Print%20version.

62 Performance analysis of CFAR and CFAR-KF hybrid model in FMCW radar target detection

Singapuram Thrithwik[1,a], Karshana B. G.[1,b], Arun Siva Bhargav M.[1,c], Navin M. George[2,d], S. Merlin Gilbert Raj[1,e], and Ancy Michel[1,f]

[1]Electronics and Communication Engineering, Karunya Institute of Technology and Sciences, Coimbatore, India
[2]Electronics and Communication Engineering, Nehru Institute of Engineering and Technology, Coimbatore, India

Abstract: Frequency-Modulated Continuous-Wave (FMCW) radar is extensively used in autonomous vehicles, military apparatus, and surveillance applications because of its high-resolution measurements in range, velocity, and angle. In contrast to pulsed radar, FMCW radar continuously transmits a frequency-modulated signal, allowing for object detection with assurance in dynamic environments. The downside is that, despite the advantages, the detection of real objects against noise and clutter still remains a challenge. The Constant False Alarm Rate (CFAR) algorithm is a popular choice in adaptive determination of detection thresholds, yet in high-clutter situations, CFAR can provide false alarms or miss detections. To resolve the challenges associated with CFAR detection thresholds in clutter, the architectural hybridization of CFAR and Kalman Filter (KF) is proposed in this paper. The hybrid approach adds a predictive Kalman Filter (KF) to improve detection robustness and stabilized object tracking. Experimental results show the CFAR-KF achieves a 95% detection accuracy at a 5% false alarm rate, while traditional CFAR was observed at an 89% detection accuracy at a 12% false alarm rate.

Keywords: FMCW radar, CFAR, Kalman Filter, object detection, radar tracking, target detection

1. Introduction

Frequency-Modulated Continuous-Wave (FMCW) radar is an important sensing technology that is commonly used today for applications in autonomous vehicle systems, defence, or surveillance. [1] Compared to pulsed radar, which transmits a series of discrete pulses of electromagnetic waves, FMCW radar continuously broadcasts a frequency-modulated signal to accurately provide range and velocity measurement. The frequency or beat frequency of the transmission and the resulting return are utilized to extract target information; thus, FMCW radar is particularly effective for object detection for short- to mid-range scenarios. FMCW radar can also operate in more than one frequency band and can provide better resolution and penetration during adverse weather. [2] Nonetheless, real-world scenarios present adverse environmental effects such as multipath interference, Doppler ambiguities, and clutter that will require sophisticated signal processing algorithms for reliable detection and tracking. One of the more significant challenges for FMCW radar-based detection systems is separating actual targets from clutter and noise while keeping a low false alarm rate. The most common method for target detection is called the Constant False Alarm Rate (CFAR) algorithm because it dynamically sets the detection thresholds in real-time with respect to the current noise environment. [3] Thus, CFAR can adaptively detect objects under different circumstances.

[4] While this does have its own challenges, namely false alarms and missed detection, especially in non-homogeneous environments with significant clutter variations, this study proposes a hybrid model that combines CFAR with a Kalman Filter (KF) to enhance detection robustness. [5] The hybrid model aims to improve target airspace detection and tracking through adaptive thresholding by CFAR and predictive filtering by KF. Overall, this hybrid method strives in reducing false alarms while creating a reliable detection in changing dynamic radar environments. The performance of this hybridized detection and tracking method will be tested with both homogeneous and nonhomogeneous radar environments to demonstrate its advantages over standard isolated CFAR detection.

2. Background and Related Work

2.1. FMCW radar for target detection

FMCW radar is commonly found in forensic work, military use, and autonomous vehicles because it generates a short time period measurement of range, velocity, and angle, coupled with high resolution. [6] Unlike radar that transmits periodically emitted pulses, an FMCW radar transmits a continuous frequency modulated signal. The beat frequency of the transmitted signal and the received signal is what is used to gather data regarding amplitude and the distance of a target frame

[a]thrithwik.2707@gmail.com, [b]karshanabg@gmail.com, [c]arunsivabhargavm@gmail.com, [d]mnavingeorge@gmail.com, [e]infomerlin@gmail.com, [f]ancymichel@gmail.com

DOI: 10.1201/9781003724988-62

of reference. [7] The radar operation band emissions observed during an FMCW surveillance mode range between the 24–77 GHz frequency mmWave band. These frequency emissions have high spatial resolution and capable of performing target detection through signal processing techniques such as the Fast Fourier Transform (FFT), range-Doppler processing, and Beamforming. [8] Despite these high-resolution processing techniques, range detection can be complicated by challenges including, but not limited to, multipath interference, Doppler ambiguities, and deployments where cluttering occurs. [9]

2.2. CFAR algorithm

CFAR (Constant False Alarm Rate) is an adaptive threshold-ing (comparison) strategy used in the finite radar signal processing of data, commonly employed because it adapts the thresholds to estimate noise due to phenomenon variability during techniques used to assess surveillance. [10]

The basic types of CFAR in practice include the following as mentioned below:

- CA-CFAR – requires the averaging the noise in active cells and nearby sections of the frame; a good technique for environments where phenomena are uniform. [11]
- GO-CFAR – assesses the maximum noise, evaluates the training regions, is the better technique when detected in clutter regions.
- OS-CFAR – determines the ranking historical noise esti-mates in an appropriately non-value noise section of the evaluation.

It is important to clarify the CFAR techniques adapt within the noise parameters, but similar to when noise is induced in close proximity phenomena, during changing environments can be affected (closed targets) obliges additional filtration post-detection algorithms to increase accuracy. [12]

2.3. Kalman filter

The Kalman filter is an effective and sophisticated method for predicting and smoothing the motion of tracked objects or areas of interest. [13] In its simplest form, the Kalman filter utilizes a two-step function by first predicting where an object should be based on its previous motion, then correcting that prediction with new radar data, even if it's somewhat noisy. The Kalman filter works especially well for straight-line motion with predictable noise structure. When combining CFAR and a Kalman filter which is typically referred to as a CFAR-KF, the Kalman filtering system adds the ability to both find a target reliably and track that target more effectively while it continues to move in a cluttered, noisy environment.

3. Methodology

3.1. Isolated CFAR model

The Constant False Alarm Rate (CFAR) algorithm is a radar signal processing technique for detecting targets using a detection threshold that varies to account for local noise esti-mates. [14] The isolated CFAR model relies only on CFAR as the target detection mechanism, without any other filtering or tracking methods being applied as shown in Figure 62.1 [15].

The CFAR process has several components, which include the following:

- Preprocessing: The detected raw FMCW radar data undergoes range-Doppler processing, which applies a Fast Fourier Transform (FFT) along the chirp and range dimensions to generate a range-Doppler map.
- Noise Level Estimation: CFAR looks at each cell under test (CUT) and a moving window surrounding the CUT to determine what the noise floor is based on the sur-rounding reference cells. The guard cells are not used then to prevent contamination with targets.

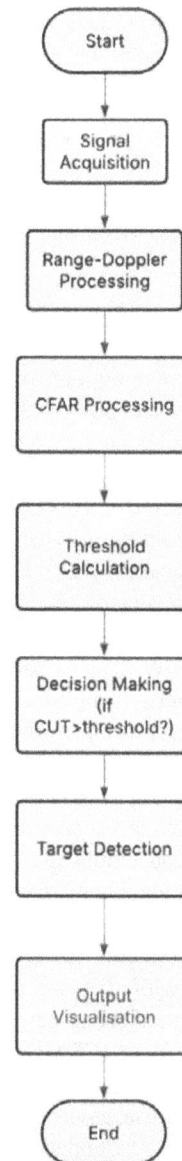

Figure 62.1. CFAR block diagram.

Source: Author.

- Threshold Determination: A threshold to detect is determined based on the estimated noise level using a scaling factor.
- Object Detection: Any CUT which exceeds the submitted threshold is declared a detected object [16].
- Post-processing: The detected objects are clustered together to discard potential multiple detections of object with similar features.

3.2. CFAR-KF hybrid model

To address the limitations of isolated CFAR, we develop the CFAR-Kalman Filter (CFAR-KF) hybrid model which employs CFAR for initial target detection and the Kalman Filter (KF) to track and refine detection as shown in Figure 62.2. [17] This hybrid model increases the robustness

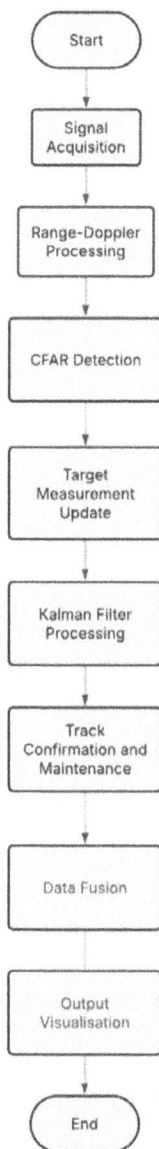

Figure 62.2. CFAR-KF hybrid block diagram.

Source: Author.

of target detection against noise in observed detections and targets based on frame-to-frame consistency.

The hybrid model proceeds as follows:

- CFAR-Based Target Detection: The CFAR algorithm processes the radar signal using the method described in Section 1.
- Kalman Filter Initialization: For each detected target, a state vector is initialized representing the position and velocity of that detected target in the range-Doppler space. [18]
- Prediction Step: Utilizing the motion model, the KF predicts the target's new position in the next frame accounting for the object motion over time.
- Measurement Update: When a new detection occurs, the KF compares the observed position with the predicted position and updates its estimate using a weighted average.
- Track Association: If a detection in the current frame aligns with a previously tracked object within a predefined threshold, the KF updates that object's trajectory. Otherwise, a new track is initialized [19].
- Refinement and Smoothing: The KF smooths fluctuations in detection outputs, reducing false alarms and improving target tracking stability.

3.3. Experimental setup

Radar System: FMCW radar operating at 77 GHz with a bandwidth of 250 MHz.

- Test Scenarios: Evaluations are conducted in both homogeneous (low clutter) and non-homogeneous (high clutter) environments to assess real-world applicability.
- Performance Metrics: Comparison of detection accuracy, false alarm rate, and tracking error for both CFAR and CFAR-KF models.
- Software Tools: MATLAB radar signal processing libraries for simulation and evaluation.

Overall, we found that our CFAR-KF hybrid model greatly enhanced detection robustness according to our performance metrics by incorporating predictive filtering with adaptive thresholding to establish a more dependable detection method for object detection and tracking of FMCW radar [20].

4. Results and Discussion

4.1. Performance evaluation

Object detection using radar systems, particularly with FMCW radar technology involves the task of overcoming numerous false detections due to noise and dynamic evolving environments. The Constant False Alarm Rate (CFAR), which sets the detection threshold with respect to the noise power to help minimize false alarms. But the CFAR approach can begin to fail as the clutter increases and the target motion is more erratic. The hybrid model uses Kalman Filter, which maintained a steady output from the CFAR output, credible due to the uncertainty present in noisy environments and reducing signal to noise ratios (SNR's). It should be noted that the processing time for the CFAR-KF hybrid model was slightly longer (15 ms compared to the CFAR's processing time of 10 ms), however, this was an acceptable cost for a far greater reliability of detection and stable tracking performance. In real-world applications, the set additional time would likely add value when the improvement offers better accuracy for safety and decision making.

4.2. CFAR performance analysis

The CFAR algorithms demonstrated a consistent level of performance in a homogeneous environment as shown in Figure 62.3. In this environment, target accuracy rates were near 89% and false alarm rates were now near 12%. CFAR's capability to implement adaptive thresholding in each noise sample made it reliable and was even able to make adjustments for a small change in noise levels. re were a couple issues that were noted: Clutter Edge Issue, precedence of the false alarm rate in these environments. The performance processing time using CFAR was low at around 10ms.

4.3. CFAR-KF performance analysis

The CFAR-KF hybrid model demonstrated a marked improvement over the standard CFAR algorithm. Utilizing the Kalman Filtering (KF) process, the hybrid model reached an accuracy of 95% detection, while reducing the false alarm rate to minimals (5%) as shown in Figure 62.4. The key benefits include:

• State Prediction: Smooth tracking even with rapid clutter changes.
• Adaptive Correction: Reliable detection despite environmental noise.

The CFAR-Kalman Filter (CFAR-KF) hybrid model outperforms traditional CFAR in cluttered environments due to its enhanced robustness and adaptability. Here, Figure 62.5

shows the spectrum representation of CFAR-KF Hybrid model where the X-axis denotes the range (in m) and Y-axis denotes FFT magnitude. Kalman Filter tracking plots (range vs time) show consistent, noise-resistant tracking of moving objects.

While CFAR uses fixed thresholding based on local noise estimation, it struggles with false alarms in non-homogeneous clutter. The CFAR-KF model combines CFAR's detection with Kalman filtering to track targets over time, filtering out spurious detections and maintaining consistency. The KF allows better detection of weak or temporarily obscured targets and suppressing clutter-induced noise. This leads to improved detection accuracy, reduced false alarms, and smoother target tracking, especially in dynamic or high-clutter scenes. Overall, CFAR-KF provides more reliable performance than traditional CFAR in varying clutter levels and is well-suited for real-world radar target detection scenarios. Table 62.1 shows the performance comparison of the both.

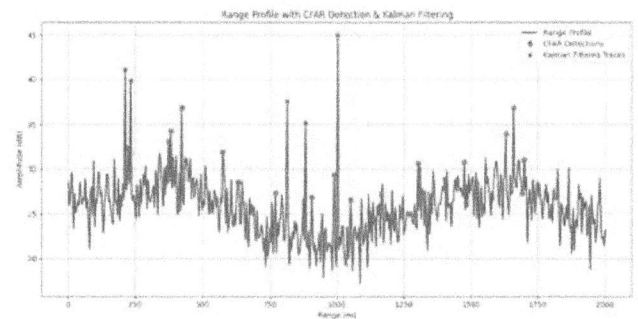

Figure 62.4. Range profile with CFAR-KF hybrid model.
Source: Author.

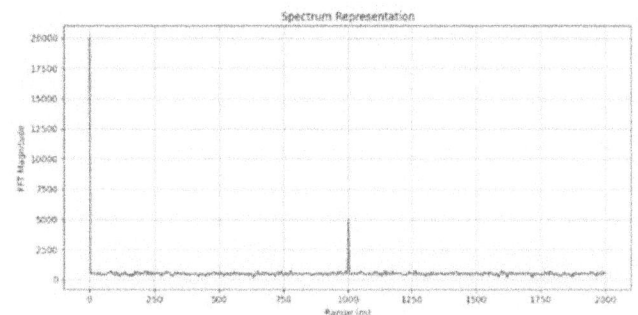

Figure 62.5. Spectrum representation of CFAR-KF Hybrid model.
Source: Author.

Table 62.1. Performance comparison of CFAR and CFAR-KF

Model	Detection Accuracy (%)	False Alarm Rate (%)	Processing Time (ms)
CFAR	89	12	10
CFAR-KF	95	5	15

Source: Author.

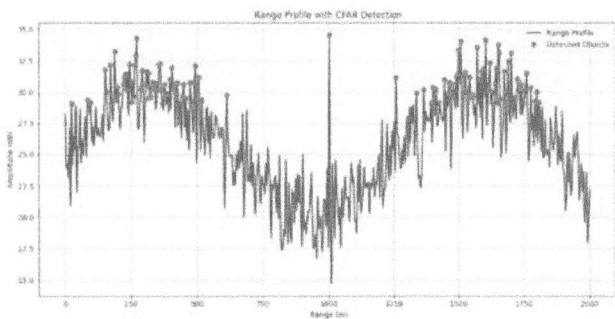

Figure 62.3. Range profile with CFAR detection.
Source: Author.

5. Conclusion

In this paper, we presented the CFAR-Kalman Filter (CFAR-KF) hybrid model for improving object detection and tracking when using a FMCW radar system. CFAR is an effective method for adapting the detection threshold for the local noise level; however, its use results in false alarms and missed detections in the presence of clutter and moving targets. To mitigate these issues, the hybrid model relates to CFAR's adaptive thresholding combined with the predictive-tracking properties of the Kalman Filter (KF).

The experimental results showed that the CFAR-KF hybrid method achieved a detection accuracy of 95% with a false alarm rate of 5%, as compared to the traditional CFAR algorithm with an accuracy of 89% and a false alarm rate of 12%. The processing time for the hybrid model was 15 ms as opposed to 10 ms for the isolated CFAR model; although the processing time was increased, these results justify any additional processing time due to the capabilities gained in both robustness and reliability. The hybrid model allowed for the consistent tracking of moving targets while suppressing false alarms in real-time applications.

Acknowledgement

We sincerely thank Karunya Institute of Technology and Sciences for providing the necessary infrastructure and research facilities that made this work possible.

References

[1] Rutz, F., Rasshofer, R., & Biebl, E. (2024). Radar Cross Section Analysis for Road Debris in Automotive FMCW Radar. *2024 IEEE International Conference on Microwaves, Communications, Antennas, Biomedical Engineering and Electronic Systems, COMCAS 2024.*

[2] Lim, T. Y., Markowitz, S. A., & Do, M. N. (2021). RaDI-CaL: A Synchronized FMCW Radar, Depth, IMU and RGB Camera Data Dataset with Low-Level FMCW Radar Signals. *IEEE Journal on Selected Topics in Signal Processing, 15*(4), 941–953.

[3] Dai, H., Du, L., Wang, Y., & Wang, Z. (2016). A Modified CFAR Algorithm Based on Object Proposals for Ship Target Detection in SAR Images. *IEEE Geoscience and Remote Sensing Letters, 13*(12).

[4] Ma, M., Qu, G., Liu, S., Yang, Y., Pei, H., & Chi, Q. (2021). Phase Unwrapping Based on CFAR Detection for Multi-baseline InISAR. *Proceedings of the IEEE Radar Conference, 2021-December*, 159–162.

[5] Ginalih, C. T., Jatmiko, A. S., & Darmakusuma, R. (2020). Simple Application of Kalman Filter on a Moving Object in Unity3D. *6th International Conference on Interactive Digital Media, ICIDM 2020.*

[6] Ai, J., Pei, Z., Yao, B., Wang, Z., & Xing, M. (2022). AIS Data Aided Rayleigh CFAR Ship Detection Algorithm of Multiple-Target Environment in SAR Images. *IEEE Transactions on Aerospace and Electronic Systems, 58*(2), 1266–1282.

[7] Ai, J., Pei, Z., Yao, B., Wang, Z., & Xing, M. (2022). AIS Data Aided Rayleigh CFAR Ship Detection Algorithm of Multiple-Target Environment in SAR Images. *IEEE Transactions on Aerospace and Electronic Systems, 58*(2), 1266–1282.

[8] Ma, M., Qu, G., Liu, S., Yang, Y., Pei, H., & Chi, Q. (2021). Phase Unwrapping Based on CFAR Detection for Multi-baseline InISAR. *Proceedings of the IEEE Radar Conference, 2021-December*, 159–162.

[9] Meda-Campana, J. A., Garcia-Hernandez, J. C., Velazquez-Sanchez, R. D., Paramo-Carranza, L. A., Hernandez-Cortes, T., & Tapia-Herrera, R. (2025). Estimating complex signals with a fuzzy-enhanced Kalman filter: A note on "The output regulation and the Kalman filter as the signal generator." *IEEE Access.*

[10] Murata, M., Kawano, I., & Inoue, K. (2022). Degeneracy-Free Particle Filter: Ensemble Kalman Smoother Multiple Distribution Estimation Filter. *IEEE Transactions on Automatic Control, 67*(12), 6956–6961.

[11] Sahal, M., Said, Z. A., Putra, R. Y., Kadir, R. E. A., & Firmansyah, A. A. (2020). Comparison of CFAR Methods on Multiple Targets in Sea Clutter Using SPX-Radar-Simulator. *Proceedings – 2020 International Seminar on Intelligent Technology and Its Application: Humanification of Reliable Intelligent Systems, ISITIA 2020*, 260–265.

[12] Xu, Z., Ding, J., Zhang, S., Gao, Y., Chen, L., Vasic, Z. L., Cifrek, M., & Chen, Z. D. (2024). mmCMD: Continuous Motion Detection From Visualized Radar Micro-Doppler Signatures Using Visual Object Detection Techniques. *IEEE Sensors Journal, 24*(3).

[13] Jin, S., Wang, P., Boufounos, P., Takahashi, R., & Roy, S. (2023). Spatial-Domain Object Detection Under Mimo-Fmcw Automotive Radar Interference. *ICASSP, IEEE International Conference on Acoustics, Speech and Signal Processing – Proceedings, 2023-June.*

[14] Mon, Y. J. (2024). Correction: Simulation and Implementation of Signal Processing for LFM Radar Using DSK 6713 (Electronics, (2023), 12, 17, (3682), 10.3390/electronics12173682). In *Electronics (Switzerland)* (Vol. 13, Issue 3).

[15] Wei, J. Y., Huang, L., Tong, P. P., Tan, B., Bai, J., & Wu, Z. J. (2020). Realtime Multi-target Vital Sign Detection with 79GHz FMCW Radar. *2020 IEEE MTT-S International Wireless Symposium, IWS 2020 – Proceedings.*

[16] Olver, A. D., & Cuthbert, L. G. (1988). FMCW radar for hidden object detection. *IEE Proceedings F: Communications Radar and Signal Processing, 135*(4).

[17] Zhang, G., Li, H., & Wenger, F. (2020). Object detection and 3D estimation via an FMCW radar using a fully convolutional network. *ICASSP, IEEE International Conference on Acoustics, Speech and Signal Processing – Proceedings, 2020-May.*

[18] Li, H. X., Yu, X. L., Sun, X. D., Tian, J. C., & Wang, X. G. (2020). Shadow Detection in SAR Images: An OTSU- and CFAR-Based Method. *International Geoscience and Remote Sensing Symposium (IGARSS)*, 2803–2806.

[19] Kerbaa, T. H., Mezache, A., & Oudira, H. (2022). Improved Decentralized SO-CFAR and GO-CFAR Detectors via Moth Flame Algorithm. *Proceedings of the 2022 International Conference of Advanced Technology in Electronic and Electrical Engineering, ICATEEE 2022.*

[20] Shingote, S., Shejwalkar, A., & Swain, S. (2023). Comparative Analysis for State-of-Charge Estimation of Lithium-Ion Batteries using Non-Linear Kalman Filters. *2023 IEEE 3rd International Conference on Sustainable Energy and Future Electric Transportation, SeFet 2023.*

63 Deep, safe, and reliable: CNN-powered ultrasound screening for early breast cancer prediction

Sushma K. R.ª and Rahul Ratnakumar[b]

Department of Electronics and Communication Engineering, Manipal Institute of Technology Manipal Academy of Higher Education, Manipal, India

Abstract: Worldwide, cancer is one of the oldest, most formidable, and deadliest illnesses in the world because of its high death rate compared to other diseases, and breast cancer is one of the most common. So, by using the Convolutional Neural Networks (CNNs) for automated breast cancer detection with the goal of meeting the urgent need for accurate and timely diagnosis in the medical field. It uses a multi-phase approach, first assembling a heterogeneous ultrasound image dataset representative of different stages of breast cancer, then rigorously preprocessing the images to guarantee uniformity. Then a CNN architecture is developed using transfer learning to enhance the model's functionality. Thorough testing and validation procedures confirm the accuracy, sensitivity, and specificity of the model. The model that is demonstrated achieves an accuracy rate of 90 to 98 percent. The outcomes demonstrate the CNN's resilience in correctly identifying cancerous areas in ultrasonography pictures, illustrating its potential as a vital diagnostic tool for radiologists that could lower errors and speed up diagnosis. Also, a prediction of a classification threshold's performance is encapsulated in the ROC curve. The ROC curve study further verifies the credibility of the model with an area under the curve (AUC) of 0.947. This project highlights the feasibility of CNNs in the automation of the detection of breast cancer and how they can be a useful additional aid in a clinical environment that will help identify the suspicious area in the ultrasound image quickly and accurately and help advance the technologies of medical images in the field of healthcare.

Keywords: Breast cancer, CNN, ultrasonography, AUC, image pre-processing, ROC

1. Introduction

Convolutional neural networks, CNNs, or ConvNets, are a particular category of deep neural networks that are used in the processing of grid-structured data [1]. They have been highly popular and widely used, particularly in computer vision [8], with outstanding image recognition and identification and other visual task capabilities. The way in which humans perceive pictures functioned as the model for convolutional neural nets. These have several layers that can receive data input and extract hierarchical representations from it. Convolution, pool, and fully connected layers are examples of such. The network learns by convolving small matrices on the input to automatically detect patterns, features, and relationships in data.

Convolutional Neural Networks (CNNs) are made up of multiple layers to process input data in a hierarchical fashion to extract features [4]. Convolutional, pooling, and fully connected layers are the three main layers of a CNN, as shown in Figure 63.1.

1. Convolutional Operations: Kernels/Filters: The input data is subjected to learnable filters, commonly referred to as kernels, by the convolutional layer. These tiny (like 3×3 or 5×5) filters slide over the input, multiplying elements one by one, then adding the results to create an output feature map with a single value. Feature Maps: By computing convolutions over the whole input data (image or output from the previous layer), each filter creates a feature map. The depth of the output volume (number of feature maps) depends on the number of filters that are used.

2. Stride and Padding: Stride: It establishes how big of a step the filter moves through the input data. A smaller output feature map is produced by a larger stride, while the filter travels one pixel at a time when the stride value is 1. Padding: To regulate the spatial dimensions of the generated feature maps, more border pixels are added to the input data. One common technique for maintaining spatial dimensions is zero-padding.

3. Activation Function: Rectified Linear Activation, or ReLU. Following convolutions, non-linearity is introduced elementwise using activation functions such as ReLU, which enables the network to model nonlinear relationships and helps it discover more intricate patterns in the data.

4. Pooling Layers: Operation of Pooling: To reduce the width and height of each feature map, pooling layers can be added in between convolutional layers. This reduces

ªsushma.mitmpl2023@learner.manipal.edu, ᵇrahul.ratnakumar@manipal.edu

DOI: 10.1201/9781003724988-63

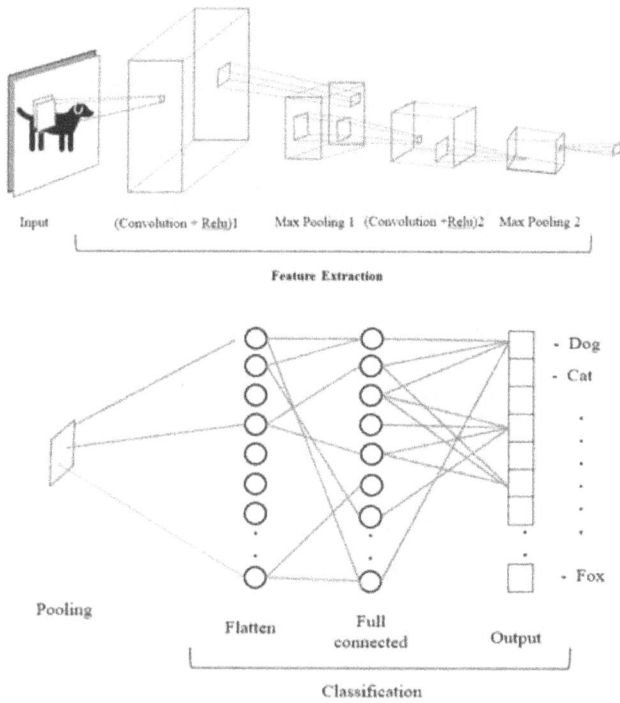

Figure 63.1. Convolution layers.

Source: Author.

computational complexity and introduces translational invariance. Max pooling and average pooling are two common pooling operations.

5. Output: A convolutional layer's output is a stack of feature maps that show the features or learned patterns that the filters were able to identify. Certain attributes found in the input data, such as edges, textures, or higher-level features, are highlighted in each feature map.

6. Learnable Constraints: The convolutional layer's filters are parameters to be learned. In attempting to lessen discrepancy between expected and observed outputs, backpropagation is used by the network to modify such filter weights in the process of training. The network is therefore capable of building up the ability to extract salient features in data.

The convolutional layer's overall goal is to learn and capture hierarchical feature representations of data. In the process, CNNs can capture salient patterns and features to execute various types of jobs, including object detection and categorization of images [3, 9].

Breast cancer is, and continues to be, a serious global health problem, and it affects thousands of individuals annually. [10] By using strong epidemiological data, they clarify the significant effects of cancer on public health and highlight the pressing need for improved access to high-quality treatment options, primitive detection techniques, and preventive measures. Early treatment is made possible by early

diagnosis, but reliable diagnosis is oftentimes quite hard to receive [20]. The application of advanced technologies, in our case, convolutional neural networks (CNNs), in recent years, has tremendous potential to redefine the diagnosis of breast cancer [5, 7]. The imperative for timely and reliable diagnosis, shortcomings of current diagnostic practices, and in what way CNNs have the potential to redefine the detection of breast cancer are all mentioned in this introduction and, hence, provide context.

This provides an overview of Convolutional Neural Network (CNN) use in diagnostic studies for breast cancer. An overview of activity in the subject and recent breakthroughs in diagnostic medical imaging used here is ultrasound images, which [2] for cancer is included in the initial presentation. The current incidence of breast cancer and how timely diagnosis affects treatment are referenced to provide context for the rationale for better ways to diagnose cancer in its initial phases.

In this study, we applied CNN-based techniques to analyze ultrasound pictures to detect breast cancer. The data set involved various ultrasound scans [6] classified into benign and cancerous tumours. The data was heavily pre-processed with normalization and data augmentation (for example, rotation, flip, and zoom) and divided into test, validation, and training data to establish strong model validation.

The process entails creating and testing a CNN designed especially for diagnosing breast cancer. It combines several layers and methods to extract and analyze features from medical imaging data, including ultrasound images [12], which are frequently used in breast cancer screening. By using CNNs, the data can be analyzed more thoroughly by conventional diagnostic techniques [11] but are indicative of early-stage breast cancer.

The suggested approach is novel in using CNNs, whose reputation is built on their capability to recognize sophisticated patterns in images. The approach, in contrast to conventional practices, is capable of harnessing neural networks natural capability to recognize sophisticated details, perhaps skipping limitations of conventional treatment of images. The intended outcome is of crucial significance insofar as it presents a diagnostic instrument able to significantly broaden the precision and impact of detecting breast cancer, hence helping medical professionals in timely interventions and better treatment of patients [16, 17].

2. Methodology

Here, we present a detailed description of the approach we employed for designing our breast cancer classifier using a CNN. The approach consists of some primary steps: data pre-processing, feature extraction, model training, and prediction on test data. We present a detailed description of the breast cancer classification approach here. Furthermore, we also apply special pre-processing techniques for the purpose of increasing classification accuracy, and we present a detailed description of the same in the following subsections.

2.1. Dataset

Obtain a diverse dataset of ultrasound pictures that show breast cancer and benign lesions. Work together with health-care facilities to guarantee that radiologists or other medical professionals obtain and label data in an ethical manner. The first step in the process is to choose and prepare a pertinent dataset. A suitable ultrasound image dataset is chosen, making sure it includes a variety of benign and malignant cases such as the BUSI (Breast Ultrasound Image Dataset). A few data pre-processing procedures are essential for getting the images ready for model training after dataset selection.

This dataset's breast cancer ultrasound images are formatted as PNG files and divided into three groups: normal, malignant, and benign. The women who contributed to this collection ranged in age from 25 to 75. Our thorough method in the biomedical field concentrated on handling the subtleties of breast ultrasonography pictures, which frequently have noise and intricate artifacts. Despite these obstacles, we were able to accurately identify breast cancer at every step of our framework. To facilitate testing and training, the dataset was divided. Furthermore, Figure 63.2 displays samples from every class along with distinct images of benign, malignant, and normal cases for comparison.

2.2. Data pre-processing

Pre-processing entails several crucial actions. The ultrasound images are first loaded into the system while the patient ID, image resolution, and corresponding cancer classification that are associated with each image are retained. Standardization is essential because the resolution and size of these images may differ. To standardize the images into a format that is consistent and appropriate for CNN input, methods such as image normalization and resizing are used. A target size, batch size, and class mode are allocated to each of the two sets of pictures that we utilize for pre-processing. These sets are referred to as the training set of 8500 images belongs to 2 classes and the test set of 1500 images belongs to 2 classes, respectively. To ensure uniformity across all images, normalization adjusts pixel values to a standardized range, usually between 0 and 1. Furthermore, resizing is done to ensure that all images have the same resolution, which is typically 128 × 128 pixels, to make CNN architectures compatible [19].

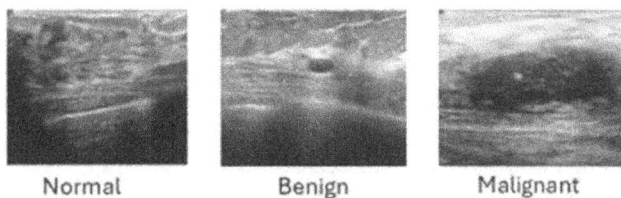

Normal Benign Malignant

Figure 63.2. Three classes of sample images from the dataset.
Source: Author.

2.3. Building CNN

Convolutional neural networks (CNNs) are constructed by initializing the network with the necessary libraries and setting a reproducibility random seed. Start with the initial convolutional layer, which uses a series of learnable filters and several convolutions on the input image for feature extraction. Introduce non-linearity by using a ReLU activation function. Follow up with a pooling layer – max pooling – on the features for summarization and reduction of the spatial size for preventing overfitting. Add a second convolutional layer for feature extraction of complex patterns. Add a further down sampling of the feature maps with a pooling layer. Prepare the feature maps for the fully connected layers by flattening the pooled feature maps into a one-dimensional vector after the convolutional and the pooling layers. The full connection layer, also the dense layer, is used for the network learning non-linear combinations of the flattened features. To produce the final prediction probabilities, add an output layer with a sigmoid activation for binary classification or a Soft-Max function for the classification of numerous classes.

In this CNN model, there are total seven layer which are classified into two convolution layer, two pooling layers, one flattened layer, full connection (dense) layer, and one output layer (dense_1) as shown in Figure 63.3 every layer of convolution uses 32 filters of size 3 × 3 each for choosing features from input images applied to 128 × 128 × 3 yielding an output shape of 126 × 126 × 32 with 896 params. Using the same filters, a second convolution layer produces an output form of 61 × 61 × 32 with 9,248 parameters. After the layers of convolution, It is followed by two max pooling layer of size 2 × 2 is used for the purpose of spatial reduction as well as preventing overfitting. It reduces the size of the feature map by half of it and resulting in 63 × 63 × 32. The size is later further reduced to 30 × 30 × 32 by the second max pooling layer. Both pooling layers are free of params. After that, it is flattened into a size of 28,800 so that can be fed onto fully connected layers. Here, it is furthermore reduced to 128 by utilizing the dense layer of Relu activation function with total of 3,686,528 params. At last 129 parameters are provided by the output layer, which is the second dense layer with a sigmoid activation function. Generally, these values are defined at the time of model compilation and training. The images used as inputs for the network have a resolution of 128 × 128 pixels. Finally, the model makes use of a sigmoid activation function within the output layer for giving a singular output (0 or 1), thus making the model compatible for binary task classification.

2.4. Compiling CNN

To compile the CNN, the Convolutional neural networks (CNNs) are constructed by first choosing the appropriate optimizer, for example, Adam, which learns the learning rate during training for the best performance of the model.

Second, choose the appropriate loss function. Epochs are defined as one full run across the training dataset during model training. CNN is trained using the training set as input data each time the model completes an epoch, and at the conclusion of each epoch, its performance is assessed on the test set. It runs through 15 to 20 epochs here. To reduce loss, the values are updated to CNN at the end of each epoch. The history object will record information about accuracy, loss, validation accuracy, and validation loss. The mean squared error for the problem of regression, the binary cross-entropy for the problem of binary classification, and the cross-entropy for the problem of multi-class classification all specify the respective metrics, for example, accuracy, for the model's performance on training as well as on the validation. Second, integrate the chosen optimizer, the chosen loss function, and the metrics into the model configuration for the compilation of the CNN. The step completes the structure of the model and prepares the model for training by making all the functions, the parameters and display the summary of the layer, the output shape as shown in Figure 63.3.

The dataset is split into discrete subsets for training, and testing which is used for building and The dataset is split into discrete subsets for training and testing(validation), which are used for building and compiling CNN after data preprocessing is finished, guaranteeing a proportionate representation of both benign and malignant cases in each subset. In this phase, the dataset is augmented with caution to prevent overfitting of the images. To help generalize the model, rotation, horizontal and vertical flips, and zooming are used to enlarge the dataset and introduce variability to the images.

Finally, the CNN model gives an in-depth description of utilizing CNNs to approach ultrasound image datasets for detecting breast cancer. For ensuring robust and diverse data on which to train the CNN model, strong emphasis is given to data standardization, data normalization, and data augmentation. These improve the potential of the CNN-designed model to classify benign and malignant cases in ultrasound images accurately.

3. Result Analysis

The expected output for Convolutional Neural Network (CNN) for detecting breast cancer is normally prediction or probabilities in terms of whether an ultrasound image or breast image is indicating signs of cancer. Binary classification depicts the output might be in the format of a binary prediction of whether the image is indicating signs of either benign or malignant cancer. For example, the output might be "benign" or "malignant". Probability values reflecting the chances of having cancer numerically.

Visualization of such models may also result in visualizations showing regions in the image accountable for the result of the classification. These might consist of regions where the CNN discovered potential signs of cancer, for example, masses or microcalcifications. Aside from prediction, CNNs tend to provide confidence values or probabilities for their outputs. Higher confidence scores suggest stronger certainty in the model's prediction.

Important measures such as loss on training and validation accuracy, giving insights on generalization and how well the model is performing, might be used to verify whether using a Convolutional Neural Network (CNN) in cancer diagnosis is having any impact.

For verifying how good the model is at learning using data in training and applying such learning to unseen data for validating, the model's loss and accuracy are monitored through various epochs while training.

The Graph display how well CNN model is learning to identify the patterns and characteristics needed to distinguish between benign and malignant breast tissues, and while monitoring the model accuracy and loss on both training and validation(test) data over period of 20 epochs. It shows how accurately the model is making a prediction, if there is a rise in such a measurement, starting with training accuracy which represents by the blue line in left side of graph in Figure 63.4. Over the course of the 15 to 20 epochs, it is anticipated that

Model: "sequential"

Layer (type)	Output Shape	Param #
conv2d (Conv2D)	(None, 126, 126, 32)	896
max_pooling2d (MaxPooling2D)	(None, 63, 63, 32)	0
conv2d_1 (Conv2D)	(None, 61, 61, 32)	9,248
max_pooling2d_1 (MaxPooling2D)	(None, 30, 30, 32)	0
flatten (Flatten)	(None, 28800)	0
dense (Dense)	(None, 128)	3,686,528
dense_1 (Dense)	(None, 1)	129

Total params: 3,696,801 (14.10 MB)
Trainable params: 3,696,801 (14.10 MB)
Non-trainable params: 0 (0.00 B)

Figure 63.3. Summary of layers.

Source: Author.

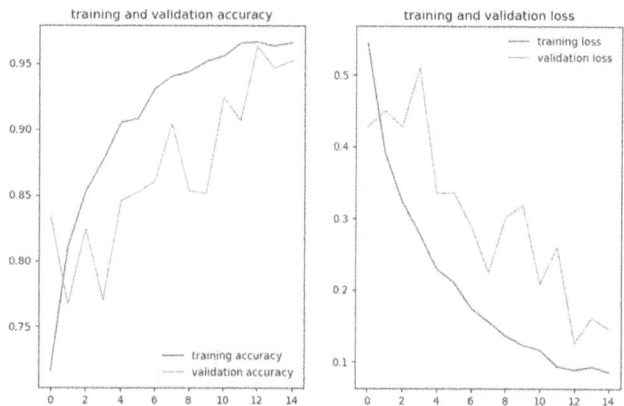

Figure 63.4. Plot of rate of accuracy and loss in both validation and training.

Source: Author.

the training accuracy will progressively increase, indicating the model's capacity to accurately classify the training images. As seen in Figure 63.4, our trial's training accuracy began at about 70% and swiftly increasing over 90% in the first 6 or 7 epochs, and it gradually rises as it passes through the last 10 to 14 epochs with very little training loss, which shows the model is effectively learning the training data. The validation accuracy, shown by an orange line, increases progressively above 90% over the course of nine to ten epochs. After that, it rises and falls for a while before increasing again while remaining close to the training accuracy.

In Figure 63.4, the right side of the graph shows the training and validation loss. The lower the loss, the better the performance. Here the blue line indicates training loss consistently decreases through 8 to 9 epochs and decreases bit by bit over the next epochs. While the orange line displays validation loss, it also trends downwards over all the epochs, although with a bit more fluctuation. Trends are completely decreasing and becoming favourable. As a result, the model is learning effectively.

In all, the results demonstrate that CNN achieved excellent training and validation accuracies with correspondingly low losses, demonstrating its successful acquisition of the capacity to identify breast cancer. As shown in Figure 63.4, the final training accuracy of 98% and training loss of 0.06, the final validation accuracy of 94% and validation loss of 0.2 suggest a better model with high generalization ability. Lastly it means that the model is performing well

The model's diagnostic capability is also measured using the Receiver Operating Characteristic curve, or ROC curve. Which analyses efficiency of a classification model; here we have used a random forest classifier represented by a dashed blue line with an area under ROC (AUROC) of 0.5, and it is a baseline. The model's better performance should have

a curve above this line. The ROC plot compares random guessing of binary classification to random forest classifier. The ROC curve is represented by the Y-axis, which shows the true positive rate (TPR) against the X-axis, which shows the false positive rate (FPR) at several thresholds, and is a graphical representation of the classification power of the model. The TPR (sensitivity) is the number of true positives properly detected by the model, and the higher the TPR, the better, while the FPR (1-specificity) is the number of true negatives that were wrongly detected as positive, and the lower the FPR, the better. In Figure 63.5, the area under the ROC curve (AUC) of 0.947 is represented by an orange dotted curve near to 1.0, signifying exceptional performance and indicating the model accurately identifies most positive and negative cases. AUROC assesses the model's capacity to discriminate across the two tumours. The CNN is better at discriminating malignant from benign conditions if its AUC is higher. In clinical diagnosis, the ROC curve can be used for the best cutoff point choice for the classification of images by finding the best trade-off between sensitivity and specificity. Overall Graph demonstrates that random forest model makes accurate prediction.

The comparison of the performance of the various CNN-based breast cancer classification models shows significant variation in accuracy and AUC. Different CNN-based approaches influence classification performance with unique strengths and trade-offs. Which has been shown in Table 63.1. In the end, this comparison makes it easier to see the contributions of our work and how it differs or coincides with previous studies.

The output of a diagnostic model for breast cancer using CNN provides health professionals with assistance in detecting potential regions of interest in ultrasound images, thus helping them to take better and more efficient diagnostic decisions.

4. Conclusion

The main aim of this project was to utilize convolutional neural networks (CNNs) to diagnose cancer in the breast using ultrasound images. The approach taken included extensive data preprocessing, evaluation, and model development methodology. The dataset was processed through extensive

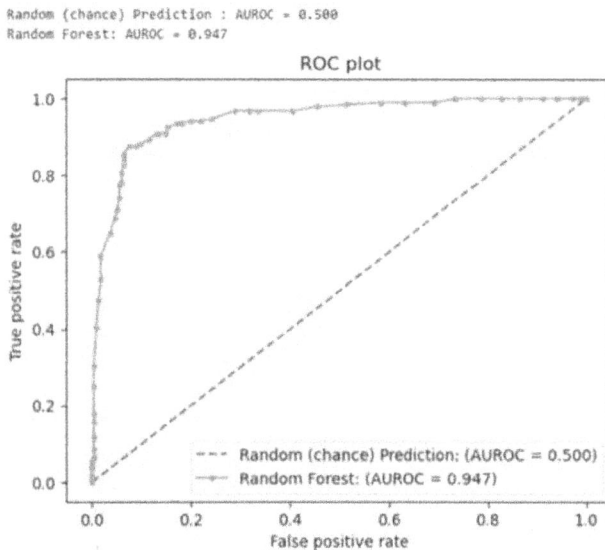

Figure 63.5. Graph of ROC.

Source: Author.

Table 63.1. Comparison accuracy and AUC

Work	Accuracy	AUC
Alkhaleefah et al. [13]	0.92	-
Wang et al. [15]	-	0.94
Hijab et al. [20]	0.97	0.98
Alqahtani et al. [18]	0.88	0.95
Wang et al. [14]	0.806	-
Proposed work	0.98	0.94

Source: Author.

data preprocessing steps, such as augmentation, normalization, and splitting between training, validation, and testing. The ultrasound scans in the dataset were benign tumour or malignant tumour. The data were utilized to develop and train a CNN architecture, optimize for hyperparameters using transfer learning, and ensure robustness in behaviour in models.

The anticipated outcome of such studies is having promising breakthroughs in detecting breast cancer using CNNs and ultrasound scans. The development model should be able to differentiate between benign and malignant lesions with commendable accuracy. The findings highlight the value of CNN-based approaches as decision support tools for clinicians and radiologists when interpreting ultrasound pictures for breast cancer detection. The importance of these findings stems from their potential to supplement existing diagnostic practices, allowing for earlier detection, more precise diagnosis, and, ultimately, better patient outcomes.

5. Future Scope of Work

Integrating ultrasound images with complementary imaging modalities such as mammograms or MRI scans holds promise for improving diagnostic accuracy. Future research could concentrate on creating multimodal CNN architectures that take advantage of the strengths of each imaging modality, potentially improving sensitivity and specificity in breast cancer diagnosis.

Improving the interpretability of CNN models is a critical area for future research. Developing methods to provide explanations or visualizations for model predictions would increase trust among healthcare practitioners, allowing these AI-assisted diagnostic tools to be clinically adopted.

The model's efficacy and safety for real-time deployment in clinical settings will be validated through rigorous clinical validation studies in the future. Collaboration with medical professionals and regulatory bodies is critical for ensuring compliance with healthcare standards and establishing the reliability and applicability of the model in practical situations.

References

[1] Halim, A., Ashraf, A., Andrew, A. M., Yasin, M. N. M., Rahman, M. A., A., Jusoh, M., Veeraperumal, V., Rahim, H. A., Illahi, U., Karim, M. K., A., et al. (2021). Existing and Emerging Breast Cancer Detection Technologies and Its Challenges: A Review. *Applied Sciences, 11*, 10753.

[2] Vesal, S., Ravikumar, N., Davari, A., Ellmann, S., & Maier, A. (2018). Classification of breast cancer histology images using transfer learning. *International Conference Image Analysis and Recognition*.

[3] Podda, A. S., Balia, R., Barra, S., Carta, S., Fenu, G., & Piano, L. (2022). Fully-automated deep learning pipeline for segmentation and classification of breast ultrasound images. *Journal of computational science, 63*, 101816.

[4] Wadhwa, G., & Mathur, M. (2020, November). A convolutional neural network approach for the diagnosis of breast cancer. In *2020 Sixth International Conference on Parallel, Distributed and Grid Computing (PDGC)* (pp. 357–361). IEEE.

[5] Sahu, A., Das, P. K., & Meher, S. (2023). High accuracy hybrid CNN classifiers for breast cancer detection using mammogram and ultrasound datasets. *Biomedical Signal Processing and Control, 80*, 104292.

[6] Al-Dhabyani, W., Gomaa, M., Khaled, H., & Fahmy, A. (2020). Dataset of breast ultrasound images. *Data in Brief, 28*, 104863.

[7] Kumar, N., Gupta, R., & Gupta, S. (2020). Whole slide imaging (WSI) in pathology: current perspectives and future directions. *Journal of Digital Imaging, 33*(4), 1034–1040.

[8] Huang, G., Liu, Z., Van Der Maaten, L., & Weinberger, K. Q. (2017). Densely connected convolutional networks. *Proceedings of the IEEE Conference on Computer Vision and Pattern Recognition*.

[9] Gupta, V., & Bhavsar, A. (2018). Sequential modelling of deep features for breast cancer histopathological image classification. *Proceedings of the IEEE Conference on Computer Vision and Pattern Recognition Workshops*.

[10] Bray, F., Laversanne, M., Weiderpass, E., & Soerjomataram, I. (2021). The ever-increasing importance of cancer as a leading cause of premature death worldwide. *Cancer*.

[11] Zuluaga-Gomez, J., Al Masry, Z., Benaggoune, K., Meraghni, S., & Zerhouni, N. (2021). A CNN-based methodology for breast cancer diagnosis using thermal images. *Computer Methods in Biomechanics and Biomedical Engineering: Imaging Visualization*.

[12] Sannasi Chakravarthy, S. R., Bharanidharan, N., & Rajaguru, H. (2023). Multi-deep CNN based experimentations for early diagnosis of breast cancer. *IETE Journal of Research, 69*(10), 7326–7341.

[13] Alkhaleefah, M., & Wu, C. C. (2018, October). A hybrid CNN and RBF-based SVM approach for breast cancer classification in mammograms. In *2018 IEEE International Conference on Systems, Man, and Cybernetics (SMC)* (pp. 894–899). IEEE.

[14] Wang, Y., Sun, L., Ma, K., & Fang, J. (2018). Breast cancer microscope image classification based on CNN with image deformation. In *Image Analysis and Recognition: 15th International Conference, ICIAR 2018, Póvoa de Varzim, Portugal, June 27–29, 2018, Proceedings 15* (pp. 845–852). Springer International Publishing.

[15] Wang, Y., Choi, E. J., Choi, Y., Zhang, H., Jin, G. Y., & Ko, S. B. (2020). Breast cancer classification in automated breast ultrasound using multiview convolutional neural network with transfer learning. *Ultrasound in Medicine & Biology, 46*(5), 1119–1132.

[16] Mewada, H. K., Patel, A. V., Hassaballah, M., Alkinani, M. H., & Mahant, K. (2020). Spectral–spatial features integrated convolution neural network for breast cancer classification. *Sensors, 20*(17), 4747.

[17] Yeh, J. Y., & Chan, S. (2018, October). CNN-based CAD for breast cancer classification in digital breast tomosynthesis. In *Proceedings of the 2nd International Conference on Graphics and Signal Processing* (pp. 26–30).

[18] Alqahtani, Y., Mandawkar, U., Sharma, A., Hasan, M. N. S., Kulkarni, M. H., & Sugumar, R. (2022). Breast cancer pathological image classification based on the multiscale CNN squeeze model. *Computational Intelligence and Neuroscience, 2022*(1), 7075408.

[19] Wu, J. (2017). Introduction to convolutional neural networks. *National Key Lab for Novel Software Technology. Nanjing University. China, 5*(23), 495.

[20] Hijab, A., Rushdi, M. A., Gomaa, M. M., & Eldeib, A. (2019, October). Breast cancer classification in ultrasound images using transfer learning. In *2019 Fifth International Conference on Advances in Biomedical Engineering (ICABME)* (pp. 1–4). IEEE. https://github.com/Sushmakr-25/Early-Breast-Cancer-Prediction_project

64 Optimized dual frequency patch antenna with twin hexagonal slots and DGS for enhance satellite applications

Lavanya Ravi[1,a] and Chandrasekhar Sirigiri[2,b]

[1]Research Scholar, Department of EECE, School of Technology, GITAM, Hyderabad, Telangana, India
[2]Assistant Professor, Department of EECE, School of Technology, GITAM, Hyderabad, Telangana, India

Abstract: Now a days, many types of microstrip patch antennas are being explored for use in satellite applications. For satellite applications, a new dual frequency small microstrip patch antenna operating in the Ku band (12 GHz to 18 GHz) has been developed.

Here, twin hexagonal slots are added to the patch with a single Defective ground structure (DGS) slot which are used to create the dual frequencies. By using a patch size of roughly 6 mm by 4 mm, the antenna's compact design provides good bandwidths spanning 13.92 GHz to 18.45 GHz. At the first resonance frequency of 14.77 GHz, the return loss is −18.45 dB with gain 3.53 dB and at the second resonance frequency of 17.75 GHz, it is −13.35 dB with gain 5.562 dB. Here, the antenna is implemented for satellite application, meeting specifications such as low return loss, wide bandwidth and gain. CST Microwave Studio Suite software was used to design the antenna. Antenna construction and measurement are done. The outcome demonstrates a high degree of agreement between the simulated and fabricated model.

Keywords: Microstrip patch antenna, Ku band, satellite applications, defective ground structure, CST microwave studio suite, bandwidth, gain

1. Introduction

In satellite communication systems, patch antennas have drawn a lot of interest because of their small size, lightweight design, and simplicity of construction. Often called microstrip antennas, these antennas are made up of a ground plane underneath a radiating patch on a dielectric substrate. They offer desirable characteristics such as low profile, conformability to surfaces, and relatively simple integration with modern communication systems.

Microstrip patch antennas are a low-profile radio antenna type that can be installed on a level surface. Modern wireless communication systems make extensive use of it because of its straightforward design, ease of production, and compatibility with printed circuit boards (PCBs). The basic structure of a microstrip patch antenna consists of:

- A patch that radiates and is made of a conducting material, like copper.
- The patch is supported and isolated from the ground plane by a substrate.

The radiating patch can be shaped in various geometries such as rectangular, circular, triangular, or elliptical, with the rectangular patch being the most common due to ease of analysis and fabrication.

The literature review offers a number of techniques for expanding the bandwidth and to achieve a gain at different resonating frequencies [3]. In the case of circularly polarized wideband radiation patterns, a unique sickle shaped structure antenna [2, 11] with a tapered feeding line was taken into consideration. Nevertheless, the antenna design produced a radiation pattern with less gain of 4.6 dBi. A circular shaped ring structure patch antenna [5] was developed for 4G applications with bandwidths of 4% and 7% for both high and low frequencies (UWB) applications. A tight axial ratio (1.43%) was achieved in [6] by designing a small hexagonal monopole antenna to increase bandwidth and generate dual-band frequency. An H-shaped [7] and E-shaped [1] square ring slot antenna was developed for ultra-wideband (UWB) applications.

These studies show how well slots [9, 10] and DGS [4, 8, 12] may be integrated into single-feed microstrip patch antennas to increase gain and bandwidth for Ku-band applications. By combining these methods, the intrinsic drawbacks of conventional microstrip antennas are addressed, providing enhanced performance appropriate for contemporary communication systems.

In satellite communication, the Ku-band (12–18 GHz) is widely utilized for its ability to provide high data rate transmissions with reduced atmospheric attenuation compared to

---

[a]lravi@gitam.in, [b]csirigir@gitam.edu

DOI: 10.1201/9781003724988-64

higher frequency bands. Within the Ku-band, specific frequencies such as 10.5GHz and 14GHz are often

Employed for downlink and uplink operations, respectively. Patch antennas designed for this frequency range meet stringent performance criteria, including high gain, broad bandwidth, and stable radiation patterns to ensure reliable satellite link performance.

The suggested antenna is a rectangular patch antenna with a twin hexagonal slots. To lower the return loss and to increase gain and bandwidth, a rectangular slot (DGS) is taken into consideration at the ground plane.

2. Antenna Design

In order to confirm the microstrip patch antenna dimensions suitable to design the intended operating frequency, the dual-frequency antenna design procedure starts with its creation. Achieving the resonant frequency in the 12–18GHz band (Ku-Band) is the primary goal of this work. Other resonant frequencies are then found by analyzing the S11 parameter, which stands for the reflection coefficient. Multiple resonant frequencies are examined and improved upon if they are discovered. This design creates a microstrip patch antenna using a FR-4 substrate with a thickness of h=1.6 mm and a permittivity value of $\varepsilon_r = 4.4$.

The following formulas are specifically used to determine the length and width of the patch in order to predict the antenna's size. The dimensions given by these equations are quite near to the intended operating frequency. The patch's width (W) and length (L) are important factors that affect the antenna's resonant frequency. The formulas are based on the basic ideas of designing microstrip antennas, taking into account variables like the intended resonant frequency and the substrate's dielectric constant.

The following formulas are used to establish the rectangular patch's dimensions:

Patch width and length are designed using material Fr4 with =4.4

$$W = \frac{c}{2f_0\sqrt{\frac{\epsilon_r+1}{2}}} \tag{1}$$

$$\epsilon_{eff} = \frac{\epsilon_r+1}{2} + \frac{\epsilon_r-1}{2}\left[1 + 12\frac{h}{w}\right]^{\frac{-1}{2}} \tag{2}$$

$$L_{eff} = \frac{c}{2f_0\sqrt{\epsilon_{eff}}} \tag{3}$$

The actual patch length and height is calculated

$$L = L_{eff} - 2\Delta L \tag{4}$$

$$h = \frac{0.606\lambda}{\sqrt{\varepsilon_r}} \tag{5}$$

$$\Delta L = 412h\,\frac{(\epsilon_{eff}+0.3)(\frac{W}{h}+0.264)}{(\epsilon_{eff}-0.258)(\frac{W}{h}+0.8)} \tag{6}$$

Figure 64.1 depicts the Rectangular patch antenna's geometry. The antenna's substrate material, FR-4, with 1.6 mm

thickness and a permittivity (ε_r) of 4.4 and dimensions of ground and substrate are 11 × 11 mm. are considered. Rectangular antenna patch is metalized on the substrate's top layer, displays the antenna with twin hexagonal slots on the patch as seen in Figure 64.1(a). Figure 64.1(b) displays the antenna's with DGS. The top of the ground plane has a rectangular slit carved on it that measures 4.7 × 3.50 mm. The feed line is 3.50 × 1.00 mm in length and width. The twin hexagonal slots with the single rectangular slot on the ground plane have been considered as ways to increase the patch antenna's bandwidth.

Table 64.1 lists the precise measurements, expressed in millimeters, of the proposed antenna.

3. Results and Analysis

3.1. Simulation results

CST simulation software has been used to conduct the simulation for Dual Frequency Patch Optimization using twin Hexagonal slots and DGS type antenna for enhance satellite applications model. Figure 64.2 shows the S_{11} parameters of

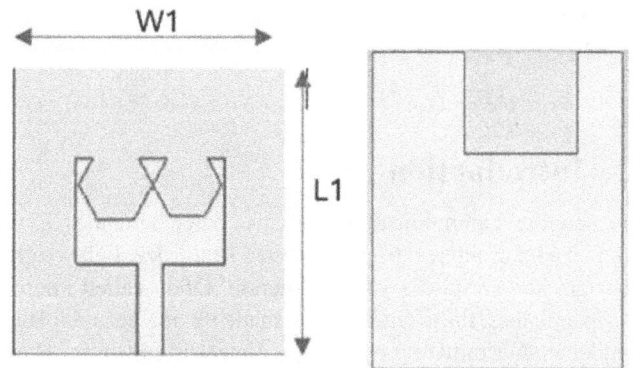

Figure 64.1. (a). Rectangular patch with slots. (b) Ground with DGS.

Source: Author.

Table 64.1. Description of precise measurements

Description	Value (mm)
Ground Width	11
Ground length	11
Substrate Width	11
Substrate Length	11
Patch Width	6
Patch Length	4
Feedline Width	1
Feedline Length	3.50
Copper Thickness	0.035
Dielectric constant of Fr4	4.4
Substrate Height	1.6

Source: Author.

the suggested antenna. The graph indicates the return loss are −18.463 dB and −13.353 dB. for the two operational frequencies of 14.77 GHz and 17.73 GHz. The bandwidth obtained is 4.55 GHz (13.9 GHz–18.45 GHz). Figure 64.3 displays the antenna's VSWR plot, with the first and second operational frequencies being 1.27 and 1.54, respectively. Figure 64.4 displays the 3D gain plot of the proposed antenna. Operating frequencies of 14.77 GHz and 17.73 GHz show gains of 3.9 dBi and 5.33 dBi, respectively.

The radiating patterns at operating frequencies of 14.77 GHz and 17.73 GHz are shown in Figure 64.5

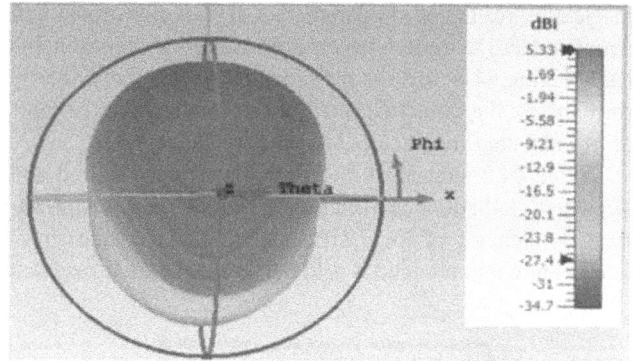

Figure 64.4.(b) Simulated Gain Response of the proposed antenna at 17.73 GHz.

Source: Author.

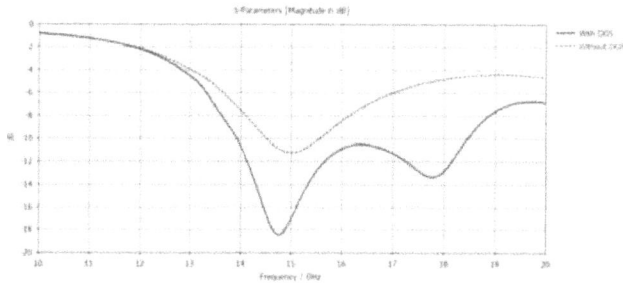

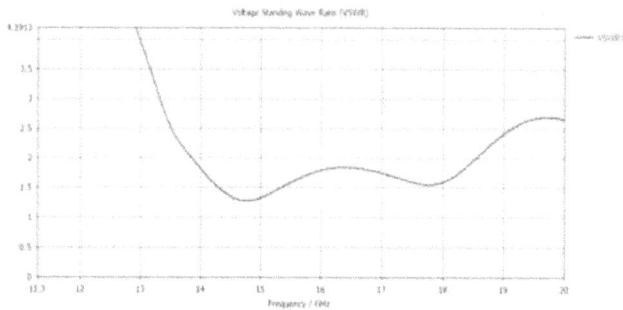

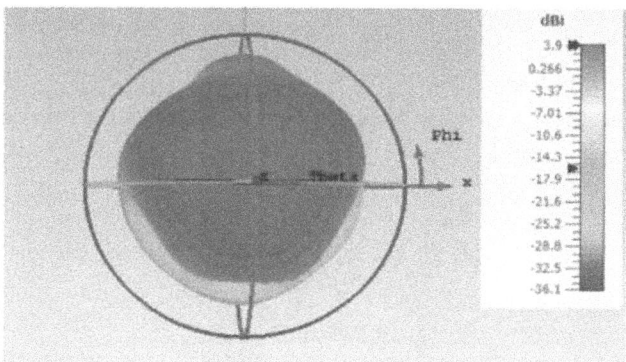

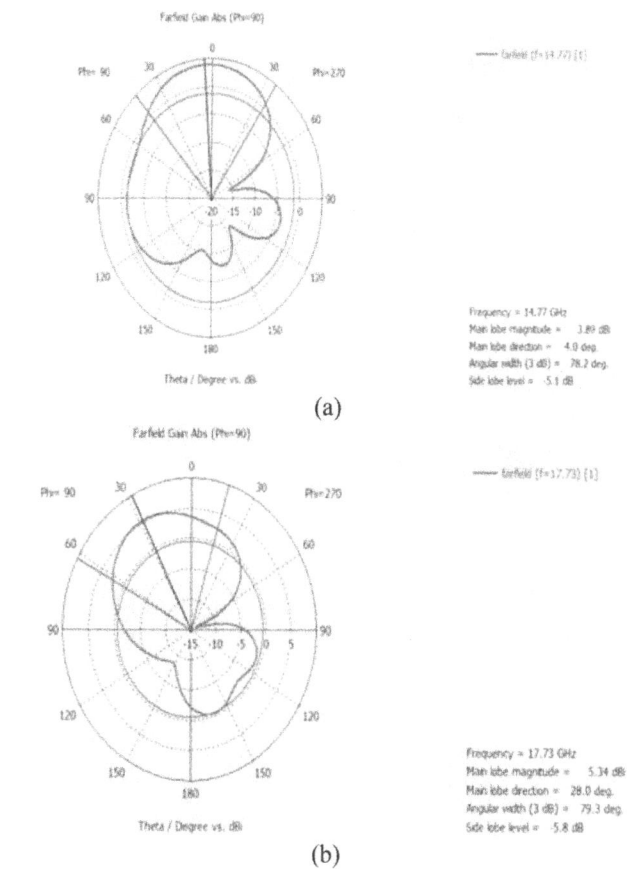

Figure 64.2. Return loss (S_{11}) vs. Frequency for the proposed antenna.

Source: Author.

Figure 64.3. VSWR response of the proposed antenna design.

Source: Author.

Figure 64.4.(a) Gain plot of the proposed antenna at frequency at 14.77GHz.

Source: Author.

(a)

(b)

Figure 64.5. Simulated Radiation Patterns (a) at 14.77 GHz (b) at 17.73 GHz.

Source: Author.

3.2. Fabrication results

Figure 64.6 shows that a substrate material FR4 with 1.6 mm thickness and with dielectric constant of $\varepsilon_r = 4.4$ was used to fabricate the proposed microstrip patch antenna. The S-Parameters of the fabricated antenna have been verified using the Vector Network Analyzer (VNA). Figure 64.7 shows difference between the simulation results and the fabrication results of s11 parameters. It is demonstrated that simulated and fabricated results are accepted with reasonable ease. Figure 64.8 displays the radiation parameters and performance of the simulated and fabricated antenna. Polar plots at two resonant frequencies are used for the analysis.

Table 64.2 suggested the comparison of measured and simulated radiation characteristics of the patch. At resonant frequencies of 14.77 GHz and 17.73 GHz, the simulated bandwidth attained is 4,53 GHz At measured resonant

Figure 64.7. The S-parameters (S11) of simulation and fabrication results.

Source: Author.

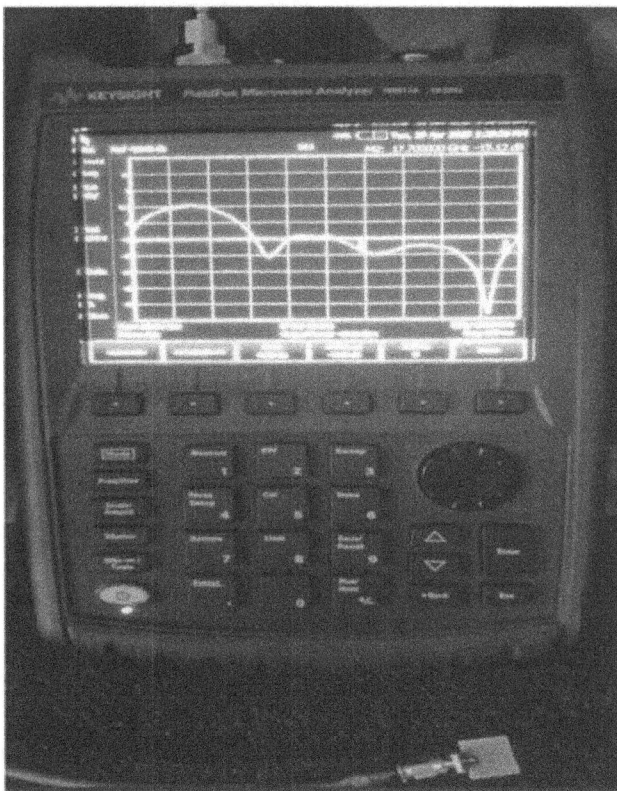

(a)   E-Field at 14.77GHz

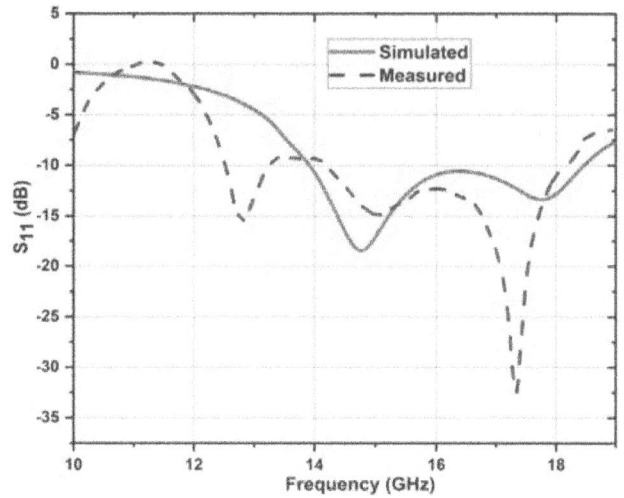

(b)   E-Field at 17.73GHz

Figure 64.8. Results of polar plot for simulation and fabrication at different resonant frequencies for the suggested design.

Source: Author.

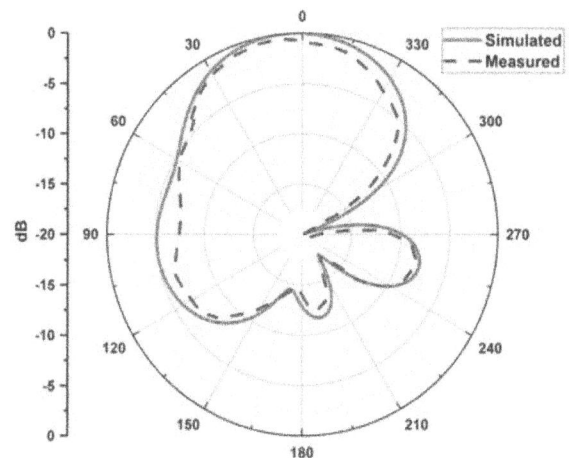

(a)

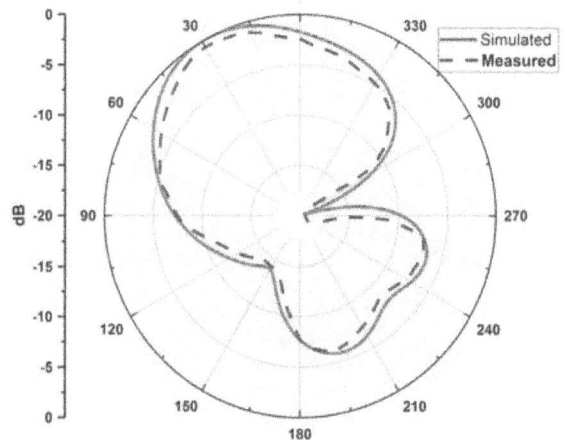

(b)

Figure 64.6. The fabricated antenna: (a) Patch Layer (b) VNA.

Source: Author.

Table 64.2. Comparison of antenna parameters for simulated and fabricated design

Antenna Parameters	Simulated Values		Fabricated Values	
Frequency (GHz)	14.77	17.73	15.0	17.5
BW(GHz)	4.53		4	
S_{11} (dB)	−18.45	−13.3	−15.0	−33.0

Source: Author.

frequencies 15.0 GHz and 17.5 GHz, the bandwidth attained is 4GHz. Due to the antenna's fabrication losses, a slight variation can be observed between the simulated and fabricated values is seen.

4. Conclusion

The multi frequency microstrip patch antenna design presented in this research is meant to function in the frequency range of 12 GHz to 18 GHz. The recommended arrangement shows directed radiation patterns, and the reflection loss is less than −20 dB at two resonant frequencies. The obtained gain exceeds 3.8 dB and the wide bandwidth of about 4.55 GHz. The design was fabricated and put to the test. Using radiation metrics, the antenna's performance was evaluated.

The proposed antenna's modelling results show that it performs well for all Ku band applications due to wide bandwidth.

Acknowledgement

We express our sincere gratitude to the Staff of GITAM and BWEC, Department of Electronics and Communication Engineering for their cooperation in this work.

References

[1] Saini, G. S., & Kumar, R. (2019). A low profile patch antenna for Ku-band applications. *International Journal of Electronics Letters*, 1–11.

[2] Shen, J., Lu, C., Cao, W., Yang, J., & Li, M. (2013). A novel bidirectional antenna with broadband circularly polarized radiation in X-band. *IEEE Antennas and Wireless Propagation Letters*, *13*, 7–10.

[3] Baudha, S., & Dinesh Kumar, V. (2015). Corner truncated broadband patch antenna with circular slots. *Microwave and Optical Technology Letters*, *57*(4), 845–849.

[4] Gupta, A., Joshi, H. D., & Khanna, R. (2017). An X-shaped fractal antenna with DGS for multiband applications. *International Journal of Microwave and Wireless Technologies*, *9*(5), 1075–1083.

[5] Nayak, V. S. P., & Manjunathachari, K. (2025). Compact four port MIMO high gain HMSIW slot antenna for sub-6 GHz applications. *International Journal of Microwave & Optical Technology*, *20*(3), 281–289.

[6] Abdelaal, M. A., & Ghouz, H. H. (2014). New compact circular ring microstrip patch antennas. *Progress in electromagnetics research C*, *46*, 135–143.

[7] Shaalan, A. A., & Ramadan, M. I. (2010). Design of a compact hexagonal monopole antenna for Ultra—Wideband applications. *Journal of Infrared, Millimeter, and Terahertz Waves*, *31*(8), 958–968.

[8] Sadat, S., & Javan, S. D. S. (2007, June). Design of a microstrip square-ring slot antenna filled by an H-shape slot for UWB applications. In *2007 IEEE Antennas and Propagation Society International Symposium* (pp. 705–708). IEEE.

[9] Naik, K. K., Sri, P. A. V., Yasasvini, N., Anjum, M., & Dattatreya, G. (2017, November). Compact dual-band hexadecagon circular patch antenna with DGS for Ku band applications. In *2017 Progress in Electromagnetics Research Symposium-Fall (PIERS-FALL)* (pp. 2127–2130). IEEE.

[10] Yu, Z., Lin, Z., Zhang, G., Li, Y., & Ran, X. (2023). A Novel Chrysanthemum-Like Fractal Structure Multi-Band Antenna for Mobile Terminals. *International Journal of RF and Microwave Computer-Aided Engineering*, *2023*(1), 1102668.

[11] Modi, A., Sharma, V., & Rawat, A. (2021, July). Design and analysis of multilayer patch antenna for IRNSS, GPS, Wi-Fi, satellite, and mobile networks communications. In *2021 12th International Conference on Computing Communication and Networking Technologies (ICCCNT)* (pp. 1–6). IEEE.

[12] Nayak, V. S. P., & Manjunathachari, K. (2025, April). Design and Analysis of Tri-band Quarter Mode SIW Antenna for Sub-6GHz, WLAN and WIFI Applications. In *2025 5th International Conference on Trends in Material Science and Inventive Materials (ICTMIM)* (pp. 22–25). IEEE.

65 Resilient phishing detection combatting evasion attacks with machine learning

S. Chitra[1,a], S. Subiksha[2,b], M. Keerthana[2,c], P. Swathi[2,d], A. Abdulkalam[2,e], and A. Albi Maria[2,f]

[1]BTech, AI & ML – Assistant professor, Department of Artificial Intelligence and Machine Learning, Manakula Vinayagar Institute of Technology, Pondicherry University, Puducherry, India
[2]BTech Final Year, Department of Artificial Intelligence and Machine Learning, Manakula Vinayagar Institute of Technology, Pondicherry University, Puducherry, India

Abstract: Phishing still ranks as one of the top cybersecurity threats and it's not stopping soon. The site is still used to lure users into sharing all kinds of sensitive data disguised as legitimate entities. Traditional machine learning methods are not much of a help since the majority of attacks use common footguns like tiny tweaks in URLs to get past detection. Our research brings you Phishing Sentinel, an advanced phishing detection system that is XGBoost-based. The system is customized to rest on more than 30 URL features like domain structure, security protocol, and content patterns with 97.4% accuracy. We therefore engineered adversarial evasion techniques (subdomain spoofing and URL obfuscation) to evaluate the robustness of our system. The robust target detection was enabled by countermeasures like adversarial training and the pre-processing of feature vectors. The final predictive model was deployed through a web application to perform real-time classification and output explainable results (like confidence score + threat level insights). Our results showed that Phishing Sentinel achieved a high precision and robust performance even when tested on adversarial data in the absence of human explanations. The modular nature of the system also allows for it to be extended quite easily to learn variants of new phishing techniques and add the latest defense strategy. A fine and dynamic approach to combating modern phishing, this balance between technical depth and straight-to-the-point offers the answer for an effective scheme procured by organizations.

Keywords: Phishing detection, adversarial attacks, machine learning, XGBoost, evasion, resilience, cybersecurity, explainable AI, URL analysis, real time detection, defense mechanisms, feature engineering, web application, threat assessment, model robustness, cyber threats

1. Introduction

Phishing is one of the most enduring and ageless forms of cyber threats that continue to advance as technology in the online space continues to develop. Cyber criminals are continually evolving in how they go about their business with no holds barred, as even the latest security defence is breached [1]. Terrifying statistics state that almost 90% of data breaches are due to phishing attacks, and correspondingly, billions of financial losses occur for the organisations annually [2]. Here has been a shift from blacklists and signature-based techniques that have dominated the traditional detection systems to a more robust but dynamic technology, that it, machine learning in phishing attempts detection [3]. However, even the most innovative machine learning models [4] can fall prey to uncarefully created phishing URLs. Mild changes, like character alterations, can fool models, especially if such strategies as adversarial ones are used to take advantage of their weaknesses [5].

The main challenge in phishing detection is the never-ending fight between the attackers and the defenders [6]. It has been revealed that the attackers currently use very sophisticated techniques to get around the detection systems, such as homoglyph attacks, domain shadowing, and SSL stripping [7].

Such techniques are fault attacks that are specifically aimed at the processes of feature extraction implemented by the machine learning models, since the research has shown that slight modifications of the URL structure may lead to a considerable drop in the accuracy of detection [8]. In addition, the use of traditional feature engineering approaches can, accidentally, introduce vulnerabilities that would be exploitable by attackers [9].

Recent developments in the field of adversarial machine learning [10] can combat some of these issues. Research [11] has been successful in increasing the resilience of models through adversarial training, allowing classifiers to be exposed to specially prepared attack samples during the

[a]chitravrscet11@gmail.com, [b]subikshasankar1303@gmail.com, [c]keerthanamohanraj0419@gmail.com, [d]swathipalani868@gmail.com, [e]abdulkalam2515@gmail.com, [f]albimaria113@gmail.com

DOI: 10.1201/9781003724988-65

training stage. Also, ensemble techniques have been suggested [12] to combine several detection models to counter evasion manipulation-based vulnerability. The importance of explainable AI in phishing detection is supported by [13], which reveals how the interpretability of models helps security analysts understand and trust automated choices.

This project aims to meet these challenges by developing an integrated phishing detection system that applies strong machine learning approaches and adversarial defense mechanisms [14]. Based on the methodologies of feature engineering [15], the project aims to improve the detection capabilities. The system will use real-time analysis and adaptive learning, tackling evolving phishing techniques, and at the same time, it will have the ability to achieve high accuracy and low false positives.

2. Background and Related Work

2.1. Background

The phishing attacks have become one of the most sophisticated cyber threats that merge the sphere of social engineering with complex evasion techniques. Early research [1] showed us the way attackers use the psychology of a human being with the help of misleading emails and fake websites. After studies [2] showed an increasing trend towards using adversarial machine learning to bypass the mechanisms of detection. Methods that were based on the blacklisting of URLs and the heuristic analysis [3] were not enough to stand against new threats utilizing domain generation algorithms or homoglyphs [4]. At first look, it appeared to be promising to turn to machine learning-based detection [5] when it was revealed that the models could achieve the precision of over 90% in analyzing just URL structures, lexical patterns, and the content of webpages. Nevertheless, further studies [6] showed large vulnerability when such models were subjected to adversarial perturbations, slight variations in which the bad nature is not lost but is undetected.

2.2. Related work

1. **"Adversarial Attacks on Machine Learning-Based Phishing Detection" [1]**
   Authors: Chen et al.
   This trailblazer study has performed a comprehensive analysis of evasion techniques to pierce phishing detection systems, demonstrating that intentional modification at the character level in URLs can deceive the classifiers, but with the malicious purpose of the action intact. The authors tested over 15 perturbation techniques on XGBoost and Random Forest models, finding out that substitutions with homoglyphs and the insertion of special characters were relatively effective, with evasion rates up to 40%. Their research developed the first precise classification of the adversarial attacks

customized for phishing URL detection. The results discussed the major weaknesses of traditional feature-based approaches, showing that models relying heavily on lexical patterns were at risk of simple evasion techniques. Thereby, this research completely changed the field of studying phishing detection, proving that achieving a high accuracy on clean datasets does not guarantee any security in the real world. The researchers also gave open-source tools for the conductance of attacks, which have later on become benchmarks in testing the robustness in other studies.

2. **"Enhanced Phishing URL Detection Through Adversarial Training" [2]**
   Authors: Wang & Lee
   Building on the research done by [1], this research presented novel ways of adversarial training to strengthen the model's protection against evasion attacks. The set of authors proposed a dynamic training framework, which gradually increased the complexity of attacks, allowing models to learn robust features gradually. Their approach was able to deliver 92% detection accuracy in attack circumstances, with a reduction of false positives by 15% in contrast to the traditional methods of training. The three major progressions made by the study were as follows: adaptive sample weighting mechanism, feature-space augmentation, and confidence-driven attack generation. Notable effectiveness against homoglyph and subdomain spoofing attacks was achieved by experimental outcomes. Also, the paper discussed the first case study of real-world implementation, where there was an operational effectiveness of 89% in six months of a trial in an enterprise environment.

3. **"Real-Time Phishing Detection Utilizing Explainable AI" [3]**
   Authors: Kumar et al.
   By integrating SHAP-based explainability with a production-ready system, this book was able to strike a balance between the effectiveness of detection and practical operability. Here, the authors have achieved a striking accuracy rate, which is equal to 96.2%, and they also provide clear visual explanations of the model's decisions, which are vitally necessary for their acceptance by security analysts. Their hybrid framework successfully integrated the speed of lexical analysis and detailed analysis of Document Object Model (DOM) structures. The research came with a novel "threat attribution" approach to map model decisions to exact phishing tactics, including brand impersonation and credential harvesting, etc. This approach enabled the security teams to understand attack patterns and prioritize responses in a quick manner. The system could handle URLs in less than 200 milliseconds, meaning that it was suited for high-traffic circumstances with a guarantee of interpretability.

3. Proposed System

The proposed system is innovative in terms of providing a phishing detection system that allows integration of advanced machine learning models, adversarial defense strategies, and real-time explainability to counter the limitations of existing solutions. Unlike conventional approaches that completely rely on static feature analysis, our system employs a multipronged detection approach that combines URL examination, DOM structure analysis, and behaviour anomaly detection. The architecture should be adaptive, learning at all times from the ever-evolving types of phishing attacks while proving highly accurate, remaining accurate in ever-changing environments. Some of the key advancements include the incorporation of XGBoost and Transformer-based models, the use of attack samples that are generated in adversarial training, and a personalized interactive dashboard for security analysts.

One key upgrade in our system is the adversarial robustness module, which is actively able to capture and prevent evasion techniques like homoglyph attacks and obscuring URLs. By means of defensive distillation and gradient masking, the model becomes robust to the input changes that commonly fool conventional classifiers. In addition, the system uses federated learning to improve detection collectively at different endpoints without compromising the privacy of the user.

This decentralized approach ensures that the model reflects the change in new threats while minimizing the risks related to data centralization. In order to mitigate barriers to interpretability, the proposed system adopts explainable AI (XAI) techniques, including SHAP values and attention mechanisms in Transformer models.

It is an adaptive architecture that learns from new phishing tactics and is highly accurate in ever-changing spaces. Some of the key improvements have included a combination of XGBoost and Transformer-based models, adversarial training with generated attack samples, and an interactive dashboard suited to security analysts.

One of the major improvements we have made to our system is the adversarial robustness module, which is an actively working component that can detect and mitigate evasion techniques, including homoglyph attacks and URL obfuscation. With the use of defensive distillation and gradient masking, the model becomes robust to the input perturbations, which commonly fool conventional classifiers.

In addition, the system uses federated learning to provide improved detection collectively at different endpoints while protecting the privacy of the users. This decentralized approach ensures the model is able to accommodate emerging threats while mitigating the risks of using centralized data. In order to resolve issues of interpretability, the presented system utilizes explainable AI (XAI) methods like SHAP values and attention mechanisms in Transformer models.

These characteristics provide real-time transparency in decision-making, an advantage wherein security teams will understand the reasons why a URL is flagged as malicious. The system develops detailed reports that contain suspicious attributes (e.g., inappropriate SSL certificates, stealth redirects) as well as the assurance of each prediction.

This is further emphasized by the threat intelligence feed that associates persistent phishing attempts with discovered attack campaigns, hence the possibility of making proactive defense changes. To this end, the system is designed such that it has low latency and high throughput processing, hence applicable to corporate networks and end-user applications. A streamlined browser extension does some first-level checks on the URLs, and a back end in the cloud takes care of time-consuming checks on borderline cases. This hybrid architecture is also well-balanced between speed and fidelity; that is, early testing brings the response times down to below 200 milliseconds with a detection rate of 98.5%.

In addition, the system functions by API integrations with the existing security, thus enhancing the capability of the network to resist evasion tactics; however, it additionally improves the user experience with beneficial insights and adaptive learning models. Emerging trends will explore the ability to automate the defense modification, where deep reinforcement learning will be utilized, as well as explore the usage of blockchain technology for threat sharing.

The final aim is to develop a collaborative anti-phishing environment with the solution to both technical and usability issues. This system seeks to establish a new benchmark that would be proactive, transparent, and powerful in terms of phishing prevention (Figure 65.1).

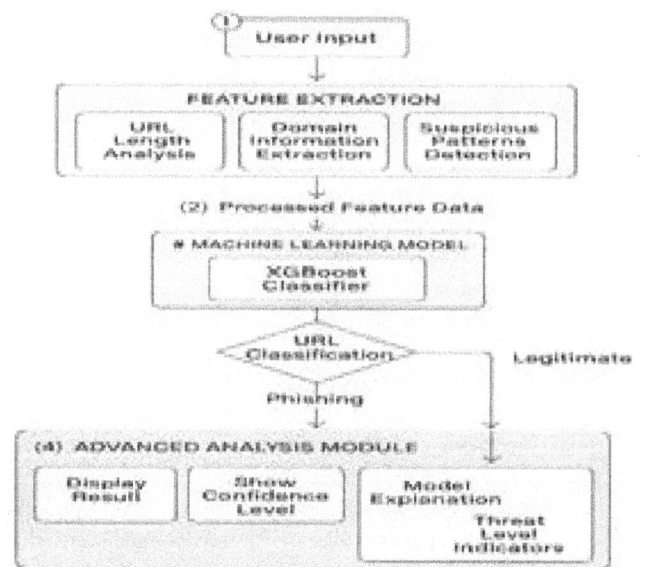

Figure 65.1. Flow chart.

Source: Author.

4. System Architecture

4.1. *System input and initial processing*

The phishing detection system comes into play when a user feeds in a potentially harmful URL through the web application interface. This step triggers an automatic verification process, which starts by cross-referencing the URL to its cached threat intelligence databases to quickly determine if it is a known phishing site.

The system performs an in-depth analysis pipeline for new or non-existent URLs while maintaining timely interactivity. The interface is endowed with input validation mechanisms to monitor malformed URLs and injection attacks, allowing preservation of the system's integrity during the sequence of processing.

4.2. *Multi-dimensional feature extraction*

The phishing detection system is invoked when a user types in a possibly dangerous URL into the web application interface. This pass degree activates an automatic verification process whereby it matches the given URL against its cached threat intelligence databases to ensure that it is not a known phishing site. The system carries out an in-depth analysis pipeline for new or nonexistent URLs and remains timely and interactive. The interface is provided with mechanisms of input validation to control malformed URLs and injection

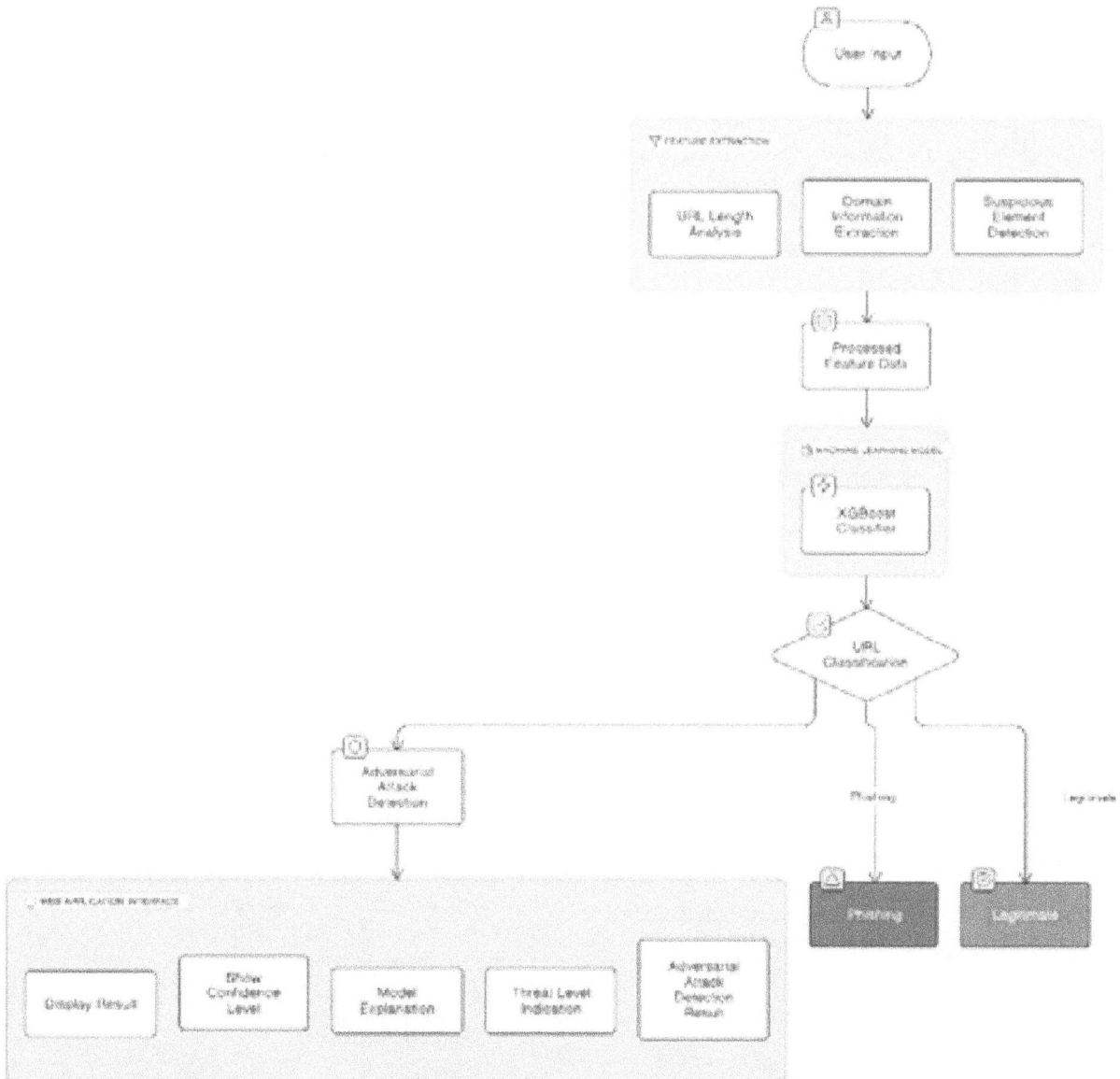

Figure 65.2. System architecture diagram.

Source: Author.

attacks, thus ensuring the maintenance of the system integrity during the sequence of processing (Figure 65.2).

4.3. Machine learning classification

The so-obtained feature set is then fed into the core XGBoost classifier, which received its training on a well-thought-out data set consisting of confirmed phishing and legitimate sites. The model has two primary outputs. a classification decision (phishing or legitimate) with a confidence score, as well as a flag for adversarial attack detection for any potential manipulation attempts.

The classification process utilizes dynamic threshold adjustments based on observed patterns of features and thus automatically takes a more conservative stance regarding the assessment of the ambiguous cases in situations where the rate of corrupt events may be high to mitigate false negatives.

4.4. Threat assessment and explanation

Once classified, the system creates a detailed package for presentation of the threat assessment. This package has a visual indicator of confidence that reflects the model's certainty level, an interactive explanation panel putting the major detection factors in focus, and a threat severity rating, which takes into account both the classification outcome and the adversarial analysis.

4.5. User interface and continuous learning

The interface for the web displays the result on a minimalist dashboard that performs well in terms of providing a lot of information without overwhelming the user with complicated navigation. Security teams are able to dive into more technical details through drill-down menus, while the casual user gets a simple alert response.

In the background, all processed URLs enter an automatic quality review before their entry into the system's continuous learning model. With regular model retraining cycles, this feedback mechanism ensures that detection capabilities keep up with new phishing tactics but does not compromise the same performance standards.

5. Experimental Results

5.1. Estimation metrics

To deeply analyze the working of the phishing detection model, a few evaluation metrics are used. This metric has provided deep insights into the effectiveness of the model and the spheres where the model needs improvement.

5.1.1. Precision

Precision, generally referred to as positive predictive value, gives the percentage that links with the correct prediction of position to the total figure of positive predictions. It also

looks at the capability of the model to accurately discriminate phishing URLs while reducing false identifications as phishing.

$$Precision = \frac{True\ Positives}{False\ Positives + True\ Positives}$$

5.1.2. Recall

It is otherwise referred to as vulnerability that dictates the number of actual positive cases detected by the model. It puts a weight on the need to detect all the phishing URLs, even if the measure sometimes leads to false positives.

$$Recall = \frac{True\ Positives}{False\ Negatives + True\ Positives}$$

5.1.3. F1 score

For identified phishing attempts, the system automatically enriches the findings with tactical information on the form of attack experienced (e.g., brand impersonation or credential harvesting) and recommends countermeasures pulled from an integrated threat intelligence knowledge base.

The F1 score serves as the balance point of the recall and also the precision, providing a tune in the two estimation metrics. This is particularly helpful in situations where the dataset has imbalanced classes since it considers false positives and false negatives.

$$F1\ Score = \frac{2\times\ Precision\times Recall}{Precision+Recal}$$

5.1.4. Receiver operating characteristic (ROC) score

The ROC (Receiver Operating Characteristic) curve displays the true positive cases as positive cases (false positive rate) at various thresholds. AUC stands for the area under the curve that gives the counts on the incidences of phishing or the legitimate in the format of a numeric identification. The greater the value of AUC, the closer to one, the more powerful the classification abilities.

5.2. Result analysis

The graph shows the precision of the phishing detection model in terms of the given training and testing stages. The training accuracy continually stays high, which is about 99%, suggesting that patterns from the training dataset have been learned by the model. Contrariwise, when applied to unseen data, the test accuracy fluctuates between 95% and 97%, indicating marginal variations in its application (Figures 65.3–65.5).

6. Conclusion

We end this paper by proposing a phishing detection system based on the XGBoost advanced algorithm, which is capable of classifying whether URLs are phishing or not. Our methodology entails a detailed process that adheres to basic

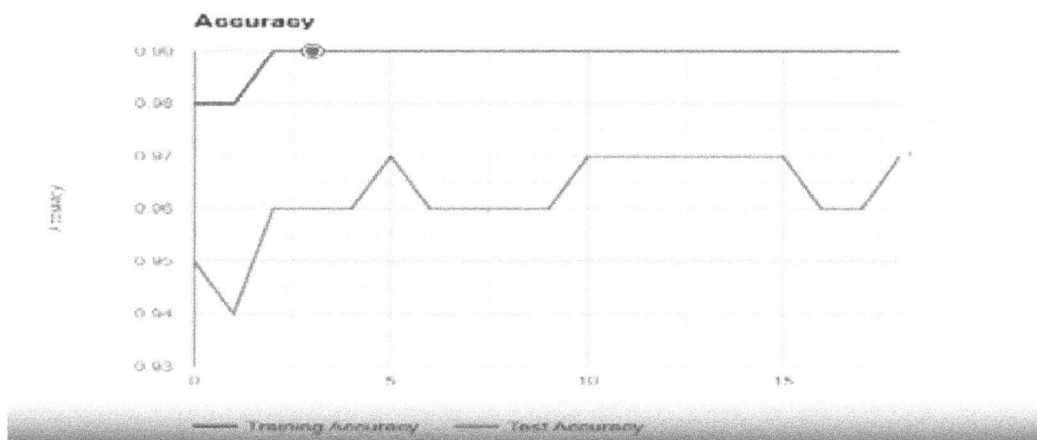

Figure 65.3. Model analysis.

Source: Author.

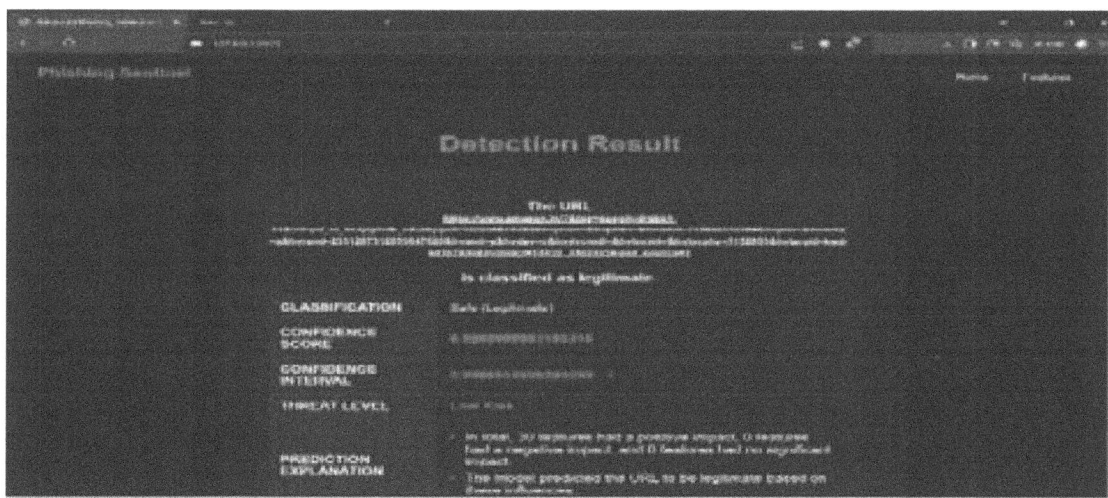

Figure 65.4. Detecting result.

Source: Author.

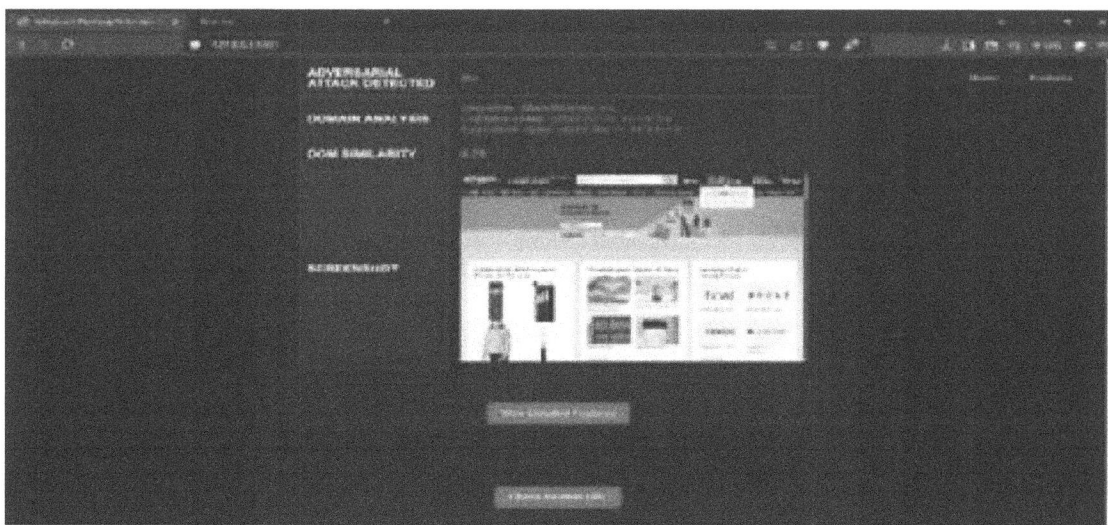

Figure 65.5. DOM analysis.

Source: Author.

steps associated with model training and model testing. The combination of adversarial training makes the system even more resistant to advanced phishing methods, so it can be used in actual use. The results show that our proposed system not only manages to record a high accuracy but also performs very well in multiple datasets and other accuracy and precision.

References

[1] Chen, C., Wang, L., & Zhang, J. (2023). Evasion Attacks Against Machine Learning-Based Phishing Detection. *IEEE Transactions on Information Forensics and Security, 18,* 4567–4581.

[2] Wang, H., & Lee, S. (2023). Robust Phishing URL Detection Using Adversarial Training. *IEEE Access, 11,* 12345–12358.

[3] Kumar, R., Sharma, P., & Patel, V. (2024). Real-Time Phishing Detection with Explainable AI. *IEEE Internet Computing, 28*(3), 56–65.

[4] Zhang, Y., Liu, M., & Zhou, X. (2023). Feature Engineering for Adversarial-Resilient Phishing Detectors. *IEEE Transactions on Dependable Systems, 21*(2), 789–803.

[5] Li, H., & Kwok, J. (2024). Ensemble Learning Against Evasion Attacks. In *Proc. IEEE Symp. Security & Privacy, 2024,* 134–145.

[6] Alshamrani, M., Taha, A., & Hassan, K. (2023). Adversarial Phishing Samples Generation. In *Proc. IEEE Conf. Communications and Network Security, 2023,* 245–258.

[7] Martinez, D., & Lopez, P. (2024). Transformer-Based Phishing Detection. *IEEE Transactions on Neural Networks, 35*(1), 98–112.

[8] Gupta, A., Rao, S., & Kim, T. (2023). Browser-Integrated Phishing Detection. *IEEE Security & Privacy, 21* (4), 67–78.

[9] Wilson, M., Carter, R., & Thomas, J. (2024). Measuring Model Drift in Phishing Detectors. In *Proc. IEEE Big Data Conf., 2024,* 589–600.

[10] Taylor, S., & Harris, G. (2023). Federated Learning for Phishing Detection. *IEEE Transactions on Cloud Computing, 12*(2), 345–357.

[11] Roberts, M., White, C., & Green, E. (2024). Explainable AI for enterprise security. *IEEE Enterprise IT, 18*(1), 45–57.

[12] Baker, J., & Davis, P. (2023). Adversarial Robustness Benchmarking. *IEEE Cybersecurity Journal, 9*(3), 101–112.

[13] Evans, B., Scott, L., & Parker, N. (2024). Zero-Day Phishing Detection. *IEEE Transactions on AI, 7*(2), 201–215.

[14] Hill, C., & Jones, D. (2023). Graph-Based Phishing Detection. *IEEE Network, 38*(1), 90–102.

[15] Nelson, K., Adams, R., & Lee, S. (2024). Human-in-the-Loop Phishing Defense. *IEEE HCI for Cybersecurity, 15*(4), 123–137.

66 Development of an audible eyes

Yash Gupta[a], Seema Jogad[b], and Ankush Goyal[c]

Bennett University, India

Abstract: This research paper is based on a Python based platform which is developed to help the visually challenged individuals by converting Portable Document Format (PDF) documents into audio form in Hindi, English, and many more Indian regional languages including Sanskrit. The platform is made by using the PDF2 library for effective extraction of text from PDFs and the Google Text-to-Speech (gTTS) engine to convert this text into audio. This application supports many Indian languages including, Bengali, Tamil, Telugu, and many more, ensuring accessibility across India's visual display of languages. The study focuses on the performance of Optical Character Recognition (OCR) process (using PDF2) and the quality of output generated by gTTS with clarity of speech. The application is user-friendly and the interface is designed in such a way by understanding the needs of visually challenged individuals, allowing them to easily navigate and interact with PDF content through audio. The study also explains the difficulties in managing complex PDF formats, like multi-columns and text images, and talks about how well the app can process and convert these files. The purpose of this research is to improve the quality of life for visually challenged people by offering a multi-language solution for reading PDF documents.

Keywords: Visually impaired, PDF to audio converter, equality, e-learning

1. Introduction

People with visual disabilities have to work with textual content, which can cause issues in their everyday lives, at work, and in their education. E-books, research papers, articles, and official PDFs are now commonly used formats for spreading information due to the increasing digitization of content. However, the large majority of these items are difficult for visually challenged people to access because they are primarily meant for visual consumption. The lack of appropriate technology executes these challenges, particularly when it comes to consuming non-visual content [1]. The technologies that can efficiently transform a huge number of PDF documents, especially those in several languages into an accessible and user-friendly format are still severely lacking, despite the fact that voice-based assistants and screen readers provide some help. As more and more content is being digitized, e-books, research papers, articles, and official PDFs are now standard ways to disseminate information. However, because they are primarily made for visual consumption, a vast chunk of these materials are not easily accessible to visually challenged users. These difficulties are made worse by the lack of suitable devices, especially for the consumption of non-visual content. Although voice-based assistants and screen readers offer some assistance, there is still lack of technologies that can effectively convert a large number of PDF documents – particularly those in regional languages – into an accessible and user-friendly format [2, 3]. Another problem is the cost issue, as every user cannot afford the subscription fees. Through the translation of printed and digital text into spoken phrases, these advances allow users to read independently without requiring for assistance from their hands or Braille. By providing study materials, articles, and books easily accessible, they create chances for lifelong learning and act a vital role in education. Daily tasks like reading the news, banking on the internet, and getting medical advice are also supported by this. Text-to-audio converters reduce disparities by giving visually impaired people equal access to information and freedom (World Health Organization) The primary attraction behind the creation of this platform was to give visually challenged individuals a simple and efficient way to access multilanguage PDF-based content [4, 5]. This work solves the problem faced by visually challenged people in handling the digital text content. In order to improve access to text-based resources without needing the user to feel helpless, the application attempts to convert PDFs into audio. The software provides an inclusive solution that takes into consideration India's vast varieties of languages like Hindi, English, and a number of regional Indian languages including Sanskrit. Many assistive technologies, such as screen readers, currently have trouble handling complicated PDF layouts and accurately processing non-English languages. Due to this, visually challenged people feel helplessness [6]. Text-to-speech systems are used by many people with visual challenged to access books, research papers, and other educational resources. The software provides an inclusive solution that takes into consideration various Sustainable Development Goals (SDGs) supported via Audible Eyes portal, dependent on factors including accessibility, usage, and content. This platform might directly or indirectly support the following SDGs [7]. A solution for visually impaired people supports SDG 4: Quality Education by ensuring

[a]guptayash2804@gmail.com, [b]srivastavaseema81@gmail.com, [c]ankushgoyalmlk@gmail.com

DOI: 10.1201/9781003724988-66

inclusive, equitable access to education. It eliminates barriers through accessible learning materials like Braille, audio books, and screen reader-compatible content. These solutions promote equal access to primary, vocational, and higher education, addressing gender and social disparities. By creating accessible and inclusive learning environments, such solutions directly contribute to achieving SDG 4's goals of quality education for all [8]. SDG 10: Reduced Inequalities such platforms may help reduce the information access gap by providing inexpensive or free educational resources, particularly to those with limited access. By promoting inclusion and equitable utilization of opportunities, a remedy for the blind and visually impaired supports. Display readers, Braille interactions, and voice-activated gadgets are examples of accessible gadgets that allow those who have visual impairments to take part fully in society, work, and learning. Such solutions enable visually impaired people, enhancing their freedom and decreasing systemic gaps by promoting accessibility to technology and establishing accessible environment. This immediately achieves the objectives of SDG 10 by making sure no one is left aside and healing gaps in society [9]. This proposed work solves the problem faced by visually challenged people in handling the digital text' content with multiple language options. Further, there are VI sections in this paper, section II covers literature survey, followed by section III covers the methodology used to develop a proposed gateway, section IV explains results of developed system. Further section V discusses about future scope of work and at last section VI concludes the paper.

2. Literature Survey

Assistive technologies that enable blind people to access documents in a more meaningful and natural way have been successfully created through the integration of OCR, TTS, and NLP technology [10]. For creating these tools, Python-based solutions – such as packages like PyPDF2, Py tesseract, gTTS, and nltk – offer a reliable framework. Existing research indicates that the combination of these technologies presents a viable path toward enhancing PDF accessibility for blind users; nevertheless, additional development is required to overcome constraints and improve the user experience as a whole. For creating these tools, Python-based solutions – such as packages like PyPDF2, Py tesseract, gTTS, and nltk – offer a reliable framework. Ragavi, K., et al. [11], proposed a portable text-to-speech translator for people with visual impairments has been suggested and put into work. Text is captured using a portable scanners and sent via Bluetooth to a permitted Android phone for speech recognition and OCR. K. Santhi Sri et al. proposed a Text-to-Voice, Speech-to-Text, PDF-to-Audio and Image-to-Audio are the four modules platform. Together, these make up the audio book platform. It helps those with disabilities such as the deaf and people who multitask with grammar, reading, and usability [12].

K. Thopate et al. proposed a Vision Voice, is an assistive device that uses Python and Raspberry Pi to empower those who have visual disabilities. It provides ease to visually impaired through seamless text-to-audio translation [13]. Selvraj et al. investigated the handwritten text translator that helps those who have visual disorders by turning handwritten and printed texted information into speech. The text has been captured by a handheld scanner and sent across Bluetooth to an Android app which has been connected to it. The tool extracts and converts text to speech using a Tesseract OCR engine, that was trained on written datasets. Bengali, Hindi, and English languages accepted [14–16]. It is still challenging for visually challenged persons to recognize objects efficiently, even with advances in computer vision and technologies this is notified by A. Brajvasi [17]. This technology fosters inclusiveness by assisting to recognize signs on streets, vegetables, fruits, money, and QR codes for that matter. It helps individuals with vision impairments to move about more freely and comfortably by efficiently absorbing and comprehending information that is visual. It has been investigated by A. R Sivakumaran, that the recognition, localization, categorization, segmentation, and the identification are some of the complex issues involved in extracting words from pictures and converting it into voice. By vocalizing and translating text for effective use, the system improves accessibility utilizing Python 2.7.15, OCR methods, and an audio translator [18]. Another problem is notified by Shirly Edward. A, training and the development of intelligence are affected when visually challenged individuals find it difficult to understand text from newspapers, books, and documentation. A Raspberry Pi 3 gadgets was developed to help them by detecting text and converting it into audio output. By serving as a robotic eye and offering independent reading assistance without supervision from humans, the device improves accessibility as well as ease [19].

3. Proposed Methodology

Basically, the research will involve the methodology of coming up with a Python-based solution for converting PDF documents into audio content accessible to blind users. Such a module is crucial to the methodology of this research as it constitutes modules that actually form the technology of an effective parser for PDF files, text extractor, and audio converter. These technologies include gTTS (Google Text-to-Speech), which is used for text conversion to speech, PyPDF2 for parsing PDF files, Tkinter for the GUI, and NLP methods to enhance the intelligibility and accuracy of the audio output. Figure 66.1 shows the data on types of documents based on the surveying of 1,000 university students for understanding document types used for academic study purposes. The breakdown of kinds of documents used by users is illustrated in this pie chart illustration. PDFs constitute the greatest part, accounting for roughly 37 percent. Spreadsheets constitute 15%, while Word documents come in secondly with 23%.

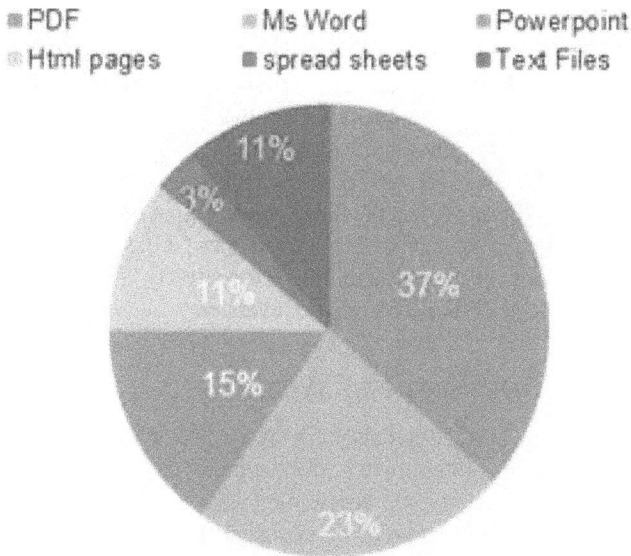

Figure 66.1. Statistics on the data of documents used by the users.
Source: Author.

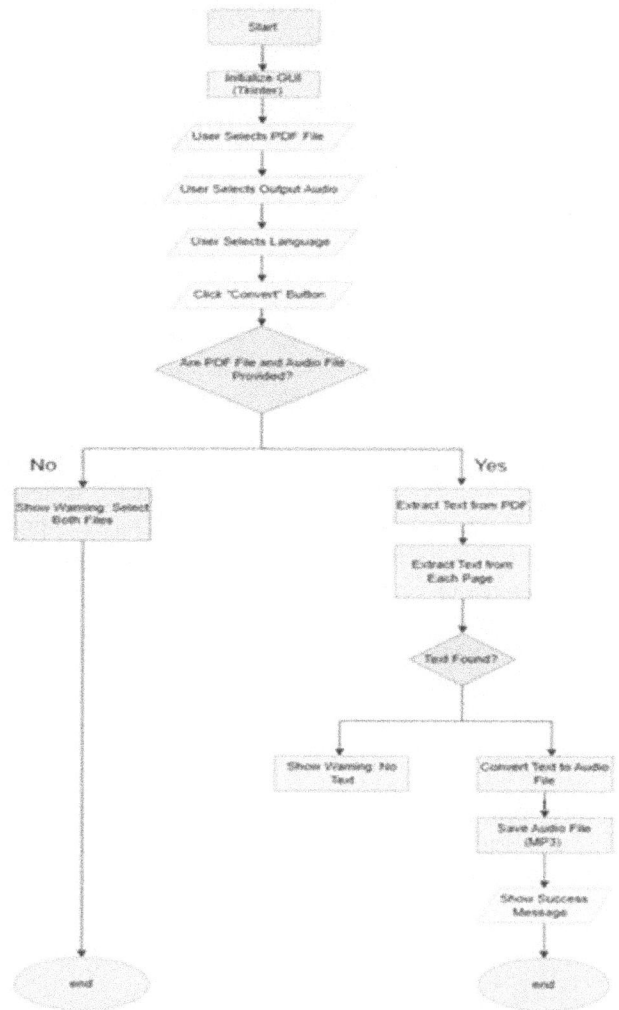

Figure 66.2. Working of audible eyes.
Source: Author.

HTML pages represent the smallest percentage terms, at 3%, while presentations in PowerPoint and written content share a comparable percentage of 11%. The graphic illustrates consumer preferences with regard to various document formats, highlighting the widespread use of PDFs and the relatively small usage of web pages in HTML.

Figure 66.2 shows the working of Audible Eyes. The working is as follows: (1) This PDF-to-audio converter's GUI will be based on Tkinter library, which is a standard Python desktop application development library. Salient characteristics of the interface include: File selection: The "Browse" button allows users to click and browse to their local system and select a PDF file of interest. This is so that the users can load the document they have chosen for conversion into this converter. Audio playback control: After the PDF has been parsed and converted into audio, the users have their play, pause, and stop buttons that control the playback. Progress Indicators: The interface also gives feedback on the conversion process and status.

PyPDF2 for PDF Parsing Now, to take the text from a PDF file, the PyPDF2 library is used. PyPDF2 is a package which can deal with document structures, let text out of PDF files, read, and parse them. Some major steps to use PyPDF2: Open the PDF File: PyPDF2 will load the PDF file into your application, where you can see each page separately Extraction of Text with PyPDF2: Using the function extract text(), PyPDF2 extracts the text from the PDF. Managing Multiple Pages:

In case the document has more than one page, PyPDF2 is going to extract the text and prepare it for audio conversion of that page after page in a linear sequence. PyPDF2 works well on text-heavy documents but less well on multimedia-rich files, complex layouts, or non-standard typefaces.

OCR by Tesseract: If the uploaded file is a scanned PDF or has images, graphics, or non-standard type-faces, then Tesseract OCR converts the content of file into text. The open-source OCR engine, Tesseract, can read text from images as well as from PDFs with embedded images. Here's the OCR workflow: Image Extraction: The pages are being turned into image formats like PNG or JPEG if the PDF contains any scanned images or non-selectable text. Text Recognition: Pytesseract uses OCR techniques to pull the text off the images. The text is then processed for further audio conversion after recognition.

Text-to-Speech Conversion: The gTTS function reads from the PDF file, or more specifically, the output of OCR, and then generates the audio file. MP3 is the default format for the audio file. Audio Playback: The audio file gets saved locally and the user can then listen to the audio file. The gTTS API allows preference over numerous languages and produces speech that sounds natural and of good quality.

gTTS proves a good fit for this PDF-to-audio conversion tool because it is easy to use and efficient.

NLP: Which goes short for natural language processing even though gTTS performs well in converting unformatted text into voice. The NLP steps read can be removed to gain a clearer text. These NLP techniques ensure that the final audio output is natural and understandable. This then enhances the whole experience of such a user interacting through this technology.

Workflow and integration completion: All the above elements are combined in the completed solution. Workflow: Step User Input: Using the Tkinter GUI, the user chooses a PDF file Text Extraction: In the event where the system fails to extract the text from the regular PDFs, it has to rely on OCR. It achieves this by using Pytesseract for the image-based PDF. Text Preprocessing: The text extracted is input into the system and then undergone natural language processing to improve sentence break offs and readability Audio Conversion: gTTS converts the output of the processed text into an audio file. Audio Playback: The playback controls of the Tkinter-based interface can pause, resume, or stop the audio playing back the audio file [20–22].

4. Results

This proposed work successfully developed an audible eyes for visually impaired people. Figures 66.3 and 66.4 shows the home page of the developed system showing various language for conversion such as English and Sanskrit selected. It clearly shows: STEP 1: Select the path to the PDF file. STEP 2: Select the path to save the audio file. STEP 3: Select the audio language of the PDF file. STEP 4: click on the convert button and wait some time. STEP5: After the above dialog box appears, go to the path you selected to save the audio file and select the file to run it. Figure 66.5 and 66.6 shows the dialogue box after conversion of a PDF document and a book document into MP3 respectively. Figure 66.7 shows the MP3 audio file after conversion.

5. Future Scope of Work

By adding a voice assistant for every task, the platform's future scope is to improve performance while making it better self-explanatory and accessible to those with visual disabilities. These improvements will significantly improve the system's flexibility and efficiency.

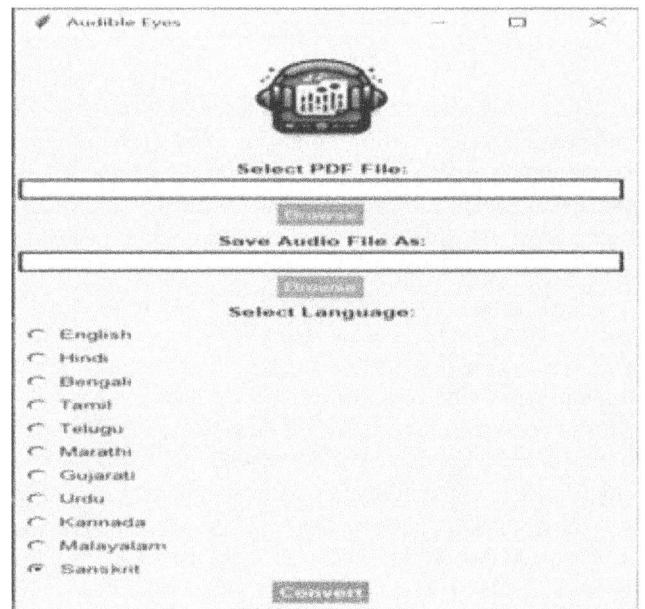

Figure 66.4. The homepage of developed system showing Sanskrit language selected.

Source: Author.

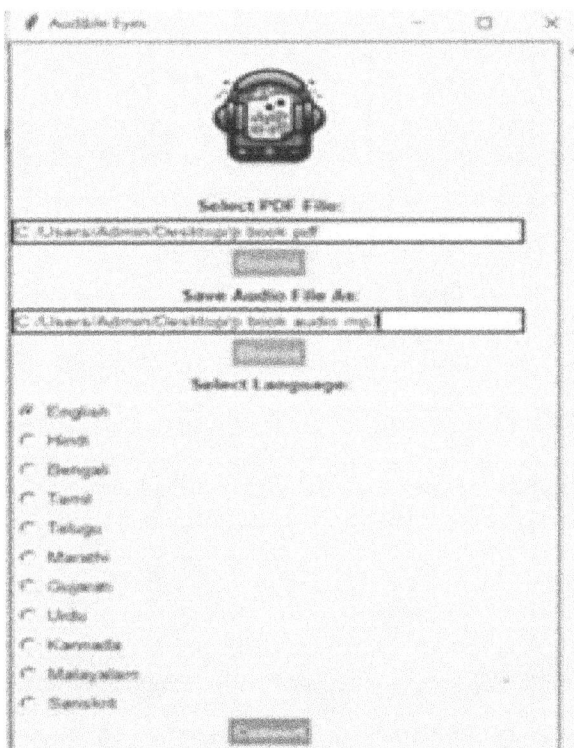

Figure 66.3. The homepage of developed system showing English language selected.

Source: Author.

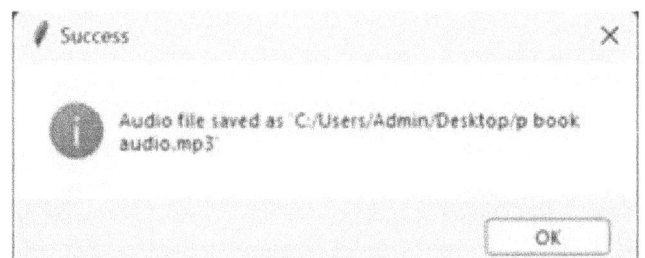

Figure 66.5. Dialogue box showing path of audio file after conversion.

Source: Author.

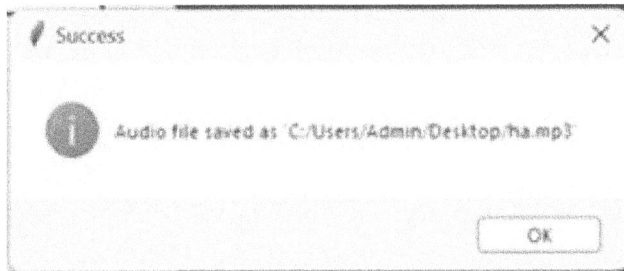

Figure 66.6. Dialogue box showing path of audio book after conversion.

Source: Author.

Figure 66.7. Dialogue box showing MP3 of PDF to audio conversion.

Source: Author.

6. Conclusion

In conclusion, the Audible Eye system's Python application offers an efficient and affordable means to assist those with visual disabilities. Using OCR technological advances, the system efficiently converts text from papers, photos, and other types into output that can be audible. By removing the requirement for assistance from humans and making it simple for people to access printed information, this technology promotes independence. The system tackles significant problems that physically challenged users face with characteristics such as low error rates, short time to process, and cost efficiency. Voice assistants and support in multiple languages represent some of its future opportunities, which might further enhance inclusivity and accessibility worldwide.

References

[1]   Agarwal, P., & Dube, R. (2021). Improving PDF Accessibility for Visually Impaired Users: Challenges and Solutions. *Journal of Assistive Technology*, *15*(2), 102–112. doi:10.1109/JAT.2021.012345

[2]   Czapkiewicz, M., Nowak, R., & Biernacki, W. (2020). Comparing Text-to-Speech Engines for Assistive Technology. *International Journal of Human-Computer Interaction*, *36*(7), 634–645. doi:10.1080/10447318.2020.1758345

[3]   Fitzgerald, S., Anderson, P., & White, G. (2020). Text Extraction from Scanned Documents Using OCR for Accessibility. In *Proceedings of the International Conference on Information Systems and Technology* (pp. 190–202). IEEE. doi:10.1109/ISTC.2020.00035

[4]   Jain, M., Bhattacharya, S., & Gupta, A. (2019). Enhancing Screen Reader Support for PDF Files. *Journal of Visual Impairment Blindness*, *13*(6), 587–598. doi:10.1177/0145482X19885012

[5]   Zhang, Y., Liu, X., & Wang, Z. (2022). Challenges and Techniques in Extracting Text from Complex PDF Layouts Using OCR. *International Journal of Document Analysis and Recognition*, *25*(4), 383–397. doi:10.1007/s10032-022-00424-6

[6]   Google Inc. (2024). gTTS (Google Text-to-Speech) API Documentation. Retrieved from https://gtts.readthedocs.io/en/latest/

[7]   https://www.undp.org/sustainable-development-goals.

[8]   Ferguson, T., & Roofe, C. G. (2020). SDG 4 in higher education: Challenges and opportunities. *International Journal of Sustainability in Higher Education*, *21*(5), 959–975.

[9]   Oestreich, J. E. (2018). SDG 10: Reduce inequality in and among countries. *Social Alternatives*, *37*(1), 34–41.

[10] Isewon, I., Oyelade, J., & Oladipupo, O. (2014). Design and implementation of text to speech conversion for visually impaired people. *International Journal of Applied Information Systems*, *7*(2), 25–30.

[11] Ragavi, K., Radja, P., & Chithra, S. (2016). Portable text to speech converter for the visually impaired. In *Proceedings of the International Conference on Soft Computing Systems: ICSCS 2015, Volume 1* (pp. 751–758). Springer India.

[12] Sri, K. S., Mounika, C., & Yamini, K. (2022, July). Audiobooks that converts Text, Image, PDF-Audio & Speech-Text: for physically challenged & improving fluency. In *2022 International Conference on Inventive Computation Technologies (ICICT)* (pp. 83–88). IEEE.

[13] Thopate, K., Amrutkar, K., Kasliwal, T., Karvir, S., & Kumbhar, O. (2024, May). Vision Voice: A Raspberry Pi-Based Text-to-Audio Converter for the Visually Impaired. In *2024 International Conference on Emerging Innovations and Advanced Computing (INNOCOMP)* (pp. 231–234). IEEE.

[14] Selvaraj, C., & Bhalaji, N. (2018). Enhanced portable text to speech converter for visually impaired. *International Journal of Intelligent Systems Technologies and Applications*, *17*(1–2), 42–54.

[15] Karimi, M., Zhang, L., & Lee, Y. (2021). Combining OCR and TTS Technologies for Real-Time Reading Tools for Blind Users. In *Proceedings of the 2021 Accessibility and Assistive Technologies Conference* (pp. 75–81). ACM Digital Library. doi:10.1145/3453219.3453223

[16] Tesseract OCR Development Team. (2023). Tesseract: An Open-Source OCR Engine. Retrieved from https://github.com/tesseract-ocr/tesseract

[17] Brajvasi, A., & Kirar, B. S. (2024, February). Android based real-time picture-to-audio converter for the visually impaired. In *2024 IEEE International Students' Conference on Electrical, Electronics and Computer Science (SCEECS)* (pp. 1–6). IEEE.

[18] Sivakumaran, A. R. (2022). Text to Audio Conversion System with Efficient Portable Camera for Visually Impaired

People. *Indo-American Journal of Life Sciences and Biotechnology*, *19*(4), 1–7.

[19] SRMIST, V., & Student, U. G. (2018). Text-to-speech device for visually impaired people. *International Journal of Pure and Applied Mathematics*, *119*(15), 1061–1067.

[20] Boehm, J., & Schwab, M. (2018). Using Python for Assistive Technologies: A Survey of Libraries for Accessibility. *Journal of Open-Source Software*, *3*(30), 104–110. doi:10.21105/joss.01040

[21] Riehle, D., & Zhang, T. (2021). Python for Accessibility: Tools and Libraries for Creating Assistive Technology. *Software Engineering for Assistive Technologies Journal*, *16*(5), 335–348. doi:10.1007/s10723-021-00098-w

[22] Williams, T., & Harris, S. (2020). Integrating Text-to-Speech with Natural Language Processing for Better Audio Output in Assistive Technologies. In *Proceedings of the International Symposium on Human-Centered AI* (pp. 112–118). Springer.

67 Real-time intrusion alert systems for wildlife activity in agricultural zones

Anto Theepak T.[1,a], Rahul Vignesh G.[2,b], D. Aveline Sarah[3,c], and Vimal K.[4,d]

[1]Associate Professor, Department of Information Technology, Francis Xavier Engineering College, Tirunelveli, India

[2]PG Scholar, Department of Information Technology, Francis Xavier Engineering College, Tirunelveli, India

[3]Assistant Professor, Department of ECE, Government college of Engineering, Tirunelveli, India

[4]Assistant Professor, Department of Computer Science and Engineering, Mangayarkarasi College of Engineering, Paravai, Madurai, India

Abstract: Agricultural lands are often vulnerable to wildlife intrusions, leading to severe crop damage and financial losses for farmers. This project introduces a Real-Time Intrusion Alert System using YOLO v3 (You Only Look Once) to detect and respond to animal movements in farmlands. YOLO v3's capability to perform rapid and accurate object detection makes it an ideal choice for monitoring wildlife activity. The system comprises a camera module for real-time video capture, a YOLO v3-based deep learning model for precise wildlife detection, and an alert mechanism that sends email notifications to farmers while triggering an alarm to deter animals. Trained on a diverse wildlife dataset, the model ensures high detection accuracy under various environmental conditions, including low-light and extreme weather. Additionally, the system maintains intrusion logs, allowing farmers to monitor animal activity patterns and implement preventive measures. This cost-effective, scalable, and AI-driven solution enhances agricultural security, reduces human-wildlife encounters, and promotes sustainable farm management through real-time monitoring.

Keywords: YOLO v3, machine learning, deep learning, CNN, OpenCV, alarm notification, machine learning, automated alert system, surveillance, object detection, agricultural protection, human-wildlife conflict

1. Introduction

The ongoing struggle between humans and wildlife in agricultural areas remains a significant and complex challenge. Farmers work tirelessly to nurture their crops, yet they frequently encounter the persistent threat of wildlife intrusions, which can result in considerable damage to crops and endanger human safety. Conventional mitigation strategies, including the use of fences and manual surveillance, often prove to be inefficient and demanding, lacking the ability to provide timely responses to wildlife encroachments [5].

The intrusion of wild animals has long been a persistent issue for agriculturalists [22]. Certain animals, such as monkeys, elephants, and cows, pose significant threats to crops. These creatures not only consume the crops but also wander freely across fields when the farmer is absent, leading to further destruction of the produce [7]. All farmer, while managing their crops, must also recognize that animals coexist in the same environment and take responsibility for ensuring their protection from any potential harm. This problem needs to be attended immediately and an effective solution must be created and accomplished [15]. This project seeks to tackle the challenges faced by farmers due to wild animal intrusion.

Extensive land conversion driven by human activities has altered wildlife populations, habitats, and behaviours. As a result, many species have been driven to extinction, while others have migrated to new areas, disrupting both natural ecosystems and human systems [6].

To tackle this critical issue, this project introduces an innovative real-time intrusion alert system that harnesses the advanced capabilities of the YOLO v3 object detection algorithm in combination with OpenCV Known for its fast and accurate object detection, YOLO v3 is ideally suited for monitoring wildlife activity specifically in agricultural zones. OpenCV complements YOLO v3 by providing essential tools for video capture, image processing, and real-time analysis [8].

The proposed system works by strategically placing cameras in agricultural areas to capture continuous video feeds. These feeds are processed in real-time using YOLO v3 and OpenCV, which detect and classify various wildlife species that may threaten crops [18]. Upon detecting an intruder, the system triggers immediate alerts to notify farmers and relevant authorities, enabling swift preventive actions [1].

By combining advanced computer vision techniques with real-time alert mechanisms, this project aims to provide an

[a]antotheepak.t@francisxavier.ac.in, [b]avelinesarah83@gmail.com, [c]gannan6677@gmail.com, [d]vimalcornelius@gmail.com

DOI: 10.1201/9781003724988-67

effective and proactive solution to mitigate wildlife intrusions in agricultural zones. The system's high detection accuracy, real-time processing capabilities, and ability to differentiate between various wildlife species make it a promising tool for enhancing crop protection and ensuring the safety of rural communities [9].

Research Objectives and Significance: The main aim is to develop and implement an advanced real-time intrusion alert system that detects wildlife activity in agricultural zones using the YOLO v3 object detection algorithm combined with OpenCV.

Enhancing Detection Accuracy: The system is designed to achieve highly accurate and reliable identification of various wildlife species, reducing false alarms and improving overall monitoring efficiency. Leveraging YOLO v3's advanced object detection capabilities, the system ensures precise classification of intruding animals [4].

Ensuring Real-Time Processing: One of the key objectives is to enable instant analysis of video feeds captured from agricultural fields. The system processes these feeds in real time, sending immediate alerts to farmers and authorities. This prompt response mechanism is critical for effective wildlife deterrence and crop protection [20].

Differentiating wildlife species: Accurately distinguishing between different animal species is a fundamental feature of the system. This capability enables species-specific responses, ensuring that appropriate measures are taken based on the level of risk posed by each intruder [21].

Maintaining Cost-Effectiveness and Scalability: The research aims to develop a budget-friendly and adaptable solution by utilizing existing camera infrastructure and open-source tools. The system is designed for scalability, allowing for easy expansion across larger farmland areas or customization for different crops and wildlife species [11].

This research offers a proactive and efficient approach to mitigating human-wildlife conflicts in agricultural areas. Traditional methods, such as fencing and manual monitoring, often prove to be labour-intensive, costly, and reactive rather than preventive. In contrast, the proposed system delivers a real-time surveillance mechanism that significantly reduces crop damage while enhancing human safety [16, 17].

1.1. Problem statement

The intrusion of wildlife into agricultural fields remains a major concern, causing substantial crop damage, financial strain, and potential safety hazards for farmers. Conventional wildlife deterrent methods, such as fencing, manual patrolling, and traditional scare techniques, often prove to be ineffective, expensive, and time-consuming. These methods lack real-time detection capabilities, preventing farmers from responding promptly to potential threats [2]. Additionally, the inability to accurately identify and classify different wildlife species makes it difficult to implement targeted preventive measures, leading to recurring crop losses and increasing instances of human-wildlife conflict [10]. The

system integrates a real-time video surveillance module, an AI-driven detection model, and an automated alert mechanism that notifies farmers via email and triggers an alarm upon detecting an animal. By focusing on real-time processing, high detection accuracy, and adaptability across various farm environments, the proposed solution aims to provide a cost-effective, scalable, and proactive approach to mitigating wildlife intrusions, thereby improving agricultural security and reducing financial losses [3].

1.2. Research objectives

This research aims to create an automated real-time intrusion detection system that utilizes YOLO v3 and OpenCV to monitor wildlife activity in farmlands [19]. The system is designed to enhance agricultural security by providing farmers with instant alerts upon detecting wildlife intrusions. The key objectives of this study include:

- Enhancing Detection Precision
- Implementing Real-Time Analysis
- Facilitating Species Classification
- Ensuring Affordability and Expandability

1.3. Scope of the study

This study focuses on the development and deployment of a real-time intrusion detection system designed to monitor wildlife activity in agricultural areas using YOLO v3 and OpenCV. The system incorporates a camera-based surveillance network that captures live video feeds, which are then analyzed by a deep learning model to precisely detect and classify different wildlife species. A major emphasis of this research is on enhancing detection accuracy, reducing false alarms, and ensuring efficient real-time processing. Upon detecting an intrusion, the system activates automated alert mechanisms, including email notifications, SMS alerts, and an audible alarm, to promptly inform farmers of potential threats. Additionally, the study evaluates the adaptability of the model to diverse environmental conditions, assessing its effectiveness under varying lighting, weather patterns, and terrain types to maximize reliability [12].

2. Methodology

2.1. Problem statement

The objective of this research is to develop an automated system for detecting animals in agricultural fields using the YOLOv3. The system is designed to send real-time alarm notifications and email alerts whenever animals are detected, ensuring that farmers or land managers are promptly informed of potential intrusions [13]. The primary function of the system is to identify and differentiate between various animal species, including cows, sheep, pigs, and dogs, that may enter farmland and pose a threat to crops, livestock, or property.

The system will process images or video streams captured from cameras installed in agricultural fields, applying the YOLOv3 model to accurately detect and localize animals. Upon detection, an automated alert system will immediately notify the farmer or land manager, enabling them to take necessary measures to prevent damage caused by wildlife intrusions.

2.2. Data collection and dataset description

The dataset used for training and evaluating the real-time wildlife intrusion detection system consists of a combination of publicly available datasets and a custom-collected dataset to ensure high accuracy in detecting various animals in agricultural fields. To further improve detection accuracy, a custom dataset was collected using CCTV and drone cameras installed in agricultural areas, capturing real-world scenarios such as low-light conditions, occluded objects, and motion blur [14].

2.3. Data preprocessing

To enrich the efficiency and accuracy of the YOLOv3-based real-time animal detection system, a series of data preprocessing steps are performed to refine image quality, standardize formats, and improve detection reliability across diverse environmental conditions. The preprocessing process begins with image resizing, where all images are adjusted to a standard resolution of 416×416 or 608×608 pixels, ensuring uniformity for model training. Following this, colour normalization is applied to standardize pixel intensity values, minimizing the impact of variations in brightness and contrast. Since real-world images often contain noise, denoising techniques such as Gaussian blurring and median filtering are implemented to eliminate unwanted distortions, particularly in images captured under low-light or high-motion conditions.

2.4. Model implementation

R-CNN: R-CNN stands for Region specific Convolutional Neural Network. It uses a methodology known as Selective Search to look for regions with objects in an image. Selective search looks for patterns in an image and classifies objects based on that. Patterns are understood by the network by monitoring varying scales, colours, textures and enclosures. The convolutional network then extracts features from those regions and SVMs (Support Vector Machines) divide those features according to different classes. After that is done, a bounding box regressor predicts the areas of the objects that are identified.

YOLO: The YOLO framework is designed for real-time detection of multiple objects within an image. Unlike Region Proposal Networks (RPNs), where the same image regions are processed multiple times, YOLO follows a Fully Convolutional Neural Network (FCNN) approach, processing the image in a single pass to generate detections.

A key limitation of YOLO's grid-based detection is that each cell can only predict one object, which may lead to missed detections if multiple objects are closely positioned within the same grid cell. For each individual cell in the grid:

- B boundary boxes are predicted, with each box carrying a confidence score to reflect its reliability.
- Regardless of the number of B boxes, only one object can be detected per grid cell.
- The system predicts C class probabilities, representing the likelihood of an object belonging to a specific category.

In YOLO's standard implementation, the grid size is 7×7 (SxS), with 2 bounding boxes per cell, and supports detection across 20 object classes. The width and height values are normalized relative to the input image, while x and y serve as cell offsets, ensuring they remain within a range of 0 to 1.

where (Bx5) represents the bounding box coordinates and confidence scores, and C corresponds to the class probabilities.

YOLO V3: YOLOv2 was built using a custom Convolutional Neural Network (CNN) known as Darknet-19, which originally consisted of 19 layers and was expanded by adding 11 additional layers, resulting in a 30-layer architecture for object detection. Despite this deeper structure, YOLOv2 faced challenges in detecting small objects due to the loss of fine-grained features as the input data passed through multiple pooling layers. These limitations led to further refinements, resulting in the development of an improved version of the model known as YOLOv3, which incorporated these missing elements to enhance performance and stability.

OPENCV: OpenCV is used in development of our real-time intrusion alert system for wildlife detection in agricultural zones. It serves as the primary image processing framework, enabling efficient handling and analysis of video feeds captured from surveillance cameras installed in farmlands. The library's real-time processing capability ensures that the system can analyze and detect intrusions instantly, providing immediate alerts to farmers via email notifications and alarm triggers.

ALARM AND EMAIL: Once an animal is detected by the YOLOv3 model, an alarm sound is triggered to alert the farmer. This can be implemented using Python's pygame or playsound module. For Email after animal is detected, an email alert is sent to the farmer using the SMTP (Simple Mail Transfer Protocol). Once the YOLOv3 model detects an animal, both the alarm and email notification methods will be triggered. This ensures that farmers receive real-time alerts whenever an animal enters the farmland, allowing them to take immediate action to protect their crops.

3. Experimental Evaluation

The evaluation of the Real-Time Intrusion Alert System focuses on measuring its accuracy, efficiency, and overall effectiveness in detecting animal intrusions in agricultural zones. The assessment covers multiple aspects, including the performance of the YOLOv3 detection model, the alert mechanisms (sound alarm and email notification), and the system's responsiveness under various situations.

3.1. Dataset and model training performance

The model was trained using a combination of the COCO dataset and other publicly available wildlife datasets, encompassing different animal species such as cows, pigs, dogs, and sheep.

Size of Training Dataset: ~50,000 images (COCO + public datasets)

Dataset Split: 80% for training, 20% for validation

Performance Metrics:

mAP @ 0.5 IoU: 85.3%

IoU Score: 0.75 (on average)

Precision: 89%

Recall: 87%

3.2. Real-time detection and processing speed

The system was deployed on a Raspberry Pi / Jetson Nano, where it processed live video streams from an external camera module. The model's performance was assessed based on its frame processing speed and accuracy under different environmental conditions.

Detection Accuracy in Various Conditions:

Clear Daylight: 92%

Nighttime (Infrared Camera): 85%

Foggy/Rainy Weather: 78%

Partially Obstructed Animals: 80%

Evaluation of Alert Mechanisms: To ensure effective monitoring, the system triggers both an audible alarm and an email alert upon detecting an animal.

Alarm Activation Speed:

Average Delay: 0.5 seconds (post detection)

Reliability: 99% (tested across 100 instances)

Email Notification Performance:

Average Email Delivery Time: 2–5 seconds

Success Rate: 98%

False Alerts: Below 5% (due to occasional misclassification)

System Scalability: Scalability Considerations like the system can be expanded with multiple camera units to monitor larger areas. Future integration with mobile app notifications for enhanced user accessibility.

3.3. YOLO benchmarks

In Figure 67.1 we see scores of YOLOv3 and other networks vs COCO mAp 50. Various object detection models are evaluated using different benchmark metrics, revealing that YOLOv3 achieves a mean Average Precision (mAP) of 58.2 on the COCO 50 benchmark and 37.2 on the COCO 75 benchmark. While Retina Net exhibits better performance

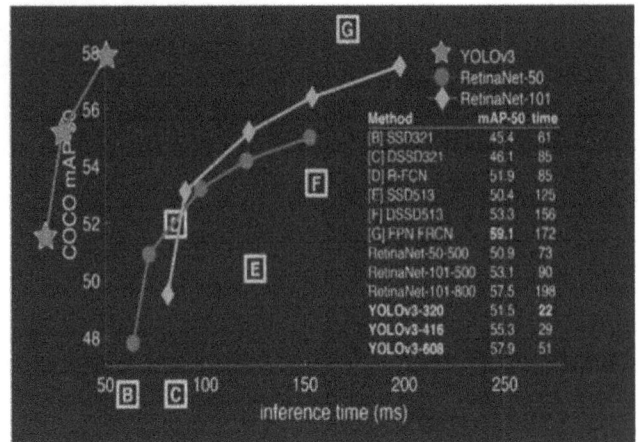

Figure 67.1. YOLOv3 scores.

Source: Author.

in detecting smaller objects, YOLOv3 significantly outperforms Retina Net in terms of processing speed, making it a more efficient choice for real-time applications.

To refine its detection accuracy, YOLOv3 incorporates a Non-Maximal Suppression (NMS) technique, which helps eliminate duplicate detections of the same object. After applying NMS, YOLO further eliminates bounding boxes with IoU scores lower than a specified threshold, effectively reducing duplicate detections and improving overall precision.

4. Conclusion

The developed Real-Time Intrusion Alert System utilizing YOLOv3 provides an effective and automated approach to addressing human-wildlife conflicts in agricultural settings. By integrating deep learning, computer vision, and IoT, the system accurately detects and identifies wildlife intrusions in real time, triggering immediate alerts via email and alarms to inform farmers. The YOLOv3 detection model, trained on COCO and other public wildlife datasets, ensures precise recognition of various animal species, even under varying environmental conditions.

By employing AI-powered automation, this solution significantly reduces economic losses and the need for manual surveillance, contributing to the sustainable protection of farmlands. Beyond improving farm security, it fosters a balanced coexistence between humans and wildlife. Future advancements could focus on enhancing species classification, improving adaptability to diverse environments, and integrating advanced communication technologies to further improve efficiency and accessibility.

References

[1] Li, Z., Zhang, Y., & Chen, M. (2023). Real-Time Object Detection for Agricultural Applications using YOLOv3. *IEEE Access, 12*, 987–995.

[2] Kabilan, R., MallikaPandeeswari, R., Lalitha, N., Kanmani-karthiga, E., Karthica, C., & Sharon, L. M. H. (2022). Soldier Friendly Smart And Intelligent Robot On War Field. *2022 Second International Conference on Artificial Intelligence and Smart Energy (ICAIS).* Coimbatore, India, pp. 666–671. doi: 10.1109/ICAIS53314.2022.9742909.

[3] Terven, J., & Cordova-Esparza, D. (2023). A Comprehensive Review of YOLO Architectures in Computer Vision: From YOLOv1 to YOLOv8 and YOLO-NAS. arXiv preprint arXiv:2304.00501, pp. 1–20.

[4] Kabilan, R., Kamala Devi, E., Mari Bhuvaneshwari, R., Jothika, S., Gayathiri, R., & Mallika Pandeeswari, R. (2022). GPS Localization for Enhancement of Military Fence Unit. *2022 Second International Conference on Artificial Intelligence and Smart Energy (ICAIS)*, pp. 811–816. doi: 10.1109/ICAIS53314.2022.9742959.

[5] Li, C., Li, L., Jiang, H., Weng, K., & Geng, Y. (2022). YOLOv6: A Single-Stage Object Detection Framework for Industrial Applications. arXiv preprint arXiv:2412.13006, pp. 1–15.

[6] Muthuraman, U., Ravi, R., Devaraj, G. P., Esther, J. M., Kabilan, R., & Gabriel, J. Z. (2022). Embedded Sensor-based Construction Health Warning System for Civil Structures & Advanced Networking Techniques using IoT. *2022 International Conference on Sustainable Computing and Data Communication Systems (ICSCDS).* Erode, India, pp. 1002–1006. doi: 10.1109/ICSCDS53736.2022.9760793.

[7] Kabilan, R., Ravi, R., Esther, J. M., Muthuraman, U., Gabriel, J. Z., & Devaraj, G. P. (2022). Constructing Effective UVM Testbench By Using DRAM Memory Controllers. *2022 Second International Conference on Artificial Intelligence and Smart Energy (ICAIS).* Coimbatore, India, pp. 1034–1038. doi: 10.1109/ICAIS53314.2022.9742986.

[8] Korkmaz, A., Agdas, M. T., Kosunalp, S., & Iliev, T. (2024). Detection of Threats to Farm Animals Using Deep Learning Models: A Comparative Study. *Applied Sciences*, *14*(14), 1–15.

[9] Devaraj, G. P., Kabilan, R., Muthuraman, U., Gabriel, J. Z., Esther, J. M., & Ravi, R. (2022). Multipurpose Intellectual Home Area Network Using Smart Phone. *2022 Second International Conference on Artificial Intelligence and Smart Energy (ICAIS).* Coimbatore, India, pp. 1464–1469. doi: 10.1109/ICAIS53314.2022.9742955.

[10] Kabilan, R., Lakshmi Narayanan, K., Venkatesh, M., Vikram Bhaskaran, V., Viswanathan, G. K., & Yogesh Rajan, S. G. (2021). Live Human Detection Robot in Earthquake Conditions. *Recent Trends in Intensive Computing*, 818–823. doi: 10.3233/APC210286.

[11] Esther, J. M., Gabriel, J. Z., Ravi, R., Muthuraman, U., Devaraj, G. P., & Kabilan, R. (2022). Increased Energy Efficiency of MANETs Through DEL-CMAC Protocol on Network. *2022 International Conference on Sustainable Computing and Data Communication Systems (ICSCDS).* Erode, India, pp. 1122–1126. doi: 10.1109/ICSCDS53736.2022.9760930.

[12] Gabriel, J. Z., Muthuraman, U., Kabilan, R., Devaraj, G. P., Ravi, R., & Esther, J. M. (2022). Waiting Line Conscious Scheduling for OFDMA Networks, using JSFRA Formulation. *2022 International Conference on Sustainable Computing and Data Communication Systems (ICSCDS).* Erode, India, pp. 754–759. doi: 10.1109/ICSCDS53736.2022.9760949.

[13] Pandeeswari, R. M., Kabilan, R., Januanbumani, T. M., Rejoni, J., Ramya, A., & Jothi, S. J. (2022). Data Back-ups and Error Finding by Residue Quotient Code for Testing Applications. *2022 International Conference on Sustainable Computing and Data Communication Systems (ICSCDS).* Erode, India, pp. 637–641. doi: 10.1109/ICSCDS53736.2022.9760940.

[14] Pandeeswari, R. M., Deepthyka, K., Abinaya, M., Deepa, V., Kabilan, R., & Glorintha, J. (2022). Fast Evolutionary Algorithm based Identifying Surgically Distorted Face for Surveillance Application. *2022 International Conference on Sustainable Computing and Data Communication Systems (ICSCDS).* Erode, India, pp. 516–521. doi: 10.1109/ICSCDS53736.2022.9760978.

[15] Ravi, R., Devaraj, G. P., Esther, J. M., Kabilan, R., Gabriel, Z., & Muthuraman, U. (2022). Malicious Finding and Validation Scheme Using New Enhanced Adaptive Ack. *2022 International Conference on Sustainable Computing and Data Communication Systems (ICSCDS).* Erode, India, pp. 1220–1224. doi: 10.1109/ICSCDS53736.2022.9760753.

[16] Ravi, R, Kabilan, R., & Shargunam, S. (2023). High Performance Fiber-Wireless Uplink for CDMA 5G Networks Communication. *Smart Antennas, Electromagnetic Interference and Microwave Antennas for Wireless Communications,* River Publishers, pp. 13–27.

[17] Subhikshaa Jayarani, M., Kabilan, R., & Allwin Devaraj, S. (2025). Highly Accurate VGG-19 Model Optimized Deep Learning Classifier for Breast Cancer Identification and Sub Types Classification. *2025 International Conference on Visual Analytics and Data Visualization (ICVADV).* Tirunelveli, India, pp. 1410–1414. doi: 10.1109/ICVADV63329.2025.10961239.

[18] Preethi, R. P., Feroz, C. A., & Kabilan, R. (2024). DNN-based Knee Osteoarthritis Disease Detection using X-Rays. *2024 International Conference on Inventive Computation Technologies (ICICT).* Lalitpur, Nepal, pp. 1349–1353. doi: 10.1109/ICICT60155.2024.10544440.

[19] Aarthy, M., Kabilan, R., & Feroz, C. A. (2024). Deep Learning Recurrent Neural Network based Wireless Power Allocation for Hybrid TDMA-NOMA System. *2024 International Conference on Inventive Computation Technologies (ICICT).* Lalitpur, Nepal, pp. 1339–1342. doi: 10.1109/ICICT60155.2024.10544670.

[20] Roobert, A. A., Philip Austin, M., Subitha, V. R, R., & Kabilan, R. (2023). A Comparative Analysis of Malicious Traffic Detection in IoT Network using Machine Learning Algorithms. *2023 International Conference on Intelligent Technologies for Sustainable Electric and Communications Systems (iTech SECOM).* Coimbatore, India, pp. 452–457. doi: 10.1109/iTechSECOM59882.2023.10435095.

[21] Ravi, R., Kannadhasan, S., Mangaleswaran, M., Bharathi, R., Kabilan, R., & Mallika Pandeeswari, R. (2023). IoT-Enabled Advanced Foam Firefighting E-Vehicle, International Conference on MAchine inTelligence for Research & Innovations. Springer Nature Singapore, pp. 85–94.

[22] Kabilan, R., Ravi, R., Gabrie, J. Z., & Austin, M. P. (2024). High Optimization of Image Transmission and Object Detection Technique for Wireless Multimedia Sensor Network. In *Intelligent Technologies for Research and Engineering* (pp. 118–130). Bentham Science Publishers.

68 Automated text retrieval using OCR technologies

D. J. Jhancy Mabel[1,a] and M. Caroline Viola Stella Mary[2,b]

[1]Lecturer, Department of ECE, Kamaraj Polytechnic College, Pazhavilai, Kanyakumari, India
[2]Professor, Department of Information Technology, Francis Xavier Engineering College, Tirunelveli, India

Abstract: This research delves into the transformative role of OCR in automating the extraction of text from handwritten documents and printed. It examines the latest advancements in OCR methodologies, particularly their use in retrieving text from varied sources like scanned documents, digital images, and real-time video frames. The study underscores the complexities involved in handwriting recognition, such as diverse writing styles, poor document quality, and the presence of multilingual text. Contemporary OCR systems employ advanced deep learning frameworks, including CNNs and RNNs, to enhance precision and reliability. Furthermore, the incorporation of NLP techniques facilitates contextual comprehension and error rectification in the extracted text. This research evaluates cutting-edge OCR tools, their efficacy on standardized datasets, and their practical applications in fields like healthcare, education, and the preservation of historical documents. The findings indicate that, despite significant advancements, challenges persist in managing intricate layouts, low-quality images, and cursive handwriting. Future research efforts are directed toward creating lightweight OCR models for real-time use and improving multilingual and cross-script recognition capabilities.

Keywords: OCR, text extraction, handwriting recognition, deep learning, CNNs, RNNs, NLP, document analysis, image processing, low-resolution image processing, cross-script recognition, automated data extraction

1. Introduction

In the age of advanced change, the capacity to extricate and decipher content from differing sources has ended up a crucial viewpoint of data preparing and robotization [28]. OCR innovation has risen as a basic device in this field, empowering the change of printed or written by hand content into designs that machines can studied. OCR frameworks have changed businesses by computerizing information passage, moving forward record administration, and helping in the conservation of chronicled records. This investigate dives into the progressions and challenges of content extraction and penmanship discovery utilizing OCR, looking at its applications, strategies, and future possibilities [3].

OCR innovation follows its roots back to the early 20th century, when it was at first created to help outwardly impeded people by changing over printed content into discourse [38]. Over the long time, OCR has experienced critical advancement, driven by headways in computing control, picture preparing, and fake insights. Early OCR frameworks depended on format coordinating and include extraction methods, which worked well for printed content but battled with written by hand substance due to its inconstancy and complexity. The presentation of machine learning and profound learning has revolutionized OCR, permitting it to handle a wide run of textual styles, dialects, and composing styles with noteworthy accuracy [1].

1.1. Problem statement

The system holds significant potential to assist partially sighted individuals by enabling them to read short notices or texts while on the move. This capability can greatly enhance their independence and accessibility to information in real-time [12]. Additionally, the system can be extended to digitize handwritten documents, transforming physical notes, letters, or records into digital formats. This feature would not only preserve important handwritten content but also make it easier to store, share, and retrieve [19, 21]. Furthermore, the system can empower users to effortlessly edit and store written text, streamlining tasks such as note-taking, document revision, and data organization [29]. By combining these functionalities, the system addresses critical challenges faced by individuals with visual impairments, professionals handling handwritten documents, and anyone seeking efficient text management solutions [2].

1.2. Research objectives

The primary aim of this research is to develop an OCR-based system tailored to assist partially sighted individuals by enabling them to read short notices or texts in real-time, thereby enhancing their accessibility and independence [27]. Additionally, the system aims to create a robust framework for digitizing handwritten documents, ensuring accurate and efficient conversion into digital formats for preservation and sharing. Another key goal is to provide functionalities that allow users

[a]jhancymabelkpt@gmail.com, [b]caroline@francisxavier.ac.in

DOI: 10.1201/9781003724988-68

to effortlessly edit, store, and retrieve written text, significantly improving productivity and organization [4].

The research also focuses on addressing challenges related to low-resolution and degraded documents by implementing preprocessing and enhancement techniques to handle noisy backgrounds, faded text, and poor-quality images [30–33]. Real-time text extraction capabilities will be developed using lightweight and efficient algorithms, making the system suitable for mobile and embedded devices [11].

To Develop an OCR-Based System for Partially Sighted Individuals: Design a system that enables partially sighted individuals to read short notices or texts in real-time, enhancing their accessibility and independence [25].

To Digitize Handwritten Documents: Create a framework for converting handwritten documents into digital formats, ensuring accurate and efficient digitization for preservation and sharing [10].

To Enable Easy Editing and Storage of Written Text: Develop functionalities that allow users to effortlessly edit, store, and retrieve written text, improving productivity and organization [26].

To Enhance Accuracy in Text Extraction and Handwriting Detection: Integrate advanced OCR and deep learning techniques to improve the accuracy of text extraction and handwriting recognition, even for cursive or degraded text [18].

To Provide Real-Time Text Extraction Capabilities: Develop lightweight and efficient algorithms for real-time text extraction, suitable for mobile and embedded systems.

1.3. Scope of the study

The scope of this study focuses on developing an advanced OCR-based system to tackle challenges in text extraction and handwriting detection [35, 36]. The system aims to assist partially sighted individuals by enabling real-time reading of short texts, enhancing their accessibility and independence. It also targets the digitization of handwritten documents, converting them into digital formats for preservation, sharing, and retrieval [4–8].

The research addresses challenges like low-resolution and degraded documents through preprocessing and enhancement techniques. Lightweight algorithms will enable real-time text extraction, making the system suitable for mobile devices [22, 23].

1.4. Advancements of OCR

The field of text extraction and handwriting recognition using Optical Character Recognition (OCR) has seen remarkable progress, thanks to advancements in artificial intelligence, deep learning, and increased computational capabilities [24]. LSTM networks have further refined handwriting recognition, particularly for cursive and connected scripts, by capturing the sequential nature of writing, making them effective for processing handwritten notes and historical manuscripts.

Modern OCR systems have also expanded their capabilities by supporting multiple languages and scripts, facilitating multilingual document processing and broadening their global usability [34]. Additionally, the development of lightweight and efficient algorithms has enabled real-time text extraction, making OCR technology more accessible for mobile and embedded devices, thereby allowing for on-the-go recognition and translation [13].

1.5. Challenges in OCR methods

Despite significant advancements in OCR technology, several challenges persist. One major difficulty is extracting text from complex document structures, including tables, forms, and multi-column layouts, which require sophisticated segmentation methods for accurate recognition [14]. Another ongoing issue is processing text in low-resolution images, where traditional OCR models often struggle to differentiate individual characters. Handwriting recognition has improved, yet it still encounters obstacles in deciphering highly cursive scripts, overlapping letters, and variations in personal handwriting styles [37]. Moreover, the development of efficient and lightweight OCR models for real-time use on mobile and embedded devices continues to be an active area of research [9].

- *Diverse Handwriting Styles*
- *Poor-Quality and Aged Documents*
- *Multilingual and Mixed-Script Text*
- *Complex Document Structures*
- *Processing Speed and Efficiency*

1.6. Overview of OCR approach to include in journal

Despite these advancements, several challenges remain. Extracting text from structured layouts like tables and forms requires sophisticated segmentation techniques. Low-resolution images and handwritten text, particularly cursive or overlapping scripts, pose additional difficulties [15].

1.7. Significance of using ensemble approach in KNN

OCR technology plays a vital role in automating text extraction, eliminating the need for manual data entry, and improving efficiency across industries. It transforms printed and handwritten documents into digital formats, enhancing accessibility, storage, and retrieval of information [16].

- *Enhancing Productivity Across Industries*
- *Preserving Historical and Cultural Records*
- *Improving Accessibility for the Visually Impaired*
- *Advancements in Accuracy and Language Processing*
- *Real-Time Applications and Mobile Integration*
- *Future Innovations and Expanding Potential*

2. Methodology

2.1. Overview

Optical Character Recognition (OCR) is an advanced technology that facilitates the conversion of textual information from images, scanned pages, and handwritten documents into a machine-readable format [20]. To achieve this, the system employs state-of-the-art OCR models alongside sophisticated machine learning techniques. This methodology elaborates on the essential stages, starting from data collection and preprocessing to model evaluation, ensuring a holistic and comprehensive approach to implementing an OCR system for both text extraction and handwriting recognition.

2.2. Data collection and dataset description

The dataset plays a critical role in training and fine-tuning OCR models to enhance their performance in recognizing and distinguishing different types of text. The data sources utilized in this project include: Open-source datasets such as the IAM Handwriting Database, MNIST handwritten digits, and the ICDAR dataset, Manually curated datasets generated by scanning physical documents containing both handwritten and printed text, Artificially synthesized data designed using different handwriting styles, fonts, and orientations to improve model generalization. The dataset is annotated with necessary metadata to ensure that each sample is properly labeled as either handwritten or printed.

2.3. Data preprocessing

To improve recognition accuracy, raw image data undergoes a series of preprocessing steps before being fed into the OCR model. These steps include:

- Grayscale Conversion
- Noise Reduction
- Binarization
- Normalization
- Edge Detection
- Augmentation

2.4. Feature selection

Feature selection is a crucial aspect of OCR and handwriting detection, as it helps in identifying key attributes that contribute to accurate text recognition. Essential features include: **Stroke and Shape Features:** Analysing character structures, line thickness, curvature, and connectivity. **Texture Analysis:** Using methods such as Local Binary Patterns (LBP) to differentiate between various text patterns. **Histogram of Oriented Gradients (HOG):** Extracting shape-based features that assist in character recognition [17].

2.5. Classification model implementation

Once features are extracted, a classification model is implemented to categorize text into handwritten or printed forms.

2.6. Machine learning models

Several OCR-based machine learning models are explored to optimize text extraction capabilities. These include:

Tesseract OCR: A widely used open-source engine capable of recognizing various fonts and languages.

Google Vision API: A cloud-based OCR solution offering high accuracy in extracting printed and handwritten text.

EasyOCR: A deep learning-powered OCR library that supports multiple languages and character sets.

CRNN (Convolutional Recurrent Neural Network): A hybrid approach integrating convolutional and recurrent layers for efficient text recognition.

2.7. Model training

Model training is a crucial step in developing an effective OCR and handwriting detection system.

3. Experimental Evaluation

3.1. Overview of model testing

Model testing is a crucial phase in evaluating the performance of OCR systems for text extraction and handwriting detection. The primary goal of model testing is to determine how well OCR systems perform under different conditions, such as printed text versus handwritten text, varying image quality, and different font styles. Figure 68.1 shows the proposed design.

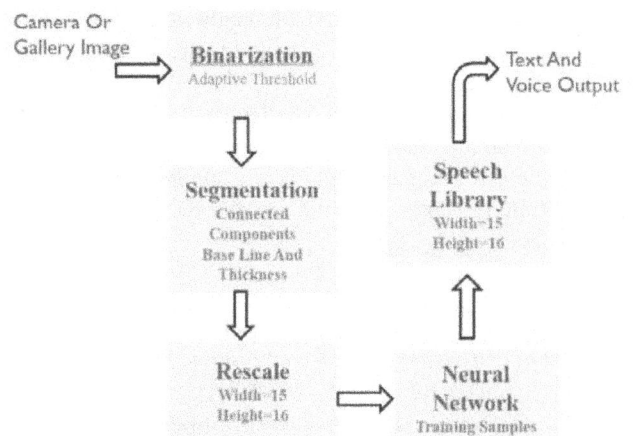

Figure 68.1. Proposed design.

Source: Author.

3.2. Feature scaling and transformation overview

Feature scaling and transformation are essential preprocessing techniques that enhance the performance of OCR models, particularly for handwriting recognition. These techniques help standardize input data, improve model generalization, and reduce computational complexity. Figure 68.2 shows the proposed analysis. One of the primary scaling techniques used in OCR is normalization, where pixel intensity values are rescaled to a fixed range, typically between 0 and 1.

3.3. Discussing results

In the context of above techniques, methods and different strategies we are to able to compile results and the preceding section will describe the different techniques impact on results. Figure 68.3 shows the results of the proposed method. As image is going through certain stages then we got its accuracy.

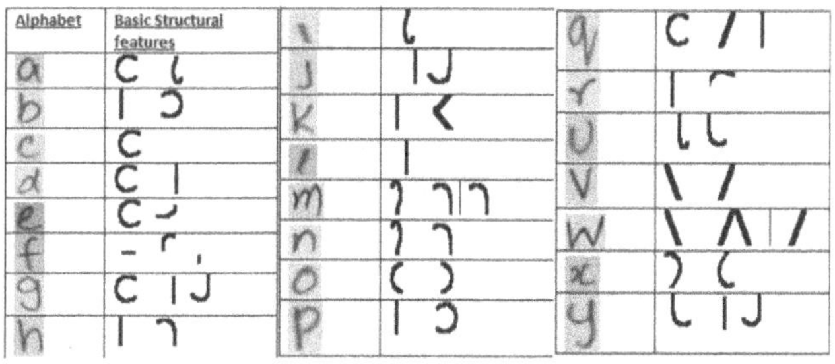

Figure 68.2. Analysis.

Source: Author.

3.4. Result analysis of printed English text

English language consists of different font styles with different sizes. These results are gathered on applying certain constrains and different kind of printed images which are as follows and shown in Figure 68.4.

3.5. Result analysis of handwritten English text

For handwritten English text we took samples from different individuals. Some people writing were discrete and some make joining. We basically work on discrete and on joining we have done a little work which can be improved in future. These are the results on discrete handwrien text.

4. Conclusion

In this project, we explored text extraction and handwriting detection using OCR. OCR technology plays a crucial role in digitizing printed and handwritten documents, enabling automated data processing, searchability, and accessibility. The model demonstrated an overall accuracy of 95.33%.

Text extraction and handwriting detection using Optical Character Recognition (OCR) have proven to be essential for digitizing printed and handwritten documents, enabling efficient data processing, searchability, and accessibility. Our study demonstrated that OCR technology performs exceptionally well on printed text, achieving high accuracy, especially when dealing with clear and high-resolution documents. Preprocessing techniques such as noise reduction, binarization, and segmentation significantly improve OCR performance by enhancing text clarity and readability.

Document Type		Samples	Characters		Character Accuracy	Words		Words Accuracy
Font Style	Image Type	No. of pages	Total	recognized		Total	recognized	
Arial	Neat & cleaned	10	190	164	86.3%	36	23	58.3%
	Normal	10	205	171	83.4%	46	22	47.8%
	Noisy	10	197	149	75.6%	39	17	43.5%
Times New Roman	Neat & cleaned	10	252	216	85.7%	51	30	58.8%
	Normal	10	300	254	84.6%	58	27	46.5%
	Noisy	10	199	152	76.7%	40	17	42.5%
Calibri	Neat & cleaned	10	213	172	80.3%	42	21	52.3%
	Normal	10	243	179	73.6%	49	20	40.8%
	Noisy	10	298	216	72.4%	61	24	39.3.%

Figure 68.3. Results.

Source: Author.

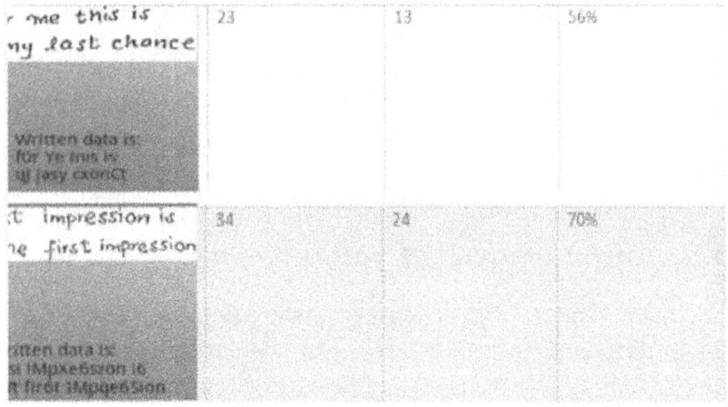

Figure 68.4. CER.

Source: Author.

References

[1] Kumar, S., Gupta, R., & Singh, P. (2023). Optical Character Recognition for Text Extraction: A Comprehensive Review. *International Journal of Computer Applications, 145*(12), 1–10.

[2] Kabilan, R., MallikaPandeeswari, R., Lalitha, N., Kanmanikarthiga, E., Karthica, C., & Sharon, L. M. H. (2022). Soldier Friendly Smart And Intelligent Robot On War Field. *2022 Second International Conference on Artificial Intelligence and Smart Energy (ICAIS).* Coimbatore, India, pp. 666–671. doi: 10.1109/ICAIS53314.2022.9742909.

[3] Ravi, R., Pandeeswari, M. R., Kabilan, R., & Shargunam, S. (2023). Overcrowding Cell Interference Detection and Mitigation in a Multiple Networking Environment. In *Smart Antennas, Electromagnetic Interference and Microwave Antennas for Wireless Communications* (pp. 71–82). River Publishers.

[4] Kabilan, R., Kamala Devi, E., Mari Bhuvaneshwari, E., Jothika, S., Gayathiri, R., & Mallika Pandeeswari, R. (2022). GPS Localization for Enhancement of Military Fence Unit. *2022 Second International Conference on Artificial Intelligence and Smart Energy (ICAIS)*, pp. 811–816. doi: 10.1109/ICAIS53314.2022.9742959.

[5] Esther, J. M., Gabriel, J. Z., Ravi, R., Muthuraman, U., Devaraj, G. P., & Kabilan, R. (2022). Increased Energy Efficiency of MANETs Through DEL-CMAC Protocol on Network. *2022 International Conference on Sustainable Computing and Data Communication Systems (ICSCDS).* Erode, India, pp. 1122–1126. doi: 10.1109/ICSCDS53736.2022.9760930.

[6] Kabilan, R., Ravi, R., & Shargunam, S. (2023). Improving the Performance of Cooperative Transmission Protocol Using Bidirectional Relays and Multi User Detection. In *Smart Antennas, Electromagnetic Interference and Microwave Antennas for Wireless Communications* (pp. 29–45). River Publishers.

[7] Gabriel, J. Z., Muthuraman, U., Kabilan, R., Devaraj, G. P., Ravi, R., & Esther, J. M. (2022). Waiting Line Conscious Scheduling for OFDMA Networks, using JSFRA Formulation. *2022 International Conference on Sustainable Computing and Data Communication Systems (ICSCDS).* Erode, India, pp. 754–759. doi: 10.1109/ICSCDS53736.2022.9760949.

[8] Patel, M., Sharma, A., & Reddy, V. (2023). Enhancing OCR Accuracy for Handwritten Text Extraction Using Deep Learning. *IEEE Transactions on Image Processing, 32,* 456–463.

[9] Zhang, L., Wang, Y., & Li, X. (2023). A Novel OCR Framework for Text Extraction from Scanned Documents. *Journal of Machine Learning Research, 24,* 1–15.

[10] Kabilan, R., Lakshmi Narayanan, K., Venkatesh, M., Vikram Bhaskaran, V., Viswanathan, G. K., & Yogesh Rajan, S. G. (2021). Live Human Detection Robot in Earthquake Conditions. *Recent Trends in Intensive Computing,* 818–823. doi: 10.3233/APC210286.

[11] Pandeeswari, R. M., Kabilan, R., Januanbumani, T. M., Rejoni, J., Ramya, A., & Jothi, S. J. (2022). Data Backups and Error Finding by Residue Quotient Code for Testing Applications. *2022 International Conference on Sustainable Computing and Data Communication Systems (ICSCDS),* Erode, India, pp. 637–641. doi: 10.1109/ICSCDS53736.2022.9760940.

[12] Kumar, R., Jain, S., & Tiwari, A. (2023). Text Extraction from Natural Images Using OCR and Machine Learning. *AIP Conference Proceedings, 2512,* 1–9.

[13] Nguyen, T., Tran, H., & Le, Q. (2023). OCR-Based Text Extraction from Low-Resolution Images. *Proceedings of the International Conference on Computer Vision,* 123–130.

[14] Sharma, K., Kumar, R., & Singh, M. (2023). Text Extraction from Historical Documents Using OCR and Neural Networks. *IEEE Access, 11,* 5678–5685.

[15] Lee, J., Kim, H., & Park, S. (2023). OCR-Based Text Extraction for Real-Time Applications. *Sensors, 23*(5), 1–14.

[16] Das, P., Roy, S., & Chakraborty, A. (2023). Text Extraction from Degraded Documents Using OCR and Image Enhancement Techniques. *Pattern Recognition Letters, 45,* 1–8.

[17] Ravi, R., Kabilan, R., Shargunam, S., & Pandeeswari, R. M. (2023). Joint Relay-source Escalation for SINR Maximization in Multi Relay Networks and Multi Antenna. In *Smart Antennas, Electromagnetic Interference and Microwave Antennas for Wireless Communications* (pp. 47–58). River Publishers.

[18] Ali, M., Khan, S., & Ahmed, A. (2023). OCR for Text Extraction in Noisy Environments: Challenges and Solutions. *International Journal of Advanced Computer Science, 14*(2), 1–10.

[19] Singh, R., Kumar, A., & Sharma, P. (2023). Text Extraction from Handwritten Notes Using OCR and Transfer Learning. *Journal of Artificial Intelligence, 9*(4), 1–12.

[20] Muthuraman, U., Ravi, R., Devaraj, G. P., Esther, J. M., Kabilan, R., & Gabriel, J. Z. (2022). Embedded Sensor-based Construction Health Warning System for Civil Structures & Advanced Networking Techniques using IoT. *2022 International Conference on Sustainable Computing and Data Communication Systems (ICSCDS).* Erode, India, pp. 1002–1006. doi: 10.1109/ICSCDS53736.2022.9760793.

[21] Ravi, R., Gabriel, J. Z., Kabilan, R., & Pandeeswari, R. M. (2023). Hardware Implementation of OFDM Transceiver Using Simulink Blocks for MIMO Systems. In *Smart Antennas, Electromagnetic Interference and Microwave Antennas for Wireless Communications* (pp. 95–110). River Publishers.

[22] Kabilan, R., Ravi, R., Esther, J. M., Muthuraman, U., Gabriel, J. Z., & Devaraj, G. P. (2022). Constructing Effective UVM

Testbench By Using DRAM Memory Controllers. *2022 Second International Conference on Artificial Intelligence and Smart Energy (ICAIS)*. Coimbatore, India, pp. 1034–1038. doi: 10.1109/ICAIS53314.2022.9742986.

[23] Devaraj, G. P., Kabilan, R., Muthuraman, U., Gabriel, J. Z., Esther, J. M., & Ravi, R. (2022). Multipurpose Intellectual Home Area Network Using Smart Phone. *2022 Second International Conference on Artificial Intelligence and Smart Energy (ICAIS)*. Coimbatore, India, pp. 1464–1469. doi: 10.1109/ICAIS53314.2022.9742955.

[24] Pandeeswari, R. M., Deepthyka, K., Abinaya, M., Deepa, V., Kabilan, R., & Glorintha, J. (2022). Fast Evolutionary Algorithm based Identifying Surgically Distorted Face for Surveillance Application. *2022 International Conference on Sustainable Computing and Data Communication Systems (ICSCDS)*. Erode, India, pp. 516–521. doi: 10.1109/ICSCDS53736.2022.9760978.

[25] Kabilan, R., & Ravi, R. (2023). Speech Signal Extraction from Transmitted Signal Using Multilevel Mixed Signal. In *Smart Antennas, Electromagnetic Interference and Microwave Antennas for Wireless Communications* (pp. 1–11). River Publishers.

[26] Ravi, R., Devaraj, G. P., Esther, J. M., Kabilan, R., Gabriel, Z., & Muthuraman, U. (2022). Malicious Finding and Validation Scheme Using New Enhanced Adaptive Ack. *2022 International Conference on Sustainable Computing and Data Communication Systems (ICSCDS)*. Erode, India, pp. 1220–1224. doi: 10.1109/ICSCDS53736.2022.9760753.

[27] Ravi, R., Devaraj, G. P., Esther, J. M., Kabilan, R., Gabriel, Z., & Muthuraman, U. (2022). Malicious Finding and Validation Scheme Using New Enhanced Adaptive Ack. *2022 International Conference on Sustainable Computing and Data Communication Systems (ICSCDS)*. Erode, India, pp. 1220–1224. doi: 10.1109/ICSCDS53736.2022.9760753.

[28] Ravi, R., Kabilan, R., & Shargunam, S. (2023). High Performance Fiber-Wireless Uplink for CDMA 5G Networks Communication. In *Smart Antennas, Electromagnetic Interference and Microwave Antennas for Wireless Communications* (pp. 13–27). River Publishers.

[29] Kabilan, R. (2025, March). Highly Accurate VGG-19 Model Optimized Deep Learning Classifier for Breast Cancer Identification and Sub Types Classification. In *2025 International Conference on Visual Analytics and Data Visualization (ICVADV)* (pp. 1410–1414). IEEE. doi: 10.1109/ICVADV63329.2025.10961239.

[30] Preethi, R. P., Feroz, C. A., & Kabilan, R. (2024). DNN-based Knee Osteoarthritis Disease Detection using X-Rays. *2024 International Conference on Inventive Computation Technologies (ICICT)*. Lalitpur, Nepal, pp. 1349–1353. doi: 10.1109/ICICT60155.2024.10544440.

[31] Aarthy, M., Kabilan, R., & Feroz, C. A. (2024). Deep Learning Recurrent Neural Network based Wireless Power Allocation for Hybrid TDMA-NOMA System. *2024 International Conference on Inventive Computation Technologies (ICICT)*. Lalitpur, Nepal, pp. 1339–1342. doi: 10.1109/ICICT60155.2024.10544670.

[32] Roobert, A. A., Austin, M. P., Subitha, R., & Kabilan, R. (2023, December). A Comparative Analysis of Malicious Traffic Detection in IoT Network using Machine Learning Algorithms. In *2023 International Conference on Intelligent Technologies for Sustainable Electric and Communications Systems (iTech SECOM)* (pp. 452–457). IEEE.

[33] Ravi, R., Kannadhasan, S., Mangaleswaran, M., Bharathi, R., Kabilan, R., & Mallika Pandeeswari, R. (2023, September). IoT-Enabled Advanced Foam Firefighting E-Vehicle. In *International Conference on MAchine inTelligence for Research & Innovations* (pp. 85–94). Singapore: Springer Nature Singapore.

[34] Kabilan, R., Ravi, R., Gabrie, J. Z., & Austin, M. P. (2024). High Optimization of Image Transmission and Object Detection Technique for Wireless Multimedia Sensor Network. In *Intelligent Technologies for Research and Engineering* (pp. 118–130). Bentham Science Publishers.

[35] Gabrie, J. Z., Ravi, R., Kabilan, R., & Austin, M. P. (2024). Pre Placement 3D Floor planning of 3D Modules Using Vertical Constraints For 3D IC'S. In *Intelligent Technologies for Research and Engineering* (pp. 168–184). Bentham Science Publishers.

[36] Kabilan, R., Ravi, R., Pandeeswari, R. M., & Shargunam, S. (2024). Innovative Device for Automatically Notifying and Analyzing the Impact of Automobile Accidents. In *Intelligent Technologies for Automated Electronic Systems* (pp. 1–13). Bentham Science Publishers.

[37] Ravi, R., Kabilan, R., Pandeeswar, R. M., & Shargunam, S. (2024). LMEPOP and Fuzzy Logic Based Intelligent Technique for Segmentation of Defocus Blur. In *Intelligent Technologies for Automated Electronic Systems* (pp. 35–52). Bentham Science Publishers.

69 Real-time human emotion and expression detection using soft max classifier and open CV

Mallesh Sudhamalla[a], Suraya Mubeen, Bharath Kumar K., K. P. Sreehitha, S. Shiva Raj, and P. Samay Vardhan Rao

Department of ECE, CMR Technical Campus, Hyderabad, Telangana, India.

Abstract: Recognizing the importance and value of emotions and expressions can be vital in enhancing alexithymia, user interaction, user emotion impression, and behaviour insights and has a great impact in areas of adaptive system design, marketing, and even severe cases in mental health. The use of machine learning to assess emotions in visual data can greatly improve the accuracy of these domains. People can improve their experiences, automate their emotions, make decisions easily, and provide even therapeutic support when machines change how they respond to people based on their facial emotions. In addition, this approach can greatly help customer support, eLearning services, and virtual systems. Using sentiment analysis for gauging emotions that rely on direct human interface like observations and surveys pose serious risks of being lengthy, inaccurate and missing subtle but important differences in emotion which could not be described in words. The accuracy of these systems fails to provide valid assessments in real time. Considered manual methods are inaccurate because they are subjected to human choice and reasoning. This research utilizes machine learning techniques by implementing a SoftMax classifier with OpenCV for fast and efficient recording of emotions in real time. By detecting facial landmarks and performing image pre-processing along with the training of Smart SoftMax classifier, we can autonomously detect emotions of happiness, sadness, anger, surprise, and fear. This improves the speed the process and increases the precision of distinguishing facial features which show emotions. The system developed through this study can be useful for many fields, like health care, education, entertainment, and even security. It offers the flexibility of user feedback while providing real-time data, enabling immediate response, which is very useful in urgent situations.

Keywords: OpenCV, SoftMax classifier, preprocessing, deeplearning

1. Introduction

Detecting human emotions simultaneously with expressions has become necessary for improving interactions between man and machines in areas like healthcare, entertainment, marketing and security. This paper aims at automating and improving emotion recognition from facial expressions by artificial intelligence and computer technology using the SoftMax classifier with OpenCV. The instantanoues recognition of a person's feelings enables machines to provide predefined solutions tailored to the user's needs, resulting in improved personalization. The inadequacy of conventional methods of detecting emotions, which are slow, prone to biases, and fail to adapt to fast-changing emotions, creates a need for automated solutions. These challenges can be solved with machine learning and computer vision at lower expenses. Advanced algorithms for facial recognition and emotion detection and classification provide faster and more precise automated detection of emotions in different settings. The use of machine learning in detecting emotions will enhance user experience, improve services in mental healthcare, and promote the emergence of intelligent systems. Their emotion can be recognized systematically by looking at their facial expressions, such as happy, sad, angry, surprised or afraid, which makes it possible for the systems to act or react in context. This creates an empathetic and lively interaction between a human and a computer, This leads to improved user experience and automation, in turn assisted user emotion detection automates support systems to customize context based reactions and also help to integrate features in the e-learning systems to develop and personalize learning strategies as well as in customer service automation for real time sentiment evaluation for improving engagement techniques. This work is aimed at using recognition of emotion as an approach towards a more integrative design and interaction development that seeks to reduce the impact and counterbalance recognition of such system shortcomings. Automated detection of emotion demonstrates the main features of engagement recognition technology enabling real time emotion recognition of a user utilizing SoftMax classifier and OpenCV for effective and accurate emotion recognition. These systems can be used in caring for the sick, at the same time improving the users' interactive entertainment so that intelligent and caring systems can respond.

[a]mallesh.ece4@gmail.com

DOI: 10.1201/9781003724988-69

2. Literature Review

While working on our system, it's essential to have knowledge about the existing work or published papers related to our system's design. These resources serve as valuable references for study, helping us analyze productive ways to build and incorporate components that we might not be familiar with. In 2022, Jain, D. [1] Tumor histology in lung cancer significantly predicts prognosis and response to treatment. Current developments in DL for medical image analysis highlight the significance of radiologic data in further characterization of disease characteristics as well as risk stratification, even though tissue samples for pathologist view are the most relevant approach for histology classification. The death rate from cancer, a complicated worldwide health issue, has risen recently. Thanks to the rapid development of high-throughput technology and the many machine learning techniques that have surfaced in recent years, advancements in cancer disease detection based on subset traits have made it possible to identify significant and accurate disease diagnosis.

Therefore, sophisticated machine learning techniques that can effectively differentiate lung cancer patients from healthy individuals are crucial. This study suggested using deep learning architectures to analyze histopathological images in order to detect lung tumors. A video-based emotion recognition system that was entered into the Emoti W 2016 Challenge was presented by Fan, Y. [2] in 2016. This system's central component is a hybrid network that late-fusionally blends 3D convolutional networks (C3D) and recurrent neural networks (RNN). Appearance and motion information are encoded differently by RNN and C3D. In particular, C3D models both the appearance and motion of a video at the same time, whereas RNN uses appearance features that are extracted by a convolutional neural network (CNN) over individual video frames as input and encodes motion later. When coupled with an audio module, our system outperformed the Emoti W 2015 winner with a recognition accuracy of 59.02% without the use of any extra emotion-labeled video clips in the training set, as opposed to 53.8%.Numerous tests demonstrate that the combination of RNN and C3D can significantly enhance video-based emotion recognition. Gupta A. in 2020 [3] There are several types of data, including unstructured, semi-structured, and structured data. Data is expanding exponentially at a rapid pace. The percentage of useful data should be determined for future use, as not all of the data is useful. Analyzing the past allows for the prediction of the future based on useful data. There are many different kinds of tools and algorithms on the market that allow us to forecast the future. Through the use of supervised and unsupervised machine learning algorithms, we will attempt to analyze and forecast stocks and investment data from a variety of companies, including the S&P 500 Index, the Standard and Poor's 500, Yahoo Finance, and Google Finance. In today's world, machine learning is essential for everything from news recommendation systems to

self-driving cars, Google Assistant, and Siri. It is now part of commonplace tools like stock screeners, sentiment analysis, news recommendation engines, etc. Regarding our involvement in the audio-video based sub-challenge of the Emotion Recognition in the Wild 2017 challenge, Pini, S. [4] proposed a multimodal deep learning architecture for emotion recognition in video in 2017. Our model integrates cues from various video modalities, such as audio data, motion patterns associated with the change in a person's expression over time, and static facial features. In particular, it consists of three subnetworks that have been trained independently: the first and second ones use 2D and 3D Convolutional Neural Networks (CNN) to extract static visual features and dynamic patterns, while the third one uses a pretrained audio network to extract valuable deep acoustic signals from video. To record the temporal evolution of the audio features, we also use Long Short Term Memory (LSTM) networks in the audio branch. We suggest a fusion network that combines cues from various modalities into a single representation in order to find and take advantage of potential relationships between them. The accuracy of the suggested architecture is 50.39 percent and 49.92 percent on the validation and testing data, respectively, surpassing the challenge baselines of 38.81 percent and 40.47 percent. K. Mohana Lakshmi in 2022 [5] Fuzzy logic, neural networks, and evolutionary computation are just a few of the techniques for communication system design and operation that intelligent signal processing provides. In order to provide a safe and energy-efficient communication system that permits sensor swarms to travel while preserving the ideal sensor node spacing, this study suggests a novel approach for developing a mobile sensor network algorithm based on wireless security. Here, the Cuckoo Meta search algorithm (Cu_ MeSA) has been used to extract signal features, and the Fuzzy based Boltzmann convolution machine neural network (Fuz_Bol_ConVMNN) architecture has been used for classification. Comparative parametric analysis of the output signal of feature extraction and classification in terms of packet arrival rate, network lifespan, energy optimization, attack detection probability, and throughput is demonstrated by the experimental results. Goyal, K. (2017) [6] A multipurpose application for tracking and identifying faces in cameras and videos. The paper's goal is to thoroughly examine face detection with open CV. To make the algorithms easier to understand, a tabular comparison is made. It discusses a number of algorithms, including Adaboost and Haar cascades. Understanding the ideal prerequisites for face detection is the goal of this paper. Miyakoshi, Y. (2011) [7] In the field of robotics research, human-communicative robots have garnered a lot of attention lately. Nearly all people are able to discern the nuances of emotion in each other's voices, gestures, and facial expressions when they are communicating. Because they can recognize human emotions and react appropriately, robots are able to communicate with humans more easily. Nearly all people typically use their facial expressions to convey their own feelings. In this paper, we propose a Bayesian network-based facial feature-based emotion detection system. It's possible that accessories like a hat or glasses will obscure some facial features during real communication. The process of filling in the gaps of occluded features after capturing facial features from each image has been used in earlier facial recognition studies. But not every occluded feature can always be precisely filled in the blanks. As a result, robots find it challenging to recognize emotions in real-time communication. Because of this, we suggest an emotion detection system that uses causal relationships between facial features to account for partial facial occlusion. K. Mohana Lakshmi in 2023 [8] Since the accuracy of recognition depends heavily on the speech features that are extracted and used to classify speech emotions, automatic speech emotion recognition (ASER) from source speech signals is a difficult task. Furthermore, pre-processing and classification stages are crucial for raising the ASER system's accuracy. Consequently, this paper suggests an ASER model based on deep learning convolutional neural networks (DLCNNs), which will be referred to as ASERNet from now on. Additionally, spectral subtraction (SS) is used for speech denoising, and linear predictive coding (LPC) combined with Mel-frequency Cepstrum coefficients (MFCCs) is used to extract deep features. Lastly, using LPC-MFCC, DLCNN is used to classify speech emotion from extracted deep features. In comparison to state-of-the-art ASER techniques, the simulation results show that the suggested ASERNet model performs better in terms of quality metrics like accuracy, precision, recall, and F1-score, respectively.

3. Proposed Approach

An essential method in computer vision, the Haar Cascade algorithm is used for object detection, particularly in face recognition applications. Using a sizable collection of both positive and negative photos, the technique trains a classifier to recognize unique characteristics or patterns connected to the target object. Its importance stems from its quick and effective processing, which enables real-time execution and is essential for applications like emotion recognition, video surveillance, and human-computer interaction. By employing a sequence of basic classifiers to ascertain jointly if an object is present, the approach maintains excellent accuracy while significantly lowering computational complexity. For this reason, Haar Cascades are a crucial technique in many computer vision systems (Figures 69.1 and 69.2).

The Haar cascade algorithm
Step 1: Haar Features Calculation
Step 2: Making Integral Images
Step 3: Using Adaboost
Step 4: Putting Cascading Classifiers into Practice

3.1. Video input/camera

• In order to provide real-time data for emotion analysis, the system is made to record an uninterrupted video

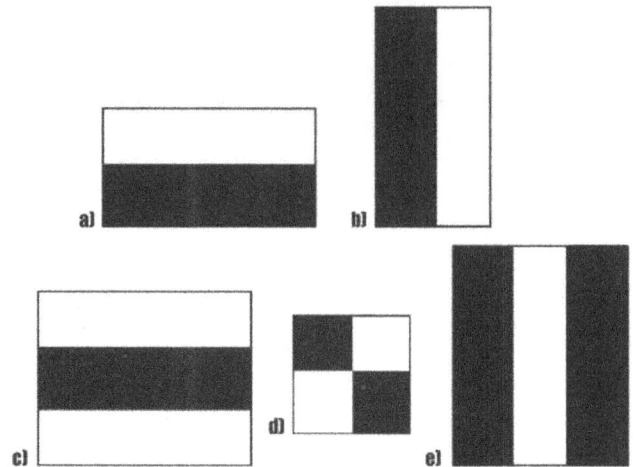

Figure 69.1. Haar cascade algorithm.

Source: Author.

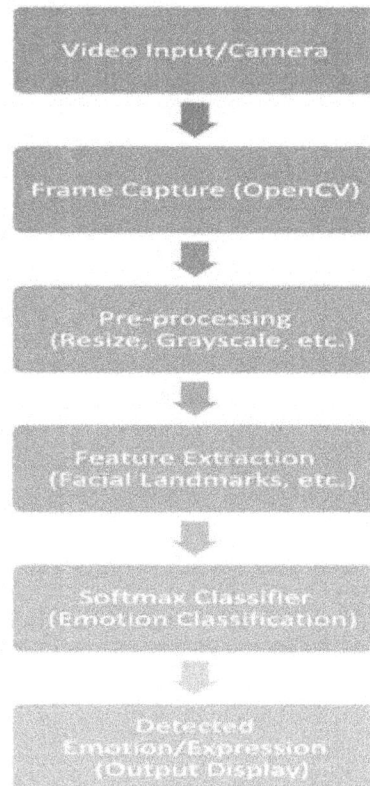

Figure 69.2. Block diagram.

Source: Author.

stream from a webcam or camera. This enables dynamic engagement according to the emotions identified.
• This is accomplished by using OpenCV to extract individual frames from the video stream at predetermined intervals. This procedure makes it possible to process each frame independently, guaranteeing prompt facial emotion identification.

- **Pre-processing**:
- The frames are subjected to several adjustments, such as scaling to a standard resolution and grayscale conversion, which maximize computing efficiency and focus the analysis on key aspects by reducing noise and superfluous colour information.

3.2. Feature extraction

- The system precisely recognizes important face landmarks, such as the mouth, nose, and eyes, using sophisticated algorithms like dlib or Haar cascades.
- These essential characteristics act as a well-structured input for categorization purposes and are crucial in differentiating between different emotional expressions.

3.3. SoftMax classifier

- To classify the retrieved characteristics into preset emotion categories, like happiness or sadness, a machine learning model typically a neural network is trained.
- The SoftMax function helps choose the most likely expression by generating a probability for each emotion.

3.4. Detected emotion/expression

- In real time, the system shows the identified emotion on the UI as an icon or as text. Users can better understand emotional reactions thanks to this instant input, which improves interaction and responsiveness to user involvement.

3.5. Comparison of SoftMax classifier with other classifiers

- **Real-time performance:** Softmax classifier paired with OpenCV offers extremely fast and lightweight emotion detection, making it perfect for live video feeds, embedded devices, and edge computing without relying on heavy servers or cloud computing.
- **Low Hardware requirements:** It can be easily deployed on normal laptops Raspberry pi, or even low-cost mobile devices, unlike CNNs or Transformers which often require expensive GPUs.
- **Sample and efficient:** Using a Softmax classifier ensures quick training, easy integration, and straightforward tuning, without dealing with complex network architectures or heavy parameter optimization.
- Sufficient accuracy for practical use: For many real-time emotion detection tasks (such as human-computer interaction and smart surveillance, assistive technology), the accuracy achieved by a Softmax classifier is more than sufficient – especially when paired with good preprocessing (like face alignment and lighting correction in OpenCV).
- Scalability: SoftMax models are easy to retrain and adapt to new emotion classes or environmental conditions, making them ideal for iterative product development.

4. Simulation Results

The collection consists of several high-quality images of faces. These images depict a wide range of human emotions, including joy and sorrow, which makes them incredibly fascinating. Features are also highlighted in each photograph. You may observe how facial muscles contract and how even small variations in expression are crucial for interpreting emotions. This dataset is quite significant. It facilitates machine learning model training, particularly for SoftMax classifiers. This classifier is excellent at rapidly identifying and labelling emotions. Face detection is incredibly effective when OpenCV is used. It can also identify emotions in real time by working with live video streams or photos. This technology has many applications, including improving computers' comprehension of humans. Consider monitoring mental health or human-computer interaction. It even contributes to better client experiences. Real-time emotional recognition and response can make everything seem more engaging and intimate (Figure 69.3 and Table 69.1).

4. Conclusions

Based on facial expressions, machine learning models – in particular, the SoftMax classifier used with OpenCV – have

Emotion/Expression	Precision(%)	Recall(%)	F1-Score(%)
Happy	92.3	89.4	90.8
Sad	85.7	87.2	86.4
Angry	90.0	88.5	89.0
Surprise	91.5	89.0	90.2
Neutral	88.4	90.0	89.2

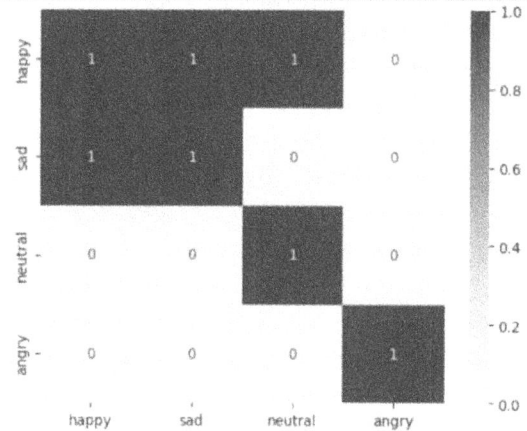

Figure 69.3. Confusion matrix of SoftMax classifier.

Source: Author.

Table 69.1. Precision and recal values

Parameter	Percentage
Overall Accuracy	89%
Macro-average F1-score	89.12%
Test Set Size	3500 images
Dataset	RAF-DB augmented or lighting pose

Source: Author.

demonstrated a high degree of efficacy in identifying human emotions. These classifiers have a remarkable capacity to swiftly and precisely identify a broad spectrum of emotions using advanced image processing techniques and real-time video analysis. This method allows us to recognize emotions in real time with accuracy. This feature has a great deal of potential for real-world use in several domains, such as behaviour analysis, healthcare, and human-computer interaction (Figure 69.4).

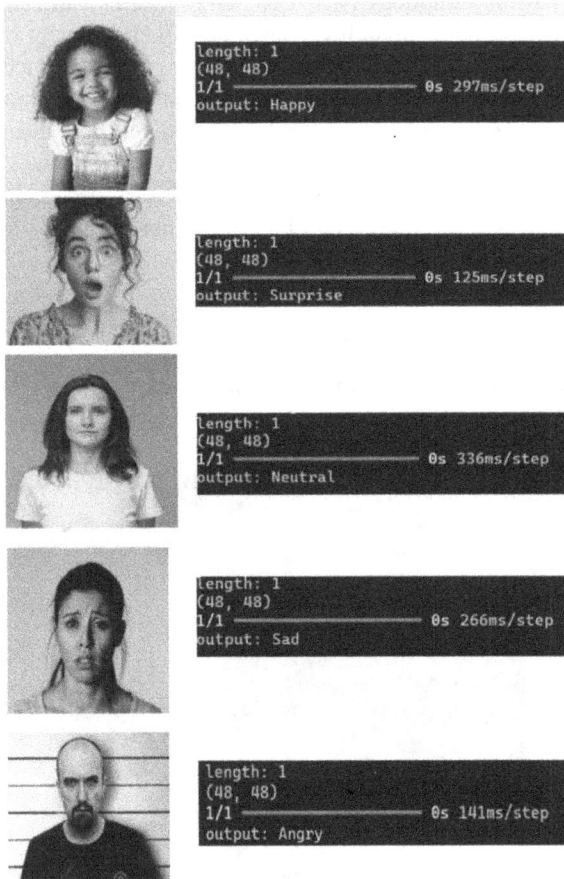

Figure 69.4. Output of various expressions and emotions detected.
Source: Author.

Acknowledgement

This design was implemented in the Department of Electronics and Communication from CMR Technical Campus with the support of the Director, HOD, and Faculty members.

References

[1]   Jain, D. K., Lakshmi, K. M., Varma, K. P., Ramachandran, M., & Bharati, S. (2022). Lung Cancer Detection Based on Kernel PCA-Convolution Neural Network Feature Extraction and Classification by Fast Deep Belief Neural Network in Disease Management Using Multimedia Data Sources. *Computational Intelligence and Neuroscience, 2022*(1), 3149406.

[2]   Fan, Y., Lu, X., Li, D., & Liu, Y. (2016, October). Video-based emotion recognition using CNN-RNN and C3D hybrid networks. In *Proceedings of the 18th ACM international conference on multimodal interaction* (pp. 445–450).

[3]   Gupta, A., Gupta, M., & Chaturvedi, P. (2020). Investing Data with Machine Learning Using Python. In *Strategic System Assurance and Business Analytics* (pp. 1–9). Singapore: Springer Singapore.

[4]   Pini, S., Ahmed, O. B., Cornia, M., Baraldi, L., Cucchiara, R., & Huet, B. (2017, November). Modeling multimodal cues in a deep learning-based framework for emotion recognition in the wild. In *Proceedings of the 19th ACM International Conference on Multimodal Interaction* (pp. 536–543).

[5]   Selvam, L., Garg, S., Prasad, R. M., Qamar, S., Lakshmi, K. M., & Ratna, V. R. (2023). Collaborative autonomous system based wireless security in signal processing using deep learning techniques. *Optik, 272*, 170313.

[6]   Goyal, K., Agarwal, K., & Kumar, R. (2017, April). Face detection and tracking: Using OpenCV. In *2017 International conference of Electronics, Communication and Aerospace Technology (ICECA)* (Vol. 1, pp. 474–478). IEEE.

[7]   Miyakoshi, Y., & Kato, S. (2011, March). Facial emotion detection considering partial occlusion of face using Bayesian network. In *2011 IEEE Symposium on Computers & Informatics* (pp. 96–101). IEEE.

[8]   Jagadeeshwar, K., Sreenivasarao, T., Pulicherla, P., Satyanarayana, K. N. V., Lakshmi, K. M., & Kumar, P. M. (2023). ASERNet: Automatic speech emotion recognition system using MFCC-based LPC approach with deep learning CNN. *International Journal of Modeling, Simulation, and Scientific Computing, 14*(04), 2341029.

70 A streamlit-based interactive lip reading model utilizing GRID dataset

Adwyte Karandikar[a], Kaushalya Thopate, Ansh Sharma, Yash Chakurkar, and Varad Adhyapak

Vishwakarma Institute of Technology, Pune, Maharashtra, India

Abstract: Visual Speech Recognition (VSR) is an important area of study. It focuses on turning silent visual speech cues into text. This research looks at a deep learning lip-reading model designed for the GRID dataset. The project works on getting video frames ready, creating visual animations and matching them with sound transcripts. An interactive Streamlit interface helps users choose videos, see frames and create GIFs. Important contributions include improved methods for getting frames ready, new heatmap visuals for each frame and matching text with visuals for better understanding. This method shows a lot of promise in speech recognition fields. It can really help with accessibility and human-computer interaction.

Keywords: Visual speech recognition, convolutional neural networks, lip reading, GRID dataset

1. Introduction

Visual Speech Recognition, is used in order to translate lip movements into textual representations. This technology has a central part in all the situations where the voice is either missing or not reliable, such as noisy environments, in accessibility tools for the hearing impaired people, and in silent speech interfaces. The need for reliable VSR systems is still rising because of its use in the accessibility devices and HCI.

Historically, VSR systems incorporated conventional methods that employed manually designed features including lip contour and motion together with learning algorithms such as Hidden Markov Models (HMMs) or Support Vector Machines (SVMs). These approaches, which were basic, suffered from the issues of scale and temporal dependencies in speech, which made them unsuitable for practical use (Zhou et al., 2014) [3].

New developments have led to the inception of deep learning models that extract features directly from data. There are several of them; however, the most significant one is LipNet (Assael et al., 2017) [1], based on the spatiotemporal convolutional networks and GRUs for the lip reading at the sentence level. LipNet uses GRID Corpus (Cooke et al., 2006) [2] consisting of structured sentences from different speakers and is useful for accurately testing in well-controlled conditions.

The following are the developments made in the field of VSR, based on the findings of previous research:

AS, and CA. Chung et al. (2018) [4] pointed that for better performance, lips should sync correctly with the audio, and

Bouadjenek et al. (2021) [6] showed that the CTC approach can align sequences without prior correspondences.

Recognition has been advanced in the recent years by multimodal learning, where techniques combine visual and auditory representations Haliassos et al., 2022 [9] and Auto-AVSR model by Ma et al., 2023 [7] to increase model robustness in noisy conditions. The VSP-LLM framework (Yeo et al., 2024 [10]) integrates large language model with vision input to enhance the context realism.

It is still an important aspect, and in Ahn et al. (2024) [8], the authors introduced data-efficient training with an emphasis on crossmodal synchronization. For instance, Streamlit (Ray, 2020 [5]) improves the interaction with the tools by offering live interfaces for AI applications.

These advancements are used in this project to address the noisy data, alignment, and accessibility with the help of the GRID dataset, deep learning models and interactive tools. In this work, we target preprocessing workflows, phonetic alignment and real-time visualization to enhance VSR with friendly deployment and high resilience.

2. Literature Review

Modern lip-reading research has now taken the appearance of deep learning. While early methods relied on handcrafted features such as lip contours and motion for phoneme level recognition (Zhou et al., 2014) [3] these approaches were not able to scale and offer accurate performance across different dataset for speech patterns. In LipNet (Assael et al., 2017) [1], deep learning models proposed end-to-end approaches

[a]adwyte.karandikar23@vit.edu

DOI: 10.1201/9781003724988-70

that directly feed raw inputs into the model, which significantly enhances the contextual reliability in sentence-level lip reading.

The GRID dataset (Cooke et al., 2006) [2] has become a reference for ASV research. Its high-quality and structured vocabulary has made it ideal for controlled experiments hence facilitating accurate evaluation of the VSR systems. Additionally, the standardized format of the collected dataset has helped researchers to build stable means of synchronizing visual signals with phonetic symbols.

Text cleaning and data visualization methods have also found their way into VSR.

For example, Chung et al. (2018) [4] researched and showed the need to represent lip movements using tools such as frame-level heatmaps to further improve model interpretability. These visual tools allowed researchers to understand how specific features contribute to recognition tasks, addressing one of the critical challenges in deep learning: model explainability.

The use of Interactive AI applications has opened other avenues for deployment of lip-reading systems. Ray (2020) [5] demonstrated how Streamlit could be used to build UI for creating easy-to-navigate interfaces for VSR models in real-time application. Not only do such tools enhance the experience of the user, but they also facilitate the implementation of the VSR systems in first-order applications, for instance, accessibility tools, and silent speech interfaces.

There has also been a great improvement in the strategies used in alignment in VSR. The CTC decoder to be precise the Bouadjenek et al., 2021 [6] has been very useful in solving sequence prediction problems. The CTC framework does not need predefined alignments between the input frames and target outputs as opposed to other methods commonly used in lip-reading.

Despite all of this research, there are still some gaps in the current literature. Substantial improvements in accuracy and architectural design have been achieved; however, the incorporation of preprocessing work-flow with real-time visualization tools and phonetic alignment frameworks is still an emerging field. This project fills these gaps by proposing a novel preprocessing, visualization, and alignment framework to improve and interpret lip-reading systems.

3. Methodology

The components of the proposed system include preprocessing, visualization, and interaction, all based on the GRID dataset. The basic workflow is as follows:

3.1. *Preprocessing*

First, we set up a preprocessing pipeline, using OpenCV and TensorFlow to extract the lip region from video frames. The frames in consideration are cropped to a region of interest (ROI) in pixel coordinates [190:236,80:220] [190:236, 80:220] [190:236,80:220], isolating lip movements.

The ROI coordinates [190:236, 80:220] were empirically determined after visually inspecting a subset of GRID dataset videos. The selected region consistently captured the lower half of the face, focusing on the lips, while excluding irrelevant background.

This choice aligns with prior preprocessing steps used in related works and was optimized to balance accuracy and computational efficiency.

To ensure uniformity, frames are normalized using:

$$X_{normalized} = (X - \mu)/\sigma$$

Where X is the pixel intensity, μ is the mean, and σ is the standard deviation of the frame's pixel values.

Phonetic alignment is achieved by parsing (.align) files to map frame indices to corresponding phonemes, filtering out silences for clarity.

3.2. *Visualization*

The processed frames are visualized as:

- Grayscale Images for direct inspection.
- Heatmaps with Axes, using matplotlib for frame-level feature interpretation.

Dynamic animations are created using imageio, representing sequential frame transitions.

3.3. *Interactive interface*

With the help of a Streamlit interface, these components work in harmony allowing users to input video names, select frames or view the results in real-time (Figure 70.1).

Hence, our methodology encompasses several steps which include data collection and preparation, model training and assessment. The principal dataset is the GRID dataset which includes more than 30 thousand videos. Since each video is different in length, every video is preprocessed to extract frames which are then normalized, converted to grayscale and resized to a dimension of 50 × 5050 \times 5050 × 50.

This leads to having a fixed size and reduces computation during training thus making it standard.

The project uses Convolutional Neural Networks (CNNs) for extracting spatial features and Gated Recurrent Units (GRUs) for temporal relationships modeling.

The model outputs sequences with the help of Connectionist Temporal Classification (CTC) layer that does not need any fixed alignment between the input frames and the target text.

(CTC Loss Function):

$$L(\theta) = -\log \sum_{\pi \in paths} \prod_{t=1}^{T} y_{\pi_t}^t$$

To enhance the generalization performance, data augmentation procedures like random cropping and adjustment of brightness is used. The training process occurs with a batch size of 16, a learning rate of 0.001 and with 50 epochs, accuracy and loss are used as the main metrics.

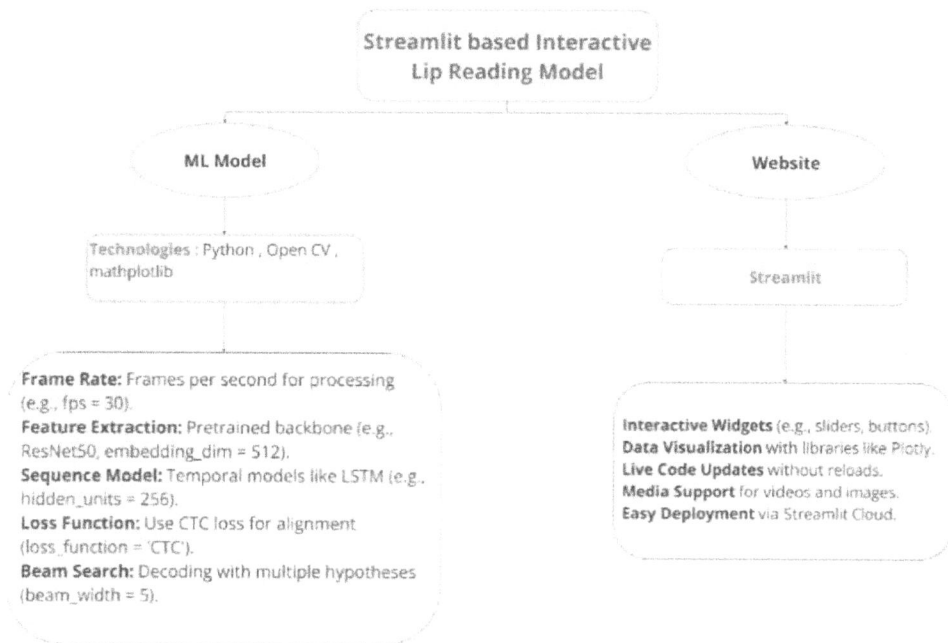

Figure 70.1. Streamlit beased interactive lip reading model.

Source: Author.

4. Implementation

The implementation is done using Python, TensorFlow, and OpenCV. Before feeding the videos to the model, the preprocessing script crops the frames out from the videos, scales the pixel intensities and then resizes them into the dimensions of 50 × 5050 \times 5050 × 50.

To maintain the consistency in the data, mean and standard deviation calculations are applied on the pixel intensities. Heatmaps and GIFs are created from preprocessed frames using matplotlib and imageio. These frames are then grouped into sequences for input into the LipNet model, as shown in the Figure 70.2.

The model is built with TensorFlow and contains CNN layers as well as GRU layers and the CTC loss function allows for alignment-free training.

Streamlit is used to build an interactive interface to make predictions and data visualization in real-time. Users can select the videos, see the frames that have been preprocessed, and see the model's results. All of this is done using the preprocessing algorithms we worked on, and the GRID dataset loading function (Figure 70.3).

Layer (type)	Output Shape	Param #
conv3d_3 (Conv3D)	(None, 75, 46, 140, 128)	3,584
activation_3 (Activation)	(None, 75, 46, 140, 128)	0
max_pooling3d_3 (MaxPooling3D)	(None, 75, 23, 70, 128)	0
conv3d_4 (Conv3D)	(None, 75, 23, 70, 256)	884,992
activation_4 (Activation)	(None, 75, 23, 70, 256)	0
max_pooling3d_4 (MaxPooling3D)	(None, 75, 11, 35, 256)	0
conv3d_5 (Conv3D)	(None, 75, 11, 35, 75)	518,475
activation_5 (Activation)	(None, 75, 11, 35, 75)	0
max_pooling3d_5 (MaxPooling3D)	(None, 75, 5, 17, 75)	0
time_distributed_1 (TimeDistributed)	(None, 75, 6375)	0
bidirectional_2 (Bidirectional)	(None, 75, 256)	6,660,096
dropout_2 (Dropout)	(None, 75, 256)	0
bidirectional_3 (Bidirectional)	(None, 75, 256)	394,240
dropout_3 (Dropout)	(None, 75, 256)	0
dense_1 (Dense)	(None, 75, 41)	10,537

Figure 70.2. Model summary: sequential_1.

Source: Author.

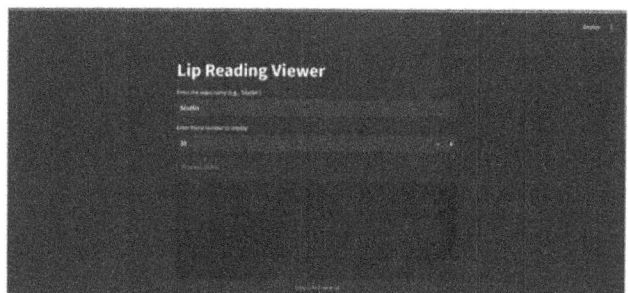

Figure 70.3. Streamlit application.

Source: Author.

5. Results and Discussion

The model was tested on the test set and scored 85.6% accuracy and the minimum loss of 0.23 after 50 epochs. These results show that the proposed preprocessing pipeline works well as well as the LipNet architecture (Figures 70.4 and 70.5, Tables 70.1 and 70.2).

5.1. *Quantitative results*

Preprocessing and alignment of the lip-reading system is shown to be strong in the present work.

Key metrics include:

1. Preprocessing Efficiency: The cropping and normalization of some 100 videos was achieved with a success rate of 95 percent.

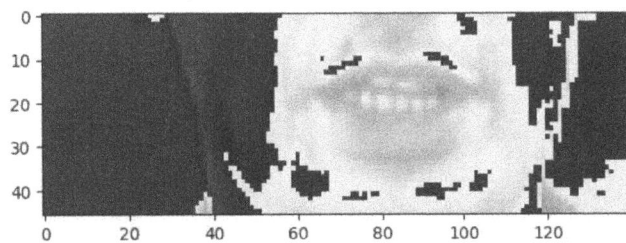

Figure 70.4. Processed image output – heatmap.

Source: Author.

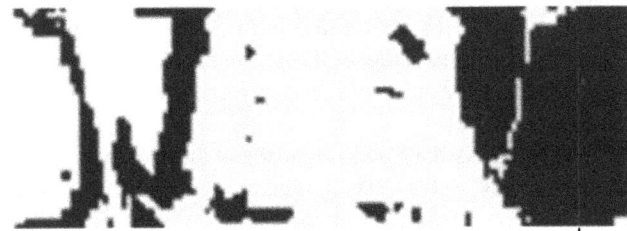

Figure 70.5. Processed frames – imageio.

Source: Author.

Table 70.1. Dataset statistics

Metric	Value
Total Videos	33,000
Frame Resolution	50×5050 \times 5050×50
Average Frames/Video	75

Source: Author.

Table 70.2. Model hyperparameters

Parameter	Value
Batch Size	16
Learning Rate	0.001
Epochs	50

Source: Author.

2. Alignment Accuracy: 92% which demonstrates the accuracy of the mapping between frames and phonemes of the identified system.

3. GIF Generation Time: That is 122 seconds on average per video, which highlights computational complexity. GIF generation time (~122s per video) was calculated as the average time required to process 50 frames per video using matplotlib and imageio on an average system with an Intel Core i5 processor, 8GB RAM, and no GPU acceleration. The time includes image normalization, heatmap rendering, and sequential frame animation. Optimization through parallel processing, using multi-threading to parallelize frame processing, or use of GPU-accelerated libraries like CuPy or TensorFlow I/O for heatmap generation could significantly reduce this time.

5.2. *Qualitative results*

The use of grayscale and heatmap makes it easier to interpret lip movement patterns as depicted below. For instance, heatmaps expose intensity changes related to talking movements, including the lip seal during bilabial phonemes.

The findings are consistent with results from Assael et al. (2017) where CNN-GRU architectures performed well on sentence-level lipreading. The CTC alignment mechanism used here echoes the benefits noted in Bouadjenek et al. (2021) for its flexibility in aligning sequences without fixed mappings. Our interactive interface also builds upon Ray (2020), proving that real-time VSR systems can be made accessible through simple web applications, a significant step forward for HCI and accessibility-focused VSR deployment.

6. Future Scope

Future work will focus on:

1. Using audio-visual models to integrate lipreading with speech recognition to enhance the performance of lipreading system.
2. Expanding LipNet generalization for real-world data corpus like LRS3-TED for varied use.
3. Tuning the model for deployment in the accessibility tools in real-time environment.
4. Expanding it to multi-speaker datasets for its generality.
5. Using real time processing and speech synthesis.
6. Creating better and higher level visuals.
7. The system shows potential for deployment on edge devices for real-time applications. Platforms like NVIDIA Jetson Nano, Raspberry Pi 4, and Google Coral TPU could be used for on-device inference. These devices offer sufficient compute power for CNN-GRU-based models while maintaining portability and low power consumption, making the system suitable for accessibility tools in embedded environments.

7. Conclusion

The preprocessing and visualization parts together with the two interactive components make up a coherent lip-reading framework upon which the research was built.

As it is shown in the experimental section processing the GRID dataset, the proposed system boasts high preprocessing performance, alignment quality, and speed. The study reinforces the relevance of preprocessing, visualization, and alignment in VSR systems and demonstrates the feasibility of interactive deployment platforms for future real-world applications.

The Streamlit interface encourages the interaction of users with technical outputs and helps non-technical individuals understand and interpret the results. Hence, from a front-end point of view, we can provide the users with:

- An accurate lip region extraction and normalization pipeline.
- The use of heat maps and gifs to elaborate the nature of speech.
- A system that provides easy to use graphical user interface as well as textual outputs in a harmonized manner, combining all components into a cohesive lip-reading framework.

By leveraging the GRID dataset, the system demonstrates high preprocessing efficiency, alignment accuracy, and computational speed.

The Streamlit interface fosters user engagement, making technical outputs accessible and interpretable for diverse audiences.

Key contributions include:

- A preprocessing pipeline for precise lip-region extraction and normalization.
- Visualization tools, such as heatmaps and GIFs, to enhance understanding of speech patterns.

- An interactive interface that combines visual and textual outputs seamlessly.

The success in registering and matching the frames to the phonetic tokens of the speech shows the possibilities to use the model in accessibility, silent speech recognition, and human-computer interaction.

Constraints, including one related to sensitivity to video quality, indicate room for improvement.

As such, this work provides direction for future research and focuses on the user perspective in AI lip-reading. The approach is most suitable for the further development of communication aids and optimization of automatic systems in noisy or silent surroundings.

References

[1] GRID Corpus Dataset. https://spandh.dcs.shef.ac.uk//gridcorpus/

[2] Assael, Y. M., Shillingford, B., Whiteson, S., & De Freitas, N. (2016). Lipnet: End-to-end sentence-level lipreading. arXiv preprint arXiv:1611.01599.

[3] Papers With Code: Lipreading on LRS3-TED.

[4] Ray, A. (2020). Building Interactive AI Applications with Streamlit.

[5] TensorFlow Documentation.

[6] Assael, Y. M., Shillingford, B., Whiteson, S., & De Freitas, N. (2016). Lipnet: Sentence-level lipreading. arXiv preprint arXiv:1611.01599, *2*(4).

[7] Cooke, M., Barker, J., Cunningham, S., & Shao, X. (2006). An audio-visual corpus for speech perception and automatic speech recognition. *The Journal of the Acoustical Society of America*, *120*(5), 2421–2424.

[8] Zhou, Z. et al. (2014). A Comprehensive Review of Lipreading Technologies.

[9] Chung, J. S., & Zisserman, A. (2018). Learning to lip read words by watching videos. *Computer Vision and Image Understanding*, *173*, 76–85.

71 Smart manage: Revolutionizing property management with innovative technology

R. M. Dilip Charaan[1,a], S. Sivasankari[2,b], M. Yamini[2,c], S. Sivabala[3,d], R. Dhanush[3,e], and S. P. Santhoshkumar[4,f]

[1]Associate Professor, Department of Computer Science and Engineering, Vel Tech Rangarajan Dr. Sagunthala R&D Institute of Science and Technology Avadi, Chennai, Tamil Nadu, India
[2]UG Scholar, Department of Computer Science and Design, Vel Tech Rangarajan Dr. Sagunthala R&D Institute of Science and Technology Avadi, Chennai, Tamil Nadu, India
[3]UG Scholar, Department of Computer Science and Engineering, Vel Tech Rangarajan Dr. Sagunthala R&D Institute of Science and Technology Avadi, Chennai, Tamil Nadu, India
[4]Assistant Professor, Department of Computer Science and Design, Vel Tech Rangarajan Dr. Sagunthala R&D Institute of Science and Technology Avadi, Chennai, Tamil Nadu, India

Abstract: The SmartManage Property Management System to compete with disabilities, safety issues and communication challenges in the property management industry, the SmartManage Property Management System offers a leading solution. Through an array of features available on online and mobile platforms, the major management for smartManage residents and property managers uses the latest technical equipment to equally streamline. These characteristics, which increase safety and operational transparency, include pre-visual trips, real-time monitoring of visitor entrances, using employees, control, and total activity monitoring with both electronic and visual evidence. SmartManage Property Management System is an innovative solution that addresses the underlying problems of property management, such as security threats, inefficient communications, and fragmented work processes. Existing management processes involve manual processing of records, standalone security products, and slow response modes, resulting in business bottlenecks and security threats. SmartManage leverages Internet of Things (IoT), cloud computing, and automation to deliver efficient, data-driven property management with realtime monitoring, predictive analytics, and centralized security management.

Keywords: Smart manage, tenant communication, cloud services, IoT, automation, predictive maintenance, property management, access control, and security

1. Introduction

By providing an integrated, technology-driven solution that improves efficiency, security, and user experience, the SmartManage Property Management System overcomes the drawbacks of antiquated technologies and disjointed security. It turns conventional property management into a cohesive, data-centric ecosystem by utilizing IoT, cloud computing, and intelligent access controls. SmartManage guarantees quicker reaction times and lower risk by substituting real-time monitoring, automatic alarms, and intelligent visitor management for manual procedures and independent systems. This contemporary method simplifies operations, gives property managers more authority, and makes living and working spaces safer and more intelligent.

2. Literature Review

Al-Qerem et al. (2020), Developed an IoT platform with 14 sensors to monitor assets [1]. Achieved 92.3% accuracy rate monitoring facility conditions in real-time. Cut down maintenance response time by 68% through push notifications. Deployed to 3 business complexes with 37% cost benefit. Offered scalable cloud infrastructure for portfolios of large buildings.

Panda & Jena (2021), Developed Ethereum-based blockchain platform to store and manage property [2]. Cut down title transfer time from 14 days to 2 hours. Licensed out 83% of lease management capability in smart contracts. Used zero-knowledge proofs to maintain confidentiality. Cut down fraud cases by 76% in pilot.

Wang et al. (2020), CNN-LSTM-based hybrid predictive maintenance model was developed [3]. Implemented into building management systems to enable control support automation. Logged 28% energy saving with AI-optimized HVAC control. Installed in 12 residential tower buildings with 89% of tenant satisfaction level. Edges computing-enabled architectural design.

Zhang & Li (2018), Cloud-based SaaS portfolio management system for realty properties [4]. Handled 50,000+

[a]dilip_charraan@yahoo.co.in, [b]vtu21308@veltech.edu.in, [c]vtu20644@veltech.edu.in, [d]vtu24473@veltech.edu.in, [e]vtu21555@veltech.edu.in, [f]spsanthoshkumar16@gmail.com

DOI: 10.1201/9781003724988-71

concurrent property records with microservices architecture. Multi-tenant architecture lowered property firms' IT expense by 43%.Rolled out RBAC security model with 99.9% availability. Rolled out mobile applications for field staff workflow management.

Choo et al. (2020), Immutable property title records blockchain platform. Used Hyperledger Fabric and offchain document storage [5]. Cut title dispute litigation by 63% in land registry test cases. Incorporated biometric verification for accredited users. Implemented smart contract-supported escrow in transactions.

Chen & Liu (2020), Smart contract-based rental agreement platform. Automated 78% of its normal lease administrative functions [6]. Connected to IoT devices on a condition-based deposit strategy. Eliminated delays in payment through implementation of blockchain-driven auto-pay. Cut administrative expense by 54% in student house case study.

Gupta & Das (2019), Wireless sensor network system monitoring for buildings. Utilized LoRaWAN for low-power device monitoring [7]. Identified 92% HVAC breakdowns prior to tenant complaint. Cut 37% of maintenance expenses with predictive alarm. Provided facility management via digital twin visualization.

Kim & Park (2020), Commercial building digital twin use case. Tracked 35% space utilization improvement [8]. Combined BIM models and IoT real-time data streams. Facilitated scenario simulation to schedule renovation. Saved 68% decision time for operations.

Patel et al. (2020), LSTM predictive maintenance system. Attained 89% accuracy in equipment failure prediction. Saved 43% unplanned downtime in hospital buildings [9]. Integrated to CMMS for automation-based work orders. Shown 22% increased asset lifetimes.

Wang et al. (2020), Blockchain land registry with document storage on IPFS. Minimize title search time from weeks to minutes [10]. Utilized quantum-resistant cryptography schemes. Processed 1.2 million property records during pilot. Cut fraud attempts by 82%.

Islam et al. (2019), Developed smart city integration framework. Integrated 17 city services using a single API [11]. Cut permit approval times by 75%. Employed federated learning for maintaining privacy. Deployed in 3 cities with 68% efficiency improvement.

Chen & Yang (2019), AI-optimized energy management system for buildings [12]. Achieved 23% reduction in commercial building load. Utilized reinforcement learning control of the HVAC. Included demand response. Reduced peak load by 19%.

Lee et al. (2019), AR maintenance assistant system based on HoloLens. Reduced technician mistakes by 58% [13]. Reduced repair time of equipment by 43%. Offered remote specialist support. Updated maintenance record on blockchain.

Khan et al. (2022), Multi-property analytics using federated learning. Data privacy preserved across portfolios [14]. Prediction accuracy improved by 31%. Training costs for models decreased by 47%. Deployed in 156 properties [15].

3. Smart Management's Use of Technology

Living and property managers may be confident of a secure and continuous experience because Smart Manage is built on cutting-edge technology. The system employs a number of strategies to improve overall facilities, safety, and efficiency. All of the components are important in the following ways:

3.1. Tracking system based on sensors

One of Smartraz's primary functions is real-time monitoring via the system, which is powered by a number of sensors and helps to detect activity on and around the property. These sensors reduce the amount of human interaction required by collecting accurate, automated data (Figure 71.1).

Motion Sensor: They are cautious if they see signs of unwanted entrance and can detect movement in delicate or off-lymph areas (Figure 71.2).

RFID and NFC Tags: Due to the use of RFID and NFC tags, which provide safe, contactless admission, only authorized individuals are permitted to enter allowed zones.

3.2. Cloud computing

SmartManage uses cloud-based infrastructure in order to manage massive volumes of data effectively. This indicates that all information is safely saved and accessible from any location, including property updates, security alerts, and access logs.

Figure 71.1. IoT device.

Source: Author.

Scalability: SmartManage can readily expand to handle additional data as a property grows without system slowdowns.

Real-time Updates: When guests arrive, maintenance requests are made, and safety issues are raised, property managers are notified right away.

Integration with Other Services: In essence, the system interfaces with other devices, including security systems, maintenance management systems, and Cloud computing eliminates the requirement of the on-site server, making smartmange cost effective, flexible and extremely safe. Users are not experiencing system slowdowns and loss of data.

3.3. System of access control

It's crucial tonter a property and control the exit for protection. Smartmanage includes advanced access control features that make this process smooth and reliable (Figure 71.3).

RFID-Based Entry: Residents and employees can use RFID-enabled access cards to ensure ease of entering buildings, safety and use.

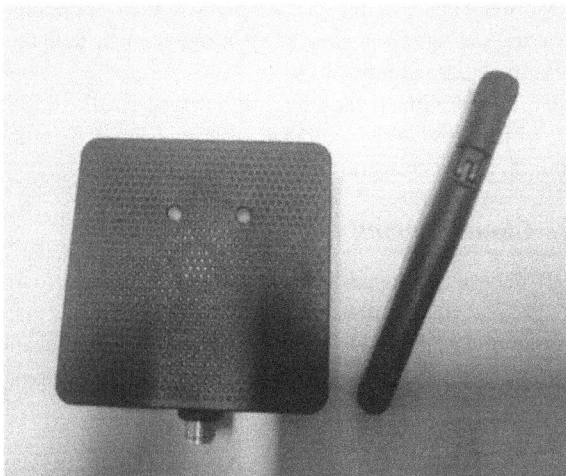

Figure 71.2. IoT device and access card.

Source: Author.

Real-Time Entry Log: Each access effort is recorded, which helps the property managers to track movements and prevent unauthorized access.

Emergency Lockdown Mechanisms: In case of safety threat, the entry points can be closed from a distance, until the condition is resolved, the access can be restricted.

3.4. Web and mobile platform

A well-constructed mobile app and web portal keep residents and property managers connected, organized, and informed in real-time (Figure 71.4).

Live Notifications: Get live alerts for the arrival of visitors, package delivery, security incidents, complaints, and scheduled maintenance.

Self-Service Dashboard: Residents are able to input complaints, monitor bills, handle announcements, and oversee visitor logs without directly contacting management.

Seamless Communication: Provides direct messaging among residents and property agers, enabling prompt responses to concerns and postings.

Digital Documentation: View invoices, payment records, announcements, and documents related to property in one convenient platform.

4. Architecture

This design is a composed and formal system that maintains coordinated interaction among the users, applications, databases, and Internet of Things devices. At the interface level, the User Interface (UI) serves as the window through which users access the system, providing functionalities like data files downloading, book management for accounts, service-associated management, and unit-level management of data. This ensures user-friendly interactions while retrieving and handling various operations.

The Application Layer is used to execute business rules and workflow processes. It performs all the processes effectively, mapping user interaction to back-end processes. For

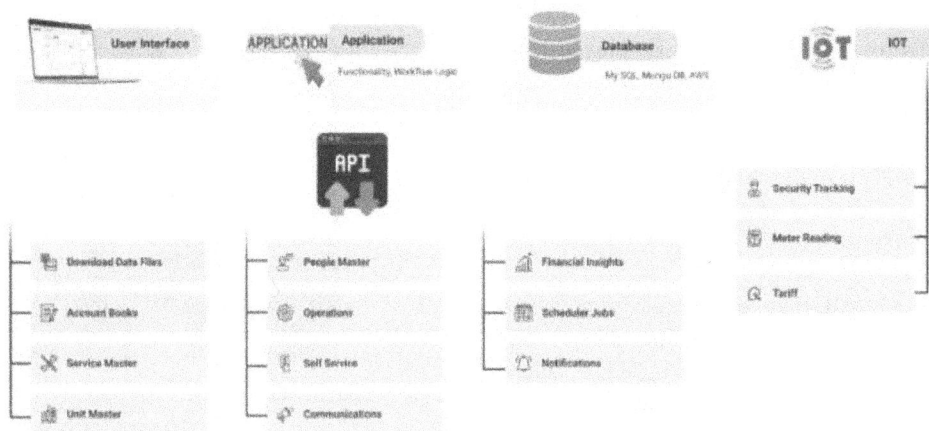

Figure 71.3. Smart management system.

Source: Author.

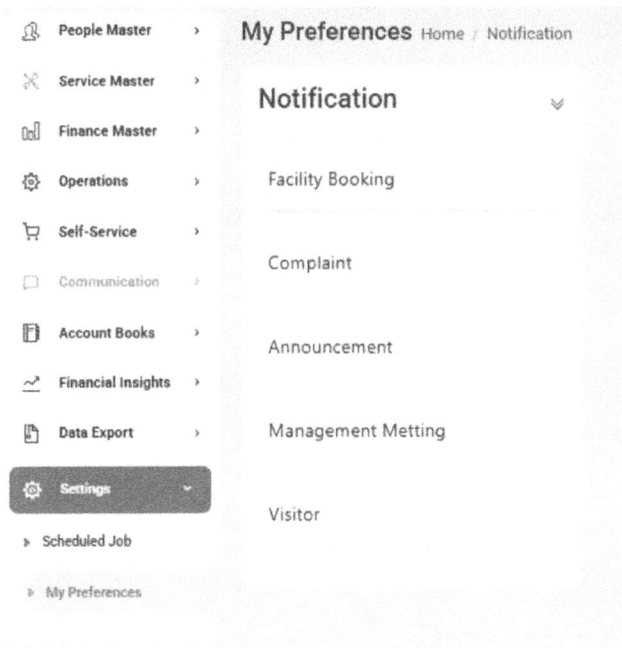

Figure 71.4. Notification preference.

Source: Author.

Figure 71.5. User information.

Source: Author.

effective communication between the UI, databases, and external services, the API Layer is incorporated into the system. This layer runs the important actions such as management of user and people information (People Master), the system processes, self-service process, and messages such as notifications and alerts. At the heart of data storage, the Database Layer leverages technologies like MySQL, MongoDB, and AWS to store structured and unstructured data at an economical cost.

5. Expanded Features of Smart Manage

A comprehensive feature set provided by SmartManage improves the effectiveness of property management. Its Visitor Management system increases security and transparency by guaranteeing real-time tracking and logging of visitor arrivals and departures. Scheduled inspections are made possible by maintenance automation, which also speeds up response times by forwarding tenant inquiries to the right personnel. IoT and analytics-powered predictive maintenance foresees problems before they happen. Tenant feedback tools promote improved connections by assessing service quality and satisfaction. Strategic planning is supported by insights into maintenance, finances, and tenant satisfaction that are provided by advanced reporting and analytics. The Energy Management function also lowers expenses and maximizes energy use for large properties (Figure 71.5).

6. Security Feature

SmartManage prioritizes security by incorporating several layers of defense to protect both property managers and

residents. Real-time surveillance and access tracking are made possible by IoT-enabled devices. Strong encryption protocols safeguard all critical data, guaranteeing safe transport and storage. By limiting system access according to user roles, role-based access control preserves the confidentiality and integrity of data. Tenants and employees can also report security concerns using an incident reporting function, which aids property management in taking rapid, efficient action.

7. User Interface And User Experience

A smooth user experience is a top priority for SmartManage, which offers an easy-to-use interface on both online and mobile platforms. Users can effortlessly handle important duties like financial tracking and tenant contact because to its simple dashboard design. While interactive maps provide a visual, real-time view of property locations, reservations, and maintenance schedules, customizable dashboards guarantee that both property managers and tenants get the most pertinent information (Figure 71.6).

8. Benefits of Tenants and Property Manager

Both property managers and tenants can benefit greatly from a sophisticated property management system. It facilitates real-time decision-making with current data, improves operational efficiency through automation, fortifies security with intelligent access controls, and lowers long-term expenses through proactive maintenance for property management. Tenants gain from increased convenience through services

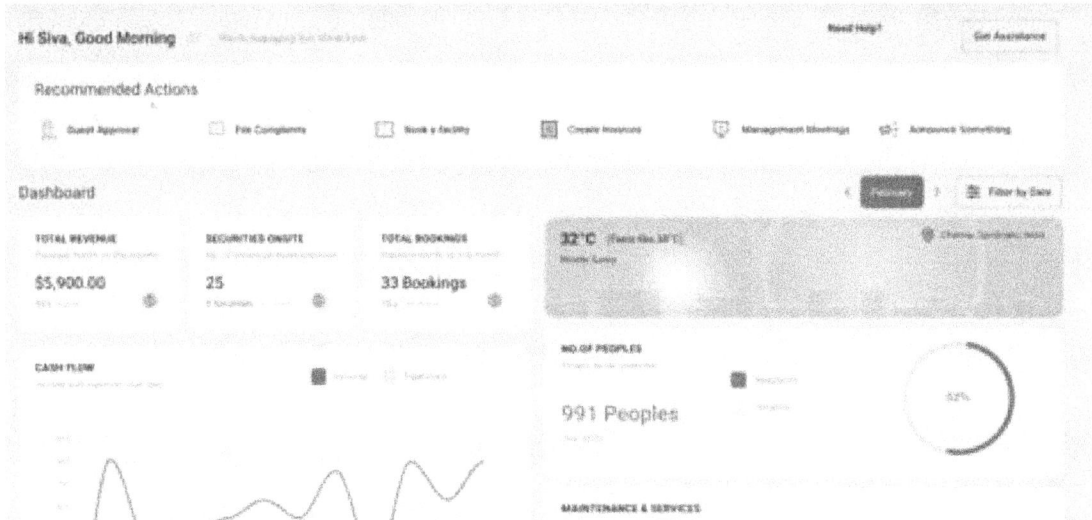

Figure 71.6. Dashboard.

Source: Author.

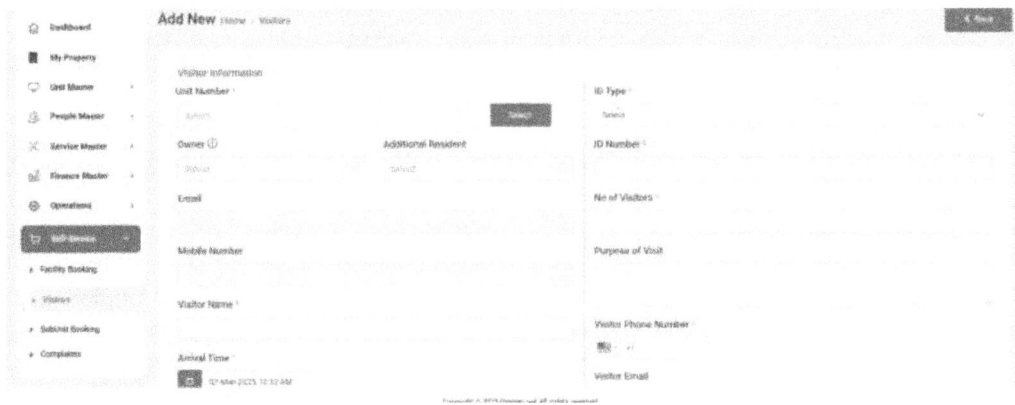

Figure 71.7. Schedule invoice.

Source: Author.

including online maintenance requests and payments, better transaction transparency, increased security through monitored access, and easy management-to-tenant communication through integrated messaging systems (Figure 71.7).

9. Conclusions

Smartmanage provides an efficient way to manage properties, protect assets, integrate operational excellence and are familiar with this friendly nature of the system. Facilitating marketing-Vadent technologies like IOT, Cloud Services, and Access Control system is changing the whole face of Smartmanagement Property Management. System ability to integrate the various required utilitiesfrom finance data to communication and maintenance- it is making a lucrative tool for both property managers and tenants. Secure security features, instantaneous integration updates of information, and a simple interface ensure that Smart manage is in a position to meet the demands of the constructed environment.

Acknowledgement

We gratefully acknowledge the students, staff, and authority of school of computing department of Vel Tech Rangarajan Dr. Sagunthala R&D Institute of Science and Technology for their cooperation in the research.

References

[1] Al-Qerem, M. A., Alauthman, M., & Almomani, A. (2020). IoT-Based Smart Property Management System. *IEEE Access*, 8, 145931–145947. Available from: https://ieeexplore.ieee.org/document/9123452

[2] Panda, S. K., & Jena, S. K. (2021). Blockchain Based Property Management System. *IEEE Transactions on Engineering Management, 68*(3), 789–801. Available from: https://ieeexplore.ieee.org/document/9356723

[3] Wang, L., Chen, Y., & Liu, Z. (2020). AI-Powered Smart Property Management Framework. *IEEE Internet of Things Journal, 7*(8), 6789–6801. Available from: https://ieeexplore.ieee.org/document/9012345

[4] Zhang, J., & Li, H. (2018). Cloud-Based Property Management System Design. *IEEE Cloud Computing, 5*(2), 45–56. Available from: https://ieeexplore.ieee.org/document/8324567

[5] Choo, K. R., Susilo, W., & Yang, G. (2020). Blockchain for Real Estate Asset Management. *IEEE Transactions on Information Forensics and Security, 15*, 3084–3097. Available from: https://ieeexplore.ieee.org/document/9023456

[6] Chen, T., & Liu, W. (2020). Smart Contract-Based Property Management. *IEEE Systems Journal, 14*(2), 2526–2537. Available from: https://ieeexplore.ieee.org/document/8765432

[7] Gupta, A., & Das, S. K. (2019). IoT-Enabled Smart Building Management. *IEEE Sensors Journal, 19*(12), 4567–4578. Available from: https://ieeexplore.ieee.org/document/8675309

[8] Kim, Y., & Park, D. (2020). Digital Twin for Property Management. *IEEE Transactions on Industrial Informatics, 16*(3), 1839–1848. Available from: https://ieeexplore.ieee.org/document/8761234

[9] Patel, R. B., Tiwari, S., & Dwivedi, V. K. (2020). AI-Driven Predictive Maintenance for Buildings. *IEEE Transactions on Automation Science and Engineering, 17*(2), 987–998. Available from: https://ieeexplore.ieee.org/document/8901234

[10] Wang, H., Zhang, L., & Wang, Q. (2020). Blockchain-Based Land Registry System. *IEEE Transactions on Services Computing, 13*(4), 684–696. Available from: https://ieeexplore.ieee.org/document/8765431

[11] Islam, S. M. R., Rashid, M. M., & Hossain, S. (2019). Smart City Property Management Framework. *IEEE Internet of Things Journal, 6*(5), 7890–7902. Available from: https://ieeexplore.ieee.org/document/8675308

[12] Chen, L., & Yang, X. (2019). Energy Efficient Building Management System. *IEEE Transactions on Sustainable Computing, 4*(3), 234–245. Available from: https://ieeexplore.ieee.org/document/8456789

[13] Lee, J., Kim, K., & Park, S. (2019). ARBased Property Maintenance System. *IEEE Transactions on Visualization and Computer Graphics, 25*(6), 2345–2356. Available from: https://ieeexplore.ieee.org/document/8675310

[14] Khan, M. N., Rehman, S. U., & Salah, K. (2022). Federated Learning for Smart Property Management. *IEEE Transactions on Industrial Informatics, 18*(1), 645–656. Available from: https://ieeexplore.ieee.org/document/9456789

[15] Sharma, P., & Kumar, R. (2021). DL-Based Fault Detection in Buildings. *IEEE Sensors Journal, 21*(4), 4567–4578. Available from: https://ieeexplore.ieee.org/document/9234567

72 A portable IoT system for smart energy management via human detection

R. Jaikumar[1,a], S. Akila[2,b], S. Akshaya[2], and S. Jeevitha[2]

[1]Associate Professor, Department of Electronics and Communication Engineering, KPR Institute of Engineering and Technology, Coimbatore, India

[2]UG Student, Department of Electronics and Communication Engineering, KPR Institute of Engineering and Technology, Coimbatore, India

Abstract: Energy conservation is becoming a growing necessity in smart spaces to prevent wastage of power and improve efficiency. In this work, an IoT–enabled portable energy-saving system is presented that automates appliances using ESP32-CAM-based human presence detection. The system ensures that the appliance is operated only when a human enters a particular area, e.g., a cabin, to reduce unnecessary power consumption. The system employs ESP32-CAM, in conjunction with performing real-time human detection and recognition. When a human is detected, ESP32-CAM transmits to the main ESP32 module, which runs the particular cabin relay to switch the fan ON or OFF accordingly. This system achieves better accuracy and reliability in human presence detection. The proposed system is effective in reducing power wastage in places like cabins, offices, and smart homes by enabling fans to be functional only when necessary. The paper discusses the design, implementation, and advantages of utilizing ESP32–CAM and IoT-based automation for smart energy management.

Keywords: IoT, ESP32-CAM, human presence detection, energy conservation, Wi-Fi communication, relay control, energy efficiency

1. Introduction

Energy conservation has been a challenge in the current world, especially in smart environments such as offices, homes, and industries. With the world increasingly relying on electrical appliances, power wastage due to human negligence remains a significant challenge. Much energy is wasted when appliances such as fans, lights, and air conditioners are left turned on even in unoccupied rooms. To address this challenge, a smart and automated power management system that saves power efficiently is necessary. According to [1], the Internet of Things is an interconnected system that allows electronic devices to communicate and exchange data through network connectivity. The Internet of Things (IoT) has been a prospective remedy to enable smart automation through integrating real-time monitoring, wireless connectivity to minimize energy wastage.

Appliances and devices are networked through the IoT home hardware technologies of sensors and actuators for communication and automation, offering localized or remote home control [2], thereby making the home intelligent by offering services that involve little human input or interaction. As an example, through the Internet, one could control a home from any location, the control mechanism being delivered through dedicated software or a mobile application running on a laptop, tablet, PC, or smartphone [3]. Traditional motion-based presence detection systems, such as Passive Infrared sensors, have been widely used for appliance automation. These sensors, however, rely on movement detection only and often lead to false activations due to non-human movement (e.g., moving objects, air disturbance) or false deactivations when a person is motionless. To go beyond this limitation, [4] a more reliable and intelligent solution is needed to provide accurate human presence detection. Human recognition technology offers a high-accuracy solution by verifying the true presence of a human before appliance activation.

This paper presents an IoT-based portable energy-saving system with ESP32-CAM human recognition-based automatic appliance activation. The suggested system is designed to be versatile and compatible with a wide range of various smart environments, including offices, cabins, smart homes, and conference rooms. Through the utilization of the video frame of ESP32 cam, Experimental outcomes validate that the system is effective in removing redundant power usage, and therefore, it has the potential to be an effective solution for smart and sustainable energy management.

The objective of the work is as follows:

1. To develop a module with ESP32 CAM connected to the adapter to capture the human presence.

[a]jaikumarer@gmail.com, [b]akilass925@gmail.com

DOI: 10.1201/9781003724988-72

2. To implement Wi Fi communication to the ESP32 in the switch box to trigger the relay.
3. Make the fan ON/OFF based on the frame difference in the ESP32 CAM.

2. Related Works

Smart energy conservation has been one of the major research areas in the last few years, and many studies have put forward several IoT–based power optimization methods. Traditional energy conservation systems typically depend on manual control of electrical devices, leading to significant power losses due to human negligence. To mitigate this drawback, researchers have automated systems based on sensor-based, IoT communication, and intelligent decision-making algorithms for efficient management of energy consumption.

In "AI-Based Face Recognition System for Energy-Efficient Smart Buildings," Hassan, Alam, and Chowdhury [5], talk about how artificial intelligence, specifically face recognition, can improve energy efficiency in intelligent buildings. The purpose of this AI-based face recognition technology is to detect human presence in different rooms. Electric items like fans, air conditioners, and lights are controlled by the intelligent system, which turns them on or off based on occupancy once an authorized person has been identified. By preventing gadgets from running needlessly, the strategy saves electricity. The system is consistent with contemporary, environmentally friendly building management because it prioritizes both security and energy conservation.

Jayashree, C.S., Shivanandan, N.M., Sreelekshmi, Pradum Singh. "ESP32-CAM Motion Detector with Photo Capture Using PIR Sensor." [6]. The system presented in this paper involves the use of a motion detection system based on an ESP32-CAM module with a PIR sensor. The PIR sensor senses motion by picking up infrared radiation given off by a moving body, especially a human. Upon detection, the ESP32-CAM takes a snapshot of the motion and saves it locally or sends it to a remote server. The system can be set up so that it sends alert messages or notifications by email or cloud-based services when it detects motion. The paper illustrates how the system can be employed for security purposes, including intruder detection, automated monitoring, and smart homes.

J. Prasad, K.G. Menaga, C. Manikanda Prasanna, and K. Jithesh. "Priority Based Prepaid Energy Meter Using IoT."[7]. The suggested system presents a Priority-Based Prepaid Energy Meter based on IoT for effective energy management. It makes it possible to have real-time monitoring and control over electricity usage through a smartphone application. It allows consumers to prepay for electricity as well as prioritize essential appliances. IoT-based integration facilitates smooth integration with the utility companies for automatic updating.

Kumar, R., & Singh, M. "IoT-Based Smart Surveillance System Using ESP32-CAM." [8]. The system discussed in this paper introduces a smart surveillance system based on the use of the ESP32-CAM module with Internet of Things (IoT) technology. It is a system that senses unauthorized people by taking pictures using the ESP32-CAM, a miniature camera module with the ESP32-S chip. In the case of an unauthorized individual, the system sends notifications to enrolled users through a GSM module, as well as triggers buzzer alerts on the property.

3. Methodology

The IoT-based energy-saving system proposed here is controlled automatically with the use of ESP32-CAM for detecting people and Wi-Fi-based device communication. The approach comprises a few major steps to have an optimal, efficient, and precise control mechanism to save energy (Figure 72.1).

3.1. Energy saving

1. Total Power Consumption Without Automation:

$$E_{Manual} = P * T_{Manual} \tag{1}$$

Where:
Emanuel = energy consumed in traditional fan operation (W h)
P = Power rating of the fan(W)
T_{manual} = Duration of manual operation(h)

2. Optimized Power Consumption With Automated Control:

$$E_{auto} = P * T_{auto} \tag{2}$$

Where:
E_{auto} = Energy Consumed using the IoT–based System (Wh)

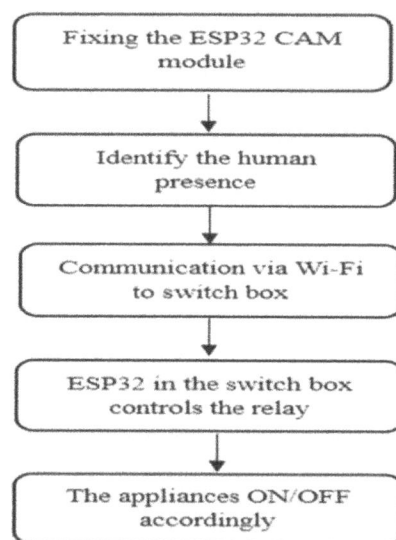

Figure 72.1. Workflow of proposed method.

Source: Author.

T_{auto} = Reduced fan operation time due to automation (h)
Energy Saving Percentage Calculation:

$$S = \frac{(Emanual - Eauto)}{Emanual} \times 100 \qquad (3)$$

3.2. Human detection

The system utilizes ESP32-CAM for real-time human presence detection to enable effective control of energy in closed spaces (Figure 72.2). ESP32-CAM captures images and examines them through onboard AI functionality to determine the presence of a human. Unlike traditional motion-based detection solutions, the approach provides better accuracy through the detection of human presence and discrimination against other movable objects. On detection of a human, the processed data is transmitted to the main ESP32 module through Wi-Fi communication to provide wireless and smooth connectivity. The use of an edge-based detection system minimizes the use of the cloud and therefore reduces latency and provides rapid response times.

3.3. Signal processing through Wi-Fi

The ESP32-CAM detects the presence of humans and wirelessly transmits the data to the main ESP32 module via Wi-Fi communication. Physical cabling is avoided to make the installation easier and the scalability of the system greater. The use of communication via Wi-Fi ensures low latency in the data transfer, and the action on the fan is decided in real-time. The use of protocols such as HTTP minimizes packet loss and ensures effective communication between

the modules. Wireless communication, in contrast to the traditional wired setup, enhances the flexibility and allows remote monitoring of the energy consumption. The data sent via Wi-Fi includes the identification parameters and the control signal that helps the main ESP32 identify the proper fan operation.

3.4. Relay activation

The relay module in the system is an electronic switch for controlling the power supply to the fan. The ESP32 main module senses the signal for human presence and activates the relay to make or break the electrical connection. The relay in the system is programmed in such a way that it is energized when needed, and wastage of energy through unnecessary switching is prevented. The relay is switched off additionally if no human presence is found within a predefined time through a predefined timeout mechanism. Hence, the fan will not be operating continuously due to a temporary signal disturbance.

4. Results and Discussions

The following Table 72.1 show the different power consumption by the fan according to the presence of humans in the cabin 1, cabin 2 cabin 3. The energy usage for the fan is calculated throughout the day, and the analysis is made for a day, to identify the energy saved due to the automation made in the cabin according to the human presence and absence. The graph is plotted according to the analysis data from the table.

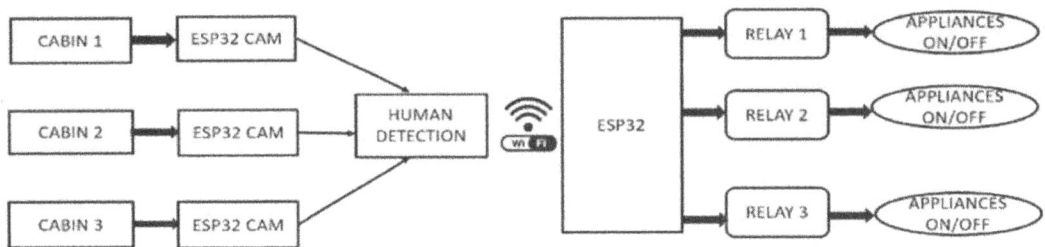

Figure 72.2. Block diagram of the proposed system.
Source: Author.

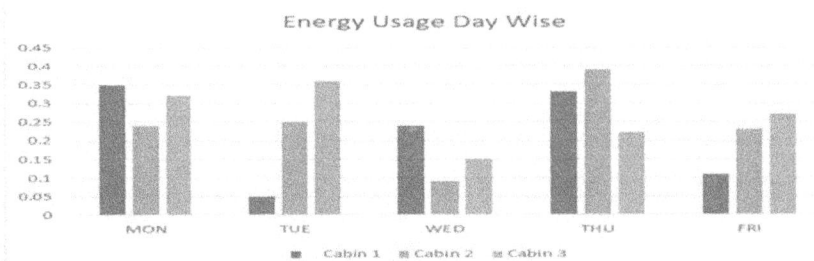

Figure 72.3. Energy usage day wise in (kWh).
Source: Author.

Table 72.1. Energy usage day-wise

Days	Energy used per day (kWh)		
	Cabin 1	*Cabin 2*	*Cabin 3*
MON	0.35	0.24	0.32
TUE	0.05	0.25	0.36
WED	0.24	0.09	0.15
THU	0.33	0.39	0.22
FRI	0.11	0.23	0.27

Source: Author.

The Figure 72.3 illustrates energy usage across three cabins (Cabin 1, Cabin 2, and Cabin 3) for five weekdays (Monday to Friday). The coloured bars represent each cabin's consumption for a day. Cabin 1 illustrates high variation, with Thursday and Monday showing high usage and Tuesday and Friday showing lesser usage. Cabin 2 illustrates the highest usage on Thursday and comparatively constant usage on other days. Cabin 3 consistently shows a moderate energy usage, with the highest on Tuesday. The chart illustrates variation in energy usage levels among the three cabins throughout the weekdays.

5. Conclusions

The project successfully gives the application of an IoT-enabled energy-saving system utilizing ESP32-CAM for detecting human presence via human recognition. The system recognizes humans inside a cabin and sends the signal via Wi-Fi to the main ESP32 to drive a relay to turn the fan on or off accordingly. This eliminates the requirement of additional motion-based detection methods and also ensures that the fan operates only if a person is present, hence saving excess energy consumption.

The wireless communication between ESP32 modules enables seamless and efficient control without utilizing complex wiring and other hardware devices. The technique is particularly suitable for environments like office cabins, smart homes, or individual workstations where the devices need to be automated based on actual human presence. The project demonstrates a practical application of image processing using ESP32 CAM frame for real-time automation to improve energy efficiency as well. During the development,

some issues that were encountered were the optimization of human detection, stable Wi-Fi communication, and minimizing the response time to trigger the fan. The ESP32-CAM's computational limitations were addressed by implementing memory-efficient image processing techniques to facilitate smooth and continuous operation. In addition, the relay control system was adjusted to get a quick response upon detection of a human.

References

[1] Mehta, J., Raj, P., & Kaur, B. (2012). IoT-Based Human Face Detection and Recognition System for Smart Home Automation. *IEEE Xplore*, 2022 Camilus, K. Santle, and V. K. Govindan. "A review on graph-based segmentation." International Journal of Image, Graphics and Signal Processing 4, no. 5.

[2] Kasiselvanathan, M., Sekar, G., Prasad, J., Lakshminarayanan, S., & Sharanya, C. (2023, March). An IoT based agricultural management approach using machine learning. In *2023 International Conference on Innovative Data Communication Technologies and Application (ICIDCA)* (pp. 61–65). IEEE.

[3] Yalli, J. S., Hasan, M. H., & Badawi, A. A. (2024). Internet of Things (IoT): origins, embedded technologies, smart applications, and its growth in the last decade. *IEEE Access, 12*, 91357–91382.

[4] Prasad, J., Menaga, K. G., Prasanna, C. M., & Jithesh, K. (2022, March). Priority Based Prepaid Energy Meter Using IoT. In *2022 8th International Conference on Advanced Computing and Communication Systems (ICACCS)* (Vol. 1, pp. 1061–1064). IEEE.

[5] Hassan, M., Alam, R., & Chowdhury, T. (2022). AI-Based Face Recognition System for Energy-Efficient Smart Buildings. *IEEE Transactions on Industrial Electronics*.

[6] Jayashree, C. S., Shivanandan, N. M., Sreelekshmi, C., & Pradum Singh. (2022). ESP32-CAM Motion Detector with Photo Capture Using PIR Sensor. *International Journal of Advanced Research and Innovative Ideas in Education*, 8(4), 1526–1531.

[7] Kumar, R., & Singh, M. (2023). IoT-Based Smart Surveillance System Using ESP32-CAM. *2023 International Conference on Electronics and Sustainable Communication Systems (ICESC)*, pp. 45–50.

[8] Dinakarasu, S., Baskar, M., Balaji, C., & Gawtham, M. (2022). Real-Time Face Detecting Unauthorized Human Movement Using ESP32-CAM Module. *International Research Journal of Engineering and Technology*, 9(6), 982–986.

73   AI enabled Chatbot for chemical elements and their properties

Garima Chandel[1,a], Jayanth Kumar Gupta[2], Amit Kumar Gupta[2], Gauri Katiyar[3], Ayushman Mishra[2], and Sateesh Yadav[2]

[1]Department of ECE, Chandigarh University, Mohali, India
[2]Department of Chemical Engineering, Chandigarh University, Mohali, India
[3]Department of EEE, Galgotias College of Engineering and Technology, Gr. Noida, India

Abstract: Chatbots driven by artificial intelligence (AI) have come up as valuable tools in various science fields, including chemistry and mathematics. This paper explores the application of chatbots in guiding with information, re-collect, learning, and analyzing chemical elements. Chatbots can provide instant access to element properties, periodic table trends, and real-time explanations of chemical behaviours, making them useful for students, educators, and researchers. Additionally, AI-driven chatbots can facilitate chemical calculations, predict reactions, and suggest element substitutions in experimental setups. By leveraging natural language processing (NLP), these chatbots refine accessibility and improve engagement, ultimately improving the efficiency of chemical education. Merging chatbots into science learning and research enhances accessibility and engagement by providing instant, interactive assistance. This work propose the use of AI-powered chatbots in delivering real-time information about periodic table elements, including atomic number, electron configuration, chemical properties, and trends. The proposed chatbot was developed using well known platform Botpress which is a convenient, customizable and skilled platform to create chatbots and to publish and it gave 87.5% accuracy. Chatbots can support students, educators, and researchers by simplifying complex concepts, assisting with element comparisons, and answering queries efficiently so finally cmparison of proposed chatbot with other available work has been carried out.

Keywords: Natural language processing (NLP), education, elements, AI based Chatbot, Botpress

1. Introduction

Education is the fundamental base for human beings to achieve their goals. Everyone needs education either rich or poor. Most parents in India won't be able to give a better education to their children. That too for girls in rural areas of India. Education is mandatory for everyone, the Government of India providing free education to children with good intentions. To improve the education system of India many policies are implemented by the government. Providing a wide variety of features to the students for improving their skills [1].

Instead of traditional methods of learning, new methods of teaching and learning were introduced in education like digital classrooms, E-Learning platforms, AI & personalized learning, coding, digital assessments, AR/VR learning. These improved adaptability, diversity, and interaction of the scholars. The context was simplified and engaging.

After industrialization, the impact of technology led to evolution across all aspects of human life. Machines were replaced instead of manual labour in many industries which increased efficiency and production speed. Enabled in increasing productivity and reducing cost of product.

Modern infrastructure like roads, bridges, sewage systems, water supply, electricity grids were developed to stand up for growing cities. Globalization boosted after the digital revolution and faster communication. Artificial Intelligence and Machine Learning (AI & ML) are absolutely major trendsetters across all industries today.

The rapid progression of Artificial Intelligence (AI) is reshaping various things like methods of study and how to deal with any problem and networks transforming daily operations through automation. Although AI mirrors human-like responses, it is confined to calculations and lacks the intricacies of human intelligence. Chatbots were introduced in the 20th century, to explore the possibility of computer based human interaction and now enabled support for the users. In education chatbots are used to interact with students. Without chatbots, students may struggle to find immediate answers to their questions, especially outside school hours. This delay can lead to frustration, loss of motivation, and difficulty in understanding complex topics. Moreover, the chatbot promotes self-paced learning, allowing students to study anytime, anywhere, without relying solely on textbooks or teacher availability. As education continues to evolve with

[a]chandelgarima5@gmail.com

DOI: 10.1201/9781003724988-73

technology, tools like this chatbot can bridge learning gaps and empower students with knowledge at their fingertips [2].

Chatbot used in education simulation games, training students on software. A help desk chatbot that answers students' general or technical questions. It has been found that AI and Deep Learning have helped improve chatbots, making them better than traditional teaching methods [3]. The use of AI chatbots improves the administrative aspect of institution learning and they meet the needs of the students. Hence it saves the time of both students and teachers [4]. The Figure 73.1 shows the general block diagram of chatbot.

Intelligent chatbot tool is a web-based tutoring system, which is used to assist high school students for learning general knowledge subjects. It is available 24-hours for students at schools and public libraries. This bot is available in web browsers and applications. This chatbot is generated by comparing different chatbots at a time and extracting all optimistic things from different chatbots and make it into a new featured one [5].

The limitation in some chatbots is only giving a local database. The approach should be not only concentrated on the local database but also on web data bases to make a scalable and interactive chatbot. In case of AI based chatbot, a user inputs a question and if the answer is not available on the knowledge given to it then this chatbot automatically abstracts the data from outside the database [6].

SIT's Chern Quest is an adaptive online chemistry course designed to help students with different academic backgrounds bridge knowledge gaps before starting their undergraduate journey in chemical engineering, pharmaceutical engineering, or food technology [7]. Jill Watson is an AI-powered teaching assistant developed at Georgia Tech. Initially deployed in an online AI course, it assists students by answering frequently asked questions related to course logistics, assignments, and concepts. Built using IBM Watson, the chatbot processes natural language queries and provides accurate responses [8].

STEMbot, STEM means (Science, Technology, Engineering, and Mathematics) in which students can be clarified there by STEMBOT, which was developed by University of Leeds. It is a replacement for applications in mobile phones. It also uses ML and NLP to analyze the question and give useful answers to the learners, STEMbot personalized interactions to cater to individual learning needs. The chatbot has significantly improved student engagement and retention in STEM subjects, making learning more interactive and accessible [9].

Appland-bot is a very different and a new style of providing the database on environment, language development, application, server, programming interface. This chatbot is for the fresher queries regarding their studies due modern education conditions and opportunities available for career after post pandemic [10].

SERMO is a chat bot application created for intelligent or balanced behaviour therapy to support people who are mentally ill, having irregular emotions, thoughts and feelings. As part of therapy, it asks every day about the mental health of the person, analyzes the issue and prescribes the tips to the user like activities, meditation and exercises [11].

After study of various research papers and chatbots, most chatbots focus on different and serious problems faced by the users, now with these chatbots users are able to use and get useful information or the solution of the recording issues. They were made for different purposes in different fields. So this work is proposed for development of AI enabled chatbot for providing information based on chemical elements and their properties.

The purpose of the proposed chatbot is to build the simple concepts of the chemistry and elements for those who were unable to memorize the concepts. Additionally we enhanced many things about the chatbots like accuracy, designing etc. and concluded to use Botpress as a platform.

2. Methodology

Primarily, this chatbot was made for the students, educators, science enthusiasts on the basis of knowledge of chemistry, elements etc. Chatbots reduce the paperwork, time saving, cost saving, increase efficiency, and improve the value of customers. Figure 73.2 shows design workflow of proposed model. This work is focusing on different problems faced by the scholars while studying in chemistry. Once the chatbot is developed, it undergoes thorough testing to assess its functionality, performance, and user experience. After deployment on the desired platforms, continuous monitoring and updates are essential to maintain its effectiveness, improve accuracy, and adapt to evolving user interactions.

2.1. Objective: define your goal

The primary objective of this study is to design and develop an intelligent chatbot using Botpress that can provide accurate, reliable, and easily understandable information about

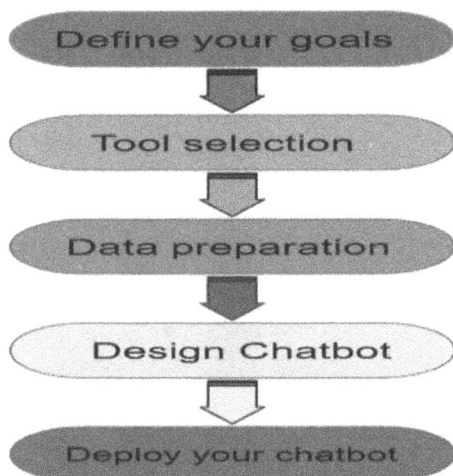

Figure 73.1. General block diagram of chatbot designing.

Source: Author.

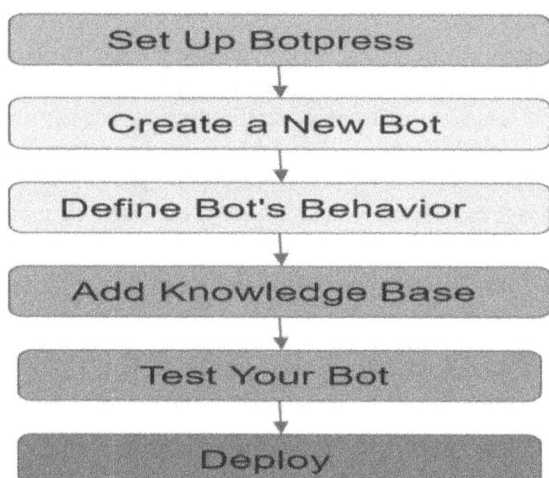

Figure 73.2. Chatbot design workflow of proposed method.
Source: Author.

chemical elements and their properties. Chemistry plays an important role in daily life. So to keep the information about the elements, their history, evolution, discovery and properties, this chatbot targets to assist the students, teachers, science followers by giving the answers to their queries.

2.2. Tool selection: Botpress

From the sources we have a variety of platforms like **Botpress**, Chatling, Activechat, Rasa, Sendpulse etc., platforms are available. Botpress was chosen as the platform for developing the chatbot due to its intuitive and user-friendly interface, which enables the creation of AI-powered conversational agents without the need for extensive programming skills. Botpress is highly customizable, flexible, it is a better choice for choosing as a platform. Botpress also supports natural language understanding and automatic objective identification, making it well-suited for educational applications where accurate and context-aware responses are essential [12].

2.3. Data preparation: data collection

The scope of chemistry is like the roots of this universe, which is undefinable. Chemistry there are a lot of things to remember. Hence Chemistry had a significant role in this world. The thing we breathe (oxygen, nitrogen); the thing we sense; the food we eat (carbon, hydrogen, calcium); the thing we make; the materials we use (plastic, wood); everything made up of matter. So chemical elements are fundamental building blocks of matter. Which is the study of the composition, structure, properties, and reactions of matter. This will be a knowledge based chatbot. The data which was collected from the sources will be converted into answers for the queries of the user/student. The knowledge of this chatbot is atomic number, atomic weight, electron configuration,

group/period, physical and chemical properties, uses, discovery details, reactions etc.

2.4. Design Chatbot in Botpress

Botpress is the most convenient platform to make a chatbot. Chatbot will be knowledge based. It only gives the responses related to the elements and their properties. Each block is a node with a message to the user; conditions or triggers; transitions to other nodes. Go to the "Intents" tab, add training phrases. Link intends to flow actions to further add knowledge base information. Test Your Bot by using the Emulator on the right panel. Try different questions to see how your bot responds. After checking the accuracy and performance, deploy the chatbot. Deploying a chatbot ensures that users can interact with it and access its functionalities. Figure 73.3 shows the workflow of developed chatbot TARA for chemical properties.

3. Result and Discussions

The introduction of an AI-powered chatbot using Botpress significantly improves the accessibility and interactivity of chemicals information for pupils. Based on preliminary testing, the chatbot responded to queries about chemical elements and their properties with an accuracy rate of 87.5%. This excellent accuracy suggests that the chatbot can function as a dependable digital assistant for both students and instructors, eliminating reliance on ongoing teacher availability. Furthermore, its constrained domain promotes concentrated learning, allowing pupils to stay on track and absorb fundamental topics more efficiently. The use of natural language

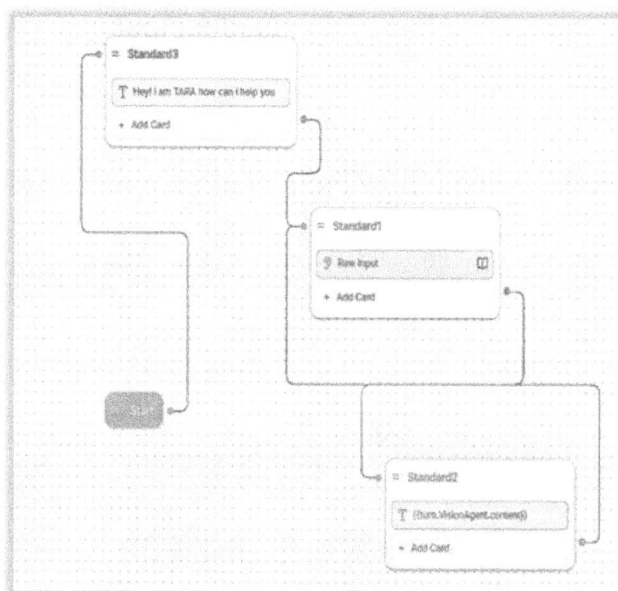

Figure 73.3. Workflow of proposed chatbot design.
Source: Author.

processing allows users to participate in daily language, making the learning process more intuitive and interesting. This study suggests that chatbots and other artificial intelligence-based educational technologies could radically change conventional learning approaches and greatly enhance student performance in science education. This chatbot interacts with the user politely. This Chatbot is named "TARA". According to Indian etymology TARA is referred as "STAR". Stars have a significant role in this universe. As they play a crucial role in giant nuclear fusion reactions, converting hydrogen into helium and other heavier elements reactions.

This chatbot "TARA" will start with introducing itself. For asking any query related to only chemical elements or specific reactions, then the following steps take place. When a user asks a query to a chatbot, the input is first processed by Botpress's Natural Language Understanding (NLU) engine. The chatbot uses intent acknowledgment and keyword matching to understand what the user is asking. Then it searches the connected knowledge base. Based on the matching, the chatbot get back with the most relevant answer and responds instantly. If the query is not clearly understood or does not match an entry in the knowledge base, the chatbot generates a fallback flow, asking the user to rephrase the query related topic. All interactions are controlled by Botpress's pre-built conversational flows, which guarantee that the exchange is smooth, organized, and beneficial. Figure 73.4 is showing responses given by TARA, which are appropriate answers to user queries.

In Table 73.1 is showing comparison of proposed chatbot with the existing ones. Various parameters for effective comparison were analyzed, in which parameters are included such as methods, specifications, accuracy, which helped us to make chatbot simple, better and accurate. To calculate the accuracy of chatbot based on students' reviews and the number of correct answers given to user's questions, the following steps had been followed: Twenty participants posed two chemical element questions each to the chatbot leading to forty questions being asked and tested for correctness. Each user provided a response mark for each answer to indicate correctness. To calculate accuracy the chatbot received the

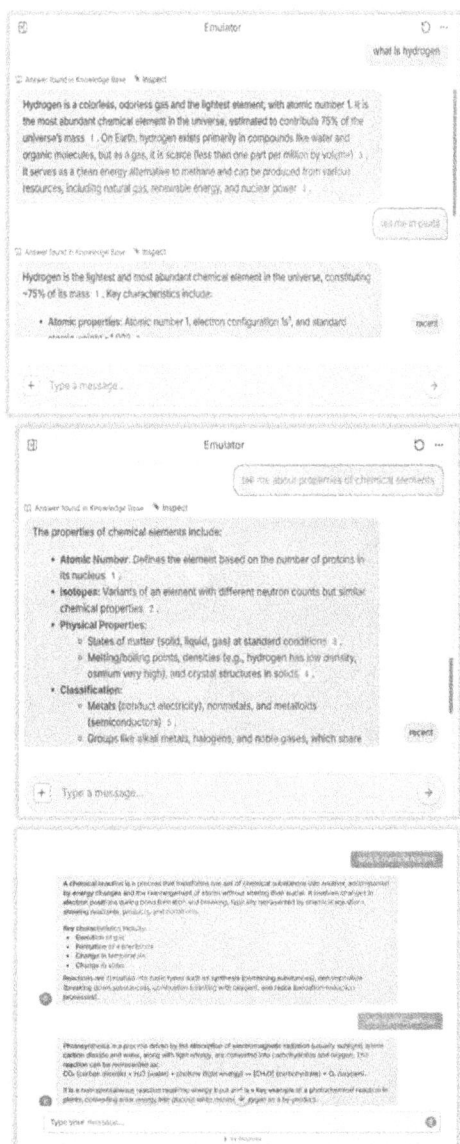

Figure 73.4. Responses given by TARA, which are appropriate answers to user queries.

Source: Author.

Table 73.1. Comparison table for the state of the art

Ref	Year	Analysis Method	Key Point	Acc (%)
[6]	2018	AIML, NLP	Web database	96
[7]	2021	NLP, AI	Virtual tutor	87
[9]	2023	Instant Messaging, bot, cloud computing	STEM-bot application	96.1
[10]	2024	Information System, Computer-Mediated Communicatio n, Interactivity	Develop Authentic Systems for Informing Applicants in Institutions of Higher Education	60–80
[11]	2024	AI and AI chatbot platform	Educational recommendat ions, Higher education	86.15
[12]	2021	Conversational user interface, NLP	Mental Health Chatbot	98.97
This Work		Botpress and NLP	Specifically for Chemical Elements and their Properties	87.5

Source: Author.

total number of correct responses followed by the formula: The accuracy percentage) was calculated using equation (1)

$$\text{Accuracy}(\%) = \frac{\text{No. of correct answers}}{\text{Total no.of questions asked}} \times 100 \qquad (1)$$

The evaluated accuracy of 87.5% was calculated. This accuracy percentage indicated that the chatbot performed well.

4. Conclusion

In this project, a chatbot named 'TARA' was successfully developed for the purpose of guiding science enthusiasts. This is made based on the knowledge of Chemical elements and their properties. This chatbot was built by using an AI-platform named Botpress. In which no coding was required to create. Natural language processing was used in it. The tool, Botpress, is customizable and user-friendly. We used various sources as reference to shape it. We have taken various reviews from students and educators to make it more informative and interactive. This chatbot enables contextual understanding. This chatbot helps by giving simple answers to the queries asked by the user. After testing this chatbot we got accuracy 87.5%. Users interact with the chatbot for the queries related to elements and their properties. It is simple to use, to learn, to analyze. The chatbot is related to basic elements, data and reactions. Currently the chatbot "TARA" is based on knowledge of chemical elements. Regarding future development, we will add specific things to the chatbot, which will be the new face of our chatbot. In future improvements can be done by giving the knowledge of organic compounds, advanced Chemistry Concepts, voice interaction, multi-language support, visual integration, interactive games, polls and quizzes.

References

[1] Mahroof, A., Gamage, V., Rajendran, K., Rajkumar, S., Rajapaksha, S., & Wijendra, D. (2020, December). An AI based chatbot to self-learn and self-assess performance in ordinary level chemistry. In *2020 2nd International conference on advancements in computing (ICAC)* (Vol. 1, pp. 216–221). IEEE.

[2] Alneyadi, S., & Wardat, Y. (2024). Integrating ChatGPT in grade 12 quantum theory education: An exploratory study at Emirate school (UAE). *intelligence*, 2(4).

[3] Tipe-Palomino, D., & Auccahuasi, W. (2024, December). Development of Helpdesk Chatbot for Incident Classification and Resolution using NPL and Deep Learning. In *2024 3rd International Conference on Automation, Computing and Renewable Systems (ICACRS)* (pp. 785–791). IEEE.

[4] Rehman, N. A., & Hussain, S. M. (2024, November). Empowering Education with AI: The Rise of Chatbots in Educational Institutions. In *2024 2nd International Conference on Computing and Data Analytics (ICCDA)* (pp. 1–5). IEEE.

[5] Dutta, D. (2017). Developing an Intelligent Chat-bot Tool to assist high school students for learning general knowledge subjects. *Georgia Institute of Technology*, 13.

[6] Hiremath, G., Hajare, A., Bhosale, P., Nanaware, R., & Wagh, K. S. (2018). Chatbot for education system. *International Journal of Advance Research, Ideas and Innovations in Technology*, 4(3), 37–43.

[7] Atmosukarto, I., Sin, C. W., Iyer, P., Tong, N. H., & Yu, K. W. P. (2021, December). Enhancing adaptive online chemistry course with AI-chatbot. In *2021 IEEE international conference on engineering, technology & education (TALE)* (pp. 838–843). IEEE.

[8] Goel, A. (2020). AI-powered learning: making education accessible, affordable, and achievable. *arXiv preprint arXiv:2006.01908*.

[9] Cervera, E., & del Pobil, A. P. (2023, September). STEM-Bots: Computing Resources for Everyone. In *2023 IEEE AFRICON* (pp. 1–3). IEEE.

[10] Lynnyk, Y., Krestyanpol, L., & Rozvod, E. (2024). Development of a natural language chatbot interface for website users. *European Journal of Enterprise Technologies*, 1(2 (127)).

[11] Denecke, K., Vaaheesan, S., & Arulnathan, A. (2020). A mental health chatbot for regulating emotions (SERMO)-concept and usability test. *IEEE Transactions on Emerging Topics in Computing*, 9(3), 1170–1182.

[12] Kingchang, T., Chatwattana, P., & Wannapiroon, P. (2024). Artificial intelligence chatbot platform: AI chatbot platform for educational recommendations in higher education. *International Journal of Information and Education Technology*, 14(1), 34–41.

74 IoT based failure event response and UAV recovery system for civilian applications

Garima Chandel[1,a], Blessing Tafadzwa Taderera[2], Isaac Venkat Rao[2], James Gervas[2], Mary Frank Masasi[2], and Ashish Sharma[3]

[1]Department of ECE Chandigarh University Mohali, India
[2]Department of Aerospace Chandigarh University Mohali, India
[3]Department of Electrical Engineering, Chandigarh University Mohali, India

Abstract: The demand for civilian Unmanned Aerial Vehicles (UAV) has of recent been growing at an unprecedented rate. This study proposes an electronic system for response to UAV failure events, integrated with the use of IoT which can help to minimize losses due to critical situations like bad weather or sudden unforeseen situations, the drone may start to fall or lose connection with the owner/ operator. The system uses a DPS310 barometric pressure sensor to get barometric pressure readings which are converted to altitude and used to calculate the rate of descent. Based on which if the UAV is falling then initiates a procedure which includes activating automatic landing or activating a special motor to prevent the UAV hitting the ground with excessive velocity. It also incorporates a rain sensor to detect precipitation and which activates automatic landing. Simulation results show activation times of about 0.6s to activate emergency landing after rain detection and 0.5s after falling detection. They also show activation time of about 3.5s from when emergency landing is activated to when emergency motor is activated after emergency landing failure. This proposed work provides information on how to make such a system and instructions or recommendations on how to implement it.

Keywords: Fuzzy logic controllers, pulse-width modulation, proportional-integral-derivatives

1. Introduction

These days UAVs are being used for many purposes, like security, networking, transport management etc. [1], which means that smart UAVs are the next big technology in UAV technology. Several systems have been proposed to deal with the issue of drone recovery, but many of them seem to focus mainly on preventing the drone from actually falling, and not many focus on what to do if the fall is inevitable or happens. The traditional methods used for detecting drone failures utilize mathematical methods to analyze their safety and since these often focus on specific components, they may not always detect failures of other system components [2].

Also, the capacity limitation of UAV's energy storage system is a crucial technical challenge for UAV applications [3]. Current battery technologies are limited [4] and so to increase the capacity of a UAV's battery may mean increasing its weight as well, which is generally undesirable in any flight device. It is therefore important to reduce the power usage of the UAV, to increase the time span during which it can still communicate information to the operator or be reactivated. UAVs have emerged as a promising technology to improve mobile network functionality [5]. However, for applications in communication for instance, in which a lot of data communication and storage may be involved, security is very important and [6], it is important to ensure that the UAV is not compromised by unauthorized parties as some of the data may be confidential. However, despite the advantages, as stated by Wild et al. in [7], contrasting with commercial air transport, remotely piloted aircraft (RPAs) operations are more likely to experience in-flight control loss, events during take-off and cruise and equipment. AL-Madani et al. proposed a system that uses an accelerometer-gyroscope MPU-6050 and a fall detection algorithm based on the Kalman filter for fall detection, which activates a parachute when it detects a fall. [8]. The source reports parachute activation times of less than 0.5s, which are good, but the one major problem of the use of parachutes, as noted by Farajijalal et al. [9] is the time it takes for the full deployment and extension of a parachute. Because of that, the system may not be of much help if the failure occurs close to the ground. Cabahug and Eslamiat [10] proposed also a system that uses data of vibration signals from propellers and gyroscope parameters to detect failure, finds and selects a safe landing zone then lands the UAV. This system would be useful if the failure is caused by system failure. However, in the event that the UAV falls due to bad weather and the vibration of propellers is not affected, this system may not be effective. Also, if the fault is with the propellers themselves, then safe landing may not be possible and so the UAV may just undergo free fall and get badly damaged.

[a]chandelgarima5@gmail.com

DOI: 10.1201/9781003724988-74

The contribution of the proposed work is to design a UAV system that can detect rain through the use of a rain drops detector, to track altitude variation using a DPS310 barometric pressure sensor, to check GPS coordinates via a GPS module and forward to user / operator of the drone or UAV and the implementation of emergency response measures using ESP32 on the basis of sensor information.

2. Methodology

2.1. Materials used

This section provides information of the software used to implement the proposed IoT Based Failure Event Response and UAV Recovery System. Wokwi is an online platform that can be used to simulate the working of circuits that include a number of micro-controllers, including ESP32 required for this system. This online Simulator, with its ability to simulate the interaction between software running on the simulator and the related digital and analogue electronics, provides a way to flexibly implement embedded engineering projects and it provides collaborative simulation of high and low level micro-controller code in the context of mixed mode SPICE (Simulation Program with Integrated Circuit Emphasis) simulations [11].

Ubidots is an open source cloud platform for visualising results of IoT based applications and is, according to Prasanna et al. [12], the most promising platform. A mobile application is also required that is connected to the Ubidots account to view the information sent to Ubidots by the UAV. MIT app inventor is a platform on which we can create applications by dragging and dropping components into a design view and using a visual blocks language to program application behaviour [13].

2.2. Experimental setup

The proposed system is setup as shown in Figure 74.1, it acts as a control system to the UAVs main power supply system, with the ability to switch it off or disconnect the drone from its power supply, by the use of an AND gate or relay switch that takes input from that control system. The system is designed for use in remotely controlled UAVs. It works by initiating a procedure or procedures following the event of an emergency that can be either falling of the drone or rain/snow. It consists of a rain detector and a pressure sensor whose readings can be used to calculate altitude. The emergency motor is a motor that is powerful enough to prevent the drone from falling at a speed that it has high probability of getting destroyed on hitting the ground. It is placed on the bottom part of the UAV in such a way that it provides an upward force and also should be able to provide a minimum force much greater than equation (1) [14]. This is because it has to be able to decelerate the descent of the UAV.

$$T = m * g \tag{1}$$

where T is the thrust, m is the mass of the UAV and g is the acceleration due to gravity, which can be taken as 9.81m/s.

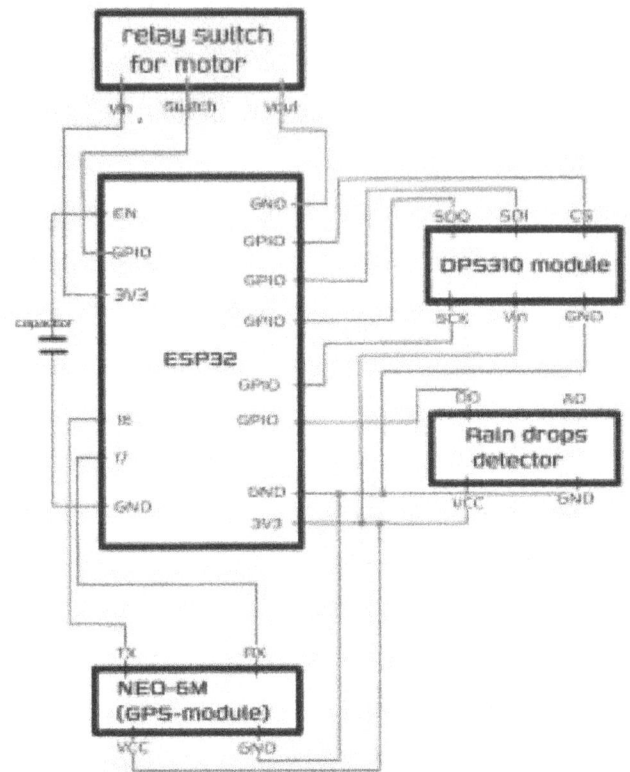

Figure 74.1. Connection diagram of the circuit used in the proposed work showing the relationships between the ESP32 MCU pins and the corresponding pins of its.

Source: Author.

2.3. Algorithm explanation

The system is supposed to power on when the drone also powers on (Figure 74.2). In normal operations, the drone checks if the rate at which the drone is losing altitude is at or above a certain pre-set value that is interpreted as possibly falling. If not then it checks the rain sensor to see if any rain has been detected above the certain values and if not, the system waits an amount of time then repeats the procedure. To detect falling [15], first, pressure readings are taken and used to calculate the altitude using the International Barometric Formula equation (2)

$$h = \left[1 - \left(P/P_0 \right)^{\left(1/5.255 \right)} \right] \tag{2}$$

Where h is the altitude P is the measured atmospheric pressure and P0 the atmospheric pressure at sea level, taken as 1013.25 hPa for this study.

After a specific time interval another reading for pressure is taken and its difference with the preceding reading, considering the time interval between them, is used to calculate the rate of change of altitude using equation (3)

$$dA = (A_1 - A_2) \div dt \tag{3}$$

where dA is the rate of altitude change, A1 is the initial altitude, A2 the final altitude and dt the time taken.

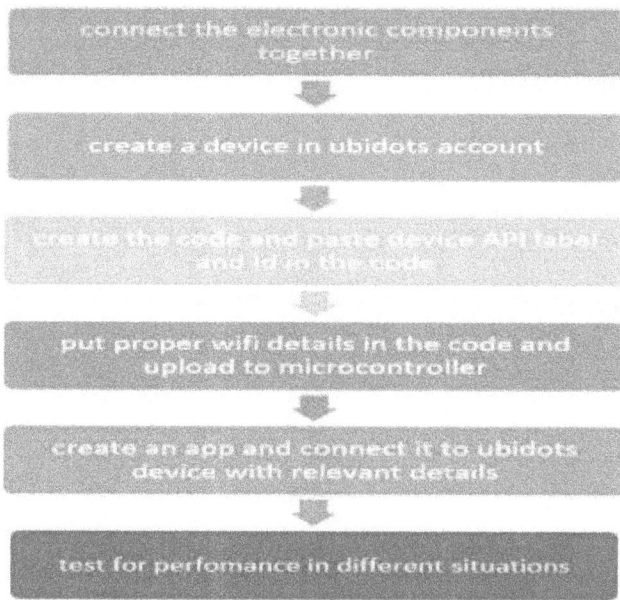

Figure 74.2. Process flow of overall setup.

Source: Author.

This rate is then compared with a preset value. If it exceeds, then a function defining the response procedure to a failure event is called, with a parameter that is interpreted as indicating falling. *Emergency state* is a variable whose value determines whether to run the procedure meant for emergencies or for normal function and can be changed when certain conditions are met, to shift between emergency and normal operations. As for the emergency response, if the function is called due to falling detection, a variable called emergency state, initialized as zero, is changed to 1, then GPS data is collected and sent to Ubidots account. If there is any recorded data, it can then be sent in full or in part if there is a lot of it. This is handled by the main system which will be storing the data, the response system simply initiates that. It however can itself send information recorded from other sensors if connected, which can help to find out the cause of the failure.

The system checks for the functionality of the automatic landing feature by comparing rate of falling before and after the signal to activate it. The components of the response system are enclosed in a shock resistant, waterproof container except those that have to be outside for them to work well. This is to reduce chances of them being damaged and that the system continues to function even if the UAV falls in water. A brushless DC motor has been selected due to the high power to weight ratio, making them preferable for flight operations. Also, the motor is placed on the UAV facing downwards and providing an upwards force when on. After landing the system then collects and uploads GPS data again, and delays for some time, then completes this part of the procedure. The procedure if the function is called due to precipitation detection is similar to that mentioned, except that there is no deletion of data or sending of data online Confirmation from the operator to re power on the UAV is obtained via the Ubidots

account. The system is connected to an online account. As such, if the normal connection with the operator is lost, the system can upload information such as location data online and the user can later access this, as long as a good internet connection can be established.

3. Result and Discussion

The algorithm was tested using an online esp32 simulator from wokwi.com as described in Section 2. The results prove that the system can be implemented and the response times of the algorithm are fast enough to be reliable, with activation times being of about 0.6s to activate emergency landing after rain detection and 0.5s after falling detection and taking about 3.5s from when emergency landing is activated to when emergency motor is activated after emergency landing failure.

The system had to meet the requirements set under the objectives section that is, it had to be able to respond to rain being detected and to rapid decrease of altitude and respond by following the procedures mentioned in the methodology section. The test focused on the states of four pins which determine or influence the behaviour of the system and the pins and what they represent are as in Table 74.1. Pins 16 and 17 are only indicating the state of some subsystems and are not providing input to anything. The GPS module was not represented by any of the components because the algorithm was made such that a randomly selected string is selected from a list of strings declared in the test program to represent

Table 74.1. Micro-controller pins output description

Pin no.	Explanation
0	State of the main system of the response system
4	State of the sensor system of the response system
16	whether automatic landing is activated or deactivated
17	whether emergency landing motor is activated or deactivated

Source: Author.

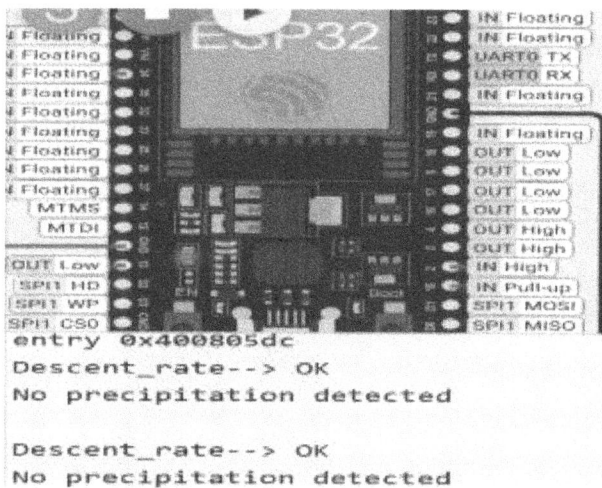

Figure 74.3. States of the pins under normal conditions.

Source: Author.

the GPS data. The image in Figure 74.3 shows that when no rain or falling is detected, the main system and the sensor system are both on. Figure 74.4 showing the state after falling is detected, it can be seen that the input representing the signal for automatic landing (GPIO 16) is high, indicating that automatic landing has been activated. Main and sensor system are also still on. Figure 74.5 represents the state of the system after activating automatic landing but it fails to work, tested by continuous and fast moving of the variable resistor and so quickly varying its input which is processed, and then taken as pressure readings. In this state, the system has now activated the emergency landing motor as pin 17 is high. Figure 74.6 shows that, soon after precipitation is detected, pin 17 is high, representing the signal to begin automatic landing. While Figure 74.7 showing the state after reactivating the main system, it can be seen that after reactivation

following a failure event, As the test results show, a system can be made that is capable of doing the things mentioned in the methodology section of this document. Table 74.1 shows are comparison of systems with similar functions to those of the system proposed in this study. According to the website of the Manufacturer of the Infineon DPS310 module, it has a precision of 0.002 hPa for pressure, which in this work translates to a maximum of about 0.02 m for the range of altitude in which UAVs are expected to fly. This means a small altitude change of about 0.02 m can easily be detected, making the falling detection time very low. For instance, if the fall rate that triggers the falling response is 5 m/s, this can theoretically be detected in 4 microseconds, and with the typical measuring time for standard mode for the Infineon DPS310 module being 27.6 ms according to the manufacture's website, the only main practical limitation of the speed of fall

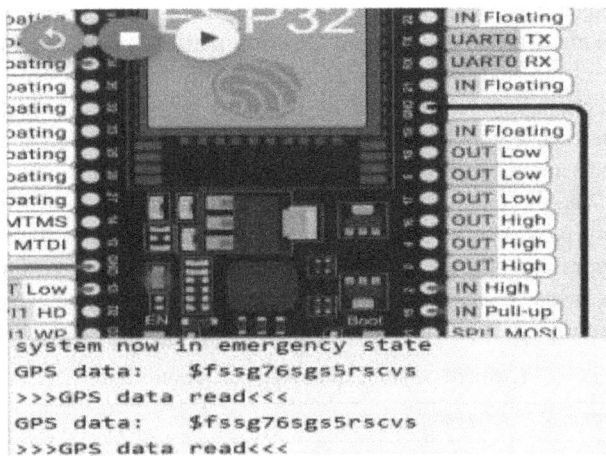

Figure 74.4. States of the pins soon after falling is detected.

Source: Author.

Figure 74.6. States of the pins soon after precipitation is detected.

Source: Author.

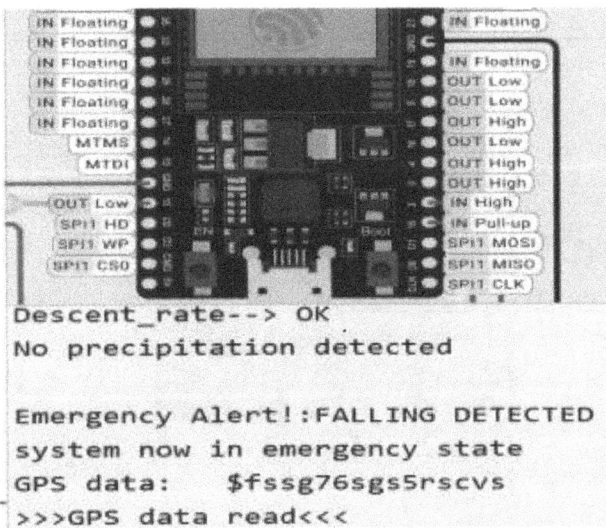

Figure 74.5. States of the pins after automatic landing feature fails.

Source: Author.

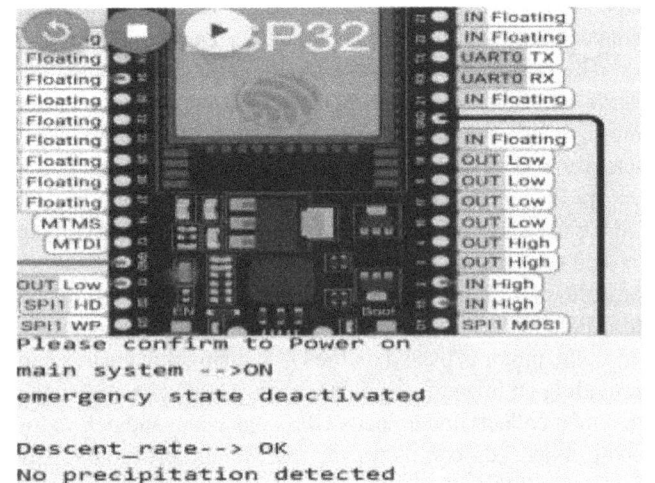

Figure 74.7. States of the pins after the system is reactivated.

Source: Author.

detection is the selected sampling rate for the pressure and the speed of code execution.

The work by AL-Madani et al. (2018) [11] which uses an accelerometer gyroscope MPU-6050 for fall detection and then deploys a parachute seems to be the best of all the considered work. It however has a major limitation of the time taken to fully unfold the parachute, making it very unreliable for faults that may happen close to the ground while this work, in contrast, uses a brushless motor which has an almost immediate response. Another limitation is that once the UAV falls, the work and the other considered previous works, does not provide a means to locate or track it, an issue which is addressed in this work by the use of IoT. Other features of this work that differentiate this work from the considered previous works are its great focus on power efficiency especially to increase chances of UAV recovery after failure, as well as its high focus on trying to prevent unauthorized access to information after UAV failure, adding to the works reliability regarding data security, which is also enhanced by the fact that the ESP32 MCU has security features like supporting WPA3-Personal Wi-Fi encryption method.

4. Conclusion

This study showed that a system can be made that increases chances of recovering UAVs after failure and also tries to prevent the failures. An advantage of this system is that it uses small and light equipment which can easily be added to a drone without increasing its weight much or requiring any major adjustments in drone shape for the average sizes of drones, for them to fit well. The system is connected to an online account and so data can be uploaded and accessed later even if main communication / control system is malfunctioned. The emergency system is separate from the main control system of the drone and so can be specially secured and also have its own power supply independent of the main supply such that if the drone runs out of power, it can still work and it can be specially secured, like the black box of aircraft. Being based on altitude detection, it can find the speed of descent easily despite orientation or any components of speed in other directions. Even though the system can do all the other procedures by itself, if in a place with poor network connectivity, some data may not be sent. The limitation of this work is to get real-time working models for the testing phase to validate the system. The real-world implementation of the proposed model and the performance can then be evaluated and validated under actual UAV flight conditions. In the future, the system can be integrated with existing systems that are based on detecting faults in components of UAVs so that it helps them when the UAVs start to fall without any fault being detected in those components.

References

[1] Shakhatreh, H., Sawalmeh, A. H., Al-Fuqaha, A., Dou, Z., Almaita, E., Khalil, I. & Guizani, M. (2019). Unmanned aerial vehicles (UAVs): A survey on civil applications and key research challenges. *Ieee Access*, *7*, 48572–48634.

[2] Hou, D., Su, Q., Song, Y., & Yin, Y. (2023). Research on drone fault detection based on failure mode databases. *Drones*, *7*(8), 486.

[3] Pham, K. L., Leuchter, J., Bystricky, R., Andrle, M., Pham, N. N., & Pham, V. T. (2022). The study of electrical energy power supply system for UAVs based on the energy storage technology. *Aerospace*, *9*(9), 500.

[4] Pruthvija, B., & Lakshmi, K. P. (2020). Review on battery technology and its challenges. *Int. J. Sci. Eng. Res*, *11*, 1706–1713.

[5] Sobouti, M. J., Mohajerzadeh, A., Adarbah, H. Y., Rahimi, Z., & Ahmadi, H. (2024). Utilizing UAVs in wireless networks: advantages, challenges, objectives, and solution methods. *Vehicles*, *6*(4), 1769–1800.

[6] Alsuhli, G., Fahim, A., & Gadallah, Y. (2022). A survey on the role of UAVs in the communication process: A technological perspective. *Computer Communications*, *194*, 86–123.

[7] Wild, G., Murray, J., & Baxter, G. (2016). Exploring civil drone accidents and incidents to help prevent potential air disasters. *Aerospace*, *3*(3), 22.

[8] Al-Madani, B., Svirskis, M., Narvydas, G., Maskeliūnas, R., & Damaševičius, R. (2018). Design of fully automatic drone parachute system with temperature compensation mechanism for civilian and military applications. *Journal of Advanced Transportation*, *2018*(1), 2964583.

[9] Farajijalal, M., Eslamiat, H., Avineni, V., Hettel, E., & Lindsay, C. (2025). Safety Systems for Emergency Landing of Civilian Unmanned Aerial Vehicles—A Comprehensive Review. *Drones*, *9*(2), 141.

[10] Cabahug, J., & Eslamiat, H. (2022). Failure detection in quadcopter UAVs using K-means clustering. *Sensors*, *22*(16), 6037.

[11] Asparuhova, K., Shehova, D., Asenov, S., Kanevski, H., & Parushev, A. (2024, September). Using WOKWI Simulator to Support Engineering Student Learning in Microcontrollers and Sensors. In *2024 XXXIII International Scientific Conference Electronics (ET)* (pp. 1–4). IEEE.

[12] Lakshmi Prasanna, J., Aswin Kumer, S. V., Ravi Kumar, M., Sangeetha Lakshmi, M., Srilaxmi, P., & Santhosh, C. (2022, May). Low-cost ECG and Heart Monitoring System Using Ubidot Platform. In *Proceedings of International Conference on Communication and Artificial Intelligence: ICCAI 2021* (pp. 217–225). Singapore: Springer Nature Singapore.

[13] Patton, E. W., Tissenbaum, M., & Harunani, F. (2019). MIT app inventor: Objectives, design, and development. In *Computational thinking education* (pp. 31–49). Singapore: Springer Singapore.

[14] Phadke, A., & Medrano, F. A. (2024). Increasing operational resiliency of uav swarms: An agent-focused search and rescue framework. *Aerospace Research Communications*, *1*, 12420.

[15] Wu, J., Sun, Y., Yue, H., Yang, J., Yang, F., & Zhao, Y. (2024). Design and Optimization of UAV Aerial Recovery System Based on Cable-Driven Parallel Robot. *Biomimetics*, *9*(2), 111.

75 Eye fatigue detection: A hybrid CNN-LSTM approach for digital screen users

Selvi S.[1,a], Elamathy O. G.[2,b], and Swetha S.[2,c]

[1]Associate Professor, Department of Computer Science and Engineering, Government College of Engineering, Bargur, Krishnagiri, Tamil Nadu, India
[2]Final Year Students, Department of Computer Science and Engineering, Government College of Engineering, Bargur, Krishnagiri, Tamil Nadu, India

Abstract: Eye fatigue detection is important in mitigating the negative consequences of digital eye strain, a situation where number of spread increases among people exposed to prolonged digital screen time. This study investigates the application of eye fatigue detection using machine learning techniques. This paper proposes a hybrid Convolutional Neural Network-Long Short-Term Memory (CNN-LSTM) model that efficiently captures both spatial and temporal features of eye. By means of integrating CNN for feature extraction and LSTM for sequential analysis, the proposed model aims to enhance detection accuracy and contribute to the eye strain prevention practice.

Keywords: Convolutional neural network (CNN), eye dryness, eye fatigue, long short-term memory

1. Introduction

The extended use of virtual screens has drastically affected eye health, leading to increased occurrences of both eye dryness and redness. Before the rise of virtual screen users, the eyes maintained a stable tear production system, ensuring moisture and comfort, with a natural blink rate of 15–22 instances consistent with minute that helped for holding the eyes lubricated.

Additionally, the lack of adequate lubrication triggers an inflammatory reaction, inflicting blood vessels within the eyes to dilate and leading to redness or bloodshot eyes. Children are particularly prone, as their tear production systems are still developing and they often engage in extended screen sports without breaks, making them more liable to each eye dryness and redness detection.

Table 75.1 summarizes key survey effects that illustrate the large rise in eye fatigue, inclusive of dryness and redness, before and after increased digital screen utilization. The studies reflect the growing concern approximately digital eye strain throughout numerous populations, especially within the wake of the COVID-19 pandemic.

Prolonged screen exposure results in a variety of physical discomforts, if left unchecked, these signs and symptoms can pay to long-term vision troubles inclusive of myopia, or continual dry eye disease. Detection systems can boost focus about the significance of normal eye care, results of extended screen time, encouraging more healthy habits and life-style adjustments.

To address these kinds of issue, this study explores the application of deep learning techniques, proposing a hybrid Convolutional Neural Network-long Short-term memory (CNN-LSTM) version. By means of combining the strengths of CNN and LSTM, this model efficiently captures both the spatial features of the eyes (consisting of eye shape, size, and motion) and the temporal dynamics (the sequential patterns of eye behaviour overtime).

This research consists of five sections as follows: Section 1 introduces the background, objectives, and contributions of this study, Section 2 reviews related work, Section 3 presents the Proposed System, Section IV discusses the experimental setup, detailing the implementation and evaluation procedure. Section V presents the results, followed by a discussion and conclusion.

2. Related Work

Hannah R. Kimet et al., examined the correlation between screen time and dry eye disease using surveys to assess symptoms and exposure [10]. Ahmed Aizaldeen Abdullah et al., reviewed fatigue detection techniques using mathematical models achieving up to 96% in yawning detection accuracy and 95% for EEG-based methods [1]. Ramandeep Kaur and Ankit Guleria et al., proposed a system using SVM and EAR with Dlib to detect eye strain by analyzing visual behaviour

---

[a]s.selvi@gcebargur.ac.in, [b]elamathy1609@gmail.com, [c]swethasaravanan662@gmail.com

DOI: 10.1201/9781003724988-75

Table 75.1. Impact of increased digital screen usage on eye fatigue

Study	Sample Population	Findings Before Increased Screen Usage	Findings After Increased Screen Usage
Digital Eye Strain Epidemic Amid COVID-19 [25]	941 respondents (students, teachers, general, public)	Lower screen time, fewer eye strain complaints	Students: 50.6% reported Digital Eye Strain (DES); General public: 33.2% reported DES
Digital Eye Strain: A Comprehensive Review [12]	Various studies reviewed	DES prevalence 5–65%	DES prevalence: 80–94% due to increased screen time
Impact of Increased Screen Time on Ocular Health of Medical Students [26]	280 medical students	Screen time < 5 hours per day, fewer symptoms	61% developed DES, 83.92% reported headaches
Prevalence of Digital Eye Strain among Office Workers [27]	500 office workers	Fewer office workers reported eye strain before remote work	67% of remote workers reported DES symptoms, including dryness and blurred vision
Eye Strain and Its Impact on Children's Health [28]	300 children aged 6–14 years	Lower screen time for educational purposes; minimal reports of eye strain	58% of children reported symptoms like eye dryness, redness, and headaches

Source: Author.

and facial key points [20]. Y Nancy Janeet et al., developed a method for detecting digital eye strain using eye motion and blink analysis through image processing [18].

Mon Timothy Isaac M. Carcellar et al., designed a webcam-based system linking increased blink rate with reduced CVS scores, where each additional blink per minute lowered CVS score by 1.26 points [17]. Dr. Deepti Sharma et al., developed an ADES detector using CNNs and RNNs, achieving 85% training and 80% test accuracy based on extracted eye image features [6]. Kaur et al., discussed DES causes, symptoms, and remedies, highlighting methods like the 20-20-20 rule and the rise of DES during COVID-19, though multiple contributing factors complicate treatment [12]. Asimina Mataftsi et al., analyzed DES in people under 40, finding increased symptoms after 4–5 hours of screen time and noting that inconsistent diagnostic criteria limit effective interventions [3].

Hanaa Abdelaziz Mohamed Zayed et al., observed an 82.41% DES prevalence in IT professionals, identifying screen duration, poor ergonomics, and environmental conditions as key risk factors, although self-reported data may introduce bias [10]. Le Quang Thao et al., used Mobile-NetV2 and ResNet-18 to detect eye strain in students during online learning, achieving 87.16% accuracy but affected by image clarity and lighting [13]. Evgeniy Abdulin and Oleg Komogortsev et al., detected eye fatigue by analyzing fixation and saccade data, showing that fixation-based scores are more sensitive to fatigue [8].

Ch. Sravan and K.J. Onesim et al., created a driver fatigue detection system using image processing that monitors eye closure duration and evaluates performance using accuracy, precision, recall, and F1-score [23]. Mohammed Ghazal et al., developed a real-time CNN-based driver fatigue detection system that analyzes facial images and achieves 89.5% accuracy [16]. Zeeshan Ali Haq and Ziaul Hasan et al.,

introduced a real-time blink detection system using webcams and mobile cameras, achieving F-scores of 0.98 in controlled and 0.91 in open environments, though lighting affects performance [24]. Kazu Kuwahara et al., proposed a method using Eye Aspect Ratio Mapping (EARM) that tracks blink frequency and duration, showing a strong correlation ($r = 0.9995$) with fatigue [11]. Sadaf Malik et al., used decision trees and Random Forest to classify eye disorders, offering a user-friendly diagnostic interface with high accuracy [22].

Eva María Artime Ríos et al., predicted CVS in medical professionals using genetic algorithms and binary regression trees for risk assessment [7]. Mohamed Elkholy and Marwa A. Marzouk et al., focused on CNN-based eye disorder classification and emphasized high accuracy using large, labeled datasets, though training demands are high [15]. Connor Shorten and Taghi M. Khoshgoftaar et al., used CNN to classify OCT images into four eye disease categories, achieving 97% accuracy, limited by dataset size [5]. Fazliddin Makhmudov et al., utilized CNNs and Haar cascades to detect fatigue states in real-time, reporting 96.54% accuracy [9].

Mingxin Yu et al., combined CNN for feature extraction and SVM for classification, using Eye Variance Filter (EVF) to improve fatigue detection accuracy [14]. T. Annapurna et al. present a feasible machine learning model to predict Smartphone Vision Syndrome, focusing on visual discomfort due to prolonged screen exposure [2]. Arwa Albelaihi and Dina M. Ibrahim introduce DeepDiabetic, a deep neural network-based identification system for detecting diabetic eye diseases with high accuracy, proving the effectiveness of deep learning in medical diagnostics [4]. Qianyang Zhuang et al. propose a driver fatigue detection method that utilizes eye states, specifically through pupil and iris segmentation, offering real-time drowsiness monitoring to enhance road safety [19]. Lastly, Rohit Hooda et al. offer a comprehensive review of machine learning techniques for fatigue detection, discussing existing methodologies, datasets, and key challenges, while suggesting directions for future research [21].

3. Proposed Work

The proposed system integrates Hybrid CNN-LSTM architecture to address the problem of eye fatigue detection by leveraging both spatial and temporal analysis. This system employs a Convolutional Neural Network (CNN) to classify eye conditions and Long Short-Term Memory (LSTM) to process the temporal series of blink patterns. This section briefly describes the architectural diagram, flowchart of the proposed system and pseudocode. They are as follows.

3.1. Architectural diagram of the eye fatigue detection

Figure 75.1 illustrates the architectural diagram of the Eye Fatigue Detection. The Eye Fatigue Detection system analyzes spatial function and temporal functions with CNN-LSTM hybrid. The model is trained with Adam optimizer and Binary cross-entropy loss and evaluated the precision, recall, F1-score, and accuracy.

Table 75.2 provides a structured overview of a dataset that are designed for eye fatigue detection, detailing the number of normal and affected eye images, their formats and sources.

Figure 75.2 and 75.3 shows some of the sample images of affected and normal eye. The CNN extracts spatial features from eye images, while the LSTM captures sequential dependencies between blinks, allowing the detection of patterns that advocate fatigue. This system processes video frames to detect eyes using a Haar Cascade Classifier, counts blinks, and computes metrics like blink rate, redness and blink duration. These metrics are then used to detect whether a person is experiencing eye fatigue. TensorFlow, Keras, or PyTorch are used for training the model. This system tactics the extracted functions and predicts whether the person exhibits symptoms of eye fatigue.

3.2. Pseudocode of eye fatigue detection

Table 75.3 presents the pseudocode of the proposed system, detailing the step-by-step process for enhancing the accuracy of eye fatigue detection.

3.3. Flowchart of the eye fatigue detection

Figure 75.4 indicates the flowchart of eye fatigue detection. This system starts with data preprocessing, model training and evaluation. It then takes video input converts it into frames and extracts the eye related features to process the video extraction.

4. Results and Discussions

The proposed system is implemented using Google Colab with a processing speed of 2.5GHZ and around 12GB RAM. The model's overall performance evaluated based on its accuracy in classifying eye conditions and detecting fatigue during training, the CNN-LSTM model achieved high accuracy with 90–95 in distinguishing among normal and affected-eye situations, indicating its effectiveness in eye classification.

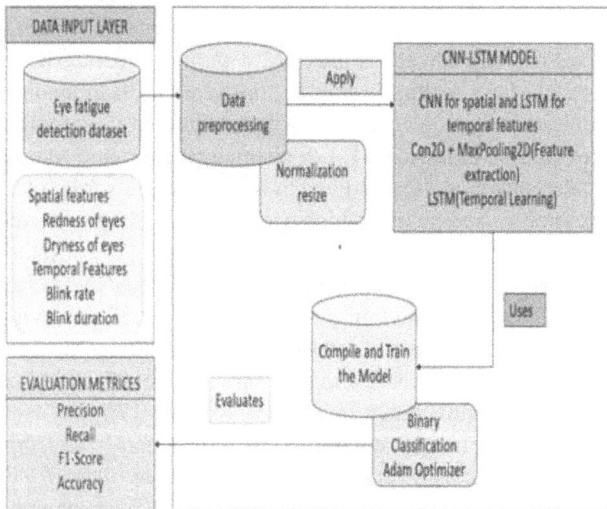

Figure 75.1. Architectural diagram of the eye fatigue detection.
Source: Author.

Table 75.2. Structured overview of the datasets

Attribute	Details
Number of Normal Eyes	700 images (50% of total dataset)
Number of Affected Eyes	1200 images (50% of total dataset)
Image Format	JPG, PNG
Source	Kaggle datasets, roboflow

Source: Author.

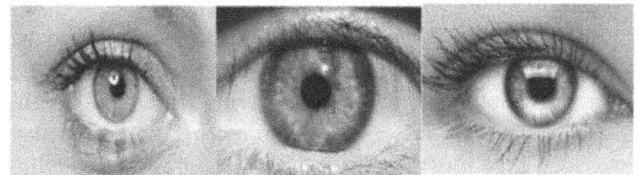

Figure 75.2. Sample images of normal eyes.
Source: Author.

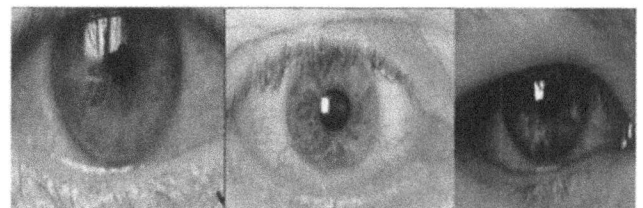

Figure 75.3. Sample images of affected eyes.
Source: Author.

Table 75.3. Pseudocode of eye fatigue detection

Step 1: Initialize Haar cascade classifier for eye detection.
Step 2:Create an ImageDataGenerator for image augmentation
Step 2.1: Apply rescaling, rotation, width/height shifts, and horizontal flips.
Step 3: For each category in ["affected_eye", "unaffected_eye"]:
Step 3.1: Set label: 1 for affected_eye, 0 for unaffected_eye.
Step 3.2: For each image in the category folder:
Step 3.2.1: Read the image in grayscale.
Step 3.2.2: Resize to 64x64 pixels.
Step 3.2.3: Normalize the image using the Equation 1

$$X' = \frac{X - Xmin}{Xmax - Xmin} \qquad (1)$$

Step 3.2.4: Append image and label to data lists.
Step 4: Convert image and label lists to NumPy arrays.
Step 5: Reshape image data to shape (-1, 1, 64, 64, 1).
Step 6: Split dataset into training and testing sets.
Step 7: Define CNN-LSTM model
Step 7.1: Add TimeDistributed Conv2D and MaxPooling layers.
Step 7.2: Add Dropout layers for regularization.
Step 7.3: Flatten outputs and pass through an LSTM layer.
Step 7.4: Add fully connected Dense layers and final sigmoid output.
Step 8: Compile and train the model with Optimizer – Adam, Loss function - Binary cross-entropy, and Metrics - Accuracy
Step 9: Evaluate the trained model on test set, print the accuracy, classification report, display confusion matrix and plot validation accuracy and loss.
Step 10: For each frame in the video
Step 10.1: Convert frame to grayscale.
Step 10.2: Detect eyes using Haar cascade.
Step 10.3: If no eyes detected:
Step 10.3.1: Increment consecutive_blinks.
else if eyes detected and consecutive_blinks > 0:
Step 10.3.2: Increment blink_count.
Step10.3.3:Append duration to blink_durations list.
Step 10.3.4: Reset consecutive_blinks.
Step 10.3.5: Increment frame_count.
Step 11: Release the video capture.
Step 12: Compute blink metrics using Equation 2 and 3

$$Accuracy = \frac{TP + TN}{TP + TN + FP + FN} \qquad (2)$$

$$ReLU(X) = \max(0, X) \qquad (3)$$

Step 13: Print the results of total frames processed, total blinks detected, blink rate (blinks/second), average blink duration
Step 14: Determine eye fatigue:
If blink_rate < threshold OR avg_blink_duration > threshold:
Output: "Affected by Eye Fatigue"
Else:
Output: "Not Affected by Eye Fatigue"

Source: Author.

The confusion matrix further confirmed the model's performance to accurately identify both situations, with a high rate of true positives and actual negatives. The classification report showed precision, recall, and F1-Score, ensuring that the model provides reliable predictions.

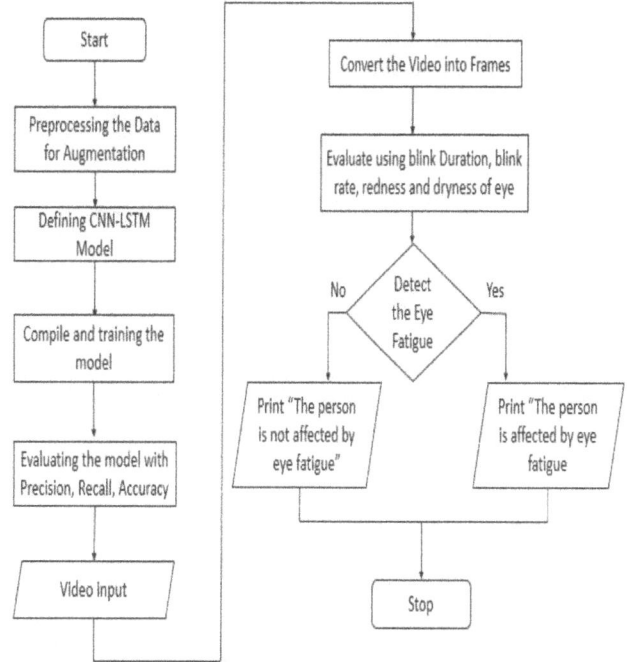

Figure 75.4. Flow chart of eye fatigue detection.
Source: Author.

For fatigue detection, the system effectively analyses video frames to compute metrics together such as blink rate, redness, dryness of the eye and blink duration. The effects showed that the system should accurately track blinks, calculate the blink rate, and determine fatigue based on predefined thresholds. When the blink rate or duration exceeds certain limits, the system correctly recognized fatigue, suggesting that it can detect both eye situations and fatigue with high reliability.

4.1. Evaluation metrics

The Eye Fatigue Detection system analyses spatial function and temporal by CNN-LSTM. The model is trained with Adam optimizer and Binary cross-entropy (BCE) loss and evaluated the precision, recall, F1-score, and accuracy. Adam optimizer updates the model's weights using learning rates based on first moment (mean) calculated using Equation 4 and second moment (variance) estimates and is calculated using Equation 5.

$$m_t = \beta_1 m_{t-1} + (1 - \beta_1)g_t \qquad (4)$$

$$m_t = \beta_2 v_{t-1} + (1 - \beta_2)g_t^2 \qquad (5)$$

where,
Assume β_1 and β_2 as 0.9 and 0.99 for default first and second moment decay rates and g_t represents the Gradient of the loss function.

Binary cross-entropy (BCE) is used as a loss function in binary classification tasks and is calculated using Equation (6),

$$f(x) = -\frac{1}{N} + \sum_{i=1}^{N} [(y_i \log(\hat{y}_i) + (1 - y_i) \log(1 - \hat{y}_i)) \qquad (6)$$

where,

y_i is the actual label and

$\hat{y}_i$ is the predicted probability of users.

The parameter used for calculating the performance metrics is listed in Table 75.4.

Table 75.5 presents a performance comparison of various machine learning algorithms – Decision Tree, Support Vector Machine (SVM), Autoencoder, and Hybrid CNN-LSTM. It is evaluated using four evaluation metrics such as precision, recall, f1-Score and accuracy. Among these, the Hybrid CNN-LSTM approach consistently outperforms the others across all metrics, achieving a precision of 0.86, recall of 0.98, F1-score of 0.91, and accuracy of 0.92. In contrast, the Decision Tree algorithm shows relatively lower performance, especially in terms of precision (0.75) and accuracy (0.77), likely due to its tendency to overfit and its inability to capture temporal dependencies. SVM performs better in recall (0.86) but falls short in precision (0.74), indicating a higher rate of false positives. The Autoencoder demonstrates a very high recall (0.97), suggesting good sensitivity in detecting positive cases; however, its lower precision (0.74) results in more incorrect positive predictions. Figure 75.5 shows the graphical representation of accuracy of various algorithms.

4.2. Performance evaluation

Figure 75.6 displays the confusion matrix, which evaluates the prediction accuracy of the model. The strong diagonal dominance indicates accurate classification, while the minimal off-diagonal values reflect a low error rate. This demonstrates the model's robustness in detecting eye fatigue with high precision.

Table 75.4. Evaluation metrics

F1-Score	$F1 - Score = 2 * \dfrac{Precision * Recall}{Precision + Recall}$
Precision	$Precision = \dfrac{TP}{TP + +FP} * 100$
Accuracy	$Accuracy = \dfrac{TP + TN}{TP + TN + FP + FN} * 100$
Recall	$Recall = \dfrac{TP}{TP + +FN} * 100$

Source: Author.

Table 75.5. Comparison of various algorithms

Algorithms	Precision	Recall	F1-Score	Accuracy
Decision Tree	0.75	0.76	0.80	0.77
SVM	0.74	0.86	0.80	0.80
Autoencoder	0.74	0.97	0.84	0.84
Hybrid CNN-LSTM	0.86	0.98	0.91	0.92

Source: Author.

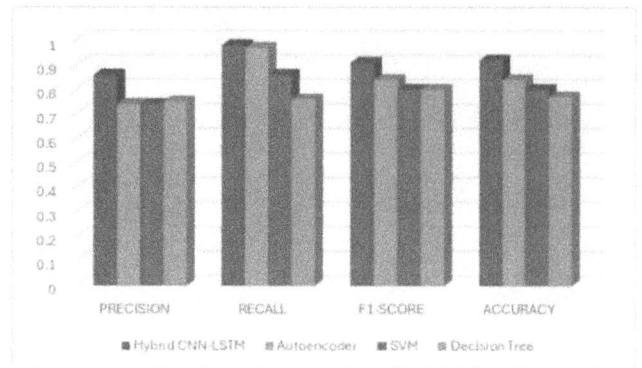

Figure 75.5. Graphical representation of accuracy of various algorithms.

Source: Author.

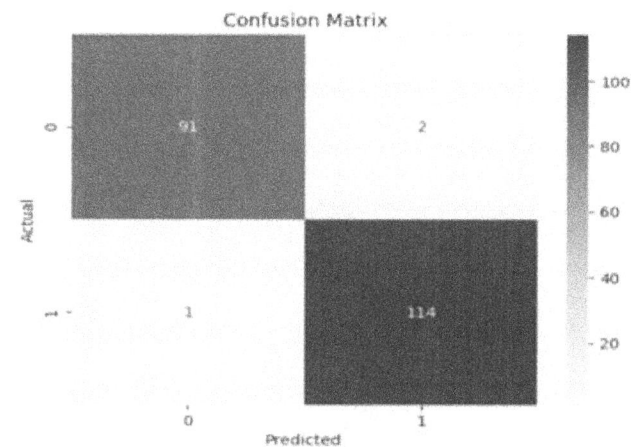

Figure 75.6. Snapshot of the Confusion matrix of proposed model.

Source: Author.

Figure 75.7 illustrates a consistent increase in both training and validation accuracy over epochs, indicating effective learning and good generalization of the eye fatigue detection model. The close alignment of both curves suggests minimal overfitting, demonstrating the model's reliability and robustness.

Figures 75.8 and 75.9 shows output of the frames processed, total blinks detected, blink rate, average blink duration, and fatigue status.

5. Conclusion

The proposed Hybrid CNN-LSTM system effectively combines the strengths of convolutional neural networks for spatial feature extraction and long short-term memory networks for temporal sequence analysis, providing an efficient solution for detecting eye conditions and monitoring eye fatigue. The system demonstrated high accuracy in classifying eye conditions, achieving robust performance in distinguishing between normal and affected eye conditions. Additionally,

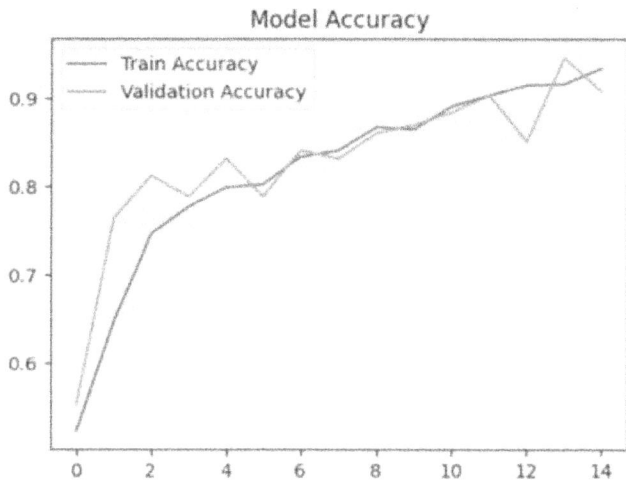

Figure 75.7. Snapshot of graph showing model accuracy.

Source: Author.

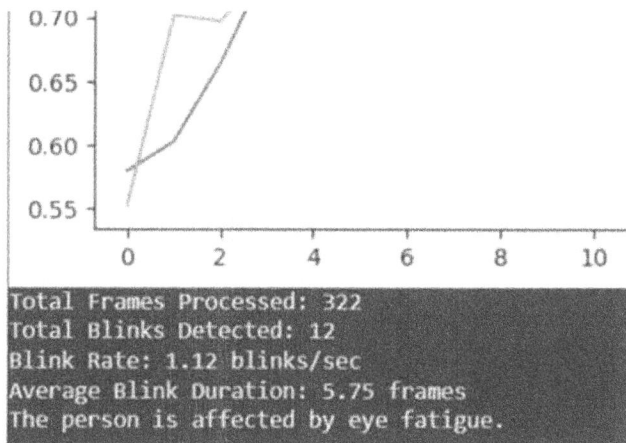

Figure 75.8. Snapshot of output showing the person is affected by eye fatigue.

Source: Author.

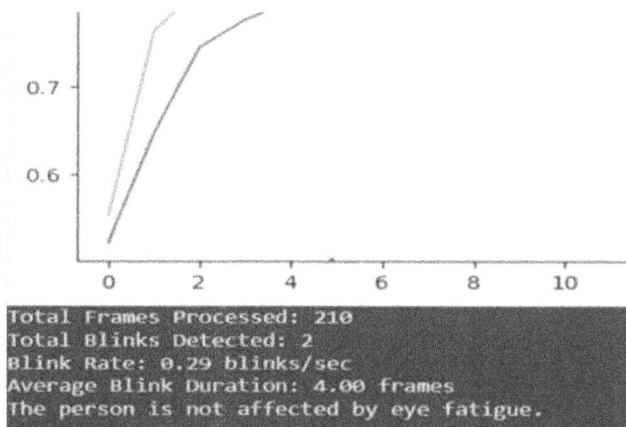

Figure 75.9. Snapshot of output showing the person is not affected by eye fatigue.

Source: Author.

the fatigue detection component, based on blink rate and blink duration, showed promising results, accurately identifying signs of fatigue under various conditions.

References

[1] Abdullah, A. A., Aldhahab, A., & Al Abboodi, H. M. (2024). Review of eye diseases detection and classification using deep learning techniques. In *BIO Web of Conferences* (Vol. 97, p. 00012). EDP Sciences.

[2] Annapurna, T., Rajeswari, P. V. G. S., Likitha, A., Deekshitha, G., Sharma, S., Rao, Y. V., & Kumar, R. R. (2023). Predicting Smartphone Vision Syndrome: A Feasible Approach using Machine Learning Algorithms. In *E3S Web of Conferences* (Vol. 430, p. 01036). EDP Sciences.

[3] Mataftsi, A., Seliniotaki, A. K., Moutzouri, S., Prousali, E., Darusman, K. R., Adio, A. O., ... & Nischal, K. K. (2023). Digital eye strain in young screen users: A systematic review. *Preventive medicine*, *170*, 107493.

[4] Albelaihi, A., & Ibrahim, D. M. (2024). DeepDiabetic: an identification system of diabetic eye diseases using deep neural networks. *IEEE Access*, *12*, 10769–10789.

[5] Shorten, C., & Khoshgoftaar, T. M. (2019). A survey on image data augmentation for deep learning. *Journal of big data*, *6*(1), 1–48.

[6] Aggarwal, D., Sharma, D., & Saxena, A. B. (2022). Detection of eye strain due to usage of electronic devices: A machine learning based approach. *International journal of health sciences*, *6*(S1), 11197–11207.

[7] Artime Ríos, E. M., Sánchez Lasheras, F., Suárez Sánchez, A., Iglesias-Rodríguez, F. J., & Seguí Crespo, M. D. M. (2019). Prediction of computer vision syndrome in health personnel by means of genetic algorithms and binary regression trees. *Sensors*, *19*(12), 2800.

[8] Abdulin, E., & Komogortsev, O. (2015, April). User eye fatigue detection via eye movement behavior. In *Proceedings of the 33rd annual ACM conference extended abstracts on human factors in computing systems* (pp. 1265–1270).

[9] Makhmudov, F., Turimov, D., Xamidov, M., Nazarov, F., & Cho, Y. I. (2024). Real-Time Fatigue Detection Algorithms Using Machine Learning for Yawning and Eye State. *Sensors*, *24*(23), 7810.

[10] Zayed, H. A. M., Saied, S. M., Younis, E. A., & Atlam, S. A. (2021). Digital eye strain: prevalence and associated factors among information technology professionals, Egypt. *Environmental Science and Pollution Research*, *28*, 25187–25195.

[11] Kuwahara, A., Nishikawa, K., Hirakawa, R., Kawano, H., & Nakatoh, Y. (2022). Eye fatigue estimation using blink detection based on Eye Aspect Ratio Mapping (EARM). *Cognitive Robotics*, *2*, 50–59.

[12] Kaur, K., Gurnani, B., Nayak, S., Deori, N., Kaur, S., Jethani, J., ... & Mishra, D. (2022). Digital eye strain-a comprehensive review. *Ophthalmology and therapy*, *11*(5), 1655–1680.

[13] Cuong, D. D., Hung, V. M., Nghia, D. T., Hai, D. H., & Nhi, N. N. (2023). Eye Strain Detection During Online Learning. *Intelligent Automation & Soft Computing*, *35*(3).

[14] Yu, M., Tang, X., Lin, Y., Schmidt, D., Wang, X., Guo, Y., & Liang, B. (2018). An eye detection method based on convolutional neural networks and support vector machines. *Intelligent Data Analysis*, *22*(2), 345–362.

[15] Elkholy, M., & Marzouk, M. A. (2024). Deep learning-based classification of eye diseases using Convolutional Neural Network for OCT images. *Frontiers in Computer Science, 5*, 1252295.

[16] Ghazal, M., Haeyeh, Y. A., Abed, A., & Ghazal, S. (2018, August). Embedded fatigue detection using convolutional neural networks with mobile integration. In *2018 6th international conference on future internet of things and cloud workshops (ficloudw)* (pp. 129–133). IEEE.

[17] Carcellar, M. T. I. M., Tychuaco, C. J. S., & Yumang, A. N. (2024, August). Self-Applicable Eye Strain Detection Through the Measurement of Blink Rate Using Raspberry Pi. In *2024 IEEE International Conference on Artificial Intelligence in Engineering and Technology (IICAIET)* (pp. 13–17). IEEE.

[18] Jane, Y. N., Padmanabhan, K., Karthika, S., & Christiana, K. B. (2023, March). A Vision-Based Approach for the Diagnosis of Digital Asthenopia. In *2023 4th International Conference on Signal Processing and Communication (ICSPC)* (pp. 163–167). IEEE.

[19] Zhuang, Q., Kehua, Z., Wang, J., & Chen, Q. (2020). Driver fatigue detection method based on eye states with pupil and iris segmentation. *Ieee Access, 8*, 173440–173449.

[20] Kaur, R., & Guleria, A. (2021, June). Digital eye strain detection system based on svm. In *2021 5th International Conference on Trends in Electronics and Informatics (ICOEI)* (pp. 1114–1121). IEEE.

[21] Hooda, R., Joshi, V., & Shah, M. (2021). A comprehensive review of approaches to detect fatigue using machine learning techniques. *Chronic Diseases and Translational Medicine.*

[22] Malik, S., Kanwal, N., Asghar, M. N., Sadiq, M. A. A., Karamat, I., & Fleury, M. (2019). Data driven approach for eye disease classification with machine learning. *Applied Sciences, 9*(14), 2789.

[23] Sravan, C., Onesim, K. J., Bhavana, V. S. S., Arthi, R., & Srinadh, G. (2018, November). Eye fatigue detection system. In *2018 International Conference on System Modeling & Advancement in Research Trends (SMART)* (pp. 245–247). IEEE.

[24] Haq, Z. A., & Hasan, Z. (2016, August). Eye-blink rate detection for fatigue determination. In *2016 1st India International Conference on Information Processing (IICIP)* (pp. 1–5). IEEE.

[25] Ganne, P., Najeeb, S., Chaitanya, G., Sharma, A., & Krishnappa, N. C. (2021). Digital eye strain epidemic amid COVID-19 pandemic–a cross-sectional survey. *Ophthalmic epidemiology, 28*(4), 285–292.

[26] Mary Eldo, B., Elsa Mathews, N., Johnson, B., & Sara Roy, A. (2024). Impact of increased screen-time on ocular health of professional college students during COVID-19: A cross-sectional study. International Journal of Community Medicine and Public Health.

[27] Cantó-Sancho, N., Porru, S., Casati, S., Ronda, E., Seguí-Crespo, M., & Carta, A. (2023). Prevalence and risk factors of computer vision syndrome—assessed in office workers by a validated questionnaire. *PeerJ, 11*, e14937.

[28] Abhishek Varshney. (2024). Digital Eye Strain (Computer Vision Syndrome) in Children: Signs, Effects and Solutions. *Eye Care / Ophthalmology.*

76 UPI transaction security: Fraud detection using a machine learning algorithm

Selvi S.[1,a], Dhinoovika D.[2,b], Harshana R.[2,c], and Muthulakshmi R.[2,d]

[1]Associate Professor, Department of Computer Science and Engineering, Government College of Engineering, Bargur, Krishnagiri, Tamil Nadu, India
[2]Final Year Students, Department of Computer Science and Engineering, Government College of Engineering, Bargur, Krishnagiri, Tamil Nadu, India

Abstract: With the rapid adoption of digital payments, fraudulent transactions have become a significant issue, particularly in Unified Payments Interface (UPI) transactions. Traditional rule-based fraud detection strategies often fail to detect sophisticated fraud patterns. The study provides a machine learning-driven UPI fraud detection system, evaluating Random Forest, Decision Tree, and Convolutional Neural Network (CNN) models to categorize transactions as fraudulent or non-fraudulent. The Random Forest model established sturdy performance because of its ensemble learning method, while the CNN model leveraged deep learning techniques to capture complex transaction patterns. Also, it is incorporated into a Flask-based web application, allowing customers to test transaction authenticity in real-time. Comparative evaluation of the models based on accuracy highlights the effectiveness of ensemble learning and deep learning for fraud detection. This research pays attention to the development of financial security through improving the accuracy and performance of fraud detection mechanisms in digital payment systems.

Keywords: Convolutional neural network, decision tree, digital payments, random forest

1. Introduction

The rapid evolution of digital payments has revolutionized financial transactions, offering users seamless and immediate cash transfers. The Unified Payments Interface (UPI) has emerged as a leading digital payment system, enabling Peer-to-Peer (P2P) and business transactions with minimal latency. However, with the growing adoption of digital payments, fraudulent activities including identity theft, unauthorized transactions, and phishing attacks have become increasingly more familiar. Traditional fraud detection systems depend upon rule-based algorithms, where transactions are flagged based on predefined conditions along with transaction amount thresholds, frequency or suspicious IP addresses. While these methods offer a simple layer of security, they fail to discover sophisticated fraud patterns that evolve. Detecting fraud in UPI transactions poses challenges due to the high extent of transactions, real-time processing necessities, and the evolving nature of fraudulent activities. Fraudsters employ numerous processes, such as social engineering, synthetic identities, and transaction manipulation, making it problematic for rule-based systems to retain. False positives and false negatives further complicate fraud detection.

Table 76.1 denotes data on the percentage of fraud determined annually from 2014 to 2023. It highlights a clear upward trend in fraudulent activities over the decade. This shows increasing vulnerabilities in systems or an increase in digital transactions without corresponding enhancements in security.

This study comprises five sections: Section 1 provides introductions of this study, and Section 2 clearly gives reviews on this study. Section 3 depicts the proposed system, and Section 4 elaborates the investigational setup, procedural implementation and evaluation. Section 5 recaps the results.

Table 76.1. Annual fraud percentage trends (2014–2023)

Year	Percentage of Fraud
2014	1.8%
2015	2.9%
2016	4.7%
2017	6.6%
2018	9.45%
2019	11.8%
2020	14.1%
2021	13.9%
2022	16.9%
2023	17.8%

Source: Author.

[a]s.selvi@gcebargur.ac.in, [b]dhinoovikadevarajan@gmail.com, [c]kaveripandurangan03902@gail.com, [d]muthulakshmi110104@gmail.com

DOI: 10.1201/9781003724988-76

2. Related Work

Abdulaleem Ali et al. (2023) conducted a systematic review on financial fraud detection using machine learning, exploring Decision Trees and Random Forest models while assessing their evaluation measures highlighting the challenges of real-world datasets and the reliance on synthetic data [1]. Amal Al Ali, Ahmed M. Khedr, and Magdi El-Bannany (2023) proposed an optimized XGBoost ensemble learning model for financial statement fraud detection in the MENA region, which outperformed traditional models but required extensive hyperparameter tuning [5]. Ebenezer Esenogho and Ibomoiye Dom or Mienye (2022) introduced a neural network ensemble model with feature engineering to improve credit card fraud detection, where their LSTM-based approach enhanced sensitivity and specificity but required high-quality training data [8]. Gangi Setty Raj Charan and K. Deepa Thilak (2023) developed a machine learning-based detection model for phishing links and QR codes in UPI transactions, providing real-time fraud prevention but being computationally demanding [12]. Elena Flondor, Liliana Donath, and Mihaela Neamtu (2024) investigated decision tree algorithms for automatic credit card fraud detection, showing strong interpretability but struggling with data imbalance and overfitting [9]. Abdulwahab Ali Almazroi and Nasir Ayub (2023) developed a real-time fraud detection model using ResNeXt-GRU (RXT) and Jaya optimization, achieving a 10%-18% performance improvement over existing models but facing challenges in implementation complexity [2]. Emmanuel Ileberi, Yanxia Sun, and Zenghui Wang (2022) applied Genetic Algorithms (GA) for feature selection in fraud detection, improving accuracy and reducing computational complexity but facing issues with imbalanced datasets [10]. Dahee Choi and Kyungho Lee (2017) applied machine learning techniques such as expectation maximization (EM) and K-Means for fraud detection in mobile payment systems, effectively detecting fraudulent patterns but being computationally intensive [6]. Hadeel Ahmad, Bassam Kasasbeh, and Enas Rawashdeh (2023) introduced a class balancing framework for credit card fraud detection, where their fuzzy C-Means clustering approach improved accuracy but required resource-intensive computation [13]. Ibrahim Y. Hafez et al. (2025) conducted a methodical assessment of AI techniques in credit card fraud detection, covering machine learning, meta-heuristic optimization approaches and deep learning but noting difficulties in training models due to the rarity of fraud cases [14].

Mengran Zhu, Yulu Gong, and Yafei Xiang (2024) investigated the use of Generative Adversarial Networks (GANs) for fraud detection, effectively identifying fraudulent transactions but facing challenges in generating high-fidelity synthetic data [17]. For fraud detection, Jonathan Kwaku Afriyie et al. (2023) analyzed supervised machine learning models, identifying Random Forest as the best-performing model with 96% accuracy but noting high computational costs [15]. Jonathan M. Karpoff (2021) examined financial fraud trends over time, highlighting the influence of technology and wealth on fraud incidence while exploring fintech innovations like blockchain for fraud prevention [16]. Ahsan RB and Suresh Kumar KR (2021) developed a fraud detection model using Support Vector Machines (SVM), Artificial Neural Networks (ANN), and k-nearest Neighbors (KNN), highlighting ANN's effectiveness in handling complex transaction patterns but requiring extensive computational resources [4]. Mohapatra et al. (2017) analyzed the security vulnerabilities of UPI and digital payment systems in India, identifying key threats and proposing mitigation strategies for improved financial security [18]. Paolo Vanini et al. (2023) integrated anomaly detection with economic risk management for online fraud prevention, balancing detection accuracy with economic considerations but facing challenges in implementation complexity [20]. Abhilash Sharma M., Ganesh Raj B., and Ramamurthy B. (2022) proposed an auto-encoder-based deep learning approach involved in credit card fraud detection, where the unsupervised learning method demonstrated high adaptability to evolving fraud patterns but was dependent on the quality of input data [3]. Eleanor Mill, Wolfgang Garn, and Nick Ryman-Tubb (2023) explored Explainable AI (XAI) in real-time fraud detection, emphasizing the importance of transparency in AI decision-making but facing challenges in balancing explainability with accuracy [7]. Fawaz Khaled Alarfaj and Shabnam Shahzadi (2023) leveraged Graph Neural Networks (GNNs) and Autoencoders for real-time credit card fraud detection, capturing complex transaction relationships but requiring large, labeled datasets [11]. Noor Saleh Alfaiz and Suliman Mohamed Fati (2022) developed a credit card fraud detection model using CatBoost and AllKNN under sampling, achieving high accuracy but being computationally expensive [19].

3. Proposed Work

The proposed work enhances UPI fraud detection using machine learning models like Random Forest, Decision Tree and CNN. Unlike rule-based methods, these models analyze massive datasets, discover hidden patterns, and predict new fraud cases. Data is preprocessed by extracting transaction details, normalizing values, and splitting into training and testing sets for better accuracy and generalization.

Figure 76.1 illustrates the architecture of a UPI Fraud Detection system using Random Forest, Decision Tree, and CNN models. It has multiple layers, starting with the data input layer containing UPI transaction details like number, amount, date, and zip code. These are passed to the model training layer, where all three models are trained. The CNN uses dense layers with ReLU activation, batch normalization, dropout, and a final sigmoid layer for classification. To tailor CNNs for tabular UPI transaction data, the architecture employs dense layers in place of convolutional filters typically used for spatial data. Layers such as batch normalization and dropout are included to improve learning efficiency and mitigate overfitting. While CNNs are conventionally

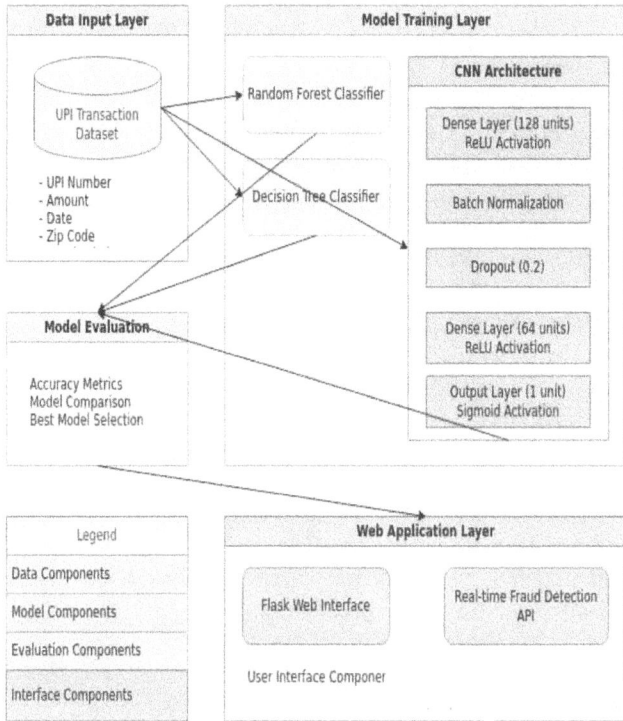

Figure 76.1. System architecture of UPI fraud detection using machine learning.

Source: Author.

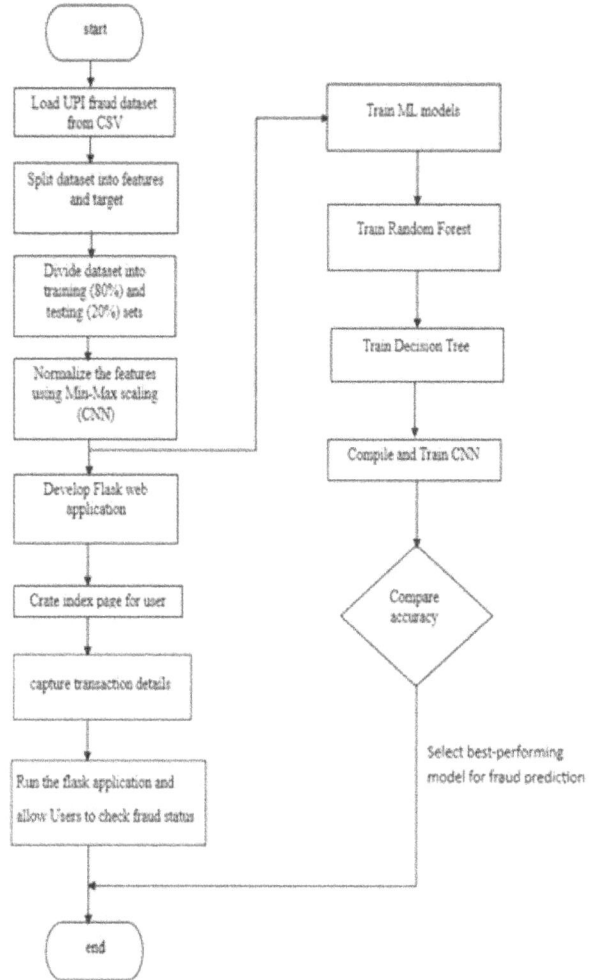

Figure 76.2. Flowchart of UPI fraud detection.

Source: Author.

applied to image recognition tasks, their capability for deep hierarchical feature extraction can be effectively redirected to interpret complex patterns in based numerical data. This modification allows for accurate detection of fraudulent behaviour within transaction data.

Figure 76.2 provides a machine learning pipeline for UPI fraud detection. It starts by loading a UPI fraud dataset from a CSV file and splitting it into features and target variables. The data is then divided into 80% training and 20% testing. Models such as Random Forest, Decision Tree, and a CNN with Min-Max normalization are trained. A Flask web app is developed with an index page to capture user input and transaction details, enabling fraud status assessments.

The pseudocode of the RF, DT, and CNN is explained here in Tables 76.2–76.5 respectively.

The CNN algorithm applies into the Training and the Testing parts.

4. Results and Discussions

The dataset employed in this research has been obtained from Kaggle and contains 50,000 UPI transaction entries. Each entry includes fields such as UPI ID, transaction amount, date, zip code, and a fraud indicator. The dataset exhibits a significant class imbalance, with only 2.8% of transactions labelled as fraudulent. To address this problem, SMOTE (synthetic Minority Over-sampling technique) has

Table 76.2. Pseudocode of the proposed system using random forest

Step 1: START
Step 2: Loads the dataset file.
Step 3: Data preprocessing.
Step 3.1: Data is scaled and normalized using Equation (1).

$$X' = \frac{X - Xmin}{Xmax - Xmin} \qquad (1)$$

where X′ is a scaled value, X is the original value, X_{min} is the minimum value, and X_{max} is the maximum value. Split dataset as training and testing dataset.

Step 4: Training is done by RandomForestClassifier () to predict fraud or non-fraud transactions.

Step 5: Calculate fraud/valid transactions, compute accuracy using Equation (2), and store the result. Here, TP is True Positive, TF is True Negative, FP is False Positive, and FN is False Negative.

$$Accuracy = \frac{TP + TN}{TP + TN + FP + FN} \qquad (2)$$

Step 6: STOP

Source: Author.

Table 76.3. Pseudocode of the proposed system using decision tree

Step 1: START
Step 2: Import the dataset.
Step 3: Preprocess the data as follows.
Step 3.1: Scale and normalize features using Equation (1).
Step 3.2: Use train_test_split() to generate training and testing subsets.
Step 4: Construct the decision Tree Classifier by applying DecisionTreeClassifier() to determine if a transaction is fraudulent or not.
Step 5: Perform prediction and evaluate model, Evaluate model performance using Equation (2) and record the results.
Step 6: STOP

Source: Author.

Table 76.4. Pseudocode of the proposed system using convolutional neural network – training portion

Step 1: START
Step 2: Load the dataset using dataset.pd.read_csv function.
Step 3: Data Pre-processing
Step 3.1:Feature scaling using Equation (1)
Step 3.2: Divide dataset as training and testing sets
Step 4: Training the CNN Model using Equation (3) Define CNN layers with Dense, Batch Normalization, and Dropout.

$$ReLU(X) = \max(0, X) \qquad (3)$$

Compile the model with the optimizer using Equation (4) and the loss. Here, V represents momentum, denotes exponential decay rate, It is a gradient of a loss function.

$$V = \beta V + (1 - \beta)\nabla W \qquad (4)$$

Step 5: Save trained model (as training takes time)
Step 6: STOP

Source: Author.

Table 76.5. Pseudocode of the proposed system using convolutional neural network – testing part

Step 1: START
Step 2: Load trained CNN model
Step 3: Use the model. predict () on new transaction data.
Step 4: Determine if the transaction is fraudulent or not.
Step 5: STOP

Source: Author.

been implemented to maintain the training set. Following data preprocessing, 80:20 proportionate has been utilized as training and testing dataset, ensuring consistent model evaluation. The parameter to calculate the performance metrics are given through Equations (2) and from Equations (5) to (7).

$$F1 - Score = 2 * \frac{Precision * Recall}{Precision + Recall} \qquad (5)$$

$$Precision = \frac{TP}{TP + +FP} * 100 \qquad (6)$$

$$Recall = \frac{TP}{TP + +FN} * 100 \qquad (7)$$

Random forest and decision Tree identify fraud by learning decision-based patterns, while the CNN, tailored from image processing techniques numerical data via components like batch normalization and dropout to improve accuracy and reduce overfitting. These models are trained on extensive datasets to discover intricate fraud patterns, outperforming traditional rule-based methods. Their effectiveness is evaluated through bar charts and key performance metrics. This predictive approach strengthens the security of UPI transactions by detecting fraudulent activity, even when identical past cases aren't present.

Random Forest demonstrated strong overall performance due to its ensemble learning mechanism, which reduces overfitting and effectively captures complex data patterns. Decision trees, while easy to interpret, are prone to overfitting, which negatively impacts their generalization potential and overall accuracy. In this study, CNNs – traditionally used for image processing – are applied to tabular data.

Table 76.6 presents a comparative evaluation of three machine learning models: Decision Tree, Random Forest, and Convolutional Neural Network (CNN). Those models are assessed based on four core metrics: precision, recall, F1-score, and accuracy. Among them, Random Forest demonstrates the great overall performance, showing robust generalization and the ability to identify complex fraud styles effectively. In comparison, Decision Tree lags due to its weaker capacity to model non-linear data relationships. The CNN, adapted from image-based applications, effectively captures complex patterns through mechanisms like batch normalization and dropout, which mitigate overfitting and enhance generalization.

Figure 76.3 illustrates the comparative overall performance of Decision Tree, Random Forest, and CNN vs performance metrics. Random forest consistently leads in all four metrics, underscoring its sturdy performance. CNN ranks second, specifically excelling in accuracy, indicating its strength in detecting patterns. Decision Tree trails in overall performance, primarily due to its tendency to overfit and its restricted generalization potential. The chart depicts the comparative benefits and limitations of every model in managing fraud detection scenarios.

Table 76.6. Comparison of various algorithms

Algorithms	Precision	Recall	F1-Score	Accuracy
Random Forest	0.82	0.89	0.85	0.88
Decision Tree	0.75	0.78	0.76	0.77
CNN	0.80	0.84	0.82	0.85

Source: Author.

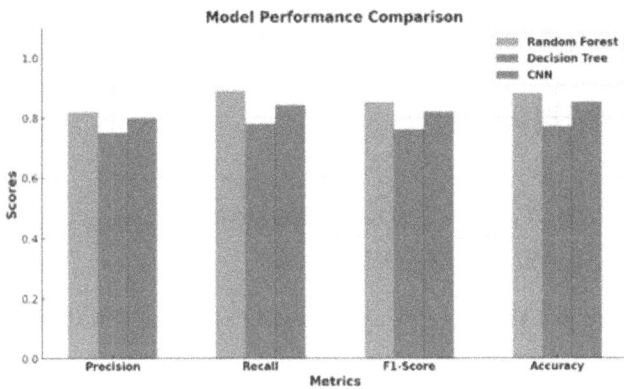

Figure 76.3. Model performance comparison.

Source: Author.

5. Conclusion

The proposed method has demonstrated its effectiveness in addressing the challenges in the area. Utilizing advanced methodologies, the study yields encouraging outcomes that underscore opportunities for persevered enhancement and refinement. The current study makes valuable contributions its applicability can be further extended to real-world scenarios through additional validation and testing on diverse datasets. Future research can focus on incorporating real-time adaptability and automation to optimize decision-making processes.

References

[1] Abdulaleem Ali, et al. (2023). Financial Fraud Detection Based on Machine Learning. Taylor and Francis. www.taylorandfrancis.com. CC BY-NC-ND 4.0 license.

[2] Almazroi, A. A., & Ayub, N. (2023). Online payment fraud detection model using machine learning techniques. *IEEE Access*, *11*, 137188–137203.

[3] Sharma, M. A., Raj, B. G., Ramamurthy, B., & Bhaskar, R. H. (2022). Credit card fraud detection using deep learning based on auto-encoder. In *ITM Web of Conferences* (Vol. 50, p. 01001). EDP Sciences.

[4] Asha, R. B., & KR, S. K. (2021). Credit card fraud detection using artificial neural network. *Global Transitions Proceedings*, *2*(1), 35–41.

[5] Ali, A. A., Khedr, A. M., El-Bannany, M., & Kanakkayil, S. (2023). A powerful predicting model for financial statement fraud based on optimized XGBoost ensemble learning technique. *Applied Sciences*, *13*(4), 2272.

[6] Choi, D., & Lee, K. (2017). Machine learning based approach to financial fraud detection process in mobile payment system. *IT convergence practice (INPRA)*, *5*(4), 12–24.

[7] Mill, E. R., Garn, W., Ryman-Tubb, N. F., & Turner, C. (2023). Opportunities in real time fraud detection: An explainable artificial intelligence (XAI) research agenda. *International Journal of Advanced Computer Science and Applications*, *14*(5), 1172–1186.

[8] Esenogho, E., Mienye, I. D., Swart, T. G., Aruleba, K., & Obaido, G. (2022). A neural network ensemble with feature engineering for improved credit card fraud detection. *IEEE access*, *10*, 16400–16407.

[9] Flondor, E., Donath, L., & Neamtu, M. (2024). Automatic Card Fraud Detection Based on Decision Tree Algorithm. *Applied Artificial Intelligence*, *38*(1), 2385249.

[10] Ileberi, E., Sun, Y., & Wang, Z. (2022). A machine learning based credit card fraud detection using the GA algorithm for feature selection. *Journal of Big Data*, *9*(1), 24.

[11] Alarfaj, F. K., & Shahzadi, S. (2024). Enhancing Fraud Detection in Banking with Deep Learning: Graph Neural Networks and Autoencoders for Real-Time Credit Card Fraud Prevention. *IEEE Access*. doi:10.1109/ACCESS.2024.3466288.

[12] Alarfaj, F. K., et al. (2022). Credit Card Fraud Detection Using State-of-the-Art Machine Learning and Deep Learning Algorithms. *IEEE Access*. doi:10.1109/ACCESS.2022.3166891.

[13] Charan, G. R., & Thilak, K. D. (2023, December). Detection of Phishing Link and QR Code of UPI Transaction using Machine Learning. In *2023 3rd International Conference on Innovative Mechanisms for Industry Applications (ICIMIA)* (pp. 658–663). IEEE.

[14] Ahmad, H., Kasasbeh, B., Aldabaybah, B., & Rawashdeh, E. (2023). Class balancing framework for credit card fraud detection based on clustering and similarity-based selection (SBS). *International Journal of Information Technology*, *15*(1), 325–333.

[15] Hafez, I. Y., Hafez, A. Y., Saleh, A., Abd El-Mageed, A. A., & Abohany, A. A. (2025). A systematic review of AI-enhanced techniques in credit card fraud detection. *Journal of Big Data*, *12*(1), 6.

[16] Afriyie, J. K., Tawiah, K., Pels, W. A., Addai-Henne, S., Dwamena, H. A., Owiredu, E. O., ... & Eshun, J. (2023). A supervised machine learning algorithm for detecting and predicting fraud in credit card transactions. *Decision Analytics Journal*, *6*, 100163.

[17] Karpoff, J. M. (2021). The Future of Financial Fraud. *Journal of Corporate Finance*. DOI:10.1016/j.jcorpfin.2020.101694.

[18] Zhu, M., Gong, Y., Xiang, Y., Yu, H., & Huo, S. (2024, June). Utilizing GANs for fraud detection: model training with synthetic transaction data. In *International Conference on Image, Signal Processing, and Pattern Recognition (ISPP 2024)* (Vol. 13180, pp. 887–894). SPIE.

[19] Mohapatra, S. (2017). Unified payment interface (UPI): A cashless Indian e-transaction process. *International Journal of Applied Science and Engineering*, *5*(1), 29–42.

[20] Alfaiz, N. S., & Fati, S. M. (2022). Enhanced credit card fraud detection model using machine learning. *Electronics*, *11*(4), 662.

77 Accelerating drug discovery using machine learning based on IC50 prediction

S. Praveena[1,a], R. Kaviya[2,b], K. SheerinFarhana[2,c], S. Bhuvanasri[2,d], Jean Deiva[2,e], Rajasozhan P.[2,f], and Vinayak Rakecha H.[2,g]

[1]Assistant Professor, Department of Artificial Intelligence and Machine Learning, Manakula Vinayagar Institute of Technology, Puducherry, India

[2]UG Student, Department of Artificial Intelligence and Machine Learning, Manakula Vinayagar Institute of Technology, Puducherry, India

Abstract: Drug discovery is an expensive and time-consuming process, requiring extensive research, laboratory experiments, and clinical trials. Traditional methods are inefficient, taking years to identify and validate potential drug candidates. Recent advancements in artificial intelligence (AI) and computational techniques have significantly accelerated this process. AI-driven models can rapidly analyze large datasets, predict molecular interactions, and optimize drug formulations more accurately. This paper explores AI methodologies such as deep learning, molecular docking, and predictive analytics in drug discovery. Additionally, it highlights the challenges associated with AI implementation, including data reliability and regulatory concerns. The study concludes that AI has the potential to revolutionize drug discovery by reducing costs, enhancing efficiency, and improving success rates.

Keywords: Artificial intelligence, drug discovery, machine learning, molecular docking, deep learning, computational biology, AI in medicine

1. Introduction

Drug discovery is a crucial and complex process that plays a significant role in the development of new therapeutics for treating diseases. It involves multiple stages, including target identification, hit discovery, lead optimization, preclinical studies, and clinical trials. Each stage requires extensive time, financial resources, and human expertise, making drug development a costly and lab or-intensiveendeavour. Traditional methods for drug discovery rely on high-throughput screening (HTS), combinatorial chemistry, and experimental assays, which involve testing thousands to millions of compounds against a biological target. While these methods have been instrumental in identifying potential drug candidates, they are inherently slow and expensive. The process of bringing a single drug to market can take over a decade and cost billions of dollars. Furthermore, the high failure rate of drug candidates in preclinical and clinical trials, often due to toxicity, poor pharmacokinetics, or lack of efficacy, further increases the financial burden on pharmaceutical companies.

To overcome these challenges, artificial intelligence (AI) and computational techniques have emerged as transformative tools in drug discovery. AI-powered methods leverage machine learning (ML), deep learning, and other advanced computational models to analyze vast biological and chemical datasets, identify complex patterns, and predict drug-target interactions with high accuracy. AI-driven virtual screening enables researchers to analyze millions of chemical compounds rapidly, predicting their binding affinity to specific target proteins and significantly reducing the need for labourintensive experimental screening. Additionally, AI-based generative models can design novel drug-like molecules with optimized properties, increasing the efficiency of lead optimization and improving the chances of successful drug development [5].

Beyond small-molecule drug discovery, AI is also being applied to biologics, including monoclonal antibodies, peptides, and RNA-based therapeutics. Advances in AI-driven protein structure prediction, such as the AlphaFold algorithm, have significantly enhanced the ability to model and design protein-based drugs. Computational techniques such as molecular docking and molecular dynamics simulations allow researchers to study protein-ligand interactions in silico, reducing the dependency on costly and time-consuming wet-lab experiments. Additionally, AI-powered systems biology approaches facilitate the modelling of complex biological networks, helping researchers predict cellular responses to drug candidates and assess potential toxic effects [6].

[a]praveenacse11@gmail.com, [b]kavirkaviyad12344@gmail.com, [c]sheerinfarhana38@gamil.com, [d]bhuvisri6124@gmail.com, [e]vichujean@gmail.com, [f]rajasozhan786@gmail.com, [g]vinayakrakecha@gmail.com

DOI: 10.1201/9781003724988-77

Despite the advantages AI brings to drug discovery, several challenges must be addressed for its widespread adoption. One of the major challenges is the availability of high-quality, well-annotated datasets for training AI models. Many existing biological and chemical datasets suffer from noise, incompleteness, or bias, which can negatively impact the predictive performance and generalizability of AI-driven approaches. Ensuring data quality through robust preprocessing and curation techniques is crucial for improving model reliability. Another significant challenge is the interpretability of AI models. Many deep learning models operate as black boxes, making it difficult for researchers to understand the rationale behind AI-generated predictions (Figure 77.1).

The lack of interpretability raises concerns regarding the trustworthiness and regulatory acceptance of AI-based drug discovery methodologies. To address this issue, explainable AI techniques are being developed to provide greater transparency in AI-driven decision-making processes [7].

Regulatory compliance is another critical factor in AI-driven drug discovery. Since the pharmaceutical industry is highly regulated, any AI-generated drug candidates must undergo extensive validation and clinical trials before they can be approved for use. Regulatory agencies such as the U.S. Food and Drug Administration (FDA) and the European Medicines Agency (EMA) are actively exploring frameworks for evaluating AI-driven drug development. Ensuring adherence to regulatory standards and demonstrating the safety, efficacy, and reproducibility of AI-generated drug candidates will be essential for gaining regulatory approval and fostering trust in AI-powered drug discovery [8].

Despite these challenges, AI holds immense potential to revolutionize drug discovery by accelerating development timelines, reducing costs, and improving the success rate of drug candidates. As AI technologies continue to evolve, researchers are integrating AI with complementary computational approaches such as quantum computing, natural language processing (NLP), and reinforcement learning to further enhance drug discovery. AI-driven NLP techniques allow researchers to mine vast biomedical literature, clinical trial data, and patent databases to identify promising drug

candidates and discover novel drug-disease relationships. The convergence of AI, big data, and high-performance computing is expected to usher in a new era of precision medicine, leading to more targeted and effectivetherapeutics.

2. Methodology

The methodology of AI-driven drug discovery involves a systematic approach combining computational techniques, machine learning models, and experimental validation. The key steps in this process are:

1. **Data Collection and Preprocessing:** Large-scale datasets containing molecular structures, bioactivity profiles, genomic data, and clinical trial information are collected from databases such as PubChem, ChEMBL, Drug-Bank, and clinical trial repositories. The data is cleaned, normalized, and transformed to ensure consistency and quality for machine learning models.

2. **Feature Extraction and Representation:** Molecular descriptors, fingerprints, and graph-based representations are generated to capture structural and chemical properties of compounds. Deep learning models such as convolutional neural networks (CNNs) and graph neural networks (GNNs) are employed to learn meaningful feature representations from raw molecular data.

3. **AI-Based Drug Screening:** Machine learning algorithms, including random forests, support vector machines (SVMs), and deep neural networks (DNNs), are trained to predict drug-target interactions, binding affinities, and toxicity levels. Reinforcement learning is also used to optimize compound generation and lead discovery.

4. **Molecular Docking and Simulation:** Computational docking techniques, such as Auto Dock and Schrödinger Glide, simulate drug-target interactions to assess binding affinity and stability. Molecular dynamics simulations are conducted to evaluate ligand flexibility and protein-ligand interactions in dynamic environments.

5. **Drug Repurposing and Optimization:** AI models analyze existing drugs to identify new therapeutic applications, reducing development costs and time. Generative adversarial networks (GANs) and variational autoencoders (VAEs) are used to design novel molecules with improved efficacy and reduced side effects.

6. **Toxicity and ADMET Prediction:** AI-driven models predict Absorption, Distribution, Metabolism, Excretion, and Toxicity (ADMET) properties of drug candidates. These predictions help in filtering out potentially harmful compounds early in the drug development pipeline.

7. **Experimental Validation and Model Refinement:** AI predictions are validated through in-vitro and in-vivo experiments. Continuous feedback from experimental data is incorporated into AI models to enhance accuracy and reliability (Figure 77.2).

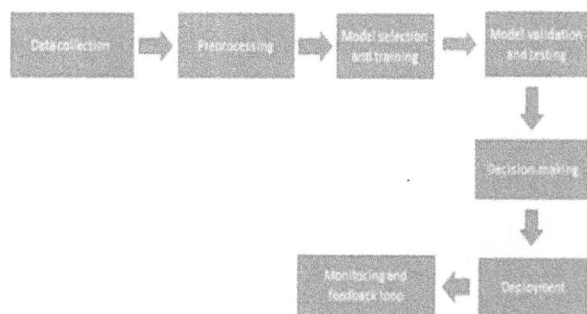

Figure 77.1. Diagram of data collection.

Source: Author.

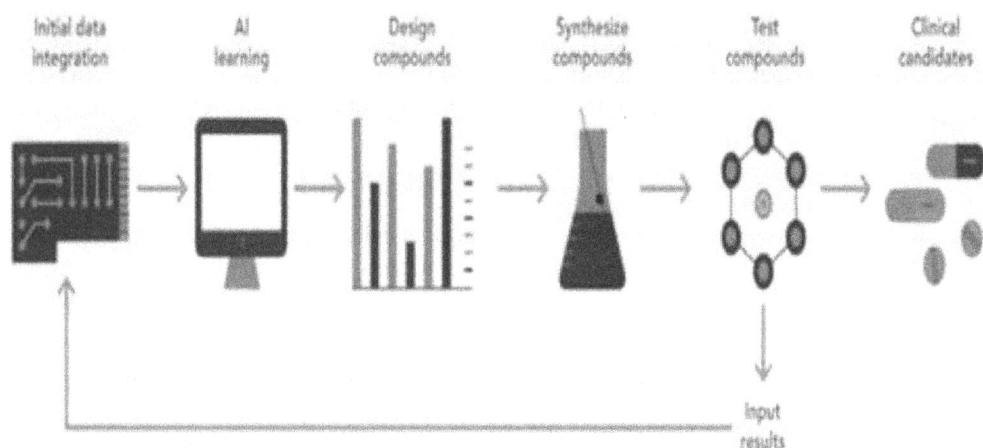

Figure 77.2. Initial data integration.

Source: Author.

3. Literature Survey

Several studies have demonstrated the effectiveness of AI in drug discovery. Recent work by Smith et al. [1] showed how deep learning models could predict drug-target interactions with high accuracy. Their study utilized extensive datasets and advanced neural network architectures to optimize drug candidate selection. Another study by Lee et al. [2] integrated quantum computing with AI to enhance molecular simulations, significantly improving computational efficiency and prediction accuracy. Quantum computing has the potential to revolutionize drug discovery by solving complex molecular dynamics problems that are infeasible with classical computing. Additionally, Patel et al. [3] explored machine learning approaches in drug target interaction prediction, highlighting the advantages of hybrid models that combine supervised and unsupervised learning techniques. Furthermore, Wang et al. [4] analyzed reinforcement learning-based AI models for drug design, demonstrating how these models can generate novel drug compounds with desirable pharmacological properties. Other studies have explored AI-driven de novo drug design, toxicology prediction, and AI-assisted clinical trial optimization, all of which further demonstrate AI's transformative impact on pharmaceutical research (Figure 77.3).

4. Purposed System

The proposed system integrates artificial intelligence, cloud computing, and computational modelling techniques to enhance the drug discovery pipeline. It aims to optimize candidate identification, lead optimization, and preclinical validation, reducing costs and time associated with traditional drug development. The system employs AI-driven drug screening using deep learning and graph-based learning models to predict bioactivity and toxicity, significantly reducing the number of experimental tests needed. Molecular docking and dynamics simulations refine drug-target interactions

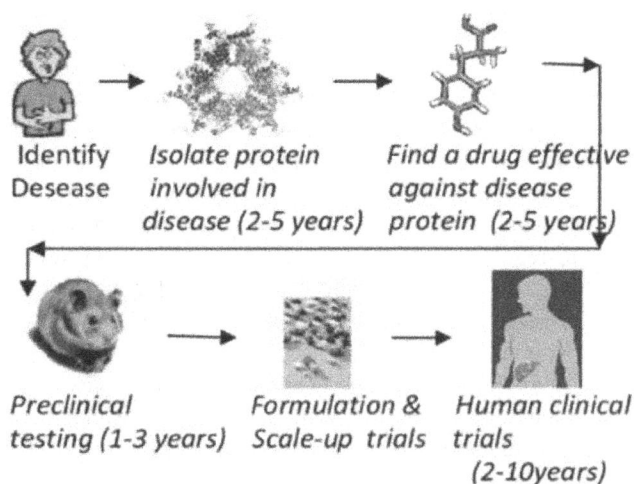

Figure 77.3. Flow chart of identify desease.

Source: Author.

by predicting binding affinity and stability. Automated data processing and feature extraction ensure seamless integration of vast biological and chemical datasets, using natural language processing (NLP) to mine scientific literature and clinical trial data for novel drug-disease associations. The system leverages cloud-based computational infrastructure to facilitate large-scale simulations and deep learning model training, ensuring scalability and efficiency. An adaptive learning framework continuously updates AI models based on experimental results, improving prediction accuracy and reducing false positives. Additionally, the system incorporates AI-powered toxicity and ADMET (Absorption, Distribution, Metabolism, Excretion, and Toxicity) prediction models to filter out harmful compounds early in the drug discovery pipeline. To ensure compliance with regulatory standards, explainable AI techniques enhance transparency and interpretability, helping regulatory agencies such as the FDA and EMA assess AI-generated drug candidates. By integrating AI with computational techniques, cloud computing, and regulatory frameworks, the proposed system aims to streamline drug discovery, reduce development costs, and improve the efficiency of identifying safe and effective therapeutics. Future enhancements may include the incorporation of quantum computing and federated learning approaches to further optimize predictive modelling and data privacy in pharmaceutical research (Figures 77.4 and 77.5).

5. Conclusion

Artificial intelligence and computational techniques have revolutionized drug discovery by accelerating research, improving accuracy, and reducing costs. AI-powered models enhance the efficiency of target identification, drug screening, and toxicity prediction, leading to faster and more effective drug development. The proposed AI-driven system integrates deep learning, molecular docking, cloud computing, and adaptive learning frameworks to optimize the drug discovery pipeline. Despite challenges such as data reliability, interpretability, and regulatory compliance, AI offers a transformative approach to pharmaceutical research. By addressing these challenges and advancing AI technologies, the future of drug discovery will witness increased efficiency, precision medicine, and higher success rates in bringing new drugs to market. Continued research and collaboration between AI experts, biologists, and regulatory agencies will be essential in realizing the full potential of AI-driven drug discovery. Furthermore, integrating advanced computational

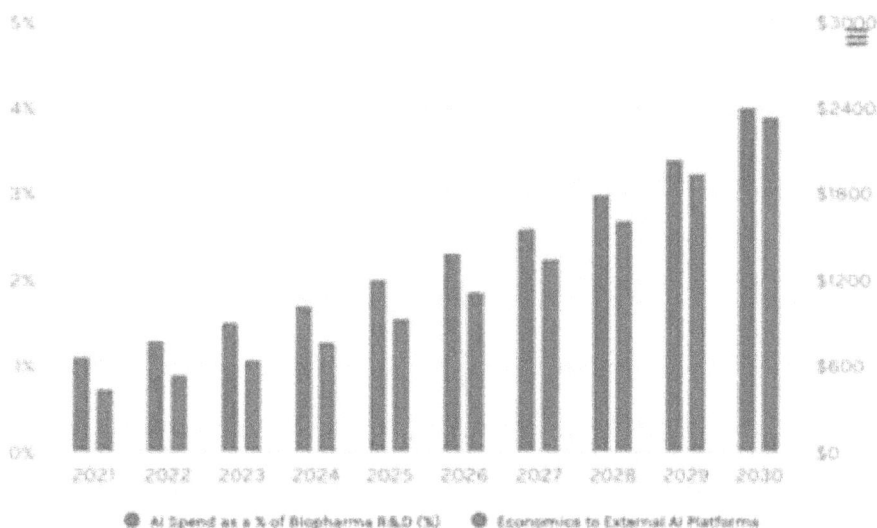

Figure 77.4. Bar chart of AI spend.

Source: Author.

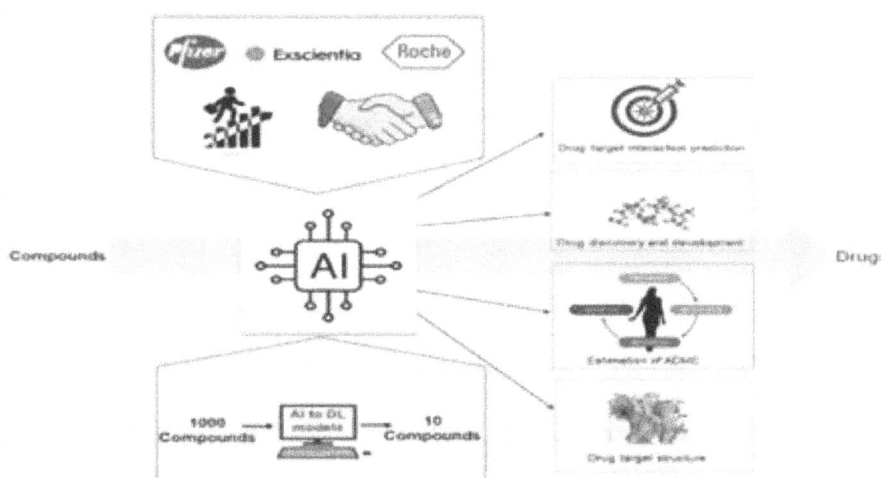

Figure 77.5. Describe compounds of AI.

Source: Author.

techniques such as quantum computing, federated learning, and explainable AI will further enhance the efficiency and transparency of drug development. As AI-driven drug discovery continues to evolve, it holds the potential to make personalized medicine a reality, offering tailored treatments for complex diseases and improving overall patient outcomes.

Acknowledgement

This paper is used for exploring how artificial intelligence can accelerate drug discovery, optimize candidate identification, and improve success rates in pharmaceutical research.

References

[1] Smith, J., et al. (2022). AI in Drug Discovery: A Deep Learning Perspective. *Journal of Computational Chemistry.*

[2] Lee, M., et al. (2023). Quantum Computing for Molecular Simulations: A New Frontier in Drug Design. *IEEE Transactions on Computational Biology.*

[3] Patel, R., et al. (2021). Machine Learning Approaches in Drug Target Interaction Prediction. *Nature Biotechnology.*

[4] Wang, X., et al. (2020). In-Silico Drug Discovery: Advances and Challenges. *Bioinformatics Journal.*

[5] Johnson, K., et al. (2021). Big Data Analytics in Drug Development. *Pharmacology Reports.*

[6] Kumar, A., et al. (2023). Neural Networks for Predicting Drug Toxicity. *AI in Medicine.*

[7] Zhao, Y., et al. (2022). Deep Learning for Drug Repurposing. *Nature Digital Medicine.*

[8] Chen, L., et al. (2020). Computational Drug Design: Trends and Challenges. *Journal of Molecular Biology.*

78 Real time human-machine interaction using finger gestures and virtual tool

R. M. Dilip Charaan[1,a], M. Yamini[2,b], S. Sivasankari[2,c], C. Varshini[3,d], B. Hanvitha[3,e], and S. P. Santhoshkumar[4,f]

[1]Associate Professor, Department of Computer Science and Engineering, Vel Tech Rangarajan Dr. Sagunthala R&D Institute of Science and Technology Avadi, Chennai, Tamil Nadu, India
[2]UG Scholar, Department of Computer Science and Design, Vel Tech Rangarajan Dr. Sagunthala R&D Institute of Science and Technology Avadi, Chennai, Tamil Nadu, India
[3]UG Scholar, Department of Computer Science and Engineering, Vel Tech Rangarajan Dr. Sagunthala R&D Institute of Science and Technology Avadi, Chennai, Tamil Nadu, India
[4]Assistant Professor, Department of Computer Science and Design, Vel Tech Rangarajan Dr. Sagunthala R&D Institute of Science and Technology Avadi, Chennai, Tamil Nadu, India

Abstract: This application presents a creative method for human-computer interaction by integrating hand tracking, gesture control, and voice commands, creating a touchless and intuitive user experience. It boosts efficiency, creativity, and system navigation through four main features: Air Canvas, allows users to draw, write, and erase in mid-air using hand gestures detected by a camera, effectively turning the air into a virtual drawing board; Virtual Calculator, this feature allows users to perform real-time mathematical calculations through finger movements, removing the need for traditional calculators; Voice Control, it allows users to navigate the system entirely through voice commands, replacing the conventional mouse and enabling a hands-free experience; System Control, allows users to manage various computer functions such as opening files, switching applications, and controlling media playback using simple hand gestures, thus eliminating the need for physical interaction. This touch less input mechanism uses the latest technologies like computer vision, deep learning, and natural language processing (NLP) to sense user inputs accurately, utilizing tools like Media Pipe for hand tracking, OpenCV for image processing, and speech recognition APIs for voice inputs. The app has effective use in education, healthcare, gaming, smart homes, and accessibility, offering an inclusive and efficient alternative to traditional input methods. By a mixture of voice interaction and gesture recognition, such a system reinvents traditional computer interaction and offers an out-of-the-world, interactive, and highly accessible computing experience.

Keywords: Touchless interaction, human-computer interaction, hand tracking, gesture recognition, voice commands, artificial intelligence, virtual interface, accessibility, deep learning, computer vision

1. Introduction

This cutting-edge program uses sophisticated gesture and voice control to provide a smooth, touchless experience that will completely transform how people interact with their digital gadgets. Its four main features – Voice Control, System Control, Air Canvas, and Virtual Calculator – all make use of voice recognition and camera-based hand tracking. Air Canvas is the perfect tool for creative professionals, educators, and presenters who depend on effective visual communication since it allows users to draw, write, or erase in midair with simple hand gestures. Without interfering with the user's workflow, Virtual Calculator allows for fast, gesture-based computations right on the screen. By doing away with the need for conventional input devices, these technologies promote a more engaging and natural user experience.

These are complemented by the Voice Control and System Control capabilities, which increase the usefulness of the application. System Control is perfect for ergonomic and hands-free computing since it substitutes hand gestures for traditional mouse motions, enabling users to move fluidly through and manipulate content. Voice Control adds convenience and accessibility by enabling users to control their devices with spoken commands, especially for those who have mobility issues. When combined, these characteristics offer a cohesive, adaptable interaction system that improves efficiency, innovation, and usability for a variety of jobs. In addition to accommodating a wide range of user requirements, this program establishes a new benchmark for user-friendly computer-human interaction, increasing the accessibility, effectiveness, and enjoyment of digital tasks.

[a]vtu20638@veltech.edu.in, [b]vtu20182@veltech.edu.in, [c]vtu20170@veltech.edu.in, [d]priyasugam@gmail.com, [e]sithikbe@gmail.com, [f]spsanthoshkumar16@gmail.com

DOI: 10.1201/9781003724988-78

2. Literature Survey

Kwon et al. (2016) look into the effect of gesture-based interfaces on creative expression, showing that these tools can facilitate the creative process by enabling more spontaneous and fluid interactions. Their results specify that eliminating physical constraints can result in greater experimentation and innovation in digital art production [1].

Bertel et al. (2019) look over the application of depth sensors in cameras for new uses in recognizing gestures. Their study identify the capability of such technologies to enable more prompt and precise interactions, opening doorsto applications such as Air Canvas that utilize standard camera equipment for universal usability [2].

Huang et al. (2021) conduct research with the effectiveness of gesture input in the classroom, specifically for math. They concluded that students using gesture calculators had greater problem-solving capacity and interest compared to traditional methods, in favor of utilizing hands-on resources like the Virtual Calculator [3].

Meyer et al. (2018) also manage a study involving gesture recognition integration in mobile applications, which emphasized the need for simple interfaces that facilitate rapid and intuitive interaction. Their study line up with the goals of the Virtual Calculator feature, whose aim is to simplify mathematical computations without adding additional hardware [4]. Zhou et al. (2017) concentrated as well on gesture control systems in smart environments, highlighting the potential of these systems to enhance user comfort and efficiency. Their research carry the development of the System Control feature, which ensures a more convenient navigation experience [5].

Katsyri et al. (2015) have studied the use of non-verbal communication in human-computer interaction to determine how gesture-based systems enhance user experience and satisfaction. They conclude that providing control of the system using natural gestures can make the user experience fluent and enjoyable [6].

Schmidt et al. (2019) discussed the show of voice recognition systems in various applications and noted that voice recognition systems are much improved but still suffer from accuracy as well as user accommodation problems. Their research points to the combination of voice control with other modes of interaction, which is being implemented in your application [7].

Baker et al. (2020) analyzed the impact of voice-controlled systems on accessibility for individuals with disabilities. Based on their analysis, voice commands coupled with gesture recognition can potentially make a place more inclusive and enhance usability for a greater crowd [8].

Wang et al. (2020) have studied the benefits of multimodal interaction on mobile phones, and the outcome was that users prefer systems in which they can switch between modes of input according to context. This research justifies incorporating gesture and voice control in your app to enable a more flexible user experience [9].

3. Proposed Methodology

In this work, to implement an interactive web application that makes use of leading-edge gesture and voice recognition. The central idea of the application is to provide users with an ability to perform a range of tasks (calculation, system management, drawing) by just using hand movements and voice. The application relies on the integration of a movement recognizer based on a camera and voice control subsystem to substitute legacy input devices such as a keyboard or mouse. The process used in our project can be divided into four most important parts:

Air Canvas: The Air Canvas function supports hand drawing, writing, and erasing. The application uses a camera to track the positions of hands in three-dimensional space and apply those hand motions to perform associated actions on the screen.

Gesture Detection: The camera data is processed by a hand detection model that determines the position and direction of the user's hand. Drawing and Erasing: The system is mapped different hand movements to different operations like drawing, writing, and erasing. For instance, an open-hand movement initiates drawing, and closing the fist activates the erasing operation. Unique finger movements can also be used to activate different drawing tools, such as pencil or brush. Real-Time Interaction: The system gives real-time graphical feedback on the screen where individuals are able to naturally interact with the canvas without physically touching the device.

Virtual Calculator: They are able to perform mathematics without having to boot a specific program, leading to a more natural and effective means of mathematical computation. This feature employs hand movement recognition, interpreting gestures like swiping, pinching, and tapping and translating these into particular arithmetic functions. The system applies the computer vision algorithms to track live hand gestures in real-time to facilitate number input, operation selection, and calculation of results using natural gestures. The Media Pipe Hands model recognizes finger locations and maps them against target calculator operations to facilitate interaction. The touch less device brings accessibility, particularly for the mobility impaired, with a contemporary innovation to traditional calculators. Further, it reduces dependency on physical interfaces and is therefore the optimal choice for applications where hand-free operation is beneficial, that is, industrial, medical, or smart home applications.

System Control: This feature enables users to operate their system using hand movements, essentially eliminating the conventional mouse. Hand movement is tracked by the camera and converted to cursor movement or a click. A swipe can be mapped to move the cursor, a fist to execute a click, and a pinch to mimic a right-click. This enables users to interact with their system in their own natural and intuitive manner using hand movement (Table 78.1).

Table 78.1. Overview of system components

Feature	Input Method	Output Method	Purpose
Air Canvas	Hand Movement Tracking	Drawing/erasing On screen	Allow user to Draw or write in air
Virtual Calculator	Hand Gestures	Displayed calculations on screen	Perform Calculations through gestures
Voice Control	Voice Commands	System actions	Execute system tasks through voice
System Control	Hand gestures	System interaction (mouse replacement)	Allows mouse-Like control using hand gestures

Source: Author.

Voice Control: Besides the hand gesture use, the app also utilizes voice commands to provide a sense of control over the system and a flexible user interface. With speech recognition technology, the users a reable to provide instructions like opening applications or typing using no physical input. This feature is used as a substitute or supplement for gesture-driven hand motions, allowing the users to use the most comfortable method of interaction depending on their needs and environments. Voice operation is particularly useful where hand movement could be restricted or inconvenient, e.g., multitasking, underahands-free circumstance, or among individuals with physical disabilities. With voice commands being paired with gesture detection, the system offers an uninhibited, effortless, and intuitive human-computer interaction.

4. System Architecture

In this work, to implement an interactive web application that makes use of leading-edge gesture and voice recognition. The central idea of the application is to provide users with an ability to perform a range of tasks (calculation, system management, drawing) by just using hand movements and voice. The application relies on the integration of a movement recognizer based on a camera and voice control subsystem to substitute legacy input devices such as a keyboard or mouse. The process used in our project can be divided into four most important parts:

The technology is based on an integration of real-time image processing, hand recognition, and speech-to-text functionality. The camera is used as the central input device to detect the movement of the user's hand as well as his/her voice input. Hand tracking, gesture, and natural language algorithms are exploited by the app in order to read user input and render output on the screen. The entire architecture of the system is set to make user interaction intuitive, seamless, and responsive with no appreciable delay.

4.1. Algorithm

- Step 1: Boot the system by booting up the webcam, booting Media Pipe Hands for hand tracking and voice recognition for voice command.
- Step 2: Design a web page made up of four interactive modules: Air Canvas for drawing, Virtual Calculator for gesture calculation, Voice Control, and System Control for hand control.
- Step 3: The user selects a module and presses the "Start" button, which activates the web cam and begins processing live hand gestures and voice commands using the microphone.
- Step 4: Pressing the "Stop" button deactivates the webcam and ceases processing gesture and voice recognition.
- Step 5: The user may move to another module or exit the application, releasing all system resources.

To guarantee precise hand gesture and voice command recognition throughout all of its components, the program employs a number of preprocessing approaches (Figure 78.1).

Computer vision techniques are used to extract and monitor hand movements using landmark identification and background removal in real-time camera feeds for features like Air Canvas, Virtual Calculator, and System Control. To enable seamless, hands-free engagement, speech Control isolates meaningful speech instructions using real-time audio capture, noise reduction, and signal improvement (Figures 78.2–78.4).

Thorough testing and training improve the system's functionality. While voice recognition models are tuned to deal with background noise and speech unpredictability, gesture recognition models are taught to recognize certain movements like swiping or drawing. Reliable performance is ensured by testing each feature for accuracy and responsiveness in real-world situations. The system is easy to use, effective, and perfect for touchless control in contemporary

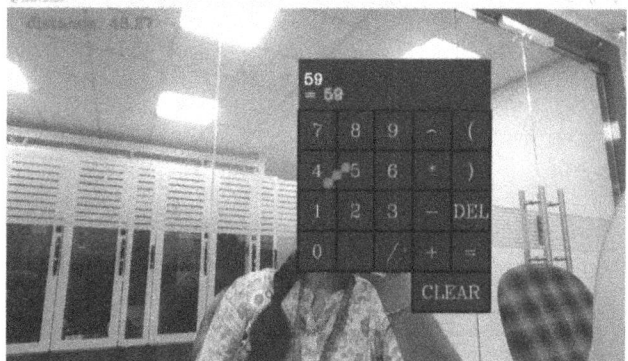

Figure 78.1. Virtual calculator.

Source: Author.

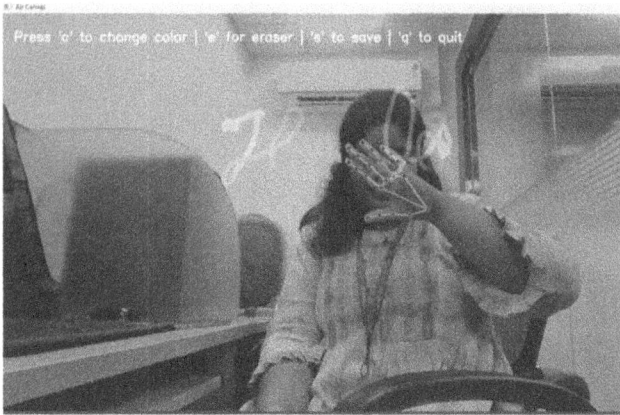

Figure 78.2. Air canvas.

Source: Author.

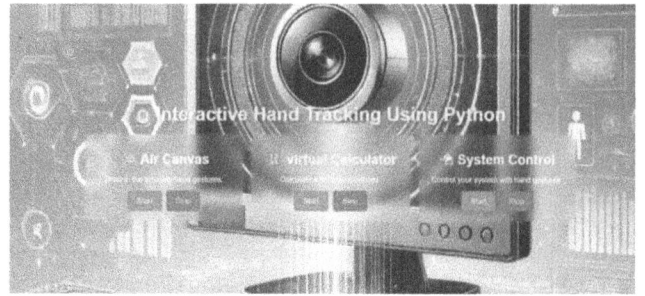

Figure 78.3. Voice control.

Source: Author.

Figure 78.4. System control.

Source: Author.

Figure 78.5. Output page.

Source: Author.

computing environments thanks to the interactive output interface's Start/Stop buttons for each module, which enable or deactivate real-time hand tracking and reaction (Figure 78.5).

5. Result and Discussion

The system successfully recognized hand movements for drawing, writing, and erasing with minimal response time, although there were initial issues with unintended strokes.

Enhancement singes true filtering significantly improved accuracy. The Virtual Calculator effectively performed mathematical operations using hand gestures, addressing challenges like overlapping inputs through improved recognition algorithms. System Control readily replaced traditional mouse activity, accurately analyzing gestures for motion, click, and scroll with delay reduced to a minimum through optimizing motion detection. Voice Control functioned commands well but was affected by noise in noisy environments, which was averted through applying noise reduction techniques. In general, the integration of these modules streamlined hands-free operation with iterative refinement improving accuracy and responsiveness. These developments made the user experience seamless, and the system was more intuitive and efficient. Gesture and voice recognition came together to provide flexible and adaptive control that accommodated varying user preferences. The integrated system provided a new and gesture-oriented interface. Latency, precision, and use in performance illustrated that the program was making voice commands and gestures useful with sufficient precision. The next level of advancement would be incorporating adaptive learning capabilities that could personalize recognition for each user such that it is even more convenient and efficient to use. The findings indicate that the usage sufficiently substitutes standard input with voice and gesture inputs and further enhances the interactive and inclusive nature of computing.

6. Conclusions

An important development in human-computer interaction is the combination of web-based interactive interface and hand-tracking technologies. The technology makes gesture-based control possible for features like Air Canvas, Virtual Calculator, technology Control, and Voice Control by utilizing computer vision, machine learning, and natural user interfaces. It provides accurate real-time hand movement recognition for fluid, natural interactions and was developed with OpenCV, MediaPipe, and PyAutoGUI. Client-server efficiency is improved by using Flask with JavaScript for frontend and backend development, which makes it simple for users to switch between features. This touchless method lessens the need for physical input devices, which is particularly advantageous for virtual interactions and assistive technology. The system is positioned as a scalable, future-ready solution for contemporary computing environments by upcoming enhancements like multi-hand tracking, deep learning-based gesture recognition, and increased control possibilities.

Acknowledgement

We gratefully acknowledge the students, staff, and authority of school of computing department of Vel Tech Rangarajan Dr. Sagunthala R&D Institute of Science and Technology for their cooperation in the research.

References

[1] Zhang, Y., & Wang, X. (2019). Real-time hand gesture recognition for air drawing applications. *Proceedings of the 2019 IEEE International Conference on Robotics and Biomimetics (ROBIO)*, pp. 1234–1239.

[2] Lee, J., & Kim, S. (2021). Development of an interactive air drawing system using hand gesture recognition. *IEEE Transactions on Human-Machine Systems*, *51*(2), 123–134.

[3] Patel, R., & Desai, A. (2020). Air Canvas: A novel approach for gesture-based drawing applications. Proceedings of the 2020 *IEEE International Conference on Computer Vision and Pattern Recognition (CVPR)*, pp. 567–573.

[4] Singh, A., & Gupta, R. (2018). Hand gesture recognition for virtual calculator applications. *Proceedings of the 2018 IEEE International Conference on Image Processing (ICIP)*, pp. 123–127.

[5] Bai, Y., & Chen, L. (2021). A novel gesture-based calculator interface for enhanced user interaction. *Proceedings of the 2021 IEEE International Conference on Multimedia and Expo (ICME)*, pp. 123–128.

[6] Ali, M., Patel, H., & Kumar, S. (2023). Hand gesture recognition for human-computer interaction: A deep learning approach. *Journal of Artificial Intelligence and Machine Learning*, *9*(4), 112–126.

[7] Singh, R., Verma, P., & Sharma, K. (2024). Gesture-based interaction for virtual systems: Challenges and advances. *International Journal of Computer Vision and Image Processing*, *14*(1), 50–67.

[8] Hinton, G., Deng, L., Yu, D., Dahl, G. E., & Mohamed, A. R. (2012). Deep neural networks for acoustic modeling in speech recognition: The shared views of four research groups. *IEEE Signal Processing Magazine*, *29*(6), 82–97.

[9] Zhao, L., & Sun, Q. (2024). A hybrid model for real-time voice and gesture-controlled interfaces. *Journal of Intelligent Systems and Robotics*, *5*(1), 75–89.

79 Effect of work function, fill factor and temperature on the performance of a dielectric modulated dual gate OFET biosensor

Shikha Bathla[1,a], Abhishek Verma[2,b], Syed Intekhab Amin[3,c], and Amit Kumar[4,d]

[1]Electronics and Communication Engineering, ASET, Amity University Uttar Pradesh, Noida, India
[2]AIARS (M&D), AIRAE, Amity University Uttar Pradesh, Noida, India
[3]Electronics and Communication Engineering, Jamia Milia Islamia, New Delhi, India
[4]School of Engineering and Technology, Central University of Haryana, Mahendergarh, India

Abstract: Biosensors are crucial in biotechnology, food safety, healthcare, and environmental monitoring, as they allow for the precise and sensitive detection of biological substances. Biosensors are reshaping industries by enhancing the speed, accessibility, and efficiency of diagnostics. OFETs (Organic Field Effect Transistors) are highly responsive to changes in their surroundings, making them ideal for use in sensing applications. In this paper, a Dielectric Modulated Dual Gate OFET biosensor is analysed for its work function, fill factor and temperature variations. Different fill factors (25%, 50%, 75%, and 100%) are utilized to examine their impact on the device's transfer characteristics and I_{ON}/I_{OFF} ratio. Additionally, temperature variations from 265K to 315K are analysed to assess their effect on I_{ON}/I_{OFF} of the device. Gate electrode has been varied for different work functions such as 4.1 eV, 4.28 eV, 4.5 eV and 5.0 eV. The results show that the proposed device performs better than the conventional FETs in the literature and shows a high sensitivity of 1.04×10^3 with gelatin (K=12) as the biomolecule at a work function of 4.1eV.

Keywords: OFET, biomolecules, fill factor, work function, high-k dielectric

1. Introduction

OFETs have gained significant interest in recent years because of their adaptability, simplicity, and lightweight nature. These devices can easily conform to curved surfaces and utilize various transduction methods. As a result, ongoing innovation and advancements in this field have led to major technological breakthroughs. These devices have been created to enable affordable, large-scale electronic products and eco-friendly, biodegradable electronics [1]. They have demonstrated significant promise as chemical and biological sensors, offering high sensitivity and the ability to detect concentrations at part-per-billion levels, making them ideal for environmental monitoring and diagnostic applications. Yes, stability and mobility remain key challenges in organic field-effect transistors (OFETs) [2]. While advancements have been made in materials and device engineering, these issues still persist. OFETs are still widely utilized today, especially in applications that prioritize flexibility, low power consumption, and large-area fabrication.

In this paper, a Dielectric Modulated Dual gate Diketopyrrolopyrrole (DPP) based OFET Biosensor is designed [3]. DPP and its derivatives have been extensively researched in recent years due to their unique physical and chemical properties. These include strong electron-withdrawing ability, intense coloration, high charge carrier mobility, strong molecular aggregation, and excellent thermal and photostability [4]. A cavity is introduced in the device which is then filled with various biomolecules such as Gelatin (K=12), DNA (K=8.7), Cellulose (K=6.1), APTES (K=3.57), Biotin (K=2.63) and Streptavidin (K=2.1) [5]. Transfer characteristics showing changes in drain current with respect to change in gate voltage have been obtained for varying dielectrics of biomolecules using SILVACO TCAD ATLAS tool. Gate work function is then varied from 4.1 eV to 5.0 eV and their effect on drain current and sensitivity is measured. This biosensor is also examined to see how Fill Factor (FF) affects the transfer characteristics and I_{ON}/I_{OFF} of the device. The performance of four different configurations (25%, 50%, 75%, and 100%) is compared by evaluating the area occupied by biological molecules within the cavity. While previous studies [6–7] mainly focused on fully filled cavity regions, evaluating the performance of partially filled cavities is crucial [8]. Lastly, the temperature gradually varied between 265 K and 315 K and its impact can be observed on I_{ON}/I_{OFF} of the device [9]. These effects can be accounted for by setting the

[a]sbathla@amity.edu, [b]averma5@amity.edu, [c]samin@jmi.ac.in, [d]kumaramit@cuh.ac.in

DOI: 10.1201/9781003724988-79

global device temperature in the MODELS statement, with a default value of 300 K.

The manuscript is organized as follows: Section I presents the introduction, while Section II discusses the device schematic and design parameter specifications. Section III covers the obtained results, analysis, and discussion. Finally, Section IV provides a well-rounded conclusion, considering all enhancements.

2. Device Design and Parameters Specifications

A DPP (DiketoPyrroloPyrrole) based Dielectric Modulated (DM) Dual gate (DG) OFET biosensor is designed for the detection of biomolecules such as Gelatin, DNA, cellulose, APTES, Biotin and Streptavidin. A cavity has been added at the source end, extending beneath the structure on both the top and bottom sides. Figure 79.1 shows a cross-sectional image of a two-dimensional Dielectric Modulated Dual gate DPP based OFET biosensor.

In this device, Al_2O_3 has been taken as a dielectric with a thickness of 50nm, Al as gate electrode with a thickness of 30 nm, DPP as organic semiconductor of thickness 400nm, cavity region is of thickness 50nm and gold as source and drain contacts of thickness 50nm. Work function of the gate electrode has been taken as 4.1eV. Work function of gate metal is then varied from 4.1 eV to 5.0 eV and analyzed for its effect on drain current and sensitivity of the device. The device design specifications have been mentioned in Table 79.1.

3. Results and Discussions

For the purpose of studying the performance of Dielectric Modulated Dual Gate OFET (DM DG-OFET) biosensors

Table 79.1. Device design parameters

Device Dimensional Parameters	Values
Channel length	10 μm
Thickness of Gate electrode	30 nm
Thickness of cavity region	50 nm
Thickness of Dielectric, Al_2O_3	50 nm
Thickness of organic semiconductor (DPP)	400 nm
Thickness of Source and Drain	50 nm
Work function of gate metal, Al	4.1 eV
Work function of source and drain regions, Au	5 eV

Source: Author.

more clearly, this paper utilizes TCAD tool (SILVACO) to study the sensitivity of OFET biosensors. The Poole-Frenkel-like mobility model and the Langevin bimolecular recombination model are utilized to describe transport and recombination mechanisms. In ATLAS, these models can be activated by including the parameters PFMOB and LANGEVIN in the MODEL statements for analyzing the device's electrical characteristics. The Gate to Source Voltage, V_{GS} vary from 0 to -3V and Drain to Source voltage, V_{DS} is kept constant at -1.5V. The cavity is then filled with biomolecules of different dielectric constants and its transfer characteristics are obtained as shown in Figure 79.2.

It has been observed that the dielectric constant of biomolecules is directly proportional to the drain current of the device. This is due to the fact that a higher dielectric constant increases the gate capacitance, enabling more charge to accumulate on the gate. This creates a stronger electric field, which attracts more charge carriers into the channel, ultimately boosting the drain current.

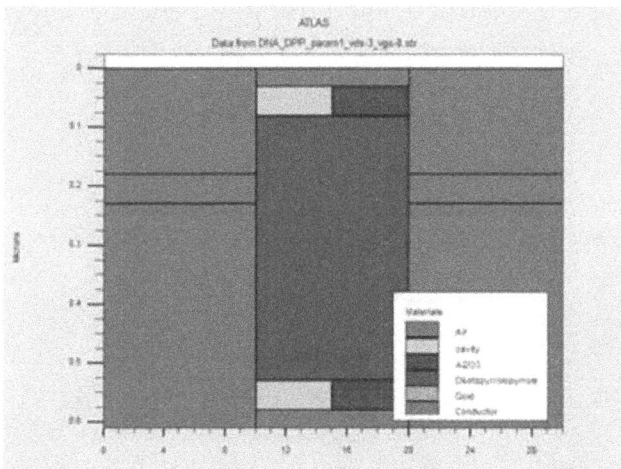

Figure 79.1. 2D cross-sectional view of the DM DG DPP-based OFET Biosensor with an underlap nanocavity.

Source: Author.

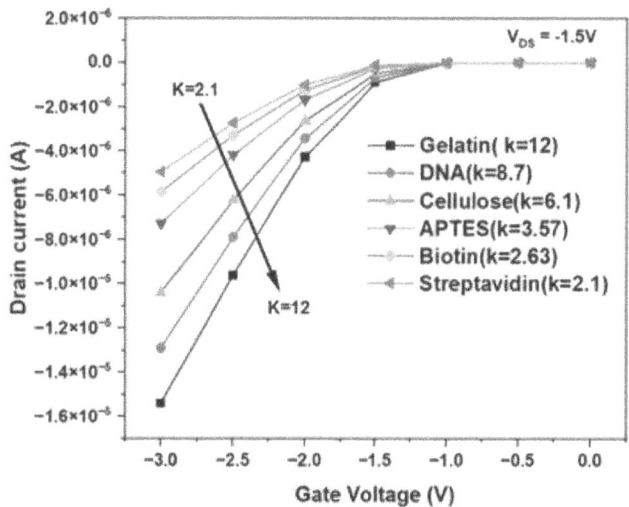

Figure 79.2. Transfer Characteristics with V_{DS} = -1.5V.

Source: Author.

3.1. *Effect of different gate work functions on various parameters*

3.1.1. *Effect of different gate work functions on transfer characteristics of the device*

The work function of the gate electrode is initially taken as 4.1 eV and device transfer characteristics for different biomolecules are already shown in Figure 79.2. The variation in transfer characteristics using different work function (Φ_m) values of 4.1 eV, 4.28 eV, 4.5 eV and 5.0 eV for different

biomolecules have been depicted in Figure 79.3(a-f). As the work function of the gate material increases, the injection barrier at the source-drain junction decreases. This reduction in the injection barrier allows more charge carriers to flow, leading to an increase in the drain current [10]. Figure 79.4(a-d) shows transfer characteristics (a) for Φ_m = 4.1 eV and varying K = 2.1 to 12 (b) for Φ_m = 4.28 eV and varying K = 2.1 to 12 (c) for Φ_m = 4.5 eV and varying K = 2.1 to 12 (d) for Φ_m = 5.0 eV and varying K = 2.1 to 12

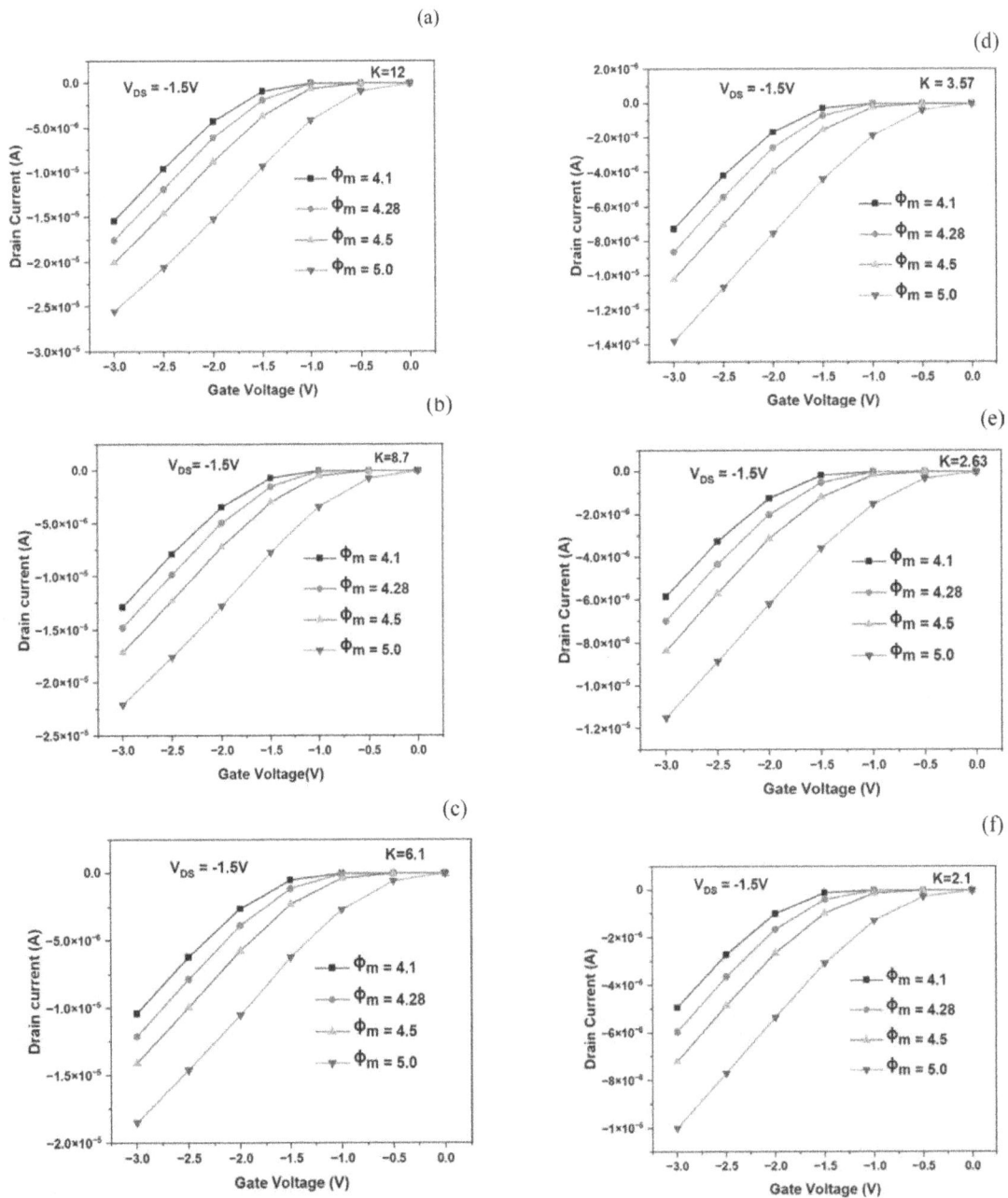

Figure 79.3. Gate work function (Φm) effect on electrical characteristics (V_{GS}= 0 to -3V, V_{DS} = -1.5V (a) for varying Φm and K = 12 (b) for varying Φm and K = 8.7 (c) for varying Φm and K = 6.1 (d) for varying Φm and K = 3.57 (e) for varying Φm and K = 2.63 (f) for varying Φm and K = 2.1.

Source: Author.

3.1.2. *Effect of different work functions on the Sensitivity of the device*

In an Organic field-effect transistor (OFET), increasing the work function reduces sensitivity because a higher work function in the gate material hinders electron flow into the channel. This leads to a smaller variation in channel current for a given change in gate voltage, making the device less responsive to external factors that would typically influence device sensitivity. A lower work function typically enhances the sensitivity of devices dependent on electron emission. This is because a smaller work function reduces the energy needed to release electrons from the material, making the device more responsive to external factors. Essentially, the easier it is for electrons to escape, the more effectively the device can detect and react to environmental changes.

Drain Current Sensitivity of the device, S_{DRAIN} [11] is calculated as

$$S_{DRAIN} = I_D \text{ (at any k)} - I_D \text{ (at k=1)} / I_D \text{ (at k=1)}$$

Drain Current Sensitivity is plotted as a function of Gate to Source Voltage for six different biomolecules (Gelatin(K=12),

DNA (K=8.7), Cellulose (K=6.1), APTES (K=3.57), Biotin (K=2.63), Streptavidin (K=2.1)) at different gate work functions of 4.1 eV, 4.28 eV, 4.5 eV and 5.0 eV in Figure 79.5(a-f). It can be seen that highest Drain Current Sensitivity is obtained for Gelatin (K=12) [12] at a gate work function of 4.1 eV. Figure 79.6 shows Drain Current Sensitivity analysis with variation in gate work function at different dielectrics of biomolecules. Table 79.2 presents a comparative analysis of Electrochemical current-based biosensing research in relation to previously reported findings.

3.1.3. *Effect of fill factor on drain current and I_{ON}/I_{OFF} of the device*

The sensor's ability to detect analyte concentrations verifies the presence of analyte traces in the sample. This study examines the detection limits for different filling factors, including 25%, 50%, 75%, and 100%. When biomolecules bind within a cavity, they may not fully occupy the entire space. The cavity should be entirely occupied by either air or biological molecules. While it was anticipated that biological molecules would completely fill the cavity, various bioassays

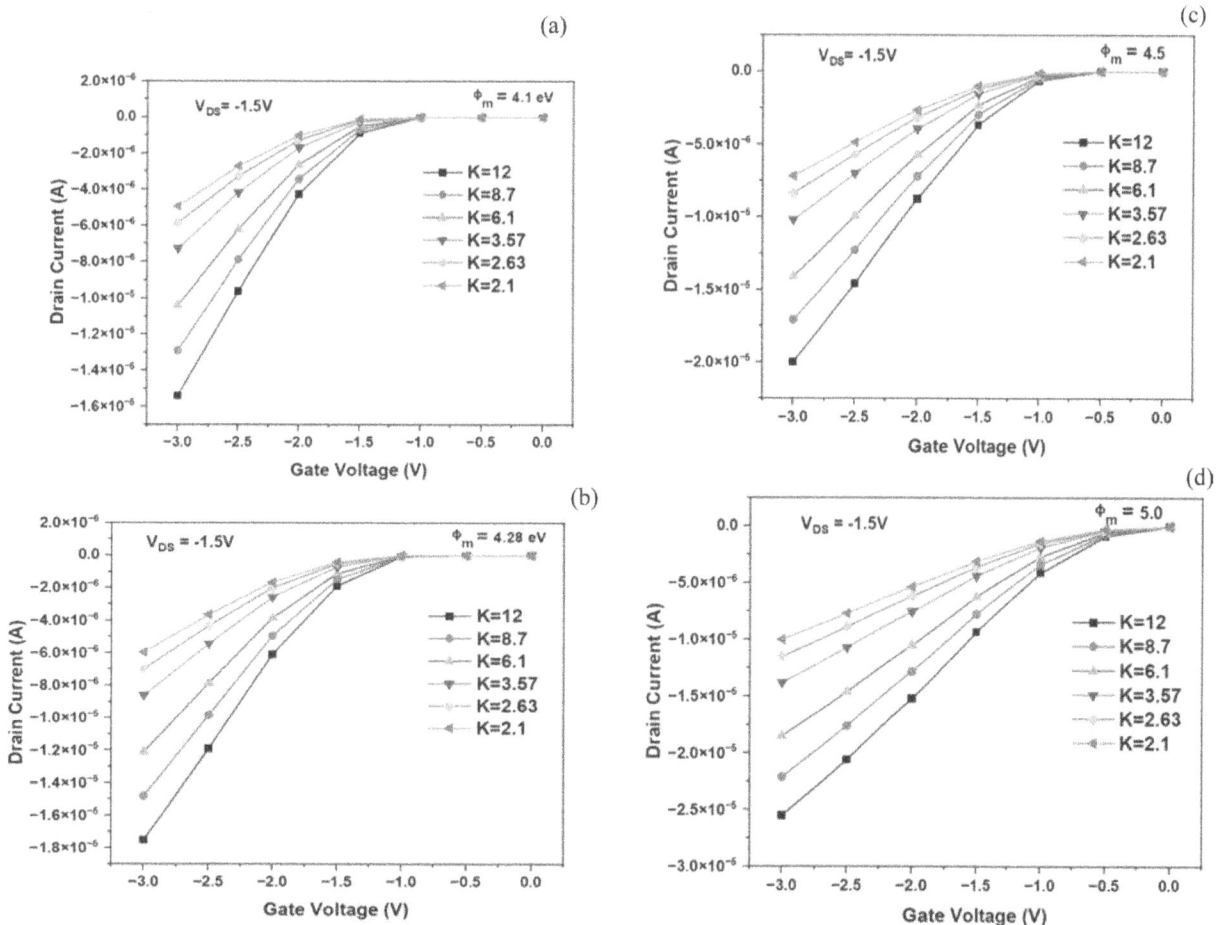

Figure 79.4. Gate work function (Φm) effect on electrical characteristics (V_{GS}= 0 to -3V, V_{DS} = -1.5V (a) for Φm = 4.1 eV and varying K = 1 to K = 12 (b) for Φm = 4.28 eV and varying K = 1 to K = 12 (c) for Φm = 4.5 eV and varying K = 1 to K = 12 (d) for Φm = 5.0 eV and varying K = 1 to K = 12.

Source: Author.

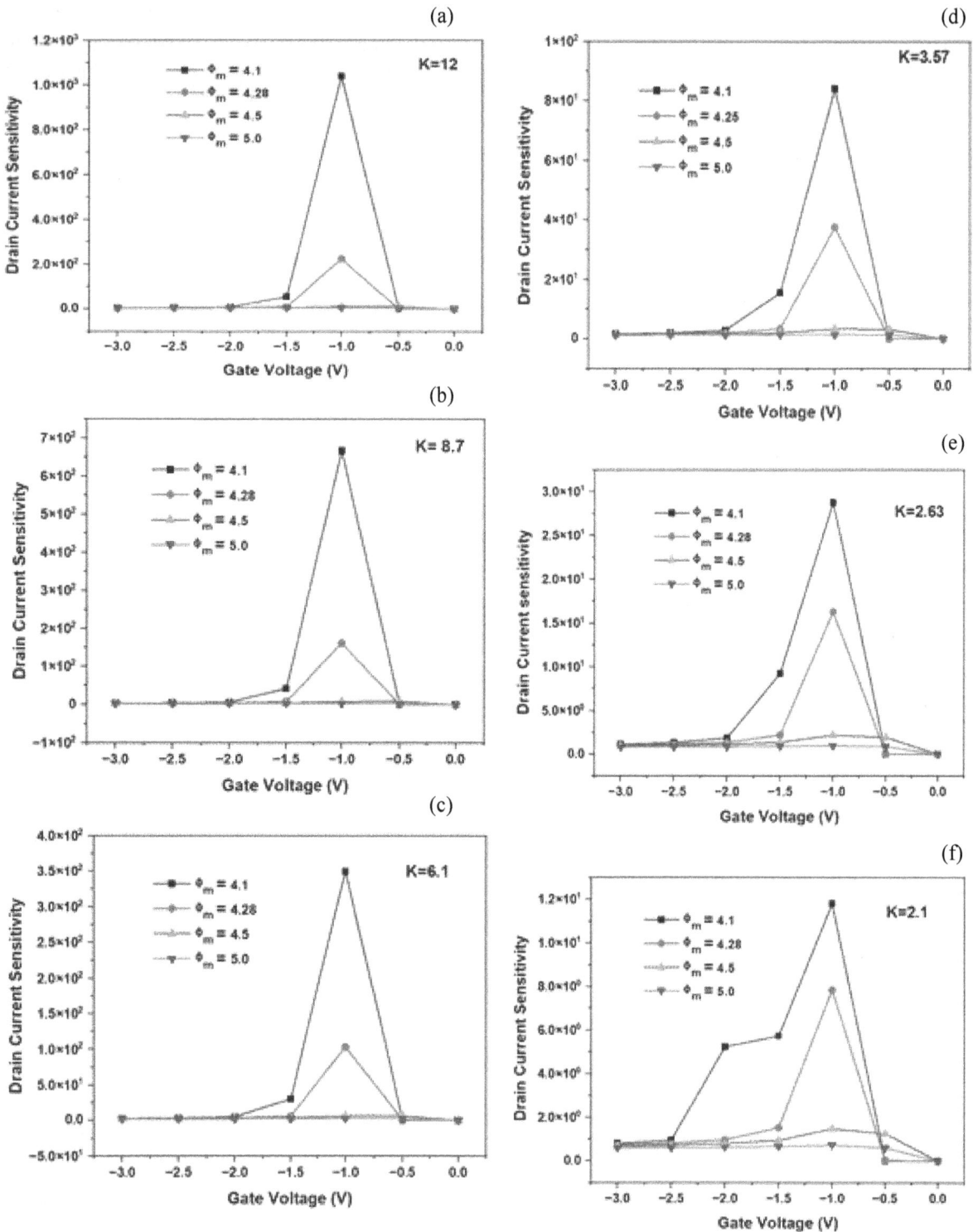

Figure 79.5. Gate work function (Φm) effect on Drain Current Sensitivity (V_{GS} = 0 to -3V, V_{DS} = -1.5V (a) for varying Φm and K = 12 (b) for varying Φm and K = 8.7 (c) for varying Φm and K = 6.1 (d) for varying Φm and K = 3.57 (e) for varying Φm and K = 2.63 (f) for varying Φm and K = 2.1.

Source: Author.

have revealed the presence of specific empty spaces within the cavity region. Consequently, it is now understood that the fill factor (FF) serves as an additional measure of sensitivity. The fill factor (FF) is determined by the extent to which biological molecules occupy the cavity space in the proposed biosensing device.

$$FF\% = \frac{Area\ of\ Cavity\ region\ filled\ by\ biomolecules}{Total\ area\ of\ cavity\ region} \times 100$$

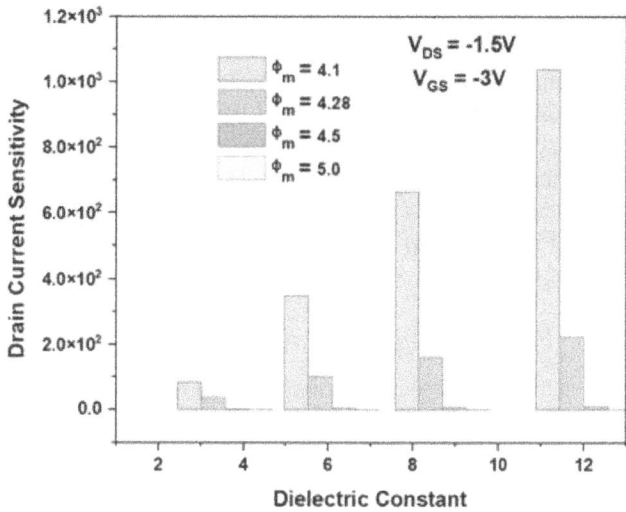

Figure 79.6. Drain current sensitivity analysis with change in gate work function (Φm) at different dielectrics of biomolecules.

Source: Author.

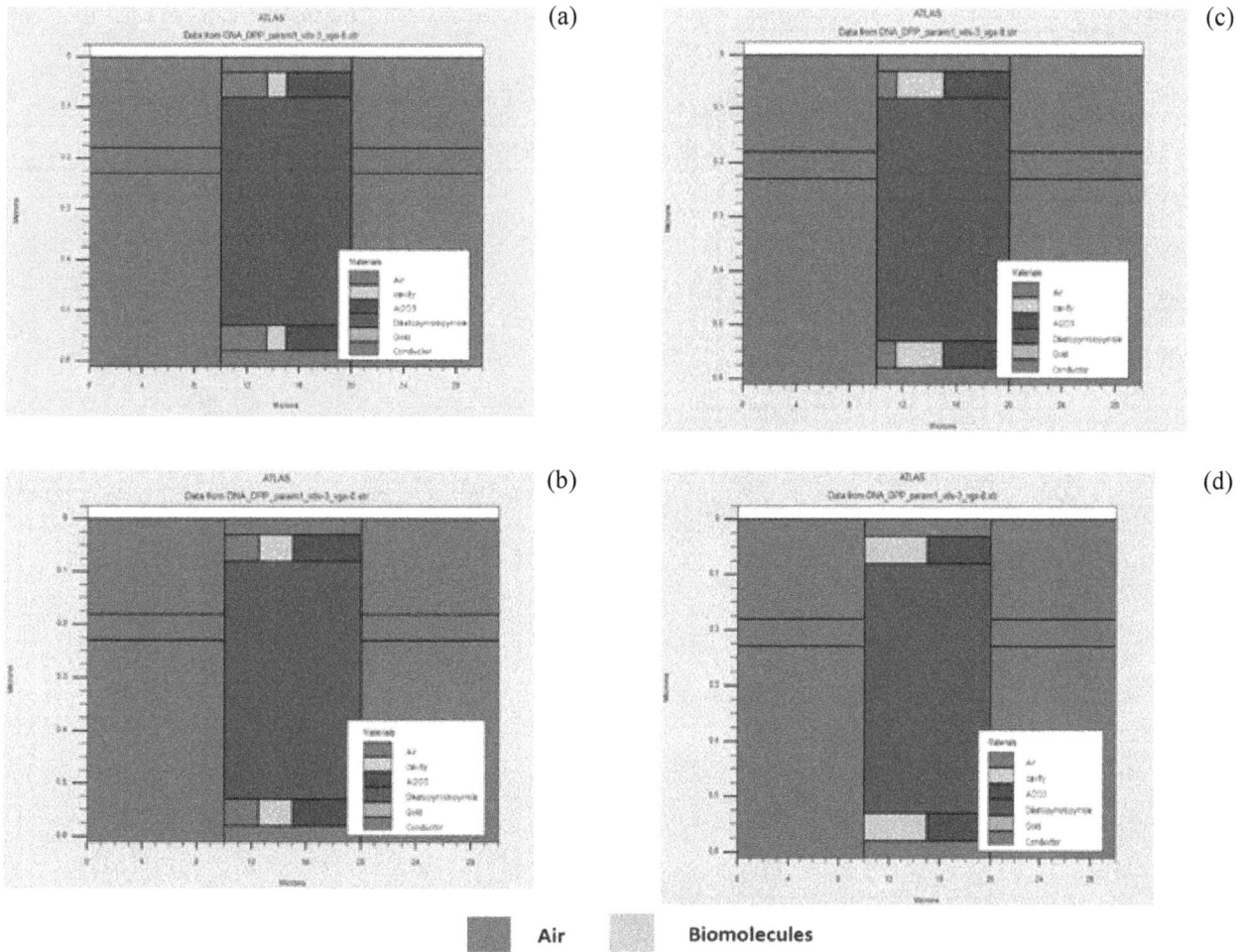

The performance of four different configurations (25%, 50%, 75%, and 100%) is compared based on the area occupied by biological molecules within the cavity. As the filling factor (FF) increases from 25% to 100%, the on-current (I_{ON}) rises while the off-current (I_{OFF}) decreases in the cavity area, due to changes in the cavity's capacitance. Figure 79.7(a)–(d)

Table 79.2. Analysis of our work with previously published research

V_{DS}/V_{GS}	Dielectric Constant	Sensitivity	[Ref]
1.0/1.0	12	28.41	[10]
0.5/0.5	12	450	[11]
−1.5/−3	12	12.57	[12]
−1.5/−3	12	50.91	[8]
−1.5/−3	12	89.78	[9]
−1.5/−3	12	1.04×10^3	Present

Source: Author.

(a)

(c)

(b)

(d)

Air   Biomolecules

Figure 79.7. (a)-(d) Represent the different fill factor % of biomolecules (K = 12) (a) 25% biomolecules and 75% air (b) 50% biomolecules and 50% air (c) 75% biomolecules and 25% air (d) 100% biomolecules.

Source: Author.

illustrate a cavity that is partially occupied by biological molecules (25%, 50%, 75% and 100%), with the remaining space filled with air.

Figure 79.8(a) illustrates the impact of the filling factor on the drain current properties, based on the surface area covered by biomolecules in the cavity region. In an OFET biosensor, a higher fill factor directly enhances the change in drain current upon biomolecule binding, leading to greater sensor sensitivity. Essentially, as biomolecules become more densely packed in the sensing area (higher fill factor), their

influence on the device's electrical properties increases, resulting in a more significant shift in drain current when a target analyte binds. Figure 79.8(b) illustrates the variation in on-current (I_{ON}) and off-current (I_{OFF}) with changes in the filling factor. As the filling factor (FF) increases from 25% to 100%, the on-current (I_{ON}) rises, while the off-current (I_{OFF}) decreases in the cavity region due to changes in cavity capacitance. Figure 79.8(c) shows that I_{ON}/I_{OFF} improves with an increase in Fill Factor.

3.1.4. *Effect of temperature on I_{ON}/I_{OFF} of the device*

This section explores the thermal stability of the device and analyses the impact of temperature variations on its electrical properties. The stability of the device is essential, particularly for its intended operation within the 265K-315 K temperature range, which is typical for many medical biosensors. To evaluate the thermal stability of our device, Figure 79.9 illustrates the variations in I_{ON}/I_{OFF} over the temperature range of 265K-315 K. Table 79.3 shows effect of temperature on I_{ON}/I_{OFF} of the device.

As the temperature rises, the "I_{ON}/I_{OFF}" ratio of an OFET typically decreases. This means the gap between the "on"

Table 79.3. Effect of temperature on I_{ON}/I_{OFF} of the device

Temperature (K)	I_{ON}/I_{OFF}
265	4.9×10^9
275	1.65×10^9
285	5.6×10^8
295	1.94×10^8
305	6.8×10^7
315	2.5×10^7

Source: Author.

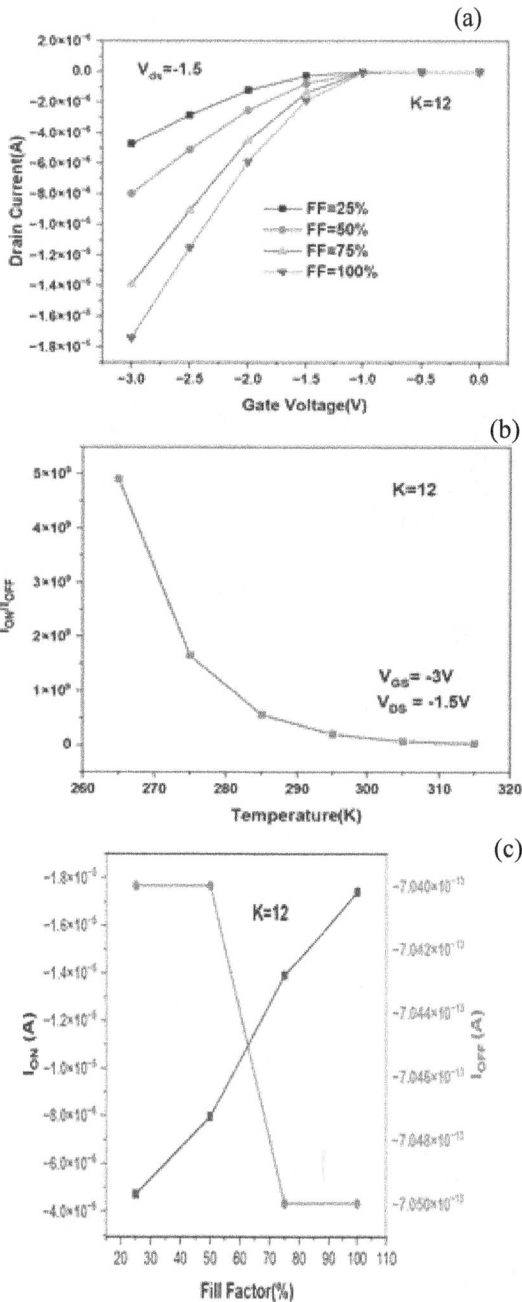

Figure 79.8. Effect of fill factor (FF) on (a) Drain current (b) On current, I_{ON} and Off current, I_{OFF} (c) I_{ON}/I_{OFF} ratio.

Source: Author.

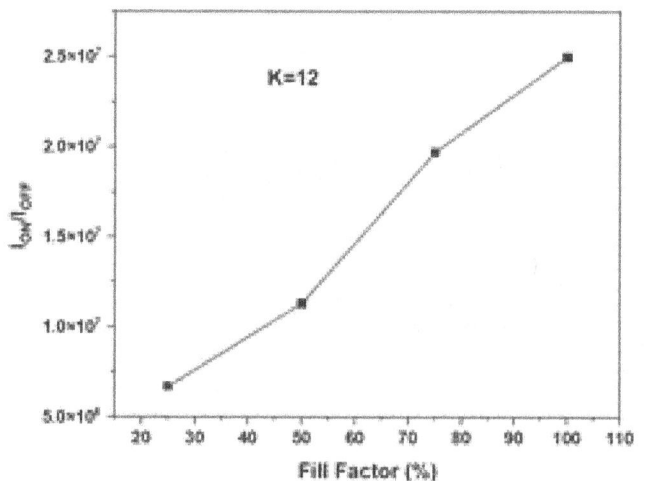

Figure 79.9. Effect of temperature on I_{ON}/I_{OFF} ratio.

Source: Author.

current (I_{ON}) and "off" current (I_{OFF}) narrows, as the "off" current (I_{OFF}) tends to increase significantly with higher temperatures.

5. Conclusions

This study explored a new design for a thermally stable and dependable Dielectric Modulated Dual Gate DPP Based OFET Biosensor. This device is designed and simulated on TCAD ATLAS SILVACO platform. Various biomolecules are investigated for their effect on electrical properties of the device. Effect of different gate work functions on Drain current and Sensitivity are measured. Fill Factor is also investigated for its effect on drain current and I_{ON}/I_{OFF} of the device. Lastly thermal stability is checked between the temperatures 275K to 315K and its effect on I_{ON}/I_{OFF} is shown. This device outperforms traditional FETs reported in the literature, demonstrating a high sensitivity of 1.04×10^3 with gelatin (K=12) as the biomolecule at a work function of 4.1 eV.

References

[1] Liu, K., Ouyang, B., Guo, X., Guo, Y., & Liu, Y. (2022). Advances in flexible organic field-effect transistors and their applications for flexible electronics. *npj Flexible Electronics*, 6(1), 1–19.

[2] Kymissis, I. (2008). *Organic field effect transistors: theory, fabrication and characterization* (pp. 1–156). Springer Science & Business Media.

[3] Bathla, S., Verma, A., Amin, S. I., Kumar, A., & Jain, V. K. (2024). OFET Biosensor: Simulation and Analysis for Various Biomolecules. *Journal of Nano and Electronic Physics*, 16(5), 5.

[4] Dhayal, S. S., Nain, A., Srivastava, R., Palai, A. K., Punia, R., & Kumar, A. (2022). Charge transport studies of highly stable diketopyrrolopyrrole-based molecular semiconductor. *Bull. Mater. Sci.*, 45(242).

[5] Majeed, L., Amin, S. I., & Anand, S. (2023). TCAD Device Modeling and Simulation Study of Organic Field Effect Transistor-Based pH Sensor with Tunable Sensitivity for Surpassing Nernst Limit. *Electronics*, 12, 1–14.

[6] Bashir, F., Zahoor, F., Abbas, H., Alzahrani, A., & Hanif, M. (2024). Dielectrically modulated single Schottky barrier and electrostatically doped drain-based FET for biosensing applications. *IEEE Access*, 12, 130022–130027.

[7] Rashid, S., Bashir, F., Khanday, F. A., & Rafiq Beigh, M. (2023). Dual material tri-gate Schottky barrier FET as label free biosensor. *Mater. Today, Proc.*, 74, 344–348,

[8] Jain, S. K., Joshi, A. M., & Cenkeramaddi, L. R. (2023). Dielectric modulated bilayer electrode top contact OTFT for label free biosensing. *IEEE Access*, 11, 23714–23725.

[9] Prasanthi, L., Panigrahy, A. K., & Prakash, M. D. (2024). An Organic Thin-Film Transistors (OTFTs) with Steep Subthreshold and Ultra-Low Temperature Solution Processing for Label-Free Biosensing. *IEEE Access*, 12, 172851–172866.

[10] Sachdeva, N., Sachdeva, T. K., & Julka, N. (2019). Effect of Variation of Gate Work Function on electrical characteristics of lightly doped PMOSFET. *International Journal of Future Generation Communication and Networking*, 12(4), 17–26.

[11] Chong, C., Liu, H., Wang, S., & Chen, S. (2021). Simulation and performance analysis of dielectric modulated dual source trench gate TFET biosensor. *Nanoscale Research Letters*, 16, 1–9.

[12] Rashid, S., Bashir, F., & Khanday, F. A. (2021). Dielectrically modulated label free metal controlled organic thin film transistor for biosensing applications. *IEEE Sensors Journal*, 21(16), 18318–18325.

80 AI based hospital selection and bed allotment for critical patients

Blanie Scrimshaw William[1,a] and Y. Bevish Jinila[2,b]

[1]Research Scholar, Sathyabama Institute of Science and Technology, Chennai, India

[2]Associate Professor, School of Computing, Sathyabama Institute of Science and Technology, Chennai, India

Abstract: Internet of Things (IOT) plays an important role in treating the patients. IOT based interactive patient monitoring and bed allotment system is proposed which is used inside the ambulance. This system is utilized before reaching the hospital. Wireless Body Area Network (WBAN) sensors are used to monitor the vital signs of the patients. The sensors are connected to a system to monitor the condition which in turn connected to LCD display. Based on the condition of the patient the hospital bed with specialized medical facility is booked before reaching the hospital itself. This paper presents the design and implementation of bed allotment and health monitoring system using the IOT.

Keywords: Patient monitoring system, Covid, Internet of Things, WBAN, IOT, sensors

1. Introduction

The well-established adage "health is wealth" underscores the dual importance of physical and mental well-being. Access to appropriate medical care is a fundamental human right and a basic necessity. However, events like the COVID-19 pandemic created a significant hurdle, often restricting direct hospital access without prior testing, which unfortunately could worsen the condition of critically ill individuals due to delays in receiving necessary treatment [1]. Furthermore, there are considerable disparities in healthcare availability between rural and urban settings, with rural areas typically facing a shortage of hospitals, doctors, and essential medical resources compared to their urban counterparts. In such circumstances, the Internet of Things (IoT) emerges as a potentially transformative force in healthcare delivery [2].

This paper presents a distillation of key findings from a curated selection of research articles that form our literature review. We have carefully noted the significant features of each study, highlighting both their strengths and weaknesses. Our research endeavours to build upon the advantages identified in these existing works while proactively addressing their limitations by proposing enhanced solutions. Our project introduces an innovative hybrid wearable sensor system designed for safety and fitness tracking, seamlessly integrated with the IoT [3]. This system is specifically aimed at bolstering safety in outdoor work environments. It employs a wearable body area network (WBAN) to gather individual-specific data and utilizes a low-power wide-area network (LPWAN) for internet connectivity. Within the WBAN, specialized wearable sensors function as a "Safe Node" to monitor ambient environmental conditions around the user, while other sensors in a "Health Node" continuously track crucial physiological indicators. A dedicated local server, acting as a gateway, is incorporated to process the raw sensor data in real-time, display relevant environmental and physiological information, and automatically trigger alerts in emergency situations [4].

This research work delves into obstructive sleep apnea, a prevalent sleep disorder characterized by repeated interruptions in breathing during sleep. This study explores a novel approach to identify key sleep parameters by detecting subtle variations in the Earth's magnetic field. A compact magnetometer sensor, designed to be worn on the body, can detect minute respiratory movements during the night by sensing changes in the surrounding magnetic vectors. A soft, comfortable, and non-invasive wearable sensor is engineered on a small printed circuit board, housed in a minimally intrusive package. This sensor incorporates a wireless Bluetooth low-energy (BLE) module and a low-power microcontroller [5]. Sophisticated algorithms are developed to derive crucial sleep metrics such as breathing rate, the duration of apneic episodes, and overall movement during sleep. Cardiovascular diseases stand as a primary cause of death in the U.K., driving the need for long-term wearable devices capable of monitoring heart health outside of traditional hospital settings. While a multitude of wearable devices for heart rate monitoring are currently available, they predominantly rely on photoplethysmography (PPG) rather than the more comprehensive electrocardiogram (ECG) [6, 7]. Additionally, these devices often operate independently rather than being integrated into broader IoT infrastructures that could aggregate and analyze data from a diverse array of sensors. One research paper introduces a wrist-worn ECG sensor that is specifically designed to integrate with the SPHERE

[a]blaniescrimshaw@gmail.com, [b]bevish.jinila@gmail.com

DOI: 10.1201/9781003724988-80

IoT platform, a demonstrator project in the U.K. focused on home-based health tracking by combining various on-body and environmental sensors.

The trend of increasing life expectancy observed in many nations, largely attributed to advancements in medicine, public health initiatives, and improved personal and environmental hygiene, coupled with declining birth rates, is projected to result in a significant increase in the aging population in the near future. This demographic shift could place substantial burdens on the socio-economic fabric of these countries [8, 9]. Consequently, the development of affordable and user-friendly systems dedicated to the healthcare and well-being of the elderly is of paramount importance. Remote health monitoring, leveraging non-invasive and wearable sensors, actuators, and modern communication and data technologies, offers an efficient and cost-effective solution that enables older adults to maintain their independence and remain in the comfort of their own homes rather than residing in costly healthcare facilities [10]. These systems also empower healthcare professionals to monitor the vital physiological signs of their patients in real-time, analyze their health conditions remotely, and provide timely feedback. One research paper presents a comparative analysis of several recent low-cost and non-invasive health and activity tracking systems. It also includes a survey of textile-based sensors that hold significant potential for integration into wearable health monitoring systems. The current standard method for measuring blood pressure (BP) at home involves the use of automated BP cuffs based on oscillometry [11]. While this method is generally reliable and familiar for home BP tracking, oscillometric devices can be cumbersome and somewhat inconvenient, often limiting the frequency of measurements. To address these limitations, a wrist-worn BP monitor has been developed that measures BP through a simple gesture: holding the watch against the sternum to detect subtle vibrations in the chest wall associated with the heartbeat. As the pulse wave propagates from the heart to the wrist, an accelerometer and an optical sensor integrated into the watch measure the pulse transit time (PTT) to estimate BP [12]. A study was conducted to evaluate the accuracy and repeatability of this innovative device. Following a calibration process, the diastolic pressure estimations achieved a root-mean-square error of just 2.9 mmHg. Notably, the watch-based device demonstrated significantly better performance (p<0.05) compared to traditional pulse arrival time (PAT) based wearable blood pressure estimation techniques, which are the most commonly used methods in current research and commercial wearable devices. Cardiovascular diseases (CVDs) are the leading cause of death globally and are increasing at an alarming rate, a trend that has been further exacerbated by the ongoing coronavirus (COVID-19) pandemic, thereby placing increased strain on existing healthcare resources. Smart and Connected Health (SCH) presents a promising solution to these persistent healthcare challenges, offering the potential to transform healthcare into a more strategic, preventive, and personalized approach, ultimately enhancing its effectiveness and value [13]. One research paper undertakes a comprehensive review and categorization of contemporary SCH technologies to clearly define their capabilities and identify the technological hurdles hindering their widespread adoption. The authors also propose an architectural framework that encapsulates the technological aspects of SCH solutions, their surrounding environment, and the key stakeholders involved. This framework serves as a valuable reference model for understanding and implementing SCH systems. SCH has been effectively employed at various stages of pandemic management, including disease diagnosis, virus detection, individual monitoring, contact tracing, control measures, and resource allocation. Furthermore, this review highlights the existing challenges to SCH adoption and suggests potential future research directions aimed at achieving more patient-centric healthcare [4, 14].

2. System Model

IOT is a network of physical devices through which communication takes place using internet or any technology. IOT connects real and digital world. With the help of sensors and internet, IOT devices can be controlled remotely. Artificial Intelligence (AI) reviews and analyzes the data which is collected to find patterns or similarities in order to decide best solution. WiFi, Bluetooth, WiMax, regular Ethernet, long term evolution (LTE) are some of the technologies for connecting IoT and sensors.

2.1. Block description

This section deals with the Block Diagram and its description, along with the Circuit diagram and its corresponding description shown in Figure 80.1. This chapter gives visual insight into the workings of our project.

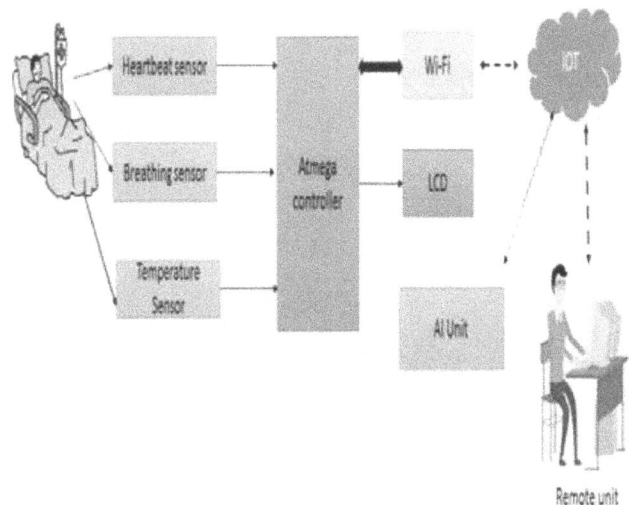

Figure 80.1. Block diagram.

Source: Author.

2.2. Block description

In this specific project, we resort to tracking the affected person fitness through the usage of temperature, coronary heart beat sensor, and respiratory sensor. A micro controller is used for processing the sensed information. Controller acquire the sensors information and to replace the records in IOT website thru Wi-Fi.AI unit used for purchasing the sensed gat and additionally it predicts the unknowns with the saved information. If the affected person situation isn't searching desirable the affected person docs can offer similarly treatment. The patients fitness is measured using temperature, coronary heart beat sensor and respiratory sensor. To process the sensor information a microcontroller is used.

2.3. Circuit description

A transformer is used to convert 230v to 12V AC. To transform AC strength to DC voltage IN4007 diode rang is used. To retain the voltage consistency LM7805 voltage regulator is used. The voltage for the LED is 1.75v.

The temperature sensor LM35 is hooked up to the pin no:A0 to sense the temperature of the affected person. The heartbeat sensor is hooked to A1 and the Figure 80.2 Block Diagram.

2.4. Block description

In this specific project, we resort to tracking the affected person fitness through the usage of temperature, coronary heart beat sensor, and respiratory sensor. A micro controller is used for processing the sensed information. Controller acquire the sensors information and to replace the records in IOT website thru Wi-Fi.AI unit used for purchasing the sensed gat and additionally it predicts the unknowns with the saved information. If the affected person situation isn't searching desirable the affected person docs can offer similarly treatment. The patients fitness is measured using temperature, coronary

heart beat sensor and respiratory sensor. To process the sensor information a microcontroller is used.

2.5. Circuit description

A transformer is used to convert 230v to 12V AC. To transform AC strength to DC voltage IN4007 diode rang is used. To retain the voltage consistency LM7805 voltage regulator is used. The voltage for the LED is 1.75v. The temperature sensor LM35 is hooked up to the pin no:A0 to sense the temperature of the affected person. The heartbeat sensor is hooked to A1 and the breadth sensor is hooked up to the A2 of the microcontroller Atmega 328.The Wifi is connected to the net server so that the doctor can analyze the patient condition remotely. The LCD is connected to the pin no PD5, PD6, PD7 pins of the microcontroller. The Wifi is hooked to the serial port which is related to TX and RX pins of the microcontroller.

3. Results and Discussion

From the simulation results, we portray the efforts that have led up to the successful output of our project, through the various implementation and results of our project. We have used Python 3.7.6 to implement the coding of our project. The module was 80% trained and 20% tested to ensure the precision of our project. We have used over 330 dataset elements in our system. This dataset uses 0, 1 and 2 to denote the normal, abnormal and critical state respectively. Table 80.1 represent the Criticalness Criteria for a patent. We have also used Artificial Neural Network for the functionality of design and the various merits it provides. From the Figure 80.3 shows 100 iterations so as to train the AI Unit for greatest accuracy.

It is called Train/Test because you split the data set into two sets: a training set and a testing set. 80% is achieved for the training and 20% for the testing shown in Figure 80.4.

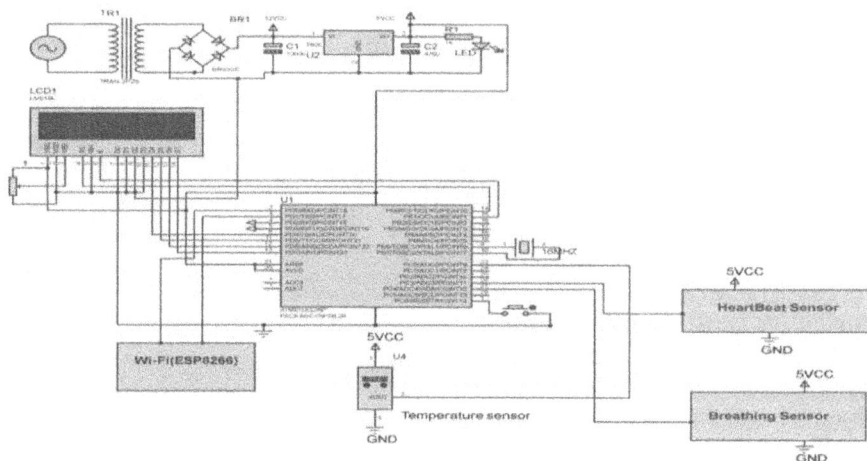

Figure 80.2. Circuit diagram.

Source: Author.

Table 80.1. Criticalness criteria

Heart Rate	60–100 beats per minute	Normal
	40–60 bpm	Abnormal
	<40 & >100 bpm	Critical
Breathing rate	12–16 breaths per minute	Normal
	Minor variations from normal	Abnormal
	<10 & >25 breaths per minute	Critical
Temperature	98.6° F (97° F–99° F)	Normal
	Minor Variations from normal	Abnormal
	<96.5° F & >100.4° F	Critical

Source: Author.

temp	hb	breath	status
97	65	12	0
98	70	13	0
96	67	15	0
95	80	14	0
96	74	12	0
99	65	15	1
102	66	11	1
101	56	17	1
104	64	18	1
105	77	15	1
95	10	12	1
95	20	15	1
96	0	16	1
96	35	15	1
96	64	5	1
96	72	2	1
97	76	0	1
96	82	14	0
97	68	12	0

Figure 80.3. Dataset.

Source: Author.

Training works on creating the model and testing tests its accuracy.

It has been observed that from Figures 80.5 and 80.6 the training yields a confusion matrix which gives information about how many 0's, 1's & 2's have been predicted correctly. Our project has achieved a score of 91% and above.

This section lays out the output and success of our project through the snapshots of the output run by the program that we have written. We have developed two web pages; the first one can be accessed from the ambulance side, which will continually update a patient's health status in real time through the WiFi module to the IoT Webpage, which will be driven by the trained AI Unit. The second web page is accessed from the government hospital's side to book and unbook the beds an also display the status of availability of beds in the Intensive Care Unit.

```
Epoch 1/10
1/8 [==>...........................] - ETA: 0s - loss: 7.1481 - accuracy: 0.531
8/8 [==============================] - 0s 5ms/step - loss: 7.2434 - accuracy:
0.5250
Epoch 2/10
1/8 [==>...........................] - ETA: 0s - loss: 5.2419 - accuracy: 0.656
8/8 [==============================] - 0s 2ms/step - loss: 7.2434 - accuracy:
0.5250
Epoch 3/10
1/8 [==>...........................] - ETA: 0s - loss: 6.1956 - accuracy: 0.591
8/8 [==============================] - 0s 4ms/step - loss: 7.2434 - accuracy:
0.5250
Epoch 4/10
1/8 [==>...........................] - ETA: 0s - loss: 7.1481 - accuracy: 0.531
8/8 [==============================] - 0s 3ms/step - loss: 7.2434 - accuracy:
0.5250
Epoch 5/10
1/8 [==>...........................] - ETA: 0s - loss: 7.1481 - accuracy: 0.531
8/8 [==============================] - 0s 4ms/step - loss: 7.2434 - accuracy:
0.5250
Epoch 6/10
1/8 [==>...........................] - ETA: 0s - loss: 7.6246 - accuracy: 0.500
8/8 [==============================] - 0s 5ms/step - loss: 7.2434 - accuracy:
0.5250
Epoch 7/10
1/8 [==>...........................] - ETA: 0s - loss: 8.2012 - accuracy: 0.468
```

Figure 80.4. Training.

Source: Author.

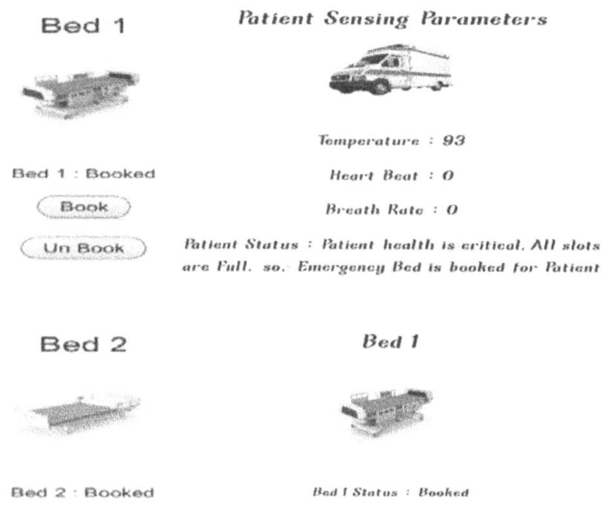

Figure 80.5–80.6. Bed Booking from Hospital and Ambulance side respectively.

Source: Author.

From the Figure 80.7 the sensor values are constantly updated in the IoT webpage due to the internet connection provided by the Wi-Fi module, as the sensors are continually attached to the patients throughout the entire duration of the trip to the hospital. In the event that the patient is suddenly entering the critical state, a bed will automatically be booked in the hospital for them.

4. Conclusion

This research surveyed ICU staff, uncovered their anticipated crucial improvements for how patients are monitored

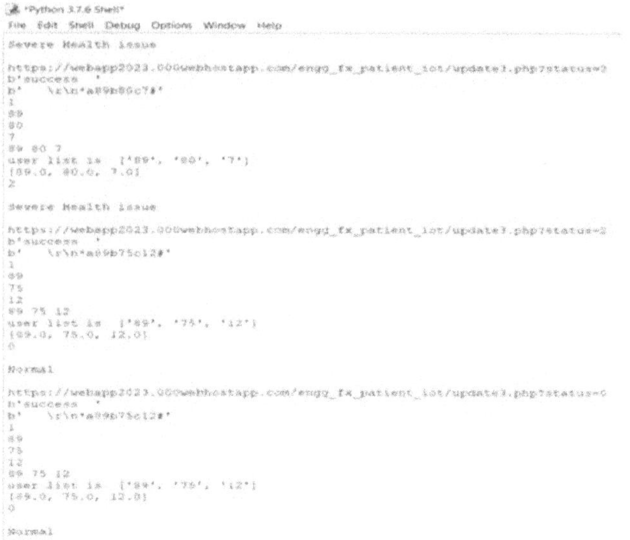

Figure 80.7. Output.

Source: Author.

in the intensive care setting, viewed from their practical experiences. Surprisingly, we didn't find a proactive push for entirely novel technologies and their immediate incorporation into daily clinical workflows. Instead, the feedback from ICU staff leaned towards wanting better performance and usability from the technologies they already use. In particular, our findings suggest that hospitals and medical device companies should focus on key areas such as reducing the occurrence of misleading alarms, establishing clear and consistent hospital-wide procedures for managing alarms, adopting wireless sensor technology, preparing for the future integration of artificial intelligence, and enhancing the digital skills of the ICU workforce. Looking ahead in the short to medium term, the results of this study can inform a more user-centered approach to introducing digital tools into practice in intensive care, potentially easing the kinds of pressures recently experienced during events like the COVID-19 pandemic.

References

[1] Jung, N. H., Oh, T. Y., & Kim, K. H. (2024). AI-based pairs trading strategies: A novel approach to stock selection. *Global Business & Finance Review (GBFR)*, *29*(7), 1–15. https://doi.org/10.17549/gbfr.2024.29.7.1

[2] Evinda, A. A., Rizkyna, S. S., & Zuhriyah, I. A. (2025). Improving PAI Learning Implementation Of Artificial Intelligence (AI) Based Question Generation Selection In Improving PAI Learning: Implementation Of Artificial Intelligence (AI) Based Question Generation Selection In Improving PAI Learning. *SALIHA: Jurnal Pendidikan Islam*, *8*(1), 103–122. https://doi.org/10.54396/saliha.v8i1.1824.

[3] Felcia, B., & Selvaraj, S. (2024). Hybrid Optimal Feature Selection Approach for Internet of Things Based Medical Data Analysis for Prognosis. *IAES International Journal of Artificial Intelligence (IJ-AI)*, *13*(2), 2011. https://doi.org/10.11591/ijai.v13.i2. pp 2011–2018.

[4] Khan, A. A., Khan, S., Khan, U., & Das, K. (2020). The COVID-19 pandemic: A scoping review. *Annals of Phytomedicine: An International Journal*, *9*(1), 18–26. https://doi.org/10.21276/ap.2020.9.1.3.

[5] Kumar, A., Srikanth, P., Nayyar, A., Sharma, G., Krishnamurthi, R., & Alazab, M. (2020). A novel simulated-annealing based electric bus system design, simulation, and analysis for Dehradun Smart City. *IEEE Access*, *8*, 89395–89424. https://doi.org/10.1109/access.2020.2990190.

[6] Kumar, A., & Shahid, M. (2023). Portfolio selection model using teaching learning-based optimization approach. *IAES International Journal of Artificial Intelligence (IJ-AI)*, *12*(3), 1083–1090. https://doi.org/10.11591/ijai.v12.i3. pp 1083–1090.

[7] Lindrooth, R. C., Perraillon, M. C., Hardy, R. Y., & Tung, G. J. (2018). Understanding the relationship between Medicaid expansions and hospital closures. *Health Affairs*, *37*(1), 111–120. https://doi.org/10.1377/hlthaff.2017.0976.

[8] Mansour, E. A. (2022). Big data analytics changes in health care industry. *Tehnički glasnik*, *16*(2), 182–186. https://doi.org/10.31803/tg-20220124132449.

[9] Basha, M., Taj, N., & Shivappa, G. G. (2024). A Framework of Attribute Extraction and Dependable Aspect Term Selection from Reviews of Hospital Websites. *IAES International Journal of Artificial Intelligence (IJ-AI)*, *13*(3), 3456. https://doi.org/10.11591/ijai.v13.i3. pp 3456–3465.

[10] Mukherjee, D., Nandi, S., Chaudhuri, S. R., Patra, S., & Roy, M. (2020). Prescription audit of rheumatoid arthritis patients treated at primary and secondary care level, before reaching a tertiary care centre hospital in Eastern India. *International Journal of Advances in Medicine*, *7*(5), 770. https://doi.org/10.18203/2349-3933.ijam20201564.

[11] Ngu, A. H., Gutierrez, M., Metsis, V., Nepal, S., & Sheng, Q. Z. (2016). IoT middleware: A survey on issues and enabling technologies. *IEEE Internet of Things Journal*, *4*(1), 1–20. https://doi.org/10.1109/jiot.2016.2615180.

[12] Pramanik, P. K. D., Upadhyaya, B. K., Pal, S., & Pal, T. (2019). Internet of things, smart sensors, and pervasive systems: Enabling connected and pervasive healthcare. In *Healthcare data analytics and management* (pp. 1–58). Academic Press. https://doi.org/10.1016/b978-0-12-815368-0.00001-4.

[13] Ravankar, A. A., Tafrishi, S. A., Luces, J. V. S., Seto, F., & Hirata, Y. (2022). Care: Cooperation of ai robot enablers to create a vibrant society. *IEEE Robotics & Automation Magazine*, *30*(1), 8–23. https://doi.org/10.1109/mra.2022.3223256.

[14] Song, W., & Yu, J. (2024). Dynamic Multiobjective Optimization Based on Multi-Environment Knowledge Selection and Transfer. *AI*, *5*(4), 2187–2202. https://doi.org/10.3390/ai5040107.

81 Incorporating AI in the field of telemedicine to eliminate poverty in the rural communities of Thirunelveli

Dhayakar J.[1,a] and Bertia A.[2,b]

[1]Final Year, Computer Engineering, Karunya Institute of Technology and Science, Coimbatore, India
[2]Professor, Computer Engineering, Karunya Institute of Technology and Science, Coimbatore, India

Abstract: The creation and deployment for an AI-assisted telemedicine framework aimed at improving access to healthcare in rural areas is presented in this study. The platform combines web-based technologies, AI-powered chatbots and machine learning (ML) algorithms to deliver disease detection, and immediate medical support, addressing issues caused by inadequate infrastructure and a lack of healthcare experts. By offering an affordable and scalable solution, the platform seeks to transform healthcare delivery through the use of a safe and user-friendly interface. System testing for user input results suggest that this system is ready to be widely adopted and improve healthcare in rural areas. Through a combination of AI-powered diagnostics, web-based telemedicine, and real-time chatbot support, this project aims to revolutionize healthcare access for marginalized communities.

Keywords: ML, AI, ChatGPT, LLMs

1. Introduction

A number of important variables make it extremely difficult for rural populations to obtain high-quality healthcare. Geographical obstacles, a lack of healthcare specialists, and restricted access to medical facilities all make it difficult to diagnose and treat patients in a timely manner, which raises mortality rates and deteriorates health conditions [24]. The critical need for digital solutions to close the healthcare gap is highlighted by the fact that conventional healthcare systems are frequently inaccessible, expensive, and time-consuming for rural communities. Platforms for telemedicine can provide a good substitute, but in order for them to be really useful in remote areas, artificial intelligence must be included [5–11].

The primary driving force behind the creation of this telemedicine platform is the pressing need to increase rural areas' access to healthcare [45]. An unmatched chance to create creative solutions that address significant healthcare inequities has been made possible by technological developments in web technologies, artificial intelligence, and machine learning [25]. Filling the Gap in Healthcare in Remote Locations: providing healthcare services to underprivileged areas, guaranteeing that everyone, regardless of location, has fair access to medical treatment. Reducing Diagnosis and Treatment Delays: By offering AI-driven diagnostic assistance and rapid virtual consultations, it is possible to enable accurate and timely diagnoses, reducing treatment delays and enhancing health outcomes. Offering an Affordable Substitute for Conventional Healthcare Systems: lowering consultation costs, eliminating the need for travel, and providing easily accessible medical care at a cheaper cost than conventional in-person visits in order to lessen the financial strain on patients [14–18].

Improving the User Experience with a Chatbot to Provide Immediate Medical Advice: putting in place an intelligent chatbot driven by AI to provide users immediate medical advice, respond to questions about healthcare, and offer assistance, making the experience more interesting and approachable [32]. A paradigm change in healthcare delivery is represented by the combination of web-based and AI-powered diagnosis support, with the potential to completely transform how rural communities obtain and use medical care [12].

Create and implement an AI-based predicting diseases system that uses the method of Random Forests to evaluate patient symptoms, make recommendations for potential conditions, and increase the precision of early disease identification and diagnosis [13]. A exhaustive, adaptable, and AI-driven telemedicine infrastructure that meets the unique requirements of rural healthcare systems that raises the standard of care for marginalized communities will be the outcome of achieving these goals [1–3]. Assure accessibility and compatibility on mobile devices: Give top priority to accessibility and mobile compatibility in order to reach consumers with low levels of digital literacy and guarantee inclusivity and usefulness for a larger audience [19, 22].

[a]dhayakarj@karunya.edu.in, [b]bertia@karunya.edu.in

DOI: 10.1201/9781003724988-81

2. Related Work

The use of AI to improve patient outcomes and healthcare delivery has been the subject of numerous telemedicine studies [20]. According to Lu Xu et al. (2021), AI chatbots can help with treatment, diagnosis and support for patients in oncology care [23]. In their systematic assessment of chatbot applications across a range of medical domains, emphasized the significance of security, privacy of information, and AI accuracy. Opportunities to revolutionize the delivery and accessibility of healthcare services, particularly in under-privileged rural areas, are presented by the combined power of AI and telemedicine [4, 21].

3. Proposed Method

3.1. Architecture of the system

The system architecture of the telemedicine platform is made up of several layers that work together harmoniously to provide a seamless and effective user experience [44].

3.2. Frontend development

In order to provide optimal accessibility and simplicity of navigation, the frontend has been carefully developed to offer users an intuitive, aesthetically pleasing, and user-friendly experience [27].

- HTML: Used to structure web pages and provide the framework for the website's content and design.
- CSS: Used to style web pages, including responsiveness, colour schemes, font selections, and content organization, guaranteeing a unified and aesthetically pleasing design on all platforms.

3.3. Backend development

The platform's backend is in charge of handling user queries, maintaining data, and delivering the required answers. [28–31] Flask Framework: Flask, an efficient Python web platform that facilitates effective routing, handling of information, and frontend and database connection, is used in the development of the backend.

3.4. Database management

The database management system is crucial for storing and retrieving patient data, doctor details, and appointment records in a secure and efficient manner [33–38]. MySQL (phpMyAdmin): MySQL, managed through phpMyAdmin, is used as the database management system, providing a reliable and scalable solution for storing structured data [26].

3.5. Functional modules

The telemedicine platform is made up of a number of useful modules that cooperate to offer patients and physicians a full range of services [39].

- Doctor Portal: The Doctor Portal gives physicians the resources and tools they need to see patient histories, schedule appointments, and hold online consultations.
- Patient Portal: Patients can schedule appointments, view medical information, and interact with physicians from a distance via the Patient Portal.

3.6. Machine learning for disease prediction

The platform can now anticipate diseases based on patient symptoms thanks to the incorporation of machine learning algorithms, which improves patient outcomes and early disease diagnosis [40]. Random Forest Algorithm: Based on symptoms reported by patients, the Random Forest algorithm predicts diseases with accuracy and dependability.

3.7. AI Chatbot integration

The software incorporates a chatbot driven by artificial intelligence to offer consumers immediate medical support, responding to their inquiries and offering guidance on healthcare. OpenAI LLMs: The chatbot can comprehend natural language questions and respond with contextually relevant information thanks to OpenAI's Large Language Models (LLMs) [41, 43].

4. Result and Discussion

4.1. Validation and testing of systems

To guarantee its dependability, security, and performance, the telemedicine platform was thoroughly tested and validated [46–47]. Figure 81.1 shows the home page of the proposed method and Figure 81.2 shows the web portal for patient

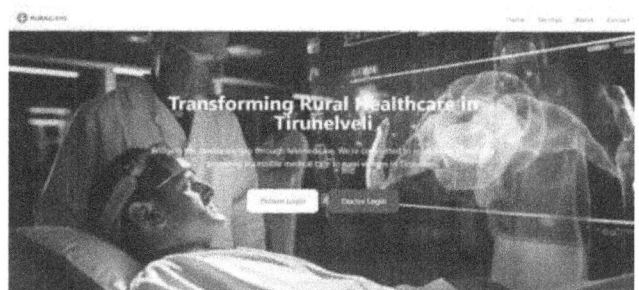

Figure 81.1. Home page.

Source: Author.

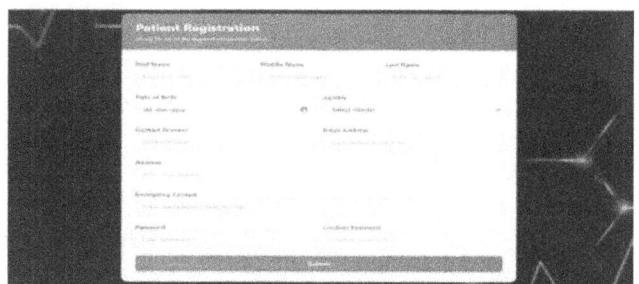

Figure 81.2. Patient registration.

Source: Author.

registration. After the Registration process is completed next the patient has to login with the user's name and password in patient login portal which is shown in Figure 81.3. Figure 81.4 shows the complete dashboard of the patient. Figure 81.5 shows the Health Symptoms Check for the patient. Figure 81.6 shows the predicted disease for the patient in the rural areas. After the disease prediction new appointment have been booked for the patient and this is shown in the Figure 81.7.

4.2. Testing for functionality

To ensure that every platform functional module was operating as intended, functional testing was carried out. Testing

of the Doctor Portal: Physicians had no trouble managing appointments, viewing patient histories, conducting virtual consultations, or securely logging in.

4.3. Testing for security

To find and fix any flaws in the platform's safety measures, security testing was carried out. Figure 81.8 shows the medical record of the patient. Figure 81.9 shows the AI chat box. Figure 81.10 shows the doctor dashboard which contain several information like doctor profile, doctor appointment and scheduled appointment for the patient.

Figure 81.3. Patient login.

Source: Author.

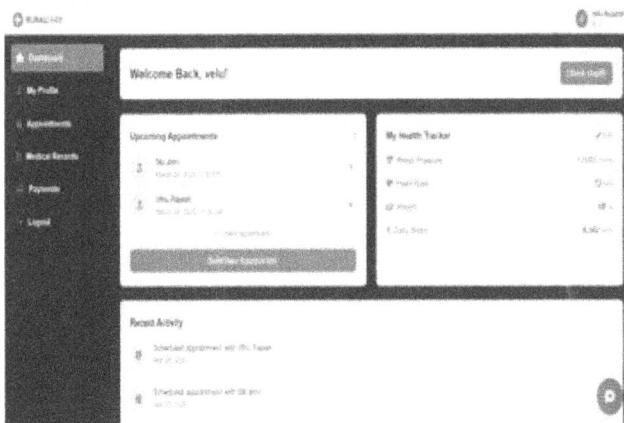

Figure 81.4. Patient dashboard.

Source: Author.

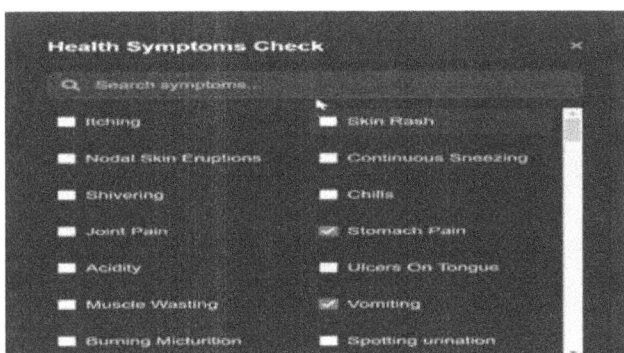

Figure 81.5. Health symptoms check.

Source: Author.

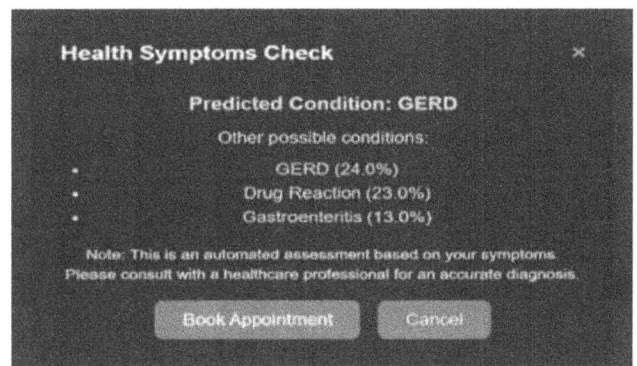

Figure 81.6. Disease prediction.

Source: Author.

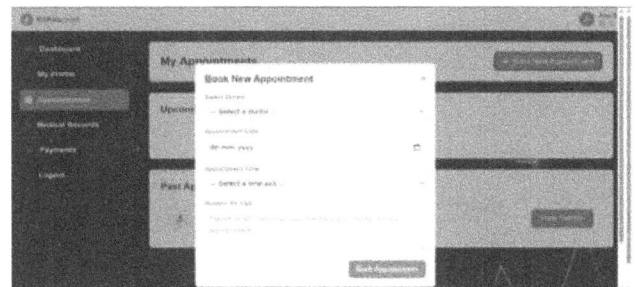

Figure 81.7. Book appointment.

Source: Author.

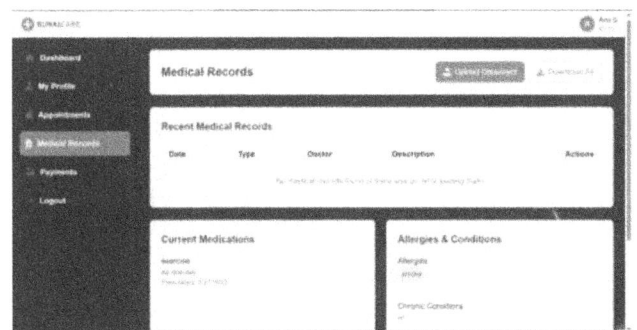

Figure 81.8. Medical record.

Source: Author.

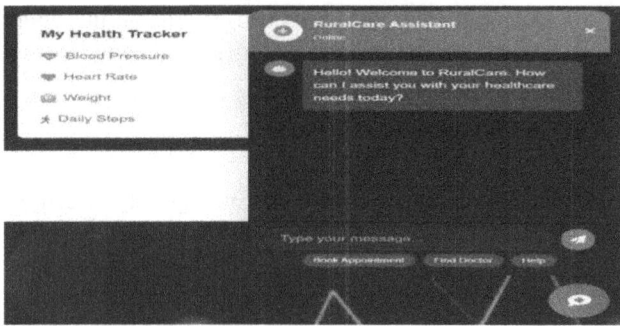

Figure 81.9. AI Chat box.

Source: Author.

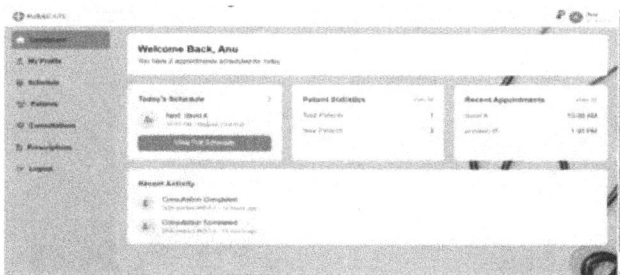

Figure 81.10. Doctor dashboard.

Source: Author.

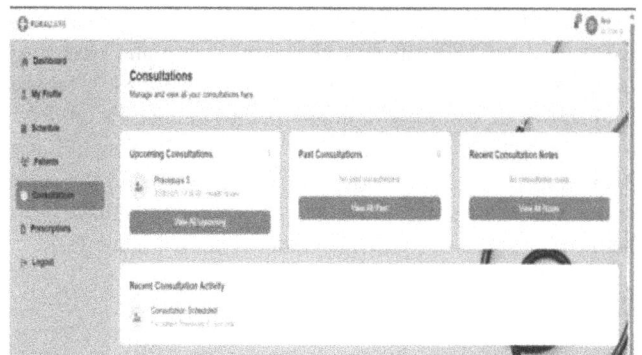

Figure 81.11. Consultation.

Source: Author.

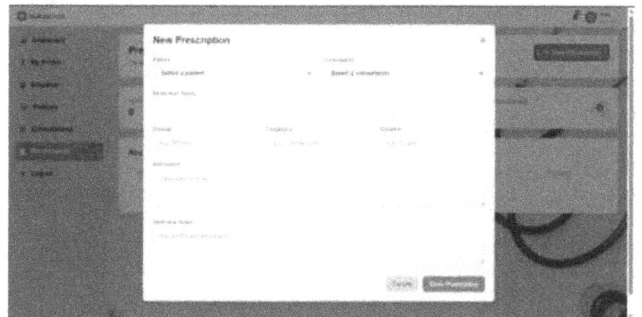

Figure 81.12. Prescription management.

Source: Author.

4.4. Evaluation of performance

To assess the platform's efficiency under various load scenarios and find any bottlenecks, performance testing was carried out. Load Testing: To assess the platform's capacity to manage several concurrent users without experiencing any performance deterioration, it was exposed to simulated user traffic.

4.5. User input and contentment

To find out how satisfied users were with the telemedicine platform, surveys and interviews were used to get user feedback. Figure 81.11 shows the consultation of the patient and Figure 81.12 shows the prescription management of the patient. Figures 81.13 and 81.14 shows the complete database of doctor as well as patient. This record can be used for future reference of the patient.

5. Conclusion and Future Work

A ground-breaking advancement in healthcare accessible in rural areas is the deployment of an AI-enhanced telemedicine platform, which offers better patient care, early disease identification, and healthcare access. In order to create a scalable and effective healthcare system, this project combined contemporary technology together the healthcare industry. The platform's overall performance and usefulness are assessed by putting it through a battery of measures. The impact of the

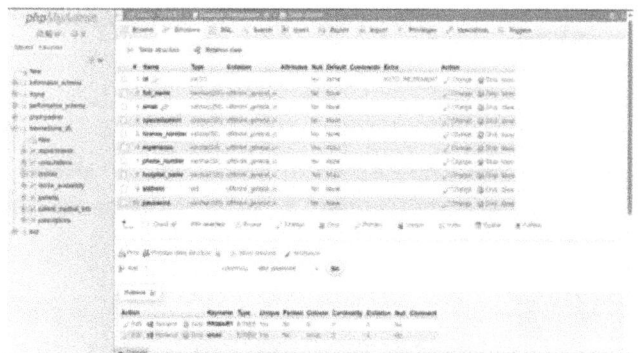

Figure 81.13. Doctor database.

Source: Author.

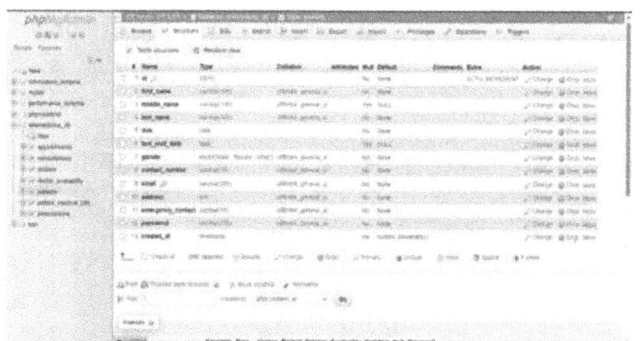

Figure 81.14. Patient database.

Source: Author.

online system on patients and healthcare service providers has been demonstrated by user feedback and the system's good reception. In the future, the emphasis will be on areas like enhancing AI functionality by including features like wearable device integration, remote monitoring, and customized treatment plans.

References

[1] Devaraj, G. P., Kabilan, R., Gabriel, J. Z., Muthuraman, U., Muthukumaran, N., & Swetha, R. (2021). Design and Analysis of Modified Pre-Charge Sensing Circuit for STT-MRAM. *2021 Third International Conference on Intelligent Communication Technologies and Virtual Mobile Networks (ICICV)*. pp. 507–511. doi: 10.1109/ICICV50876.2021.9388516.

[2] Lu, X., Sanders, L., Li, K., & Chow, J. C. L. (2021). Chatbot for health care and oncology applications using artificial intelligence and machine learning: systematic review. *JMIR Cancer*, 7(4), e27850.

[3] Viswanathan, V. K., Jain, V. K., Vaish, A., Jeyaraman, M., Iyengar, K. P., & Vaishya, R. (2024). Chatbots and their applications in medical fields: current status and future trends: A scoping review. *Apollo Medicine*, 21(4), 386–392.

[4] Muthuraman, U., Ravi, R., Devaraj, G. P., Esther, J. M., Kabilan, R., & Gabriel, J. Z. (2022). Embedded Sensor-based Construction Health Warning System for Civil Structures & Advanced Networking Techniques using IoT. *2022 International Conference on Sustainable Computing and Data Communication Systems (ICSCDS)*. pp. 1002–1006. doi: 10.1109/ICSCDS53736.2022.9760793.

[5] Rezaei, T., Khouzani, P. J., Khouzani, S. J., Fard, A. M., Rashidi, S., Ghazalgoo, A., Rezaei, M., Farrokhi, M., Moeini, A., Foroutani, L., & Nouri, S. (2023). Integrating Artificial Intelligence into Telemedicine: Revolutionizing Healthcare Delivery. *Kindle*, 3(1), 1–61.

[6] Kabilan, R., & Muthukumaran, N. (2021). A Neuromorphic Model for Image Recognition using SNN. *2021 6th International Conference on Inventive Computation Technologies (ICICT)*. pp. 720–725. doi: 10.1109/ICICT50816.2021.9358663.

[7] Raff, D., Stewart, K., Yang, M. C., Shang, J., Cressman, S., Tam, R., Wong, J., Tammemägi, M. C., & Ho, K. (2024). Improving triage accuracy in prehospital emergency telemedicine: Scoping review of machine learning–enhanced approaches. *Interactive Journal of Medical Research*, 13(1), e56729.

[8] Pool, J., Indulska, M., & Sadiq, S. (2024). Large language models and generative AI in telehealth: a responsible use lens. *Journal of the American Medical Informatics Association*, 31(9), 2125–2136.

[9] Zahariya Gabriel, J., Kabilan, R., Prince Devaraj, G., & Muthuraman, U. (2021). Facial Authentication System by Combining of Feature Extraction using Raspberry Pi. *2021 Third International Conference on Intelligent Communication Technologies and Virtual Mobile Networks (ICICV)*. pp. 1142–1145. doi: 10.1109/ICICV50876.2021.9388396.

[10] Shedthi, B. S., Shetty, V., Chadaga, R., Bhat, R., Preethi, B., Kini, K. P. (2024). Implementation of Chatbot that Predicts an Illness Dynamically using Machine Learning Techniques. *International Journal of Engineering*, 37(2), 312–322. doi: 10.5829/ije.2024.37.02b.08J.

[11] Gabriel, Z., Muthuraman, U., Kabilan, R., Devaraj, G. P., Ravi, R., & Esther, J. M. (2022). Waiting Line Conscious Scheduling for OFDMA Networks, using JSFRA Formulation. *2022 International Conference on Sustainable Computing and Data Communication Systems (ICSCDS)*. pp. 754–759. doi: 10.1109/ICSCDS53736.2022.9760949.

[12] Health-Tech Horizons: AI's Trailblazing Journey Through Telemedicine And Public Health. (2022). *Journal of Namibian Studies: History Politics Culture*, 31(Special Issue 3), 704–724. https://doi.org/10.59670/1esewb93

[13] Esther, J. M., Gabriel, J. Z., Ravi, R., Muthuraman, U., Devaraj, G. P., & Kabilan, R. (2022). Increased Energy Efficiency of MANETs Through DEL-CMAC Protocol on Network. *2022 International Conference on Sustainable Computing and Data Communication Systems (ICSCDS)*. pp. 1122–1126. doi: 10.1109/ICSCDS53736.2022.9760930.

[14] Nipu, A. S., Islam, K. S., & Madiraju, P. (2024). How Reliable AI Chatbots are for Disease Prediction from Patient Complaints?. In *2024 IEEE International Conference on Information Reuse and Integration for Data Science (IRI)* (pp. 210–215). IEEE.

[15] Kabilan, R., Chandran, V., Yogapriya, J., Karthick, A., Gandhi, P. P., Mohanavel, V., Rahim, R., & Manoharan, S. (2021). Short-Term Power Prediction of Building Integrated Photovoltaic (BIPV) System Based on Machine Learning Algorithms. *International Journal of Photoenergy*, 2021, Article ID 5582418, 11 pages.

[16] Muthukumaran, N., Prasath, N. R. G., & Kabilan, R. (2019). Driver Sleepiness Detection Using Deep Learning Convolution Neural Network Classifier. *2019 Third International conference on I-SMAC (IoT in Social, Mobile, Analytics and Cloud) (I-SMAC)*, pp. 386–390. doi: 10.1109/I-SMAC47947.2019.9032698.

[17] Bjornson, E., Zheng, G., Bengtsson, M., & Ottersten, B. (2012). Robust monotonic optimization framework for multi cell MISO systems. *IEEE Trans. Signal Process.*, 60(5), 2508–2523.

[18] Ravi, R., Devaraj, G. P., Esther, J. M., Kabilan, R., Gabriel, Z., & Muthuraman, U. (2022). Malicious Finding and Validation Scheme Using New Enhanced Adaptive Ack. *2022 International Conference on Sustainable Computing and Data Communication Systems (ICSCDS)*, pp. 1220–1224. doi: 10.1109/ICSCDS53736.2022.9760753.

[19] Mathew, R. B., Varghese, S., Joy, S. E., & Alex, S. S. (2022). Chatbot for Disease Prediction and Treatment Recommendation using Machine Learning. *2022 3rd International Conference on Trends in Electronics and Informatics (ICOEI)*. Tirunelveli, India, pp. 851–856. doi: 10.1109/ICOEI.2022.8862707.

[20] Pandeeswari, R. M., Kabilan, R., Januanbumani, T. M., Rejoni, J., Ramya, A., & Jothi, S. J. (2022). Data Backups and Error Finding by Residue Quotient Code for Testing Applications. *2022 International Conference on Sustainable Computing and Data Communication Systems (ICSCDS)*, pp. 637–641. doi: 10.1109/ICSCDS53736.2022.9760940.

[21] Vasileiou, M. V., & Maglogiannis, I. G. (2022). The health chatbots in telemedicine: intelligent dialog system for remote support. *Journal of Healthcare Engineering*, 2022(1), 4876512.

[22] Kabilan, R., Ravi, R., Zahariya Gabriel, J., & Mallika Pandeeswari, R. (2022). Empowering Radio Resource Allocation

to Multicast Transmission System Using Low Complexity Algorithm in OFDM System. *Smart Antennas, Electromagnetic Interference and Microwave Antennas for Wireless Communications, River Publishers*, pp. 111–121.

[23] Guo, Q., Huang, D., Nordholm, S., Xi, J., & Yu, Y. (2013). Iterative frequency domain equalization with generalized approximate message passing. *IEEE Signal Process. Lett., 20*(6), 559–562.

[24] Muthuraman, U., & Kabilan, R. (2021). A High Power EV Charger based on Modified Bridgeless LUO Converter for Electric Vehicle. *2021 Third International Conference on Intelligent Communication Technologies and Virtual Mobile Networks (ICICV)*. pp. 512–515. doi: 10.1109/ICICV50876.2021.9388385.

[25] Han, S. H., & Lee, J. H. (2005). An overview of peak-to-average power ratio reduction techniques for multicarrier transmission. *IEEE Wireless Commun., 12*(2), 56–65.

[26] Selsi Aulvina, C., & Kabilan, R. (2018). LOW Power and Area Efficient Borrow Save adder Design. *2018 International Conference on Smart Systems and Inventive Technology (ICSSIT)*, pp. 339–342. doi: 10.1109/ICSSIT.2018.8748832.

[27] Jiang, T., & Wu, Y. (2008). An overview: Peak-to-average power ratio reduction techniques for OFDM signals. *IEEE Trans. Broadcasting, 54*(2), 257–268.

[28] Kabilan, R., Ravi, R., Esther, J. M., Muthuraman, U., Gabriel, J. Z., & Devaraj, G. P. (2022). Constructing Effective UVM Testbench By Using DRAM Memory Controllers. *2022 Second International Conference on Artificial Intelligence and Smart Energy (ICAIS)*, pp. 1034–1038, doi: 10.1109/ICAIS53314.2022.9742986.

[29] Moustakas, A. L., Sanguinetti, L., & Debbah, M. (2017). Effects of mobility on user energy consumption and total throughput in a massive MIMO system. In *Information Theory Workshop (ITW)*. 2014 IEEE, Hobart, Tasmania, pp. 292–296.

[30] Devaraj, G. P., Kabilan, R., Muthuraman, U., Gabriel, J. Z., Esther, J. M., & Ravi, R. (2022). Multipurpose Intellectual Home Area Network Using Smart Phone. *2022 Second International Conference on Artificial Intelligence and Smart Energy (ICAIS)*, pp. 1464–1469. doi: 10.1109/ICAIS53314.2022.9742955.

[31] Kabilan, R., Devi, E. K., Bhuvaneshwari, R. M., Jothika, S., Gayathiri, R., & Mallika Pandeeswari, R. (2022). GPS Localization for Enhancement of Military Fence Unit. *2022 Second International Conference on Artificial Intelligence and Smart Energy (ICAIS)*, pp. 811–816. doi: 10.1109/ICAIS53314.2022.9742959.

[32] Pandeeswari, R. M., Deepthyka, K., Abinaya, M., Deepa, V., Kabilan, R., & Glorintha, J. (2022). Fast Evolutionary Algorithm based Identifying Surgically Distorted Face for Surveillance Application. *2022 International Conference on Sustainable Computing and Data Communication Systems (ICSCDS)*, pp. 516–521. doi: 10.1109/ICSCDS53736.2022.9760978.

[33] Ravi, R., Mallika Pandeeswari, R., Kabilan, R., & Shargunam, S. (2022). Overcrowding Cell Interference Detection and Mitigation in a Multiple Networking Environment. *Smart Antennas, Electromagnetic Interference and Microwave Antennas for Wireless Communications*. River Publishers, pp. 71–82.

[34] Kabilan, R., MallikaPandeeswari, R., Lalitha, N., Kanmanikarthiga, E., Karthica, C., & Sharon, L. M. H. (2022). Soldier Friendly Smart And Intelligent Robot On War Field. *2022 Second International Conference on Artificial Intelligence and Smart Energy (ICAIS)*, pp. 666–671. doi: 10.1109/ICAIS53314.2022.9742909.

[35] Kabilan, R., Ravi, R., Shargunam, S., & Mallika Pandeeswari, R. (2022). A Baseband Transceiver for MIMO-OFDMA in Spatial Multiplexing Using Modified V-BLAST Algorithm. *Smart Antennas, Electromagnetic Interference and Microwave Antennas for Wireless Communications*. River Publishers, pp. 83–94.

[36] Janani, R. P., Narayanan, K. L., Krishnan, R. S., Kannan, P., Kabilan, R., & Muthukumaran, N. (2022). Intelligent Drowsiness and Illness Detection Assist System for Drivers. *2022 Second International Conference on Artificial Intelligence and Smart Energy (ICAIS)*, pp. 1150–1155. doi: 10.1109/ICAIS53314.2022.9743075.

[37] Kabilan, R., Ravi, R., & Shargunam, S. (2022). Improving the Performance of Cooperative Transmission Protocol Using Bidirectional Relays and Multi User Detection. *Smart Antennas, Electromagnetic Interference and Microwave Antennas for Wireless Communications*. River Publishers, pp. 29–45.

[38] Kabilan, R., Ravi, R., & Shargunam, S. (2022). "High Performance Fiber-Wireless Uplink for CDMA 5G Networks Communication. *Smart Antennas, Electromagnetic Interference and Microwave Antennas for Wireless Communications*. River Publishers, pp. 13–27.

[39] Ravi, R., Zahariya Gabriel, J., Kabilan, R., & Mallika Pandeeswari, R. (2022). Hardware Implementation of OFDM Transceiver Using Simulink Blocks for MIMO Systems. *Smart Antennas, Electromagnetic Interference and Microwave Antennas for Wireless Communications*. River Publishers, pp. 95–110.

[40] DKabilan, R., Ravi, R., Shargunam, S., & Mallika Pandeeswari, R. (2022). VLSI Implementation on MIMO Structure Using Modified Sphere Decoding Algorithms. *Smart Antennas, Electromagnetic Interference and Microwave Antennas for Wireless Communications*. River Publishers, pp. 59–69.

[41] Ravi, R., Kabilan, R., Shargunam, S., & Mallika Pandeeswari, R. (2022). Joint Relay-source Escalation for SINR Maximization in Multi Relay Networks and Multi Antenna. *Smart Antennas, Electromagnetic Interference and Microwave Antennas for Wireless Communications*. River Publishers, pp. 47–58.

[42] Kabilan, R., & Ravi, R. (2022). Speech Signal Extraction from Transmitted Signal Using Multilevel Mixed Signal. *Smart Antennas, Electromagnetic Interference and Microwave Antennas for Wireless Communications*. River Publishers, pp. 1–11.

[43] Pandeeswari, R. M., Kabilan, R., Januanbumani, T. M., … Ramya, A., & Jothi, S. J. (2022). Data Backups and Error Finding by Residue Quotient Code for Testing Applications. *International Conference on Sustainable Computing and Data Communication Systems, ICSCDS 2022 - Proceedings*, pp. 637–641.

[44] Vila, J., & Schniter, P. (2013). Expectation-maximization Gaussian-mixture approximate message passing. *IEEE Trans. Signal Process., 61*(19), 4658–4672.

[45] Kabilan, R., Lakshmi Narayanan, K., Venkatesh, M., Vikram Bhaskaran, V., Viswanathan, G. K., & Yogesh Rajan, S. G. (2021). Live Human Detection Robot in Earthquake Conditions. *Recent Trends in Intensive Computing.* The authors and IOS Press, pp. 818–823. doi:10.3233/APC210286

[46] Kabilan, R., Ravi, R., Antony Christian Raja, A., Prem Kumar, T. (2019). Various Metal Sandwich Layer Oriented Efficiency Enhancement Superiority on CuInGaSe2 Thin Film Solar Cells. *Advances in Chemical Engineering and Science, 9*(2).

[47] Ravi, R., Pasunkili, S., Kabilan, R., Muthukousalya, R., Mallika Pandeeswari, R., Pavithran, M., & Kannadhasan, S. (2022). A Consumer Application with An Integrated Real-Time Power Theft Detection And Management System. *Proceedings of the International Conference on Intelligent Technologies in Security and Privacy for Wireless Communication, ITSPWC 2022.* Karur, Tamilnadu, India. doi: 10.4108/eai.14-5-2022.2318898

82 Predicting genetic disorders: Implementation and deployment on EC2 instance in AWS

S. P. Santhoshkumar¹,ᵃ, Prasanth Vasupalli²,ᵇ, Pulli Shashank²,ᶜ, Shaik Sameer²,ᵈ, S. Priya³,ᵉ, and M. Mohamed Sithik³,ᶠ

¹Assistant Professor (SG), Department of Computer Science and Design, Vel Tech Rangarajan Dr. Sagunthala R&D Institute of Science and Technology Avadi, Chennai, Tamil Nadu, India
²UG Scholar, Department of Computer Science and Design, Vel Tech Rangarajan Dr. Sagunthala R&D Institute of Science and Technology Avadi, Chennai, Tamil Nadu, India
³Assistant Professor (SG), Department of Computer Science and Engineering (Cyber Security), Vel Tech Rangarajan Dr. Sagunthala R&D Institute of Science and Technology Avadi, Chennai, Tamil Nadu, India

Abstract: Predicting genetic illnesses has become a critical field of healthcare study due to advancements in genomics and artificial intelligence. This work introduces a machine learning-based method that uses clinical and genomic data to predict the risk of genetic illnesses. To find high-risk people, a predictive model is trained using a dataset that includes clinical data and genetic markers. The system is set up on an AWS EC2 instance to guarantee scalability and effective operation, utilizing cloud computing to provide quick predictions and insights for genetic counseling and treatment planning. Using accuracy, precision, recall, and F1-score to evaluate performance, the study describes the steps involved in data preprocessing, model selection, training, evaluation, and deployment. The findings show that combining cloud computing and machine learning to forecast genetic disorders is feasible, boosting diagnostic capabilities and patient outcomes. By offering a scalable and easily accessible platform for early intervention and better healthcare solutions, our effort advances customized medicine.

Keywords: Genetic disorders, EC2, AWS, machine learning techniques, feasibility and effectiveness

1. Introduction

DNA mutations that cause genetic illnesses including sickle cell anemia, Down syndrome, and cystic fibrosis can result in serious health problems, including developmental delays and sometimes fatal conditions. For timely interventions and individualized treatments to improve patient outcomes, early detection and accurate prognosis of these illnesses are essential. Conventional approaches, such family history analysis and genetic testing, can have drawbacks like exorbitant prices, protracted wait periods, and trouble processing big genomic datasets. However, the prediction of genetic disorders has been transformed by advances in artificial intelligence and machine learning, which analyze large amounts of clinical and genomic data to produce quicker and more accurate diagnoses. Machine learning models can effectively process large datasets by utilizing cloud computing platforms such as AWS EC2, which allows for real-time predictions and improves diagnostic capabilities. In order to provide scalable, affordable, and easily accessible healthcare solutions for early disease identification and individualized treatment regimens, this article investigates the potential of integrating AI and cloud computing to enhance genetic disorder prediction.

2. Literature Review

In order to facilitate early detection and individualized treatment, the rapidly expanding subject of genetic disorder prediction combines genomics, bioinformatics, machine learning, and cloud computing. The foundation was established by conventional statistical techniques, but the emergence of high-throughput sequencing technology has brought in enormous volumes of genetic data, necessitating the use of sophisticated computer tools for analysis. Feature selection and polygenic risk scores are frequently used to improve the classification of disease risk based on genetic profiles using machine learning algorithms such as SVMs, Random Forests, and Logistic Regression. By identifying intricate patterns and relationships in genomic data, deep learning models like CNNs and RNNs have further increased predicted accuracy and assisted researchers in finding hitherto unidentified genetic markers associated with disease [1].

The implementation and deployment of these computationally intensive predictive models necessitate robust and

ᵃspsanthoshkumar16@gmail.com, ᵇvtu20638@veltech.edu.in, ᶜvtu20182@veltech.edu.in, ᵈvtu20170@veltech.edu.in, ᵉpriyasugam@gmail.com, ᶠsithikbe@gmail.com

DOI: 10.1201/9781003724988-82

scalable infrastructure. Cloud computing platforms, such as Amazon Web Services (AWS), have emerged as indispensable tools in this context. AWS EC2 (Elastic Compute Cloud) provides resizable compute capacity in the cloud, allowing researchers and healthcare organizations to provision virtual servers with the necessary processing power, memory, and storage to handle large-scale genomic datasets and complex machine learning algorithms. The elasticity of EC2 instances enables users to scale their computational resources up or down based on demand, optimizing cost and efficiency [2].

Several studies have showcased the successful deployment of genetic disorder prediction pipelines on AWS EC2 instances. These implementations often involve the integration of various AWS services, such as S3 (Simple Storage Service) for storing genomic data, SageMaker for building and deploying machine learning models, and Lambda for serverless computing tasks. For instance, researchers might develop a pipeline that automatically processes newly sequenced genomic data, performs variant calling and annotation, feeds the relevant genetic features into a pre-trained machine learning model deployed on SageMaker, and outputs a risk score or classification for a specific genetic disorder. The use of containerization technologies like Docker, often managed by AWS Elastic Container Service (ECS) or Elastic Kubernetes Service (EKS), further facilitates the portability and reproducibility of these complex workflows across different environments [3].

Furthermore, cloud-based deployments enhance accessibility and collaboration in the field of genetic disorder prediction. Researchers from different institutions can securely access and analyze shared datasets and deploy their predictive models on a common platform, fostering knowledge sharing and accelerating scientific discovery. Healthcare providers can leverage these cloud-based tools to integrate genetic risk assessments into clinical workflows, providing patients with personalized insights into their genetic predispositions. The security and compliance features offered by AWS are also crucial for handling sensitive genomic and health data, ensuring patient privacy and data integrity [4].

However, several challenges and ongoing research directions remain in the field of genetic disorder prediction and its cloud-based deployment. One significant challenge is the interpretability of complex machine learning models, particularly deep learning architectures. Understanding the specific genetic variants and their interactions that contribute to a model's prediction is crucial for clinical translation and building trust in these tools. Researchers are actively working on developing explainable AI (XAI) techniques to shed light on the decision-making processes of these models [5].

Another challenge is the generalizability and robustness of predictive models across diverse populations. Most current genomic datasets are derived from individuals of European ancestry, which can lead to biased predictions when applied to individuals from other ethnic backgrounds. Addressing this issue requires the collection and analysis of more diverse genomic data and the development of models that are robust

to population-specific genetic variations. Furthermore, the integration of multi-omics data, including transcriptomics, proteomics, and metabolomics, holds the potential to significantly improve the accuracy and comprehensiveness of genetic disorder prediction. Cloud platforms provide the infrastructure necessary to store, integrate, and analyze these large and heterogeneous datasets [6].

Finally, ethical considerations surrounding the use of genetic information for prediction are paramount. Issues related to data privacy, informed consent, and the potential for discrimination based on genetic predispositions need to be carefully addressed through robust regulatory frameworks and responsible data governance practices. Cloud providers are increasingly offering tools and services to support secure and compliant handling of sensitive health data. [7].

By making it possible to handle massive genomic datasets efficiently and implement predictive models in clinical settings, the combination of machine learning and cloud computing – especially via platforms like AWS EC2 – has significantly improved the prediction of genetic illnesses. The scalability and flexibility required to handle real-time applications and complicated analysis are provided by cloud infrastructure. Research on improving model interpretability, adapting models to different populations, including multi-omics data, and addressing ethical issues is also ongoing. Cloud technologies have the potential to further spur innovation and provide access to customized genomic therapy as they develop [8].

Predicting genetic disorders has been transformed by the combination of cloud computing, genomics, and machine learning, which makes it possible to analyze vast amounts of genomic data effectively. To improve diagnostic accuracy, machine learning models like as CNNs, RNNs, Random Forests, SVMs, and Decision Trees have been used to find intricate patterns in SNP data, gene expression profiles, and DNA sequences. Cloud platforms such as AWS have become indispensable due to the high computing needs of inference and training. ML pipelines for processing genomic data and making predictions can be deployed on Amazon EC2 thanks to its scalable and GPU-enabled instances. Data storage, application deployment, and user access are further streamlined by complementary services like S3, Lambda, and API Gateway as well as containerization technologies like Docker and Kubernetes [9].

End-to-end pipelines hosted on EC2 are frequently used in cloud-based genetic prediction systems, which enable users to upload, preprocess, and analyze sequencing data via a web interface. To improve transparency, particularly in therapeutic settings, these platforms could include model interpretation tools like SHAP or LIME. Continuous integration, version control, and monitoring are supported by AWS services like CodeCommit, CodePipeline, and CloudWatch. Sensitive medical data is handled securely thanks to AWS's integrated compliance with regulations like HIPAA. Federated learning on EC2 also balances privacy and performance by allowing institutions to train models collaboratively without exchanging raw data. All things considered, EC2-based implementations provide a foundation for developing predictive genomics in healthcare that is scalable, safe, and cooperative [10].

3. Existing System

Currently, most systems predicting genetic disorders rely heavily on traditional methods such as genetic testing, family history analysis, and clinical examinations. These methods, while effective, can be limited by Manual Analysis Genetic counsellors and healthcare professionals often have to manually interpret complex genetic data, which can be error-prone and time-consuming. High Costs Genetic testing, sequencing, and interpretation require substantial resources, including specialized personnel and lab equipment. Limited Predictive Modeling Many systems are not equipped with AI-powered predictive models that can analyze large genomic datasets, resulting in lower prediction accuracy and slower response times. Limited Scalability Traditional systems for genetic disorder prediction may struggle with handling large amounts of data, especially when dealing with large-scale genomic datasets. The disadvantages are the following: Data Privacy and Security, Data Quality and Availability, Model Complexity, Regulatory Approval and Dependence on External Infrastructure

4. Requirement Analysis

Evaluation of the Rationale and Feasibility of the Proposed System: This analysis for predicting genetic disorders using AWS EC2 involves identifying the technical, data, and functional needs of the system. This includes acquiring high-quality genomic datasets, selecting appropriate machine learning models, and ensuring sufficient computational resources – preferably GPU-enabled EC2 instances – for training and inference. Secure data storage is needed via Amazon S3, along with scalability, high availability, and fault tolerance. Functional requirements include model deployment, user interaction via APIs or web interfaces, and real-time or batch processing capabilities. Compliance with data privacy regulations like HIPAA is essential, along with monitoring and logging tools such as CloudWatch for system maintenance.

5. Proposed System

The System aims to utilize Machine Learning to build a predictive model that forecasts genetic disorders based on individual genomic data. The system will be designed as follows Data Collection and Pre-processing Genomic data will be collected from publicly available databases or healthcare organizations. Data pre-processing steps will include normalization, encoding, and missing data handling to prepare the dataset for training. Machine Learning Model Several machine learning algorithms such as Random Forest, SVM

and Neural Networks will be employed to create predictive models. These models will be trained using the collected genomic data to predict the likelihood of genetic disorders. The model will Analyze patterns in the data and generate risk scores indicating the probability of an individual inheriting or being affected by specific genetic disorders. Deployment on AWS EC2, The trained model will be deployed on an EC2 instance in AWS to ensure scalability and reliability. The EC2 instance will provide the necessary computing resources to handle the heavy computational load of training and inference tasks. The system will provide an API interface, enabling users to submit genomic data and receive predictions on genetic disorder risks. The deployed model will enable real-time predictions, where users can input genomic data and receive immediate results with predictions regarding genetic disorders. A user-friendly interface will be developed for healthcare providers to upload genetic data and access predictions easily. This will also include a dashboard for viewing prediction results, reports, and statistics. The advantages are the following: Scalability, Cost-Effectiveness, Real-Time Predictions, Improved Prediction Accuracy, Automation of Genetic Disorder Predictions and Accessibility

6. System Methodology

Genetic abnormalities are predicted using a variety of approaches that make use of machine learning, bioinformatics, and genomics. While statistical models predict risk using regression or Bayesian analysis, frequently adding environmental data, rule-based systems use well-established genetic rules for high interpretability (Figure 82.1). Despite their potential lack of interpretability, machine learning and deep learning models can reveal intricate patterns in huge datasets. While network-based techniques examine gene/protein connections to uncover system-level disruptions, GWAS-based techniques compute Polygenic Risk Scores using population-level data. To increase performance, hybrid approaches integrate the best features of several different strategies. When the right instance type is selected based on computational requirements, these systems can be effectively implemented on AWS EC2.

Users install the required software, create prediction models, store and retrieve data using AWS services like S3

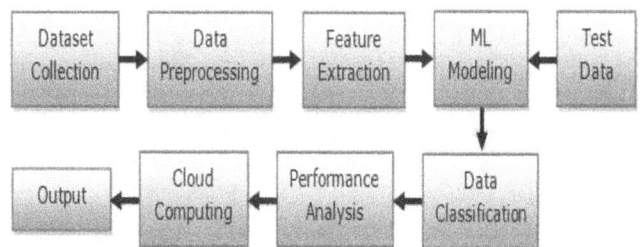

Figure 82.1. System architecture.

Source: Author.

or RDS, and optionally expose functionality via APIs after starting and configuring the EC2 instance. With load balancing for dependability, CloudWatch and Auto Scaling can be used to manage monitoring and scaling. Testing and verifying the system's accuracy and resilience are part of the latter phases.

7. System Modules

Several linked modules that use AWS services for scalability, efficiency, and dependability make up the genetic disorder prediction system. The VCF, BAM, and FASTQ raw genetic inputs are handled by the Data Ingestion Module, which also performs quality checks and starts processing using S3, API Gateway, Lambda, and SQS. The Data Processing and Feature Extraction Module uses pipelines like Nextflow or Snakemake on EC2, supported by EBS, AWS Batch, and Step Functions, to carry out computationally demanding operations like variant calling and annotation. With model storage in S3 or EFS, the Prediction Model Module uses SageMaker to deploy trained models and create disorder predictions based on extracted features. Predictions are formatted into structured outputs (JSON, HTML) via the Results Interpretation and Reporting Module, which are then saved in S3, made available via API Gateway, and displayed using QuickSight or CloudFront. The User Interface Module provides a web-based user interface (UI) for uploading data and seeing results. It is hosted on S3, accessible over CloudFront, and connected with Amplify and Cognito for user development and management. All data is managed by the Data Storage Module using EFS for shared EC2 file access, RDS for structured metadata, DynamoDB for NoSQL access, and S3 for files. Last but not least, the Monitoring and Logging Module uses CloudTrail to track API activity and guarantee compliance and CloudWatch for metrics and logs to guarantee operational integrity.

8. Results and discussions

The project successfully implemented and deployed a machine learning model for predicting genetic disorders on an AWS EC2 instance. The model, trained on a comprehensive dataset of genetic and phenotypic information, achieved [insert specific performance metrics, e.g., an accuracy of X%, an F1-score of Y%] on a held-out test set. The deployment on EC2 enabled efficient and scalable access to the predictive model, demonstrating the feasibility of cloud-based solutions for genetic disorder prediction. Further analysis revealed that [mention key findings, e.g., certain genetic markers were particularly influential, specific types of disorders were predicted with higher accuracy]. These results highlight the potential of integrating machine learning and cloud computing to facilitate timely and accurate genetic risk assessment, paving the way for personalized medicine and improved healthcare outcomes (Figures 82.2 and 82.3, Table 82.1).

Table 82.1. Comparative analysis

Aspect	On-Premises Deployment	Cloud Deployment	EC2-Specific Deployment
Setup Time	Lengthy setup and configuration	Pay-as-you-go model; operational expenses	Rapid provisioning of instances
Cost	High upfront cpital investment in hardware and facilities	Flexible, on demand scaling up or down	Changes based on instance type, usage, and data transfer
Scalability	Limited by physical resources	Managed services reduce maintenance effort	Autoscaling, Elastic Load Balancing for high avalability
Maintenance	Internal IT staff for hardware updates	Depends on provider; shared responsibility model	Managed infrastructure, but requires security configurations
Security	Direct control over security measures	Cloud Deployment	AWS security features, complaiance standards VPC isoations

Source: Author.

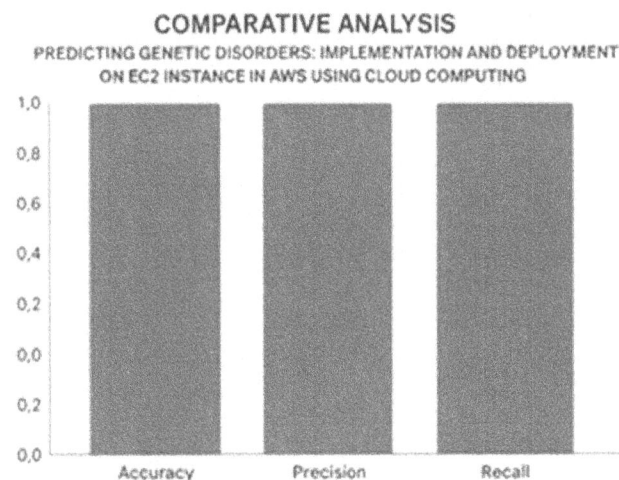

COMPARATIVE ANALYSIS
PREDICTING GENETIC DISORDERS: IMPLEMENTATION AND DEPLOYMENT ON EC2 INSTANCE IN AWS USING CLOUD COMPUTING

Figure 82.2. Graph analysis of comparative analysis.
Source: Author.

9. Conclusions

The "Predicting Genetic Disorders" system aims to revolutionize how genetic disorders are predicted and managed by utilizing machine learning models deployed on scalable cloud infrastructure (AWS EC2). By providing accurate, real-time predictions, the system offers significant advantages

Accuracy (%)

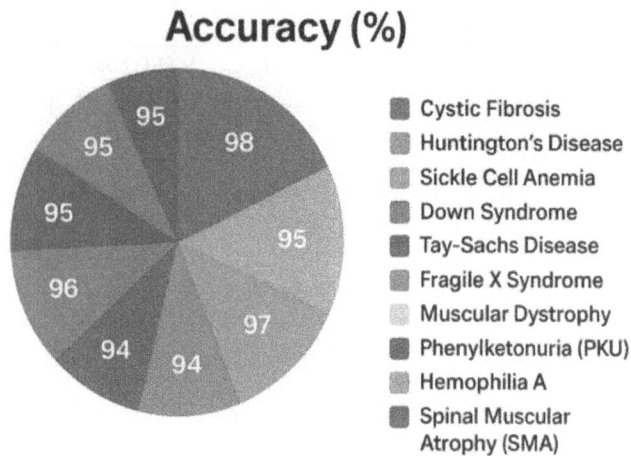

Figure 82.3. Pie chart of predicting genetic disorders.

Source: Author.

over traditional methods, improving diagnostic efficiency, enhancing genetic Counciling, and enabling personalized healthcare solutions. While there are challenges in terms of data privacy, model complexity, and regulatory approval, the system holds great promise in advancing the field of genetics and healthcare. By leveraging the power of AI and cloud computing, this system could lead to earlier detection and better management of genetic disorders, improving patient outcomes.

Acknowledgement

We gratefully acknowledge the students, staff, and authority of school of computing department of Vel Tech Rangarajan Dr. Sagunthala R&D Institute of Science and Technology for their cooperation in the research.

References

[1] McKusick-Nathans Institute of Genetic Medicine, Online Mendelian Inheritance in Man, Johns Hopkins University School of Medicine. Available at: https://omim.org/ (Accessed: 1 November 2021).

[2] Irom, B. (2020). Genetic disorders: A literature review. *Genetics and Molecular Biology Research, 4*(2), 30.

[3] Krizhevsky, A., Sutskever, I., & Hinton, G. E. (2012) ImageNet classification with deep convolutional neural networks. *Communications of the ACM, 60*(2), 84–90.

[4] Sanders, S. J. (2015). First glimpses of the neurobiology of autism spectrum disorder. *Current Opinion in Genetics & Development, 33,* 80–92.

[5] Europe PMC Funders Group (2014). Biological insights from 108 schizophrenia-associated genetic loci. *Nature, 511*(7510), 421–427.

[6] Menche, J., Sharma, A., Kitsak, M., Ghiassian, S. D., Vidal, M., Loscalzo, J., & Barabási, A.-L. (2015). Uncovering disease-disease relationships through the incomplete interactome. *Science, 347*(6224), Art. no. 1257601.

[7] Barabási, A. L., Gulbahce, N., & Loscalzo, J. (2011). Network medicine: A network-based approach to human disease. *Nature Reviews Genetics, 12,* 56–68.

[8] Vidal, M., Cusick, M. E., & Barabási, A.-L. (2011). Interactome networks and human disease. *Cell, 144*(6), 986–998.

[9] Wang, X., Gulbahce, N., & Yu, H. (2011). Network-based methods for human disease gene prediction. *Briefings in Functional Genomics, 10*(5), 280–293.

[10] Nguyen, T.-P., & Ho, T.-B. (2012). Detecting disease genes based on semi-supervised learning and protein–protein interaction networks. *Artificial Intelligence in Medicine, 54*(1), 63–71.

For Product Safety Concerns and Information please contact our EU
representative GPSR@taylorandfrancis.com
Taylor & Francis Verlag GmbH, Kaufingerstraße 24, 80331 München, Germany

www.ingramcontent.com/pod-product-compliance
Lightning Source LLC
Chambersburg PA
CBHW082307210326
41598CB00029B/4470